MACROECONOMICS

Principles & Applications

MACROECONOMICS
Principles & Applications

Robert P. Thomas
University of Washington — Seattle

in collaboration with

William V. Weber
Eastern Illinois University

THE DRYDEN PRESS
Chicago Fort Worth San Francisco Philadelphia
Montreal Toronto London Sydney Tokyo

Acquisitions Editor: Rebecca Ryan
Ancillary Development: Eric Elvekrog
Project Editor: Karen Steib
Production Manager: Barb Bahnsen
Director of Editing, Design, and Production: Jane Perkins

Text and Cover Designer: Jeanne Calabrese
Copy Editor: Mary Englehart
Indexer: Sheila Ary
Compositor: York Graphic Services
Text Type: 10/12 Bodoni

Library of Congress Cataloging-in-Publication Data
Thomas, Robert Paul, 1938–
    Macroeconomics: principles and applications.
    1. Macroeconomics.   I. Weber, William V.
II. Title.
HB172.5.T473 1990   339   89-25961
ISBN 0-03-013158-8

Printed in the United States of America
901-032-987654321
Copyright © 1990 by The Dryden Press, a division of Holt,
Rinehart and Winston, Inc.

Address orders:
The Dryden Press
Orlando, FL 32887

Address editorial correspondence:
The Dryden Press
908 N. Elm Street
Hinsdale, IL 60521

The Dryden Press
Holt, Rinehart and Winston
Saunders College Publishing

Cover Source: © 1984 Art Kane/The Stock Market.

THE DRYDEN PRESS SERIES IN ECONOMICS

ABOUT THE AUTHOR

Robert Thomas lives with his wife and two children on Camano Island, Washington. He received his undergraduate degree from Carleton College and his M.A. and Ph.D. from Northwestern University. He is currently Professor of Economics at the University of Washington where he teaches principles of economics and economic history. He has written several books, and published numerous scholarly articles. Thomas served for three years as the economic advisor for a United States senator, and for three years as the University of Washington's faculty representative to the Washington State legislature. This experience proved to him the value of economics in formulating public policy.

In addition to his academic career, the author has briefly owned and operated both a radio station and gasoline station, built his own house and barn, cleared and fenced his land, grown grapes, and raised cattle, sheep, donkeys, and collie dogs — all of which have taught him patience and the ultimate value of specialization. His ventures have been rewarding experiences, if not always financially profitable. But none have been as rewarding as teaching the principles of economics course, which remains his favorite professional activity.

PREFACE
TO THE INSTRUCTOR

• A NEW APPROACH TO TEACHING •

Every economics teacher has felt frustrated by how little students retain from their principles course. Sometimes students might vaguely recall a concept. At other times they can even push a curve around. But when we ask them to apply a concept to a real-world problem, inevitably the results are disappointing. In part, this is because we are unable to convey the relevance of economics to everyday life. Years of experience in teaching principles has shown me that there are two levels of economic understanding that a first course must achieve. The first is a basic understanding of the logic of economics. The second is a rudimentary ability to apply economic principles to real-world problems. By the end of a course students often have mastered the first, but seldom the second. Yet unless they are able to apply the basic concepts to the world around them, the technical tools recently mastered are forgotten soon after the final exam is over.

The goal of this book is to help you take your students one step further along the road toward mastering economics. By learning basic economic principles and applications of these principles, your students will come to appreciate that the economic way of thinking helps them to think consistently and coherently about a wide range of social problems. Professors of economics know that the principles of economics can help make sense out of confusion, tie together a seemingly unrelated group of facts, suggest alternatives that are not readily apparent, and uncover implications that would otherwise remain hidden. Students in the principles course should, at the very least, come to appreciate the power of economic thinking. This appreciation will give them an incentive to learn the principles because they are useful, to retain what they have learned, and, perhaps, to take more economics courses. •

• HOW THIS TEXT USES APPLICATIONS •

This book is not an issues book in the traditional sense. It is a principles of economics text that extensively employs applications. Teaching economic theory in a principles course is essential. Without the theoretical foundations, students can at best read opinions on all sides of an issue, look at statistics, and learn that there are apparently good arguments supported by statistics on both sides of any important issue. But they will not be able to take a clear position themselves, to sort sense from nonsense. The principles of economics in this book are taught as the tools of analysis. This is accomplished by first raising certain problems or issues (in the chapter *previews*), teaching the tools necessary for analysis (in the chapter body), and finally applying these tools to analyze the problem (in the *preview*

analyses). Along the way there are also shorter, self-contained boxed applications to help keep students interested. The problems that the chapter previews raise have been carefully selected so that a basic economic analysis will require no more than the tools covered in that chapter. Newspaper or magazine articles are often unsuitable for this purpose, because most require too much prior knowledge.

Existing textbooks do an excellent job of preparing students to acquire the first level of economic thinking — mastery of economic concepts — but they do little to help them attain the ability to apply the theory learned. While "applications" are now appearing more frequently in principles textbooks, their purpose is primarily to illustrate a theoretical principle. Though better than nothing, this is just the opposite of the way I believe they should be employed. Using theory to clarify a problem gives students an opportunity to appreciate the power of economic analysis and to begin using economic reasoning themselves. This technique provides a motivation for mastering abstract economic concepts by demonstrating that economic principles are useful for more than answering questions on examinations.

In *Economics: Principles and Applications*, no economic principle or concept is taught unless it can be put to work immediately. Because economic analysis is so widely applicable, following this precept does no serious injury to the traditional way economic theory is presented in the principles course. The overall text organization and the topic coverage within chapters do not depart radically from the organization and coverage found in current leading texts. What is different is that each chapter begins with two or three previews of real-world problems that beg for economic analysis. The economic concepts are then presented in the traditional manner and fleshed out

through the use of relevant illustrations. The final step consists of applying the newly learned concepts to the previews, exploring the implications, and outlining possible resolutions or new ways of understanding economic phenomena based on the relationship between concepts and events.

There are over 200 applications in this book, some short and some more extended. Because time is already too short in a one-semester micro or macro course, I have written the chapters in such a way that none of the applications is mandatory. This built-in flexibility allows the instructor to assign only those applications you feel are most important or that you have time to discuss. Because the applications require no more explanation of concepts than the chapter itself provides, they may even be recommended as optional reading! Instructors who enjoy a heavier focus on applications can build their class presentation around them, although an understanding of the basic text concepts in no way presumes that the students have read the applications. ●

● THE CONTENT ●

The Introduction (Chapters 1–5) The book begins with a set of fundamental economic ideas. The purpose of this first section is to show students the types of problems that economic theory can help them understand and to instill a sense of how economics can provide answers to real-world problems.

The book is constructed to split into separate micro and macro texts, both sharing this common introductory section with the combined volume. These five chapters focus on how the market determines relative values and allocates scarce resources. Besides serving as the beginning section of a course devoted to microeconomics, the first section provides the basic microeconomic framework necessary for the study of macroeconomics. In addition to the traditional topics, there are two unique appendixes, "Economics of Information" (Chapter 3) and "Government Expenditures and Revenues" (Chapter 5).

Microeconomics (Chapters 6–19 in Both the Combined Volume and the Micro Split) A high degree of consensus exists among economists as to the theoretical content of a principles course in microeconomics. The book thus follows a traditional pattern of presentation. Part 2, "Pure Competition," is devoted to considering the determinants of demand and supply and to presenting the theory of pure competition. Part 3, "Price Searching," takes up price searching, or imperfectly competitive markets. For those instructors who want to incorporate some elementary game theory into their principles course, the appendix to Chapter 12 presents an introduction to using the game theory approach to oligopoly. Part 4, "Factor Mar-

kets," consists of three chapters on this important topic. The final section is Part 5, "Market Failure and Public Policy."

Macroeconomics (Chapters 20–32 of the Combined Volume and Chapters 6–18 of the Macro Split) There are two special features of the macroeconomic section: the consensus that exists among economists about macroeconomics is emphasized over differences, and international trade topics are integrated into each chapter where relevant.

Because macroeconomic theory has undergone great changes in recent years, there is less agreement among teachers of economics about how to teach macroeconomics than about how to teach microeconomics. However, this book assumes that we are beyond the point where it is useful to pigeonhole theories. Modern macroeconomics has emerged from the recent decades more balanced — both less activist and less conservative — than in the past. Although important differences continue to exist among economists over macroeconomic models and policy, it is important for first-time students of macroeconomics to realize that a substantial degree of consensus does exist. *Economics: Principles and Applications* does not neglect or gloss over the differences among various modern macroeconomic schools of thought. Instead, these differences are discussed when appropriate within the context of those general principles of macroeconomics on which there is consensus.

Part 5, "Introduction to Macroeconomics," consists of three chapters that lay the foundation for studying the macroeconomy. The first chapter of this sequence covers national income accounting. It introduces basic macroeconomic variables. Chapter 21 (macro split Chapter 7) then introduces the basic macroeconomic model used throughout the book: the aggregate-demand/aggregate-supply model. The analytical similarity between this model and the supply/demand model of price theory, combined with the advantages of being able to deal directly with changes in the price level and to be able to handle supply shocks explicitly, makes this a superior pedagogical approach. The section concludes with a chapter on the key macroeconomic problems: growth, unemployment, and inflation. The appendix to this chapter, "How You Can Keep Track of the Macroeconomy — A Do-It-Yourself Kit," introduces students to the statistical series that track the performance of the economy.

Part 7, "The Real Sector" (combined volume Chapters 23–26, macro split Chapters 9–12), covers the subject of aggregate supply and demand in more depth. Chapter 23 (macro split Chapter 9) covers the Keynesian cross as a theory of aggregate demand, applicable when the price level is fixed. In the next chapter we learn that Keynesian economic theory reveals much of what lies behind aggregate demand. This section ends with a chapter on fiscal policy. Part 8, "The Monetary Sector" (combined volume Chapters 27–29, macro split Chapters 13–15), covers the essentials of money, banking, and monetary policy. Finally, Part 9, "Macroeconomic Problems" (combined volume Chapters 30–32, macro split Chapters 16–18), provides an in-depth look at inflation, unemployment, and growth and productivity. A special appendix to Chapter 31 (macro split Chapter 17) discusses and contrasts the various schools of macroeconomic thought.

Applications in Macroeconomics As in the microeconomics portion, numerous applications help motivate the theoretical discussions. It is clearly more difficult to provide macro applications because of the more limited number of examples available for analysis. To overcome this problem, macro applications often turn to historical developments in macroeconomic theory. The purpose of these applications is to show the relevance of macroeconomic theory to the real world and to build an appreciation for the difficulties of developing and implementing economic policy in both the past and the present.

Integration of International Topics Many domestic economic events can best be understood within the context of the international economy. The United States can no longer be usefully treated for most purposes as separate unto itself. Discussions of the federal budget deficit today are likely to include the balance of payments deficit, and discussions of monetary policy often refer to the international value of the dollar. For this reason the text contains special sections devoted to the implications of the international economy for the topic being discussed. There is another reason for this integration. Many instructors run out of time before they can adequately cover international trade. The integration of trade and trade theory into the basic discussion of macroeconomics is a partial remedy to the time constraint.

International Topics (Combined Volume Chapters 33–36, Macro Split Chapters 19–22) The concluding section is devoted to international trade and economic development. These topics are presented within the context of the increasing importance of international trade, the cyclical problems of the value of the dollar, the growth of protectionist sentiment, the persistent balance of payments deficit, and the international debt crisis. •

• P E D A G O G Y •

In addition to the previews/analyses and boxed applications, each chapter of this text offers these learning aids:

Learning objectives
Chapter introductions
Set-off in-text definitions
Full-color graphs, many with detailed teaching captions
Numbered summaries
Listing of required economic concepts
Review questions
Problems
Application problems

Please turn to page xvi for a visual introduction to these features. •

• P A C K A G E •

Economics: Principles and Applications comes with a full range of teaching and study-support items. Every component of this package has been developed to complement the text and to help the instructor and students maximize the time spent on the course.

Test Bank Available in two separate volumes, Test Bank I (micro) and Test Bank II (macro) offer a combined total of more than 3,600 test questions. These are divided into true/false and multiple-choice questions, which are identified by topic and level of difficulty. The test bank is also available in a state-of-the-art, computerized version for IBM PC, Apple II, and Macintosh microcomputers.

Test Bank I was written by Colleen Cameron of the University of Southern Mississippi, and Test Bank II was written by Gary Burbridge of Grand Rapids Junior College. All questions have been independently checked and their answers verified for accuracy and consistency with the text.

Study Guide Designed to help students review important chapter concepts, extend their ability to apply economic analysis, and prepare for exams, the *Study Guide* to accompany *Economics: Principles and Applications* will be useful for students at all levels of ability. Each chapter contains: learning objectives; a review of required economic concepts; a chapter review with incorporated exercises; graphing exercises; a practice test with multiple-choice and true/false questions; applications exercises; a "common mistakes" section that highlights errors students often make and shows how to avoid them; and full answers to all exercises and practice-test questions.

The *Study Guide* was written by Dale W. Warnke and Edward J. Starshak of the College of Lake County. It is available both in a combined volume and in separate micro and macro volumes.

Instructor's Manual Because switching texts is so often a time-consuming project, the *Instructor's Manual* to accompany *Economics: Principles and Applications* is structured to help simplify course planning. In addition to the special section "Teaching with Applications," for each text chapter the *Instructor's Manual* provides: learning objectives; required economic concepts; a list of applications and the concepts that each application utilizes; detailed lecture notes; full answers to all end-of-chapter questions and problems; additional exercises and discussion questions; and additional application exercises

The manual is packaged in a three-ring binder to make it easier for you to incorporate your own lecture notes. It is also available on floppy disk in ASCII format for those instructors who prefer to create a personalized version. The *Instructor's Manual* was written by the author and William Knight of Prince George's Community College.

Computerized Graphing Tutorial Developed for use with an IBM PC or compatible, the graphing tutorial contains two disks of lessons related to core topics in the textbook. Simple enough for students to use without supervision, this valuable learning aid focuses on important concepts in each chapter and enables students to utilize the computer to practice using graphs in the solution of problems. The tutorial includes the following features: 300 questions arranged by chapter; a drawing program that allows students to draw and manipulate graphs in response to questions (no special equipment beyond a graphics card is necessary); and a built-in error-catching routine that tells students if an answer is incorrect and why it is incorrect.

The graphing tutorial was written and programed by Tod Porter and Teresa Riley of Youngstown State University. It is available free to instructors upon adoption and may be copied for students.

HyperCard Tutorial Developed specifically for use with *Economics: Principles and Applications*, the *HyperCard Macintosh Tutorial* brings key concepts to life through high-interest animation. Ideal for use as a classroom demonstration or in a student lab, the tutorial works through 50 text graphs as it discusses key concepts. All the images and text in the tutorial are designed for use in a large lecture room and can be projected with a Macintosh computer, standard overhead projector, and a projection pad hook-up. The disk is available free to instructors and may be copied for students. The *HyperCard Macintosh Tutorial* was written by John Pisciotta of Baylor University.

The Electronic Scorecard Macro Simulation The *Electronic Scorecard* encourages students to develop their economic decision-making skills by tracking and manipulating current macro data. Ideal as part of any macroeconomics course, this unique simulation sets up, in spreadsheet fashion, an organized listing of important economic and financial variables. Students can then monitor the economy by inputting real data — available from the business section of a national newspaper — on a weekly basis and manipulating it in response to exercises assigned by the instructor. An accompanying *Instructor's Manual* includes suggested exercises and ideas for incorporating the software into the course.

Available for use with an IBM PC and suitable for use with any macroeconomics text, the simulation is available free to all adopters and to students at a nominal charge. *The Electronic Scorecard* was developed and written by J. Richard Aronson of Lehigh University.

Graphing Video Because an understanding of the nature of graphs is essential to students' grasp of economic principles, a unique graphing video is offered free to each adopter of *Economics: Principles and Applications*. Intended for use as a student introduction to graphs, this ten-minute animated video reviews the basics of how graphs are used in economics and explores such key concepts as how shifts occur and how slopes are calculated. Ideal for showing in a first class, the video was produced especially for The Dryden Press to accompany our principles of economics texts.

Transparency Acetates *Economics: Principles and Applications* is accompanied by a set of color overhead transparencies designed for classroom use. The complete acetate set features: more than 150 graphs taken from the book; large print for easier classroom projection; and consistency of colors used in the transparencies and in the text graphs so that students can more easily follow along with lectures ●

TO THE STUDENT

I hear and I forget
I see and I remember
I do and I understand
- Confucius

I am looking at your picture. Well, perhaps not yours, but a group of students in a class like yours. I have it pinned up over my Macintosh. Economics is often considered, at best, to be a difficult course to take, and at worst a boring and difficult one. This is reflected in the picture. Some students are religiously writing down every word the professor is saying as if afraid of missing a vital point. Some, however, clearly wish they were somewhere else. One male is reading a newspaper, and another is looking at an attractive female. Neither has his mind on economics.

Every morning when I sat down to write this book, I looked at the picture and asked myself how I could present that day's topic in a way that would both interest you as a student and best help you to master the subject. Getting your attention is important because both the author and your professor believe that the course in the principles of economics you are just beginning is the most important course you will take in college.

The main reason for this belief is that economics as a way of thinking has proven to be so useful. The economic way of thinking, once you have acquired the skill, will allow you to derive sense from nonsense and to clarify and think consistently about a wide range of social and personal problems. Indeed, the range of applicability for economic thinking is practically unlimited. Acquire the ability to think like an economist and a whole new world will open up for you. That is an exciting prospect. We want you to make the most of this opportunity.

So why is economics often considered difficult and boring? The main reason, I believe, is that many students get little more out of taking the subject than a grade and credit hours. They never acquire the ability to apply the economics they learn. There appear to be two stages to learning how to think like an economist: The first is to be able to understand the logic of economic theory; the second, to be able to apply that logic to real-world problems. You must master both stages if you are going to obtain the most benefits, or perhaps any benefit at all, from your study of economics.

There is a way to do this and to avoid the pitfalls that have claimed many of your fellow students: Combine the learning of economic theory with the direct application of that theory to real-world problems. This book is designed to allow you to do just that.

It is almost as simple as one, two, three.

One. Each chapter begins with two or more previews of problems which hopefully you will recognize as interesting and/or important enough to require analysis. These are problems that you would like to be able to analyze for yourself as an economist would. But before you can do this you must have the necessary economic tools — the tools that you will acquire in the chapter. Mastering these tools is Step Two.

Two. The body of the chapter presents the economic concepts (tools) needed to correctly analyze the problems. Unless you master these tools you will not be able to understand how economists reach the conclusions they do. Reading the text is not enough. You will soon forget what you read. Once you have finished studying the chapter, check your level of mastery by reviewing the key terms and answering at least some of the questions at the end of the chapter. Now, you are ready for Step Three, which is the crucial step in mastering economics.

Three. You must read each application to see how the tools you have just acquired can be used to analyze the problems set forth in the previews. Seeing how the tools are applied will not only show you the power of the economic way of thinking, but will help you reach the second stage of economic knowledge — the ability to apply economics for yourself. After all, why else should you spend the time studying economics? When you see how the tools can be used, you will remember them. Finally, begin to apply your newly acquired knowledge by attempting one or more of the application problems presented at the end of the chapter. When you begin to use economics, you will begin to understand the discipline.

You recall that we said above that learning economics is almost as easy as one, two, three. There is something else that is required: *consistency of effort.* Economics is a cumulative discipline. Each succeeding chapter, or lesson, builds upon the previous one. You will save yourself a lot of grief if you keep up with your assignments. Learning to think like an economist is a substantial, but not an impossible, undertaking. It is something like setting the goal of doing 1,000 sit-ups or push-ups during the academic term. It's not hard if you religiously do 10 a day but it's very difficult, perhaps impossible, if you try to do all 1,000 the last day of the term.

You are now ready to begin. I envy you. There is a thrill to intellectual discovery that can't be obtained in any other way. I hope that learning economics from this book is as interesting for you as it was for me to write it. ●

ACKNOWLEDGMENTS

The writing of a textbook this size is a giant undertaking, at least it was for me. What started out as a leisurely hike through the mountains quickly turned into the writing equivalent of the Bataan death march. Fortunately, I was not alone. That I survived the ordeal and the book is finished is due in large measure to *Becky Ryan*, Acquisitions Editor at The Dryden Press. Becky combined the qualities of a sympathetic listener with a frequent, but judicious, use of the bayonet to prod me toward completion. Becky also served as the developmental editor for the project even after receiving a well-deserved promotion to her current position. Her contribution to the book goes far beyond the role of editor. It was Becky who first recognized the possibilities of a rough outline and sample chapters I submitted. It was Becky who sponsored the project within her company, took the heat when things didn't go according to schedule, and saw to it that my vision actually materialized into a book. Becky's contribution appears on every page of this book.

Becky did not work alone. *Eric Elvekrog* served as developmental editor for the supplementary materials. *Jeanne Calabrese* was responsible for the design of the book and its cover. She designed a book that is at the same time functional and beautiful. *Dan Swanson* turned my graphs into a publishable form. *Karen Steib* served as the project editor, keeping in order the thousands of details that make up a book, often creating order out of apparent disorder. *Mary Englehart* did such a skillful job of copyediting that I would often read her corrections and say to myself, "That's how I should have written it in the first place." *Kathy Pruno* and *Pat Lewis* also assisted at this stage. *Karen Vertovec, JoAnn Learman, Marcia LaBrenz, Linda Melton*, and *Nancy Dietz* did the proofreading. *Susan Jansen* was in charge of producing the supplementary materials package. *Barb Bahnsen, Katie Mattingly*, and *Jan Doty* round out the production team that made this text and package possible.

Finally, three economists deserve mention. *Charles Nelson* listened patiently to problems and offered numerous helpful suggestions while the book was being written. *Nic Nigro* helped me formulate the questions at the end of each chapter. *Bill Weber*, in addition to his contributions as an author, carefully read the manuscript for errors. For the hours of time he put into this project, both the Dryden staff and I are deeply indebted.

My family was supportive of my efforts. My wife, Bonnie, patiently suffered through the writing of this book as did, with somewhat less patience, my children, Robert and Megan, both of whom experienced the opportunity cost of an author/father in terms of less time together. Finally, my friend Jim Schwab came to my rescue by repairing a failing hard disk without losing a single page of text. My thanks to all of you.

We also gratefully acknowledge the contributions of the following academic reviewers.

Ted Amato *University of North Carolina*
Robert Baade *Lake Forest College*
Richard Ballman *Augustana College*
Jeffrey Baser *Murray State University*
Steve Beckman *University of Colorado — Denver*
Charles Bertz *Cerritos College*
Gary Burbridge *Grand Rapids Junior College*
Colleen Cameron *University of Southern Mississippi*
Richard Edwards *Saint Bonaventure University*
Carl Enomoto *New Mexico State University*
Rod Erfani *Transylvania University*
John Farrell *Oregon State University*
Michael Ferrantino *Southern Methodist University*
Roger Goldberg *Ohio Northern University*
John Gross *University of Wisconsin — Milwaukee*
Mary Hirschfeld *Occidental College*
John Kaatz *Georgia Institute of Technology*
Taghi Kermani *Youngstown State University*
Philip King *San Francisco State University*
Bill Knight *Prince George's Community College*
James Kyle *Indiana State University*
Joe B. Lear *Cuesta College*
Robert Marshal *Duke University*
Mathias Mbah *Bowie State College*
Joseph Meskey *East Carolina University*
Manouchehr Mokhtari *University of Houston*
Mike Neiswiadomy *University of North Texas*
Charles Nelson *University of Washington*
James O'Toole *California State University, Chico*
Martin Perline *Wichita State University*
Tod Porter *Youngstown State University*
Carol Rankin *Xavier University*
Chris Rhoden *Solano Community College*
Teresa Riley *Youngstown State University*
Dick Robertson *Hinds Community College*
Nancy Rumore *University of Southwest Louisiana*
Ben Russo *University of North Carolina — Charlotte*
Gerald Shilling *Richland College*
James E. Sondgeroth *Austin Community College*
John Sondey *University of Idaho*
Lee Specter *Ball State University*
Nancy Spillman *Los Angeles Trade Tech*
Daniel Teferra *Ferris State University*
A.M. Turay *Mississippi State University*
Dale Warnke *College of Lake County*
Harold Warren *East Tennessee State University*
Darwin Wassink *University of Wisconsin — Eau Claire*
Dale Wasson *Southwest Missouri State University*
James Watson *Jefferson College*
Janice Weaver *Drake University*
Don Wells *University of Arizona*
Walter Wessels *North Carolina State University*
Charles Wishart *Indiana State University*

Robert Thomas
Seattle   *December 1989* ●

ABOUT THE
COLORS USED
IN THE GRAPHS

The design of this book is colorful. This helps to hold interest and reflects the real-world nature of the applications. But most importantly, the colors have a pedagogical function in the graphs. Each curve has its own assigned color that is used consistently throughout the text. This helps students sort out and remember the many new concepts they are learning. It also makes graphing more understandable for students who have a harder time making the connection between written explanations and visual representation.

Below is a list of the color coding used throughout the text.

- Supply
- Marginal cost
- Marginal physical product
- Total product
- Average physical product
- Short-run aggregate supply
- Leakages/injections approach for determining real GNP
- GNP statistics time series

- Total cost
- Average total cost
- Isocosts
- Indifference curves
- Time series for M1
- Short-run Phillips curve

- Demand
- Marginal revenue
- Aggregate demand
- Aggregate expenditures
- Consumption function
- Time series for price indices

- Isoquants
- Time series for natural rate of unemployment
- Time series for M2

- Long-run average total cost
- Average variable cost
- Total variable cost
- Production possibilities frontiers
- Laffer curves
- Treasury bill interest rates

- Perfectly inelastic supply
- Long-run aggregate supply
- Long-run Phillips curve

In addition, all shifts move from lighter shades to darker shades.

INTRODUCING
THE BOOK

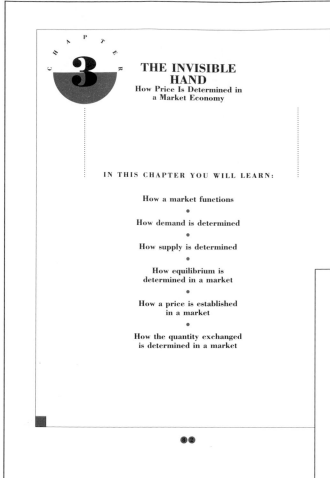

C H A P T E R

3

THE INVISIBLE HAND
How Price Is Determined in
a Market Economy

IN THIS CHAPTER YOU WILL LEARN:

How a market functions

•

How demand is determined

•

How supply is determined

•

How equilibrium is
determined in a market

•

How a price is established
in a market

•

How the quantity exchanged
is determined in a market

82

▲
Chapter opening outlines the key topics to be covered.

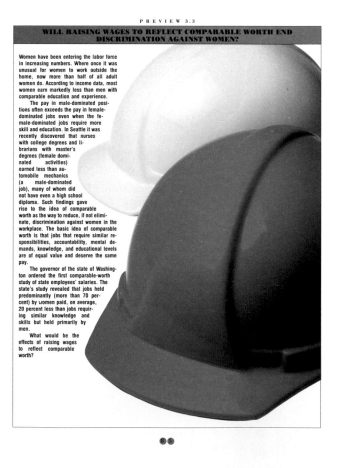

PREVIEW 3.3

**WILL RAISING WAGES TO REFLECT COMPARABLE WORTH END
DISCRIMINATION AGAINST WOMEN?**

Women have been entering the labor force in increasing numbers. Where once it was unusual for women to work outside the home, now more than half of all adult women do. According to income data, most women earn markedly less than men with comparable education and experience.

The pay in male-dominated positions often exceeds the pay in female-dominated jobs even when the female-dominated jobs require more skill and education. In Seattle it was recently discovered that nurses with college degrees and librarians with master's degrees (female dominated activities) earned less than automobile mechanics (a male-dominated job), many of whom did not have even a high school diploma. Such findings gave rise to the idea of comparable worth as the way to reduce, if not eliminate, discrimination against women in the workplace. The basic idea of comparable worth is that jobs that require similar responsibilities, accountability, mental demands, knowledge, and educational levels are of equal value and deserve the same pay.

The governor of the state of Washington ordered the first comparable-worth study of state employees' salaries. The state's study revealed that jobs held predominantly (more than 70 percent) by women paid, on average, 20 percent less than jobs requiring similar knowledge and skills but held primarily by men.

What would be the effects of raising wages to reflect comparable worth?

83

▲
*Chapter previews set up economic problems that will be
analyzed at the end of the chapter using chapter
concepts.*

Boxed applications provide brief examples of how economic concepts help make sense of real-world situations.

▼

A P P L I C A T I O N

3.1

MOTHERS TO BE AND
THE LAW OF DEMAND

Just before midnight on a cold, rainy Seattle night, a TV news reporter and cameramen from a local TV news program arrived at the parking lot of a hospital for a fast-breaking story. In each of several cars in the lot sat a pregnant woman with her husband. The reporter tried to interview several of the soon-to-be mothers, all of whom were clearly in labor and equally clearly didn't want to talk about it. The reporter then spoke with two of the husbands, who said they didn't have insurance that covered maternity care.

Then at the stroke of midnight, in front of the cameras, all of the car doors opened at the same time, and each expectant woman made her way slowly across the parking lot and through the emergency room door. The TV cameras following the procession into the hospital revealed pandemonium. Each husband was demanding that his wife be admitted first, and most wives were asking only to be allowed to lie down. The reporter managed a hurried interview with a harried hospital worker, who stated in no uncertain terms, "This happens every night, and I am getting real tired of it."

The very next night, the TV reporter interviewed the mothers, each holding her newborn child. These interviews revealed that since none of the families involved had medical insurance, each family would have to pay all the costs of delivery. The hospital charged $240 a day and counted any part of a day as a whole day. If an expectant mother checked in at 11 p.m., she was charged for that entire day. Rather than pay $240 for one hour of care, the new mothers had elected to tough it out in the parking lot until after midnight.

The TV reporter also interviewed the hospital administrator, who announced that the hospital would be changing its pricing policy and would now charge an hourly rate of $10 per hour for less than a full day. When the price of one hour of care fell from $240 to $10 for women who found themselves in labor at 11:00 p.m., there was an increase in the quantity of hospital care demanded.

Women whose labor was still manageable were no longer likely to wait the extra hour if they were already at the hospital, because the cost of the one hour of care they would receive between 11:00 p.m. and midnight was now only $10 rather than $240. Thus, to the extent that conditions allow, even women in labor can reduce or expand their consumption of hospital care by an hour in response to a price change, providing another example of the working of the law of demand.

For a high-rise apartment, the additional cost of providing two exits to the outside may exceed the additional benefits of reducing the risk of injury or death from fire. Lower-cost substitutes for an extra door, such as smoke alarms, fire extinguishers, or "No Smoking" signs, may also reduce the risk of injury or death from fire.

Similarly, the statement that everyone should have the medical care he or she needs appears to be a sound statement, but how much medical care does a person need? Most people would agree that persons seriously injured in automobile accidents should have immediate medical attention whether they can pay for it or not. Also, a person suffering from a heart attack or cancer is clearly in need of medical care. How about the man with influenza or the woman with athlete's foot? Are they also in need? The costs of treating influenza and athlete's foot are real. There is, and always will be, a limited number of physicians. If their time is used treating the needs of flu sufferers and persons with itchy feet, they are not available to treat patients with heart disease and lung cancer.

If medical care, like any scarce good, is made free to consumers, there is no incentive to economize on its use, even if the doctors do not charge a fee. Flu sufferers will be tempted to substitute a trip to the doctor for taking two aspirins and going to bed. Persons with itchy feet might well decide they need professional attention rather than purchasing an over-the-counter medication from their pharmacist.

For purposes of economic analysis, a need turns out to be a want when closely examined. The question then becomes: To what degree are

TABLE 3.2
The Supply Schedule for Wheat

PRICE (DOLLARS PER BUSHEL)	QUANTITY SUPPLIED (MILLIONS OF BUSHELS PER YEAR)
0	0
1	10
2	20
3	30
4	40
5	50
6	60
7	70

Demand, which reflects the forces operating on buyers in a market, represents one-half of the forces that affect market price. Supply, which reflects the forces operating on sellers, makes up the other half.

FACTORS AFFECTING SUPPLY IN A MARKET
As in the case of demand schedules, there are both price and nonprice factors that affect supply.

PRICE AND SUPPLY
The quantities of goods and services that sellers are willing to supply to the market also depend on the price of the good. Suppliers, like demanders, also follow the fundamental postulate of economics as illustrated by the **law of supply.**

The law of supply is the principle that as the price at which a good can be sold increases, more of that good will be offered for sale when other things are held constant.

The market price represents the benefit that suppliers receive from selling in the market. As the benefit to suppliers increases with a rise in the price, sellers will respond by offering more in the market. Thus a positive relationship exists between price and the quantity supplied. More will be supplied as the price of the good increases. When economists discuss the relationship between price and supply along a given supply curve, they use the term *quantity supplied.*

A **supply schedule** shows the amounts of a good or service that individuals or firms will offer for sale at various prices. A higher price will induce suppliers to offer more of a good for sale in the market.

A supply schedule is a tabulation of the relationship between price and the quantity of a good offered for sale; as price increases, the quantity supplied increases.

A possible supply schedule for wheat is shown in Table 3.2. If the price of wheat is $1 per bushel, the quantity offered in the market will be 10 million bushels. If the price of wheat is $2 per bushel, the quantity supplied in the market will be 20 million bushels. A further price increase to $5 per bushel will increase the quantity supplied to 50 million bushels.

▲
In-text definitions are highlighted for easy reference.

Full-color graphs, many with detailed teaching captions, help students use graphs to understand economic concepts.
▼

FIGURE 3.7
Disequilibrium in the Wheat Market

Disequilibrium exists when a market does not clear because the quantity demanded does not equal the quantity supplied. This will happen when the price is not equal to the equilibrium price. Suppose, as shown in Part A, that the market price for wheat is initially $6 per bushel, which exceeds the equilibrium price of $3.50. In this case the quantity demanded will be 10 million bushels and the quantity supplied will be 60 million bushels. The quantity supplied exceeds the quantity demanded, creating a *surplus*. As long as a surplus exists, there will be an incentive for some suppliers to offer lower prices, and price will fall to the equilibrium value.

Part B shows the case in which the price is below the equilibrium price. Suppose the price is $2 per bushel, in which case the quantity demanded will exceed the quantity supplied, creating a *shortage*. When a shortage exists, some buyers will have an incentive to offer higher prices rather than do without, and the price will rise to the equilibrium price of $3.50 per bushel.

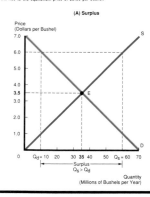
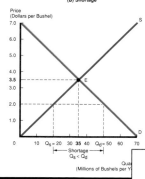

amount of the shortage. Nevertheless, a shortage will continue to exist until the price reaches the equilibrium price of $3.50, for only at the equilibrium price will the quantity demanded just equal the quantity supplied.

The equilibrium price is discovered in the market by this process of bidding by persons who are dissatisfied with the existing price. Only at the equilibrium price will all buyers and sellers be satisfied with the existing quantities. When no person has any incentive to buy or sell more, the market has reached the equilibrium price.

BENEFITS OF A MARKET

Adam Smith, generally considered to be the first great economist, described the benefits of a market (or industry, as he called it) in a famous passage in his book *The Wealth of Nations*. He likened the workings of a market to an invisible hand:

> He generally, indeed neither intends to promote the public interest, nor knows how much he is promoting it. . . . He intends only his own security;

PREVIEW 3.3 ANALYSIS

RAISING WAGES TO REFLECT COMPARABLE WORTH

"**B**eep, Beep! Yale's Cheap" read one sign carried by a picket from Local 34 of the Federation of University Employees during a strike of staff workers at Yale University. The picket didn't mean tuition — she meant the wages Yale paid female employees. Her local had determined that the University paid truck drivers, gardeners, cooks, and campus police — all male-dominated occupations that did not require a college degree — more than was paid to staff workers, such as administrative assistants, secretaries, and librarians, which at Yale are all female-dominated occupations. Many of the female-dominated occupations actually were held by persons with college degrees. Local 34 had had enough and demanded comparable wages for jobs of comparable worth. Yale replied that raising wages to reflect comparable worth was not in women's best interest. Raising wages in female-dominated jobs to match the wages of male-dominated occupations would, by increasing the incentives to stay in their present occupations, mire women in dead-end jobs. On the basis of this statement, Local 34 went on strike, supported by many students and faculty.

The strike at Yale occurred two decades after the passage of the Equal Pay Act of 1963 and the 1964 Civil Rights Act, which made illegal sex discrimination on the job or in access to employment opportunities. Yet today females earn less than males on the average, not because these laws are widely ignored, but because women and men are not distributed uniformly throughout the work force. The occupations dominated by women tend to pay less than those dominated by men.

In Seattle, for example, mechanics (a male-dominated occupation) are paid more than nurses or librarians (female-dominated professions), even though these female-dominated professions require more education and entail higher levels of responsibility than does the occupation of fixing cars. Moreover, nurses and librarians often have advanced professional degrees, while some mechanics do not even possess high school diplomas.

Frustrations at market outcomes like these have led to pressure to adjust wages according to the principle of comparable worth. Proponents of paying according to comparable worth assert that within a firm, jobs should be valued in terms of the skill, effort, and responsibilities required. If two jobs are comparable in these characteristics, they should receive equal compensation. According to advocates of the principle of comparable worth, the interaction of the supply and demand for workers in labor markets results in such obvious inequities that it should be replaced with a more equitable system based on comparable worth.

Supporters of the comparable-worth principle have made some progress toward its adoption. Several bills have been introduced in Congress and at state and local levels. More than 30 states have passed comparable-worth laws regulating state employment practices, but many states have been slow to take action. Only two states, Minnesota and Washington, have actually appropriated funds to remove pay inequities at the state level.

Several city governments have also adopted comparable-worth policies. In Colorado Springs 36 female city hall secretaries complained that the city auto mechanics (all men) were scheduled to get much larger raises than they were. Although the Equal Pay Act requires equal pay for the same job, it does not apply to workers doing different jobs. The secre-

▲
Preview analyses use chapter concepts to evaluate the problems presented in the chapter previews.

The list of required economic concepts helps students review important ideas presented in the chapter. Key questions review basic chapter content. Problems ask students to use chapter concepts.
▼

REQUIRED ECONOMIC CONCEPTS

Market	Substitution effect
Industry	Income effect
Competitive (price-taker) market	Demand schedule
Imperfectly competitive (price-searcher) market	Demand curve
	Market demand curve
Purely competitive market	Law of supply
Externalities	Supply schedule
Wants	Supply curve
Demands	Market supply curve
Fundamental postulate of economics	Equilibrium price
Law of demand	Surplus
Law of diminishing marginal value	Shortage
(or utility)	Equilibrium quantity

KEY QUESTIONS

1. How does a market facilitate trade?
2. What are the characteristics of a purely competitive market?
3. What are market externalities?
4. What does equilibrium in the market signify?
5. What is the law of demand? What variables affect demand?
6. What factors affect the quantity demanded?
7. What is the law of diminishing marginal value?
8. What is the substitution effect? The income effect?
9. What is the difference between need and demand?
10. What is the law of supply?
11. How is the market demand curve derived from individual demand curves? The supply curve from individual supply curves?
12. What is the law of increasing costs? What relation does it have to the supply?
13. What does a shortage or excess demand indicate?
14. What does surplus or excess supply indicate?

PROBLEMS

Price per Unit

1. Refer to the accompanying graph depicting the U.S. sugar market in answering questions below.
   a. What is the market situation at price P_2?
   b. Suppose the government sets a floor price on sugar at P_1, that is, a price which a lower price cannot be charged by the farmer. Which will be larger, quantity demanded or quantity supplied?
   c. Suppose, instead, a ceiling price of P_3 is set by the government, that is, above which it is illegal to charge. Will quantity supplied be greater or quantity demanded?
   d. Suppose the floor-price regulation is removed. Assuming the market is competitive, what will be the final market price be?

---

10. A two-good economy produces ballpoint pens and loose-leaf notebooks, as shown in the illustration.
    a. What is the opportunity cost of producing three loose-leaf notebooks? Of producing the third loose-leaf notebook?
    b. Derive the supply curve for loose-leaf notebooks from the illustration.
11. How can one argue that it is more efficient for a firm to produce another bookcase when it is already operating at a loss? Or is the statement ridiculous?
12. How can demand increase and supply increase and yet the price of grapes increase as the quantity of grapes produced expands over a period of several years?
13. It is common to see or hear about long lines of people waiting — sometimes overnight — to buy tickets for rock concerts.
    a. What does this fact tell you about the costs of waiting in line to these people? To support your answer, what casual evidence can you gather from observing who is standing in these lines?
    b. What do the waiting lines tell you about the price of the tickets?
    c. What reasons do managers of rock groups have for setting ticket prices at the levels they do? Are live concerts the only source of revenue to rock groups? Explain.
    d. Why would an airline pilot not be likely to stand in line to buy a rock concert ticket? How would he or she probably try to obtain a ticket?
14. Scalping tickets is illegal nearly everywhere in the United States. Scalpers have sold bowl tickets at prices ranging from $400 to $600 each. They buy the tickets from the players themselves and from cashiers who acquire them at the printed price and then resell them at a markup.
    a. What can you conclude about the official price of the bowl tickets?
    b. Are scalpers violating the law of demand by selling the tickets for $500 each?
    c. In general, can scalpers lose money scalping? What are other risks they take? Is their activity costless?
    d. Do scalpers actually provide benefits to customers? Or do they increase transaction costs to people desiring otherwise unavailable tickets?
    e. Do scalpers cheat buyers because they charge more than they "ought" to, or do they allocate resources in a more efficient manner?

APPLICATION ANALYSIS

1. In the thirteenth century the famous scholastic philosopher Thomas Aquinas argued for a "just price" based on "the cost of raw materials and labor." He also spoke about a "just wage," with workers being paid in accordance with their social position, their skills, and the nature of the work. In the 1980s the issue of a fair wage for women emerged along with the concept of comparable worth discussed in the chapter. Dissimilar jobs that are of equal "intrinsic value" should be equally compensated, the argument goes, based on a point system of evaluating occupations. Thus in Minnesota a librarian's job was valued as equal to a firefighter's. Thus a policy that started out as "equal pay for equal work" (in the same job) became "equal pay for equal value."
    a. Is there a similarity between the views of Aquinas and today's comparable-worth advocates?
    b. As the problem is stated, how do you believe the cost of raw materials and labor in the thirteenth century and the wage of the auto mechanic today were determined? Is the auto mechanic's wage a "fair wage"? How do you know?
    c. What is "intrinsic value"? Do you think your assessment of it may differ from others' assessment? Will the point-determination level of various jobs be affected by who is on the point evaluation board?

▲
The application analysis gives students an opportunity to test their ability to use economic reasoning.

CONTENTS IN BRIEF

CONTENTS

Appendix to Chapter 3   The Economics of Information 122

4

How Competitive Markets Function 132

5

The Economics of the Public Sector   174

Appendix to Chapter 5   Government Expenditures and Revenues 211

11

Aggregate Supply, National Income, and the Price Level 436

12

Fiscal Policy 462

MACROECONOMICS
Principles & Applications

P A R T 1

INTRODUCING
ECONOMICS

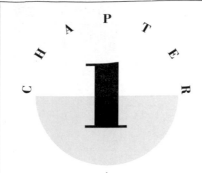

C H A P T E R

1

BEGINNING TO APPLY ECONOMICS
Scarcity and Choice

IN THIS CHAPTER YOU WILL LEARN:

That scarcity is the source of economic problems

•

Why all economic problems involve choice

•

How economists study economic problems

•

How to do your first formal economic thinking

•

How to apply the basic postulates of economics to economic problems

WHY IS A VAN GOGH PAINTING OF A SUNFLOWER WORTH $40 MILLION?

On March 30, 1987, the art world was stunned when a bid of $39.9 million won the auction contest for one of the seven sunflower paintings Vincent van Gogh produced. The breathtaking winning bid was at that time triple the highest price ever paid for a painting at auction. The painting was offered by a family named Beatty that had purchased it in 1934 for $10,000. Reportedly, the painting's original chrome yellow had darkened to ocher and brown over the years, and the painting's surface had calloused. However, the deteriorating condition of the painting did not discourage bidders. There were about a dozen serious bidders in the running until the bidding reached $25 million, after which point there were only two. Finally, at $39.9 million, there was only one bidder — a man who had just paid a record price for a work of art.

What sense can we make of such a sale? Why would anyone pay for a painting an amount of money that would buy a 40-story building in most metropolitan areas of the country or a Boeing 747 jumbo jet airliner? How would an economist explain the events that took place that evening at the auction?

HOW SHOULD AN AVERAGE CITIZEN EVALUATE "STAR WARS"?

In 1983 President Ronald Reagan announced a new national defense program called the Strategic Defense Initiative (the SDI program). The nation's press quickly renamed it "Star Wars." The purpose of the SDI program is to develop and deploy an antiballistic-missile system to intercept and destroy intercontinental missiles aimed at the United States. If such a system existed, it would be possible to abandon the nation's current defensive strategy of mutual assured destruction (MAD), which is based on guaranteed massive nuclear retaliation *after* an attack.

The president believed that the SDI program was preferable to MAD, was technologically feasible, and was worth the $100 billion or more that it would cost. This belief was not universally shared. Many detractors did not think it was possible to develop such a system at that time, and, even if it were, they believed the SDI program would not improve U.S. national security.

The decision on whether or not to develop the SDI program is a political one. How should an ordinary citizen, one who is neither a scientist nor a military person, form an opinion about such a program? What are the economic implications of proceeding with this project?

IS THE 55 MPH SPEED LIMIT GOOD ECONOMIC POLICY?

Every driver of an automobile is familiar with the federal 55 MPH speed limit. The law limiting highway speeds to a maximum of 55 MPH was passed in 1974 in an attempt to conserve on gasoline during the energy crisis. Besides reducing the nation's consumption of petroleum, the 55 MPH speed limit had the pleasant additional effect of significantly reducing the number of highway traffic fatalities. This effect led to a bumper sticker that reads: "55 miles per hour: A law we can live with."

The federal 55 MPH speed limit has its opponents. Many people can remember when the highway speed limit was set by the states and averaged 70 MPH. You could get where you were going much faster at 70 MPH than at 55 MPH. In 1987 opponents won a partial repeal of the law. It is now legally permissible to drive 65 MPH in rural areas of the nation's interstate highway system, but the speed limit remains 55 MPH in urban areas and on noninterstate highways.

Is the 55 MPH speed limit good economic policy? Are the gasoline and lives saved worth more than the additional travel time a lowered speed limit requires? The tools you will learn about in this chapter will help you answer these questions.

• INTRODUCTION •

What do such diverse phenomena as an auction of a van Gogh painting, "Star Wars," and the effects of the 55 MPH speed limit have in common? Each of the problems they present, plus some others we shall encounter, requires economic analysis for a solution or an evaluation. In this chapter we shall begin the study of economics by developing the basic tools of the economic way of thinking. With these tools, each of us can learn to evaluate alternatives and to become a more rational economic-decision maker. •

THE SCARCITY PROBLEM

It may be possible to imagine a society in which all wants can be satisfied, but such a society has never existed. Many societies have among their myths and traditions a belief that there once was a golden age, an earlier period of human history when humanity wanted for nothing — a period when scarcity was unknown. In Greek and Roman mythology, the golden age was a period of innocence and abundance. All manner of food was available for the taking. Milk and honey reportedly flowed in the rivers. In the Bible, the Garden of Eden is described as providing within its borders everything that God thought Adam and Eve could possibly desire. The golden age of Greco-Roman tradition and the Garden of Eden of Christianity both depicted a world in which scarcity did not exist — a period of time when wants could always be immediately satisfied.

In both traditions the extent of humanity's wants appears to have been underestimated. The human beings in both situations wanted to possess more knowledge than was available. The natural curiosity of human beings led to havoc. Pandora, according to Roman legend, opened the famous box from which sprang all of humanity's ills. Adam and Eve ate of the forbidden fruit of knowledge and were expelled from their garden paradise. Thereafter, according to legend, people have had to labor and to suffer to provide for their wants. The world after the fall has had a perpetual problem with scarcity — there has not been enough resources to satisfy all the demands of individuals and societies.

Take a moment and list some of the things you would like that you don't now have — a list of your unsatisfied wants. Perhaps you would like a new compact-disc player, some new clothes, a new car, more time, a straight-A grade average, and/or a new friend. If your list of wants at the moment exceeds your capacity to satisfy those wants, as it surely does, you have a scarcity problem. Moreover, this will always be the case.

You may think your scarcity problem exists only because you are relatively poor, but it also exists for persons whom we normally think of as very rich. Joanna Carson, the ex-wife of TV personality Johnny Carson, was awarded $36,000 *a month* in her divorce settlement. She soon found that it was not enough, and she returned to court to ask for $12,000 more a month.

Michael Nesmith, now a video producer, was one of the original Monkees, a rock group that imitated the Beatles. During the peak of the Monkees' popularity, Nesmith had more than $2 million in his checking account and was concerned that he would run out of spaces on the accounting form to record his growing bank balance. He needn't have worried. Within a few years he was broke and in debt to the Internal Revenue

GETTING BY ON
$1 MILLION A YEAR

You have to be very good at what you do to make $1 million or more a year, especially if you did not inherit wealth. Fewer than one-half of 1 percent of all U.S. taxpayers (16,662 in 1985) report incomes of more than $1 million. Would making seven figures a year free you from the scarcity problems that plague everyone else? *Forbes*, in its October 27, 1986, issue, investigated how several self-made millionaires actually live.

Dan, an East Coast stockbroker who makes several million dollars a year, says that someone in his situation is "wealthy enough to have an expensive life-style but not so wealthy that your money is inexhaustible." Susan, a millionaire of two years standing, earns her income selling real estate. "It's true I make more money, much more," Susan says. "But the nature of my business — and without my business I wouldn't make the money — is that expenses are higher. In real estate you need a certain image, from what you wear to what you drive." Susan, who is a single parent, owns two $30,000 automobiles even though she is the family's only licensed driver.

Dan has earned more than $1 million in each of the last ten years. He is married with two children. In a good year he earns $5 million, in a poor year about $3 million. Dan says: "I always feel insecure because I'm in the stock market. My family is used to a certain life-style. We shop in certain places, go to certain resorts. It's all very expensive. I'm supporting homes, people who work for me, cars. In the stock market, it's not a guaranteed income."

Dan manages a disposable income of between $1.8 and $2.4 million a year. Maintenance on his 18-room apartment, for which he paid $1 million five years ago, is $3,500 a month. Servants cost him $50,000 a year. He owns a 20-room home in the Hamptons on Long Island that costs $100,000 a year to maintain plus another $6,000 in taxes. A cottage in France costs him $20,000 a year to keep up. His private jet costs $20,000 a year to maintain. The family spends $200,000 a year on vacations, gives $100,000 to charity, and spends another $100,000 on art. Dan's two children, both in private schools, are thoroughly used to the rich life and assume that the best is all there is. "They wouldn't know what not sitting middle orchestra for an event was," Dan says. Is there anything else he would like to have besides a more secure source of income? Yes, if Dan had more money, he would like to have a yacht. Dan, despite his relative affluence, has not satisfied his material wants.

Susan is a divorced mother with three children. She is still concentrating on acquiring the basics: a home, cars, and an education for her children. She recently purchased a $300,000 house with wooded acreage. She bought $40,000 worth of furniture and plans to buy $60,000 more. She has begun to collect antiques, and she has a $50,000 collection of Waterford crystal. She spent $30,000 to install a swimming pool, but she figures it will save her the $21,000 she used to spend sending her kids to camp during the summer. She spent $12,000 to put braces on her children's teeth, and child care runs $11,000 a year.

Susan spends $300 a week on business clothes and more for fun clothes (she bought a $7,000 mink and several $1,000 evening dresses). "I just buy what I want and when the bills come I pay them," she says. Children's clothing is budgeted for $4,000 a year. Susan spends $400 a week in restaurants, $1,000 a month on phone calls, and $1,200 a month in car payments. She is saving up for her children's prep school and college educations, which she figures will cost a total of about $1 million. What would she like to buy but can't at the moment? She would like, as did Dan, a more secure source of income; real estate is a cyclical business. And like Dan, she wants to purchase a cabin cruiser, something small, about 40 feet! Also a second home would be nice.

Susan and Dan are rich by most standards, but they still don't have enough. They live well, but they still worry about money — or rather the lack of it. If $1 million a year isn't enough to solve the scarcity problem, then few of us will escape the problems created by scarcity.[1]

---

[1] *Forbes*, October 27, 1986, 48–50.

Service. He was forced to sell his Hollywood mansion and his expensive automobiles and moved into the building he had purchased to house his chauffeur.

Malcolm S. Forbes, owner of *Forbes* magazine, would like to have a major painting by van Gogh, but, despite the fact that he is very rich, he has not been able to satisfy this desire. All individuals are dissatisfied with their material lives in the sense that they would always like more. There is never enough. Everyone has a scarcity problem.

What is true for individuals is, in the case of scarcity, also true for society. The federal government has great trouble balancing its budget. The demands placed upon the government greatly exceed the willingness of our elected officials to tax the voters. There are always worthwhile social projects that could be undertaken: The condition of the poor could be improved; more schools could be constructed and more teachers trained; more highways could be built or rebuilt; more air traffic controllers, police officers, and fire fighters could be hired; more could be spent on national defense. The list could go on and on.

THE LAW OF SCARCITY

Because of what economists call the **law of scarcity**, humanity has a problem with **scarce goods** that cannot be avoided.

> *The law of scarcity states that for every person and society some goods are scarce. These goods are not available in sufficient amounts to satisfy existing wants.*

Not all good things in the world are scarce goods. Some goods are available in sufficient abundance that they are **free goods** — everyone has as much of them as they desire. They can use as much of a free good as they like without diminishing the amount of this good that is available for others to enjoy. A beautiful summer day, while it lasts, is a free good, as is a scenic view. A good is free only if it is not scarce.

> *A free good is a good that is available in sufficient abundance to satisfy the wants of all who wish to consume it.*

Most goods are not available in nature in sufficient abundance to be free; most goods are scarce. When you consume one unit of a scarce good, there is generally one less unit of it available. Apples are scarce goods. Eat an apple, and there is one less available for you and others to consume. Buy an automobile, and there is one less automobile that your neighbor could potentially enjoy.

SCARCITY OF RESOURCES

We have seen that wants are unlimited but that goods and services are scarce. Resources are valuable to a society because they can be used to produce goods and services. The ultimate source of scarcity lies in the limited availability of resources. Productive resources are sometimes called the **factors of production.**

> *The factors of production are the land, labor, capital, and entrepreneurial ability that can be used to produce goods and services.*

Productive resources are valuable because they can be combined to produce goods and services. They serve as inputs into the production process out of which come the final goods and services we wish to consume. The more resources that are available, the more goods and services there are that can be produced. Resources are always owned by someone who must be paid to allow their use in the production process.

When we speak of resources in economic theory, we generally do so abstractly. We talk of land, labor, capital, and entrepreneurship as if all units of each of these categories were identical — one unit of land, for example, is the same as any other unit of land. Economists, of course, know that one acre of land is uniquely different from any other in its location. As accurate as this distinction is in reality, it serves only to needlessly complicate the analysis for most purposes. When the unique properties of land, or of any of the other factors of production for that matter, are required for an analysis, as they are on occasion, the crucial differences will be explicitly taken into account. So:

Land includes all the natural resources — the gifts of nature — that are useful in producing goods. Arable land, forests, mineral resources, and oil deposits, all of which are useful in the production process, are included in the category. Land is necessary for farming, for building factories and residences, and for constructing highways, railways, and airports. Until recently, all productive activities employed land to a greater (farming) or lesser (industry) extent. Only with the advent of the space shuttle and the proposed space station can some productive activities like manufacturing pure medicines take place without land as an input.

Land, including natural resources, is relatively fixed in amount — only so much exists in nature. Land will be owned by someone who must be paid to allow the land to be used in the production process. The payments to land are called *rents*. Generally, land, together with its natural resources, must be improved over its natural state to be useful for production. This improvement involves the application of another factor of production — labor.

Labor represents the human content of resources. Almost every individual is a potential supplier of labor. Labor is an inclusive term that refers to the physical talents of men and women that can be directed to produce goods and services. The services of production line workers, teachers, farmers, as well as those of physicians, economists, and professional athletes, are all considered labor. To induce individuals to supply their labor, they must be paid. The payment to labor is known as *wages*, which vary among occupations. Generally, the labor force increases with population growth, but its quality can also be improved by education. The variation in wages earned by occupation is due in large measure to the skills that workers have acquired. That is where the third factor of production — capital — comes in.

Capital refers to manufactured inputs that augment the production process. It is generally thought of as being composed of the buildings, equipment, machines, and inventories that are used to augment land and labor in the production of goods and services. Such things comprise physical capital. Capital is important because the quantity of goods and services that a given amount of land and labor can produce can be increased by adding capital. Suppose you wish to paint a wall. It will be finished faster and better if you acquire a brush and a ladder than if you use your hand to apply the paint and your legs to jump up the wall.

The same is true if capital is embodied in human beings through training. Education and job-related training can improve the efficiency of labor. If you can read the instructions on the paint can label and have acquired some competence with the paint brush, you will be able to paint the wall both faster and better than if you do not possess these abilities. Capital embodied in human beings is called *human capital*.

Capital is created and amassed from the savings of the economy. Capital can be invested either in machines or in human beings to make land and labor more productive. The increased output that results from applying capital allows the owners of capital to be paid for its use. The payment to capital is called *interest*. It is important to distinguish between capital and money. Money is not capital, although it is sometimes used to acquire capital goods. Money facilitates trades, but it does not enter directly into the production process as resources do.

Finally, land, labor, and capital must be combined and directed to produce goods and services. That is where entrepreneurship, the fourth factor of production, comes in.

Entrepreneurship refers to the special human abilities needed to employ the other resources to produce goods and services. It is the entrepreneur who bears the risk of hiring the other factors of production to produce goods and services. There is usually no guarantee that an economic venture will be profitable, other than that provided by the entrepreneur. It is the entrepreneur who hires laborers and guarantees that their wages will be paid, who rents the land and guarantees that the rent will be paid, who obtains the capital and contracts to pay a rate of interest. It is the entrepreneur who organizes the factors of production in the production process and sells the product, who decides what to produce and how much, what factors of production to employ, and how much of each to hire. The entrepreneur's goal is to gain a profit by selling the firm's output for more than the total costs that must be paid to the owners of the factors of production. But there is no guarantee that this goal will be achieved — it may or it may not. The entrepreneur thus bears the risks involved while performing the necessary task of organizing production.

Entrepreneurs not only bear the risks of organizing production, but they also look for opportunities to introduce new products and production techniques and assume the risks of making them work. Entrepreneurs are the driving force in the economy, organizing the production process in a never-ending search for profitable opportunities.

None of the productive resources discussed above are available in sufficient amounts to be free. All are scarce.

SCARCITY AND CHOICE

Scarcity presents a major problem for society. If there is never enough, as in the case of a scarce good, then from among the many good things we could possibly have we must choose the few goods we will actually acquire. *Scarcity requires choice.* A child learns early in life that a quarter will not buy a pack of gum, a candy bar, and a package of mints, and that he or she will have to choose one thing from among these three good things. College students soon learn that they cannot get a good grade on their economics test and spend the weekend partying. They will have to choose. Society cannot have more schools, parks, and aircraft and at the same time allow its individual members to have more goods of their own. Society must choose.

Only scarce goods involve choices. Free goods, because they are so abundant, do not require a choice.

DEFINITION OF ECONOMICS

Economics is the study of how choices are made in the face of scarcity.

Economics is the study of how and with what consequences individuals and society, when faced with a scarcity problem, choose (1) from among scarce goods, (2) to employ scarce resources, and (3) to distribute scarce goods and resources.

Because of scarcity, every society must devise an economic system that provides a means of determining (1) what goods among the many desirable scarce goods will be produced, (2) how scarce resources will be employed to produce these goods, and (3) who will receive the limited amount of goods that are produced. These decisions are based on the "what, how, and for whom" questions, each of which implies that choices must be made. Sometimes economists reduce these three questions to one: How are resources to be allocated? Whatever the form of the question, society cannot avoid the choices that are required.

AN ECONOMIC SYSTEM: A UNIVERSAL REQUIREMENT

Each society must develop an **economic system** that will enable it to make the required choices.

An economic system is the institutional means by which scarce resources are allocated to satisfy the wants of society.

The institutions of a society are made up of the nation's laws, habits, ethics, and customs. Institutions govern the economic system and direct its behavior. The goal of any economic system is to obtain the greatest possible benefits from the scarce resources available and to distribute the output in a way that is acceptable to the members of the society.

Economic systems are classified sometimes according to the way decisions are made, and sometimes according to the ownership of resources. When grouped in terms of the ownership of the means of production, there are two types of systems: **capitalism** and **socialism**.

Capitalism is an economic system based on private ownership of the factors of production and on decentralized decision making in free markets.

Socialism is an economic system in which property is collectively owned and decision making is in the hands of the community, generally the government.

When characterized in terms of decision making, there are again two basic types of economic systems: a laissez-faire system (translated *free-market system*), which is sometimes referred to as the *price system* or the *free-enterprise system*, and a command system, sometimes called a *planned system*, which relies on collective decision making to allocate resources.

A laissez-faire system is a system that relies on the initiative of individual decision makers as they exchange goods and services in markets.

A *market* is an arrangement through which buyers and sellers trade goods and resources. The U.S. economy relies mainly on individual decision making within a market economy to allocate resources. Since there are not sufficient goods and services to satisfy everyone's desires, prices are used to allocate the scarce goods. Prices are determined in the markets and measure the scarcity of goods. The market-determined price encourages suppliers to offer for sale the amount of a good that buyers are prepared to buy. When a price increases, it provides an incentive for buyers to voluntarily conserve on the use of the scarce good and for suppliers to increase its availability. In the final analysis, scarce goods and resources flow to those who are willing to pay the most for them.

> *A command system is one that allocates resources by means of communal joint decisions.*

A command economy can range from primitive communism, in which all decisions are taken collectively, to a planned national economy in which the government passes laws and sets regulations compelling behavior and in which the government taxes and spends to provide goods and services directly to the society. In both cases decisions are made collectively rather than by individuals and must necessarily be political in nature. Primitive communism may exist in families that collectively make household decisions. When entire economies take the form of a command system, the government owns the means of production and makes most of the decisions on how resources will be allocated. The economies of the U.S.S.R. and mainland China provide examples of a command system.

In the U.S. economy, the allocative decisions are mostly left to individuals operating in markets, with the government providing those functions that the market performs poorly or not at all. Because the economic system employed in the United States is a combination of the laissez-faire and the command types, it can be called a *mixed economy*.

COMPETITION, RATIONING, AND DISCRIMINATION

All economic systems must deal with three inevitable consequences of scarcity: competition, rationing, and discrimination. The existence of scarcity necessarily implies that individuals burdened with unlimited wants will compete among themselves to obtain as many of the scarce goods and resources as possible. The nature of this *competition* will be influenced by the institutions that govern the economic system, as we shall see later in this chapter. Competition can have both constructive and destructive effects, but it cannot be avoided if scarcity is present. The goal of any economic system should be to channel competition into constructive practices and away from destructive pursuits.

Since there will never be enough scarce goods to go around, the economic system will have to ration these scarce goods in some manner. Some persons will obtain goods that others also desire. The economic system must establish a method for rationing scarce goods and resources among the many competing interests. *Rationing* is implied by scarcity and in turn implies that discrimination will exist. If there is not enough to satisfy all wants, those who remain unsatisfied have been discriminated against. Any economic system will therefore be forced to discriminate among individuals in the society.

Since *discrimination* cannot be avoided, an acceptable basis for discrimination must be established. In U.S. society it is illegal to discriminate on the basis of sex, creed, race, or age, but it is legal to discriminate on the basis of ability, performance, or knowledge.

The kind of economic system selected will influence the direction competition will take, the nature of the rationing system, and the forms of discrimination. All economic systems must take into account the reality that the methods chosen to allocate scarce goods will influence the performance of the economy.

Compare, for example, the various ways that grades could be assigned in your economics class. Most colleges and universities employ a grading system to evaluate how students are doing in their course work and to provide information to graduate and professional schools and to prospective employers on the intellectual qualifications and achievements of students. Grades are generally assigned on the basis of relative performance in class, but they could be distributed in some other way. Each alternative method will uniquely influence the competitive behavior of students, will ration the best grades differently, and will discriminate among students according to different criteria.

First, let us describe the economic system that your instructor probably employs. By design, good grades are scarce at your school. There are limited numbers of A's and B's available, a larger number of C's is available, D's are not very scarce, and failing grades are free. To qualify for a good grade, you will have to do better on the exams than most of the other students in the class. This means that you will have to learn relatively more economics than they do. Since the other students in the class also desire to share among the good grades and avoid the poor ones, they will be similarly motivated. Competition with your classmates will direct your behavior in a way that maximizes the amount of learning that takes place. Those students who learn the most economics will receive the better grades. Those who learn relatively less will receive the poorer grades.

A kind of market system is generally involved in awarding grades. Those students who are willing to put forth the most effort will generally perform best on the tests and receive the better grades. In a sense, those who are willing to pay the most in terms of learning the most economics will receive the better grades. This system channels competitive behavior into increasing the students' knowledge of economics instead of leading to less desirable results. Since the purpose of attending college is to obtain knowledge, most students recognize the fairness of the results from allocating resources in this manner. That doesn't mean that everyone is satisfied with the results, as almost everyone would like to have been awarded better grades. The law of scarcity is still at work.

To see why colleges employ this system, consider the experience of a former economics professor who decided to give all of his students A's and told them so at the beginning of the term. Student attendance at his lectures immediately began to decline and continued to decline until one day no one came. His students did not learn much economics that term, but they probably learned more history, mathematics, chemistry, and French, and they no doubt enjoyed more leisure than they would have if the economics course had been graded in a normal fashion. A's in the economics course became a free good, but A's in the other subjects the students were taking remained scarce goods. The economics students rationally reallocated their study efforts toward their other subjects where the added time could earn them better grades — but at the cost of a failure to learn economics.

Some of you may still not be convinced that competing for good grades is desirable. Just as scarce goods can be allocated in several ways other than through a market system, so also can scarce grades be distrib-

WHO MAKES THE COFFEE IN YOUR OFFICE?

Every society has to establish an economic system to organize the production and distribution of goods. Some systems seem to work better than others. Just as every society must organize the production and distribution of goods, almost every office must provide and distribute coffee. Who makes the coffee in your office?

Many of you have worked in an office and more will do so in the not too distant future. Anyone who works in an office will readily agree that the provision and distribution of coffee is a serious matter. Office coffee systems break down with monotonous frequency and when they do, tempers flare. The production and distribution of the office coffee can be an office manager's nightmare.

But it also provides the economist with a unique opportunity to observe how different economic systems, each designed to supply the office with a basic good — a cup of coffee — actually work in practice. In reality, the variety of systems for supplying the American office with coffee closely mirrors the variety of economic systems that exist throughout the world. Just as every economic system must answer the *what, how,* and *for whom* questions, so also must any system designed to supply the office with coffee.

The first of the fundamental questions is: *What to produce?* Should the coffee be regular or dark roast, with caffeine or decaffeinated? Should the coffee be brewed or instant? Should sugar be available and, if so, should it be real sugar or a sugar substitute? Should the cream be real cream, half and half, milk, or a nondairy substitute? If coffee is to be supplied, shouldn't tea also be available? How about hot chocolate?

How to produce the office coffee is no easier to decide. There are many ways to prepare coffee: percolate it, boil it, drip hot water through it, or add instant coffee to hot water. Each process requires a specialized piece of capital equipment that can be obtained in various sizes. Further complicating the *how* problem is that each method requires a different amount of labor to produce a pot of coffee. There are clearly economies to be considered in producing the office coffee. The more that is brewed at one time, the fewer noncoffee inputs are required per cup of coffee. Finally, in order to produce coffee, all of the necessary components must be brought together: ground or instant coffee, water, energy, capital, and labor. All must be available simultaneously, and their application to the task must be directed by someone.

Providing the labor to make the coffee is one of the major problems in every office. Making the coffee is often a mark of low status and has even been an issue in sex discrimination charges. Because relying on volunteers to make the coffee seldom works, some rule is usually employed. One such rule might be that the person who takes the last cup of coffee must make a fresh pot. Or a rotating list of coffee-making assignments may be employed. Often one person is assigned to make coffee and another to perform the clean-up chores.

Each possible rule creates incentives for behavior. Under a voluntary system, for example, some coffee drinkers carefully time their trips to the coffee bar and thereby never have to make a pot of coffee. The time they spend observing coffee consumption in order to be able to time their trips takes time away from their work. Other workers soon catch on to this behavior and start to keep track of who actually makes the coffee. The result is expressed ill will toward the shirkers and more time away from work in order to monitor the behavior of the suspected shirkers.

The final question is: *For whom will the coffee be produced?* Office coffee, like any scarce good, can be allocated to those who are willing to pay the price in either money or labor, to those who are willing to wait in line, or to those who have influence, offer bribes, or issue threats. Some of these methods are used more often than others, and variations on each have been repeatedly tried in offices throughout the country.

There are two functions that must be performed to produce coffee in an office. First, the ground or instant coffee itself, which is a scarce good, must be obtained. Second, the coffee must be brewed and distributed in some way among the office workers. Sometimes the employer buys the coffee, but more often the employees must rely on their own devices. In the economics department at the University of Washington, a monthly assessment purchased coffee, tea, and hot chocolate from a local supplier. This system broke down when noncoffee drinkers objected to subsidizing their coffee-drinking colleagues.

Next came a voluntary pay-as-you-go system, in which the coffee drinkers put a dime for each cup of coffee in a little dish next to the coffee pot. Tea and hot chocolate drinkers were too few in number to be included in this system and were left on their own. Unfortunately, not everyone paid every time he or she took a cup of coffee, and the dish repeatedly went broke. Moreover, there were arguments between the faculty and the secretarial staff about who should actually make the coffee.

uted in another way. Queuing (standing in line), favoritism, bribery, lottery, or violence are other ways that scarce goods can be allocated. Each of these methods is or has been used in our society to allocate scarce goods. Each could also be used to allocate the scarce grades in your economics class. Consider how each of these methods would influence the nature of student behavior, ration the good grades, and discriminate among students. How might each method, if it were used, affect the amount of economics learned in the class? Would you consider the results fair?

Have you ever stood in line to register for a class or to buy a movie or concert ticket? Has a class ever been closed before you got a chance to register? The scarce goods in these cases are provided to those who get

When a reporter for the student newspaper wrote a story on the problems the economics department was having in devising an economic system to distribute office coffee, the department created a committee to study the problem and to suggest a solution. The committee explored the following alternative systems:

1. *Primitive communism.* In a small office a few persons can agree to share the responsibilities of providing the office coffee. They can agree to share the cost and the duties involved. Communal decisions can answer the *what, how,* and *for whom* questions. The shirking of responsibility is always a potential problem, but when it happens, it can be quickly detected and peer pressure exerted to correct the problem.

What works in small groups often breaks down if it is tried in large offices. The problem of detecting shirking increases, and the coffee distribution system breaks down more frequently. The disturbance that this creates attracts the attention of the office manager or, as in this case, the department chairperson, who then sometimes takes direct control of the system. In this way a planned economy is substituted for the original communal effort.

2. *Command (planned) economy.* In a command economy, the administrative assistant or office manager usually takes charge. He or she decides what is to be produced and how it will be produced, designates the person responsible, and decides who qualifies for coffee. The administrative assistant may decide that only decaffeinated coffee and a cream substitute will be available, that the mail clerk will make a pot of coffee every two hours, and that only those persons who pay $2 a month to the coffee fund can take a cup. The preferences of the administrative assistant dictate *what* will be produced, *how* it will be produced, and ultimately *for whom* the coffee will be available. This system breaks down when people object to the limited choices available or when infrequent coffee drinkers object to subsidizing their more serious coffee-drinking co-workers.

3. *Laissez-faire (free-enterprise) system.* Under this type of economic system, individuals work out their own arrangements for acquiring coffee. A large number of diverse possibilities arise. Some persons will make their own; others will buy theirs either from a commercial establishment or from someone in the office. One of the virtues of this system is that, if the customers are willing to pay the price, a market system can satisfy a variety of intensities of desire. If coffee is wanted at a particular time, it will be provided, as will a choice of real cream or cream substitute. Tea, coffee, and hot chocolate drinkers will be accommodated. The extra cost of decentralized production involving more coffee pots than centralized production is more than outweighed by the reduced cost of less shirking and the increased benefit of more variety.

This system sometimes breaks down when some office members think there must be a better way and decide to supply coffee communally. After all, there are economies in making coffee for the entire office staff. If the office had a big coffee maker in a centrally located place, everyone could use it at a lower cost than if individuals acquired their own coffee. Collective memories are short. Many coffee drinkers don't remember

that the office has already tried to do this in the past.

The economics department committee that investigated the coffee problem found that the laissez-faire (free-enterprise) system was the best alternative and recommended that supplying coffee be the individual faculty member's responsibility. The system seems to have worked well. Coffee is still consumed by the faculty in their offices, and the coffee problem, if it exists, has at least stayed out of the student newspaper. Still, some economists are heard from time to time suggesting that if there were only a large communally owned coffee pot in a central place, then. . . .[2]

_____

[2] The author was reminded of this experience by Jane Shaw's article, "Who Makes the Coffee in Your Office?" *The Wall Street Journal,* March 10, 1986, 16.

there first. Suppose a first-come first-served (queuing) method were used to allocate the grades in your economics class. The first few students standing in front of your professor's door would receive A's, the next several would receive B's, and so on. *Queuing* would clearly reward those patient students with little else to do and penalize those for whom time was more precious, such as those who had jobs. Moreover, queuing would provide little incentive for a student to learn economics. Would you consider the allocation of grades to be fair in this case?

Another way to allocate scarce goods is through *favoritism.* Favoritism occurs when scarce goods are awarded on the basis of personal preference. Favoritism, if used in your class, would award good grades to those students who were most attractive to the professor and poor grades to those who were less attractive. The professor would be free to express through grades whatever biases he or she possessed. Favoritism would provide an incentive for students to behave in ways that would please the professor. Learning economics may or may not be a way of winning a high grade in this case. Being polite, attractive in appearance, and even reverential during lectures might be more effective. It is sometimes, wrongly, alleged that favoritism is employed in awarding grades. Have you ever heard a fellow student exclaim: "The instructor didn't like me!" as an explanation for a poor showing in a class? If this were true, would you think it fair?

Another way to allocate scarce goods is to bribe the decision maker to allow you to have it. *Bribery* is a way of obtaining a scarce grade by paying the professor for it. Those who would obtain the good grades under this system would be those who were willing to pay the most; the grades would have little to do with how well the highest payers had learned economics. A student looking for an A in economics would be advised to find a job to earn the money required to offer the biggest bribe rather than spend time studying. Being a good automobile mechanic, window washer, or baby-sitter might be a better way to obtain a good grade. If grades were actually distributed in this way, would you be satisfied with the outcome?

Some form of *lottery* is another way scarce goods can be allocated. A lottery allocates the scarce good by chance. Assigning good grades by chance would also destroy any incentive for students to learn economics. Whether a student received a good grade or a bad grade would depend entirely on the luck of the draw. Imagine what would happen if, when first attending an economics class, a student was given a card on which was recorded his or her course grade. Do you think such a student would be highly motivated to study economics that term? Would the outcome be satisfactory to you? Would your opinion change depending on the grade you received?

Finally, *violence* is sometimes used to allocate scarce goods. The famous phrase from the *Godfather* movies "Make them an offer they can't refuse" did not refer to an irresistibly attractive proposition but rather to the dire consequences of refusing. If violence against the economics professor were threatened or, heaven forbid, employed, the most vicious and the physically strongest students would no doubt receive the higher grades. Violence could also, of course, be used against fellow students to keep them from pressing rival claims for a good grade. Violence as a method of allocating scarce grades would not create a positive incentive for learning economics. Time would perhaps be better spent in learning self-defense. Employing violence as a method of allocating grades would also seriously reduce the likelihood of economics classes being offered in the future!

While you were reading the preceding paragraphs, you may have thought of other implications of the various systems for allocating scarce goods. If so, while performing this simple-minded experiment, you have just had your first experience in economic analysis. By analyzing how students would behave when faced with different situations, you have made your first economic predictions. You have determined how and with what consequences individual students, when faced with different economic systems, would choose among scarce goods and would employ their scarce resources. In so doing, you have predicted which kinds of students would receive the better grades under each system and how they would behave in the process.

The ability to do economics can be significantly extended by acquiring a few basic economic propositions, a task to which we shall now turn our attention.

ECONOMIC ANALYSIS

Economics is a way of thinking. We have seen that scarcity requires choices and that economics is the science of choice. The heart of economics is analysis, sometimes referred to as *economic theory*. The basis of almost all economic theory is the assumption that an individual will, when all costs have been reckoned, select the option that promises the largest net benefit — that is, the most satisfaction. This assumption can be expanded through a set of economic postulates. Nearly all of economic theory is an extension of these postulates.

THREE POSTULATES OF ECONOMIC ANALYSIS

The fundamental postulate of economics is that *as the personal benefits of selecting an alternative increase, the decision maker is more likely to select that alternative; conversely, as the personal costs of selecting an alternative increase, the decision maker is more likely to reject that alternative.*

This postulate assumes that individuals are able to estimate both benefits and costs. Imagine yourself in the position of Bob, whose favorite musical group is going to give a benefit concert in his city. Bob really wants to attend that concert. Then it is announced that Bruce Springsteen is also going to appear in the concert. Bruce Springsteen is Bob's favorite entertainer. The fact that Bruce Springsteen is also on the program increases the benefits of Bob's attending the concert and makes it more likely that he will choose to attend. Then it is announced that center-stage seats will cost $100 a ticket. Since Bob wants to take his wife with him, he will need two tickets. The higher-than-expected cost of the concert makes it more likely that Bob will choose not to attend. When the date of the concert is announced as the same night that Bob's boss has invited Bob and his wife to dinner, the cost of going to the concert is substantially increased, making it even more unlikely that Bob will buy tickets.

Have you ever watched a video marketing show? The auctioneer first offers a diamond-encrusted watch to attract your interest. Then he throws in a matching necklace, which entices you to buy the pair. Then to clinch the deal, a matching diamond ring is tossed in "absolutely free." Each time an additional item is included in the deal, it becomes more likely that you will call in an order. However, when the price is finally announced, the higher the price, the less likely it is that you will actually order the watch, necklace, and ring combination. As the benefits of an alternative increase, the more likely it is that a decision maker will select that alternative. Conversely, the higher the cost of an alternative, the less likely it is that the alternative will be chosen. We shall repeatedly apply, refine, and extend the fundamental postulate throughout this introduction to economic analysis.

Benefit is the personal satisfaction that results from selecting one alternative rather than another. But to understand economic costs, one must understand **opportunity cost.**

> *The opportunity cost is the highest-valued alternative that must be sacrificed when an action is selected; it is what the decision maker could have had instead.*

Since the opportunity cost of an action is the highest-valued alternative that must be sacrificed, the opportunity cost is to be found in an examination of the alternatives that must be sacrificed. The opportunity cost, or the opportunity that is lost, is the true cost of choosing one alternative over another.

The second postulate of economics is that *all economic costs are opportunity costs*. Suppose that a young girl with a quarter purchased a roll of mints but very much wanted a candy bar as well. If those mints had not been available, she would have chosen the candy bar. The sacrificed candy bar is the opportunity cost of selecting the mints. The student who had to choose between partying and gaining a better understanding of economics by studying paid for his increased knowledge by denying himself the pleasure of a weekend's entertainment. It is easy to explain why attendance at lectures is low on the first nice day of spring. The opportunity cost of being inside listening to a professor is just too high for many students to pay.

If, in our earlier example, Bob had purchased two tickets to the concert, it would have cost him $200. The opportunity cost of this expense was a set of tires for his car, which, before the concert was announced, he had been saving up to buy. It might have been a new color TV set, a compact-disc player, an airline ticket to New York City or to Hawaii, half of a hard disk drive for his Macintosh computer, or any one of many other things that $200 would buy. The opportunity cost of going to the concert was not all of these things, just the highest-valued alternative given up, which was the set of new tires.

Every college student knows from firsthand experience that college is not free. For example, one state university estimates in its catalog that the cost of attending the university for a year is $4,362, itemized as follows:

Tuition	$1,308
Books	399
Room and board	1,101
Transportation	555
Personal expenses	999
Total	$4,362

The interesting thing about this estimate is not that it is inaccurate for most students, but that several items included as expenses are not really opportunity costs of attending the university. Even so, the university's estimate of the total cost is much too low because it doesn't consider the biggest opportunity cost of all.

An opportunity cost is an expense that would be avoided if the alternative under consideration were not chosen. If you did not attend the university, you would not have to bear that cost. For example, tuition and book fees are actually opportunity costs because if you did not attend the university, you would not have to pay tuition and probably would not voluntarily buy the required textbooks. But how about room and board? If you did not attend the university, you would still have to pay for a place to live and for food to eat. Room and board is not an opportunity cost of attending the university unless it costs more at the university than you would have to spend elsewhere — and then only the difference in cost

SCARCITY, OPPORTUNITY COST, AND THE SEARCH FOR A FREE LUNCH

"There is no such thing as a free lunch" is a saying that reflects one of the basic tenets of economics: Scarce resources have alternative uses. If a resource is used for one purpose, it is unavailable to be used for another purpose. If resources are employed to make lunch, they cannot be used to make dinner, feed the cat, or manufacture a computer. Lunches have opportunity costs in the form of the lost goods that could have been produced instead.

Not everyone sees it precisely this way. The Nobel-prize-winning economist Paul Samuelson has written:

No free lunch? What nonsense. That is a scientific law with only 4 billion exceptions. If it were true, no member of the human species would survive for even a week.[3]

Professor Samuelson had in mind the example of the family where the parents provide free of charge the food necessary for their children to survive.

A lot of restaurant owners would agree with Professor Samuelson, since they benefit from providing lunches for a lot of people who are paying for someone else's lunch. Isn't the guest receiving a "free lunch"?

It used to be a traditional first assignment for beginning students of economics at a certain university to try to find a free lunch and to report back to the class if they succeeded. If the class agreed that a student had

---

[3] *Newsweek*, December 1969.

indeed found a free lunch, the student would receive as a reward an A on the first mid-term exam. It was a noble quest the students were undertaking. If a free lunch could be found, the basic tenet of economics could be disproved and the very foundation of the entire discipline undermined.

In order to ensure that each student knew what he or she was to look for, the term *free lunch* was defined at the start. Webster's unabridged dictionary defines *free* in 21 different ways. The ninth definition seemed to best fit our purposes: "without cost or payment, as a free ticket." Lunch was more directly defined as: "a light meal, usually in the middle of the day." So what the students were searching for was a light meal available between the hours of 10 a.m. and 2 p.m. without cost or payment.

One young man reported that a local tavern served free peanuts beginning precisely at 2 p.m. The class made him check it out, stipulating that he could not purchase anything and had to dump all of the peanuts in his book bag and ask for more, for if the peanuts were truly free, he should be able to have as many as he wished. He tried but failed in his attempt to fill his book bag with peanuts, and he was asked to leave when he refused to buy something to drink.

Another young man, a prelaw student, tried a different approach. This time he rested his case on an impeccable authority, the *American Economic Review,* which in the year 1887 reported in an article that it was common practice among the bars in Chicago to offer a free lunch to attract customers. The student believed that he had won his case. The most important journal of the economics profession stated that not only did free lunches exist, they were also a common practice. The class asked to see the article, read and discussed it, and decided that there was an implied cost to the customer, who had to purchase a beer or two to qualify for the free food.

The students also decided that the economics profession had made great strides since 1887. Today it would not be enough to find costless food at midday to disprove the famous saying. Even if the food were a gift, a

meal provided by parents for their children, or food from a food bank, it is not free to society. Parents generally have to sacrifice other goods to obtain food for their family. Even if the food comes from a food bank, it still isn't free to society. Food banks periodically run out of food and ask their donors for more. If the food were really free, that would not happen. Goods are free precisely because they are not scarce and do not have opportunity costs.

Our dispute with the Nobel-prize-winning economist is definitional. A good may well be free to an individual, as when a gift is presented. This is what Professor Samuelson had in mind. At the same time, the gift is not free to society because the gift has an opportunity cost in terms of the resources employed to produce it. When you encounter the saying "There is no such thing as a free lunch," you will now know what it means. It means that when scarce resources are used to produce a good, those resources could have been used to make something else instead. It is the loss of that something else that represents the opportunity cost involved and that takes the "free" out of "free lunch."

---

should be considered an opportunity cost. Also, if you did not attend the university, you would still have transportation and personal expenses. The university catalog thus overstates the cost of a year at college by including costs that are not true economic costs. Only tuition and books are clearly opportunity costs, and they total $1,707 a year, not $4,362.

Before you begin to think of college as a better deal than when you first read the catalog, it must be pointed out that the university's estimate of costs is incomplete.

The catalog also understates the cost of a college education by not including the biggest opportunity cost of all: If you did not go to college, chances are you would choose to work instead. If you were working and made $5 per hour, you would earn $10,000 a year. That $10,000 is an opportunity cost of attending the university full time. A four-year education at the state university costs at least $40,000 more than the cost for tuition and books!

Many students work to pay for books, tuition, and fees. But some also work for another reason. The opportunity cost of being a full-time student is too high — not because of the fees listed in the catalog, but because the opportunity cost of not working is too great to forgo.

The third postulate of economic analysis derives directly from the existence of scarcity. If there is never enough, economic decision makers will always attempt to do as well as possible with what they do have. Economic decision makers are assumed to choose with care, because they are forced by scarcity to do so.

The third postulate of economic analysis is that *economic decision makers choose purposefully and always economize. Decision makers always attempt to achieve a goal at the lowest possible cost. Conversely, they always attempt to obtain the maximum satisfaction for a given cost.*

Economists assume that economic decision makers can evaluate the benefit or satisfaction to be obtained from an alternative. Decision makers can recognize opportunities that will make them better off and pitfalls that will make them worse off, and they can choose between them. Since resources are scarce, decision makers do not consciously waste resources but try to make the most of every situation. An economic decision maker always attempts to achieve a goal at the lowest possible cost.

During the 1970s and early 1980s, for instance, prices were rising rapidly because of inflation (a general increase in the level of prices in an economy). Stores were frequently marking up the sticker prices on goods. Sometimes stores marked up the prices only on replacement goods, leaving the old stock at the old price. Consumers responded to this practice by sorting through the merchandise in search of those items marked with a lower price — a prime example of decision makers attempting to achieve a goal at the lowest possible cost.

ECONOMIC THINKING AND MARGINAL ANALYSIS

One of the most important tools employed by economists is **marginal analysis**. Almost all economic decisions involve making marginal changes; that is, making net additions to or subtractions from the status quo. In fact, the word *additional* is synonymous with *marginal*.

> *Marginal analysis is the study of the effect of small changes relative to an existing situation.*

All economic decisions can usefully be analyzed as marginal decisions and put in the context of comparing changes in costs with changes in benefits. Buyers at auctions, in deciding whether or not to bid higher, compare the increase in the bid price with their personal valuations of the good. Producers, in deciding how much to supply, compare the addition to cost of offering one more unit with the addition to revenue gained from that unit's sale.

Perhaps you have at some time attended an auction. An auction provides a good example of marginal analysis in action. The auctioneer introduces the good to be sold and asks for an opening bid. Each bidder mentally calculates how much that good is worth to him or her and will continue to bid as long as the bid is below that figure. The bid price continues to rise as bidders compete for the good, until finally the highest bid is obtained. The auctioneer pronounces: "Going, going, gone! Sold to the person with the green backpack!"

Only one person will be the highest bidder. Suppose that person to be Jane. Jane feels that the good is worth at least as much to her as the bid price, and that probably it is worth somewhat more. She has compared the benefits with the costs and decided on balance that the good is worth the price that must be paid. Jim, the next-to-last bidder — the one who did not win the good — is not dissatisfied with the result. He voluntarily withdrew from the bidding because the sales price was greater than the value he placed on the good. The marginal increase in price from the last bid made this decision possible. It was the marginal increase in price that caused the price to exceed Jim's personal valuation of its worth, leading him to voluntarily withdraw from further bidding.

Marginal analysis can make sense out of apparently questionable behavior. Airlines regularly offer a fare to standby passengers that is below the total cost of carrying a passenger. Suppose that the full cost of flying a passenger from Denver to New York City is $250, calculated by dividing the total cost of flying the plane that distance by the number of seats available. Yet an airline frequently offers to carry standby passengers for less than this amount. How can the airline profit by selling available seats for $125 to passengers standing by at the gate in the hope that the plane will not be full?

The answer lies in applying marginal analysis. Most of the costs associated with the flight do not depend on whether the plane is full or not. The costs of owning and maintaining the airplane, the pilot and crew salaries, and the landing and takeoff charges are costs that must be paid if the plane flies at all. These costs remain the same whether the plane carries 50 or 150 passengers.

Suppose that when departure time arrives, that the plane still has room for more passengers. If it departs partially empty, the airline will earn nothing from the empty seats. If it sells the seats for anything more than the costs involved in carrying the extra passengers, it will profit from doing so. So the relevant costs to consider are the additional, or marginal, costs associated with carrying a few more passengers. These costs are the extra costs associated with issuing more tickets, handling more baggage, burning extra fuel, and preparing additional meals and refreshments. These particular costs are probably quite small, and certainly less than the $125 that will be gained from selling standby tickets. So if the airline can fill its plane by selling standby tickets for more than the extra costs involved, it will profit. It is more profitable to let the standbys fly than to depart with empty seats because the additional (marginal) cost incurred is less than the additional (marginal) revenue earned. So in this case total profits are increased by the practice of selling for less than the full cost of production.

The idea of marginal analysis allows us to formulate a decision rule for making economic decisions.

DECISION RULE

The three postulates of economic analysis allow us to derive a decision rule that will govern how individuals make choices. All economic choices are made at the margin, or point of change. The marginal decision rule is called the **principle of rational behavior:**

> *The principle of rational behavior is a rule stating that an economic decision maker should take any action from which there is a positive net benefit. A positive net benefit exists when the addition to benefits exceeds the addition to costs.*

Economists often refer to the benefit or satisfaction from selecting an alternative as the *utility* that is derived from the decision. The benefit from selecting one alternative over another is the **marginal benefit** or **marginal utility** of the action.

> *The marginal benefit, or marginal utility, is the additional benefit obtained from taking an action.*

An economic decision maker will select any alternative in which the marginal utility exceeds the **marginal (additional) cost** and, conversely, will reject any alternative in which the marginal utility is less than the marginal cost.

> *Marginal cost is the addition to costs that results from taking an action. Marginal costs are always opportunity costs.*

As long as the marginal benefit exceeds the marginal cost, a proposed action should be taken. However, if the marginal benefit is less than the marginal cost, the proposed action should be rejected.

In our earlier illustration of an auction, Jim, the potential buyer of the good, dropped out when the marginal cost of the good exceeded his valuation of the marginal benefit of owning it. Only for Jane, who made the winning bid, was there a net benefit in owning the good. For her, the marginal benefit of taking the action of making the winning bid exceeded the marginal cost. For everyone else, the marginal cost represented by that bid exceeded the marginal benefit of owning the good. In the same way, the airline that offers standby tickets does so because the marginal cost of flying these passengers is less than the marginal benefit of the extra ticket sales. Thus a net benefit exists that makes it profitable for the airline to offer standby tickets. Any action should be undertaken if there is a net benefit in doing so.

The concepts of scarcity, opportunity cost, and economizing can be graphically demonstrated by the production possibilities frontier.

THE PRODUCTION POSSIBILITIES SCHEDULE

The iron law of scarcity, the necessity for choice, and the concept of opportunity costs can be demonstrated by the **production possibilities schedule.**

> *A production possibilities schedule is a schedule that shows the various combinations of the amounts of any two goods that can be produced from the resources available and the given state of technology.*

TABLE 1.1
Production Possibilities Relating Time Spent Studying to Expected Grades

TIME SPENT STUDYING ECONOMICS (HOURS/WEEK)	EXPECTED GRADE IN ECONOMICS	TIME SPENT STUDYING HISTORY (HOURS/WEEK)	EXPECTED GRADE IN HISTORY
10.0	A	0.0	F
7.5	B	2.5	D
5.0	C	5.0	C
2.5	D	7.5	B
0.0	F	10.0	A

The production possibilities schedule can be shown in a simple diagram called the *production possibilities frontier.*

Table 1.1 presents the grade-production possibilities for a student taking both economics and history. The student has 10 hours a week available to study the two subjects. The grades the student can expect in each course depend on how much time is devoted to studying the subject. If all 10 hours are devoted to studying economics, for example, the student could expect to receive an A in that course — but at the opportunity cost of receiving a failing grade in history, for which no study time would be available. Conversely, if all the study time is spent on history, the expected grade in that course would be an A, but the expected grade in economics would be an F. If the student devotes half of the available study time to economics and half to history, the expected grade in both courses would be a C. Table 1.1 assumes that the student has average intellectual abilities, a fixed amount of study time available (10 hours in this case), and uses that time efficiently. The table shows the maximum grade combinations that can be expected for each allocation of the 10-hour study time. Because study time is a scarce resource, it is not possible for the student to earn an A in both subjects, given the study time available and the efficiency with which he or she studies.

This same information can be displayed in graphic form. In Figure 1.1 the line that runs from point A on the vertical axis to point A on the horizontal axis is the production possibilities frontier (PPF). The PPF shows all possible combinations of the maximum amount of any two goods that can be produced from a fixed amount of resources. The student can choose to operate at any point on the PPF. He or she could choose to produce an A in economics and an F in history or any combination on the frontier, such as a B in economics and a D in history. The PPF depicts the choices available and the opportunity cost of each choice.

All students would like to do better than the possibilities displayed. Unfortunately, achieving an A in each course (represented by point AA) is not possible with the available resources. Any point on the production possibilities frontier is the best that can be achieved. The frontier cannot be exceeded unless more resources become available or the student becomes more efficient at studying. The student might be able to find more resources — perhaps by allotting more time to studying and less to sleeping, or by buying the course workbook instead of attending a concert — or might be able in some way to improve the efficiency of studying — perhaps by learning speed reading, which is an improvement in technology. In this case the quantity of resources and the state of technology are not fixed, and the entire PPF will shift out. If enough resources are obtained or the technology of learning is sufficiently improved, it might be

FIGURE 1.1
Production Possibilities Frontier for Expected Grades in Economics and History

This figure shows the grades that can be expected from allocating the 10 hours a week of available study time between the study of economics and history. The points T, W, X, Y, and Z indicate five possible ways of allocating the available study time and the expected grades that go with each allocation. All students would like to do better than these alternatives, since with them at best only a C average can be achieved. Everyone would like to operate at a point like AA and earn an A average. But this is impossible given the amount of available study time (10 hours) and the student's existing learning ability. It might be possible to reach a point like AA if the student could find more study time (obtain more resources) or improve his or her learning ability (a technological improvement). It is possible to do worse by wasting the available resources. If study time is wasted, the student could operate at a point like DD inside the PPF, or even FF.

10 Hours Is the Total Study Time Available

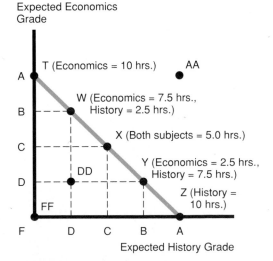

FIGURE 1.2

Production Possibilities Frontier Used to
Display Choices Available to Society

The production possibilities frontier reveals the possible efficient combinations of outputs given the level of resources and the state of technology. Society may choose to operate at any point along the PPF. Society would prefer to operate at a point like A, which would allow society to have more of both goods than at any point along the PPF, but the state of technology and the amounts of resources available make this impossible. The best society can do is to operate at some point on the PPF. Society can do worse. When resources are unemployed or when they are allocated inefficiently, the economy will be operating inside the PPF at a point such as U. Resources are being wasted; society could have more of both goods by moving to the frontier. Once at the frontier, however, having more of one good involves having less of the other good. Suppose the economy is operating at point Y on the PPF. If society decides to move to point X to obtain more military goods ($M_3 - M_2$), it will have to sacrifice some consumer goods ($C_2 - C_1$), a sacrifice that represents the opportunity cost of obtaining more military goods.

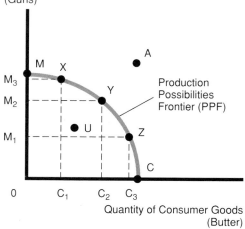

Quantity of Military Goods
(Guns)

Quantity of Consumer Goods
(Butter)

possible to shift the PPF out by enough to reach point AA. But this is speculation. As long as the quantity of resources and the state of technology are fixed, the combinations of grades on the PPF are the best that can be achieved.

However, it is possible to do worse. If the student wastes the available alloted study time partying or sleeping, it is possible to earn a D in both subjects (a situation represented by point DD) or even to fail (point FF). In either case, the student would be operating inside the production possibilities frontier.

The production possibilities frontier can also display the choices available to an entire society.

THE CHOICES AVAILABLE TO SOCIETY

The resources available to society are limited. In its desire to economize, society will attempt to obtain the most satisfaction from the available resources. For example, every society or nation must decide how to allot its production between military and civilian goods. This decision is often referred to as the *guns versus butter* choice, with *guns* referring to the quantity of military goods a society can have and *butter* referring to the quantity of consumer goods it can have. Figure 1.2 shows a production possibilities frontier that displays the various maximum combinations of military and consumer goods that society might have. Every nation will try to operate somewhere on the PPF curve. (The PPF is truly a curve in this case, bowed out when viewed from the origin. Later we shall explain why this shape is more typical than the straight-line shape of the PPF used in the student-grade example.)

Society may produce any combination of military and consumer goods that lies on the production possibilities frontier. Almost every nation — Costa Rica being the sole exception — chooses to produce some of both goods. Costa Rica does not have a military (although it does have a police force), and it has chosen to operate at point C in Figure 1.2. Any other nation desiring some of both goods could, for example, select combination X, Y, or Z, or any other point on the PPF.

Ronald Reagan was elected president after promising to increase U.S. military capabilities. If the United States had been operating at point Y on the production possibilities frontier, the economy would have been producing M_2 military goods and C_2 consumer goods. The implications of the president's program would have been to shift the United States to point X, increasing the quantity of military goods produced from M_2 to M_3, at the cost of reducing the quantity of consumer goods produced from C_2 to C_1. Any move along the PPF requires a trade-off. More military goods can be produced only at the expense of producing fewer civilian goods.

The law of scarcity cannot be ignored. If an economy is operating efficiently and employing all the available resources, producing more of one good means sacrificing the production of some of the other good. Thus when you hear, as was stated during a recent presidential campaign, that a country cannot have both more guns and more butter, this is what is meant. If more resources are devoted to the production of military goods, less will be available to produce consumer goods.

Society would, of course, prefer to operate at point A, but it cannot because it is constrained by scarcity to operate at some point on the production possibilities frontier. Given the available resources and the state of technology, a point on the PPF is the best that can be achieved.

Society could also operate at any point inside the PPF, such as at U, in which case the economy would not be obtaining the best possible output from the available resources. When the economy is experiencing excess unemployment or is allocating its resources inefficiently, it is operating inside its production possibilities frontier.

In summary, the production possibilities frontier at any point in time is determined by two constraints: the available quantity of resources and the state of existing technology. If an economy is to operate on the PPF, it must efficiently use all the available resources. If the economy is operating efficiently, the PPF shows the various combinations of goods that can be obtained.

Now we shall examine why the production possibilities frontier is often a curve and not a straight line.

THE LAW OF INCREASING COSTS

The production possibilities frontier is a straight line if all resources are equally good at producing both goods. In this case the opportunity cost of producing more of one good remains the same no matter how much of the good, up to the maximum amount, is produced. Thus in Figure 1.1 the opportunity cost of obtaining one letter grade better in economics is always receiving one letter grade worse in history.

Typically, however, not all resources available to a society are equally good at producing all goods. Some are typically better at producing one type of good than they are at producing another type. A steel forge, for example, is better at producing tanks and aircraft carriers than at producing wine, whereas a vineyard is better at producing wine than at producing bombers. Suppose an economy were operating at point A on the production possibilities frontier depicted in Figure 1.3, producing only consumer goods. It would be able to produce 7 units of consumer goods, if the economy were operating efficiently, and no military goods.

Now suppose a military threat were perceived and that in response decision makers decided to produce one unit of military goods. If the economy continued to operate efficiently, it would move from point A to point B on the production possibilities frontier. In order to do this, in accordance with the economizing postulate, the resources that were least productive in producing consumer goods and most productive in producing military goods would be transferred first. Although they were relatively poor at producing consumer goods and hence produced relatively few consumer goods, these resources could nevertheless produce an entire unit of military goods. The output of military goods would therefore increase by one unit at the expense of less than a unit of consumer goods.

In an economy producing only two types of goods, the opportunity cost of one type is expressed in terms of the other type. For example, the opportunity cost of one unit of military goods is expressed in units of consumer goods. The opportunity cost of the first unit of military goods in Figure 1.3 would be quite small in terms of the civilian goods sacrificed, perhaps no more than one-fourth of a unit of civilian goods as read off the horizontal axis. The movement from point A to point B involves the sacrifice of one-fourth unit of consumer goods. Where previously 7 units of consumer goods were produced and now military goods are also produced, 6.75 units of consumer goods are now available as well as one unit of military goods. The opportunity cost of one unit of military goods, when moving from point A to point B, is 0.25 unit of consumer goods sacrificed.

FIGURE 1.3
The Law of Increasing Costs

The law of increasing costs implies a production possibilities frontier that is bowed out when viewed from the origin (point 0). The law of increasing costs derives from the assumption that not all resources are equally good at producing both military and consumer goods. The opportunity cost increases for each additional unit of military goods desired because its production employs resources that are increasingly better able to produce consumer goods than were the previously transferred resources.

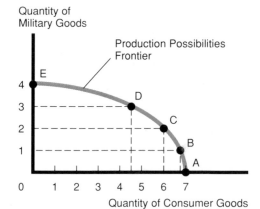

Each production possibilities frontier, such as PPF_1, is constructed for a moment in time during which the quantity of resources available is fixed, as is the state of technology. Over time, as more resources become available and/or the state of technology improves, the PPF will shift out from PPF_1 to PPF_2. This process is known as economic growth. Economic growth expands the PPF and allows the economy to consume more of both goods. Suppose that when the economy was operating on PPF_1, it was operating at point A. Now suppose that economic growth occurs and the PPF shifts to PPF_2. The economy can now produce the same amount of consumer goods C_1 and more military goods M_2, or the same amount of military goods M_1 as before and more consumer goods C_2, or any combination of both more consumer goods and more military goods that lies along the new PPF from B_1 to B_2, such as at point A'.

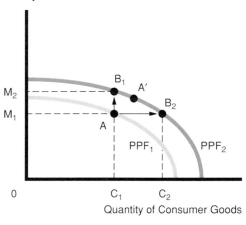

Quantity of Consumer Goods

A second unit of military goods, a movement from point B to point C, is more expensive. It requires the sacrifice of more consumer goods — perhaps 0.75 unit — because the resources transferred this time are relatively better suited to the production of civilian goods than were the resources that were first transferred to the production of military goods. For the same reason, a third unit of military goods, represented by a shift from point C to point D, would cost even more (about 1.5 units) than the second unit in terms of consumer goods given up. A fourth unit of military goods would cost still more — fully 4.5 units of civilian goods — as resources that were very good in producing consumer goods are transferred to the production of military goods, for which they are ill suited.

The increase in opportunity cost to produce each succeeding unit of a good is explained by the **law of increasing costs**.

The law of increasing costs states that as the economy attempts to produce more⸝of a good, the opportunity cost of additional units expressed in terms of other goods sacrificed will increase.

As a result, a production possibilities frontier is generally bowed out when viewed from the origin (point 0) of a graph, as shown in Figure 1.3.

ECONOMIC GROWTH

The production possibilities frontier is always drawn for a particular point in time. At any instant in time, the amount of available resources is fixed, as is the state of technology. Over time, however, as more resources become available and as the state of technology improves, the PPF shifts out. Figure 1.4 shows that the effect of increasing the available resources or of technological improvement is to shift the entire curve out from PPF_1 to PPF_2. If the economy was initially operating at point A on PPF_1 (producing C_1 consumer goods and M_1 military goods), it becomes possible to produce more of both goods after economic growth occurs.

The process of economic growth shifts the entire production possibilities frontier from PPF_1 to PPF_2. The economy can now choose to produce the same amount of consumer goods (C_1) and have more military goods (M_2 instead of M_1), or it could produce more consumer goods (C_2 instead of C_1) and the same amount of military goods (M_1) as before, or it could produce more of both goods by operating at a point such as A', somewhere between B_1 and B_2. Economic growth thus allows society to have more goods than before.

Economic growth can occur for one of two reasons: (1) More resources become available — a growing population might provide more labor, new land might be reclaimed, or the society might have saved to provide more physical and human capital; (2) technology improves — new knowledge might be acquired that allows more goods to be produced with the same amount of resources. For example, we are currently experiencing the computer revolution. As new and better computers are produced, the economy becomes more productive. Economic growth is not free, however. Resources have to be employed to bring it about. The society must limit its current consumption in order to increase the quantity and quality of the resources that will be available in the future or to fund the research and development necessary to bring about technological change.

The production possibilities frontier is a useful tool for depicting what we have learned so far about the economic way of thinking. In terms of the postulates of economic thinking, what we have learned is that: (1) the *law of scarcity* establishes the boundary of the PPF — at any point in time the PPF curve indicates the best that society can do; (2) on the PPF, the *opportunity cost* of increasing the output of one good can be measured in terms of the output of the other good that is sacrificed; and (3) the *economizing postulate* ensures that society will always attempt to operate on the PPF.

SUMMARY

1. Scarcity is the source of economic problems. Because wants are un-limited, there can never be enough goods and resources to satisfy society's wants. Scarcity exists because resources are limited relative to human wants. Resources are the land, labor, capital, and entrepreneurial ability that can be used to produce want-satisfying goods.
2. The law of scarcity states that for every person and for society as a whole, some goods are scarce. A good is scarce if there is not enough of it to satisfy all of the demands for it. A good is free if it exists in such abundance that it can satisfy the wants of all who wish to consume it.
3. The existence of scarcity requires that economic agents make choices.
4. Economics can be defined as the study of how and with what conse-quences individuals and society, when faced with a scarcity problem, choose (1) from among scarce goods, (2) to employ scarce resources, and (3) to distribute scarce goods and resources.
5. Scarcity implies competition, rationing, and discrimination.
6. Every society must devise an economic system that will answer the *what, how,* and *for whom* questions.
7. Economic theory rests upon three postulates of economic analysis:
   a. The fundamental postulate of economics is that as the personal benefits of choosing an alternative increase, the decision maker will be more likely to select that alternative; conversely, as the personal costs of selecting an alternative increase, the decision maker is more likely to reject that alternative.
   b. The true cost of any action is the opportunity cost, the highest-valued alternative that is sacrificed in making a choice. Opportu-nity costs are sometimes referred to as marginal costs.
   c. Economic decision makers always *economize* by trying to achieve a goal at the lowest possible cost. Conversely, they always at-tempt to obtain the maximum benefits at a given cost.
8. The postulates of economic thinking imply a simple decision rule called the *rule of rational behavior*. This rule states that an economic decision maker should take any action in which the additional (marginal) benefits exceed the addition to costs (the marginal or opportunity costs). All possible actions that create net benefits should be undertaken.
9. The production possibilities frontier shows the maximum combina-tions of goods that an economy is able to produce from its limited re-sources and given the existing state of technology.
10. The law of increasing cost is that as more of one good is produced, its opportunity cost (cost in terms of other goods sacrificed) will increase. The law of increasing cost is operative when not all resources are equally good at producing all goods.

11. Economic growth occurs when a society obtains more resources or experiences technological progress. When economic growth occurs, the production possibilities frontier shifts out, allowing the society to have more of both goods. Economic growth is not free because resources have to be used to bring it about.

PREVIEW 1.1 ANALYSIS

WHY IS A VAN GOGH PAINTING OF A SUNFLOWER WORTH $40 MILLION?

R ecord auction prices for fine paintings became a common occurrence in the late 1980s. In 1987 the art world was stunned when a painting by Vincent van Gogh was sold for three times the greatest price previously paid for a painting sold at auction. Almost as flabbergasting, there were an estimated dozen serious bidders in the running up to $25 million, and only later did the ranks thin to two bidders. Amazing as it was, the auction of March 30, 1987, was probably not very different from another auction of a van Gogh painting that had occurred 18 years earlier.

This similar auction, fully reported by *Auction Magazine* and headlined in newspapers, saw the sale of the van Gogh painting "Le Cypres et l'arbe en fleurs" for $1.3 million to Aristotle Onassis, who was acting at the behest of his wife Jacqueline. The next-to-last bidder was also a famous man, Malcolm Forbes, owner and publisher of the business magazine that bears his name. In a *Forbes* article the story of Forbes' attempt to secure the painting for his very own is recounted:

> Malcolm Forbes is a rich man, one of the 400 richest men in the United States by his own magazine's calculation, worth over $500 million in 1987. He is a famous balloonist as well as a collector of art whose collection is well known for its imperial eggs made by Fabergé. He also has a famous collection of toy soldiers that has made him the envy of many toy collectors. But at the time he bid $1.25 million for the van Gogh, he had never participated in a major art auction and had not previously bid over five figures for any work of art at auction.
>
> When the van Gogh painting was announced for auction, Forbes established a personal value to him based on recent private sales of similar paintings and his own instincts and preferences. He decided that he wanted that painting and was willing to bid seven figures ($1 million) to obtain it. When auction night came, Forbes, his wife, and two of his sons were in attendance, along with about 50 other persons, many of them potential purchasers. The painting was displayed on the stage alongside the auctioneer's podium. Circulating in front of the auctioneer was a bid caller whose job it was to notice, shout out, and record all bids. If a person wanted to bid, all he or she had to do was nod a head, raise a hand, or make some other positive gesture and the bid caller would shout out the bid. If you attend such an auction and you do not want to bid, you had best sit very still.
>
> The auctioneer opened the bidding. About one dozen persons entered into the competition at one time or another. But when the price reached $1 million, only Forbes and Onassis were still active. Forbes bid $1,100,000, and Onassis quickly upped the bid to $1,200,000.[4]

The account concluded with the following description of the final minutes of the bidding:

---

[4] "The Van Gogh Was Almost His," *Forbes.*

"One million two against you, sir," the bid caller said. Malcolm S. Forbes, editor-in-chief and owner of *Forbes* magazine, his face flushed with excitement, stared hard at the vibrant swirls of van Gogh's *Le Cypres et l'arbe en fleurs*, which was displayed on the stage. He thought about how he had wanted a van Gogh ever since reading *Lust for Life*, how it might be years before another such van Gogh became available to a private collector like himself, how with perhaps just one more bid the work could be his.

"One million two against you, sir," the bid caller repeated insistently. The auctioneer prepared to gavel the knockdown. At the last instant, Forbes nodded. "Fifty!" cried the bid caller. But it was not enough. The auctioneer quickly received a bid of a million three. The bid caller looked at Forbes. Forbes looked at his wife, who with two of their sons was sitting next to him. She shook her head vigorously. Forbes smiled resignedly, and shrugged his shoulders at the bid caller. He had lost. "The other guy just didn't pause at all before raising his bid," Forbes says. "I saw that I just wasn't going to be able to get it."[5]

Forbes reported mixed feelings about becoming that season's " . . . most notable underbidder." He had gone to the auction willing to pay one million dollars for the van Gogh. Then having been caught up in "auction fever," he had gone two bids higher than he had intended. He felt that the van Gogh was probably worth $1.3 million, but he wasn't going to be able to get it for that price. The other bidder appeared to be very determined. So Forbes willingly dropped out of the bidding, and the van Gogh was sold to Onassis.

What can we say about this auction on the basis of the economics we now know? Clearly, the van Gogh painting was a scarce good that had to be allocated in some manner. Whatever the method chosen, there would be competition to obtain the painting. Its owner, trying to maximize the net benefit from the sale, decided to convey it at auction to the person willing to pay the most for it.

The auctioneer started the bidding at a low price and the prospective purchasers increased the bid price in increments, each attempting to buy the painting at the lowest possible price. Initially, the bidding went rapidly, as there were a number of persons willing to pay a relatively low price for the painting. In the above description of the auction, each participant continued to bid as long as the marginal benefit of the painting exceeded the existing bid price. The existing bid price reflects the marginal, or opportunity, cost of the good.

The behavior of each bidder followed the fundamental postulate of economics. As the auction price increased, some bidders began to drop out, precisely as the fundamental postulate predicts: *As the personal costs of selecting an alternative increase, the decision maker is more likely to reject that alternative*. This rejection would have occurred, according to the decision rule, when the bid price reached and exceeded each bidder's personal valuation of the marginal utility of the good. Finally, only the winner, Aristotle Onassis, was left, the only person whose valuation of the marginal utility of the painting exceeded his valuation of the opportunity cost. The person who wanted the work of art the most, in the sense that he was willing to pay the most for it, got the painting. The process of bidding had increased the opportunity cost of owning the painting until only the person who made the winning bid still enjoyed a net benefit from owning the painting.

Why did Malcolm Forbes drop out of the bidding? He clearly wanted that van Gogh painting, and he is one of the richest men in America. He

[5] Chris Wells, *Auction Magazine*, reprinted in the *Forbes* article.

didn't drop out because he could not afford to pay over $1 million for it. He could have easily done that. He dropped out because, rich as he had become, he still had a scarcity problem.

Forbes was not able to acquire all of the works of art that he desired to own. If he had bought that painting, he would not have been able to acquire other works of art that, collectively, he desired more than one great van Gogh. He might have had to sacrifice some of the numerous paintings he subsequently acquired — paintings by Renoir, Vlaminck, Warhol, and Stella, as well as 75 jeweled art objects by Fabergé, collections of kinetic art and Oriental china, and 10,000 toy soldiers. Forbes did later manage to acquire, some time after the auction, a small "wash" by van Gogh for only $63,750, which didn't interfere with his other collecting activities nearly as much as buying the painting would have.

The opportunity cost of the "Le Cypres et l'arbe en fleurs" in terms of the other works of art that had to be sacrificed was simply too high a price for Forbes to pay. The opportunity cost to Forbes exceeded the marginal benefit of owning the van Gogh painting. He stopped bidding when the opportunity cost exceeded the marginal benefit. It doesn't pay, even for one of the world's richest men, to take an action in which there are no net benefits.

HOW SHOULD AN AVERAGE CITIZEN EVALUATE "STAR WARS"?

Defense expenditures in real terms have been rising since the end of World War II. The United States today spends substantially more on national defense than it did in the 1970s. These expenditures have opportunity costs in terms of fewer consumer goods available. Consequently, everyone would like to reduce defense expenditures. In 1983 when President Reagan announced the Strategic Defense Initiative (the SDI program), he was proposing a strategy the goal of which was to make it possible to reduce future defense spending.

SDI is a research program to develop a defensive shield against incoming intercontinental ballistic missiles. The press quickly labeled the program "Star Wars." The cost of this program was estimated to be more than $100 billion over and above the substantial military buildup that was already under way. The purpose of the program was to develop a system that would allow an active defense of the country against a nuclear missile attack. Currently, our only defense is the deterrent effect of the nation's ability to retaliate in kind after a nuclear attack.

President Reagan suggested that if the United States had an effective space shield, we could substantially reduce the future level of defense expenditures. A second possible benefit of the program is that the existence of the SDI program would make the U.S.S.R., the chief U.S. adversary, more willing than it otherwise would be to negotiate an arms control treaty. If this benefit were realized, the level of defense spending could be lower in the future.

The critics of the SDI program contended that such a system was impossible to develop and could not work. They recommended that the United States continue to rely on a doctrine of mutual assured destruction (MAD) to keep the country from nuclear war. Continuing to maintain the status quo means devoting in the future approximately the same proportion of the nation's resources to defense as we do now.

The production possibilities frontier (PPF) can be used to show the potential economic costs and benefits of pursuing the SDI program. Most people in the United States agree that it is necessary to employ some resources for national defense and that to do so involves the sacrifice of some consumer goods. Also, most people agree that the country should spend enough to avoid a nuclear war, which would collapse the PPF shown in Figure 1.5 toward zero.

The American people do not agree, however, on how much is enough to spend on defense. Everyone wants to be strong enough to deter a war, but they disagree about how much is enough to accomplish this goal. In effect, they do not agree about exactly where on the production possibilities frontier to operate. This conflict is resolved through the political process by elected officials. Suppose that through the political process we are currently operating at point B on the PPF shown in Figure 1.5.

Implications for the SDI program flow directly from the law of scarcity. If the United States uses more of its limited resources for defense, it will have less to use for consumer goods. In Figure 1.5 the production possibilities frontier shows the trade-off between military goods (measured along the vertical axis) and consumer goods (measured along the horizontal axis). If the United States is currently operating at point B on the PPF (producing X' of military goods and Y' of consumer goods), then an increase in military spending (from X' to X) can come only at the expense of fewer consumer goods (a decline from Y' to Y). The opportunity cost of more military goods is the amount of consumer goods that must be sacrificed. This reduction in consumer goods is the immediate effect of pursuing the SDI program.

The SDI program will also have future effects. Investing in the SDI program will not only cause a shift in current output, but it will also affect the future production possibilities frontier as well. In its initial stages, the SDI program is almost all research and development (R&D). This R&D will almost certainly lead to technological advances in the production of military goods, which will have some spillover into the production of consumer goods. The PPF will thus shift out to PPF_{sdi}, as shown in Figure 1.6. The shift is biased toward the production of military goods, so the production possibilities for producing military goods increase more rapidly over time than do the production possibilities for producing consumer goods.

In the absence of the SDI program, the production possibilities frontier would have shifted (to PPF_{sq}) because of technological change and resource growth, but in this status quo case the shift would have been relatively more biased toward the production of consumer goods. The shift in the PPF if the status quo is continued would allow a greater maximum amount of consumer goods (Z on the horizontal axis) and relatively fewer military goods (N on the vertical axis) than would be possible if the SDI program is pursued (Y consumer goods measured on the horizontal axis and M military goods measured on the vertical axis).

The SDI program strategy is that the sacrifice of current consumer goods involved in moving from point B to point A on the current production possibilities frontier (PPF_c) will either create a defensive shield against ballistic missiles or bring about an arms control treaty. Either of these outcomes will allow the United States to reduce its military spending as a proportion of the economy's total output. The United States would then be able to move to a point like C' on PPF_{sdi}. Hence, in the future the country would have more consumer goods, not fewer.

FIGURE 1.5
Production Possibilities Frontier Showing
Trade-off between Military and
Consumer Goods

The United States is currently operating at point B on the production possibilities frontier, producing X' military goods and Y' consumer goods. The proposal to undertake SDI requires that additional resources be devoted to military goods. This involves the shift from point B to point A and the transfer of resources that currently are producing $Y' - Y$ consumer goods. This reduction in consumer goods is the immediate effect of undertaking the SDI program.

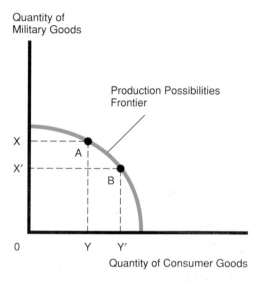

FIGURE 1.6
Relative Changes in Production Possibilities
Frontier with SDI Compared with Changes
that Occur with Status Quo

Three production possibilities frontiers are shown in this
figure: PPF$_e$ is the existing PPF, PPF$_{sdi}$ is the future PPF if
the SDI program is pursued, and PPF$_{sq}$ is the future PPF
if SDI is not undertaken. On PPF$_e$ the movement from
point B to point A shows the sacrifice of some consumer
goods today required to pursue SDI. If SDI is undertaken, the PPF in the future will, as economic growth
occurs, shift to PPF$_{sdi}$ and the economy will move to
point A''. Proponents of SDI suggest that if the program
is successful or if its development leads to an arms reduction treaty, then military spending can be reduced and
the economy can move to a point such as C' where less
is spent on the military and more consumer goods are
enjoyed. Instead, if the status quo is maintained, the PPF
will in the future shift to PPF$_{sq}$ and the economy will
move to point B''. Critics of SDI point out if SDI fails and
the United States returns to the past level of defense
expenditures, the country will be on PPF$_{sdi}$, not PPF$_{sq}$.
Thus it will be able to produce only at point B'. The loss
in output represented by the distance between B'' and B'
represents the cost of pursuing a program that its opponents think is certain to fail.

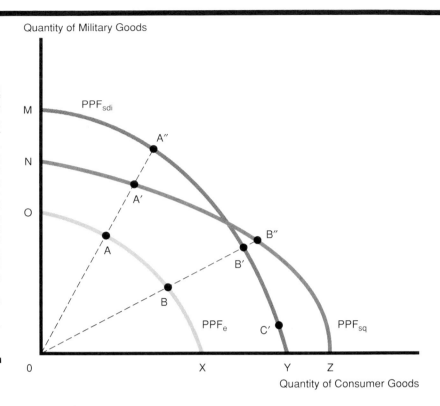

The argument runs as follows. In Figure 1.6 the movement from point
B to point A will eventually shift the future production possibilities frontier to PPF$_{sdi}$, rather than PPF$_{sq}$, where the economy would operate at
point A''. Once the SDI program proved effective or once an arms control
treaty was negotiated, the United States could move to point C', reducing
its military spending as a proportion of total output and increasing its
production of consumer goods.

Opponents of SDI believe that the program will not work and that
once this is recognized the United States will return to spending the same
proportion of national output on defense that proved successful in deter-
ring war in the past (shown by the line from the origin that runs through
the B's on the graph). Had the United States not undertaken SDI, the
production possibilities frontier would have shifted to PPF$_{sq}$. The economy would operate at B'' on this frontier. However, the resources wasted
in unsuccessfully trying to develop SDI have put the economy on production possibility frontier PPF$_{sdi}$ so that the economy will operate at point
B'. Instead of B'' the economy will be able to produce only B'. The difference between B'' and B' represents the cost of the failed program.

Some critics see an even worse potential result. They suggest that the
Russians will counter SDI by increasing their own defense expenditures.
It will be necessary, when SDI fails, for the United States to continue to
devote the same proportion of its output to defense spending that it did
with SDI. Thus the nation will continue to devote the proportion of its
output that lies along the line connecting the origin and the A points in
Figure 1.6. So the nation could end up at A'' on PPF$_{sdi}$ with fewer consumer goods than are currently enjoyed.

The use of the concept of the production possibilities frontier to illustrate some of the implications of the SDI program has allowed us to pin-

point the critical questions. The key issue is whether or not you believe an effective space shield can be developed with today's technology that will lead to an eventual reduction in the proportion of U.S. output that goes to defense spending. Believing that it can work is a necessary condition for supporting the program, but not a sufficient condition, because you must still decide whether the SDI program is the most efficient (least-cost) way of achieving the desired result of reducing the proportion of the nation's output devoted to military expenditures. If you believe that SDI cannot work or that it will not lead to the desired results, you have an argument for opposing the SDI program.

IS THE 55 MPH SPEED LIMIT GOOD ECONOMIC POLICY?

PREVIEW 1.3 ANALYSIS

The 55 MPH speed limit is now part of everyday experience for young Americans, most of whom probably don't remember when the speed limit was 70 MPH. The national speed limit must be a bitter pill for many Americans, for it seems to be frequently violated. The limitations of a national speed limit were somewhat reduced in 1987, when the federal government raised the speed limit on rural interstate highways to 65 MPH, but this concession was scant help for most commuters on the urban sections of the interstate highways and for travelers on state highways where the limit remained 55 MPH.

Even this partial lifting of the speed limit was difficult to get through Congress. A lot of people still support a reduced speed limit because reduced highway speeds save lives and conserve gasoline. The 55 MPH speed limit was first imposed in response to the energy crisis of 1974. Its purpose was to conserve gasoline; the miles per gallon an automobile gets declines as speed increases. Once imposed, the 55 MPH speed limit resulted in an unanticipated additional benefit — traffic fatalities were significantly reduced. The decline in highway deaths was so significant, by as much as 5,000 a year — that for many this benefit became the main reason for keeping the law once the energy crisis had abated.

Despite increased efforts by state law-enforcement personnel, general compliance with the speed limit has not been achieved, as anyone who drives the nation's highways can attest. The reason that the speed limit is not voluntarily observed is that going slower requires the expenditure of more time traveling, and time, like any other scarce good, has an opportunity cost.

An individual's time is a precious good because it is scarce — but life is also precious, as is gasoline. Either we save lives and gasoline at the expense of spending more time traveling, or we spend less time in our automobiles by going faster and in the process lose more lives on highways and consume more gasoline. We cannot have more of all three goods.

We must choose among these scarce goods. To choose well, we need to know the opportunity costs of the alternatives. One way to calculate the opportunity cost of saving lives by driving slower is to compare the extra time spent driving with the time saved by having fewer traffic deaths. It has been estimated that the 55 MPH speed limit requires the nation's drivers to collectively spend an additional 2,710 million hours in their cars. If we compare the extra travel time with the reduction in traffic fatalities, we find that it costs 102 years of extra driving time to save the life of one person who can be expected to live another 35.2 years. This finding may suggest that the 55 MPH speed limit is not a very efficient way to save lives.

A more precise way to estimate opportunity cost in this case is to obtain the dollar cost for saving a life by driving slower. Studies have shown that drivers are willing to pay up to 42 percent of their hourly wage to avoid an extra hour of traveling. When the 2,710 million extra hours are evaluated at 42 percent of the average wage rate, the opportunity cost is $6 billion, or $1.3 million for each life saved.

Is this exchange worthwhile? Is the life of a human being worth more than $1.3 million? How can one put a price on a human life? As difficult as putting a dollar value on life is to accept in principle, in practice such valuations are made every day. Law courts are often called on to place a value on a human life that has been lost due to negligence on someone's part. In supporting a 55 MPH speed limit, the federal government implicitly recognized that the value of traveling at this speed is worth the 50,000 traffic deaths that still occur. After all, the speed limit could be set at 1 MPH and, if the law could be enforced, very few persons would die in traffic accidents. Few people would advocate this as a way to save lives because the cost of the extra travel time would be immense.

There have been numerous attempts to determine the value of a human life. Most economists agree that the value of anything is the maximum amount a person is willing to pay to acquire it. The best estimates of the value of a human life, then, should be derived from information on how much individuals are willing to pay to save a life. One study, based on what car buyers are willing to pay for increased automobile safety, estimates the value of a life at $500,000. This study is supported by another study that draws on data on how often seatbelts are used by drivers. This study also found that when driving a car, individuals behave as if they valued a life at $500,000.

If these studies are accurate, it would appear that by employing the 55 MPH speed limit to save lives, we spend $1.3 million to save a life valued at $500,000. The opportunity cost of the time lost in extra travel is more than the value of the lives saved. No wonder that less than half of all freeway drivers obey the speed limit. We now know that there are two kinds of inefficiencies that will cause an economy to operate inside the production possibilities frontier: the unemployment of resources and the misallocation of resources. Paying an excessive amount for a good (saving a life) is an example of the latter.

It is possible that you value a human life, especially your own, more than the economists say you do and that you are still in favor of the reduced speed limit. Consider this argument: We have seen that decision makers choose purposefully and always attempt to achieve a goal at the lowest possible cost. Is a reduced speed limit the most cost-effective way of saving a life?

People die in many ways: starvation, disease, accident, by their own hand, or at the hand of others. About 2 million die each year, and 99 percent of all deaths are not traffic-related. To determine if traveling at the reduced speed limit is the most efficient way to save a life, we need to investigate the cost of alternative life-saving measures. About as many persons die from fire as die in automobile accidents. It is estimated that a life could be saved for between $40,000 and $80,000 each by placing a smoke detector in every home. Heart disease accounts for 40 percent of all deaths. Adding additional mobile cardiac-care units to the nation's health care systems would cost only $2,000 per life saved. Reducing roadside hazards would save the lives of automobile drivers and passengers for between $20,000 and $100,000 each. The opportunity cost of saving lives by requiring a reduced speed limit appears to be too high by these comparisons. It is too high because there are alternative means of accomplishing the same goal at a lower cost.

The efficiency of a reduced speed limit in conserving gasoline can be evaluated in the same way. Are there alternatives that will conserve gas for a lower cost than reducing the speed limit? The government estimates that traveling at 55 MPH has reduced our gasoline consumption by 1 to 2 percent. The same amount of gasoline could be saved by ensuring that each car owner switches to radial tires when the present tires wear out, or keeps the present tires properly inflated, or changes spark plugs regularly. Each of these alternatives would conserve as much gas at a cost that is trivial compared to the cost of the 55 MPH speed limit. Another alternative that would save as much gas is to induce American drivers to buy fuel-efficient automobiles. If just 4 percent of drivers switched, it would save as much gas as the speed reduction.

How could society induce people to reduce their consumption of gasoline? What means does society have to change human behavior? According to the fundamental postulate of economics, increasing the benefits of taking an action increases the chances that the action will be selected by decision makers. Conversely, increasing the costs of the action will decrease its chances of being selected.

The type of economic system that exists will influence how the fundamental postulate will be employed. We have seen that there are two basic ways to organize an economic system: (1) the laissez-faire (free-market) system and (2) the command (planned) system, which takes the form of government directives. The U.S. economy, being a mixed economy, employs both systems. Human behavior can be influenced either by passing a law that makes the desired behavior compulsory, together with penalties for disobedience, or by increasing the personal incentives to behave in the desired way. Both methods rely on the fundamental theorem of economics to achieve the objective — the first by imposing costs on the existing undesirable behavior in the form of penalties for not complying with the new law, and the second by increasing the benefits of selecting the alternative desired behavior. The first method commands the desired behavior, whereas the second method provides an incentive for decision makers to choose to act in the desired manner.

In responding to the energy crisis, for example, the federal government generally chose to employ commands rather than incentives. It passed a law reducing the speed limit to 55 MPH, and it required automobile manufacturers to increase the fuel efficiency of new cars. Speeding tickets were issued to violators of the reduced speed limit, and large fines awaited the automobile manufacturers who did not comply with the fuel-efficiency regulation.

The government was aided in its efforts by the free-market system. The increased scarcity of energy meant substantially higher gasoline prices; prices more than doubled between 1975 and 1982. Drivers responded, as the fundamental postulate suggests, by reducing their consumption of gasoline, driving slower, eliminating unnecessary trips, keeping their cars tuned, car pooling, and using public transportation. When it came time to buy a new car, fuel economy was high on the buyers' priority lists. No laws had to be passed to encourage this behavior — the higher price of gasoline and the consumers' desire to economize were sufficient motivation.

The effect of this combination of the free-market and command systems was to reduce substantially the nation's consumption of gasoline. While some applauded the government's action, others said that the stick wielded by the command economy was unnecessary, because higher gas prices alone could make the free-market economy adjust to the new conditions.[6]

REQUIRED ECONOMIC CONCEPTS

Law of scarcity	Command system
Scarce good	Opportunity cost
Free good	Marginal analysis
Factors of production	Principle of rational behavior
Economics	Marginal benefit (marginal utility)
Economic system	Marginal cost
Capitalism	Production possibilities schedule
Socialism	Law of increasing costs
Laissez-faire system	

KEY QUESTIONS

1. What is the law of scarcity?
2. How do free goods differ from scarce goods?
3. What are factors of production? Specify the four factors of production.
4. Why does scarcity imply that choices must be made?
5. Briefly, what are economic systems? Name three types of economic systems.
6. Define *economics*.
7. What are the three consequences of scarcity?
8. How can the allocation of resources occur without using relative prices?
9. Define *opportunity cost*.
10. What is meant by the statement that economic choices are made at the margin? What is the decision rule that is consistent with such choices?
11. What is the law of increasing cost?
12. Is the economic value of human life infinite and therefore immeasurable?

PROBLEMS

1. A letter to a national magazine (*U.S. News & World Report*, Feb. 5, 1979) said: "Your catchy title 'Guns and Butter' is an oversimplification of national needs. It presumes that good defense and social programs come at each other's expense. In fact, national defense is itself a crucial social need. It makes no more sense to contend that defense comes at the expense of other social needs than it does to contend that education comes at the expense of

---

[6] Charles A. Lave, "The Costs of Going 55," *Newsweek*, October 23, 1978; Steven E. Rhoads, "How Much Should We Spend to Save a Life?" *The Public Interest*, Spring, 1978.

health. Be hopeful, all the nation's needs are important." Do you agree with the writer's analysis? Why or why not?

2.   Is air a free good or a scarce good? What about clean air in U.S. cities? Are worms a scarce good? Why or why not?

3.   You take an extra 20 minutes driving around the block looking for a free parking space before getting to your 9 a.m. class. Is the free parking space you find free? Why or why not?

4.   During and after World War II, the wages of domestic servants increased greatly. Did the former servants price themselves out of domestic jobs? Is that why there are so few of them today?

5.   Why are laundromats and wash-and-wear clothes so popular these days? Is it only because they are convenient? Can you relate your answer to Problem 4? Can you relate your answer to one of the economic postulates discussed in the chapter? Also, are we a wasteful society because we throw away things rather than have them repaired? Give an argument for the negative viewpoint.

6.   Someone has said: "The scarcity concept does not apply in the case of renewable timber resources where the concept of 'sustainable yield' is applied on government lands. Namely, cut trees at such a rate as to ensure a constant supply of lumber forever." Is the concept of scarcity thereby avoided here? Why or why not?

7.   "Take a bus and leave the driving to us" was the familiar tag line of Greyhound advertising. Explain why it might be cheaper to take a plane rather than a bus to see your grandmother in another city.

8.   By 1985 federal student loans had an 18 percent default rate. Should the government drop the program because of the apparent waste of resources involved? What has to be weighed against what?

9.   Suppose you take 3 hours off one evening to watch TV and forgo tutoring a student at $12 an hour for 3 hours. You could also have used the time to do $30 worth of typing. What were the costs to you of watching TV, if any?

APPLICATION ANALYSIS

1.   The owner of a parcel of land and of a store on that land is trying to decide whether to (a) lease the land to a developer for $6,000 a year, (b) rent the store to a business for $5,000 a year, or (c) continue to operate the store himself, where annual costs are $11,000 and expected revenues are $18,000. What is the opportunity cost to the owner of operating the store himself?

2.   The issue of "Star Wars" was discussed in the analysis for Preview 1.2. Referring to the following figure, answer the questions that follow:

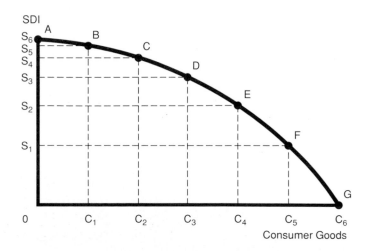

a.   If the economy is currently operating at point F, what is the level of consumer-goods production and the level of SDI spending?

b.   What is the opportunity cost if the economy moves from point D to point C?

c.   What would be the total cost to the economy of the SDI program if the economy is operating at point D?

d.   Suppose the SDI program is technically successful and leads to some technological spillover in the production of consumer goods. Roughly, what would the PPF curve tend to look like, assuming technological improvements are greater in the military realm than in the consumer goods realm?

e.   If there are increasing costs in the development of SDI technology, does it follow that there are decreasing costs in the production of consumer goods?

f.   Substitute the label *AIDS Research* for *Consumer Goods* on the horizontal axis of the figure. Suppose AIDS, by analogy, becomes the bubonic plague of the 1990s. How would this affect the PPF curve? Suppose World War III breaks out due to insufficient development of SDI and the Russians are encouraged to attack. How would this affect the PPF curve? Suppose SDI is fully developed and World War III breaks out. What do *you* think the PPF curve will look like?

APPENDIX TO CHAPTER 1

USING GRAPHS

To learn how the economy works, we must deal with many different relationships. For example, the relationships between interest rates and investment, between price and the amount people want to buy, and between cost and the amount firms want to produce are all important to a basic understanding of our economy. We use graphs to summarize and analyze the data underlying these types of economic relationships.

Graphs need not be mysterious, nor are they only for the mathematically inclined. Graphs are merely a tool to help us see the consequences of economic events — they literally allow us to draw pictures of the economy in order to visualize its workings. Analysis using graphs is not difficult. By following a few basic rules, we can find graphs to be an easy and powerful tool in the study of our economy.

USING GRAPHS TO SHOW ECONOMIC TRENDS

The simple economic graph in Figure 1A.1 shows the relationship between household income and the amount spent on consumable goods. To make this graph, we place a scale running left to right to measure income — this scale is called the *horizontal axis*. We use a second scale running bottom to top — the *vertical axis* — to measure the amount spent by households. (In your basic mathematics courses, you would usually label the horizontal axis "*x*" and the vertical axis "*y*.") We always label the two axes so that there is no confusion about the relationship shown by the graph.

In Figure 1A.1 we want to show how the amount of money people earn is related to the amount they plan to spend. (These amounts may not be the same, of course, since people borrow and save.) One way of doing this is by plotting *points* to develop a picture of the economic data. The actual data for several years are given in the table in Figure 1A.1. To plot the data for one year, we simply measure the income for that year on the horizontal axis and the spending for that year on the vertical axis, which gives us a point. For example, the point labeled "A" in Figure 1A.1 represents the first set of data in the table — a national income of $0.69 trillion and spending of $0.43 trillion in 1965. Similarly, the point labeled "B" represents the second set of data given in the table. *Notice that a single point gives two pieces of information: (1) the information obtained from*

This appendix was written by William V. Weber.

FIGURE 1A.1

By plotting points on a graph, we can visualize the trend in economic data.

Year	U.S. National Income (Trillions of Dollars)	U.S. Consumer Spending (Trillions of Dollars)
1965	0.69	0.43
1970	0.99	0.62
1975	1.55	0.98
1978	2.16	1.35
1980	2.63	1.67

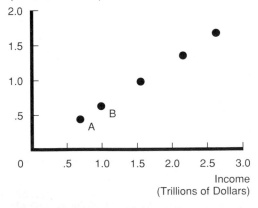

FIGURE 1A.2

A line or curve can be drawn to represent the trend observed in economic data.

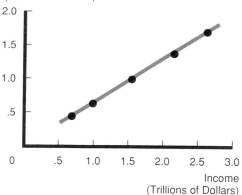

FIGURE 1A.3

In economic analysis we often work only with the line or curve that represents the trend observed in the data.

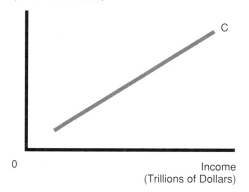

FIGURE 1A.4

Letters with subscripts are often used to label specific points on a trend line when the actual numbers are unavailable.

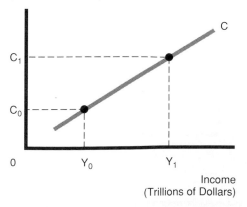

measuring left to right using the scale on the horizontal axis, and (2) the information obtained from measuring bottom to top on the vertical axis.

At this point you should verify that the other points are correctly plotted and that the graph shows a picture of the data. By now you have probably noticed a trend in the data. We see that the points are lining up in the northeast direction. We can visualize this trend by drawing a line through the data, as shown in Figure 1A.2. As we move left to right along this line, we are also moving up. This says that as income increases the amount spent is also increasing. The trend line we have drawn summarizes the basic relationship between income and consumer spending — as one goes up, the other also goes up.

In most economic analysis, we work only with the lines and curves representing the basic trends. In other words, we don't need to work with the specific numbers appearing in the actual data. We can learn a lot about the economy by looking only at the basic trends in the data. This is called *qualitative analysis.* (Working with the actual numbers would be called *quantitative analysis.*) The type of graph used for qualitative analysis is shown in Figure 1A.3. As you can see, this graph shows only the basic trend; the numbers representing the data behind the graph have simply been erased. The trend line itself is usually labeled with an abbreviation. The one in Figure 1A.3 is labeled "C," for "consumer spending."

Occasionally, we want to refer to some specific numbers in the economic relationship even when we have only the trend line. Sometimes we might simply make up numbers to illustrate the situation; at other times we might use letters or letters with subscripts to represent numbers in the graph. The latter situation is shown in Figure 1A.4. Do not be intimidated by the labeling in this graph. The notations "Y_0" and "Y_1" simply represent two different levels of income, with Y_1 being larger than Y_0. "Y_0" and "Y_1" are simply names for numbers that we don't have at the moment. Similarly, the notations "C_0" and "C_1" are just stand-ins for two different numbers on the vertical axis. The subscripts simply help us to see which names go together to represent a point in the graph.

THE CONCEPT OF SLOPE

Slope is often an important factor to consider when interpreting the trend in an economic graph. For example, consider the two income/spending graphs shown in Figure 1A.5. The one on the left is clearly steeper — it goes up faster than the other line as we go from left to right. We say that the steeper line has the greater slope.

There is a simple formula for the calculation of slope. First choose two points on the trend line. Then calculate the vertical distance and the horizontal distance between the two points. The slope of the line is then the vertical distance between the points divided by the horizontal distance between them. If the line is upward-sloping as we move from left to right, the resulting number is positive. If the line is downward-sloping, we put a negative sign on the slope to indicate this.

In the graph on the left of Figure 1A.5, the slope is calculated to be 0.90. This is because the horizontal distance between the two points shown on the graph is 1.0 and the vertical distance is 0.9. Dividing these two numbers gives a slope of 9/10, or 0.90. In other words, consumer spending (on the vertical axis) rises nine-tenths as fast as income (on the horizontal axis). Notice that the slope is positive, showing that the trend line is upward-sloping. You should do a similar calculation to show that the slope in the graph on the right is 0.70. Notice that steeper trend lines give larger numbers in the slope calculation.

F I G U R E   1 A . 5

Slope is used to measure how quickly a trend is rising or falling.

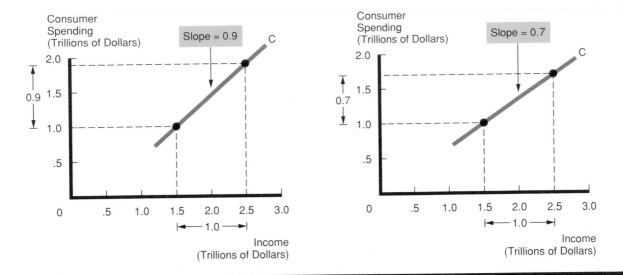

The slope of a trend line describes how the quantity on the vertical axis changes as the quantity on the horizontal axis changes. In Figure 1A.5 the slopes describe how fast the country's consumer spending rises as its income rises. In the graph on the left the slope is 0.90. This says that households spend 90 cents of every additional dollar of income. In the graph on the right the slope is smaller — only 0.70. This group of households spends only 70 cents of every additional dollar of income, saving the other 30 cents.

So the slopes in Figure 1A.5 represent how fast households spend additional income. The steeper slope in the left graph shows households that spend a relatively large amount of any extra income. In the right graph additional income is spent less quickly — the households represented in this graph tend to be savers. This set of graphs could be used, for example, to help analyze differences between the American economy (where personal saving tends to be relatively low, as in the left graph) and the Japanese economy (where personal saving tends to be high, as in the right graph).

We often have need of the economic interpretations of the slopes of trend lines. Economists usually use the word *marginal* in this context. (For example, you will see in Chapter 23 that the slope of the income/ spending relationship just discussed is called the *marginal propensity to consume.*) Don't let the terminology that economists use confuse you — just remember that *slope* (and the "marginal" name economists give it) *simply tells us how fast something is changing.*

SHIFTING CURVES VERSUS MOVING ALONG CURVES

Suppose we are working with a line or curve showing an economic relationship. (We usually use the word *curve* to mean *curve or line.* Thus we call the trend a *curve,* even when the trend falls in a line.) There are two

FIGURE 1A.6

No matter what the current level of income is, lower interest rates will stimulate consumer spending. Since a background parameter has changed, there is an entirely new trend and the curve shifts up.

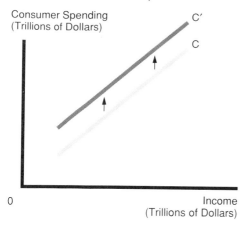

FIGURE 1A.7

A rise in prices in the economy will shift down the income/spending trend.

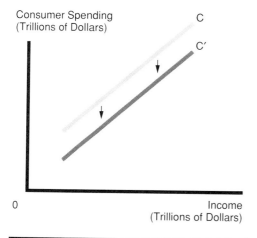

FIGURE 1A.8

When household income rises, we can simply follow the trend to see how consumer spending will change.

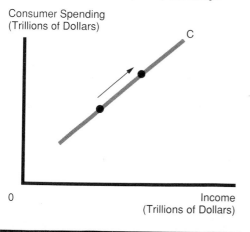

basic ways of showing changes in a graph: (1) shifting the curve that shows the trend and (2) moving from one point to another on the curve. The difference in the interpretation of these two methods often appears in economic analysis.

Let us return to our example of the income/spending graph. Clearly, there are many economic factors that can affect the trend between income and spending. Households' desire to save, the level of prices in the economy, the average size of families, and the interest rate that must be paid on loans and mortgages are just a few of the factors that affect the trend shown in the graph. But these other factors are not shown directly in the graph — they are not measured on the axes. Instead, these factors are in the background of the graph — they affect the trend but are not shown on either of the axes. These "background variables" underlying the trend are often called *parameters*.

The way that these underlying factors affect a graph is worth memorizing now, for it is used throughout this textbook. *When a variable in the background changes, the entire trend shown in the graph changes; we illustrate these changes in parameters by shifting the curve.*

Let us consider some examples. Suppose that there is a substantial fall in interest rates. Since mortgages, automobile loans, and credit card purchases would be less expensive and, in the case of loans, easier to obtain, we should expect this to stimulate household spending. How would these lower interest rates affect the trend shown in our income/spending line?

The answer is shown in Figure 1A.6. Whether households have low or high incomes, they will be buying more cars, houses, and durable goods when interest rates are lower. So consumer spending will have gone up, whether we are looking at the left side or the right side of the graph. In other words, we shall see an entirely new trend when interest rates fall — there has been a *shift* in the trend. Because all income levels have greater consumer spending, all points in the trend line have moved up. Notice the underlying principle here: A change in a background parameter completely changes the trend and shifts the curve.

Changes in other parameters would be illustrated by other shifts in the curve. For example, suppose there is a general increase in prices in the economy. How would we show this in the graph? We can reason that households will tend to cut back their purchases when prices rise. This is because their financial assets (like their checking accounts) can't buy as many goods, making the households less wealthy. Since decreased spending is in the downward direction in our graph (as shown on the vertical axis), this change is represented by a downward shift in the trend line. This is shown in Figure 1A.7.

There is one type of change that is shown with a movement along the curve instead of a shift in the curve. Suppose household income rises during an economic recovery. How would this affect the basic economic trend shown in our graph?

Here we have to be careful. Looking at the axes of our graph, we see that the curve shows how income and consumption are related. The upward slope of the curve shows that consumer spending rises when income rises. To illustrate the effects of higher income, we move along the trend as shown in Figure 1A.8. Using the horizontal axis, we represent the higher income by moving to the right. Since we are moving up along the trend as we go to the right, using the vertical axis we see that consumer spending rises when income rises.

Notice the difference in this case. *When the economic factors identifying the axes of a graph are the only factors that are changing, this is illustrated as a movement along the curve. The trend itself is unchanged;*

only the particular data selected from the trend are different. Always remember that a curve illustrates a relationship between two economic variables. If only those two variables change, we are simply changing the point we are looking at on the trend. Only changes in the underlying parameters of the trend can shift the curve.

When working with a graph, use the following steps to determine when to shift a curve. First determine if any background factors not directly shown on the graph have changed. If only the variables on the axes have changed, then only the location in the graph is different and you will show a movement along the curve. If a background factor has indeed changed, you will show a shift in the curve. In that case, you must figure out the directions in which the factors on the axes will change in order to determine the exact way that the curve shifts.

We conclude with three examples to further illustrate the ideas presented here.

AN EXAMPLE —
THE BUDGET LINE

Suppose you have $15 to spend on hamburgers and French fries for yourself and a group of friends. A burger costs $1.00 and an order of fries costs $0.50. In this situation you have a simple economic choice: How many burgers and fries can you buy with your $15?

Figure 1A.9 summarizes the answer. We choose to measure the number of burgers purchased on the horizontal axis and the number of orders of fries purchased on the vertical axis. The point labeled "A" shows one of your possible purchases — you could buy no burgers and 30 orders of fries. The point "B" shows another possibility — you could buy 15 burgers and no fries. The other points represent other possible combinations of burgers and fries you could purchase — 5 burgers and 20 fries, and 10 burgers and 10 fries.

In this case, the trend is downward as we move from left to right. Using the horizontal and vertical axes, we see that this simply means that the number of orders of fries you can buy with your $15 falls as the number of burgers you purchase rises. This trend line is often called a *budget line.*

Suppose that on the way to the burger stand you decide to buy more burgers and fewer fries than you had originally planned. How would this be shown on the graph? Figure 1A.10 shows the correct answer. (Notice that we have again deleted the numbers and show only the trend on the graph.) Since only the factors on the two axes have changed, we move along the budget line. We move down to show fewer fries and to the right to show more burgers.

On the other hand, suppose you discover that you have lost $3 and have only $12 when you get to the burger stand. How would this affect the budget line? This time a background factor affecting the number of burgers and fries you can purchase — the money you have to spend — has changed. Notice that this factor is not on either axis, so the curve shifts in this case. Since less money will decrease the amount of burgers and/or fries you can choose to buy, the budget line should move down (to show fewer fries) and to the left (to show fewer burgers). This is shown in Figure 1A.11.

We shall learn more about the budget line in the appendix to Chapter 6.

FIGURE 1A.9

This trend line — called a *budget line* — shows the possible purchases a person can make with $30 when a burger costs $1.00 and an order of fries costs $0.50.

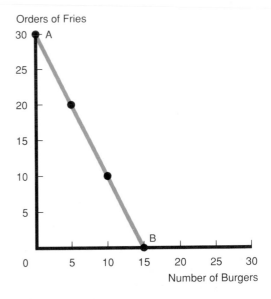

FIGURE 1A.10

If a person chooses to buy more burgers and fewer fries with the money available, only the variables on the axes have changed. This is shown with a movement down the curve.

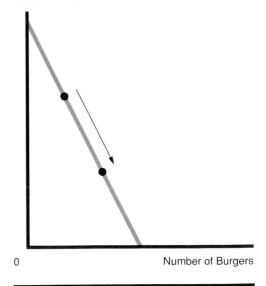

FIGURE 1A.11

With less money, a person can now buy fewer burgers and/or fewer fries. Since a parameter in the background of the graph has changed, this is shown by shifting the curve down and to the left.

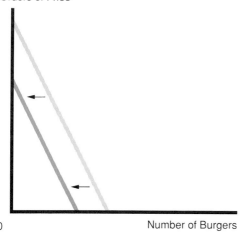

Orders of Fries

0   Number of Burgers

FIGURE 1A.12

This curve shows what the trend between the number of hours you study and your exam grade might look like.

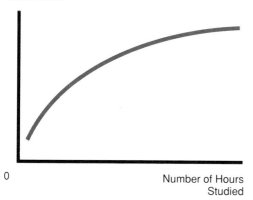

Exam Score

0   Number of Hours
                               Studied

FIGURE 1A.13

If you study more hours, to raise your exam grade, this would be diagramed with a movement along the curve.

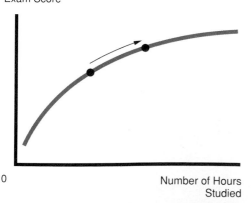

Exam Score

0   Number of Hours
                               Studied

AN EXAMPLE —

STUDYING AND GRADES

If life in college is at all fair, we would expect that the grades you get on exams will rise as you study more. Figure 1A.12 shows what this trend might look like.

To show this trend, we first need to set up the axes of our graph. For this example we shall measure the number of hours you study for an exam on the horizontal axis. The grade you get on the exam will be measured on the vertical axis.

If you have mastered the material in the earlier sections of this appendix, it should be easy to see why we have drawn an upward-sloping curve for this graph. As the amount of studying increases (i.e., as we move to the right along the curve), the grade you can expect to earn on your exam should also increase (i.e., we also move up along the curve).

What may not be obvious is why we have drawn a curve instead of a straight line to represent this trend. To see why, first recall what slope in a graph represents. In general, slope simply tells us how fast things are changing. Using the axes we have set up for this graph, we determine that the slope of the curve in Figure 1A.12 tells us how fast your exam score rises as you increase the amount of studying. (Economists might call this your "marginal" exam score.)

We have drawn the studying/grade trend so that it gets flatter as we move from left to right. This expresses the idea that your studying is becoming less and less productive as you study more and more. To see this, begin by considering those first two or three hours of studying. Those hours are usually very productive — often they are just enough to squeak out that C grade (as many procrastinators have discovered during their college careers). This is shown by the steep trend at the beginning of the graph in Figure 1A.12. For those first few hours of studying, your potential grade (measured on the vertical axis) rises quickly as you study more hours (measured on the horizontal axis).

Now consider those later hours of studying shown on the right side of the graph. Just because the first three hours of studying brought you from an F to a C does not mean that another three hours of studying will raise you from a C to an A. Instead, another three hours of studying might raise you to a B. Three more hours might get you to a low A, and it might take another three hours of studying to make that a solid A. You can't expect these additional hours of studying to be as productive with respect to your exam performance. You could probably rely on memorization to pull the C. But you usually need some skill and intuition in addition to memorized knowledge to pull the higher grades, for these require practice and frequent review which are more time-consuming than simple memorization.

We can therefore predict that your potential grade will increase less quickly with additional studying, and we want to have this trend reflected in our graph. We do this by drawing the curve in Figure 1A.12 so that it gets flatter and flatter as we move from left to right. Since the slope in this diagram represents how fast your grade (shown on the vertical axis) rises with additional studying (shown on the horizontal axis), the flatter trend shows the diminishing productivity of your studying.

Of course, the distinction between shifting the curve and moving along the curve also applies to this example. If you decide to increase your grade by studying more hours, this would be diagramed as a movement along the curve. Because only the two factors on the axes have changed, there is no change in the overall trend. We are simply following the trend in this case, as shown in Figure 1A.13.

On the other hand, suppose you get a new computer and have access to software tutorials that supplement your studying. Now because a background factor affecting the trend has changed, the curve will shift. Since we expect your exam grades to increase and this is shown by the upward direction in the graph, we shift the study/grade curve upward, as shown in Figure 1A.14.

AN EXAMPLE —
THE PRODUCTION POSSIBILITIES FRONTIER

To conclude our survey of graphs, we shall reexamine the production possibilities frontier (PPF) graphs of Chapter 1. As you will see, the basic ideas introduced in this appendix — slope, moving along trends, and shifting trends — appear throughout the discussion of those graphs.

Recall that the production possibilities frontier shows the various combinations of goods that a society could choose to produce with its available resources and technology. For example, the graph in Figure 1A.15 (which is similar to the PPF graphs discussed in Chapter 1) shows the trend formed by a nation's potential production of military and consumer goods.

We shall begin by considering the slope in the production possibilities frontier curve. First of all, the trend in the PPF is drawn downward-sloping. This shows the idea of opportunity cost. If we want more consumer goods (if we move to the right), then we must sacrifice some military goods (we must also move down).

Notice that the magnitude of the production possibilities frontier's slope is increasing — the PPF is getting steeper as we move from left to right. To understand what this represents, recall that, in general, slope measures how fast things are changing. In this specific case, the slope of the PPF shows how quickly we lose military goods when we choose to have more consumer goods. In other words, the PPF's slope measures how large a sacrifice of military goods is necessary to get extra consumer goods. By drawing the PPF steeper and steeper as we move from left to right, we are showing that we must sacrifice more and more military goods to get additional consumer goods. As discussed in Chapter 1, this idea is called the *law of increasing costs*.

The distinction between moving along the curve and shifting the curve is also important when working with the production possibilities frontier. For example, consider the story we told with Figure 1.3 (reproduced here as Figure 1A.16). We wanted to show what would happen in the economy as people perceived a military threat. We reasoned that they would have to sacrifice consumer goods in order to obtain more military goods. Since only the variables on the two axes of the PPF graph had changed, this was illustrated by moving along the curve from A to B to C to D to E.

The story was different in Figure 1.4 (reproduced here as Figure 1A.17). In that example we looked at economic growth. When there is economic growth, more resources become available and/or the technology improves. Since these factors are in the background of the graph and therefore not measured on the graph's axes, these caused the PPF to shift. Since both the amount of military goods produced (measured on the vertical axis) and the amount of consumer goods produced (measured on the horizontal axis) could be increased by economic growth, the PPF shifts up and to the left.

FIGURE 1A.14

If you try to raise your exam grade by using a new computer and software tutorials, this would be diagrammed as a shift of the curve

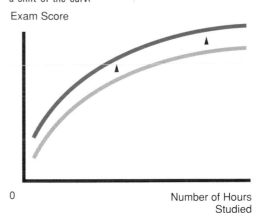

Exam Score

0   Number of Hours Studied

FIGURE 1A.15

The slope of the PPF curve measures the sacrifice in military goods required to get extra consumer goods.

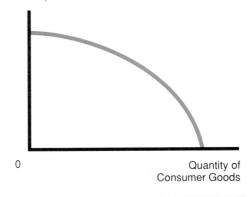

Quantity of Military Goods

0   Quantity of Consumer Goods

FIGURE 1A.16

If a society wants to produce more military goods (and hence fewer consumer goods) in response to a perceived military threat, this would be shown with a movement along the PPF curve.

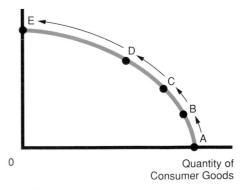

Quantity of Military Goods

0   Quantity of Consumer Goods

FIGURE 1A.17

When more resources become available and/or technology improves due to economic growth, this would be diagramed as a shift of the PPF curve.

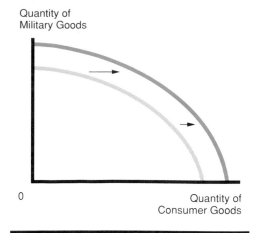

Quantity of
Military Goods

0   Quantity of
                                      Consumer Goods

SUMMARY

1. Graphs are simply pictures of trends that appear in economic data. It is often easier to work with the lines and curves representing the trends than with the actual data.

2. A graph shows the trend or relationship between two variables — one on the horizontal axis and one on the vertical axis. Any other factors that affect the trend are in the background of the graph and are called parameters.

3. Slope measures how quickly a trend line is rising or falling. A positive slope represents a rising trend, and a negative slope represents a falling trend. The steeper a trend is, the faster the variable on the vertical axis is changing.

4. A trend can have constant slope (as in the income/spending trend), it can start steep and become flatter and flatter (as in the studying/grade trend), or it can start flat and become steeper and steeper (as in the production possibilities curve). The pattern in the slope is chosen to best represent the trend to be expected between the two variables measured on the axes.

5. There are two different ways to show changes on a graph: (a) If only the factors measured on the axes are changing, then we are simply following the trend. This is shown by moving along the curve. (b) If one of the background parameters affecting the trend changes, then we have a totally new trend to consider. This is shown by shifting the curve representing the trend.

THE FUNDAMENTALS OF EXCHANGE

IN THIS CHAPTER YOU WILL LEARN:

How trade organizes the economy

●

How trade benefits producers and consumers

●

How trade makes specialization possible

●

How trade encourages low-cost production

IS THERE A WINNER AND A LOSER IN EVERY TRADE?

On March 7, 1778, Captain Cook sailed into Nootka Sound, off the coast of present-day British Columbia. There he and his crew met and established friendly relations with the Indians of the region. "They seemed to be a mild, inoffensive people more desirous of iron than anything else . . . ." The English exchanged iron products for the Indians' masks, cedar cloth, skins, and furs.

Midshipman Trevenen of Cook's crew was about to throw away a broken iron belt buckle, which he had placed upon his wrist as a sort of bracelet, when he saw an Indian eyeing him enviously. A bargain was struck, and the buckle was exchanged for a sea otter pelt.

When the explorers returned to China, Trevenen was able to sell the single pelt for $300 (more than $6,000 in today's dollars). He was able to purchase everything he personally required, plus silk gowns, tea, fans, and other items that he took home as presents for his family — all as proceeds from the trade of a "worthless" broken metal belt buckle. Trevenen was certain that he had much the best of the bargain. But had he? Why was the Indian so anxious to enter into such an uneven exchange?

Source: *The Journals of Captain Cook* (Seattle: University of Washington Press, 1976), 26.

SUBURBAN SERFDOM

Every Saturday morning, if the weather permits, Bob and Ralph can be found outside their homes caring for their lawns, plants, and shrubs. They are neighbors who occupy adjacent houses with lawns and gardens nearly identical in size and layout. Ralph is an insurance agent and Bob is an economist. Both of them dislike their lawn and garden chores and would much rather do something else, but both have surrendered to the neighborhood social pressure to keep up appearances and property values. Bob complains incessantly about his fate to whoever will listen, claiming that he is little more than a suburban serf. Ralph is more stoical about his circumstances, doggedly but quickly pursuing his tasks until they are finished.

Ralph is quite a bit older than Bob and hates to stoop over. Nevertheless, despite his age, he is able to perform the tasks of lawn and garden maintenance much more quickly than Bob, finishing each task in less time than Bob. Saturday mornings improved for both, however, when Bob and Ralph made the following deal.

Under the agreement, Ralph mows his own lawn and then part of Bob's lawn in exchange for which Bob weeds Ralph's entire garden. Ralph spends the same amount of time on his outdoor tasks as he always has, but he spends all of it mowing. Ralph agreed to the plan because he didn't like to bend over to weed. Bob agreed to it not because he preferred to weed (he hated both tasks equally!) but because he wanted to be finished with the onerous tasks of gardening and lawn mowing as quickly as possible. Bob knew that if he and Ralph specialized, with Ralph doing most of the mowing and Bob doing all of the weeding, he would finish sooner. Why is this so?

FAMINES — THE ULTIMATE CONSEQUENCE OF SCARCITY

Famines have received much public attention in recent decades because they have continued to plague some Third World countries despite the general prosperity of most of the world's economies. The great Biafran famine of 1968, for example, was followed by a severe famine in Bangladesh in 1974 and by recurrent famines in Ethiopia and sub-Saharan Africa during the 1970s and 1980s. The more fortunate countries of the world have responded by sending relief. These well-intentioned efforts have been less than a total success, however, in part because the nature of famines is not well understood either by the persons in charge of relief efforts or by the general public whose charity provides the relief.

It is generally assumed that famines occur because of a sudden, unforeseen decline in the availability of food in a particular area. Certainly it is reasonable to conclude that the cause of starvation is a shortage of food that results from a natural or man-made catastrophe.

This picture of famine, however, is not entirely accurate. When famines have occurred in the twentieth century, not all segments of the population have suffered equally. Urban populations have fared the best, and among the rural populations agricultural workers, as distinct from farmers who own their own land, have suffered the most. Starvation is the result of *some* people not having enough to eat, rather than a matter of there not being enough food for all to eat.

While food shortage may be one cause of starvation among certain population segments, it is not the only cause and in fact may not be the main cause of most famines. During several famines, food was actually exported from the area where people were starving. During the great Irish potato famine of the 1840s, for example, large quantities of food were exported from Ireland, where people were starving, to England, where people were not starving. There is also evidence that food was shipped from Bangladesh to India during the Bangladesh famine and out of Ethiopia during the 1970s famine.

Because famines still occur, and because conscience requires that help be sent when they do, it is imperative to understand their true causes in order to deliver effective relief.

• INTRODUCTION •

The greatest improvement in the productive powers of labor, and the greater part of the skill, dexterity, and judgment with which it is any where directed, or applied, seem to have been the effects of the division of labor.

Adam Smith, *The Wealth of Nations*

Consider the enormous task of organizing the American economy. There are more than 240 million individuals living in 85 million household-consumer groups, each with its own tastes and preferences. The labor force is composed of more than 115 million individuals, each with different skills and ambitions. These individuals work for more than 16 million business firms, producing thousands of different goods and services that are eventually consumed by the millions of individuals.

How and by whom is this enormous economy organized? The answer is surprisingly simple and straightforward. Each individual, in cooperation with every other individual in the economy, organizes the economy through the process of **exchange**. Persons exchanging what they have for other things that they want is the basis for economic organization. Literally millions of exchanges take place every day in the United States, and the sum total of these exchanges organizes the nation's economy.

Exchange is the act of giving or taking one thing in return for another. •

EXCHANGE AND ECONOMIC ORGANIZATION

Three types of exchange influence economic organization: trade, gift giving, and theft. Each is undertaken because the individual initiating the exchange expects to be better off once it is completed, but each of these exchanges has a different effect on economic organization.

The first and most important type of exchange is **trade**. What is exchanged is the legal ownership of the goods involved. Trades are two-way exchanges. Each trader gives up something but also receives something.

1. A trade takes place when a good moves from a person who values it less to a person who values it more.
2. Both persons engage in the trade because they expect to be better off after the exchange, or, at the very least, one person expects to be better off and the other expects to be no worse off.

No doubt you are already familiar with the process of trading. Most persons begin to trade when they are very young. Young children regularly trade toys or baseball cards. Such exchanges contain the basic elements of all trade.

A trade is the exchange of the legal right to a good or service for the legal right to something that another person owns.

The basic purpose of trade is to increase the participants' well-being by making them better off.

The second form of exchange is **gift giving**.

Gift giving is a one-way exchange wherein one person transfers the legal ownership of a good to another person and receives in return the satisfaction resulting from making that person better off.

Gift giving is a very important social activity in the U.S. economy. Numerous days are set aside for personal gift giving: Christmas, birthdays, anniversaries, and similar occasions. Individuals also give more than $50 billion in charitable contributions each year. Private gift giving, if it is truly voluntary, also makes everyone better off. The recipient now has more goods than before, making the giver feel better as a result.

There are two main purposes for giving gifts: (1) to express affection and (2) to transfer wealth. When you give a gift to a person you love, it is given as a token of your affection. When you give to United Way or a similar charity, you do so to improve the material well-being of less fortunate persons. The U.S. government is deeply involved in gift giving of the second type. More than half of the federal government's expenditures are in the form of income transferred from taxpayers to those individuals who are by law entitled. Social security, aid to families with dependent children, national student loans, and farm price-support programs are examples of government gift giving.

The recipient of an entitlement may have had to perform some service to qualify. Social security recipients, having spent their working lives paying social security taxes, may object to having their social security checks referred to as *gifts*. But the truth is that most social security recipients receive much more than they ever paid in taxes. Public gift giving, because it has an element of compulsion (you must pay your taxes whether or not you agree with how they are spent), may or may not make everyone better off, depending on the circumstances.

Theft is the third type of exchange.

> *Theft is an involuntary transfer in which one person confiscates a good belonging to another person.*

Theft can be considered involuntary gift giving in that the thief expects to become better off; the victim, however, is clearly made worse off. Theft is an important negative influence in the process of organizing the economy. Surprisingly, there is actually a holiday devoted to theft: on Halloween youngsters are encouraged to practice extortion, in the form of trick or treat. Children in disguise offer adults a deal they dare not refuse lest some malicious act make them worse off. What is important about theft, from society's point of view, is the need to minimize this form of exchange.

TRADE

Trade is the most significant form of exchange because it conserves resources and allows traders to achieve their goals at the lowest possible cost. Society, of course, discovered the benefits of trade long before there were any economists. The contribution of economics is the formal demonstration of the benefits of trade.

Its benefits make trade one of the most important concepts in economics:

1. Trade itself creates wealth.
2. Trade encourages the low-cost producer to supply the goods.

In the following section we shall examine how the process of trading creates wealth. Then, after we consider theft and gift giving, we shall see how trade creates wealth by encouraging the low-cost producer to supply the goods.

CREATION OF WEALTH THROUGH TRADE You probably would agree that it is better to be wealthy than to be poor. But of what does **wealth** consist? If you respond: "Wealth consists of material possessions," you would be only partially correct. The more accurate response would be:

APPLICATION

2.1

WHAT CONSTITUTES
WEALTH?

When most persons are asked to define wealth, they list material goods or measures of the ability to acquire material goods. Wealth, they believe, consists of houses, cars, electronic goods, jewelry, or the money to buy such things. Material things can contribute to wealth, but there is no necessary relationship between an increase in the quantity of material things and an increase in wealth. A garbage dump is a collection of material things, but to most persons it is not an accumulation of wealth. What is the difference between the material things in a garbage dump and those in a safety deposit box at the local bank? The difference lies in the valuation people place on the two types of contents.

In fact, wealth can exist without the presence of any material goods. It is possible, for example, to purchase at auction the English title of lord of a manor without actually purchasing any physical property within the manor itself. Originally, in the Middle Ages, an English manor was an area of land with a few serfs granted by the Crown to a loyal servant. In addition to the land, the lord of the manor received various rights and privileges, such as the rights to hold a market, to cut firewood, and to use some of the labor of the manor's inhabitants. There were only two ways to acquire such a title. The first and surest way was to pick the right parents, make sure you were the firstborn male, and wait for your father to go to his final reward. The second way was to do so many highly conspicuous good works that the only appropriate earthly reward was a title granted by the king.

There is now another way. In the early 1920s Parliament, without intending to do so, created another avenue to a title. An act that stripped the manor lords of most of their rights and privileges made it legally possible to separate the title itself from the manorial real estate. Initially, no one thought the title would have any value without the real estate.

Then in 1960 a Lord Huntington asked a real estate firm to determine whether there was any monetary value in a dozen lordships of manors he had inherited. All that was to be transferred were the titles — the Lordship of Beedon in Berkshire or the Lordship of Stratford St. Andrews near Ipswich, for example. No physical property was involved, the real estate having been sold and the other rights nullified long ago. To everyone's surprise, the lordships were snatched up at auction for an average of £3,500 each.

What was the buyer buying? The lordships of manors are property. They are incorporeal (property without body) as distinguished from land, which is corporeal property. What the buyer actually obtained was the right to use the title John Jones, Lord of the Manor of Thistledown on Thames on his stationery, business cards, automobile, or anywhere else he wished to use it. The owner of this title would probably find it convenient to shorten it to Lord Thistledown. This title, while it wouldn't qualify for a seat in the House of Lords, might well obtain a better seat in a restaurant. A buyer of a title may believe that it conveys a certain prestige that could not be obtained in any other way.

The ownership of manorial titles has actually proved to be a fairly good investment. The prices of lordships of manors have been steadily increasing over time. The price of the cheapest manorial title at the most recent auction was £6,000. All titles offered were quickly sold. The auctioneer is even thinking of holding a similar auction in the United States — at Disney World!

The fact that titles have a value of their own proves that wealth is not confined to the ownership of material goods. Instead, wealth consists of whatever people value. Owning a title of lordship of a manor is wealth precisely because other people also place a value on it.

Wealth is whatever people value.

Wealth is related to material things only if people value those things. Pork is of value to a Christian, but not to a Muslim. Increasing the number of pigs would increase wealth in the United States, but not in a Muslim country such as Iran. It is not the material object itself that creates wealth, but the fact that people value that item.

Consider the following situation. Mary has a Bruce Springsteen album and a brother named Aaron. Mary values the album highly, a sentiment not shared by Aaron. Aaron would gladly give it away, but Mary would not. The album is wealth to Mary precisely because she values it, but it is not wealth to Aaron. On the other hand, Aaron has some video games that he values highly, but they are completely worthless to Mary. If Aaron received another video game, he would consider himself wealthier. But if Mary received a video game, she would not consider herself wealthier. Wealth, therefore, does not consist of material things alone, but is determined by the value an individual places on them.

Suppose Mary exchanges her Bruce Springsteen album for Sue's Madonna album. This type of trade is called a **barter exchange**.

A barter exchange is one in which one good is directly traded for another good.

Under what circumstances would this type of exchange take place?

First, the exchange would occur only if Mary had something that Sue wanted and Sue had something that Mary wanted. In our example this condition was satisfied. Mary possessed a Springsteen album that Sue wanted, and Sue had a Madonna album that Mary coveted. Second, such an exchange would occur only if Mary valued the Madonna album more than she valued her Springsteen album. Conversely, Sue would agree to the exchange only if she valued the Springsteen album more than her Madonna album. *Thus trade never takes place between goods valued equally by either one of the traders.*

This type of trade demonstrates that when preferences differ there is a basis for profitable trade. The trade was possible only because the two trading parties had different preferences when it came to record albums. *When preferences differ, there may be a basis for trade.*

When the trade in record albums occurred, Mary surrendered what she valued less for what she valued more, and so did Sue. The same amount of material goods exists after the trade — one Springsteen album and one Madonna album — but the persons who have these items value them more than did their previous owners. Because valuations have increased, wealth has been created. *Trade creates wealth precisely because it allocates goods to those who value them the most.*

Record albums may not be items of crucial importance, but the exchange demonstrates the gains that result from trade. Most trades are more complicated and less direct than the simple barter exchange described above. Perhaps a more typical trade would involve the exchange of your labor for money. After you have accumulated enough money, you can exchange that money at a grocery store for food or at a car dealership for a new car.

What has been exchanged when you purchase a car? A partially correct answer would be that the car dealer gave up the car that was valued less than the things that the money received in exchange would buy, which were valued more. You, in return for the car, gave up the thing(s) that you would have purchased had you not bought the car. You did this because you desired the car more than the highest-valued alternative that the money spent for the car could buy. Both you and the car dealer benefited because you gave up something you valued less for something you valued more. Thus wealth has been created because goods have been transferred to those who value them most.

In the above trade, money was exchanged for a car, but more than the physical reality of the car was involved. What was exchanged was the *legal ownership* of the money and of the automobile. You, the purchaser of the car, received a legal title along with the car. The title guarantees to you certain rights, known as **private-property rights,** that govern the possession and use of the car.

> *Private-property rights are rights granting the owner exclusive control over the use and sale of the property.*

Private-property rights give the owner the sole right to exclude others from using the good, the exclusive right to enjoy the good, and the exclusive right to sell the good.

The value of private-property rights can easily be seen in the car purchase example above. Suppose the car did not come with these rights. Would the car have been worth as much in trade as it was with these rights? Suppose the car you obtained in trade could be used by anyone else without your permission. When you left your parked car, for example, you could never be certain that it would be there on your return because someone else could be using it in the meantime. Clearly, such a car is worth less to you than one that is yours exclusively. How much would you pay to purchase a car without a legal title? The answer is not very much!

The private-property rights that come with the purchase of a car in the form of a title to the car and the registration of ownership are responsible for much of the value you place on the car. The government has determined that the car is private property, has specified the owner of that property, and has guaranteed the owner the security of his or her property.

THEFT

Theft has exactly the opposite result of trade. A theft occurs when one person confiscates a good whose legal ownership belongs to another person. Theft has the advantage of being a simple, direct way to become better off without giving up something in return. Many people, it seems, cannot resist the attractions of theft. Almost 10 million acts of robbery, burglary, and larceny take place every year in the United States, resulting in nearly $5 billion in property losses.

Theft destroys wealth. Thieves expect to be better off, but they will not be if they are caught. Victims are clearly worse off. If they had wanted the thieves to have the goods stolen from them, the victims would have presented the goods to the thieves in the first place. In the case of theft, goods generally go from persons who value them more to persons who value them less. This is because the value of goods is reduced when they are stolen. Theft in this way destroys wealth.

Goods that have been stolen cannot be legally resold, because legal rights in property are not transferred with the stolen goods when they are traded. Because they do not possess rights in property, stolen goods resell for much less than they originally sold for, perhaps only about one-third of their price as legally owned goods. Thus the $5 billion worth of legally owned goods is reduced in value by two-thirds when they become stolen goods. Theft destroys wealth because it severs the legal property rights that are responsible for much of the value of goods. When a thief steals a good for which you paid $100, he or she knows that it can be resold for only about $33.

Theft destroys wealth in still another way. If there is a threat that you will lose your private possessions to a thief, you will take steps to minimize

APPLICATION

2.2

FREE BICYCLES AND PRIVATE-PROPERTY RIGHTS

Traffic congestion has become a major problem in many of the urban centers of Europe, especially in the older parts of the cities. It has become difficult to get around in these cities and almost impossible to find a place to park an automobile. Public transportation is always crowded and often inconvenient. A number of youth groups in Geneva, Switzerland, decided to do something positive about the problem. Banding together, they purchased 150 new pink bicycles and placed them on the streets of Geneva for anybody to ride. These bicycles were owned by the groups but declared to be available for all to use. The youth groups expected the young people of the city to use the free bicycles whenever they wanted to travel in the downtown areas.

Economic theory would predict that this social experiment was doomed to failure, because it separated private-property rights from the bicycles. The bicycles were simply worth less when they were available for all to use than when they were the exclusive property of an individual owner. The reduced value of the collectively owned bicycles would have serious consequences for the success of the pink bicycles.

All went according to plan for a few months, and then trouble developed. The number of pink bicycles in working order noticeably declined. An inventory showed that only 127 bicycles could be found, and 75 of these were not in working order. Many of the broken bicycles were the result of too many riders at one time, because it had become popular to see how many persons could pile on a bike at one time. None of the riders had felt obligated to interfere with this behavior or to repair the damaged bicycles. Instead, the bicycles were simply abandoned where they had broken down. Some of the missing bicycles, which, it was discovered, had been repainted, were later retrieved. All of these stolen bicycles were in working order.

An additional problem was also uncovered. Some persons, those who were not up to actually stealing and repainting a pink bicycle but tired of not finding a bicycle available, would use a bicycle lock. They would ride a pink bicycle to a destination and then lock the bicycle in order to ensure its presence when they returned.

These results are not surprising. In fact, they are predictable behavior in the absence of private-property rights. No one has sufficient incentive to maintain and protect goods that have to be shared with everyone else. Why maintain a bicycle when other people would obtain most of the benefits of any repairs you made? If it were your bicycle, you would probably keep it in good repair. But if it is everybody's bicycle, why bother?

A bicycle that is your private property is simply worth more to you than a bicycle that can be used by everyone. The persons who stole and repainted the pink bicycles instinctively knew this. Paint the bike blue and everyone else would leave it alone. The persons who carried bicycle locks were trying to reserve a bike for their exclusive use. They were attempting to assert private-property rights because goods held as private property are worth more to individuals than goods available for all to use. Private-property rights create wealth.

that threat. You may install locks or a burglar alarm, buy a large dog, hire a private security guard, and take out an insurance policy. These expenses have an opportunity cost. You have sacrificed the potential ownership of more goods in order to protect the goods you now own. In fact, if the threat of loss is high, you may react by purchasing goods that you desire less but that cannot be easily stolen. Leisure is such a good. If what you produce is likely to be taken without your permission, why work so hard? Thus theft has serious disincentive effects.

In order to reduce the loss of wealth through theft and to counter the disincentives theft creates, every society has laws against stealing and spends resources enforcing these laws.

GIFT GIVING

Gift giving does not create wealth in quite the same way as trade. Gift giving creates wealth because the giver feels better off (wealthier) knowing that the recipient now has more material goods — the highest valued use for the gift is its possession by the recipient. The recipient is obviously better off because he or she has more wealth than before receiving the gift.

Gift giving is consistent with the third postulate of economic analysis that was discussed in Chapter 1: Economic decision makers always choose purposefully and always economize. Economic analysis does not assume that people act selfishly; rather it assumes that they always act in a way that maximizes individual satisfaction. Presenting a gift to a friend or relation is a purposeful act designed to express your regard for that person. You are made better off because you have expressed your affection and/or respect in a concrete act. Gift giving is consistent with choosing purposefully, whereas selfish behavior is not.

Gift giving is, however, not always self-sacrificing. Sometimes gift giving contains elements of both trading and stealing. Some people give presents on gift-giving days in part because they expect to receive gifts in return. Thus gift giving has some aspects of trading, but it may also have aspects of extortion. Suppose you fail to give any gifts at all this Christmas. What will be the reaction of your family and friends? Gift giving when the present is expected is not a purely voluntary expression in that it has an element of compulsion about it.

It is important to distinguish gifts that are given to express affection from gifts that are given to transfer wealth. It may be totally inappropriate to give a loved one a check for a sum of money when a personally selected gift would be preferred and expected. A carefully selected gift conveys its own message of affection. However, when giving gifts to transfer wealth, gifts in kind can be an inefficient way to accomplish this task, as Application 2.3 demonstrates.

The possibility of receiving a gift designed to transfer wealth creates incentives of your own. How do you behave in order to maximize your chances of receiving a gift? The answer is to appear the most worthy of the potential recipients. In order to do this, you must surpass your rivals. You must become Aunt Alberta's favorite niece or nephew, you must write the best grant proposal, or you must lobby most effectively to have your group receive a transfer from the government. Each of these activities requires resources that have opportunity costs. The resources that you spend becoming the most worthy cannot be used to produce goods and services for trading purposes. Gift giving can therefore result in behavior that reduces wealth if individuals employ resources to curry favor with gift givers instead of producing goods for trade. Is this the best use of those resources?

TRADE AND PRODUCTION AT THE LOWEST COST

As important as gifts and thefts are in our society, trade is the exchange that governs the process of organizing the economy. The process of trading, as we have seen, creates wealth, but perhaps even more important, trade encourages efficiency in the production of goods and services. Trading encourages the low-cost producer to do the work.

A P P L I C A T I O N

2.3

THE PECULIAR ECONOMICS OF GIFT GIVING

A service station located in a major metropolitan area has in its service bay a large tank of kerosene, a fuel not widely used in that locality. The station sells very little of the fuel in this tank even though the tank takes up quite a bit of room. A curious customer asked the station's owner why he didn't get rid of the tank. The owner replied that kerosene was one of his most profitable products, a puzzling reply since he obviously sold so little.

The puzzle was resolved sometime later when the curious customer observed a man enter the station and seek out the owner. Together both men went to the cash register, and the owner took out $2.50 and gave it to the man in exchange for a coupon. The cou-

pon was from the Salvation Army and was good for five gallons of kerosene to be used for home-heating purposes. Because the Salvation Army wished to make the poor better off and more comfortable during the cold winter months, if offered to pay the service station $5 if the station would give the bearer of such a coupon five gallons of kerosene. The bearer in this case didn't want kerosene, he wanted cash. He was willing to discount the coupon, receiving half of its value in return for cash. The service station owner was happy to oblige the man, because he made $2.50 in the transaction and didn't have to surrender a drop of kerosene in return.

This transaction reveals something very important about gift giving designed to transfer wealth. Suppose that A is the cost of the gift to the donor, B is the value of the gift to the recipient, and C is the cost to the recipient of obtaining the gift. Then:

$$A - B = \text{Waste involved in giving the gift}$$
$$B - C = \text{Increase in the recipient's well-being}$$

In this case A is $5, which is the amount that the coupon cost the Salvation Army, and B is $2.50, which is the amount that the recipient was willing to take for the coupon. The waste $(A - B)$ is

$2.50. The Salvation Army thus paid $5 to increase the welfare of the recipient by $2.50.

The gift was not totally free to the recipient, of course. He had to qualify for the gift by demonstrating need. Perhaps he had to go to the Salvation Army's shelter and stand in line for a while to obtain the coupon. The opportunity cost of the time thus spent is equal to C, and $B - C$ is the net value of the gift to the recipient. Therefore the value of the gift was somewhat less than $2.50, depending on the value of C.

How could the Salvation Army achieve its goal more efficiently and economically? It could have given money directly rather than as a gift in kind. By giving the man $2.50 in cash and making him equally as well off, the Salvation Army would have saved $2.50, which then could be used to make some other poor person better off. Or it could have given the man $5 and made him twice as well off. In either case, the service station operator, whom the Salvation Army never intended to help, would have been cut out of the gift.

People value goods differently. What you consider the most valuable good to obtain if you had more income is likely to be different from what your neighbor would choose. The busiest day of the year for many U.S. retailers is the day after Christmas when people exchange the presents they received for goods they would prefer to have. Although it may be appropriate for individuals to give gifts in kind as tokens of affection, it is inefficient for the Salvation Army to do so.

Since valuations are likely to differ among people — the Salvation Army valuing kerosene at $5 and the recipient valuing it at less than $2.50, for example — the only way to ensure that there is no waste in gift giving is to give cash. Only in this case is A (cost of gift to donor) certain to be equal to B (value of gift to recipient) and the possibility of waste thus eliminated.

The implication of this example for the economics of gift giving for gifts designed to transfer wealth is that the well-being of a recipient of a gift can be improved at lower cost by giving cash than by giving a gift in kind. Thus, when deciding how to improve the welfare of a particular group, governments and charitable organizations should directly transfer money rather than provide particular goods, coupons, or even food stamps.

SPECIALIZATION
FOSTERED BY TRADE

Trade creates wealth by fostering **specialization**.

Specialization is the process of concentrating production in the hands of the most efficient producer.

When the relatively efficient producer is encouraged to undertake a task, goods are produced at a lower cost than would otherwise be the case. In the quotation in the introduction to this chapter, Adam Smith, the great eighteenth-century economist, noted the effect that specialization has upon productivity.

In a famous passage in the first chapter of his book *The Wealth of Nations*, Smith described a pin factory:

> One man draws out the wire, another straightens it, a third cuts it, a fourth points it, a fifth grinds it at the top for receiving the head; to make the head requires two or three distinct operations; to put it on is a peculiar business, to whiten the pins another; it is even a trade by itself to put them into the paper; and the important business of making a pin is, in this manner, divided into about eighteen distinct operations. . . .[1]

Smith observed that by dividing the process of manufacturing pins into a number of distinct steps, the efficiency of pin production was enormously increased. Productivity is enhanced by specialization because each worker becomes proficient at a narrowly defined, specific task, and less time is wasted moving between tasks.

> I have seen a small manufactory of this kind where ten men only were employed . . . . They could, when they exerted themselves, make among them about . . . forty-eight thousand pins in a day. . . . But if they had all wrought separately, . . . they certainly could not each of them have made twenty. . . .[2]

Specialization, according to Smith, increased the output per person from 20 pins a day to 48,000 — a remarkable increase!

Smith credited most of the increases in economic productivity to specialization, or "the division of labor." Specialization increased productivity by increasing the skills of labor, by reducing the time spent on changing tasks, and by encouraging the invention of new cost-reducing processes. First, when labor is specialized in doing only one task, workers become very proficient in performing this single function and the task becomes routine. Second, when workers perform the same task constantly, time is not spent putting away the tools needed for one task and setting up for another task. Third, when workers' attention is focused on narrowly defined tasks, ways to perform the tasks more easily and quickly become apparent. Thus technological change can occur through specialization.

The possibility of trade makes specialization possible. Because all people wish to consume a variety of goods, they will not voluntarily concentrate exclusively on producing one particular good unless they can trade the resulting excess output for a variety of goods that are more desirable to them. The workers in the pin factory that Adam Smith observed no doubt desired food, clothing, and shelter more than thousands of straight pins. These workers would specialize in producing pins only if

---

[1]Adam Smith, *The Wealth of Nations* (Cannan edition, 1937), 4.
[2]Ibid., 5.

these pins could be profitably exchanged for other goods. *The gains in productivity that specialization allows can be obtained only if the resulting output can be traded.*

SPECIALIZATION AND COMPARATIVE ADVANTAGE

Trade makes specialization possible, but **comparative advantage** determines which individual, business firm, or nation will specialize in which products and who will be the low-cost producer. Comparative advantage is the ability of an individual, firm, or nation to produce a good at the lowest opportunity cost.

Comparative advantage is the principle which states that total output will be greatest when the output of each good is produced by the low-opportunity-cost producer and is exchanged for other, more desirable goods for which that individual, firm, or nation is not the low-cost producer.

Comparative advantage is not the same as **absolute advantage.**

Absolute advantage is the ability of an individual, firm, or nation to produce more of a good than rival producers can produce, given similar resources and the same state of technology.

Suppose that two geographic regions — such as Japan and that part of the United States known as the Northeast — are similar in size and have the same technology. Each area produces two goods: steel and computers. Assume that the United States can produce more of these goods than Japan. The United States, then, has an absolute advantage in the production of both steel and computers.

Table 2.1 summarizes the production possibilities for the two countries. Assuming that both countries have the same amount of resources, the United States can produce more computers and more steel than Japan. If the United States produced only computers, it could produce 30, while Japan could produce only 10. If, alternatively, the United States produced only steel, it could produce 30 tons, while Japan could produce only 20 tons. Suppose that the United States devoted half of its resources to producing computers and half to producing steel, and suppose that Japan did likewise. In this case, the United States would produce 15 computers and 15 tons of steel, while Japan would produce 5 computers and 10 tons of steel.

TABLE 2.1
Production Possibilities for the United States and Japan

	UNITED STATES		JAPAN	
PRODUCTION POSSIBILITIES	COMPUTERS PRODUCED	STEEL PRODUCED (TONS)	COMPUTERS PRODUCED	STEEL PRODUCED (TONS)
Computers only	30	0	10	0
Half and half	15	15	5	10
Steel only	0	30	0	20
Opportunity cost	1 Computer = 1 Ton of steel		1 Computer = 2 Tons of steel	

FIGURE 2.1
Production Possibilities for the United States and Japan

In the absence of trade, the United States chooses to produce the combination represented by point A on its PPF — 18 computers and 12 tons of steel — and consumes the same quantities it produces. In the absence of trade, Japan chooses to produce the combination represented by point B — 8 computers and 4 tons of steel — and similarly consumes what it produces. Point A′ and point B′ represent combinations for each country that are more desirable than the combination the country has chosen but that are unattainable, given existing resources and technology and given the absence of trade. A comparison of the two graphs shows that the United States has an absolute advantage in the production of both goods, because the United States can produce more of both goods than Japan can.

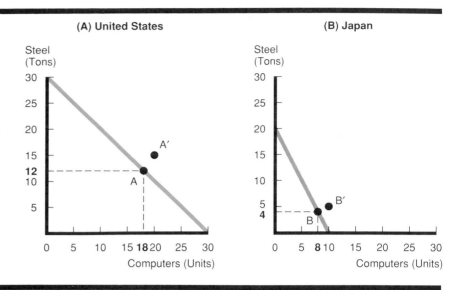

Figure 2.1 shows the production possibilities frontiers (PPFs) for both the United States and Japan. The production possibilities for the United States clearly dominate those of Japan, reflecting the absolute advantage of the United States in producing both computers and steel. Let us reasonably assume that both countries desire some of both goods. Each PPF shows the maximum combination that each country can produce and consume. The United States chooses to operate at point A on its PPF, producing and consuming 12 tons of steel and 18 computers. The United States would like to produce and consume more of both goods — say, at point A′ (20 computers and 15 tons of steel) — but this combination is unattainable given the available resources and state of technology. Japan chooses to produce and consume at point B, producing and consuming 4 tons of steel and 8 computers. Japan would also like to produce and consume more of both goods — say, at point B′ (10 computers and 5 tons of steel) — but is constrained by its production possibilities from doing so.

It might appear that no possibilities for trade exist between the U.S. Northeast and Japan because the United States can produce more of both goods, *but absolute advantage tells us nothing about the possibilities for profitable exchanges.* Comparative advantage governs trade and arises out of relative, not absolute, efficiency. As long as the **opportunity cost** of doing the same task differs between two individuals, firms, or countries, each will have a comparative advantage in producing some good. Opportunity costs, then, determine comparative advantage.

> *The opportunity cost of an economic action is the value of the best forgone alternative.*

Differences in opportunity cost determine whether or not comparative advantage exists. As long as the opportunity cost of producing a computer in terms of steel sacrificed differs between the United States and Japan, one country will have a comparative advantage in computers and the other will have a comparative advantage in steel. As Table 2.1 shows, the United States can increase its output of computers by one unit at the sacrifice of one ton of steel, whereas Japan can produce one more computer only be sacrificing two tons of steel.

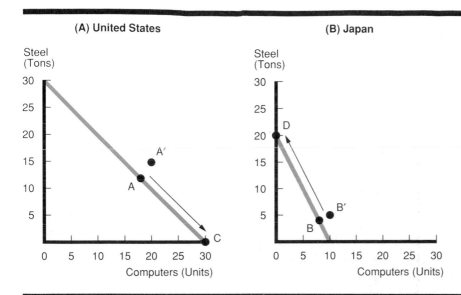

(A) United States

(B) Japan

FIGURE 2.2
Production with Complete Specialization

The opportunity cost of each good — the cost of the one good in terms of the amount of the other that must be given up to produce the first good — determines a country's comparative advantage. The slope of the U.S. production possibilities frontier shows that the U.S. cost of one computer is one ton of steel, and the slope of the Japanese PPF shows that the Japanese cost of one computer is two tons of steel. Thus the United States has a comparative advantage in computers, and Japan has a comparative advantage in steel. If each country specializes in the production of the good in which it has a comparative advantage, the United States will produce 30 computers (at point C) and no steel, and Japan will produce 20 tons of steel (at point D) and no computers. By specializing, the total two-country output of computers increases from 26 to 30, and the total output of steel increases from 16 to 20 tons.

Because opportunity costs differ, comparative advantage must exist. The United States has a comparative advantage in producing computers because in the United States a computer costs one ton of steel but in Japan a computer costs two tons of steel. Japan thus has a comparative *disadvantage* in producing computers. However, with a disadvantage in producing computers, Japan has a comparative advantage in producing steel. One ton of steel costs Japan the loss of only one-half of a computer, whereas one ton of steel costs the United States an entire computer.

Because economic agents seek to obtain the most from their scarce resources (recall the economizing postulate in Chapter 1), each task should be undertaken at the lowest possible cost. In a world with more than one nation, the production of each good should be undertaken by the nation that has both the lowest opportunity cost and a comparative advantage in producing the product.

Suppose both countries in Figure 2.2 specialize in the production of the goods in which they have a comparative advantage. In the United States, production would move from point A to point C at the lower tip of the production possibilities frontier. The United States would then produce 30 computers and zero tons of steel. Similarly, Japan would move from point B to point D at the upper tip of its PPF, producing 20 tons of steel and zero computers.

Before specialization, the total output for the two countries (see Table 2.2) is 26 computers (18 in the United States and 8 in Japan) and 16 tons of steel (12 tons in the United States and 4 tons in Japan). When the two countries specialize according to comparative advantage, the combined output of the two is 30 computers, all produced in the United States, and 20 tons of steel, all produced in Japan. Specialization has allowed the combined output of the two countries to increase by 4 computers and 4 tons of steel.

TERMS OF TRADE

The United States and Japan would specialize in the production of computers or steel only if they could also trade, because both countries want to consume some of both goods. If trade were not a possibility, the United

TABLE 2.2
Comparative Advantage Directs Specialization

GOOD	OUTPUT BEFORE SPECIALIZATION	OUTPUT AFTER SPECIALIZATION	TRADE EXPORTS (−) AND IMPORTS (+)	CONSUMPTION AFTER TRADE	GAINS FROM TRADE
United States					
Computers	18	30	−10	20	+2
Steel	12	0	+15	15	+3
Japan					
Computers	8	0	+10	10	+2
Steel	4	20	−15	5	+1
Total for Two Countries					
Total computers	26	30	—	30	+4
Total steel	16	20	—	20	+4

States would not choose to produce only computers, because it would then be unable to consume steel. Similarly, without trade, Japan would not choose to produce only steel because it wishes to be able to consume computers as well. If the gains from specialization are to be enjoyed, the two countries must be able to exchange some of the good each produces for some of the good the other produces. The United States must be able to exchange some of the computers it produces for some of the steel produced in Japan. The reverse must be true for Japan.

Whether or not trade between the two countries will be profitable depends on the price, or **terms of trade**, at which computers can be exchanged for steel.

> *Terms of trade are reflections of the relative prices of two goods. It is the rate at which one good can be exchanged for another good.*

The production possibilities schedule tells us that the United States can convert one computer (c) into one ton of steel (s). The United States, then, must be able to get more than a ton of steel for each computer if it is to gain from trade. Conversely, Japan can convert two tons of steel domestically into one computer, so it must be able to obtain a computer for less than two tons of steel. The international price, or terms of trade, must lie between the U.S. opportunity cost of 1c = 1s and the Japanese opportunity cost of 1c = 2s. What the actual price, or terms of trade, will be depends on the forces of competition, a subject we shall consider in Chapter 3. For convenience, let us choose the midpoint between the two possibilities and set the terms of trade at 1c = 1.5s.

GAINS FROM TRADE

Given the terms of trade 1c = 1.5s, Table 2.2 shows how it is possible for the United States and Japan to consume both more computers and more steel by sharing in the gains from specialization. In Figure 2.3 point A′ is preferred to point A because at A′ the United States is able to have more of both goods than at point A. Point A′ can be achieved by trading 10 of the 30 computers produced by specialization (leaving 20 computers for home use). The 10 computers are exchanged for 15 tons of steel at the

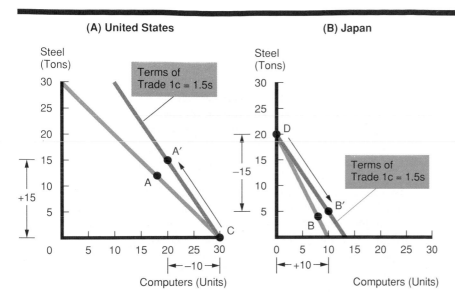

FIGURE 2.3
Consumption after Trade and Specialization

By specializing in the production of a good in which it has a comparative advantage and then trading some of that good for the other good, each country will be able to consume more of each good. The terms of trade, as indicated in the figure, reflect the rate at which one good can be exchanged for the other. In this example, the terms of trade are assumed to be "1 computer = 1.5 tons of steel." Thus, by producing 30 computers and trading 10 of them for 15 tons of steel, the United States can consume 20 computers and 15 tons of steel — a consumption combination, represented by point A', that is beyond its production possibilities frontier. Similarly, by producing 20 tons of steel and trading 15 of those for 10 computers, Japan can consume 5 tons of steel and 10 computers — a consumption combination, represented by point B', that is beyond its PPF.

existing terms of trade (1c = 1.5s). The terms of trade indicated in Figure 2.3 represent the possibilities of exchanging computers for steel.

After trade, the United States can consume 20 computers and 15 tons of steel (point A'). Prior to specialization and trade, the United States could consume only 18 computers and 12 tons of steel (point A), so the gains from specialization and trade for the United States are 2 computers and 3 tons of steel.

What works for the United States also works for Japan. Prior to specialization, Japan could consume only 8 computers and 4 tons of steel (point B in Figure 2.3). After specializing and producing 20 tons of steel, Japan exchanges 15 of the 20 tons of steel for 10 computers along the terms-of-trade line. Thus, after trade, Japan can consume 10 computers and 5 tons of steel (Point B'), for gains of 2 computers and 1 ton of steel.

Both the United States and Japan therefore benefit from specialization and trade. Each country has succeeded in moving beyond its production possibilities frontier. The United States can consume at point A' and Japan at B'.

We now see that there are two ways to make a society better off: (1) expand the production possibilities frontier itself and (2) engage in foreign trade. As discussed in Chapter 1, to extend a nation's consumption possibilities, the PPF may be expanded through an increase in the quantity or quality of the nation's resources or through technological progress. Consumption possibilities can also be extended *without* shifting the PPF curve by means of specialization and trade according to comparative advantage. In its effect on the consumption possibilities of individuals or nations, specialization and trade is functionally equivalent to having more resources or experiencing technological advances. Comparative advantage is not limited to trade between countries but extends to regions, firms, and individuals.

Comparative advantage determines the most efficient way for an economy to employ scarce resources. The pursuit of comparative advantage leads producers to consider the opportunity costs of the resources under their command so that they may choose the most valuable alternative available. *The pursuit of comparative advantage means the sacrifice of that which is less valuable for that which is more valuable.* We saw in the preceding example the importance of relative prices, or terms of trade, in determining comparative advantage. Had the relative price of computers been outside the range of 1 to 2 tons of steel per computer, there would have been no basis for trade. Relative prices therefore help to determine comparative advantage.

Consider another example. Suppose a physician is also a champion typist. While in medical school, the physician typed her own research papers and class notes. Now that she has graduated and is setting up her own medical practice, should she employ a secretary to do her typing for her, even though she could do the work faster herself? Here the concept of relative prices can be used to find the answer to this question.

The physician finds that she has 40 pages of typing each day. She could do it herself in 1 hour or she could hire a secretary to do it in 4 hours. The physician therefore has an absolute advantage of 4 to 1 over the secretary in typing. But if she is typing, she can't be seeing patients. If she practiced medicine instead of spending an hour typing, she could earn $100. Thus typing involves a sacrifice of $100 per hour. Alternatively, the physician could employ a secretary for 4 hours at $5 per hour. If she employed a secretary, the typing would cost $20; if she did it herself, it would cost $100. Clearly, the physician has a comparative advantage in practicing medicine for the extra hour, and a secretary has a comparative advantage in doing the typing. If the physician follows comparative advantage, she will gain $80 as a result.

If each agent produces according to its comparative advantage, the most profitable alternative is to allow the low-cost producer to do the work, with the low-cost producer identified by relative prices. Even though the physician has a 4-to-1 advantage in typing speed, she has an even greater 20-to-1 advantage in relative prices. The relative-price advantage far outweighs the relative-speed advantage and determines where the comparative advantage lies. Producing according to comparative advantage, then, requires the sacrifice of that which is less valuable — typing in this case — for that which is more valuable — practicing medicine — and requires selection of the most profitable available alternative.

This example demonstrates that it is possible for countries with high wages to trade profitably with low-wage countries. Even though the United States has high wages compared to Mexico, it is still profitable for trade to take place between the two countries. U.S. producers pay higher wages than Mexican firms precisely because U.S. workers are more productive. The United States probably has an absolute advantage in most goods imported from Mexico. But it is comparative advantage and not absolute advantage that governs trade. The United States is in the position of the physician in the preceding example who is also a champion typist. It still pays to specialize according to comparative advantage: Stick to doctoring and hire a secretary.

The importance of terms of trade in determining comparative advantage also explains why there is such concern over the value of the dollar in the international currency markets. When the dollar declines in value relative to the Japanese yen or the West German mark, some U.S. industries gain comparative advantage and exports increase. Conversely, when the dollar appreciates in value relative to these currencies, some U.S. industries lose comparative advantage.

The terms of trade thus have the effect of setting limits on trade. There are other factors that also limit specialization and trade, as we shall discuss in the following section.

LIMITS OF SPECIALIZATION AND TRADE

Obviously, when all workers, firms, and nations are completely specialized, there will be no further gains to be had from trade. But since every task can be divided into many smaller tasks, there must be other limiting factors at work. We return once again to Adam Smith for the answer:

> As it is the power of exchanging that gives occasion to the division of labor, so the extent of this division must always be limited . . . by the extent of the market.[3]

The size of the **market,** then, limits specialization.

> *A market is any established arrangement that brings buyers and sellers together to trade goods and services.*

What determines the size of the market? Trading is an activity that requires scarce resources. Individuals must find other persons and business firms with which to trade. They must then negotiate the terms at which the exchanges will occur and agree to some way of enforcing these agreements. The costs of making trades, referred to as **transaction costs,** limit their occurrence.

> *Transaction costs are the cost involved in searching out trades, the cost of negotiating an agreement, and the cost of enforcing that agreement.*

Organized markets are a way of reducing transaction costs. The first markets were geographic places where buyers and sellers would come together on specific dates to trade. If a buyer wanted a cow, that person would come to town on market day. If a seller wanted to sell a cow, that person would bring the animal to town on market day. An announced time and place would attract all potential buyers and sellers, thereby reducing the search costs of trading.

We shall discuss markets in more detail in Chapter 3, but for now we shall examine how an organized market reduces transaction costs. Search costs will naturally be lower when markets exist because most potential buyers and sellers would be attracted to the markets. The costs of negotiating an agreement will also be reduced as the results of previous transactions become known to all potential traders. The worth of one cow will be close to the worth of other cows traded on the same day.

The larger the market, the lower will be the transaction costs. As markets expand in size, it becomes possible for individuals and firms to follow their comparative advantage and act as intermediaries whose sole function is to lower transaction costs. Perhaps these intermediaries will buy and sell the goods, or perhaps they will only act as agents for buyers and sellers. A real estate agent's chief function is to try to find buyers for clients' houses. A stockbroker facilitates the exchange of shares for clients. The larger the market, the more efficient these agents will be.

The local real estate market is much smaller than the New York Stock Exchange, of course. As a result, it may cost the seller of a house 10 percent of the house's value in real estate commissions to sell, whereas it will cost the seller of IBM stock only 1 or 2 percent of the stock's value to

---

[3]Ibid., 17.

sell. Again, the larger the market, the more efficiently trades will be made.

Transaction costs are also reduced by the use of money in the trade. In the barter exchange between Mary and Sue that we discussed earlier, Mary had to find someone who had a Madonna record and who also wanted a Springsteen album more than his or her Madonna album. In other words, the trade required a **mutual coincidence of wants.**

> *Mutual coincidence of wants is a condition of a barter exchange requiring that each person (1) have what a potential trader wants and (2) desires what that potential trader has to exchange.*

Searching for such a person is likely to be a costly undertaking. If trading were confined to barter exchanges, relatively few trades would take place.

Suppose, instead, that Mary could sell her Springsteen album to the first person who wanted it in exchange for something everyone else would also want. Then she could trade that something else with the first person she found with a Madonna record for trade. Clearly, the costs of trading would be reduced if that something else could be found. What would that something else be? **Money.**

> *Money is any commodity that all people will accept in trade because they know that everyone else will in turn accept that commodity in trade.*

In the United States the dollar serves as money. All people will accept it in trade because they know that everyone else will also accept it.

The use of money reduces transaction costs by reducing search costs. In this regard, money oils the mechanism of exchange. Money serves as the means of overcoming the restrictions imposed by the mutual coincidence of wants.

Money also allows more complicated exchanges to occur. Suppose Mary would like to trade her Springsteen album today but she does not want to acquire the Madonna album until later, after she returns from her family vacation. If barter exchanges were the only kind available, she would have to get Sue to agree to keep the Madonna record in good condition and surrender it later. She would have to trust Sue to keep her word, and she would have to figure out a way to enforce the agreement.

The availability of money makes it unnecessary either to trust Sue or to negotiate a way to enforce the agreement. Mary sells her album for money and holds on to the money until she returns from her vacation. Thus money also serves the function of a store of value. Trades can be made today and the purchasing power received from the trade can be stored by holding money to be used in the future. Money also serves as a unit of account, allowing wealth to be evaluated in terms of a common unit. A unit of account is an amount that can be used to measure the value of things. Thus we have millionaires, persons who have accumulated wealth the value of which totals a million dollars.

Money serving as a unit of account allows opportunity costs to be reckoned in dollars rather than in lists of the goods that represent the highest-valued alternatives. The prices of goods can be represented in terms of money rather than in terms of other goods given up. In the trade of computers for steel between the United States and Japan, instead of expressing the terms of trade as 1.5 tons of steel for a computer, the relative price can more easily be expressed in dollars. In order to appreciate the importance of money as a unit of account, imagine what the consequences would be if the next time you go to a store, instead of prices being expressed in terms of money, each good came with a tag listing the other goods the store would accept in trade.

Transaction costs limit the quantity of potential trades, which in turn determines the extent of specialization. Money and markets are economic innovations that jointly reduce transaction costs and hence encourage specialization.

CHANGES IN COMPARATIVE ADVANTAGE

Comparative advantage is not carved in stone but inevitably changes over time. Changes in comparative advantage will always require the reallocation of resources from less productive to more productive uses.

In the textile industry, comparative advantage has a history of moving westward. Historically, the low-cost producers of textiles were initially in Belgium. Then comparative advantage moved to England, from there to the United States, from there to Japan, and from there to other Far Eastern countries. Each time comparative advantage moved, the textile industry was born anew, becoming a growth industry in its new country. Meanwhile, it died in the country that had lost the comparative advantage, forcing workers there to move to other jobs in industries where comparative advantage did exist.

Changing comparative advantage also affects regions and states. For example, Wisconsin initially held a comparative advantage in mining lead, lost that to several Western states, became the largest producer of wheat in the country, and soon lost that comparative advantage to the prairie states. Wisconsin then became a dairy state and a producer of machine tools. Each time comparative advantage was lost in one area of the United States, it was gained in another.

Each country, region, or individual will always have a comparative advantage in producing certain products. When comparative advantage is lost in one activity, it is created in another. For example, the United States today has lost comparative advantage in producing television sets, and it may be in the process of losing comparative advantage in producing steel and textiles and perhaps automobiles. Meanwhile, it has gained comparative advantage in producing high-technology goods, such as airplanes and computers.

What changes comparative advantage? Comparative advantage is determined by opportunity costs and relative prices. Anything that changes opportunity costs or relative prices will also change comparative advantage. In Chapter 1 we discovered that the production possibilities frontier curve that measured opportunity costs was itself determined by the availability of the factors of production and the current state of technology. A change in the quantity or quality of the factors of production or in the state of technology corresponding to a production possibilities schedule also changes comparative advantage. Comparative advantage may also change when there is a change in population, when a nation's rate of saving changes, or when more natural resources are discovered.

When comparative advantage changes, the economy must reallocate resources to take advantage of the new situation. Since the forces that determine comparative advantage are always changing, all economies must be in the constant process of reallocating their resources from less productive to more productive uses.

OTHER BARRIERS TO TRADE

It should be apparent from the discussion above that anything that impedes trade reduces the extent of specialization and thereby makes the economy poorer. Transaction costs are not the only barriers to trade. Historically, for political reasons, many legal barriers to trade have been erected. In international trade, tariffs and quotas have been imposed. Tariffs are taxes that are levied on imported goods. Quotas are legal restrictions on the total quantity of foreign goods that can be annually imported into a country. Domestically, wage and price controls have at times been implemented. Licenses and patents limit entrance to certain professions. Some taxes, like sales taxes, actually derive directly from trades.

The effect of these interferences with free trade is reduction of the gains from trade and of the amount of specialization in the economy. By reducing the extent of specialization in the economy, noneconomic barriers to trade impoverish the economy. It may still be worthwhile to impose these restrictions, but the cost in terms of lost opportunities for trade and specialization should be explicitly recognized.

SUMMARY

1. The three types of exchanges are trade, gift giving, and theft.
    a. Trade involves the voluntary legal transfer of property in return for an acceptable payment. A voluntary trade always makes both parties to the trade better off; hence wealth is created.
    b. Gift giving is the voluntary legal transfer of property in return for the satisfaction of having made someone else better off. Since gifts make both parties better off, wealth is created.
    c. Theft is the involuntary transfer of property from the victim to the thief. Because it severs the link between the stolen good and legal property rights, theft destroys wealth.
2. Trade organizes the economy.
3. Wealth consists of whatever people value.
4. Private-property rights are legal rights of ownership that convey to the owner of a good the sole right to use and dispose of that good. By increasing the value of goods to their owners, private-property rights contribute to wealth.
5. Voluntary exchange always creates wealth, because voluntary exchange involves giving up what is less valuable for what is more valuable. Trade is as much a wealth-creating activity as the production of more goods due to technological change or the discovery of more resources.
6. Individuals and businesses specialize in order to engage in trade, which allows them to increase their wealth. They specialize in activities in which they have a comparative advantage. Whenever comparative advantage exists, profitable exchange is possible.
7. The basis for trade may lie in a difference in preferences or in comparative advantage.
8. Comparative advantage is determined by opportunity cost. As long as opportunity costs differ between two individuals, business firms, or countries, each will have a comparative advantage in the production of some good.
9. As long as opportunity costs differ, comparative advantage will exist even if one individual, firm, or country has an absolute advantage in the production of all goods.

10. Relative prices, because they reflect opportunity costs, help to determine comparative advantage.

11. Money and markets also help to create wealth by reducing transaction costs and thereby increasing the possibilities for profitable trades.

12. Comparative advantage will change if opportunity costs change. Since opportunity costs are determined by the quantity and quality of the factors of production and by the state of technology, changes in these variables may change comparative advantage.

13. To produce according to its comparative advantage, an economy must be constantly in the process of reallocating resources from less productive uses to more productive uses.

14. Anything that prevents voluntary exchange promotes inefficiency by interfering with specialization according to comparative advantage.

IS THERE A WINNER AND A LOSER IN EVERY TRADE?

PREVIEW 2.1 ANALYSIS

"In every trade there is a winner and a loser," stated John Madden, former football coach turned TV announcer. Madden was talking about the voluntary exchange of players in professional sports, but his statement could be generalized to refer to all types of trades. Have you ever heard anybody say about a transaction that "she certainly got the best of that deal" or "he was really taken this time"? Instinctively, some people feel that if someone profits handsomely from a trade, someone else must have lost out.

The trade described in Preview 2.1 is documented by historical account. Midshipman Trevenen of Captain Cook's crew was able to trade a seemingly worthless belt buckle for a valuable sea otter pelt. Trevenen believed that he had much the best of that bargain. But had he? Why was the Indian so anxious to enter into such an uneven exchange? Trevenen himself was puzzled by the Indian's behavior. He wrote: "The Indian thought that he had made a very advantageous bargain."

We now know that goods of equal value to both parties are never exchanged. A trade takes place because the persons exchanging the goods value them differently. The belt buckle that was worthless to the sailor was of great value to the Indian. The sea otter pelt that was of great value to Trevenen was a commonplace possession of the Indian. When valuations differ, trade can benefit both parties.

Iron objects could not be manufactured by the Indian no matter how many resources were devoted to the task. Possessing any iron at all, even a broken belt buckle, would distinguish the Indian as a wealthy man within his tribe. Sea otter pelts were so common among Indians that no such distinction would be attached to the possession of the pelt. Trevenen, on the other hand, lived in a society for which the Industrial Revolution had made iron a commonplace commodity. Sea otter pelts were quite scarce and therefore valuable, particularly since distinctive items of clothing could be fashioned from them. Trevenen was able to exchange his pelt for a large amount of valuable goods. Both parties to the trade thus benefited from the exchange.

Why did John Madden believe that in a trade of professional sports players, one team is a winner and the other a loser? He was evaluating such trades with the benefit of hindsight, of course. In a world full of uncertainty, no one can see the future perfectly. The teams participating

in a specific trade may have misjudged the abilities of the players involved, or one of the traded players may later have sustained an injury
that affected his performance. After the trade, one of the teams involved
might have wished that it had not made the deal, but at the time of the
trade, there were only prospective winners. Each of the trading teams
expected that it would benefit from the trade. Traders do not enter into
deals with the expectation that the trade will make them worse off.

PREVIEW 2.2 ANALYSIS

SUBURBAN SERFDOM

Bob and Ralph, whom we met in Preview 2.2, are next-door neighbors who have nearly identical lawns and gardens. Both men spend
Saturday mornings maintaining their property, and both dislike their
chores. Ralph, who is older than Bob, particularly dislikes weeding because it requires much bending over.

Ralph is able to perform the maintenance tasks much more quickly
than Bob. When Bob timed himself and Ralph one day, he found that
Ralph generally requires 60 minutes to weed and 90 minutes to mow,
while Bob takes 120 minutes to weed and 240 minutes to mow. Ralph thus
gets his work done in 150 minutes, while Bob requires 360 minutes. Not
only does Ralph finish more quickly, he also completes each task in less
time than Bob.

Bob offered Ralph a deal. He first suggested that Ralph mow both
lawns and that he, Bob, weed both flower beds. Ralph declined, pointing
out that it would take him 90 minutes to mow Bob's lawn and only 60
minutes to weed his own flower bed. Ralph wanted to be a good neighbor,
but he didn't want to subsidize Bob. After all, he also hated gardening
and lawn chores.

Ralph countered with another offer. Suppose Ralph mowed his own
lawn and then used his 60 minutes of weeding time to mow two-thirds of
Bob's lawn instead. Ralph would spend the same amount of time as before
but he would spend it all mowing, which he preferred since he was now of
an age when he hated to bend over. In exchange, Bob would weed all of
Ralph's flower beds. Bob agreed to the plan. He knew that if he and
Ralph traded according to comparative advantage, Bob would finish
sooner than if they did not trade.

Table 2.3, which presents the production possibilities before and
after the trade, shows that Ralph has an absolute advantage over Bob in

TABLE 2.3
Production Possibilities of the Suburban Serfs before Trade

ACTIVITY	BOB	RALPH
Weeding	120 minutes	60 minutes
Mowing	240 minutes	90 minutes
Total	360 minutes	150 minutes

T A B L E   2 . 4
Ralph's and Bob's Production Possibilities before and after Trade

	BOB	RALPH
Before Trade	120 minutes weeding 240 minutes mowing	60 minutes weeding 90 minutes mowing
	360 minutes total	150 minutes total

After Trade	120 minutes weeding Ralph's
	    garden
	120 minutes weeding own
	    garden
	80 minutes mowing 1/3 of
	    own lawn
		90 minutes mowing own
		    lawn
		60 minutes mowing 2/3
		    of Bob's lawn

	320 minutes total	150 minutes total
Gains from Trade	40 minutes total	0 minutes total

doing both tasks. It takes him less time to do either task. But it is comparative advantage, not absolute advantage, that determines the possibilities of a profitable trade. Because Ralph is not equally superior in doing both tasks, a comparative advantage exists.

To determine comparative advantage, it is necessary first to consider the two men's opportunity cost for doing each task. In the time it takes Bob to weed his garden, he could have mowed one-half (120 minutes/240 minutes) of his lawn. *Bob's opportunity cost is 1 weeded garden = ½ mowed lawn.* Similarly, while Ralph is weeding his garden, he is sacrificing two-thirds (60 minutes/90 minutes) of his lawn being mowed. *Ralph's opportunity cost is 1 weeded garden = ⅔ mowed lawn.* Since the opportunity cost of weeding relative to mowing is different for the two men, comparative advantages exist.

Bob is the low-cost producer of weeding since while weeding he sacrifices less of a mowed lawn than does Ralph. So *Bob has a comparative advantage in weeding.* Conversely, *Ralph has a comparative advantage in mowing.* The opportunity cost to Ralph of mowing is less in terms of a weeded garden sacrificed than it is for Bob.

Bob takes advantage of comparative advantage in striking the deal with Ralph. He gets Ralph to agree to specialize in mowing, a task in which Ralph is the low-cost producer and a task that he happens to prefer to weeding. So Ralph mows his own lawn and two-thirds of Bob's. Bob weeds Ralph's garden, then weeds his own garden and mows the one-third of his lawn that Ralph left unmowed. Table 2.4 shows that Ralph spends the same amount of time gardening as before the exchange, but he spends it doing the task he prefers. Bob, however, spends less total time, saving 40 minutes overall.

Producing according to comparative advantage creates wealth (whatever people value). Avoiding weeding is valuable to Ralph. Saving time is valuable to Bob.

FAMINES — THE ULTIMATE CONSEQUENCE OF SCARCITY

he theory of exchange can be used to explore the reasons why famine occurs.[4] A simple view is that people starve because there is not enough to eat. When crops fail, farmers eat what they produce, leaving city dwellers and tradesmen to starve. When all the food is consumed, the farmers in turn suffer. In reality, this description fits no known famines. No famine is as simple as this. It is a fact that some famines have occurred despite the fact that there was *more*, not less, food available in the region. Furthermore, during modern famines urban dwellers almost never starve; instead, it is rural dwellers who are most adversely affected.

The starvation that occurs in a famine is generally a matter of *some* persons not having enough to eat, rather than there not being enough for all to eat. Famines within a group occur because there is (1) a sudden decline in the availability of food, (2) a sudden decline in the availability of the goods used to obtain food in trade, or (3) a sudden rise in the relative price of food. The latter may happen either because of a decline in the price of the goods used to obtain food in trade, or because of a rise in the price of food itself. If relief is to be effective when famines occur, it is important to be able to identify both the causes of the famine and the groups affected.

Figure 2.4 shows the outputs produced by a particular group of people, together with the terms of trade prior to the advent of a famine. Perhaps this group might be composed of rural laborers or craft workers who have small garden plots whose output is supplemented by income earned by working for farmers or by making handicrafts. This group is potentially vulnerable to famine because it is not self-sufficient in food production.

FIGURE 2.4
Trading to Avoid Starvation

Trade is routinely used to avoid starvation in every country of the world. Suppose the combination of goods produced by a particular group of people is represented by point X, with N_e of nonfood and F_e of food being produced. However, a minimum food consumption equal to F_m is required to survive. The group depicted in this figure is short of food by an amount equal to $F_m - F_e$. The terms-of-trade line T_1 shows the rate at which nonfood can be exchanged for food. To meet the minimum food requirement, $N_e - N_t$ nonfood units must be exchanged to make up the shortage. By making this trade, the group can move from point X, where there is not enough to eat, to point Y, where there is enough to eat.

This particular group annually produces the combination X, composed of N_e of nonfood and F_e of food. The vertical line F_m represents the group's minimum food requirement. If this group fails to obtain F_m, it will starve. Usually this group can obtain at least F_m amounts of food by trading some of its nonfood endowment for food in the market. The line T_1 represents the terms of trade available to this group. The group can exchange its initial endowment X for any other point on this line. In this illustration, the group exchanges at least $N_e - N_t$ of its nonfood endowment for $F_t - F_e$ of food and thereby manages to avoid starvation, since F_t is equal to F_m. The effect of the trade is to move from point X to point Y on the terms-of-trade line T_1.

Figure 2.5 shows how a crop failure might shift the group's endowment from X to X′, with the food portion of the endowment collapsing from F_e to F_y and the nonfood endowment remaining the same. When this shift occurs, the terms-of-trade line collapses from T_1 to T_2 but maintains the same slope because the price of food relative to nonfood has not changed. Even if the relative price of food does not change, it now becomes impossible for the group to avoid starvation. Even if the group trades all of its nonfood endowment for food, the most food it can obtain is F′, which is less than the minimum food requirement, F_m.

The problem that exists when a local area suffers a crop failure is not a lack of food, but rather a lack of wealth to purchase sufficient food. It

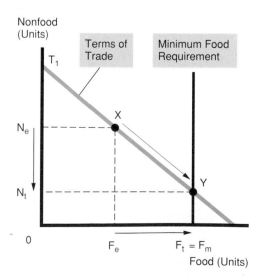

Nonfood
(Units)

Terms of Trade

Minimum Food Requirement

T_1

N_e

X

N_t

Y

0

F_e

$F_t = F_m$

Food (Units)

---

[4]This analysis draws on Amarty Sen, *Resources, Values and Development* (Cambridge, MA: 1984), 452–484.

is the sudden inability of a particular family or group to purchase enough food to avoid starvation. The ability to purchase food is in reality not limited to current endowments. Since food can be purchased using a family's savings, families with wealth can and do escape the ravages of famines. Urban areas, which are generally wealthier than rural areas, often escape the worst effects of famine. Moreover, urban areas are directly linked by trade to other regions. When a city's traditional food suppliers suffer crop failures, other areas with food surpluses make up the difference. In the recent Ethiopian famines, starvation occurred in rural areas but not in urban areas.

Crop failure famine may in this manner affect an entire region or just one family. If a particular group, for example, suffers a crop failure while the rest of the regional economy is enjoying good crops, starvation may take place in an isolated area in the midst of general prosperity, as in the case of the Ethiopian famine of 1973 and the Bangladesh famine of 1974. Once again the problem is the sudden decline in income that a crop failure creates.

A decline in the availability of food to a family or group is, however, not the only way starvation can occur. If the nonfood endowment collapses while the food endowment remains stable, starvation can still occur. If the endowment combination moves from X to X″ in Figure 2.5 so that nonfood production falls to N_x while food output remains at F_e, the group will again be unable to escape starvation. The best that the group can do by trading away all of its nonfood production for food is to obtain a food quantity of F', which is less than the minimum food requirement, F_m. This group can starve without a general decline in the availability of food in the area because the group can no longer afford to buy sufficient food.

During the great Bengalese famine of 1943, for example, starvation occurred despite the fact that total food availability did not decline. During World War II the British, fearing a Japanese invasion of India, confiscated all boats in the area to deny the invaders transportation. The Japanese never came, but because the lack of boats denied Bengalese fishermen the means of making a living, they starved. Other groups not affected by the confiscation of boats managed to avoid starvation.

Finally, Figure 2.6 shows how famine can occur without a change in domestic output if the terms of trade change. The terms of trade will change if the relative price of food increases. The previous terms of trade, represented by the line T_1, allow 1 unit of nonfood output to be traded for 2 units of food. Now suppose the price of food increases relative to the price of nonfood. This could occur because of a crop failure in a nearby region with which trade occurs or because of a general rise in the world price of agricultural commodities. After this price increase, 1 unit of nonfood will purchase only 1 unit of food, as shown by the new, steeper terms-of-trade line, T_2.

The nonfood endowment can no longer be exchanged for sufficient food to avoid starvation. Where previously $N_e - N_t$ nonfood could be traded for enough food to move from X to Y in the figure, now an exchange of all nonfood produced will allow the group to acquire a total amount of food equal only to F', which is not sufficient to avoid starvation. This same result could occur if the price of nonfood goods declined because of increased foreign competition or industrialization of the region. However, if the price of nonfood output rises sufficiently, the family or group will starve no longer, since it is able to exchange its nonfood output for the minimum required amount of food.

Thus starvation may occur without crop failures. Persons who own food sell it to the highest bidders who happen to live elsewhere. This

FIGURE 2.5
Famine That Results When Output Collapses

Famine can occur when the production of either food or nonfood goods declines. Initially, the group was producing at point X with outputs equal to F_e amounts of food and N_e amounts of nonfood. Now suppose that food production declines to F_y while nonfood production remains at N_e, as shown by a shift from X to X′. The terms of trade remain the same (the slope does not change), but because of the decline in food output, the line shifts to T_1'. The most food that can be obtained by trading all of the nonfood output is F', which is less than the minimum food requirement, F_m. If, on the other hand, nonfood production declines from N_e to N_x while food production remains the same, the output combination declines from X to X″. The same results are obtained. The group can no longer trade its diminished output for sufficient food to escape starvation.

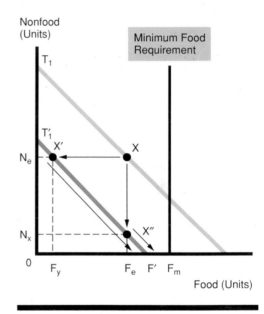

FIGURE 2.6

Famine That Results from a Change in the Terms of Trade

This figure demonstrates that famine can occur without a change in total production if the terms of trade change adversely. Suppose the combination of food and nonfood outputs remains the same. The group escapes starvation with the initial terms of trade, T_1, by exchanging the amount $N_e - N_t$ of nonfood for an additional $F_m - F_e$ of food. If, however, the terms of trade shift from T_1 to T_2, the total amount of nonfood production becomes insufficient to purchase enough additional food ($F_m - F_e$) to avoid starvation. The best that the group can now do by trading all of its nonfood production is to acquire a total of F' food, which is less than F_m, the minimum required.

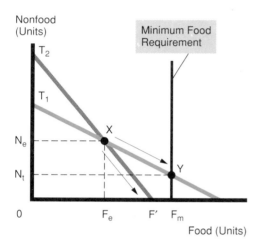

exportation may leave particular groups within the exporting region — such as craft workers and agricultural laborers — with insufficient means to purchase enough food to avoid starvation.

The economic theory of famines suggests that starvation can occur for two general reasons: (1) Either the total production of a particular group collapses, or (2) the terms of trade change to make it impossible for a group to use its nonfood production to acquire sufficient food to avoid starvation. Both causes could also of course be at work at the same time.

The Irish famine of the 1840s provides a good example. Prior to the famine, Ireland was an exporter of food to England. Cereal grains were grown for export, while the general population consumed the potato as its staple food. Cereal grains were reportedly too expensive to make up the balance of the diet in good times. When the potato crop failed, the Irish poor, who in good times could not afford to buy the grain that was grown, certainly couldn't afford to buy it when times were bad. Grain continued to be shipped to England as the Irish poor starved.

> In the long troubled history of England and Ireland no issue has provoked so much anger or so embittered relations between the two countries as the indisputable fact that huge quantities of food were exported from Ireland to England through the period when people in Ireland were dying of starvation.[5]

It may well have been that throughout the famine Ireland continued to produce enough food to feed its people, but the existing economic and political system did not allow the food to reach the people who required it. The export of food from famine areas is, in fact, not uncommon. It happened repeatedly during famines in China and was alleged to occur during the 1974 famine in Bangladesh.

The causes of a specific famine must be identified if relief efforts are to be effective. If the cause of the famine is a change in the terms of trade that reflects a rise in the relative price of food, then it may be sufficient to counter the price rise by temporarily increasing the supply of food from foreign sources. An increase in food imports would reverse the change in the terms of trade (from T_2 to T_1 in Figure 2.6). Donations and the temporary distribution of free food may not be necessary or even desirable in such a case. Distributing free goods that are scarce is difficult even for developed economies to carry off. Instead of relieving the poor, the attempt to distribute free food may result in increased corruption. Even if it is successful, providing a scarce good for free creates a powerful disincentive for existing agriculture.

The theory of famines suggests, however, that not all groups in a famine area may be affected equally. Simply increasing by donations the availability of food within the famine area may not solve the problem of starvation unless the means can also be found to ensure that starving people are the sole recipients. Because a temporary collapse of food output will affect some groups more than others, some way of targeting the groups in need is required.

The history of efforts to rush food to famine areas for free distribution is not reassuring. Food has rotted on receiving docks due to the lack of an effective distribution system; it has disappeared due to corruption to be resold, often in another country; or it has frequently been distributed to persons who were not starving. The theory of famines suggests that foreign-subsidized sales of food designed to alter the terms of trade and thus allow starving families to continue to exchange their nonfood production for the minimum amount of food needed to survive might prove a better way.

---

[5]C. Woodham-Smith, *The Great Hunger: Ireland 1845–9* (London: 1975), 700.

REQUIRED ECONOMIC CONCEPTS

Exchange	Comparative advantage
Trade	Absolute advantage
Gift giving	Opportunity cost
Theft	Terms of trade
Wealth	Market
Barter exchange	Transaction costs
Private-property rights	Mutual coincidence of wants
Specialization	Money

KEY QUESTIONS

1. What is a market? What is an example of an involuntary exchange?
2. When trade occurs, what characteristic of a good other than its physical properties is exchanged?
3. What is an example of a voluntary one-way exchange?
4. What kind of trade occurs when goods are exchanged for other goods? What is required for such a trade to be possible?
5. What is wealth? Why isn't garbage normally considered wealth? For whom might garbage be considered wealth?
6. Name two rights that private ownership confers upon the holder.
7. Why does trading stocks on the New York Stock Exchange take place in a more efficient market than buying and selling houses locally?
8. Why does absolute advantage not exclude the possibility of trade taking place?
9. Why is specialization more efficient than the jack-of-all-trades approach to economic activity?
10. If two traders have the same opportunity cost of production, might there still be a basis for trade? What determines whether comparative advantage exists or not?
11. What are transaction costs?
12. What specific cost is involved in buying stamps at the post office other than the price of the stamps themselves?
13. What costs are involved in finding a "good" car mechanic?
14. Give a reason for some people starving even when there is no crop failure.
15. What functions does money serve? What effect does it have on transaction costs, particularly negotiating costs?

PROBLEMS

1. Why did the pink bicycles of Geneva, Switzerland, decline in number and deteriorate? What essential characteristic was missing? Who owned these bicycles?
2. When Bolivia trades its valuable tin to the United States for its surplus grain, is this an example of the United States more or less getting something for nothing? Explain.

APPLICATION

2.4

RITA'S LIFE COMPARED WITH THE LIVES OF HER GRANDPARENTS

The forces that have worked to change the quality of life over the past 50 years can readily be seen by comparing the life that economics major Rita Stone will lead after college with the lives of her grandparents. Some of the striking difference is apparent from national economic statistics — for example, Rita will probably live a longer, healthier life and be several times richer. Statistics, however, do not reveal the changes in life-styles that accompany economic changes, nor do they reveal the forces that are at work shaping lives.

When Rita's grandparents married, her grandfather went to work and her grandmother stayed home to raise the children. Grandpa worked for the same company doing roughly the same thing all of his life. Grandma ran the household, tended a garden, preserved food, made quilts, cleaned house, and watched over several children as they grew up. She worked hard, but she never held a job outside the home. Rita's father was raised to take her grandfather's place in the job market, and her mother was brought up to run a household and to raise a family of her own.

How different Rita's life will be! She will accomplish many of the same things, but she will do it in a way much different from her grandparents' way. She will likely marry later and raise fewer children. Both she and her spouse will probably work — significantly more than half of all families of her generation will have two income earners. The jobs she and her spouse will hold may not even have existed in her grandparents' day — one-third of all current job titles did not exist ten years ago. Her grandfather and grandmother labored with their hands and did not require additional exercise. Rita will work with her mind, and she will have to schedule a regular workout to keep in physical shape. To keep up with the times, she will have to change careers several times in her working life. Moreover, Rita and her family will be much more mobile geographically than her grandparents were; she and her husband will probably, while pursuing their various careers, live in several states during their lifetimes.

Rita's family life will also be markedly different from that of her grandparents. The strict division of tasks wherein her grandfather brought home the paycheck and her grandmother ran the household is gone forever. When both partners work, there is little time to do the chores. Even in her grandparents' day, there was never enough time, but during Rita's lifetime there will be a serious time shortage. The solution to this shortage is to rely more on trading in markets to get the household work done. Two incomes in a family make this possible.

The same forces that have drawn women out of the home and into the workplace are operating to see that the household chores are performed. We have entered the conven-

ience age. Business firms offer products and services that will save Rita time. Where food preparation took up a large portion of her grandmother's time, now there are numerous ways to cut down on the time it takes to feed a family. Fast-food restaurants like McDonald's, pizza shops, and delicatessens provide alternatives to preparing meals at home. In a typical supermarket today, the space devoted to microwave dinners and gourmet take-out meals has been greatly expanded. Food represents a big share of the convenience boom, but there is also a surge of firms offering to take over other household chores: lawn work, car maintenance, child care, pet care, care of elderly family members, and so on. More and more shopping can be done at home by means of catalogs and telemarketing.

The appearance of our cities is consequently changing as Minute Lubes and 7-11 stores move into abandoned service stations; 7-11 stores themselves are being made over into 24-hour convenience markets offering fast and packaged food. The retail function of downtown business districts is rapidly being replaced by suburban shopping malls. The department store may soon become a thing of

3. Suppose John and Jane each possess an equal endowment of 8 chocolate kisses and 12 shell peanuts. John is indifferent between consuming 1 kiss and 3 peanuts; that is, he is willing to give up 3 peanuts to get 1 kiss. Jane, however, is indifferent between consuming 1 kiss and 1 peanut. She is willing to give up 1 kiss to get 1 peanut and vice versa.

   a. What is the opportunity cost to John of consuming 1 peanut? To Jane of consuming 1 peanut?

   b. Would trade occur between John and Jane if the exchange ratio were 1 chocolate to 4 peanuts? Explain.

   c. Would trade occur between John and Jane if the exchange ratio were 1 chocolate to 2 peanuts? Explain.

4. Suppose that you receive in the mail an advertisement that includes sample cloth for trousers. The trousers are offered at a discount. Why would you, even at the cut rate price,

the past, with retail business taken over by discount stores and specialty shops. The hardware store of old has been replaced by the home-maintenance store, complete with garden department, which now offers complete installation of the products it sells.

What are the forces that are determining that Rita's life will be very different from the lives of her parents and grandparents? The differences will have resulted in large part from the factors that determine comparative advantage: new-product development, changes in the quantity and quality of the factors of production, and technological progress. Changes in comparative advantage alter people's lives by requiring the reallocation of resources.

Market size, for example, has increased significantly over the past two generations. Typically, markets today are not limited to regions or nations as in Rita's grandparents' day, but are international in scope. When her grandparents were Rita's age, oil came from Kansas and Texas; now much of it is imported — some from as far away as the Persian Gulf. The United States at that time imported only 5 percent of the goods it consumed, most of which were raw materials. Today about 25 percent of total U.S. consumption is imported, including many types of manufactured goods ranging from consumer electronics to automobiles.

The world has become more specialized as international trade has grown, and the United States is no exception. As a consequence, most production processes have become much more specialized, which accounts for the creation of new kinds of jobs that did not exist previously. Astronauts as well as computer and microchip designers were science fiction characters when Rita's grandparents were young. Most of the new jobs that exist today, however, are subdivisions of tasks that formerly were performed for her grandparents. Lawyers, for example, served her grandparents, but today lawyers specialize in particular aspects of the law. They are tax lawyers, tort lawyers, environmental lawyers, corporate lawyers, and so on. The same is true of most other professions. Some architects specialize in the design of schools, others in commercial buildings, and still others in residences.

The manufacturing process itself has undergone radical changes. The principles that governed the organization of Adam Smith's pin factory have been replicated and applied throughout the world in ways he could never have imagined. The division of labor has been systematically pursued, with tasks so narrowly defined that robots can be designed to do them. The manufacturing revolution was going on during Rita's grandparents' adult lives, and it was during that time that mass production techniques were reorganizing the economy.

The service revolution is another factor that is changing comparative advantage. The vast majority of workers today toil in the service sector. The service sector is that part of the economy that runs on trade and information. In 1985 there were 76 million Americans working in the service sector, while there were only 25 million in manufacturing and 3 million in agriculture. Finance, insurance, and real estate comprise the category that is the largest employer within the service sector, followed by retail trade, wholesale trade, transportation and utilities, and communications.

The forces that determine comparative advantage seem to be changing more rapidly than ever before. As a result, regions and countries are gaining and losing comparative advantage just as rapidly. Rita must be prepared for the consequences. She will, either by plan or necessity, change jobs and even occupations much more often than did her grandfather.

The same forces of specialization that have changed the world of work have made it possible to run a household with less personal involvement, thereby allowing both spouses to be gainfully employed. The convenience age was created by the pursuit of comparative advantage. It is simply more efficient for many women to work and to trade for many of the goods and services that their grandmothers produced within the home. Using prepared and precooked meals, periodically hiring a person to clean the house or to do the gardening, using a laundry or dry cleaner, and buying wash-and-wear clothing are all examples of the reorganization of our personal lives made possible by following comparative advantage and trade.

Trade organizes our economy and with it our personal lives. The pursuit of comparative advantage accounts for many of the changes that have occurred since Rita's grandparents' years of employment. When comparative advantage changes, so do our professional and personal lives.

be less inclined to order the trousers, preferring instead to pay more at a local clothing store?

5. Mr. Byte is the best computer programmer in the company. He was, nevertheless, promoted to a vice presidency in the company. Was this not a waste of his talents? Explain.

6. During the protests of the late 1960s, did the rock singers who toured the country giving concerts with their multiwatt amplifiers — over which they blasted protest songs about the war, pollution (noise too?), materialism, the evils of technology and hypocrisy — ever have to deal with intermediaries (middlemen)? Did they willingly choose to? Comment.

7. Is it likely that prices at various garage sales will vary more than prices at local retail outlets? Does it follow that prices at auto salvage yards will vary as much for the same car parts as they do at swap meets?

APPLICATION ANALYSIS

1. Jack Brown of the United States and Bill Jones of Canada both operate backyard auto repair shops. Suppose the property line separating them coincides with the U.S.–Canadian border. Assume that the following times apply to performing standard brake replacements and tune-ups:

	BROWN	JONES
(T) Tune-ups	60 minutes	80 minutes
(B) Brakes	30 minutes	60 minutes
Total	90 minutes	140 minutes

   a. Who, if either, has a comparative advantage in performing tune-ups? In repairing brakes? Is there a basis for specialization and trade?

   b. Which one, if any, of the following exchange ratios signifies there is a beneficial basis for trading tasks? 1B to 1/2 T, 1B to 1/4 T, 1B to 5/8 T, 1B to 3/4 T. Work out the calculations for the trade-off that increases the wealth (leisure) of each of the two mechanics.

   c. Why do you think the problem was set up with the dividing line between Brown and Jones's yards also lying along the U.S.–Canadian border?

2. The graphs below depict the production possibilities frontiers for the U.S. West and Japan and their respective productions of logs and television sets. Before trade the United States produces 100 logs and 200 TV sets, shown by point A, and Japan produces 10 logs and 200 TV sets, shown by point B.

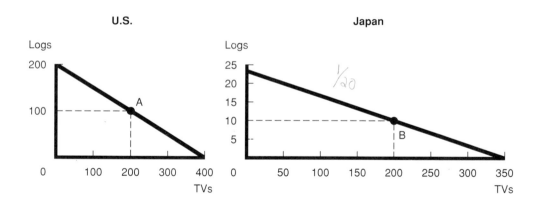

   a. What is the opportunity cost for Japan to produce logs? For the United States to produce TV sets?

   b. Which country has a comparative advantage in the production of logs? In the production of TV sets?

   c. Suppose the foreign exchange ratio between the U.S. West and Japan is 1 log to 10 TVs. Will the United States export or import TVs? How many? Will Japan export or import logs? How many? To answer this question, assume that the United States starts at point A and Japan at point B, with each country desiring to increase its wealth; also assume that Japan after trade intends to consume 22 logs.

   d. If the United States offers terms of trade equal to Japan's opportunity cost, will Japan export TVs or logs? How many?

3

THE INVISIBLE HAND

How Price Is Determined in a Market Economy

IN THIS CHAPTER YOU WILL LEARN:

How a market functions

•

How demand is determined

•

How supply is determined

•

How equilibrium is determined in a market

•

How a price is established in a market

•

How the quantity exchanged is determined in a market

WHY DO THINGS COST SO MUCH AROUND DISNEYLAND?

Recently, a middle-aged couple from Indianapolis made a trip to Disneyland. On their way from the airport to their hotel, the bus driver pointed out that Orange County, in which Disneyland is located, held the distinction of being the most expensive place in the country to live. As the bus passed a row of houses, the driver pointed out that the average price of a house was $180,000, and that a house rents for $600 a month. Many people, he said, chose to live 45 minutes further up the freeway, where housing prices were half as much. The woman from Indianapolis remarked to her husband that back home a house like that would sell for $45,000. She asked her husband why the Orange County houses cost so much. He replied, "It's southern California, dear," to which she countered, "What does that mean?"

When the couple arrived at the hotel, they were told that their double room would cost $189 a day. The woman was astonished at the high price. Back in Indianapolis, she told the desk clerk, the very best hotel allows children to stay free and costs only $69 a day. "I suppose it costs so much because it's southern California," she added. "The bus driver was right," she told her husband as they walked to their room. "Orange County is an expensive place even to visit. We certainly couldn't afford to live here."

Why does shelter cost so much more around Disneyland than it does in Indianapolis?

GETTING ALONG IN BERKELEY

During the 1960s and early 1970s, Berkeley, California, where the University of California at Berkeley is located, had all the appearances of a university town. Students made up the most obvious segment of the population, supporting the merchants and landlords. There was little need for dormitories because most of the 30,000 students could find suitable quarters in the town within easy walking or biking distance of the university. Today many of Cal's students don't live in Berkeley any more because there's no place for them. The university has only 6,000 dorm rooms, and there are few apartments available in the town.

Neighborhoods around other state colleges and universities have experienced an unprecedented level of apartment construction in recent years, but there has been little or no increase in the number of apartments in Berkeley. Those apartments that are still rentable have taken on a shabby, run-down appearance because landlords refuse to make even minor repairs. Even these poorly maintained apartments are difficult to find. Students intent on living near the campus are often forced to offer rewards and bribes to find a place to live. Most of the students have resorted to living in high-rise apartments in nearby cities and commuting to classes.

Why has Berkeley suffered a rental-housing shortage?

WILL RAISING WAGES TO REFLECT COMPARABLE WORTH END DISCRIMINATION AGAINST WOMEN?

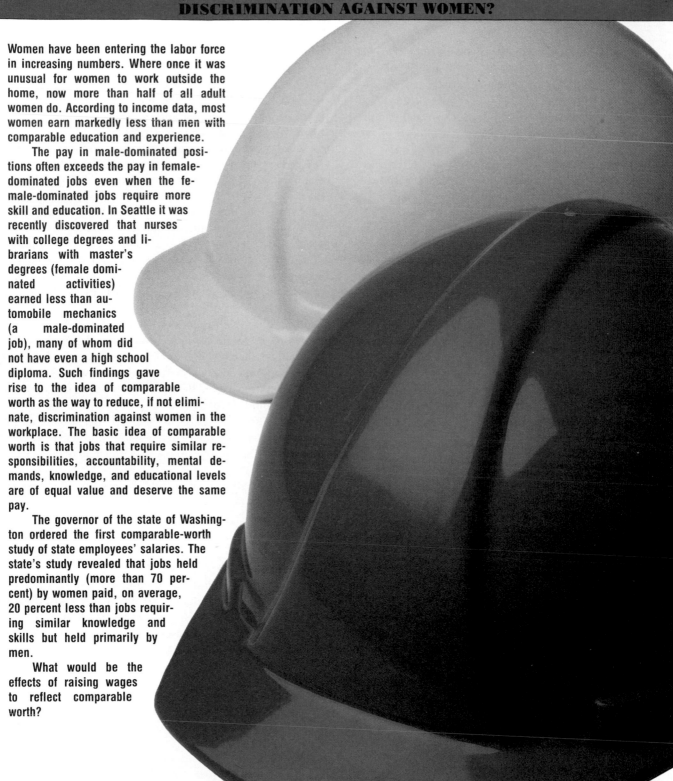

Women have been entering the labor force in increasing numbers. Where once it was unusual for women to work outside the home, now more than half of all adult women do. According to income data, most women earn markedly less than men with comparable education and experience.

The pay in male-dominated positions often exceeds the pay in female-dominated jobs even when the female-dominated jobs require more skill and education. In Seattle it was recently discovered that nurses with college degrees and librarians with master's degrees (female dominated activities) earned less than automobile mechanics (a male-dominated job), many of whom did not have even a high school diploma. Such findings gave rise to the idea of comparable worth as the way to reduce, if not eliminate, discrimination against women in the workplace. The basic idea of comparable worth is that jobs that require similar responsibilities, accountability, mental demands, knowledge, and educational levels are of equal value and deserve the same pay.

The governor of the state of Washington ordered the first comparable-worth study of state employees' salaries. The state's study revealed that jobs held predominantly (more than 70 percent) by women paid, on average, 20 percent less than jobs requiring similar knowledge and skills but held primarily by men.

What would be the effects of raising wages to reflect comparable worth?

• INTRODUCTION •

One of the activities you most frequently engage in is trading. Literally millions of goods and services are exchanged every day in the United States. These exchanges are generally aided by the existence of markets, which were introduced in Chapter 2. It is difficult to exaggerate the importance of markets in the organization of our economy.

An easy way to comprehend the advantages that markets convey to society is to compare the performance of the free-market economies, such as the United States, Western Europe, and Japan, with that of the centrally planned economies of the U.S.S.R. and its allies. Such a comparison would reveal not only that free-market economies have provided a higher standard of living but also that they function more smoothly on a daily basis. While a Soviet housewife spends much time trudging from waiting line to waiting line and may end up resorting to an illegal black market to find what she wants, her American counterpart almost always finds amply stocked shelves offering a variety of alternatives. Apparently, market economies are much better than centrally planned economies at finding out what people want and then providing it. Why?

We are said to be living in the age of information processing, and markets excel at this task. Markets provide the information required for millions of economic decision makers to make appropriate decisions. Markets process two kinds of information: (1) information about what people want and (2) information about the economic costs of meeting these wants. Markets then send out economic signals in the form of prices that guide producers in deciding what and how much to make and that guide consumers in deciding what and how much to buy.

Market-determined prices occupy center stage in this process, providing the necessary information for decentralized decision making and ensuring that the actions of producers and consumers mesh. All of this happens simultaneously for thousands of producers, millions of consumers, and billions of different trades. Central planners, in comparison, are deprived of much of the information that markets provide. One Soviet economist has been quoted as stating that one issue of *The Wall Street Journal* provides more information about the United States economy than Soviet central planners have available annually to plan the entire economy. It is as if planned economies are groping in an information darkness while decentralized market economies are performing without direction in the light of day.

By their performance, markets have demonstrated the value of the information they provide. So important are markets in the U.S. economy that an entire branch of economics called *microeconomics* is devoted to explaining how markets behave. Because of the importance of markets, we shall devote two chapters to introducing you to how they function. This chapter will concentrate on how markets determine the prices of goods and services. Chapter 4 will focus on the forces that cause market prices to change.

We shall begin our study by asking the question: What is a market? •

WHAT IS A MARKET?

The purpose of a **market** is to facilitate trades and exchanges. Chapter 2 explained how specialization and exchange create wealth and how markets encourage specialization and exchange. In markets the prices of goods and services, wages and salaries, interest rates and rents are determined. These prices guide individuals in buying and selling. Market prices provide the information necessary for a free-enterprise economy to function efficiently.

> *A market is an institutional arrangement that brings together buyers and sellers and facilitates exchanges.*

Markets can assume many forms — swap meets, arts and crafts fairs, stock markets, commodity markets, auction houses, even a college placement service. All of these markets bring people together for the purpose of making trades and exchanges. One of the great advantages of markets is that they allow people to trade without having to meet in person. Stock can be bought, for example, without ever having to meet the person who sold it. Stockbrokers, real estate salespersons, and insurance agents are all engaged in facilitating the work of markets. Markets are not defined by geography; some are local, some regional, some national, and some international in scope. Nor are they limited by time; futures markets, for example, allow a person to buy or sell commodities that do not yet exist. The scope of a market is determined by the area over which a single price exists for the good or service being traded. The critical characteristic of a market is not its form but its function, which is to facilitate trading.

The concept of a market allows economists to divide economic activities into **industries.**

> *An industry is composed of the firms that supply goods and services to a particular market.*

Thus when we speak of an industry, we are discussing a specific collection of firms that produce similar if not identical products. When we talk of the apple industry, we are concerned with the specific group of farmers who grow apples and not the farmers who grow wheat. When we speak of the automobile industry, we are talking about the manufacturers that supply automobiles to the automobile market and not the manufacturers of other goods. Each industry has its own market in which the output of that industry is traded.

Economists are interested in how the organization of markets influences the price and quantity of goods sold. Economists divide markets into two basic types: (1) **competitive,** or **price-taker markets,** and (2) **imperfectly competitive,** or **price-searcher markets.**

> *A competitive (price-taker) market exists when both buyers and sellers accept the market-determined price in making their decisions to buy or sell.*

> *An imperfectly competitive (price-searcher) market exists when either the buyer or the seller (or both) has sufficient market power to influence the market price, in which case the decision maker with market power searches for the best price to charge for the good or service.*

We shall begin our discussion of markets by studying competitive markets.

COMPETITIVE MARKETS

In competitive markets both buyers and sellers face so much competition that neither has any control over the market price. Any buyer or seller can buy or sell as little or as much as desired at the existing market price without affecting that price. When this situation exists, the market is said to be a **purely competitive market.**

> *A purely competitive market is a market in which there are many buyers and sellers, a homogeneous product is traded, and there is easy entry and exit of buyers and sellers from the market.*

This definition could use some explanation. You may well be wondering: How many buyers and sellers are many? *Many* in this case is defined operationally, not numerically. *Many* is whatever number is required to ensure that no buyer or seller has any control over the market price. It may be as few as seven, as one study determined, or several more, depending on the circumstances. The largest egg producer does not produce sufficient eggs to affect the market price of eggs, and the largest egg buyer does not purchase sufficient eggs to determine the selling price of eggs. If either does not sell or buy, the market price will not change. Both must accept the market price. They are price takers. This is not true for all markets, of course. If General Motors, for example, decides not to sell cars, the market price of automobiles will clearly be affected.

A homogeneous product exists when buyers do not care which firm produced the good, because all products in that industry are considered identical. When you buy eggs, chickens, apples, or oranges you do not usually care which farm produced them; they are therefore examples of homogeneous products. Not all markets trade homogeneous products. When you shop for a pair of jeans, for example, you will be offered a variety of styles and colors. You probably do not consider all jeans to be identical.

Easy entry and exit means that no barriers keep a supplier or buyer from trading in the market. If you want to produce eggs, raise chickens, or grow apples, you can do so, provided you have the necessary funds. There are no legal barriers to stop you from entering these industries. If you currently own a firm that is operating in one of these industries, nothing can stop you from deciding to sell out or to simply stop producing. Entry and exit are not free for all industries, however. You cannot decide today to become a physician tomorrow. There are significant legal requirements for the practice of medicine. Also, if you own a public utility such as a telephone or an electrical company, you cannot stop producing. You are generally required by law to supply your product or service to all demanders.

Another qualification is sometimes added to the definition of pure competition: Significant **externalities** must be absent.

> *Externalities are external costs (or benefits) of an economic activity imposed on (or received by) someone other than the economic agent making the decision to engage in the activity.*

Air or water pollution that results from producing or consuming a good is an example of an externality. Some economic activities currently generate externalities: oil refineries, steel mills, paper mills, for example. Others, like most agricultural activities and almost all services, do not.

IMPORTANCE OF PURE COMPETITION   There are three good reasons for beginning our study of price theory with pure competition. First, pure competition is useful for analyzing a number of actual markets. Almost all agricultural and many commodity markets are purely competitive, as are most service industries as well as some manufacturing markets. To understand the perennial farm crisis in the United States, for instance, it is necessary to understand how a purely competitive market works.

Second, examining the theory of pure competition is a good starting point for the study of microeconomics. Every other market structure has some elements in common with pure competition. By learning the theory behind pure competition, we shall also be mastering some of the important elements of the other market structures.

Third, pure competition is unique in that it is the only market structure that in theory efficiently allocates society's scarce resources, thereby obtaining the maximum consumer satisfaction from a given amount of resources. When a market meets the conditions for a competitive market, the price that is determined in the market will be the result of the competitive process. In such a market the information generated about prices guides individual decision makers, each seeking to further his or her own interests, to jointly make the best use of the available scarce resources.

The resulting price, as we shall see below, will be precisely the price that reflects the value of the resources to society. Pure competition is therefore useful for judging the behavior of existing markets.

A competitive industry must meet all of the characteristics described above. To understand the importance of these characteristics for the operation of competitive markets, let us examine the U.S. wheat market, which closely approximates the conditions for a competitive industry.

First, the market for wheat facilitates trade between the many buyers and the many sellers of wheat. Thousands of farmers grow wheat in every state in the continental United States west of the Mississippi River. The wheat produced is ultimately sold to hundreds of buyers through organized commodity exchanges. The wheat farmer with the largest acreage doesn't supply one-thousandth of a percent of the annual sales on these exchanges. Nor does the largest buyer purchase more than a very small percentage of the total crop. No buyer or seller in the wheat market is large enough to influence the price, and therefore all have no choice but to accept the market-determined price.

Second, the wheat market trades a homogeneous product. Wheat is graded and sold to a standard. A buyer doesn't have to inspect his or her purchase. One farmer's wheat of a particular grade is identical to that of any other farmer. A baker, for instance, does not care which farm produced the wheat that is going to be used as long as it meets the standards that have been set.

Third, there are no legal barriers to stop anyone from buying or selling wheat or from ceasing to do so. Hundreds of new farmers began growing wheat last year and even more stopped growing wheat. The condition for easy entry does not mean that anybody can do it, only that many can. When it becomes profitable to produce wheat, more farmers will plant wheat, and when wheat becomes unprofitable, some wheat farmers will plant other crops instead.

Finally, there are no significant externalities in the wheat market. No person who is uninvolved in the trading of wheat is either harmed or benefited by its production, trade, and consumption. Also, growing wheat does not contribute to pollution.

DETERMINING MARKET EQUILIBRIUM

The basic question of microeconomics is: How is price determined in a free-market economy? In answering this fundamental question, economists divide the forces acting within a market into (1) the demand factors influencing buyers and (2) the supply factors influencing sellers. Both demand and supply determine the value, or price, of a good or service. According to Alfred Marshall, the great English economist who did much to develop the theory of how markets behave, asking which force — demand or supply — is more important in the determination of price is like asking which blade of a scissors — the upper or the lower — cuts a piece of paper. Neither demand nor supply is more important than the other in establishing the market price; both must be considered together.

FACTORS AFFECTING DEMAND IN A MARKET

All economics is based on the iron law of scarcity, which we discussed in Chapter 1. The law of scarcity states that wants are unlimited while the means of satisfying those wants are strictly limited. Because of scarcity, individuals and society must choose those few goods they will actually buy from among the unlimited number of things they would like to have.

The difference between **wants** and **demands** is critical.

> *Wants are the totality of goods people would have if scarcity did not exist, including all of the goods people would want if the goods were free.*

> *Demand refers to those goods that consumers choose in the face of scarcity and for which they are actually prepared to pay a price.*

The list of goods that people want is obviously much larger than the list of goods that they demand. This section examines the role that price plays in the demand for goods and services.

If you were asked what factors affect your demand for a good, say cheeseburgers, you would probably respond by listing several things — how you currently felt about cheeseburgers, how much money you had, the prices of chicken sandwiches and hamburgers, and how much cheeseburgers cost. You would be correct, for several factors do affect your demand for cheeseburgers. We shall begin our investigation of demand by focusing on the role of price in the demand for goods and services.

THE LAW OF DEMAND

How do consumers choose which goods to purchase? We already know from Chapter 1 that consumers choose purposefully. First, they economize. They endeavor to spend their scarce resources in the way that will bring them the most satisfaction. Second, they follow the **fundamental postulate of economics:**

> *The fundamental postulate of economics states that as the personal gain from choosing an alternative increases, other things held constant, a person is more likely to choose that alternative. Conversely, as the cost associated with choosing a particular alternative increases, other things held constant, a person will be less likely to select that alternative.*

Therefore, as the price of a good increases, buyers choose either not to buy it or to buy less of it than before. This behavior is governed by the **law of demand:**

> *The law of demand states that as the price of a good increases, the quantity demanded of that good will decline when other things are held constant.*

The quantity of a good that buyers desire at a particular price is the *quantity demanded* at that price. The law of demand also holds true in reverse. As the price of a good decreases, the *quantity demanded* increases.

Underlying the law of demand is the **law of diminishing marginal value or utility,** which is based on the observation that the more of any good one has, the less one values an additional unit of that good.

> *The law of diminishing marginal value states that the marginal benefit of a good declines as more of that good is consumed.*

Marginal benefit is the additional benefit or satisfaction that an individual receives from consuming one more unit of a good or service. Marginal benefit declines as more of a good is consumed. Thus the more of any good you have, the less you will value and be willing to pay for another unit of it.

For example, think how hungry you can get waiting for a holiday dinner. It smells so good that you can hardly wait a moment longer. When it is finally time to eat, you rush to your seat at the table. The dishes are passed, and you heap your plate high. The food tastes as good as it smells. You begin to eat with enthusiasm, then you eat more slowly, and finally you have had enough. When asked if you would like to have seconds, you decline!

Barely 20 minutes earlier, you could hardly wait to be asked to the table, but now that you have eaten your fill, the last thing you desire is more food. The reason is simple: The more of any good you have consumed, the less you value another unit of that good. The marginal (additional) value provided by another unit of a good is always less than the value of the preceding unit. This law of diminishing marginal value explains why the law of demand accurately describes the behavior of buyers. Another unit of a good is worth less to the buyer, so he or she will buy more only if the price is lower than the preceding unit's price. Conversely, for the same reasons, a buyer will purchase less if the price increases.

Diminishing marginal value thus implies the law of demand: The quantity demanded of a good will increase only if its price falls, because additional units of a good are worth less than previous units. Thus the price of a good will determine the quantity of the good demanded. When its market price changes, so will the quantity demanded of a good.

A change in the price a consumer must pay for a good has two effects on the quantity of that good the consumer will wish to purchase: (1) a substitution effect and (2) an income effect. First, when the price of one good increases relative to the prices of all other goods, some of the other goods, because they are now relatively less expensive, will appear to be more desirable than before. Thus, following the fundamental postulate of economics, people will be more likely to reject the good that has become relatively more expensive and to substitute instead some of the goods that have become relatively less expensive. Thus when a good increases in price relative to the prices of other goods, consumers will buy less of the now more expensive good and substitute instead more of other goods. This is the **substitution effect.**

> *The substitution effect is the decrease in quantity demanded for a good whose price has risen that is caused by the substitution of this more-expensive good for other goods that are now relatively less expensive.*

In the 1970s when the price of coffee increased substantially, consumers responded by drinking less coffee and substituting instead more tea and soft drinks. While all coffee drinkers responded in the same way — reducing coffee consumption and substituting more of other goods — not all responded to the same extent. Devoted coffee drinkers probably reduced their consumption less than casual coffee drinkers, and some casual drinkers may have stopped drinking coffee altogether. The overall effect in the market was to reduce the quantity of coffee purchased and to increase the quantities of other goods traded. When the price of a specific good rises relative to the prices of other goods, it is a universal tendency for consumers to substitute by buying less of the now relatively more expensive good and buying more of other goods that are now relatively less expensive.

The second result of an increase in the price of a good is that the consumer will have less money left to spend if he or she buys the good than before the price increase. A change in the relative price of a good is similar to a change in income. When, for example, the price of coffee increased from $2 a pound to $6, a family that consumed a pound of coffee a week would need an annual increase in income of $208 to maintain their coffee consumption. Without an increase in income, the family cannot continue to buy both the same amount of coffee and the same amount of other goods as before the price rise. Thus a price increase can be considered a decline in income. When a family's income falls, it will be forced to reduce the quantity of all goods purchased, including the amount of coffee. When a good increases in price relative to the prices of other goods, consumers are poorer and buy less of all goods, including the good whose price has risen. This is the **income effect.**

> *The income effect is the change in quantity demanded of a good whose price has risen that is caused by the decrease in real income resulting from the price change.*

Thus, as the law of demand states, when the relative price of a good increases, the quantity demanded will decrease. The income effect also works in reverse: When the relative price of a good decreases, people become richer and can buy more of all goods.

When the price of a good rises relative to the prices of all other goods, the substitution effect and the income effect combine to reduce the quantity demanded of the now more expensive good. Conversely, when the relative price of a good falls, the quantity demanded of the good will increase.

NEED VERSUS DEMAND

In relation to the law of demand, the concept of *need* is not very useful for economic analysis. Because need implies an absolute necessity for a good, the following apparently reasonable statements are seriously misleading:

> Every dwelling must have at least two exits to the outside of the building capable of allowing the occupants to escape in case of fire.

> Health care should be a right; everyone should be able to obtain the medical care he or she needs.

Consider the first statement. Will everyone who occupies a dwelling that does not have two exits to the outside be injured or killed in a fire? Clearly not, but the risk of death or injury is greater with only one exit. But why stop there? Why not require an outside exit from every room in a dwelling? The answer is that fire safety is not the only good in which people are interested. They are also interested in low costs of construction, in low heating and cooling costs, in reducing the risk of burglary, and so on. The more exits that are required, the higher these other costs will be.

The above statement about required dwelling exits ignores three important facts:

1. Economic goods are not free and can be obtained only by sacrificing something else that is also a good.
2. There are substitutes for nearly everything.
3. The efficient way to choose among substitutes is to compare additional costs with additional benefits.

APPLICATION

3.1

MOTHERS TO BE AND THE LAW OF DEMAND

Just before midnight on a cold, rainy Seattle night, a TV news reporter and cameramen from a local TV news program arrived at the parking lot of a hospital for a fast-breaking story. In each of several cars in the lot sat a pregnant woman with her husband. The reporter tried to interview several of the soon-to-be mothers, all of whom were clearly in labor and equally clearly didn't want to talk about it. The reporter then spoke with two of the husbands, who said they didn't have insurance that covered maternity care.

Then at the stroke of midnight, in front of the cameras, all of the car doors opened at the same time, and each expectant woman made her way slowly across the parking lot and through the emergency room door. The

TV cameras following the procession into the hospital revealed pandemonium. Each husband was demanding that his wife be admitted first, and most wives were asking only to be allowed to lie down. The reporter managed a hurried interview with a harried hospital worker, who stated in no uncertain terms, "This happens every night, and I am getting real tired of it."

The very next night, the TV reporter interviewed the mothers, each holding her newborn child. These interviews revealed that since none of the families involved had medical insurance, each family would have to pay all the costs of delivery.The hospital charged $240 a day and counted any part of a day as a whole day. If an expectant mother checked in at 11 p.m., she was charged for that entire day. Rather than pay $240 for one hour of care, the new mothers had elected to tough it out in the parking lot until after midnight.

The TV reporter also interviewed the hospital administrator, who announced that the hospital would be changing its pricing policy and would now charge an hourly rate of $10 per hour for less than a full day. When the price of one hour of care fell from $240 to $10 for women who found themselves in labor at 11:00 p.m., there was an increase in the quantity of hospital care demanded.

Women whose labor was still manageable were no longer likely to wait the extra hour if they were already at the hospital, because the cost of the one hour of care they would receive between 11:00 p.m. and midnight was now only $10 rather than $240. Thus, to the extent that conditions allow, even women in labor can reduce or expand their consumption of hospital care by an hour in response to a price change, providing another example of the working of the law of demand.

For a high-rise apartment, the additional cost of providing two exits to the outside may exceed the additional benefits of reducing the risk of injury or death from fire. Lower-cost substitutes for an extra door, such as smoke alarms, fire extinguishers, or "No Smoking" signs, may also reduce the risk of injury or death from fire.

Similarly, the statement that everyone should have the medical care he or she needs appears to be a sound statement, but how much medical care does a person need? Most people would agree that persons seriously injured in automobile accidents should have immediate medical attention whether they can pay for it or not. Also, a person suffering from a heart attack or cancer is clearly in need of medical care. How about the man with influenza or the woman with athlete's foot? Are they also in need? The costs of treating influenza and athlete's foot are real. There is, and always will be, a limited number of physicians. If their time is used treating the needs of flu sufferers and persons with itchy feet, they are not available to treat patients with heart disease and lung cancer.

If medical care, like any scarce good, is made free to consumers, there is no incentive to economize on its use, even if the doctors do not charge a fee. Flu sufferers will be tempted to substitute a trip to the doctor for taking two aspirins and going to bed. Persons with itchy feet might well decide they need professional attention rather than purchasing an over-the-counter medication from their pharmacist.

For purposes of economic analysis, a need turns out to be a want when closely examined. The question then becomes: To what degree are

TABLE 3.1
The Demand Schedule for Wheat

PRICE (DOLLARS PER BUSHEL)	QUANTITY DEMANDED (MILLIONS OF BUSHELS PER YEAR)
7	0
6	10
5	20
4	30
3	40
2	50
1	60
0	70

these goods wanted? Are they desirable enough to pay for them? If so, then these wants become demands, and the higher their price, the less will be the quantity demanded.

THE DEMAND SCHEDULE

A **demand schedule** depicts the relationship between price and quantity demanded, showing that as price decreases, the quantity demanded increases.

> *A demand schedule is a tabulation of the relationship between price and the quantity demanded of a good; as price increases, the quantity demanded decreases.*

Table 3.1 shows a possible demand schedule for wheat. Wheat buyers will decide not to purchase the wheat if the price is $7 per bushel, not because they do not want wheat but because the price is too high. Instead, they will use their limited income to buy goods that, at existing prices, they desire more. If the price of wheat should decline to $6 per bushel, buyers will respond to the lower relative price by purchasing 10 million bushels. Should the price fall still further — say, to $3 — buyers will respond by increasing the quantity demanded to 40 million bushels. Thus, in compliance with the law of demand, reducing the price of a good coaxes buyers to purchase more of that good.

For a demand schedule to be meaningful, the units of measurement of both the price and the quantity and the time period under study must be stated. Generally, the price is in dollars per unit and the quantity is units per time period. The units could be bushels (as in Table 3.1), pounds, or simply the number that would be sold. The time period could be days, weeks, months, or years.

A demand schedule is constructed holding constant all of the other factors that influence demand. It answers the question: If all of these other factors remain the same while price is allowed to vary, what will be the effect on the quantity demanded of the good?

A demand schedule always exhibits a negative relationship between price and the quantity demanded, as suggested by the law of demand. This is owing to the operation of the law of diminishing marginal value, which, you will recall, postulates that the marginal benefit of consuming another unit of a good will be less than the marginal benefit derived from consuming previous units of that good. The demand schedule thus reflects the marginal benefits of consuming additional units of a good. In Table 3.1 the marginal benefit of consuming 10 million bushels is equal to $6, the marginal benefit of consuming 10 million more bushels for a total of 20 million is $5, the marginal benefit of 30 million bushels is equal to $4, and so on.

THE DEMAND CURVE

A **demand curve** graphically displays the information from a demand schedule. It shows the relationship between price and quantity demanded in graphic form.

> *A demand curve is a graphic presentation of the relationship between price and the quantity demanded of a good.*

The information from Table 3.1 is shown graphically in Figure 3.1. Price is measured in dollars per bushel on the vertical axis and quantity demanded is measured in millions of bushels per year on the horizontal axis. The demand curve, D, shows the various price/quantity-demanded combinations from Table 3.1. The curve is drawn through points A to H, which have been plotted from the data provided in the table.

When discussing the relationship between price and quantity along an existing demand curve, economists use the term *quantity demanded*. A demand curve is downward-sloping, showing the negative relationship between price and the quantity demanded. When the price is $5 per bushel on the vertical axis, the quantity demanded (as represented by point C on the demand curve) will be 20 million bushels. If the price declines to $2, the quantity demanded (point F) will increase to 50 million bushels. The demand curve shows that as more units are put on the market, lower prices are required to induce buyers to acquire them.

The demand curve in Figure 3.1 could be the demand curve for an individual or it could be a **market demand curve.** Since we are interested in what determines the market price of a good, we shall be interested in the market demand curve. A market demand curve is composed of all the demand curves of individual buyers.

> *The market demand curve is the horizontal summation of the demand curves of all of the individuals participating in the market; it is obtained by summing the quantities demanded by all individuals at each possible price.*

Figure 3.2 shows how the market demand curve for a market with two consumers, Person A and Person B, is derived from the individual demand curves for those two persons. The market demand curve is obtained by summing the individual quantities demanded at each price. Picking a price and moving horizontally, we then add together the individual demand curves. If the price is $0, Person A would acquire 50 units, as would Person B; hence the market demand will be 100 units at a price of $0. If the price increases to $2, then Person A will buy 25 units and Person B will buy the same amount. The total quantity demanded is thus 50 units at the $2 price. If the price increases to $4 per unit, both individuals will drop out of the market, and there will be zero quantity demanded in the market. Since the demand curve of each individual is downward-sloping, the market demand curve is also downward-sloping. Thus we see that all market demand curves also obey the law of demand.

Price, of course, is not the only thing that determines the quantity of a good that will be purchased.

FIGURE 3.1
Demand Curve for Wheat

The demand curve for wheat is plotted from the data in Table 3.1. It shows the various quantities demanded by buyers at every possible price. Each point on the demand curve represents a possible price/quantity-demanded combination. If, for example, the price of wheat is $2 per bushel, the quantity that buyers desire will be 50 million bushels. If the price is higher, say $5 a bushel, the quantity demanded would be 20 million bushels. Thus the demand curve reflects the law of demand, and so demand curves therefore always slope downward to the right.

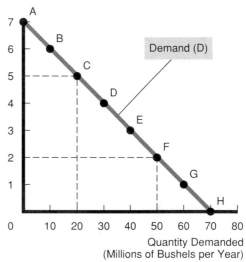

FIGURE 3.2
Deriving the Market Demand Curve

The market demand curve is composed of the demand curves of all of the individual buyers. In the figure there are two buyers: Person A and Person B. When the price is $2, the quantity demanded in the market is 50 units, made up of the 25 units that Person A desires and the 25 units that Person B wants. The market demand curve for each possible price is the sum of the quantities demanded by Person A and Person B. The market demand curve can be thought of as the horizontal summation of the individual demand curves because it is derived by adding together the individual quantities demanded at each price while not adding together the prices paid by each individual.

NONPRICE FACTORS THAT AFFECT DEMAND

When we began our discussion of demand, you were asked to list the factors that affected demand for a good. A number of factors other than price were listed. How do these factors affect the demand for a good? They determine the position of the demand curve — whether it will be far to the right, close to the origin, or somewhere in between.

Some of the nonprice factors that influence the position of the demand curve are the prices of other goods, population, and per capita income. In Chapter 4 we shall examine in more detail the role these factors play in the market. It will suffice for now to examine the influence of a few of them on the demand for wheat. The position of the demand curve will be influenced by the prices of other goods. Some of these other goods will be substitutes for wheat. If their prices are relatively high, there will be a corresponding strong demand for wheat. The entire demand curve for wheat will be positioned further from the origin than if the prices of the substitute goods were lower.

Generally, the larger the population and the higher the per capita income, the greater will be the demand for wheat. The more people, the greater the total demand for products made from wheat will be, since there will be more individual demand curves represented in the market demand curve. The higher the average income of each person, the greater will be each individual demand for wheat. The demand curve will therefore lie further from the origin as the population increases and individual incomes rise.

The role played by the nonprice factors that affect demand is to determine the position of the demand curve. The demand curve will still slope downward, but where it is located will be determined by these nonprice factors.

TABLE 3.2
The Supply Schedule for Wheat

PRICE (DOLLARS PER BUSHEL)	QUANTITY SUPPLIED (MILLIONS OF BUSHELS PER YEAR)
0	0
1	10
2	20
3	30
4	40
5	50
6	60
7	70

Demand, which reflects the forces operating on buyers in a market, represents one-half of the forces that affect market price. Supply, which reflects the forces operating on sellers, makes up the other half.

FACTORS AFFECTING SUPPLY IN A MARKET

As in the case of demand schedules, there are both price and nonprice factors that affect supply.

PRICE AND SUPPLY

The quantities of goods and services that sellers are willing to supply to the market also depend on the price of the good. Suppliers, like demanders, also follow the fundamental postulate of economics as illustrated by the **law of supply.**

The law of supply is the principle that as the price at which a good can be sold increases, more of that good will be offered for sale when other things are held constant.

The market price represents the benefit that suppliers receive from selling in the market. As the benefit to suppliers increases with a rise in the price, sellers will respond by offering more in the market. Thus a positive relationship exists between price and the quantity supplied. More will be supplied as the price of the good increases. When economists discuss the relationship between price and supply along a given supply curve, they use the term *quantity supplied.*

A **supply schedule** shows the amounts of a good or service that individuals or firms will offer for sale at various prices. A higher price will induce suppliers to offer more of a good for sale in the market.

A supply schedule is a tabulation of the relationship between price and the quantity of a good offered for sale; as price increases, the quantity supplied increases.

A possible supply schedule for wheat is shown in Table 3.2. If the price of wheat is $1 per bushel, the quantity offered in the market will be 10 million bushels. If the price of wheat is $2 per bushel, the quantity supplied in the market will be 20 million bushels. A further price increase to $5 per bushel will increase the quantity supplied to 50 million bushels.

FIGURE 3.3
Supply Curve for Wheat

This supply curve is plotted from the data in Table 3.2 and shows the quantity of wheat that suppliers are willing to offer for sale at each price. Each of points A–H on the curve represents a possible price/quantity-supplied combination. At a price of $3, suppliers will offer for sale 30 million bushels of wheat (point D). If the price is $5, suppliers will offer 50 million bushels of wheat for sale (point F). The supply curve slopes upward because suppliers are willing to offer more wheat at higher prices.

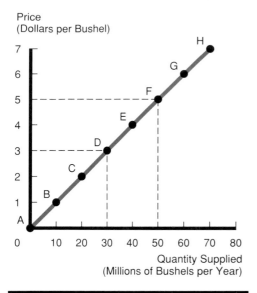

THE SUPPLY CURVE

The information contained in Table 3.2 can be presented as a **supply curve.** A supply curve shows in graphic form how the quantity supplied of a good responds to all possible prices.

> *A supply curve is a graphic presentation of the relationship between price and the quantity supplied of a good.*

The relationship between price and quantity supplied is positive; to induce suppliers to offer more in the market, a higher price is required. In Figure 3.3 a price of $0 will not induce any supply (point A). If the price increases to $3, the quantity supplied will be 30 million bushels (point D). If the price increases further to $5, the quantity supplied would increase to 50 million bushels (point F).

WHY SUPPLY CURVES SLOPE UPWARD The positive relationship that exists between price and quantity supplied is based on the law of increasing costs, which was discussed in Chapter 1. Figure 3.4 demonstrates how the law of supply is implied by the law of increasing costs and why the supply schedule reflects the opportunity or marginal cost of supplying a good to the market.

It is possible to derive a supply curve directly from the production possibilities frontier (PPF) and thereby demonstrate why supply curves slope upward. Every PPF, like those we studied in Chapter 1, implies a supply curve. When the PPF reflects the law of increasing costs, as it does in Figure 3.4, the resulting supply curve will slope upward.

The production possibilities frontier in Part A of Figure 3.4 shows the combinations of two goods, X and Y, that can be produced when all resources are fully employed. Points A–E indicate some of these combinations. If society chooses point A, it will produce 3.7 units of Y and no units of X. If society instead decides that it would like to produce 1 unit of X (by moving to point B on the frontier), 0.2 unit of Y must be sacrificed to obtain the first unit of X. If a second unit of X is produced by moving to point C on the frontier, the opportunity or marginal cost would increase to 0.5 unit of Y. The opportunity cost of a third unit of X would be 1.0 unit of Y, and so on, until obtaining the fourth unit of X requires the sacrifice of 2.0 units of Y. The marginal cost of each succeeding unit increases in accordance with the law of increasing costs.

This information is reproduced as a supply curve in Part B of Figure 3.4. The vertical axis of the production possibilities frontier measures the quantity of Good Y *acquired*, and the vertical axis of the supply curve measures the price of Good X as the quantity of Y that must be *sacrificed* to obtain each unit of X. Thus the vertical axis of the supply curve measures the sacrifice, or the marginal cost, that is necessary to obtain another unit of X.

Point A on the production possibilities frontier (3.7 units of Y, 0 units of X) corresponds to point A on the supply curve. Since zero units of X are produced in Part A, zero units of X are supplied in Part B and zero units of Y are forgone. To produce 1 unit of X in Part A, the economy had to move from point A (where 3.7 units of Y were produced) to point B (where 3.5 units of Y would be produced). Thus the marginal cost of producing the first unit of X would be 3.7 − 3.5 = 0.2 unit of Y. Thus point B in Part B represents the quantity of X (1 unit) plotted against the price of X in terms of 0.2 unit of Y forgone. Point C in Part B shows that the sacrifice or marginal cost of obtaining the second unit of X is 0.5 unit

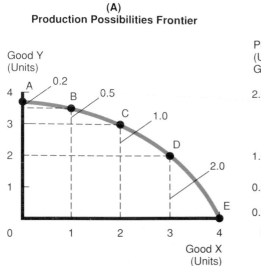

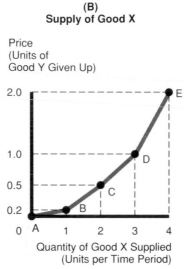

FIGURE 3.4
Deriving the Supply Curve from the
Production Possibilities Frontier

The supply curve can be derived directly from a production possibilities frontier. The production possibilities frontier (PPF) shown in Part A reveals the various possible combinations of good X and good Y that can be efficiently produced by the economy. The supply curve shows the opportunity cost of supplying various quantities of a good. Thus the information contained in the PPF is sufficient to derive a supply curve. Both graphs show that the opportunity costs of the first, second, third, and fourth units of good X are 0.2, 0.5, 1.0, and 2.0 units of good Y, respectively. The supply curve is upward-sloping because the opportunity cost of each succeeding unit increases in terms of the amount of Y that must be given up.

of Y. Similarly, points D and E on the supply curve represent the marginal cost of additional units of X in terms of the increasing amounts of Y that must be given up.

The supply curve thus represents the marginal cost of supplying additional units of a good — an important point to remember. The quantity of the good supplied is measured on the horizontal axis, and the marginal cost, or price, is measured on the vertical axis. In Part B of Figure 3.4, the marginal or additional cost is measured in terms of the amount of the other good that was given up. The supply curve, therefore, directly measures the sacrifice (in terms of other goods) that must be made in order to obtain the quantities supplied in the market.

The marginal costs of production represented by the supply curve reflect the opportunity cost of using resources to produce a particular good rather than producing the next best alternative. The marginal or opportunity cost of obtaining more of X in terms of the amount of Y that must be sacrificed can be considered the price of X. When marginal costs are expressed in dollars rather than in specific units of the goods that must be sacrificed, it is done so for convenience. It is simply more convenient to speak of $100 as the opportunity cost of the resources used to produce a good than to list the quantities of other goods that must be sacrificed.

Since marginal costs increase as output of a good grows, in accordance with the law of increasing costs, suppliers require a higher price to be induced to offer more of that good for sale. Thus the supply curve will exhibit a positive relationship between price and the quantity supplied. Supply curves therefore generally slope upward.

DERIVING THE MARKET SUPPLY CURVE The market supply curve is the aggregation of all the supply curves of individual suppliers. It is obtained in a way similar to the market demand curve, by summing at each possible price the quantities supplied by all suppliers.

FIGURE 3.5
Deriving the Market Supply Curve

The total quantity offered in the market is the sum of the individual offerings of suppliers. The total supply in this figure is made up of the quantities offered by two persons: Person A and Person B. When the price is $3, for example, Person A will offer 25 units and Person B another 25 units, for a total of 50 units. If the price were higher, say $6, then both persons will offer more. The quantity supplied by Person A will increase to 50 units, as will the quantity supplied by Person B, for a total quantity supplied of 100 units. The market supply curve will be upward-sloping because the individual supply curves are upward-sloping. The market supply curve is the horizontal summation of the individual supply curves; it is obtained by summing the quantities supplied by all individual suppliers at each possible price.

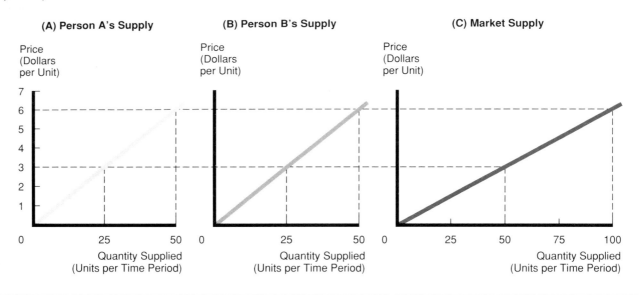

The market supply curve is the horizontal summation of the supply curves of all of the individual suppliers participating in the market; it is obtained by summing the quantities supplied by all suppliers at each possible price.

In Figure 3.5, when the price is $0, both Person A and Person B will offer zero units for sale. If the price is $3, Person A will supply 25 units, as will Person B. Thus the total quantity supplied to the market when the price is $3 is 50 units. When the market price is $6, both persons will supply more units than they did at $3. Person A will supply 50 units, and Person B will also supply 50 units, for a total quantity supplied in the market of 100 units. Because the individual supply curves all slope upward, the market supply curve will also slope upward.

NONPRICE FACTORS INFLUENCING SUPPLY

As with demand, there are factors other than price that influence supply, and, as with demand, these factors influence the position of the supply curve. These factors include the prices of the factors of production used to produce the good and the state of technology and expectations about future prices. The higher the prices of the factors of production, the closer the supply curve will be to the origin. If the prices of land, labor, and capital employed to produce a good are high, then obviously smaller amounts can be produced at each price than if the prices of inputs were lower. Similarly, the more advanced the state of technology, the larger the amounts that can be produced from given sets of inputs and that can be supplied at each price. The prices of the factors of production and the state of technology thus determine the position of the supply curve, which will continue to be upward-sloping with respect to price.

Now that you have been introduced to the concepts of demand and supply, it is time to combine these concepts to see how market prices are determined.

EQUILIBRIUM OF SUPPLY AND DEMAND

The interaction of the market supply and demand curves determines the market price and the quantity sold of a good or service. This interaction helps to coordinate the decisions of buyers and sellers, who have competing and opposing interests. Buyers want to purchase goods at the lowest possible price, whereas sellers want to sell goods at the highest possible price.

Consider the market for wheat, which approximates the conditions of pure competition. The demand and supply curves in Figure 3.6 represent conditions in the wheat market. Along a given demand curve (D in the figure), there are many possible price/quantity combinations reflecting the demand for wheat, while the supply curve similarly offers as many possible price/quantity combinations reflecting the supply of wheat. Neither the demand curve nor the supply curve is in itself sufficient to determine the market price and quantity sold.

How is the market price determined? There is only one price/quantity combination in Figure 3.6 that lies on both the demand and supply curves. This unique combination occurs at point E, where the supply curve intersects, or cuts, the demand curve from below. Point E corresponds to a price of $3.50 and a quantity of 35 million bushels per year. Only at this **equilibrium price** does the amount that suppliers want to sell equal the amount that buyers want to purchase.

> *The equilibrium (or market-clearing) price is the price at which the quantity demanded by buyers just equals the quantity supplied by sellers.*

Because at the equilibrium price the amount of a good that buyers want to buy just equals the amount that suppliers wish to sell, the market is said to clear.

The equilibrium, or market-clearing, price can also be found in Table 3.3. Column 1 lists the possible equilibrium prices, Column 2 shows the quantity of wheat that will be demanded at each price, and Column 3 gives the quantity that will be supplied at each price. If you search down Columns 2 and 3, you will discover that the quantity of wheat demanded is equal to the quantity supplied at a quantity of 35 million bushels. Now consult Column 1 to find the market-clearing price, which is $3.50 a bushel.

Suppose the price initially happens to be different from the market-clearing price. Part A of Figure 3.7 shows what happens when the price rises above the equilibrium price — $6, say, rather than $3.50. In this case the quantity demanded will decline from 35 million bushels to 10 million bushels. The quantity supplied will respond in the opposite direc-

FIGURE 3.6
Establishing Equilibrium Price and Quantity in the Wheat Market

The actual quantity of wheat exchanged and the price at which it is sold are determined by the interaction of the demand and supply curves in the wheat market. These curves are plotted from the data in Table 3.3. Both the equilibrium price and the quantity exchanged are determined by the intersection of the supply curve and the demand curve, shown by point E. The equilibrium price in this example is $3.50 per bushel, and the equilibrium quantity exchanged is 35 million bushels. Point E is the only point where a possible price/quantity-demanded point on the demand curve is matched by a price/quantity-supplied point on the supply curve. So at this point the market clears: The amount that buyers wish to purchase just equals the amount that sellers wish to supply. At no other price will this occur.

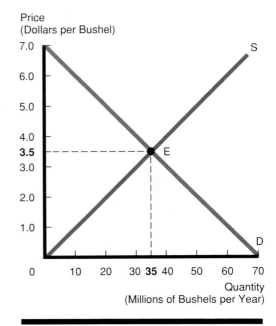

TABLE 3.3
Equilibrium in the Wheat Market

PRICE (DOLLARS PER BUSHEL) (1)	QUANTITY DEMANDED (MILLIONS OF BUSHELS PER YEAR) (2)	QUANTITY SUPPLIED (MILLIONS OF BUSHELS PER YEAR) (3)
7.00	0	70
6.00	10	60
5.00	20	50
4.00	30	40
3.50	**35**	**35**
3.00	40	30
2.00	50	20
1.00	60	10
0.00	70	0

tion, increasing from 35 million bushels to 60 million bushels. A **surplus** of 60 − 10 = 50 million bushels will exist. Many sellers who are willing to sell wheat will not be able to find a buyer.

> *A surplus, or excess supply, is a condition in which, at the existing price, the quantity supplied is greater than the quantity demanded. A surplus occurs when the existing price is higher than the equilibrium price.*

Rather than be shut off from trading when a surplus exists, some suppliers will offer wheat at a lower price. At a lower price — say, $5 — some suppliers will reduce the amount they want to sell and perhaps some will drop out of the market altogether. Consequently, the quantity supplied in the market will fall. The lower price has the opposite effect on buyers. Some buyers will want to buy more at the now lower price, and some buyers who had dropped out of the market at $6 will now want to buy some wheat, which will increase the quantity demanded. The net effect of the increase in quantity demanded and the decrease in quantity supplied is a reduction in the surplus, although a surplus will still exist at $5. The process of suppliers offering lower prices will continue until the surplus is eliminated at the equilibrium price of $3.50, for only at this price will the market clear.

Part B of Figure 3.7 shows what happens when the price falls below the equilibrium price — say, to $2. Buyers will want to buy 50 million bushels of wheat, while sellers will want to sell only 20 million bushels. A **shortage** will exist, because the quantity demanded exceeds the quantity supplied by 50 − 20 = 30 million bushels.

> *A shortage, or excess demand, is a condition in which, at the existing price, the quantity demanded exceeds the quantity supplied. A shortage occurs when the existing price is lower than the equilibrium price.*

Rather than do without when a shortage exists, some buyers will offer sellers a higher price. The higher price will motivate suppliers to increase the quantity supplied and will discourage some buyers, thereby having the opposite effect on the quantity demanded. Thus the quantity supplied increases while the quantity demanded decreases, thereby reducing the

FIGURE 3.7
Disequilibrium in the Wheat Market

Disequilibrium exists when a market does not clear because the quantity demanded does not equal the quantity supplied. This will happen when the price is not equal to the equilibrium price. Suppose, as shown in Part A, that the market price for wheat is initially $6 per bushel, which exceeds the equilibrium price of $3.50. In this case the quantity demanded will be 10 million bushels and the quantity supplied will be 60 million bushels. The quantity supplied exceeds the quantity demanded, creating a *surplus*. As long as a surplus exists, there will be an incentive for some suppliers to offer lower prices, and price will fall to the equilibrium value.

Part B shows the case in which the price is below the equilibrium price. Suppose the price is $2 per bushel, in which case the quantity demanded will exceed the quantity supplied, creating a *shortage*. When a shortage exists, some buyers will have an incentive to offer higher prices rather than do without, and the price will rise to the equilibrium price of $3.50 per bushel.

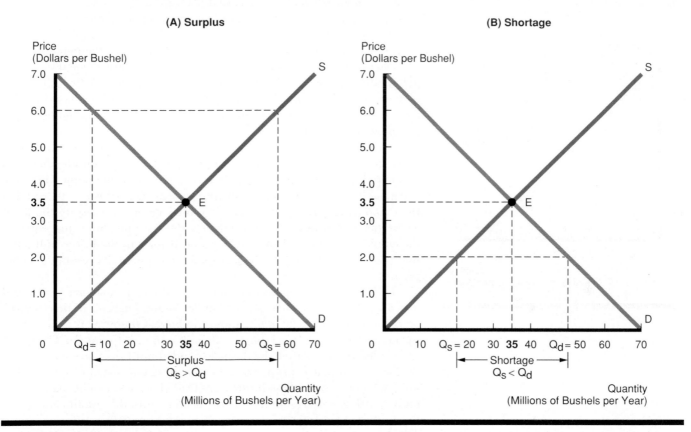

amount of the shortage. Nevertheless, a shortage will continue to exist until the price reaches the equilibrium price of $3.50, for only at the equilibrium price will the quantity demanded just equal the quantity supplied.

The equilibrium price is discovered in the market by this process of bidding by persons who are dissatisfied with the existing price. Only at the equilibrium price will all buyers and sellers be satisfied with the existing quantities. When no person has any incentive to buy or sell more, the market has reached the equilibrium price.

BENEFITS OF A MARKET

Adam Smith, generally considered to be the first great economist, described the benefits of a market (or industry, as he called it) in a famous passage in his book *The Wealth of Nations*. He likened the workings of a market to an invisible hand:

> He generally, indeed neither intends to promote the public interest, nor knows how much he is promoting it. . . . He intends only his own security;

FIGURE 3.8
Equilibrium in the Wheat Market

A competitive market in equilibrium allocates resources efficiently. The demand curve, which reflects the buyers' marginal valuation of the good, declines as additional units are obtained. The supply curve reflects the rising marginal (opportunity) cost of producing additional units of the good. When the market is in equilibrium, the marginal benefit to buyers of the last unit purchased is equal to the marginal cost of producing it, and the market price provides a measure of both.

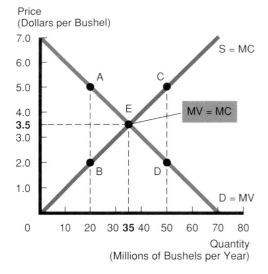

and by directing that industry in such a manner as its produce may be of the greatest value, he intends only his own gain and he is in this, as in many other cases, led by an invisible hand to promote an end which was no part of his intention. . . . By pursuing his own interest he frequently promotes that of society more effectively than when he really intends to promote it.[1]

Today we would consider that a market in equilibrium accomplishes three important social functions: (1) It allows the peaceful resolution of the potential conflict that exists between buyers who desire a low price and sellers who desire a high price; (2) it allows scarce resources to be allocated in an efficient manner; and (3) it provides the information necessary to allow economic decision makers to allocate efficiently the resources under their command.

First, a market in equilibrium peacefully resolves the potential conflicts between buyers and sellers, whose interests are diametrically opposed, through the voluntary actions of both parties. Both buyers and sellers are satisfied with the quantity traded at the equilibrium price. The market thus provides a mechanism for voluntarily solving conflicts over the allocation of scarce goods and resources.

Second, a market in equilibrium allocates scarce goods and resources efficiently, allowing society to obtain the most satisfaction possible from its limited resources. Buyers purchase a good up to the point where the marginal benefit achieved from the last unit purchased is exactly equal to the equilibrium price. Suppliers offer for sale amounts up to the point where the opportunity cost of producing the last unit sold is just equal to the equilibrium price. Thus the marginal benefit to the buyer of the last unit traded is just equal to the marginal, or opportunity, cost of producing it.

In Figure 3.8 suppose that only 20 million bushels are exchanged instead of the equilibrium quantity of 35 million bushels. In this case the marginal value of the 20 millionth unit to buyers (point A) is greater than the marginal cost of supplying the 20 millionth unit (point B). The quantity traded in the market should be expanded until the marginal value of the last unit exchanged is just equal to the marginal cost of producing that unit. When only 20 million bushels are traded, society can be made better off by putting more resources into the market until the equilibrium quantity is exchanged.

If more than the equilibrium quantity is traded — say, 50 million bushels in Figure 3.8 — rather than the equilibrium quantity of 35 million bushels, then too many resources will be employed in this market. The marginal cost of producing the 50 millionth unit (point C) exceeds the marginal benefit that consumers receive from buying it (point D). Society would be better off consuming less of the good (the equilibrium quantity) and transferring the resources used to produce the excess 15 units (50 − 35 = 15) to other industries to allow the production of other goods.

The market at equilibrium allocates resources efficiently, ensuring that the quantity traded is the amount that will provide the maximum satisfaction from the available resources. The **equilibrium quantity** is the amount that will equate the marginal value consumers receive from consuming the last unit of the good with the marginal cost of producing that last unit.

---

[1] Adam Smith, *The Wealth of Nations*, 423.

The equilibrium quantity is the amount that equates the marginal value of the last unit of a good exchanged in the market with the marginal, or opportunity, cost of producing it. Thus the value of the last unit traded is just equal to the value of using the same resources to produce the best alternative.

The third social function the market in equilibrium accomplishes is to economize on the information required for buyers and sellers to employ their scarce resources effectively. All that buyers and sellers must know are the existing market prices and how to access the markets. It is as if an *invisible hand* does the rest. It is not necessary for the buyer to know how to produce the good or even to know who produced it. Nor is it necessary for the seller to know anything about the buyer. The beauty of the market is that no one person must know everything, for no one decision maker is in charge. Buyers and sellers are led by an invisible hand to benefit society while trying to benefit themselves.

SUMMARY

1. Trades take place in markets. A market is an institutional arrangement that brings buyers and sellers together and facilitates exchanges. The main economic function of markets is to establish the price at which goods can be traded.

2. There are two basic types of markets: price-taker markets and price-searcher markets. In price-taker markets, both buyers and sellers accept the market-determined price. In price-searcher markets, either the buyer or the seller must determine the market price.

3. Purely competitive markets are price-taker markets. A competitive market is characterized by many buyers and sellers, a homogeneous product, easy entry into and exit from the market, and the absence of externalities.

4. The fundamental question of microeconomics is: How is value, or price, determined? The market provides the answer. The market price is determined by the competition between buyers, who act as the demanders of goods, and sellers, who supply goods. To understand how price is determined, it is necessary to consider the forces acting on both demand and supply.

5. The law of demand describes the behavior of buyers with respect to price: The quantity demanded will increase as price decreases, and vice versa. The law of demand is based on the law of diminishing marginal value.

6. The relationship between price and quantity demanded by buyers is given by the demand schedule. A demand schedule reveals a negative relationship between price and quantity, as the law of demand requires. The demand schedule can be depicted graphically as a demand curve that slopes downward to the right.

7. The law of supply describes the behavior of suppliers with respect to price: The quantity supplied will increase as price increases. The law of supply is derived from the law of increasing costs.

8. The relationship between price and quantity supplied by sellers is given by the supply schedule. A supply schedule reveals a positive relationship between price and quantity. A supply schedule can be depicted graphically as a supply curve that slopes upward to the right.

9. The equilibrium price and the quantity traded are determined by the interaction of the demand and supply schedules. Equilibrium occurs at the price where the quantity demanded equals the quantity supplied.

10. The equilibrium price and quantity can be determined graphically by the intersection of the demand and supply curves. Equilibrium is established where the two curves cross.

11. If price rises higher than the equilibrium price, a surplus will exist. If price is free to fluctuate, then forces will be at work to return the price to the equilibrium level, eliminating the surplus in the process.

12. If price falls below the equilibrium price, a shortage will exist. If price is free to fluctuate, competitive forces will return the price to the equilibrium level, and the shortage will disappear.

13. A competitive market accomplishes three important economic functions: It peacefully resolves the potential conflict between buyers and sellers who have different goals, it allocates resources efficiently, and it provides the information that both buyers and sellers require to make economic decisions.

PREVIEW 3.1 ANALYSIS

WHY DO THINGS COST SO MUCH AROUND DISNEYLAND?

Preview 3.1 pointed out that shelter — whether a house for purchase or rent or a hotel room for the night — costs a lot more around Disneyland than it does in Indianapolis. Many visitors to Disneyland are astonished at how much more housing costs near there than back home. Why? You are now in a position to provide a better explanation than "It's southern California, dear."

The economic tools of how markets determine the equilibrium price of a good or service can provide the reason. The price of any good traded in competitive markets is determined by the interaction of the forces of supply and demand. The point at which the supply curve intersects the demand curve establishes the equilibrium price. If the price of shelter around Disneyland is higher than elsewhere, it is because the demand for shelter there relative to its supply is greater than elsewhere. Thus the equilibrium price will be higher there than in other locations.

This can be seen in Figure 3.9. In Part A the supply and demand for shelter around Disneyland is shown. In Part B the same information is provided for Indianapolis. You can readily see that the equilibrium position in the two markets occurs at different prices. The equilibrium position in Part A occurs at point E, establishing a price of P_d. The equilibrium position (point E) in Part B establishes a lower price of P_i. The price of shelter is higher around Disneyland as a result.

Although this explanation is correct as far as it goes, it probably would not satisfy the woman who asked her husband why housing costs more around Disneyland than back home any more than did "It's southern California, dear." A more complete explanation would point out the relative positions of the supply and demand curves in the two geographic areas.

A higher price for shelter around Disneyland could come about in three different ways: If the demand for housing in the two areas were the same but supply was restricted in southern California, or if the supply of housing was the same in both areas but the demand for shelter was rela-

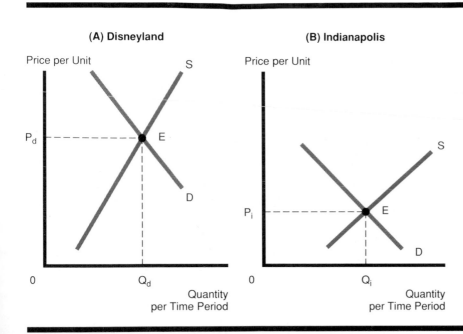

(A) Disneyland

Price per Unit

P_d

E

S

D

0   Q_d

Quantity
per Time Period

(B) Indianapolis

Price per Unit

P_i

E

S

D

0   Q_i

Quantity
per Time Period

FIGURE 3.9
The Price of Shelter

Two independent markets for shelter (houses, apartments, hotels, and motels) are depicted in this figure — the market for the area around Disneyland and the market for the area around Indianapolis. The price of shelter is different in the two geographic areas because the supply curves intersect the demand curves at different prices. The equilibrium price of shelter around Disneyland is therefore greater than the equilibrium price in Indianapolis.

tively greater in southern California, or if there were a combination of the two circumstances. The first two possibilities are graphed in Figure 3.10.

Even if the demand for housing were the same in the two areas, as long as the supply of housing was relatively less in southern California, the price of shelter would be higher around Disneyland. This can be seen by comparing Part A of Figure 3.10 with Part B. The demand curves are the same in the two areas, but the supply of housing is less around Disneyland than in the Indianapolis area. As a result the supply curve in Part A intersects the demand curve at a higher price than in Part B.

Another possibility that would produce a higher price for shelter in southern California would be if demand for housing were relatively greater there than in Indianapolis. Suppose that the supply of housing was the same in both areas but that demand was greater around Disneyland. This situation is shown in Parts C and D, where identical supply curves appear but demand is greater in Part C than in Part D. In this case the supply curve will intersect the demand curve in Part C at a higher price than in Part D.

The higher price for housing in southern California can be explained either by a more restricted supply of housing or by an increased demand for housing around Disneyland relative to the supply and demand conditions that exist in Indianapolis. There is, of course, a third possibility made up of a combination of these two explanations. It is possible that both a relatively restricted supply and a greater demand could exist at the same time to produce higher prices for shelter in southern California than exists in Indianapolis.

This still leaves unanswered the question of why these conditions are more prevalent in southern California than in Indianapolis. You will recall from our chapter discussion that there are specific factors that determine the position of the supply and demand curves. In the case of supply, the availability of the factors of production, the state of technology, and expectations about future prices were listed. Housing requires land, materials, and labor, as well as the technology to efficiently combine these factors in the construction of housing.

FIGURE 3.10
Why Prices of Shelter May Differ

The price of shelter around Disneyland could be higher than in Indianapolis either because of supply conditions or because of demand conditions. Price may vary because of supply conditions if the supply of shelter is more restricted in one area than in the other. The demand curves are identical in Parts A and B of this figure, for instance, but the supply curve is more restricted in Part A than in Part B. Thus the equilibrium price is higher in Part A than in Part B. The price of shelter could also be higher in one area than in the other because of demand conditions. The supply curves in Parts C and D are identical, but the demand curves differ. Because demand is greater in Part C at every possible price than in Part D, the equilibrium price is higher in Part C than in Part D.

Differences in Supply

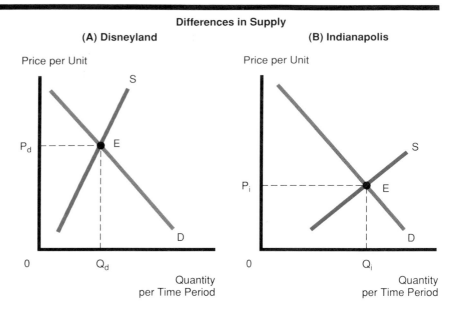

Differences in Demand

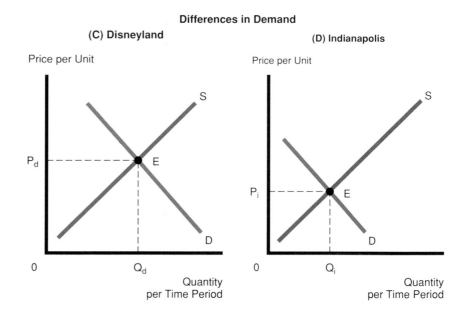

Among these factors, only the availability of land is likely to be significantly different in the two geographic areas. Consider the need for land on which to put hotels and motels. There is a limited amount of land close to Disneyland for such use, whereas there are many suitable locations in Indianapolis. The same thing is probably true of suitable residential housing locations. Indianapolis is located on the north-central plains and can expand in any direction. Los Angeles, in contrast, is located on the West Coast surrounded by steeply rising hills and canyons, which severely restrict the availability of suitable locations for homes. There is thus reason to believe that the supply of housing around Disneyland is restricted relative to the supply of housing around Indianapolis.

The forces that determine the location of the demand curve are probably an even more important reason why housing costs are so high in southern California. Even if the supply of housing were the same in the two areas, it is probable that housing prices would be higher around

Disneyland because of demand conditions. In our chapter discussion we discovered that population and income were among the forces that determine the location of the demand curve. The population of the Los Angeles area is over twelve times greater than that of Indianapolis. The population density per square mile in the Los Angeles area is three times greater than in Indianapolis. This alone would cause the demand for shelter to be significantly greater in southern California.

Not only are there more people, and more people per square mile, in Los Angeles than in Indianapolis, but per capita income is also higher. The average per capita income in Los Angeles is fully 10 percent greater than in Indianapolis. The higher the per capita income, the more of all goods, including housing, that individuals will demand. The higher per capita income existing in Los Angeles reinforces the relatively greater demand for housing in southern California that is in turn caused by a larger population. Thus we should expect that the demand for housing around Disneyland will be relatively greater than in Indianapolis. There are therefore reasons to believe that a relatively restricted supply of housing along with a relatively greater demand for housing explains why the position of the demand and supply curves for housing in southern California is different from the position of the curves that represent the housing market in Indianapolis.

All of the differences we have discussed here combine to account for the high prices for shelter around Disneyland. Do you think that this was what the man from Indianapolis meant when he told his wife: "It's southern California, dear"?

⎯⎯⎯⎯⎯⎯⎯⎯⎯⎯⎯⎯⎯⎯⎯⎯⎯⎯⎯⎯⎯⎯⎯ ●

RENT CONTROLS AT BERKELEY

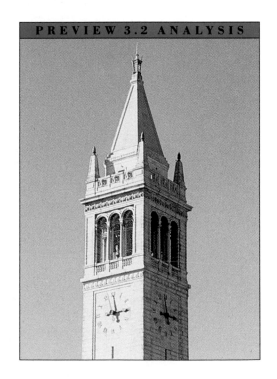

PREVIEW 3.2 ANALYSIS

The effect of rent controls in Berkeley, California, has been to reduce the supply of housing. Students at the University of California at Berkeley often pay fees to find an apartment and sometimes offer bribes and rewards to obtain housing near the university campus. A finder's fee of $300 is not uncommon for a tip that leads to an available apartment. Leasing agents often charge a $60 registration fee to allow students to see their listings, with no guarantee that the apartments listed are still available. Vacancy rates approach zero. People who are lucky enough to have rent-controlled apartments don't move. One former student who has a rent-controlled detached bungalow has lived there for 12 years and has commuted daily into San Francisco since graduation. She would like to live closer to her job, but she can't find anything closer for the rent she now pays. She paid $200 a month when she first moved in and pays only $241 12 years later. She would have to pay between $450 and $500 a month to find anything comparable outside of Berkeley. If former students do not leave, then present students have a hard time finding housing.

Most students simply cannot find housing near the university. Even if they succeed in locating a vacant apartment, they frequently find that the landlord is reluctant to rent to them. Most landlords think that students do not make the best tenants — they are sometimes loud and disturb other tenants, are often messy, and tend to move out at the end of the academic year. Landlords would rather rent to more stable and reliable tenants, which they can easily find. The shortage of housing has forced students to live in nearby, non-rent-controlled cities and to commute to classes, creating traffic and parking problems near the university.

The University of California at Berkeley is the only institution of higher learning in California to be located in a city that has imposed rent controls. The other state universities and colleges in California do not have the housing problems that Berkeley faces, because the private sector has provided plenty of housing for their students. The situation created by rent controls is, however, not unique to Berkeley. The same consequences have been observed in New York City, Washington, DC, and San Francisco, all of which have rent control laws.

Applying the economics of supply and demand helps us to predict the effects of rent control. Rent controls interfere with the normal functioning of the market by imposing a price for rental housing that is below the equilibrium price. In Figure 3.11 the controlled price, P_c, is lower than the equilibrium price, P_e. Persons who are lucky enough to live in a rent-controlled dwelling pay less than they would in a free market ($P_c < P_e$), but not everyone who would like an apartment at rent P_c is able to find one. At rent P_c the quantity demanded is Q_d (see point E'), a quantity of housing that is significantly greater than the quantity that is supplied (Q_s) at that rent. In a free market for rental housing, equilibrium would have occurred at point E, where the quantity demanded and supplied would have been Q and the rent would have been P_e. A shortage of rental housing (equal to $Q_d - Q_s$) exists at the rent-controlled price.

The quantity supplied, Q_s, is less than the equilibrium quantity, Q, because landlords seeking to obtain the highest return possible from their investments look for alternative uses for their properties, uses that are not price-regulated. Condominium conversion is one possible alternative. Conversion to commercial use is another. In Berkeley the city government had to prohibit condominium conversions and had to extend rent controls to commercial properties in order to keep the supply of available housing from completely drying up.

Despite such attempts, the quantity supplied of available rental housing will always be less than the quantity demanded if the rent-controlled price (P_c) is below the equilibrium price (P_e), resulting in a shortage. There will not be sufficient housing for all who would like it at the rent-controlled price; some people will be forced to look elsewhere.

If prices were free to rise to P_e, the shortage would be eliminated as buyers offered and suppliers accepted higher prices. The quantity supplied would increase and the quantity demanded would decrease as the price rose until the two quantities were equal at the equilibrium price. When price is not free to rise, some other way must be found to allocate the too few goods among the too many demanders.

Possible allocation methods include: waiting in line or being placed on a waiting list, favoritism, bribery, lottery, or even violence. These alternatives to the price system were discussed in Chapter 1. In Berkeley's rental-housing market, all of these have been used at one time or another instead of the market to allocate resources.

Being at the top of a waiting list may not qualify a person for a rent-controlled apartment when one becomes available. Rent controls increase landlords' incentives to indulge their individual prejudices when choosing tenants. Discrimination by race, sex, age, or other characteristics becomes more frequent. In a free housing market in equilibrium, there is only one tenant for each apartment. Landlords do not have the luxury of discriminating among applicants on any basis other than ability to pay. If they do, they must pay the price of leaving their dwellings vacant for a longer time while they search for "acceptable" tenants. With rent control there are usually a number of applicants for each vacant apartment, so landlords can practice favoritism.

The reduction in the quantity supplied that occurs whenever the regulated price is below the market-clearing price creates a situation in which the available goods, Q_s in Figure 3.11, are worth more to buyers (in this case, renters) than landlords can legally charge. As the figure shows, the marginal benefit, or value, of Q_s units of housing (point E'') is P_v. Thus some potential renters will be willing to pay up to P_v to obtain an apartment, a price that is greater than the equilibrium price, P_e.

The difference between what buyers are willing to pay and what landlords can legally charge provides the incentive for illegal side payments. One practice that has developed is for tenants to rent a dwelling at the controlled price, but only after first buying the key to the dwelling for a substantial sum of money. Another form of "key money" is the requirement of a large security deposit that the renter will find very hard to get back at the end of the lease. Such practices are essentially ways of making side payments for the right to rent dwellings. Renters are willing to make these side payments rather than do without, and landlords always like to have more income. It is very difficult to police such transactions, for it is in the interest of both parties to evade the law.

To the extent that side payments are blocked and opportunities to convert to alternative non-rent-controlled uses are prohibited, landlords will attempt to maximize their cash flows by reducing the amount of maintenance performed. A rent control board, like the one created in Berkeley, with the power to order repairs is one possible tenant response, but such boards are not always effective. A landlord may resist legal demands to make unprofitable repairs, refuse to pay the fines, and even stop paying taxes, eventually choosing to abandon the run-down building altogether. Because of such abandonments, New York City itself has become the largest single owner of apartment buildings in the city. Wherever rent control has been established, the city inevitably takes on a shabby, run-down appearance.

The lesson to be learned from rent controls in Berkeley, or in any other city where they have been established and enforced, is that a vote of the city council cannot repeal the law of scarcity. Rent control may allow present tenants to enjoy lower rents, but this blessing comes at the expense of the inevitable deterioration of the urban environment. While present tenants may end up paying less, persons searching for a place to live will probably pay more. The scarcity of housing will become greater, not less. There will never be sufficient housing for everyone willing to pay the rent control price. Some persons will search in vain, with nothing to show for the time and money spent. Others may be forced to pay bribes, finder's fees, key money, or large security deposits to obtain housing, possibly paying more than what the market would have charged.

Furthermore, if the market is not allowed to allocate scarce goods, then some other method must be selected. Whatever the method chosen, discrimination will exist. A free market discriminates against those unwilling to pay the market-determined price. Rent controls allow landlords to discriminate according to their own prejudices.[2]

---

² Sources for this analysis: Dan Walters, "Even Liberals Shudder at Berkeley Now," *The Wall Street Journal*, December 13, 1985; "Protracted Rent Control War Takes Toll on Housing Stock," *Insight*, April 13, 1987, 38–40.

FIGURE 3.11
Effects of Rent Controls

When governments impose rent controls on local housing markets, causing the maximum rental price to be below the equilibrium price, a shortage of housing will be created. If, instead of allowing the equilibrium price (P_e) to allocate housing units, the government sets a ceiling price of P_c, the quantity supplied of housing will be Q_s and the quantity demanded will be Q_d. Since the quantity demanded exceeds the quantity supplied, a shortage will exist. Those persons who succeed in finding a place to live may obtain it at less than the market price ($P_c < P_e$). But they could end up paying more to obtain a rent-controlled unit. The marginal value of the Q_s housing units available (point E'') is P_v, so some potential renters will be willing to pay even more than the equilibrium price (P_e) to obtain a housing unit. Since there are more units demanded than supplied, the available housing units will be allocated on some basis other than willingness to pay. Thus the possibility exists that potential tenants willing to pay up to P_v to obtain a housing unit will find some way to buy their way into a rent-controlled dwelling.

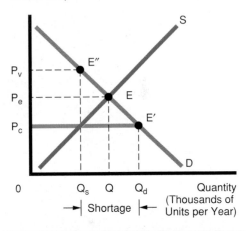

Price
(Dollars per
Rental Unit)

RAISING WAGES TO REFLECT COMPARABLE WORTH

"Beep, Beep! Yale's Cheap" read one sign carried by a picket from Local 34 of the Federation of University Employees during a strike of staff workers at Yale University. The picket didn't mean tuition — she meant the wages Yale paid female employees. Her local had determined that the University paid truck drivers, gardeners, cooks, and campus police — all male-dominated occupations that did not require a college degree — more than was paid to staff workers, such as administrative assistants, secretaries, and librarians, which at Yale are all female-dominated occupations. Many of the female-dominated occupations actually were held by persons with college degrees. Local 34 had had enough and demanded comparable wages for jobs of comparable worth. Yale replied that raising wages to reflect comparable worth was not in women's best interest. Raising wages in female-dominated jobs to match the wages of male-dominated occupations would, by increasing the incentives to stay in their present occupations, mire women in dead-end jobs. On the basis of this statement, Local 34 went on strike, supported by many students and faculty.

The strike at Yale occurred two decades after the passage of the Equal Pay Act of 1963 and the 1964 Civil Rights Act, which made illegal sex discrimination on the job or in access to employment opportunities. Yet today females earn less than males on the average, not because these laws are widely ignored, but because women and men are not distributed uniformly throughout the work force. The occupations dominated by women tend to pay less than those dominated by men.

In Seattle, for example, mechanics (a male-dominated occupation) are paid more than nurses or librarians (female-dominated professions), even though these female-dominated professions require more education and entail higher levels of responsibility than does the occupation of fixing cars. Moreover, nurses and librarians often have advanced professional degrees, while some mechanics do not even possess high school diplomas.

Frustrations at market outcomes like these have led to pressure to adjust wages according to the principle of comparable worth. Proponents of paying according to comparable worth assert that within a firm, jobs should be valued in terms of the skill, effort, and responsibilities required. If two jobs are comparable in these characteristics, they should receive equal compensation. According to advocates of the principle of comparable worth, the interaction of the supply and demand for workers in labor markets results in such obvious inequities that it should be replaced with a more equitable system based on comparable worth.

Supporters of the comparable-worth principle have made some progress toward its adoption. Several bills have been introduced in Congress and at state and local levels. More than 30 states have passed comparable-worth laws regulating state employment practices, but many states have been slow to take action. Only two states, Minnesota and Washington, have actually appropriated funds to remove pay inequities at the state level.

Several city governments have also adopted comparable-worth policies. In Colorado Springs 36 female city hall secretaries complained that the city auto mechanics (all men) were scheduled to get much larger raises than they were. Although the Equal Pay Act requires equal pay for the same job, it does not apply to workers doing different jobs. The secretaries' protest, therefore, was not a question of law but a moral issue. The city elders decided that the secretaries' jobs were just as difficult and as important as the mechanics' jobs but paid $300 a month less. They concluded that the wage discrepancy was basically unfair. The city's personnel director, a male, explained:

> It was basically a moral issue. Sure, supply and demand would have provided us a clerical force at lower salaries, but that market fact was a result of years of discrimination against women workers. We felt we had no right to take advantage of it.

Once the decision was made to adjust wages on the basis of comparable worth, the problem became *how* to implement that decision. The difficulty was how to judge the value of a job. Previously, the labor market had decided the matter. The city had to pay the market wage in order to hire workers. If the city offered less, it would not be able to fill all the positions available; if it offered more, it would have too many applicants. Since the market was no longer allowed to provide this information, an independent judgment was required.

Colorado Springs drew its answers from the Hay Guide-Chart Profile. This scale assigns points to each job in four areas: know-how, problem solving, accountability, and working conditions. The Hay scale found that the jobs performed by a secretarial supervisor and a probation counselor each totaled 208 points. However, the probation job, which was traditionally male, paid 23 percent more than the secretarial job, which was traditionally female. Thus the probation counselor received 23 percent more pay for comparable work. Adjustment of wages according to comparable worth brought significant raises for about 500 city employees in female-dominated jobs. Although in Colorado Springs or Minnesota or Washington State, the labor market has been overthrown in establishing employee pay, the concept of supply and demand continues to be useful in predicting the effects of this new pay principle on the allocation of resources in the labor market.

Figure 3.12 attempts to show why the market values the services of nurses or secretaries (female-dominated occupations) less than the services of mechanics (a male-dominated occupation). The supply and demand for mechanics is shown in Part A, and the supply and demand for nurses or secretaries is shown in Part B. The equilibrium market-clearing price is W_m for mechanics and W_n for nurses. The wages paid mechanics are higher than the wages received by nurses or secretaries. This figure assumes that mechanics are paid more because the supply of mechanics relative to the demand for mechanics is lower than the supply of nurses and secretaries relative to the demand for nurses and secretaries.

One explanation for the relatively higher supply of nurses and secretaries would be that women are systematically denied access to certain occupations (in violation of the law). Another hypothesis is that women, for rational reasons, systematically choose occupations where continuity of service is not critically important — occupations in which a person can enter and leave the labor market without great difficulty. Studies have shown that females, during the child-rearing years, participate less in the labor market than their male counterparts. To the extent that they plan to spend time raising children, women choose occupations that allow them to work by the hour or part-time, that do not require overtime or travel away from home, and that they can leave for prolonged periods and easily return to later in life. Thus many occupations that involve climbing up the corporate ladder, where prolonged absences are not possible, are not as attractive to women as to men. Another possibility is that women could be

FIGURE 3.12
Initial Effects of Implementing the Comparable-Worth Principle

One explanation for the observation that women-dominated occupations pay less than male-dominated occupations is the hypothesis that the supply of workers relative to the demand in male-dominated occupations is lower than in female-dominated occupations. Thus male-dominated occupations such as mechanics (Part A) will pay a higher wage (W_m) than is paid in female-dominated occupations such as nurses or secretaries (W_n in Part B). Now suppose that comparable worth is used to determine wages in female-dominated occupations and that a nursing or secretarial job is determined to be comparable to a mechanic's job. The wages of nurses and secretaries are raised to the level of mechanics' wages, from W_n to $W' = W_m$. The result will be that the quantity supplied of workers in these labor markets will increase from Q_n to Q_s, while the quantity demanded will shrink from Q_n to Q_d, as some current workers lose their jobs. Consequently, a surplus of willing but unemployed workers will be created.

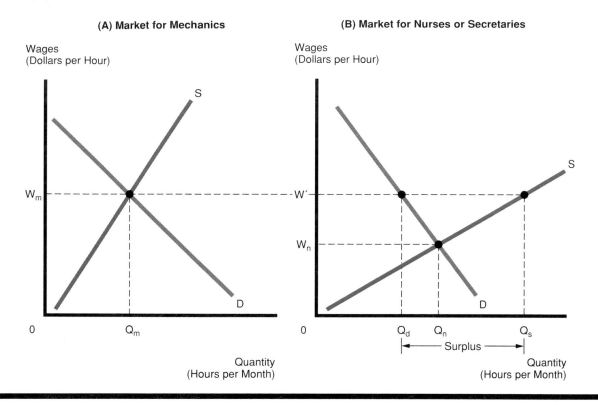

denied access, either in the hiring process or the promotion process, to jobs that benefit from continuity because the person doing the hiring or promoting believes a woman is more likely to leave the job. Jobs in which continuity of service is not of vital importance are less available in the modern economy than full-time, career occupations. These occupations tend to become female-dominated occupations and are relatively oversupplied.

The increase in female participation in the job market over the past several decades does not mean that more women have decided to forgo marriage and children; rather it means that more women have become mothers who also work outside the home. This dual responsibility is a consideration for women in their selection of an occupation (but is growing to be a consideration also for men who are married to working mothers). The increase in the numbers of women who are or who plan to be working mothers increases the supply of workers in female-dominated occupations, whose wages tend to be lower than wages in male-dominated occupations.

In this hypothesis, women who choose not to form families and are therefore less likely to be absent from the labor force for extended periods of time would not be as restricted in their choice of occupation and would earn wages comparable to those of males. Several studies confirm this hypothesis: Women who have never been married have earnings, when adjusted for educational levels and other economic variables, that are virtually identical to the earnings of their male counterparts.

What will be the consequence of adopting the comparable-worth principle instead of relying on market-determined wages? Suppose that a state government decides to rely on a comparable-worth determination to set the wages of state employees. The Hay scale determines that the jobs of secretaries (a female-dominated occupation) and the jobs of mechanics (a male-dominated occupation) are of comparable worth and should pay the same wages. The effect of raising the wages of secretaries to the level of mechanics is shown in Part B of Figure 3.12. When the wages of secretaries increase from W_n to W', the quantity of secretaries demanded will decline from Q_n to Q_d, while the quantity supplied will increase from Q_n to Q_s, creating a surplus of secretaries. The number of persons who would like to work in the female-dominated occupation exceeds the number of jobs available. By the same token, the secretarial supervisor in Colorado Springs will have the pick of the crop when a vacancy occurs. Vacancies there will be relatively rare, however, for workers will hold onto these jobs because they know that they are paid more than they could earn outside of the city government. Not all the people who hold the wage-adjusted jobs will be able to keep them. The quantity demanded of secretaries will actually decline from Q_n to Q_d. Thus one of the major effects of paying according to the comparable-worth principle is to reduce the employment opportunities in female-dominated occupations in state government. This decline in employment opportunities will occur even if comparable-worth adjustments are made in the private sector. An employer will hire an additional worker up to the point where the value of the output of that worker is just equal to the cost of the employee to the firm. If the wage of the employee is increased, then the employer will respond by hiring fewer workers.

There is a secondary effect of raising wages in female-dominated activities. Workers in female-dominated occupations who cannot find wage-adjusted jobs will find jobs in occupations where wages have not been adjusted. Some of the persons who make up the labor surplus in Figure 3.13 will seek and find jobs in the private-sector labor market where the supply of labor will increase, as represented in Part A by a shift in the supply curve of labor from S to S'. This supply shift will lower wages from W to W'', a decline that will permit the employment of the surplus workers.

Suppose wages are adjusted in all female-dominated occupations in both the private and the public sectors. In this case Part B of Figure 3.13 represents any occupation in which wages will be adjusted. A surplus of applicants will result and the existing number of jobs, most of which are currently held by women, will decline in number. The unsuccessful applicants for a wage-adjusted job will be forced either to go without a job or to seek work for lower wages in that part of the labor market not affected by wage adjustment. These women will then have to seek employment in occupations that are currently male-dominated, that may be less suitable to them, and that pay lower wages than they currently receive.

FIGURE 3.13
Secondary Effects of Implementing the Comparable-Worth Principle

Increasing wages in female-dominated occupations such as nursing to reflect comparable worth will create a surplus of willing workers, as shown in Part B. Where previously Q_n nurses were employed, the higher wages (W' instead of W_n) result in a reduction in available jobs from Q_n to Q_d at the same time that more willing workers ($Q_s - Q_n$) are attracted by the higher pay to seek jobs in nursing. Hospitals will always have several applicants for each available position. Those who succeed in finding jobs will receive better pay than in the absence of comparable worth. But what of the $Q_s - Q_d$ unsuccessful applicants? These workers will not remain unemployed forever but will seek jobs in the nonnursing labor market (Part A), causing the supply of labor in that market to shift to the right from S to S'. As a result, the equilibrium wage in these occupations will decline from W to W'' in order to employ Q' - Q more workers. Thus the effect of comparable worth is (1) to raise the wages of workers who manage to retain jobs as nurses, and (2) to lower the wages received by those persons who are forced to seek employment outside of nursing.

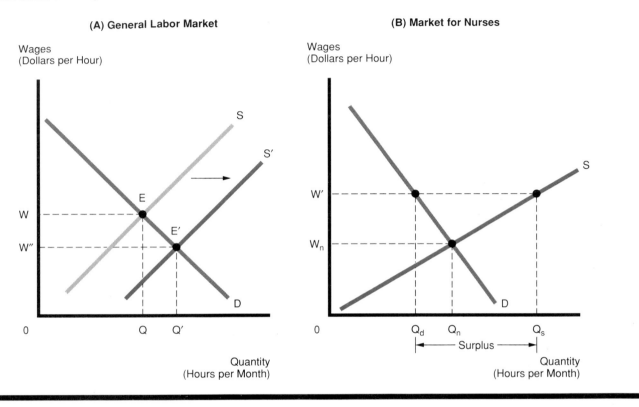

Adjustment of wages on the basis of comparable worth, if it is implemented on a wide scale, will have mixed effects on the economic well-being of the women it is intended to help. Those women who have and can keep the jobs that receive pay increases will be better off, but their good fortune will come at the expense of those women who lose their jobs or who must accept employment in occupations that are less suitable to their preferred life-style and/or pay lower wages than they now receive.[3]

[3] Sources for this analysis: Randall J. Pozdena, "Women's Wages," *Bulletin, Federal Reserve Bank of San Francisco*, June 8, 1984; T. R. Reid, "Comparable Worth Bowls Over Conservative City," *Los Angeles Times*; Gary Becker, "Productivity Is the Best Affirmative Action Plan," *Business Week*, April 27, 1987, 28.

REQUIRED ECONOMIC CONCEPTS

Market

Industry

Competitive (price-taker) market

Imperfectly competitive (price-searcher)
 market

Purely competitive market

Externalities

Wants

Demands

Fundamental postulate of economics

Law of demand

Law of diminishing marginal value
 (or utility)

Substitution effect

Income effect

Demand schedule

Demand curve

Market demand curve

Law of supply

Supply schedule

Supply curve

Market supply curve

Equilibrium price

Surplus

Shortage

Equilibrium quantity

KEY QUESTIONS

1. How does a market facilitate trade?
2. What are the characteristics of a purely competitive market?
3. What are market externalities?
4. What does equilibrium in the market signify?
5. What is the law of demand? What variables affect demand?
6. What factors affect the quantity demanded?
7. What is the law of diminishing marginal value?
8. What is the substitution effect? The income effect?
9. What is the difference between need and demand?
10. What is the law of supply?
11. How is the market demand curve derived from individual demand curves? The market supply curve from individual supply curves?
12. What is the law of increasing costs? What relation does it have to the supply curve?
13. What does a shortage or excess demand indicate?
14. What does surplus or excess supply indicate?

PROBLEMS

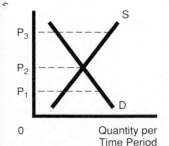

Price per Unit

0   Quantity per
    Time Period

1. Refer to the accompanying graph depicting the U.S. sugar market in answering the questions below.

   a.   What is the market situation at price P_2?

   b.   Suppose the government sets a floor price on sugar at P_1, that is, a price below which a lower price cannot be charged by the farmer. Which will be larger, quantity demanded or quantity supplied?

   c.   Suppose, instead, a ceiling price of P_3 is set by the government, that is, a price above which it is illegal to charge. Will quantity supplied be greater or less than quantity demanded?

   d.   Suppose the floor-price regulation is removed. Assuming the market is competitive, what will the final market price be?

2. Refer to the accompanying table in answering the questions below.

Market for Your College's Sweaters

PRICE	QUANTITY DEMANDED PER MONTH	QUANTITY SUPPLIED PER MONTH
$80	0	30
70	2	27
65	3	24
60	4	21
55	5	18
50	7	15
45	8	14
40	10	10
35	12	8
30	16	5
25	20	3
20	25	0

    a.   What is the equilibrium price?

    b.   Is there a shortage or a surplus at the price of $30? How much?

    c.   Is there a shortage or a surplus at the price of $60? How much?

3. Assume that Kim and Fred constitute the market for cassette tapes and that they have the demand schedules shown in the accompanying table.

Market Demand for Cassette Tapes

PRICE	KIM: QUANTITY PER MONTH	FRED: QUANTITY PER MONTH	MARKET: QUANTITY PER MONTH
$15	2	0	
13	3	2	
12	4	3	
10	5	4	
8	7	5	
6	10	6	
5	12	7	

    a.   Fill in the quantity for each price in the market demand column.

    b.   Suppose the market price was $8 and there were 15 cassettes in stock. How many would remain unsold?

    c.   Graph Kim's and Fred's demand schedules and from them graph the market demand schedule.

4. Sally and Sid have each managed to acquire four tickets to the Boston Celtics basketball playoff game. Their preference for tickets is shown below (Q = quantity, MV = marginal value in dollars).

SALLY		SID	
Q	MV	Q	MV
1	$57	1	$85
2	52	2	80
3	47	3	75
4	42	4	70
5	37	5	65
6	32	6	61
7	27	7	58
8	22	8	52

a. If there are no transaction costs when Sally and Sid decide to exchange tickets, who would buy tickets from whom? How many?

b. Suppose Sally incurs $3 and Sid incurs $5 worth of transaction costs per ticket exchanged. Who would buy tickets from whom? How many?

c. In Part b above, under what conditions would an intermediary (middleman) make it worthwhile for Sally and Sid to trade? (Numbers are not necessary.)

5. The chapter discusses the relationship between the law of demand and diminishing marginal benefit or value. Explain how you would also relate the notion of opportunity cost to the law of demand.

6. When an oil executive says, "Tell me the price of oil and I'll tell you the supply of oil," what does he mean? Does his statement have any relation to a price control ceiling that could cause rather than ease a gasoline shortage?

7. It has been said: "You cannot measure physicians' services in terms of economics." Does the physician? Evaluate the comment (keeping in mind the discussion on near-term women waiting in the hospital parking lot): "If it were clear that people seek medical care only out of need, then everything doctors do is necessary, and the issue would be settled."

8. A newspaper columnist has written: "Television used to be in the business of producing entertainment, and along the way made money. But increasingly television is in the business of making money, with entertainment little more than a by-product." Is this statement consistent with demand theory? Why or why not?

9. Draw a graph that represents the government's imposition of rent controls on rental units in your city or town.

a. How might the landlords behave? Name two actions they might take and explain why they would do so.

b. How might the renters behave? Name two actions they might take and explain why they would do so.

c. Which transaction costs for persons looking for rental units would be affected?

d. Do you think rents on any unregulated units would be affected? Why or why not?

e. Would the opportunity cost of renting units now appear to be relatively more or less attractive to landlords than before rent controls? Explain.

f. Would rent controls have any effect on the level of transaction costs to those looking for rental units?

g. How does the city or town lose as a result of rent controls?

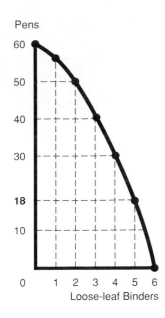

10. A two-good economy produces ballpoint pens and loose-leaf notebooks, as shown in the illustration.

a.   What is the opportunity cost of producing three loose-leaf notebooks? Of producing the third loose-leaf notebook?

b.   Derive the supply curve for loose-leaf notebooks from the illustration.

11. How can one argue that it is more efficient for a firm to produce another bookcase when it is already operating at a loss? Or is the statement ridiculous?

12. How can demand increase and supply increase and yet the price of grapes increase as the quantity of grapes produced expands over a period of several years?

13. It is common to see or hear about long lines of people waiting — sometimes overnight — to buy tickets for rock concerts.

a.   What does this fact tell you about the costs of waiting in line to these people? To support your answer, what casual evidence can you gather from observing who is standing in these lines?

b.   What do the waiting lines tell you about the price of the tickets?

c.   What reasons do managers of rock groups have for setting ticket prices at the levels they do? Are live concerts the only source of revenue to rock groups? Explain.

d.   Why would an airline pilot not be likely to stand in line to buy a rock concert ticket? How would he or she probably try to obtain a ticket?

14. Scalping tickets is illegal nearly everywhere in the United States. Scalpers have sold bowl tickets at prices ranging from $400 to $600 each. They buy the tickets from the players themselves and from cashiers who acquire them at the printed price and then resell them at a markup.

a.   What can you conclude about the official price of the bowl tickets?

b.   Are scalpers violating the law of demand by selling the tickets for $500 each?

c.   In general, can scalpers lose money scalping? What are other risks they take? Is their activity costless?

d.   Do scalpers actually provide benefits to customers? Or do they increase transaction costs to people desiring otherwise unavailable tickets?

e.   Do scalpers cheat buyers because they charge more than they "ought" to, or do they allocate resources in a more efficient manner?

APPLICATION ANALYSIS

1.   In the thirteenth century the famous scholastic philosopher Thomas Aquinas argued for a "just price" based on "the cost of raw materials and labor." He also spoke about a "just wage," with workers being paid in accordance with their social position, their skills, and the nature of the work. In the 1980s the issue of a fair wage for women emerged along with the concept of comparable worth discussed in the chapter. Dissimilar jobs that are of equal "intrinsic value" should be equally compensated, the argument goes, based on a point system of evaluating occupations. Thus in Minnesota a librarian's job was valued as equal to a firefighter's. Thus a policy that started out as "equal pay for equal work" (in the same job) became "equal pay for equal value."

a.   Is there a similarity between the views of Aquinas and today's comparable-worth advocates?

b.   As the problem is stated, how do you believe the cost of raw materials and labor in the thirteenth century and the wage of the auto mechanic today were determined? Is the auto mechanic's wage a "fair wage"? How do you know?

c.   What is "intrinsic value"? Do you think your assessment of it may differ from others' assessment? Will the point-determination level of various jobs be affected by who is on the point evaluation board?

d. In Washington State a registered nurse was assigned 573 points in an occupation evaluation, while a computer analyst received 426 points, although in the market computer analysts were being paid 56 percent more than registered nurses. In your opinion, was the point assignment fair? Define *fair*. Can you arrive at an objective definition of *fair?*

e. Why do you think "equal pay for equal work" evolved to "equal pay for equal value"? Do you believe it is because full-time, year-round earnings of women are about 70 percent that of full-time men? Can you think of any variables this raw comparison may be overlooking?

f. Why do you think comparable worth has made most of its inroads into the government sector but has gained little in the private sector? Should the revenue sources of the government sector versus the private sector be considered in answering this question?

g. Do you believe that comparable worth represents an argument that is emotionally comforting to supporters as well as a political necessity for politicians, or do you believe it is a compassionate antidote to the cold, indifferent, analytic apparatus of the heartless marketplace? That is, do you think women in the labor force should be removed from the realm of competitive pricing? Is the concept of comparable worth "fair"?

h. Is it a testable hypothesis to state that any real productivity differences between the sexes in certain occupations simply reflect cultural differences? Or is this circular reasoning and therefore an error in logic?

2. Before May 1976 Minnesota had a usury law that limited the interest rate to a maximum of 8 percent on *in-state* mortgage loans, loans to individuals, incorporated businesses, and farmers. Draw a graph with the interest rate along the vertical axis and mortgage loans along the horizontal axis. Assume the market rate of interest was 8 percent. From October 1973 to April 1976 the market interest rate rose above 8 percent, reaching 10.4 percent in September 1974. Show this change on your graph.

a. At a 10.4 percent market interest rate, is the quantity demanded for mortgage loans greater or less than the quantity supplied when the legal rate is 8 percent?

b. Can you think of ways that lenders (banks, savings and loans) found to charge an interest rate effectively higher than the legal rate of 8 percent?

c. Do you think that people who could not obtain loans in Minnesota were willing to pay 10.4 percent outside Minnesota for the unregulated federal FHA and VA mortgages?

d. Because builders also borrow, interest fees to builders went up. Since this cost to builders went up, did the law achieve the purpose of protecting house buyers?

122

APPENDIX TO CHAPTER 3

THE ECONOMICS OF INFORMATION

PREVIEW

MIKE MILKIN, BRAND X, AND THE FEDERAL DEPOSIT INSURANCE CORPORATION

What could Mike Milkin (a former employee of a major stock and bond broker), Brand X (a bathroom cleanser), and the Federal Deposit Insurance Corporation (the FDIC — the agency of the federal government that guarantees the safety of bank deposits) have in common? Mike Milkin was the highest-paid employee in history, Brand X was a commercial failure and was withdrawn from the market, and the FDIC and its sister agency, the Federal Savings and Loan Insurance Corporation (FSLIC), are in serious financial trouble. The FSLIC is broke and may be merged into the barely solvent FDIC.

Michael R. Milkin, formerly of the financial firm Drexel Burnham Lambert Inc., was paid a salary and bonus of $550 million in 1987 for the work he did for the firm in 1986. Drexel paid Milkin more than the firm itself earned in profits in 1986. This makes him the highest-paid employee in history. Think of it, a half-billion dollars a year is $1.5 million a day, or $107,000 per hour, based on his usual 14-hour work day. In the time it took him to drive to work, Mr. Milkin would earn more than most Americans earn in a year. His income for 1986 exceeded that earned by John D. Rockefeller (calculated in today's dollars) in his prime. Milkin's 1987 earnings may have been exceeded by only one other American, Al Capone, who in 1927 reportedly earned $105,000, which would be worth more than $600 million in today's dollars. Capone, however, was self-employed. Why would any business firm pay an employee $550 million for one year's work?

Brand X (not the actual brand name) attempted to compete directly with the best-selling bathroom cleanser by copying the same chemical formula, packaging the cleanser in an identical bottle, and labeling it in the same colors as the leading brand. Its salespeople were instructed to see that Brand X was placed next to the leading brand on store shelves. The clincher that would close the sale was that Brand X was priced at half the price of the leading brand. How could it miss? Who could pass up the chance to pay only half the price for virtually the same product? The answer: almost everybody. Brand X never caught on. After a year of miserable sales, it was quietly withdrawn from the market. Why did Brand X fail when it had so much going for it?

The FDIC and FSLIC are the agencies which guarantee that when you deposit money in a bank or savings and loan association, you will always, even if the bank goes broke, be able to get your money back. The FDIC was established by the federal government in 1933 to restore confidence in the national banking system that had been badly shaken by numerous bank failures. When a bank failed prior to 1933, depositors could lose part or all of the money they had on deposit. The FDIC solved this problem. Each financial institution pays a premium to insure the money it has on deposit. These accumulated premiums are used to make good all deposits of less than $100,000 should a financial institution fail. The system worked well enough for 50 years, but during the 1980s the failure of so many savings and loans bankrupted the FSLIC and left the taxpayers holding the bag for $200 billion in deposit guarantees. The FDIC is in better shape, but it has also been hard hit by hundreds of bank failures. What led to this crisis in deposit insurance?

What Mike Milkin, Brand X, and the FDIC have in common is that the question we have asked about each can be answered by using the economics of information.

THE ECONOMIC THEORY OF INFORMATION

In this chapter you discovered how a purely competitive market determines the price of a good or service. In the real world the conditions for pure competition are not always met. One of the problems that plagues markets is lack of information. Consumers and business firms make decisions on the basis of expected costs and benefits. Consumers decide to purchase a good because they expect that the benefits of ownership will exceed the opportunity costs of the purchase. Business firms decide to supply goods because the expected costs of the resources required are less than the expected receipts for the products' sale. But nothing is certain in the real world, and expectations may turn out to be wrong.

In the Analysis of Preview 2.1 in Chapter 2, TV sports commentator John Madden was quoted as saying, with respect to professional football, "In every trade there is a winner and a loser." He was surely wrong if we consider the expectations of the participants when the trade is made: Both parties expect to be made better off or they never would have agreed to the exchange. But he may be right in hindsight. If the player you traded becomes an All-Pro while the player you obtained suffers a career-ending injury, you will no doubt wish that you had never made the deal.

Mistaken expectations are costly, so people try to avoid them. Discovering that the compact disc you have just paid list price for is available at a discount at another store is annoying, an automobile whose transmission fails soon after you bought it is expensive, a disk drive on a computer that fails when you are writing a book or term paper can be a disaster, and working around asbestos can be fatal.

The way to eliminate mistakes is to obtain more information before taking an action. But information is itself a scarce good and obtaining more information can be costly. If information were free no one would ever make a mistake. But even though information is expensive, it may turn out to be less costly to suffer some mistakes than to obtain the information necessary to avoid them.

Since information is costly it will require the expenditure of resources to make trades. The costs associated with trades are known as transaction costs.

TRANSACTION COSTS

Buyers and sellers do not go to market without bearing certain costs. These are called transaction costs — the costs associated with attempts to buy or sell. Transaction costs fall into three categories:

- Search costs are the information costs associated with the discovery of profitable trading opportunities.
- Bargaining costs are the costs of negotiating a trade.
- Enforcement costs are the costs of ensuring that the other party to a trade lives up to the agreement.

Search costs are the costs of obtaining information about the qualities of rival products and the terms on which they are available for sale. They include the costs of reading or watching advertisements, telephoning, and shopping around. If you wish to buy a car, you must decide which make, model, and year to buy. Then you will have to find cars available for sale that meet your specifications and attempt to assess the quality of those available cars.

Bargaining costs include the costs of negotiating a trade and making offers and counteroffers. The seller of a car you might like to buy will have an asking price. You will naturally attempt to buy at a lower price, but you are also interested in the quality of the car. Perhaps you will ask for certain repairs or for the seller to guarantee the vehicle's performance.

After you conclude a deal, you still must make sure that the other party lives up to the agreement. Was the car satisfactorily repaired? Had the odometer been turned back to a lower mileage? Our nation's law courts are filled with lawsuits seeking to compel buyers and sellers to live up to their past agreements.

SEARCH COSTS

If information were free, the price of a good would not vary from store to store or place to place by more than the costs of transportation. But information is not free, and resources must be devoted to acquiring information. In deciding how much information to gather, individuals will follow the principle of rational behavior first introduced in Chapter 1.

The principle of rational behavior states that an economic decision maker should take any action from which there is a positive net benefit. A positive net benefit exists when the addition to benefits exceeds the addition to costs.

A person will acquire more information as long as the benefits of additional knowledge exceed the costs of acquiring it.

This idea is more reasonable than it may at first appear. Suppose that you decide to buy a new personal computer. The more information you possess about the technical qualities of the available computers, their reliability, warranties, and available prices, the better the choice you will eventually make. But it is costly in terms of time to read all of the product-specification and test reports, to talk with owners, and to comparison-shop. Your time is valuable and the time you spend searching cannot be used for other valuable activities. You will at some point decide that you have enough information and will make your decision. When you reach that point, you will have decided that the benefit of additional information is not worth the additional cost. You have been following the rule of rational behavior.

Anything that reduces search costs will improve the economic decisions you make, because it will allow you to obtain more information than would be rational if information costs were greater, and anything that reduces transaction costs will make it possible to conduct trades at lower cost.

MARKETS

Markets exist because they reduce transaction costs. They lower the costs of bringing buyers and sellers together, of negotiating trades, and of enforcing the terms of an agreement. Markets are among the most efficient mechanisms we have for creating high-quality information at low cost. Markets place prices on goods and resources that economic decision makers can use to make economic decisions.

Sometimes we associate markets with physical places, but this is misleading. It is more productive to focus on the functions that markets perform. A market exists wherever there is present a set of personal interrelationships that generates competing bids and offers to make exchanges. Some markets are considered to be "well organized" in that they continuously and comprehensively assemble the bids and offers of buyers and sellers, facilitating trades so that a single market price for a uniform good is established over a wide geographic area. The New York Stock Exchange is an excellent example. The price of a share of IBM is established for the whole world in this market. A local grocery store competes in a fairly well organized market. Buyers and sellers are in frequent contact so that neither the price of bread nor its quality will vary much from store to store. Negotiation costs are small, since a buyer either accepts the deal offered by the store or shops elsewhere. Enforcement costs are reduced by the store guarantee of quality.

A used-car lot is a less organized market. Buyers and sellers do not come into contact very often. Both price and quality must be negotiated for each trade, and enforcement costs can be high, often depending on the seller's reputation. The local bulletin board at the student union or the classified ads in the local newspaper are examples of poorly organized markets. Search costs are high, the exact good being exchanged along with its price must be negotiated, and enforcement costs are likely to be very high.

Each of the above markets, whether well organized or not, allows competing bids and offers to establish prices. Each such price is a piece of valuable information to other people about the terms on which trades are available. Markets thus generate vast quantities of clear and accurate information about available opportunities. The more prices generated by markets and the more widely they are known, the more opportunities there will be available to people to improve their material condition.

Markets reduce search costs by producing information. Middlemen do the same thing.

MIDDLEMEN

Middlemen, brokers, and professional traders are specialists in organizing markets to facilitate transactions.

Middlemen function as intermediaries by bringing together buyers and sellers or by buying goods themselves for resale.

Everyone is familiar with some middleman. Stockbrokers, real estate agents, insurance agents, and travel agents are middlemen, but so are retail stores, automobile and equipment dealers, convenience stores, and service stations. All function as intermediaries. They link producer suppliers with consumer buyers. When you purchased your car insurance, you dealt with an agent who placed your insurance with a company in return for a fee paid by the company. When you last bought milk, the retail grocer matched your demand for milk with the dairy's supply.

Middlemen often get a bad rap, being considered by some as parasites on the economy. Farmers often complain that they receive only a small portion of the amount that consumers ultimately pay for food. Middlemen, in the form of processors, wholesalers, and retail grocery stores that produce no food and whose combined efforts couldn't feed a single person, end up with most of the revenues. Other people view real estate agents in a similar way, claiming that they buy up the best property and charge excessive fees for their efforts. According to one critic, "The only person who wins in the real estate game is the agent who gets paid when you buy and when you sell." Lawyers, who often function as middlemen writing the contracts for complicated deals, are generally not held in high esteem by the public.

The problem may be that middlemen do not produce a product like bread that you can see, feel, and eat. Instead, middlemen specialize in producing information about existing exchange opportunities and the qualities of rival goods. Middlemen are subject to such criticisms mainly because many people do not recognize that information is scarce in the same way that bread is scarce. Those people who wrongly believe (see Application 2.1 in Chapter 2) that wealth consists of material things will be skeptical of the productivity of intermediaries.

By reducing transaction costs, middlemen expand the range of exchange opportunities available to individuals. Middlemen produce opportunities that are valuable in the same way that bread is valuable. If the price of bread falls, everyone who consumes bread will be wealthier. They can now buy the same amount of bread and have money left over to buy other things.

Now consider what middlemen do. Suppose you wish to buy 100 shares of IBM. You could approach your friends to see if they have any IBM shares for sale, or you could place a request in the classified ads or on a community bulletin board. Eventually, no doubt, you will find someone with shares to sell. You still must bargain before coming to an agreement on an acceptable price.

If you stick with it, you will be able to acquire 100 shares of IBM. But you will not have acquired them as cheaply as if you had directly called a stockbroker, placed an order, and paid a commission for the right to buy the shares. Not only will the price per share that you pay through the broker probably be less, but the commission cost will almost certainly be less than your costs of search among your friends or via the newspaper and bulletin board. The existence of a middleman has allowed you to buy shares of stock for less, leaving you with money left over to buy other things, exactly as occurred when the price of bread declined.

You have a house for sale, and somewhere there is a person who would like to buy the house. But you do not know each other. You could advertise your house, answer repeated telephone calls, and hold open houses every Sunday. Meanwhile your potential buyer is reading the Sunday paper, answering the interesting ads, and visiting the most promising possibilities. Your prospective buyer will, with luck, eventually find your house. Bargaining will begin, with first the buyer making an offer and then you countering until you have a deal that will require a contract. A house can be a complicated good to sell in that it involves the negotiation of product quality, warranties, drawing up and checking legal documents, arranging payment, the transfer of the title, and so on.

Alternatively, you could list your house with a real estate agent. The agent would screen all prospective buyers, offering each an inventory of listings along with information about each house. On the basis of knowledge of the current market, the agent will advise you on how much to ask for your house, show your house to interested qualified buyers, help prepare the offer, write the contract, arrange the financing, and close the deal. In return you will pay the agent a percentage of the purchase price.

Depending on the opportunity cost of your time, your expectations about the difficulty of finding a buyer, and your own knowledge of the real estate market, it may pay you to engage a real estate agent. By bringing prospective buyers and sellers together, the agent reduces the transaction costs of buying and selling real estate. The agent works for the seller but finds buyers by providing them with valuable information.

Real estate agents, like all middlemen, reduce transaction costs and thus expand trading opportunities. Without middlemen the range of trading opportunities would be much more restricted than it actually is.

THE ADVERSE SELECTION PROBLEM

Since information is costly to obtain, it is possible that buyers and sellers will possess different amounts of knowledge and that the party with superior knowledge could trap the other party into a disadvantageous agreement. This is known as the **adverse selection problem**.

> *The adverse selection problem is a situation that occurs when the cost of information is lower for one of the participants in a trade, allowing the participant with more information, either the buyer or the seller, to negotiate a particularly advantageous agreement.*

The used-car market suffers from problems of adverse selection. Consider a used-car market composed only of owners who bought their cars new and who now wish to sell them, and of potential buyers who want to buy a used car. Neither buyers nor sellers make a living trading automobiles. If both the buyer and the seller had the same information about the quality of the car being traded, the exchange price would adequately reflect the quality of the vehicle. All qualities of automobiles would be traded, with well-cared-for used cars selling for a higher price than well-worn used cars.

But this is never the case. The seller has owned the vehicle and knows its performance capabilities and mechanical history. The buyer does not possess this information and can only superficially judge the car's quality. Thus the seller has an information advantage over the potential buyer that the buyer cannot inexpensively overcome. Suppose the seller asks a price that suggests the car is of average quality. Should the buyer pay the asking price? If the car is of average quality, it would be worth the price, but the buyer cannot judge the car's actual quality. If the buyer assumes

27

· · · · · · · · · · · · · · ·

A P P L I C A T I O N

3a.1

·:·

MIKE MILKIN AS MIDDLEMAN

Mike Milkin was paid $550 million because he almost single-handedly changed the financial face of corporate America. Milkin did this by recognizing the possibilities for using **bonds** to finance the expansion of small companies.

A bond is a financial obligation that binds the borrower, in return for the use of borrowed money, to repay the sum (called the principal) *in full at a certain future date (called the* maturity) *and to make a fixed annual payment (called the* yield *or* interest) *until maturity.*

As security, bondholders receive first claim on the assets of the company should it default on its promise to pay either interest or principal.

Bonds historically were used to finance the activities of highly creditworthy institutions such as the government (federal, state, and local), as well as large corporations. Because buyers of bonds were thought to be searching for relatively safe investments, bond financing was reserved to the above in-stitutions. Smaller, less creditworthy corporations were generally excluded from the bond market and had to rely on banks or the sale of stock for their financing.

Milkin discovered that the risk of default for smaller corporations was not much greater than that for large corporations, and that this greater risk could be adequately compensated for by higher interest payments. He also discovered that there were buyers for bonds of greater risk if the bonds paid sufficiently higher interest rates. Thus the "junk bond" market, which traded high-yield/higher-risk securities, was created.

Milkin, working for his employer, Drexel Burnham Lambert, approached smaller corporations and offered to sell their bonds through his contacts. Smaller corporations could now receive financing for expansion that they could not previously obtain else-where at comparable interest rates. Junk bond buyers obtained assets that paid a higher rate of return than was available else-where. The junk bond market during the 1980s financed the activities of hundreds of small companies that previously had not been deemed sufficiently creditworthy to issue bonds.

The junk bond market also financed the activities of some corporate raiders. For bet-ter or for worse, raiders have used junk bonds to finance the takeover of some of the country's largest corporations. Junk bonds have also been used for leveraged buy-outs that allowed individuals to turn corporations into private companies. In both cases the new owners thought they could manage the ac-quired companies more profitably than the previous managements had. An additional benefit was derived from the fact that take-overs and leveraged buy-outs increased the share prices of the firms involved. Thousands of shareholders became wealthier because of these activities.

Milkin was indicted by the federal gov-ernment and charged with using insider infor-mation to make advantageous stock pur-chases and sales for his own benefit. These are precisely the charges that are often levied at middlemen, who are widely thought to take advantage of others. Milkin, however, turned out to be the most popular middleman since Robin Hood. His supporters, often from the companies that he had helped to obtain fi-nancing, took out full-page ads in the nation's leading newspapers bearing the headline "Mike Milkin, We Believe in You." *The Wall Street Journal* received angry letters pointing out Milkin's accomplishments and denounc-ing the paper for not supporting him.

His supporters believed that Milkin was paid exactly what he was worth. Milkin was responsible for up to 80 percent of his em-ployer's business. Drexel Burnham Lambert was not run by fools. The firm did not pay Milkin one cent more than he earned. He re-portedly helped to raise tens of billions of dol-lars to finance the expansion of smaller busi-nesses, which in turn increased the nation's output and employment and earned commis-sions for his firm. Milkin, according to his supporters, was paid only a small portion of the wealth that his activities created.

The junk bond market has been invaded by competitors and the idea of high-yield bond financing has become a major tool for financing business in the United States today. Guilty or innocent, the market Mike Milkin created has expanded the opportunities avail-able to U.S. business.[1]

the car to be of average quality but the seller is getting rid of the car because it is of poor quality, the seller will have entered into an advanta-geous contract and the buyer into a disadvantageous contract.

The buyer is not without possible defenses and will tend to assume that the car is of poor quality. After all, a good reason to sell a car is that it is unsatisfactory in some way. Should the potential buyer offer a lower price? If the car is of average quality, the seller will not accept the offer since the car is worth more. If the car is of low quality and worth less than the offer, the seller will accept the offer, but in this event the buyer would be making a bad deal. If his offer is accepted, the buyer will be paying more than the car is worth. So the buyer probably won't make a lower

---

[1] Steve Swartz, "Why Mike Milkin Stands to Qualify for Guinness Book," *The Wall Street Journal*, March 31, 1989; Letters to the Editor, *The Wall Street Journal*, April 18, 1989.

offer for fear he will be locked into a bad deal. Therefore the seller of a car of average quality will find few buyers.

Adverse selection in the used-car market can thus lead to market failure — possible profitable trades in quality used cars exist, but the trades cannot be made. Buyers will assume that used cars are lemons and will pay only low prices, so sellers will respond by actually supplying only low-quality cars.[2]

It is in such situations that middlemen can expand the possibilities for trade. Enter, in the role of used-car dealer, a middleman who has acquired the ability to judge the quality of automobiles and who will serve as an intermediary between seller and buyer. The used-car dealer will recognize that the car in the above example is of average quality or is worn out and will make an offer for the car based on its actual quality. The dealer will in turn price the car according to its quality, with a markup included to pay for his services. Buyers are willing to pay the markup to avoid purchasing a "lemon."

Buyers may therefore be able to rely on the dealer's asking price as a measure of quality. What stops the dealer from selling poor-quality cars for high prices and creating an adverse selection problem? Generally, it is because the dealer has a reputation to uphold, a reputation that is the foundation of his business. The dealer makes a living selling cars, and future sales depend on the firm's reputation for honesty.

In the real world, of course, there exist both disreputable, fly-by-night used-car dealers who create adverse selection problems, and reputable dealers who earn their living certifying quality. Middlemen who serve as intermediaries guaranteeing quality are not limited to the used-car business. They exist everywhere there is an imbalance of information between potential traders. Major retail chain stores, such as Sears Roebuck, K mart, and Safeway, serve as the certifiers of quality for their customers. Such stores depend on repeat sales and will stand behind the products they sell. Brand names, such as Maytag, IBM, Xerox, and Coca-Cola, also certify quality to buyers. In this way markets respond to the adverse selection problem. Middlemen and intermediaries enter the market to overcome the consumer's lack of information.

THE MORAL HAZARD PROBLEM

One of the elements of transaction costs is the cost of enforcing an agreement. When information is costly, it can be expensive to track the actual performance of the other party in an exchange. Also, it can be difficult to verify the claims made by individuals trying to obtain a favorable trade or contract. The cost of obtaining information gives rise to the **moral hazard problem.**

> *The moral hazard problem is a problem that arises when one party to an exchange alters his or her performance in order to take advantage of the contract at the other party's expense.*

A moral hazard exists when a person falsifies a claim in order to make a trade that will take advantage of the other party's lack of information. A

---

[2] George Akerlof, "The Market for 'Lemons': Quality, Uncertainty, and the Market Mechanism," *Quarterly Journal of Economics* (August 1970).

3a.2

**HOW COULD BRAND X
FAIL TO BE A WINNER?**

Brand X attempted to compete directly with the best-selling bathroom cleanser by copying the same chemical formula, packaging the cleanser in an identical bottle, and labeling it in the same colors as the leading brand. Its

salespeople were instructed to see that Brand X was placed next to the leading brand on store shelves. The clincher that the manufacturer relied on to close the sale was that Brand X was priced at half the price of the leading brand. How could it miss? Who could pass up the chance to pay only half the price for a virtually identical product?

The answer: almost everybody. Brand X never caught on and after a year of miserable sales was withdrawn from the market. Brand X fell victim to adverse selection. Consumers viewed the price of the product as a proxy for product quality. A low price suggested corresponding low quality. Consumers were simply not willing to use a lower-quality product at half the price to clean their bathrooms.

And for good reason! If you have ever scrubbed a bathtub or shower stall, you know that the cost of the cleanser is a small part of the total cost of accomplishing the job. If a lower-quality cleanser means that more time and physical effort would be required to save a dollar, most consumers weren't going to buy it. In fact, had consumers taken the chance, they would have discovered that Brand X performed identically to the leading brand. It cleaned just as well with no additional effort required. After all, it was chemically identical to the leading brand. But so few were willing to take the risk that Brand X was a financial failure. Adverse selection was at work limiting the trading opportunities of consumers.

person who has just discovered that he has a serious illness will be tempted to apply for health insurance, and perhaps for life insurance as well. If accepted, he would be taking advantage of the contract, since he would never have been accepted if the insurance company had known about his illness.

The moral hazard problem also applies to persons who change their behavior because of a contract they have entered into. Persons with health insurance are likely to go to the doctor more often than persons without health insurance. Drivers with collision insurance are likely to be less careful than drivers without insurance.

Insurance companies cover themselves by requiring customers to pass a medical examination and by refusing to cover preexisting illnesses. They also require that insured persons share in the loss. Automobile insurance and health insurance are issued with deductibles and copayments. If you have an automobile accident, you have to pay the first $250 or $500 of the cost of repair. If you go to a doctor, you have to pay the first $100 each year and 20 percent of the bill thereafter. Since you share in the loss, you are more likely to drive carefully and less likely to visit a doctor for minor illnesses.

But not all instances of moral hazard can be so easily dealt with. Fires in homes and businesses occur most frequently in the winter months of December and January. The incidence of fire in dwellings is about the same for each of the two months, but not of fires in commercial establishments. More than twice as many fires occur in business firms in January than occur in December.

There is a ready explanation for this observation and it involves the moral hazard problem. Arson is a possible way for a failing business to recover its losses. For many businesses December is the most profitable month of the year. Even a failing business does not want to miss this opportunity. So arson is resorted to in January, after the Christmas rush is over. The moral hazard problem thus explains why insurance companies investigate more thoroughly the claims of fire damage from business firms than from households, particularly the claims for fires that occur early in the new year.

The moral hazard problem also explains why some possible trades do not take place. If it is impossible to write a contract that keeps people from changing their behavior as a consequence of a transaction, it may be

HOW DID THE FDIC AND FSLIC GET INTO THEIR CURRENT STRAITS?

President Franklin D. Roosevelt, in his first news conference in 1933, rejected the idea of federally supplied deposit insurance to guarantee the nation's bank depositors against loss. He stated: "We do not wish to make the United States government liable for the mistakes and errors of individual banks, and put a premium on unsound banking in the future." The president was describing the moral hazard problem discussed above. If all deposits are insured, depositors will have no incentive to closely monitor the practices of their banks to ensure that they will be able to repay the deposits. A major constraint on imprudent lending practices by financial institutions is removed by federal deposit insurance.

A series of bank runs, with depositors simultaneously demanding their money, occurred in 1933. These runs led to the failure of over 4,000 banks, which changed the president's mind about deposit insurance. Congress later in the year instituted federally sponsored deposit insurance. President Roosevelt may have changed his mind about deposit insurance, but he did not forget the moral hazard problem. Along with deposit insurance went increased government regulation of financial institutions. The FDIC and FSLIC, coupled with stricter regulation of the activities of financial institutions, were successful in stopping bank runs. The nation's banking system functioned fairly well for a number of decades. The moral hazard problem that worried President Roosevelt had not been eliminated, just held in check.

mortgages at fixed rates of interest. When inflation caused interest rates to rise, these institutions were in trouble. To attract deposits, many had to pay a higher rate of interest than their existing mortgages were paying them. These S&Ls were slowly bleeding to death.

Congress tried to patch things up, but nothing worked very well, including giving the S&Ls expanded powers to make loans and the right to offer interest-paying checking deposits. These allowances were extended in the vain hope that the S&Ls could increase their earnings and remain solvent.

The savings and loans are not the only financial institutions in trouble. A lot of banks have failed during the 1980s, including 200 in 1988. The rash of bank failures, according to some, is due to a decline in regulation. In order to maintain a level playing field, the amount of government regulation of banks was reduced as the S&Ls were given expanded powers. A decline in regulation, while deposit insurance continued, provided the opportunity for the moral hazard problem to reappear.

If deposits are guaranteed, depositors will have no incentive to monitor the practices of the financial institutions. Banks make money lending out their customers' deposits and pocketing the difference between what is paid out in interest to attract deposits and what is earned on loans. Customer deposits make up most of a bank's assets. The capital the owners have at risk in a bank is a small part, typically less than 5 percent, of the bank's loans.

If it is not regulated, a bank has an incentive to attract as many deposits as possible by paying a slightly higher rate of interest than its competitors and to lend these deposits at as high a rate of interest as possible. This means making more risky loans. Depositors don't care what the bank does because

cial institutions as to high-risk institutions. If the high-risk strategy works, the bank makes a lot of money; if it doesn't work, the owners of the bank don't lose very much because they didn't have much of their own money at risk. Many commercial banks were willing to take the chance, along with almost all failing S&Ls.

Needless to say, for many institutions the high-risk strategy produced losses, not profits, as borrowers defaulted on their loans. The insurers were called upon to make good billions of dollars in deposits. As a result, the FSLIC is itself insolvent and the U.S. taxpayer is stuck with making good $200 billion worth of deposits.

A number of solutions have been proposed to solve the moral hazard problem created by deposit insurance. One proposal is for the insurance agency to charge institutions with risky-loan portfolios more in insurance premiums than it charges conservatively run institutions. This would reduce the incentive to make risky loans. Another proposal is to require financial institutions to have more capital invested in the banks so that more of the owners' money is at risk. Another proposed solution is to require co-insurance: The first $10,000 of deposits would be fully insured, but coverage would apply to only 90 percent of additional deposits up to $100,000. Thus if a bank were to fail, larger deposits would be only partially repaid. Depositors would therefore have an incentive to obtain information about the institution's financial practices, and management would have an incentive to behave conservatively in order to attract larger deposits. Finally, it has been suggested that government get out of the deposit insurance business and leave it to the private sector. Private insurers would certainly base their rates for deposit insurance on the riskiness of the banks' loans.[3]

---

unprofitable for the party that is being taken advantage of to trade at all. Small businesses in some areas, for example, can no longer buy fire insurance because arson has made it unprofitable for insurance companies to assume the risk.

---

[3] Lindley H. Clark, "The Outlook: Perils of Insuring Bank Deposits," *The Wall Street Journal*, May 8, 1989.

HOW COMPETITIVE MARKETS FUNCTION

IN THIS CHAPTER YOU WILL LEARN:

More about how a competitive market functions

•

Why a competitive market allocates resources efficiently

•

Why demand changes

•

Why supply changes

•

Why prices change

•

Why quantities change

ALL IS NOT WELL IN THE HEALTH CARE INDUSTRY

John had not felt well all day. While he was working at the body shop, his left arm had pained him. That night while watching TV, his chest felt tight. Then it felt as if an elephant were sitting on him. He was having a heart attack. John was rushed to a hospital, where he spent three days in intensive care and another three days in the recovery ward. He survived, but he almost had another heart attack when he was presented with the bill for medical services, for he did not have medical insurance. The bill came to $12,000 for hospital care and tests, and it did not include the fee for doctor's services. John's experience is not unusual. A serious accident or illness can mean financial ruin if one survives. The cost of a hospital room currently is well over $200 a day; intensive care can cost $700 a day.

The nation has become increasingly concerned about the rising costs of medical care. Health care costs increased 8 percent in 1986, when the rate of inflation was about 1 percent. Between 1980 and 1988 the number of persons qualifying for Medicare, the government-financed health care program, increased 14 percent, but the costs of the program increased 127 percent.

In 1960 the cost of health care absorbed 6 percent of national income; today it absorbs 12 percent and is rising. The proportion of national income going to health care is expected to reach 13 percent by 1992. Health care costs the nation more than the combined federal expenditures on social security and national defense. Although the importance of high-quality health care is recognized, there is a growing consensus that health care costs are out of control. Recent attempts to curtail these growing costs have met with little success.

Health care in the United States is delivered primarily by the free market. How can a free market be out of control? How can the rapid relative increase in the costs of health care be explained? Can anything be done about it?

SUPPLY MEETS DEMAND IN THE COCAINE BUSINESS

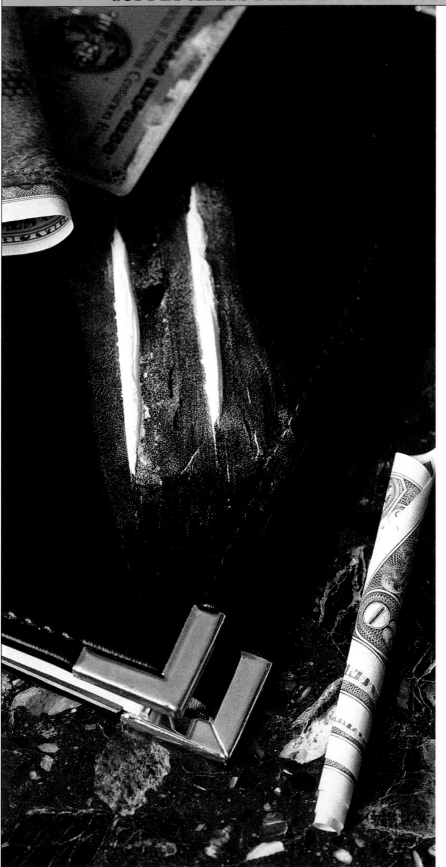

"More than any other business that I know, the drug business is pure capitalism, pure supply and demand," a Miami defense lawyer is reported to have said. Peddling cocaine is not, of course, just another business. Selling the drug is illegal and will land the dealer in jail when and if caught, but producing and distributing cocaine is a multibillion dollar industry that is, despite its illegality, subject to the forces of supply and demand.

Ten years ago cocaine was a cottage industry. Since then it has progressed far from its entrepreneurial origins to become an efficiently managed, giant industry that has saturated its main market, the United States, and seen its profit margins narrow. In response to these changes, the industry has innovated new products, such as "crack," and has sought new markets in Europe.

Although distributing cocaine is subject to the laws of economics, some of its practices are shaped by its outlaw character, which endows it with enormous risks for both dealers and consumers and with commensurately high profits for its suppliers. The industry, for example, is probably plagued with higher labor turnover than most legitimate businesses — at least one would like to think so.

Its illegitimacy also makes it difficult to track. The only consistent statistics available on prices, measured in thousands of dollars per ounce, are reported regularly by *Hi Times* magazine. Statistics on the volume of the illegal trade, estimated in tons, can only be inferred from federal government estimates, based on successful interceptions, or from suggestive statistics on the cash surplus of the Miami branch of the Federal Reserve Bank.

These statistics are sufficient to allow the tools of supply and demand to be used to analyze the cocaine trade. What can be inferred from an economic analysis of this illegal trade? What does the pattern of prices and quantities of cocaine over time tell us is going on in the cocaine trade?[1]

---

[1] *The Wall Street Journal*, June 30, 1986, 1.

COMPETITION IN THE WINE-GRAPE INDUSTRY

The rows of vines stretch nearly a quarter-mile, rising slightly with the land, then falling away to the south. This section contains 80 rows, and each row's end post is neatly numbered in black on white. In the distance a thin cloud of mist moves slowly above the vines; a spray against mildew is applied by a tractor and sprayer that are hidden by foliage. The vines, which were planted eight years ago, are reaching their peak in productivity. Already, in late June, the clusters of grapes are well formed and numerous, promising a bumper crop.

These vines, if conditions do not improve, will be pulled out next year, a victim not of blight but of economics. The price of grapes has fallen so low that it no longer pays the farmer to grow wine grapes. When these grapes were planted eight years ago, grape prices were so high that those farmers who were in the business made small fortunes. These profits attracted new farmers to the business. Now conditions are different. There has been an abundance of wine grapes on the market for several years. If prices do not improve, the farmer will have no choice but to rip out the vines and use the land for a more profitable crop.

The current grape market confounds the farmer. Each year he has done his job and produced good sound grapes that have been made into fine wines. He thinks of his grapes as being identical from one year to the next, but they have sold for widely varying prices. Sometimes prices were high enough to earn a fine profit, but more often he just managed to break even, and recently he has suffered losses. Why has the price of grapes fluctuated so widely?

• I N T R O D U C T I O N •

I n Chapter 3 you discovered how in competitive markets the equilibrium price and quantity exchanged were determined. In this chapter we shall begin with a discussion of how competitive markets result in the efficient allocation of resources. We shall then discuss two ways that economists employ the theory of competitive markets, and finally we shall turn to an investigation of why equilibrium prices may change. •

ECONOMIC EFFICIENCY

One of the primary virtues of competitive markets — a virtue that makes these markets so appealing to economists — is that they allocate resources in an economically efficient manner. Economic efficiency was taken up in Chapter 1, where we learned that efficient production meant that the economy was operating on the production possibilities frontier. Economic efficiency was again considered at the end of Chapter 2, where the concept was extended to the process of exchange. We shall now extend the concept still further.

The concept of **economic efficiency** means that nothing valuable is wasted.

> *Economic efficiency is a condition that exists when the economy's resources are so organized that no reallocation of resources can make one person better off without harming another person.*

In other words, all possibilities for profitable exchanges have been met.

An economy is operating inefficiently if any potential opportunities for trade are not being utilized. Consider the hot lunch served in the Lincoln School District on February 11:

Hamburger on a Bun
Tater Tots
Tossed Salad
Dixie Cup
Milk

The teacher of the first-grade class at the primary school does not allow her students to trade lunch items. Suppose Megan loves Tater Tots but hates tossed salad while Josh likes tossed salad but will not eat Tater Tots. If the situation remains unchanged, some Tater Tots and some salad will be returned uneaten. An inefficient situation thus exists. If the teacher would allow these two students to exchange Tater Tots for salad, both of the lunches would be consumed, both youngsters would consider themselves better off, and nothing would be wasted.

Across the street at the high school, nothing stops food trades from taking place. Tater Tots and tossed salads are freely exchanged for whatever they will bring. As a result, less food is wasted. Despite the fact that larger portions are served at the high school, the district's dietitian attributes the lower wastage there to bigger appetites, but you now know there is also another reason — trades are taking place.

Consider another example. Suppose wheat is being sold in two different markets for two different prices. Wheat is sold in Denver for $15 a bushel and in Kansas City for $1 a bushel. Bread made from wheat will be very expensive in Denver and eaten only on special occasions. At the same time in Kansas City, in addition to being an everyday food for human consumption, wheat is used to feed livestock. If, ignoring the costs of transporting wheat, the two markets can be linked, such a situation would be inefficient because a profitable opportunity exists for traders to buy wheat in Kansas City and sell it in Denver. As traders take advantage of this opportunity, the price of wheat will rise in Kansas City and fall in Denver. These trades will continue until the price of wheat is the same in both markets. After trade, wheat will be used for the same purpose in both cities, probably to produce relatively inexpensive bread for human consumption.

Inefficiency is present as long as any profitable trading opportunities still exist. If a competitive market exists, competition between traders will eventually take advantage of all profitable opportunities for exchange. In efficient markets in equilibrium, all opportunities to gain from trade will have disappeared.

Competitive markets are efficient markets precisely because no further profitable opportunities exist when the market is in equilibrium. Consider the competitive market diagramed in Figure 4.1. In this market the forces of supply and demand have achieved in an equilibrium a price P and a quantity Q. The demand curve, D, slopes downward, reflecting the law of diminishing marginal value, and the supply curve, S, slopes upward, reflecting the law of increasing costs. The equilibrium price, P, limits the quantity that is demanded in the market. Purchasers will acquire the good up to the point where, for the last unit purchased, the marginal benefit, or marginal value (MV), to the buyer just equals the price (P) that must be paid, or until MV = P.

This condition holds for the last unit purchased. The marginal value for all previous units bought will be greater than the equilibrium price, which is why they were purchased. Thus when the equilibrium quantity has been purchased, no further profitable purchases can be made.

The equilibrium price also limits the quantity that will be supplied to the market. Sellers will agree to sell units only up to the point where the marginal, or opportunity, cost of the last unit supplied is equal to the price received, or until MC = P. The amount received (P) for the last unit sold is just equal to the marginal cost (MC) of that unit. If one more unit were sold, the marginal cost would exceed the price received, so the exchange of another unit would be unprofitable. When the equilibrium quantity of the good has been sold, no more profitable opportunities remain for suppliers to exploit. Only at the equilibrium price and quantity will the marginal value of the last unit sold to buyers equal the marginal cost of that unit to sellers. The point of equilibrium is the point where all profitable exchanges have been made. This point is represented by point E in Figure 4.1.

To understand why all profitable trades are undertaken at equilibrium, consider what would happen if fewer than the equilibrium quantity of trades were made. Suppose that the quantity Q_1 were traded in the market instead of the equilibrium quantity Q. In this case, the buyer's position would be point A, where the marginal value to the buyer would be P_2 instead of P, and the marginal cost to the seller would be indicated by point B. When only Q_1 trades are made, the marginal value is greater than the marginal cost of supplying the good and there still exist profitable opportunities for trade. Suppliers could offer more for sale at marginal costs that were below the price some buyers would pay.

If trades were limited to Q_1, society would suffer in lost trading opportunities an amount equal to the light salmon triangle in Figure 4.1.

FIGURE 4.1
Economic Efficiency in a Competitive Market

When a competitive market is in equilibrium at point E on the graph, traders have taken advantage of all profitable exchange opportunities and no one can be made better off without making someone else worse off. In equilibrium the marginal cost of producing the last unit traded (unit Q), as shown on the supply curve S, is just equal to the equilibrium price, P. The marginal value of the last unit purchased (unit Q) to the buyer, as shown on the demand curve D, is also equal to the equilibrium price, P. Thus in equilibrium the market price is equal to both the marginal cost and the marginal value of the last unit traded.

If only Q_1 units are traded, then the marginal value is greater than the marginal cost, and some profitable opportunities for trade are not being exploited. The shaded triangle AEB represents the value of these lost opportunities.

If more than the equilibrium quantity is exchanged, say Q_2 instead of Q, then the marginal cost exceeds the marginal value. Consumers value the last unit they purchase less than the opportunity cost of producing it. Too much of the good ($Q_2 - Q$) is being produced. The triangle CED measures the social loss involved in producing too much of the good.

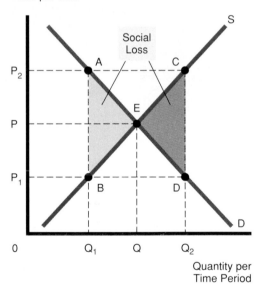

Such a situation was created when the first-graders in our lunchroom example lost trading opportunities because the teacher refused to allow Megan and Josh to exchange Tater Tots and salad. In our wheat sale example, a similar loss would occur if traders were barred from shipping wheat from Kansas City to Denver.

It is also possible for the process of exchange to go too far. Suppose that in Figure 4.1 the quantity Q_2 were traded instead of the equilibrium quantity Q. In this case the opportunity cost of the last unit exchanged is P_2 as indicated by point C, and the marginal value of the last unit exchanged is P_1 as shown at point D. Clearly, at quantity Q_2 the marginal value to buyers falls far short of its marginal cost to produce.

Since the supply curve represents the opportunity cost of the resources if they were applied to their best alternative use, the resources used to produce the last unit traded (Q_2), and indeed all units greater than Q, would have a higher value to society if they were employed *outside* the industry. It is therefore always inefficient to exchange in the market a quantity greater than the equilibrium quantity.

The shaded triangle CED represents the social loss from exchanging Q_2 units instead of Q units in the market. The social loss in this case results from the trade of units whose opportunity cost exceeds their marginal value. In the previous case the social loss represented by the light salmon triangle resulted from too few units being exchanged. The marginal value of the last unit traded exceeded its marginal (opportunity) cost because too few units were exchanged.

Only when the equilibrium quantity, Q, is exchanged at price P will there be no further possibility for profitable trades. Efficiency will exist only when the price of the last unit of the good exchanged equals both the marginal (or opportunity) cost of production and the marginal value to the buyer — that is, when $P = MC = MV$. If price is greater or less than marginal cost, there is inefficiency, and by reallocating resources some persons could be made better off with no persons being made worse off.

We now know how value is determined in competitive markets. In addition, we have seen that competitive markets have the advantage of operating efficiently and wasting no scarce resources. We shall now look at how economists use this model to examine economic conditions in the real world.

POSITIVE AND NORMATIVE ECONOMIC MODELS

An economic model, such as the theory of competitive markets, can be employed in either of two different ways: as a *positive model* or as a *normative model*. Briefly, a positive model describes conditions as they actually exist, and a normative model describes ideal conditions, or conditions as they should exist.

POSITIVE ECONOMIC MODELS

The competitive model that we have been examining can be used to analyze how markets actually work and to make predictions about what will happen if certain changes occur in the markets. The use of economic models to analyze *what is* is an example of **positive economics**.

Positive economics is the study of what is *in the economy. Positive economic statements can, in principle, be tested and proven false.*

Positive economic models can be employed to make statements explaining past events: "Because X occurred, Y happened." They can also be used to make statements about future events in the form of a forecast: "If X occurs, then Y will happen."

The law of demand is an example of a positive statement. The law of demand states that if the price of a good increases, the quantity demanded will decrease, assuming other factors have not changed. Positive economics is therefore limited to making statements about facts and about the relationship among facts, statements that analyze actual situations in the economy.

Positive economic statements can, in principle at least, be tested by comparing them with the facts. The relationship between the quantity demanded of a good and its price can be empirically investigated to see if the statement is consistent with the facts. In the previous chapter the analyses of comparable worth, rent controls, and the price of shelter are examples of positive economics. The end-of-chapter analyses of the markets for cocaine and wine grapes also employ positive economic statements to explain how these markets function.

NORMATIVE ECONOMIC MODELS

Economic models can be, and often are, used in another way. **Normative economics** looks for the ideal and tries to determine *what ought to be*. Any discussion of what ought to be *implies value judgments*.

> *Normative economics is the study of* what ought to be *and involves value judgments. Normative economic statements cannot be proven false.*

Normative economic statements, which often continue from where positive economics leaves off, take the following form: "If Policy X is followed, it will result in Y occurring. Y is a desirable outcome, so we *should* pursue Policy X." The first sentence is an example of positive economics. The second statement is a normative statement because it makes a value judgment when it implies that Y is desirable and should be pursued.

The Analysis of Preview 4.1 at the end of the chapter, which examines the way health care is delivered in the United States, will contain both positive and normative statements. Positive economics is used to trace the ways in which the health care industry operates and fails to meet the conditions for a competitive market, whereas normative economics is used to make policy prescriptions that, if adopted, would make the health care market operate more efficiently. The analysis as a whole, however, is a normative analysis because not everyone may agree that a more efficient health care market is a good thing. Some people may disagree about whether in this case it is worthwhile to make the changes necessary to obtain a more efficient market. Others may view health care as a right, believing that everyone should have as much as they desire.

Suppose that as the result of a positive analysis of the health care industry, it is determined that the industry is producing Q_2 in Figure 4.1. The marginal value of the last unit is at point D while the marginal cost is at point C and the recommendation is made to reduce the output of health care. Less health care would be produced, an outcome that runs counter to the belief that everyone should have as much as they want.

Before we can investigate the health care industry or the markets for cocaine and wine grapes, we need to understand why the prices of goods change. The prices of goods determined in markets are not carved in stone. Why do prices sometimes rise and at other times fall, and why do the quantities of goods exchanged in the market also vary?

FIGURE 4.2
Price Changes in a Competitive Market

The equilibrium price and quantity in a market will change if either demand or supply changes. In Part A an increase in demand is represented by a shift of the demand curve from D to D_1. The supply curve does not change. As a result, the equilibrium position shifts from E to E_1, the equilibrium price increases from P to P_1, and the equilibrium quantity exchanged increases from Q to Q_1. A decrease in demand is represented by a shift of the demand curve from D to D_2. The market price falls from P to P_2 and the quantity traded in the market declines from Q to Q_2.

Changes in supply as shown in Part B will also affect the equilibrium price and quantity. A decrease in supply, shown as a shift of the supply curve from S to S_1, causes the equilibrium position to shift from E to E_1. As a result, the equilibrium price increases from P to P_1, while the equilibrium quantity exchanged falls from Q to Q_1. An increase in supply, shown as a shift of the supply curve from S to S_2 has the opposite effect on price and quantity.

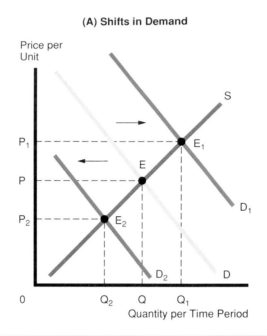

(A) Shifts in Demand

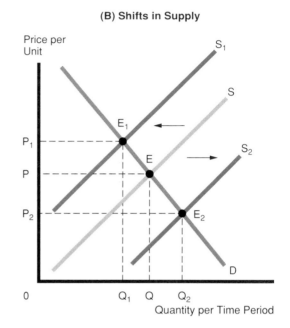

(B) Shifts in Supply

WHY PRICES CHANGE

We discovered in Chapter 3 how the forces of demand and supply acting within a competitive market determine the price of a good or service. We are now ready to discover why prices change.

Why, for example, has the relative price of health care increased so rapidly over the past decade compared with the prices of other goods? Why has the price of cocaine or wine grapes fluctuated over the same time period?

To answer the question of why relative prices change, we shall build on our knowledge of how price is determined in the market. We know that the value of a good is determined when the forces of supply and demand are in equilibrium. Only the equilibrium price equates the quantity supplied with the quantity demanded, allowing the market to clear.

The equilibrium price will change only if the forces that determine market equilibrium change. *The equilibrium price will change only if either the forces affecting the demand schedule or the forces affecting the supply schedule change.* Either the demand curve or the supply curve must actually shift if the equilibrium price of a good is to change. When either a demand or a supply curve shifts, the entire curve moves its position in the graph to the right or left. Figure 4.2 diagrams the effects of shifts in the demand and supply curves.

A change in demand will change both the equilibrium price and the quantity. Whether price and quantity increase or decrease depends on

TABLE 4.1
Effects of Shifts in Demand and Supply Curves

TYPE OF SHIFT	EFFECT ON EQUILIBRIUM PRICE	EFFECT ON EQUILIBRIUM QUANTITY TRADED
Increase in demand (Demand curve shifts right)	Price rises	Quantity rises
Decrease in demand (Demand curve shifts left)	Price falls	Quantity falls
Increase in supply (Supply curve shifts right)	Price falls	Quantity rises
Decrease in supply (Supply curve shifts left)	Price rises	Quantity falls

whether demand increases or decreases. Part A shows a market initially in equilibrium with demand curve D and supply curve S at a price of P and a quantity exchanged of Q. An increase in demand is shown by a shift of the demand curve to the right from D to D_1. The entire demand curve has moved to the right. The new demand curve, D_1, now intersects the supply curve at equilibrium point E_1 instead of E. The equilibrium price has risen to P_1 and the quantity traded has increased to Q_1. Returning to the initial supply (S) and demand (D) curves, we see that a decline in demand is represented by a leftward shift in the demand curve from D to D_2. The effect of a decline in demand is to shift the equilibrium point from E to E_2, causing the equilibrium price to fall from P to P_2 and the equilibrium quantity to decline from Q to Q_2.

A change in supply will also change the equilibrium price and quantity. Part B of Figure 4.2 shows the effects of shifts in the supply curve. A decrease in supply is shown as a leftward shift of the supply curve from S to S_1. The effect of such a shift is to move the equilibrium point from E to E_1, where the equilibrium price has risen from P to P_1 and the equilibrium quantity has fallen from Q to Q_1. An increase in supply is represented as a shift of the supply curve from S to S_2. This shift moves the equilibrium point from E to E_2, which causes a lower equilibrium price of P_2 but a higher quantity exchanged of Q_2.

Table 4.1 summarizes the effects of shifts in the demand and supply curves on the equilibrium price and quantity. With this information it is possible to predict the effects on prices and quantities of a given change in demand or supply. If we know that the demand for wheat is going to increase because the Soviets have had a poor harvest and must enter the world market to purchase additional supplies, we can predict that both the price and the quantity of wheat sold are going to increase. If we learn that the orange supply will decline because a frost has damaged orange trees in Florida, we can predict that the price of orange juice will increase while the quantity sold will decrease.

By applying the information in Figure 4.2 and Table 4.1, we can also determine the source of a known change in price and quantity. Economic theory can be used to explain past events. Here are a few examples. Both the price of cast-iron skillets and the quantity sold increased between 1985 and 1987. Consulting either Figure 4.2 or Table 4.1, we find that only an increase in demand would increase both price and quantity. Between 1985 and 1986 the price of Cabbage Patch dolls declined as did the number sold, so clearly the explanation is a decline in demand. The price of blank videotapes fell from $10 in 1984 to $4 in 1986, while sales doubled and redoubled. The cause of the change in price and quantity had to be an increase in supply. Finally, the price of pork increased 40 percent during 1986 as the quantity sold declined. The cause was a decline in supply.

As informative as Table 4.1 and Figure 4.2 are in identifying the causes of changes in prices and quantities in a competitive market, knowing what causes demand and supply curves to shift would significantly expand our ability to predict and explain economic events.

CHANGES IN DEMAND

Although price is the sole determinant of the *quantity demanded* chosen from a fixed demand curve, other things besides price affect the *demand* for a good, such as how much income a person has or what other goods cost. This semantic distinction between a *change in demand* and a *change in quantity demanded* allows an economist to isolate the effect, one factor at a time, of those things that affect the quantity of a good that buyers will purchase. It is important to remember that when we are discussing a change in demand or supply, we allow only one determinant to change at a time and hold all other possible determinants constant.

A change in the price of a good, according to the law of demand, will induce a **change in the quantity demanded** but will not change the location of the good's demand curve. In Part A of Figure 4.3 a decline in price from P_1 to P_2 will increase the quantity demanded from Q_1 to Q_2. When the price falls, the consumer's position on the demand curve *moves along* the curve from point A to point B, where the corresponding quantity demanded is greater.

> *A change in quantity demanded is a movement along a fixed demand curve caused by a change in the price of the good.*

This effect of a change in price assumes no change in those other things that affect demand. What are those other things, and what happens if they do change?

The *determinants of demand* are: the price of related goods, the size of the population, income, the tastes of consumers, and buyers' expectations about future prices.[2] When the determinants of demand are held constant and the price of the good is allowed to vary, a demand curve that obeys the law of demand will be traced out, as shown in Part A of Figure 4.3, where a decline in price from P_1 to P_2 leads to an increase in the quantity demanded from Q_1 to Q_2.

However, when any of the determinants of demand changes in value, there will be a **change in demand** and the location in space of the entire demand curve will change. Demand can either increase (the demand curve shifts out to the right) or decrease (the demand curve shifts back to the left). Which way the demand curve shifts depends on the determinant that changes and the way it changes.

---

[2] The quantity of a good that will be demanded (Q_d) can be conveniently written as a function of the price of the product (P_p) and the determinants of demand:

$$Q_d = Q\,(P_p,\ \overline{P_r},\ \overline{P},\ \overline{I_p},\ \overline{T},\ \overline{E})$$

where the quantity demanded (Q_d, the dependent variable) is a function of the independent variable, the price of the product (P_p), and the parameters of demand: the price of related goods (P_r), population (P), income (I_p), tastes (T), and expectations about future prices (E). The bar over each of these parameters in the above equation indicates that the parameter is being held constant while we determine the demand curve.

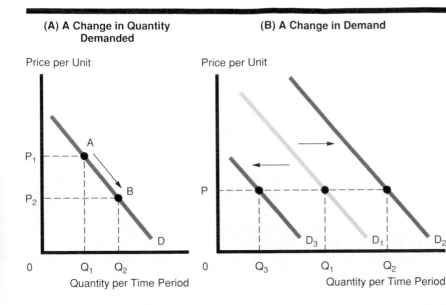

(A) A Change in Quantity Demanded

Price per Unit

(B) A Change in Demand

Price per Unit

Quantity per Time Period

Quantity per Time Period

FIGURE 4.3
A Change in Quantity Demanded versus a Change in Demand

In Part A a demand curve is drawn holding constant the determinants of demand: the prices of related goods, income, population, tastes, and expectations of future prices of the good. A change in the price of the good from the initial price P_1 to P_2, holding the determinants of demand constant, will cause a change in the *quantity demanded* from Q_1 to Q_2. This is represented in Part A as a movement along the demand curve, D, from point A to point B. The term *quantity demanded* refers to a movement along a given demand curve.

If any of the determinants of demand changes, the entire demand curve will shift, as shown in Part B. An increase in demand in response to a change in a determinant is shown as a shift from D_1 to D_2. When an increase in demand occurs, the quantity desired at the existing price, P, will increase from Q_1 to Q_2. A decline in demand is shown by a shift of the demand curve from D_1 to D_3. When demand declines, the amount desired at the existing price, P, will decline from Q_1 to Q_3.

A change in demand is a shift of the entire demand curve caused by a change in one of the determinants of demand.

If a demand determinant changes, the demand curve will shift. When a determinant changes, it affects the demand for a good by shifting the entire demand curve. The effect on a demand curve when a determinant changes is shown in Part B of Figure 4.3. If the demand curve shifts out to the right from D_1 to D_2, as shown by the arrow, the quantity demanded of the good will increase from Q_1 to Q_2 even though the price does not change. If demand decreases from D_1 to D_3, as shown by the arrow, purchases will decline from Q_1 to Q_3 without a change in price.

Which way will the demand curve shift when a determinant changes? The direction of the demand shift depends on which determinant changes and whether that determinant increases or decreases.

PRICE OF RELATED GOODS The demand for a good is affected by the prices of other goods a consumer purchases. The prices of two types of related goods — substitutes and complements — influence the location of the demand curve.

Substitutes Substitutes are goods that are rivals in consumption. A substitute is a good that consumers would consider acceptable in the place of the good whose demand we are investigating. When the price of a substitute increases, the demand for the good being studied will also increase. The reverse is also true: When the price of a substitute declines, the demand for the good under study will also decline.

Substitutes are two goods for which an increase in the price of one causes an increase in demand for the other, and vice versa.

One example of a set of substitutes can be found on the menu board of any fast-food restaurant: hamburgers, cheeseburgers, and chicken sandwiches are all substitutes for one another. If the price of hamburgers alone is reduced, the demand for cheeseburgers and chicken sandwiches will decrease. When a local McDonald's offered 29-cent hamburgers one Valentine's Day, it sold thousands of them, but it sold hardly any Big Macs or McDLTs or chicken nuggets. The basic hamburger was a substitute for the other items on the menu; when its price declined, so too did the demand for goods that are substitutes for a hamburger.

Substitutes are everywhere: Coke, Pepsi, and 7-Up substitute for each other as soft drinks; oil, gas, electricity, and wood substitute for each other as sources of energy to heat your home; beef, pork, lamb, and chicken substitute for each other as meat to eat; movies, theater, sports events, and television substitute for each other as entertainment; automobiles, bicycles, buses, railroads, and airplanes substitute for each other as means of transportation.

When the price of a substitute increases, the demand curve for the good under investigation will shift to the right, from D_1 to D_2, in Part B of Figure 4.3. If the price of the good does not change, more will be purchased after the price of a substitute increases: Q_2 instead of Q_1 in Figure 4.3. If the price of a substitute falls, the demand curve of the good being studied will shift back, from D_1 to D_3, and the quantity purchased at price P will decrease to Q_3.

Complements **Complements** are goods that are consumed jointly. Hamburgers and French fries are complements, as are hamburgers and catsup, automobiles and tires, automobiles and gasoline, dress shirts and neckties, socks and shoes, eggs and salt. When you consume one, most people also tend to consume the other. Automobiles and tires and gasoline are consumed together; when the price of one of these goods increases, the cost of jointly consuming the package also increases, and less of all three will be consumed. Thus an increase in the price of a good tends to reduce the demand for its complements.

> *Complements are two goods for which an increase in the price of one results in a decrease in demand for the other, and vice versa.*

If the price of a complement increases, the demand curve of the good being examined will shift to the left, from D_1 to D_3, in Figure 4.3, and the quantity purchased at price P will decrease from Q_1 to Q_3. The reverse will be true if the price of a complement falls.

SIZE OF THE POPULATION The demand for a good also depends on the size of the **population**, that is, on how many people are in the market. The more people there are buying the good, other things held constant, the greater will be the demand. As more people enter the market for a particular product, the demand for that product will increase, and the demand curve will shift to the right. If population declines, the demand for most products will decline, and demand curves will shift to the left.

The number of people in a market can change for several reasons. Population can grow or decline, persons can migrate, trade barriers between countries can be erected or dismantled, and the legal age for consuming the product can be raised or lowered. Recently the federal government passed a law reducing federal funding for highways to states that do not have a legal minimum drinking age of 21. In those states that subsequently raised the legal minimum drinking age, the demand for alcoholic beverages declined.

INCOME Changes in income can affect the demand for a good in two ways. As your income increases, you will tend to buy more of most goods. If, for example, your income were to double, you will surely spend more on housing, transportation, clothing, food, and entertainment than you do now. Such goods are known as **income-normal goods,** or, sometimes, simply as *normal goods.*

> *An income-normal good is a good whose demand increases when, other things held constant, per capita income increases.*

The demand curve will shift out for a normal good when per capita income increases and will shift back when per capita income decreases. Automobiles are income-normal goods; when income increases, so does the demand for automobiles (from D_1 to D_2 in Part B of Figure 4.3). The reverse is true when per capita income declines.

Although most goods are income-normal goods, the demand for some goods will actually decline when per capita income increases. When per capita income increases, people will cut back on their purchases of day-old bread and used clothing. When you graduate, you will probably buy fewer hamburgers, fewer bus rides, fewer retread tires, and no black-and-white television sets. Such goods are **income-inferior goods,** sometimes referred to simply as *inferior goods.*

> *An income-inferior good is a good for which demand decreases when per capita income increases.*

Bus rides are an income-inferior good. If per capita income increases, the demand for bus rides decreases and the demand curve for bus rides shifts back to the left. If per capita income decreases, the demand curve for income-inferior goods, such as bus rides and black-and-white television sets, shifts to the right.

TASTES OF CONSUMERS Tastes refer to the likes and dislikes of consumers. You may like asparagus and positively dislike or even hate brussels sprouts. When tastes change in favor of a particular good, the demand for that good will increase. When tastes change against a good, the demand for that good will decrease. Hit records and videotapes have a limited life span because people tire of them. The demands for all fashion goods, such as clothing and entertainment, are influenced by taste changes. A particular style of dress will be very much in fashion one year and very much out of fashion the next year.

> *Tastes are a reflection of consumers' preferences for and aversions to different goods and are based on consumer likes and dislikes.*

Take the example of men's undershirts. Prior to the 1930s almost every man wore a tank-top knit undershirt — until Clark Gable appeared in the movie "It Happened One Night." The movie won five Academy Awards and was viewed by millions of people. In that movie Gable arose one morning, and as he got dressed he put on his dress shirt over his bare chest — no undershirt. The men's undershirt industry immediately went into a depression as the men of America shed their undershirts. Almost overnight the tastes of men had turned against undershirts, and demand for undershirts declined drastically. When tastes change to favor a good,

FIGURE 4.4
Effect of a Change in Demand on
Equilibrium Price and Quantity

When demand changes, so will, other things held constant, the equilibrium price and quantity exchanged in a
market. As Part A shows, a decline in demand will shift
the demand curve to the left from D_1 to D_2. The existing
unchanged supply curve, S, will now intersect the new
demand curve, D_2, at a point (E_2) that is lower and to the
left of the previous equilibrium point (E_1). A new equilibrium price (P_2) will be established, which will be lower
than the previous price (P_1), while the quantity traded in
the market will decline from Q_1 to Q_2.

An increase in demand has the opposite effect. In
Part B the demand curve shifts from D_1 to D_2. The equilibrium point moves from E_1 to E_2, causing the equilibrium price to rise from P_1 to P_2 and the equilibrium quantity exchanged to increase from Q_1 to Q_2.

(A) A Decline in Demand

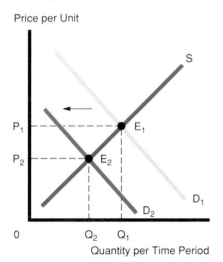

(B) An Increase in Demand

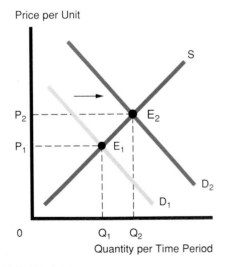

the demand for that good increases. When tastes go against a good, the
demand for that good decreases.

EXPECTATIONS ABOUT FUTURE PRICES Expectations about
future prices also affect the location of the demand curve. If buyers think
that the price of a good will be higher in the future or that the good will be
increasingly scarce in the future, they will attempt to buy more of that
good now. Today's demand for the good will increase. Conversely, if buyers expect that the price of a good will be lower in the future, they will
tend to buy less now in order to buy more in the future.

In 1973 the Nixon administration imposed price controls on most
goods, and exactly as economic theory would predict, shortages developed. One month there was a meat shortage, another month a paper clip
shortage, the next month there was a shortage somewhere else. During
one of his late-night monologues, Johnny Carson joked about the critical
shortage of toilet tissue. He was only kidding, but the possibility that it
could be true was only too believable to many viewers. There may be
substitutes for everything, but apparently there are limits. The thought of
finding substitutes for toilet paper from among other household paper
products was not at all appealing to millions of Americans. The morning
following Carson's monologue there was a run on toilet tissue throughout
the nation. Stores quickly ran out, and a real shortage developed. That
night Carson opened his show by announcing that he had been joking
about the lack of toilet tissue, and the critical shortage was over. Some
persons, however, had already acquired several months' supply.

Expectations of higher future prices or limited future availability can
shift the location of a demand curve. If future prices are expected to be
higher, the demand for goods today will increase and the demand curve
will shift out. If prices are expected to be lower in the future, the demand
for current goods will decrease and the demand curve will shift in.

**EFFECTS OF CHANGE IN DEMAND ON THE ALLOCATION OF
RESOURCES** So far you have discovered that when one of the determinants of demand changes, so will the entire demand curve. Changes in
demand will change the equilibrium price and quantity sold in a competitive market.

Decrease in Demand Demand will decline and the demand curve will
shift to the left if:

1. The price of a substitute falls.
2. The price of a complement increases.
3. Income declines for a normal good.
4. Income increases for an inferior good.
5. Population decreases.
6. Tastes change against the good.
7. The price of the good is expected to be lower in the future.

The effect of a decline in demand is shown in Part A of Figure 4.4.
The demand curve shifts to the left from D_1 to D_2. Assume that the market
contains an upward-sloping supply curve, in which case the shift in demand moves the equilibrium point from E_1 to E_2, lowering the equilibrium price from P_1 to P_2 and lowering the equilibrium quantity from Q_1
to Q_2. The effect of a decrease in demand is to decrease both price and
quantity. The market responds to the desires of buyers. When one of the
determinants of demand changes in a way that reduces demand, the result

is a decrease in the equilibrium price and a reduction in the quantity of the good exchanged. This is exactly what buyers had in mind.

Increase in Demand Demand will increase and the demand curve will shift to the right if:

1. The price of a substitute increases.
2. The price of a complement declines.
3. Income increases for a normal good.
4. Income declines for an inferior good.
5. Population increases.
6. Tastes change in favor of the good.
7. The price of the good is expected to be higher in the future.

The effect of an increase in demand is shown in Part B of Figure 4.4. The effect of shifting the demand curve out from D_1 to D_2 is to move the equilibrium point from E_1 to E_2, increasing the equilibrium price from P_1 to P_2 and increasing the equilibrium quantity from Q_1 to Q_2. The effect of an increase in demand is to increase both price and quantity. A competitive market thus responds to the desires of buyers. When buyers desire more of a good because one of the determinants of demand has changed, the result will be that more of the good will be provided, albeit at a higher price. Thus both the market price and the quantity exchanged will change if any of the determinants of demand change. Which way price and quantity change depends on which determinant changes and on the direction of that change.

The market price and quantity exchanged will also change if the conditions affecting the supply curve change.

CHANGES IN SUPPLY

The amount of a good that is offered in the market depends on the price of the good and also on a variety of other factors known as the determinants of supply. Economists distinguish between movements along a supply curve and shifts in the position of the supply curve by calling the former a **change in the quantity supplied** and the latter a **change in supply**.

> *A change in the quantity supplied is a movement along a fixed supply curve caused by a change in the price of the product.*

> *A change in supply is a shift of the entire supply curve caused by a change in one of the determinants of supply.*

The quantity supplied is a function of the price of the product, which is the independent variable, and a number of determinants of supply. The *determinants of supply* are: the prices of the factors of production, the prices of production-related goods, the state of technology, taxes and subsidies, the number of sellers, and expectations about future prices.[3]

---

[3] The quantity of a good to be supplied can, like the quantity of a good demanded, be written as a function of the price of the product and the determinants of supply:

$$Q_s = Q(P_p, \overline{P_f}, \overline{P_r}, \overline{T}, \overline{T_x}, \overline{N}, \overline{E})$$

where the quantity supplied (Q_s) is the dependent variable, P_p the price of the product, P_f the price of the factors of production, P_r the price of related goods in production, T the state of technology, T_x taxes, N the number of sellers, and E the suppliers' expectations about the future level of prices.

FIGURE 4.5

A Change in Quantity Supplied versus a
Change in Supply

When price changes, as in Part A, there will be a *change
in the quantity supplied*. If price increases from P_1 to P_2,
the quantity supplied will increase from Q_1 to Q_2, reflecting a movement along the supply curve from point A to
point B. The term *quantity supplied* describes a movement along a given supply curve.

The determinants that affect the position of the supply curve are: the prices of the factors of production, the
prices of production-related goods, the state of technology, the number of sellers, taxes and subsidies, and expectations about future prices. When one of the determinants changes, the entire supply curve will shift, as
shown in Part B. A shift of the entire supply curve is
described as a *change in supply*. If one of the determinants of supply changes in a way that causes a decrease
in supply, the entire supply curve will shift to the left from
S_1 to S_2 as indicated by the arrow in Part B. The quantity
supplied of the good at the existing price, P, will decline
from Q_1 to Q_2. If, instead, a determinant changes to
cause an increase in supply, the entire supply curve will
shift to the right from S_1 to S_3. The quantity supplied at
the existing price, P, will increase from Q_1 to Q_3.

(A) A Change in Quantity Supplied

(B) A Change in Supply

When these determinants of supply are held constant and the price of the
product is allowed to vary, changes in the *quantity supplied* will trace out
the supply curve. When a determinant changes, the entire supply curve
will shift in response.

This distinction can be seen in Figure 4.5. In Part A of Figure 4.5,
when the price of the product changes from P_1 to P_2, the quantity supplied, as measured along a fixed supply curve, will change, moving from
point A to point B. The quantity supplied will increase from Q_1 to Q_2.
Conversely, when the price of a product falls, the quantity supplied will
also fall, in accordance with the law of supply.

The entire supply curve will change its location when any of the determinants of supply changes. If supply increases, the supply curve will shift
to the right, as shown in Part B, from S_1 to S_3. After the shift, the amount
offered for sale at the existing price (P) will increase from Q_1 to Q_3. If
supply declines, the entire supply curve will shift to the left, from S_1 to S_2,
and the amount offered for sale at the existing price will decline from Q_1
to Q_2.

PRICES OF THE FACTORS OF PRODUCTION   In order to produce a good, firms must acquire resources in *factor markets*. When the
price of a factor of production changes, so will the firm's costs of production. The higher the costs of producing the good, the smaller is the amount
the firm is willing to offer in the product market at the existing price. Most
firms employ land, labor, capital, and entrepreneurship in the production process. When the price of one of these factors changes, so does the
cost of producing the good. When the price of labor increases, for example, the cost of producing clothing will increase and the amount of clothing that a producer is willing to supply at the existing price will decline. As
a result, the supply curve will shift to the left from S_1 to S_2 in Part B of
Figure 4.5.

If the price of a factor of production declines, the costs of producing
goods that employ that factor will also decline. When the costs of production decline, firms will be willing to offer more goods for sale at the existing price. The supply curve will shift to the right from S_1 to S_3.

If new resources are discovered — for example, a new oil field — the
price of that resource will decline, and the supply curves for goods that
use the resource will shift to the right. If the availability of a resource
decreases, its price will rise, and the supply of goods that use the resource
will decline. When the oil crisis developed in the last half of the 1970s, the
costs of production of goods, such as plastics, that used a large amount of
oil increased dramatically, and the supply of these goods declined substantially. The supply of a good will increase and the supply curve will
shift to the right if the price of a factor of production declines. Conversely, the supply of a good will decrease and the supply curve will shift
to the left if the price of a factor of production increases.

PRICES OF PRODUCTION-RELATED GOODS   The prices of production-related goods also affect the position of the supply curve. Production-related goods are goods that use the same or similar resources as the
good whose supply we are studying. Production-related goods can be separated into substitutes and complements.

A *substitute in production* is a good that competes for resources with
the good under study. Wheat and corn can be grown on the same land and
both require labor and fertilizer. If farmers are interested in supplying

wheat, the price of corn will be important. If the price of corn rises relative to the price of wheat, farmers will tend to shift some of their resources that are now devoted to wheat production to the production of more corn. As this substitution occurs, the supply of wheat will decline and the supply curve of wheat will shift to the left. Thus the supply of a good will decrease and the supply curve will shift to the left if the price of another good which is a substitute in production increases. Conversely, supply will increase and the supply curve will shift to the right if the price of a substitute in production declines.

A *complement in production* is a good that is produced jointly with another good. When you successfully drill for oil, you will generally also find natural gas. When you raise cattle for meat, you will inevitably also produce leather hides. When you raise sheep, besides meat you will produce wool. The price of complements in production is an important determinant of the supply of a good because it affects the profitability of the joint production effort. Thus the supply of a good will increase and the supply curve will shift to the right if the price of another good that is a complement in production increases. Conversely, supply will decline and the supply curve will shift to the left if the price of a complement in production decreases.

STATE OF TECHNOLOGY   The state of technology reflects existing knowledge about the relationship between a quantity of inputs and the amount of output that will result. The state of technology sets the upper limit on the amount of goods and services that can be produced from a given amount of resources. When technology improves, more goods and services can be produced from a given amount of resources. Technological progress lowers the costs of producing a good. A firm will therefore be willing to offer more goods at the same price if technological progress has been made. When transistors replaced vacuum tubes and when microchips later replaced transistors, the costs of producing computers declined. The supply of computers consequently increased, and the supply curve shifted to the right. When technological progress occurs, the cost of producing a good will decline, and the supply curve of the good will shift out to the right.

Technological progress occurs more or less regularly in most sectors of the economy. Because technological knowledge, once discovered, is easy to preserve and difficult to lose, examples of technological regression are fairly rare. One example can be found, however. The stained-glass windows of the medieval cathedrals of Europe cannot be identically duplicated today, because the exact process has been lost to the ages. We can produce approximate, but not identical, replacements.

TAXES AND SUBSIDIES   There are governmental actions that affect the supply of goods. The kind and the amount of taxes levied upon or subsidies granted to producers will affect the amount of goods supplied at a certain price. In particular, excise taxes, such as the sales tax, will affect the supply curve. An *excise tax* is a tax that is paid on each unit of a good or service sold. In the late 1980s a value-added tax — another form of excise tax — was proposed at the federal level. If a value-added tax were imposed on a good, it would increase the costs of supplying the good, and the supply curve would shift to the left.

Some activities have, from time to time, been granted subsidies by the federal government. A *subsidy* is a payment to produce. Until recently, the federal government paid operating subsidies to American owners of merchant marine vessels and offered grants to have these ships built in American shipyards. Today many communities and states compete with each other to attract industry by granting tax breaks and/or providing free land. Where a tax increases the cost of production and reduces supply, subsidies reduce the cost of production and increase supply. If taxes that affect the costs of production increase (or if subsidies decrease), supply will decrease and the supply curve will shift to the left. If taxes are reduced (or if subsidies increase), supply will increase and the supply curve will shift out to the right.

NUMBER OF SELLERS   When more producers enter a market to offer a good for sale, the supply of that good will increase. Firms enter a market in anticipation of earning profits. When they begin production, they increase the supply of the good. The more firms, other things held constant, the larger will be the supply of a good. In addition, the existence of a large number of firms meets one of the major requirements for a competitive industry. If there are fewer than the number of firms required for a competitive industry, supply will be restricted. Restrictions on the entry of potential firms into an industry generally mean a restricted supply. Whenever restrictions on the entry of firms into a market are lowered, we can expect an increase in the supply of goods in those markets. An increase in the number of firms in a market will increase the supply of the good and shift the supply curve to the right. Conversely, if the number of firms in a market decreases, the supply of the good will decrease and the supply curve will shift to the left.

EXPECTATIONS   The current supply of a good also depends on the expected level of the future prices of the good. If the price of the good is expected to be higher in the future, less of the good will be supplied today than if the future price were expected to remain the same. If the price of oil is expected to be higher in the future, persons or firms that own oil reserves will tend to supply less today in order to be able to supply more at the higher future price. Conversely, if future oil prices are expected to be lower, the owners of the resource will try to supply more today (to take advantage of today's higher price) and less in the future. Thus when expectations about the level of future prices change, so will the supply curve. If prices are expected to be higher in the future, the supply of the good today will decrease and the supply curve will shift to the left. If future prices are expected to be lower, the supply today will increase and the supply curve will shift to the right.

EFFECTS OF CHANGES IN SUPPLY ON THE ALLOCATION OF RESOURCES   What will happen to the equilibrium price and quantity when supply changes? The effect on both will depend on whether there is an increase or a decrease in supply.

Decrease in Supply   Supply will decrease and the supply curve will shift to the left if:

1.   There is an increase in the price of a good that is a substitute in production.

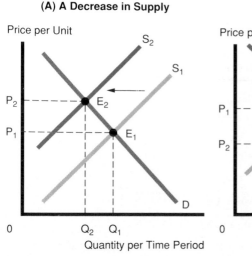

(A) A Decrease in Supply

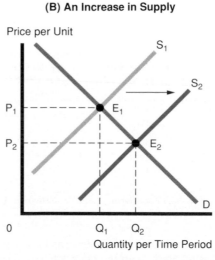

(B) An Increase in Supply

FIGURE 4.6

Effect of a Change in Supply on Equilibrium Price and Quantity

When supply increases or decreases, the equilibrium price and quantity, other things held constant, will change. In Part A a decrease in supply is represented by a shift of the supply curve from S_1 to S_2. The equilibrium point will shift from E_1 to E_2, and as a result the equilibrium price will increase from P_1 to P_2 and the equilibrium quantity will decrease from Q_1 to Q_2. In Part B an increase in supply causes the supply curve to shift to the right from S_1 to S_2. The equilibrium point moves from E_1 to E_2, causing the equilibrium price to decrease from P_1 to P_2 and the quantity to increase from Q_1 to Q_2.

2. There is a decrease in the price of a good that is a complement in production.
3. The price of a factor of production increases.
4. The state of technology deteriorates.
5. The number of suppliers declines.
6. Taxes are increased or subsidies are decreased.
7. Future prices are expected to be higher than current prices.

When one of the above determinant changes occurs, the supply curve shown in Part A of Figure 4.6 will shift to the left from S_1 to S_2, moving the equilibrium point from E_1 to E_2. The equilibrium price will increase from P_1 to P_2, and the equilibrium quantity will decline from Q_1 to Q_2. When any of the determinants changes in a way to reduce supply, the result in the market will be a decline in the amount of goods exchanged and a rise in the equilibrium price.

Increase in Supply Supply will increase and the supply curve will shift to the right if:

1. There is a decrease in the price of a good that is a substitute in production.
2. There is an increase in the price of a good that is a complement in production.
3. The price of a factor of production declines.
4. The state of technology improves.
5. The number of suppliers increases.
6. Taxes are reduced or subsidies are increased.
7. Prices in the future are expected to be lower than current prices.

When one of the above determinant changes occurs, the supply curve shown in Part B of Figure 4.6 will shift to the right from S_1 to S_2. The increase in supply will shift the equilibrium point from E_1 to E_2, the equilibrium price will fall from P_1 to P_2, and the equilibrium quantity will increase from Q_1 to Q_2. Thus when one of the determinants changes in a way to encourage more supply, the market responds by lowering the equilibrium price to encourage an increase in the quantity of the good traded.

APPLICATION

4.1

DEMAND AND SUPPLY CHANGES IN THE CONCORD GRAPE INDUSTRY

TABLE 4.2
Prices and Quantities of Concord Grapes, 1982–1986

YEAR (1)	PRICE OF GRAPES (DOLLARS PER TON) (2)	DIRECTION OF PRICE CHANGE (3)	QUANTITY OF GRAPES (THOUSANDS OF TONS) (4)	DIRECTION OF QUANTITY CHANGE (5)
1982	140	•	372	•
1983	110	−	466	+
1984	80	−	407	−
1985	105	+	316	−
1986	174	+	338	+

Source: *The Northwest Grape Grower*, February 1987.

The price and quantity statistics for the Concord grape industry from 1982 to 1986 reflect all four of the possible shifts in supply and demand (see Table 4.2). Concord grape juice is responsible for the familiar taste of frozen or bottled grape juice. The processor mixes to taste the unfermented juice of these grapes with the unfermented juice of red wine grapes. There are 16 grape juice processors in the U.S. grape juice industry plus processors in Canada who also buy American-grown Concord grapes, and there are hundreds of growers of the grape. In the recent past, both

processors and growers have entered and left the industry. Fresh Concord grapes are also sold to producers of jams and jellies as well as directly to consumers. Altogether there are numerous buyers and sellers in this market, all producing an identical product, and there is free entry and easy exit from this competitive industry.

Table 4.2 and Figure 4.7 can be used to analyze the shifts in supply and demand that have taken place over the five-year period from 1982 to 1986. Between 1982 and 1983 the price of Concord grapes fell (−) and the quantity sold increased (+). When this price/quantity pattern (−P, +Q) appears, it suggests that supply has increased relative to demand.

This can readily be seen in Figure 4.7. In this figure the initial equilibrium **E** is determined where the initial supply curve **S** intersects the initial demand curve **D**. The equilibrium price **P** and quantity exchanged **Q** represent the price and quantity, respectively, of Concord grapes in 1982. In order to see what must have happened during 1983, we trace out the new pattern of prices that emerged during that year. Table 4.2 provides the price (column 2) and quantity data (column 4) for this market, along with the direction of change from the previous year (columns 3 and 5). The price of grapes between 1982 and 1983 declined (−P), as shown by

arrow 1, and the quantity of grapes exchanged increased (+Q), as shown by arrow 2, bringing us to a new equilibrium point, E_1. What can account for the shift in the equilibrium point from **E** to E_1? Supply must have increased relative to demand as represented by a shift of the supply curve from **S** to +S. No other shift of the supply curve or the demand curve would result in a decline in price while simultaneously allowing the quantity exchanged to increase.

Now, what happened in this market during 1984? Table 4.2 reveals that between 1983 and 1984 both price and quantity declined. This pattern (−P, −Q) indicates a decline in demand. In order to see why, we do the same type of analysis that we did for the changes that occurred during the previous year. This time the initial supply **(S)** and demand **(D)** curves represent conditions in 1983, and the initial price **(P)** and quantity **(Q)** represent the price and quantity data for 1983. Between 1983 and 1984 price declined, a movement indicated by arrow 3, and so did quantity, a movement indicated by arrow 4. The new equilibrium point is represented by E_2. There is only one shift of supply and demand curves that during 1984 could cause the equilibrium point to move from **E** to E_2, and that is a decline in demand as represented by the shift in the demand curve from **D** to −D.

SIMULTANEOUS CHANGES IN SUPPLY AND DEMAND

Economic theory, as we have seen, yields precise predictions and explanations as to how the equilibrium price and quantity will change when either the supply curve alone or the demand curve alone shifts. In the real world, changes in the values of the determinants of supply and demand often occur simultaneously. When this happens, it is not possible to make

FIGURE 4.7
Using the Change in Price and Quantity to Identify the Shift in Demand or Supply

This figure summarizes the effects that shifts in demand and supply have on the equilibrium price and quantity in a market, allowing an inference to be drawn as to the cause of a change in price and quantity. The initial supply curve, **S**, and demand curve, **D**, establish an equilibrium point at **E**.

Assume it is known that the market price of the good decreases when the quantity traded increases. A decline in price is a movement described by arrow 1. Combine this with a simultaneous increase in quantity, a movement described by arrow 2, and you reach a new equilibrium point E_1. A change in equilibrium positions from **E** to E_1, other things held constant, can be caused only by an increase in supply. The supply curve must have shifted from **S** to +S. When price falls and quantity rises, other things being equal, an increase in supply must have occurred.

Suppose you observe instead that both price and quantity decline. Again starting at **E**, a decline in price is represented by arrow 3, which when combined with a decline in quantity indicated by arrow 4, suggests that the equilibrium point has moved from **E** to E_2. Such a movement, other things being equal, is consistent only with a decline in demand. The demand curve must have moved from **D** to −D.

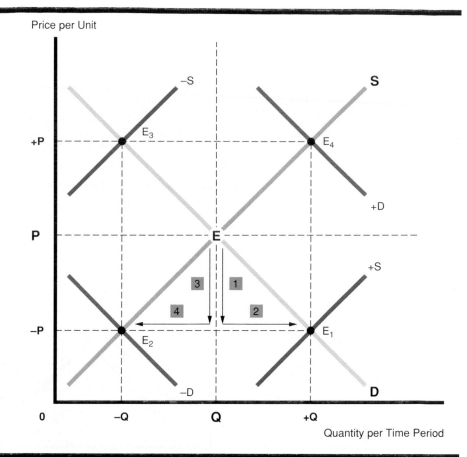

Between 1984 and 1985 price increased and quantity declined. There is again only one shift of the supply and demand curves that can explain this occurrence. Repeating the same procedure as before, we allow **E** to represent the equilibrium price and quantity in 1984 and we trace out the change in the pattern of price and quantity that occurred during 1985. We find that the equilibrium moves from **E** to E_3. Only one shift can account for this movement — a decline in supply from **S** to −S. Finally, between the years 1985 and 1986 price increased and quantity also increased. The equilibrium point thus moved from **E** to E_4 during 1986. Only an increase in demand can account for this change.

By analyzing changes in the pattern of prices and quantities in this way, we can determine what has happened in a market. The theory of shifts in demand and supply can be used to analyze the historical pattern of prices and quantities in a market. The shift that has been identified in this way, however, is only the dominant shift that has occurred. The increase in demand between 1985 and 1986 does not necessarily mean that supply remained unchanged, only that the demand shift dominated whatever shift in supply might also have occurred. The dominant shift in demand has alone left its imprint on the pattern of price and quantity.

Identifying the dominant demand or supply shifts that have taken place in a market is only the first step in explaining the changes in price and quantity that take place, but it is a necessary first step. A more complete explanation would entail a further investigation into which determinant shifts actually caused the changes.[4]

_____
[4] *The Northwest Grape Grower*, February 1987.

precise predictions about the direction of change of one of the two variables — price or quantity — without knowing the relative strengths of the two shifts. Figures 4.8 and 4.9 show the possible combinations of simultaneous shifts in supply and demand and the possible outcomes.

In Figure 4.8 Parts A, B, and C show what happens to the equilibrium price and quantity when both demand and supply increase together. An increase in demand by itself will tend to cause price to rise along with

FIGURE 4.8
Simultaneous Increases or Decreases in Demand and Supply

It is not unusual for both demand and supply curves to shift at the same time. When attempting to predict what will happen to the equilibrium price and quantity when demand and supply curves shift simultaneously, it is necessary also to know the relative strengths of the two shifts.

In Parts A, B, and C, both demand and supply increase together. The increase in demand or the increase in supply both cause the quantity exchanged to increase. But an increase in demand will tend to cause price to rise, whereas an increase in supply will cause price to fall. The actual direction of the change in price depends on the relative strengths of the two shifts.

Parts D, E, and F show the effects of a simultaneous decrease in demand and supply. Both a decrease in demand and a decrease in supply will tend to cause the quantity exchanged to decline. But a decrease in demand, other things being equal, will cause price to fall, whereas a decrease in supply will have the opposite effect and cause price to rise. To predict the direction of change in price when this happens, it is necessary to know the relative strengths of the two shifts.

Simultaneous Increases in Demand and Supply

(A)

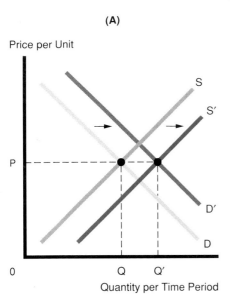

(B)

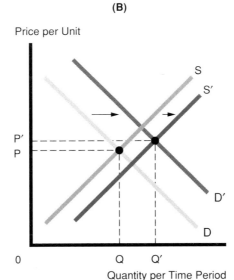

(C)

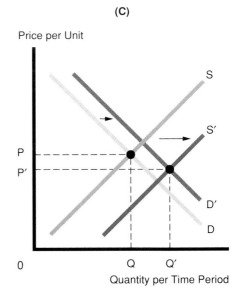

Simultaneous Decreases in Demand and Supply

(D)

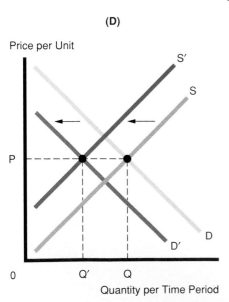

(E)

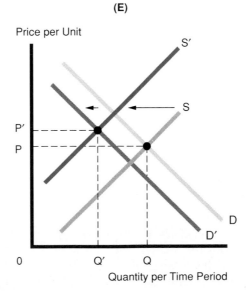

(F)

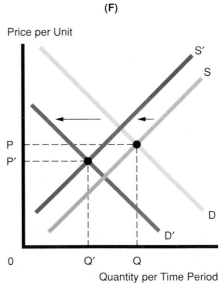

quantity, whereas an increase in supply by itself will tend to cause price to fall along with an increase in quantity exchanged. When supply and demand increase together, it is clear that the quantity exchanged will increase (Q′ is greater than Q in each case), but the effect on price depends on the relative strengths of the two shifts. If, as in Part A, the two shifts are of equal strength, then price will not change. The tendency for price to rise due to an increase in demand is just canceled out by the tendency for price to fall due to an increase in supply. If, as in Part B, the increase in demand exceeds the increase in supply, then the equilibrium price will increase from P to P′. If, however, the increase in supply is greater than the increase in demand, the effect will be to lower the equilibrium price as the relatively greater increase in supply overcomes the tendency for an increase in demand to raise price. The equilibrium price will fall from P to P′, as shown in Part C.

When *both* supply and demand decrease simultaneously, as shown in Parts D, E, and F, the effect on the equilibrium quantity exchanged is clear. A decline in both supply and demand will cause the quantity of the good exchanged to decrease. What happens to the equilibrium price depends on which — the decrease in supply or the decrease in demand — dominates. If the two shifts are of equal strength, as shown in Part D, then the equilibrium price will not change as the quantity traded decreases. Suppose, however, the decline in supply is greater than the decline in demand, as shown in Part E. In this case the equilibrium price will rise from P to P′ as the effect of a decline in supply to raise price overcomes the tendency of a decline in demand to lower price. Conversely, if the decline in demand is greater than the decline in supply, as shown in Part F, a fall in the equilibrium price from P to P′ will result, because the decline in demand dominates.

Suppose the shift in demand is in the opposite direction from the shift in supply, a possibility shown in Figure 4.9. When this happens, the effect on the equilibrium price remains predictable, but the effect on the equilibrium quantity does not. It is easy to see why this is so by examining Parts A, B, and C, which show the three possible outcomes when demand increases along with a simultaneous decline in supply. In each case the equilibrium price will rise from P to P′, because both an increase in demand and a decrease in supply imply a rise in price. But an increase in demand will by itself cause the equilibrium quantity to rise, whereas a decrease in supply will cause the equilibrium quantity to fall. What happens to the equilibrium quantity traded cannot be predicted unless the relative strengths of the two shifts are known.

Whether the quantity exchanged increases or decreases or remains the same depends on the relative strengths of the two shifts. If the increase in demand and the decrease in supply are of equal strengths, as in Part A, then the quantity traded will remain unchanged. If, however, the increase in demand is greater than the decline in supply, as in Part B, then the equilibrium quantity will increase. If that situation is reversed, with the decrease in supply dominating the increase in demand, then the equilibrium quantity will decline.

Suppose the reverse occurs and demand declines while supply increases. Again it is possible to predict the effect on the equilibrium price, which will decline because both a decline in demand and an increase in supply will tend to cause the equilibrium price to fall. But the impact on quantity is unpredictable unless the relative strengths of the two shifts are known. Once again, three possible outcomes exist, as shown in Parts D,

FIGURE 4.9
Simultaneous but Opposite Changes in Demand and Supply

When supply changes in one direction while demand changes in the other direction, it is possible to predict the direction of change in price. But in order to predict the change in quantity, it is necessary to know the relative strengths of the two shifts.

Parts A, B, and C show the possible outcomes from a simultaneous increase in demand and decrease in supply. An increase in demand will, other things being equal, cause the equilibrium price to increase, as also would a decrease in supply. But each would have the opposite effect on the quantity exchanged. So the ultimate outcome of such simultaneous shifts in terms of quantity exchanged depends on the relative strength of each change.

Parts D, E, and F show the possible effects of a simultaneous decline in demand and increase in supply. The two shifts will reinforce each other in causing price to fall, but they have opposite effects on quantity. An increase in supply will tend to cause quantity to increase, while a decline in demand will cause quantity to fall. The net effect on quantity depends on the relative strengths of the two shifts.

Simultaneous Increase in Demand and Decrease in Supply

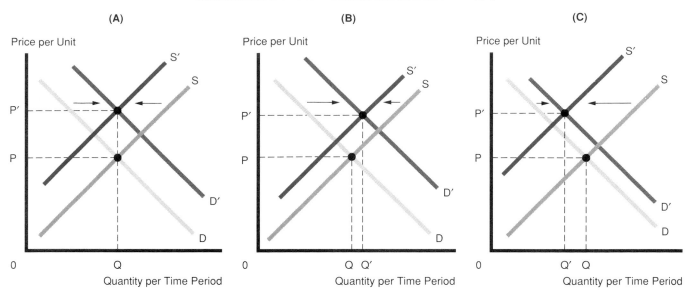

Simultaneous Decrease in Demand and Increase in Supply

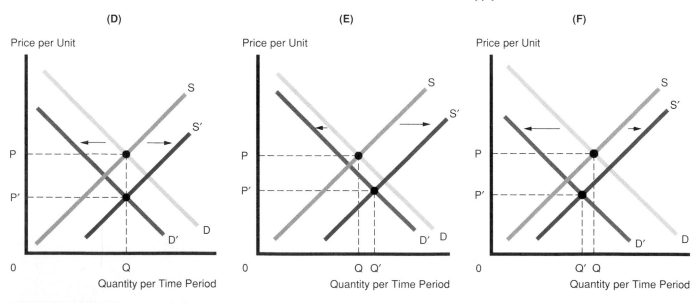

E, and F of Figure 4.9. If the two shifts are of equal strength, then the equilibrium price will fall and the equilibrium quantity will be unchanged as the two opposing forces cancel each other out, as shown in Part D. If, however, the increase in supply is greater than the decrease in demand, as in Part E, then the equilibrium quantity will increase as the equilibrium price declines. Conversely, if the decline in demand overwhelms the increase in supply, the equilibrium quantity will decline, as shown in Part F. What we have observed, then, is that when both the supply and demand curves shift simultaneously, the effect on either the equilibrium price or the equilibrium quantity becomes unpredictable unless the relative strengths of the two shifts are known.

It is possible, of course, to determine after the fact which shift was dominant by examining the pattern of prices and quantities. If we observe a historical pattern showing that both the price and the quantity of a good have increased over time, we can definitely say that the increase in demand has dominated the changes that have taken place in the market. In this way, price and quantity can be used to explain historical economic events.

SUMMARY

1. A competitive market will allocate resources efficiently by allowing all profitable trades to occur.
2. Positive economics is the study of the economy as it is, theoretically free of value judgments.
3. Normative economics is the study of what should be in the economy as judged from the individual economist's point of view.
4. Changes in the value of goods and services result from changes in the conditions of supply and demand.
5. A change in demand is a shift in the location of the demand curve. A change in the quantity demanded is a movement along a fixed demand curve in response to a change in price.
6. A change in demand results from a change in one of the determinants of demand: the price of related goods, the size of the population, income, the tastes of consumers, and buyers' expectations about future prices.
7. When demand for a good increases, both the price and quantity of the good will increase. When demand declines, both the price and quantity of the good will decrease.
8. A change in supply is a shift in the location of the supply curve. A change in the quantity supplied is a movement along a fixed supply curve caused by a change in price.
9. A change in supply results from a change in one of the determinants of supply: the prices of the factors of production, the prices of production-related goods, the state of technology, taxes and subsidies, the number of sellers, and expectations about future prices.
10. When supply increases, the supply curve will shift to the right and the price of the product will decline as the quantity traded increases. When supply decreases, the supply curve will shift to the left and the price will increase as the quantity traded decreases.
11. When both the supply and demand curves shift simultaneously, the effect on either the equilibrium price or the equilibrium quantity becomes unpredictable unless the relative strengths of the two shifts are known.

ALL IS NOT WELL IN THE HEALTH CARE INDUSTRY

Preview 4.1 pointed out that rapidly rising health care costs have become a serious national problem. One way to approach the problem of health care costs is to compare how health care is actually produced with how it would ideally be produced in a competitive market. A competitive market is used as an ideal market because in theory such a market allocates resources efficiently. This comparison will allow us to predict how deviations from a competitive market will affect the equilibrium price and quantity in the market.

As outlined in Chapter 3, a competitive market:

1. Contains many knowledgeable buyers and many sellers.
2. Trades a homogeneous product.
3. Allows easy entry and exit from the market.

When these conditions are met, the economic incentives that govern the behavior of buyers and sellers will establish an equilibrium price and quantity that efficiently allocates economic resources.

In practice, however, the fact that few of these conditions are actually met in the health care industry may account for its reputed poor performance. To identify problem areas in the industry, we shall compare the ideal competitive model with conditions that exist in the health care industry. This application combines both positive and normative economic analysis. We are assuming that if the health care industry were organized as a competitive industry, it would operate efficiently. Positive statements, which are used to explain how the health care industry actually operates, are blended with normative statements, which are used to compare the actual operation of the current health care industry with its projected operation if the industry could be organized as a competitive market.

How close does the health care delivery system in operation in the United States come to a competitive industry? Although there are certainly many buyers of medical services, few of the demanders are knowledgeable about the nature of the care they receive. In fact, the reason most people go to a doctor in the first place is their relative ignorance of medical science and consequent lack of knowledge about how to treat themselves. The physician–patient relationship is typical of the industry; the patient employs the physician to diagnose and treat his or her illness. Often the patient does not directly pay the physician for services rendered. Instead, some third party — an insurance company or the government — pays the bill. In the health care industry, typically, the doctor prescribes the treatment, the patient takes the medicine, and a third party pays the bill.

There appear to be numerous providers of medical care, but appearances in this case are deceiving. Because the typical patient lacks the ability to judge the quality of medical care, every state in the union has strict requirements limiting the practice of medicine to persons who meet certain qualifications. Even so, medical services are not homogeneous; there are differences among physicians, types of equipment, and facilities. The imposition of professional standards is designed to ensure a minimum level of competence among health care practitioners. Critics have charged that the American Medical Association — the professional organization of physicians — has used these professional standards to actually restrict entry into medical practice. The standards, it is argued, are set too high and/or bear little relation to the practice of medicine. As a result, there are fewer doctors practicing medicine today than would be the case if entry into the industry were not restricted.

We see, then, that our current health care delivery system deviates rather widely from the operation of a competitive industry, because many buyers are not knowledgeable, because third parties pay the bill, because there are fewer providers of medical care than necessary for perfect competition, because health care is a nonhomogeneous product, and because entry into the industry is restricted.

To some degree, the differences between the health care industry and a competitive industry can be attributed to the unique nature of medical care and, to some degree, to the way we have chosen to provide health care.

Let us examine separately the effects of these differences on the supply and demand for medical care.

THE SUPPLY OF MEDICAL CARE

Unlike most industries, the health care industry is, with the government's approval, largely self-regulated. Prior to 1850 the industry was virtually unregulated, with unrestricted entry for physicians and hospitals. In 1847 the American Medical Association (AMA) was formed to ensure that the industry did not produce low-quality health care. Over the years, the AMA has acquired the legal authority to accredit medical schools and to oversee the licensing of physicians and health care facilities.

Critics charge that this authority has permitted the industry to go beyond the concern for minimum quality and to control prices by limiting entry into the health care field. They point to the unusually high financial rewards enjoyed by doctors. Today physicians are the highest paid of all the professions, earning on average $110,000 a year. Such high incomes should attract the best and brightest students, and they do. Each year twice as many students apply to medical school as can be accepted.

The main reason that so many students are turned away is the lack of space for them in medical schools approved by the AMA. During the first century of the AMA's control over school accreditation, the number of medical schools declined by two-thirds. The number of doctors per 1,000 population also declined. Thus at a time when the demand for medical care was increasing because of rising per capita incomes, the number of physicians per capita was actually falling. The supply curve, in economic terms, was shifting to the left at a time when the demand curve was shifting to the right. The result, as you can now predict, was a significant increase in the income of doctors relative to the other professions. Recently the per capita supply of doctors has been increasing, due to a federal government subsidy to medical schools that encourages them to train more doctors. The relative growth of physicians' incomes has leveled off as supply has increased, but physicians still head the list of best-paid professionals.

The AMA has resisted any attempt to increase competition within the industry that would lower the cost of medical care. Until recently, doctors were prohibited from advertising by the AMA. Currently, advertising is limited in practice to doctors opening up new offices. The AMA has generally resisted innovations in health care delivery that promoted competition. The Kaiser Foundation, for example, in the 1940s set up the first health maintenance organization (HMO), which offered prepaid, rather than fee-for-service, health care. A local AMA chapter found the Kaiser

FIGURE 4.10
Effect of Reducing the Number of Physicians

The supply curve S_c represents the supply of physicians that would exist if all qualified students were admitted to medical school. The interaction of this supply curve with the demand curve for physicians, D, would result in an equilibrium position Y, establishing a price of medical care P_c and a quantity exchanged Q_c. The supply of physicians is restricted, however. Not all qualified students can find a space in a medical school. As a result, the actual supply curve, S_a, lies to the left of supply curve S_c, and the actual equilibrium occurs at point X rather than at point Y. The actual equilibrium price is P_a, which is higher than P_c, and the quantity exchanged is less, Q_a rather than Q_c. Not all of the possible exchanges can be made in the existing market, and a social loss equal to the triangle XYZ results from the restricted supply.

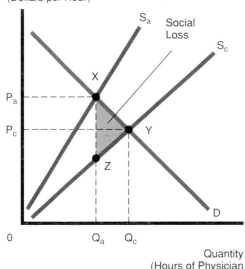

Price of Physicians' Services
(Dollars per Hour)

Quantity
(Hours of Physician
Care per Time Period)

Plan's medical director guilty of unethical medical practices and barred Kaiser physicians from membership in the AMA. It took a U.S. Supreme Court ruling to overturn the authority of organized medicine in this area and to permit HMOs to exist.

The evidence suggests that entry into the medical profession is very difficult and that there are fewer doctors today than there would be if all qualified students had been admitted to medical schools. The effect of reducing the number of physicians on the price of medical care is shown in Figure 4.10. The supply curve S_c represents the supply of doctors that would exist if all qualified students could attend medical school. The equilibrium price for medical care, given supply S_c, is P_c and the equilibrium quantity is Q_c.

The actual restricted supply of physicians is represented by the supply curve S_a, which lies to the left of the supply curve S_c. The actual equilibrium price is P_a, which is greater than P_c, and the actual equilibrium quantity is Q_a, which is less than Q_c. The effect of restricting the supply of physicians is an increase in the price of medical care and a reduction in the amount of medical care provided.

Restricting the supply of doctors creates a social loss, which is absent in a competitive market. The relatively high price of physicians' services lowers the quantity demanded of those services from Q_c to Q_a. At Q_a the marginal benefits of physicians' services exceed their marginal costs. There are possible gains from trade (the salmon triangle in Figure 4.10) that are not being achieved. The shaded triangle XYZ represents the social loss that results from producing too few physicians' services.

THE DEMAND FOR MEDICAL CARE

Two factors have increased the demand for medical care in the United States over time. The first is that real per capita income has increased, roughly doubling every generation. Medical care is an income-normal good, and the effect of an increase in per capita income on a normal good is to increase the demand for that good. An increase in demand for medical care, represented in Figure 4.11 as a shift to the right of the demand curve, results in an increase in the equilibrium price of health care from P_c to P_a and in an increase in the quantity of health care provided from Q_c to Q_a.

The second factor that has increased demand for medical care is the spread of private health care insurance plans and government Medicare and Medicaid programs. These programs are known as prepaid, or third-party payment, systems. The employee or the employer pays a fixed premium to an insurance company and the insurance company in turn agrees to pay the employee's health care costs. The employee decides when to visit a doctor, but the bill is paid by a third party, generally the insurance company. These programs began during World War II when employers began to offer their employees prepaid health care insurance, supplied by nonprofit insurers like Blue Cross and Blue Shield, instead of wage increases.

These fringe benefits had the advantage to the worker that they were not taxed as income. Thus the employer could offer workers an increase in income by paying for health insurance that was tax-deductible to the firm as a business expense and tax-free to the worker. Such plans quickly spread throughout the private sector.

The use of third-party payers has two effects on the cost of medical care. The first effect is to reinforce the effect of the increase in income by expanding the number of persons who demand medical care. When the number of persons in the market increases, the demand for the good will increase. In Figure 4.11 the demand curve for medical care shifts out from D_1 to D_2, increasing the equilibrium quantity from Q_c to Q_a and raising the price from P_c to P_a.

As health care insurance became increasingly linked to employment, the cost of medical care has increased, and the poor and the elderly have had a difficult time acquiring low-cost health care. To remedy this perceived inequity, the federal government in 1965 enacted Medicare, which obligated the government to pay for health care for the elderly. Recently some states have also begun to offer health care insurance for the nonelderly poor. In 1950, 80 percent of all medical expenditures were paid directly by the patient. Today less than 35 percent are paid by the patient, and more than 65 percent are paid by third parties.

The second effect of third-party payment plans is to lower the perceived marginal cost of medical care to the insured person. When a person without health insurance faces a decision about whether or not to go to a doctor, he or she must consider the opportunity cost of the visit. Is paying the doctor bill worth the sacrifice of a new pair of shoes for the child or a night out at the movies with the spouse plus the implicit cost of visiting the doctor's office? This opportunity cost is significantly less when the person is insured and the insurance covers all medical costs, being limited to the opportunity cost of the time spent in seeing a doctor.

For a person with full-coverage health insurance, the opportunity cost of visiting a doctor is fairly low, but the actual cost of providing the health care is not. If you decide not to go, the physician can see another patient instead. Full-coverage health insurance provides an incentive to overuse medical facilities by encouraging those with insurance to seek medical care that they would reject if they had to pay directly the full opportunity cost of a visit.

Figure 4.12 diagrams the effect of the incentives created by third-party payment plans. If the individual had to consider the opportunity cost of a visit to the doctor, he or she would purchase medical care up to the quantity Q_c, at which the marginal cost equals the marginal benefit, as shown by the demand curve, and would pay the equilibrium price P_c.

If, however, the individual's opportunity cost of seeing a doctor is lower than P_c, as it is for a fully insured patient, the quantity demanded will increase to Q_a, where the marginal benefit is equal to the individual's opportunity cost of P_i. The marginal cost of supplying Q_a medical services is P_a, which is substantially greater than the individual's opportunity cost, and also greater than P_c, the equilibrium price for a competitive industry. Thus third-party payment plans create an incentive to overutilize the health care system by the amount $Q_a - Q_c$.

To the extent that patients consume more than Q_c units of health care, the marginal cost of producing medical care will exceed the marginal benefit to the last users. When the marginal cost of supplying a good exceeds the marginal benefit, the resources used to produce the good could have, from society's point of view, been better used elsewhere. The total social loss of producing too much health care is shown by the salmon triangle.

In summary, the high costs that exist in the health care industry can be attributed in part to a tangle of inappropriate economic structures and incentives combined with the increase in demand for health care. The above analysis suggests that some of the increase in cost is economic waste.

FIGURE 4.11
Effect of Increases in Income on the Demand for Medical Care

The level of income is a determinant of the demand for medical care. When per capita income increases, the demand curve shifts from D_1 to D_2, and the equilibrium point moves from E_1 to E_2. The increase in demand results in an increase in the quantity supplied. As a result, both the equilibrium price and the quantity of health care increase. The price of health care increases from P_c to P_a, and the quantity consumed increases from Q_c to Q_a.

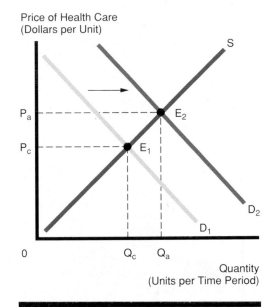

F I G U R E 4.12
Effect of Prepaid Health Care on the
Quantity Demanded of Health Care

The supply and demand for health care are represented
by supply curve S and demand curve D. The equilibrium
price is P_c, and the quantity exchanged is Q_c. An uninsured individual who decides to seek health care does so
only if the expected marginal value is equal to the opportunity cost measured by the market price P_c. When an
individual purchases a prepaid health insurance policy,
he or she no longer has to pay the full marginal cost of
each visit, since the insurance company pays the bill.
Instead of an opportunity cost of P_c, the individual's opportunity cost falls to P_i, which measures only the time
cost of seeking medical care. The quantity demanded
thus increases, from Q_c to Q_a, to the point where the
marginal value of the last unit consumed (Q_a) equals the
now lower opportunity cost P_i. But the marginal cost of
providing Q_a amount of health care is measured at point
X and is equal to P_a. Thus the effect of prepaid health
insurance is to cause the marginal value of the last unit
consumed to be less than the marginal cost. A social loss
equal to the triangle XYZ is the result.

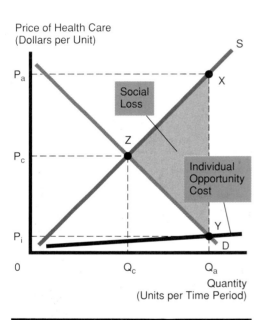

Price of Health Care
(Dollars per Unit)

POLICY PRESCRIPTIONS

The nation's health care system is sick, but it is not dead. Much can and is
being done to raise the level of economic efficiency with which the medical
industry operates. It is clear from the diagnosis that the problems that
afflict the medical profession originate from a variety of causes on both
the supply and demand sides. Solutions must therefore address both
sides.

SUPPLY-SIDE POLICY RECOMMENDATIONS   First, the supply
of physicians could be increased still more. Currently, twice as many
persons apply for medical school as places exist for them, and most are
capable of becoming physicians. A federal subsidy initiated in 1963 has
helped to increase the supply of doctors. This increased domestic supply
of doctors has been augmented by the immigration of foreign-trained doctors, some of them Americans who went abroad for training. A continued
increase in the supply of doctors should lower the price of physicians'
services.

It has been suggested that doctors could respond to a decline in price
by abusing their physician–patient relationship and ordering the additional tests, procedures, and surgery necessary to maintain their standard of living. Simply increasing the number of doctors may not be
enough. Measures must be taken to increase competition within the profession.

Encouraging physicians to advertise might help. When the ban
against the advertising of contact lenses was discontinued in 1975, the
price of contact lenses fell by 30 percent. Physician advertising, although
legal, is still discouraged by local medical associations. Generally, only
physicians who are starting new practices advertise.

Perhaps the best way to improve the doctor's incentive to perform
efficiently is provided by health maintenance organizations (HMOs). For
a fixed fee, HMOs, such as the Kaiser Plan, provide complete health care
for the enrolled individual. HMOs supply doctors with incentives to practice preventive medicine and to perform efficiently only those medical
procedures that are actually required. Studies have shown that an HMO
can deliver health care with savings of up to 40 percent compared with the
traditional fee-for-service method.

As an alternative, some large health insurance companies and corporations are using their bargaining power to negotiate lower prices with
preferred-provider organizations (PPOs) — doctors and hospitals that
agree to discount their services. The employer then provides a financial
incentive for employees to use these providers. Costs savings of 10 to 30
percent can result from using PPOs.

The continued growth of health maintenance organizations (HMOs)
and preferred-provider organizations (PPOs) will increase competition
for the traditional fee-for-service physicians. The lack of competition in
the past may have been responsible in large part for the rapid rise in
health care costs.

DEMAND-SIDE POLICY RECOMMENDATIONS   On the demand
side, medical insurance that guarantees full reimbursement for all medical expenses creates an incentive for the quantity of health care demanded to exceed the optimal amount. The obvious solution is to increase
the copayment portion of medical costs. *Copayment* refers to that portion
of health care costs that are actually borne by the patient. For example,
the patient pays the first several hundred dollars of medical expenses per

year, and the insurance company pays the rest. In this way the first visits to the doctor each year still impose a significant opportunity cost on the patient. Yet if the patient has a serious accident or illness, most of the medical bills will be covered by insurance.

Unfortunately, the public has strongly resisted this idea. When an increase in the copayments of Medicare was suggested as a cost-reducing measure, the proposal was met with a fire storm of opposition. Similarly, private health insurers have found it difficult to market high-copayment plans. One of the reasons for this opposition is that people view high copayments as a reduction in their medical benefits.

However, if more employers offered their employees a choice of medical plans and allowed the employees to pocket the difference in premiums if they select a lower-cost, high-copayment plan, then perhaps high-copayment plans would become more popular. Also, the tax deductibility of employer-provided health insurance could be repealed, thereby reducing the incentives for employees to prefer employer-provided health insurance over higher wages.

Some of these policy recommendations are already being tried. Others are still being considered. One thing is clear: The high and rising cost of health care can be reduced if the health care delivery system in the United States were changed to behave more like a competitive industry.

SUPPLY MEETS DEMAND IN THE COCAINE BUSINESS

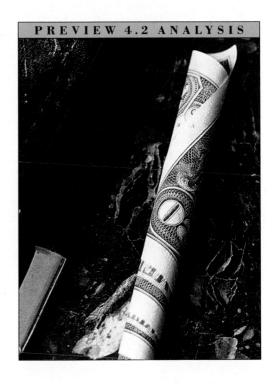

Cocaine is an illegal drug; to possess it or trade it without license is against the law. Nevertheless, in the last decade or so the market for cocaine has evolved from a cottage enterprise to a giant industry, annually doing more than an estimated $15 billion worth of business in the United States alone. Economic analysis can be used to account for the growth of this illegal industry.

Figure 4.13 reproduces the data on prices and quantities of cocaine traded in the United States for the years 1976 to 1986 found in Table 4.3. Figure 4.14 provides a vehicle with which to analyze the price and quantity patterns exhibited during those years. Between 1976 and 1978, both the price of the drug and the quantity sold increased. Starting at equilibrium, E, in Figure 4.14, an increase in both price and quantity reflects an increase in demand. During the years 1979 and 1980, the price of cocaine fell while the quantity sold increased. This suggests, again referring to Figure 4.14, an increase in supply during those years. From 1981 to 1982, the price of cocaine increased while the quantity sold fell, indicating a decline in supply. During 1983 demand increased, since both price and quantity increased. Finally, from 1984 to 1986, the price fell while the quantity expanded, reflecting an increase in supply.

Identifying the dominant shifts in the supply and demand for cocaine over time is the first step in our investigation of the causes of the industry's growth. The next step is to investigate the determinants of demand or supply that caused a particular shift. Generally, when economists investigate a market, they undertake a quantitative analysis. In our present analysis, we shall confine our investigation to a qualitative discussion of those determinants that changed in a manner consistent with the identified change in demand or supply.

FIGURE 4.13
Price and Quantity in the Cocaine
Market

The price and quantity data for the cocaine market
in the United States for the years 1976 through
1986 are presented in this chart. These data can be
divided into subperiods according to consistent
price and quantity patterns, thereby allowing the
relevant shifts in supply and demand that have occurred in this market to be identified.

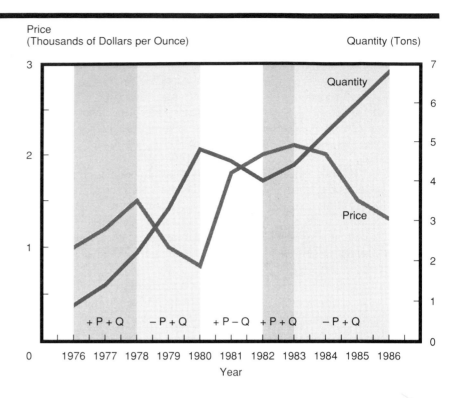

TABLE 4.3
Prices and Quantities of Cocaine: 1976–1986

YEAR	PRICE OF COCAINE (THOUSANDS OF DOLLARS PER TON)	DIRECTION OF PRICE CHANGE	QUANTITY OF COCAINE (TONS)	DIRECTION OF QUANTITY CHANGE	IMPLIED SHIFT IN SUPPLY OR DEMAND
1976	1.0	•	0.9	•	—
1977	1.2	+	1.4	+	Increase in demand
1978	1.5	+	2.2	+	Increase in demand
1979	1.0	−	3.3	+	Increase in supply
1980	0.8	−	4.8	+	Increase in supply
1981	1.8	+	4.5	−	Decrease in supply
1982	2.0	+	4.0	−	Decrease in supply
1983	2.1	+	4.4	+	Increase in demand
1984	2.0	−	5.2	+	Increase in supply
1985	1.5	−	6.0	+	Increase in supply
1986	1.3	−	6.8	+	Increase in supply

Source: *The Wall Street Journal*, June 30, 1986, 1.

1976–1978:
AN INCREASE IN DEMAND

Demand must have increased during the 1976–1978 period, because both
the price of the drug and the quantity traded increased. Prior to the
mid-1970s, cocaine was not a major drug in the United States. Marijuana
was the choice of American drug users. In the early 1970s, the U.S. gov-

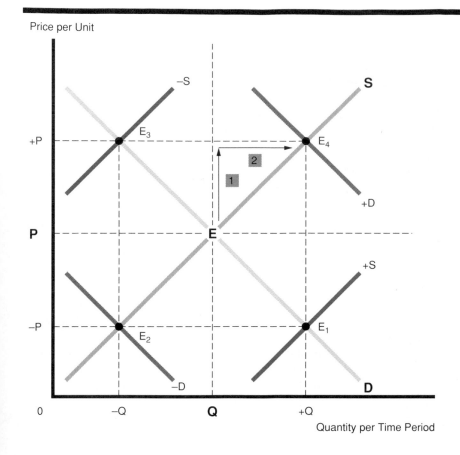

Price per Unit

Quantity per Time Period

FIGURE 4.14
Using the Change in Price and Quantity to
Identify the Shift in Demand and Supply

This graph allows analysis of the data presented in Figure
4.13 in order to determine which curve — the supply or
demand curve — has shifted. For example, between
1976 and 1978, both the price of cocaine and the quantity traded increased, which is consistent with an increase in demand. This can be seen by studying the
graph. Initially, the supply and demand curves for cocaine are represented by **S** and **D**, respectively. The initial
equilibrium point is **E**. Between 1976 and 1978, both
price and quantity increased. An increase in price is indicated by arrow 1. This change is coupled with the increase in quantity, indicated by arrow 2, bringing the new
equilibrium point to E_4. Only an increase in demand, a
shift of the demand curve from **D** to +D, is consistent
with this new price and quantity pattern. In this way each
of the subperiods in Figure 4.13 can be analyzed to identify the dominant shift that has occurred in the cocaine
market.

ernment began to take steps to reduce the smuggling of marijuana. Mexico
was the source of 95 percent of the marijuana consumed in the United
States. In 1975 the Mexican government, at the behest of the American
government, began to eradicate marijuana crops with the herbicide para-
quat. Colombia was another source of marijuana. Colombian marijuana
was mainly transported by sea because of its bulk. The U.S. Coast Guard
and drug enforcement agencies became increasingly effective in stopping
the shipments from Colombia. Where previously nine out of ten boats had
been successful in getting through to the United States, by late 1975 it was
estimated that only half that number were making it. The price of marijuana rose sharply, reflecting the decline in supply that was taking place.
Marijuana is bulky relative to its value when compared to cocaine. A
suitcase of cocaine is equal in value to a boatload of marijuana. Thus it is
much easier for drug enforcement officials to curtail the marijuana trade
than it is to reduce the cocaine traffic.

   Marijuana and cocaine are substitutes for each other. When the price
of one good increases — in this case, marijuana — the demand for its
substitute good increases. Thus the demand for cocaine increased as the
price of marijuana increased. Per capita income, another demand determinant, was also increasing during these years, as was the number of
persons in the age groups that characterized the heavy drug users. These
two determinant changes were probably of small consequence, however,
compared to the change in taste that was occurring as drug users began to
experiment with cocaine.

   The rise in the price of marijuana motivated drug users to try cocaine, and many liked it. Many drug users mistakenly believed at the time

that cocaine was a safe and nonaddicting drug. The fact that it was relatively expensive, however, somewhat limited its market. Cocaine first became fashionable among young and wealthy entertainers and sports stars. Then usage spread among the young in general. The number of high school seniors who had tried the drug increased every year during the last half of the 1970s. Cocaine became the chosen drug of drug users, and Miami became the center of the cocaine trade. The increase in demand for cocaine increased both the price and quantity sold in 1977 and 1978.

1979–1980:
AN INCREASE IN SUPPLY

In 1979 and 1980, the price of cocaine fell while the quantity sold roughly doubled. Clearly, a significant increase in supply occurred during these years. When price is falling and quantity increasing, the supply curve is shifting to the right relative to the demand curve.

The rapid rise in the price of cocaine that had occurred between 1976 and 1978 attracted more drug producers and dealers to the trade. As drug dealers switched from marijuana to cocaine, competition heated up. Competition in an illegal market can take brutal forms, and the number of drug-related homicides in the Miami area increased sharply.

Murder is one way of dealing with competition; offering a lower price is another. To lower prices, dealers had to become more efficient. It paid to reorganize the trade along more efficient lines. Contracts were made with growers, modern laboratories were constructed in safe locations, and airplanes were acquired for transport. The effects of the entry of more suppliers into the market and of employing modern technology allowed the supply curve to shift to the right. The result of the supply increase was that the price of cocaine fell while the quantity sold increased substantially.

1981–1982:
A DECLINE IN SUPPLY

By the end of the 1970s, the public and the federal government recognized that cocaine had become a major problem. The resources of drug enforcement agencies were redirected to hunt for cocaine, and a program of eradicating drugs at the source began. A record amount of cocaine was seized by enforcement officers in 1981. Peru, Bolivia, and Colombia began in 1981 to implement effective plant eradication programs. These law enforcement efforts were apparently effective in reducing the supply of cocaine, because the price increased while the quantity sold declined.

1983:
AN INCREASE IN DEMAND

Apparently demand increased again during 1983 as the price of cocaine increased, as did the estimated quantity traded. The use of cocaine was depicted as acceptable in TV programs and in movies at this time, perhaps encouraging an expansion of use.

1984–1986:
ANOTHER INCREASE IN SUPPLY

Cocaine suppliers were quick to adjust to these developments. After 1983 the price of cocaine began to fall and the volume of cocaine sales increased, indicating an increase in supply. Drug dealers went underground, and the previous conspicuous displays of affluence on their part disappeared. Shipments were broken down into many small cargos that were shipped separately. Ports other than Miami were increasingly used, with Los Angeles becoming an important center of the trade.

The growing of cocaine was moved into remote areas of Central America. Laboratories were dispersed and better concealed. The local eradication programs met with increased resistance. Drug dealers even assassinated the Colombian minister of justice, who had been in charge of the eradication program. The production of coca leaf, after the initial success of the eradication programs, actually increased significantly in these years. Colombian production was estimated to have increased from 5,000 metric tons in 1983 to 12,800 metric tons in 1984. The potentially high profits to be made in cocaine provided the incentive to counter the movements of drug enforcement.

The increase in supply was reflected in the price and quantity pattern in the U.S. cocaine market. The price fell while the quantity traded increased.

THE FUTURE

In the last few years, the cocaine industry appears to have reached a plateau. Cocaine is now widely recognized to be a dangerous, very addictive drug. It is no longer portrayed as fashionable by the entertainment media; rather, it is treated as a social problem. Widespread appreciation of this fact surely limits its potential market. The fact that supply developments have dominated the market in the recent past suggests that the industry is maturing and will not rapidly expand in the future. The decline in the market price along with a rise in quantity exchanged is disturbing, because it suggests that current enforcement efforts are not very effective. Another disturbing recent development is the innovation of a new, relatively inexpensive form of cocaine called "crack." It is possible that in this form cocaine use will spread to lower-income groups and that demand for the drug will begin to grow again in the future.[5]

COMPETITION IN THE WINE-GRAPE INDUSTRY

PREVIEW 4.3 ANALYSIS

The growers of wine grapes have experienced good times and bad. Sometimes mother nature plays a mean hand, bringing early frosts or droughts, but mainly whether a year is good or bad depends on the market price received for the grapes. The price of grapes has fluctuated significantly over the past decade or so. Booms followed by busts are typical of this industry.

The recent economic history of grape growing shows two such cycles, each roughly a decade long, which are clearly depicted in the price and quantity history shown in Table 4.4 and charted in Figure 4.15. The years 1966–1975 comprise one cycle, and the years 1976–1985 make up the second cycle. During the boom phase of a typical cycle, price rises for a

[5] Sources for this analysis: *Annual Report of the Organized Crime and Drug Enforcement Task Force* (Washington, DC: Various issues); Drug Enforcement Administration, *Narcotics Intelligence Estimate* (Washington, DC: Various issues); Thomas E. Ricks, "Inside Dope: The Cocaine Business," *The Wall Street Journal*, June 30, 1986, 1.

TABLE 4.4
Prices and Quantities of Bulk Wine Grapes: 1966–1985

YEAR	PRICE OF GRAPES (DOLLARS PER TON)	DIRECTION OF PRICE CHANGE	QUANTITY OF GRAPES (THOUSANDS OF TONS)	DIRECTION OF QUANTITY CHANGE
1966	40	•	0.7	•
1967	60	+	0.9	+
1968	63	+	1.0	+
1969	70	+	1.2	+
1970	79	+	1.5	+
1971	85	+	1.9	+
1972	151	+	1.5	−
1973	133	−	1.9	+
1974	110	−	2.0	+
1975	92	−	2.2	+
1976	115	+	2.3	+
1977	149	+	2.4	+
1978	182	+	2.6	+
1979	195	+	2.7	+
1980	201	+	2.9	+
1981	250	+	2.5	−
1982	195	−	3.0	+
1983	184	−	3.4	+
1984	174	−	3.6	+
1985	162	−	3.9	+

few years, as does the quantity sold in the market. This boom phase occurred in the wine-grape industry in the years 1966–1971 and again in the years 1975–1980. Since both price and quantity were rising, the demand for wine grapes was increasing in these periods.

During the bust phase of each cycle, the quantity sold continues to increase but price decreases. Busts occurred in the years 1973–1975 and again in 1982–1985. Clearly, the supply of wine grapes was increasing relative to the demand for grapes in these periods.

Two years seem to defy this pattern: 1972 and 1981. In both of these years, price increased while quantity fell, indicating that the supply of wine grapes had declined. Grapes are an agricultural product whose output is dependent on the favor of nature. Most wine grapes are grown in California, where the climate is mild and stable, but even in California nature sometimes fails the farmer. In 1972 a drought occurred, and in 1982 a late spring frost occurred. Both reduced the size of the grape crop, causing a decline in supply during those years.

The booms and busts revealed in the price and quantity statistics are readily explained by economic theory when the relevant facts about how grapes are produced are considered. An increase in demand can stimulate an increase in the quantity supplied. The rise in the price of grapes due to an increase in demand increases the profitability of grape growing, creating an incentive for growers to produce more grapes. Suppliers initially work the vineyards harder and more intensively. Their ability to increase production quickly is limited, however, since it takes a vine to grow a grape and growing a vine takes time. Existing suppliers will begin to expand their vineyards, and new firms will enter the industry. As these

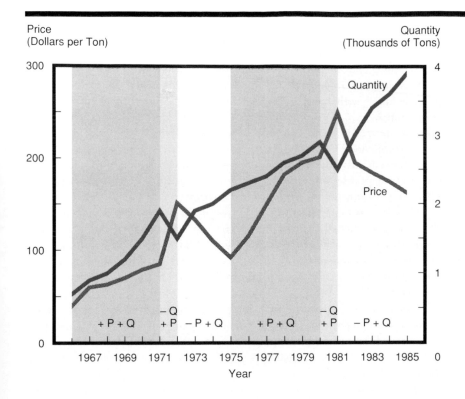

Price
(Dollars per Ton)

Quantity
(Thousands of Tons)

−Q
+P −P +Q

−Q
+P −P +Q

+P +Q

+P +Q

1967 1969 1971 1973 1975 1977 1979 1981 1983 1985

Year

FIGURE 4.15
Price and Quantity of Wine Grapes

The annual price and quantity of wine grapes sold in the United States in the years 1966–1985 are presented in this figure. These years can be divided into six periods, which form a cyclical pattern. Between 1966 and 1971, for example, both the price of wine grapes and the quantity produced increased, and a boom period again occurred in 1975–1980. This figure can be used to analyze these data in order to identify the dominant shifts that have occurred in this market and discover the causes of the cycle.

adjustments occur over time, the supply curve will shift to the right. When supply increases, prices will fall as the quantities traded expand. The supply curve will continue to shift out until all the profitable trades generated by the increases in demand are exhausted.

Notice the pattern of prices and quantities generated in this process. Initially, in response to the increase in demand, the market price increases, as does the quantity exchanged as growers move along the existing supply curve. This pattern of prices and quantities is exactly like the one experienced in the wine-grape market during the boom phase. When the newly planted vines begin to produce, supply increases and the supply curve shifts to the right. If the increase in supply is great enough, even if demand continues to increase, it will cause price to decline as the quantity traded in the market expands and the market enters a bust phase. During the bust phase, increases in supply catch up with the previous increases in demand, and the price of grapes declines, while the quantities grown and traded continue to expand.

If the prices and quantities of wine grapes sold in the market at the end of the roughly two decades under study here are compared with the price and quantity at the beginning, it is clear that there has been a substantial increase in demand. The price in 1985 was four times greater than it was in 1966, and the quantities of grapes traded are more than five times greater. Demand has clearly been increasing over time. But the changes that have occurred in the grape industry have not been confined to demand alone. Prices, instead of increasing steadily, have fluctuated, while quantity has increased fairly steadily, indicating that changes in supply have also occurred. Sometimes increases in demand have dominated the grape market and the prices of grapes have increased, and at other times increases in supply have dominated and grape prices have declined.

Why did demand increase over the past two decades? The demand for wine grapes is derived from the demand for wine. When the demand for wine increases, so too does the demand for wine grapes. In the middle 1960s, Americans began to take a serious interest in wine as a complement to their interest in French cuisine. The trend toward gourmet cooking carried along with it an increased interest in consuming wine. Grocery stores put in expanded wine sections, the number of specialty wine shops grew, restaurants began to feature wine lists, wine clubs and magazines were established. Coinciding with the gourmet-cooking fad was a trend away from highly alcoholic beverages and toward lighter drinks. Wine was an acceptable substitute for the martini, and white wine and brie gatherings began to replace cocktail parties.

Changes in tastes do not occur overnight but over a period of time. The change in taste in favor of wine no doubt reinforced the increase in demand that was occurring in this 1966–1985 period. Per capita income increased in a cyclical fashion, and as the distribution system developed throughout the country, the number of persons that would purchase wine increased.

The increase in demand for wine grapes during the two decades under study derived from the desire of consumers to consume more wine. This desire was transmitted to grape growers by means of the market and was accommodated by an increase in supply. The price system coordinated these developments.

The demand for wine grapes increased relative to the supply from 1966 to 1971 and again from 1975 to 1980. As a result, the price of wine grapes increased. Growing wine grapes became more profitable than growing other crops. Existing vineyard owners, attempting to obtain more output from existing vines, began to expand, and producers of other crops began to plant vines. There is a substantial lag between planting vines and the first harvest. After a minimum of three years, a newly planted vine produces only a partial crop. After five years, a full crop is realized. Thus three to five years after the market signals consumers' desire for more grapes, grapes from the new vines actually come to the market.

This lag in supply accounts for the cyclical pattern of prices in the wine-grape industry. Even if demand increases continuously over the period, the supply response will be very uneven. The vines planted in response to the increase in price in 1966 began to produce in 1970, and so on. Thus the supply curve will begin to shift out three to five years after vines are planted in response to the higher prices for grapes.

REQUIRED ECONOMIC CONCEPTS

Economic efficiency	Complements
Positive economics	Income-normal good
Normative economics	Income-inferior good
Change in quantity demanded	Tastes
Change in demand	Change in quantity supplied
Substitutes	Change in supply

KEY QUESTIONS

1. What is meant by economic efficiency?
2. What implication do competitive markets have for profits?
3. How do positive statements differ from normative ones?
4. What causes prices to change in competitive markets?
5. What determinants cause the demand curve to shift? The supply curve?
6. What is the difference between demand and quantity demanded?
7. How does an inferior good differ from a normal good?
8. Doctors claim medical care should operate as a system of free enterprise. In this case, why did the AMA resist creation of Health Maintenance Organizations (HMOs)?
9. How have third-party payments affected the cost of medical care in the United States?

PROBLEMS

1. Which of the following statements are normative? Which are positive?
   a. Democracy is the best form of government.
   b. Raising the minimum wage will cause an increase in unemployment among teenagers.
   c. The end justifies the means.
   d. A majority of U.S. citizens believe nuclear testing is wrong.
   e. Scientists should not create human life in the laboratory.
   f. "If at 20 you are not a liberal, you have no heart; if at 40 you are not a conservative, you have no sense." *(Winston Churchill)*
   g. There are mental differences between men and women.
   h. Scientists can create life in the laboratory.
   i. Price controls cause shortages and illegal markets.
2. What is the difference, if any, between scarcity and shortage?
3. In a letter to a magazine, Mr. Smith wrote: "If people would buy less gasoline, the supply would increase and the price would fall. Simple — but fundamental economics." Do you agree with Mr. Smith? Why or why not?
4. Suppose the market for Mickey Mouse T-shirts is in equilibrium. A new technology appears that reduces the costs of making the shirts. At the same time, a successful advertising campaign for the shirts is launched on children's TV shows. Do you believe the new equilibrium in this market will result in higher or lower prices? In higher or lower quantities? Or will both prices and quantities be indeterminant? Explain.
5. A letter to the editor stated: "Rents in this city are so high no one can afford to rent apartments." Does the comment make sense? Explain.
6. Given supply and demand, what direct changes in either supply or demand would you expect in the following situations, and for what reason?
   a. It used to take us an hour to build a smoke detector. Now it takes from 6 to 10 minutes. What happens in the market for smoke detectors?
   b. The price of seedless grapes doubles. What happens in the nonseedless grape market?
   c. Beer prices leap. What happens in the pizza market?
   d. Prices of baseball tickets have risen over the last 20 years, yet attendance continues to rise. Whas has happened in the market for baseball games?
   e. For dietary reasons, the U.S. public reduces substantially its consumption of candy and pastry. What happens in the sugar market? (Assume the sugar market is competitive. Actually, there is a floor price on sugar.)

f.   It is announced on the news during the fall season that there will be a shortage of tire chains this coming winter. What happens in the market for tire chains?

g.   The city announces that it will impose rent controls at the end of the month. What will happen to housing starts and building permits?

7.   A mother on welfare finally lands a good job. When she gets her paycheck, she switches from buying low-priced whitefish twice a week to buying more expensive trout. Why wouldn't she buy more whitefish?

8.   Assume an economy consists of five related markets initially in equilibrium: corn, cattle, retail beef, hamburger buns, and fish and chips. Draw a graph for each of these markets. Now suppose drought destroys half the corn crop. Corn is used to feed and fatten cattle. Starting with the corn market, indicate the consequences of the drought by drawing in either a new demand curve or a new supply curve (but not both) in each graph. Label all the curves and indicate the initial and final equilibrium prices and quantities along the appropriate axes in each graph. (*Hint:* Ranchers reduce the size of their breeding herds when corn prices rise sharply.)

APPLICATION ANALYSIS

1.   During the oil crisis of 1973 and 1978, when price controls existed on gasoline (they were lifted in the early 1980s), drivers waited in horrendously long lines to buy gasoline and the public was exhorted to conserve energy. From time to time, one would see a newspaper or magazine article containing the following graph that projected into the future the supply and demand for oil, while gloomily discussing the future shortage of oil.

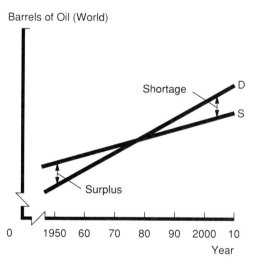

a.   What would an economist see that is fundamentally wrong with this graph? What essential variable is missing?

b.   What government policies would ensure a repetition of the long lines of 1973 and 1978 if world oil production dropped sharply again?

c.   For those drivers who waited in line in 1973 and 1978, did the pump price of gasoline reflect the full cost of their buying gasoline? Explain.

2.   Data from *Medical Economics* reported the following average net income (after expenses) for doctors in 1985:

Neurosurgeons	$192,000
Radiologists	150,000
OBs-gynecologists	121,410
General surgeons	120,830

Internists	89,630
Pediatricians	79,110
General practitioners	71,540

From three to five years after starting practice, the *median* net income for doctors in 1985 was $99,300.

The 1988 *Statistical Abstract of the United States* records that the nation's consumer price index rose from 42.0 in 1970 to 114.1 in 1986, an increase of 172 percent, whereas the medical price index increased from 120 to 435, an increase of 262.5 percent. Medical expenses as a percentage of national expenditures rose from 7.4 percent of gross national expenditures in 1970 to 11.7 percent in 1986. For Austria in 1986 it was 7.8 percent, for Canada 8.4 percent, for Italy 7.2 percent, for Belgium 6.2 percent, for Japan 6.6 percent, for the U.K. 5.9 percent, for West Germany 8.1 percent, and for Sweden 9.4 percent. Moreover, the number of per capita visits per year to doctors in the United States was the lowest among these countries, and the U.S. infant mortality rate was the highest. In 1987 there were 37 million Americans without medical coverage. Given this, former head of HEW (now HHS) Joseph Califano bought the argument that there is a surplus of doctors in the United States, an argument also put forth by sociologist Paul Starr, who said, "Physicians can only gain by taking business away from other physicians." Another doctor says, "There's no way we can avoid charging more and more and *expect to make what any doctor considers a fair return* on his time and knowledge. Doctors should be able to make a 50 percent profit or it just isn't worthwhile."

a. Why do you think the number of per capita visits per year to doctors in the United States is lowest among the listed countries? What economic concept does this fact reflect?

b. One critic argues that the federal government must bear a large share of the blame for inflated medical costs. Given an aging U.S. population, what part of the scissors of supply and demand was strongly affected here? What policies caused this effect?

c. What is implied about the earnings doctors should make in light of the statements about there being an oversupply of doctors? Do the restaurants and record shops near your college enter the market with an assurance of earning a planned or guaranteed profit? Do shoemakers take sales away from other shoemakers? Should such a practice be disallowed? Thus, what institutional arrangements help to ensure high earnings for doctors? How do they affect the scissors of supply and demand? With what result? Do similar institutional arrangements exist for accountants, dentists, and lawyers? In what way?

d. The average rate of return on investment for United States business firms is about 11 to 12 percent. On the basis of the last quote in the introduction above, is a 12 percent return a "fair return"? Is it too low?

e. In 1975 the chairman of the AMA's board of trustees said, "It's ironic that the FTC [Federal Trade Commission] should attack a code devised and operated as a standard of conduct in the best interest of the patient. . . . [Price] advertising by a professional is the very antithesis of professionalism. . . . We think there's enough hucksterism without huckstering medicine." Do you find these statements to be somewhat ironic? If so, why? What do you think is the major impact in a market where price competition is discouraged? What evidence do you have for your answer? Do you believe that if doctors and hospitals were required to list their hourly rates, prices would fall? Do you believe the AMA would fight this requirement? Why has the AMA resisted HMOs? Is doctoring a profession or a business?

THE ECONOMICS OF THE PUBLIC SECTOR

WHAT HAPPENS TO AN ECONOMY WHEN A GOVERNMENT COLLAPSES?

Lebanon is an example of economic development in reverse. At one time its free-enterprise economy was the jewel of the Middle East. Today Lebanon is an economic desert and a political jungle. Once an international banking center with trade and commerce providing two-thirds of the national income, a center for tourism, and a country with rich agricultural acreage, Lebanon is now more famous for foreign hostages held captive somewhere within its borders. Foreigners are kidnapped for political reasons, but native Lebanese are kidnapped for economic reasons. Hostage taking for ransom may now rank among the major economic activities of the country. Certainly, the narcotics trade ranks among the leading economic activities.

Banking has ceased to exist, and trade and commerce have been essentially reduced to barter. The average worker exists by trading personal possessions, by buying subsidized food, and by hiring out as a militiaman, a smuggler, or a gangster. The weakened central government still attempts to provide subsidized staple consumer products, but cannot perform efficiently even this basic function. Enterprising Lebanese buy up the cheap food and fuel and smuggle them to neighboring countries where they will fetch higher prices. Meanwhile some Lebanese, especially in the urban areas, go hungry. People regularly pick over garbage heaps for edible scraps (garbage-disposal services have ceased to exist).

Beirut, the capital of Lebanon, was once considered the Paris of the Middle East for its beauty and the gracious life it offered both visitors and residents. It now lies in ruins, its numerous damaged buildings unrepaired. The basic services of water, sewage, electricity, and telephone are available only part of the time, if at all.

The people of Lebanon have fallen victim to the worst kind of warfare — a civil war. Warring factions have reduced the power of the central government until it functions as a government in name only. Lebanon's decline provides an excellent example of the effects of failed government. When government fails to perform its basic functions, so does the economy. What are these basic functions of government? How do these functions interact with a country's economy?

EDUCATION AT RISK

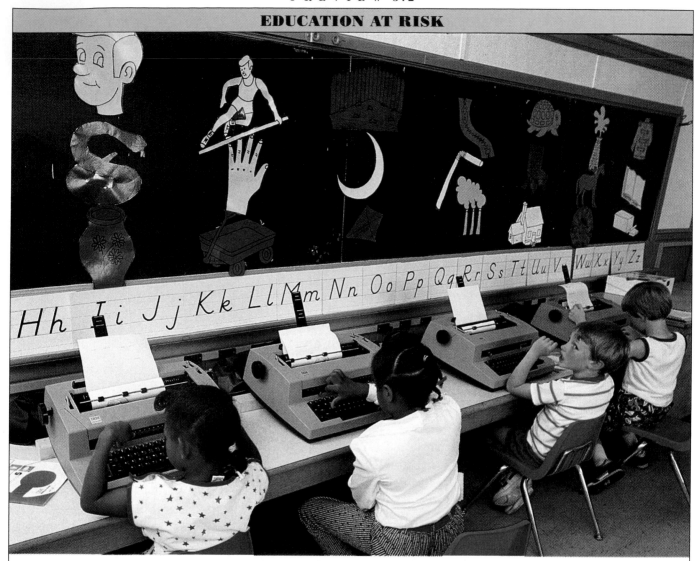

In 1983, through a publication entitled *A Nation at Risk* issued by the National Commission of Excellence, Americans first came to know just how bad their schools had become. This report and others that followed demonstrated just how far short the U.S. educational system had fallen in providing the most basic aspects of education. They revealed that 23 million Americans and 13 percent of all 17-year-olds were functional illiterates. College-bound high school students' scores on the Scholastic Aptitude Test declined for a decade before rising slightly recently. About one-quarter of the nation's youth fail to complete high school, and in the worst schools more than half fail to do so. Investigators found that when compared with the school systems of other countries, the U.S. educational system did nothing particularly well and a number of things poorly.

These reports moved education up to a higher place on the agendas of the nation's politicians. Several state governors pushed for more funding for schools and for reform programs. Requirements for education were increased. Proposals to upgrade the quality of teachers abounded. Programs addressing the problem of high school dropouts were created.

Several years after the call for educational reform, the government was spending more and taxing more for education. In 1980 the nation spent $104 billion for its elementary and secondary schools. In 1987 it spent $167 billion. Between 1979 and 1983 spending for primary and secondary education grew at the inflation-adjusted rate of 7 percent. Since 1983 it has grown twice as fast. The nation now spends a substantially higher percentage of its national income on education than do other countries with better educational systems. One study found, however, that less than 1 percent of the funding for primary and secondary education has been used for educational reform.

The failure of the nation's school systems is not an example of the failure of the free market, because most elementary and secondary education is provided by the government. The failure of the American public school system is an example of the failure of collective action. How can our democratic governments fail to accomplish social goals widely supported by the nation's citizens?

• I N T R O D U C T I O N •

Every society must establish an economic system. Chapter 1 explained that there are two basic ways for an economy to solve the allocation problem created by the persistence of scarcity: (1) a system of laissez-faire allocation by the private sector, often called a *market economy*, and (2) a command system in which the government, or public sector, makes the necessary decisions. In the United States most economic decisions are made by individuals trading in markets, but government does allocate some resources directly and plays a critical role in providing an alternative way to allocate resources.

The government defines and enforces property rights, provides for the national defense and for police and fire protection, manages the money supply, operates the mail service, supplies much of the education, and in some places produces the electricity and provides the waste disposal. Government in the United States not only directly provides various goods and services in the economy, but it also transfers income among various groups in the economy and regulates the economic activities of the private sector. Because of this, our economy is often called a **mixed economy**.

> A mixed economy is one in which economic decisions are made partly by the private sector and partly by the public sector.

In this chapter we shall review the fundamental role that government plays in the economy, a role that has been discussed in prior chapters. We shall examine some of the shortcomings of the market system that create a demand for government intervention and then evaluate the potential for government action to rectify these defects. Finally, we shall briefly examine the economics of how the public sector works and discuss the potential of government action as an alternative way of solving fundamental economic problems. •

CRITERIA FOR JUDGING ECONOMIC PERFORMANCE

One of the basic principles of the economic way of thinking is that economic decision makers must economize: *Economic decision makers attempt to obtain the most out of the available scarce resources.* Efficiency is the criterion by which economists judge both the free market and the public sector.

Economic efficiency is simply obtaining the most from the available resources. The rule of rational behavior introduced in Chapter 1 provides a decision rule for attaining economic efficiency: *A decision maker should take any action in which the addition to benefits (the marginal benefit) exceeds the addition to costs (the marginal cost).*

As we saw in Chapter 4, an economy is operating efficiently only if all the profitable trades have been exhausted. In Figure 5.1 a competitive market with supply curve S and demand curve D is drawn. According to this decision rule, buyers should continue to buy and suppliers should continue to sell up to point E, where quantity Q_e is traded at price P_e. In Figure 5.1 if less than quantity Q_e, say Q_1, is exchanged, some profitable trades have not been made. Because the marginal cost of supplying Q_1 (at point B) is less than the price buyers would be willing to pay (point A), a social cost in a form of a loss in the possible gains from trade would occur equal to the triangle AEB.

- *Social cost* is the total of all costs that society bears when an economic action is taken. Social costs include private costs as well as any costs that society as a whole must bear.
- *Social benefit* is the total benefit that society receives when an economic action is taken. Social benefits include private benefits as well as any benefits that society as a whole receives.
- A *social loss* occurs when the social costs of an economic action exceed the social benefits.

FIGURE 5.1
Ideal Economic Efficiency

Economic efficiency is obtained in a market when the marginal cost of producing the last unit exchanged is just equal to the marginal value, or marginal benefit, of the last unit traded. This occurs where the supply curve, S, intersects the demand curve, D, at point E. The price P_e is equal to both the marginal cost of supplying the unit Q_e and the marginal benefit from consuming it. If less than Q_e is produced, say Q_1, then the marginal benefit measured at point A is greater than the marginal cost measured at point B. The triangle AEB measures the social loss involved in exchanging Q_1 rather than Q_e. A social loss is also incurred if too much is exchanged. If Q_2 is exchanged instead of Q_e, the marginal cost of producing Q_2 measured at point C exceeds the marginal value or benefit of that quantity measured at point D. The social loss of producing Q_2 rather than Q_e is measured by the triangle CED.

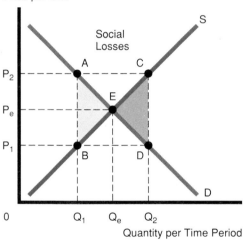

Exchanging less than the optimal quantity of goods and services imposes a social cost because all of the gains from trade have not been obtained. If quantity exchanged increases to Q_e, society would gain an amount equal to the triangle AEB. The social loss in this case is the loss of potential output.

If more than quantity Q_e is traded, a similar loss is incurred. Suppose the quantity exchanged is Q_2 rather than Q_e. The marginal cost of producing Q_2 is measured at point C and will be greater than the marginal value or benefit measured at point D. A social loss equal to the area of triangle CED will occur. In this case the social loss occurs because society pays more for all units produced greater than the amount Q_e. Only at point E, when Q_e is produced, will the marginal value of the last unit exchanged just equal the marginal cost of producing that unit.

A competitive market, as we saw in Chapter 3, will reach an equilibrium at precisely point E. Suppliers will continue to supply a good as long as the market price is greater than the marginal cost. Buyers will continue to buy a good as long as the market price is less than the marginal benefit, or marginal value, of another unit of that good. Market forces will therefore push the quantity exchanged to Q_e and establish a market price of P_e. Suppliers will find it unprofitable to supply more than Q_e, and buyers will find it uneconomic to purchase more than that amount. All profitable trades will therefore be exhausted in a competitive market. The invisible hand makes sure that a competitive market exchanges the correct amount of the good to achieve economic efficiency.

The invisible hand does not function efficiently by itself, however. A market requires assistance from government (the visible hand) to allocate scarce goods and resources efficiently. There is thus both a demand for government services and a supply of government services. In the following discussion of the economic role that government plays in the U.S. economy, we shall first focus on the demand by the body politic for government action to increase the efficiency with which the market operates. We shall then consider the supply response on the part of government.

DEMAND FOR GOVERNMENT SERVICES

The value of any good is composed of the benefits from consuming the good itself and from the private-property rights that are attached to the good.

DEFINING PRIVATE-PROPERTY RIGHTS

Private-property rights were defined in Chapter 2. Private-property rights grant to owners the exclusive right to use, enjoy, and sell their privately owned possessions, subject only to the limitations imposed by law.

Government is the source of private-property rights. Through the legal system, government defines and specifies the kind and extent of property rights, assigns them to individuals and institutions, and sets the conditions under which they may be transferred to others. When you buy a piece of real estate, you acquire a deed of ownership. The deed describes the geographic location of the property and identifies you as the legal owner. Your property will no doubt be zoned, which will limit the activities in which you can engage on your land. The deed may include easements, which give others specified rights to use your land, traverse it, or enter onto it to maintain public utilities.

The same is true for types of property other than real estate. The government determines the extent and kind of property rights attached to a good and determines who is the legal owner. For example, if you were to design and build your own car, you would have to legally register and obtain a license for it before you could operate it on public roads or sell it. To obtain a license, you would need to bring receipts for all the parts to an official state agency to obtain a title of ownership. The *title* protects your property, creating much of its value, and allows you to sell the car.

ENFORCING PRIVATE-PROPERTY RIGHTS

The government not only determines who is the legal owner of property but also attempts to make the owner's property secure. In the United States the government has police powers to enforce human and property rights, and it uses these powers to protect human rights and to discourage theft of property. In Chapter 2 we explained that theft destroys wealth by separating goods from their property rights.

In Chapter 2 we also explained that every trade implies a contract that specifies what is to be exchanged. The U.S. government, through its legal system, defines the nature of permissible contracts and limits their extent. It is illegal, for example, to sell oneself into slavery or to exchange certain commodities, such as prohibited drugs. A contract may be as simple as the exchange of money for milk and a grocery store receipt or as complicated as a lengthy document for the construction of a nuclear power plant. Legal contracts that govern trades are often the subject of disputes. Thus one of the important functions of government is to adjudicate contract disputes and then to enforce the terms of those contracts.

Why is government given the responsibility in our society for specifying and enforcing private-property rights? Why can't the market perform this function? The basic reason is that these necessary activities are pure public goods, and the market cannot allocate *pure public goods* efficiently, as you will discover below.

PRIVATE AND PUBLIC GOODS

Before we define a public good, it will be useful to discover its opposite — a private good. The market, as we have seen in previous chapters, can efficiently allocate a **private good.**

> *A private good has three important features: it is a rival in consumption, it is divisible, and nonowners can be excluded from using it.*

First, a good is a rival in consumption if a limited amount of the good is available and the consumption of some of the good diminishes the amount available for others to consume. At any point in time, there is a given quantity of apples in existence. If you eat one, there is one less apple available for others to consume. The second characteristic is that a private good is divisible. A bushel of apples can be divided into individual apples each of which can be cut up into pieces. The third characteristic is the ease with which nonowners can be excluded from enjoying the good. It is possible at low cost to restrict others from enjoying a private good. Your toothbrush is an example of a private good with low exclusion costs: Once you have used it, its usefulness to others is rather limited. Many, if not most, of the goods in your possession are private goods.

The market is not able, however, to efficiently allocate a **pure public good.**

> *A pure public good is a good that is a nonrival in consumption, that is not divisible, and that nonpaying persons cannot be easily excluded from using once it has been produced.*

Once it has been produced, a pure public good can be consumed by a person without significantly reducing the amount available for others to consume; it cannot easily be divided into smaller units; and people cannot be kept from consuming the good even if they refuse to pay for it.

Examples of pure public goods are the legal and judicial system, national defense, and the monetary system. The legal and judicial system defines and enforces property rights. Once a law establishing private property has been passed, it benefits everyone — no matter how many persons are covered. When one person benefits from private property, no fewer benefits are available to others. The law obviously cannot be subdivided, and people cannot be easily excluded because they do not pay for the benefits.

Similarly, national defense, which protects the entire country, protects everyone in the country equally, and no one can be placed outside the system. National defense meets all the criteria of a pure public good. National defense, unlike apples, is not a rival in consumption. Everyone's property is protected by national defense, and one person's benefits do not diminish the amount of protection available to other citizens. Unlike apples, national defense cannot be divided and parceled out piecemeal to consumers. It must be provided in one activity. And unlike apples, national defense cannot be provided to some persons and not to others. No one living in this country can be excluded from enjoying the benefits of national defense. If the city of Detroit is protected, everyone living in the city and their property is protected equally.

The nation's monetary system is also a pure public good. The monetary system provides a means of payment to avoid the costs of barter, a unit of account that allows diverse goods to be valued in terms of a common unit and allows wealth to be easily measured, and a store of value that allows individuals to make trades today and store the proceeds to be spent in the future. If such a system is to work efficiently, there must be only one national system, whose use by another person does not diminish the usefulness of the system for others, and from which no one can be excluded. If a monetary system is to work, it must be available to all.

Not all the goods supplied by government are pure public goods. Some goods are private goods that a government has chosen to allocate for political reasons. All goods provided by government, whether they are pure public goods or private goods, are **political goods.**

> *A political good is any good supplied by the political process. Political goods can be either public or private goods.*

Public parks and recreational areas, school milk programs, and surplus-commodity programs are all government-supplied goods, but the goods provided are private goods, not pure public goods. These goods are rivals in consumption and are divisible, and people can easily be excluded from enjoying the goods. The political process has decided to supply these private goods for political, not economic, reasons. The recipients of these politically supplied goods could easily, for example, be excluded if they did not pay or did not meet some other criteria. Indeed, many school lunch programs require a partial payment from students. Students who forget their lunch money are provided a peanut butter sandwich instead of a full lunch.

The political goods, both private goods and pure public goods, that government supplies are not *free goods*. Scarce resources with opportunity costs must be employed to produce all of them. Providing more political goods comes at the expense of having fewer goods provided through the market.

PROVIDING PUBLIC GOODS

The provision of pure public goods requires collective action because pure public goods are difficult for the market to provide. The market either will not provide a public good at all or will supply too little of it. The basic problem is that if others cannot be excluded from enjoying a good once it is produced, there will be no one willing to pay for it. A rational decision maker would therefore prefer to let others pay for the good. Suppliers will not produce a good for which there is no market, and because few paying customers will be found, no market will exist to allocate a pure public good.

A sufficient amount of national defense probably would not exist if its production were left entirely to the private sector. A free market trading in private goods functions because there is a direct link between consumption and payment. If a buyer does not pay for a good, he or she will probably not obtain it. Thus there is an incentive for buyers to pay. Suppliers rely on the buyers' payment for their incentive to produce and supply that good. If suppliers cannot be assured of payment, they will not supply enough. If national defense is provided, it is provided to all, whether the individuals who benefit pay or not. When this happens, the tendency is for people to opt out of paying their share, since whether they pay or not does not influence the availability of the good. The upshot is that the free market will not provide a sufficient amount of national defense or any other pure public good.

The need for public goods provides a sufficient reason for government intervention in an economic system. What the private sector cannot do, the government will surely be called upon to attempt. National defense is both necessary and a public good. If the correct amount is to be provided, we cannot rely on the market to provide it. In the case of a pure public good, the government decides how much to produce and how to produce it, and then it taxes individuals to pay for it.

The same is true for defining and protecting human and property rights, which are public goods. Not enough of either can or will be produced by a free market. It is up to society to act collectively to produce the necessary amount of public goods. Public goods cannot be efficiently supplied by the private sector, because once these goods are produced, no one can be excluded from enjoying the benefits for nonpayment.

There exists a simple but persuasive way to demonstrate why individual choice will lead to the production of too few public goods. It is known as the *prisoner's dilemma*.

FIGURE 5.2
The Prisoner's Dilemma

This table illustrates the "prisoner's dilemma," revealing the choices and resulting outcomes for two participants — you and your partner. You have both committed a crime and have been arrested. The evidence against you is weak, and the prosecutor needs a confession to ensure a conviction. You are separated from your partner and each of you independently is offered the opportunity to go free on probation if you confess and testify against your partner. This deal is conditional upon your partner not also confessing. If he or she does, you will receive a life sentence whether you confess or not. Your partner faces the same choices.

In the figure the column at the left shows the two choices available to you as one of the participants. In the row at the top are the two choices available to your partner in crime. The quadrant at the intersection of each row and column shows the outcome for you (top half) and for your partner (lower half) for each combination of decisions. For example, if you decide to remain silent while your partner decides to confess, the outcome is revealed in the upper right-hand quadrant. You will receive a life sentence while your partner goes free. What should you do?

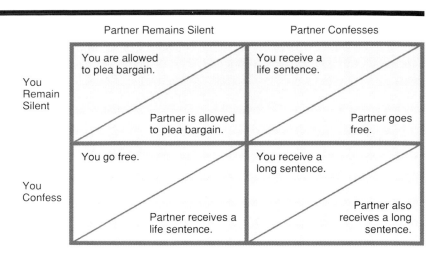

FIGURE 5.3
Why Lives Are Lost in Fires

Suppose you are attending a public function when a fire breaks out. In the left-hand column of this figure are the alternatives available to you, and in the top row are the alternatives available to everyone else. In the quadrants are the outcomes that correspond to each combination of choices. Consider your alternatives. Suppose you and everyone else decide to walk; the result is that you will probably get out. However, if you decide to run while everyone else walks, you will certainly get out. If everyone else decides to run, but you decide to walk, you will not get out of the burning building alive. If you decide to run, you may get out. Since running is the superior personal choice, everyone decides to run. The outcome of this is found in the lower right-hand quadrant: A panic will occur and some lives will be lost. Notice, however, that if everyone chooses to walk instead, the outcome will be as shown in the upper left-hand quadrant — everyone will probably get out alive. In this case self-interest produces the worst possible outcome.

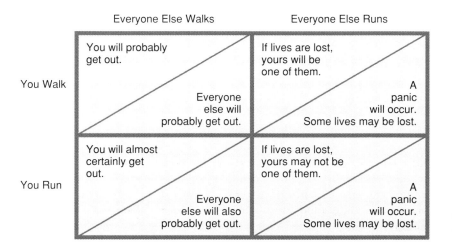

THE PRISONER'S DILEMMA Economists are interested in prediction and explanation. One approach to the theory of government that has proven promising in this regard comes from the theory of games. It is called the **prisoner's dilemma.**

The prisoner's dilemma is a framework for analyzing the choices and outcomes for a decision-making process in which the combination of the choices made by two decision makers determines the outcome.

The prisoner's dilemma was initially designed to explain the behavior of two prisoners who have been arrested and are being interrogated in separate rooms. Both are guilty, but the police have a weak case and need a confession to ensure a conviction. Without a confession, the two prisoners will each be allowed to plea-bargain to a lesser charge.

The police offer each prisoner the following deal: Confess and agree to turn state's evidence against your partner and go free on probation,

APPLICATION

5.1

WHY LIVES ARE LOST DUE TO FIRES IN PUBLIC PLACES

The prisoner's dilemma can be used to describe a number of actual situations. It can, for example, explain the instances of deaths that occur from fires in public places. In the 1970s a nightclub in Cincinnati caught fire while it was filled with people. When the fire was extinguished, the fire fighters found masses of dead bodies heaped in front of the exits, indicating that a panic had occurred. In the fire marshal's opinion, they all could have gotten out if the evacuation had proceeded in an orderly fashion. In 1984 there was a simi-

lar occurrence at an English soccer match during a live telecast, when more than 100 persons perished. Again the bodies were found in heaps in front of the stadium exits.

What caused these avoidable deaths? The prisoner's dilemma can help to explain this socially undesirable behavior. Suppose you are in a crowded building when a fire breaks out. Figure 5.3 provides a table showing the results of different combinations of decisions in this circumstance. The choice is whether to walk or to run to the exits. If everyone, including you, decides to walk to the exits in an orderly manner, everyone will probably get out. This outcome is shown in the upper left-hand quadrant.

Probability is not certainty. If everyone else decides to walk and you decide to run, you will almost *certainly* get out, and as long as everyone else remains calm and walks, they will also probably get out. Selfish behavior on your part, reinforced by a natural flight response, leads to a decision to run. This decision is strengthened by a consideration of what will happen if you walk and everyone else

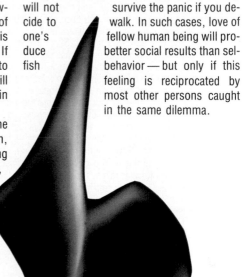

runs. In this case, your life will be among the lives that will be lost — so you decide to run.

What occurs to you as appropriate behavior, however, will also occur to almost everyone else. Most will also run, causing a panic during which some lives will be lost. You may survive the panic if you run along with everyone else, but you certainly will not survive the panic if you decide to walk. In such cases, love of one's fellow human being will produce better social results than selfish behavior — but only if this feeling is reciprocated by most other persons caught in the same dilemma.

provided your partner, who is being offered the same deal, doesn't also confess. If your partner also confesses, the deal is off. If you decide not to confess but your partner turns state's evidence, you will get a life sentence while your partner goes free. The reverse is also true. If both of you confess, both will be convicted and both will receive long jail sentences.

The simplest way to keep these options straight is to construct a table as shown in Figure 5.2. Suppose you are one of the prisoners in this unfortunate situation. What should you do? Clearly the outcome, whatever you decide, depends on what your partner in crime decides to do. There is an interdependence between the two decisions. The best outcome would appear to be for both of you to remain silent, in which case both of you will be allowed to plea-bargain to a lesser charge. This outcome is shown in the upper left-hand quadrant of the table. Both of you would certainly remain silent *if* you could trust your partner.

But you don't know for certain what your partner will do. If you choose to remain silent and your partner talks, you will get a life sentence and your partner will go free. This outcome is found in the upper right-hand quadrant. Thus if you remain silent, you will get to plea-bargain or you will receive a life sentence. Suppose, however, you decide to confess. These options are obviously better. If you confess and your partner remains silent, you will go free. If your partner also confesses, you will receive a long jail sentence, which, bad as it is, is clearly better than a life sentence.

No matter what your partner does, you will be better off if you confess. You avoid the possibility of a life sentence, and you actually might go

FIGURE 5.4
Why National Defense Is Provided by Government

This table shows the possible outcomes if national defense were paid for voluntarily by you and by all those persons who receive its benefits. The left-hand column presents the two choices available to you: to cooperate and pay your share of $1,053, or to cheat and pay nothing. The top row shows that the same two alternatives are available to everyone else. If you decide to cooperate and so does everyone else, the government will have ($1,053 + $252,699,998,947), or $252.7 billion, to spend on defense. If you decide to cheat but everyone else cooperates and pays, the government will have only $1,053 less, which is still sufficient for an adequate defense. Because your contribution is not required to defend the country, you have an incentive to be a free rider and not to cooperate. However, everyone else will face the same alternatives and reach the same conclusion, and the government will receive zero revenues — the outcome shown in the lower right-hand quadrant. To solve the free-rider problem, the government compels contributions in the form of taxes, thereby obtaining the outcome shown in the upper left-hand quadrant.

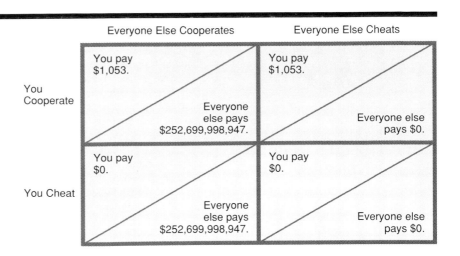

free. A selfish person will therefore always choose to confess. The police are offering your partner the same deal, and if your partner is selfishly motivated, a confession will also be forthcoming. Both of you are most likely to confess and convict each other into a long jail sentence, so the equilibrium will occur in the lower right-hand quadrant, even though the outcome is not the best that could have been achieved. The best combined result would have occurred if both of you *had remained silent*. In that case, you would both have been allowed to plea-bargain and would have received lesser sentences. This decision, however, requires a selfless act on the part of *both of you*.

REQUIREMENT FOR COLLECTIVE ACTION How does the prisoner's dilemma reveal the need for government to replace the market in providing certain goods? Let us take the case of a public good such as national defense. Given the history of the world, almost everyone would agree that some level of national defense is necessary even if there is no agreement on how much is enough. Yet no country relies on its citizens' willingness to pay to provide national defense. Each country compels its citizens to pay taxes for defense. Consider the table in Figure 5.4, which depicts the situation an average U.S. citizen would have faced in 1985 if each could have decided whether or not to voluntarily pay for the nation's defense. The United States spent $252.7 billion in 1985 for national defense, of which each citizen paid an average of $1,053. You paid on average $1,053 and everyone else paid a total of $252,699,998,947.

Suppose you had a choice of whether to pay your share or not. If everyone, including yourself, cooperated, the nation could spend the entire amount that Congress had appropriated. This outcome is shown in the upper left-hand quadrant of the figure. However, if you alone cooperated and everyone else cheated and didn't pay, the amount available for national defense would be limited to your contribution of $1,053. Few people would think that amount sufficient.

On the other hand, suppose that everyone else cooperated and you alone cheated. In this case, the amount available for national defense would be only $1,053 less than the amount Congress deemed necessary, or

$252,699,998,947. This outcome is shown in the lower left-hand quadrant. Will the United States be placed at risk if the nation spends $1,053 less? Hardly! The Department of Defense daily probably wastes much more than that. Now consider your position. Do you have a good use for the $1,053? You bet! Think of the things you could buy with an extra $1,053. So if contributing to national defense were voluntary, you would rationally decide not to contribute, assuming (hoping) that everyone else will do his or her civic duty. After all, your contribution alone in 1985 did not affect the security of the country one bit; it was the contributions of everyone else that made the difference.

Realizing this fact, if given a choice, you have every incentive to be a **free rider.**

> *A free rider is a person who receives the benefits of a good without contributing to its costs of production.*

If you figured this out, so would other people. Each would in turn choose not to contribute. The equilibrium result, as shown in the lower right-hand quadrant of Figure 5.4, is that no money would be available to spend on national defense if providing national defense were left to voluntary action.

The government solves the free-rider problem by compelling each taxpayer to contribute to national defense and to the general support of the government. If you refuse to pay your taxes, the government will force you to do so and, in addition, will impose a fine or a prison term or both. The purpose of the penalty is to make paying your share of the cost of national defense, or the cost of operating the government, a more attractive option than cheating.

Indeed, the solution to the prisoner's dilemma is to change the incentive either to confess or to be a free rider (to cheat) by changing the outcomes in the upper and lower right-hand quadrants to be less desirable than the outcomes in the upper and lower left-hand quadrants. Fines and possible prison terms for evasion increase your incentive to pay your taxes. In small groups, peer group pressure may be sufficient incentive: Confess or free ride and your peers will ruin your reputation and social standing.

The prisoner's dilemma shows why public goods will not be produced in sufficient amount, or at all, if left to the free market. The solution to the prisoner's dilemma is to compel individuals to act collectively in ways that further society's interests but violate the individual's perceived self-interests.

The necessity to provide public goods provides one reason why the government must be active in the economy. The failure of the market to perform satisfactorily provides another.

WHY THE MARKET MIGHT FAIL

Four other important circumstances can lead the invisible hand astray and keep the market from attaining economic efficiency. When these circumstances arise, there will be a demand for government intervention to allow the market to function efficiently either by regulating the behavior of market forces or by replacing the market altogether with collective action. These circumstances are: (1) a lack of competition, (2) the presence of externalities, (3) macroeconomic fluctuations, and (4) a socially unacceptable distribution of income.

FIGURE 5.5
Effect of a Lack of Competition on
Economic Efficiency

If the market depicted in this figure were competitive, equilibrium would occur at point E_c, the market price would be P_c, and Q_c would be the quantity exchanged. If, however, fewer than the required number of firms for a competitive market existed, these firms could increase their profits by restricting output below Q_c, say to Q_m. At Q_m the market price would be P_m, which measures the marginal benefit, and the marginal cost of production would be MC. Restricting output below the level that would be exchanged in a competitive market reduces the gains from trade, causing a social loss equal to the salmon triangle. Society thus suffers a social loss if output is restricted below the competitive level.

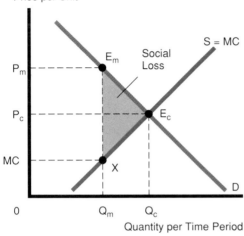

LACK OF COMPETITION   Competition among suppliers and among buyers is critical to the efficient operation of a market-based economy. Competition drives the market price to the level of the cost of production. Every seller would like to charge a higher price for goods, and every buyer would like to pay less. Because competition forces each supplier to meet the offer of each competitor, the market price will be forced to the level that just covers the cost of production. In Figure 5.5 the equilibrium will occur at E_c, where the market price equals the marginal cost of production.

Suppose instead that only a single firm exists in a market or that a few large firms collude and act as if they were a single firm. If competition among the firms within an industry can be eliminated, then higher prices can be charged, to the benefit of existing suppliers and to the detriment of consumers. The resulting lack of competition is known as the **monopoly problem**.

> *The monopoly problem arises when, due to the lack of competition in a market, producers act as if they were a single firm and restrict output in order to increase price.*

Monopoly literally means one firm. If the existing suppliers, for example, could agree among themselves to collectively collude to act as one firm and offer fewer goods for sale, they could charge a higher price and earn larger profits. Consider Figure 5.5 where the supply curve, S, and the demand curve, D, represent market forces. If competition exists, the equilibrium will be at E_c, with a price of P_c and a quantity exchanged of Q_c. If, however, the suppliers agreed among themselves to restrict output to Q_m instead of Q_c, then the market price would be P_m instead of P_c. Producers have an incentive to collude in this way because their profits will increase.

Since the restricted supply violates the conditions for economic efficiency, some potentially profitable trades will not be made. The social loss that results is indicated in Figure 5.5 by the salmon triangle $E_m E_c X$. This social loss stems from a monopolist offering too few goods, Q_m, rather than the equilibrium quantity, Q_c, in the market. A monopoly problem can exist only if there is one supplier in the market or few enough firms in the market to act as a single firm would. When many firms exist in a market, collusion is impossible and competition will prevail.

When a monopoly problem exists, there will be a conflict between the best interest of the supplier and the best interest of society. In this case, there is a possibility for government action to improve the situation by (1) promoting competition, or (2) regulating the monopoly and forcing it to charge a price of P_c, or (3) establishing direct government ownership of the industry on the assumption that a publicly owned firm will act in the public interest.

The U.S. government has established a series of laws, known as the antitrust laws, to promote competition when all of the conditions for pure competition are not met. The most important of the antitrust laws are the Sherman Antitrust Act and the Clayton Act (outlawing anticompetitive mergers), which make it illegal for firms to collude or attempt to monopolize a market. The federal government has also established the Federal Trade Commission to police unfair competitive practices. To promote competition, some large firms that were guilty of violating the antitrust laws have been split into a number of smaller firms by court action. The most recent example was the dissolution of American Telephone and Telegraph (AT&T) into a separate long-distance carrier and a number of independent regional telephone companies.

The presence of monopoly may also stimulate a demand for direct regulation of an industry or for government ownership. Telephone service, cable TV systems, and natural gas companies are considered to be monopolies and are regulated by public authorities. Some electric-power companies are owned by the federal government, as is the U.S. post office for example.

EXTERNALITIES   The production and consumption of goods can sometimes affect persons who are not directly involved in the market. **Externalities** are benefits or costs that spill over to affect other persons who are not parties to the exchange.

> *An externality is present when, as a result of a trade or action, a third party not directly involved in the trade is either harmed or benefited.*

When an externality is present, social costs and benefits are different from the private costs and benefits considered by the traders. A trade involves a buyer and a seller who must mutually agree to an exchange. Both agree because each will be better off after the trade, but some trades involve externalities, which are not taken into account by the market participants. In such a case, a third party is affected by the trade without the party's consent. The presence of externalities leads the free market to exchange either too much or too little of a good.

Externalities can take the form of imposing either costs or benefits on third parties. When you drive during rush hour, your presence increases the level of congestion, imposing costs on other drivers in the form of slower speeds. At the same time, the exhaust from your automobile increases the level of air pollution, damaging all other users of air without their consent. The emission into the atmosphere of by-products from the production of chemicals, paper, or steel has similar side effects. Government at the federal and state levels has responded with a set of environmental laws and regulations that limit emissions and impose fines on violators.

These laws have not always worked exactly as they were intended. In the state of Washington, for example, the excrement from dairy cattle is a major source of pollution for neighboring streams and rivers, destroying fish and wildlife that other persons value. The government responded by requiring dairy farmers to construct manure lagoons to hold cattle waste until it can be safely applied to pastures as fertilizer. One such lagoon was constructed just outside the city limits of the town of Stanwood. The stench from the lagoon permeated the entire downtown shopping area, to the complete disgust of the residents. Here one **negative externality** was exchanged for another.

> *A negative externality is a cost imposed on a third party to a trade or action without the party's consent.*

Some externalities have beneficial effects on others: a new road or bridge often increases the value of nearby land; an attractively dressed person provides pleasurable viewing for others; a neighbor who paints her house and keeps a beautiful garden improves the entire neighborhood. Positive externalities also lead the free market to misallocate

FIGURE 5.6
Effect of Externalities on Economic Efficiency

When an externality exists, some third party not directly involved in the trade is either harmed or benefited. Part A shows the effect of a negative externality, and Part B shows the effect of a positive externality.

Part A — Negative externality: The private-cost supply curve, S_a, represents only the costs that sellers bear. In addition to these costs are the costs of the externality X that fall on third parties. Thus the social-cost supply curve that reflects all costs is $S_a + X$. It can readily be seen that too much of a good (Q_a instead of Q_i) is exchanged and that the market price is too low (P_a rather than P_i) when a negative externality is present.

Part B — Positive externality: The private-cost demand curve in this case will be D_a but this demand curve does not reflect all of the benefits associated with obtaining the good. There also exists a positive external benefit equal to X that is enjoyed by third parties. The social demand curve $D_a + X$, which includes all the benefits from exchanging the good, will be made up of the private demand curve D_a plus the external positive benefit X. The effect of a positive externality can be determined by comparing the equilibrium points E_a and E_i. When a positive externality exists, the market will trade too few units of the good (Q_a instead of Q_i) at too low a price (P_a instead of P_i).

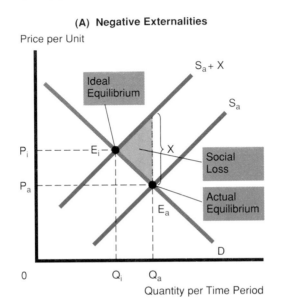 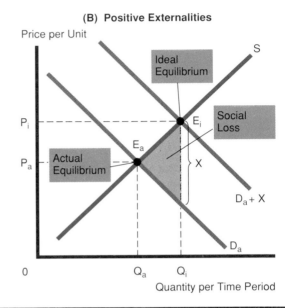

resources. When Walt Disney purchased an orange grove outside Los Angeles to build Disneyland, the result was a substantial increase in the value of the surrounding orange groves. Out came the trees and up went fast-food restaurants and motels. Disneyland created a **positive externality** for its neighbors.

A positive externality is a benefit to a third party for which the party does not pay.

Externalities, whether positive or negative, cause problems for a market economy. Consider the case of the paper industry. A paper-producing firm must acquire wood pulp, labor, capital, and energy. These resources must be obtained in resource markets, and the firm must pay its opportunity costs in order to obtain them. These costs will be reflected in the firm's supply curve, S_a, in Part A of Figure 5.6. The supply curve intersects the demand curve, D, for paper at E_a, establishing a market price of P_a and a quantity of Q_a.

The firm must also dispose of the waste by-products of paper manufacture. Because the producer does not have to pay if the firm exhausts these products directly into the air or discharges them into a nearby stream, the cost of disposal is not reflected by the supply curve, S_a. Discharging pollutants into the environment is not free to society, however, even if it is free to the firm. Society pays in the form of a decline in environmental quality. In Part A of Figure 5.6, the opportunity cost to society of disposing waste by-products equals X dollars. The supply curve that reflects all the costs of producing paper — both social costs as well as private costs — is therefore $S_a + X$. The intersection of the adjusted supply curve with the demand curve establishes an ideal equilibrium at point E_i, where a smaller quantity, Q_i, is produced at a higher price, P_i.

From society's point of view, the ideal output is Q_i and the ideal price is P_i. If the ideal price and quantity are compared with the actual price and quantity, it appears that when a negative externality is present, too much of a good is produced at too low a price. The social loss is indicated by the salmon triangle and represents the extent to which the marginal cost to society of the output produced exceeds the marginal value of paper to consumers. Thus when negative externalities are present, the market provides too much of a good because producers are free to ignore some costs that are real costs to society. Also, some trades are made that would not be profitable if all true costs were considered by suppliers.

Positive externalities also create problems for efficient market allocation. In this case, the market demand curve (D_a in Part B of Figure 5.6) does not reflect all of the benefits that are present, because some of the benefits flow to people who are directly involved in taking the economic action. The true social demand curve that reflects all of the benefits is $D_a + X$, where X represents the value of the external benefits to those who are receiving the positive externality. Expansion of output beyond Q_a to Q_i would result in a net gain to society equal to the salmon triangle. Thus when positive externalities are present, the market provides too little of the good.

Many foreign nations have taken advantage of the technological gains made by the United States since World War II. Until 1987 Korea, for example, did not recognize U.S. copyrights and patents. In other areas of the Far East, U.S. copyrights and patents are recognized but are ignored in practice. Publishers there feel free to reproduce U.S. books, microchips, and even Levi jeans without paying the U.S. owners for the right to do so. Thus U.S. publishers did not capture all the benefits of their publications, nor did U.S. microchip manufacturers receive all of the benefits of their research, nor did Levi jeans manufacturers garner all of the benefits of their copyrights. The result was fewer books published, fewer high-technology products developed, and fewer jeans produced in the United States than would have been the case had our producers been able to capture all of the social benefits that their efforts created.

Consider the case of French *haute couture*. In the past, Paris was the center of high fashion for women's clothing. The major fashion houses would stage shows twice a year to exhibit their new collections. Some persons with photographic minds and a talent for sketching made their livelihood by attending these shows and later selling their sketches to clothing manufacturers, who were able, in a matter of days, to offer copies, called *knock-offs*, for sale at much lower prices. As a result, the major fashion houses were always fewer in number and never as profitable as they would have been had they been able to capture all the benefits they created with their designs.

The development of new technology, so necessary if the United States is to maintain a high standard of living, can be seriously handicapped if

FIGURE 5.7
Unemployment, Inefficiency, and Economic Growth

Part A—The effects of unemployment, inefficiency, and unexpected price level changes: The production possibilities frontier (PPF) shows the maximum possible combinations of the output of two goods, Good Y and Good X, that can be produced given the available resources and technology. When the economy is operating inside this frontier (as at point U) because monopoly is present or externalities exist, it is not making the most efficient use of the available resources. By improving efficiency, the economy could operate anywhere between points A and B on PPF₁. The possibility of obtaining more goods when the economy is operating at point U creates a demand for government action.

Part B—The benefits of economic growth: Suppose the economy is operating efficiently at point A on PPF₁. Economic growth is represented by a shift of the production possibilities frontier to the right from PPF₁ to PPF₂. When this happens, the economy can have more of both goods by operating somewhere between points B and C on PPF₂. The economy gains when economic growth occurs, and this gain in turn generates demand for government policies that foster economic growth.

(A) The Effects of Unemployment, Inefficiency, and Unexpected Price Level Changes

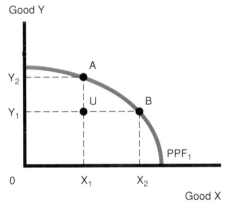

(B) The Benefits of Economic Growth

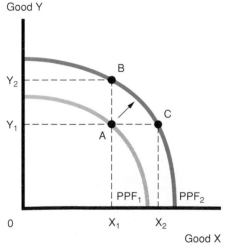

the new knowledge cannot be legally protected. A company is not likely to go to the expense of researching and developing new products and processes if its rivals can freely copy the innovations. The firm would simply have created a positive externality for its rivals to profitably exploit. Thus the incentive for firms to invest in research and development is either reduced or eliminated. Recognizing this possibility, most governments allow innovating firms to patent or copyright new technology to ensure that they alone will gain from their efforts.

Competitive markets fail to allocate resources efficiently when externalities are present. A market tends to underproduce when positive externalities exist and to overproduce when negative externalities exist. The presence of externalities often leads to a demand for government action. Negative externalities are the reason for the environmental legislation of the 1960s and 1970s. Positive externalities are the reason for the existence of patent and copyright laws and the recent changes that have taken place in them.

The production possibilities frontier, first introduced in Chapter 1, can be used to summarize the losses to the economy that result from either a lack of competition or the presence of externalities. When an economy operates inside the production possibilities frontier, it is wasting scarce resources. This waste is shown in Part A of Figure 5.7 as operating at point U. It is possible, if the economy could allocate its resources more efficiently, to have more of one good without sacrificing any of the second good. If it could eliminate waste, the economy could have the same amount of Good X (X_1) and more of Good Y (Y_2 instead of Y_1), or the same amount of Good Y (Y_1) and more of Good X (X_2 instead of X_1), or some combination of more of both goods, such as any of the points between A and B on the production possibilities frontier. If an economy is operating inefficiently either because of the monopoly problem or because of externalities, it will be operating inside the production possibilities frontier.

MACROECONOMIC FLUCTUATIONS   Historically, all economic systems have been subject to fluctuations in the level of economic activity. Economic recession and recovery seem to follow a cyclical path over time. During these fluctuations, the level of unemployment falls, rises, and then falls again, the rate of economic growth is at times positive and at other times negative, and the price level increases and sometimes even declines. The only constant, it seems, is change. The study of the overall economy is called **macroeconomics.**

> *Macroeconomics is the study of the economy as a whole. It is concerned with the aggregate level of employment, economic growth, and the price level.*

A fluctuating economy greatly complicates the task of economic decision makers.

If the economy is to obtain the greatest benefits from its scarce resources, it must fully employ those resources. If an economy suffers from unemployment resulting from macroeconomic instability, it will operate inside the production possibilities frontier. Unemployment can result when the overall demand for the economy's goods is insufficient to employ all the factors of production, including labor. When unemployment occurs, there will be a strong demand for the government to act to remedy the situation.

Similarly, if the market system is to function well, a stable price level is desirable. Business decisions relating to investment in new plants and capital goods as well as personal investment decisions are influenced by the decision makers' perceptions of the future price level of the output of the economy. Whether to buy a new house or car may well be contingent on the individual's perception about future prices. An unstable price level increases the uncertainty involved in making exchanges that unfold in the future. The effect of unexpected changes in the price level is a less efficient market system because some resources are wasted. When the price level becomes unpredictably unstable, the economy will operate inside the production possibilities frontier, as at point U in Part A of Figure 5.7.

Another macroeconomic problem, in addition to a fluctuating economy, is the rate of economic growth. Economic growth allows an economy to expand its production capabilities. Economic growth occurs in response to an improvement in technology that allows more goods and services to be produced from an existing amount of resources. Or it may occur in response to an increase in the availability of resources.

In Part B of Figure 5.7 when economic growth occurs, the production possibilities frontier shifts out. An economy operating at point A prior to economic growth can, when economic growth occurs, have more goods and services than before. Economic growth expands the production possibilities frontier from PPF_1 to PPF_2. By operating at some point between points B and C, the economy can have more of both goods than it could have had without economic growth.

The policies of government exert a powerful influence on the level of economic activity. Properly conducted and coordinated, these policies can contribute to economic stability and growth by encouraging price stability and the full and efficient utilization of resources. Problems that develop within the macroeconomic economy can give impetus to the demand for government action.

Finally, the distribution of income can be a source of demand for government action.

SOCIALLY UNACCEPTABLE DISTRIBUTION OF INCOME In a market-based economy, the distribution of income is determined by the exchange of resources. The incomes of individuals are determined by what they receive from others. The prices of the factors of production, the extent of individuals' resources, and the choices made by individuals in employing their resources will determine their income. Since the abilities, opportunities, luck, inheritances, and preferences of individuals differ, there will inevitably be an unequal distribution of income.

The distribution of income that results from a free-market system may not be acceptable to the society. Individuals acting alone cannot affect the distribution of income significantly. Even the richest person in an economy cannot give away enough wealth to alter the distribution of income appreciably. But collective action can make a difference. Government has the power to alter the distribution of income, and it is called on frequently to do so.

The prisoner's dilemma demonstrates why voluntary actions by individuals are unlikely to solve a problem with the distribution of income. The reasoning is the same as for the problem of why national defense cannot be obtained by voluntary contributions. Even if everyone agreed that the existing distribution of income is socially unacceptable, it is unlikely to be changed if left to individual action. If everyone above a certain income level agreed to contribute, the problem would be solved, but the contribution of a person acting alone would be too small to make much difference. Thus we have the classic free-rider problem. Most individuals, while hoping that everyone else will contribute, will decide to opt out of giving. The result is that only a few give, and the distribution of income remains unacceptably unequal. If the distribution of income is to be significantly changed, it will require collective, not voluntary, action.

The inequitable distribution of income is a consistent source of demand for government action. One solution is to compel giving by using the powers of the government to tax and redistribute income. Over half of the federal government's budget is currently devoted to redistributing income.

We began our discussion of the role of government with a consideration of pure public goods. For the market system to operate efficiently, it is necessary for certain pure public goods to be produced: Private-property rights must exist for efficient exchanges to occur, the society must be defended, and a money supply must be available. The private sector either will not produce pure public goods at all or it will not produce them in sufficient amounts.

Moreover, the market system will fail to allocate resources efficiently if there is a lack of competition, or if externalities exist, or if macroeconomic fluctuations occur. Finally, the distribution of income that results from a free market may be unacceptable to the society. Each of these sources of inefficiency or social dissatisfaction may be a source of the demand for public-sector action providing the possibility for society to gain from government intervention.

THE ECONOMICS OF COLLECTIVE DECISION MAKING

Collective action through government is an alternative to allocating resources by means of the market. By responding to the demand for collective action in a free-enterprise economy, the visible hand of government can improve the performance of the economy. Government action can be the source of economic gains when the action corrects the shortcomings of the market process.

Government action can (1) directly produce or cause to be produced both private and public goods, (2) create new or different property rights, (3) regulate economic behavior, and (4) employ its powers to create money and to tax and spend in ways that promote the general welfare.

GOVERNMENT-DIRECTED PRODUCTION

The government can either undertake directly the production of pure public goods, such as the national defense, the legal system, and the provision of police protection, or it can pay the private sector to produce the pure public goods, paying for these services with compulsory taxes. In this way the free-rider problem that hobbles the market system's provision of such goods can be overcome.

COMMON PROPERTY

Sometimes incomplete or inappropriately specified property rights can cause a problem that requires government action. Steel factories and chemical plants, for example, exhausted refuse into the environment until the 1960s, because everyone had the right to use the atmosphere and waterways in any way they chose. The natural environment was held as **common property:**

> *Common property is property that belongs to all citizens. All have the right to use such property resources in any way they see fit. No one can be excluded from enjoying a common-property resource.*

Since no one can be excluded from using a common-property resource, no market can ration its use. A resource cannot be sold to a person who already has the right to use it. Thus there is no incentive to supply the resource or to conserve on its use. A steel plant, for example, pays the opportunity costs of all the resources it acquires in markets, but it fails to pay the costs of disposing of its waste products because it has the right to use the environment in any way it chooses. Since no market exists to ration the use of the scarce environment, no market price is available to guide economic decision making.

Common-property rights work fine until the demand for the resource becomes too great. With population growth and economic development has come a significant increase in environmental utilization and a consequent decline in environmental quality from overuse.

The lack of private ownership of environmental resources, therefore, lies at the heart of most environmental problems. The solution to these problems could require a change in property rights. Common-property resources that have become scarce could be converted to private property, in which case a market would develop to exchange the resource as owners seek the most profitable use. If a common-property resource is converted to private property, a competitive market would ensure its efficient utilization. Changing the nature of property rights, however, is not always technically possible or politically feasible.

REGULATION

When common-property resources are overused, the government has another alternative. It can use its legal power to coerce individuals into altering the behavior that creates the problem. Laws can be passed and penalties imposed for disobedience. When monopoly exists, antitrust laws can be passed and enforced. When pollution becomes a problem, government can impose regulations governing the use of the resource that is being overutilized.

COUNTERCYCLICAL ACTIVITIES

The power of the government to create money and to spend and tax can be employed to stabilize the macroeconomic economy. The size of the federal government makes it an important participant in the national economy. Besides directing the production of social capital (such as roads, dams, and public buildings) and providing social services (such as public health, education, and law enforcement), government spending also plays an important role in the macroeconomic economy. The very size of the government makes it a potentially stabilizing force in the economy.

Should the economy fall into recession, an increase in the quantity of money and the level of government expenditures can help revive the economy. The power to tax can be used in a similar way. A tax reduction during a recession will, by increasing the average consumer's spendable income, also help the economy to revive. The tax system can also be employed to alter economic behavior. Taxes can be used to encourage or discourage specific activities. Consumption, savings, and investment can be encouraged or discouraged by the way taxes are levied.

The ways taxes are imposed can also influence the distribution of income. Any tax system can be used to favor or penalize specific groups. If the distribution of income is considered to be too unequal, the richest taxpayers can be forced to pay more taxes and the poorer ones less or none.

The power of government to define and enforce property rights, to regulate, and to spend and tax provides it with powerful weapons to correct the problems that are created when the invisible hand fails. When the market fails to allocate resources efficiently, there is the possibility of gaining from government action. If collective action can be employed to solve these problems, then there can be a net gain from public policy.

Although collective, or public-sector, action can be used to improve economic efficiency, collective action can itself be a source of inefficiency. Collective activity is simply an alternative form of economic organization and cannot escape the constraints imposed by scarcity. Public-sector actions, like market-directed activities, will always be the product of competition, will be required to ration scarce goods, and will discriminate in some fashion.

Collective action is undertaken by individuals who understand their own best interests. Self-interest is an important motivator in the marketplace, and it is also a powerful motivator in making collective decisions. If market decisions are influenced by changes in perceived self-interest, so too are the decisions made by the public sector.

THE MARKET VERSUS COLLECTIVE ACTION

There are both similarities and differences between decision making in the market and collective decision making.

SIMILARITIES BETWEEN THE PRIVATE AND PUBLIC SECTORS

The motivations of all decision makers, both private and public, are similar, and all decision makers are constrained by the existence of scarcity. The law of scarcity imposes constraints on the public sector similar to those it places on the private sector. The production of both public and private goods incurs opportunity costs. If more public goods are produced, fewer private goods will be available. Producing more public goods means higher taxes, now or in the future, and less disposable income for consumers to spend on private goods. The link between consumption and payment cannot be broken at the aggregate level. If scarcity exists, more public goods can be acquired only by having fewer private goods.

Nor is competition absent. There can never be enough political goods. Politicians compete for votes by offering government programs. Bureaucrats compete for larger budgets and for promotions. In their quest to obtain favorable legislation, special-interest groups compete for the attention of elected officials by offering contributions and votes. The problem of rationing political goods cannot be avoided. Where there is rationing, discrimination necessarily will exist. Some persons will receive more than others.

DIFFERENCES BETWEEN THE PRIVATE AND PUBLIC SECTORS

The differences in the ways that private-sector and public-sector goods are supplied are found in the nature of the consumption/payment link, in the nature of the goods themselves, in the way decision-making abilities are distributed, and in the use of dollars versus votes. An examination of these differences leads to an understanding of why citizens are always somewhat dissatisfied with their government.

THE INDIVIDUAL CONSUMPTION/PAYMENT LINK A consumer wishing to purchase a private good, such as an apple, must be willing to pay the price. Acquiring an apple requires that it be paid for and requires the direct sacrifice of what could have been obtained instead. A direct link between consumption and payment exists. The person consuming the good typically is the person paying for the good.

Things are different for politically supplied goods. Once the government produces a pure public good, by the very nature of that good it is available to all persons without regard to the amount of taxes those individuals pay. Your tax bill will be the same whether or not your children attend a public school, whether or not you sue in small-claims court, visit a public park, attend government-subsidized cultural events, grow hops or wheat that benefit from government agricultural programs, receive social security benefits, or take out a federal student loan. You will be taxed to support such programs whether you use them or not. For most politically supplied goods, the individual consumption/payment link is broken.

The severed link between consumption and payment explains a paradox that has often baffled public pollsters. When people are asked whether total federal spending should be reduced, more than two-thirds respond in the affirmative. But when the same people are asked whether government spending should be reduced for particular programs, such as health care, education, social security, student loans, or national defense, a majority answer no. A contradiction thus exists, for while individuals believe that total government spending is too great, they do not believe that spending for particular programs is excessive. This presents politicians with a dilemma: They cannot cut total federal spending without cutting spending on individual programs.

This paradox can be understood by considering the implications of breaking the individual's consumption/payment link for politically supplied goods. In Figure 5.8, if each individual had to pay for each government program directly, he or she would demand the quantity Q and pay price P. These amounts are determined by the equilibrium point E, which

FIGURE 5.8
Demand for Publicly Produced Goods When the Individual Consumption/Payment Link Has Been Severed

If each individual had to pay directly for the goods and services provided by the government, equilibrium would occur at point E, the price would be P, and the quantity provided would be Q. At Q the marginal cost of producing the last unit is just equal to the marginal benefit or value of the good to the consumer-citizen. The total expenditure on these goods is shown by rectangle PEQ0.

When the government produces goods that are available to all and raises the necessary funds by taxation, the consumption/payment link is broken. The amount of taxes an individual pays will be the same whether the individual consumes a little or a lot of government-supplied goods. The effective price of such goods to the consumer becomes zero and the consumer responds by demanding the amount Q_a, where the marginal benefit is zero. The government responds by supplying Q_a. The marginal cost of supplying Q_a instead of Q increases to point A and the total expenditure on government-provided goods increases to rectangle P_aAQ_a0. Too many government-supplied goods are provided, because the marginal benefit of Q_a is less than the marginal cost. Thus a waste equal to triangle AEE_a is generated. When the consumption/payment link is broken, as in the case of many government-supplied goods and services, the result will be that too many publicly provided goods will be supplied.

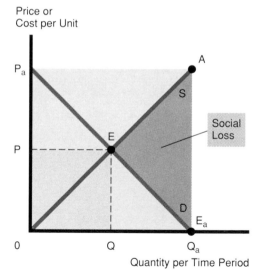

Price or
Cost per Unit

is established where the demand curve intersects the supply curve. The total expenditure on the quantity Q is equal to the rectangle PEQ0.

Because individuals do not pay directly for most publicly produced goods, the amount of these goods consumed is independent of the cost of producing them. The price that individuals pay for each publicly produced good or service is essentially zero, since whether they consume them or not, their taxes remain the same. Each person responds to a zero price by publicly demanding Q_a, where the marginal benefit or value is equal to zero.

If the government responds fully to voters' demands, it will offer Q_a of the good, which will cost P_a to produce. The total expenditure on the quantity Q_a is equal to P_aAQ_a0, shown as the entire shaded area. Part of this area is waste, because the marginal cost exceeds the marginal benefit. This is the case for all of the units produced beyond Q. Thus the triangle AEE_a is waste.

This result occurs because the individual consumption/payment link has been broken. Since voters do not directly pay for the benefits they receive, they rationally view the individual political good as having a cost of zero to them. But the cost to society is not zero but is equal to P_a. When voters consider the total tax bill, they are of a different mind. Voters respond to the total cost by rightly considering it too high for the total benefits they receive. The paradox of public polls is thus clarified.

Combining the polling paradox with the prisoner's dilemma yields yet another paradox. The prisoner's dilemma suggests that if provision for public goods were left to the market, too few would be produced. The collective response is to let government provide such goods as well as some private goods. In the process of the government's supplying these political goods, the consumption/payment link is broken. The severing of the consumption/payment link suggests in turn that when left to the political process, too many political goods will be supplied. It appears that the choice may be between either too few or too many political goods.

INDIVIDUAL PRODUCTS VERSUS A BUNDLE OF COLLECTIVE GOODS When you go to a grocery store, you can choose from among thousands of products the ones you desire most. Every person in the store takes advantage of this opportunity. If you examine individual shopping carts at the checkout counter, you will quickly discover that no two baskets contain exactly the same items. The private sector allows individuals to select from a wide variety of goods and services the precise bundle of goods that they want most, given the market price that must be paid for each item and the incomes consumers have to spend.

In the political arena, the choice is much more limited. In a representative government, each voter votes for one official who in turn, along with other elected officials, will be called on to select for you the bundle of political goods that you will receive. You cannot choose the defense policy of one candidate, the social programs of another, and the foreign policy of a third, if indeed there is a third candidate. Instead, you must select the candidate whose positions on all the issues combined are closest to your own. It is unlikely that the candidate's views will match precisely your own views.

The bundling of political goods explains in part why most people are somewhat dissatisfied with government. It is very unlikely that any candidate will precisely reflect a voter's views on everything.

DISTRIBUTION OF DECISION-MAKING ABILITIES The ability to influence decision making differs between the public and private sectors. The answers to the *what, how,* and *for whom* questions that every economy must ask will be different depending on whether the decisions are made privately or publicly. In the private sector, goods will go to the person who is willing to pay the most for them. Whether or not a specific good will be produced depends on whether there are enough dollar votes to pay the opportunity costs of the resources required to produce the good. Who will obtain the goods that are produced depends on who is willing to cast the most dollar votes. The number of dollar votes an individual possesses is a function of the distribution of income, which in turn depends on the individual's abilities, skills, willingness to work, past savings, inheritances, and luck. As we have seen, an unequal distribution of dollar votes is certain to occur as a consequence of an uneven distribution of income.

In the U.S. political arena, each citizen has one vote. In theory, the decision-making power is much more equally distributed in the public sector than it is in the private sector. In practice, however, everyone does not have equal access to political goods. The political process will favor those persons who have the ability to organize and deliver a block of votes. Such persons will inevitably have more decision-making power than the single, nonaligned voters.

DOLLARS VERSUS VOTES In the market for private goods, consumers employ their dollar votes to demand goods and services. Producers respond to the demands of consumers in order to obtain those dollar votes. The actions of both consumers and producers are directed by self-interest. In our political system, voters are the counterparts of consumers, and politicians the counterparts of producers. Voters employ their votes, contributions, and organizing abilities to demand political goods. Politicians respond by supplying these goods to the groups that helped get them elected. Voters are interested in obtaining the bundle of political goods they desire at the lowest possible vote cost, and politicians are interested in supplying enough political goods to ensure job security.

Voters tend to support political candidates who reflect their vision of what society should be. Included in the voters' vision are the political benefits they will receive balanced against the personal cost of achieving those benefits. Other things being equal, voters tend to support candidates who they expect to deliver the largest net personal benefits to them. The greater the expected gains from a candidate's election, the more voters will do to support that candidate's election. Politicians thus have an incentive to cater to politically active voters.

Unfortunately, as in free-market decision making, there is nothing to guarantee that the distribution of income resulting from the political process will itself be socially desirable. After all, individual self-interest is not absent from the political area. The power of government can be used to further individual or group interests as well as the interests of the general public. Sometimes the goal of a group is to obtain direct income transfers; sometimes it is a price support, a government guarantee of a loan, a monopoly, or a tax break or preference. It would be surprising if the distribution of income resulting from the tug and pull of politics is the one that the body politic collectively desires.

WHY GOVERNMENT ACTION MIGHT FAIL

The public sector, as well as the market, has inherent weaknesses that may lead to failure on its part. These weaknesses are: (1) the rational ignorance of voters, (2) the efforts of special-interest groups, (3) the shortsighted effect, and (4) the lack of incentives to perform efficiently.

THE RATIONALLY IGNORANT VOTER

Can you name your state's two senators and the congressional representative for your district? If you can't, you are in good company. Neither can a majority of voters. Did you vote in the last general election? Approximately half of all eligible voters did not. These lamentable facts are the result of **rational ignorance** on the part of voters.

> *The rational ignorance of voters arises from the lack of incentives for individual voters to become informed and to participate in public affairs.*

It simply doesn't pay for the average voter to be fully informed on political issues.

The lack of incentives to fully participate in the political arena derives directly from the nature of representative government. Numerous voters elect a few representatives. Given this situation, it is unlikely that the vote of a specific individual will be decisive. The outcome of the election will be the same whether a specific person votes or not. Moreover, it is not costless to vote. Time and transportation costs are involved. Voting for a candidate becomes more an act of patriotism than participation in a decision-making process.

Nor does the individual voter have much of an incentive to be informed on political issues or on differences between rival candidates. Since the opinions and decisions of one individual are not likely to be decisive, no individual has an incentive other than personal curiosity to be well-informed on political issues.

Since information is costly and the individual voter has little incentive to bear this cost, the burden of informing voters falls on candidates, political parties, and the media. Voters acquire information through newspaper stories, news broadcasts, the endorsements of political figures and newspaper editors, the opinions of friends, and political advertising — seldom from serious research into the issues. The voter has little incentive to spend time gathering information.

Contrast the little effort individuals expend becoming well-informed on political decisions with the effort they expend on making a major purchase. Would you be surprised to learn that almost all people can identify the make of automobile they own or plan to buy? It pays to investigate the qualities of the automobiles available prior to making a purchase. Unlike in the political arena, the choice of a particular make of automobile will be decisive. If you decide to buy a Chevrolet, it is a Chevrolet you will get. In the political arena you will get the winner of the election, who will be the same person whether or not you voted.

Because voters do not have much incentive to acquire adequate information to make rational political decisions, they may not make wise choices. This possible defect is at least partially overcome by competition between rival candidates and political parties, but a poorly informed electorate makes possible the special-interest effect.

SPECIAL-INTEREST GROUPS — THE PASSIONATE MINORITY

A **special-interest group** exists when a small group of voters has a large stake in a political outcome that is of only minor consequence to most voters. The special interest binds these voters together as they select candidates solely on the basis of their views on a single issue. Every political party and candidate has an incentive to listen to special-interest groups.

> *A special-interest group is one in which a minority of voters have a large stake in a particular political outcome. Members of this group stand to gain substantially if their position is adopted. Conversely, the majority of voters neither gain nor lose much if the special interest predominates.*

Sometimes special-interest groups are called a *passionate minority*, because the members of such groups will decide which candidate to support on the basis of one narrow issue alone.

Politicians who must win elections are attracted to special-interest groups. Special-interest groups have an incentive to vote and to make financial contributions to candidates who support their cause. Because elections in the United States are generally close, attaining the support of a passionate minority may make the difference between winning and losing for a candidate.

Supporting a special-interest group may even be costless to a politician in terms of votes lost, even if allowing the special-interest group to dominate imposes costs on all other voters. As long as the costs are small and widely dispersed, most voters will remain uninformed about the effects and not care very much about the issue. If a politician resists the special-interest group, he or she will surely lose its support without gaining appreciable support in return from the majority who care little about the issue.

Consider the case of agricultural price supports that keep the price of many food products above the free-market price. These supports harm a majority of Americans, who must pay both higher prices for food and higher taxes to finance the support programs. The losses to society as a whole are not trivial, running into many billions of dollars, but the cost per family is fairly small. The benefits of price-support programs are concentrated among farmers, who make up only a small minority of Americans. Price supports are vital to maintaining the farmers' standard of living, and they act accordingly. Farmers as a group will turn against any candidate who opposes a price-support program and will support with votes and contributions candidates who promise to promote price-support programs.

When the political process upholds the interests of passionate minorities even when their goals are costly to society as a whole, government itself becomes a source of inefficiency in the market. The special-interest effect explains many of the actions of government that economists view as inefficient: farm programs, rent controls, and protectionist international trade legislation. These policies may not be good for the country, but they are good for special-interest groups — and good for the politicians they support.

SHORTSIGHTED EFFECT

Because voters have so little incentive to be well-informed on political issues, they often make judgments about candidates on the basis of the current state of affairs. Politicians respond to this tendency by favoring programs that have immediate benefits and low current costs. Programs that have immediate costs and future benefits are slighted. This tendency narrows the planning horizon of government to the period before the next election. Economists call this inherent bias the **shortsighted effect:**

> *The shortsighted effect is the tendency for government to favor actions having immediate benefits and future costs and to neglect actions having immediate costs and future benefits.*

Long-term solutions to problems that impose costs on today's voters tend to be rejected in favor of patchwork solutions that have low current costs. If things go wrong after the next election, a politician is better off being in office trying to correct the situation than out of office saying "I told you so."

The shortsighted effect can explain why the nation's highways, bridges, dams, canals, and locks are falling into disrepair. The gain from maintaining these structures accrues slowly over time, but the costs of maintaining them must be paid today. The political benefits were accrued earlier, and the costs are occurring now. For the same reason, education and public health are underfunded.

OPERATIONAL INEFFICIENCY

Government bashing is a popular spectator sport. No one associates the words *government* and *bureaucrat* with efficiency. Cost overruns, boondoggles, pork barrels, waste, and mismanagement are more likely associations. There is some truth in these associations, not because politicians and bureaucrats are not well-meaning and hard-working but because of the incentives they face.

In the private sector, wasteful and inefficient actions are penalized by a loss of profits, or by a loss of jobs, or even by bankruptcy. Efficiency is rewarded with profits, promotions, and higher salaries. Nothing similar occurs in the public sector. When inefficiency occurs in the public sector, the burden falls not on the decision maker, as it does in the private sector, but upon the taxpayer. Conversely, any saving achieved by a bureaucrat is not a personal benefit but accrues to the taxpayer. A business person who achieves cost reductions will be rewarded by a bigger bank account. A bureaucrat who accomplishes the same thing will have shown that less money was actually needed all along and is likely to be penalized by having the department's budget reduced.

The incentive for efficient behavior on the part of government officials is further reduced by the lack of any means of judging efficiency. The market test is absent. In the private sector, inefficiency brings immediate penalties — reduced profits or losses and the threat of bankruptcy. In the public sector, no such test exists. In the private sector, decision makers are risking their own or their stockholders' money, with those involved taking a keen interest in the results. In the public sector, politicians and bureaucrats are risking the taxpayers' money, but even disgruntled individual taxpayers have little incentive to closely monitor government expenditures.

Increasingly, the lack of incentives for the public sector to attain operational efficiency is being recognized. One of the ways to address the problem is to privatize government operations. Municipal services, such as garbage collection and fire protection, can be contracted out to the private sector, with the government providing the funds for private firms to produce the public goods. In Great Britain and France, many of the industries that had in the past been nationalized have recently been returned to private ownership.

When market failure occurs, collective action by the government may correct the defect, but the government itself suffers from defects that can lead to failure. Voter ignorance, special-interest groups, the shortsighted effect, and the lack of incentives to perform efficiently may lead to collective actions that make the economy less efficient in dealing with the scarcity problem.

SUMMARY

1. Economic efficiency occurs when the economy is obtaining the most output possible from a given quantity of resources. This efficiency is achieved when all possible profitable trades have been made, and the gains from trade are maximized.

2. To attain economic efficiency in the private sector, human and private property rights must be defined and enforced.

3. Pure public goods are goods that are not rivals in consumption, that are indivisible, and that nonpaying consumers cannot be easily excluded from using once the good has been produced.

4. The prisoner's dilemma demonstrates why a free market will not produce the optimal amount of pure public goods. Each citizen will have the incentive to act as a free rider when deciding to pay for a pure public good.

5. In addition to the inability of the free market to provide the optimal amount of pure public goods, the market will fail to allocate resources efficiently or acceptably if: (a) there is a lack of competition, (b) externalities are present, (c) there is macroeconomic instability, or (d) an unacceptable distribution of income results.

6. When market failure occurs, there is always the potential for collective action by government to correct it.

7. Collective action is a form of economic organization that is always an alternative to the market economy. Public-sector actions reflect the desires of voters and the competition among political candidates. Self-interest is the guiding principle in political decision making, as it is in private decision making.

8. Voters seek collective action (a) to correct market failures that lead to inefficiency and (b) to change the distribution of income.

9. The similarities between private decision making and collective action are: The law of scarcity applies to both, implying that the aggregate consumption/payment link cannot be broken, and competition exists in both sectors.

10. The differences between private decision making and collective action are: (a) The individual consumption/payment link can be broken in the public sector but not in the private sector. (b) Individuals are free to select from among individual goods the ones they wish to consume in the private sector, but in the public sector they must accept a bundle of goods

selected for them. (c) The ability to influence decision making is distributed differently between the two sectors. (d) Resources are allocated on the basis of dollar votes in the private sector and on the basis of political votes in the public sector.

11. The possibility that government collective action may fail to allocate resources efficiently arises from: (a) rational voter ignorance, (b) the existence of special-interest groups, (c) the shortsighted effect, and (d) the lack of incentives to operate efficiently.

PREVIEW 5.1 ANALYSIS

WHAT HAPPENS TO AN ECONOMY WHEN A GOVERNMENT COLLAPSES?

The functions of government are often taken for granted. The most important function of government is to define and protect human rights and private-property rights. The government of Lebanon has failed to perform this most basic function for more than a decade. The frequency of hostage taking and of random deaths from car bombs demonstrates that the most basic human rights are no longer protected there. If human rights are precarious in Lebanon, private-property rights hardly exist at all. The country has been divided by civil war into sections controlled by warring militias, with each militia governing the area under its control as it sees fit.

The civil war resulted from the unwillingness of the group in power to share that power with others. When the French left Lebanon in 1943, they established a National Pact that divided power among the various religious groups according to population. The National Pact spelled out that the president would be a Meronite Christian, the prime minister a Sunni Muslim, the speaker of parliament a Shia Muslim. The army would be commanded by a Meronite with a Druze as chief of staff. At every level of government, Christians and Muslims would be represented in a ratio of six to five. This arrangement fell apart because population growth changed the relative size of the various religious groups, with the Shias forging ahead of the rest.

The Shias demanded political power in proportion to their increased numbers, but their demands were resisted. In 1974 their leaders called for a giant political rally to protest. The civil war in Lebanon dates from this rally and has scarcely let up since. Violence rapidly became a way of life. Private militia armies were created by the various religious groups to support and defend their interests. These groups appealed successfully to foreign interests for military and financial support.

The Lebanese government, as a result, has all but ceased to function, and with it the Lebanese economy. The cabinet is so politically divided that it seldom meets, government officials of all religious persuasions have been frequently assassinated, and the national government has lost control of much of the country and of its main source of revenue — tariffs levied on imports. Local militias rule the country's half-dozen Mediterranean ports. The Lebanese eventually gave up on their own leadership as hopeless and turned to foreign governments — first Israel and then Syria — to maintain order. Neither succeeded in controlling the militias and warlords who govern local areas.

A modern economy based on specialization and trade cannot function unless human rights and private-property rights are secured by a viable government. Lebanon was once the financial and merchant capital of the Middle East. Both finance and trade, being incompatible with chaos and anarchy, quickly dissipated when law and order broke down. Tourism, once a major industry, quickly dried up for the same reason. The next economic casualty was industry, once a rapidly growing sector. Factories that initially continued to function frequently had their output hijacked, were subject to extortion by local warlords, or could not obtain needed supplies. Many factories were destroyed or abandoned because of the fighting. These factories were never rebuilt. As a consequence, almost no private or public investment has been made in Lebanon for more than a decade.

Photographs of Beirut reveal that buildings badly damaged in the civil war, like the nation's factories, remain unrepaired. Persons who were able left for other countries, taking with them as many of their assets as possible. Those unable to flee remained, trying to cope as best they could. The average wage earner survives only by holding two or more jobs, by selling off personal possessions, or by hiring out as a militia soldier, gangster, or smuggler. The main economic activities are producing and smuggling opium and hashish and taking and trading hostages.

The average monthly wage, when converted to dollars, amounts to less than $10. Everyone with Lebanese pounds has tried to convert them into U.S. dollars. The Lebanese pound that traded 2.3 to the U.S. dollar in 1975 traded 300 to the dollar in 1987. Traders have almost stopped taking the local currency altogether, insisting on foreign currency.

Inflation has ravaged the economy. The price of food doubled during the first half of 1987 and continued doubling every month during the last half of that year. The result has been mass protests that are related not to the issues of the civil war but to the prevailing incidence of hunger.

Food riots have occurred. Despite efforts to keep the price of fuel, flour, and bread artificially low through government subsidy, food is in short supply. Lebanon, once an exporter of agricultural products, now imports 75 percent of its food. Any farmer with a surplus quickly exports it to a neighboring country where it can be sold for a stable currency.

When a government dies, the economy dies with it. Governments are needed to define and protect human rights and private-property rights. When government fails to provide these basic functions, an economy based on specialization and exchange cannot exist. The example of Lebanon provides a sad illustration of the need for a stable, functioning government.[1]

---

[1]Sources for this analysis: *The Economist*, September 12–18, 1987, 44; and December 26–January 8, 1988, 64.

EDUCATION AT RISK

The American public school system is in trouble, under attack from both the right and the left of the political spectrum. Despite increases in the amount of public funds devoted to education, student achievement scores have not improved significantly and have even declined in many areas of the country. Parents complain that they have little input into the educational process of their children. More and more parents are sending their children to private schools or are even educating their children themselves at home. Many taxpayers complain that the public schools are needlessly expensive and that devoting more public money to schools has not resulted in better performance.

This dissatisfaction has arisen despite the fact that providing education is one of the primary functions of government. More public employees are employed in education than in any other government function, including national defense. Since the colonial period, the U.S. government has recognized that a literate, educated population is essential to the successful functioning of democracy. In colonial Massachusetts, for example, in order to qualify for a land grant to form a township, it was necessary for the colonists to provide both a church and a school. A population, it was thought, had to be literate in order to fully participate in religious and state activities.

Education has always provided benefits for the individual. Being able to read and write and do mathematics makes the individual more productive and allows him or her to earn higher wages. These private benefits will be expressed in the individual's demand for education. If the state did not provide public education, there still would be schools — but probably not enough of them, because education is believed by many to provide significant positive externalities.

The benefits to society that arise from making an individual better qualified to perform the role of a citizen in our democratic republic also make an individual a more productive worker in the economy. Other benefits of education take the form of greater participation in democracy and lower public costs for both welfare and the criminal justice system. These social benefits represent a positive externality that no single citizen can individually capture but that all citizens can collectively enjoy. Such external benefits will not be reflected in the individual's demand for education.

Since it represents society as a whole, the government is just as interested in securing these public benefits as it is in gaining the private benefits. The full range of public and private benefits, however, will not be enjoyed if the provision of education is left entirely to the private sector. In Figure 5.9 the private-sector demand curve is represented by D_a and the marginal cost of providing education is represented by the supply curve S. The equilibrium price and quantity of education, in the absence of intervention by the government, is determined by the intersection of the private demand curve and the supply curve at point E_a. The equilibrium price is P_a and the quantity consumed is Q_a.

The demand curve, D_a, does not represent all of the benefits provided by education, only the private benefits. In addition, there exist social benefits, which, since they accrue to everyone, will not be represented in the private demand for education. Suppose these positive externalities are of the amount X in the figure. If we add X to the private demand curve D_a, we obtain the social demand curve $D_a + X$. The optimal amount of education is determined where the supply curve S intersects the demand curve $D_a + X$ at point E_i, which establishes the optimal price P_i and quantity Q_i. It can readily be seen that when a positive externality is present, the market will produce too little of the good, Q_a in this case instead of Q_i. If the provision of education is left to the private sector alone, too little will be provided. The loss to society is equal to the salmon triangle. More education should be supplied than the private sector will voluntarily provide.

If the optimal amount of education is to be produced, the government will have to provide increased access to education. But increasing access does not imply that the state must actually supply the education by directly operating schools. Rather than operate the schools directly, the government could contract with the private sector in some way to supply education. The federal government requires airplanes and tanks for the national defense, but it does not itself manufacture either. Instead, it contracts with private companies to supply military hardware built to its specifications. As another example, the federal government provides veterans with educational benefits in the form of various GI bills. The education itself is not produced by the federal government. Instead, the government gives the veteran a voucher to spend at the college of his or her choice.

Nevertheless, government provides basic education in this country by operating schools. Most education, especially in the elementary and secondary grades, is provided at the local level and paid for out of property taxes. Most college education is provided by the individual states and paid for out of state tax revenues supplemented by tuition payments.

Although private schools exist at every level of education, they educate only a small, but growing, portion of the student population. Since they are not subsidized by the state, private schools are relatively more expensive for students and parents to utilize, thus ensuring that they will never become the major suppliers of education. The existence of private schools, however, provides a basis for comparing how well public schools are doing. Let us compare how the public schools at the elementary and secondary levels function relative to the country's private schools in order to obtain some idea of the difference between publicly supplied and privately supplied education.

Both public and private schools feel the constraint that scarcity places on the availability of resources. In the aggregate, the consumption/payment link cannot be broken. Private schools must attract enough students/parents willing to pay tuition and donors of private gifts to supply sufficient funds to cover the costs of production. The public schools must obtain sufficient revenues from the government to cover their costs — an activity that often requires a favorable vote by local residents. Scarcity always implies competition. Private schools compete for students who will pay; public schools compete for public funds.

Private schools compete by offering educational programs that will attract students and gifts. Public schools compete with the other functions of government for taxpayer funds. In the case of public schools, the competitive behavior generated by scarcity may not be the behavior desired by the consumers of education. Public schools are ultimately answerable to the taxpayer and to legislators, a wider group than the parents and students. Nonparent taxpayers have opinions about how schools should be operated that may be different from those of parent taxpayers.

Because there are positive externalities associated with education, individuals may seek less education than is socially optimal. To deal with this possibility, the government requires that each child obtain a mini-

FIGURE 5.9
Positive External Benefits Provided by Education

Education is widely considered to provide benefits to society as a whole in addition to the private benefits enjoyed by individuals. Thus education provides a positive externality, indicated by X, that is not reflected in the market demand curve, D_a. If the provision of education is left to the private sector, the quantity provided would be determined by the intersection of the supply curve, S, with the market demand curve, D_a. The equilibrium point will be at E_a, the equilibrium quantity would be Q_a and the market price would be P_a. The social demand curve, $D_a + X$, is composed of the market demand curve plus the positive externality X. The ideal equilibrium would be at E_i, where the supply curve, S, intersects the social demand curve, $D_a + X$, with Q_i produced at a price of P_i. If E_i is compared with E_a, it is clear that too little education (Q_a instead of Q_i) is provided by the private sector alone. The result of leaving the provision of education to the private sector would be a social loss, as shown by the shaded triangle.

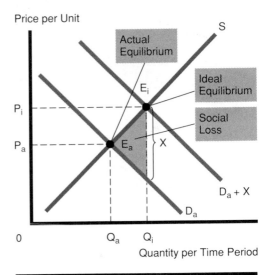

mum amount of education. Currently, a child must achieve at least an eighth-grade education or the age of 16 before leaving school.

The family of the student in a private school pays the tuition. The family will, accordingly, select from among the alternatives the school that offers the educational mix it is willing to purchase. The family thus has an incentive to search out the school that best meets its requirements. In the public schools, the student is assigned to a school and a teacher. The local public school has a monopoly on providing free education within its district. The student/parent must accept the mix that the public school offers. Because it is unlikely that the school will offer exactly the mix that the family desires, most families will be somewhat dissatisfied with public schooling.

The families with children in the public schools do not directly pay for their children's education. They pay as taxpayers and are joined in paying by families who do not have children in the public schools. Families with children look upon education as costing less than its true price, since any increase in cost is shared with taxpayers without school-age children. Parents with children in school therefore have an incentive to ask schools to take on more functions and to provide more education. Taxpayers without school-age children consider basic education to be needlessly expensive and often would like to have less of it provided. In practice, some compromise between the two views is struck, leaving neither group totally satisfied.

Thus the way public education is supplied in this country is bound to lead to dissatisfaction. In the case of public schools, this dissatisfaction is partially justified by the measured poor performance of public school children as revealed in the studies that led to the educational-reform movement. The poor performance is a reflection not of educators' lack of dedication to their professions, but of the kinds of incentives the system provides. Incentives are important in determining behavior, and in the case of politically supplied goods, few incentives exist for efficient behavior on the part of teachers and administrators.

Compare the incentives present in the private school with those present in the public school. The private school obtains most of its funds by offering educational services that will attract students who are willing to pay the necessary tuition. The public school receives its revenues on the basis of the number of students assigned to it. The private school administrator has ample incentive, therefore, to respond to the desires of parents; the public school administrator has much less incentive.

To attract students, the private school has the incentive to offer the educational programs that the families of school-age children desire. The public school has no such incentive. The professional administrator is free to offer any mix of educational programs he or she chooses, subject to the laws of the state and the approval of a volunteer school board. The approval of students and parents matters less than the administrator's opinion or the laws of the state.

The administrator of a private school has the incentive to manage the school's resources carefully. Any savings that are achieved can be applied to improving the educational programs or to reducing tuition, either of which will attract more students. The administrator of a public school who achieves savings or manages efficiently is likely to be rewarded by a reduction in next year's budget.

What is true for administrators is also true for teachers. Teachers are paid according to their years of experience and academic attainments, and not according to the performance of their pupils. The way to a higher salary, if you are a teacher, is not to work to improve the skills of your students, but to improve your own skills, by obtaining a master's degree, for example, and surviving for a few more years in the classroom.

In fact, the level of education and the experience of teachers do not seem to be related to the performance of students, as measured by achievement tests. Public school teachers are more or less free to follow their preferences in the classroom. They may choose, without penalty, to devote less attention to reading, writing, and arithmetic and more time to discipline, socialization, ethics, and good citizenship. Or teachers may "baby-sit" the students until it is time to go home. Choosing more leisure has no cost in terms of salary or promotion.

Administrators of private schools have an incentive to monitor the performance of their teachers, because a lack of achievement on the part of the students is likely to lead to a loss of students and tuition revenues. Public school administrators have no such incentive. The students belong to the schools until they either graduate or reach the age of 16. In fact, poor performance may lead to increased, not decreased, budgets as politicians try to win elections by being known as supporters of education.

All teachers do not behave irresponsibly, of course. There are many public school teachers who make a real difference and who are dedicated to their students, but these teachers are rewarded no differently from the teachers who shirk. Good teaching in a public school is an act of charity on the part of dedicated teachers. If good teaching were rewarded and poor performance penalized, there would be more good teaching.

How can parents or taxpayers influence the behavior of public school teachers and administrators in ways that would increase their satisfaction with public schools? One policy would be to pay teachers and administrators according to their output as measured by achievement tests, peer reviews, or some other evaluation system, instead of by educational attainments and seniority. Such a policy would provide the incentive for teachers to expend the effort to teach the basic skills required in modern society.

A second possible policy would be to increase the family's range of choice of schools by reducing the size of school districts to increase the number of different schools available and by allowing families to choose which public school their children will attend. In such a system, each student would be given a voucher to spend at the government-certified school of the family's choice, thereby restoring the individual consumption/payment link. Schools would then have to compete to attract students. Those that were successful would benefit from increased revenues, and those that were unsuccessful would have an incentive to change. A test of performance would exist. Good schools would attract students; poorer schools would lose students. The results would be there for all to see. Public schools would then have a set of incentives much the same as exists today for private schools.

The poor performance of our public school system may be more the result of the way we have chosen to supply education than of a lack of resources. We have selected a method that creates the incentive for students, teachers, and administrators to fail. Reforming public education may not require more money but rather a change in incentives.[2]

---

[2] Sources for this analysis: *The Economist*, October 31, 1987, 19–22; Dwight R. Lee, "An Alternative to the Public School: Educational Vouchers," *Current*, October 1986, 26–31; Norman Macrae, "What Works in Education: Competition and Schooling," *Current*, February 1987, 15–21; Lawrence A. Uzzell, "More Money Isn't Buying Better Schools," *The Wall Street Journal*, November 3, 1987, 31.

REQUIRED ECONOMIC CONCEPTS

Mixed economy   Macroeconomics
Private-property rights   Common property
Private good   Rational ignorance
Pure public good   Special-interest group
Political good   Shortsighted effect
Prisoner's dilemma
Free rider
Monopoly problem
Externalities
Negative externality
Positive externality

KEY QUESTIONS

1. What is a government?
2. What are private-property rights? Who creates and grants them?
3. What is the difference between a private good, a public good, and a political (publicly provided) good?
4. What is a free rider?
5. What are positive and negative externalities?
6. What is a common-property resource? Is the ocean a common-property resource?
7. How can markets fail to allocate resources efficiently?
8. How does the consumption/payment link or its lack affect the allocation of scarce resources?
9. What four factors can cause government to fail to efficiently allocate resources?
10. How does rational ignorance lead to uninformed voters and low voter turnout at elections?
11. How is the status of public education in the United States related to the consumption/payment link?

PROBLEMS

1.   You may have observed that some books in your college library have been underlined, highlighted, scribbled in, or otherwise deliberately abused. Can you give a reason for this that is consistent with the concepts of this chapter?
2.   Why does the FCC (Federal Communications Commission) license radio stations and assign them frequencies? In the early days of radio this was not done. Why do you think the policy was changed? Is your TV set a public or private good? What about the program you are watching on your TV set? Would you say that most goods are mixed goods — a combination of private and public goods? Explain.
3.   Which of the following fit or nearly fit the definition of a politically (publicly) provided good? Also indicate whether each is a private, public, or mixed good (i.e., a combination of private and public goods).
   a.   National defense
   b.   A polio vaccination

    c.   A book on a city library shelf

    d.   An F-16 jet fighter plane

    e.   A lighthouse

4.   Given the free-rider effect, answer the following:

    a.   Explain why a voter would understate his or her preference for a political (or publicly provided) good rather than reveal his or her true preference for it.

    b.   Explain why a voter would overstate his or her preference for a political good rather than reveal his or her true preference for it. (*Hint:* Consider who pays for the good and who receives the benefits.)

5.   If an instructor of a small class grades on a curve, is there an externality imposed on others by the best student? By the worst student? Explain. Also, if the class is half-filled, what is the marginal cost to the college of an unregistered person sitting in on the class? What is the marginal cost if the class is completely filled with registered students?

6.   Aside from the contributions they make to politicians, why are lobbies and special-interest groups often so influential in Congress?

7.   Should we conclude from the chapter discussion that the average citizen is lazy and that is why voters have little knowledge about the issues and why voter turnout is usually low? Can you use the concept of opportunity cost in formulating your answer? Do you believe that voter turnout would be higher if elections were held on Sundays instead of Tuesdays? Why or why not?

8.   The farm lobby is one of the most powerful lobbies in the domain of Congress. Why do you think this is so? How has the traditional farm policy of the U.S. government affected consumers? How has it affected taxpayers? Is low-income homesteading for farmers different in kind from low-income housing subsidies for the poor? Can you argue that one group is on welfare and the other is not because society benefits much more from farm subsidies than from housing subsidies? What arguments can you give to support your position? (*Hint:* Think in terms of benefits, costs, and externalities.) What are farmers maximizing? What are politicians maximizing?

APPLICATION ANALYSIS

1.   The discussion on education in this chapter does not mention the cultural and social problems that today's students bring to the schools and that the schools are not prepared to handle. Considering these problems and the consumption/payment linkage or nonlinkage in U.S. schools, answer the following:

    a.   We have often heard about the shortage of math and science teachers in the nation's schools. The solution of pay differentials has been suggested. Why? Who would resist the paying of differential salaries to teachers based on the subjects they teach?

    b.   Also suggested is an unhampered voucher system for education, in which families are given government coupons worth a certain amount of tuition that are cashed in by the school the student chooses to attend or is sent to. Would resistance to a voucher system come from the same people who strongly dislike the lack of selection of teachers available to the average public school student? Explain.

    c.   What nonteacher groups or individuals would be likely to resist a system in which vouchers can be used to attend any school — public or private? Why? Before answering, consider that after World War II, returning U.S. military personnel were paid for attending any college — public or private — of their choosing under the GI bill. What is the difference between the GI bill and a voucher system?

    d.   The SAT scores of students majoring in education are at or near the bottom of the scale measured across different majors. Education majors scored significantly below the national average on SAT tests. Can you specify several things that could be done to reverse this fact? Why might your ideas not be accepted by the profession?

    e.   Evaluate this statement: "When it comes to education, no costs are too high."

2.   The philosopher-mathematician Bertrand Russell once said, "A fanatical belief in democracy makes democratic institutions impossible." What did he mean by this statement? Can you apply his quote to the United States today?

APPENDIX TO CHAPTER 5

GOVERNMENT EXPENDITURES AND REVENUES

Government is an important sector of the economy, both in terms of its effect and influence on the economy and as a player in its own right. Government at the federal, state, and local levels combined allocates over one-third of the national output. This has not always been the case. In the United States only 50 years ago, the government was a relatively minor player on the economic scene. In 1929 total combined government expenditures were slightly less than 10 percent of the total national output. By the middle 1980s combined government expenditures exceeded 35 percent of the national output. In 1929 the average person worked 52 minutes in each 8-hour day to pay federal, state, and local taxes. By 1985 that individual was working 2 hours and 38 minutes of each working day to pay taxes: 55 minutes to pay state and local government taxes, and 1 hour and 43 minutes to pay federal taxes. In 1987 the 1 federal, 50 state governments, and the more than 82,000 local governments in the United States collectively spent nearly $1,571.4 billion, which was $107.2 billion more than they took in taxes. Total expenditures amounted to $6,440 per person.

In this appendix we shall first look at how governments spend the resources under their control and then consider how governments obtain the resources they spend.

TOTAL GOVERNMENT EXPENDITURES AND REVENUES

There is a division of responsibility among the various levels of the U.S. government. This division of responsibility causes the different levels of government both to spend resources in different ways and to obtain revenues from different sources.

- Government expenditure is the total of all spending activities that government agencies make to purchase goods and services and to transfer income between citizen groups or to other countries.
- Government revenue is the income of government received mainly in the form of tax payments. Government revenue does not include government borrowing.

All government expenditures and revenues can be divided into a few categories. Table 5A.1 reports both total expenditures and total revenues

TABLE 5A.1
Federal, State, and Local Government Revenues and Expenditures: 1987
(Billions of Dollars)

A: FEDERAL, STATE, AND LOCAL GOVERNMENT REVENUES AND EXPENDITURES

Revenues		$1,464.2
Personal taxes	$564.7	
Corporate taxes	137.5	
Indirect business taxes	367.6	
Social insurance contributions	394.4	
Expenditures		1,571.4
Purchases of goods and services	923.8	
Transfer payments	531.2	
Net interest payments	109.7	
Less dividends received	6.3	
Subsidies	13.1	
Surplus (+) or Deficit (−)		−107.2

B: FEDERAL REVENUES AND EXPENDITURES

Revenues		$916.5
Personal taxes	$403.8	
Corporate taxes	110.3	
Indirect business taxes	54.0	
Social insurance contributions	348.4	
Expenditures		1,069.1
Purchases of goods and services	380.6	
Transfer payments	413.2	
Grants to state and local governments	104.7	
Net interest payments	142.6	
Subsidies	28.1	
Surplus (+) or Deficit (−)		−152.6

C: STATE AND LOCAL GOVERNMENT REVENUES AND EXPENDITURES

Revenues		$652.3
Personal taxes	$160.9	
Corporate taxes	27.2	
Indirect business taxes	313.6	
Social insurance contributions	46.1	
Federal grants in aid	104.7	
Expenditures		607.0
Purchases of goods and services	543.2	
Transfer payments	118.0	
Net interest payments	−39.3	
Subsidies	−15.0	
Surplus (+) or Deficit (−)		45.4

for all levels of government and for the federal government and the state and local governments separately. Government revenues do not always equal expenditures. To understand the mechanics of government budgeting, a few definitions are needed:

- When government revenues equal government expenditures, the government's budget is said to be balanced.
- When government expenditures exceed government revenues, the government is said to be running a budget deficit. When revenues exceed expenditures, the government is said to be running a budget surplus.
- The national debt is the total of the IOUs owed by the federal government on which interest and principal payments must be made annually. When the federal government's budget is in deficit, the national debt expands. When the federal government runs a surplus, the national debt decreases.

Government revenues at all levels in 1987 totaled almost $1.5 trillion. Total expenditures exceeded this amount, leaving a deficit. Personal taxes, such as the personal income tax, was the largest source of government funds, followed by social insurance contributions, indirect business taxes, and corporate taxes, in that order. The social security tax was the main source of revenue for social insurance contributions, as was the corporate income tax for corporate taxes. Purchases of goods and services is the largest item in total government expenditures, followed by transfer payments and net interest payments, with government subsidies being a minor item.

In 1987 the public sector ran a deficit of $107.2 billion. This deficit was covered by borrowing from the private sector. Governments issued debt obligations (bonds) that promised to repay the sums borrowed at some future date and that paid interest in the meantime.

State and local governments are generally required by their constitutions to run balanced budgets, in which current revenues must equal current expenditures. States, however, can borrow to finance capital expenditures, paying the interest and repaying the principal out of future revenues. The federal government does not have to run a balanced budget and is free to run deficits as long as lenders are willing to provide funds. Deficits have become expected procedure for the federal government, and the result has been a national debt. The national debt in 1987 totaled $2,355.3 billion.

FEDERAL GOVERNMENT REVENUES AND EXPENDITURES

The expenditures of the federal government have increased significantly over the last four decades. Figure 5A.1 plots total federal government expenditures from 1948 through 1987. The expenditures of the federal government in 1987 (see Table 5A.1) totaled $1,069.1 billion, of which $916.5 billion was raised in revenues and $152.6 was borrowed. Personal taxes were the largest source of revenue, followed by social insurance contributions, corporate taxes, and indirect business taxes, in that order. Transfer payments made up the largest category of federal expenditures, followed by the purchase of goods and services, net interest payments on the national debt, and grants to state and local governments.

Part A of Figure 5A.2 plots federal government expenditures and revenues. It is clear that while both expenditures and revenues increased between 1968 and 1987, expenditures increased more rapidly than revenues. A good way to put the size and growth of the federal government in perspective is to plot federal expenditures and revenues as a percentage of

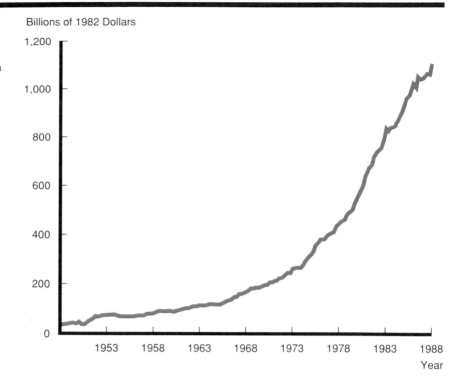

Billions of 1982 Dollars

total national output. Part B of Figure 5A.2 charts federal expenditures and revenues as percentages of national output. When federal expenditures as a percentage of total national output increases, the federal government is growing relative to the economy as a whole. The federal government in effect is controlling more of the nation's output, and the private sector is controlling less. If you follow the line that measures government expenditures in the figure, you will discover that although it fluctuated, the trend was clearly upward. In 1968 the share of total output controlled by the federal government was about 19 percent. By 1987 the federal government's share had increased to about 24 percent.

Now consider revenues as a percentage of total output over the same time period. Revenues also fluctuated but did not grow over time. Revenues fluctuated between 18 and 20 percent of total national output. The result was a persistent budget deficit. Since 1969, when the federal budget was last in balance, deficits have been a problem. Part C of Figure 5A.2 presents the budget deficit as a percentage of total national output for the years 1968 through 1987. You can readily see from the chart that federal revenues did not keep up with expenditures and that the federal government increasingly resorted to deficit financing to pay for government activities.

WHAT DOES THE FEDERAL GOVERNMENT DO?

The activities of the federal government can be determined from considering the more detailed breakdown of federal government expenditures. Table 5A.2 presents the composition of federal government expenditures for two years, 1960 and 1988, for nine categories of federal spending. The

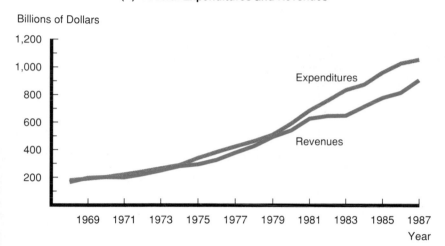

(A) Federal Expenditures and Revenues

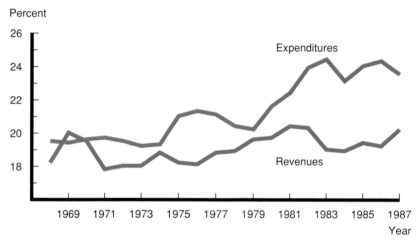

(B) Revenues and Expenditures as a Percent of National Income

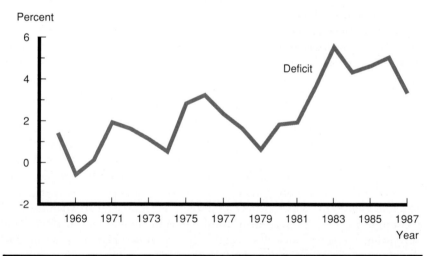

(C) Federal Budget Deficit as a Percent of National Income

FIGURE 5A.2

Expenditures and Revenues of the Federal Government: 1968–1987

A: Expenditures and Revenues of the Federal Government

B: Expenditures and Revenues of the Federal Government as Percentages of National Income

C: Federal Budget Deficit as a Percentage of National Income

TABLE 5A.2
Composition of Federal Budget Outlays: 1960 and 1988

	FISCAL 1960		FISCAL 1988	
CATEGORY	AMOUNT (BILLIONS OF DOLLARS)	PERCENT OF TOTAL	AMOUNT (BILLIONS OF DOLLARS)	PERCENT OF TOTAL
Defense, space, foreign affairs	49.5	53.7%	297.6	28.1%
Transfers of income	20.6	22.3	312.1	29.4
Transfers in kind	1.1	1.2	136.5	12.9
Social programs	1.3	1.4	44.4	4.2
Investment in transportation, water, and recreation	5.4	5.8	15.7	1.5
Revenue sharing	0.1	—	1.8	0.2
Subsidies to producers	4.5	4.9	80.9	7.6
Net interest	6.9	7.7	139.0	13.1
Other	2.8	3.0	32.0	3.0
Total	$92.2	100.0	$1,060.0	100.0

Source: Budget of United States Government.

category of *defense, space, and foreign affairs* includes outlays for military and space programs and for military and nonmilitary foreign assistance. *Transfers of income* includes cash outlays for social security payments, unemployment compensation, aid to families with dependent children, and other public-assistance payments to the poor or disabled. *Transfers in kind* refers to outlays made to help people purchase specific goods and services, such as medical care and housing. These outlays include expenditures for Medicare, Medicaid, food stamps, and housing allowances. *Social programs* includes payments to state and local governments to support education, job-retraining programs, and community development programs. *Investment in transportation, water, and recreation* includes outlays for highways, airports, water projects, national parks, and wilderness areas (sometimes this category is called *social infrastructure*). *Revenue sharing* is the transfer of revenues by the federal government to state and local governments in unrestricted grants to use as they see fit. *Subsidies to producers* includes outlays made directly to producers in certain industries, such as agriculture, the postal service, and the merchant marine. *Net interest* includes the payments made to holders of the national debt. *Other programs* includes the cost of the legislative and judicial branches of the federal government.

A comparison of federal expenditures for fiscal 1960 with fiscal 1988 reveals that not only did total federal expenditures increase tenfold, but the composition of federal spending significantly changed. *National defense, space, and foreign affairs* increased only sixfold, and has thus declined in relative importance in the federal budget. This category, which in 1960 represented nearly 54 percent of total federal expenditures, accounted for only 28 percent of total federal expenditures in 1988. The only other category to decline relatively was *investment in transportation, water, and recreation*, which declined from 5.8 percent to 1.5 percent of total expenditures.

The relative declines in these two categories were offset by increases in the other categories. *Transfers of income, transfers in kind*, and *social programs* combined almost doubled in relative importance between 1960

TABLE 5A.3
State and Local Government Revenues and Expenditures:
1986 (Billions of Dollars)

Revenues by Source		$641
Property taxes	$112	
Sales taxes	135	
Individual income taxes	74	
Corporate income taxes	20	
Grants from federal government	113	
All other	187	
Expenditures by Function		606
Education	211	
Highways	49	
Public welfare	76	
All other	270	
Surplus (+) or Deficit (−)		35

Source: *Economic Report of the President*, 1988.

and 1988, as did *net interest* and *subsidies to producers*. The conclusion
that can be reached from these comparisons is that the priorities of the
federal government have changed significantly over the past three decades. In 1960 the major functions were to promote the national defense,
maintain the infrastructure, and fund an existing social security program.
By 1988 social programs and the redistribution of income via transfer
programs were of equal importance.

STATE AND LOCAL EXPENDITURES

State and local governments perform functions different from those of the
federal government. This can be seen in Table 5A.1 by comparing the
expenditures of state and local governments (Part C) with the expenditures of the federal government (Part B). State and local governments
spend a higher portion of their resources for goods and services and
transfer a smaller portion than does the federal government. The federal
government runs a deficit, while state and local governments combined
run a surplus. Consequently, while the federal government is a net payer
of interest, state and local governments are net receivers of interest payments.

Table 5A.3 shows a breakdown of state and local government expenditures by function. Providing public education is the biggest single expense of state and local governments, followed by public welfare payments and spending for highways. State and local governments, however,
spend more in total on the other functions of government than they do for
education. These other functions include expenditures for law enforcement, fire protection, land use controls, public health, and so on.

The current division of tasks that exists between the federal level and
the state and local levels is apparently intended to allow the federal government to provide for the national defense and to transfer income, and
the state and local governments to deliver the services that communities
require — law and order, the protection of property, basic education,
and the administration of federal programs at the local level.

HOW GOVERNMENT OBTAINS
THE RESOURCES IT ALLOCATES

How do governments obtain the resources they allocate? There are three sources: taxes, borrowing, and the creation of money.

- Taxes are sums of money accounting for a portion of income or property that legally a person or business must periodically pay to the government.
- Borrowing is the receipt of resources with the understanding that the resources will be returned to the lender at some future date.
- Creation of money is an addition to the total supply of money.

Let us first consider taxation. The first recorded taxes took the form of tithes, with a given percentage of a crop each year being owed to public officials. Suppose an economy produces 100 bushels of wheat. The tithe means that 10 percent of the crop, or ten bushels, is due the government. Thus the private sector has 90 bushels of wheat and the public sector has 10 bushels. When money came to be widely employed, money payments were substituted for payments in kind. Suppose that $100 in money exists so that a bushel of wheat will sell for a dollar: 100 bushels of wheat are worth $100. The government now receives $10 annually from farmers. Thus the public sector has $10 to purchase 10 bushels of wheat in the market and the private sector has $90 to purchase 90 bushels.

Government's control over resources is not limited to its ability to tax: It can also borrow and, at the federal level, create money. Suppose the government desires to spend $11 and that the economy still is producing $100 worth of wheat, out of which the government receives $10 in tax revenues. Further suppose that the government cannot or will not raise taxes. A deficit now exists of $1.

One alternative is to borrow $1 from the private sector. The government issues a $1 bond that pays interest. The bond represents the government's promise to return the $1 at some future date and to pay interest in the meantime. One citizen will prefer the interest that can now be earned to $1 worth of current consumption and will supply the government with the $1 it requires in exchange for the bond. The government can now pay for all of its expenditures, as the deficit is covered by the loan. The public sector has 11 bushels of wheat and the private sector has 89 bushels.

A second alternative for covering the $1 deficit without raising taxes is to print an extra $1 and use it to cover the deficit. The government prints the $1 and uses it to cover its deficit in purchasing goods. The government now controls 11 bushels of wheat and the private sector 89. There is still a total of 100 bushels of wheat, but now there is $101. So the price of wheat increases to $1.01. The price level has increased to reduce the number of bushels available to the private sector. The result is that the public sector has acquired more resources and the private sector has fewer resources. The actual process of money supply creation in the United States is somewhat less direct and more complicated, but the results are the same.

GOVERNMENT REVENUES

Most government revenues come from taxes. Table 5A.1 reveals that personal taxes — taxes on individuals — are the largest single source of revenues, followed by social insurance contributions, indirect business taxes, and corporate taxes, in that order. Actually, this table reports the sources of the revenues, identifying the parties in society that collected the taxes and forwarded them to the government. It does not report who really pays the tax.

In fact, all taxes are ultimately paid by individuals. Business firms do not pay taxes, but they do collect taxes. Business firms are, after all, owned by individuals. When a tax is levied on a business, if the tax cannot be passed on to customers, then the business's owners, who are individuals, have to pay the tax. Thus Table 5A.1 reveals not who bears the burden of the tax but who collects it for the government and the type of economic activity that is being taxed.

Table 5A.1 also shows that the federal government (Part B) relies much more heavily on personal taxes, social insurance contributions, and corporate taxes than do state and local governments (Part C) and less heavily on indirect business taxes. A more detailed breakdown of the sources of revenues for state and local governments is found in Table 5A.3. Sales taxes, property taxes, and other sources such as license fees are, along with grants from the federal government, the main sources of state and local revenues.

PRINCIPLES OF TAXATION

There are three types of tax systems: proportional, progressive, and regressive, depending on how an individual's tax burden responds to changes in income.

Proportional taxation exists when an individual's taxes change in direct proportion to a change in income. With this system, all taxpayers pay the same proportion of their income in taxes. If the tax rate were 15 percent, an individual with an income of $10,000 would pay .15 × $10,000, or $1,500 in taxes, while an individual with an income of $50,000 would pay .15 × $50,000, or $7,500.

Proportional taxes exist when the percentage of income paid in taxes is the same regardless of the level of income. A proportional tax system is often called a *flat tax*, since the percentage paid does not change with income.

Progressive taxation exists when the percentage of a person's income paid in taxes increases as personal income increases. A progressive tax system makes use of different marginal tax rates. The marginal or incremental tax rate is determined by:

$$\text{Marginal tax rate} = \frac{\text{Change in tax bill}}{\text{Change in income}}$$

The marginal tax rate is not the same as the average tax rate. The average tax rate is:

$$\text{Average tax rate} = \frac{\text{Total tax bill}}{\text{Total income}}$$

The difference between the marginal tax rate and the average tax rate can be seen in the following example. Suppose that the first $30,000 in income is taxed at a marginal rate of 15 percent, and that income above $30,000 is taxed at a marginal rate of 28 percent. A person with an income of $30,000 will pay .15 × $30,000, or $4,500, in taxes. A person with an income of $60,000 will pay 15 percent on the first $30,000 in income and 28 percent on all income above $30,000, or (.15 × $30,000) + (.28 × $30,000) = $12,900. In the first case the marginal and average tax rate is the same, but in the second case the marginal tax rate on the last dollar earned is 28 percent, whereas the average tax rate on all of the income is ($12,900/$60,000), or 21.5 percent.

There is a common misconception about marginal tax rates. Consider the woman who says that she does not want a raise because it would put her in a higher tax bracket. She is implying that the increase in salary would be more than wiped out by a corresponding increase in taxes as her salary moved her into a higher marginal tax bracket. Not so, because the higher marginal tax rate applies only to *additional* income and not to all income. She is confusing marginal tax rates with average tax rates.

Suppose, as in the example above, that a person was making $30,000 and paid a marginal tax rate of 15 percent on that amount, or $4,500. Now suppose the individual received a $5,000 raise and now makes $35,000 a year. How much would her taxes go up? Income over $30,000 is taxed at a rate of 28 percent. Her tax bill would *not* be 28 percent of $35,000, or $9,800, as she expects. She would still pay 15 percent on the first $30,000, or $4,500, but she would now pay 28 percent on the $5,000 raise, or $1,400, for a total of $5,900. Only the increase in income is taxed at the higher marginal rate, not the entire amount of income.

It is important to keep in mind that the average tax rate is always less than the marginal tax rate in a progressive tax system, and that the marginal rate and the average rate are always the same in a proportional tax system.

A *regressive tax system* is one in which the percentage of income paid in taxes actually declines as income increases. In a regressive tax system, the marginal rate is always below the average rate. The social security tax is a regressive tax. It is levied only up to a certain income. If an individual earns more than that level of income, he or she will not pay the social security tax on the additional income. The marginal tax rate on income above the legislated amount is zero. So a person whose income exceeds the legislated minimum will pay a lower percentage of total income for social security than will a person with a lower income.

THEORIES OF A FAIR TAX

> Don't tax you
> Don't tax me
> Tax that other fellow under the tree!
> *Motto of a Washington, D.C.,*
> *tax lobbyist*

No one likes to pay taxes. Each individual's idea of a fair tax probably is for the other person to pay it. Nevertheless, economists have long struggled with the idea of a fair tax. The two most widely accepted criteria for fairness are vertical and horizontal equity.

Horizontal equity refers to the method of taxation in which persons who make the same income pay the same amount of tax regardless of how the income was earned. Thus a person with a small business who earns $30,000 a year should pay the same tax as a person who teaches school and makes the same amount of money.

Vertical equity refers to the method of taxation in which persons with different levels of income are taxed differently. Thus a rich person would be taxed differently than a poor person. Even if you agree with the principle of vertical equity, there remains the question of how unequals should be treated. The two most widely discussed principles that are consistent with vertical equity are the ability-to-pay and the benefits-received principles.

ABILITY-TO-PAY PRINCIPLE The ability-to-pay principle states that as income increases, so should the average tax rate. The ability-to-pay principle is often used to argue for a progressive tax system. According to this principle, a man with $10,000 in income should pay a smaller portion of his income in taxes than a man with an income of $100,000 a year. Regressive taxes are therefore unfair. The question remains how much more should a richer person pay than a poorer person? When this question arises, the ability-to-pay principle of taxation boils down to a political rather than an economic question.

BENEFITS-RECEIVED PRINCIPLE The benefits-received principle of taxation states that an individual's taxes should be in proportion to the benefits received. Thus those who receive numerous benefits should pay more than those who receive fewer benefits. Wealth, for example, may provide a measure of the benefits received. A person who owns property receives more benefits from national defense, protection, and justice than a person who does not own any property; that property owner should therefore pay more in taxes. The federal and state gasoline tax, for example, is levied on the benefits-received principle. People who use the public roads more frequently should pay more, and they do; every time they drive they consume taxed gasoline, in effect paying a user fee. But how about retired people living on social security or people on welfare? Clearly, they are receiving important benefits. Should they be taxed accordingly?

Neither the ability-to-pay nor the benefits-received principle can be anything more than a rough guide for tax policy. Nevertheless, taxes are collected by governments. How have taxes been levied in the United States? Has the tax system been proportional, progressive, or regressive?

You can see from Tables 5A.1 and 5A.3 that a variety of taxes are collected in the United States: personal and corporate income taxes, social security taxes, sales taxes, excise taxes, property taxes, and so on. When all taxes are considered, how progressive, proportional, or regressive is the total tax system? In the past, the income tax was designed to be progressive, with 15 marginal rates existing until 1986. But the social security tax is regressive. Perhaps the sales tax is also. So how about the tax system as a whole?

Several studies have been made of the incidence of the tax system. The most recent study found that tax burdens in 1985 were roughly proportional to income. Joseph Pechman concluded that under the most progressive assumptions possible the tax system as a whole was mildly progressive, with an average tax rate on the low end of the income scale of 20 percent rising to 25 percent at the high end of the income scale. Using assumptions that would tend to produce the most regressive results, the system becomes only mildly regressive. It is most likely, Pechman concluded, that the tax system is basically proportional.[1] Not all studies agree with this conclusion. Another study found that the tax system in 1972 was progressive.[2] The bottom 10 percent of the income earners paid 11.7 percent of their income in taxes. The average tax rate increased with

---

[1] Joseph Pechman, *Who Paid the Taxes, 1966–1985?* (Washington, D.C.: Brookings Institution, 1985).

[2] Edgar K. Browning and William R. Johnson, *The Distribution of the Tax Burden* (American Enterprise Institute, 1979).

each 10 percent of the population, with the top 10 percent paying 38.3 percent of their income in taxes. These studies may now be obsolete due to the federal tax reform of 1986.

THE 1986 TAX REFORM ACT

In 1986 the tax code was completely rewritten for the first time since 1957. This tax reform was designed to remedy many of the horizontal and vertical equity problems that previously existed. Prior to 1986 there were 15 marginal tax rates, ranging from 11 to 50 percent. These rates were repealed and replaced by three marginal rates: 15 percent on income up to $29,750, a marginal rate of 28 percent on income between $29,750 and $71,900, and a rate of 33 percent on income between $71,900 and $149,250. Above $149,250 additional income would be taxed at 28 percent.

The personal exemption was increased from $1,080 to $2,000, and the standard deduction was increased. The increased exemptions and standard deductions meant that millions of poorer Americans were now exempt from paying the federal income tax. In order to lower marginal tax rates and increase both exemptions and the standard deduction, a number of other deductions that had been previously allowed for tax purposes were modified or repealed. The effect that the Tax Reform Act of 1986 has had on the incidence of the tax structure remains to be studied.

SUMMARY

1. Government has become a significant factor in the U.S. economy over the last several decades, allocating over a third of the nation's total output. The government sector is composed of the federal government, the state governments, and the local (county and city) governments.

2. There is a division of tasks among the federal, state, and local governments that is revealed in their expenditure patterns. The federal government specializes in providing national defense and, in recent years, in transferring income. State and local governments specialize in providing to local areas services such as education, highways, public assistance, law and order, justice, and the like.

3. Governments obtain the resources they allocate from three sources: taxes, borrowing, and the creation of money. The federal government is the only authority with the right to create money.

4. The federal government is allowed to run a deficit, but state and local governments are not. State and local governments can, however, borrow for capital improvements, paying the principal and interest out of future revenues.

5. The federal government relies heavily on the personal income tax and the social security tax as sources of revenue, whereas state and local governments rely more heavily on property taxes and indirect business taxes such as the sales tax. The federal government is currently running a deficit, and state and local governments are running surpluses. Overall, the government sector was in deficit in 1987.

6. There are three types of tax systems in relation to income: proportional, progressive, and regressive. When the marginal tax rate is the same as the average tax rate, the system is proportional to income. When the marginal rate is greater than the average rate, the system is progressive. When the marginal rate is lower than the average rate, the system is regressive.

7. A marginal tax bracket is a range of income over which a tax of a certain percentage is levied. Typically, the marginal tax rate increases as income increases. When a person's income increases so that he or she is placed in a higher tax bracket, the higher marginal tax rate is computed only on the income above a certain level, not on all of the income. To assume that a higher tax bracket means a higher tax rate on all income is to confuse average tax rates with marginal tax rates.

8. Businesses do not pay taxes; only individuals pay taxes. A suggestion to increase business taxes is in reality a suggestion to tax either the business's customers or the business's owners, or both.

9. A fair tax system may involve horizontal and vertical equity. Horizontal equity means that individuals with the same income should pay the same amount of taxes. Vertical equity means that individuals with different incomes should be taxed differently. The ability-to-pay and the benefits-received principles are methods of achieving vertical equity. These principles are simply guides, not rules, for levying taxes.

10. Economists disagree over the incidence of the tax system of the United States. The most recent research suggests that the tax system is roughly proportional to income. Earlier research found it to be progressive. The Tax Reform Act of 1986 may have made both findings obsolete.

PART 2

INTRODUCTION TO MACROECONOMICS

6 KEEPING SCORE
National Income Accounting

IN THIS CHAPTER YOU WILL LEARN:

The concept of national income accounting

•

The concept of gross national product and gross domestic product

•

The ways that gross national product can be calculated

•

The benefits and defects of gross national product

•

The adjustments that can be made to gross national product

•

The various categories in the national income accounts

•

Some of the uses for the national income accounts

THE SHIFT TO SERVICES: WHERE WILL YOU WORK?

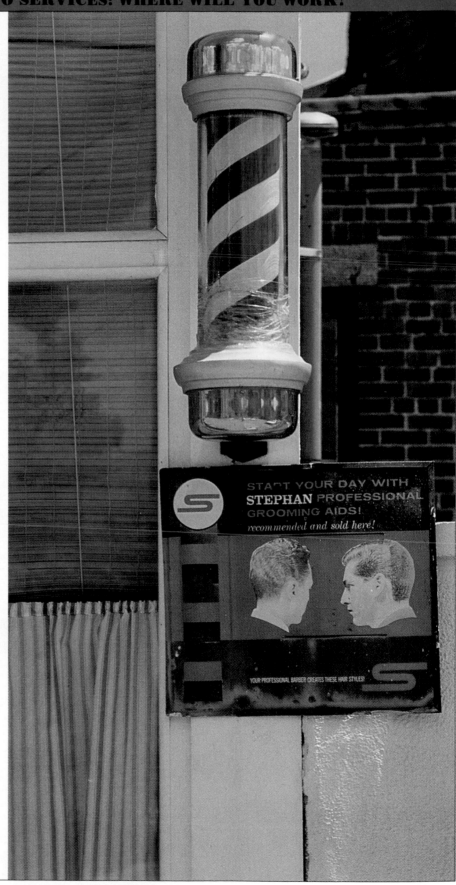

> Surely the American people are not willing to become merely a service economy. The American character is as much built around the sinews and muscle of the factory line as the white-collar office.
> — Editorial, *Christian Science Monitor* (1987)

In recent years, jobs have grown in the service sector and declined in the manufacturing sector. When manufacturing industries such as the steel, automobile, textile, and farm machinery industries contract, the nation loses some of its capacity to produce goods and some of its workers lose their jobs. Between 1980 and 1985 the United States lost 800,000 manufacturing jobs. During the same period of time, however, the economy added 7.5 million jobs in the service sector.

The loss of manufacturing jobs has led to concerns that the United States is losing its industrial base. This worries some people who do not believe that you can eat a haircut or drive an investment plan. Some fear that concentrating on services will lead to slow economic growth and a lower standard of living as Americans take turns producing fast food for a minimum wage. Others worry that the national wealth cannot grow indefinitely when the economy is mainly based on producing intangible goods like health care and communications. Others worry about the implications for national security when the economy shifts out of producing the steel necessary for a variety of defense concerns such as weapons and into information processing. Still others either see no meaningful distinction between services and manufacturing in regard to the issues raised above or do not see the adverse consequences that the doubters predict. Such observers see the shift to services as the hallmark of a healthy economy, not the harbinger of economic retreat.

Which view is correct? Has there been, and is there now, a relative expansion of the service sector at the expense of manufacturing?[1]

[1]Sources: *Business Week*, May 16, 1988, 84; June 20, 1988, 8; July 11, 1988, 5.

THE SELLING OF AMERICA

Have you wondered about the extent to which foreigners are buying up America's real assets? Certainly, the media has been concerned of late with a rash of stories and reports on the selling of America. Reportedly, one-quarter of all the downtown commercial real estate in Los Angeles is now owned by Japanese nationals, and similar estimates have been made for other large urban centers in the United States. Are these worries well founded? Are we selling our nation's resources?

WHICH COUNTRY HAS THE LARGEST AND RICHEST ECONOMY?

There used to be no doubt which country was the largest and richest. The United States was clearly the world leader. But no longer. Everywhere these days there is head shaking and hand wringing over the decline of America. Headlines in national newspapers and magazines like: "Kiss No. 1 Goodbye, Folks," "America, Europe Is Coming," and "Emergence of Superrich Japan as Major Superpower" ring warnings of the relative decline of the United States and the rise of its rivals.

Clearly, pessimism about America is in vogue. The sudden emergence of the United States as the world's largest debtor, of Japan as the richest creditor, and the soon-to-occur creation of a united European economy have raised doubts that America is still the world's leader. But does this pessimistic view bear scrutiny? The national income accounts to which you will be introduced in this chapter can help answer these questions: Is the U.S. economy still the largest in the world?

Does it provide on average the most goods and services to its citizens? Is the U.S. economy growing at significantly lower rates than its rivals' so that it is just a matter of time before America becomes a second-rate power?[2]

[2]Source: Karen Elliot House, "The '90s & Beyond," *The Wall Street Journal*, January 23, 1989, 1.

• I N T R O D U C T I O N •

Macroeconomics is the branch of economics that studies the economy as a whole. Macroeconomics is interesting because it deals with the major economic problems of the times. It has to do with economic expansions, recessions, and depressions, the level of aggregate output, the rate of price inflation or deflation, unemployment, and the balance of payments, the federal budget deficit, and the international trade deficit. The interests of macroeconomics can perhaps be summarized into a concern with the overall performance of the economy: Is the economy growing or contracting? Is the overall price level rising or falling? Are employment conditions becoming better or worse?

Many, if not most, of the terms in the paragraph above are probably only somewhat familiar to you — you have heard them in newscasts and seen them in print, but their exact meaning until now has possibly escaped you. Do not be concerned, for these terms are the subject of macroeconomics, and their exact meanings will become clear as you proceed in your study. You will find that these are issues of both personal and national concern. Being the study of the economy as a whole, macroeconomics deals with phenomena that affect all markets and all economic decision makers. •

HOW MACROECONOMICS DIFFERS FROM MICROECONOMICS

Macroeconomics not only deals with important issues, but it is also a fascinating intellectual pursuit because of its unique approach. In order to deal with the entire economy, macroeconomics reduces complicated economic concepts to manageable essentials. Macroeconomics disregards details such as how individuals and business firms behave, or how prices and quantities are determined in individual markets. These are the subject matter of microeconomics discussed in the previous chapters of this book. We now leave these topics behind to concentrate on totals such as the total output of the economy, the overall price level, the economywide level of employment, consumption, investment, and government spending. These are aggregates, obtained by the process of **aggregation:**

> *Aggregation is the process of combining many individual microeconomic markets into one overall market to determine the total output of the economy and the overall price level.*

Disregarding precise definitions, can you imagine the total output of the economy obtained from adding up the output of individual markets? If so, you are engaging in aggregation. Can you form a mental image of common tendencies that might affect the output and/or the prices of all products? If so, you are doing macroeconomics.

Macroeconomics proceeds on the assumptions that:

1. The concerns of microeconomics with the determination of the relative price and output of particular markets are of limited consequences for most issues that affect the overall economy.

2. The behavior of individual markets can be aggregated to obtain meaningful measures of the performance of the economy as a whole.
3. There are forces that affect the overall economy which affect all individual markets so that these markets, when subjected to macroeconomic forces, tend to move together.

Thus the many individual markets in the economy can be considered as one when the question concerns the economy as a whole. Macroeconomics is more abstract than microeconomics. The benefit of increased abstraction is the ability to handle and understand the vital interaction between macroeconomic variables.

Because macroeconomics is also vitally concerned with assessing the overall performance of the economy, the basic relationships that exist between macroeconomic variables must be identified. But our study does not stop there. The behavior of the economy is affected by the economic policies of the federal government. How macroeconomic relationships are affected by economic policy must also be discovered. In this pursuit macroeconomists, as you will discover in succeeding chapters, are interested in such things as the money supply and interest rates, which are the variables of monetary policy, and in fiscal policy in the form of the tax and expenditure decisions of the government as incorporated in the federal budget. Again, do not fret if you do not know the precise meanings of these terms — you soon will!

Despite the differences in subject and approach between macro and microeconomics, there is no basic conflict between the two. The overall economy is, after all, composed of its individual microeconomic markets. The difference is one of level and emphasis. Both fields of study are concerned with economic policy, but macroeconomics has been particularly influenced by the economic problems of the day. Microeconomic problems may or may not lead to changes in government policy, but major macroeconomic problems, because so much is at stake, always lead to demands for changes in government policy.

Economists are therefore concerned not only with assessing the performance of the economy but with being able to predict the consequences of the various policy options. As the modern world economy has evolved, the range of macroeconomic problems has evolved in tandem. Modern macroeconomic theory began with attempts to explain the Great Depression and has been affected by successive recessions, inflations, and combinations of the two that have occurred in the recent past. Macroeconomic theory is not set in stone but is still developing and evolving as the problems with which it has to deal have changed.

CONTENDING MACROECONOMIC THEORIES

In the past several decades many contending macroeconomic theories have developed, leading to the belief that modern macroeconomics is nothing more than a battleground for rival economic doctrines. But macroeconomists, like microeconomists, essentially agree on the scope and method of macroeconomics. The areas of disagreement are like interesting, highly visible islands of discord within a great sea of theoretical agreement. In the following sections we shall mainly concentrate on exploring the sea of agreement, describing the islands of disagreement as they appear on the horizon.

The three chapters of this part are designed to provide an introduction to the study of macroeconomics. Chapter 6 will introduce you to the concepts of national income accounting, the process of aggregation used to produce economic statistics that measure the behavior of the overall economy. The national income accounts allow economic decision makers to track the overall performance of the economy. When the Great Depression began, national income accounting did not exist. No one was sure just how bad the downturn in 1929 was because no one was keeping score. Today we have in place the national income accounts, which allow interested individuals to keep track of how the economy is doing.

Statistics without theory to explain their interrelationships are valueless. In Chapter 7 the basic macroeconomic model of aggregate demand and aggregate supply will be presented. This theory represents the foundation on which modern macroeconomics is built. It is so general that all contending theories can be explored using the model. The basic model can and will be used first to explain the theory of classical economics, the view that existed at the time of the Great Depression. We shall then see where classical economics went wrong. Throughout your study of macroeconomics the basic model will be extended and modified in the light of empirical investigations of how the economy actually behaves, and it will be used as a vehicle to show how contending macroeconomic theories work.

The purpose of macroeconomic theory is to explain how the economy operates. That the overall economy does not always work satisfactorily surely is not news to you. In Chapter 8 the aggregate-demand/aggregate-supply model presented in Chapter 7 will be employed to discuss the trilogy of macroeconomic problems: growth, unemployment, and inflation. Often these problems are initially presented only as descriptions to beginning students. But one of the primary uses of economic theory is in framing economic problems so that only the essential elements will be considered. The use of the basic model to describe the trilogy of economic problems will allow you to comprehend better not only what a recession is but also what causes recessions to occur, not only how inflation is defined but how inflation happens, and not only what economic growth is but how it occurs.

WHAT ARE THE NATIONAL INCOME ACCOUNTS?

The main goals of macroeconomics are to explain the current performance of the macroeconomy and to foretell its future state. This is done by developing theories that are tested by measuring levels of economic activity. In this chapter you will be introduced to the concept of the national income accounts, which are the main means of keeping track of important economic variables. You will discover what gross national product and related national income concepts represent and how they are measured. As a result you will be able to assess both the virtues and the defects of these concepts as measures of overall economic activity.

A BRIEF HISTORY OF NATIONAL INCOME ACCOUNTING

In 1929 the world economy went into a tailspin from which it would not recover for a decade. The Great Depression, besides creating untold suffering, altered the world. But when the economy fell into the Great Depression, no one knew it was happening until well after it had begun. Furthermore, it was impossible to know at the time just how bad the

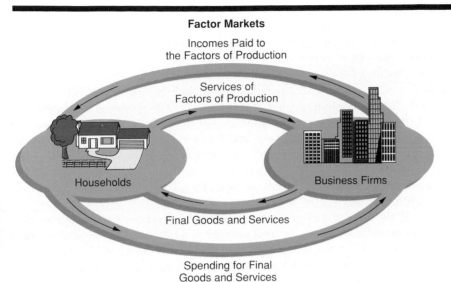

Factor Markets

Incomes Paid to
the Factors of Production

Services of
Factors of Production

Households

Business Firms

Final Goods and Services

Spending for Final
Goods and Services

Product Markets

FIGURE 6.1
Circular Flow of Income and Spending

The simple circular flow diagram in this figure shows the interrelationship between households and business firms through exchanges in factor and product markets. The outer loop shows money flows and the inner loop shows the flows of factors and products. The circular flow in the upper loop reveals that the value of the services of the factors of production equals the money income these factors receive. The flow in the lower loop shows that the value of the final goods and services exchanged equals the total amount of money expenditures on those goods and services. If households spend the entire amount of their income, then the total income paid to the factors of production (outside upper loop) will equal the total value of the final goods and services produced in the economy (outside lower loop).

economic situation had become because no one kept statistical track of the overall economy. President Hoover even thought the situation was turning around at the very time the economy was in a free fall. What was missing at that time was a way to measure the overall performance of the economy.

Surprisingly, it was the representative branch of government, not the executive branch as you might expect, that first felt the need for a measure of overall economic activity. The U.S. Senate's Finance Committee early in the Depression decade commissioned Professor Simon Kuznets to develop and construct a measure of the aggregate output of the country. In 1933 he reported the first national income statistics for the years 1929 to 1932. Only then was it clear just how bad the economic situation of the country had become. Professor Kuznets was later awarded the Nobel Prize in economics for his efforts.

In order to measure the economy's aggregate output, Professor Kuznets pioneered a set of statistics known as **national income accounts.** These accounts have subsequently been refined, and they are now widely used internationally.

> *National income accounts are a set of statistics measuring aggregate output and its components; they provide a way of measuring and evaluating the performance of the whole economy.*

National income accounting is central to any endeavor to apply macroeconomic theories or to make economic policy.

National income accounts are based on the concept of the circular flow of income. The basic circular flow model depicted in Figure 6.1 indicates the flow of money payments in the outer loop and the flow of the factors of production and the goods and services they produce in the inner loop. This simple model includes only the private sector composed of households and business firms and assumes that households spend all of their income and businesses produce only consumer goods. Households provide business firms with the services of the factors of production (labor, capital, and resources), shown in the inner loop of the top part of the diagram, in return for income payments shown in the outer loop. The value of the services provided by households is equal to the income payments they receive.

Business firms employ the factors of production to produce the goods and services on which households spend their income, as depicted in the inner loop of the bottom part of the diagram. The spending of households for final goods and services (outer loop of the bottom part of the diagram) is equal to the value of the goods and services they purchase. Finally, if we initially assume that households spend all of their income, then the total payments to the factors of production must be equal to the value of the goods and services produced, an equality on which national income accounting rests.

If the total value of the final goods and services produced in the economy is $1,000, then a total income of $1,000 will be created for the owners of the factors of production. This is so because production involves costs. Workers must be paid, capital rewarded, and resources purchased — all to allow firms the chance to earn profits. The act of production thus generates income for the households that own the factors of production as well as for the business firms. The total value of what is produced is in turn paid out to the owners of the factors of production.

What ensures that the total value of what is produced will equal the total factor payments? Suppose that in creating $1,000 worth of goods the labor employed is paid $750, land rents absorb $50 and capital rental another $100, for a total of $900, which leaves $100 for which we have yet to account. This $100 is profit. Profits are equal to the residual, what is left over after all other factors are paid. Profits flow to business firms, which are themselves owned by households. If total factor payments had exceeded the $1,000 value of the goods and services produced, then profits would be negative and the firm would have suffered a loss sufficient to maintain the identity. In either event the value of what is produced is always equal to the income received by households, which are the owners of the factors of production and all business firms.

GROSS NATIONAL PRODUCT (GNP)

The broadest and most famous measure of national income is **gross national product,** or **GNP.** GNP may be the best known of all acronyms. Newly released GNP figures make headlines in the papers and are announced as a matter of great importance on national TV. It is doubtful if any statistic has ever been treated with more respect or has been considered of more significance than GNP.

Gross national product is the total market value of the final goods and services produced during a year by domestically owned factors of production.

GNP is the result of the efforts of domestically owned factors of production. Not all of the factors of production are owned by the nationals of a country; some are owned by citizens of other countries. Television sets are produced in the United States in factories owned by Japanese nationals. The profits and payments to the invested capital of these factories are not included in the GNP of the United States. U.S. citizens own factories in other countries. Ford and General Motors, for example, own plants in Europe. The profits and payments to American-owned capital are included in U.S. GNP.

If you are interested in the value of national output produced within a country's borders, the national income account you require is **gross domestic product (GDP).**

Gross domestic product measures the value of the final goods and services produced by all of the factors of production located within an economy regardless of who owns them.

In the United States there is currently little difference between GNP and GDP. This means that income earned abroad is roughly balanced by income earned domestically by foreign nationals. The difference between GNP and GDP does provide a measure of the importance of foreign ownership of the production resources within a country (see Preview 6.2 Analysis). When making comparisons of the size of international economies, you will find that GDP is often employed instead of GNP.

It is important to note that neither GNP nor GDP measures the total value of all goods and services produced in the economy; they measure only the total value of the *final* goods and services produced. **Final goods and services** are goods that are not used up in the production process and that are ultimately received by the final users of the products or services or are exported.

Final goods and services are those goods and services that are actually consumed or retained by the ultimate user or are exported.

Goods and services that are totally used up when producing final goods and services are not included in gross national product. Such goods are classified as **intermediate goods.**

Intermediate goods are goods that are completely used up in the production of final goods and services.

The value of intermediate goods is not included in calculating GNP to avoid double-counting the value of the final goods and services produced. Double-counting would overstate the actual amount of goods available in the economy. An automobile, for example, is composed of steel and other metals, paint, rubber, and plastic, which are purchased by automobile manufacturers from suppliers and used to produce automobiles. These goods are intermediate goods because they are not delivered directly to the final user but to the manufacturers of automobiles. The value of these intermediate goods is ignored in constructing GNP precisely because it is already included in the value of the cars produced. An automobile that costs $10,000 has included in its value the cost of the intermediate goods used in its manufacture.

The existence of intermediate goods does allow GNP to be calculated in another way by adding together the **value added** from each firm in the economy.

Value added is the amount of value contributed to a product by a firm at a given stage of the production process.

Value added is equal to a firm's sales less the value of the intermediate goods it uses to produce its products. Thus, to continue the example of automobile manufacturing, either the total value of automobiles produced can be summed and included annually in GNP, or the value added of all automobile producers plus the value added of each of the industry's suppliers can be totaled. The results of the two procedures will be the same.

TABLE 6.1
Gross National Product by Industrial Category: 1986

INDUSTRIAL CATEGORY	VALUE ADDED (BILLIONS OF 1986 DOLLARS)	PERCENTAGE OF GNP
Agriculture, forestry, fisheries	$ 93	2.2%
Mining	131	3.1
Construction	194	4.6
Manufacturing	838	19.9
Transportation and utilities	396	9.4
Distribution (wholesale and retail)	686	16.3
Finance, insurance, real estate	657	15.6
Services	673	16.0
Government	501	11.9
Other (rest of world)	40	1.0
GNP	$4,209	100.0%

Source: *Survey of Current Business.*

The U.S. Department of Commerce collects GNP statistics using the value-added approach. The value added by industrial categories is shown in Table 6.1.

PER CAPITA GROSS NATIONAL PRODUCT

In 1986 GNP in the United States was $4.2 trillion — a number so astronomical that it is difficult to comprehend. A statistic that is more easily grasped is **per capita gross national product.**

> *Per capita gross national product measures the value per person of the final goods and services produced by domestically owned factors of production in a given year.*

It is calculated by dividing gross national product by the population of the country, so for 1986:

$$\text{Per capita GNP} = \frac{\text{Gross national product}}{\text{Population}} = \frac{\$4.208 \text{ trillion}}{241.5 \text{ million}} = \$17,420$$

Per capita income in the United States in 1986 was $17,420 for every man, woman, and child. A family of four's share of GNP, if GNP was equally divided among the whole population, totaled almost $70,000! Do not despair if you didn't receive this amount. Gross national product does not represent the flow of income to households, as you will discover below.

WHAT GROSS NATIONAL PRODUCT DOES NOT MEASURE

GNP measures the value of the final goods and services produced during a particular year. Some goods and services that are exchanged during a particular year were not produced during the year for which the GNP estimate applies. Used cars, previously owned houses and buildings, some art objects, and all antiques are examples. The costs of such goods are excluded because they are not currently produced goods but were the products of some previous year. They were included in that year's GNP. The costs of making the trades of previously produced goods, such as commissions and fees, are, however, current services and are counted in this year's GNP.

The national income accounts attempt to measure the total value of the flow of all final goods and services to consumers. Ideally, all final goods would be valued at market-determined prices, but not all can be. The fact that not all final goods and services are exchanged in markets complicates the task of national income estimators. There are no market-determined prices to value the outputs produced. Although many government services are supplied free of charge to all citizens, estimators are forced to impute a value to these goods and services. One way to do this is to estimate a market value; another way is to value the goods and services at their costs of production. Government services, for example, are valued at the costs of production. Home owners, for example, live in houses that provide a service that has an opportunity cost. If it were not owned, the house would be rented for a fee. Gross national product contains an estimate of the amount of this imputed rent. Thus the value of some components of GNP are not derived from market prices but are estimated.

It is also difficult for GNP estimators to adjust for quality changes that occur in final goods and services over time. A black-and-white television set produced in 1965 is clearly inferior to the remote-controlled color television set of 1988. The services performed by a doctor today are superior to the services of a doctor two decades ago. If you compare GNP today with GNP two decades ago, you are not comparing the same goods. The growth of GNP over the last two decades will be understated by the extent that the quality of goods and services has increased.

All final goods should be included in GNP, but not all are. Some nonmarket activities are excluded from GNP because of the difficulty of measuring their imputed value. The activities of homemakers, volunteer services, and do-it-yourselfers are excluded for this reason. If the value of these activities were imputed, GNP would be substantially larger.

Also excluded are illegal activities and production that is undertaken to escape taxation. Illegal activities such as the drug trade, illegal gambling, and the numbers racket are excluded, while legal gambling and state lotteries, which are similar legal activities, are included. Illegal activities are excluded on practical grounds; because they are hidden activities, it is difficult to measure their extent. Underground activities, such as when a worker is paid in cash and doesn't report all income when he or she pays income taxes, are also excluded for practical reasons. Such goods and services are indistinguishable from similar "aboveground" activities, except that no taxes are paid. The final value of such activities is excluded because of the difficulty in estimating their value. There are, however, unofficial estimates of these activities that provide some idea of the extent that GNP is underestimated. The value of the goods and services produced in the underground economy may range from a low of 3–5 percent of GNP up to several times these amounts.

GNP also does not attempt to value the leisure consumed by Americans. The number of hours worked per year has declined considerably over the last half-century as workers have decided to consume part of their increased productivity in time off from work rather than in more goods and services. In 1900 workers averaged a 60-hour workweek; by 1987 this had fallen to a 40-hour workweek. If workers today worked as long as they did in 1900, real output would be considerably higher. The fact that workers have chosen more time off rather than more goods and services suggests that they place a higher value on leisure than on the goods and services sacrificed.

However, leisure is not valued in national income accounts because GNP values only tangible goods and services. The omission of leisure in these accounts seriously understates GNP if we wish to use it as a measure of economic well-being. The omission becomes very important when we attempt to compare GNP over time. The average workweek has declined over time, so the quantity of leisure consumed has increased. Comparing the output of tangible goods and services will therefore understate the true growth in economic well-being.

But GNP is not designed to be a measure of economic well-being, although it is often used for that purpose. It is simply a measure of the value of the final goods and services produced in the economy. It is designed to track what is happening to the output of final goods and services and thereby to provide a scorecard for the economy.

There are other problems associated with using GNP as a measure of economic well-being. Some of the goods measured in GNP may, in fact, be "bads" or have bad consequences that remain unaccounted for. Industry, for example, often produces pollution along with manufactured goods. Acid rain created by burning fossil fuels is destroying the nation's timber and lakes. Yet the value added of the manufactured goods is included at full value in GNP, not at the value net of external costs. External costs are not taken into account when estimating GNP.

The errors of omission and commission of national income accounting should serve as a warning about using GNP indiscriminately. GNP in practice makes some use of imputed values in place of market-determined prices, excludes some final goods and services including leisure, and counts all goods at their market value even when some of those goods impose external costs on society. GNP was not designed as a measure of economic well-being. But items designed for one purpose can often usefully be employed for another purpose. Despite these defects, GNP ranks among the best indicators of the overall performance of the economy available. The above criticisms do not suggest that GNP cannot be used to evaluate economic welfare, only that the estimates must be used with care.

MEASURING GROSS NATIONAL PRODUCT

A look at Figure 6.1 reveals that GNP can be calculated in one of two ways: the expenditure approach or the flow-of-income approach. The **expenditure approach** involves adding up the money expenditures of households for final goods and services as measured along the outer loop at the bottom of the diagram.

> *The expenditure approach to calculating gross national product is the practice of summing the total dollar values of all final products sold in a given year.*

The expenditure approach can also be calculated as the sum of the value added by each firm in the economy during one year.

The circular flow diagram also suggests a second way that GNP can be calculated. The process of producing the final goods and services creates at the same time an equivalent amount of income for the owners of the factors of production. The value of final goods and services produced therefore equals the total amount of factor income. The approach is

FIGURE 6.2

Calculating GNP from the Expenditures Approach and the Breakdown of the National Income Accounts

The circular flow diagram in this figure shows the interrelationship among five sectors of the economy: households, government, business firms, foreign trade, and financial markets. It shows how these sectors are related by the flow of income and in the process, along the upper loop, how GNP is calculated and, along the lower loop, how the various national income statistics are calculated. Beginning with households at point 1 consumers decide how much of their disposable income to consume (C) and to save (S). Consumption expenditures flow directly to business firms while savings flow to financial markets and in turn are used to fund investment expenditures (I), point 2, or as part of government expenditures, point 3. Point 4 introduces the foreign-trade sector. GNP, measured at point 5, is composed of the flows of income from consumption, investment, government expenditures, and net exports.

The lower loop of the diagram reveals how the various national income statistics are derived from GNP. When depreciation is subtracted in the form of capital consumption allowance at point 6, the result is net national product (NNP). When indirect business taxes are subtracted at point 7, the result is national income. Subtracting other taxes and adding government transfers gives personal income at point 8. Deducting personal taxes leaves at point 9 personal disposable income, which is the amount that consumers have to allocate between consumption and saving, the amount of income with which we began the explanation.

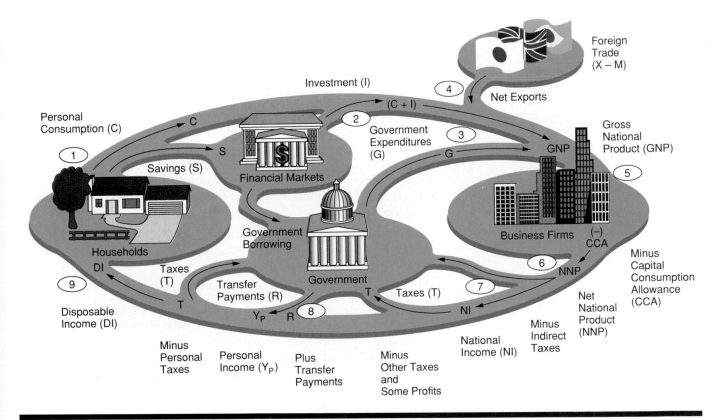

known as the **flow-of-income approach** and measures GNP along the outside loop at the top of the circular flow diagram in Figure 6.1.

> *The flow-of-income approach to calculating gross national product is the practice of summing the flow of income to the owners of all factors of production in the economy in a given year.*

Whether calculated by the flow-of-income approach or by the expenditures approach, GNP will be the same. The value of total expenditures for final goods and services will be the same as the total income of the factors of production. The two methods are often used as checks on one another.

THE EXPENDITURES APPROACH The expenditures, or flow-of-products, approach adds together the dollar values of all final goods and services produced during one year. The real world is more complicated than the simple circular flow diagram in Figure 6.1 suggests. Figure 6.2

TABLE 6.2
Gross National Product Calculated by the Expenditure Approach: 1986
(Billions of Dollars)

EXPENDITURE CATEGORY		VALUE IN 1986	PERCENTAGE OF TOTAL
Personal consumption		$2,762	65.6%
Nondurable goods	$933		
Durable goods	388		
Services	441		
Gross private domestic investment		686	16.3
Nonresidential structures	144		
Equipment	315		
Residential structures	217		
Inventory adjustment	11		
Government purchases		865	20.6
Federal	367		
State and local	498		
Exports minus imports		−106	−2.5
Gross national product		$4,209	100.0%

Source: *Survey of Current Business.*

presents a more complete circular flow diagram. GNP is composed of all of the final goods produced in one year. There are four categories of final goods and services:

1. Personal consumption expenditures
2. Government expenditures for goods and services
3. Investment expenditures
4. Balance of foreign trade (exports minus imports)

Each of these categories is included in the figure, along with a decision-making unit that determines the amount of each expenditure. The household sector determines the amount of consumption and saving (point 1), financial markets the amount of investment (point 2), government the amount of government expenditures (point 3), and the foreign-trade sector (point 4) the balance of foreign trade. The relative importance of each category in determining GNP can be seen from the data in Table 6.2.

Personal Consumption Expenditures Personal consumption expenditures are final goods and services purchased by households. Consumption goods (point 1) are either consumed immediately (food, soft drinks, movies, and haircuts) and are known as *nondurable goods*, or are consumed over time (VCRs, automobiles, and refrigerators) and are called *durable goods*. Services, like nondurable goods, are also consumed immediately. These expenditures are made by households for their enjoyment and are not used to produce other goods. Personal consumption expenditures comprise the largest single category in GNP — over 65 percent.

Investment Expenditures Investment expenditures are made to increase or replace the nation's capital stock. Investment expenditures are used to purchase capital goods, which, because they are final goods, are added to consumption expenditures at point 2 in the circular flow diagram in Figure 6.2. Capital is composed of buildings, equipment, and inventories, all of which will be used in the future to produce more goods and services.

Investment is not classified as an intermediate good because capital is not completely used up in producing final products. The steel used for a car body is an intermediate good because it is totally embodied in a vehicle and sold to a consumer in the course of the year being evaluated. Steel used to produce a metal press, however, helps to build automobile bodies for an extended period of time and is therefore classified as a capital good.

Capital goods are only partly used up in a year. The part that is consumed is called *depreciation*. **Depreciation,** like wages or rents, is a current cost of production.

> *Depreciation is the value of the capital stock that has been consumed or used up in a given year in the process of producing goods and services.*

Capital stock is acquired by investing. Investment is divided into two subcategories in national income accounting: inventory investment and fixed investment. **Inventory investment** consists of goods waiting to be sold. Because business firms cannot precisely predict the amount and timing of orders they will receive, they produce some goods in advance and store them while awaiting buyers. Retail stores, for example, place inventories on shelves from which customers can select the goods they desire.

> *Inventory investment is investment that reflects the increase or decrease over a year of the size of inventories that firms keep on hand.*

Fixed investment is the other category of investment.

> *Fixed investment is composed of the addition of new plant, equipment, and buildings to the capital stock.*

Fixed investment is also usefully subdivided into two other categories: residential and nonresidential. Residential investment is the value of the private housing that is built in a year. Nonresidential investment measures the value of the plants, equipment, and commercial buildings that are constructed in a year. Private-sector investment in 1986 amounted to 16.3 percent of GNP. Thus consumption expenditures plus investment expenditures account for nearly 82 percent of GNP.

Government Expenditures Governments at every level purchase final goods and services. Governments purchase weapons, hire military personnel, operate schools, and support police and fire departments. These expenditures are included in GNP. Some government activities may appear to be intermediate goods, such as government regulatory agencies, but by convention nearly all government purchases of goods and services are counted in GNP as if they were final goods.

However, only government expenditures for goods and services are counted in GNP. Governments are also involved in redistributing income, but transfers are not included, because no additional goods or services are produced by transfer payments.

The largest transfer program is social security, but the government also transfers income to the unemployed, the poor, and to groups that are considered deserving, such as students and farmers. Government is not the only institution involved in transferring income, however. Individuals and businesses also engage in charitable giving. These amounts are also not included in GNP, because no goods or services have been produced as a consequence of the transfers.

Despite the exclusion of a significant part of government activities, the government sector is still the second largest contributor to GNP when it is calculated according to the flow-of-products method. The government sector — federal, state, and local — accounted for 20.6 percent of GNP in 1986. When government expenditures are added to consumption and investment expenditures (point 3 on the circular flow diagram), we have expenditures that total 102.5 percent of GNP. How can this be? The answer lies in the foreign-trade sector.

Balance of Trade: Exports minus Imports   Not all of the goods produced in the United States are purchased domestically, and not all of the goods purchased here are made here. GNP, if it is to give an accurate portrayal of the total output of final goods and services, must include foreign trade. This is accomplished by adding the value of domestically produced goods that are exported and subtracting the value of foreign-made goods that are imported. The value of exports minus the value of imports is referred to as net exports, which is shown as point 4 on the circular flow diagram in Figure 6.2.

Net exports may be positive, as when the United States sells abroad more than it purchases there, or negative, as has lately been the case. The foreign-trade balance is negative when the United States purchases more from foreign countries than it sells abroad. In 1986 the foreign-trade sector contributed to GNP a negative amount equal to 2.5 percent of GNP. Thus if we subtract the negative contribution of the foreign-trade sector in 1986, we shall have accounted for precisely 100 percent of GNP, according to the expenditures or flow-of-products method.

In the expenditures approach, adding together the amounts of personal consumption expenditures, investment expenditures, government expenditures, and net exports gives GNP of $4.2 trillion in 1986, as shown in Table 6.2.

THE FLOW-OF-INCOME APPROACH   The circular flow diagram in Figure 6.2 demonstrates that the value of the final goods and services produced in the economy in one year must also be equal to the flow of income to the owners of the factors of production. When the flow of income is totaled, it is called **gross national income (GNI).**

> *Gross national income is the sum of all the income earned by the owners of the factors of production. It is calculated by adding together the incomes earned by labor, land, and capital, and the profits that are received by entrepreneurs.*

Since GNI must equal GNP, it can be used as a separate check on the accuracy of GNP calculations.

Factor Incomes   The incomes of the owners of the factors of production depend on the payments those owners receive in the course of producing GNP. Unfortunately, the flow of income that can be measured in the economy does not closely correspond to the four factors of production: labor, land, capital, and entrepreneurship, as you can see from Table 6.3. This table relates the amount of these payments, along with the percentage of GNI each provided in 1986.

Payments directly made to labor are called *compensation of employees* and accounted for 59.3 percent of GNI in 1986. Payments to land are shown in the table as *rental income of persons* and equaled 1.4 percent of

T A B L E   6 . 3
Gross National Income by Source of Income: 1986

SOURCE OF INCOME	INCOME (BILLIONS OF DOLLARS)	PERCENTAGE
Compensation of employees	$2,498	59.3%
Proprietor's income	279	6.6
Rental income of persons	61	1.4
Corporate profits	300	7.1
Net interest	295	7.0
Depreciation and other	776	18.6
Total	$4,209	100.0%

Source: *Survey of Current Business*.

GNI. *Proprietor's income* is part payment for the labor of the self-employed, part payment to the capital they have invested in their businesses, and part profit. Proprietor's income accounted for 6.6 percent of GNI. *Corporate profits* do not measure all of the profits earned in the economy, but only the profits of incorporated firms and not the profits of partnerships and sole proprietors. Corporate profits equaled 7.1 percent of GNI in 1986. *Depreciation* is payment for the capital used up during the year, and *net interest* represents payments for the use of credit, some of which was borrowed to acquire capital goods and some to buy consumer durables. Depreciation and miscellaneous payments accounted for 18.6 percent of GNI, while net interest payments amounted to 7.0 percent.

BREAKDOWN OF THE NATIONAL INCOME ACCOUNTS

Gross national product and gross national income are the broadest measures of national income. There are times when less comprehensive measures are required. GNP includes a capital consumption allowance to account for the depreciation of the capital stock during the year. The capital consumption allowance amounted to $455 billion in 1986, or nearly 11 percent of GNP. But this expenditure simply replaced the capital that was used up during the year and did not represent the production of any goods and services. When depreciation is subtracted from GNP, a different statistic called *net national product* is obtained.

NET NATIONAL PRODUCT

If economists are interested in a measure that indicates the actual amount of final goods and services available in the economy during a year, they exclude the capital consumption allowance. When they do this, they are using a concept for aggregate output that is called **net national product (NNP).**

> *Net national product is the measure of the total value of final goods and services actually available in the economy in a given year.*

Net national product is calculated by subtracting the capital consumption allowance (CCA), which measures the total depreciation during the year, from GNP:

$$NNP = GNP - CCA$$

NNP is shown in Figure 6.2 at point 6. What is left after CCA is subtracted from GNP measures the total amount of new goods and services available to the economy.

NATIONAL INCOME

Both GNP and NNP are determined by the prices that buyers pay for final goods and services. Included in these prices are numerous excise and sales taxes, such as the retail sales tax levied in several states and the federal excise tax on liquor and cigarettes. These tax payments are called indirect business taxes and although they add to government revenues, they do not generate income for businesses and individuals. A measure that indicates the total income available in the economy to purchase goods and services should exclude such taxes. Such a measure is called **national income (NI).**

> *National income is the measure of the total value of the payments to the owners of the factors of production.*

National income is calculated from net national product by subtracting the amount of indirect business taxes:

$$NI = NNP - \text{Indirect business taxes}$$

NI is shown in Figure 6.2 at point 7.

Not all income that is earned by the factors of production is actually paid to them during a given year, nor is earned income the sole determinant of the gross amount of money households have to spend. To determine the gross value of what households have to spend, some adjustments must be made to national income to obtain personal income.

PERSONAL INCOME

Not all income that is earned is actually received during the year under study. Included in national income are three sources that should be excluded from **personal income.** These are (1) undistributed corporate profits, (2) corporate income taxes, and (3) social security contributions. Corporations do not pay out all of their earnings as dividends but usually retain part for purposes of reinvestment. Moreover, corporations, if they are profitable, must pay corporate income taxes. Households also must pay social security taxes on their earnings, which are deducted from their paychecks and never received. All three are subtracted from national income to obtain personal income.

But there are also additions to national income that must be made to obtain personal income. Transfer payments (gifts from any source whatever) are not included in GNP; they are not payments for goods and services but they do add to personal income. Similarly interest payments by governments are excluded from GNP and considered transfers. Transfers do add to household income and should be added to NNP to obtain personal income (Y_P).

> *Personal income is the gross amount of income available to households. It is obtained from national income by subtracting undistributed corporate profits, corporate taxes, and social security contributions and adding back the amount of transfers, including government interest payments.*

Personal income is obtained from national income using the following calculation:

$$Y_P = NI - \text{Undistributed corporate profits, corporate taxes,}$$
$$\text{social security contributions}$$
$$+ \text{Transfers, including government interest payments}$$

Y_P is measured at point 8 on the circular flow diagram in Figure 6.2.

Finally, personal income measures the gross amount of income that households receive. It does not measure the actual amount they have to spend or save. Personal disposable income measures this amount.

PERSONAL DISPOSABLE INCOME

To determine the amount of income that households actually have available to spend or save, individual taxes, such as state and federal income taxes, must be subtracted from personal income to obtain **personal disposable income (DI)**.

> *Personal disposable income is the amount of income households have at their disposal to spend or save.*

Personal disposable income, or disposable income, is calculated by subtracting personal taxes from personal income:

$$DI = Y_P - \text{Personal taxes}$$

DI is measured at point 9 on the circular flow diagram in Figure 6.2.

When all of the adjustments to GNP have been made to obtain personal disposable income for 1986, the result is a personal disposable income of $2.97 billion out of the $4.21 billion in GNP. Personal disposable income measures the amount of income that households have to spend or save. Per capita disposable income in 1986 was $12,300, or over $5,122 less than per capita GNP. The personal income of a family of four was $49,200. Actually, households have quite a bit less to spend or save than GNP suggests.

Table 6.4 summarizes the various national income statistics for 1986. Each account gives users a different perspective on the aggregate economy and each is useful for answering a variety of different questions. If you are interested in the value of the goods and services produced for final demand, then GNP provides the answer. If instead you wish to know by how much the national aggregate output exceeded the amount necessary to replace the worn-out portion of the capital stock, NNP provides that answer. If, however, you are interested in determining the amount of personal consumption and personal saving, personal disposable income is the most useful national income category. Table 6.4 summarizes how the various national income statistics are calculated and provides the 1986 values for each category.

TABLE 6.4
Breakdown of the National Income Accounts: 1986

ITEM	INCOME (BILLIONS OF DOLLARS)
Gross national product (GNP) = Gross national income (GNI)	$4,209
− Capital consumption allowance (depreciation)	−455
= Net national product (NNP)	$3,754
− Indirect business taxes	−367
= National income (NI)	$3,387
− Corporate taxes, undistributed corporate profits, social security contributions	−595
+ Transfer payments and government interest payments	+695
= Personal income (Y_P)	$3,487
− Personal taxes	−513
= Personal disposable income (DI)	$2,974

Source: Department of Commerce.

What do households do with their disposable income? **Consumption expenditure** accounts for most personal disposable income.

> *Consumption expenditure is all of the spending by households except the purchase of housing.*

In 1986 personal disposable income was $2,974 billion, of which $2,762 billion, or nearly 93 percent, was spent on consumption. Interest payments absorbed $94 billion, and the remaining $116 billion represented **personal saving.**

> *Personal saving is the proportion of personal disposable income that is saved.*

The share of personal savings in personal disposable income is called the *personal savings rate.* The personal savings rate in the United States in 1986 was around 4 percent, which was the lowest savings rate among the major industrial countries. This low rate is a cause of concern for some economists, as we shall see in subsequent chapters.

It should be noted that households are not the only economic institutions that save. Business firms also save. Businesses save by not distributing all of their profits to their owners (the undistributed corporate profits we discussed above exemplify business saving) and by setting aside funds to replace their depreciating capital stock. The sum of personal saving and business saving is termed **private saving.**

> *Private saving is the total of personal saving plus business saving out of retained earnings and funds set aside for depreciation expenses.*

Billions of U.S. Dollars

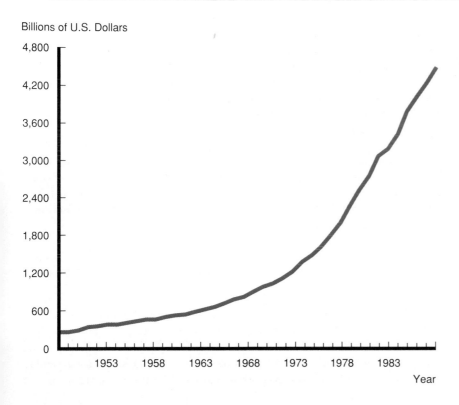

FIGURE 6.3
Nominal Gross National Product in the
United States: 1948–1987

In 1948 nominal GNP was $252 billion; by 1987 it was
$4.6 trillion. It is clear that nominal GNP has significantly
increased over time, but not at a constant rate. The rate
of increase fluctuates over time and beginning in 1970
appears to have increased. Much of this increase was
due to increases in the price level rather than to increases
in the output of final goods and services.

GROSS NATIONAL PRODUCT OVER TIME

What do we mean when we state that gross national product was $4.2
trillion in 1986, personal disposable income was $2.97 trillion, consump-
tion $2.76 trillion, and personal savings $116 billion? Such amounts are
often most useful when compared to similar amounts from other years.
Figure 6.3 graphically displays the value of GNP for the years 1948–
1987. GNP is measured in the prices that prevailed in each of the years.
This is called **nominal gross national product.**

> *Nominal gross national product is the value of final goods
> and services for a given year measured in terms of the pre-
> vailing market prices in that year.*

It can readily be seen from the graph that the trend of nominal GNP
is upward over time, indicating that the overall size of the economy has
increased over time. This implication may be misleading, however. Nominal GNP can rise between years either because the production of final
goods and services increases, or because the prices of all final goods have
increased, or because both occur at the same time. To determine how
much the production of final goods and services has changed over time, it
is important to be certain that the differences between the years are actually due to changes in the output of goods and services and not merely to
price-level changes.

REAL GROSS NATIONAL PRODUCT

Because GNP is widely used to measure the performance of the economy,
it is important that it measure the change in the output of goods and
services only. As mentioned above there are two ways that nominal GNP

can increase: through an increase in the quantities of final goods and services, or through an increase in the prices of these goods and services. Frequently, both of these increases occur together. An increase in the quantity of goods and services means that the society as a whole has more goods and services available to satisfy the wants of its members. But when nominal GNP increases due to a general rise in prices, more goods and services are not available to satisfy wants; there are just higher prices for the same amount of goods. It is important to be able to distinguish between the two types of increases.

So far we have discussed GNP measured in current dollar prices, called nominal GNP. When nominal GNP increases, it is not clear whether we have more goods and services, or just higher prices, or some of both. It is possible to eliminate the effect of changing prices in GNP. When this is done, the resulting measure is called **real gross national product** to distinguish the measure from nominal GNP.

> *Real gross national product is the measure of the actual quantity of final goods and services produced in the economy; it is determined by removing the effects of price changes.*

Real GNP measures aggregate output in constant dollar prices, using the prices from some base year to eliminate the effect of price-level changes between years. Real GNP answers the question: What would be the value of the final goods and services produced by the economy in a particular year if those goods and services were evaluated by the prices that existed in a base year?

Economists employ a price index known as the **GNP deflator** to eliminate price-level changes from nominal GNP. The GNP deflator measures the extent to which the prices of the goods included in GNP on average change from year to year. The formula for calculating the GNP deflator is:

$$\text{GNP deflator} = \frac{\text{Price level in year}}{\text{Price level in base year}} \times 100$$

> *The GNP deflator is a price index that measures price changes in the economy from year to year.*

Figure 6.4 displays the GNP deflator for the years 1948 to 1987. The year 1982 has been arbitrarily chosen as the base year in this index and given a weight of 100. When the general level of prices for a year was lower than in 1982, the GNP deflator will have a value less than 100 for those years. Conversely, when the overall price level for a year is greater than prevailed in 1982, the GNP deflator for that year will have a value greater than 100. It is clear that the price level has increased since 1948 and has increased more rapidly after 1970. The rate of increase has slowed during the 1980s.

The GNP deflator provides the means of converting nominal GNP to real GNP. The differences between the two can be striking. Nominal GNP in 1980, for example, was \$2,732 billion, and in 1986 it was \$4,209 billion, or 54 percent greater. How much of this increase was real and how much was due to increases in the price level?

The GNP deflator in 1982, chosen as the base year and valued at 100, in 1980 stood at 85.7, and in 1986 was 114.5. The price level therefore increased from 85.7 to 114.5 over the years from 1980 to 1986. So some portion of the increase in nominal GNP was due to an increase in the price level.

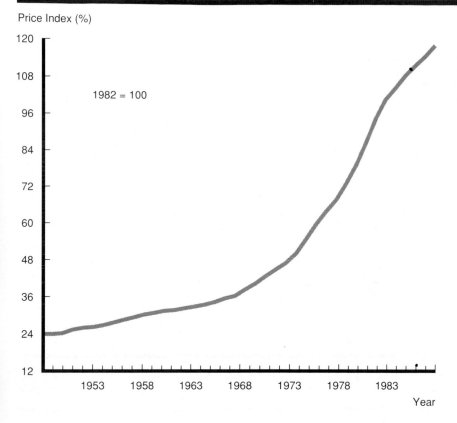

Price Index (%)

1982 = 100

FIGURE 6.4
Implicit Price Index in the Gross National Products Accounts: The GNP Deflator

This figure charts the GNP deflator, which is the price index used to convert nominal GNP to real GNP. The year 1982 has been selected as the base year and set at 100. A GNP deflator of less than 100 indicates that the price level is lower than in the base year 1982, and a number greater than 100 indicates that the price level is higher than in the base year. It is clear that the GNP deflator increased roughly in step with nominal GNP from 1948 through 1987, as shown in Figure 6.3. This suggests that much of the increase in nominal GNP was due to inflation and not to an increase in the output of final goods and services.

How much was due to an increase in the production of goods? Consider:

$$\frac{\text{Nominal GNP in 1980}}{\text{GNP deflator in 1980}} = \frac{\$2,732}{.857} = \$3,188 \text{ billion in 1982 dollars}$$

and

$$\frac{\text{Nominal GNP in 1986}}{\text{GNP deflator in 1986}} = \frac{\$4,209}{1.145} = \$3,676 \text{ billion in 1982 dollars}$$

$$\frac{\text{Real 1986 GNP in 1982 dollars}}{\text{Real 1980 GNP in 1982 dollars}} = \frac{\$3,676}{\$3,188} = 1.15$$

In sum, real GNP increased by 15 percent between 1980 and 1986, while nominal GNP was rising by 54 percent. Most of the increase in nominal GNP was due to price-level increases.

The difference between real and nominal GNP can be quite large in percentage terms, particularly during periods of high inflation. The historical difference between nominal and real GNP can be seen in Figure 6.5. It is clear from this figure that real GNP has grown much more slowly than nominal GNP. Moreover, the fluctuations in real GNP are apparently greater than occur in nominal GNP. The production of real goods and services is much more variable than measurement in nominal value reveals. The fluctuations in real GNP appear even more pronounced when displayed as per capita GNP, as in Figure 6.6.

Real GNP is a particularly valuable tool for economists, because it measures the total quantity of goods and services the economy is actually

FIGURE 6.5
Real and Nominal Gross National Product in
the United States: 1948–1987

This figure allows the comparison of real and nominal
GNP. Real GNP measures the amount of physical goods
and services the economy is producing after the effects
of price-level changes have been removed by employing
the GNP deflator. Since 1982 is the base year, real and
nominal GNP are the same in that year. A comparison of
the two figures reveals that nominal GNP has grown at a
more rapid rate than real GNP, reflecting the effect of
inflation in determining nominal GNP. A second conclusion is evident: Real GNP fluctuates much more significantly than nominal GNP.

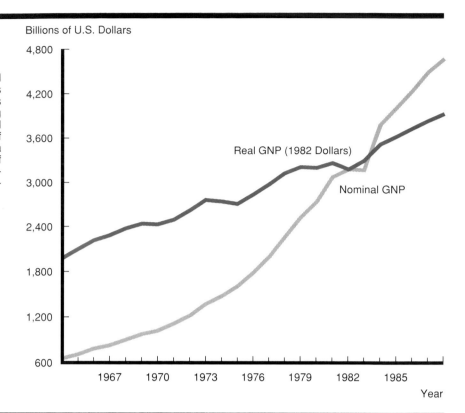

FIGURE 6.6
Real Per Capita Income in the United States,
Measured in 1982 Dollars: 1948–1987

Real per capita income is obtained by dividing real GNP
by the size of the population. It provides a measure of the
average amount of final real goods and services available
to each citizen. Real per capita income has increased
significantly over the last four decades, increasing from
$7,400 in 1948 (measured in 1982 dollars) to $15,900 in
1987. The increase has not been smooth: Although real
per capita income has generally increased over time, it
has actually declined in some years.

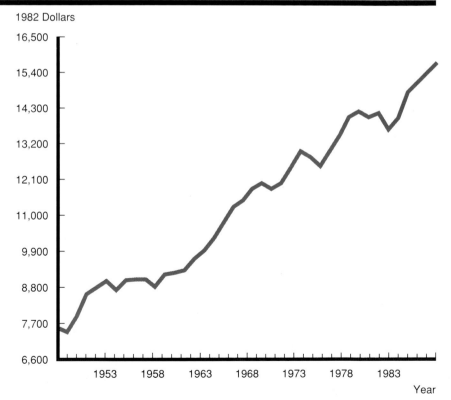

producing. Comparing real GNP over time allows an estimation of how
the economy is performing and reveals fluctuations in the real output of
the economy. It is evident from these figures that real GNP does not
advance smoothly but with significant fluctuations.

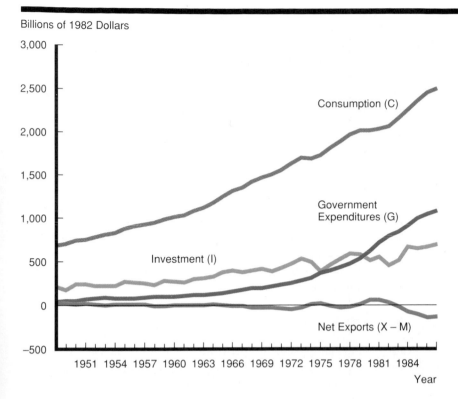

Billions of 1982 Dollars

Consumption (C)

Government Expenditures (G)

Investment (I)

Net Exports (X – M)

Year

FIGURE 6.7
Components of Real Gross National Product, Measured in 1982 Dollars: 1948–1987

This figure charts the four components of GNP: consumption, investment, government expenditures for goods and services, and net exports (exports minus imports). In 1987 consumption was the largest component of GNP, followed by government expenditures, investment, and net exports.

COMPONENTS OF GROSS NATIONAL PRODUCT RECONSIDERED

Examining the components of GNP reveals much about its composition and about the trends in the macroeconomy over time. Figure 6.7 displays the components of real GNP when it is constructed according to the flow-of-products method. It is clear that consumption is the main component of GNP, that government expenditures for goods and services have been expanding more rapidly than the other components, that investment is more variable from year to year than the other components, and that foreign trade has always been a rather small component of real GNP, although it has lately become relatively more important as a negative contribution. Net exports have been sharply negative since 1982.

FINAL THOUGHTS ON GROSS NATIONAL PRODUCT

GNP is valuable precisely because it is so all-encompassing, taking into account the activities of both profit-seeking businesses and nonprofit-making institutions such as government at all levels. This breadth generates serious conceptual problems as well as practical problems in assembling and collecting the huge amount of data required. You discovered above that in computing national income statistics, GNP estimators (1) have chosen to ignore leisure as well as household services and the value of voluntary activities, (2) have had serious problems with dealing with quality improvements over time, and (3) are forced to impute the value of many economic activities to obtain estimates. These difficulties suggest that GNP figures must be used with care.

Because of the size of the task of estimating GNP, it is attempted only every three months on a quarterly basis. During the third week of the month following the end of a calendar quarter, the Department of Commerce releases preliminary estimates of that quarter's GNP. Anything preliminary suggests that a final figure that may be significantly different will be forthcoming. For example, in January 1985 it was announced that the economy had expanded at an inflation-adjusted rate of 3.9 percent during the last quarter of 1984. This was good news since the economy had apparently been growing at a rate above the historical pace since World War II. Unfortunately, that 3.9 percent growth rate was only a preliminary estimate. When all of the data were in, the GNP growth rate was revised to only 0.6 percent. Instead of growing fairly rapidly as initially indicated, the economy was expanding very slowly. Had the preliminary estimate been more accurate, economic decision makers would have been alerted much more quickly that 1985 was going to be a year of slow, not rapid, economic expansion.

GNP has many uses, but its lack of timeliness means that economists and economic decision makers must watch other measures of economic performance as well. In succeeding chapters you will discover that other kinds of information are necessary to keep current track of the economy.

SUMMARY

1. National income accounting provides the means for measuring the total output of goods and services in the economy. The basic concept of national income accounting rests on the concept of the circular flow of income and output. The value of the final output produced in the economy is equal to the value of the total income created, because the very act of production creates a corresponding equivalent amount of income for the owners of the factors of production.

2. Gross national product (GNP) is the key measure of economic activity, because it is the broadest measure of total output. GNP is defined as the final value of all goods and services produced by domestically owned factors of production in a given year. Only final goods and services are included, to avoid the problem of double counting. Intermediate goods are therefore not included in GNP.

3. GNP can be calculated in two basic ways. It can be calculated by adding up the values of the final goods and services produced, or by measuring the value added of each firm in the economy.

4. GNP can also be derived by measuring the total income of the factors of production. When calculated according to this method, it is sometimes called gross national income (GNI). GNP should always equal GNI.

5. There are therefore three separate ways to arrive at the value of GNP:

    a. GNP = Personal consumption expenditures + Investment expenditures + Government expenditures for goods and services + Net exports (Exports − Imports).

    b. GNP = Sum of the value added of each firm in the economy. Value added equals the payments to the factors of production made by each firm minus the purchases of intermediate goods.

    c. GNP = GNI = Compensation of employees + Proprietor's income + Rental income + Corporate profits + Net interest payments + Depreciation + Other miscellaneous payments.

6. There are both conceptual and measurement problems with estimating GNP. The actual measurement of GNP excludes some final goods and services, imputes the value of other goods and services, and ignores leisure in the calculation. Also adequately estimating quality improvement

in goods and services presents a serious problem when comparing GNP over time.

7. The national income accounts can be broken down into subcategories:

- GNP − Depreciation = Net national product (NNP)
- NNP − Indirect business taxes = National income (NI)
- NI − Factor payments not received by individuals and social security contributions + Transfer payments = Personal income (Y_P)
- Y_P − Personal taxes = Personal disposable income (DI)

8. Nominal GNP is the value of final goods and services measured using current prices. Nominal GNP can change, due either to a change in the output of goods and services or to a change in the overall price level.

9. Real GNP eliminates changes in the price level from nominal GNP. Real GNP is obtained by using a price index known as the GNP deflator. Real GNP provides a better measure of the goods and services produced for final consumption than does nominal GNP.

10. Real GNP is often used as a measure of economic well-being although it was not designed for this purpose and has several deficiencies when so used. At the very least, the cost of externalities such as pollution should be excluded, the value of leisure should be included, and adjustments for improvement in the quality of goods and services should be made.

11. GNP is available quarterly, with a preliminary estimate issued the third week after the calendar quarter ends. This estimate is subject to subsequent revision, and sometimes the corrections are significant. In order to keep score on the macroeconomy, it is necessary to track more than just GNP.

THE SHIFT TO SERVICES: WHERE WILL YOU WORK?

PREVIEW 6.1 ANALYSIS

Since World War II the proportion of services in GNP has increased from 58 percent to 68 percent. The accompanying shift in the distribution of the labor force has been much larger. In 1948 about half of all U.S. workers were employed in the service sector; in 1987 it was about three-quarters. These significant changes have given rise to fears that the United States is fast becoming a nation whose workers are serving each other hamburgers and taking in other people's laundry, a nation that can no longer compete in manufacturing and is being reduced to performing services.

Americans apparently have just recently awakened to these changes in the structure of the economy. In actuality, the trend to services is at least a century old. The current fear of services also reveals a profound misinterpretation of American economic history. The rise of the service sector is most likely due to the strength, not the weakness, of the economy's manufacturing sector combined with the rise of international specialization. It is precisely the high productivity of the manufacturing and agricultural sectors that has made the fast growth of the service sector possible. Moreover, these forces have been active not just in the 1970s and 1980s but throughout our nation's history.

The national income accounts allow changes within the various sectors of the economy to be compared. The purpose of this analysis is to

FIGURE 6.8
Distribution of Real Gross National Product:
1948–1985

This figure shows that the percentage of real GNP contributed by manufacturing has remained relatively constant over time. Manufacturing contributed about 21 percent of real GNP in 1948 and about the same percentage in 1985. The contribution of the service sector has increased over time from less than 60 percent to almost 70 percent. This expansion has taken place at the expense of the primary sector (agriculture, mining, and construction), which has declined by approximately as much as the service sector has expanded.

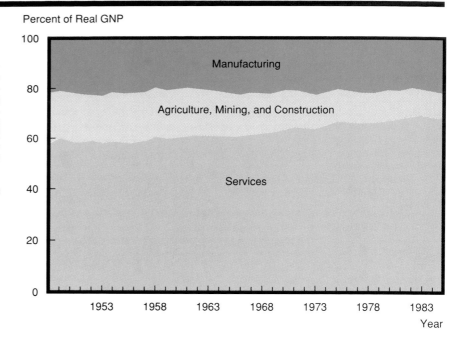

document these long-range trends employing the national income accounts and to indicate some of the forces that are responsible for them.

The shift to services is not of recent origin. This is clear from Figure 6.8. This graph presents the percentage of real GNP produced by three sectors of the economy: (1) services, (2) manufacturing, and (3) agriculture, mining, and construction. The percentage of real GNP produced in the service sector has increased over time from 58 percent in 1947 to about 68 percent in 1987. This rise was not at the expense of the manufacturing sector, as is often assumed, but at the expense of agriculture, mining, and construction. The value of manufacturing output has remained relatively constant as a percentage of real GNP. Manufacturing accounted for about 22 percent of real GNP in 1947 and for about the same amount in 1987, while that of agriculture, mining, and construction declined from 20 percent to 12 percent.

In order to understand the implications of these findings, it is important to understand what is included in the service sector. Services are more broadly defined than is generally realized. More than fast foods and laundries are included. The service sector is composed of the retail and wholesale trades, transportation and communications, finance, insurance and real estate, and miscellaneous services, such as business and personal services, health care, and education.

Figure 6.9 shows the shares of services and manufacturing measured both as the percentage of real GNP and as the percentage of the labor force employed in each activity. The service sector is clearly growing whether measured in terms of relative output or relative employment. The upward trend in services output, shown in Part A of Figure 6.9, seems to have been fairly constant over time. The trend in both real GNP and employment does, however, appear to have been a bit more rapid since the last half of the 1960s, but the development is not of recent origin.

The trends in real GNP and employment in manufacturing (Part B of Figure 6.9) are perhaps more interesting. There is no apparent trend in the real value of manufacturing output as a percentage of real GNP, with the share fluctuating between 21 percent and 23 percent. In terms of employment, however, there is a definite declining trend. Employment in manufacturing as a percentage of the labor force has declined from over 30 percent to about 20 percent. Thus although manufacturing has maintained a constant percentage of GNP, it has over time employed a declining proportion of the labor force. Clearly, the productivity of labor in manufacturing has been increasing, allowing over time a smaller proportion of the labor force to produce a constant share of real GNP.

If you compare the fluctuations of output in manufacturing with those in services, it is clear that the variations in manufacturing output are much greater than in services. Service-sector output and employment do not vary from year to year nearly as much as they do in manufacturing.

In sum, services as a percentage of GNP represent a growing proportion of GNP mainly at the expense of agriculture, mining, and construction, not manufacturing. In terms of employment, however, manufacturing has been surrendering workers to be reemployed in the service sector. The fact that employment and output in the service sector have both grown at similar rates, while employment has declined relative to output in the manufacturing sector, suggests that productivity growth in the service sector has lagged behind growth in manufacturing. If there is cause for alarm, it is that productivity growth in services does not seem to increase as rapidly as in manufacturing.

The existing data suggest that the relative decline in employment in manufacturing has occurred while the relative value of manufacturing output has remained constant. This provides a clue to what is happening in our economy. The technological dynamics of the manufacturing sector have increased the productivity of labor in manufacturing, which has resulted in an increase in the incomes of workers employed in manufacturing as well as in the incomes of all Americans as the relative prices of manufacturing goods have declined. Consumers have chosen to take the greater proportion of their increased incomes in the purchase of relatively more services and relatively fewer goods. Americans today, because they are wealthier than their parents, consume relatively more education, information processing, and health care, eat out more often, send their clothes to dry cleaners more frequently, and spend more on vacations and entertainment and relatively less, though still more in absolute terms, for automobiles, food, refrigerators, and fountain pens than did their parents.

The relatively greater demand for services provides profitable opportunities for businesses and workers, while at the same time the increased productivity of workers in manufacturing frees labor for employment in the service sector. The American economy is simply following the natural pattern of consumer demands in an advancing economy. The increase in per capita GNP is itself the reason for the relative rise of the service sector.

You will recall that the decline in manufacturing has been confined to a decline in relative employment. The United States produces many more manufactured goods domestically today than it did four decades ago, or one decade ago, or even five years ago. The real output of manufactured goods has continued to rise, and manufacturing is not a declining industry in the sense that fewer goods are being produced in the United States. The service sector is simply increasing relative to the manufacturing sector, but both are increasing in real terms.

The apparent decline in manufacturing may reflect the decline of certain industries. The American economy may no longer have a comparative advantage (see Chapter 2) in producing some industrial products like steel, textiles, or even automobiles. It would be a mistake to identify the decline of these industries with the decline in manufacturing in general. Instead of a comparative advantage in basic manufacturing, our

FIGURE 6.9
Shares of the Service and Manufacturing Sectors in Real Gross National Product and Employment: 1951–1985

Because the service sector is defined in this figure more narrowly than in Figure 6.8, its percentage contribution, shown in Part A, is somewhat less. Nevertheless, the rise of the service sector as a percentage of real GNP is apparent, along with a corresponding percentage increase in employment in this sector. In Part B the percentage contribution of manufacturing to real GNP is charted, along with manufacturing's share of total employment. Note that while the percentage of GNP contributed by manufacturing remained constant over time, employment in this sector did not. The percentage of the labor force employed in manufacturing declined significantly from 1951 to 1985.

(A) Share of Service Industries in Real GNP and Employment

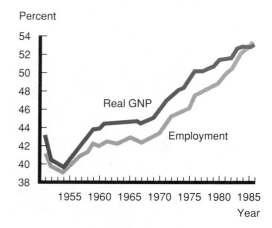

(B) Share of Manufacturing in Real GNP and Employment

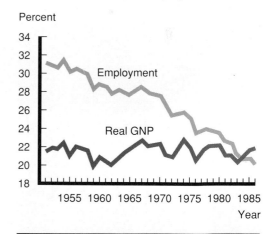

economy increasingly has a comparative advantage in high-tech industries like computers, biomedical technology, and airplanes.

The United States also has a comparative advantage in some services, such as research and development, information processing, medical technology — all of the things that fall under the heading of high technology — as well as in finance and insurance. The decline in basic industry and the rise of high-tech industries coupled with the rising share of services in GNP is more indicative of a successful economy than of a failing one.

In conclusion, contrary to popular opinion, there has not been a noticeable acceleration in the gradual trend from producing goods to producing services. The trend over the past five years has been consistent with the trend over the last several decades. Nor does the gradual shift toward services necessarily mean future declines in the rate of economic growth throughout the economy. It depends on which service-sector industries expand the most. Productivity increases in some service-sector activities are among the highest in the country. The secular shift toward services in the U.S. economy probably represents a sign of strength in the economy rather than a sign of decline. The trend toward services simply reflects the ability of the economy to reallocate resources consistent with increasing productivity, incomes, and consumer demands.

So where will you work? The service sector, like manufacturing, will continue to offer high-paying as well as low-paying jobs. The best-paying and most attractive jobs always go to the individuals who possess the skills that are in demand. The best jobs are therefore usually in the expanding sector of the economy, and the service sector will continue to be it. If you want one of the best jobs, it is highly likely that the "sinews and muscle" mentioned in the quotation at the beginning of the preview will be less in demand than well-developed "gray matter." There will still be jobs in manufacturing, but these jobs will be held increasingly by the mentally skilled, not the physically skilled. So you are on the right track: A college education is and will continue to be a necessary qualification for the better career opportunities in this country.[3]

THE SELLING OF AMERICA

A re you worried by the recent newspaper accounts reporting the selling of America to foreigners? The recent decline in the international value of the dollar, coupled with the huge dollar holdings of foreigners resulting from our large continuing balance of payments deficits, has led to recent highly publicized foreign purchases of American firms and real estate and to foreign firms building plants in the United States. This is, of course, just a reversal of what American firms have done in the past when they invested heavily abroad. But now that the shoe is on the other foot, many Americans are concerned. How much of America is already in the hands of foreign owners? Nobody really knows, because until recently nobody cared. But now politicians are putting pressure on government agencies to find out.

[3]Sources for this analysis: Brian Motley, "The Shift to Services," *Weekly Letter, Federal Reserve Bank of San Francisco,* January 16, 1987; Mack Ott, "The Growing Share of Services in the U.S. Economy — Degeneration or Evolution?" *Review, Federal Reserve Bank of St. Louis,* June/July, 1987.

TABLE 6.5
U.S. Gross National Product and Gross Domestic Product: 1981–1988
(Billions of Dollars)

	1981	1982	1983	1984	1985	1986	1987	1988
GDP	$3,001	$3,115	$3,356	$3,725	$3,971	$4,195	$4,484	$4,795
Net factor income from abroad	52	51	50	40	40	41	29	25
GNP	3,053	3,166	3,406	3,765	4,010	4,235	4,513	4,820
GNP/GDP	1.017	1.016	1.015	1.011	1.010	1.010	1.006	1.005

Source: *International Financial Statistics*, January 1989, 546–547.

One way to find out already exists. This information is part of the national income accounts. The importance of foreign-owned investments in the United States relative to U.S. investments abroad can be determined by comparing gross national product (GNP) with gross domestic product (GDP). Gross national product measures the value of the output produced by domestically owned factors of production. Part of the GNP of the United States is earned abroad from prior international investments. The income earned by an American in Paris as well as the profits of an American-owned firm in Brazil are counted in the U.S. GNP, whereas the profits earned by a Japanese-owned factory in the United States are not included in America's GNP, but in Japan's. The income earned by American workers in a foreign-owned factory in the United States is, however, included in the GNP of the United States. For many economies there is little difference between GNP and GDP. This is true for the United States. This means either that the income earned abroad is relatively small or that activities undertaken abroad by a country are roughly balanced by foreign business activities within that country's borders.

Clearly, we should be more interested in the difference between GNP and GDP than in how much of America is owned by foreigners. As long as Americans own about as much abroad as foreigners own here, the difference between the two national income statistics will remain small. If foreigners are buying up large amounts of America's assets and Americans are not similarly investing abroad, the difference between the two statistics will widen in the future. Gross domestic product exceeds gross national product in most countries located to the south of the United States, reflecting the fact that foreign nationals own more production resources in those countries than their citizens own in other countries. The same situation exists for our neighbor to the north, Canada.

In the United States GDP is less than GNP. American citizens earn more abroad from their ownership of resources in other countries than foreign nationals earn from their ownership of resources located in the United States. This has been true throughout the 1980s, as can be seen in Table 6.5, but the difference between GNP and GDP is narrowing over time.

Recently, in 1987 or 1988, depending on the source, the United States became a debtor nation for the first time since World War I, which suggests that GDP may soon exceed GNP, but the difference is likely for a time to remain small. There seems little need, as yet, to become exercised about the selling of America. Foreign ownership of productive resources is more important in most other countries than in the United States; the difference, for example, between GNP and GDP for Luxembourg is over 10 percent. If you are still worried about the future, just keep track of the difference between GNP and GDP.

PREVIEW 6.3 ANALYSIS

WHICH COUNTRY HAS THE LARGEST AND RICHEST ECONOMY?

Recently it has become fashionable to bemoan the decline of the United States as a world power. The decline is attributable to the recent performance of the American economy, which has seemingly lagged behind its major rivals. The spectacular performance of the Japanese economy, the soon-to-emerge united European Community, the huge population and rapid growth of the Chinese economy, and the reform of the struggling Russian economy are all seen as real threats to America's dominance. There are several dimensions to the argument that America is in decline: military, political, cultural, and economic. But world power is not simply the result of money, might, market size, or masses of people.

Economics can contribute to the part of this debate that focuses on the size and performance of the economies of the world. Below we shall compare the five major economies of the world, each of which has some claim to be a world leader: the United States, Japan, the Soviet Union, the European Community, and mainland China.

Economists have developed a concept called national income accounting that is relevant to this argument. GNP, for example, can be used for comparing the size of the economies throughout the world and for calculating the size of the world economy. When the GNP of each country in the world was tabulated and totaled for 1987, it exceeded 17 trillion U.S. dollars. Each country's GNP was calculated in terms of its own currency and then converted to U.S. dollars according to the prevailing foreign exchange rates.

Comparing the levels of GNP between countries is difficult to do accurately. The proper exchange rate to convert one country's currency into dollars must be found. Exchange rates can change significantly over time, thereby influencing the statistical comparisons. Different countries are likely to produce different goods and certainly a different mix of goods. Consider the GNP of China compared to the GNP of the United States. A large portion of China's GNP is composed of agricultural products, whereas U.S. agricultural output is a small part of GNP. In the United States computers, automobiles, and jet airliners are produced, but not in China. The quality of goods produced in the United States is probably higher than in China, and certainly more leisure is available to Americans than to the Chinese. Moreover, there are a great many more Chinese than there are Americans. Thus GNP cannot exactly measure the levels of economic welfare in the two countries.

Figure 6.10 shows as a pie chart how the world's GNP was distributed by country in 1987. The United States produced 26 percent of the world's GNP, followed by the new European Community with 22.2 percent, the Soviet Union with 13.9 percent, and Japan with 9.4 percent.

Eastern Europe contributed 5.3 percent and mainland China only 1.7 percent. All the remaining countries of the world together accounted for 21.5 percent. The four major economies of the world — the United States, the Soviet Union, the European Community, and Japan — account for more than three-quarters of the world's GNP.

The nominal GNP by country for the United States, the Soviet Union, Japan, the European Community, and mainland China can be found in Table 6.6. The United States was the largest national economy in 1987, followed by the European Community, Soviet Union, Japan, and China. The united European Community represents the closest rival to the United States in terms of total output of final goods and services. The Soviet Union's economy is half the size of the United States' and the Japanese economy is a little more than one-third the size of the United States'. Mainland China isn't even in the running.

The overall level of GNP that measures the size of an economy may be a misleading indicator of the economy's performance because population size varies significantly among the five countries. China's population, as can be seen in the table, is greater than the combined populations of the other four countries. There are 80 million more Europeans than Americans, 40 million more Soviets, and 122 million fewer Japanese. Per capita GNP takes population differences into account.

Per capita GNP provides a better measure of the average availability of final goods and services in each country. Per capita GNP is obtained by dividing nominal GNP by the size of the population. When this is done,

FIGURE 6.10
Relative Share of the World's Gross National Product Produced by Country or Region: 1987

The total world GNP in 1987 expressed in United States dollars was $17 trillion. The percentages of this total produced by individual countries and regions are shown in this figure.

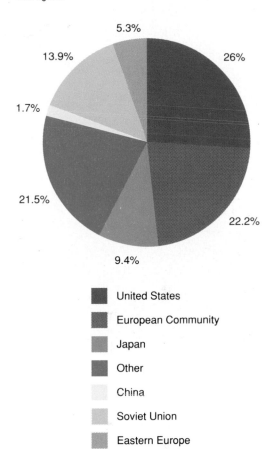

- United States
- European Community
- Japan
- Other
- China
- Soviet Union
- Eastern Europe

TABLE 6.6
Comparison of the Size and Performance of the Major World Economies: 1987

	UNITED STATES	SOVIET UNION	JAPAN	EUROPEAN COMMUNITY	CHINA
Gross National Product (Billions of 1987 U.S. dollars)	$4,436	$2,375	$1,608	$3,782	$294
Population (Millions)	244	284	122	324	1,074
Per Capita GNP (1987 U.S. dollars)	$18,200	$8,360	$13,180	$11,690	$270
1987 Inflation (Percent change in price level)	3.7	−0.9	0.1	3.1	9.2
Real GNP Growth Rate (Annual average in percent)					
1966–1970	2.8%	5.1%	11.0%	4.6%	N.A.
1971–1975	2.3	3.1	4.3	3.0	5.5%
1976–1980	3.3	2.2	5.0	3.0	6.1
1981–1985	3.0	1.8	3.9	1.5	9.2
1987	2.9	0.5	4.2	2.9	9.4

Source: *The Wall Street Journal*, January 23, 1987, A8.

the ranking of the five countries changes. Per capita income in the United States at $18,200 is still the highest among the largest world economies, but now Japan is second, the European Community third, the Soviet Union fourth, and China remains the lowest by a very large amount. Per capita income in Japan is less than three-quarters the per capita income in the United States, per capita income in Europe is less than two-thirds the level in the United States, and the Soviet Union's per capita income is less than half that of the United States'.

The United States may be the largest economy in terms of GNP and it may provide the largest amount of final goods and services to each citizen, but unless its economy is growing at a rate comparable to the growth rates of its rivals, its preeminence will be a short-term affair. In the long run the country with the fastest growth rate will have the largest economy. In comparing growth rates among countries, it is important to compare changes in real GNP. Nominal GNP can increase either because the output of final goods and services increases or because the prices of these goods increase due to inflation. You can see in Table 6.6 that the percentage change in the overall price level varies significantly among countries. China's inflation was the highest in 1987, with the United States second, the European Community third, and Japan fourth, while the Soviet Union actually experienced a decline in the price level, which is known as deflation. Varying rates of change in the overall price levels would over time distort any comparison of growth rates among countries.

The GNP deflator for each country has been used to correct for price level changes and thereby to obtain the real growth rate. In Table 6.6 the average growth rates of the five economies are shown for five-year periods from 1966 to 1985, along with the annual growth rate for 1987, the most recent single year available. A glance at this information reveals that the United States has experienced the most stable rate of growth over time, ranging from 2.3 percent to 3.0 percent, but not the fastest growth rate. That distinction belongs to China, which by any national income measure has the smallest economy on the list. The growth rate of the Japanese economy has consistently been higher than the growth rate in the United States. The average growth rate of real GNP in the Soviet Union has been steadily declining since 1965, and the average growth rates in Japan and the European Community may be declining.

Clearly, the only country that represents a threat to the preeminence of the United States is Japan. Yet the Japanese economy is today much smaller than the economy of the United States and will remain so, even if it continues to grow at relatively rapid rates in the future. The relatively slow growth rate of the American economy is troublesome, but as other major economies have developed their growth rates have slowed. Perhaps economic growth rates of around 3 percent are the price of being at the forefront of economic development.

The national income accounts have allowed us to put the "national decline" argument in empirical perspective. GNP, real GNP, and per capita GNP allow the comparison of the size and performance of countries around the world — a comparison that would be impossible without national income accounts.[4]

---

[4]Source: Karen Elliot House, "The '90s & Beyond," *The Wall Street Journal*, January 23, 1989, 1.

REQUIRED ECONOMIC CONCEPTS

Aggregation
National income accounts
Gross national product (GNP)
Gross domestic product (GDP)
Final goods and services
Intermediate goods
Value added
Per capita gross national product
Expenditure approach
Flow-of-income approach
Depreciation
Inventory investment

Fixed investment
Gross national income
Net national product
National income
Personal income
Personal disposable income
Consumption expenditure
Personal saving
Private saving
Nominal gross national product
Real gross national product
GNP deflator

KEY QUESTIONS

1. How does macroeconomics differ from microeconomics?
2. What are two ways to calculate gross national product (GNP)? What is a third way that results in an equivalent measure of total output?
3. What are transfer payments?
4. How does personal disposable income differ from personal income?
5. Why might GNP be a better measure of economic activity than NNP?
6. Why are homemakers' services not included in GNP?
7. In what way does GNP accounting understate the economy's production in a given year?
8. Why is per capita GNP a better measure of economic well-being than the level of GNP alone?
9. What difficulties are encountered in measuring the value of output of the service sector of the economy and, in particular, the public sector compared to the private sector?
10. Has the United States become a debtor nation? Explain how the national accounts can be used to answer this question.
11. Why are comparisons of per capita income among countries difficult to make?

PROBLEMS

1. Which of the following are primarily microeconomic phenomena and which are macroeconomic phenomena?
    a. The state sales tax on cigarettes is raised.
    b. OPEC agrees to increase the price of a barrel of oil by $5, raising the fear of a round of inflation.
    c. The Federal Reserve reduces growth in the money supply.
    d. The Midwest farm drought of 1988 reduced corn and grain production by 20 percent.
    e. GNP is predicted to grow by only 2 percent.
    f. The auto and steel unions negotiate wage increases greater than productivity increases, which threaten to render U.S. products less price competitive in world markets.
    g. A decline in the U.S. unemployment rate to 5.2 percent spurs the Federal Reserve to raise interest rates.

2. According to the GNP accounts, which contributes more to GNP — an illegal zip gun sold on the street for $30 or a hit of cocaine purchased for $40? What about $30 for a zip gun compared to two secondhand physics books you buy for a total of $45 at the bookstore?

3. Why are profits included as part of costs in the GNP accounts?

4. Suppose a political fanatic blows up the campus NROTC building, which is then rebuilt. Did GNP go down after the bombing and then return up to its original level when it was rebuilt, assuming everything else was unchanged?

5. Which GNP classification does each of the following come under — consumption, investment, government expenditures, net exports, or none of these if the item is not included in GNP?

    a. $20 you pay an unlicensed gypsy fortune-teller.
    b. Monthly rent for an apartment.
    c. A house you buy in the year it was built.
    d. $2 million won in a state lottery.
    e. A 20-year-old condominium that you buy.
    f. The decline in business inventories over the year.
    g. A $3,000 purchase of AT&T stock made by citizen Smith.
    h. A new fighter-bomber plane.
    i. Social security payments.
    j. $10,000 won on a TV quiz show.
    k. Purchase of new trucks by U-Haul Truck Rental Company.
    l. Purchase of new golf clubs by a golf instructor.

6. A 1977 all-time movie money-maker list had *Star Wars* at the top with earnings of $127 million in 1977 alone. The 1939 film *Gone with the Wind*, in seventh place, had accumulated earnings of $76.7 million. Since "money talks," one might presume that by 1977 *Star Wars* was the biggest all-time revenue earner. Is this presumption correct? What alternative ways would you use to compare the box office appeal of films? Addendum: By 1983, the film *E.T.* took the lead with earnings of $194 million. Use the GNP deflator to compare the earnings of *Stars Wars* in 1977 with *E.T.*, assuming for simplicity that all of *E.T.*'s earnings occurred in 1983.

7. a. GNP for the United States in 1987 was approximately $3,800 billion and in 1980 it was $3,190 billion. The GNP deflator in 1987 was 100.2 and in 1980 it was 90.2. Was real GNP in 1987 in 1982 constant dollars greater or smaller than real GNP in 1980? By how much?

    b. In 1980 the population of the United States was approximately 227,757,000. In 1987 it was around 243,770,000. What was the percentage change in *real* GNP per capita from 1980 to 1987?

8. The Horse's Mouth Company on campus printed and sold $100,000 worth of faculty lecture notes to students last year. The company paid $50,000 to a manager and student helpers, and it also paid $35,000 for paper, ink, electricity, tape, and other inputs. Its machines depreciated $4,000 over the year.

    a. Calculate the company's contribution to GNP.
    b. How much was value added?
    c. What were its pretax profits, excluding opportunity costs?

9. Gross investment = Net investment + Depreciation.

    a. Suppose that during the year depreciated capital is replaced and there are additional expenditures for some new capital formation. What happens to the level of the total capital stock of the economy at the end of the year compared to the beginning of the year?

    b. Suppose no new capital is created during the year and only depreciated capital is replaced. What happens to net investment? Is gross investment therefore up or down? Explain.

    c. If not all of the depreciated capital is replaced and no new capital is created, what happens to net investment? Is gross investment negative? Explain.

    d. Can gross investment ever be less than zero? Explain.

APPLICATION ANALYSIS

Using the following items, answer questions 1 through 5 below:

+ a. Consumption
  b. Wages
  c. Depreciation
  d. Gross investment
  e. Corporate profits (before taxes)
  f. Business transfer payments
+ g. Government expenditures
  h. Indirect business tax

  i. Government transfer payments
  j. Personal savings
  k. Corporate income tax
  l. Interest paid by the government
  m. Net corporate savings
  n. Dividends
  o. Social security taxes paid by employers
  p. Personal Taxes
+ q. exports

1. Using the expenditures approach and the lettered items (e.g., a + b − c) in the list above, what is GNP?
2. What is NNP?
3. What are two ways to calculate NI?
4. What is net investment?
5. What is GNI (i.e., GNP from the income side)?

CHAPTER 7

THE BASIC MODEL OF MACROECONOMICS

IN THIS CHAPTER YOU WILL LEARN:

The basic model of
macroeconomics that will
be used to study the major
problems of
macroeconomics

How the forces of aggregate
demand and aggregate
supply determine the
equilibrium price level and
the level of aggregate output

What causes the equilibrium position
of the macroeconomy to change

The concept of potential national
income and why the economy might
not produce at this level

How the self-correcting mechanism
tends to move the economy to the
level of potential national income

THE GREAT DEPRESSION

It happened again on Monday, October 19, 1987 — the stock market crashed! The Dow Jones Industrial Average, the most frequently consulted stock market average, plummeted 508 points, losing 22.6 percent of its total value. It was the largest one-day percentage loss in the history of the New York Stock Exchange. This market debacle wiped out over $1 trillion in wealth in one day of trading. Bad as this was for Americans, the stock market crash raised an even worse specter — the possibility of a depression like the Great Depression, which had been signaled by a stock market crash that occurred on October 28, 1929. Did this mean that America was headed toward another Great Depression? *The Wall Street Journal* asked and answered this question in a front-page headline of its October 20, 1987, issue: "A Repeat of '29? Depression in '87 Is Not Expected."

What was the Great Depression? You have to be fairly old to have lived through the first one, which roughly spanned the decade of the 1930s. Statistics tell the story. The real value of the gross national product fell 36 percent between 1929 and 1933 and declined even more on a per capita basis. By 1933 one in four Americans was out of work, and many who still had jobs were able to work only part-time. Nine thousand banks failed during the decade, and millions lost all of their savings. Between 1929 and 1932 manufacturing output fell by half. Thereafter the situation got slowly better. It wasn't until 1937 that national output exceeded the level attained in 1929, and it wasn't until the advent of World War II that the economy fully recovered. The Great Depression demonstrated that the macroeconomy did not always perform adequately.

Statistics tell a cold story. They do not reveal the experience of those who lived through the Great Depression. The Depression was a curiously silent event. You could not just look out the window and see it happening. You had to know where to look. Men who lost their jobs dropped out of sight, as did shopkeepers who lost their businesses. "For Rent" signs appeared in shop windows and in front of vacant houses. Many Americans escaped

Continued

the worst of the Depression, but everyone was touched by it. Everyone knew of someone who was engaged in a desperate struggle, but the struggle went on behind closed doors.

That is, it did while there were doors for the desperate to close. When a man first lost his job, his family lived on savings while he looked for work. If he didn't find work before the savings were exhausted, they cashed in their life insurance for its loan value. When that was gone, they moved in with relatives. Eviction became so common that children made a game of it. They would pile dollhouse furniture in front of the playhouse door, and then carry it away.

If relatives could not help, a destitute family was forced to move into dwellings constructed of salvage lumber and packing crates. These dwellings were located in shantytowns called Hoovervilles (after the president of the United States at that time). Every big city had its Hooverville.

People took whatever work they could get. Apple stands, behind which the unemployed tried to sell fruit to the employed, became a common sight along the city streets. Hundreds of men lined up in front of hiring halls seeking a day's work. Generally, they waited in vain. When work could not be found, people panhandled — another word for begged. A hit song of the era contains the words "Brother, can you spare a dime?" which describes the situation many Americans found themselves in during the 1930s.

The numbers of the poor simply overwhelmed private charities. There were at the time no national charities that could help to relieve mass poverty. There was initially no federal relief effort. Many people went hungry. Some starved. How could this happen in America, the breadbasket of the world? In truth, the country, its governing bodies, and its economists were not ready for the consequences of the collapse of the economy. It simply had happened, it was unexpected, and the causes remained mysterious.

The silent nature of the Great Depression made it difficult to grasp the extent of

the economy's collapse. As difficult as it is to comprehend in our statistical age, the government then kept few economic statistics. Although we now know that gross national product was falling by 12 percent during the first year of the decline, economists at the time were talking about how mild the decline was! It was even left up to national business magazines to fill the information gap. *Fortune* reported late in 1932 that it thought that 34 million persons, more than one-fourth of the population, belonged to families with no full-time breadwinner. Everyone by this time knew that it was bad, but no one knew how bad. It wasn't until 1933 that the first national income statistics were published to show the enormous decline in the nation's real output since 1929.

If the extent of the Depression was unknown during the early 1930s, there was equal confusion about what had caused the Depression, and even more disagreement over what should be done about it. By the election of 1932 it was clear that the country wanted the federal government to do something, even if it was the wrong thing. Franklin D. Roosevelt was overwhelmingly elected president, and he ushered in the "New Deal," which proposed that the federal government intervene in the economy in a number of ways.

The New Deal lacked a well-formulated foundation precisely because the economics profession was unprepared to deal with a prolonged collapse of the economy. The prevailing view at the time, now known as classical economics, was that the overall economy contained a self-correcting mechanism that would quickly restore full employment. All that was required was time for this mechanism to work. Most economists of the time were surprised at both the extent of the economy's collapse and the duration of the Depression, which called into question the economy's self-correcting mechanism.

It wasn't until 1936 that a Cambridge University professor named John Maynard Keynes published *The General Theory of Employment, Interest, and Money*, a book that revolutionized the economics profession and provided the intellectual basis for modern macroeconomics. Modern macroeconomics, the study of the economy as a whole, was developed in response to the Great Depression and has grown substantially beyond the original contribution of Keynes. Although modern macroeconomics came too late to help guide public policy during the Great Depression, it can be used to explain to us what happened during the 1930s. In this chapter you shall see how classical economics went wrong and how modern macroeconomics has been modified to take into account the possibilities of a depression.

Sources: Gerald Gunderson, *A New Economic History of America* (New York: McGraw-Hill, 1976), 475–491; Jonathan Hughes, *American Economic History* (Glenview, IL: Scott Foresman, 1983), Chap. 25.

• INTRODUCTION •

The Great Depression focused the country's attention on the national economy. The nation became, and has remained, intensely concerned with the level of overall output, the level of employment, the general direction of prices. These are the concerns of macroeconomics.

How the macroeconomic economy is functioning can be read from the behavior of two key variables — the aggregate price level and the aggregate output. •

TWO KEY MACROECONOMIC VARIABLES

It is the purpose of macroeconomic theory to explore the forces that determine the level of national economic output and the overall level of prices.

AGGREGATE OUTPUT

Macroeconomists are interested in the total physical output of goods and services in the economy, called **aggregate output.**

> *Aggregate output is the sum total of the final goods and services produced, evaluated in constant prices.*

The most frequently used measure of aggregate output is real gross national product, to which you were introduced in Chapter 6.

AGGREGATE PRICE LEVEL

The **aggregate price level** measures the tendency of all prices in the economy to move together.

> *The aggregate price level is the average price of all goods and services included in the gross national product, expressed as a price index.*

A price index is a number that shows the average percentage change that has occurred in some group of prices over a period of time. The most commonly used price indexes for this purpose are the gross national product deflator (GNP_d) and the consumer price index (CPI). The consumer price index is a measure of the change in consumer prices only, and as such it is less inconclusive than the GNP deflator, which was discussed in Chapter 6. Price indexes thus measure the extent to which all prices in the economy tend to rise or fall together.

The two key variables in macroeconomics are the aggregate price level and the aggregate output. A price index, such as the GNP deflator or the consumer price index, is used to measure the aggregate price level. The change in the price level indicates whether the economy is experiencing inflation or deflation. The aggregate output is measured by the real gross national product. Changes in the level of real GNP between years indicate whether the economy is expanding or contracting.

EXPLANATION AND PREDICTION IN MACROECONOMICS

Macroeconomics views the entire economy as a whole, as if it were composed of one giant market that produced an output called aggregate output at a price called the aggregate price level. When viewed this way, it is extremely useful to employ the tools of aggregate supply and aggregate demand to determine the level of aggregate output and the aggregate price level. Employing the aggregate-supply/aggregate-demand model allows the determination of the equilibrium level of aggregate output and the aggregate price level, and it also explains why the values of these variables might change.

Observed changes in the aggregate price level and in aggregate output can be explained by shifts in the aggregate-supply and aggregate-demand curves. Conversely, the future levels of aggregate supply and aggregate output can be predicted from known shifts in the aggregate-supply and aggregate-demand schedules. Mastering the tools of aggregate supply and aggregate demand will allow you to investigate the major macroeconomic problems of the past and present.

THE BASIC AGGREGATE-SUPPLY/ AGGREGATE-DEMAND MODEL

The first step in solving macroeconomic problems is to understand how the equilibrium level of aggregate output and the aggregate price level are determined. In macroeconomics the aggregate level of prices and the aggregate output are determined by the interaction of **aggregate demand** and **aggregate supply**.

> *Aggregate demand is the quantity of aggregate output that is demanded at every price level; it can be expressed graphically as the aggregate demand curve.*

> *Aggregate supply is the quantity of aggregate output that will be supplied at every price level; it can be expressed graphically as the aggregate supply curve.*

There are many similarities, as well as important differences, between the basic model of macroeconomics and the basic supply and demand model of microeconomics.

SIMILARITIES AND DIFFERENCES BETWEEN MICROECONOMIC AND MACROECONOMIC MODELS

Aggregate demand schedules, like the demand schedules of microeconomics, slope downward but for different reasons. Aggregate supply schedules, in the short run, like market supply schedules, slope upward. The equilibrium price level and aggregate output occur where the quantity of aggregate output demanded just equals the quantity of aggregate output supplied.

This is shown in Figure 7.1. The graphs appear the same as in microeconomics except for different labels. The vertical axis measures the price level and the horizontal axis measures the quantity of aggregate output produced. The price level is measured by a price index like the GNP deflator and the aggregate output by a measure of national income like

FIGURE 7.1

Aggregate Demand, Aggregate Supply, and the Determination of Equilibrium

The price level and the quantity of aggregate output demanded are inversely related, so aggregate demand curves slope downward. A typical aggregate demand curve is depicted in Part A. The price level and the quantity of aggregate output supplied are directly related in the short run, so aggregate supply curves slope upward. A typical aggregate supply curve is shown in Part B. Equilibrium is determined in Part C where the aggregate supply curve intersects the aggregate demand curve. This occurs at point E, where the quantity of aggregate output supplied just equals the quantity of aggregate output demanded.

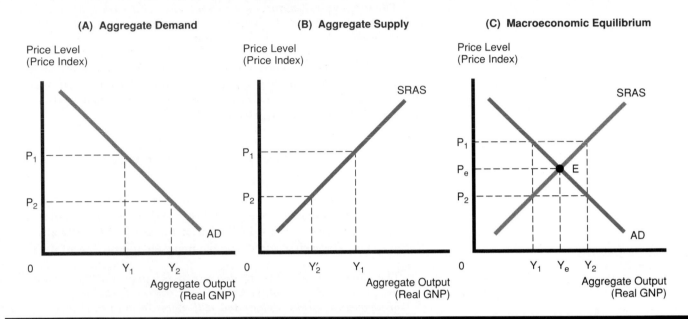

gross national product. Part A shows the downward-sloping aggregate demand curve, Part B shows the upward-sloping aggregate supply curve, and Part C reveals how the combination of the two determines the equilibrium price level and aggregate output.

There are also non-price-level determinants that affect the amount of aggregate supply and aggregate demand at every price level and that are handled in the same way as in microeconomics. The aggregate-supply/aggregate-demand model assumes that all nonprice determinants that influence the amounts of aggregate supply or aggregate demand are held constant as we derive the aggregate supply and aggregate demand schedules.

The determinants of aggregate demand and aggregate supply are different from their microeconomic counterparts, but they function in the same manner. When the value of one of the determinants changes, either the entire aggregate supply schedule or the entire aggregate demand schedule will also change. As in microeconomics, a change in a determinant will cause a shift in either the aggregate demand or the aggregate supply curve.

The convention that we adopted in microeconomics to distinguish movements along a demand or supply curve from a shift of the curve is continued in macroeconomics.

- A movement along an existing aggregate demand curve is referred to as a *change in the quantity of aggregate output demanded*. A shift in the aggregate demand curve is called a *change in aggregate demand*.
- A movement along an existing aggregate supply curve is referred to as a *change in the quantity of aggregate output supplied*. A shift in the aggregate supply curve is called a *change in aggregate supply*.

AGGREGATE DEMAND

Aggregate demand is crucial to the determination of the equilibrium level of national income and the overall level of prices. The **aggregate demand (AD) curve** relates the quantity demanded of aggregate output at every price level.

> *The aggregate demand curve shows the relationship between the price level and the quantity of aggregate output demanded, other things held constant.*

Part A of Figure 7.1 shows an aggregate demand curve, which has a negative slope. The quantity of aggregate output demanded increases as the price level falls. The quantity of real GNP demanded is greater at price level P_2 than it is at price level P_1.

WHY AGGREGATE DEMAND CURVES SLOPE DOWNWARD

Aggregate demand curves slope downward because of the impact of price level on the real value of money, and because there are also interest rate effects and changes in the substitution of foreign for domestically produced goods. These effects underlie the **macroeconomic law of demand**.

> *The macroeconomic law of demand is the principle that when the price level falls, other things held constant, the quantity of aggregate output demanded will increase, and that when the price level increases, the quantity of aggregate output demanded will decline.*

The aggregate demand curve thus slopes downward and to the right just like microeconomic demand curves, but for somewhat different reasons.

The macroeconomic aggregate demand curve, shown in Part A of Figure 7.1, slopes downward and to the right in obedience to the macroeconomic law of demand. The aggregate demand curve is drawn holding constant the non-price-level determinants of aggregate demand and allowing the price level to vary. When the price level falls from P_1 to P_2, the quantity of aggregate output demanded will increase from Y_1 to Y_2. Conversely, if the price level were to increase, other things held constant, the quantity of aggregate output demanded would decline.

Why do aggregate demand curves observe the macroeconomic law of demand?

INCOME AND WEALTH EFFECT When the price level changes, so does the real value of money and of all other assets whose value is measured in money. If the price level increases, the real value of a person's wealth held in money-denominated assets, such as cash, bank accounts, bonds, and debt obligations, declines. The owners of these money-denominated assets become poorer. When people become poorer, they spend less on goods and services. Thus the quantity of real gross national income demanded will decline as the price level increases.

Suppose you have $2,000 in the bank when the price level is 1.00. If the price level doubles to 2.00, the real purchasing power of your money in the bank will be cut in half. You will be able to purchase one-half as many goods after the price level increase than you could before it occurred. Your consumption expenditures will probably decline as a consequence. So consumption expenditures, which are an important part of aggregate demand, will decline when the price index rises, because some of your income and wealth is held in dollars.

If the price level falls, the effect on aggregate demand works in reverse: The real value of a person's money-denominated income and wealth will increase and consumption expenditures will also increase. Thus we have the **wealth and income effect** to explain why aggregate demand curves slope downward.

> *The wealth and income effect is the change in the purchasing power of a given amount of money-denominated wealth that results from a change in the price level, causing individuals to alter their consumption expenditures.*

The quantity of aggregate output demanded will increase when the price level falls and decrease when the price level rises. The wealth effect is sometimes called the *real-balances effect*. The wealth or real-balances effect thus helps to explain why aggregate demand curves obey the macroeconomic law of demand.

INTEREST RATE EFFECT When the price level changes, it will affect interest rates, which will in turn affect the demand for interest-sensitive goods, such as business and household direct investment that is part of aggregate demand. When the price of everything increases, firms and households will demand more money to carry on normal economic activities. But if the actual quantity of money remains unchanged, the increase in demand relative to supply will cause the price of borrowed money (the rate of interest) to rise. When interest rates rise, the quantity demanded of interest-sensitive goods purchased with borrowed money, such as houses, automobiles, and capital goods, declines. Because an increase in the rate of interest will cause fewer goods to be demanded, the quantity of aggregate output demanded will decline.

The **interest rate effect** works in reverse if the price level falls, in which case the interest rate falls, and the quantity demanded of interest-sensitive goods increases, causing the quantity of aggregate output demanded to increase.

> *The interest rate effect is the effect the interest rate has on the quantity demanded of interest-sensitive goods, thereby affecting the quantity of aggregate output demanded.*

SUBSTITUTION OF FOREIGN GOODS EFFECT The substitution effect, so important in the theory of demand in microeconomics, plays a less important role in the macroeconomic theory of aggregate demand, but it does play a role. When the price level increases, the prices of all domestically produced goods rise in unison, so the relative prices of domestically produced goods do not change. There is consequently no substitution effect in macroeconomics such as occurs when relative prices change in microeconomics.

Instead, the substitution effect in macroeconomics takes place between domestically produced goods and foreign-produced goods. It is known as the **substitution of foreign goods effect.**

> *The substitution of foreign goods effect is the effect that an increase or decrease in price level has on the demand for foreign and domestic goods.*

In the U.S. economy an increase in the general price level causes American-made goods to become more expensive and foreign-made goods to become relatively less expensive. Because foreigners will purchase fewer American-made goods, exports will fall, and because Americans will tend to substitute foreign-made imported goods for domestically produced goods, imports will rise. Since aggregate demand represents the demand for American goods from all sources, the quantity of aggregate output demanded will tend to decline as the price level increases, as the macroeconomic law of demand predicts.

The reverse is true for a decline in the overall price level. When the domestic price level falls, exports will tend to increase and imports to fall as both Americans and our trading partners tend to substitute American-made goods for foreign-made goods. When the price level changes, the substitution effect acts to make the aggregate demand curve slope downward. When the price level rises, the quantity of aggregate output demanded declines as foreign-made goods are substituted for domestically produced goods. The reverse happens when the overall price level falls.

The aggregate demand curve slopes downward and to the right for three reasons: the wealth effect, the interest rate effect, and the substitution of foreign goods effect.

AGGREGATE SUPPLY IN THE SHORT RUN

The **short-run aggregate supply (SRAS) curve** slopes upward and to the right. This results in an increase in the quantity of aggregate output supplied as the price level increases and in less aggregate output as the price level decreases.

> *The short-run aggregate supply (SRAS) curve shows a positive relationship between the quantity of aggregate output supplied in the short run and the price level, other things being equal, including the expected price level.*

The phrase "short run" refers to a period during which consumers and businesses have not fully adjusted to unexpected changes in the economy. Since expectations are held fixed along an SRAS curve, SRAS shows how the quantity of aggregate output supplied reacts to unexpected changes in the price level. *When the price level unexpectedly increases, the quantity of aggregate output supplied will also increase in the short run. When the price level unexpectedly falls, the reverse will happen.*

The short-run aggregate supply schedule assumes that the nonprice factors that affect the level of aggregate supply are held constant. These other things, known as the determinants of supply, are the prices of the factors of production, the state of technology, and expectations about the future state of the economy. When the determinants of supply are held constant and the price level is allowed to vary, the short-run aggregate supply curve will be traced out.

The aggregate short-run supply curve will show a positive relationship between the price level and the quantity of aggregate output supplied, because in the short run as the quantity of aggregate output supplied increases so do the costs of production. To produce more, firms will have to hire more but less productive workers at the existing wage rates. Thus costs will rise with increased output, but not as much as the price level. The wage rate was determined at the lower expected price level, as were the costs of nonlabor inputs.

It is easy to see why a profit-seeking business firm would increase output when the price level unexpectedly increases. The profits from producing additional output are equal to the price of the additional units produced minus the additions to cost. Since prices of goods increase more than production cost, output will rise with the price level.

In Part B of Figure 7.1 a decrease in the price level from P_1 to P_2 (other things being equal) will bring about a decrease in the quantity of aggregate output supplied from Y_1 to Y_2'. An increase in the price level from P_2 to P_1 will bring about an increase from Y_2' to Y_1 in the quantity of aggregate output supplied.

MACROECONOMIC EQUILIBRIUM IN THE SHORT RUN

The forces of aggregate demand and aggregate supply combine to establish the equilibrium price level and aggregate output, as shown in Part C of Figure 7.1. **Macroeconomic equilibrium** in the short run is established when the aggregate macroeconomic market clears. This occurs when the quantity of aggregate output supplied just equals the quantity of aggregate output demanded.

> *The macroeconomic equilibrium is the only price level at which the quantity of aggregate output supplied just equals the quantity of aggregate output demanded; at this price level the macroeconomic market is said to clear.*

This condition is fulfilled at only one point (point E), where the aggregate supply curve crosses the aggregate demand curve. The point of equilibrium determines the price level (P_e) and aggregate output (Y_e) that will be produced.

In order to see that the macroeconomic equilibrium established by the aggregate-supply/aggregate-demand model is a unique position, consider what would happen if a price higher than P_e, say P_1, were initially established. In this case the combined output of all business firms in the economy, the quantity of aggregate output supplied, would be Y_2, but the quantity demanded would be only Y_1. Businesses in this situation would find that their sales were less than their production and unsold inventories would accumulate. These firms would have an incentive to cut back production and lower prices to reduce their inventories.

The quantity of aggregate output supplied would decline while the quantity of aggregate output demanded would increase as the price level falls. This process would continue until business firms found that their combined rate of production just equaled sales (the level of aggregate output Y_e), which will occur only at the equilibrium price level.

Consider the case where the price level is initially lower than the equilibrium price level. Suppose P_2 was initially established as the price level. In this case the quantity of aggregate output demanded (Y_2) would be greater than the quantity supplied (Y_1). Businesses would find that their inventories were declining, and buyers would discover shortages. This experience would produce forces causing the price level to increase as buyers offered and firms demanded higher prices for their products. A higher price level would both stimulate greater total output and reduce the quantity of aggregate output demanded. This process would continue until the aggregate production level just equaled the quantity of aggregate output demanded. Again, the equilibrium position would be established at point E.

TABLE 7.1
Changes in Determinants and Resulting Changes in Aggregate Demand

PARAMETER	DIRECTION OF PARAMETER CHANGE	SHIFT IN AGGREGATE DEMAND	DIRECTION OF PARAMETER CHANGE	SHIFT IN AGGREGATE DEMAND
Government Expenditures	Increase	Right	Decrease	Left
Taxes	Increase	Left	Decrease	Right
Money in Circulation	Increases	Right	Decreases	Left
Population	Increases	Right	Decreases	Left
Expectations	Improve	Right	Deteriorate	Left

Once achieved, a macroeconomic equilibrium is not carved in stone but changes when and if one of the determinants of aggregate supply or of aggregate demand changes.

WHY AGGREGATE DEMAND CURVES SHIFT

Aggregate demand curves shift when one of the non-price-level determinants of aggregate demand changes in value. The determinants of aggregate demand are the "other things held constant" in the definition of aggregate demand. The non-price-level determinants of aggregate demand include: government expenditures and taxation, the money supply, expectations about the future state of the economy, and the size of the population. These determinants affect the level of aggregate demand at every price level. When the value of a determinant changes, other things held constant, the entire aggregate demand schedule is altered and the aggregate demand curve shifts. Table 7.1 relates the direction of change of the determinants of demand with the resulting changes in aggregate demand.

GOVERNMENT EXPENDITURES AND TAXATION The fiscal actions of government will affect the quantity of aggregate output demanded at every price level. How and how much the government taxes its citizens and what it does with the tax revenues will also affect aggregate demand. Generally, when government expenditures increase, so will aggregate demand and the aggregate demand curve will shift to the right, from AD_1 to AD_2 in Figure 7.2. If the price level remains at P_1, the quantity of aggregate output demanded will increase from Y_1 to Y_2. If government expenditures decline generally, aggregate demand will shift to the left from AD_1 to AD_3, and the quantity of aggregate output demanded will fall from Y_1 to Y_3 if the price level remains fixed at P_1.

An increase in taxes, other things being equal, will cause aggregate demand to decline. So when taxes increase, the aggregate demand curve shifts to the left from AD_1 to AD_3, and when taxes are reduced aggregate demand will increase, as shown by a shift to the right from AD_1 to AD_2. The government can therefore affect the behavior of the economy through the effect of its fiscal actions on aggregate demand.

MONEY SUPPLY The amount of money in circulation also affects aggregate demand. When the amount of money increases, so will aggregate demand. One way to look at the effect of an increase in the money supply is to consider what your reaction would be if you suddenly found yourself with more money than you wanted to hold. What would you do? Surely you would get rid of the excess. Perhaps you would spend it directly for goods and services, or lend it to someone else at interest. The person, business, or bank that you lent the money to would certainly spend it. So in either case an increase in the money supply results in an increase in the aggregate demand for goods and services. An increase in the money supply will therefore cause the aggregate demand curve to shift to the right from AD_1 to AD_2. A decrease in the money supply will have the opposite effect, causing the demand curve to shift from AD_1 to AD_3.

EXPECTATIONS Expectations about the future state of the economy will affect the position of the aggregate demand curve. The amount of goods and services that households and business firms plan to purchase depends on their views of future prospects. When expectations change, so will the amount of planned purchases by economic decision makers, and consequently the aggregate demand schedule changes. Suppose that expectations change so that economic decision makers now think the future looks brighter. Business firms will now wish to invest more in new products, inventories of current products, and new plant and equipment. Consumers will now be more likely to make that purchase of a new car or house. Aggregate demand will expand as expectations improve, and the aggregate demand curve will shift to the right from AD_1 to AD_2.

Conversely, if future prospects begin to look worse, both businesses and households are likely to reduce their current purchases of goods and services. When expectations worsen, current aggregate demand will decline, and the aggregate demand curve will shift to the left from AD_1 to AD_3.

POPULATION The larger the population, other things being equal, the greater the amount of aggregate demand. When population increases, so will aggregate demand, and the aggregate demand curve will shift to the right from AD_1 to AD_2. Conversely, when population declines, so will aggregate demand, and the demand curve will shift to the left from AD_1 to AD_3.

CONSEQUENCES OF A CHANGE IN DEMAND

Changes in aggregate demand will bring about changes in the equilibrium price level and aggregate output. When aggregate demand increases, the aggregate demand curve will shift out along the short-run aggregate supply curve. This is shown in Part A of Figure 7.3. The aggregate demand curve shifts to the right from AD_1 to AD_2, causing the equilibrium point to shift from E_1 to E_2. The equilibrium price level increases from P_1 to P_2, and the level of aggregate output increases from Y_1 to Y_2. If aggregate demand declines, the aggregate demand curve shifts to the left from AD_1 to AD_2 in Part B of Figure 7.3. The equilibrium point moves from E_1 to E_2, with the equilibrium price level falling from P_1 to P_2 and the aggregate output falling from Y_1 to Y_2.

When aggregate demand changes, so will the equilibrium price level and the level of real aggregate output. The same is true for changes in short-run aggregate supply.

FIGURE 7.2
Change in Aggregate Demand When One of the Non-Price-Level Determinants Changes

When the non-price-level determinants are held constant and the price level changes, an aggregate demand curve like AD_1 is derived. When the price level remains constant but one of the determinants changes, the entire aggregate demand curve will shift. An increase in aggregate demand is shown by a shift to the right of the AD curve, like the shift from AD_1 to AD_2. A decrease in aggregate demand is shown by a shift to the left, as from AD_1 to AD_3. Table 7.1 summarizes the factors that can cause these shifts.

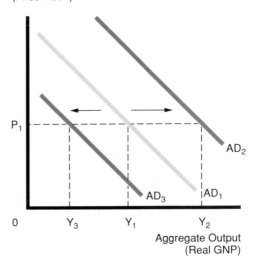

FIGURE 7.3
Effect of a Change in Aggregate Demand

An increase in aggregate demand results in an increase in both the price level and aggregate output. A decline in aggregate demand results in a decline in the price level coupled with a decline in aggregate output.

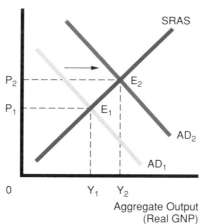

(A) An Increase in Aggregate Demand

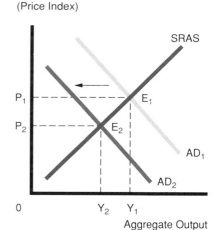

(B) A Decrease in Aggregate Demand

CHANGES IN THE SHORT-RUN AGGREGATE SUPPLY

The short-run aggregate supply curve can also shift if one of the non-price-level determinants of aggregate supply changes in value. The determinants of aggregate supply include the prices of the factors of production, the state of technology, productivity, and expectations about the future state of the economy.

FACTORS OF PRODUCTION The factors of production are labor, land, capital, and entrepreneurship. Wage payments are the price of labor, rent is the price of land, interest is the payment for the use of capital, and profits accrue to entrepreneurs. If the prices of the factors of production increase, so too do the costs of production, causing the short-run supply curve to shift to the left. If the costs of the factors of production decline, the short-run aggregate supply curve will shift to the right.

Changes in the prices of the factors of production can occur quickly or slowly. Wages, which are quantitatively the most important factor of production, generally are negotiated annually, and sometimes labor contracts have multiyear durations. The prices of the other factors of production may change quickly. Agricultural goods, which depend on the cooperation of nature, are subject to feasts and famines. Crude oil prices have changed significantly three times in the last fifteen years.

When the prices of the factors of production change quickly and significantly it is called a **supply shock.**

> *A supply shock is a situation that develops when the costs of production increase throughout the economy because of an increase in the price of a factor of production.*

Supply shocks will be adverse when the price of a factor of production increases, causing the short-run aggregate supply to decline and shift to the left. The oil price shocks of 1974 and 1980 were adverse supply shocks. Supply shocks will be beneficial when the price of a factor of production declines. The decline in world oil prices in the mid-1980s provided a beneficial supply shock. Short-run aggregate supply increases as a result of a beneficial supply shock.

TECHNOLOGY AND PRODUCTIVITY Technology and productivity are also nonprice determinants of aggregate supply. Technology refers to the pool of existing knowledge of how goods and services can be produced. The current computer and information-processing revolution has resulted in ongoing technological improvements. When technological knowledge improves, it becomes possible for productivity to also improve. Productivity, which measures output per unit of input, can increase or decrease within a given state of technology. Just-in-time production is an example of a productivity improvement within the existing state of technology. Just-in-time production involves scheduling the arrival of materials at the production line just as they are required, thereby cutting down on inventories and warehouse space. Technological and productivity changes generally occur slowly but regularly.

If either technology or productivity improves, the costs of production will decline and the short-run aggregate supply (SRAS) curve will increase (shift to the right). If technology or productivity deteriorates, then costs will increase, and the SRAS curve will fall (shift to the left).

EXPECTATIONS Finally, if expectations about the future state of the economy improve, the short-run aggregate supply curve will shift to the right, but if expectations become more pessimistic, the SRAS will shift to the left. Expectations are as important to determining aggregate supply as they are to determining aggregate demand. When the short-run aggregate supply curve is constructed, it is assumed that the expected price level will remain constant.

Expected changes in the price level constitute a major factor in determining the outcome of wage negotiations. Workers and businesses agree to wage contracts on the basis of present expectations about the future price level. If workers and business leaders expect the price level to increase over the time period covered by the contract, a cost-of-living pay increase will be included in the contract. If these expectations prove incorrect, then as they change so will wages.

Suppose a stable price level was expected when wage contracts were initially negotiated, but during the course of the contract inflation unexpectedly occurs and is expected to continue. When the contract expires, workers will demand that they be compensated in the future not only for the existing increase in the cost of living, but also for future expected price level increases. Employers, if they hold the same expectations, will agree to the wage increases. The same is true for suppliers of the other factors of production. When expectations change, so will the short-run aggregate supply curve.

Table 7.2 relates the direction of change of the determinants of supply with the direction of shift of the short-run aggregate supply curve. The effect of a change in the determinants of supply, other things being equal, is to cause the short-run aggregate supply curve to shift. This effect is shown in Figure 7.4. If the price of a factor of production declines, the state of technology improves, productivity improves, or expectations about the future state of the economy become more positive, then the short-run aggregate supply curve will shift to the right from $SRAS_1$ to $SRAS_2$. The amount of aggregate output supplied will increase at the existing price level (P_1) from Y_1 to Y_2. However, if the price of one of the factors of production increases, if technology deteriorates, if productivity

TABLE 7.2
Changes in Determinants and Resulting Changes in Aggregate Supply

PARAMETER	DIRECTION OF PARAMETER CHANGE	SHIFT IN AGGREGATE SUPPLY	DIRECTION OF PARAMETER CHANGE	SHIFT IN AGGREGATE SUPPLY
Prices of the Factors of Production	Increase	Left	Decrease	Right
State of Technology	Improves	Right	Deteriorates	Left
Productivity Change	Improves	Right	Deteriorates	Left
Expectations	Positive	Right	Negative	Left

declines, or if expectations about the future become negative, then the aggregate supply curve will shift to the left from $SRAS_1$ to $SRAS_3$. The amount of aggregate output supplied will decline at the existing price level (P_1) from Y_1 to Y_3.

CONSEQUENCES OF CHANGES IN THE SHORT-RUN AGGREGATE SUPPLY

A shift in the short-run aggregate supply curve (assuming no change in the aggregate demand curve) will result in a change in the equilibrium price level and in aggregate output. In Figure 7.5 the effects of a change in aggregate supply are depicted. In Part A the effects of an increase in the short-run aggregate supply curve are shown. When the short-run aggregate supply curve shifts to the right from $SRAS_1$ to $SRAS_2$, the equilibrium point moves from E_1 to E_2, causing the price level to decline from P_1 to P_2 and the equilibrium value of aggregate output to expand from Y_1 to Y_2. If the short-run aggregate supply curve shifts to the left from $SRAS_1$ to $SRAS_2$, as shown in Part B, equilibrium will move from E_1 to E_2. The price level will rise as a consequence and the level of aggregate output will fall.

It is possible to infer from observed changes in the price level and aggregate output which schedule (the aggregate demand curve or the short-run aggregate supply curve) has shifted. Figure 7.6 will help us make this distinction. The figure depicts the macroeconomic economy in equilibrium with aggregate demand, **AD**, and short-run aggregate supply, **SRAS**, generating a price level of P_e and an aggregate output of Y_e.

Suppose that it is then observed that the price level increases at the same time that aggregate output falls. How can this be explained in terms of a shift in either the aggregate demand curve or the aggregate supply curve? The equilibrium point has obviously changed. A movement from **E** to E_1 accurately describes what has occurred. A decline in aggregate supply accounts for the change in equilibrium positions. Thus the observed changes in the price level and aggregate output were caused by a shift in the short-run aggregate supply curve from **SRAS** to $SRAS_1$.

If, instead, it were observed that the general price level increased while aggregate output also expanded, the equilibrium point has obviously moved from **E** to E_2, which could only be caused by an increase in the aggregate demand curve, a shift from **AD** to AD_2. If it were observed that the price level fell while aggregate output increased, then the equilibrium has shifted from **E** to E_3. Such a change is consistent with an in-

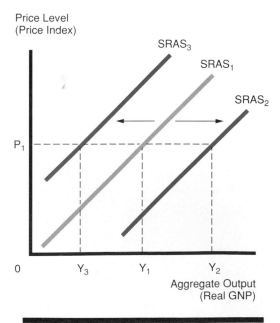

FIGURE 7.4
Changes in the Short-Run Aggregate Supply When One of the Non-Price-Level Determinants Changes

Table 7.2 summarizes the factors that can change short-run aggregate supply. If a non-price–level determinant changes in a way that stimulates firms' output, $SRAS_1$ shifts to the right to $SRAS_2$. If a parameter changes to discourage production by firms, $SRAS_1$ shifts to the left to $SRAS_3$.

Price Level
(Price Index)

(A) An Increase in Aggregate Supply   **(B) A Decrease in Aggregate Supply**

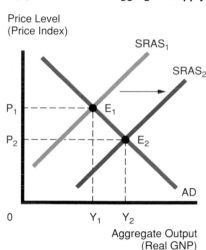 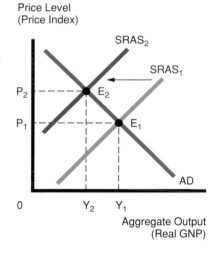

FIGURE 7.5
Effects of a Change in Aggregate Supply

An increase in short-run aggregate supply will result in a decline in the price level and an increase in the aggregate output. A decrease in short-run aggregate supply will cause the price level to rise and aggregate output to fall.

FIGURE 7.6
Identifying the Shifts in Aggregate Supply and Demand Curves

A decline in aggregate output coupled with an increase in the price level would result only from a decline in short-run aggregate supply. An increase in the price level associated with an increase in aggregate output would result only from an increase in aggregate demand. A decline in the price level coupled with an increase in aggregate output would come about only as a result of an increase in short-run aggregate supply. If both the price level and aggregate output decline, the cause is a decline in aggregate demand.

crease in aggregate supply from **SRAS** to $SRAS_3$. Finally, if the price level were observed to fall while aggregate output also declined, then the equilibrium point would have moved from **E** to E_4. Such a movement would be caused by a decline in aggregate demand, a shift from **AD** to AD_4.

When a change in the price level and aggregate output is observed, it is possible in this way to explain what has happened in terms of a shift in either the aggregate supply curve or the aggregate demand curve. Now it

A P P L I C A T I O N

7.1

WHAT CAUSED THE GREAT DEPRESSION?

The Great Depression was an extremely unusual economic event. It was so severe and it lasted so long that no one who lived through it ever forgot it. The Great Depression began in 1929 and reached its nadir in 1933. During these four years the economy measured by real GNP suffered in percentage terms its most drastic sustained drop in history, falling by over 30 percent. At the same time the price level also substantially declined, falling by nearly 25 percent.

The rapid decline in the economy can be read from Table 7.3. Real GNP and the associated price level are provided for each year of the Great Depression. The precipitous decline

TABLE 7.3

Determining the Shifts in Aggregate Supply and Aggregate Demand from Price Level and Aggregate Output Data: 1929–1939

YEAR (1)	PRICE LEVEL (CPI) (1947 = 100) (2)	DIRECTION OF CHANGE (3)	AGGREGATE OUTPUT (REAL GNP) (1947 = 100) (4)	DIRECTION OF CHANGE (5)	OBSERVED SHIFT (6)
1929	73.3		149.3		
1930	71.4	−	135.2	−	−AD
1931	65.0	−	126.6	−	−AD
1932	58.4	−	107.6	−	−AD
1933	55.3	−	103.7	−	−AD
1934	57.2	+	113.4	+	+AD
1935	58.7	+	127.8	+	+AD
1936	59.3	+	142.5	+	+AD
1937	61.4	+	153.5	+	+AD
1938	60.3	−	145.9	−	−AD
1939	59.4	−	157.5	+	+AS

Source: *Historical Statistics*, Series E113; E. Cary Brown, "Fiscal Policy in the Thirties: A Reappraisal," *American Economic Review* (December 1956): 857–879.

in the economy from 1929 to 1933 can readily be seen in the table. Thereafter, from 1934 to 1941, the economy, with the exception of 1938, revived, expanding rapidly at an average rate of around 10 percent per year. But the revival began from such a low level that it is not until 1937 that real GNP matched the output obtained in 1929. The economy had not fully recovered by 1937, as real GNP per person did not obtain the 1929 level until 1940. Thus national income statistics show that the Great Depression lingered on for an entire decade.

It is possible to determine from Table 7.3 the direction of change of aggregate output and the price level during the years of the Great Depression. From this information it is possible to infer whether it was the aggregate demand curve or the aggregate supply curve that shifted in a way that accounts for the observed changes in the major macroeconomic variables. During each year between 1929 and 1933 both aggregate output and the overall price level declined, indicating that a decline in aggregate demand had occurred. Thus the Great Depression was caused by a persistent decline in aggregate demand that lasted for four years.

From 1933 to 1937 the pattern created by aggregate output and the price level reversed, with both aggregate output and the price level increasing. This implies that aggregate demand was increasing. The expansion that occurred between 1934 and 1937 was dominated by an increase in aggregate demand.

During 1938 both the price level and the level of aggregate output declined, suggesting that aggregate demand had declined. The year 1938 thus experienced a recession in the middle of the recovery. This was followed by an outward shift in the short-run aggregate supply curve during 1939. Exactly such a shift would be expected due to the self-correcting forces operating in the macroeconomic economy, as you will soon discover below.

The use of the observed pattern of aggregate output and the price level explains the concentration of a generation of economists and economic historians on aggregate demand in their attempts to explain the Great Depression. In every year save one it was shifts in the aggregate demand curve that explain the observed pattern of the major macroeconomic variables.

is possible for simultaneous shifts in both schedules to occur. In this case, it is possible to identify the dominant shift — the one that determined the observed price-level/aggregate-output change. This identification allows economists to focus their attention on which of the determinants shifted to cause the observed event.

THE SHORT RUN AND THE LONG RUN

So far we have discussed the effects of shifts in the short-run aggregate supply curve and the aggregate demand curve on the equilibrium price level and aggregate output. The *short run* is a time period that is insufficient for economic decision makers to fully adjust expectations to reality. In the short run wages and prices are not perfectly flexible.

The short-run aggregate supply curve slopes upward because economic decision makers have not accurately anticipated the price level. If the price level is higher than expected, workers are stuck with wage contracts that do not fully compensate them for the unexpected increase in prices. Business firms thus have contracts for the purchase of the factors of production that do not increase as rapidly as the price level, making it profitable to increase production when the price level unexpectedly increases.

Conversely, if the price level unexpectedly falls, workers will, in the short run, still be paid the previously agreed-upon wage. So the costs of production do not fall as much as product prices measured by the price level. As it becomes less profitable, production will be reduced in the short run.

In the long run, however, the economy will adjust to the reality of any situation. The *long run* is a period of time sufficient for expectations and all wages and prices to fully adjust to a new situation. In the long run the economy will always operate at the level of potential national income, which is the output the economy will produce when all the factors of production are fully employed.

POTENTIAL NATIONAL INCOME

How much aggregate output would the economy produce if all of the factors of production were fully employed? The concept of **potential national income** answers this question.

> *Potential national income is the real gross national product that would be produced if all of the factors of production were fully employed.*

Potential national income, sometimes called the *natural level of output*, does not depend on the price level, but on the state of technology and on the quantity and quality of the available factors of production. Thus once the level of potential national income is established, it will appear as a vertical line, labeled Y_p, in aggregate supply/demand diagrams.

POTENTIAL NATIONAL INCOME AND SHORT-RUN EQUILIBRIUM

Will the short-run equilibrium always occur at a level that will ensure that the potential national income will be produced by the economy? The answer is regrettably no, neither in theory nor in reality, as the Great Depression demonstrated. Macroeconomic short-run equilibrium may occur at a point where aggregate output is either above, below, or equal to potential national income. When short-run equilibrium occurs at a level below potential GNP, a **deflationary gap** is said to exist.

> *A deflationary gap is a situation in which short-run equilibrium aggregate output is less than potential national income.*

FIGURE 7.7
Deflationary and Inflationary Gaps

It is possible for the economy to operate in the short run at a level of aggregate output that is lower than the level of potential national income. Part A depicts a deflationary gap, which exists when aggregate output in the short run is less than potential national income. It is also possible for the economy in the short run to produce at a level of aggregate output that exceeds potential national income. This case is shown in Part B and is known as an inflationary gap.

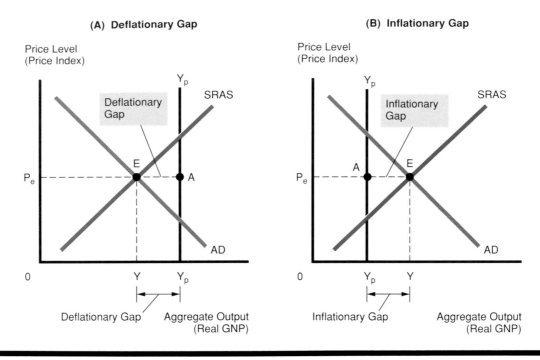

FIGURE 7.8
An Economy at Full Employment

When the aggregate demand curve is intersected by the short-run aggregate supply curve at the level of potential national income, the economy will be operating at full employment. Aggregate output (Y) is equal to potential national income (Y_p) when the price level is P_e. The equilibrium position (point E) is also known as the long-run equilibrium.

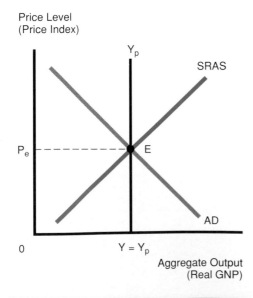

A deflationary gap is shown in Part A of Figure 7.7. Short-run equilibrium occurs at point E, causing aggregate output to be Y, while potential national income is Y_p. Since Y_p is greater than Y, a deflationary gap exists equal to the distance EA or $(Y_p - Y)$. The deflationary gap measures the extent of the loss the economy as a whole suffers when the economy operates at less than full employment.

Just as it is possible for the economy to operate at less than full employment, it is also possible for the economy to operate for a time at a level of aggregate output that exceeds potential national income. When this happens, it is called an **inflationary gap**.

> *An inflationary gap is a situation in which short-run equilibrium aggregate output exceeds potential national income.*

Part B of Figure 7.7 depicts an inflationary gap. The short-run equilibrium level of output occurs at point E, where the short-run aggregate supply curve intersects the aggregate demand curve. This results in a level of aggregate output, Y, that exceeds potential national income, Y_p. The difference between Y and Y_p (the distance AE) measures the inflationary gap.

It may appear that an inflationary gap is a good thing after all, for the economy is actually producing more goods than its long-run potential will allow. But this is not the case. When an inflationary gap appears, it is because some workers are supplying more labor than they would like to supply in an ideal macroeconomic world. They are caught in labor contracts based on previous expectations that do not reflect the new reality.

APPLICATION
7.2

THE ECONOMIC COSTS OF THE GREAT DEPRESSION

The concept of potential national income allows the calculation of the lost economic output during the Great Depression. Table 7.4 compares the actual GNP with the potential national income that could have been produced during the depression years 1929 through 1939. Column 2 shows the actual real GNP during the depression decade, column 3 estimates the potential national income that could have been produced, and column 4 shows the difference between what could have been produced and what was actually produced, representing the difference as a percentage of potential national income. The extent of the losses suffered by the economy during this decade of depression can readily be seen in the table. By 1933 almost 40 percent of the possible output of the economy was lost through unemployment.

Overall, the economy throughout the decade sacrificed almost a quarter of the output that could have been produced. The total loss of output amounts to $464 billion in 1947 dollars, which is the equivalent of three years' total output for the economy in terms

TABLE 7.4
Actual GNP and Potential National Income: 1929–1939

YEAR (1)	ACTUAL REAL GNP (BILLIONS OF DOLLARS) (1947 = 100) (2)	POTENTIAL NATIONAL INCOME (BILLIONS OF DOLLARS) (1947 = 100) (3)	LOSS IN OUTPUT (BILLIONS OF DOLLARS) (4)	LOSS AS A PERCENTAGE OF GNP (5)
1929	149.3	149.3	—	—
1930	135.2	154.0	18.8	12%
1931	126.6	158.0	31.4	20
1932	107.6	163.9	56.3	34
1933	103.7	169.1	65.4	39
1934	113.4	174.4	61.0	35
1935	127.8	179.9	52.1	29
1936	142.5	185.6	43.1	23
1937	153.5	191.5	38.0	20
1938	145.9	197.5	51.6	26
1939	157.5	203.7	46.2	23

Source: E. Cary Brown, "Fiscal Policy in the Thirties: A Reappraisal," *American Economic Review* (December 1956): 857–879.

of the potential output in 1929, or two years in terms of the potential output in 1939. The lost output would have been able to provide a new average-size house plus a new Ford or Chevrolet for every man, woman, and child in the country, with enough money left over to take a two-week vacation in the new car.

Potential national income depends on the quantity of the factors of production and on the state of technological knowledge. When the quantity of the factors of production available to the economy increases or when

technological progress occurs, potential national income will increase.

Even during the 1930s the level of potential national income continued to increase as the labor force continued to grow and technological progress occurred. Thus potential national income increased throughout the decade, growing from $149.3 billion in 1929 to $203.7 billion in 1939. Despite the rapid growth of the economy from 1933 on, real GNP did not catch up with potential GNP until the United States entered World War II.

FULL EMPLOYMENT

The remaining possibility is for the short-run equilibrium to occur at a point where the equilibrium level of aggregate output is just equal to potential national income. When this occurs, the economy is operating at **full employment.**

> *Full employment is a situation in which the short-run equilibrium level of aggregate output equals the potential level of national income.*

This possibility is shown in Figure 7.8. Equilibrium occurs at point E, where the short-run aggregate supply curve intersects the aggregate demand curve. In this case the equilibrium level of output Y is also equal to the level of potential national income, Y_p. Thus neither a deflationary nor an inflationary gap exists. The economy is operating efficiently, obtaining the maximum amount of output from the available resources.

THE LONG-RUN AUTOMATIC ADJUSTMENT PROCESS

FIGURE 7.9
Short-Run and Long-Run Adjustment to an Increase in Aggregate Demand

Suppose the economy is at full employment. An unexpected increase in aggregate demand puts upward pressure on the price level and aggregate output as shown in Part A. This inflationary gap cannot last in the long run. Wages will rise, causing short-run aggregate supply to fall to SRAS', as shown in Part B. The price level continues to rise while the economy returns to full employment in the long run.

(A) Short-Run Adjustment

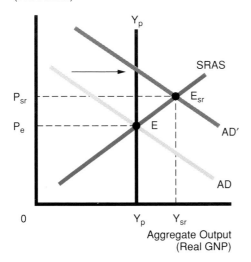

(B) Long-Run Adjustment

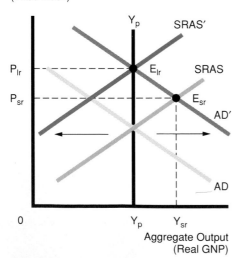

Suppose that either a deflationary or an inflationary gap exists. Are there forces operating in the macroeconomic economy that will tend to move the economy to full employment so that the potential national income can be realized? It may appear from the experiences of the Great Depression that the answer is no. After all, the economy operated at levels greatly below potential national income for an entire decade. Despite this dismal performance, the answer is definitely yes!

Most economists would agree that there are forces at work in the macroeconomic economy that will eventually cause aggregate output to return to the level of potential national income if either a deflationary or inflationary gap appears. But there is a great deal of uncertainty about the length of time required for these forces to bring the economy to full employment. Some economists believe that these self-correcting forces operate quickly in the case of an inflationary gap but slowly when a deflationary gap appears. This debate will be taken up more extensively later in this book.

Suppose the economy is operating at full employment (aggregate output is equal to potential national income) and there is an increase in aggregate demand due to a change in one of the non-price-level determinants of demand. Prices will increase and business firms will respond by attempting to increase output. Firms will strive to hire more workers at the prevailing wage rate. The additional workers who can be hired at existing wages will be less productive than previously hired workers, since the more productive workers will already be employed. That is one of the reasons, as revealed above, why the short-run aggregate supply curve slopes upward. Hiring less productive workers means higher marginal (or additional) costs for producing the additional output.

This situation is shown in Part A of Figure 7.9. The increase in aggregate demand is shown as a shift from AD to AD', as indicated by the arrow. The result is that the short-run macroeconomic equilibrium moves from E to E_{sr}, with aggregate output increasing from Y_p to Y_{sr} and the price level rising from P_e to P_{sr}. The increase in aggregate demand has stimulated an increase in the quantity of aggregate output supplied, and an inflationary gap equal to $Y_{sr} - Y_p$ appears.

This situation cannot last forever. The price level has increased from P_e to P_{sr} and is higher than workers anticipated when they agreed to existing labor contracts. Real wages will have declined as a result of the increases in the price level and money wages. Workers in this situation, when their contracts expire, will demand higher wages to keep up with the rising prices. Business firms, in order to keep their labor forces, will eventually have to grant wage increases. But when the cost of labor increases, so does the cost of production at every level of output, so the short-run aggregate supply curve shifts to the left.

The shift in the aggregate supply curve will continue until the SRAS curve intersects the AD curve at the point of potential national income. This is shown in Part B of Figure 7.9. Thus, in the long run, the point of equilibrium will move from E_{sr} to E_{lr}. Aggregate output declines to the level of potential national income (from Y_{sr} to Y_p) while the price level increases still further (from P_{sr} to P_{lr}). The shift of the short-run aggregate supply curve, representing a decline in aggregate supply, results in a movement back along the aggregate demand curve AD', causing a decline in the quantity of aggregate output demanded. In this way an inflationary gap is reduced by the self-correcting forces acting in the macroeconomic economy. Thus the upward adjustment of wages when an inflationary gap appears provides an automatic adjustment mechanism that will, in the long run, push aggregate output back to the level of potential national income.

In summary, if an increase in aggregate demand disturbs an economy from a full-employment equilibrium, the result is an increase in the level of aggregate output and in the overall price level. This creates an inflationary gap in the short run. The inflationary gap, however, contains within it the seeds of its own destruction. The price level has increased while the level of money wages has not. Thus real wages have declined. Workers insist that the level of real wages be increased if they are to continue to offer the same quantity of labor as they did before aggregate demand increased.

When money wages increase, the short-run aggregate supply curve shifts to the left. The long-run equilibrium position is reached when the short-run aggregate supply curve intersects the aggregate demand curve at the level of potential national income. When the macroeconomic economy is in long-run equilibrium, each business firm is producing the output it desires, and each person who desires work can find a job at a wage he or she will accept.

It is important to note the long-run consequences of the result of an increase in the level of aggregate demand when the economy is operating at full employment. The price level increases but the level of aggregate output remains the same. Thus in the long run the price level is determined by the level of aggregate demand, and the level of aggregate output is determined by the position of potential national income.

DEFLATIONARY GAP

Automatic self-correcting forces are also at work when a deflationary gap appears. This time let us assume that there has been a change in one of the determinants of aggregate demand that causes it to decline. In Part A of Figure 7.10 aggregate demand declines from AD to AD', as shown by the arrow, causing the point of equilibrium to shift from E to E_{sr}. The result is that aggregate output in the short run (Y_{sr}) declines below the level of potential national income (Y_p) and a deflationary gap appears. Firms, facing a decline in sales due to lower demand, begin to lay off workers. The less productive workers are the first to go, so costs and prices decline as the equilibrium position moves down along the SRAS curve. Thus the price level falls to P_{sr}. That is the short-run adjustment.

The decline in prices means an increase in real wages. But some workers who were willing to work at the previous lower level of real wages will not be able to find jobs. They will offer to work at the previous level of real wages, which means accepting lower money wages. As wage contracts expire, they are renegotiated downward and the SRAS curve shifts to the right, from SRAS to SRAS', because of the lower costs of production. Thus the price level falls further, but the level of aggregate output increases toward the level of potential national income. The shift in the SRAS curve will continue until the long-run equilibrium is reestablished at potential national income. Thus the downward adjustment of wages and prices will provide a self-correcting mechanism whenever a deflationary gap appears, pushing aggregate output toward the level of potential national income.

FIGURE 7.10
Short-Run and Long-Run Adjustment to a Decline in Aggregate Demand

When aggregate demand unexpectedly declines, as shown in Part A by the leftward shift of the aggregate demand curve, there is a decline in the price level and in aggregate output, creating a deflationary gap. The decline in aggregate output means that some workers will be laid off. Money wages will fall until real wages are at the same level as before the unexpected decline in aggregate demand. The decline in money wages will cause the SRAS curve in Part B to shift to the right in the long run. The price level will decline and aggregate output will expand as the unemployed workers are called back to their jobs.

(A) Short-Run Adjustment

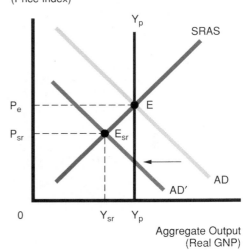

(B) Long-Run Adjustment

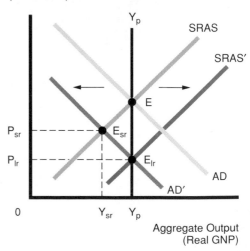

In Application 7.1 the downturn that occurred in 1938 in the midst of the economy's recovery from the Great Depression was briefly discussed. Both the price level and real aggregate output declined during 1938, extending the deflationary gap that already existed. A decline in both the price level and aggregate output signals that a decline in aggregate demand occurred during the year, like in Part A of Figure 7.10. In the long run the automatic adjustment process will cause the short-run aggregate supply curve to increase as wages fall, as shown in Part B of the figure. This process was already occurring by 1939, as shown by the decline in the price level coupled with a rise in real aggregate output. That the automatic adjustment process was not of sufficient strength in 1939 to restore full employment is indicated by the substantial deflationary gap that existed during that year.

Given the experience of the economy during the Great Depression, there is some question about the strength of this self-correcting mechanism in dealing with a deflationary gap. Many economists believe that there exists an asymmetry in the reaction time of the macroeconomic adjustment mechanism: The economy adjusts fairly quickly to the appearance of an inflationary gap but less quickly to the onset of a deflationary gap. But this opinion is not shared by all economists.

Inflationary and deflationary gaps can also be created by shifts in the short-run aggregate supply curve, called *supply shocks*, and will generate a self-correcting process similar to the one we have been describing. Supply shocks will be discussed in detail in later chapters.

LONG-RUN AGGREGATE SUPPLY CURVE

The possibility of an automatic adjustment mechanism naturally leads to a discussion of another important macroeconomic concept: the long-run aggregate supply curve. We have already been employing this concept in the guise of potential national income. The vertical potential national income curve, Y_p, is the long-run aggregate supply curve of the basic macroeconomic model. We have seen above that when the macroeconomy is in long-run equilibrium, aggregate output will occur at the level of potential national income. Since the level of potential national income does not depend on the price level, neither will the long-run aggregate supply curve.

The **long-run aggregate supply (LRAS) curve** can be identified by asking the following question. Suppose that prices and wages were flexible enough to adjust instantly to the appearance of a deflationary or an inflationary gap. The short-run aggregate supply curve would instantaneously adjust upward or downward as the case demanded. Full employment would always prevail and aggregate output would be at the level of potential national income. There would be no need for an SRAS curve; only the vertical LRAS curve at the level of potential national income would be required. Thus the LRAS curve shows that potential national income is compatible with any price level when prices and wages are fully adjusted.

> *The long-run aggregate supply curve is a curve showing the aggregate output that occurs when the macroeconomy has fully adjusted to any unexpected changes in the price level.*

Long-run equilibrium represents the world that classical economists saw. It is a world in which prices and wages are so flexible that the self-correcting mechanism would immediately return the economy to full employment should an inflationary gap or a deflationary gap occur.

SUMMARY

1.   The two key variables in macroeconomics are the aggregate price level and the level of aggregate output. The aggregate price level is measured by a price index such as the GNP deflator, and aggregate output is measured by real national income statistics, such as the real gross national product.

2.   The equilibrium level of aggregate output and the price level are determined by the basic macroeconomic model of aggregate supply and aggregate demand. Equilibrium occurs when the macroeconomic market clears, which occurs when the quantity of aggregate output supplied equals the quantity of aggregate output demanded.

3.   The macroeconomic law of demand states that as the aggregate price level increases, the quantity of aggregate output demanded will decline when other things are held constant. Aggregate demand curves thus slope downward. They do so for three reasons: the income and wealth effect, the interest rate effect, and the substitution of foreign goods effect.

4.   There exists in the short run a positive relationship between the quantity of aggregate output supplied and the price level, assuming other things are held constant. Macroeconomic supply curves in the short run slope upward, because as the price level unexpectedly increases, the profitability of producing more output increases along with the costs of production for all firms in the economy.

5.   When the determinants of aggregate supply or of aggregate demand change, the result will be a new equilibrium position with the price level and level of aggregate output changing.

6.   Potential national income is the level of real aggregate output that would be produced if the economy were at full employment. Potential national income does not depend on the price level. Potential national income determines the position of the long-run aggregate supply curve, which also does not depend on the price level.

7.   An inflationary gap occurs when the economy is operating in the short run at a level of aggregate output that exceeds potential national income. A deflationary gap exists when the economy is operating in the short run at less than the level of potential national income.

8.   When either a deflationary or inflationary gap occurs, there will be forces at work to return the economy to the level of potential national income. The strength of this self-correcting mechanism is a subject of debate among economists.

9.   In the long run the aggregate price level is determined by the level of aggregate demand and the level of aggregate output by the position of the long-run aggregate supply curve. In the short run the overall price level and the level of aggregate output are determined by the aggregate demand and the short-run aggregate supply schedule.

THE GREAT DEPRESSION

A single definitive explanation for the Great Depression does not exist. There are perhaps as many explanations as there have been investigators. Most explanations for the Depression, for the reasons stated in Application 7.1, concentrate on explaining the decline in aggregate demand. An explanation for the decline in demand must focus on changes in one or more of the determinants of demand. The determinants of aggregate demand are: government expenditures and taxes, the money supply, population, and expectations.

The existing explanations can be conveniently divided into two categories: (1) those that concentrate on financial sources, such as the money supply and the banks, and (2) those that concentrate on disturbances in the real sector, focusing on changes in consumption and investment, foreign trade, or expectations. In this analysis we shall discuss these explanations briefly, and we shall return to them later in the book as we extend our knowledge of macroeconomics.

The financial-sector explanations for the Great Depression center on the stock market collapse that occurred late in 1929. These explanations suggest that the loss of wealth suffered by investors was of sufficient magnitude to severely reduce personal consumption expenditures and to alter expectations about the future state of the macroeconomy. If it reflected a change in expectations, the stock market can explain why consumption and investment declined.

It may also be that the stock market collapse foretold the advent of the Great Depression by acting as a leading indicator. The stock market crashed because investors foresaw that the economy was about to enter a severe recession. The crash was followed by a brief recovery in stock prices, and then by further declines. An average of stock prices that stood at 260.2 in 1929 had fallen to 69.3 by 1932. Perhaps this decline mirrored the state of expectations about the economy, reinforcing the tendency for aggregate demand to decline.

The stock market collapse may also serve to explain the Great Depression to the extent that the market crash led to a banking crisis that occurred during the first few years of the Great Depression and that affected the money supply. One of the more widely accepted explanations for the Great Depression focuses on the behavior of the money supply during the 1930s. A decline in the money supply would by itself cause aggregate demand to decline. The money supply, as shown in Table 7.5, contracted every year between 1929 and 1933, declining by over 25 percent over the period. Thereafter it expanded, but the damage had been done. One of the major causes of the decline in the money supply was the collapse of the nation's banking system. Almost 6,000 banks failed between 1929 and 1933.

The real-sector explanations for the Great Depression hold that the decline in aggregate demand was caused by declines in the components that make up the gross national product. In particular, consumption expenditures and/or declines in the quantity of investment have been singled out as causes by some economic historians. It can readily be seen from Table 7.5 that both consumption and investment declined during the 1930s. But it is not clear whether these changes were the cause or the consequence of the Great Depression.

If GNP declines, one would expect that consumption and investment would also fall as a consequence. It is also to be expected that a decline in

TABLE 7.5
Money Supply, Consumption, Investment, Government, and Foreign Trade
Statistics: 1929–1941 (Billions of Dollars)

YEAR (1)	FINANCIAL SECTOR MONEY SUPPLY (CASH + DEMAND DEPOSITS) (2)	REAL SECTOR CONSUMPTION EXPENDITURES (3)	INVESTMENT EXPENDITURES (4)	GOVERNMENT EXPENDITURES (5)	FOREIGN TRADE BALANCE (6)
1929	$26.2	$79.0	$16.2	$8.5	$1.1
1930	25.1	71.0	10.3	9.2	1.0
1931	23.5	61.3	5.5	9.2	.5
1932	20.2	49.3	0.9	8.1	.4
1933	19.2	46.4	1.4	8.0	.4
1934	21.4	51.9	2.9	9.8	.6
1935	25.2	56.3	6.3	10.0	.1
1936	29.0	62.6	8.4	11.8	.1
1937	30.7	67.3	11.9	11.7	.3
1938	29.7	64.5	6.7	12.8	1.3
1939	33.4	67.6	9.3	13.3	1.1
1940	38.7	71.9	13.2	14.2	1.7
1941	45.5	81.9	18.1	24.9	2.4

Source: *Economic Report of the President*, Statistical Tables Relating to Income, Employment, and Production (various years); *Historical Statistics*, Series U-182.

consumption or investment would cause GNP to fall. It is not clear whether the figures in the table reflect an exogenous decline in consumption and investment that caused GNP to fall or whether they reflect the effects of a decline in GNP that induced a decline in consumption and investment.

Another school of thought suggests that it was the passage of the Smoot-Hawley Tariff Act of 1930 that turned a recession into a depression by erecting substantial barriers to international trade. The Smoot-Hawley tariff significantly raised the price of imports and led to retaliation by the nation's trading partners that resulted in much reduced levels of foreign trade. It can be seen from the table that foreign trade almost disappeared during the Depression.

We must also consider the reaction of the federal government during the early years of the Depression. The decline in GNP meant a decline in tax receipts, to which the government responded by raising taxes — not just a little but a lot. The tax increases that occurred in the early 1930s were up to that point the largest in U.S. fiscal history. An increase in taxes will also cause a decline in aggregate demand. Finally, government expenditures remained fairly steady between 1929 and 1934, as shown in column 5 of Table 7.5, probably having little effect on the level of aggregate demand.

In summary, there is evidence that many of the determinants of aggregate demand changed in a way that would have caused a decline in aggregate demand between 1929 and 1933. Consumption, investment, and the foreign trade balance declined, as real gross national product declined. Taxes were increased, and government expenditures remained constant, while the money supply fell sharply.

Whether these declines were a consequence or cause of the decline in real GNP cannot at this point be determined. It is difficult to determine whether, for example, the decline in consumption, investment, foreign trade, or even the money supply, was the cause or the consequence of the decline in aggregate demand. This difficulty lies at the heart of the problem of determining what actually caused the Great Depression. It is little wonder that no consensus exists.

Just as most determinants of aggregate demand changed in a way that could cause a decline in aggregate demand between 1929 and 1933, most of these same determinants changed in a way to cause aggregate demand to grow from 1934 onward. The money supply more than doubled, consumption and investment grew (although the foreign trade balance did not start to recover until 1937), government expenditures grew but taxes were not increased, and the stock market began to recover, suggesting that expectations were improving. Nevertheless, as pointed out above, the recovery, rapid as it was, began from such a low level that the economy had not fully recovered by the end of the decade.

The absence of a consensus explanation for what actually caused the Great Depression does not preclude the learning of valuable lessons. One major lesson learned from the Great Depression is that a decline as rapid and steep as that which occurred between 1929 and 1933 will be very difficult to correct quickly. It is therefore very important not to allow such a sharp decline to recur. A second lesson that some members of the economics profession believe they have learned is that the self-correcting forces operating to restore the economy to full employment may be weak, especially for large declines in aggregate demand. Other economists disagree, pointing to evidence that the self-correcting forces were at work but suggesting that they were simply overwhelmed by a series of negative aggregate demand shocks.

Another important lesson, perhaps the most important one, is that when an economy is entering a recession, the federal government should not take actions that will further decrease aggregate demand. Between 1929 and 1932 the federal government not only allowed the money supply to fall substantially when the appropriate policy would have been to increase the money supply, but the government substantially raised taxes when taxes should have been lowered, and it passed substantial tariff barriers when the opposite would have been appropriate.

REQUIRED ECONOMIC CONCEPTS

Aggregate output	**Supply shock**
Aggregate price level	**Potential national income**
Aggregate supply	**Deflationary gap**
Aggregate demand	**Inflationary gap**
Aggregate demand curve	**Full employment**
Macroeconomic law of demand	**Long-run aggregate supply curve**
Wealth and income effect	
Interest rate effect	
Substitution of foreign goods effect	
Short-run aggregate supply curve	
Macroeconomic equilibrium	

KEY QUESTIONS

1. What is the great economic slump of the 1930s called?
2. Name the three major effects that explain why the aggregate demand curve has a negative slope. Why does the short-run aggregate supply curve have a positive slope?
3. What are the determinants that can cause the aggregate demand curve to shift?
4. What are the determinants that can cause the short-run aggregate supply curve to shift?
5. What is meant by potential national income?
6. Under what circumstances does an inflationary gap occur? A deflationary gap?
7. Why is the long-run aggregate supply curve vertical?
8. What is the difference between the short run and long run in macroeconomics?

PROBLEMS

1. In the following indicate whether the initial effect is on the aggregate supply or aggregate demand curve or both, state whether there is a shift, and, if there is a shift, tell what its direction is.
    a. The income tax to households increases.
    b. The income tax to corporations decreases.
    c. "There is concern that high factory operating rates and a tight labor market are exerting inflationary pressure."
    d. The federal government reduces its level of spending.
    e. Consumers substitute more foreign goods for domestically produced goods.
    f. Former economic adviser Charles Schultze says, "Between 1965 and 1980 we had three great shocks to fight: the two OPEC oil embargoes (1973 and 1978) and the Vietnam War." Also, describe what these shocks did to the price level.
    g. Schultze also said, "Only the sharp recession of 1981–1982, which resulted from the Federal Reserve's tight-money policies, was enough to break inflation's back." Also, explain this statement. (Note: By "tight-money policies," Schultze means policies that decrease the available money supply.)
    h. "Debt-burdened consumers will spend more cautiously and tax reform will hobble business investment. But the dollar's decline in the foreign exchange markets will spur sales of U.S. goods abroad and have a moderating effect."
    i. The interest rate declines significantly, spurring business investment spending.
    j. The new OPEC oil agreement of 1988 raised the price of a barrel of crude oil (32 gallons) from $14 to $22.
2. Suppose the economy is at its potential full-employment level of output. What might cause both the price level and employment to increase? Do you think this will lead to a permanent long-run increase in output? If not, what would you predict would happen? Explain.
3. Suppose the short-run aggregate supply (SRAS) curve is given by the following data. Output is measured in billions of real dollars. Assume that real potential income is $880 billion.

PRICE INDEX	QUANTITY OF AGGREGATE OUTPUT SUPPLIED
120	$920
115	900
110	880
105	860
100	840
90	820

a.   At what price levels would aggregate demand have to intersect short-run aggregate supply for inflationary gaps to occur?

b.   At what price levels would aggregate demand have to intersect short-run aggregate supply for deflationary gaps to occur?

c.   At what price level would AD have to intersect SRAS for there to be no gap?

d.   If SRAS intersects AD at a point on the LRAS curve, what statement can you make about the actual price level and the price level that workers and producers expect will occur in the future?

4.   The demand curve for a given product is the horizontal summation of individual demand curves for that product. Explain why the aggregate demand curve is *not* the horizontal summation of all the demand curves of different products in the economy.

THE CLASSICAL MODEL AND SOME EMPIRICAL TESTS

PREVIEW
HYPERINFLATION IN THE UNITED STATES

The very rapid rise in the prices of all goods and services is called *hyperinflation*. Hyperinflation is the price-level counterpart of a depression. Although today generally considered a problem that afflicts only foreign countries, hyperinflation has been experienced two times in the United States, both during wartimes. The first occurred during the American Revolution; the phrase "Not worth a Continental" reflected the decline in value of the currency issued by the Continental Congress. The second occurred during the Civil War when the Confederacy experienced a runaway inflation. On the day the war ended in 1865, the value of a Confederate dollar was about 1 percent of its value in 1860.

During both hyperinflations prices rose first slowly, then more rapidly, until finally the value of the currency was depreciating so fast that the people refused to accept money in trade. The result was mass hardship as the monetary economy broke down. Domestic currencies ceased to circulate, being replaced by barter and/or the circulation of foreign currencies. The hyperinflation during the American Revolution ended with a currency reform, and in the South it ended when the North emerged victorious.

During both hyperinflations people blamed speculators for their problems and price controls were imposed in vain attempts to curb the accelerating price level. George Washington's army starved at Valley Forge during 1777 because price controls were imposed on the theory that they would reduce the expense of provisioning the army. Instead the controls reduced the availability of supplies. Farmers refused to accept the Continental currency at the artificially low prices. Price controls were repealed the following year. During both wars the public did not concentrate on the prime cause of inflation; hence they were not able to formulate an effective program of reform that would have mitigated the hardships.

That inflation was the consequence of excessive growth in the money supply was known to the economists of the eighteenth century. Adam

Smith, David Ricardo, J. B. Say, J. S. Mill, and David Hume had formulated a theory, known as the quantity theory, to explain the relationship between the quantity of money and the overall price level. The quantity theory was half of a two-part theory designed to explain how the overall economy operated. That theory is now known as *classical economics*.

Although the quantity theory was a powerful if simplified theory of how the price level was determined, it proved somewhat inaccurate in predicting the overall effect of an increased money supply on the price level during hyperinflations. Yet the theory was adequate to inform economic decision makers in the Confederacy, had they paid attention, that the root cause of inflation was not speculation but the growth of the money supply.

The second half of the classical theory rested on Say's law, which states that "supply creates its own demand" and implies that the economy will tend always to operate with the full employment of the factors of production. Extended periods of unemployment were not to be expected.

The biggest test of classical economics came with the Great Depression — a test that it obviously failed. Classical economics is currently making a comeback, modified and refined in the light of what the economics profession has learned about inflations and depressions. Modern macroeconomic theory began with the Great Depression, but it has been built on the foundation provided by the classical economists.

THE CLASSICAL MODEL OF MACROECONOMICS

The classical model was the first systematic attempt to explain how the macroeconomy operated. The classical model was developed through the efforts of several eighteenth-century economists. Adam Smith, J. S. Mill, and Thomas Malthus all contributed, and in particular the work of David Hume, David Ricardo, and J. B. Say proved instrumental. These economists were interested in explaining how the overall price level and the real value of national output were determined.

The classical economists started with three assumptions about the economy:

1. The economy is competitive: No one buyer or seller can affect the price of a good or factor of production. All prices and wages are assumed to be flexible and free to seek the equilibrium level determined by the market forces of supply and demand.
2. People are motivated by self-interest: Economic decision makers attempt to maximize their economic welfare.
3. Economic decision makers are not fooled by money illusion. Buyers and sellers react to changes in relative prices, not absolute prices. Consumers would not change their behavior if just the absolute level of prices changes, as when all prices and wages double. But they would change their behavior when relative prices change, as when the price of one good doubles while all other prices and wages remain the same.

The third assumption requires some explanation. Workers are assumed to decide how much labor to supply on the basis of the real wage. The real wage is determined by how many goods and services the money wage can buy. If the price level falls and money wages decline proportionately, then a worker can still buy the same quantity of goods and services as before. The absence-of-money-illusion assumption states that workers will not be fooled into changing their behavior by a change in the price level matched by a corresponding change in money wages. Only actual changes in real wages will affect the amount of labor workers will supply.

Given these assumptions, the classical economists were able to work out a consistent theory of the macroeconomic economy. The classical model can be interpreted within the basic macroeconomic model.

The classical model divided the forces that affected aggregate output and the overall price level into factors that determined the aggregate demand for gross national product and the forces that determined the aggregate output of GNP. The price level and real national output were determined when the quantity of aggregate demand (AD) equaled the quantity of aggregate supply (AS).

Classical economists argued that aggregate supply had a particular shape. Aggregate supply was believed to be totally unresponsive to changes in the price level. They believed that aggregate supply was determined by the quantity and quality of the factors of production and by the state of technology, but not by the price level. Thus the same quantity of aggregate output would be supplied at every price level. The classical model thus contains only the long-run aggregate supply curve of the basic macroeconomic model.

This assumption is crucial to the classical economic theory. Consider Figure 7A.1, where both an aggregate demand (AD_1) curve and an aggregate supply (AS) curve are drawn. The AD_1 curve is downward-sloping, reflecting the inverse relationship between the quantity of real national output demanded and the price level. The AS curve is drawn as a vertical line reflecting the classical assumption that the quantity of national output supplied is not responsive to changes in the price level. Macroeconomic equilibrium occurs at point E_1, where the quantity of aggregate output demanded equals the quantity of aggregate output supplied. The equilibrium price level will be P_e and real national output will be Y_e.

It can readily be seen that the vertical AS curve determines the level of real national output. No matter what the level of aggregate demand, real national output will always be equal to Y_e. Moreover, the price level is determined only by the level of aggregate demand. If aggregate demand increased from AD_1 to AD_2, the price level would increase to P_e' as equilibrium shifts from E_1 to E_2 while real national output remained the same. The classical economists thus concluded that real national output was determined by factors that affected aggregate supply, and that the price level was determined by the level of aggregate demand.

AGGREGATE DEMAND IN THE CLASSICAL MODEL

What could cause aggregate demand to increase in the classical model? The classical economists had a straightforward answer: the quantity of money. Money was defined in Chapter 2 as a good that serves as a medium of exchange. Since it can be exchanged for every other good, money allows the economy to escape the bondage of barter exchanges. Classical economists discovered the relationship between the quantity of money and the macroeconomy known as the *equation of exchange*. The equation of exchange is:

$$MV = PQ$$

FIGURE 7A.1
Classical Model of Macroeconomics

The classical model divides the economy into two sectors, a monetary sector that determines the level of aggregate demand and a real-goods sector that determines the level of aggregate output. An increase in the quantity of money in circulation will cause aggregate demand to increase. The aggregate supply curve of the classical model is not dependent on the price level but on the quantity and quality of the factors of production and the state of technology. Aggregate supply therefore is constant. When aggregate demand changes, the entire effect on the economy is to cause the price level to change while aggregate output remains unchanged.

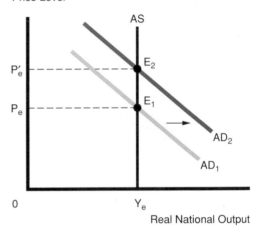

where M is the quantity of money, V is the velocity of circulation, P is the price level, and Q is real national output. You have been previously introduced to all of the variables except the **velocity of circulation.**

The velocity of circulation is the average number of times that a unit of money is spent on final goods and services during a period of one year.

The velocity of circulation is defined as the ratio of nominal national output to the money supply, or V = PQ/M. The higher the value of V, the more rapidly people turn over, via exchanges, the existing stock of money. A velocity of 10 means that on average each unit of money, say a dollar, is spent 10 times each year.

The definition of velocity makes the equation of exchange an identity. It must be true. It says that the total value of what is spent (MV) must be equal to the total value of what is produced (PQ). The money supply times the average number of times a dollar is spent equals the total value of what is spent to purchase nominal national output. Since the price level times real national output equals nominal national output, the two sides of the equation must be equal to each other.

The equation of exchange allows the determination of the relationship between the quantity of national output demanded and the price level. Rewrite the equation of exchange as:

$$Q = \frac{MV}{P}$$

The quantity of real national output demanded will be inversely related to the price level. When the price level increases, holding M and V constant, the quantity of real national output demanded will decline. So the aggregate demand curve will slope downward and to the right, just as microeconomic demand curves do.

The rewritten equation of exchange also reveals why the classical aggregate demand curve might shift. The AD curve will shift when the quantity of money changes. If the quantity of money increases, so will the quantity of real national output demanded and the AD curve will shift to the right from AD_1 to AD_2 in Figure 7A.1. Conversely, if the quantity of money declines, so will the quantity of real national output demanded and the AD curve will shift to the left. Theoretically, the AD curve should also shift if the velocity of circulation changes, but this is not the case in the classical model. Classical economists assumed that velocity was fixed, and in doing so, converted the equation of exchange from an identity into a theory.

The equation of exchange can be turned from an identity, which must be true, into a theory, which may be proven false, by making restrictive assumptions about the behavior of the variables and testing the predictions. Classical economists assumed that both the velocity of circulation and real national output were fixed at any point in time. This allowed them to derive the following relationship between the quantity of money and the price level that is known as the **classical quantity theory.**

The equation of exchange can be rewritten to isolate the determinants of the price level:

$$P = M\frac{V}{Q}$$

If V and Q are both fixed by assumption, then V/Q will be a constant, and a change in the price level will be proportional to the change in the money supply. Whenever the money supply increases by 5 percent, for example,

FIGURE 7A.2

Say's Law and the Circular Flow Diagram

Say's Law states that supply creates its own demand. Aggregate demand would always be sufficient to purchase the economy's potential national income. In Part A, the process of producing $1,000 in goods creates an equal amount of income for the factors of production. Thus households have $1,000 in income with which to purchase the $1,000 worth of goods. If households desire to spend $900 for goods and services and to save $100, as shown in Part B, these savings are deposited with financial institutions, which in turn loan the savings to business firms that desire to invest in new capital goods. The composition of output will now be $900 in consumer goods and $100 in investment goods. According to Say's law, $1,000 in production will still generate $1,000 in demand for goods.

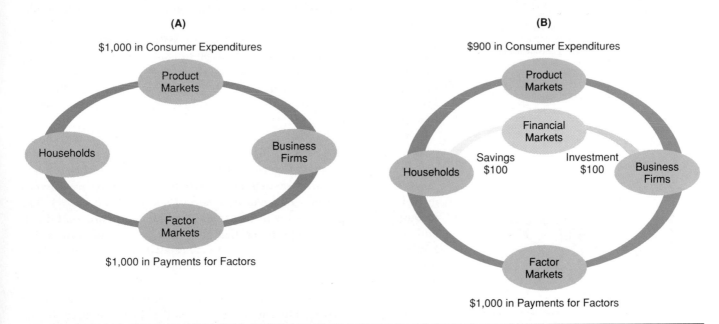

so will the price level. Inflation in the classical model is thus purely a monetary phenomenon.

> *The classical quantity theory is a theory stating that the change in the price level will be proportional to the change in the quantity of money.*

This prediction rests on the assumption that velocity and real national output are fixed. Classical economists believed that velocity was determined by habits and institutions of a country that changed only very slowly, and that it could be assumed to be effectively constant at any point in time.

Classical economists also assumed that the level of real national output was fixed at the maximum that could be produced with the available resources and state of technology. They did not believe that it was possible for the economy to depart from producing the maximum amount of national output. They believed that the process of production created an offsetting demand for goods and services. J. B. Say said it best when he coined the phrase "Supply creates its own demand," which is now known as *Say's Law*.

Say thought that the very process of supplying goods proved the desire to consume other goods. Individuals produce more of a good than they desire to consume only because they wish to exchange the excess for other goods they desire to consume. A person desires to supply something only because he or she has a demand for some other good. The implication of this is that there can never be goods produced for which a demand does not exist.

A circular flow diagram can be used to illustrate Say's Law. If, as in Part A of Figure 7A.2, an economy produces $1,000 worth of goods, it

FIGURE 7A.3
Financial and Labor Markets in the Classical Model

Part A shows the working of financial markets, which in the classical model ensure that the amount of desired savings by households will just equal the amount of desired investment by business firms. The quantity of desired savings will equal the quantity of desired investment at the equilibrium rate of interest.

Part B shows that a change in the price level does not affect the amount of aggregate output in the classical model because money wages will change along with the price level to keep real wages constant.

(A) Financial Markets

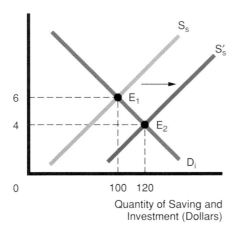

(B) Labor Markets

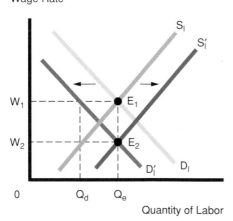

must acquire the necessary factors of production, and in the process of doing so $1,000 is paid out to households, which are the ultimate owners of the factors of production. The workers and resource owners allow business firms to use their resources because they desire to use the income earned to purchase goods and services. The $1,000 worth of goods produced precisely equals the $1,000 in income necessary to buy the goods. Thus supply will create its own demand. The economy will always operate at the level of maximum real national output and all resources will be fully employed.

But suppose households desire to save $100 out of their $1,000 in income and choose to purchase only $900 in consumer goods. According to Say's Law, the $100 in savings will be exactly offset by $100 in business investment. In Part B consumer-goods production will equal $900 and investment goods will equal $100, for a total that equals the $1,000 in household income.

What ensures that the amount of savings will always equal the amount of investment? The answer is the rate of interest that is the price of credit as determined in competitive financial markets. The rate of interest will operate to make desired savings by households equal to desired investment by business firms. This can be seen in Part A of Figure 7A.3. The amount of savings and investment is measured along the horizontal axis and the interest rate along the vertical axis. The amount of savings that households desire to supply (S_s) is positively related to the rate of interest. The higher the rate of interest, the more households will desire to save. The quantity of investment that business firms desire (D_i) is negatively related to the interest rate. The higher the rate of interest, the less credit that will be demanded. The rate of interest will adjust to equate the desired quantity of savings with the desired quantity of investment. The desired quantity of savings of $100 will equal the desired quantity of investment at 6 percent.

If households desire to save more, the supply of savings will shift from S_s to S_s'. Consumption will decline as savings increase. In competitive financial markets with flexible prices, the interest rate will decline to 4 percent so that the quantity of investment demanded will increase to $120. In this way the quantity of investment automatically increases to make up for the decline in consumption goods. Changes in desired savings will not cause the economy to deviate from producing the maximum national output.

The only unemployment that can exist in the classical model is voluntary. If the demand for labor declines in a competitive market with flexible wages, so will the wage rate. In Part B of Figure 7A.3 the classical labor market is illustrated. The supply of labor (S_l) is determined by the real wage rate and is positively related to the money wage rate. The demand for labor (D_l) also depends on the real wage rate and varies inversely with the money wage rate. The equilibrium wage is determined by the intersection of the supply and demand curves and initially takes place at point E_1. The equilibrium money wage is W_1 and the quantity of labor employed is Q_e.

Suppose aggregate demand declines, causing the price level to fall in Figure 7A.1. The decline in the price level causes the real wage to rise in the labor market. The demand for labor at the existing money wage W_1 thus declines from D_l to D_l'. Employers will continue to hire the same quantity of labor only if the money wage falls by the same amount as the price level.

Workers are assumed not to suffer from money illusion. They will recognize that the real wage has increased and that unemployment will occur unless money wages fall. In order to avoid unemployment, workers will readily accept a decline in money wages as long as real wages do not fall. The supply of labor will therefore shift automatically from S_1 to S'_1. The equilibrium will move from E_1 to E_2, the money wage will fall from W_1 to W_2, the real wage will remain the same, and the quantity of labor employed will remain the same. The only unemployment will be voluntary, composed of persons who do not wish to work at the prevailing real wage.

Unemployment will exist only if money wages are not flexible and do not decline with the fall in the price level. If money wages do not fall when the demand for labor declines because the supply of labor does not shift, then unemployment will occur. If the money wage remains at W_1, the quantity demanded of labor (Q_d) will be less than the quantity supplied (Q_e), and unemployment will be created. The classical model assumes this will not occur. Thus extended periods of unemployment are not expected to occur.

Classical economists believed that the macroeconomy would take care of itself. Changes in relative prices, interest rates, and money wages would allow the economy to adjust to maintain equilibrium at the maximum level of national output. There was no need for government to intervene in the economy except to ensure that the assumptions of competitive markets with flexible wages and prices were maintained. There was no cause to worry that aggregate demand would be insufficient to ensure full employment — Say's Law would see to that. The classical model provided a rationale for a laissez-faire governmental policy.

In summary, we have shown that the classical model proceeded by dividing the macroeconomy into two sectors: a monetary sector that determined the price level and a real sector that determined real national output. The price level will change only if the money supply changes. The level of real national output will be altered only if the state of technology or the quantity or quality of the factors of production changes. The classical model makes two predictions that can be tested:

1. The price level will be proportional to the money supply.
2. The economy will operate at a level of real national output that ensures the full employment of all resources.

P R E V I E W   A N A L Y S I S
HYPERINFLATION IN THE UNITED STATES

The United States has experienced two periods of hyperinflation: during the Revolutionary War and in the South during the Civil War. In each case the increase in the price level was preceded by an increase in the money supply as the government issued money to purchase supplies to fight the war. Figure 7A.4 charts the relationship between the money supply and the price level for the two hyperinflations.

The classical quantity theory predicts that the rise in the price level will be proportional to the increase in the money supply. In Part A of Figure 7A.4 the increases in the money supply and corresponding increases in the price level for the Confederacy are available on a quarterly basis from 1861 to 1864, when the statistical series ends. It appears that the classical quantity theory predicts quite well up to the fourth quarter of 1862: Both price level and the money supply rise in lockstep. Beginning

FIGURE 7A.4
Inflation and the Money Supply: A Test of the Classical Quantity Theory

The classical quantity theory predicts that changes in the price level should be proportional to changes in the money supply. In both the Confederacy in 1861–1864 and the colonies during the American Revolution, the predictions of the classical quantity theory broke down as the rate of inflation accelerated due to the disproportionately rapid increase in the price level.

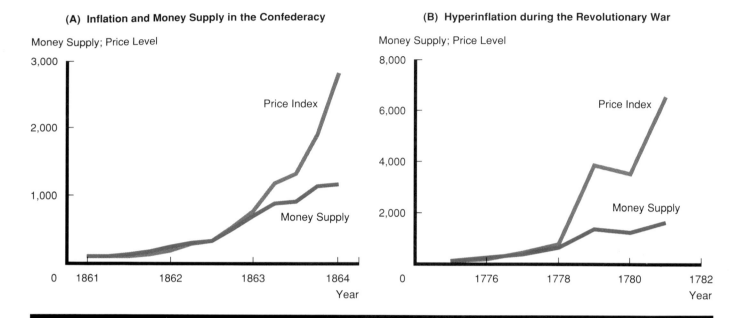

in 1863, this relationship begins to break down. The price level increases more rapidly than the money supply.

The same phenomenon was true during the American Revolution. Part B of Figure 7A.4 provides information on the increase in the money supply and the price level on an annual basis for the years 1775–1781. The increase in the price level corresponds closely with the increase in the money supply through 1779, as the classical quantity theory predicts. But after that date the relationship breaks down, with the price level outstripping the growth of the money supply.

The classical quantity theory breaks down during hyperinflations. When an economic theory does not correspond with observed economic behavior, that theory must be modified. The limitations of the classical quantity theory are now widely recognized. Modern quantity theorists have modified the quantity theory, as you will see in a later chapter, to make it more closely correspond with the observed behavior of the economy.

The Great Depression produced an even more significant test of classical economics. According to classical theory, the Depression should never have occurred. The decline in the money supply that took place between 1929 and 1933 (see Table 7.5) would have caused the aggregate demand to decline, but this should not have affected aggregate output. If you look again at Figure 7A.1, the decline in the money supply should have caused the aggregate demand curve to shift down from AD_2 to AD_1 and the sole effect should have been a decline in the price level without a change in aggregate output. The price level did decline, but so did aggregate output.

According to classical theory, the decline in the price level should have been accompanied by a decline in money wages to keep the real wage constant. If this happens, employment and output should not change. The

TABLE 7A.1
Labor Market Statistics: 1929–1941

YEAR (1)	UNEMPLOYMENT RATE (2)	UNEMPLOYMENT RATE ADJUSTED FOR GOVERNMENT WORK PROJECTS (3)	ANNUAL MONEY EARNINGS (4)	AVERAGE HOURLY MONEY WAGES (5)	REAL WAGES (1947 = 100) (6)
1929	3.2	3.2	$1,462	$0.57	$0.77
1930	8.7	8.7	1,294	0.55	0.77
1931	15.9	15.9	1,068	0.52	0.80
1932	23.6	23.6	807	0.45	0.77
1933	25.2	20.9	722	0.44	0.80
1934	22.0	16.2	789	0.53	0.93
1935	20.3	14.4	851	0.55	0.94
1936	17.0	10.0	932	0.56	0.94
1937	14.3	9.2	1,072	0.56	0.91
1938	19.1	12.5	956	0.62	1.03
1939	17.2	11.3	1,029	0.63	1.06
1940	14.6	N.A.	1,113	0.66	1.11
1941	9.9	N.A.	1,561	0.66	1.05

Sources: Joseph Swanson and Samuel Williamson, "Estimates of National Product and Income for the United States Economy, 1914–1941," *Explorations in Economic History* (Fall 1972): Table 1; Stanley Lebergott, "The American Labor Force," in L. E. Davis et al., *American Economic Growth* (New York, 1972), 213; and Michael Darby, "Three and a Half Million U.S. Employees Have Been Mislaid," *Journal of Political Economy* (February 1976), 8.

fact that aggregate output declined and unemployment appeared during the Great Depression suggests that this did not happen. Table 7A.1 confirms this suspicion. This table contains information on the unemployment rate, real average annual earnings, the hourly money wages, and the real wages. Average hourly earnings, shown in column 5, did decline, but not by as much as the price level fell. This can be seen by comparing column 6, which reports average real wages, with column 5. Average real wages are calculated by adjusting money wages by a price index. Column 6 reveals that real wages actually increased despite the decline in money wages. Thus money wages, though declining, did not fall as much as the price level. The result was growing unemployment, as can be seen in columns 2 and 3.

When a theory fails to predict, it must be modified. A good place to start is with the assumptions. The failure of money wages to decline by as much as the price level suggests that some of the assumptions of the classical model may be inappropriate. Perhaps workers do suffer from money illusion, or financial markets do not always equate desired savings with desired investment, or money wages are not flexible downward. In this regard, Keynesian economic theory departed from classical economics in an attempt to improve macroeconomic theory, as you shall see in the following chapters.[1]

[1]Sources for this analysis: Eugene M. Lerner, "Money, Prices, and Wages in the Confederacy, 1861–65," *Journal of Political Economy* (February 1955); and Herbert Runyon, "Fiscal 1777 and 1977," *Business & Financial Letter, Federal Reserve Bank of San Francisco,* October 1, 1976.

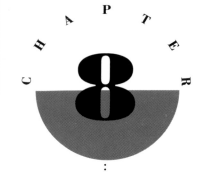

8

A TRILOGY OF MACROECONOMIC PROBLEMS
Growth, Unemployment, and Inflation

IN THIS CHAPTER YOU WILL LEARN:

**That the ideal
macroeconomic world does
not exist**

●

**How economic growth,
unemployment, and
inflation affect the
macroeconomy**

●

**How growth,
unemployment, and
inflation are measured**

THREE PROBLEMS OF THE MACROECONOMY

There are three major macroeconomic problems: recession and the resulting unemployment, inflation, and slow economic growth. Each in its own way disrupts the lives of people, creating hardship and disappointment. Here's a sample of the difficulties these problems can or have created.

1. The rate of economic growth, for as long as the United States has had national income statistics, has allowed the standard of living of the average American to double each generation. This means that your grandfather probably lived twice as well as your great-grandfather, and your father twice as well as your grandfather. This phenomenon has become known as the American dream.

But the chances are that you cannot expect to do as well. The rate of economic growth apparently has slowed since 1973. Between 1870 and 1985 the average annual percentage increase in per capita income was 3.47 percent; however, between 1973 and 1985 the average percentage increase was only 2.24, a decline of 35 percent. The long-term growth rate in labor productivity, which averaged slightly over 2 percent from 1900 to 1986, declined to 1.5 percent for the years 1973–1986, a decline of 25 percent. If these recent trends in the rate of growth of labor productivity and of per capita income continue over your working life, your standard of living will not increase nearly so rapidly as that of your forebears.

Surely this is an exaggeration. How can a drop of only 1.2 percent in the per capita economic growth rate have such a large impact on future standards of living?

2. During the 1981–1982 recession factories were closed all over the country. Here's a sample. The A&P food-processing plant in Horseheads, New York, the world's largest, closed its doors and sent home 1,100 workers. GAF shut down 13 roofing plants located throughout the country and laid off 1,800 workers. Wrangler stopped making jeans in North Carolina; another 320 people lost their jobs. Ford shut down its Lorain, Ohio, assembly plant and added another 2,250 to the unemployment rolls. General Tire provided another 1,500 in Akron, Ohio, when it closed its plant, and Texaco laid off 304
continued

THREE PROBLEMS OF THE MACROECONOMY Continued

workers at its refinery in Tulsa, Oklahoma, as the shutdowns proceeded.

Every month for nearly two years hundreds of thousands of Americans were let go by their employers. The unemployment rate reached its peak at 10.6 percent in the fourth quarter of 1982, with 12.2 million Americans out of work. Only 4.4 million of these unfortunates were eligible for unemployment benefits. Also another four to five million were no longer counted among the unemployed, because they had become discouraged from continuing to seek employment. Another group probably as large was working short hours, but it was not counted as unemployed by the government. All in all, the number of Americans whose jobs were affected by the recession numbered perhaps as many as 20 million, or 18 percent of the labor force.

The economic loss borne by the nation was estimated by the Urban Institute to be $570 billion, of which $336 billion was borne directly by workers and their families. The rest was felt by the owners of other factors of production that were idled by the recession.

The average loss per household was $3,309, but this cost was, of course, not spread evenly across the nation. The millions of unemployed were concentrated in the industrial sector and they bore a disproportionate share of the burden. The unemployment rate in steel and primary-metal production was 29 percent, in automobiles 23 percent, in construction 22

percent, in appliances 19 percent, in rubber and plastics 15 percent, and in apparel and textiles 13 percent. Thus the average cost of the recession in terms of unemployment was misleading. Most Americans kept their jobs, although millions were worried that their turn to be unemployed would come. Those 20 million who were directly affected paid a disproportionate price.

What are recessions? Why does the unemployment rate rise during recessions? Are the enormous costs of the 1982–1983 recession accurately reported above?

3. Aerotech was a company founded during World War II to supply the rapidly expanding aircraft industry with electronic components. The firm had prospered after the war both as a defense contractor and

as a supplier to producers of commercial jet airliners, because it produced products known for their superb engineering and construction. During the 1970s the uncertainty of a fluctuating inflation rate had several effects on Aerotech.

Sam Taft left his old job to find a better-paying one. Because he wanted to buy a house, he needed a higher income to qualify for a home loan. When he had last searched for a job, it had taken him three months to find one. He was prepared for a long search. He was pleasantly surprised to find in just one week a new position at Aerotech that paid an acceptable salary. Even with a higher-paying job, it didn't seem that his family actually lived any better than before. Jill Montgomery, who had just received her MBA, was also offered a job at Aerotech in marketing, but she decided instead to accept a job as a financial planner. Bill Thompson, the executive vice president of the firm, was not so lucky. He was an engineer, as had been all the past presidents of Aerotech. The president was retiring and had recommended Bill to replace him. But Bill didn't get the job. The board of directors instead selected the company treasurer, citing the need for a financial man to lead the company in such uncertain economic times. How was each of these decisions influenced by the inflationary conditions of the times?

Source: William Greider, *Secrets of the Temple*, 452–455.

• INTRODUCTION •

Five conversations you would never hear in an ideal macroeconomic world:

1. "I'm sorry dear. I know it's just before Christmas, but the plant's closing, and all of the guys were laid off, just like me. It's happening all over the country — nothing I can do about it."
2. "We were doing just fine until interest rates kept going up and up. Finally the bank just said: Pay up! It was all over. In came the auctioneer and he sold everything: tractor, livestock, the car, even the kids' 4-H lambs — everything!"
3. "I was sure that $1,000 a month was enough to live on comfortably when I retired. I told Mabel if we can't live on a thousand a month, we'd better quit. Now, how do you quit living?"
4. "I had it all planned out. We had the best product. It was years ahead of the competition. Then, bang, everybody quit buying. I guess it was the recession. Well, you know, no sales, no dollars, and I had to let everybody go and just shut down."
5. "It's not like I got a degree in history, speech, or something that prepares you for a job in the food-service industry. I got a degree in economics! People I interview tell me: Last year we would have hired you for $24,000 a year and put you in our management-training program, but the way business is, we're even letting our experienced managers with MBAs go. If this keeps up, I'll be out there competing with the historians for a job under the Golden Arches."

No doubt you would like to live in an economy that provides ample opportunities for personal success, with no unpleasant surprises that could threaten your future — at least none beyond your control. Such a world would avoid wide swings in economic activity, would provide acceptable jobs for everyone who wants to work, would sustain stable price levels, and would produce steadily rising standards of living. Inflations, recessions, and depressions would not threaten your future. Absent also would be adverse acts of nature, such as droughts and floods, and wide swings in raw material prices. Individuals could be confident of enjoying a prosperous and predictable future where their own decisions and actions alone determined their individual fortunes.

The real world certainly does not approach this ideal. The macroeconomy is characterized by expansions and contractions that directly affect the fortunes of individuals and businesses. Unexpected events frequently occur, which, though they may benefit some people, generally harm others. Unemployment rises and falls with the fluctuations of the economy, adversely affecting the economic opportunities of many persons. The price level sometimes falls but more often it increases at widely varying rates, making economic decision making difficult for all. Frequently of late, high levels of unemployment have been associated with price inflation, combining two of the worst macroeconomic problems.

The three basic macroeconomic problems are slow economic growth, unemployment, and inflation. Slow economic growth results when the increase in real output of the economy does not increase as rapidly as it should, and when future standards of living do not increase as rapidly as could be expected. Unemployment results from a reduction in job opportunities that forces some workers who would like to work at existing wage rates to go without a job. The nation therefore loses the output that the unemployed could have produced. Inflation involves the rise in the general price level, reducing the value of money, imposing a cost on holders of money, and possibly redistributing wealth.

None of these problems would exist in an ideal macroeconomic world. Everyone would welcome the ideal world of ample jobs, steady prices, and a steadily rising standard of living. Although this ideal world is not yet with us, economic policymakers constantly strive to create conditions that will allow the economy to come as close to it as possible. In order to do this, we must first understand why the economy in the real world may diverge from the ideal. This chapter will introduce you to the three problems and begin to explore their interrelationship. •

ECONOMIC GROWTH

Economic growth is a signal of a macroeconomy's health. It refers to the increase in aggregate output that occurs over time.

Economic growth occurs when aggregate output, measured as real gross national product, increases.

The economic growth rate is the annual percentage increase in real gross national product (GNP$_r$) and measures the observed rate of increase in aggregate economic output. Economic growth between two years, such as between 1985 and 1986, can be measured as follows:

FIGURE 8.1
Real Gross National Product and Its Trend:
1948–1987

It is clear from this figure that the trend of GNP is upward. Real GNP over time tends to increase annually at a
rate of about 3 percent. But actual real GNP does not
increase smoothly like its trend; rather it increases with
significant fluctuations. There are periods in which actual
real GNP has been above the trend and other times when
it has been below the trend. Although real GNP generally
increases, sometimes it has actually declined.

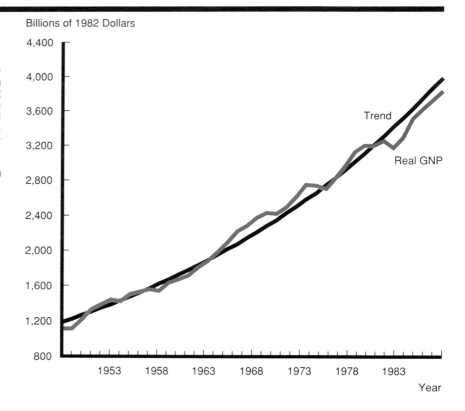

Billions of 1982 Dollars

$$\text{Real growth in 1986} = \frac{1986\ \text{GNP}_r - 1985\ \text{GNP}_r}{1985\ \text{GNP}_r} \times 100\%$$

$$= \frac{\$3{,}677\ \text{billion} - \$3{,}585\ \text{billion}}{\$3{,}585\ \text{billion}} \times 100\% = 2.5\%$$

FLUCTUATIONS IN THE GROWTH RATE

Real GNP typically has not remained the same from year to year. The
historical trend is for it to increase over time. Economic growth has historically not proceeded at a constant pace, as can be seen in Figure 8.1,
which charts real GNP measured quarterly (every three months) in 1982
dollars for the years 1948–1987. A trend line is included. The trend is
clearly upward. If the past is any guide to the future, it is to be expected
that real GNP will grow over time.

While this will be true on average, it may not be true for any particular year. It is clear from the graph that real GNP fluctuates significantly
around the trend line. The rate of growth of real GNP has been both
above and below the trend line for a number of years in succession. The
pace of economic growth has not been smooth in the past and probably
will not be in the future.

The extent of the fluctuations in real GNP can be seen in Figure 8.2,
which charts the quarterly growth rate of real GNP for the years 1948–
1987 along with the trend in the growth rate. It is clear that there are wide
swings in quarterly growth rates and that the trend is slightly downward.
The downward trend is troublesome to many and will be considered in a
later chapter.

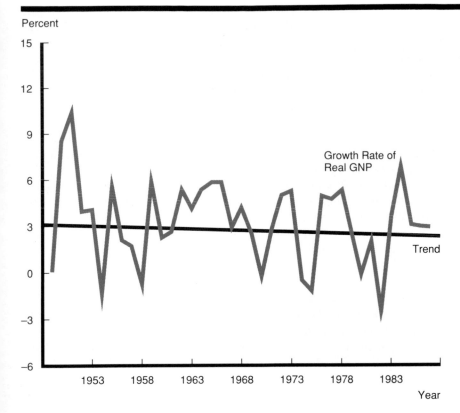

Percent

Growth Rate of
Real GNP

Trend

1953   1958   1963   1968   1973   1978   1983

Year

FIGURE 8.2
Growth Rates of Real Gross National
Product and Its Trend: 1948–1987

The GNP trend line in this figure declines slightly from a
bit more than 3 percent in 1948 to a bit less than this
amount in 1987. It is clear from the graph that the rate of
change in real GNP fluctuates a great deal.

Over a long period of time real GNP has tended to grow at a rate of
a little above 3 percent. This growth has been allowed by the increase in
the nation's potential level of real national income. Potential national
income depends on the size and quality of the labor force, on the quantity
of the other factors of production (capital and resources) available, and
on the state of technology. When one of these determinants increases,
other things being equal, so will the potential level of real GNP. The
economy will then have the capability of producing a larger real GNP.

The determinants of potential national income generally change only
slowly over time. The quantities of the factors of production change only
slowly. Population, for example, one of the main determinants of the
quantity of labor in the economy, grows slowly. The capital stock also
historically has expanded slowly, and technological change is a gradual
process. Potential national income therefore probably grows slowly and
fairly regularly over time.

Growing potential national income is not the same thing as economic
growth, however. In order for economic growth to occur, it is necessary
that potential national income increase, but this is not in itself sufficient
to ensure growth. For example, potential national income increased
throughout the Great Depression but economic growth certainly did not
occur. The macroeconomy must also operate at its potential if economic
growth is to take place. Aggregate demand and the short-run aggregate
supply must make it possible for the economy to take advantage of the
increased potential. Thus two elements are necessary for economic growth
to occur over time: potential real GNP must expand and the macroeconomic situation must take advantage of the increased potential.

Potential economic growth can be shown in the basic macroeconomic
model as a shift to the right of potential national income, which positions

FIGURE 8.3
Actual and Potential National Income:
1948 and 1987

Both 1948 and 1987 were years when the economy operated near its capacity. In 1948 the short-run aggregate supply curve SRAS$_{48}$ intersects the aggregate demand curve AD$_{48}$ at the level of potential national income, which was $1,109 billion measured in 1982 dollars. The price level measured by the GNP deflator was 23.6. Between that year and 1987 the level of potential national income increased to $3,820, an increase of 3.4 times, and the short-run aggregate supply curve SRAS$_{87}$ intersected the aggregate demand curve AD$_{87}$ at this level. From the fact that the price level had increased to 117.5, a fivefold increase since 1948, it can be inferred that aggregate demand had expanded much more than potential national income.

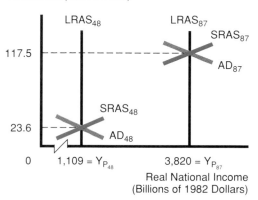

Price Level (1982 Dollars)

the long-run aggregate supply (LRAS) curve. Thus the long-run aggregate supply schedule is determined by the level of potential national income and is unrelated to the price level. The LRAS is represented as a vertical line in a graph of the basic macroeconomic model as shown in Figure 8.3. The basic inference to be drawn from the LRAS is that in the long run the economy will tend to produce at the level of potential national income whatever the price level.

As depicted in Figure 8.3, the LRAS curve has shifted to the right as the potential level of real national income has increased. If the economy is to enjoy the fruits of economic growth, it must continue to operate on the LRAS curve as it shifts to the right.

Between 1948 and 1987 the nation's production capacity and actual real GNP increased 3.4 times as a result of economic growth. In both 1948 and 1987 the economy was operating close to its potential levels, so actual and potential real GNP were approximately the same. Meanwhile the price level increased fivefold.

In Figure 8.3 changes in the basic macroeconomic model that must have occurred between 1948 and 1987 are graphed. As the LRAS curve shifted to the right, so must have both the short-run aggregate supply (SRAS) curve and the aggregate demand curve if the economy was to continue to operate at the level of potential national income. Moreover, if the overall price level increased fivefold, aggregate demand must have increased by more than the increase in potential national income, as shown in Figure 8.3.

ASSESSING THE CURRENT PERFORMANCE OF THE ECONOMY: THE BUSINESS CYCLE

A glance at Figure 8.2 is sufficient to demonstrate that the actual annual rates of economic growth have been highly variable. Economists refer to the fluctuating path of real GNP as the **business cycle**, because of the predominant up-and-down pattern that real GNP has historically followed.

The business cycle is the historical pattern of cyclical up-and-down movements in real gross national product.

The typical pattern of the business cycle is shown in Figure 8.4. The four phases of the business cycle are trough, expansion, peak, and recession. The trough occurs at the bottom of the preceding recession when real GNP reaches its lowest level in that business cycle. The trough is followed by a period of **expansion** that typically features substantial increases in real GNP and employment. Every expansion inevitably reaches a peak where the maximum real GNP for that cycle is produced. The peak is followed by a **recession** in which real GNP and the level of employment decline until reaching a new trough. Recessions are recognized as having occurred when real GNP has declined for two quarters in succession. Eventually the recession reaches its trough. Then a new business cycle begins to trace out the same pattern.

A **depression**, such as the one that occurred in the 1930s, is an extended severe recession that may encompass several business cycles. During depressions the recession phase is stronger than the following recovery phase. During the Great Depression decade recessions occurred between 1929 and 1933, and again in 1938, with recoveries occurring between 1934 and 1937, and from 1939 to the outbreak of World War II. It was not until

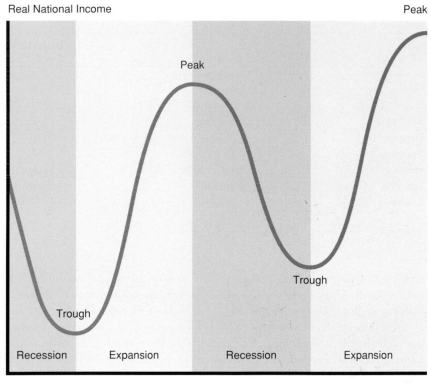

Real National Income

Peak

Peak

Trough

Trough

Recession   Expansion   Recession   Expansion

Time

FIGURE 8.4
Four Phases of a Business Cycle

A business cycle is composed of four phases: trough, expansion, peak, and recession, each measured by the level of real GNP. The cycle begins at the trough, at which point the lowest real GNP is recorded. The trough is followed by the expansion, during which real GNP expands until it reaches its peak, the highest level of real GNP during the cycle. Thereafter the economy falls into recession and real GNP declines until it reaches a new trough and enters a new business cycle. Generally, each succeeding trough and peak occurs at a higher level of real GNP than its predecessor.

the 1940s that the economy recovered to the level of potential national income.

> *An expansion is a phase of the business cycle that is characterized by increasing real GNP and total employment in the economy.*

> *A recession is a phase of the business cycle that is characterized by a decline in real GNP lasting for two or more quarters.*

> *A depression is a very severe recession that lasts for a prolonged period of time.*

Although depressions are infrequent, recessions are unfortunately all too frequent occurrences. There have been numerous recessions but only three depressions since the United States became a nation.

Business cycles, contrary to what the term may imply, are in reality neither regular nor symmetrical. The average business cycle lasts about five years from trough to trough, with the typical expansion lasting for about four years and the typical recession for about one year. There is also nothing regular about the business cycle, and averages in this case may be misleading. Some complete cycles have lasted only a year, while others have lasted as long as nine years. Because the level of potential national income will have increased over the business cycle, the typical business-cycle peak occurs at a higher level of real GNP than the preceding peak.

During expansions numerous economic indicators signal economic growth. Real GNP, industrial production, new-business formations, new

TABLE 8.1
Business Cycles: 1945–1987

TROUGH	PEAK	DURATION (MONTHS)
October 1945	November 1948	45
October 1949	July 1953	56
May 1954	August 1957	49
April 1958	April 1960	32
February 1961	December 1969	116
November 1970	November 1973	47
March 1975	January 1980	62
July 1980	July 1981	18
November 1982	—	—

Source: U.S. Department of Commerce.

orders, building permits, and corporate profits all rise, along with total employment. Meanwhile the unemployment rate and the rate of business failures decline. During recessions these indicators reverse their signals. It used to be thought that the price level increased during an expansion and fell during a recession. But there have been numerous exceptions. During recent recessions the price level has continued to rise, although at a reduced rate. This phenomenon of recession with rising prices has been labeled **stagflation.**

> *Stagflation is the simultaneous existence of recession and inflation.*

Stagflation combines the worst of all possible macroeconomic situations: inflation, high unemployment, and negative economic growth. The existence of stagflation, which will be dealt with later in this book, has presented a major challenge to economists.

Business cycles are a fact of life that complicates everyone's life. The prosperity of both businesses and individuals increases during expansions and declines during recessions. Employment opportunities, profits, new-business formations, and even the federal government's budget deficit — all follow the swings of the business cycle.

TIMING OF BUSINESS CYCLES The duration of a business cycle refers to the length of time it takes to move through one complete business cycle from trough to trough. No two business cycles are alike. One expansion lasted only 18 months and another 116 months (see Table 8.1). The average duration has been five years, of which four years are expansion and one year is recession.

CAUSES OF BUSINESS CYCLES What causes business cycles? The basic macroeconomic model can provide clues. If aggregate demand and the short-run aggregate supply (SRAS) curve always kept pace with the change in potential national income, there would be no business cycles. The defining characteristic of a recession or depression is a sustained decline in real GNP. Aggregate output as measured by observed real GNP departs from the level of potential national income. The basic macroeconomic model suggests that there could be two causes for a decline in real

GNP: a decline in aggregate demand or a decline in short-run aggregate supply.

Consider first the effect of a decline in aggregate demand. Suppose the macroeconomy is initially in short-run and long-run equilibrium at E_1 in Part A of Figure 8.5. If aggregate demand declines as shown from AD to AD', the short-run equilibrium will move from E_1 to E_2. Real national income will decline from Y_P to Y_A and the price level will fall from PL_1 to PL_2. A recessionary gap appears that is equal to Y_P minus Y_A.

A decline in the SRAS curve can also cause real national income to decline. This is shown in Part B of Figure 8.5. Again starting at long-run equilibrium E_1, a decline in SRAS will cause the SRAS curve to shift to the left from SRAS to SRAS'. The new equilibrium position is E_2. Real national income will decline from Y_P to Y_A and a deflationary gap will be created. The price level in this case will also rise.

In both cases a deflationary gap will appear. The appearance of a deflationary gap is perhaps the main characteristic of a recession. A deflationary gap signals that the economy is wasting resources, since the actual aggregate output is less than the level of potential national income.

UNEMPLOYMENT

A deflationary gap caused by a decline in real GNP is the main characteristic of a recession. Because a decline in aggregate output below the level of potential national income means fewer workers are required, unemployment increases during a recession. People lose their jobs, and their lives are disrupted. The economy as a whole loses the output that could have been produced by the newly unemployed, while the unemployed lose the income they could have earned. When it occurs, unemployment does not fall equally on everyone in the economy. The burden instead falls disproportionately on those unlucky enough to lose their jobs, and on the owners of the other factors of production that are now redundant. Because of the significant social costs involved, both the public and politicians are naturally sensitive to rising unemployment.

In Chapter 1 you discovered that there are never enough goods and services to satisfy all the wants of society. There will therefore always be useful work to be done to satisfy the unlimited wants of society. How, then, given the existence of scarcity, is it possible for a person willing to work to be without a job? The definition of **unemployment** provides a clue.

> *Unemployment is a condition that exists when people who wish to work are searching for acceptable job opportunities.*

The labor market in the United States is composed of millions of employers and even more workers. There is an almost bewildering variety of jobs that must be filled, requiring a variety of different talents, skills, and experiences from workers. A list of job titles would fill a book the size of a medium-sized telephone directory. Clearly, it is a major task to match jobs with workers. How is this task accomplished?

If every job seeker knew about every job, the qualifications required, and what it paid, and every employer knew the qualifications of every job seeker, there would be little, if any, unemployment. The principle of comparative advantage would ensure a job for each willing worker. In a world in which everyone has complete information about job opportunities and worker skills, the task of matching workers and jobs would be

FIGURE 8.5
Two Causes of a Recession

There are two causes of a recession: A demand-side recession stemming from a decline in aggregate demand or a supply-side recession caused by a decline in short-run aggregate supply. Initially, the economy is in long-run equilibrium at E_1, producing aggregate output equal to the level of potential national income with a price level of PL_1. Part A reveals the effect of a decline in aggregate demand. Part B shows the effect of a decline in short-run aggregate supply. A demand-side recession can be distinguished from a supply-side recession by the price level effect. A demand-side inflation results in a decline in the price level, whereas a supply-side recession causes the price level to increase.

(A) Demand-Induced Recession

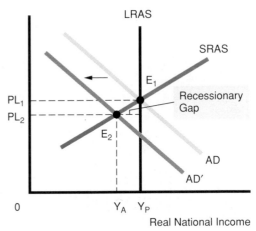

(B) Supply-Induced Recession

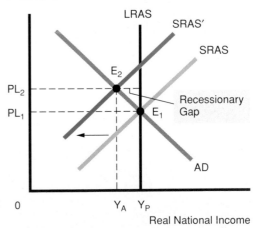

FIGURE 8.6
Natural Rate of Unemployment

The natural rate of unemployment is the rate of unemployment to which the economy will tend in the long run as the economy moves to the level of potential national income. There is no government estimate of the natural rate such as the BLS unemployment rate, but there are private estimates such as the one reproduced in this figure. You can readily see that from 1940 to 1980 the natural rate tended to increase. Some economists believe that the natural rate has declined somewhat since 1980, as the author's extension of this series indicates.

Source: R. A. Gordon, *Macroeconomics*, 3rd ed. (Boston: Little, Brown, 1984).

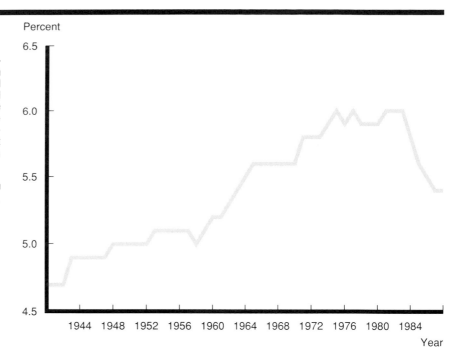

relatively easy. Workers could select the best jobs available to them and employers could choose the best workers.

Complete information about job opportunities does not exist. A person looking for work has to acquire information about the available job openings. Business firms must search for suitable workers to hire. Unemployment exists because it requires time as well as other resources to match workers with jobs. Workers must search for job opportunities and employers must look for suitable workers.

Moreover, the task is never finished. Every day young people enter the labor force for the first time and older workers retire. Some workers do not stay put, but are constantly in the process of changing jobs and careers. New firms are constantly being formed, new products introduced, new technologies innovated. Unprofitable firms die, old products and processes are phased out. Each change means a change in the pattern of employment. In the process of reallocating resources, unemployment is a natural occurrence as persons move from less productive to more productive occupations.

Individuals who are unemployed are searching for acceptable job opportunities. Although there is always useful work to be done, an unemployed worker may find that what is immediately available is unsuitable. When an engineer is laid off, there will be many immediate job opportunities available, but they may not be in the field of engineering or they may be located too far from home. The engineer may decide to remain unemployed rather than deliver telephone books or become a telephone solicitor, and instead choose to search for an acceptable job opportunity. Similarly, a laid-off automobile worker may find his or her next best alternative less worthwhile than waiting for the plant to reopen. Or an unemployed stockbroker may choose to spend time looking for another job in the financial sector rather than sell automobiles or insurance.

DEFINING FULL EMPLOYMENT

Full employment in a dynamic economy cannot mean zero unemployment. Some persons will always be unemployed as the economy carries out the

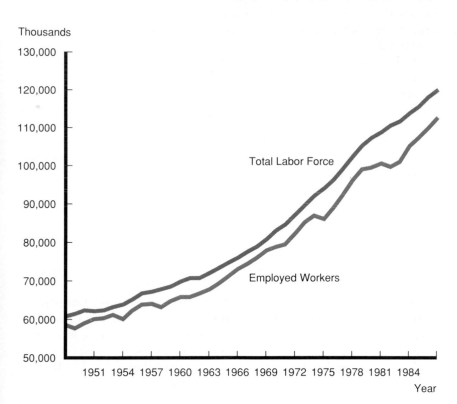

Thousands

FIGURE 8.7
Growth of the Labor Force and of Employed
Workers: 1948–1987

In this figure the labor force is charted along with the total number of persons employed. The difference between the two equals the total number of persons unemployed. It is clear from the graph that both the labor force and the total number of persons employed have grown significantly, with both the labor force and total employed doubling over the last 40 years. The labor force has grown much more regularly than the number of employed, which has fluctuated with the business cycle.

necessary process of reallocating resources. As comparative advantage changes, it will be necessary, if the economy is to continue to grow, for workers and other resources to be transferred between occupations and industries.

Consistent with this ongoing reallocation of resources and with the characteristics of the labor force is a rate of unemployment that corresponds to the level of potential real national income. This rate is often referred to as the **natural rate of unemployment.**

> *The natural rate of unemployment is the unemployment rate at which there is an approximate balance between the number of unfilled jobs and the number of qualified job seekers.*

Often the natural rate of unemployment is referred to as the full-employment rate of unemployment. There is a job for all job seekers — all they have to do is find it, and while they are searching they are unemployed. The natural rate of unemployment is the rate of unemployment from which potential national income is calculated.

The natural rate of unemployment is not a constant but changes over time as labor force characteristics change. One estimate of the natural rate of unemployment is shown in Figure 8.6. According to this estimate, the natural rate of unemployment has increased from the 1940s to the present.

THE MEASURED UNEMPLOYMENT RATE

The size of the labor force and the number of employed workers are shown in Figure 8.7. The labor force is composed of all persons over the age of 16 who hold a regular job or are seeking one. The employed are composed of persons who hold a job. It can be seen from the figure that the number of employed persons increased almost as much as did the labor force. Millions more new workers have entered the labor force than have left it over the last three decades. The size of the total labor force in the United States has roughly doubled between 1948 and 1987. Almost 20 million additional workers were added in the last decade alone.

The increase in the size of the labor force is due partly to population growth, partly to the aging of the population, and partly to increased participation rates. The population of the United States increased from 147 million in 1948 to 244 million in 1987, adding new workers in the process. There are currently relatively more persons of working age and relatively fewer persons below the age of 16 than there used to be. More women are now part of the labor force than was the case in the past.

The growing American economy has produced millions of new jobs, providing employment for most but not all workers. The difference between the labor force and the number of employed persons measures the number of the unemployed. In 1987 the size of the labor force was 120.6 million, the total number of employed persons was 113.5 million, and the total number of unemployed persons was 7.1 million.

Perhaps a better way to look at the relative importance of unemployment is to calculate the unemployment rate. The unemployment rate measures the percentage of the labor force that is unemployed at a point in time. Every month the Bureau of the Census surveys thousands of households on labor market participation over the preceding week. The Bureau of Labor Statistics (BLS) uses this information to estimate the number of Americans who were employed and unemployed during the preceding month. Each individual 16 years or older in the survey group is classified as either employed, unemployed, or not in the labor force. The labor force is composed of the first two groups, the employed and the unemployed, which are used to calculate the **unemployment rate.**

> *The unemployment rate is the number of unemployed divided by the number of persons in the labor force.*

A person is classified as unemployed if he or she did not work during the preceding week, was looking for work during the previous four months, and is currently available for work. Part-time workers, even if they would like a full-time job, are classified as employed. Persons without jobs but who do not meet these conditions are classified as not in the labor force.

A person who is not in the labor force is in this category for one of two reasons. Either the person has decided not to work or is a discouraged worker. Millions of Americans have consciously decided not to work for a variety of reasons. They are students, retired or disabled persons, discouraged workers, or they have young children. A **discouraged worker** has decided not to look for work because past efforts to find a job have been unsuccessful.

> *A discouraged worker is a person who has decided not to search for work in the belief that there are no acceptable jobs available.*

Discouraged workers remain out of the labor force because past experience has convinced them that it will be fruitless to keep trying. Discouraged workers often possess few skills, or the skills they have are no longer in demand in a changing economy.

The unemployment rate thus may understate the number of persons who could be classified as unemployed at any point in time. Discouraged

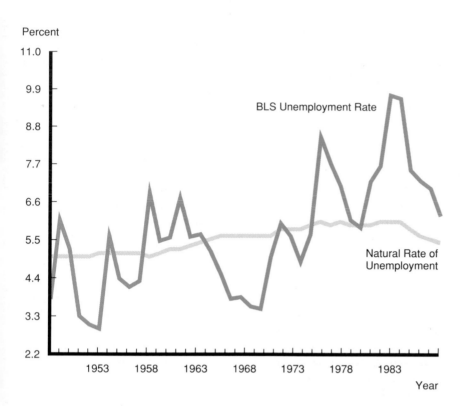

Percent

FIGURE 8.8
Unemployment Rate and Natural Rate of
Unemployment: 1948–1987

It is apparent from this figure that the unemployment rate
has been rising over time and has fluctuated much more
than the natural rate of unemployment. Part of the recent
rise in the unemployment rate is due to a corresponding
rise of the natural rate. The fluctuation in the unemployment rate is partly due to fluctuation in the economic
growth of the economy. These fluctuations account for
the fact that the unemployment rate is sometimes above
and sometimes below the natural rate.

workers who most likely would like to work are excluded, and persons
able to find only part-time work are counted as fully employed.

Despite the defects, the unemployment rate is one of the most widely
used and widely quoted economic statistics. Figure 8.8 shows the unemployment rate for the years 1948–1987. It is clear that the unemployment
rate has fluctuated widely, ranging from a low of 2.6 in the second quarter
of 1953 to a high of 10.7 percent in the fourth quarter of 1982. Moreover,
the unemployment rate has trended upward since 1968.

What accounts for the fluctuations and upward trend in the unemployment rate? Fluctuations in the unemployment rate are influenced by
the rate of growth of the economy as a whole. If you compare Figure 8.8
with Figure 8.2, you can see that the measured unemployment rate is
inversely related to the rate of change in real GNP. When the rate of
economic growth is high, the unemployment rate is low, and when the rate
of change in real GNP is negative, the rate of unemployment is high.

The relationship between the rate of economic growth and the unemployment rate is called **Okun's Law,** after the economist Arthur Okun,
who first discovered it.

> *Okun's Law is a principle stating that the unemployment rate
> will rise by one percentage point for every two-percentage-
> point decline in real gross national product below 3 percent,
> and will decline by one percentage point for every two-
> percentage-point increase in real gross national product.*

This principle sounds complicated, but it is not. The economy, as you
discovered above, grows on average at a rate of about 3 percent per year.
Suppose the unemployment rate is 5 percent. A decline to 1 percent
growth will result in a rise in the unemployment rate by one percentage
point to 6 percent.

The upward trend in the unemployment rate can be partially explained by the natural rate of unemployment. If you compare the unemployment rate with the natural rate of unemployment in Figure 8.8, you will see that the trend in the unemployment rate roughly mirrors the rise in the natural rate of unemployment. The determinants of the natural rate of unemployment will be taken up in later chapters.

Because the natural rate and the measured rate have increased together over time, economists are concerned not so much with the absolute level of the BLS unemployment rate as with the difference between the employment rate and the natural rate of unemployment. Look again at Figure 8.8. It is clear that there are periods of time when the official unemployment rate has been above the natural rate of unemployment and periods when it has been below. Comparing the natural rate of unemployment with the BLS official unemployment rate allows the calculation at any point in time of **excess unemployment.**

> *Excess unemployment exists when the official rate of unemployment exceeds the natural rate of unemployment.*

Excess unemployment represents a cost to society in terms of lost output.

There have also been times when the unemployment rate has been less than the natural rate of unemployment. When the measured unemployment is less than the natural rate, there is too little unemployment. How can there be too little unemployment? In answering this question and in considering the costs of excess unemployment, it is useful to distinguish between the various kinds of unemployment.

KINDS OF UNEMPLOYMENT

The official unemployment rate does not provide information on the causes of unemployment nor the degree to which employment is voluntary. Consider the aspiring actor who remains unemployed, refusing to become a truck driver, until an acceptable acting job is available. Isn't there a strong aspect of voluntariness in this person's unemployment? Now consider the unemployed steel worker, head of a household, who, despite considerable efforts, cannot find a job that will keep house and home together. Is this person voluntarily unemployed?

At times the number of jobs in the economy simply declines. There have been periods in American economic history when the unemployed have not found even menial jobs to be easily available. During the Great Depression many of the unemployed found that few jobs of any description could be found. The degree to which unemployment is voluntary thus varies with the person and with economic conditions.

Economists have found it useful to identify three kinds of unemployment: frictional unemployment, cyclical unemployment, and structural unemployment.

FRICTIONAL UNEMPLOYMENT As the economy is constantly in the process of change, new employment opportunities appear in one business, industry, or region and disappear in others. People are constantly entering the labor force, looking for better jobs, or leaving the labor force. The result of this constant change is **frictional unemployment.**

> *Frictional unemployment is the unemployment associated with the constant reallocation of resources in our economy.*

Frictional unemployment provides benefits as well as costs. In this case unemployment occurs because individuals are in the process of searching out and taking up more productive (higher-paying) jobs. The economy becomes more efficient as this process continues. Workers invest the opportunity cost of unemployment to find a better job and are rewarded with higher pay when they find it. Society benefits as resources are reallocated. Frictional unemployment is the price society pays for an efficient economy. It will always be with us and roughly corresponds to the concept of the natural rate of unemployment.

If frictional unemployment is a necessary cost for the efficient allocation of resources, there are ways to reduce its magnitude, some better than others. Any measure that improves the flow of information about job opportunities or reduces the time spent in job searching will reduce frictional unemployment. Such measures can be viewed as investing in a more efficient economy.

There is another way to reduce frictional unemployment — fool workers into taking jobs too early. This happens when unexpected inflation causes nominal, but not real, wages to rise and workers confuse nominal with real wages. When this **wage illusion** happens, workers take up new jobs too soon, believing that the higher nominal wages offered represent higher real wages.

Wage illusion occurs when workers wrongly equate higher nominal wages with higher real wages.

Suppose a worker leaves his or her job, which pays $5 per hour, to search for a better-paying one. Meanwhile the price level unexpectedly increases by 10 percent. The worker is offered a job at $5.50, which he or she takes, thinking that the real wage has increased in the process. But the real wage is the same as earned in the prior job, since both prices and wages have increased by 10 percent. The search time invested in finding a better-paying job has been wasted.

Inflation and wage illusion provide an explanation for how the economy can operate at over full employment. Workers who are frictionally unemployed while seeking higher-paying jobs are fooled by unexpected inflation into taking jobs too soon. In the process the economy does not become more efficient, which is the general result of frictional unemployment, and the worker who has invested time in job searching will have invested in unemployment for nothing. When this happens, the economy has too little unemployment to reallocate resources efficiently.

CYCLICAL UNEMPLOYMENT Unemployment is not a simple phenomenon. Not all unemployment is frictional unemployment. **Cyclical unemployment** provides no benefits to the economy, only costs. During cyclical downturns the economy produces fewer goods and services and hence provides fewer jobs.

Cyclical unemployment is the unemployment that results from declines in aggregate economic activity, which causes a decline in the number of jobs available.

The industrial sector is particularly affected during cyclical downturns. The purchases of many industrial goods can be delayed, which is exactly what happens when a recession occurs. Cyclical unemployment is not voluntary. During economic downturns some individuals become unemployed because their jobs are temporarily or permanently eliminated.

Cyclical unemployment imposes costs on both individuals and society. The unemployed bear the cost of lost wages, the owners of the other factors of production that are idled do not receive factor payments, and society is deprived of the output the idled workers could have produced. Cyclical unemployment thus represents a clear loss to the economy.

STRUCTURAL UNEMPLOYMENT In a growing, developing economy some regions, industries, and companies will be expanding and some contracting. Expanding industries will be hiring more workers, while contracting industries will be laying off workers. When entire industries decline, workers are likely to suffer **structural unemployment.**

> *Structural unemployment is the unemployment that occurs when the skills a worker possesses are no longer in demand, as when industries decline because the product produced either becomes obsolete or is replaced by a lower-cost source.*

An industry declines when it loses its comparative advantage because of rising local costs, technological change, changes in consumer preferences, or the increased availability of lower-cost substitutes.

Structural unemployment is especially costly when it is concentrated in a particular region. The switch from coal to oil made many Appalachian coal miners structurally unemployed. The decline of the steel industry owing to lower-cost foreign producers was particularly hard on the industrial Northeast. Similarly, the decline of the forest products industry owing to foreign competition and a decline in the use of wood in buildings has hurt the Northwest.

There is little that is voluntary about structural unemployment. Workers who are affected are likely to be older persons who have deep ties to the locality in which they live and used to work. It is costly for them to move to areas where jobs are available and expensive for them to acquire new skills. Meanwhile, the next best alternative they face locally may be unacceptable.

Structural unemployment is a difficult problem for policymakers. Economic efficiency requires that industries that lose their comparative advantage should be allowed to disappear and the resources they employ transferred to industries that retain a comparative advantage. But in the process some individuals who had valuable skills when the old industry was flourishing now find little demand for their skills. They bear a high cost for the reallocation of resources. An unemployed forest products worker generally does not possess and cannot easily acquire the skills required to work for a computer software producer.

All unemployment is costly to the economy. Frictional unemployment, which has a large voluntary component, however, produces both costs and benefits for the economy. The optimum level of frictional unemployment can be reduced by policies that make the labor market more efficient.

Involuntary unemployment, whether cyclical or structural, is costly without having any redeeming features. Cyclical unemployment, which would not exist in the ideal macroeconomic world, can potentially be reduced by policies that smooth out the cyclical fluctuations of the economy. Structural unemployment would still exist in the ideal macroeconomic world. The incidence of structural unemployment cannot be reduced without reducing the efficiency of resource allocation in the economy, but its duration can potentially be reduced by job-retraining programs.

POTENTIAL NATIONAL INCOME

The concept of the natural rate of unemployment allows the redefinition of **potential national income.**

> *Potential national income is the level of gross national product that would be produced if the economy were operating at the natural rate of unemployment.*

The combination of actual GNP and potential national income thus allows the costs of excess unemployment to be measured.

When real GNP is less than the level of potential national income, the economy is not operating up to its potential. Real output is being lost and profitable opportunities wasted. The difference between real GNP and potential national income, known as the deflationary gap, is a measure of the loss in national income due to unemployed resources.

A deflationary gap is shown in Part A of Figure 8.9. When the equilibrium position is E_{SR}, real GNP will be Y_A, which is less than potential national income Y_P. The difference between Y_P and Y_A is a measure of the loss due to a recession. The short-run equilibrium E_{SR} is not a long-run equilibrium. Forces will be at work to return the economy to a long-run equilibrium position. These automatic adjustment forces will result in shifting the short-run aggregate supply curve from $SRAS_1$ to $SRAS_2$ and the equilibrium position from E_{SR} to E_{LR}. As this occurs, the price level will decline from PL_{SR} to PL_{LR}. When a recessionary gap exists, the economy will be operating at less than the level of potential national income. In the long run the price level will fall and the recessionary gap will disappear.

Another possibility exists. Suppose real GNP exceeds the level of potential national income. This possibility is shown in Part B of Figure 8.9. Equilibrium occurs at E_{SR}, with real GNP equal to Y_A, which is greater than Y_P. You will recognize this situation as an inflationary gap.

An inflationary gap indicates that (1) the employment level is too high to ensure the efficient allocation of resources, and (2) the price level will rise in the long run. It is not possible to calculate directly the social costs of an inflationary gap in the same way that the social costs of a recessionary gap can be estimated. The costs of inflation are less direct than the costs of recession, but they are no less real.

This naturally brings us to the third major macroeconomic problem: inflation.

INFLATION

Economic decision makers fear inflation sometimes more and sometimes less than they do unemployment, depending on the circumstances. Inflation was the country's major economic concern according to numerous national polls taken in the late 1970s and early 1980s. People are concerned about inflation for a variety of reasons. Basically they are afraid that their incomes will fall behind the rise in prices and cause their standard of living to erode, and that their personal wealth will decline as inflation proceeds.

Whether or not these fears are justified depends on the circumstances, as we shall see in future chapters. But it is clear that inflation complicates economic decision making as the level of future prices becomes uncertain. This makes it difficult to confidently make decisions about purchases that occur over time, such as buying a house, a factory, or a piece of capital equipment. A number of economists believe that the

FIGURE 8.9
Inflationary and Recessionary Gaps

Part A shows a recessionary gap. A recessionary gap exists when the short-run aggregate supply curve $SRAS_1$ intersects the aggregate demand curve AD at a short-run equilibrium position E_{SR} that determines a level of aggregate output Y_A that is less than the level of potential national income Y_P. In the long run the short-run aggregate supply curve will shift to the right from $SRAS_1$ to $SRAS_2$, moving the economy to a long-run position and causing the price level to fall from P_{SR} to PL_{LR}, with aggregate output returning to the level of potential national income.

Part B illustrates an inflationary gap. An inflationary gap exists when the short-run aggregate supply curve intersects the aggregate demand curve at a position E_{SR} that determines a level of aggregate output Y_A that exceeds the level of potential national income Y_P. In the long run the short-run aggregate supply curve will shift to the left from $SRAS_1$ to $SRAS_2$, causing the price level to rise to PL_{LR} and the level of aggregate output to decline to the level of potential national income.

(A) Recessionary Gap

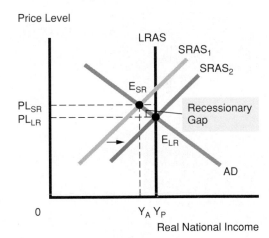

(B) Inflationary Gap

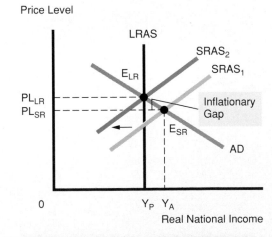

inflation of the 1970s was a major cause of the poor performance of the economy during that decade, precisely because it interfered in making long-term decisions.

There does not exist a simple measure for the costs of inflation as exists for a recession. The lack of a direct measure of the costs of inflation complicates the task of assessing the damage inflation inflicts on the economy. While **inflation** may be difficult to assess, it is simple to define and identify statistically.

> *Inflation is an increase in the overall level of prices.*

The price level increases when prices throughout the economy are, on average, increasing. If all prices increased at the same rate during inflations, it would be simple to measure the rate of inflation. If, for example, all prices increased by 5 percent, the rate of inflation would obviously be 5 percent.

But during inflations relative prices continue to change due to microeconomic adjustments between individual markets. Thus some prices rise faster than others, and some may even fall during an inflationary period. During the inflation of the 1970s, for example, the dollar price of electronic components and many electronic goods fell, while energy prices and the costs of medical care increased more rapidly than the average. Because relative prices are also changing, it is necessary to construct a **price index** to measure the general tendency of all prices.

> *A price index relates the current year's cost of a market basket of goods and services as a percentage of the cost of the same goods in some base year.*

You are already familiar with one particular price index — the GNP deflator. Another price index, the **consumer price index (CPI)**, is probably more widely employed than the GNP deflator.

> *The consumer price index measures changes in the prices of consumption goods and services.*

The CPI is the price index that measures the cost of living for consumers. In the CPI the market basket is the combination of goods and services consumed by a typical family. This market basket was derived by studying the buying habits of about 24,000 households in 85 urban areas. The CPI (or any other price index) is calculated by:

$$\frac{\text{Price}}{\text{index}} = \frac{\text{Cost of a specified market basket in the current year}}{\text{Cost of a specified market basket in the base year} \times 100}$$

The base year of the CPI for the figures used in this chapter is 1982. The CPI for that year is set at 100. In 1987 the value of the CPI had increased to 114, which suggests that the cost of purchasing the typical market basket of goods and services had increased over the five-year period by 14 percent.

The rise in the CPI from 1948 to 1987 is shown in Figure 8.10. It is clear that between these years the overall price level increased significantly, from 24 to 114. In 1948 the CPI for the same market basket cost was 24, indicating that goods that would generally cost more than a dollar in 1987 could have been purchased for less than a quarter in 1948.

The graph allows you to track inflation over time. The rate of inflation was fairly low between 1948 and the middle 1960s; thereafter it accel-

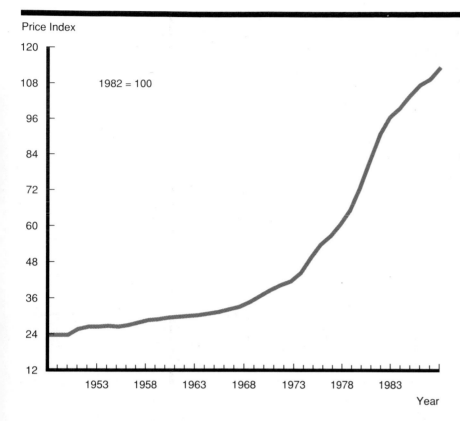

Price Index

1982 = 100

Year

FIGURE 8.10
Consumer Price Index: 1948–1987

The consumer price index, which measures the price level of a typical household's market basket of goods, is available monthly and measures inflation at the retail level. This graph reveals that in the late 1960s the rate of inflation in the economy began to increase, that in the 1970s it continued to rise, and that it moderated a bit during the 1980s.

erated until the 1980s, when it slowed. However, a chart such as Figure 8.10 tends to hide the wide variations in inflation rates that have occurred over time. A chart of the inflation rate itself would be more revealing in this respect. The inflation rate from year to year can be calculated from a price index according to the following equation:

$$\text{Inflation rate in 1987} = \frac{\text{1987 CPI} - \text{1986 CPI}}{\text{1986 CPI}} \times 100\%$$

The CPI during the first quarter of 1987 was 111.8 and during the same period in 1986 it was 109.3. Thus:

$$\frac{111.8 - 109.3}{109.3} \times 100\% = 2.2\%$$

The rate of inflation from the first quarter of 1986 to the first quarter of 1987 was 2.2 percent.

There has historically been a great deal of variation in the rate of inflation. The quarterly rate of inflation from 1948 to 1987 is shown in Figure 8.11. This graph of the inflation rate pinpoints the last half of the 1960s as the time period when the rate of inflation began to accelerate, reaching double-digit levels in the first quarters of both 1975 and 1981. The inflation that occurred over this period has been labeled the "Great Inflation" by the nation's press. Beginning in 1981, the rate of inflation subsided even more rapidly than it had accelerated. The Great Inflation is apparently over, as the rate of inflation has fluctuated between 3 and 5 percent in recent years — but it is not forgotten.

FIGURE 8.11
Inflation Rate: 1948–1987

The inflation rate can be measured by the rate of change in the consumer price index. It is clear from this figure that the rate of inflation has fluctuated significantly over time, rising while fluctuating widely during the 1970s. The rate of inflation declined significantly in the early 1980s and has remained at a rate significantly below the rates recorded in the 1970s.

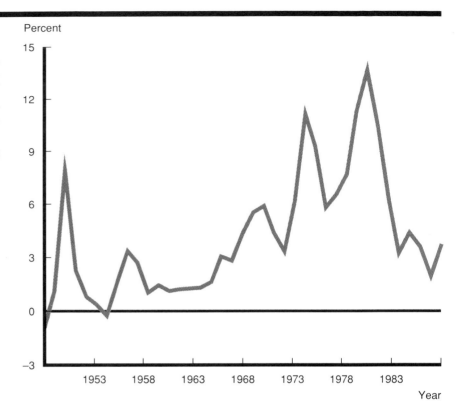

A close look at Figure 8.11 is revealing. It is readily seen that since 1948 there has generally been a positive increase in the price level. Except for 1949 and briefly in 1953, in every quarter the price level rose. Between 1948 and 1965 the annual rate of inflation was modest. But thereafter it began to rise, and the variations in the inflation rate became wider. Although Figure 8.10 shows a fairly smooth rate of increase for the overall price index, when you look closer at the inflation rate itself (Figure 8.11), it is clear that the rate of inflation is subject to wide variability. Some inflation apparently is a fact of modern life, but the rate of inflation has been highly variable over time.

CAUSES OF INFLATION

A rise in the overall price level, as determined through use of the basic macroeconomic model, can occur for two reasons: an increase in aggregate demand, called *demand-side inflation,* and a decline in the short-run aggregate supply (SRAS) curve, called *supply-side inflation.* We shall first discuss **demand-side inflation.**

> *Demand-side inflation occurs when aggregate demand increases, causing the aggregate demand curve to shift to the right and the price level to increase.*

Both types of inflation are shown in Figure 8.12. Suppose initially the economy depicted in Part A is in long-run equilibrium at E_1. Demand-side inflation can be illustrated by a shift to the right of the aggregate demand curve, from AD_1 to AD_2. The equilibrium position in the short run moves from E_1 to E_{SR}, the price level rises from PL_1 to PL_{SR}, and thus inflation occurs. In the case of demand-side inflation, real national

FIGURE 8.12
Two Causes of Inflation

Inflation can arise from either the demand side or the supply side. Part A illustrates demand-side inflation. The increases in the price level will be made permanent as short-run aggregate supply changes in reaction to the inflationary gap. Part B illustrates supply-side inflation, which will be temporary if the economy's automatic adjustment forces affect SRAS and will restore the long-run equilibrium.

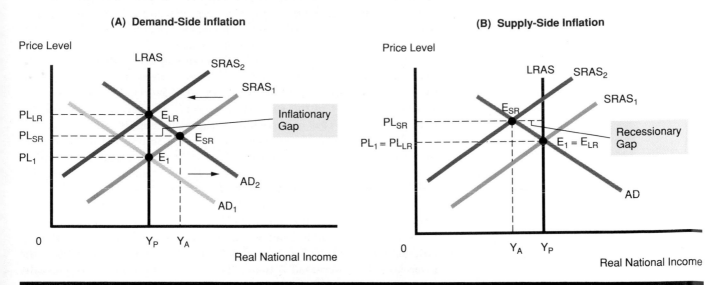

income will temporarily increase from Y_P to Y_A, and the economy will for a time operate at above full employment as an inflationary gap is created.

In this case the unemployment rate will be temporarily below the natural rate of unemployment. The rise in the price level will have fooled some of the people who are frictionally unemployed into taking jobs too soon. When the economy is operating at this level, resources are not being efficiently allocated. This condition will not persist. Workers will eventually realize that the price level has risen and seek compensating wage increases. When this happens, the SRAS curve will shift to the left to $SRAS_2$. The economy will return to long-run equilibrium with aggregate output equal to potential national income, and the price level will increase to PL_{LR}. Thus inflation can occur due to an increase in aggregate demand, in which case an economy initially in long-run equilibrium will experience a rise in the price level and an inflationary gap in the short run, which will disappear as the price level further permanently increases in the long run.

The second type of inflation is **supply-side inflation.**

Supply-side inflation occurs when the short-run aggregate supply declines, causing the short-run aggregate supply curve to shift to the left and the price level to increase.

This possibility is illustrated in Part B. The economy is initially in long-run equilibrium at E_1, when a decline in the short-run aggregate supply occurs and the SRAS curve shifts to the left from $SRAS_1$ to $SRAS_2$. The short-run equilibrium moves from E_1 to E_{SR} and the price level rises from PL_1 to PL_{SR}. In the case of supply-side inflation, the level of real GNP produced declines below the level of potential national income. The rate of unemployment will exceed the natural rate and excess unemployment, which characterizes a recessionary gap, will exist.

Supply-side inflation may be temporary rather than permanent. The long-run solution to any recessionary gap is for the price level to fall as SRAS rises to restore full employment, shifting from SRAS₂ back to SRAS₁. In the long run the price level will decline, eliminating the initial inflation caused by the decline in aggregate supply. Thus inflation can occur due to a decline in aggregate supply. The price level will increase when short-run aggregate supply shifts up, causing a recessionary gap to occur. But the increase will prove temporary, for in the long run the price level will fall to remove the recessionary gap.

We have seen, then, that both an increase in aggregate demand and a decrease in aggregate supply will result in an increase in the price level in the short run. Inflation will be the result. The increase in the price level will be permanent in the case of an increase in aggregate demand and temporary in the case of a decline in aggregate supply.

The basic model of macroeconomics can also be used to distinguish between the two possible causes of inflation. Demand-side inflation will be accompanied by an *increase* in real national income, and supply-side inflation will be associated with a *decline* in real national income. One of the important implications of our discussion so far is that persistent inflations must stem from the demand side.

First, it was pointed out when we discussed economic growth that although real GNP had increased 3.4 times between 1948 and 1987, the price level had increased 5 times. Thus aggregate output was generally increasing as the price level increased, suggesting that relative increases in aggregate demand were occurring.

Second, if the price level permanently increases over time, it must be due to demand-side influences. Declines in aggregate supply would be accompanied by a rising price level in the short run, followed by a decline in the price level as long-run adjustments took effect. A glance back at Figure 8.10 reveals that increases in the CPI were generally permanent in nature. Supply-side inflation does occur, however, but its effects are temporary. If you look again at Figure 8.11, where the rate of inflation is charted, whenever you observe a sharp upward spike in the inflation rate followed by an equally sharp drop, a suspicion of supply-side effects is a good place to start. The sharp rise and fall in the rate of inflation between 1973 and 1975 and again between 1979 and 1982 were both caused by adverse aggregate supply shocks.

Once it has been established which kind of inflation is occurring, the next step is to investigate the causes of either the increase in aggregate demand or the decline in aggregate supply, whichever is responsible. This step will be taken in the subsequent chapters that consider the problem of inflation.

CONSEQUENCES OF INFLATION

Many people fear inflation because they believe that their incomes will fall behind the rise in prices and their standard of living will decline. Casual observation tends to confirm this belief: Prices rise fairly continuously, while wages increase only periodically. Thus people observe prices rising all the time while their wages increase much less frequently — they naturally believe that wages always trail inflation. Actually, the evidence suggests that during inflations the prices of goods and services and the prices of the factors of production, wages, interest, and rent generally rise together. Thus both the prices of the things people buy and the things they sell rise together. Whether they rise in unison depends on the circumstances. Inflation generally affects all prices, both the prices of goods and services and the prices of the factors of production. Inflation does not automatically lower standards of living.

One consequence of inflation that is unavoidable is the decline in the value of money. Anyone holding money, or contracts fixed in money terms, will find that the real purchasing power of their money or fixed-price contract will decline. Economic decision makers, when faced with inflation, will therefore conserve on their money holdings, reducing the gains from trade that money provides.

Inflation can also affect the economy in three other undesirable ways: (1) Inflation can adversely affect the level of real output, (2) it can cause a reduction in economic efficiency, and (3) it can redistribute income and wealth in the economy. Inflation can but doesn't necessarily have to cause these undesirable consequences. Whether inflation will have these consequences depends on whether the rate of inflation is expected or comes as a surprise.

A perfectly anticipated inflation exists if economic decision makers accurately foresee the future rate of increase in the price level and incorporate these expectations in their economic actions. If the rate of inflation is correctly anticipated, the effects of future inflation on the value of goods and services exchanged will be incorporated in all economic contracts, thus avoiding the undesirable effects. If the rate of inflation is widely expected to be 5 percent per year, all future prices will be automatically marked up by 5 percent per year, interest rates will increase to account for the decline in the real value of money, wages will go up by 5 percent per year, property leases will contain a 5-percent-per-year escalator clause, and income tax rates will be altered to take into account the rise in nominal income.

The macroeconomy in this way adjusts to mitigate the undesirable consequences of inflation. All contracts will incorporate inflation premiums to protect economic decision makers from the undesirable effects of inflation. Thus perfectly anticipated inflation will not affect the level of aggregate output or redistribute income and wealth, because the future increase in prices will be taken into account in making economic decisions.

Consider Part A of Figure 8.13. The economy is initially in long-run equilibrium at E_1. Suppose aggregate demand is accurately expected to increase from AD_1 to AD_2. What will be the effect of this change in expectations? Individuals expecting the increase in aggregate demand will correctly anticipate that the long-run effect will be to cause the price level to rise from PL_1 to PL_2. If individual workers and business firms are not to be harmed by the increase in the price level, they will immediately demand higher wages and raise prices. The short-run aggregate supply curve will therefore shift to the left from $SRAS_1$ to $SRAS_2$ simultaneously with the increase in aggregate demand.

The economy automatically moves from one long-run equilibrium to another, the price level rises from PL_1 to PL_2, and real output and employment are not affected. A perfectly anticipated inflation does not affect the output of the economy. Since economic decision makers are aware in advance of the rise in prices, they will insist that the expected increase in the price level be taken into account in all their dealings. Perfectly anticipated inflation will not redistribute wealth, nor will it lead to significant amounts of inefficient behavior. It will result solely in an increase in the price level with no effect on real GNP.

Perfectly anticipated inflation does not lead to serious economic consequences, but this is not true for unanticipated inflation. If the future rate of inflation is not perfectly anticipated and some economic decision

FIGURE 8.13
Anticipated and Unanticipated Inflation

The effect that inflation has on the economy depends to a large extent on whether inflation is anticipated or unanticipated. Part A illustrates the case of a perfectly anticipated inflation, which affects only the price level. Part B shows the case of an unanticipated inflation, which affects aggregate output in the short run as well as the price level.

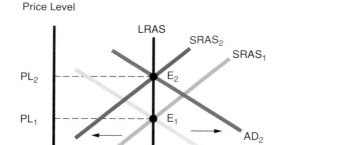

(A) Perfectly Anticipated Inflation

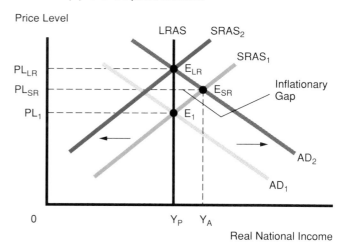

(B) Unanticipated Inflation

makers are surprised, many of the undesirable possible consequences of inflation will occur. Real economic output will be affected, inefficient behavior will be encouraged, and income and wealth will be redistributed.

Suppose an unanticipated increase in aggregate demand occurs. What effect will this have on aggregate output and price level? Consider Part B of Figure 8.13. Suppose aggregate demand suddenly increases and the increase is not expected by economic decision makers. Aggregate demand increases from AD_1 to AD_2, while the SRAS curve remains unchanged. Equilibrium in the short run moves from E_1 to E_{SR}, the price level increases to PL_{SR}, and aggregate output increases from Y_P to Y_A. Since Y_A is greater than Y_P, an inflationary gap is created. An unanticipated increase in aggregate demand in the short run causes the price level to rise and aggregate output to increase.

The unexpected increase in aggregate demand has fooled some workers into accepting jobs too soon, causing them to confuse the rise in money wages with a rise in real wages. Once it becomes clear to all (expectations adjust to the new reality) that the price level is increasing above the level previously expected, the short-run aggregate supply curve will shift to the left from $SRAS_1$ to $SRAS_2$.

The economy will eventually move from the short-run equilibrium E_{SR} to the long-run equilibrium E_{LR}. The price level will increase to PL_{LR} and real output will decline from Y_A to Y_P to eliminate the inflationary gap. Thus unanticipated inflation will affect the level of economic output. When the rate of inflation cannot be anticipated, the real sector of the economy will be affected. Not only will aggregate output be affected but so will the efficiency with which resources are allocated.

REDUCTION IN ECONOMIC EFFICIENCY
Whether inflation will lead to inefficient behavior also depends on whether future inflation rates can be anticipated. When the inflation rate

surprises economic decision makers, they will adjust their behavior. If the rate of inflation is erratic and variable, the success of a business depends as much on its ability to accurately forecast future inflation rates as on its ability to see and exploit other profitable opportunities. The result is that resources are devoted to the task of predicting inflation and away from more socially profitable activities.

The fear of future inflation at rates that defy prediction leads decision makers to engage in speculative activities. Speculation occurs in real estate, precious metals, art objects, and foreign currencies — all in an attempt to do well in an inflationary environment. These economically sterile investments replace investments in new factories, machines, and research and development that would add to the production capacity of the economy.

If the future rate of inflation could be predicted, such behavior would not take place. Ignoring changes in relative prices that would certainly occur, all prices would tend to rise together by the amounts anticipated. Few resources would have to be devoted to predicting future inflation rates, and relative prices would reveal profitable opportunities, as they do when inflation is absent.

REDISTRIBUTION OF INCOME AND WEALTH

Inflation can redistribute income and wealth by decreasing the real value of the incomes of some while increasing the real value of the incomes of others. How can this happen?

It will happen only if future inflation rates cannot be accurately predicted. Suppose the United Auto Workers enters into a three-year wage contract with Ford Motor Company. The union, whose workers are currently making $20 per hour, expects the rate of inflation to be 5 percent over the three years. So, ignoring increases in pay for increases in productivity, the union enters into a contract calling for 5 percent per year in wage increases. If the actual rate of inflation is the expected 5 percent, the workers' real income and standard of living will not change.

But suppose the rate of inflation is higher than expected, say 10 percent per year. The 5 percent annual increase will not compensate the workers for the rise in the price level. Their standard of living will fall while the profits, hence the incomes of the Ford stockholders, will increase. Workers lose in this case and the company gains, because the rate of inflation was surprisingly high.

Consider another example. You buy a house for $100,000 with a fixed-rate mortgage obtained from your local savings and loan association. The rate of interest is 7 percent. The 7 percent is the sum of the real rate of interest, say 2 percent, and an inflation premium of 5 percent, determined by the anticipated rate of inflation of 5 percent over the life of the loan. Suppose, however, that the rate of inflation turns out to be 10 percent. Your income and the value of your house will probably appreciate by 10 percent per year, but your mortgage payment will remain the same. As you make your fixed monthly payments, the value of the dollars you pay will decline by 10 percent per year, not the 5 percent that the savings and loan expected. The savings and loan is repaid in dollars that are worth less than it expected. Wealth will therefore be transferred from the savings and loan to you. The real value of the payments you make to the savings and loan is less than was expected at the time the loan was made. You are consequently richer than you expected to be, and the savings and loan is poorer. Hundreds of savings and loans are in deep financial trouble precisely because the rate of inflation during the 1970s and early 1980s was higher than they expected when they made fixed-rate loans.

In the above examples both the United Auto Workers and the savings and loan associations lost out to inflation because the value of the money payments they received declined by more than was expected. This transfer of income could, of course, have been avoided if future rates of inflation had been accurately anticipated and wage and loan contracts had been appropriately adjusted.

The costs of inflation that society fears are those that are associated with the consequences of unanticipated inflations. Do people anticipate inflation? Can they do it? Clearly, it would pay for them to try to do so. The appendix for this chapter and a more detailed application in Chapter 16 will show you how you can participate in inflation forecasting. Steady inflation rates would obviously make this task easier, whereas erratic and sporadic inflation rates will complicate the task. Unfortunately, in the real world inflation rates have not been steady and easily predictable, as another glance at Figure 8.11 will attest. When inflation rates are not, or cannot, be anticipated, inflation will result in undesirable changes in the level of real output, in inefficient behavior, and in the redistribution of income and wealth.

By concentrating on aggregate demand and aggregate supply, the basic model of macroeconomics can explain the behavior of the key variables of macroeconomic theory. What remains to be understood is what causes the various shifts in aggregate demand and supply that result in economic growth, recession, unemployment, and inflation. In subsequent chapters the basic model will be elaborated upon, and the causes of shifts in aggregate demand and supply will be discussed.

SUMMARY

1. The ideal macroeconomic world does not exist. Instead, the world is characterized by business cycles causing the pace of economic growth to vary, along with periodic recessions and inflations. Macroeconomics is particularly concerned with the rate of economic growth, the current performance of the economy, and the rate of inflation.

2. The basic macroeconomic model can be usefully employed to identify and explain each of these concerns. There are two basic measures of macroeconomic performance: real GNP to measure aggregate output, and the GNP deflator to measure changes in the price level. These two primary variables of the basic macroeconomic model allow an observer to track the behavior of the economy.

3. Economic growth occurs when potential national income increases along with an accommodating increase both in the SRAS curve and in aggregate demand.

4. Economic growth is measured by the annual percentage change in real GNP.

5. Historically, the path of long-term economic growth has not been smooth but rather has been characterized by business cycles. A business cycle is characterized by trough, recovery, peak, and recession phases. The performance of the economy varies over the business cycle.

6. The current performance of the economy can be measured by comparing actual real GNP with potential GNP. If actual real GNP exceeds potential national income, an inflationary gap exists. If potential national income exceeds actual real GNP, a recessionary gap exists.

7. Potential national income positions the long-run aggregate supply curve, which does not vary when the price level changes. Potential na-

tional income is the aggregate income that would be produced when the unemployment rate is equal to the natural rate of unemployment, which is the rate that corresponds to full employment in the economy.

8. Unemployment is measured by the unemployment rate. Historically, the unemployment rate has varied substantially and is closely related to the level of real GNP and the natural rate of unemployment. Excess unemployment exists when the unemployment rate exceeds the natural rate of unemployment.

9. There are three kinds of unemployment: frictional, cyclical, and structural. Frictional unemployment roughly corresponds to the natural rate of unemployment.

10. Unemployment can result from either an insufficiency of aggregate demand or a decline in the SRAS curve. Unemployment occurs when equilibrium occurs to the left of the LRAS curve.

11. Inflation is measured by the annual percentage increase in a price index. The GNP deflator is the most comprehensive price index. The consumer price index measures changes in the cost of living for a typical consumer.

12. Inflation has been the norm in the United States since World War II, but the rate of inflation has varied widely over time.

13. Inflation can originate from either the demand side or the supply side. Demand-side inflation starts from an increase in aggregate demand. Supply-side inflation stems from a decline in short-run aggregate supply. Demand-side inflation is permanent, whereas supply-side inflation is temporary.

14. Inflation is a problem because of its undesirable potential to alter aggregate output, to create economic inefficiency, and to redistribute income and wealth. Whether any of these in fact happen depends on whether the inflation comes as a surprise or is anticipated. Perfectly anticipated inflation does result in the above undesirable consequences being limited to causing a decline in the value of money.

THREE PROBLEMS OF THE MACROECONOMY

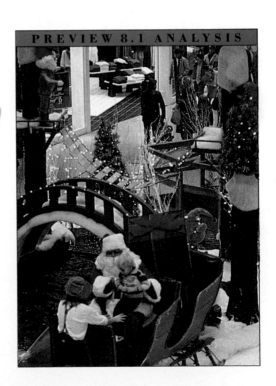

I n Preview 8.1 you were introduced to the three major macroeconomic problems: recession and excess unemployment, inflation, and slow economic growth, all of which would be absent in an ideal macroeconomic world. It is possible, by employing the tools acquired in this chapter, to begin the process of assessing the social costs of each, a process that will continue throughout our discussion of macroeconomics.

THE COSTS OF RECESSION AND UNEMPLOYMENT

Recessions would be absent in an ideal macroeconomic world. Recessions are a concern because they impose costs on society. The basic macroeconomic model suggests a direct way to measure these costs. The extent of the social costs caused by recession can be measured by comparing the actual level of real GNP with the level of potential national income.

Table 8.2 provides both real GNP (column 2) and an estimate of potential national income for the years 1980–1986 (column 3). The loss of real output is calculated in column 4 as the difference between column 3

TABLE 8.2
Real and Potential Gross National Product: 1980–1986

YEAR (1)	ACTUAL REAL GNP (2)	POTENTIAL GNP (3)	DIFFERENCE (2) − (3) (4)	PERCENTAGE OF POTENTIAL GNP (5)
1980	$1,475	$1,525	−$50	3.2%
1981	1,514	1,571	−57	3.6
1982	1,485	1,618	−133	8.2
1983	1,538	1,667	−129	7.7
1984	1,637	1,718	−81	4.7
1985	1,681	1,768	−87	4.9
1986	1,724	1,821	−97	5.3

Source: R. A. Gordon, *Macroeconomics*, 3rd ed. (Boston: Little, Brown, 1986). Series extended by the author.

and column 2, and this difference is expressed as a percentage of potential national income in column 5.

This period contained two recessions: a minor recession in 1980 and a much more serious one in 1982–1983. It is clear, according to these estimates, that throughout the period the economy continuously operated below the level of potential national income.

The total loss suffered from 1980 to 1986 equaled $634 billion in 1972 dollars. This was roughly $1,554 trillion in current dollars, or 37 percent of 1986 GNP. Another way to figure the loss is that in current dollars it amounted to $24,125 per family spread over the seven-year period. The costs of the persistent recessionary gap suffered from 1980 to 1986 were significant.

You should interpret these results with some caution. You are already familiar with the problems involved in accurately estimating real GNP. The difficulties of estimating the level of potential national income are perhaps even greater. Nevertheless, the losses recorded in Table 8.2 suggest that recession is costly to society.

Accompanying a recessionary gap will be excess unemployment. Table 8.3 provides an estimate of the excess unemployment that existed during the 1980s. Column 2 reports the observed BLS unemployment rate, column 3 the estimated natural rate of unemployment, column 4 excess unemployment as a percentage of the labor force, and column 5 excess unemployment as the number of persons. During the recession of 1982–1983 excess unemployment reached 3.5 percent of the labor force, which meant that about 3.5 million persons were involuntarily unemployed. Since the average duration of unemployment even during recession is considerably less than a year, many persons experienced periods of unemployment during these years. People are right to fear recessions. Recession and excess unemployment will be considered in much more detail in Chapter 17.

Inflation, the second macroeconomic problem on our list, also imposes costs on society that would be absent in an ideal macroeconomic world.

INFLATION

Like recession, inflation has few supporters. It is, however, difficult to explain simply why inflation is bad for the economic health of the coun-

TABLE 8.3
Unemployment, Natural Rate of Unemployment, and Excess Unemployment:
1980–1987

YEAR (1)	UNEMPLOYMENT RATE (2)	NATURAL RATE OF UNEMPLOYMENT (3)	EXCESS UNEMPLOYMENT (4)	NUMBER OF EXCESS UNEMPLOYED (MILLIONS) (5)
1980	7.0%	5.9%	1.1%	1.09
1981	7.5	6.0	1.5	1.51
1982	9.5	6.0	3.5	3.48
1983	9.5	6.0	3.5	3.53
1984	7.4	5.8	1.6	1.68
1985	7.1	5.6	1.5	1.61
1986	6.9	5.5	1.4	1.53
1987	6.1	5.4	0.7	0.79

Source: *Economic Report of the President, 1988*; R. A. Gordon, *Macroeconomics*, 3rd ed. (Boston: Little, Brown, 1986). Series extended by the author.

try. In this chapter you discovered that it makes a difference whether the rate of inflation is anticipated or not. Unanticipated inflation imposes costs that are absent when the rate of inflation is expected by economic decision makers. Both anticipated and unanticipated inflation impose real costs on society, but because of the differences in the effects, the magnitudes involved are different. So when discussing the social costs of inflation, a distinction must be drawn between the two types.

It is, unfortunately, not possible to simply measure the inflationary gap to determine the costs of inflation. The economy apparently has more goods and services as a result of an inflationary gap, but this increased output is produced by persons who have been fooled into working and producing more. Unanticipated inflation misleads economic decision makers into confusing an increase in nominal wages with an increase in real wages.

Job seekers, like Sam Taft to whom you were introduced in the preview, are fooled into taking jobs when they would have preferred to either enjoy more leisure or spend the time off from work searching for a truly better-paying job. The alternatives to work for persons like Sam are of higher value than the wages earned. The inflationary gap does not measure the costs of inflation in the same way that a recessionary gap represents the costs of recession.

The crux of the arguments against inflation is that it leads to inefficient behavior. Unanticipated inflation leads Sam Taft to misallocate his resources until he recognizes that he has been fooled. Sam was not alone in being fooled in this way. Aerotech itself had misinterpreted the rising prices it received for its products as due to an increase in demand for its products. That is why it was so anxious to hire both Sam and Jill Montgomery. You will recall that while Sam accepted the job offered, Jill did not.

Jill Montgomery took a job as a financial planner instead of working for Aerotech, because the variable inflation rate had heightened insecurity among the nation's economic decision makers. A demand for Jill's services was created by persons concerned with protecting their investments from inflation risk. Persons who have contracts written in nominal terms — whether real estate contracts, wage contracts, or retirement plans — suffer losses when inflation is incorrectly anticipated. They thus have an incentive to try to forecast future inflation rates. Therefore attractive jobs in financial planning, like the one Jill Montgomery accepted, are created. Instead of contributing to the production and sale of electronic components, Jill is helping people protect existing assets. Uncertainty about future inflation rates can lead to the establishment of socially inefficient institutions, institutions that would not exist in an ideal macroeconomic world.

Some of the costs of inflation occur whether inflation is anticipated or unanticipated. Inflation combined with a tax system that taxes nominal not real incomes, for example, distorts profits, leading economic decision makers to socially inefficient behavior. Inflation coupled with the existing tax structure, for example, encourages individuals like Sam Taft to buy a house rather than continue to rent. Interest payments are deductible for income tax purposes. As inflation causes nominal interest rates to rise, the deductible portion of the monthly house payment increases. This favors home ownership over renting not because of the merits of home ownership but simply because of inflation.

A similar incentive was created for firms like Aerotech to invest in longer-lived capital assets and to prefer debt to equity as sources of financing for their businesses. Interest payments are tax deductible, but dividends are not. Inflation makes business firms, like individual investors, devote scarce resources to financial planning. The rising importance of financial matters also cost Bill Thompson his shot at the presidency of Aerotech. Engineering was no longer the most important area in determining Aerotech's future; inflation caused financial problems to become the major concern of the board of directors. So the company treasurer got the job instead.

Inflation also leads to a decline in the value of money and of assets denominated in dollars. Persons who hold money balances to conduct future transactions find that the purchasing power of the money they hold will decline. Persons have an incentive to conserve on their money balances. The economy is less liquid than it would be in the absence of inflation. Money, as you discovered in Chapter 2, oils the mechanism of exchange, encouraging specialization and exchange. Money also serves the function of a temporary store of value. When economic decision makers are encouraged to conserve on money balances, they hold less than the optimal quantity of money. Decision makers will not be as capable of taking advantage of profitable opportunities as they would if inflation were absent. Some of these potential benefits will be lost.

The decline in liquidity is the cost that is always mentioned when the costs of inflation are discussed. It is only one of the costs of inflation and probably one of the least important. Inflation is costly to the society because it leads to inefficient behavior. It encourages inefficient institutions to develop. When combined with the existing tax system, inflation affects the amount and composition of the nation's capital stock and causes the value of money to decline. These costs exist whether or not the rate of inflation is correctly anticipated.

Inflation also increases uncertainty about the future. Once it gets started, inflation has a tendency to accelerate. The higher the level of inflation, the greater the variability in the inflation rate, thus making it more difficult to formulate accurate inflationary expectations. As a consequence, unanticipated inflation redistributes income and wealth. The total amount of financial assets such as bank accounts, currency, and bonds in the United States exceeds $12 trillion. A 1 percent increase in unanticipated inflation reduces the real value of financial assets by over $120 billion.

Although it is not possible to measure directly the costs of inflation in the same way as the costs of recession can be determined, the costs of inflation are no less real. The causes and consequences of inflation will be considered in more detail in Chapter 16.

SLOW ECONOMIC GROWTH

Inflation has also been shown empirically to be associated with slower economic growth. Studies that have compared the rate of inflation with the rate of economic growth for a large number of countries have generally found a negative relationship between the rate of inflation and the rate of increase in national income. The slowdown in the rate of economic growth that often accompanies accelerating inflation is probably the result of all of the costs discussed above: the formation of inefficient institutions, the burden of a nominal tax system, the costs of reduced liquidity, and the increase in uncertainty, as well as the misallocation of resources that results from the distortion of nominal prices.

Slow economic growth would not happen in the ideal macroeconomic world. Slow economic growth is currently a problem in the U.S. economy. The regular improvement in the standard of living that is associated with the American experience is dependent on rapid economic growth. It was believed until recently that the American economy had institutionalized economic growth. Economic growth was something that, though not well understood, just regularly happened.

Potential national income serves as the measure for full employment, positions the long-run aggregate supply curve, and allows the determination of inflationary and recessionary gaps. No such device exists to determine the optimal rate of economic growth. Rapid and slow growth must be determined by reference to historical experience. As the preview suggested, since 1973 the rate of economic progress seems to have slowed. The rate of increase in the productivity of labor has also declined from the long-term average, as has the rate of increase in national income.

The cause of this decline is not as yet well understood by economists. This problem will be taken up in detail in Chapter 18. It may be the result of the Great Inflation that occurred during those years, or more narrowly the result of repeated increases in the price of crude oil that were unique to that era, or of something even more insidious because it may still be operating on the economy.

If the cause of this slowdown in economic growth is not well understood, the consequences can be easily determined. The decline in the average rate of increase in national income from the long-term average of 3.47 percent to 2.24 percent is more serious than it may appear.

Over the last century national income has doubled roughly every 21 years because of the long-term growth rate of 3.47 percent. Since 1973, however, as a consequence of the decline in the rate of growth, it will take 32 years for national income to double. The average standard of living is not improving of late as rapidly as it did during your parents' and grandparents' days. The recent decline in the rate of growth clearly has serious implications for your future.

The three major macroeconomic problems — recession, inflation, and slow economic growth — all impose serious costs on society that would be absent in the ideal macroeconomic world. All economists agree about this, and all concur that it is a desirable goal to reduce or eliminate these costs. But economists, as you will discover in subsequent sections of this book, remain divided about which of these problems is the most serious and about the best approach to achieving the goal.

REQUIRED ECONOMIC CONCEPTS

Economic growth	**Excess unemployment**
Business cycle	**Frictional unemployment**
Expansion	**Wage illusion**
Recession	**Cyclical unemployment**
Depression	**Structural unemployment**
Stagflation	**Potential national income**
Unemployment	**Inflation**
Natural rate of unemployment	**Price index**
Unemployment rate	**Consumer price index**
Discouraged worker	**Demand-side inflation**
Okun's Law	**Supply-side inflation**

KEY QUESTIONS

1. What are the three major concerns of macroeconomics?
2. What are the four phases of a business cycle?
3. How is the duration of a business cycle measured?
4. What are some indicators that decline during a recession? Does employment necessarily decline? Explain.
5. Can we immediately know when the economy has entered a recession? Explain.
6. How long has the average business cycle in the United States lasted?
7. What are three reasons why an individual would not be included in the labor force?
8. What are the three major kinds of unemployment?
9. Why can the measured unemployment rate understate the true unemployment rate?
10. Does full employment signify there is zero unemployment? Explain.
11. What is the natural rate of unemployment?
12. What are the social costs that can be associated with a recession?
13. What are at least two possible effects of inflation?
14. Is there almost no redistribution of income and wealth in the economy if everyone perfectly anticipates an inflation? Explain.
15. What is the problem associated with future rates of inflation being substantially unpredictable?

PROBLEMS

1. "Business history repeats itself, but always with a difference." Interpret this statement. Would the increase in sales of air-conditioners in May through July and the increase in the sales of cars during the winter months be considered part of the business cycle?

2. Suppose real GNP drops sharply in one quarter, climbs a small amount in the next quarter, then drops again in the third quarter. Does this nine-month pattern signify a recession is upon the economy? What additional information is needed before a conclusion can be reached about a recession beginning to take hold?

3. For each of the following state whether the fluctuation in real GNP is associated with a shift in aggregate demand or in short-run aggregate supply.

   a. Personal income is expected to decline.

   b. OPEC imposes an oil embargo on the United States.

   c. Average productivity of the labor force goes down.

   d. Housing starts go down.

   e. The economy begins to experience a rise in its capacity utilization.

4. Identify the type of unemployment associated with each of the following, and state whether it is primarily voluntary or involuntary.

   a. "Just as the country once moved from agriculture to industry, it is now moving from industry to services."

   b. Cindy is a college graduate with a B.A. in English. She has been looking for work as an editor while turning down waitress jobs.

   c. "White-collar and blue-collar workers join the jobless as the economy drags into the new year."

   d. Loggers are laid off for two weeks because of a dry spell.

   e. The growth of automated industries will provide few opportunities for the unskilled, uneducated job applicant, even if the economy goes into a period of strong growth.

   f. Elevator operators lost their jobs in the High Tower building when the elevators were automated.

5. A business executive says, "A weak economy is likely to be more devastating to workers' aspirations than technological change." What kinds of unemployment are being referred to here?

6. A BLS official says, "The CPI does not attempt to delineate changes in the lifestyle of Americans." What did he mean?

7. Use the data below to perform the following calculations. [*Note:* The participation rate is equal to the ratio of the total labor force to the total noninstitutional population (those not in jails, nursing homes, hospitals, the military, and the like).]

Total population	202 million
Civilian noninstitutional population	200 million
Civilian labor force	100 million
Employed civilians	90 million

   a. Calculate the unemployment rate.

   b. Calculate the participation rate.

   c. How many employed people are not in the civilian labor force? What are they?

8. Can structural unemployment perhaps be considered frictional unemployment with a hangover? Explain.

9. a. In regard to an economy, does it make sense to say, "Inflation does not cause the pie to get smaller, it just cuts it up differently"? Do you agree? Why or why not?

   b. Assume that OPEC can raise the world price of crude oil by $5 a barrel while the United States imports 30 to 40 percent of its oil from OPEC. How does the answer to Part a change?

10. In each situation below, assume that the asset mentioned is the only asset that is owned (an unrealistic assumption). Is the owner worse or better off if the economy experiences an unanticipated inflationary surge?

   a. Participants in unindexed private pension plans.

   b. A person repaying a fixed-rate mortgage.

   c. Bondholders.

   d. Misers and paranoids who shun banks and keep their cash hidden.

   e. The government as holder of the national debt.

    f.   Those whose money income rises faster than the inflation rate.

    g.   Those who own real assets whose prices rise faster than the CPI.

    h.   Families whose holdings of variably priced assets such as cars, land, housing, and the like are greater than their holdings of monetary assets.

    i.   Social Security recipients.

11. Why would an unanticipated inflation be likely to transfer more wealth from the elderly to young families rather than the other way around? When you consider Social Security funding and payments, might your answer change?

12. Consider the four income classes: the poor, the middle class, the upper middle class, and the very rich. The poor are more likely to have fewer debts, since they are not homeowners and because it is generally harder for them to get loans. The middle class are likely to be heavily in debt because they hold mortgages, but they also tend to hold a greater percentage of their wealth in physical assets like cars and tools than the very rich. The very rich are savers and therefore lenders to a much greater degree than the middle class. The very rich are likely to hold a larger percentage of their wealth in monetary assets like bonds and stock than the middle class. When an unanticipated inflation occurs, which group(s) would benefit most and which group(s) would benefit least from income and wealth transfers?

APPLICATION ANALYSIS

1.   In reality, families do not own one kind of physical asset, such as a car, or one kind of monetary asset, such as cash or a checking account. They hold a mixed bag of assets. Therefore the final effect of unanticipated inflation on the real wealth of families depends on the mix of their asset holdings. The prices of many physical assets often go up in money terms when there is inflation. It is one reason why the price level rises to begin with. However, money assets that are fixed in nominal terms, such as the yield on a bond, are fixed in money terms. The yield is worth less in real terms when the price level rises. Since wealth is equal to real assets plus monetary assets, it can be shown that real net wealth is equal to nominal net wealth divided by the price level index. From common practice in accounting, we also know that net wealth (or net worth) is equal to assets minus liabilities. Assets are things you own, and liabilities are what you owe someone else. That is, assets are things on which you have an ownership claim, whereas liabilities are claims others have on you. For instance, a loan you have taken out at the bank is a liability to you — a claim on you by the bank, whereas it is an asset to the bank.

    Consider the following account of the John Doe family when the rate of inflation is zero in Year 1.

ASSETS		LIABILITIES AND NET WORTH	
House	$90,000	Mortgage outstanding	$60,000
Bond	10,000	Net worth	40,000
Total	$100,000	Total	$100,000

    a.   Is the Doe family a net monetary debtor or a net monetary creditor? That is, on net, does it owe money or is money owed to it? How much? (*Hint:* Consider monetary assets versus monetary liabilities.)

    b.   What is the Doe family's nominal net wealth if:

Net wealth = (Real assets − Real liabilities)
               + (Monetary assets − Monetary liabilities)

and we let real liabilities be zero throughout this problem?

c. Suppose the price level rises unexpectedly by 20 percent in Year 2. What is the value of the Doe family's net wealth in money or nominal dollars in Year 2?

d. What is the value of the Doe family's real net wealth? By how much has it risen or fallen?

e. Go back to Year 1 and assume this time that the price level falls unexpectedly by 10 percent. What is the value of the Doe family's real wealth in Year 2? By how much has it risen or fallen?

HOW YOU CAN KEEP TRACK OF THE MACROECONOMY — A DO-IT-YOURSELF KIT

Human beings have a keen desire to foresee the future. The ancient Greeks and Romans consulted oracles, some read the entrails of sacrificed animals, and others checked the position of stars in the heavens in attempts to devine the future. Animal sacrifice seems to have fallen out of style, but not so astrology. The schedule of a former president of the United States was reportedly based on the advice of an astrologer.

This desire for knowledge of future economic events has led to the practice of economic forecasting. Professional economists do not consult star charts, but they do frequently employ charts of economic statistics that are interpreted using economic theory, sometimes in the form of large econometric models run on computers. But economic forecasting is not all science. There is always an element of intuition involved, which we shall call the art of economic forecasting.

Why try to divine the economic future? Why not just consult the national income accounts and see how the economy is doing? Many economic decisions require a knowledge of the future as well as the present. The macroeconomy does not proceed smoothly, as you discovered in this chapter. The past performance of the economy has included many recessions, a few depressions, periods of inflation, and eras of both rapid and slow growth. What is happening in the future in the macroeconomy is bound to affect your fortunes as well as those of everybody else.

Where is the economy today? Where is it headed? It will be too late for many purposes if you wait for gross national product to answer these questions. Estimates of GNP are available only quarterly, and it is often fully six months after the fact that a reliable figure is available. Fortunately, there is an abundance of other more timely information to allow you to keep track of the economy.

All forecasts of the future require an accurate assessment of the present state of the economy. In order to ascertain the present state of the economy, it is necessary to consult the relevant statistical measures. There are three tests a statistical measure must pass. An economic statistic must be relevant (must measure what it is supposed to), must be widely available (cannot be a secret), and must be available on a timely basis.

Certainly GNP, even with its deficiencies, passes the test of relevance, for it is the best measure of the performance of the overall economy. When GNP is available in both nominal and real terms, we have a mea-

sure of real output and, in the GNP deflator, we have a measure of inflation. Why do we need anything else?

There are still two other tests an economic indicator must pass. To be
useful, an economic indicator must also be widely available and released
in a timely fashion. Certainly, GNP estimates are readily available, being
announced nationwide in the press and over the airways. The main problem with GNP is its lack of timeliness. GNP is available only on a quarterly basis and then is subject to periodic revision.

The initially released GNP figure is a preliminary estimate. As more
complete information becomes available, the estimate is revised. Sometimes the revisions are substantial and not completed prior to the announcement of the next quarter's estimate. In the case of the fourth-
quarter 1984 estimate, for example, it was later revised downward to only
0.6 percent, which reflects very sluggish economic growth. In fact, the
fourth-quarter slow-growth rate was a harbinger of below-average growth
for the next three years. GNP estimates in final form are simply not
available in timely enough fashion to chart the present state of the economy. Why is this?

This is why: The business cycle, which lasts on average about five
years, is composed of an expansionary phase that lasts about four years
and a recessionary phase that lasts about one year. These averages can be
misleading. One recent business cycle downturn lasted only six months,
from January 1980 to July 1980. In this case the recession was half over
before the preliminary estimate was issued showing an economic downturn was happening. It took several more months before the initial estimates could be confirmed by additional data, and by that time the economy was expanding again. If you relied only on GNP statistics, the
recession would have been over before you were certain that it had begun.

Economic indicators more timely than the national income accounts
are needed to keep track of the current rates of aggregate output and the
overall price level.

Professional economists are constantly at work trying to forecast the
future. The results of their efforts are widely published. *Business Week* in
its January issue traditionally carries a story that lists the predictions of
many leading economists for the new year. Although professional economists follow dozens of economic indicators, it will be sufficient for you to
keep your eye on a few timely measures. These statistics will allow you to
make your own educated guesses about where the economy is and where it
is headed.

It is not difficult to find this information. Each Monday *The Wall
Street Journal* publishes a story on the key indicators released during the
prior week, complete with a summary table and a list of the indicators
that will appear during the current week. *The Wall Street Journal* generally publishes these statistics on the front page at the top of column 4,
along with a graph, the day after they are announced. A written report
will also appear elsewhere in the paper commenting on the new information. This information, if you follow it regularly, will alert you to significant changes that are occurring in the economy.

If you spend a few minutes on each of these reports, you will develop
a feel for what is happening and in time will find that you are making your
own predictions. When preliminary GNP figures are released on a quarterly basis, you can use them to check your predictions. The preliminary
GNP figures, as they become available, are also published on the front
page of *The Wall Street Journal*.

KEEPING TRACK OF THE PRESENT STATE OF THE ECONOMY

If you want current information about the state of the economy, *The Wall Street Journal* is the first place to look. In each issue you will find an almost bewildering amount of information on the current economy. Which specific statistics are important for you? Let us consider indicators of real output first.

One of the more important economic indicators is the *index of industrial production,* which tracks the output of the industrial sector. This monthly index reflects the changes in the physical output of U.S. factories, mines, and electric and gas utilities. This index tends to move in the same direction as GNP but with wider swings. Industrial production increases more rapidly than GNP when the economy is expanding and falls more rapidly when the economy is in recession, which makes it a good index for tracking the economy between reports on GNP. The industrial production index is usually announced on the third Monday of the month and provides information on the preceding month.

The *capacity utilization index,* which is generally announced the day after the index of industrial production, provides an indication of how close to full employment the economy is operating. A word of warning: It is not clear what the full-employment level of capacity utilization is in this index, other than that it is significantly below 100.

Personal income is announced monthly by the Commerce Department, usually during the fourth week of the month. Personal income, as you know from Chapter 6, shows the before-tax income received by households in the form of wages and salaries, interest, and dividend payments, as well as transfer payments, such as Social Security, unemployment compensation, and pension payments. Personal-income data will allow you to track what is happening to the consumption capacity of households, the major portion of GNP. When personal income increases, it generally means that consumption spending is also rising. When personal income falls, especially if it falls for several months in a row, it is a bad sign for the economy.

Retail sales will also allow you to keep track of what is happening to consumption expenditures. Retail sales data are available the second Friday of the month. The Commerce Department's retail sales estimates include everything from automobiles to groceries. The course of retail sales provides a direct clue to consumer attitudes. A systematic slowdown in retail sales often foreshadows a decline in real GNP.

Housing starts measures the number of residential buildings on which construction was started during the month. Housing starts provides an indicator of the level of investment spending that is occurring. Housing starts are available monthly on Wednesday of the third week. A pickup in the pace of housing construction usually accompanies a spurt of rapid economic growth, whereas a decline in housing starts is an ominous sign for the economy.

In the chapter we discussed the *unemployment rate* as a measure of the extent to which the macroeconomy was making good use of its available resources. *Total employment,* however, may be a better indicator for spotting changes in economic conditions. Total employment is generally announced, along with the unemployment rate, on the first Friday of the month. A decrease in total employment is an indication that employers are reducing the number of jobs available and are cutting production. A rise in total employment coupled with a decline in the unemployment rate is a sign of growing strength of the overall economy.

Changes in the price level can be tracked monthly by two widely announced price indexes: the *producer price index (PPI)* and the *consumer price index (CPI)*. The producer price index measures changes in the prices of goods at stages in the production process, from crude materials to finished goods sold to retailers. An increase in this index may mean higher prices later at the consumer level. The producer price index is widely followed as a predictor of future inflation at the retail level.

Prices at the consumer level are measured by the consumer price index. The consumer price index tracks the prices of 360 goods and services. There are a number of separate CPIs. The most often referred to is the one for urban consumers, but a second variation, covering urban wage earners and clerical workers, is widely employed in labor contracts to measure cost-of-living wage increases. Neither the PPI nor the CPI is as inclusive as the GNP deflator, but both can point to inflationary trends before the GNP deflator is available.

Following these economic statistics will allow you to keep track of the performance of the overall economy during the periods between the publication of GNP estimates. But what about the future?

FORECASTING THE FUTURE STATE OF THE ECONOMY

What about the future state of the economy? While professional economists attempt to make quantitative predictions of macroeconomic variables, all that you need to do for most purposes is forecast the direction of change. Will real GNP be up or down? Will the unemployment rate rise or fall? Will the rate of inflation increase or decrease?

Where do you start? Let's start with three indicators of the future state of the economy: the money supply, the stock market, and the index of leading indicators. The *money supply* is an important shift determinant for aggregate demand and an important determinant of the various interest rates in the economy. Changes in the money supply are announced weekly. The money-supply figures are eagerly anticipated by Wall Street, which often reacts sharply to their announcement.

Unfortunately, the money supply fluctuates widely from week to week — some would say it fluctuates wildly. Fortunately, changes in the money supply, as will be discussed in a subsequent chapter, seem to affect the economy only with a lag. It is the rate of growth of the money supply six months to a year ago that is affecting the economy today. So current changes in the money-supply growth are a good way for you to forecast the future.

But because week-to-week changes are misleading, the weekly changes reported in the nation's press are of little use. What is needed is a statistical series. Fortunately, this information is easily available. The Federal Reserve Bank of St. Louis puts out two reports on money supply, one of which is called *National Economic Trends* and the other *U.S. Financial Data*. *U.S. Financial Data* is published weekly and provides current information on the money supply and interest rates over the past several years. *National Economic Trends* does the same thing for the real sector, charting most of the information we shall discuss below. These reports are free for the asking. Just write to the Federal Reserve Bank of St. Louis, and you will be put on its mailing list. The Federal Reserve Bank of Cleveland also publishes monthly *Economic Trends* (also available free), which reviews recent economic information. These publications will save you the trouble of making your own charts and tables.

If the money supply has been rising at a rapid rate over the past year or two, then probably so will nominal GNP in the future. But if the rate of growth has slowed for a period of time, it may signal a coming slowdown for the economy. Changes in the money supply have been a good though not an infallible predictor of the future.

A second indicator that often foresees future developments in the overall economy is the *stock market*. When the stock market is rising, it often foretells a rise in real GNP. When the stock market declines, it often does so in advance of the turn to recession for the overall economy. Economists prefer the Standard and Poor's index as a measure of stock market performance to the more famous Dow Jones industrial index because it is more comprehensive. Like the money supply, the stock market has not been infallible. Professor Paul Samuelson, a Nobel Prize–winning economist, once remarked that the stock market has predicted seven of the last four recessions. The great Wall Street crash of 1987, for example, the most dramatic financial event of the 1980s, signaled for many economists the advent of a recession in 1988 — a recession that did not occur.

Finally, the *index of leading indicators* is specifically designed to foretell movements in real GNP. This index reduces to a single number the movements of a dozen statistics that generally lead developments in real GNP. This index is issued monthly by the Commerce Department and includes such data as stock prices, new orders placed by manufacturers, changes in the money supply, and the prices of raw materials. If the index moves in the same direction for several months, it is a good sign that total output will move in the same direction in the near future. If the index turns down for three months in a row, it generally foretells a coming recession. But you should be aware that the index of leading indicators does not perfectly foretell the future path of real GNP. In the past it has given a number of misleading signals.

There are indexes other than the producer price index that economists watch to foretell future inflation rates. The *commodities price index* is often watched, as the prices of commodities (raw materials and agricultural products) often rise and fall prior to increases and decreases in the CPI. Also, the price of gold is often watched, because gold is considered to be a hedge against inflation. When economic decision makers begin to fear inflation, the demand for gold increases, causing its price to rise. The rise in price is a signal that many investors are forecasting an increase in the inflation rate.[1]

If you keep an eye on these statistics, you will probably not be fooled by changes in the macroeconomy. You are just beginning your study of macroeconomics; as your knowledge increases, you will have a better understanding of what changes in the indicators discussed above mean. However, be aware that economic forecasting still remains part art and part science. No one can foretell the future perfectly. What you can do is to arm yourself with the necessary macroeconomic theory and the latest statistics, and you can probably do as well as anybody else.

---

[1] Source: Charles R. Nelson, *The Investor's Guide to Economic Indicators* (New York: Wiley, 1987).

P A R T 3

THE REAL SECTOR

C H A P T E R

9

NATIONAL INCOME, AGGREGATE EXPENDITURES, AND AGGREGATE DEMAND
The Keynesian Model

IN THIS CHAPTER YOU WILL LEARN:

How the income/ expenditure model determines the equilibrium level of real national income in the economy

●

The components of aggregate expenditures and the relationship between aggregate expenditures and aggregate demand

●

The effects that consumption, investment, and government spending have on the equilibrium level of real national income

●

How the income/ expenditure model can be applied to diagnose the health of the economy

THE ECONOMIC SITUATION IN 1961 AND IN 1989

John F. Kennedy was elected president of the United States in 1960 and immediately upon taking office in January 1961 began to grapple with the existing economic situation. Nearly three decades later, in 1988, George Bush was elected president. He too had an economic problem with which his administration had to deal.

In April 1960 the economy had slipped into recession and the unemployment rate had increased from 5.5 percent to 6.7 percent. President Kennedy had promised during the election campaign to get " . . . the economy moving again." To do this, the youngest president in our country's history was determined to install a new economic philosophy in the federal government.

George Bush became president in the midst of the nation's longest recovery. Inflation was more or less contained, but there were disturbing signs that inflation was heating up when the Bush administration assumed office. The producer price index rose at an annual rate of 12.7 during January and February, and the consumer price index was increasing at an annual rate of 6.1 percent during these same months. The Bush administration believed that it must act to restrain inflation and maintain public confidence.

Kennedy's economic advisors applied, for the first time in the United States, modern macroeconomic theory based on Keynesian analysis. This theory had been widely taught in the economics departments of the nation's colleges and universities since World War II, but it had never systematically been put into practice by the federal government.

The economists of the Bush administration would probably deny they were practicing Keynesian economists, but they would not deny the influence Keynesian economics has had on modern macroeconomics. Macroeconomics has evolved, developed, and changed in the three decades that separated the two administrations. Yet the methods these economists employed, and the statistics they used, bore a strong Keynesian imprint. How were the tools of Keynesian macroeconomics used to diagnose and treat the ills of the economies of the Kennedy and Bush administrations?

THE GREAT DEPRESSION AND THE KEYNESIAN EXPLANATION

The Great Depression that began in 1929 was the worst in U.S. history. Economic historians have compared it with the downturns of the 1840s and 1890s, but the comparisons only show the severity of the Great Depression, which was unparalleled in the extent and duration of the underemployment of labor and resources. Economists, who were at the time generally influenced by the classical school of economic thought, were initially confounded by the Great Depression.

Out of this confusion came a revolution in economic thought, which began when the great British economist J. M. Keynes published his *General Theory of Employment, Interest, and Money*. In this book Keynes created the foundation for the innovative macroeconomic theory that bears his name.

Keynesian theory was primarily designed to explain how a prolonged period of underemployment of resources could occur. Keynes employed broad macroeconomic aggregates along with some assumptions about the nature of the economy that differed from the assumptions of the classical school. The Keynesian explanation of prolonged underemployment naturally contained implications for why the Depression occurred, and what should have been done about it at the time. Keynes and his followers suggested that among the participants in the economy only government had both the incentive and the ability to effectively counter a recession or depression. The intellectual stage was set for a major expansion of the role of government in the economy that took place in the 1960s following the election of President Kennedy.

There are several contending explanations for the cause of the Great Depression, two of which stand out: the spending hypothesis and the money hypothesis. The spending hypothesis is founded in Keynesian theory, and the money hypothesis is based on monetarist economics. In this part of this book we shall concentrate on the spending hypothesis. The money hypothesis will be taken up in the next part.

What happened in the U.S. economy during the early 1930s, and what were the variables that the spending hypothesis suggests were instrumental in causing the Great Depression?

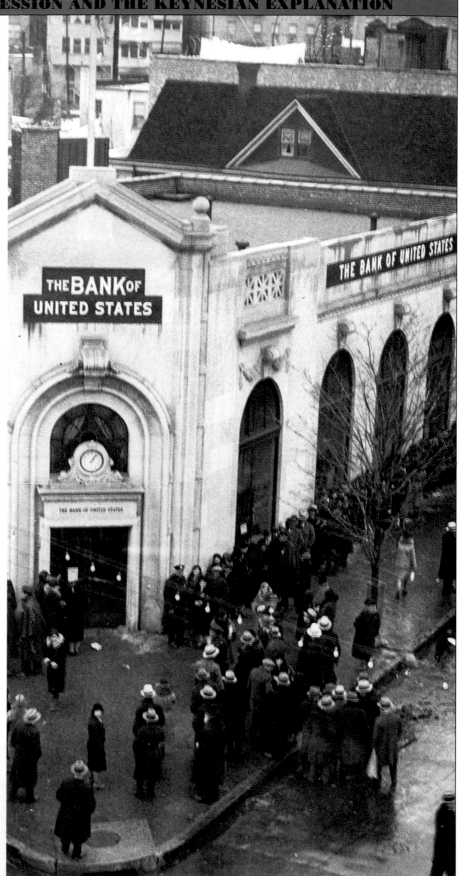

• INTRODUCTION •

When asked if he was a Keynesian, Paul Volcker, former Chairman of the Federal Reserve Board, replied: "I'll give you a Nixonian answer: We're all Keynesians now — in terms of the way we look at things. National income statistics are a Keynesian view of the world, and the language of economists tends to be Keynesian."[1]

If you pick up a business magazine like *Business Week* or *Fortune* or a newspaper like *The Wall Street Journal*, you will find articles describing the state of the economy. These articles report either on the health of the overall economy or on a particular aspect of it. Headlines appear such as "Consumers Are Still Spending Up a Storm," "Investment Is Booming," and "Exports Rise but Imports Still Dominate" or the opposite "Consumers Take Wait-and-See Attitude"

and "Investment Slows." Everyone in business, it seems, is interested in two things: what the current state of the economy is and where it is headed.

But did you ever wonder why business writers focus on consumption, investment, government spending and the deficit, and the balance of foreign trade when discussing the macroeconomy? What you are seeing is the influence of Keynesian economics. The variables that the income/expenditure model, as the basic Keynesian model is called, considers crucial have not only influenced the way economic statistics are collected but have come to frame the way we think about macroeconomics in general. The purpose of this chapter is to discover how the equilibrium level of real national income is determined in the income/expenditure model. •

INCOME/EXPENDITURE APPROACH TO DETERMINING NATIONAL INCOME

Keynes first developed his theory to explain how an economy could settle on a level of output that was less than the economy's potential output. This was the main theoretical problem presented by the Great Depression. In Keynes' opinion there were two major flaws in classical economics (discussed in the appendix to Chapter 7) that prevented that theory from explaining the occurrence and duration of the Great Depression. First, the classical model assumed that wages and prices were sufficiently flexible to eliminate quickly shortages and surpluses in both the product and labor markets. When conditions change, the classical model assumed that prices and wages also quickly change to reestablish equilibrium at full employment. Keynes doubted that this was so. He especially distrusted the assumption that wages were sufficiently flexible to eliminate quickly any unemployment that occurred.

Second, Keynes rejected outright Say's Law, which states: "Supply creates its own demand." He did not feel that a change in the rate of interest was the only mechanism working to equate the amount of investment with the amount of saving. He believed, instead, that the amount of savings depended more on the level of national income than on interest rates. Thus changes in the level of income were more likely to equate the level of saving with the level of investment than were changes in interest rates. Supply did not therefore automatically create its own demand. Rather, the level of economic activity would adjust, suggesting the possibility of prolonged unemployment in the labor markets such as occurred during the Great Depression.

Keynesian theory models the economy in the short run. In the long run Keynes and his followers accept the classical proposition that wages and the price level will adjust to restore full employment. Keynes did not believe this to be a source of solace for the economy. In one of his most famous statements, he reportedly said: "In the long run we are all dead,"

---

[1]William R. Neikirk, *Volcker: Portrait of the Money Man* (New York: Congdon & Weed, 1987), 77–78.

348

FIGURE 9.1

Keynesian Short-Run Aggregate Supply
Curve

The Keynesian short-run aggregate supply (SRAS) curve
shown in this figure exhibits a particular shape. Reading
from left to right, the SRAS curve has a horizontal component that runs from A to B. Within this segment aggregate demand can increase, such as from AD_1 to AD_2, and
the single outcome will be an increase in real national
income from AD_1 to AD_2. The price level will not be affected by changes in aggregate demand within this
range. If aggregate demand increases further to AD_3, the
response along the SRAS will be an increase in real national income from Y_{N_2} to Y_{N_3} along with an increase in
the price level from PL to PL'. The segment of the SRAS
curve from point B to point C is an intermediate range in
which both real national income and the price level will be
affected by changes in aggregate demand. Beyond point
C the SRAS curve enters the classical range in which
changes in aggregate demand affect only the price level,
with real national income remaining fixed at Y_{N_4}.

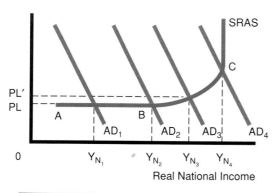

suggesting that in the present the economy is always operating in the short
run.

Keynesian theory begins by assuming that the short-run aggregate
supply curve will have a particular shape.

THE KEYNESIAN SHORT-RUN
AGGREGATE SUPPLY CURVE

The aggregate supply curve shows the level of real national income (real
GNP) that will be supplied at each price level. Consider the economic
situation that concerned Keynes. A number of people are out of work and
are willing, indeed searching, for work at existing wage rates. These idle
workers are involuntarily unemployed because they are willing to work at
existing wage rates. Some business firms, at the same time, are not operating at capacity, and idle plants and equipment exist. It is therefore possible to expand national output without raising either prices or wages by
simply bringing the existing unemployed workers back to work with the
existing underutilized capital equipment. The basic problem is that aggregate demand is insufficient to allow the economy to operate at full employment, and the solution is to increase aggregate demand.

The short-run aggregate supply (SRAS) curve, according to Keynesian analysis, is a true curve containing a horizontal segment at the existing
price level. This segment continues as long as there are involuntarily unemployed workers willing to work at the existing wage rates. If aggregate
demand increases within this range, real national income will increase
with no corresponding increase in the price level. Once the level of aggregate demand is sufficient for all the involuntarily unemployed to be back
at work and the economy has reached full employment, the short-run
aggregate supply becomes upward sloping and eventually becomes vertical. Additional attempts to increase output by increasing aggregate demand will increase both real national income and the price level. If aggregate demand continues to expand, eventually the only result will be
increases in the price level.

Figure 9.1 shows a Keynesian SRAS curve. The horizontal segment
running from A to B depicts the Keynesian range, which is caused by the
existence of involuntarily unemployed workers and idle resources. As
long as the aggregate demand curve intersects the aggregate supply curve
within this region, real national income (output) can expand or contract
without causing the price level (PL) to change. An increase in aggregate
demand, for example, as reflected by a shift from AD_1 to AD_2, will expand
national income from Y_{N_1} to Y_{N_2} without changing the price level. Thus
the price level can be initially ignored by assuming that it is fixed, when
employing the Keynesian model to analyze an economy operating at less
than full employment. But if the level of aggregate demand were to increase again, from AD_2 to AD_3, output will increase but so will the price
level, because the economy is approaching the full-employment level. Beyond AD_4 the economy will have reached the classical region on the SRAS
curve, and changes in the price level will be the consequence of any
change in aggregate demand.

In our discussion below we shall assume, except where explicitly
noted, that the economy is operating in the Keynesian range of the SRAS
curve. Thus changes in aggregate demand will result in proportional
changes in real national income. The SRAS curve thus becomes irrelevant
to the determination of real national income. The Keynesian model is a
theory about aggregate demand. It provides the foundation for the mod-

ern theory of aggregate demand, which is the main reason we are examining it in detail in this chapter. Today it is widely recognized that a complete macroeconomic model must also consider aggregate supply. This was less important in the 1930s and the 1960s than it is today.

This is not to suggest that the Keynesian model cannot explain changes that occur in the economy when it is operating beyond point B in Figure 9.1. It can, but it wasn't explicitly designed to deal with an economy operating in this region. In the model presented below, the price level is assumed to be fixed and the economy is assumed to be operating in the short run.

CIRCULAR FLOW OF INCOME AND PRODUCTION

The most important question that the income/expenditure model attempts to answer is what determines the level of real national income. A circular flow diagram is helpful in order to acquire an intuitive feel for the way equilibrium real national income is determined. Such a diagram allows an appreciation of the leakages and injections that occur in the flows of income that are generated in an economy. The relative sizes of the leakages and injections are crucial for the determination of equilibrium real national income.

The circular flow diagram is presented as a graphic description of the important macroeconomic relationships in the economy. Figure 9.2 depicts a system of tunnels in which economic income flows in a clockwise direction. In Part A the private sector of the economy is modeled. The impact of government is temporarily ignored. The main tunnel connects consumers with business firms, which engage in trades with each other by exchanging consumption (C) and investment goods (I). Real national income, measured as real net national product (Y_N), flows from business firms to consumers in the form of payments made to the owners of the factors of production. Consumers can do two things with the income they receive: consume or save. Consumers return much of the real national income directly to business firms in the form of consumption payments.

There is, however, a one-way branch off the main tunnel. Into this branch flows part of the real national income that consumers receive. This flow represents savings that flow to the financial sector, thereby creating a leakage out of the circular flow. This branch tunnel continues from the financial sector back to the main tunnel, representing the injection of investment into the circular flow of income.

The circular flow of income allows an observer to grasp the main determinants of real national income. Real national income (Y_N) is flowing from business firms to consumers as payment for the use of the factors of production. Part of this income continues within the main tunnel as consumption expenditures (C), and part leaks out by being diverted into a branch tunnel (point 1 in the diagram) in the form of savings (S), which flow to the financial system. Because consumers save as well as consume, consumption expenditures (C) will be less than national income. The leakage of savings is not lost to the economy, but is reinjected as investment (I) (point 2) to the main tunnel.

The amount of aggregate expenditures for consumption and investment (C + I) flowing to business firms is equal to the value of the output produced by these firms. Since consumers own the businesses as well as the factors of production, the flow of income returns from the businesses

FIGURE 9.2
The Circular Flow of Income and Production

In Part A the circular flow diagram links the business sector with consumers via the flow of income. Consumers receive the flow of real national income (Y_N) in the form of factor payments and directly return much of it to business firms in the form of spending for consumption (C) goods. Consumers, however, do not spend all of their income for consumption, because they save part of it (S). Savings, which represent a leakage out of the circular flow at point 1, are diverted to the financial sector where they are borrowed to purchase investment goods (I) thus rejoining the circular flow as an injection at point 2. Thus business firms receive the amount of consumption expenditures plus the amount of investment expenditures (C + I) at point 3, which equals real national income (Y_N), which flows as factor payments to consumers at point 4. Thus at equilibrium the amount of the leakages (savings) will equal the amount of investment (injection). Real national income will adjust to ensure that saving equals investment.

Part B presents the same circular flow diagram as Part A but with government and the foreign-trade sector added. Government represents both a source of injection in the form of transfers and expenditures, and a source of leakage in the form of taxes. The foreign-trade sector is a source of leakage in the form of imports and a source of injection in the form of exports.

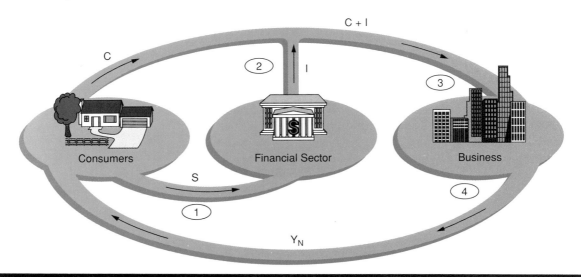

to consumers. Thus the amount of aggregate expenditures must equal the amount of national income:

$$C + I = Y_N$$

Aggregate expenditures is equal to the final demands for real national income. In this case aggregate expenditures equals the amount of consumption expenditures plus the amount of investment expenditures. Since there are only two things that consumers can do with income — consume or save — consumption plus savings must also equal national income:

$$C + S = Y_N$$

Therefore:

$$C + S = Y_N = C + I$$

Hence:

$$S = I$$

The amount actually saved must equal at the equilibrium level of national income the amount that is invested. The leakages out of the circular flow must equal the injections into it. What ensures that this is so? The size of the flow of national income in the Keynesian model plays this role. The level of national income will adjust until the amount saved equals the amount invested.

The decision to divert part of national income into savings is made by consumers (at point 1 in Part A of Figure 9.2). The decision to inject income into the main tunnel is made by investors (at point 2) in conjunc-

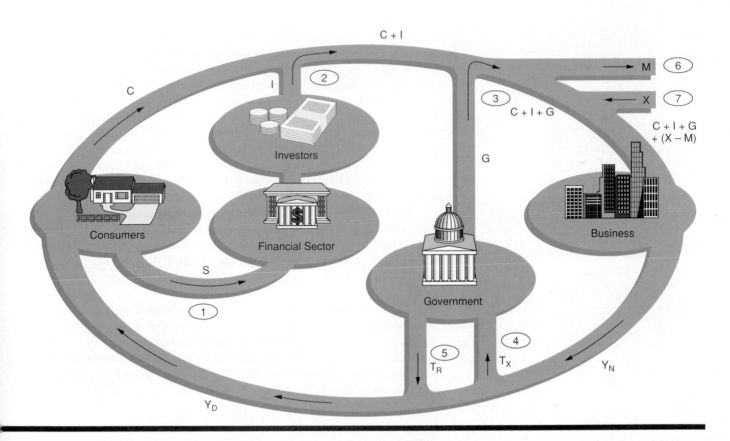

tion with the financial sector. The decision to save and the decision to invest are therefore generally made by two different groups. Thus planned or desired saving refers to the amount consumers wish to save at every level of real national income, and planned or desired investment refers to the amount investors wish to invest at every level of real national income.

What ensures that the amount that consumers desire to save is equal to the amount that investors want to invest? This is the same as asking: Is the amount of leakage out of the system always the same as the amount of injection into it? Suppose consumers initially plan to save more than investors plan to invest. In the Keynesian model the flow of income in the main tunnel will adjust until the leakage out via desired saving just equals the injection in the form of desired investment. If consumers initially want to save more than investors want to invest, then the flow of income will be reduced. Consumers will respond to the decline in income at their disposal by reducing both the amount of consumption and the amount of saving they do. Equilibrium will be established when the amount of desired saving adjusts to equal the amount of desired investment. The flow of real national income in the main tunnel will consequently fall.

The decline in income and saving will continue until the amount of saving is just equal to the amount of investment. When this happens, the leakages out of the main tunnel will just equal the injections, and the flow of income in the upper loop will equal the flow of income in the lower loop. Thus saving and investment plans may differ, but the level of national income will always adjust to make the level of actual saving equal to the level of actual investment. The macroeconomy will have adjusted to establish the equilibrium flow of national income at which actual saving equals actual investment. Thus the level of national income will be influenced by the desires of consumers to save and by the investment plans of business.

Saving and investment decisions represent one source of leakages and injections into the circular flow of income. Government decisions provide another. The role of government is added to the circular flow in Part B of Figure 9.2. Government expenditures (G) through its spending decisions provides an injection into the circular flow (point 3), and via its tax policy (T_X) it provides another source of leakage out of the circular flow (point 4). Government also transfers income directly to consumers by taxing some consumers and giving that money to others. This injection occurs at point 5. The government can influence the level of national income by varying expenditures and transfers (injections) and taxes (leakages), which affects real national income the same way as changes in investment and saving decisions.

What determines the equilibrium level of national income in the circular flow model when government is added? The answer is the same as without government. The equilibrium level of national income will adjust to equate the total leakages out of the circular flow (savings and taxes) with the total injections into the flow (investment and government spending).

The foreign-trade sector is yet another source of injection and leakage into the macroeconomy. These sources are also shown in Part B. The foreign-trade sector is composed of imports (M) that represent a leakage out of the circular flow (point 6) and of exports (X) that represent another injection (point 7). Imports reduce the circular flow of income and exports increase the circular flow. Thus:

$$C + I + G + X = Y_N$$

and

$$C + S + T + M = Y_N$$

Therefore:

$$C + I + G + X = C + S + T + M$$

Thus the total of consumption plus injections (investment plus government expenditures plus exports) will equal national income, and so will consumption plus the total of leakages (savings plus tax revenues plus imports). Although the amount of leakage must equal the amount of injection, the amount of savings no longer has to equal the amount of investment, or the amount of taxes the amount of government spending, or the amount of exports the amount of imports — as long as the totals match.

The circular flow model provides an intuitive look at how the macroeconomy functions. When employing the Keynesian model, always keep in mind that the equilibrium level of national income will adjust to maintain the equality between total leakages and total injections.

We shall now examine the Keynesian model in a more systematic fashion.

HOW EQUILIBRIUM NATIONAL INCOME IS DETERMINED

Keynes' explanation of how an economy determines the amount of real output that will be produced in the short run depends entirely on the desired level of **aggregate expenditures**. This approach is often referred to as the income/expenditure model. In the Keynesian model aggregate expenditures determine the demand for national income.

> *Aggregate expenditures is the total of expenditures for consumption, investment, government, and the difference between the value of exports and imports.*

It is no accident that the major expenditure categories of gross national product (GNP) as identified in the national income accounts are private consumption expenditures (C), private investment (I), government expenditures (G), and net exports (X − M), which is the level of exports minus the level of imports. They were designed to correspond to the Keynesian model, as the quotation at the beginning of this chapter suggests.

Keynesian theory's income/expenditure approach explains how the desired level of expenditure in each of these categories is determined and, as a consequence of the sum of these actions, how the equilibrium level of national income is established. *Aggregate demand,* which is the relationship between price level and real national income, is replaced by the concept of aggregate expenditures, which reflects the relationship between total expenditures and real national income.

When graphed, aggregate demand has the price level on the vertical axis and real national income on the horizontal axis. The aggregate demand curve slopes downward, implying that the level of real national income demanded will increase when the price level declines. The aggregate demand (AD) schedule is graphed in Part B of Figure 9.3. The Keynesian model assumes a constant price level, so when graphing the income/expenditure model the vertical axis measures the level of desired aggregate expenditure and the horizontal axis measures the level of real national income. Aggregate expenditures will increase as real national income increases. So the aggregate expenditures (AE) schedule when graphed, as in Part A of Figure 9.3, slopes upward.

The SRAS curve is also ignored in Keynesian analysis, because only the horizontal segment is relevant. As was discussed above, within this segment any increase in aggregate demand automatically generates a proportional increase in national income without a price level change. In place of the SRAS curve, a 45° line (see Part A of Figure 9.3) is substituted. The 45° line includes all points on a graph at which the value of the variable measured on the vertical axis is equal to the value of the variable measured on the horizontal axis. Thus in the income/expenditure approach a 45° line replaces the SRAS curve. The 45° line indicates all of the points at which aggregate expenditures will equal real national income. The 45° line therefore represents all of the possible points at which the macroeconomic economy can possibly be at equilibrium.

The 45° line corresponds to the Keynesian segment of the SRAS curve in Figure 9.1. It signifies that in determining real national income within the Keynesian model, all that matters is the level of aggregate expenditures. Any change in the level of aggregate expenditures will result in a proportional change in real national income. If, as in Part A of Figure 9.3, the level of aggregate expenditures is $100 billion, then so will the level of real national income equal $100 billion. If the level of aggregate expenditures increases to $200 billion, the level of real national income will increase to the same amount.

The actual equilibrium level of real national income is determined where the aggregate expenditures function intersects the 45° line. In Part A of Figure 9.3 the aggregate expenditure curve AE intersects the 45° line at point E, establishing the equilibrium level of national income to be Y_N, which happens to correspond to the level of potential national income

FIGURE 9.3
Equilibrium Level of National Income

This figure allows the income/expenditure model in Part A to be directly compared with the basic macroeconomic model in Part B. Both models will predict the same level (Y_N) of equilibrium real national income. The income/expenditure model allows the components of aggregate expenditures to be considered, whereas the aggregate-demand/aggregate-supply model allows the price level to be determined.

(A) Income/Expenditure Model

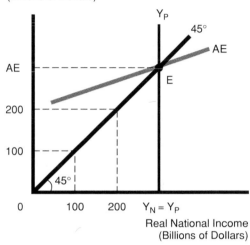

(B) AD/AS Model

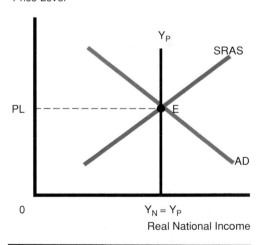

(Y_P). The economy at Y_P is operating at full employment. At this point the actual real national income is drawn equal to potential national income.

The aggregate expenditures schedule is drawn for a given price level. The price level is a determinant of aggregate expenditures. When a determinant changes, the entire schedule shifts. It is not possible to directly read the price level from this graph. When the price level changes, the entire aggregate expenditures schedule shifts up or down.

How does the income/expenditure model compare with the basic model of macroeconomics? The aggregate-demand/aggregate-supply model establishes the equilibrium level of national income by the intersection of the two curves. The income/expenditure model uses the intersection of the aggregate expenditures curve with the 45° line to find the equilibrium level of national income. The two are equivalent — both models yield the same results, real national income equal to Y_N, as can be seen in Figure 9.3.

Why employ two models that yield the same results? Each model has certain advantages over the other. The aggregate-demand/aggregate-supply model has the advantage of allowing the price level to be determined and the SRAS curve to shift. The income/expenditure model assumes that the price level is constant but allows the components of aggregate expenditures (which are determinants of aggregate demand) to be examined.

Until relatively recently, aggregate expenditures or aggregate demand was considered to be the main determinant of real national income. After all, as was revealed in Chapter 7, it was the collapse of aggregate demand that caused the Great Depression. Moreover, if you look again at the circular flow diagram, it is aggregate expenditures (aggregate demand) that can be adjusted by government action if macroeconomic decision makers decide to intervene in the macroeconomy. Changing government expenditures, transfers, and/or taxes directly will affect aggregate expenditures and therefore real national income.

Both models are useful. A consideration of aggregate expenditures allows the determinants of the level of aggregate demand to be considered individually and collectively as variables, but at the expense of assuming that the price level is constant. Aggregate demand allows the price level to be determined but at the expense of concealing the role of the individual determinants of aggregate demand.

Now let us turn to the individual determinants of aggregate expenditures.

AGGREGATE EXPENDITURES

Aggregate expenditures is equal to the total of consumption spending, investment spending, government expenditures, and the balance of foreign trade. All are equally important as theoretical categories, but not in the quantitative amounts that they contribute to aggregate expenditures. Consumption expenditures are quantitatively far and away the most important. Moreover, the relationship between consumption expenditures and national income lies at the heart of aggregate expenditures.

THE CONSUMPTION/INCOME RELATIONSHIP

The heart of the income/expenditure model is the relationship between national income and the level of consumer spending. We shall make the

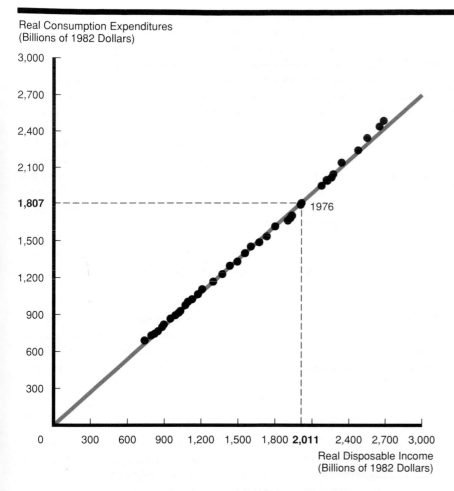

Real Consumption Expenditures
(Billions of 1982 Dollars)

FIGURE 9.4
Real Consumer Expenditures and Real
Disposable Income: 1949–1987

In this figure each point on the graph represents the combination of real consumption spending, measured on the vertical axis, and real disposable income, measured on the horizontal axis. In 1976, for example, the point on the graph indicates that real consumption expenditure was $1,807 billion when real disposable income was $2,011 billion. If you were to stretch a string in such a way that each point on the graph was as close to it as possible (the string represented on the graph by a straight line), you can see that while most points are very near the string, not all lie on it. This suggests that while the relationship between consumption expenditures and disposable income is very close it is not perfect.

simplifying assumption in the discussion below that real disposable income is equal to real national income minus taxes plus transfers. If you look again at Part B of Figure 9.2, you will see that consumers receive disposable income (Y_D), which is what is left after taxes are subtracted and transfers are added to net national product (Y_N).

Consumers have only two things to do with the disposable income they receive: save or spend. They generally do some of both, spending most of their disposable income on consumption and saving the rest. Economists are very interested in this decision, because in the final analysis the decision of how much to consume and how much to save has a strong effect on the equilibrium level of real national income.

In Figure 9.4 real disposable income is charted along with real consumption spending for the years 1949–1987. The correspondence between the two series is remarkably close, suggesting that consumption will rise when income increases and will fall when income decreases. The difference between the two time series is the amount of personal saving. The relationship between disposable income and consumption, though strongly positive, does not, however, exhibit a perfect correspondence.

Knowing that consumption will move in the same direction as disposable income is helpful but not sufficient for our purposes. Economists would like to know by *how much* consumption will change when disposable income changes. The scatter diagram in Figure 9.4 will be helpful in answering this question. Each dot on the chart represents the data for both consumer spending and disposable income for a single year.

If you place an imaginary piece of string and stretch it along the scatter so you have about as many dots above the string as below the string, you can obtain a picture of the consumption/disposable-income relationship. Let the solid line on the graph take the place of the string. Most dots lie very close to the string, suggesting that the consumption/income relationship is very close and stable over time. The relationship between disposable income and consumption expenditures thus appears almost to fit a straight line — almost but not quite.

If you calculate the slope of the line, you will find the relationship between an increase in disposable income and the resulting increase in consumption spending. The slope of the line is 0.90. This means that for every $100 billion change in disposable income, as measured on the horizontal axis, there will be associated with it about $90 billion in additional consumption, as measured on the vertical axis:

$$\text{Slope} = \frac{\text{Vertical change of \$90 billion}}{\text{Horizontal change of \$100 billion}} = 0.90$$

The slope of the line is very important. If you know what it is, you can predict that a dollar's increase in disposable income will lead to an increase in consumption of approximately 90 cents, with about 10 cents in additional savings. But you can do even better than this approximation if you expand your theory of consumption somewhat.

THE CONSUMPTION FUNCTION

What do we know about the relationship between consumption and disposable income so far? We know that there is a close and fairly stable relationship between consumer expenditures and disposable income. This relationship is called the **consumption function.**

> *The consumption function is the relationship between total consumer spending and total disposable income, other things being equal.*

Table 9.1 shows a hypothetical short-run consumption function. In column 1 the level of real disposable income is presented. The amount of consumption associated with each level of disposable income is found in column 2, and the amount of saving associated with each level of disposable income is shown in column 3.

Since people can only save or spend their current income:

$$Y_D = C + S$$

Thus the amount in column 2 plus the amount in column 3 must always equal the amount in column 1. There is one unusual feature in Table 9.1. When disposable income is zero, people still consume $50 worth of goods and services. Rather than starve, this consumption is financed out of past savings, so savings this period is a negative $50. The consumption function represented in this table shows the positive relationship between consumption and disposable income.

There is more that we can learn from Table 9.1. We know from the line that was constructed in the scatter diagram in Figure 9.4 that the slope of the consumption function is constant. This fact allows us to make predictions about how an additional amount of disposable income will be

TABLE 9.1
Consumption and Savings as a Function of Disposable Income
(Billions of Dollars)

DISPOSABLE INCOME[a] (1)	DESIRED CONSUMPTION EXPENDITURES (2)	DESIRED SAVINGS (1) – (2) (3)	MARGINAL PROPENSITY TO CONSUME (4)	AVERAGE PROPENSITY TO CONSUME (5)
0	50	−50	—	—
100	125	−25	0.75	1.25
200	200	0	0.75	1.00
300	275	25	0.75	0.92
400	350	50	0.75	0.86
500	425	75	0.75	0.85
600	500	100	0.75	0.83
700	575	125	0.75	0.82
800	650	150	0.75	0.81

[a]Equal, in the absence of a government sector, to national income.

allocated by consumers between consumption and savings. The slope of the consumption function is known as the **marginal propensity to consume (MPC)**.

> The marginal propensity to consume is the ratio of the change in consumption to the change in disposable income, other things being equal.
>
> $$MPC = \frac{\text{Change in consumption}}{\text{Change in disposable income}}$$

The marginal propensity to consume thus tells us the proportion of an additional dollar of disposable income that will be spent for consumption. When disposable income increases by $100 billion in column 1, desired consumption expenditures always increases by $75 billion; thus the MPC is 0.75, as shown in column 4 of Table 9.1.

The portion of an additional dollar of disposable income that is not spent will be saved. Thus we can obtain the **marginal propensity to save (MPS)** by subtracting the MPC from 1:

$$1 - MPC = MPS$$

> The marginal propensity to save is the ratio of the change in savings to the change in disposable income, other things being equal.
>
> $$MPS = \frac{\text{Change in savings}}{\text{Change in disposable income}}$$

The marginal propensity to save associated with the information given in Table 9.1 will therefore be 0.25.

The marginal propensity to consume is not equal to the **average propensity to consume (APC)**. There is a crucial difference between the

FIGURE 9.5
Consumption and Savings Functions

A consumption function together with the 45° line is graphed in Part A. The consumption function initially lies above the 45° line, then crosses it at the point where consumption expenditures are equal to disposable income. Thereafter the consumption function lies below the 45° line. When the consumption function is above the 45° line, the economy is dissaving, paying for present consumption out of past savings. When consumption expenditures equal disposable income, as they do at $200 billion, savings will be zero. When consumption is less than disposable income, as it is when disposable income exceeds $200 billion, savings will be positive. In Part B a savings function is derived from the consumption function shown in Part A by subtracting the consumption function from the 45° line for all levels of disposable income. When disposable income is zero, savings will be a negative $50 billion. As disposable income increases, savings remain negative until disposable income is equal to $200 billion, at which point savings will be zero. Thereafter as disposable income increases, savings will be positive.

(A) Consumption Function

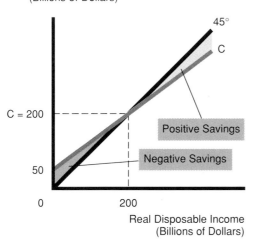

(B) Savings Function

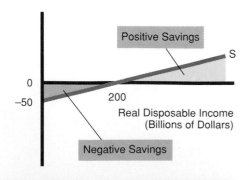

marginal propensity to consume (MPC) and the average propensity to consume. The MPC gives the amount of consumption that will be generated for each additional dollar of disposable income, while the APC gives the average consumption per dollar of disposable income.

The average propensity to consume is the amount of consumption divided by the amount of disposable income.

$$APC = \frac{Consumption}{Disposable\ income}$$

This can also be readily seen in Table 9.1. The marginal propensity to consume remains constant at 0.75 throughout the table as income increases in increments of $100 billion from zero to $800 billion, while the average propensity to consume declines from 1.25 to 0.81. It is important to keep this distinction in mind, since using the APC to predict what will happen to consumption if disposable income increases is likely to give misleading results.

The consumption function, the values for which are shown in Table 9.1, can be written algebraically as:

$$C = \$50\ billion + 0.75Y_D$$

where C is consumption, Y_D is disposable income, $50 billion is the constant term, and 0.75 is the marginal propensity to consume. You will probably recognize it as the equation for a straight line. When disposable income is zero, consumption will be $50 billion. This $50 billion is the amount of **autonomous consumption.**

Autonomous consumption is the amount of consumption expenditure that would occur if disposable income were zero.

If disposable income were zero, consumption, financed out of past savings, would still be equal to the amount of autonomous consumption, or $50 billion. If disposable income were positive, 75 cents out of every additional dollar of disposable income would be spent for consumption and 25 cents would be saved.

The information contained in Table 9.1 is graphed in Figure 9.5. In Part A consumption expenditures are measured along the vertical axis and disposable income along the horizontal axis. The consumption function is graphed along with the 45° line, which shows points where expenditures are equal to income. Since there is no government in this model, there can be no taxes or transfers, so real disposable income is also equal to national income. When income is below $200 billion, consumption is greater than income and saving is negative; at $200 billion, consumption equals income, so saving is zero. When income is above $200 billion, consumption is less than income and saving is positive.

The amount of savings at each level of disposable income is shown in Part B of Figure 9.5. The information depicted in Part A can also be found in Part B. The 45° line is not used in this part because the graph must provide for negative values that never occur when considering consumption. The vertical axis of Part B measures the amount of saving, positive or negative; the horizontal axis, identical to the one used in Part A, shows real disposable income.

The saving function can be obtained from the consumption function by subtracting the amount of consumption expenditures at every level of disposable income from the 45° line. This procedure relies on the equality:

$$C + S = Y_D$$

The amount of consumption expenditures (C) plus the amount of savings (S) must equal the amount of disposable income (Y_D) that consumers receive.

When income is zero, consumption is $50 billion, so saving must be a negative $50 billion. Consumers will spend past savings, reducing their wealth, to maintain consumption at this level. When disposable income increases to $200 billion, consumption, according to the consumption function, will also be $200 billion, so saving is zero. Saving at levels of disposable income below $200 billion will be negative, and will be zero at $200 billion. If disposable income is greater than $200 billion, consumption expenditures will be less than income, so savings will be positive. Savings will be positive at all levels of disposable income above $200 billion.

MOVEMENTS ALONG VERSUS SHIFTS IN THE CONSUMPTION FUNCTION

Income is not the only factor that affects the level of consumption. A person's consumption decision is also influenced by his or her own wealth, the amount of taxes paid, and the price level, among other things. Changes in these things obviously will affect how much one desires to consume. But they affect the consumption function in a different way than changes in disposable income. Changes in these things alter the amount of consumption at all levels of disposable income. In short, such changes affect the level of autonomous consumption expenditures. Factors other than disposable income that affect consumption expenditures are called the determinants of the consumption function. If any of the determinants changes, the consumption/income relationship changes.

The determinants of the aggregate consumption function include the level of wealth, the price level, the extent of taxation, as well as the age structure of the population, the distribution of income, the attitudes of the people toward thrift, and expectations about future levels of prices and income. If any of these factors changes, the entire consumption function itself will change. That is, consumption at every level of income will be affected. Such a change represents a shift in the consumption function as the level of autonomous consumption expenditures changes.

It is important to distinguish between a **shift in the consumption function** and a **movement along a consumption function.**

A shift in the consumption function occurs when a determinant affecting the consumption function changes.

A movement along the consumption function occurs when disposable income changes and all other factors that affect consumption are held constant.

In Figure 9.6 a change in real disposable income from $200 billion to $400 billion will cause consumption to increase from $200 billion to $350 billion, reflecting a *movement along* an existing consumption function C as indicated by the arrow in Part A. Savings will increase from zero to $50 billion in value as a movement along savings function S in Part B. An

FIGURE 9.6

Comparing a Movement along a Given
Consumption Function with a Shift in
the Consumption Function

This figure demonstrates the distinction to be made between a movement along the consumption function and a
shift of the function itself. In Part A as disposable income
increases from zero, consumption expenditures will also
increase, as is shown along the consumption function C.
When the level of disposable income is $200 billion, con-
sumption expenditures will also be $200 billion, and sav-
ing will be zero. When disposable income is $400 billion,
consumption will be $350 billion. When one of the deter-
minants of consumption changes, the entire consumption function will shift, as here from C to C'. The increase
in autonomous consumption from $50 billion to $100
billion causes consumption expenditures to increase by
$50 billion at every level of disposable income. Note,
however, what happens to the level of disposable income
at which zero saving occurs: This point has moved from
$200 billion to $400 billion. An autonomous increase in
consumption of $50 billion results in an increase in con-
sumption expenditures of $200 billion, composed of the
$50 billion increase in autonomous consumption plus the
$150 billion induced increase. In Part B the effect of an
upward shift in the consumption function is shown. An
increase in consumption will cause the savings function
to shift down from S to S'. The zero savings point increases from $200 billion to $400 billion, showing that
the effect of an increase in consumption is the same in
Parts A and B.

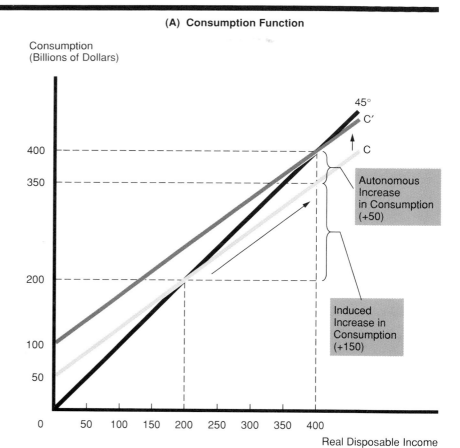

(A) Consumption Function

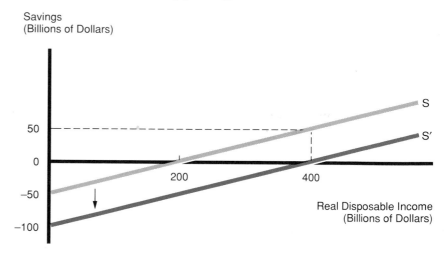

(B) Savings Function

increase in disposable income will therefore induce an increase in both the
amount of consumption and the amount of savings.

Now suppose one of the determinants of the consumption function
changes in value. Suppose the price level falls or taxes are reduced, both
of which will affect the amount of autonomous consumption. How would
such changes affect the consumption function? A change in the determinants of the consumption function will cause *the entire consumption func-*

TABLE 9.2
Consumption and Savings as a Function of National Income
(Billions of Dollars)

DISPOSABLE INCOME (1)	CONSUMPTION FUNCTION C		CONSUMPTION FUNCTION C'	
	DESIRED CONSUMPTION EXPENDITURES (2)	DESIRED SAVINGS (1) − (2) (3)	DESIRED CONSUMPTION EXPENDITURES (4)	DESIRED SAVINGS (1) − (4) (5)
$ 0	$ 50	−$50	$100	−$100
100	125	−25	175	−75
200	200	0	250	−50
300	275	25	325	−25
400	350	50	400	0
500	425	75	475	25
600	500	100	550	50
700	575	125	625	75
800	650	150	700	100

tion to shift.[2] In Part A of Figure 9.6 the consumption function shifts up from C to C', in response to consumers' greater wealth. When this happens, consumption expenditures will increase at all levels of disposable income. When disposable income is equal to $200 billion, consumption expenditures will increase from $200 billion to $250 billion. When disposable income is $400 billion, consumption will increase from $350 billion to $400 billion.

There is another important implication that can be drawn from Figure 9.6. Suppose that the consumption function is initially C, with autonomous consumption equal to $50 billion and a marginal propensity to consume of 0.75. The consumption function crosses the 45° line at a level of real national income of $200 billion. Now suppose the consumption function shifts up by $50 billion to a total of $100 billion and maintains the same marginal propensity to consume. The consumption function now represented by C' crosses the 45° line at a level of real national income of $400 billion, an increase of $200 billion. The effect of a $50 billion increase in autonomous consumption was to induce $150 billion in additional consumption.

Coincident with the shift up in the consumption function will be a downward shift in the savings function from S to S', as indicated by the arrow in Part B. Savings is what is left over from disposable income after consumption occurs. If you now desire to consume more at every level of disposable income, you simply will have to save less. The zero savings point thus moves from $200 billion to $400 billion. Similar information is contained in Table 9.2. Consumption function C' reflects an increase in

---

[2]The consumption function can be written in a symbolic shorthand form as:

$$C = C(Y_D, W, E, PL, T, O)$$

where the dependent variable C is consumption, the independent variable Y_D is disposable income, and the determinants are respectively W for wealth, E for expectations, PL for the price level, T for taxes, and O for other nonincome factors that affect the level of consumption. If disposable income changes from $200 billion to $400 billion, as it does in Figure 9.6, then the level of consumption as measured along the existing consumption function C will increase from $200 billion to $350 billion. However, should any of the nonincome determinants, from W to O, change, then the entire consumption function will either move up (a shift from C to C') or down (a shift from C' to C).

autonomous consumption over consumption function C of $50 billion at every level of disposable income. Thus when disposable income is zero, consumption will be $100 billion instead of $50 billion. The level of disposable income where consumption is equal to disposable income and savings is zero increases from $200 billion to $400 billion.

HOW THE CONSUMPTION FUNCTION IS AFFECTED BY A DETERMINANT CHANGE

Now let us consider how the determinants will affect the consumption function when they change. People consume in order to obtain present satisfaction. Yet most people do not spend all of their current disposable income for consumption. People save by not consuming all of their current income. They save for a variety of reasons. They save in order to make a future major purchase such as the down payment on a house or an automobile, for their retirement years, or to leave an estate for their children. Anything that affects the reasons for saving, or the amount necessary to meet a savings goal, will affect the consumption function.

WEALTH One factor affecting consumption is the existing amount of consumers' wealth. People hold their wealth in a variety of forms: stocks, bonds, real estate, and the like. When the real value of the wealth owned by consumers changes, people feel either richer or poorer and may as a consequence change the amount of current consumption they desire. When the stock market rallies and share prices increase, stockholders feel richer and may therefore decide to consume more and to save less out of current income. When stock prices are high, for example, consumers may decide that they don't have to save as much for retirement this year as they had previously thought and/or that now is the time to take that long overdue vacation. Thus rising stock prices reduce the amount of savings out of current income and increase the amount of consumption.

If wealth increases, then, autonomous consumption will increase and the consumption function will shift up. Conversely, if wealth decreases, the autonomous consumption will decline, and the consumption function will shift down. The effect of an increase in wealth on the consumption function can be seen in Figure 9.6. An increase in wealth will cause consumers to save less out of current income and to consume more. The consumption function will therefore shift up from C to C' in Part A and the savings function will shift down as shown in Part B by the shift from S to S'.

The stock market crashed on October 17, 1987. The decline in stock prices destroyed about $1 trillion in wealth. This loss of wealth caused the consumption function to shift down. One model of the consumption function predicted at the time that for every $1 decline in wealth consumption would decline by between 3 and 6 cents. This would mean a decline in annual consumption of $30 billion to $60 billion, or about 1 to 2 percent of consumption expenditures. This prediction was based on the consumption function shifting down like a shift from consumption function C' to C in Part A of Figure 9.6.

EXPECTATIONS Expectations about the future also affect consumption decisions. People form expectations about future levels of income and prices and they adjust current consumption decisions on the basis of these expectations. It has been said that people felt during the 1920s that "there were the rich and those who were going to be rich" and during the Great Depression they believed that " . . . there were the unemployed and those who were going to be unemployed." The desire to consume out of a given level of income would have been higher during the 1920s than it was during the 1930s purely as a result of the difference in expectations. Thus if expectations about future levels of national income and employment opportunities become more positive, the consumption function will shift up as households try to consume more at all levels of current income. If expectations become increasingly negative, the consumption function will shift down.

Similarly, expectations about the future level of prices affect current consumption. If the price level is expected to be higher in the future, people may rush to make purchases now in order to obtain the expected relatively lower current prices. Alternatively, if prices are expected to be lower in the future, people may choose to defer consumption today by saving more out of current income in order to buy at the expected lower future prices. Thus if expectations about the future level of prices change so that households now believe that future prices will be higher, the consumption function will shift up as consumers try to consume more currently. If expectations about the future level of prices change so that households now believe that in the future prices will be lower, the consumption function will shift down. Suppose expectations about the future become more positive. In this case the consumption function in Part A of Figure 9.6 will shift up from C to C'. If expectations become more pessimistic, the consumption function will shift down from C' to C.

PRICE LEVEL The actual level of prices also affects the level of current consumption by affecting the real value of financial assets fixed in nominal or dollar values. Households always maintain some of their wealth in money, as well as in savings accounts and perhaps bonds. When the price level changes, the real value of these financial assets changes in inverse proportion. When the price level falls, for example, the real value of these assets increases. Households are now wealthier than they were and are likely to desire to increase their consumption at every level of real national income. When the price level increases during inflation, the real value of nominal assets (assets denominated in dollars) will fall, making households poorer and causing them to reduce current consumption. Thus an increase in the actual price level will cause the consumption function to shift down, because holders of nominal (money-denominated) assets are made poorer. A decrease in the price level will cause the consumption function to shift up, because holders of nominal assets are now wealthier.

The effect that changes in the price level have on the consumption function is very important. Much of the discussion later in this chapter is based on this effect.

TAXATION Suppose we relax for now the assumption that government does not exist and consider the question of taxes. When there are governments, there will be taxes. How do taxes affect the consumption function? Recall that disposable income is equal to national income minus taxes plus transfers. Assume that transfers are zero but taxes are not; thus disposable income is smaller than national income by the amount of taxes. An increase in taxes will therefore reduce disposable income at all levels of national income. If disposable income falls at every level of national income, so will current consumption at all levels of national income. The entire consumption function shifts down if taxes are increased.

Conversely, if taxes are lowered, disposable income at all levels of national income will increase and the consumption function will shift up accordingly. It is easy to confuse this shift of the consumption function with a movement along the existing consumption function, since both involve disposable income. In Part A of Figure 9.6 a decrease in taxes will shift the consumption function from C to C′, because at every level of national income real disposable income will now be $50 billion greater. Thus when disposable income is $200 billion, consumption will increase from $200 billion to $250 billion. If real disposable income is instead $400 billion, consumption, after taxes are reduced, will increase from $350 billion to $400 billion. The increase in consumption is the result of a shift of the consumption function.

If, however, taxes remain unchanged and disposable income increases from $200 billion to $400 billion, because national income has increased, consumption measured along consumption function C will increase from $200 billion to $350 billion. The increase in consumption is the result of an increase in movement along consumption function C. Thus an increase in taxes will cause the consumption function to decrease or to shift down. Conversely, a decline in taxes will cause the consumption function to increase or to shift up.

PAST LEVELS OF INCOME   Households become used to a certain level of consumption. When incomes change, consumers will be slow to adjust their standard of living to the new level. If incomes increase or decline this year, it takes time to adjust to the altered circumstances. Thus when incomes suddenly increase, consumers will respond by increasing their level of consumption only gradually. The consumption function will shift up over time. Conversely, when incomes fall, consumers for a time will attempt to maintain consumption by reducing savings. Thus past levels of income will affect the level of current consumption. Perhaps this can be called the *inertia factor*.

There is another reason why consumption does not fluctuate as much as disposable income. If consumption expenditures fluctuated with income, consumers would have to constantly change their consumption plans. Consumers know that their income will fluctuate and will adjust their consumption to an estimate of expected long-term income based on past earnings. Consumers make consumption plans that will smooth out consumption expenditures over time and try to carry them out by allowing savings to fluctuate with temporary changes in income. When income is higher than expected, consumers will save more, and when income is lower than expected, they will save less. A decline in income today will not, therefore, affect consumption today by very much, but it will affect savings. If the drop in income continues over a period of time, consumers will come to recognize that their expected long-term income is now lower and will reduce consumption accordingly. Thus consumption expenditures adjust only slowly to permanent changes in income.

OTHER NONINCOME DETERMINANTS   There are several other nonincome determinants that when they change will cause the consumption function to shift. The most important of these are conditions in the credit markets, the age distribution of the population, the distribution of income, and the population's attitude toward thrift.

Conditions in the credit markets, in particular the rate of interest consumers must pay when they borrow or receive when they save, will affect the consumption function. When interest rates increase, the reward for saving more today also increases. If consumers save more today, they can have more goods in the future than they could have had before the increase in interest rates; thus the marginal propensity to save may increase. Countering this effect is the fact that when interest rates increase, consumers will have to save less to obtain a given level of retirement income. It is difficult to predict the effect an increase in interest rates will have on the marginal propensity to save. Whatever the response of consumers to a change in interest rates, it will affect the consumption function.

Changes in the age distribution of the population will also affect the consumption function. Young people who are beginning to form families will spend a higher portion of their income than will middle-aged persons, and retired persons will probably save the least of all. Thus changes in the age distribution of the population will cause the consumption function to shift in predictable ways. For example, immediately after World War II there was a wave of family formations, followed shortly by a baby boom. The consumption function shifted up as a result of the consumption expenditures of this group.

Changes in the distribution of income will also affect the consumption function. The higher your income, the greater the proportion of your income you will save. The rich have a higher marginal propensity to save than the poor. Changes in the distribution of income that favor the poor will cause the consumption function to shift up. Changes in the distribution of income that instead favor the rich will cause the consumption function to shift down.

The final nonincome determinant is the population's attitude toward thrift. It is often said that certain nationalities are more thrifty than others. The Japanese are currently believed to be more thrifty than Americans. To the extent that this is true, the consumption function will be lower in those countries that place a high value on thrift than it will be in countries with a more prodigal attitude.

These determinants are very important in influencing the level of consumption, but, conditions in the credit markets excepted, they generally change only slowly and therefore are not likely to cause significant short-run changes in the consumption function. This partially explains why the consumption/income relationship is so stable. But these factors can be important over time, especially when comparing consumption functions between nations.

We are interested in the consumption function because we are interested in how the equilibrium level of national income is determined. Consumption expenditures are vital to this determination, as you will discover below.

DETERMINING THE EQUILIBRIUM LEVEL OF NATIONAL INCOME

The equilibrium level of national income is determined where the aggregate expenditures schedule crosses the 45° line. Using the circular flow diagram, you discovered that in an economy without government and foreign trade the equilibrium level of real national income is determined by the amount of consumption plus the amount of investment. In the

FIGURE 9.7
Importance of Investment

Part A shows that investment is a much smaller portion of GNP than is consumption and is also much more variable. Part B shows that real investment as a percentage of GNP fluctuates a great deal.

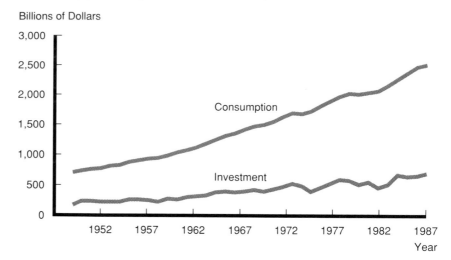

(A) Consumption and Investment Expenditures: 1949–1987

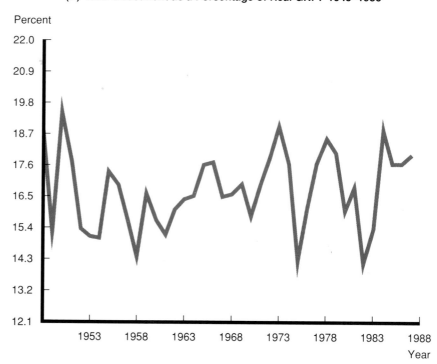

(B) Real Investment as a Percentage of Real GNP: 1948–1988

preceding section you learned that the heart of the aggregate expenditures schedule is the consumption function. In this section we shall extend our investigation into the aggregate expenditures function by briefly considering how investment decisions are made and how investment affects the equilibrium level of real national income.

Consumption and saving decisions are made by consumers. Consumption directly continues the flow of income within the main tunnel of the circular flow of national income, but savings are a leakage out of the system. Investment returns this leakage to the main tunnel of the circular flow of national income. The investment decision is therefore crucial to determining the amount of investment that will be added to consumption to determine aggregate expenditure.

After we have examined the investment decision, we shall explore how the equilibrium level of national income is affected in an economy without a government sector. Finally, we shall explore the reasons why the equilibrium level of real national income, once it is established, is stable.

THE INVESTMENT FUNCTION

The consumption function shows the level of consumption that would be desired at each level of disposable income. But consumption is not the only component of aggregate expenditures. Return to the circular flow diagram presented in Part A of Figure 9.2. The other determinant of aggregate expenditures is the amount of **investment**. The role that investment plays in the economy in the short run is to reintroduce into the flow of income the savings of households. In the long run investment provides the capital goods that allow economic growth to occur, but in the short run it helps to determine the level of real national income. Investment and savings decisions are typically made by different individuals. The savings of households are collected by financial intermediaries such as banks and in turn loaned to businesses seeking to make investments.

Economists employ the term *investment* in a more restricted sense than it is generally used.

> *Investment is the purchase of newly produced capital goods — machinery, equipment, and structures — plus changes in inventories, which are the stocks of finished goods, goods in process, and materials that firms keep on hand.*

Common usage of the term *investment* for purchases of used plants, equipment, and structures and for purely financial transactions such as the purchase of stocks and bonds is excluded from the economic definition.

Investment is a much smaller portion of aggregate expenditures than consumption, and it is much more variable. This can easily be seen in Figure 9.7, where investment and consumption expenditures over time are graphed in Part A, and investment as a percentage of real GNP is shown in Part B. In Part A it can readily be seen that investment is small relative to consumption and is more variable, and in Part B the extreme variability of investment can be clearly seen. The amount of investment, because it is so variable in relation to national income, is believed to account for much of the instability of the macroeconomic economy.

In order to include investment in the model, we shall postulate an investment function much as we did in dealing with consumption. The investment function reveals the amount of desired investment that the business community wishes to make at each level of national income. However, the investment function does not explain the high variability of investment as a percentage of national income.

The actual quantity of investment at any point in time responds to changes in expectations about the future, the expected profitability of investment, the real rate of interest that must be paid on loans, the extent of utilization of existing capital equipment, and tax provisions, besides the level of national output.

It is possible to construct an investment function that depends on the level of national income. It is reasonable to think that business firms will invest more when the level of real national income (Y_N) is high and will invest less when the level of real national income is low, as shown in Part A of Figure 9.8. The investment schedule is made up of two components:

FIGURE 9.8
The Investment Function

The investment function relates the quantity of real investment spending to the level of real national income. In Part A the investment function is composed of the level of autonomous investment ($50 billion), which is the amount of investment if real national income is zero, plus the increase in investment that is induced as real national income increases. In Part B investment expenditure is shown as a constant amount not dependent on the level of real national income. The investment function is entirely composed of the amount of autonomous investment. The effect of a shift in the investment function from I to I' illustrates the effect of an increase in autonomous investment from $50 billion to $100 billion.

(A) Investment Function

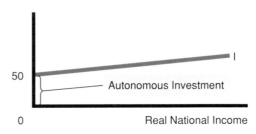

(B) Constant Investment Function

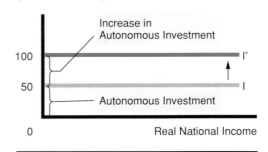

(1) **autonomous investment** equal to the amount of investment when real national income is zero, and (2) an element that depends on the level of national income.

> *Autonomous investment is the amount of desired investment expenditures that would occur if real national income were zero.*

Thus the investment function will slope upward in relation to real national income, as the consumption function does. It is possible, therefore, to make investment a function of the level of real national income and consider the other factors that influence the amount of investment as determinants of the amount of autonomous investment. When a determinant changes, it will affect the amount of autonomous investment and will cause the entire investment function to shift.

The information contained in Figure 9.7 demonstrated that real investment spending is much more variable than either consumption expenditures or real national income. This suggests that shifts in the investment function are very important in determining what happens in the macroeconomy. What are the determinants of investment, and how will the investment function shift when one of the determinants changes?

A business will invest more when it expects that the future will bring prosperity. It will also invest more the closer it is to operating at capacity, the lower the real interest rates are, and the lower taxes on invested capital are. These are the main determinants of investment. Conversely, firms will wish to invest less at every level of real national income when expectations about the future state of the economy are bleak, real interest rates are high, there is current excess production capacity, and taxes on capital are high.[3]

The macroeconomy is constantly in a state of change: Sometimes the economy is operating near capacity and at other times excess capacity exists, interest rates are in a constant state of flux, and expectations are continually being revised. When the investment function is considered in this way, it is clear that it shifts about a good deal because many of the determinants change frequently.

Because the investment function shifts about significantly, it will be helpful to make a restrictive assumption in order to explore the role that investment plays in aggregate expenditures. We shall, for now, assume that the investment function is a constant amount of real national income. That is, we shall assume that all investment is autonomous investment. This assumption makes the determination of the equilibrium level of real national income simpler to understand and focuses attention on the main characteristic of investment spending — its high variability relative to national income. A constant investment function is shown in Part B of Figure 9.8. Total investment at all levels of national income is equal to the amount of autonomous investment.

---

[3]The investment function can be written as:

$$I = I(Y_N, E, i, K, T)$$

where I is the quantity of investment and a function of the level of real income (Y_N), and where the determinants of investment are expectations (E), real interest rates (i), capacity utilization (K), and taxes (T). When real national income changes, so will the amount of investment spending as there is movement along the investment function. If one of the determinants of investment changes, so will the amount of autonomous investment and the entire investment function will shift up or down.

TABLE 9.3
Adding a Constant Amount of Investment to the Consumption Function to Determine the Aggregate Expenditures Schedule
(Billions of Dollars)

NATIONAL INCOME EQUALS DISPOSABLE INCOME (1)	DESIRED CONSUMPTION EXPENDITURES (2)	DESIRED SAVING (1) − (2) (3)	DESIRED INVESTMENT (4)	DESIRED AGGREGATE EXPENDITURES (2) + (4) (5)	UNINTENDED INVESTMENT (3) − (4) (6)
$ 0	$ 50	−$ 50	$50	$100	−$100
100	125	−25	50	175	−75
200	200	0	50	250	−50
300	275	25	50	325	−25
400	**350**	**50**	**50**	**400**	**0**
500	425	75	50	475	25
600	500	100	50	550	50
700	575	125	50	625	75
800	650	150	50	700	100

The constant amount of desired investment (I) now becomes the second private-sector component of aggregate expenditures that we have explored. Desired or planned aggregate expenditures (AE) equals the sum of desired consumption (C) and desired investment (I):

$$AE = C + I$$

Because the amount of investment is assumed to be the same at each level of national income, we can simply add the constant amount of investment to the consumption function to obtain the aggregate expenditures schedule. This has been done in Table 9.3 and is shown in graphic form in Figure 9.9.

DETERMINING EQUILIBRIUM NATIONAL INCOME IN THE PRIVATE SECTOR

The equilibrium level of national income is determined where the level of aggregate expenditures is equal to national income:

$$C + I = Y_N$$

In Table 9.3 the aggregate expenditures schedule is shown in column 5. It is obtained by adding together at every level of income the desired consumption expenditures, shown in column 2, with the desired amount of investment, shown in column 4. The equilibrium level of real national income occurs where the level of national income, found in column 1, is equal to the amount of desired aggregate expenditures, shown in column 5. This occurs at a level of national income of $400 billion, when consumption is $350 billion and investment $50 billion. Thus equilibrium in the income/expenditures model occurs at the point where the national income produced by the economy equals the level of desired aggregate expenditures.

Figure 9.9 shows how the equilibrium level of real national income can be graphically determined from the information in Table 9.3. In

FIGURE 9.9
Determining the Equilibrium Level of Real National Income in the Private Sector

In Part A equilibrium occurs at point E where the aggregate expenditures curve crosses the 45° line. When government is absent from the model, real national income equals disposable income. Equilibrium real national income in the graph is $400 billion. The equilibrium level of real national income can also be determined where total leakages (savings) equals total injections (investment). This occurs in Part B at point E, where savings equals investment. The equilibrium level of real national income is $400 billion, the same as in Part A.

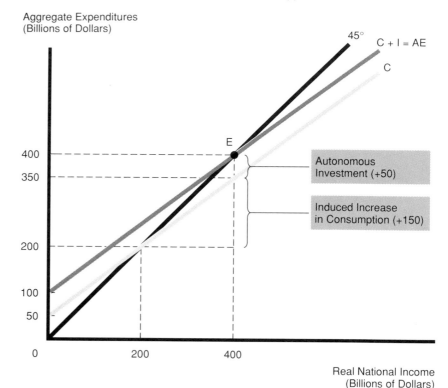

(A) Aggregate Expenditures Approach

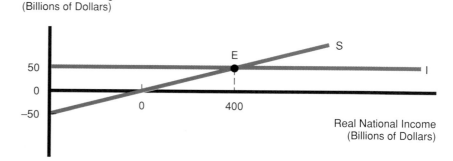

(B) Leakages/Injections Approach

Part A the vertical intercept of the aggregate expenditures schedule occurs at $100 billion. The intercept is determined by the amount of autonomous consumption represented by the constant term of the consumption function (the amount of desired consumption when income is zero, or $50 billion) plus the value of autonomous investment (the constant amount of desired investment, or $50 billion). The MPC, which is the slope of the consumption function (C), determines the slope of the aggregate expenditures schedule.

The equilibrium level of national income is determined where the aggregate expenditures curve crosses the 45° line. This occurs in Part A at point E and corresponds to a national income of $400 billion, the same result as obtained in Table 9.3. Note the effect of a $50 billion increase in autonomous consumption. Before investment was added to the model, consumption was $200 billion; after the addition of $50 billion in investment, consumption increased to $350 billion, an increase of $150 billion. The $50 billion in autonomous investment induced an increase of $150 billion in new consumption.

STABILITY OF THE EQUILIBRIUM   The equilibrium level of national income of $400 billion is stable. If national income were greater than $400 billion, there would be forces at work to reduce national income to the equilibrium level. If national income were less than the equilibrium level, similar but opposite forces would work to increase national income.

Suppose national income in Table 9.3 is initially $500 billion. In this case desired consumption will be $425 billion and desired investment $50 billion. Aggregate expenditures (C + I) will therefore be $475 billion, which is $25 billion less than national income. When national income is greater than aggregate expenditures, the economy is producing more than is being purchased. Inventories of unsold goods will build up. When the economy is producing $500 billion of real output, unintended inventories of $25 billion will be accumulated. Unintended investment is the difference between desired saving and desired investment at every level of real national income. Only at equilibrium is unintended investment zero. The amount of unintended investment is shown in column 6 of Table 9.3. Unintended investment can be either negative or positive.

A positive level of unintended investment signals business firms to reduce their output. The reduced output will in turn cause national income to decline toward the equilibrium level. This process will continue until the equilibrium level of national income ($400 billion in this case) is reached. When the economy is operating at the $400 billion level, total sales will just equal the value of total output and the amount of unintended investment will be zero.

Suppose, on the other hand, that the economy is initially operating at a level below the equilibrium level of real national income, such as $300 billion. In this case aggregate expenditures (column 5) will be greater than the value of real national income (column 1). When national income is less than aggregate expenditures, forces will be at work to increase national income to the equilibrium level. When national income is $300 billion, desired consumption is $275 billion and desired investment $50 billion. Aggregate expenditures total $325 billion, which exceeds the value of national income ($300 billion), so inventories decline by $25 billion below the level that businesses desire to hold. Unintended investment is −$25 billion. This provides the incentive for business firms to increase production, and as this happens national income increases toward the equilibrium level.

Only at the equilibrium level of national income are the forces causing national income to change at rest. At the equilibrium level of national income the combined output of business firms as reflected by real national income is just equal to the desired amounts of consumption and investment that make up aggregate expenditures.

AN ALTERNATIVE WAY TO FIND EQUILIBRIUM   You have seen above that the decisions to save and to invest are separate acts and are most likely taken by different people. Saving is done by households that consume less than their income and constitutes a withdrawal from the income stream. Investment decisions are made by businesses that invest in plants, equipment, and inventories and represent an injection into the income stream. What coordinates the two decisions? Unless there is some coordinating mechanism, there is no reason why the level of desired saving should equal the level of desired investment. Yet equilibrium can exist only if the amount of saving equals the amount of investment.

In the income/expenditure model national income will change to coordinate the independent saving and investment decisions. The level of national income will change to ensure that desired saving equals desired investment. Whenever desired saving exceeds desired investment, more is being taken out of the spending stream than is being put back and national income will tend to contract. When desired saving is less than desired investment, more is being injected into the spending stream than is being withdrawn and national income will increase. Thus equilibrium in the income/expenditure model will always occur at the level of national income that equates the desired level of saving (S) with the desired level of investment (I).

In Table 9.3 the equilibrium level of national income occurs at $400 billion, which is the level of national income at which desired saving at $50 billion equals the $50 billion of desired investment. The forces that bring about equilibrium can also be observed in this table. Suppose the level of national income (column 1) is initially $200 billion. Then desired consumption (column 2) is also $200 billion, and desired saving (column 3) is zero. Since desired investment (column 4) is equal to $50 billion, unintended investment (column 6) is −$50 billion. This is reflected in the decline in business inventories, which are being sold at a faster rate than they are being replaced by new production.

Business firms would adjust to this situation by increasing production, hiring more employees, and buying more raw materials, all of which cause national income to increase. As long as desired saving is less than desired investment, there will be an incentive in the form of negative unintended investment to increase output and as a consequence to raise national income toward the equilibrium level.

If national income were initially above the equilibrium level, the adjustment process would work in reverse. Suppose national income in Table 9.3 was initially $600 billion; in this case intended saving is $100 billion while intended investment is only $50 billion. While the economy is temporarily operating above the equilibrium level of national income, inventories will be accumulated at a rate that business never intended because the rate of production exceeds the rate of desired purchase. At $600 billion, for example, the economy is making an unintended investment of $50 billion, which is the amount that desired saving exceeds desired investment. Business will respond by cutting production, causing national income to decline toward the equilibrium level. As long as unintended investment (either positive or negative) exists, national income will adjust in the way necessary to eliminate it.

Part B of Figure 9.9 shows graphically the alternative way to determine the equilibrium level of real national income: the saving-equals-investment approach. Since saving represents a leakage out of the flow of income and investment represents an injection, equilibrium will occur when the two are equal. This occurs at a level of real national income of $400 billion, where the amount of desired investment ($50 billion) equals desired saving of $50 billion.

In the income/expenditure model there are two ways of determining the equilibrium level of national income: the first is to find where aggregate expenditures equals national income, and the second is to find the level of national income at which saving equals investment. Both methods give the same result.

Now that we have discovered how the private-sector equilibrium level of national income is determined, it is time to consider the role government plays.

DETERMINING EQUILIBRIUM NATIONAL INCOME WITH GOVERNMENT SPENDING AND TAXES ADDED

The role government plays in the macroeconomy can be seen by referring once again to the circular flow diagram. Part B of Figure 9.2 reveals how government affects the macroeconomy. Government is both a source of leakage out of the circular flow of national income and a source of injections into it. Government siphons income out of the system by levying taxes. When taxes exist, national income is no longer equal to disposable income, but is greater by the amount of tax receipts. Government also puts income back into the system by spending and through income transfers to households.

Calculating the equilibrium level of national income with the inclusion of government spending and taxes in the income/expenditure model can also be approached in two ways: by directly adding up aggregate expenditures or by following the leakage/injection method. In the aggregate expenditures approach government spending becomes the third component of aggregate expenditures. Aggregate expenditures now equals the sum of consumption expenditures (C), investment expenditures (I), and government expenditures (G):

$$AE = C + I + G$$

Consumption expenditures will be affected by the imposition of taxes. It is important to remember that consumption depends on disposable income. When taxes and transfers exist, there is a difference between national income and disposable income. We shall assume that transfers are zero but taxes are positive. In order to calculate the amount of consumption expenditures, it becomes necessary to subtract the amount of taxes from national income to obtain disposable income. Once that is done, the consumption function can be employed exactly as we did above. Because real disposable income now becomes less than real national income, the amount of consumption at every level of real national income will be correspondingly less. We shall also assume that the amount of taxes and the amount of government expenditures are constant and do not vary with real national income.

This adjustment has been made in Table 9.4. Column 1 contains real national income, column 2 shows the amount of taxes, assumed to be constant at $100 billion. Column 3 is obtained by subtracting from each row the $100 billion in column 2 from the amount in column 1 to obtain real disposable income. The marginal propensity to consume is used to calculate the amount of desired consumption for each level of real disposable income and thus provides the information found in column 4. Column 5 contains information on desired saving calculated by subtracting the amount of consumption expenditures (column 4) from disposable income (column 3). Column 6 presents the information about the levels of desired autonomous investment, and column 7 gives the amounts of autonomous government expenditures, assumed to be a constant $100 billion.

TABLE 9.4
Determining Equilibrium National Income with Government Expenditures and Taxes (Billions of Dollars)

REAL NATIONAL INCOME (1)	TAXES (2)	REAL DISPOSABLE INCOME (3)	DESIRED CONSUMPTION EXPENDITURES (4)	DESIRED SAVING (5)	INVESTMENT (6)	GOVERNMENT EXPENDITURES (7)
$ 100	$100	$ 0	$ 50	−$ 50	$50	$100
200	100	100	125	−25	50	100
300	100	200	200	0	50	100
400	100	300	275	25	50	100
500	100	400	**350**	50	**50**	**100**
600	100	500	425	75	50	100
700	100	600	500	100	50	100
800	100	700	575	125	50	100
900	100	800	650	150	50	100
1000	100	900	725	175	50	100

Equilibrium real national income can be determined by finding in Table 9.4 the level of national income that is equal to the sum of consumption (calculated from disposable income) plus investment plus government expenditures. This occurs at a level of $500 billion in the table, when consumption equals $350 billion, investment equals $50 billion, and government expenditures equal $100 billion. The aggregate expenditures schedule with government included is shown in Part A of Figure 9.10. Equilibrium occurs at point E, where real national income is $500 billion.

The leakage/injection method shown in Part B for determining the equilibrium level of national income provides an alternative approach that generates the same results. Since government spending represents an injection into the flow of income, the amount of government spending is added to the amount of investment, which is the other injection to form an investment-plus-government function (I + G). Since we have assumed that both investment and government are constant, the I + G function will be a horizontal line. Taxes represent a leakage out of the flow of income. So the amount of taxes is added to the amount of savings, which is the other leakage, to form the saving-plus-taxes function (S + T). The S + T schedule slopes upward because the savings function slopes upward.

Equilibrium occurs where the amount of leakages out of the flow of income just equals the amount of injections:

$$S + T = I + G$$

The assumed amount of investment-plus-government spending in Table 9.4 equals $150 billion. The sum of saving plus taxes equals this amount only at a level of real national income of $500 billion, where the S + T curve crosses the I + G schedule at point E. The equilibrium level of national income determined in this way will be $500 billion.

In summary, including government activities in the income/expenditure approach is straightforward. Government represents another source of leakage and injection into the flow of income. The only complication is that because consumption is a function of disposable income, an adjustment is necessary to take that fact into account when determining the equilibrium level of real national income.

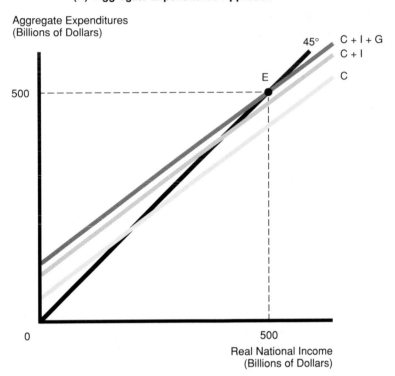

(A) Aggregate Expenditures Approach

Aggregate Expenditures
(Billions of Dollars)

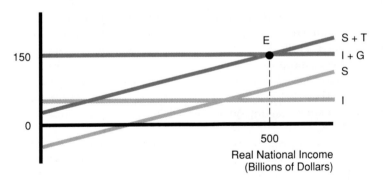

(B) Leakages/Injections Approach

Savings Plus Taxes and
Investment Plus Government

FIGURE 9.10
Equilibrium Real National Income with
Government Expenditures and Taxes Added

When government expenditures and taxes are added to the income/expenditure model, some adjustments are required. The presence of taxes (assumed to be $100 billion) drives a wedge between real national income and disposable income, on which the consumption function depends. The consumption function shifts down accordingly. Aggregate expenditures also shifts up by the amount of government expenditures (also assumed to be $100 billion). Equilibrium in Part A occurs where aggregate expenditures (C + I + G) equals real national income (point E). The equilibrium level of real national income is $500 billion. In Part B government represents both a new leakage (taxes) and a new injection (government expenditures). When $100 billion in taxes is added to the savings function, it becomes S + T, and when the $100 billion in government expenditures is added to the constant investment function, it becomes I + G. Equilibrium occurs where the quantity of leakages (S + T) equals the quantity of injections (I + G) at point E. The equilibrium level of real national income also occurs at $500 billion. In the graph and on the table savings equals investment and government expenditures equals taxes. This is a coincidence, for equilibrium requires only that total leakages equal total injections.

DETERMINING EQUILIBRIUM NATIONAL INCOME WITH THE FOREIGN-TRADE SECTOR ADDED

The final component of aggregate expenditures that represents both a leakage out of and an injection into the circular flow of income is the foreign-trade sector. Businesses in the United States sell goods to foreign buyers, exporting domestically produced products in return for income. Exports represent an injection into the circular flow of income. American consumers also buy goods produced in foreign countries that have been imported into this country. Since they are paid for out of consumer incomes, imports represent a leakage out of the circular flow of income.

How does the foreign-trade sector alter the income/expenditure approach to determining the equilibrium level of real national income? Since exports represent an injection and imports a leakage out of the circular flow, the equilibrium level of real national income will be affected by the amount of **net exports**.

Net exports is the value of exports minus the value of imports.

When the value of exports equals the value of imports, the foreign-trade sector is said to be in balance. Net exports can be positive: If the value of exports exceeds the value of imports, the balance of trade is said to be positive. Net exports can also be negative, in which case the balance of trade is negative.

One way to introduce the foreign-trade sector into the income/expenditure model is to add the amount of net exports to the aggregate expenditures function. The aggregate expenditures function discussed previously now becomes the domestic aggregate expenditures function, since it refers only to spending for domestically produced goods and services. The first step required to include foreign trade in the model is to construct both an export schedule and an import schedule as a function of real national income.

The value of exports does not depend on the level of domestic real national income. Instead, since foreign nationals are purchasing U.S. exports, it depends on the level of foreign national income and on foreign demands for U.S. exports. The U.S. export schedule will be constant with respect to U.S. national income and can be treated exactly as we treated investment spending and government expenditures.

Imports differ from exports in two crucial respects: Imports represent a leakage out of the circular flow of income, and imports depend on the level of real national income. Because part of consumer expenditures goes to buy imported goods, out of every additional dollar of real disposable income part will be spent for imports and will leak out of the circular flow of income. Suppose Americans spend ten cents of every additional dollar in real disposable income; in that case the **marginal propensity to import** (MPM) is 0.10. Thus for every increase of $100 billion in real disposable income, import spending will increase by $10 billion.

The marginal propensity to import (MPM) is the percentage of each additional dollar of real disposable income that is spent on imported goods and services.

Table 9.5 provides an illustration of how the net exports schedule is derived. Export earnings (X) are shown in column 3. Export earnings are constant relative to real national income and are assumed equal to a constant $50 billion in the table. Import spending, shown in column 4, is related to real disposable income by the marginal propensity to import. Import spending increases as real national income increases. Column 5 shows net exports, calculated by subtracting at each level of real national income the value of imports from the value of exports.

The effect of net exports on aggregate expenditures is found by adding the value of net exports to the level of domestic aggregate expenditures. This has been done in column 6. The effect of adding net exports to domestic aggregate expenditures is to increase aggregate expenditures when the balance of trade is positive and to decrease aggregate expenditures when the balance of trade is negative. Real national income is deter-

TABLE 9.5
Determining Equilibrium National Income with Foreign Trade Using the Aggregate Expenditures Approach (Billions of Dollars)

REAL NATIONAL INCOME (1)	DOMESTIC AGGREGATE EXPENDITURES (C + I + G) (TABLE 9.4) (2)	EXPORTS (X) (3)	IMPORTS (M) (4)	NET SPENDING (X − M) (3) − (4) (5)	AGGREGATE EXPENDITURES [C + I + G + (X − M)] (2) + (5) (6)
$ 100	$200	$50	$ 10	$40	$240
200	275	50	20	30	305
300	350	50	30	20	370
400	425	50	40	10	435
500	**500**	50	50	0	**500**
600	575	50	60	−10	565
700	650	50	70	−20	630
800	725	50	80	−30	695
900	800	50	90	−40	760
1,000	875	50	100	−50	825

mined where the level of aggregate expenditures with net exports added (column 6) equals real national income (column 1). This occurs at a level of $500 billion.

These results can also be obtained from graphical analysis. In Part A of Figure 9.11 net exports are added to domestic aggregate expenditures. Equilibrium occurs where aggregate expenditures [C + I + G + (X − M)] crosses the 45° line. Equilibrium in this illustration occurs at the same level of real national income as it occurred without the foreign-trade sector. This is because equilibrium occurs where foreign trade is in balance, since net exports are zero. This is a coincidence; it need not happen.[4]

Part B of Figure 9.11 shows how the foreign-trade sector affects the equilibrium level of real national income through the leakage/injection method. In this case exports are added to calculate the injection function, which becomes I + G + X. Imports are added to leakages so it becomes S + T + M. Imports increase as real national income rises by the amount of the marginal propensity to import, so the slope of the line representing total leakages changes to correspond with the new slope of the aggregate expenditures line. Equilibrium occurs where:

$$I + G + X = S + T + M$$

or at the level of $500 billion. Again, the fact that I = S, G = T, and X = M is pure coincidence. In equilibrium all that matters is that the sum of leakages equals the sum of injections.

RELATIONSHIP BETWEEN THE EQUILIBRIUM LEVEL OF AGGREGATE EXPENDITURES AND POTENTIAL REAL NATIONAL INCOME

We saw in an earlier chapter that potential real national income was the level of real GNP that the economy would produce if it fully employed all of its resources. It is possible to estimate the level of real national income

---

[4]The answer to Question 16 in the Key Questions at the end of the chapter shows that it is possible for the foreign-trade sector to affect the level of real national income.

FIGURE 9.11

Determining the Equilibrium Level of Real National Income with the Foreign-Trade Sector Added

The foreign-trade sector is included in the aggregate expenditures function by including net exports (X − M). Exports are assumed to be a constant amount since the quantity of exports does not depend on the level of domestic real national income. Imports, through the marginal propensity to import, do depend on the level of real national income. Net exports are first positive, then equal to zero, and then turn negative as real national income increases. In Part A when net exports are added to domestic aggregate expenditures (C + I + G), aggregate expenditures increase at the levels of real national income in which net exports are positive and decrease when net exports are negative. Equilibrium occurs where aggregate expenditures equals real national income at $500 billion. In Part B exports represent an injection and are added to the injection function to obtain I + G + X, and imports are added to the leakages function to obtain S + T + M. Note that the slope of the leakages function changes, because imports are related to real national income according to the marginal propensity to import, here assumed to be 0.10. Equilibrium occurs where total leakages equal total expenditures, which is at point E, where real national income is $500 billion.

(A) Aggregate Expenditures Approach

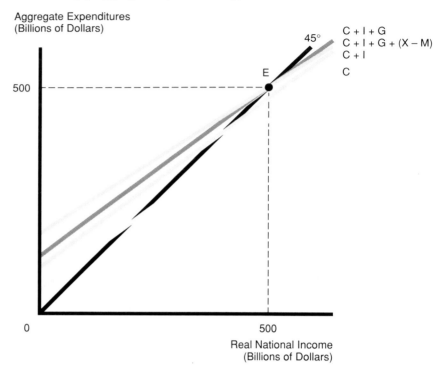

(B) Leakages/Injections Approach

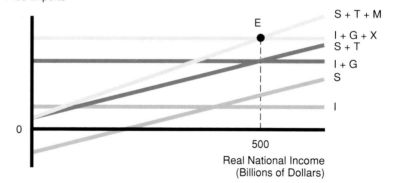

that corresponds to potential real national income and to indicate that amount, Y_P in Figure 9.12, as a vertical line from the horizontal axis on an aggregate expenditures graph. A vertical line suggests that the level of real potential national income does not depend on and will not change with the level of aggregate demand.

In Part A of Figure 9.12 the short-run equilibrium E occurs at the level of potential real national income (Y_P). The macroeconomy is in equilibrium at full employment. Sometimes the short-run equilibrium level of real national income (Y_N) occurs below the level of potential national income. This case is shown in Part B, where Y_N is less than Y_P. When this occurs, a recessionary gap equal to EA exists. A recessionary gap, some-

FIGURE 9.12

Full Employment, Recessionary Gap, and Inflationary Gap

Adding the level of potential real national income to the aggregate expenditures model allows a determination of the present state of the economy. Potential national income does not depend on the level of real national income so is shown as a vertical line (Y_P) at the level of real national income that corresponds to potential national income. In Part A when aggregate expenditures intersects the 45° line at the level of potential national income (point E), the economy is operating at full employment and is in both long-run and short-run equilibrium. There is nothing in the aggregate expenditures model that ensures that this will always be the case. It is possible, as shown in Part B, for short-run equilibrium to occur to the left (point E) of Y_P. When this happens, a recessionary gap equal to EA exists. It is also possible for short-run equilibrium to occur to the right of Y_P. This situation is shown in Part C. When this occurs, an inflationary gap equal to EA exists.

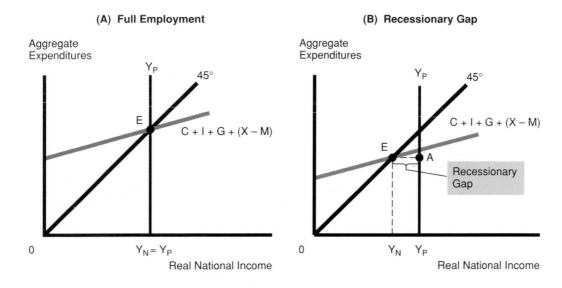

(A) Full Employment

(B) Recessionary Gap

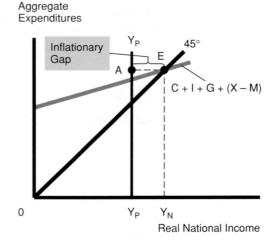

(C) Inflationary Gap

times called a deflationary gap, measures in dollars the extent to which real national income falls below potential national income.

A recessionary gap can exist if the level of aggregate expenditures intersects the 45° line to the left of potential national income. This implies that the price level is too high. You will recall that the price level is a shift parameter of the consumption function and hence of the aggregate expenditures function. If the price level falls, the consumption function will shift up; if the price level rises, the consumption function will shift down. If a **recessionary gap** exists, it can be inferred that the existing price level is too high.

> *A recessionary gap exists when the level of aggregate expenditures is too low and the price level too high to achieve equilibrium at the level of potential national income.*

It is also possible for the equilibrium level of real national income to exceed the level of potential national income. This case is shown in Part C of Figure 9.12. When this happens, an **inflationary gap** equal to EA exists. An inflationary gap exists when the level of aggregate expenditures intersects the 45° line at a level of real national income that exceeds the level of potential national income. This is equivalent to saying that the price level is too low to equate aggregate expenditures with potential national income.

> *An inflationary gap exists when the level of aggregate expenditures is too great and the price level too low to achieve equilibrium at the level of potential national income.*

Thus it is possible for the macroeconomy to establish a short-run equilibrium at either less or greater than the level of potential national income. Deflationary and inflationary gaps exist only in the short run. There is at work an automatic mechanism (see appendix) that will in the long run shift the aggregate expenditures schedule to the level of potential national income. This mechanism involves the adjustment of the price level to shift the aggregate expenditures curve to the level of potential national income.

Keynesian economists believe this adjustment occurs only slowly over time and that it takes longer for the automatic adjustment process to eliminate a recessionary gap than it does to eliminate an inflationary gap. Economists of other persuasions disagree. Probably the most important single issue dividing macroeconomists is the speed of the automatic adjustment process.

SUMMARY

1. The income/expenditure model, also known as the Keynesian model, was developed to explain how the macroeconomy could establish in the short run an equilibrium level of real national income that was below the level of potential national income. A basic assumption of the model is that wages and the price level are slow to adjust to a short-run equilibrium below the level of potential national income.

2. One of the important assumptions of the income/expenditure model is that the short-run aggregate supply schedule has a segment that is horizontal. This means that when the economy is operating within this range, any increase in aggregate demand will bring about a corresponding proportional increase in real national income without changing the price level. This assumption allows the use of a 45° line to indicate the possible equilibrium positions in the income/expenditure model.

3. The circular-flow-of-income diagram displays the relationship between real national income and its main components. This diagram shows that the level of real national income is determined either as the sum of aggregate expenditures or as the point where total leakages out of the circular flow are just equal to total injections into it.

4. Aggregate expenditures is the total of consumption expenditures, investment spending, government spending, and the balance of trade (exports minus imports). Each of these variables is assumed to be a function of real national income as well as of other factors that are considered to be determinants of the autonomous portion of expenditures. Consumption spending is the largest of these expenditures, followed by government, investment, and the balance of foreign trade in that order.

5. Consumption lies at the heart of the income/expenditure model. Consumption spending is assumed to be a function of real disposable income. A short-run consumption function that relates consumption spending to real disposable income is often constructed in the form of $C = A + bY_D$, where C is consumption, A is a constant term reflecting the level of autonomous consumption, b is the marginal propensity to consume out of disposable income, and Y_D is the level of disposable income.

6. There are only two things that a consumer can do with disposable income: spend income on consumption or save it. The marginal propensity to consume relates the proportion of an additional dollar in disposable income that will be consumed. The marginal propensity to save predicts the proportion of an additional dollar in disposable income that will be saved.

7. Consumption is the dependent variable in the consumption function and real disposable income is the independent variable. When real disposable income changes, the resulting change in consumption spending is shown as a movement along the consumption function. The level of consumption spending also depends on certain determinants. The determinants of the consumption function are wealth or past levels of income, expectations, the price level, and other things such as the age structure of the population and the population's attitude toward thrift. It is particularly important to recognize that the consumption function will shift when the price level changes.

8. Investment is a much smaller portion of aggregate expenditures than consumption but is much more variable. Investment is a function of real national income as well as of a number of determinants. The determinants are expectations, the real interest rate, capacity utilization, and taxes on capital.

9. The equilibrium level of real national income can be determined in one of two ways in the income/expenditure model: at the point where the level of aggregate expenditures equals national income, or at the point where total leakages out of the flow of income just equals total injections into it. In a private-sector model without government or foreign trade, equilibrium occurs where the amount of consumption plus the amount of investment equal real national income, or where the quantity of saving just equals the quantity of investment.

10. Including government in the model adds both a source of leakage in the form of taxes and a source of injection in the form of government expenditures equal to government spending plus transfers. When taxes exist, real national income exceeds real disposable income. This must be taken into account when calculating consumption spending as part of aggregate expenditures. Aggregate expenditures now become consumption plus investment plus government expenditures. The leakages out of the flow of income become savings plus taxes, and injections become investment plus government expenditures.

11. Equilibrium real national income can be determined as aggregate expenditures (consumption plus investment plus government expenditures) equal to real national income, or as leakages (savings plus taxes)

equal to injections (investment plus government expenditures). It is important to recognize that it is the sum of leakages and injections that must match at equilibrium. Nothing implies that when government is added investment must equal saving and government expenditures must equal tax receipts.

12. The foreign-trade sector can be included by adding the balance of trade as a component of aggregate expenditures. In this case aggregate expenditures is now equal to consumption plus investment plus government expenditures (which equals domestic aggregate expenditures) plus the balance of foreign trade (exports minus imports).

13. When equilibrium real national income is less than potential national income, a recessionary gap exists. When equilibrium real national income is greater than potential national income, an inflationary gap exists. Both are short-run occurrences.

14. When either a recessionary gap or an inflationary gap exists, there will be forces at work to restore the equilibrium to the level of potential national income by causing the price level to change. When a recessionary gap exists, there is insufficient aggregate expenditure to achieve full employment and the price level is too high to establish full employment. When an inflationary gap exists, there is too much aggregate expenditure and the price level is too low to achieve full employment.

PREVIEW 9.1 ANALYSIS

THE ECONOMIC SITUATION IN 1961 AND 1989

When the Kennedy administration took office in January 1961, the economy was suffering from unemployment and slow economic growth. Those were the symptoms, not the cause, of the economy's illness. Nearly three decades later when President Bush was inaugurated, the main worry was inflation. The economy during his predecessor's term in office had recovered from a serious bout of inflation that had lasted over a decade and a half. During the first months of Bush's presidency the price level was again rising rapidly. Was the economy about to relapse?

President Kennedy brought to the Council of Economic Advisors a group of distinguished economists who had previously been university professors. Their first task was to examine the current state of the economy. President Bush followed the Kennedy example and appointed university professors to be his economic advisors. They immediately undertook exactly the same task — an examination of the current health of the economy.

President Kennedy's economic advisors were Keynesians and employed the same income/expenditure model to analyze the economy that you have just mastered in this chapter. What the economic advisors found was not encouraging. They discovered an economy that was stagnating and a Congress that did not understand the tenets of modern macroeconomics. Kennedy's Council of Economic Advisors was determined to apply the insights of modern macroeconomics to the diagnosis and cure of the stagnating economy's problems.

The Council members believed they had three equally difficult tasks to accomplish. First, they had to analyze the economy and determine the proper corrective measures for the government to take. Second, they had to teach the president and his administration modern macroeconomics in order to obtain their support for these measures. President Kennedy him-

TABLE 9.6
Macroeconomic Variables Describing the State of the Economy:
1957–1960 and 1985–1988

VARIABLE	1957	1958	1959	1960
Rate of economic growth (percent change in GNP)	1.8%	−0.4%	6.0%	2.2%
Rate of inflation (percent change in CPI)	3.6	2.7	0.8	1.6
Unemployment rate (percent unemployed)	4.3	6.8	5.5	5.5
GNP gap (percent potential GNP)	1.6	7.1	4.6	6.3
VARIABLE	**1985**	**1986**	**1987**	**1988**
Rate of economic growth (percent change in GNP)	3.0%	2.9%	2.9%	2.7%
Rate of inflation (percent change in CPI)	3.6	1.9	3.7	4.3
Unemployment rate (percent unemployed)	7.1	6.9	6.1	5.4
GNP gap (percent potential GNP)	4.1	3.9	2.7	0.0

Source: *Economic Report of the President*, various years; *National Economic Trends, Federal Reserve Bank of St. Louis*, March 1989; *National Economic Trends, Federal Reserve Bank of Cleveland*, April 1989.

self was not a Keynesian when he took the oath of office, nor were most of the cabinet officers he appointed, especially the Secretary of the Treasury, who occupied a post vital to developing and implementing economic policy. Third, the economic advisors had to educate the Congress in order to win final approval for a policy change. It was an appropriate task for a group of academic economists to undertake. They succeeded so well that they were to affect permanently the process of macroeconomic policymaking.

Now that you have been introduced to how the equilibrium level of real national income is determined in the income/expenditure model, you can use this knowledge, much as President Kennedy's advisors did, to diagnose the state of the economy in 1961. The major macroeconomic variables that describe the state of the economy in the years immediately preceding the Kennedy administration are presented in Table 9.6. The picture painted in this table is of an economy that had suffered over the preceding several years through a recession from which it had not fully recovered.

The macroeconomy historically has averaged about 3 percent real growth annually over the last century. In only one of the four years described in the table was that average exceeded, and that was during 1959, the year immediately following the trough of the 1957–1958 recession. Typically, economic growth in the first year of a recovery is high. The next year saw a return to sluggish growth. The unemployment rate, reflecting the slow rate of economic growth, substantially exceeded what was then assumed to be the full-employment unemployment rate of 4 percent in each of the three years prior to the election of President Kennedy. Moreover the unemployment rate increased ominously during the first year of the Kennedy presidency. The rate of inflation is the only one of these measures of economic performance that did not trouble the economists of the day. The GNP gap, which is calculated as the level of potential national income (potential real GNP) minus actual national income

FIGURE 9.13
Diagnosing the Health of the Economy in
1961 and 1989

When President Kennedy assumed office in 1961, his
economic advisors discovered an economy with a recessionary gap. The situation they found is graphed in Part
A, which shows the recessionary gap. The level of aggregate expenditures is too low to attain full employment, or
the price level is too high to allow full employment to
exist. In Part B the economic situation existing when
President Bush took office in 1989 is shown. In this case
an inflationary gap, shown on the graph, was developing.
When an inflationary gap exists, either there is too large
an amount of aggregate expenditures to allow equilibrium
to occur at the level of potential national income, or the
price level is too low.

(A) 1961

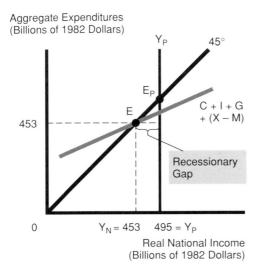

Aggregate Expenditures
(Billions of 1982 Dollars)

Real National Income
(Billions of 1982 Dollars)

(B) 1989

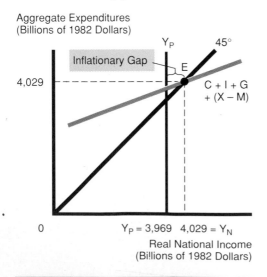

Aggregate Expenditures
(Billions of 1982 Dollars)

Real National Income
(Billions of 1982 Dollars)

(real GNP) divided by potential GNP to express the figure as a percentage, is shown as a fourth measure of economic performance. The gap had
reached 7 percent of potential GNP in 1958 and had remained high in the
succeeding years. In 1960 it was 6.3 percent and was actually increasing
during Kennedy's first year in office.

Part A of Figure 9.13 provides an explanation for the relationship
between actual and potential income for the year 1961. The vertical line
Y_P indicates the level of potential national income, which in 1961 was
$495 billion. As indicated by Y_A, the economy was producing $453 billion
of actual real national income, a gap of $42 billion, or 8.5 percent of
actual national income.

The economy was producing less than its potential because the level of
aggregate expenditures intersected the 45° line at E_A instead of E_P, which
was the level needed to enable the economy to operate at full employment.
The combination of consumption, investment, the amount of current government spending, and net exports was insufficient to employ all of the
resources available in the economy at the existing price level. The economy was operating at less than its potential, because there was an insufficient amount of aggregate expenditures and/or the price level was too
high. A recessionary gap thus existed.

President Bush's economists faced a different problem. Instead of a
sluggish economy, they discovered a vigorous one. The rate of economic
growth had over the preceding four years hovered near the historical
growth rate and as a consequence the unemployment rate had declined by
1988 to a level below most estimates of the natural rate of unemployment.
The GNP gap had disappeared as a result. One sign that the economy is
operating at a level above its potential is for the price level to rise. The
rate of inflation had been increasing over the preceding two years as the
recovery from the 1982–1983 recession continued.

During the first two months of the Bush presidency, however, the rate
of inflation suddenly jumped. The producer price index increased from
an annual rate of 4.1 percent for 1988 to 12.7 percent during the months
of January and February, and the consumer price index increased from
4.4 percent in 1988 to 6.2 percent. Inflation was back in the public spot-
light. Rising food and energy prices accounted for much of the increase in
the price indexes, but even when this influence was eliminated, both price
indexes still showed significant increases.

These signs suggested that the economy was operating at a level above
potential national income with an unemployment rate that was less than
the natural rate of unemployment. Such a situation is diagramed in Part
B of Figure 9.13. The unemployment rate in January 1989 was 5.4 percent, which is about a half of a percent below most estimates of the natural rate of unemployment. If this was the case, the actual level of real
GNP of $4,029 billion was roughly 1.5 percent greater than the level of
potential national income, which would have been $3,969 billion. The
economy was generating an inflationary gap. An inflationary gap exists
when the level of aggregate expenditures is too great and/or the price level
is too high. The problem facing the Bush administration was too high a
level of aggregate expenditures rather than too low as the Kennedy administration experienced.

Once a physician has diagnosed the patient's illness, the next questions are: How to affect a cure? Will the patient recover on his or her own,
or should treatment be undertaken? If so, what should be the course of
treatment: medication or hospitalization and surgery? Once the economists in the Kennedy administration had diagnosed the problem as an
insufficiency of aggregate demand, the questions were: What should be

done about it? Will the economy recover on its own? If so, how long will it take? Is a course of treatment advisable? If so, what are the options?

The Kennedy administration did not believe that the macroeconomy if left alone would quickly return to full employment. It hadn't happened in five years, according to the estimates of economic performance. Recent economic history argued against a quick recovery. Kennedy's economic advisors thought that the federal government should take action to effect a cure.

The Bush administration was much more inclined philosophically to allow the economy to heal itself than was the Kennedy administration. Self-healing involved a higher price level and a probable increase in the inflation rate. But President Bush was also loath to let this happen and took immediate steps to negotiate a cure with the Congress, with which he shares the responsibility for economic policy.

In both the Kennedy and Bush administrations, the recommended cure was designed to change the level of aggregate expenditures. The questions then became: How should this be done? Which elements of aggregate expenditures should be influenced? By how much? The answers to these questions will be taken up in Chapter 10, where we shall consider what causes a short-run equilibrium change.

THE GREAT DEPRESSION AND THE KEYNESIAN EXPLANATION

THE BANK OF UNITED STATES

The Great Depression began in 1929. It is now known that the downturn started near the middle of that year. Still, people then and now believed that it began with the crash of the stock market on Black Thursday, October 24, 1929. Industrial production declined slowly at first, and to contemporaries this did not appear to be out of the ordinary. Business observers predicted that 1930 would be a good year, not as good as 1929, which had been a terrific year, but about like 1928, which had been pretty good. It was not until the end of 1930, a year later, that reporters in the business press began to write about an unusual decline in business activity.

Real GNP, consumption expenditures, investment spending, government expenditures, and net exports in 1929 dollars for the years 1929–1933 are shown in Figure 9.14. You can readily see from this information that 1930 was not a typical recession year to be quickly followed by a recovery. Real GNP declined by nearly 9 percent in the first year, a sharp drop indeed. Once in motion, the decline did not stop but continued for four years until 1933. During this time the economy appeared to be in a free fall, with real GNP falling by more than 25 percent, from $104.4 billion to $74.2 billion in 1933. Something had happened to turn an expected normal economic downturn into a disaster.

What caused the Great Depression? In the introduction to Chapter 7, we identified the cause as a decline in aggregate demand. The spending hypothesis employs the income/expenditure model to explain the Great Depression. It focuses on aggregate expenditures and seeks to determine which of the components of aggregate expenditures could have changed autonomously by a sufficient amount to initiate the greatest economic decline in U.S. history.

FIGURE 9.14
Components of Aggregate Expenditures:
1929–1933 (1929 Dollars)

This figure illustrates the collapse of real GNP and how
this collapse was distributed among the components of
aggregate expenditures.

Source: Peter Temin, *Did Monetary Forces Cause
the Great Depression?* (New York: Norton, 1976), 4.

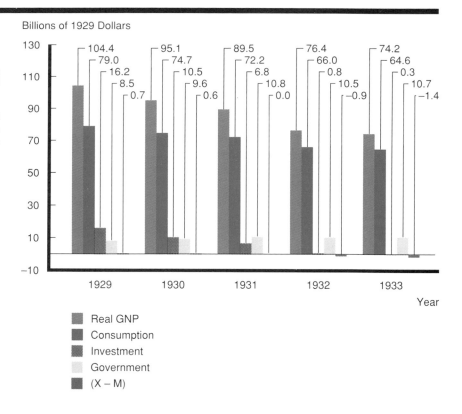

FIGURE 9.15
Diagnosing the Causes of the
Great Depression

According to the spending hypothesis, the cause of the
decline in real national income between 1929 and 1933
was a decline in the level of aggregate expenditures. The
aggregate expenditures function must have shifted down
from AE29 to AE33 and caused real national income to
fall from $104.4 billion to $74.2 billion.

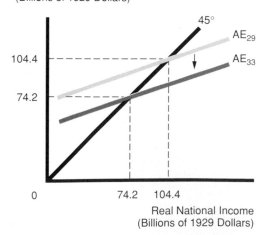

A decline in real national income, according to the spending hypothesis, is due to an autonomous decline in aggregate expenditures. Such a decline is graphed in Figure 9.15. The aggregate expenditures curve shifted down between 1929 and 1933, from AE29 to AE33, causing real national income, as a result, to fall from $104.4 billion to $74.2 billion.

This suggests that the causes of the Great Depression are to be found among the component of aggregate expenditures. The amount of aggregate expenditures is the sum of spending for consumption, investment, government, and the balance of foreign trade at every level of real national income. Figure 9.14 shows what happened to each of these variables during the free fall of real national income between 1929 and 1933. Each of the components of aggregate expenditures declined, with the sole exception of real government spending. Consumption declined relatively the least, falling by 29 percent, while investment fell to almost zero, and the contribution of the foreign-trade sector went from positive to negative.

Parts A and B of Figure 9.16 allow a visual comparison of the decline in the components of aggregate expenditures that took place between 1929 and 1933. In these graphs the foreign-trade sector is combined with government expenditures. You can easily read the amounts contributed by each component of aggregate expenditures from the graphs. Follow the vertical line down from the equilibrium position until it intersects the expenditure line for each component. In 1929 (Part A) when real national income was $104.4 billion, consumption was $79 billion, investment contributed another $16.2 billion, and government combined with the foreign-trade sector accounted for another $9.2 billion (government expenditures were $8.7 billion and net exports $.5 billion).

In 1933 (Part B) when real national income had fallen to $74.2 billion, consumption had declined to $64.6 billion, investment to only $300 million, while government expenditures combined with the foreign-trade sector had actually increased by a small amount to $9.3 billion (government expenditures had increased to $10.7 billion and net exports were a negative $1.4 billion).

Early proponents of the spending hypothesis naturally hit on the collapse of investment spending as the prime suspect. Investment spending is the most variable component of aggregate expenditures. Gross investment spending collapsed between 1929 and 1933. When depreciation charges are subtracted from gross investment of $300 million in 1933, net investment actually was negative. So bad were economic conditions that the economy was actually disinvesting. The decline in consumption was more modest in comparison. Government expenditures actually increased somewhat, and net exports played only a minor role, amounting to less than 1 percent of GNP.

You will recall from our chapter discussion that a change in value of the components of aggregate expenditures can arise from two sources: autonomous changes and induced changes. An autonomous change occurs when one of the determinants — consumption, investment, government spending, or net exports — changes. An autonomous change will then induce through its effect on national income a change in consumption expenditures as well as in any of the other variables of aggregate expenditures that are a function of real national income. So an autonomous decline in investment will induce a corresponding decline in consumption spending.

Suppose in Part B of Figure 9.16 that equilibrium national income in 1933 had been at the level of 1929. Follow the line from $104.4 billion up from the horizontal axis to the consumption function (C) and compare consumption spending at this level of income with consumption spending when real national income was at the 1933 level of $74.2 billion. Consumption spending will always be larger when real national income is greater. The greater consumption expenditures in 1929 relative to the 1933 level can be explained by the higher level of autonomous spending that existed in 1929.

Early versions of the spending hypothesis focused on an autonomous decline in investment to explain the decline in aggregate expenditures. An autonomous decline in investment can account for much of the decline in consumption spending that occurred between 1929 and 1933, but not all. According to Professor Peter Temin, a recent supporter of the spending hypothesis, the decline in investment spending early in the Great Depression cannot account for all of the decline in real national income. When he compared the decline in investment that occurred between 1929 and 1930 with the decline in investment that typically occurs during the first year of a recession, he discovered that investment declined less in 1930 than would have been expected.

The autonomous decline in investment provides only part of the explanation for why real national income declined as much as it did in 1930. Furthermore, an autonomous decline in investment cannot explain why a typical recession was converted into a depression. According to Professor Temin, the guilty party was the least likely suspect — consumption expenditures. Consumption, Temin observed, declined by more than would be expected during a typical recession and by more than can be explained by the decline in investment. He suggests that there occurred an autonomous decline in consumption spending during the early years of the 1930s. It was this autonomous decline in consumption that shifted the aggregate expenditures function down by more than usually happens during a typical recession. According to the spending hypothesis, an autonomous decline in consumption, not investment, is now the prime suspect for turning a normal recession into a depression.

FIGURE 9.16
Comparing Aggregate Expenditures:
1929 and 1933

Part A graphs the information contained in Figure 9.14 for the year 1929. Aggregate expenditures was equal to real national income when real national income was $104.4 billion. Part B shows the situation that had developed by 1933. The collapse of the investment function is evident from the graph, leading early exponents of the spending hypothesis to focus on investment as the cause of the Great Depression.

(A) 1929

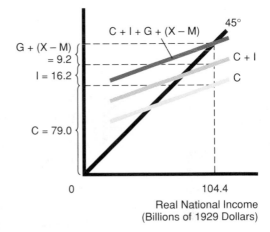

(B) 1933

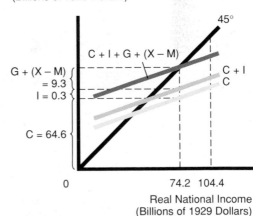

The initial decline in consumption, however, still remains unexplained. Perhaps contemporary observers who blamed it all on the stock market crash are at least partially correct. Two of the determinants of the consumption function are wealth and expectations. The decline in stock prices did not occur all at once. The crash was just the first fall in a long roller coaster ride the stock market took between 1929 and 1933. The continuous decline in stock prices just as continually reduced the wealth of households, which would have caused them to reduce consumption. The stock market is also widely held to be a barometer for future economic conditions. The prolonged decline in stock prices may have significantly reinforced negative expectations about the future, further depressing consumption spending as well as investment.[5]

—— ●

[5]Sources for this analysis: Peter Temin, *Did Monetary Sources Cause the Great Depression?* (New York: Norton, 1976); E. Cary Brown, "Fiscal Policy in the Thirties: A Reappraisal," *American Economic Review* (December 1956), 878.

REQUIRED ECONOMIC CONCEPTS

Aggregate expenditures
Consumption function
Marginal propensity to consume
Marginal propensity to save
Average propensity to consume
Autonomous consumption
Shift in the consumption function
Movement along the consumption
   function

Investment
Autonomous investment
Net exports
Marginal propensity to import
Recessionary gap
Inflationary gap

KEY QUESTIONS

1. What is Say's Law? How would Keynes phrase it?
2. Why can't there be a long-term recessionary or inflationary gap in classical theory?
3. Does Keynesian theory deny that desired saving can equal desired investment if there is a recessionary gap? Explain.
4. In Keynesian macroeconomic theory, what is the significance of the SRAS curve having a flat range?
5. What parameters are assumed to be fixed when the aggregate expenditures curve is drawn?
6. Is Keynesian theory primarily a demand-side theory or a supply-side theory? What determines the level of national income in Keynesian theory?
7. What does aggregate expenditures consist of without government in the model? With government?
8. When government is included in the model, what are the leakages out of the circular flow and injections into it?
9. What is the significance of the 45° line in the income/expenditure model?
10. What variable equilibrates saving and investment in classical theory? In Keynesian theory?

11. What is the expression for the marginal propensity to consume? For the average propensity to consume?

12. The marginal propensity to consume corresponds to what geometric property of the straight-line consumption function?

13. What variable primarily influences the amount of desired investment spending? What other variable plays an important role?

14. Which type of gap is believed to be removed more quickly — an inflationary or a recessionary (deflationary) gap? Why?

15. When government is included and macroequilibrium exists, does the leakage-equals-injection equilibrium also mean that planned or desired saving must equal planned investment?

16. According to economist Peter Temin, what was the major initiating factor in the Great Depression of the 1930s?

17. What is the spending-hypothesis explanation for the Great Depression?

PROBLEMS

1. According to the Keynesian theory of the consumption function, consumer spending increases as disposable income increases. Yet Keynes also proposed that as disposable income rises, the average propensity to consume falls. Is there an inconsistency here? Suppose the linear consumption line passes through the origin. Would the APC change as disposable income increases?

2. If the marginal propensity to save is equal to 1, would the consumption line coincide with the 45° line?

3. Would you expect the marginal propensity to consume (MPC) out of national income to be higher or lower than the MPC out of disposable income? Explain.

4. Consumption rises as disposable income rises. How then do you account for the following changes in consumption spending even though current disposable income is unchanged? In what direction are the changes?

    a. An appliance saleswoman says, "People have jobs but I've lost more than 50 sales because installment debt is now 8 percent of income compared with 5 percent a year ago."

    b. A distributor says, "I had a cancellation of 175 microwave ovens from one dealer alone. People are behaving with more caution and want a little extra in the savings account because of the way things are beginning to look."

    c. "Inflation is accelerating well into double digits. People are holding less cash and buying more things. Saving is down."

5. Given the consumption function $C_1 = 20 + 0.60Y_D$, what do 20 and 0.60 represent?

    a. Suppose C_1 changes to $C_2 = 11 + 0.75Y_D$. How does the graph of C_2 differ from the graph of C_1? What could cause this change?

    b. Assume C_2 changes to $C_3 = 11 + 0.90Y_D$. Draw a rough graph of C_2 and C_3. How does the graph of C_3 differ from the graph of C_2?

6. Investment spending increases as real income increases. How can investment spending increase if real income is decreasing and interest rates are also decreasing at the same time? Roughly graph this situation.

7. In the 1970s the Northeastern states declared the South was growing at their expense as hundreds of manufacturing firms left the North to resettle in the South. Northeastern politicians convinced the House Ways and Means Committee to extend the investment tax credit to the rehabilitation of older buildings. Why did the Northeastern politicians desire this extension? That is, how was the profit (or rate of return) on an investment affected by the extension?

8. There is an increase in government spending. What effect does this have on the aggregate expenditures curve AE? Does the price level change in the income/expenditure model?

What is the corresponding effect in the aggregate-demand/aggregate-supply model? Does it depend on the level at which actual Y_N is compared to Y_P?

9. What might be wrong with the notion that when saving equals investment in Keynesian theory, the economy must be in equilibrium at the level of potential real national income? What can you say about the saving-equals-investment relationship and its correspondence to the level of potential real national income in classical theory? What equilibrates saving to investment in the Keynesian theory? In classical theory?

10. In the accompanying figure, for which level of real national income is the system in equilibrium? Describe why equilibrium is where it is and not anywhere else by explaining the adjustments the system makes for each of two nonequilibrium levels of real national income.

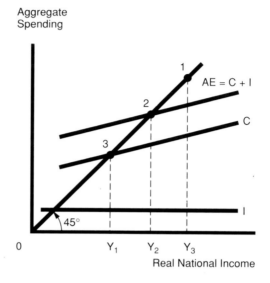

11. Does the level of investment depend on savings or does the level of savings depend on investment? Does your answer differ depending on whether you are in a classical or a Keynesian world? Explain in detail.

12. Fill in the blanks in the table below and answer the questions that follow. (I_P denotes planned or desired investment, and I_U denotes unplanned investment; figures are in billions of dollars.)

Y_N	C	S	I_P	I_U
$1,100	$1,025	— 75	$42.00	$33.00
1000 —	945	$55	38.50	16.50
900	865	—35	35.00	—0
800	—785	15	31.50	—16.50
700	705	—`5	28.00	−33.00
600	—625	−25	24.50	−49.50

a.   Calculate (1) the marginal propensity to consume and (2) the marginal propensity to save.

b.   What is the level of aggregate spending when national income is $1,100 billion? $800 billion?

c.   What is the equilibrium level of income?

d.   When income equals $1,000 billion, does a condition of underproduction or overproduction exist? Explain.

e.   Have inventories increased or decreased in the current period when income is $800 billion? Explain why income will either go up or go down in the next period.

f.   Roughly graph the problem in the income/expenditure model and in the aggregate-supply/aggregate-demand model, indicating the gap and a few basic numbers.

APPLICATION ANALYSIS

1. A Citibank study on U.S. family spending in 1973 yielded the following data:

INCOME (BEFORE TAXES)	SPENDING
$12,000–$14,999	$10,474
15,000–19,999	12,515
20,000–24,999	15,248

    a. Is the income listed in the table national income, personal income, disposable income, or none of these?

    b. What is happening to the average propensity to consume as income rises? Calculate it using $12,000, $15,000, and $20,000 as the base income for each income group.

2. The consumption-to-national income relationship (in billions of dollars) is $C = \$150 + .75Y_N$. Investment is a constant function of income and equals $10 billion.

    a. What does the $150 billion signify?

    b. Determine the equilibrium level of income.

    c. Suppose potential national income is $700 billion. Is there a gap? If so, what kind? What is the amount of the gap?

    d. At what level of income is consumption equal to income?

APPENDIX TO CHAPTER 9

LONG-RUN ADJUSTMENT IN BOTH THE AGGREGATE EXPENDITURES AND THE AGGREGATE-DEMAND/ AGGREGATE-SUPPLY MODELS

The aggregate expenditures model discussed in the chapter describes a short-run equilibrium and assumes that the price level does not change. How will the economy described by this model behave in the long run? This appendix provides the answer to this question. When the equilibrium level of aggregate expenditures occurs at the level of potential national income, the economy is also in long-run equilibrium. Nothing in the short run ensures that this will be so. Indeed, the Keynesian model was first developed to show that a recessionary gap was possible in the short run.

LONG-RUN ADJUSTMENT PROCESS IN THE INCOME/ EXPENDITURE MODEL

When a recessionary gap exists, too little output is produced to reach the potential level of national income. The result is excess unemployment. A recessionary gap exists because the price level is too high. In the long run the presence of unemployment and excess capacity will cause the price level to fall. When the price level changes, the aggregate expenditures curve will shift. A change in the price level represents a determinant of the consumption function and causes the entire consumption function to shift.

A fall in the price level will cause the consumption function to shift up, pushing up the aggregate expenditures schedule in the process. The price level will continue to fall and the aggregate expenditures curve will continue to rise as long as excess unemployment and excess capacity exist. This process will continue until the amount of aggregate expenditures equals the level of potential national income. In this way the price level adjusts to eliminate a recessionary gap.

The long-run adjustment process is illustrated in Figure 9A.1. Suppose the economy is initially operating with aggregate expenditures curve AE_1. Short-run equilibrium will occur at a level of real national income equal to Y_1, so a recessionary gap equal to EA on the graph will exist. Unemployment will exceed the natural rate, and business firms will have excess capacity. Wages and price will fall in the long run as firms seek to increase their sales and unemployed workers bargain for jobs. As the price level falls, the aggregate expenditures curve will shift up. This process will continue until the aggregate expenditures curve reaches AE_{Y_P}.

FIGURE 9A.1
Long-Run Adjustment in the Income/ Expenditure Model as the Price Level Changes

In the income/expenditure model, if the economy is experiencing either an inflationary gap or a recessionary gap, the price level will tend to change, falling in a recessionary gap and rising in an inflationary gap.

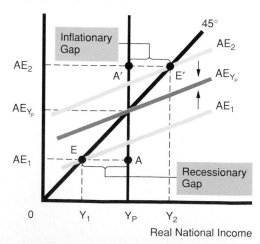

The recessionary gap is thus eventually eliminated in the long run by a falling price level and restoration of full employment.

Similarly, an inflationary gap signals that the price level is too low. Suppose in Figure 9A.1 that the economy is operating on aggregate expenditures curve AE_2. Unemployment will be less than the full-employment level, and business firms will be operating above capacity. When these conditions exist, the price level will tend to rise as firms seek price increases and workers seek raises. An increase in the price level will cause the consumption function to shift down, dragging down the aggregate expenditures function in the process. Inflation will eventually eliminate the inflationary gap as the aggregate expenditures curve shifts down to AE_{Y_P}.

How long does this take? The experience of the Great Depression suggests that it might take a long time, but economists are divided on this issue. Perhaps it is fair to say that many economists think that inflationary gaps are eliminated quicker by increases in prices and wages than recessionary gaps are eliminated by falling wages and prices. Nothing divides macroeconomists so much as the debate over the length of the long-run adjustment process.

The effect that price level changes have on aggregate expenditures also allows us to derive the aggregate demand curve of the aggregate-demand/aggregate-supply model.

RELATIONSHIP BETWEEN AGGREGATE EXPENDITURES AND AGGREGATE DEMAND

The aggregate expenditures schedule is directly related to the aggregate demand schedule. The aggregate expenditures schedule is constructed for a given price level. When the price level changes, so does the level of aggregate expenditures, because the price level is a determinant of the consumption function. Consider Figure 9A.2, where the aggregate expenditures function is shown in Part A and the related aggregate demand curve is derived in Part B. Where the aggregate expenditures function crosses the 45° line determines the equilibrium level of real national income.

When the price level is equal to 200, the aggregate expenditures function will be AE(PL = 200) and the equilibrium level of aggregate expenditure (point E_0 in Part A) will be \$300 billion. This corresponds to point E_0 on the aggregate demand schedule in Part B, where the quantity of real national income demanded when the price level is \$200 will be \$300 billion.

If the price level rises to 300, the aggregate expenditures function will shift down to AE(PL = 300) and the equilibrium level of real national income, occurring now at point E_1, will decrease to \$200 billion. The corresponding point on the aggregate demand curve will be E_1 in Part B. The quantity of real national income demanded at this point will also be \$200 billion when the price level is 300. If the price level instead falls to PL = 100, the equilibrium level of aggregate expenditures will increase to \$400 billion as the aggregate expenditures function shifts up to AE(PL = 100), and the quantity of real national income demanded will also increase to \$400 billion.

Thus there exists in theory a unique relationship between the aggregate expenditures schedule and the aggregate demand schedule. A downward-sloping aggregate demand schedule can be derived from the aggregate expenditures schedule by varying the price level.

FIGURE 9A.2
Relationship between Aggregate Expenditures and Aggregate Demand and the Price Level

The aggregate demand curve, which is a function of the price level, can be derived directly from the aggregate expenditures function by observing that a change in the price level will shift the aggregate expenditures function by shifting the consumption function. In Part A, when the price level is 200, the equilibrium level of real national income will be \$300 billion. This determines an equivalent point E_0 on the aggregate demand curve in Part B. Note that the vertical axis in Part B measures the price level, not the amount of aggregate expenditures. When the price level rises to 300 in Part A, the equilibrium level of real national income will be \$200 billion, which corresponds to point E_1 in Part B. Similarly, when the price level is \$100 billion in Part A, real national income will be equal to \$400 billion, which corresponds to point E_2 in Part B. By connecting points E_1, E_0, E_2 in Part B, a downward-sloping aggregate demand curve is constructed.

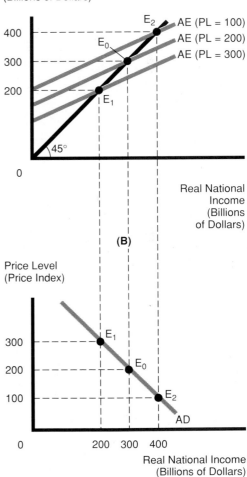

INFLATIONARY AND RECESSIONARY GAPS IN THE AGGREGATE-DEMAND/ AGGREGATE-SUPPLY MODEL RECONSIDERED

Inflationary and recessionary gaps can also be described using the aggregate-demand/aggregate-supply model. In Part A of Figure 9A.3 a macroeconomy in equilibrium at the level of potential national income is shown. The economy is in both long-run and short-run equilibrium.

Suppose short-run equilibrium occurs at a level of real national income Y_N that is less than potential national income. Such a case is shown in Part B of the figure. The level of real national income is established at E and is less than potential national income. A recessionary gap equal to EA exists. Given the level of aggregate demand, the price level is too high. Excess unemployment and excess capacity will exist. Such a situation describes a recession.

Since the price level is too high to achieve full employment, there will be forces at work to lower the price level. Firms faced with excess inventories will lower prices and some workers who are unemployed will be willing to accept lower money wages. As prices and wages fall, the short-run aggregate supply curve (SRAS) will shift to the right. This process will continue until equilibrium is established at F in Part B, where the equilibrium level of real national income is equal to potential national income and the economy is at full employment. The price level will have declined from PL_1 to PL_2, a level that will support full employment.

The same process will be at work when an inflationary gap exists. An inflationary gap is shown in Part C of Figure 9A.3. The level of aggregate demand relative to the SRAS schedule establishes equilibrium at E. Real national income exceeds the level of potential national income. The price level is too low to establish equilibrium at the level of potential national income. Business firms operating above capacity find that inventories are falling. They raise prices and attempt to increase output. Workers, sensing that prices are rising and that jobs are plentiful, demand higher wages. Thus prices and wages rise, causing the price level to rise. The SRAS curve shifts to the left as wages and costs increase. This process will continue to work until prices have increased sufficiently to increase short-run aggregate supply and shift the SRAS curve up until it reaches point F in Part C. Real national income will then be equal to potential national income and the inflationary gap will be eliminated.

Whether expressed in terms of the aggregate expenditures model or the aggregate-demand/aggregate-supply model, inflationary and recessionary gaps are short-run situations. There exist in both models forces that will in the long run return the macroeconomy to full employment. But the question remains: How long will this take? If the process takes weeks or even months, that is one thing. But if it takes years, that is a completely different matter. If the adjustment process takes place quickly, then maybe it is best to leave the macroeconomy alone. But if the adjustment process is a lengthy one, perhaps there is the potential for government to help by intervening to shorten the time involved in returning the economy to full employment.

(A) Long- and Short-Run Equilibrium

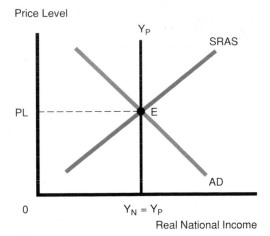

(B) Recessionary Gap

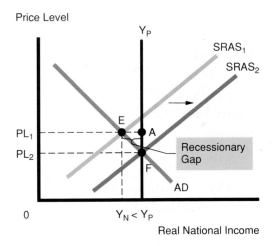

(C) Inflationary Gap

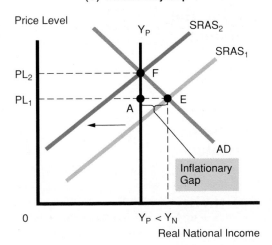

FIGURE 9A.3
Long-Run Adjustment in the Aggregate-Demand/Aggregate-Supply Model

Part A shows the macroeconomy in both short-run and long-run equilibrium, with equilibrium real national income equal to the level of potential national income (Y_P). In this case the price level allows full employment. This needn't always be the case in the short run. Suppose, as shown in Part B, that the SRAS curve SRAS$_1$ intersects the aggregate demand curve AD to the left of potential national income at point E, in which case a recessionary gap equal to EA exists. The price level (PL$_1$) is too high to allow full employment. In the long run, forces will be at work to shift the SRAS curve from SRAS$_1$ to SRAS$_2$. When the SRAS curve shifts to SRAS$_2$, the economy will have reattained long-run equilibrium at a lower price level (PL$_2$). It is also possible, as shown in Part C, for the economy to operate in the short run with an inflationary gap. In this case the existing price level (PL$_1$) is too low. Forces will be at work to shift the SRAS curve from SRAS$_1$ to SRAS$_2$. When this has occurred, the economy will again be in long-run equilibrium, but with a higher price level (PL$_2$ instead of PL$_1$).

10

AGGREGATE EXPENDITURES AND THE MULTIPLIER

IN THIS CHAPTER YOU WILL LEARN:

How an autonomous increase in aggregate expenditures will result in a multiplied expansion in real national income

How to determine the value of the expenditure multiplier

How to determine the value of the multiplier for the various government activities

How to determine the multiplier for an economy with foreign trade

The paradox of thrift

The modern theory of the consumption function

THE TAX CUTS OF 1964 AND 1981

The existence of a recessionary gap accurately describes the state of the U.S. economy in 1964 and in 1982. In both cases the federal government reduced taxes in the hope and belief that it would help to restore the economy to full employment. President Kennedy recommended a tax cut in 1963 to get the economy moving again. President Reagan convinced the Congress to pass the Economic Recovery Tax Act of 1981, which was in place when the economy fell into recession.

President Kennedy inherited an economy slowly recovering from a recession. He immediately formulated a tax reduction program designed to stimulate economic output. It began with tax cuts for business in 1961 and again in 1962. Both were designed to stimulate private business investment. The tax reduction program culminated with a large tax cut for both business and individuals, recommended in early 1963 and passed in 1964. The nation's real national income responded as Kennedy's economists had predicted, rising to the level of potential national income in 1966.

President Reagan in 1981 inherited an economy just beginning a halting recovery from recession. Despite the brief recession of 1980, inflation continued to be the major economic problem. He vigorously pursued a four-point program to ensure recovery. One of the major points of this program was the Economic Recovery Tax Act of 1981. This tax bill reduced both business and personal income taxes substantially over three years.

In 1982 the economy turned down, falling into deep recession. The Reagan administration already had in place a law to reduce taxes. Although the recession was not foreseen, an appropriate remedy was already in place. Tax rates fell by 5 percent in 1982, and by 10 percent more in each of the two succeeding years. The economy stimulated by tax reductions recovered rapidly, and real national income approached the level of potential national income by 1987.

Why do tax cuts stimulate economic output and by how much?

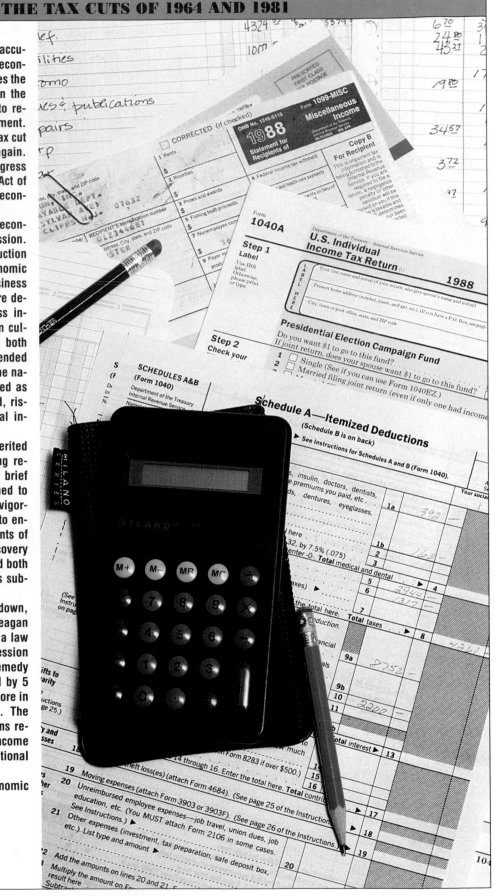

THE FAILED TAX CHANGES OF 1968 AND 1975

President Johnson succeeded President Kennedy following the Dallas assassination in November 1963. He was pledged to continue Kennedy's policies, and he led the successful fight to get Congress to pass the tax cut in 1964. President Johnson was himself elected president in 1964. Government expenditures increased rapidly during the early years of his administration, largely to finance both the Vietnam War and an expansion of social programs that the president proposed. The macroeconomic problems of 1966–1968 were the exact opposite of those of the early 1960s. The price level began to rise and inflation became a problem.

The success of tax cuts during the early 1960s suggested that the opposite was now in order. The problem was that aggregate expenditures were too high. After considerable delay President Johnson recommended that taxes be raised temporarily to lower consumption. Congress in 1968 enacted a 10 percent surcharge on personal income taxes. The results surprised both the Johnson administration and many economists. Aggregate expenditures were not significantly reduced, and inflation continued unabated.

Shortly after Gerald Ford inherited the presidency, the economy suffered a recession. In 1975, as the economy neared the bottom of the recession, President Ford recommended and Congress enacted a temporary tax reduction. Taxpayers were rebated part of the taxes paid in 1974 and had their tax bills reduced for 1975. The hope was that consumer spending would be stimulated. The result was disappointing, to say the least. The temporary tax reduction seemingly did not stimulate the economy as hoped.

What is the lesson to be learned from these failures? When do tax changes affect aggregate expenditures and when do they not?

IS THE NATION'S LOW SAVINGS RATE A CAUSE FOR CONCERN?

Many economists and policymakers have pointed to the nation's savings rate as a cause for concern. The nation's savings rates have been lower in recent years than over most of the post–World War II period. U.S. households currently save less out of their incomes than do households in other developed countries. Many observers find this development alarming, because lower savings could reduce the amounts available for investment, thereby threatening future levels of national income and labor productivity. Saving provides resources for capital formation, which in turn raises labor productivity and the standard of living. Less investment over a period of time may mean slower or even negative future growth in productivity. A permanently low savings rate could even mean a future decline in the standard of living in the United States.

A number of suggestions have been made to improve the savings rates. Both the 1981 and 1986 tax reform acts were designed in part to increase savings. Time alone will tell whether they have worked as intended. There are other policy options that were not part of the tax reform act that might be considered. But the federal government must proceed with caution. Any policy that suddenly increases the desire of households to save more out of current income carries with it the threat of recession. Consider this statement taken from a national business publication:

No one, of course, wants the savings rate to remain in the cellar. Last year's [1987] average of 3.8% was the lowest annual rate since 1947, and the savings rate has averaged below 5% since the start of 1985, compared with 6.6% in the first half of the decade and 8% in the 1970s. More saving and less consumer spending are needed if the economy is to . . . negotiate the tricky transition to an investment and export led expansion. But too rapid a return to the higher "normal" savings levels of the past could easily tip the economy into a recession.[1]

The crux of the matter is this: The nation's future prosperity requires a higher savings rate, but if this happens suddenly, the price may well be a recession. Why would a sudden increase in the nation's savings rate bring with it the threat of a recession?

[1]*Business Week*, March 14, 1988, 24.

• INTRODUCTION •

In the last chapter you learned how equilibrium real national income is determined according to the income/expenditure model. This is a necessary first step in modeling how the macroeconomy operates. The next step is to investigate what causes an equilibrium to change. Many of the interesting questions in macroeconomics are concerned with why an economy might move from one equilibrium to another. Understanding, for example, why and how the equilibrium level of real national income changes is necessary to an explanation of why an inflationary or recessionary gap can exist in the short run but not in the long run, or to the prediction and evaluation of the effects of government intervention or of a change in the behavior of consumers, business, or the foreign-trade sector on real national income. •

THE EXPENDITURE MULTIPLIER

From Chapter 9, if you studied it carefully, you already know that an autonomous increase in aggregate spending generated an even larger increase in the equilibrium level of real national income. This phenomenon is illustrated in Figure 10.1. You are already familiar with the components of aggregate expenditures. The components of aggregate expenditures (AE) are consumption (C), investment (I), government expenditures (G), and the balance of foreign trade (X − M). When aggregate expenditures [AE = C + I + G + (X − M)] increase from AE to AE′, the equilibrium moves from E_1 to E_2 and real national income increases from Y_N to Y_N'. The increase in aggregate expenditures from AE to AE′ results in a greater increase in real national income, which rises from Y_N to Y_N'.

The shift in aggregate expenditures from AE to AE′ represents an autonomous increase (an autonomous increase in one of the variables of aggregate expenditures increases aggregate expenditures at all levels of real national income). This shift results in a multiplied increase in real national income. The relationship between the magnified increase in real national income and the autonomous increase in aggregate expenditures is known as the **expenditure multiplier.**

> *The expenditure multiplier is the ratio of change in real national income to change in autonomous expenditures.*

You can easily obtain the value of the multiplier from Figure 10.1 by dividing the change in real national income by the autonomous change in aggregate expenditures:

$$\text{Multiplier} = \frac{\text{Change in real national income}}{\text{Change in autonomous expenditures}}$$

Anything that affects the slope of the aggregate expenditures line will change the value of the multiplier.

The value of the multiplier is extremely useful for predicting the resulting change in real national income when one of the components of aggregate expenditures changes.

FIGURE 10.1
Effect of an Increase in Aggregate Expenditures on Real National Income

An autonomous increase in aggregate expenditures will lead to an even greater increase in real national income. By comparing the amount of increase in aggregate expenditures with the amount of increase in real national income, we find that real national income increases by some multiple of the increase in aggregate expenditures. This relationship is the expenditure multiplier.

Aggregate Expenditures

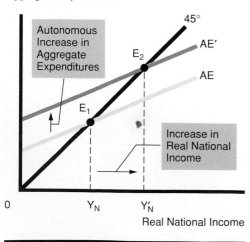

TABLE 10.1A
Determining National Income with Investment Equal to $50 Billion (Billions of Dollars)

REAL NATIONAL INCOME (1)	TAXES (2)	REAL DISPOSABLE INCOME (3)	DESIRED CONSUMPTION EXPENDITURES (4)	DESIRED SAVINGS (5)	INVESTMENT (6)	GOVERNMENT EXPENDITURES (7)
$ 100	$100	$ 0	$ 50	−$50	$50	$100
200	100	100	125	−25	50	100
300	100	200	200	0	50	100
400	100	300	275	25	50	100
500	**100**	**400**	**350**	**50**	**50**	**100**
600	100	500	425	75	50	100
700	100	600	500	100	50	100
800	100	700	575	125	50	100
900	100	800	650	150	50	100
1,000	100	900	725	175	50	100

TABLE 10.1B
Determining National Income with Investment Equal to $100 Billion (Billions of Dollars)

REAL NATIONAL INCOME (1)	TAXES (2)	REAL DISPOSABLE INCOME (3)	DESIRED CONSUMPTION EXPENDITURES (4)	DESIRED SAVINGS (5)	INVESTMENT (6)	GOVERNMENT EXPENDITURES (7)
$ 100	$100	$ 0	$ 50	−$50	$100	$100
200	100	100	125	−25	100	100
300	100	200	200	0	100	100
400	100	300	275	25	100	100
500	100	400	350	50	100	100
600	100	500	425	75	100	100
700	**100**	**600**	**500**	**100**	**100**	**100**
800	100	700	575	125	100	100
900	100	800	650	150	100	100
1,000	100	900	725	175	100	100

WHAT CAUSES THE EQUILIBRIUM LEVEL OF REAL NATIONAL INCOME TO CHANGE?

An autonomous increase in any one of these variables, the others held constant, will cause the level of aggregate expenditures to change. When aggregate expenditures change, the equilibrium level of real national income will change in the same direction by a multiplied amount.

This can readily be seen in Table 10.1A and Figure 10.2. In Table 10.1A equilibrium for a closed economy (one without foreign trade) occurs when aggregate expenditures equals real national income or when the total of consumption spending plus investment plus government spending equals real national income. Thus equilibrium exists when consumption spending is $350 billion, investment is $50 billion, and government spending is $100 billion, for a total of $500 billion.

The leakages-equal-injections method can be used to verify these results. The sum of the leakages at the equilibrium level of national income totals $150 billion (savings of $50 billion plus taxes of $100 billion), which is equal to the sum of the injections (investment of $50 billion plus government expenditures of $100 billion).

FIGURE 10.2
Effect of an Increase in Investment on
Equilibrium Real National Income

If investment increases autonomously from $50 billion to $100 billion, the aggregate expenditures curve will shift from AE (I = 50) to AE' (I = 100). Since a $200 billion increase in real national income resulted from the $50 billion autonomous increase, the value of the expenditure multiplier is 4. The same result is obtained by employing the leakages-equal-injections method. If investment increases by $50 billion, the injections function will shift from I + G (I = 50) to I' + G (I = 100). An increase of $50 billion in autonomous investment leads to an increase in real national income of $200 billion, so again the expenditure multiplier is 4.

(A) Aggregate Expenditures Approach

Aggregate Expenditures
(Billions of Dollars)

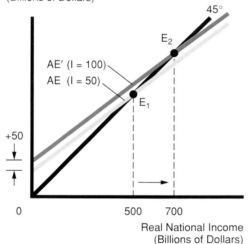

(B) Leakages/Injections Approach

Savings Plus Taxes and
Investment Plus Government
(Billions of Dollars)

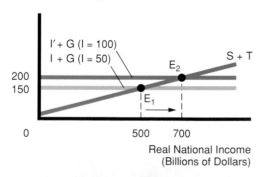

Now suppose that investment doubles, increasing to $100 billion. What happens to the equilibrium level of real national income? The answer can be found in Table 10.1B, which is identical to Table 10.1A except that investment is $100 billion instead of $50 billion. The equilibrium level of real national income has increased by more than the increase in investment spending. Equilibrium has increased to $700 billion, where real national income is equal to the total of aggregate expenditures (consumption is now $500 billion, investment $100 billion, and government spending $100 billion). An increase in investment has induced a multiplied increase in consumption expenditures. The leakages-equal-injections method yields the same results. Equilibrium occurs where the sum of savings plus taxes (the leakages) equals the sum of the increased amount of investment plus government (the injections).

These results can be read from Figure 10.2. The aggregate expenditures schedule AE (when investment is $50 billion) initially crosses the 45° line at a level of real income equal to $500 billion. Savings plus taxes is also equal to the sum of investment plus government at that level. When investment increases to $100 billion, the aggregate expenditures schedule shifts up to AE'. Equilibrium occurs at E_2 instead of E_1. The new equilibrium level of real national income increases to $700 billion.

The leakages-equal-injections approach shows the same results graphically. When investment increases, the I + G schedule shifts up by $50 billion (the amount by which investment increased) to I' + G. The equilibrium position moves from E_1 to E_2 in Part B of Figure 10.2, which corresponds to a level of real national income of $700 billion.

In each case an increase in investment of $50 billion creates an increase in the equilibrium level of real national income of $200 billion ($700 billion minus $500 billion). The multiplier relationship in this case between a change in aggregate expenditures and the resulting change in real national income is 4:

$$\text{Multiplier} = \frac{\text{Change in real national income}}{\text{Change in autonomous aggregate expenditures}} = \frac{\$200\ \text{billion}}{\$50\ \text{billion}} = 4$$

Although we used an autonomous change in investment to cause a change in aggregate expenditures, we could have used any of the components of aggregate expenditures. The multiplier works equally on any of the components. You can check this out for yourself. Suppose government spending increases by $50 billion and taxes do not change. What happens to the equilibrium level of real national income? It will increase by the multiplier (4 in this case) times the increase in government expenditures ($50 billion), or by $200 billion. The equilibrium level of real national income will increase from $700 billion to $900 billion.

This can be seen by employing the information contained in Table 10.1B. Increase government spending to $150 billion while changing nothing else. Find the level of real national income that is equal to aggregate expenditures. This occurs only at $900 billion, where consumption equals $650 billion, investment equals $100 billion, and government expenditures equals $150 billion. Add up the components of aggregate expenditures and you will find they total $900 billion, or precisely the amount of real national income. Or you could have used the leakages-equal-injections approach. Only when real national income in the table equals $900 billion will the sum of the leakages of $250 billion (savings of

$150 billion plus taxes of $100 billion) precisely equal the sum of the injections of $250 billion (investment of $100 billion plus government expenditures of $150 billion).

Moreover, the multiplier works in reverse. Suppose in Table 10.1B that government spending had declined by $50 billion (from $100 billion to $50 billion). What happens to the equilibrium level of real national income? It will fall by $200 billion (4 × (−$50 billion)). Check it out in the table. Reduce the level of government spending (column 7) by $50 billion and find the new equilibrium level of real national income. The new equilibrium level of real national income occurs at $500 billion, where consumption is $350 billion, investment $100 billion, and government spending $50 billion.

The multiplier can be calculated if you have the information contained in Table 10.1A or Table 10.1B by changing one of the components of aggregate expenditures by a known amount, finding the new equilibrium level of real national income, and dividing the change in national income by the change in aggregate expenditures.

The multiplier, once its value is known, makes it easy to calculate changes in real national income caused by changes in aggregate expenditures. Simply multiply the change in aggregate expenditures by the multiplier.

INCLUDING FOREIGN TRADE IN THE ANALYSIS

Changes in the balance of foreign trade affect the equilibrium level of real national income in exactly the same way as any other component of aggregate expenditures in the same direction as the change. An increase in the balance of trade (exports minus imports) will have a multiplied effect on increasing real national income. A decrease in the balance of trade will cause the equilibrium level of real national income to decline by a multiple amount of the decline.

THE MULTIPLIER RELATIONSHIP EXPLAINED

Why does an autonomous increase in one of the components of aggregate expenditures lead to a multiple increase in real national income? This occurs because one person's spending quickly becomes another person's income. Suppose that investment increases by $50 billion. How will this affect the flow of income in the economy? Table 10.2 tracks the flow of income. Initially, national income will increase by $50 billion. We shall call this the first-round effect because the impact of a $50 billion increase on national income does not stop here. Business firms that produce investment goods pay out the $50 billion to households as payments to the factors of production.

What will households do with this increased income? They will consume part of it and save the rest. How much they will consume is determined by the marginal propensity to consume, which we will continue to assume to be 0.75. Thus households will spend $37.5 billion out of the increase of $50 billion for consumption goods, and they will save $12.5 billion.

TABLE 10.2
How the Multiplier Works When Investment Increases by $50 Billion and the
Marginal Propensity to Consume is 0.75 (Billions of Dollars)

SPENDING ROUND (1)	INCREASE IN NATIONAL INCOME (2)	INDUCED INCREASE IN CONSUMPTION (MPC = 0.75) (3)	INDUCED INCREASE IN SAVINGS (MPS = 0.25) (4)
1	$50.00	$37.50	$12.50
2	37.50	28.10	9.40
3	28.10	21.10	7.00
4	21.10	15.80	5.30
5	15.80	11.90	3.90
6	11.90	8.90	3.00
7	8.90	6.70	2.20
8	6.70	5.00	1.70
9	5.00	3.75	1.25
10	3.75	2.80	.95
.	.	.	.
.	.	.	.
.	.	.	.
Final round	.	.	.
Total	$200.00	$150.00	$50.00

Business firms that sell consumption goods will thus receive, as Round 2 begins, payment for an extra $37.5 billion worth of goods and will raise output, increasing factor payments by this amount. Households thus receive an extra $37.5 billion in income in the form of increased factor payments, and they will spend 0.75 percent of this additional income ($28.1 billion) on more consumption goods while saving the remaining $9.4 billion.

Round 3 begins when business firms receive the $28.1 billion in consumption expenditures and increase output, paying an equal amount to households in factor payments. Households respond by consuming three-fourths ($21.1 billion) of the additional income and saving the remaining one-fourth ($7.0 billion). Thus Round 4 begins with businesses receiving $21.1 billion in additional consumption expenditures, which they pay out in turn to households that consume three-quarters and save one-quarter of the additional income.

The process continues with each subsequent round's increase in national income being smaller than the one preceding it. In the final round the increase in national income becomes very small, and the process can be assumed to have ended. What is the final result of an autonomous increase in investment of $50 billion? In the end you will find that national income has increased by $200 billion, consumption by $150 billion, and savings by $50 billion. The process ends when the entire amount of additional investment has induced an equal increase in the amount of savings. In order to do this, national income has to increase by $200 billion, or four times the amount of the addition to investment.

The multiplier process can be seen graphically in Figure 10.3. An increase of $50 billion in investment shifts the aggregate expenditures schedule up from AE to AE′. Initially, the economy was in equilibrium at $500 billion. Thus after the increase in investment, aggregate expenditures increases to $550 billion and inventories decline. Business firms

Aggregate Expenditures
(Billions of Dollars)

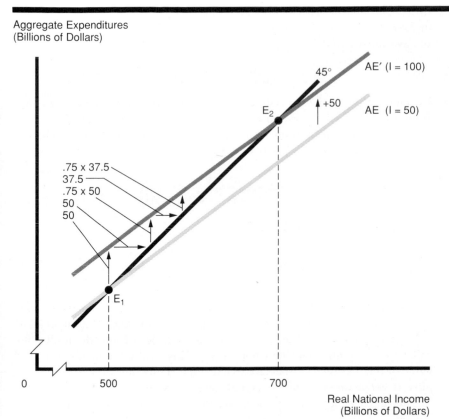

FIGURE 10.3
The Multiplier Process

An increase in autonomous investment of $50 billion, when the marginal propensity to consume is 0.75, will eventually lead to an increase in real national income of $200 billion through the multiplier process. This occurs because the initial injection spent for investment goods will induce an even greater increase in consumption expenditures. The initial injection of $50 billion is spent for investment goods. The producers of investment goods that receive this payment will, in turn, increase output by $50 billion and will pay out $50 billion to households that own the factors of production used to produce the investment goods. Households will spend 75 percent of this sum for consumption goods and save 25 percent. So consumption spending and production will increase by $37.5 billion. The producers of consumption goods that receive this payment pay it out to the owners of the factors of production used to produce the consumption goods. The owners of the factors of production will save 25 percent of the $37.5 billion and spend 75 percent of it on consumption goods. Thus the production of consumption goods and the income received by households will increase by $28.1 billion. This process will continue until at the limit $50 billion in new investment spending will have generated $200 billion in real national income, $50 billion in investment goods, and $150 billion in consumption expenditures.

respond to the decline in inventories by increasing output by $50 billion. This increases households' incomes by $50 billion, which increases their consumption by the marginal propensity to consume (0.75) times the increase in income. Thus consumption increases by $37.5 billion and savings by $12.5 billion.

Business firms receive an additional income of $37.5 billion, increase production to match, and pay out the $37.5 billion to households. Households in turn consume three-fourths of the increase in income and save one-fourth. And the process continues until a new equilibrium position is reached at $700 billion. As a result of a $50 billion increase in investment, national income has increased by $200 billion, or by a factor of 4.

The multiplier can be any positive value. Let us see how the value of the multiplier is determined.

HOW THE MULTIPLIER IS DETERMINED

The multiplier can be determined after the fact by dividing the increase in real national income by the increase in aggregate expenditures. But most of the time it would be helpful to know the value of the multiplier ahead of time.

It is possible to calculate the multiplier in advance of an increase in aggregate expenditures. In the explanation of the multiplier relationship above, the marginal propensity to consume and the marginal propensity to save played crucial roles. You will recall that since there are only two things that households can do with additional disposable income, consume or save, the marginal propensity to consume plus the marginal propensity to save must equal 1:

$$MPC + MPS = 1$$

In the example in the preceding section, the marginal propensity to consume was 0.75, so the marginal propensity to save must be 0.25.

This is the information we need to calculate the multiplier. The expenditure multiplier is always equal to:

$$Multiplier = \frac{1}{1 - MPC} = \frac{1}{MPS}$$

The multiplier can be calculated as:

$$Multiplier = \frac{1}{1 - 0.75} = \frac{1}{0.25} = 4$$

The value of the multiplier depends on the marginal propensity to consume and to save. If the marginal propensity to consume is 0.8, instead of 0.75, then the marginal propensity to save will be 0.2 and the multiplier will be 5. The multiplier can take any positive value, depending on the value of the marginal propensity to consume. Thus the value of the multiplier is determined by the marginal propensity to consume. The smaller the marginal propensity to consume, the smaller the multiplier will be, and vice versa.

If you know the value of the expenditure multiplier, you can easily calculate the resulting increase in real national income from a known change in autonomous aggregate expenditures:

Multiplier × Change in autonomous expenditures
                    = Change in real national income

The multiplier works for both increases and decreases in aggregate expenditures. If aggregate expenditures increase, then real national income will increase by the multiplied amount. If aggregate expenditures decrease, then real national income will decline by the multiplied amount.

The larger the value of the multiplier, the more a change in autonomous expenditures will affect the level of real national income. If the marginal propensity to consume is 0.5, then the multiplier will be 2. A $50 billion increase or decrease in aggregate expenditures will increase or decrease real national income by $100 billion. But if the marginal propensity to consume is 0.9, then the multiplier will be 10 and an increase or decrease in aggregate expenditures of $50 billion will increase or decrease real national income by $500 billion. When the multiplier is high, small autonomous changes in aggregate expenditures will result in larger swings in real national income than would occur if the multiplier were small. When the multiplier is high, the economy will be less stable than it would be if the multiplier were low.

In the above example we used an autonomous change in investment to describe the multiplier process. But we could have used autonomous changes in consumption as well. If an autonomous change in consumption expenditures occurs, the effect on the equilibrium level of real national income will be the same as if an equivalent change in investment has occurred.

THE MULTIPLIER WITH FOREIGN TRADE ADDED

In Chapter 9 you were introduced to the effect that including foreign trade has on the determination of real national income. The contribution of foreign trade was dependent on the level of net exports. Net exports were determined by subtracting the import function from a constant amount of exports. The marginal propensity to import (MPM), the amount out of each new dollar in disposable income that will be spent on imports, was crucial to finding the import function. You will recall that including net exports changed the slope of the aggregate expenditures function and that the slope of the aggregate expenditures function determines the value of the multiplier. The marginal propensity to import is therefore crucial to the determination of the foreign-trade or open-economy multiplier.

The expenditure multiplier value was dependent on the value of the marginal propensity to save, which indicates the proportion of each new dollar in disposable income that will leak out of the circular flow into savings. Imports are another source of leakage. Part of each additional dollar in disposable income will be spent on imported goods. This leakage is incorporated in the foreign-trade multiplier by including the marginal propensity to import.

The foreign-trade multiplier is calculated as:

$$\text{Foreign trade multiplier} = \frac{1}{\text{MPS} + \text{MPM}}$$

where MPS is the marginal propensity to save and MPM is the marginal propensity to import.

Suppose that the marginal propensity to consume is 0.75, so that the marginal propensity to save is 0.25. An additional dollar in disposable income will initially generate 75 cents in additional consumption and 25 cents in new savings. The expenditure multiplier will be 4. When foreign trade is introduced into the model, imports represent another source of leakage that is dependent on the level of real national income. Suppose that the marginal propensity to import is 0.1. Out of each new dollar in disposable income, besides the 25 cents that is saved, another 10 cents will be spent on imports. Thus the total leakage out of each new dollar in disposable income will be 35 cents and the multiplier will decline to 2.86:

$$\text{Foreign trade multiplier} = \frac{1}{.25 + .10} = 2.86$$

Because a fraction of increase in income leaks into imports in an open economy, the foreign-trade multiplier will be smaller than the expenditure multiplier for a closed economy.

GOVERNMENT ACTIVITY AND THE MULTIPLIER

Governments undertake three different kinds of fiscal actions: making payments for the purchases of goods and services, providing transfer payments, and receiving payments in the form of taxes. Government expenditures and transfers create injections into the circular flow of income, and taxes create a leakage. All three activities will have a multiplied effect on real national income, but the value of the multiplier differs in

TABLE 10.3A
Determining Real National Income with Government Expenditures Equal to $100 Billion and Taxes Equal to $100 Billion
(Billions of Dollars)

REAL NATIONAL INCOME (1)	TAXES (2)	REAL DISPOSABLE INCOME (3)	DESIRED CONSUMPTION EXPENDITURES (4)	DESIRED SAVINGS (5)	INVESTMENT (6)	GOVERNMENT EXPENDITURES (7)
$ 100	$100	$ 0	$ 50	−$50	$50	$100
200	100	100	125	−25	50	100
300	100	200	200	0	50	100
400	100	300	275	25	50	100
500	**100**	**400**	**350**	**50**	**50**	**100**
600	100	500	425	75	50	100
700	100	600	500	100	50	100
800	100	700	575	125	50	100
900	100	800	650	150	50	100
1,000	100	900	725	175	50	100

each case. The value of the multiplier for government expenditures is greater than the value of the multiplier for either taxes or transfers. Furthermore, the sign of the multiplier for expenditures and transfers is positive, while the multiplier for taxes is negative.

THE GOVERNMENT EXPENDITURES MULTIPLIER

Government spending on goods and services as a component of aggregate expenditures has the same effect on the equilibrium level of real national income that a change in investment or in the balance of foreign trade has. An increase or decrease in government expenditures will have a multiplied effect on real national income exactly as will an increase or decrease in any one of the other components of aggregate expenditures. When governments exist, there will always be government expenditures and there will be taxes, but the two do not always equal each other. Government can be added to the income/expenditure model by including the amount of government expenditures and the amount of taxes.

The effect of adding the government sector to the model is shown in Table 10.3A. Government expenditures are included (column 7) as a constant amount equal to $100 billion. The amount of government expenditures does not depend on the level of real national income but on the country's political process. Government expenditures represent an injection. Taxes are also assumed to be a constant amount equal to $100 billion (column 2) and represent a leakage.

Equilibrium occurs where aggregate expenditures (C + I + G) equals real national income. This occurs at a level of real national income of $500 billion, when consumption equals $350 billion, investment $50 billion, and government expenditures $100 billion. The leakages-equal-injections approach can also be employed. Total leakages (savings plus taxes) equal total injections (investment plus government) at the equilibrium level of real national income. This equality also occurs in the table at a level of real national income of $500 billion where leakages and injections both total $150 billion.

The effect of an increase in government expenditures can be seen by comparing Tables 10.3A and 10.3B. The two tables differ only by the

TABLE 10.3B
Determining National Income with Government Expenditures Equal to $150 Billion and Taxes Equal to $100 Billion
(Billions of Dollars)

REAL NATIONAL INCOME (1)	TAXES (2)	REAL DISPOSABLE INCOME (3)	DESIRED CONSUMPTION EXPENDITURES (4)	DESIRED SAVINGS (5)	INVESTMENT (6)	GOVERNMENT EXPENDITURES (7)
$ 100	$100	$ 0	$ 50	−$50	$50	$150
200	100	100	125	−25	50	150
300	100	200	200	0	50	150
400	100	300	275	25	50	150
500	100	400	350	50	50	150
600	100	500	425	75	50	150
700	**100**	**600**	**500**	**100**	**50**	**150**
800	100	700	575	125	50	150
900	100	800	650	150	50	150
1,000	100	900	725	175	50	150

amount of government expenditures, which is $50 billion greater in Table 10.3B than in Table 10.3A. Taxes remain the same at $100 billion. What effect will this $50 billion increase have on the equilibrium level of real national income? The answer can be easily found in Table 10.3B. Aggregate expenditures are now equal to real national income at $700 billion, when consumption equals $500 billion, investment $50 billion, and government expenditures $150 billion. Leakages now equal injections at $200 billion, which generates an equilibrium level of real national income at $700 billion.

The **government expenditure multiplier** can be derived from the above results.

> *The government expenditure multiplier is the multiplier obtained by dividing the increase in real national income by the increase in government expenditures.*

An increase in government expenditures of $50 billion generated an increase in real national income of $200 billion, implying a multiplier of 4. This is consistent with the expenditure multiplier derived directly from the consumption function. Since the marginal propensity to consume is 0.75, the marginal propensity to save is 0.25. According to the multiplier formula, the multiplier is thus 4.

$$\text{Expenditure multiplier} = \frac{1}{\text{MPS}} = \frac{1}{0.25} = 4$$

or

$$\text{Expenditure multiplier} = \frac{1}{1 - \text{MPC}} = \frac{1}{1 - 0.75} = \frac{1}{0.25} = 4$$

The multiplier for a change in government expenditures is exactly the same as the multiplier for an autonomous change in investment, consumption, or the balance of foreign trade.

If the government expenditure multiplier is the same as the private-sector multiplier, how about the multiplier associated with changes in taxes?

TABLE 10.3C
Determining National Income with Taxes Lowered by $100 Billion and Government Expenditures Held Constant at $100 Billion
(Billions of Dollars)

REAL NATIONAL INCOME (1)	TAXES (2)	REAL DISPOSABLE INCOME (3)	DESIRED CONSUMPTION EXPENDITURES $C = 50 + .75YD$ (4)	DESIRED SAVINGS (5)	INVESTMENT (6)	GOVERNMENT EXPENDITURES (7)
$ 0	$0	$ 0	$ 50	−$50	$50	$100
100	0	100	125	−25	50	100
200	0	200	200	0	50	100
300	0	300	275	25	50	100
400	0	400	350	50	50	100
500	0	500	425	75	50	100
600	0	600	500	100	50	100
700	0	700	575	125	50	100
800	**0**	**800**	**650**	**150**	**50**	**100**
900	0	900	725	175	50	100
1,000	0	1,000	800	200	50	100

THE TAXATION MULTIPLIER

Governments levy taxes to finance expenditures and transfers of income and to spread the costs of government in a known and agreed-upon way. Taxes represent a leakage from the circular flow of income. When taxes are raised, therefore, real national income will decline by some multiple of the change in taxes. Conversely, when taxes decline, real national income will increase again by some multiple of the change in taxes. The taxation multiplier carries a negative sign. When taxes are raised, real GNP will decline; when taxes are reduced, real GNP will increase.

What exact effect will an increase in taxes by itself have on the equilibrium level of real national income? The effect of decreasing taxes can be seen by comparing Table 10.3A with Table 10.3C. The marginal propensities to consume are the same as in the previous tables. Yet the tax multiplier will not be the same as the government expenditure multiplier.

In Table 10.3A the equilibrium level of real national income is $500 billion. Aggregate expenditures total $500 billion and injections equal leakages at this level of real national income. The only difference between the two tables is that taxes in Table 10.3C have been reduced to zero, so that disposable income becomes the same as real national income. When taxes are reduced by $100 billion, the equilibrium level of real national income increases by $300 billion, to $800 billion. Aggregate expenditures total $800 billion and leakages also equal injections at that level of real national income. Thus a decline in taxes of $100 billion leads to an increase in the equilibrium level of real national income of $300 billion. The **tax multiplier** is therefore −3.

> *The tax multiplier is the multiplier calculated by dividing the change in real national income by the change in taxes; it will have a negative sign.*

The multiplier for tax changes is therefore not the same as the multiplier for government expenditures. First, it operates in the opposite direction. A decrease in taxes increases, not reduces, real national income. The sign on the tax multiplier is negative. Because taxes represent a leakage out of the circular flow of income, national income will decline when taxes are increased and rise when taxes are reduced.

Second, the consumption spending at every level of national income will be affected by a change in taxes, which was not the case with a change in expenditures. The consumption function will therefore shift when taxes change. However, the consumption function, when taxes change, will not shift by the full amount of the change in taxes, but only by the amount that consumption itself changes. If taxes increase, by how much will the consumption function shift down? The answer is by the amount that consumption is reduced, which is equal to the marginal propensity to consume times the tax change.

Although this sounds complicated, it's not, but understanding how changes in taxes affect national income does require a two-step process:

1. Calculate by how much the consumption function will shift, which is equal to:

$$-\text{MPC} \times \text{Change in taxes}$$

This is the change in the consumption function.

2. Multiply the change in the consumption function calculated in Step 1 by the expenditure multiplier, which we know to be equal to the reciprocal of the marginal propensity to save:

$$\text{Change in the consumption function} \times \frac{1}{\text{MPS}}$$

We now have the resulting change in real national income from a change in taxes.

The value of the tax multiplier can be determined by combining the above two steps:

$$\text{Tax multiplier} = -\text{MPC} \times \frac{1}{\text{MPS}} = \frac{-\text{MPC}}{\text{MPS}} = \frac{-\text{MPC}}{1 - \text{MPC}}$$

We can now calculate the numerical value of the tax multiplier. Continuing with our use of a marginal propensity to consume of 0.75, the tax multiplier is equal to:

$$\text{Tax multiplier} = -0.75 \times \frac{1}{0.25} = -0.75 \times 4 = -3$$

The absolute value of the tax multiplier in this example turns out to be 1 less than the expenditure multiplier.

This finding holds generally. Whatever the expenditure multiplier is, the tax multiplier will be 1 less and will operate in the opposite direction. A reduction in taxes will increase real national income by less than an equal increase in expenditures, whereas an increase in taxes will reduce real national income by less than an equal reduction in expenditures. Thus autonomous changes in government expenditures will exert a more powerful stimulus on the equilibrium level of real national income than an equal but opposite change in taxes, because the expenditure multiplier is greater than the tax multiplier.

THE BALANCED-BUDGET MULTIPLIER

Suppose that government expenditures increase and that these expenditures are matched by an increase in taxes. What effect will these changes have on the equilibrium level of real national income? The result, which

TABLE 10.3D
Equilibrium Real National Income with Government Expenditures and Taxes Equal to $200 Billion (Billions of Dollars)

REAL NATIONAL INCOME (1)	TAXES (2)	REAL DISPOSABLE INCOME (3)	DESIRED CONSUMPTION EXPENDITURES (4)	DESIRED SAVINGS (5)	INVESTMENT (6)	GOVERNMENT EXPENDITURES (7)
$ 200	$200	$ 0	$ 50	−$50	$50	$200
300	200	100	125	−25	50	200
400	200	200	200	0	50	200
500	200	300	275	25	50	200
600	**200**	**400**	**350**	**50**	**50**	**200**
700	200	500	425	75	50	200
800	200	600	500	100	50	200
900	200	700	575	125	50	200
1,000	200	800	650	150	50	200
1,100	200	900	725	175	50	200

can be seen by comparing Table 10.3A with Table 10.3D, may be surprising. In Table 10.5A equilibrium real national income, when taxes and government expenditures are $100 billion, is $500 billion. This is true both where aggregate expenditures total $500 billion and where leakages of $150 billion equal injections of $150 billion.

Now suppose that both expenditures and taxes increase by $100 billion, as shown in Table 10.3D. Both expenditures and taxes now equal $200 billion. If we calculate the equilibrium level of real national income either via the aggregate-expenditures-equals-real-national-income method or by the leakages-equal-injections method, we find that equilibrium now occurs at $600 billion. Increasing expenditures and taxes by $100 billion has resulted in increasing the equilibrium level of real national income by an equal amount.

Why does an increase in expenditures matched by an increase in taxes result in an equal increase in the equilibrium level of real national income? The answer can be readily seen by combining the expenditure multiplier with the tax multiplier. The combination of the two is known as the **balanced-budget multiplier**.

> *The balanced-budget multiplier is the multiplier obtained by dividing the change in real national income by the amount that both government expenditures and taxes change.*

The reasoning behind this result is straightforward. The increase in real national income will be the sum of two opposite effects: The result of applying the expenditure multiplier to the increase in expenditures minus the effect in the opposite direction of the tax multiplier times the increase in taxes. Since the tax multiplier is 1 less than the expenditure multiplier and taxes increase by the amount of expenditures, the result is that real national income will increase by the same amount that taxes and expenditures increase. This can be seen by combining the formulas for the two multipliers:

$$\frac{1}{1 - \text{MPC}} - \frac{\text{MPC}}{1 - \text{MPC}} = \frac{1 - \text{MPC}}{1 - \text{MPC}} = 1$$

Thus if increased expenditures are matched by increases in taxes, national income will increase by the amount that expenditures and taxes increase. The same result will be obtained in the opposite direction if expenditures and taxes decline.

The multiplier effect of equal changes in expenditures and taxes is known as the balanced-budget multiplier. Equal increases or decreases in government expenditures and taxes will cause the equilibrium level of real national income to increase or decrease by the same amount that government expenditures and taxes change. The balanced-budget multiplier is always 1.

THE TRANSFER MULTIPLIER

Government influences the level of real national income by making expenditures for goods and services, by receiving taxes, and in one other way — by transferring income. Transfers are of increasing importance in our economy; over half of the current expenditures of the federal government are used to transfer income. Social security, aid to families with dependent children, and other welfare programs, as well as unemployment compensation, are examples of programs that transfer income.

What is the multiplier associated with transfers? Transfers are exactly the opposite of taxes. The multiplier associated with transfers therefore operates in the opposite direction from the tax multiplier. When we calculated the value of the tax multiplier in Step 1, we adjusted for the fact that taxes changed disposable income, which affected the consumption function by the marginal propensity to consume times the change in taxes. Thus an increase in taxes reduced consumption not by the full amount of the increase but by the proportion of the increase that was previously consumed. Then in Step 2 we multiplied the increase in actual consumption expenditures by the expenditure multiplier to obtain the resulting increase in real national income.

The effect of transfer payments on real national income is calculated in exactly the same way. The effect of an increase in transfer payments is to increase disposable income directly but to increase consumption by only the proportion of the increase that will be consumed. Thus Step 1 is to calculate the initial change in consumption spending by multiplying the increase in transfer payments by the marginal propensity to consume. Then in Step 2 we multiply the change in consumption by the expenditure multiplier to arrive at the resulting change in real national income.

The transfer multiplier is obtained by the following formula:

$$\text{Transfer multiplier} = \text{MPC} \times \frac{1}{\text{MPS}}$$

or, assuming the marginal propensity to consume is 0.75:

$$\text{Transfer multiplier} = 0.75 \times \frac{1}{0.25} = 0.75 \times 4 = 3$$

The absolute value of the transfer multiplier is always the same as the tax multiplier, but the two multipliers have opposite signs. If taxes rise, real national income will fall, but if transfer payments rise, real national income will increase.

THE MULTIPLIER WHEN AN INCREASE IN TRANSFERS IS BALANCED BY AN INCREASE IN TAXES When government spending takes the form of transfers rather than the purchase of goods and services, the balanced-budget multiplier no longer holds. Consider

TABLE 10.4A
Equilibrium Real National Income When Transfer Payments Are Zero (Billions of Dollars)

REAL NATIONAL INCOME (1)	TAXES (2)	TRANSFER PAYMENTS (3)	REAL DISPOSABLE INCOME (4)	DESIRED CONSUMPTION INCOME (5)	DESIRED SAVINGS EXPENDITURES (6)	INVESTMENT (7)	GOVERNMENT EXPENDITURES (8)
$ 100	$100	$0	$ 0	$ 50	−$50	$50	$100
200	100	0	100	125	−25	50	100
300	100	0	200	200	0	50	100
400	100	0	300	275	25	50	100
500	**100**	**0**	**400**	**350**	**50**	**50**	**100**
600	100	0	500	425	75	50	100
700	100	0	600	500	100	50	100
800	100	0	700	575	125	50	100
900	100	0	800	650	150	50	100
1,000	100	0	900	725	175	50	100

Table 10.4A. The equilibrium level of real national income is $500 billion when transfer payments are zero. Now suppose that transfer payments increase by $100 billion and are matched by increases in taxes of $100 billion, as shown in Table 10.4B. What will be the new equilibrium level of real national income?

We find that the equilibrium level of real national income does not change. The reason can be found in column 4 of the table. Real disposable income does not change when taxes increase by the same amount as the increase in transfer payments. Because the increase in transfers is balanced by an increase in taxes, disposable income does not change and consumption expenditures are therefore unaffected by the change.

A comparison of the two multipliers explains these results. The transfer multiplier, we saw above, is exactly the same as the tax multiplier except that the sign is different. The transfer multiplier is positive and the tax multiplier is negative. The result is that the multiplied increase in transfers is exactly canceled by the multiplied increase in taxes. The combined multiplier for an increase in transfers balanced by an increase in taxes is zero. Thus when a change in government transfer payments is matched by a corresponding change in tax payments, the multiplier will be zero.

It is important to remember that we have assumed that the marginal propensity to consume is 0.75 for taxpayers and for recipients of government expenditures and of transfers. If the MPC varies between groups, our conclusion about the balanced-transfer multiplier would be altered.

SUMMARY: THE GOVERNMENT ACTIVITY MULTIPLIERS

Government plays an important role in the economy. There are three fiscal activities of government that directly affect the level of real national income: government expenditures, transfers, and taxes. When the level of any of these activities changes, there will be a multiplied effect on the equilibrium level of real national income. But the multipliers associated with these three activities are different.

The government expenditure multiplier is the same as the aggregate expenditure multiplier. The formula for calculating the government expenditure multiplier is:

TABLE 10.4B
Equilibrium Real National Income When Both Transfers and Taxes Increase by $100 Billion (Billions of Dollars)

REAL NATIONAL INCOME (1)	TAXES (2)	TRANSFER PAYMENTS (3)	REAL DISPOSABLE INCOME (4)	DESIRED CONSUMPTION INCOME (5)	DESIRED SAVINGS EXPENDITURES (6)	INVESTMENT (7)	GOVERNMENT EXPENDITURES (8)
$ 100	$200	$100	$ 0	$ 50	−$50	$50	$100
200	200	100	100	125	−25	50	100
300	200	100	200	200	0	50	100
400	200	100	300	275	25	50	100
500	**200**	**100**	**400**	**350**	**50**	**50**	**100**
600	200	100	500	425	75	50	100
700	200	100	600	500	100	50	100
800	200	100	700	575	125	50	100
900	200	100	800	650	150	50	100
1,000	200	100	900	725	175	50	100

$$\text{Government expenditure multiplier} = \frac{1}{\text{MPS}} = \frac{1}{1 - \text{MPC}}$$

The government expenditure multiplier is thus the same as the private-sector multiplier.

This is not the case for the taxation multiplier. The taxation multiplier operates in the opposite direction from the government expenditure multiplier, and the numerical value is 1 less. The formula for the taxation multiplier is:

$$\text{Taxation multiplier} = \frac{-\text{MPC}}{1 - \text{MPC}}$$

The transfer multiplier is the same as the taxation multiplier, but has the opposite sign. The formula for the transfer multiplier is:

$$\text{Transfer multiplier} = \frac{\text{MPC}}{1 - \text{MPC}}$$

The balanced-budget multiplier applies when a change in government expenditures is exactly balanced by a change in tax payments. The value of the balanced-budget multiplier is always 1. However, when a change in transfer payments is exactly balanced by a change in taxes, the multiplier is zero.

IMPLICATIONS OF THE EXPENDITURE MULTIPLIER

EMPIRICAL ESTIMATES OF THE VALUE OF THE EXPENDITURE MULTIPLIER

The real-world value of the expenditure multiplier is likely to be considerably lower than the expenditure multipliers we have calculated in this chapter due to the probable existence of leakages out of the circular flow diagram other than savings and imports, the length of time considered,

FIGURE 10.4
The Multiplier and Aggregate Demand

In Part A a $50 billion autonomous increase in one of the components of aggregate expenditures, say investment spending, occurs, causing an upward shift in the aggregate expenditures function from AE (PL = 150) to AE′ (PL = 150). The equilibrium level of real national income increases by $200 billion, from $500 billion to $700 billion. Remember that the aggregate expenditures function is determined holding the price level constant, in this case at 150. How will the aggregate demand curve react to the same $50 billion autonomous increase in investment spending? The aggregate demand curve in Part B will shift to the right by $200 billion. When the price level is 150, the quantity of aggregate output demanded will increase from $500 billion to $700 billion — the full multiplied amount of the increase in real national income. The same changes that cause aggregate expenditures to shift will cause aggregate demand to shift. The advantage of employing the aggregate expenditures function is that the amount of the shift ($200 billion) is directly read from the graph in Part A.

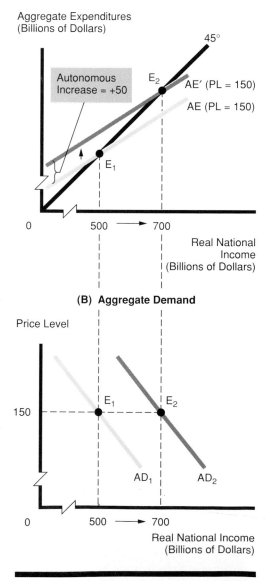

(A) Aggregate Expenditures

(B) Aggregate Demand

price level changes, and a phenomenon known as "crowding out." These effects will be considered later. It is difficult in practice to isolate multiplier effects, because in the real world other factors that also affect the level of real national income are always occurring at the same time.

One way to obtain a sense of the size of the expenditure model is to examine the multipliers generated by econometric models of the U.S. economy. Econometric models are mathematically specified economic models that are estimated statistically with the aid of computers. These models often consist of hundreds of equations that were estimated from past historical data. None of these models can predict the future exactly, but many have done a credible job and continue to be used by businesses and governments. It is possible, when using an econometric model, to change only one variable and observe the results.

The differences between the various models inevitably lead to differences in estimates of the value of the expenditure multiplier. The range of estimates for two years after the change in aggregate expenditures lies between zero (no multiplier effect) and 2.7, with most estimates falling within a range of from 1.4 to 2.2. Many economists believe that the numerical value of the expenditure multiplier is in the neighborhood of 2.0.

This does not mean that the value of the tax multiplier is exactly 1 less, as was found in our earlier theoretical discussion. As in the case of the expenditure multiplier, there are other leakages that we have not considered. Nevertheless, econometric estimates of the value of the tax multiplier are, as we would expect, generally lower. The range of empirical estimates of the value of the tax multiplier run from −1.1 to −2.1, with a majority of the estimates ranging between −1.4 and −1.6. Changes in taxes are not as potent as changes in government expenditures in affecting aggregate expenditures.

The values of the various multipliers suggested by econometric models probably provide as good a guide to the real-world values as we can obtain. But these estimates are based on the past performance of the economy and may therefore not be an accurate guide to the future.

AGGREGATE DEMAND AND THE MULTIPLIER

How does the multiplier affect aggregate demand? You now know that an autonomous increase in aggregate expenditures shifts the aggregate expenditures schedule up and has a multiplied effect on real national income. The determinants of aggregate expenditures (consumption, investment, government expenditures, and the balance of foreign trade) are the same as the determinants of the aggregate demand curve. When one of the components of aggregate expenditures autonomously changes, it will be reflected as a shift in the aggregate demand curve. When the aggregate expenditures function shifts, so will the aggregate demand curve.

How far will the aggregate demand curve shift to the right? Suppose that aggregate expenditures increase by $50 billion and the multiplier is 4. In this case the equilibrium level of real national income will increase by $200 billion, growing from $500 billion in Part A of Figure 10.4 to $700 billion. Remember that aggregate expenditures are calculated for a given price level. When the price level is 150, the aggregate demand curve will at this price level also shift to the right by the same amount that real national income has increased. In Part B the quantity of real national income demanded at a price level of 150 will increase from $500 billion to $700 billion, and the aggregate demand curve will shift to the right accordingly, from AD_1 to AD_2.

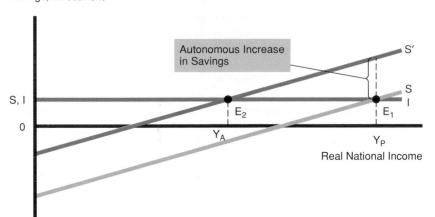

(A) Investment Constant

Savings, Investment

Autonomous Increase in Savings

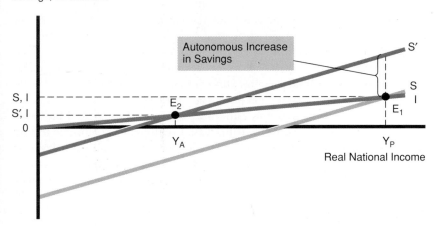

(B) Investment as a Function of Real National Income

Savings, Investment

Autonomous Increase in Savings

FIGURE 10.5
The Paradox of Thrift

The paradox of thrift in the income/expenditure model is that an increased desire to save, represented by an autonomous increase in savings, will not result in more savings and may result in less. In Part A, when people become more thrifty at every level of real national income, the savings function shifts to S'. When real national income is Y_P, the economy will now desire to save s instead of S. Equilibrium will move to E_2, where investment equals savings on the new savings function S'. Real national income will decline from Y_P to Y_A and a recessionary gap will appear. No more saving will occur at E_2 than occurred at E_1, since the lower national income has lowered the amount of savings. If investment is an increasing function of income, as in Part B, savings will actually decline.

It is possible to calculate for a given price level how much the aggregate demand curve will shift when any of the determinants of aggregate demand changes by applying the multiplier to the amount of change. Thus if consumption, investment, government, or the balance of foreign trade autonomously increases or decreases by a known amount, it is possible, if the value of the multiplier is known, to predict the extent of the shift of the aggregate demand curve.

THE PARADOX OF THRIFT

There is another important implication of the income/expenditure model. It is called the *paradox of thrift*. Suppose that households collectively decide to save more at every level of disposable income. What will be the effect on real national income? The effect will be that real national income will decline and by a multiple of the increased desire to save more. This is shown graphically in Figure 10.5, where only private savings and investment schedules are considered (the government and foreign-trade sectors are ignored for purposes of exposition). We shall employ the leakages-equal-injections method of income determination.

In Part A, prior to the decision to save more, the economy is at equilibrium at E_1, where savings equals investment (S = I) producing a real national income equal to Y_P, the level of potential national income. Now suppose that households desire to save more at every level of real national income. An autonomous increase in savings occurs and the savings function shifts up to S'. Households now desire to save more at the existing level of real national income Y_P.

The increased desire to save, however, causes the equilibrium position to change. The new equilibrium becomes E_2, where S' = I, which generates an equilibrium level of real national income of Y_A. The new equilibrium level of real national income is less by precisely the multiplier times the autonomous increase in savings. The increased desire to save has been frustrated by the decline in real national income. Households as a result end up saving the same amount as before.

It is even possible that the desire to save more collectively could result in saving less. Consider Part B of Figure 10.5, which is the same as Part A except for the investment function. Suppose that investment is a rising function of real national income. The desired amount of investment is zero when real national income is zero and rises as real national income increases. If this investment function is a better description of the economy, then a collective desire to save more will actually result in saving less. Savings measured on the vertical axis decline from S to S'.

Again, the reason is the multiplied decline in real national income that accompanies an upward shift of the savings function. Prior to the shift of the savings function, the economy is in equilibrium at E_1, where savings equals investment (S = I) and real national income is equal to the level of potential national income. However, when households collectively decide to save more at each level of income, the savings schedule shifts up to S'. This shift results in a new equilibrium at E_2, where S' = I and real national income is Y_A. Notice that because investment spending is less at lower levels of real national income, so also will the equilibrium level of savings be less. Note that at the new equilibrium actual savings is less than it was before the autonomous increase in savings. The desire to collectively save more in this case results in actually saving less. This outcome is known as the **paradox of thrift**.

> *The paradox of thrift is a principle stating that an autonomous increase in savings without a corresponding increase in investment will result in a decline in the equilibrium level of real national income, causing the quantity of savings to remain the same or even decline.*

A desire to save more will in the short run result in a decline in real national income. If the economy is at full employment or is suffering from a recessionary gap, this could be a bad thing, causing a recession or making an existing recession worse. But if the economy is experiencing an inflationary gap, an increase in the desire to save would be a good thing, moving the equilibrium level of real national income toward the level of potential national income. Moreover, an increase in the desire to save when the economy returns to full employment will provide more funds for investment. More investment means more capital goods, increased productivity, and a higher standard of living in the future.

PARADOX RESOLVED

It is frequently lamented by economists and government officials that the current savings rate is too low to support a world-class economy. How can this observation be squared with the paradox of thrift? Over time, as you will discover in Chapter 18, the rate of economic growth and the productivity of workers are dependent on the amount of capital the economy has with which to work. Capital is acquired by domestic saving or by foreign investment. The concern is that if the rate of domestic savings is too low, the size of the nation's capital stock in the future will be reduced and so will the economy's rate of economic growth.

The low level of domestic savings is a long-run concern and a threat to future living standards. Yet if efforts are made to increase savings by encouraging everyone to save more at each level of real national income, the paradox of thrift will operate to frustrate such efforts. How can the nation actually improve its savings rate? You will recall that the aggregate expenditures model is a short-run model; its predictions are for what will happen in the short run, not the long run.

We can resolve the paradox by considering both the short-run and long-run effects of an autonomous increase in savings. We shall employ the aggregate-demand/aggregate-supply model in this effort. Let us assume that the economy is in both long-run and short-run equilibrium, operating at point E_1 in Figure 10.6. In the short run an autonomous increase in savings will reduce aggregate expenditures, causing aggregate demand to decline and the aggregate demand curve to shift from AD_1 to AD_2. A new short-run equilibrium will occur at E_{SR}, real national income will decline from Y_P to Y_A, and the price level will decline from PL_1 to PL_{SR}. You will recognize this situation as a recessionary gap.

A recessionary gap will stimulate the automatic adjustment process to cause the SRAS curve to shift to the right from $SRAS_1$ to $SRAS_2$ and restore a long-run equilibrium at E_{LR}. The economy will reattain full employment and operate at the level of potential national income Y_P as the price level falls further to PL_{LR}. Thus in the long run the effect of an increase in savings is a decline in the price level. The increase in savings will allow the rate of economic growth to rise. Thus the paradox of thrift is resolved by considering the long-run implications, as well as the short-run implications, of an autonomous increase in savings. In the short run real national income will decline, but not in the long run. In the long run the entire effect will be confined to a fall in the price level.

THE CONSUMPTION FUNCTION RECONSIDERED

You have seen that the consumption and savings functions lie at the heart of the income/expenditure analysis. Not only is consumption the largest contributor to aggregate expenditures and therefore to aggregate demand, but the marginal propensity to consume influences the values of the various multipliers. So far we have considered the level of disposable income to be the main determinant of consumption. But when disposable income is compared with consumption expenditures, there is not a perfect correspondence. Over a long period of time there is a stable relationship between consumption and disposable income.

In Figure 10.7 most of the points lie very near the trend line, which has a slope and a marginal propensity to consume of 0.90. But not all points lie on the line. In fact, the actual propensity to consume jumps around a good bit from year to year. Consider the highest five points on the graph, which seem to lie above the trend line. This indicates that, although the consumption/income ratio is very stable in the long run, it is not stable in the short run. This suggested to some economists that con-

FIGURE 10.6
Paradox of Thrift Resolved

The paradox of thrift can be resolved if we employ the aggregate-demand/aggregate-supply model and remember the distinction between the short and long run. If economic decision makers decide to save more, the consumption function will shift down and the level of aggregate demand will be reduced from AD_1 to AD_2. Equilibrium in the short run will shift from E_1 to E_{SR}, the price level will fall from PL_1 to PL_{SR}, real national income will fall from Y_P to Y_A, and a recessionary gap will appear, as predicted in Figure 10.5. In the long run, however, forces will be set in motion to restore full employment. This will occur as the SRAS curve shifts to the right from $SRAS_1$ to $SRAS_2$. When this happens, equilibrium will move to E_{LR}, the economy will return to Y_P, and the price level will fall further to PL_{LR}. In the long run the entire effect of an increase in the desire to save will be a lower price level. When the economy returns to full employment, the increased savings will mean more investment and more capital goods and the level of potential national income will increase.

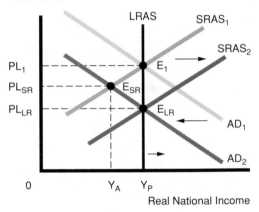

FIGURE 10.7
Real Consumption Expenditures and Real
National Income: 1947–1987

In this figure each point represents for a particular year real consumption expenditures, measured on the vertical axis, and real disposable income, measured on the horizontal axis. If consumption depended on disposable income alone, each point would lie on the trend line. Although most points lie close to the trend line, all do not lie on it, indicating that consumption expenditures for a particular year depend on something other than disposable income. Yet the long-run relationship is stable, suggesting that out of each additional dollar in disposable income 90 cents will be consumed and 10 cents saved.

Source: *Economic Report of the President, 1988* (Washington, DC: U.S. Government Printing Office, 1988).

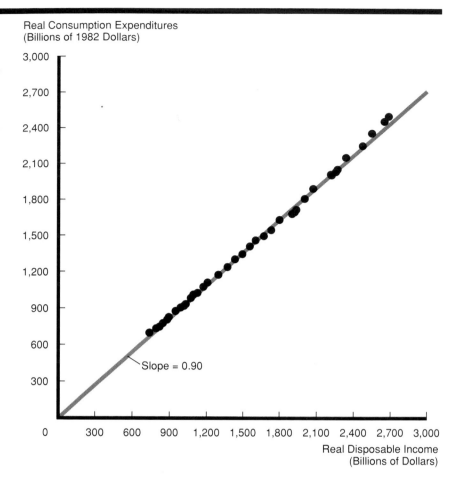

Real Consumption Expenditures
(Billions of 1982 Dollars)

Real Disposable Income
(Billions of Dollars)

sumption is also a function of some other variables that do not fluctuate as much as disposable income.

Two theories have been developed that explain the actual level of consumption expenditures better than the standard Keynesian consumption function based solely on disposable income. These theories postulate a concept of expected long-term income that replaces disposable income as the main determinant of the level of consumption expenditures. One theory is called the *life-cycle theory* and the other the *permanent-income hypothesis*.[2] The life-cycle theory postulates that individuals desire to maintain a smooth level of consumption over their lifetimes even if the flow of income they will receive is very uneven. The permanent-income hypothesis postulates that individuals develop estimates of their long-term level of income and base their consumption decisions on these estimates.

In both approaches current consumption is a function of permanent or long-term consumption rather than of current income. Although the two theories vary in detail, they are one in spirit, and we shall consider them together. Individuals know that their income will vary from year to year and they will allocate their current income in a way that allows consumption not to vary as much as income. Savings will fluctuate to allow consumption to remain stable over time.

---

[2]Franco Modigliani, Richard Brumberg, and Albert Ando formulated the life-cycle theory of the consumption function, and Milton Friedman the permanent-income hypothesis. Modigliani and Friedman were later awarded the Nobel Prize for this and other work.

Consider the example of an employed person who gets paid once a month. You would not expect this person to concentrate all consumption on payday and to consume nothing on the other days of the month. Instead, you would expect this individual to spread consumption fairly evenly over all days of the month, including payday. After all, people are regularly observed eating on days on which they receive no income. Clearly, some idea of average income longer than one day is relevant to making consumption decisions. Furthermore, there is nothing special about a month or a year in making consumption decisions. Instead, current consumption is better thought of as based on the expected level of long-term income.

The behavior of farmers provides a related example. The disposable income of farmers is highly variable, depending on the weather and on crop prices. An experienced farmer will understand this as a fact of life and, rather than live a feast-or-famine existence, will save during good years to allow his or her standard of living to be maintained during bad years. The same is true for construction workers who experience seasonal bouts of unemployment, and to some extent it is true for all of us. When making consumption decisions, individuals behave as if they had smoothed out the inevitable fluctuations in income by developing a concept of expected long-term income.

Moreover, there are reasons to believe that the planning horizon for individuals may be very long indeed. All of us, if we are lucky enough to live so long, will retire. When we do, our wage income will fall to zero. Ignoring the effects of social security, if we have not saved to finance retirement, our consumption will also decline to zero. To avoid this unhappy result, all of us save out of current income while working to finance our future retirement. We employ the possibility of saving today to allow us to smooth our consumption over our entire lifetime.

The main determinant of the level of consumption spending, therefore, is not the level of current disposable income, but the level of expected permanent income (according to the permanent-income hypothesis) or of lifetime income (according to the life-cycle theory). Although there are differences between the two theories, the main implications of both theories are similar. Recent research on the consumption function has sought to combine the two theories and has tended to confirm that temporary changes (often called *transitory changes*) in income will have little effect on consumption. Thus the modern theory of consumption states that the level of consumption expenditures depends on long-term income rather than on current disposable income.

Households seem to behave as if they adjust their consumption in accordance with estimates of long-term income. When temporary fluctuations in income occur, households maintain the level of their long-term consumption and allow the amounts that they save out of current income to adjust to the fluctuations in income. When there is, for example, a temporary increase in income, most of it will be saved. When income is temporarily lower than expected, households attempt to maintain their present level of consumption by running down accumulated savings.

Thus only changes in income that are considered permanent will affect the current level of consumption. The modern consumption function would predict that current consumption would increase less for the woman who won $10,000 by betting on the winner of the Kentucky Derby than would the current consumption of a man who held the winning lottery ticket that entitled him to an annual payment of $10,000 a year for 20 years. In both cases disposable income increases by $10,000 this year. But the $10,000 won on the horse race is a transitory increase in income, much of which will be saved, whereas the $10,000 per year in lottery winnings will increase the expected level of long-term income.

A student who worked for the parking department of a major university once remarked that medical students were obviously richer than other graduate students, basing his opinion on the observation of the different quality of the cars the two groups of students drove. The modern theory of consumption can explain the observation that medical students drive better cars than graduate students studying one of the liberal arts.

In fact, the disposable income of medical students may not be greater than that of other graduate students, even though the medical students drive better cars. What the parking attendant may have been observing was the effect of the different expectations of long-term income. Medical students can reasonably expect to enjoy significantly higher incomes over the long term than liberal-arts graduate students. The current relatively high level of consumption of medical students is consistent with their high expected long-term income. It is reasonable for them to enjoy higher levels of current consumption, even if they have to borrow to do so.

SUMMARY

1. An autonomous change in the amount of consumption, investment, the balance of foreign trade, or government expenditures will have a multiplied effect on the equilibrium level of real national income.
2. The ratio between the change in real national income and the autonomous change in one of the components of aggregate expenditures is called the *expenditures multiplier*. The value of the expenditures multiplier is the reciprocal of the marginal propensity to save.
3. The three different types of government activities will each be associated with a different value of the multiplier. The value of the multiplier for government expenditures is the same as for the expenditure multiplier generally. The tax multiplier will differ from the government expenditure multiplier by having the opposite sign and an absolute value that is less by 1. The transfer multiplier is the same as the tax multiplier but has an opposite sign. The transfer multiplier thus has the same sign as the government expenditure multiplier but a value that is lower by 1.
4. The balanced-budget multiplier is always equal to 1, and the value of the multiplier for transfers matched by tax changes is zero.
5. The paradox of thrift suggests that attempts to collectively save more will be frustrated by a multiplied fall in real national income. An attempt to collectively save more may, under certain conditions, actually result in less total savings. The paradox of thrift is a short-run phenomenon. In the long run the effect of an increase in savings will be a fall in the price level and a higher rate of economic growth, not a decline in real national income.
6. The multiplier effect can be shown, using an aggregate demand schedule, as a shift in the aggregate demand curve to the right by the multiplied amount at the existing price level.
7. The modern theory of consumption was developed to explain why consumption expenditures vary less than does disposable income. This theory postulates that current consumption depends on the expected level of income over the long term rather than on current disposable income.
8. An important implication of the modern theory of consumption is that temporary changes in the level of disposable income will produce only relatively small changes in the level of consumption and correspondingly larger changes in the level of savings.

THE TAX CUTS OF 1964 AND 1981

There were two episodes in American macroeconomic history in which taxes were successfully reduced to stimulate the economy. In the early 1960s the Kennedy and Johnson administrations cut taxes to stimulate economic activity. This tax cut was the first conscious attempt to adjust aggregate expenditures to the level required to attain full employment. Taxes were significantly reduced in 1964 and it seems to have worked, as the economy reached full employment a year or so later. In 1981 the Reagan administration obtained from Congress a series of annual tax reductions that were in effect when the economy fell into a deep recession. Some observers credit this reduction with propelling the economy out of the recession.

Why, when the economy has developed a recessionary gap, will cutting taxes improve the situation? Let us first discuss the Kennedy/Johnson tax cut, which was based on the implications of the aggregate expenditures model we have been discussing. The "New Economics" was the label used to describe the analytical and philosophical approach to economic policy employed by the Kennedy and Johnson administrations during the 1960s. The goal of the New Economics was to move the economy to the level of full employment.

In order to focus attention on the extent to which the economy was underutilizing its resources, the two administrations employed the concept of the GNP gap, which measures the extent to which real national income was below the level of potential national income. During the election year of 1960 the GNP gap was thought to equal 8 percent of potential national income, an extraordinary amount that seemed to call for the expansion of aggregate expenditures.

The 1964 tax cut was enacted a year after it was first recommended by the Kennedy administration. The GNP gap, despite previous efforts to stimulate aggregate expenditures, was estimated at the end of 1963 to still exceed 4 percent of potential national income. The tax cut was designed to increase aggregate expenditures by enough to finally close the gap. The economic situation that prevailed at the end of 1963 is shown in Figure 10.8. The equilibrium level of aggregate expenditures needed to be increased by the $36.2 billion indicated on the graph. How did Kennedy's economists calculate the amount by which taxes had to be reduced?

They employed estimates of the tax multiplier to calculate the amount of a tax reduction required to close the GNP gap. This amount is obtained by dividing the GNP gap by the value of the multiplier. The approximate estimates of the value of the tax multiplier used by Kennedy's economists was −2.58 for a personal income tax cut and −3.45 for a reduction in corporate income taxes. As shown in Table 10.5A, if the Kennedy administration had reduced only the personal income tax, the amount of the tax cut required would have been approximately $14 billion ($36.2 billion ÷ −2.58). If it had instead reduced only corporate income taxes, the amount of the tax reduction necessary would have been $10.5 billion ($36.2 billion ÷ −3.45).

President Kennedy selected a combination of the two, choosing to permanently reduce personal income taxes by $10 billion and corporate taxes by $3 billion. These were large tax cuts. The reduction in personal income taxes amounted to 20 percent of personal income tax receipts and the reduction in corporate taxes amounted to 8 percent of receipts. It was

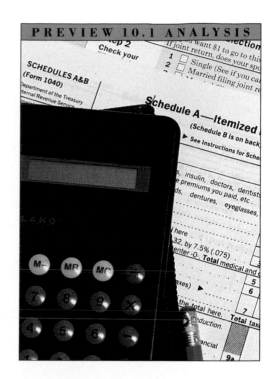

FIGURE 10.8
The Economic Situation at the End of 1963

President Kennedy's economic advisors believed that the recovery from the 1960–1961 recession was stalled. The level of potential national income was estimated to be $866.9 billion and actual real national income was $830.7 billion, so a recessionary gap equal to $36.2 billion was thought to exist. The increase in aggregate expenditures required to close this gap is indicated on the graph.

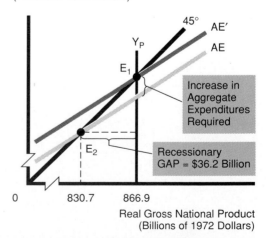

Aggregate Expenditures
(Billions of 1972 Dollars)

TABLE 10.5A
Calculating the Required Amount of Tax Reduction for 1963:
GNP Gap = $36.2 Billion

TYPE OF TAX CUT CONSIDERED	ESTIMATED VALUE OF MULTIPLIER	ACTUAL TAX REDUCTION (BILLIONS OF 1972 DOLLARS)	ESTIMATED INCREASE IN REAL GNP (BILLIONS OF 1972 DOLLARS)
Individual income tax	−2.58	−$10	$25.8
Corporate income tax	−3.45	−3	10.4
Total increase in real GNP			$36.2

Source: Arthur Okun, "Measuring the Impact of the 1964 Tax Reduction," in W. W. Heller, *Perspectives on Economic Growth* (New York: Random House, 1968).

TABLE 10.5B
Actual and Predicted Changes in Real GNP:
1963–1966 (Billions of 1972 Dollars)

	CHANGE IN GNP
1. Actual change	$152.3
2. Alternative change without tax reduction	
2A. At 3.7 percent growth path	95.9
2B. At 4.0 percent growth path	103.6
3. Difference (Row 1 − Row 2A and Row 1 − Row 2B)	48.7–56.4
4. Predicted difference	36.2

expected (see Table 10.5A) that the reduction in personal income taxes would increase real GNP by $25.8 billion and the cut in corporate income taxes would result in a $10.4 billion increase.

Did the tax reduction work as anticipated? Most people at the time thought so. The rate of economic growth significantly increased. The GNP gap (see Figure 10.9) was soon closed, and the rate of unemployment fell in 1966 to what was considered to be the natural rate of unemployment. The nation's press began to refer to the 1964 tax cut as the "magnificent tax cut."

There is no doubt that the rate of economic growth increased soon after the tax cut went into effect, but it could have been coincidence. A lot of other factors were changing at the same time. The economy may have been responding to past changes, or it may have been automatically adjusting to eliminate the existing recessionary gap. The only way to be sure that the tax cut was responsible for the recovery would be to know what would have happened to the economy if the tax cut had not been enacted. If this were known, it would be possible to compare the actual results with the tax cut against the results without the tax cut. The difference between the two would be entirely due to the effects of the tax cut.

Economists cannot rerun history, of course. The best that can be done is to construct a plausible estimate of the economy's performance in the absence of the tax cut. Table 10.5B presents one such attempt. The actual increase in real GNP that occurred with the tax cut between 1963

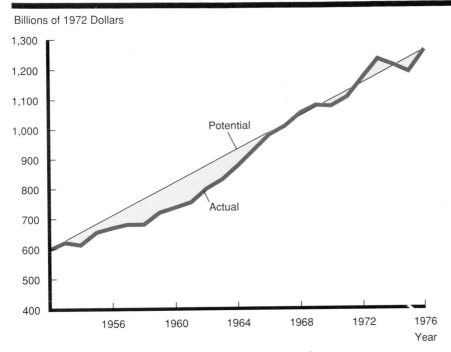

Billions of 1972 Dollars

FIGURE 10.9
Actual Real Gross National Product and
Potential National Income: 1955–1968

In this figure it is obvious that the economy had suffered from a persistent recessionary gap from 1955 through 1961, when President Kennedy took office. He responded by reducing some business taxes early in his administration. Fearing that the recovery was stalled in 1963 and that the economy could slip back, as it had in 1960, he recommended a large reduction in both the personal income tax and the corporate income tax. This reduction was passed in 1964. The recovery continued and the recessionary gap was finally closed in 1966, when the economy reached full employment.

Source: *Economic Report of the President, 1969* (Washington, DC: U.S. Government Printing Office, 1969).

(the year before the tax increase) and 1966 (by which time it is assumed the multiplier would have completed its work) was $152.3 billion, as shown in row 1. In the second entry two estimates of how much real GNP might have increased without the tax cut are presented. The economy between 1960 and 1963 had grown at an average rate of 3.7 percent. If it is assumed that it would have continued to grow at this average rate had the tax cut not been enacted, real GNP would have increased by $95.9 billion, as shown in row 2A. During this period it was estimated that potential national income was increasing at the rate of 4 percent. If instead of 3.7 percent, it is assumed that the economy would have grown at 4.0 percent, real GNP would have increased by $103.6 billion, as shown in row 2B.

Both of these alternative growth paths for the economy without a tax cut would have produced less real output at the end of the three-year period (1963–1966) than actually occurred. Real GNP was actually higher than the alternatives by between $48.7 billion and $56.4 billion (row 3). The predicted difference based on employing the multiplier was only $36.2 billion. It is certainly conceivable that the reduction in taxes was responsible for as much of the actual GNP growth as predicted above. Not all economists would agree with this conclusion, for reasons that will be discussed later in this book, nor would all accept as plausible the estimates of the alternative growth paths.

It is also possible that the tax cut may have worked too well. The economy quickly passed the level of full employment and developed an inflationary gap, as can be seen in Figure 10.5. You will see in the next analysis that the Johnson administration was slow to react and then did so inappropriately. It now appears (hindsight is 20-20) that Kennedy's economists were operating with an exaggerated estimate of the GNP gap. In 1977 the estimates of potential national income were significantly revised.

TABLE 10.6
Economic Growth, Unemployment, Inflation, and the GNP Gap during the
1981–1982 Recession

| | CHANGE IN REAL GNP | | | | UNEMPLOY-MENT RATE | INFLATION RATE | GNP GAP |
| | QUARTER | | | | | | |
YEAR	I	II	III	IV			
1981	9.0%	0.7%	3.6%	−4.9%	7.5%	10.4%	3.6%
1982	−4.6	−0.8	−0.9	−0.5	9.5	6.1	9.9
1983	3.3	9.4	6.8	5.9	9.5	3.2	9.2
1984	10.1	7.1	1.6	3.9	7.4	4.3	4.6

Source: *Economic Report of the President*, various years (Washington, DC:
U.S. Government Printing Office).

The old estimate—the one used to construct the 1964 tax cut—was found to be about $10 billion too high.

We have talked about the level of potential national income as if its true value were precisely known. This is far from the case. Potential national income is an estimate like gross national product, and probably not nearly as accurate. Potential national income has been estimated in many different ways by different persons. Each has obtained slightly different results, depending on the methods employed.

If it is true that the Kennedy administration overestimated the GNP gap, the 1964 tax cut was designed to be too stimulative. There is, however, a mitigating circumstance. The multipliers that the Kennedy administration assumed in calculating the necessary amount of the tax cut seem too high in retrospect. Current estimates of the tax cut multiplier lie within the range of −1.1 to −1.6. If these estimates are more accurate than the ones employed by Kennedy's economists, the amount by which the tax cut increased real national income in Table 10.5A is overestimated. It is possible that through offsetting errors Kennedy's economists got it right after all.

The second tax cut that is widely regarded as having been successful in altering real national income was the Economic Recovery Tax Act of 1981. This act reduced personal taxes by 5 percent in 1982 and by 10 percent in each of the next two years, while also reducing business taxes. While the tax reduction was being passed, the economy fell into a deep recession. The GNP gap that had been less than 4 percent in 1981 increased to nearly 10 percent in 1982 and remained above 9 percent during 1983 (see Table 10.6). The unemployment rate increased to nearly 10 percent during 1982 and 1983.

The only positive notes during the period were the decline in inflation, which fell from double-digit levels in 1981 to between 3 and 4 percent in 1983 and 1984, and the rapid recovery that began in 1983. The economy came out of the recession almost as rapidly as it had fallen into it. The 1981 tax cut has been given much credit for the rapid recovery. It appears to have been exactly what the economy needed. The decline in real GNP illustrated in Table 10.6 was clearly due to a lack of aggregate expenditures, since real national income and the rate of inflation both declined. The Reagan administration had urged Congress to cut government expenditures at the same time taxes were being reduced. A decline in government expenditures would, of course, have worked against increasing aggregate expenditures. But the most Congress ever did was reduce promised levels of future government expenditures. Government expenditures continued to increase throughout the recession.

Was the tax cut responsible for the rapid recovery and perhaps for keeping the recession from being worse than it was? Again, it is difficult to know because we cannot be sure what would have happened in the absence of the tax cut. Other things were going on to promote expansion, and perhaps they were responsible for the recovery. However, according to Keynesian theory, a tax reduction when the economy is in recession should improve the situation. In both 1964 and 1982 a tax cut occurred when a recessionary gap existed and economic conditions improved as the theory suggests.

THE FAILED TAX CHANGES OF 1968 AND 1975

The success of the 1964 tax cut gave rise to a brief period of euphoria among economists who believed that they had discovered a fiscal tool that would allow the management of aggregate expenditures and aggregate demand. Between 1965 and 1967 government expenditures increased rapidly to finance the war in Viet Nam and President Johnson's Great Society programs designed to widen the economic opportunities of the poor. Federal government expenditures increased from 9 percent to 11 percent of GNP. An inflationary gap rapidly developed, and the rate of inflation increased significantly as the rate of unemployment declined to below 4 percent.

Confidence in fiscal policy ran high in the Johnson administration, which recognized a need to reduce aggregate expenditures. Two options existed: reduce government expenditures or increase taxes. The president was loath to reduce government spending. Expenditures for the war could not be cut, and the president did not wish to cut his welfare programs. This left a tax increase as the most attractive option.

Increasing taxes partly to support an unpopular war was politically difficult. But in January 1967 the president asked Congress to enact a tax surcharge starting July 1. A tax surcharge is a proportional increase in taxes: Individuals and corporations continue to figure their taxes in the same way but when the tax bill is totaled, an additional percentage is added to the total. Congress delayed until June 1968 before passing the necessary legislation. The tax bill featured a 10 percent surcharge on personal income taxes, retroactive to April 1, and on corporations, retroactive to January 1.

The tax increase was designed to reduce the level of aggregate expenditures, causing the equilibrium level of real national income to decline to the level of potential national income. If a tax reduction had increased the level of aggregate expenditures in 1964, it was thought that a tax increase should reduce it. Taxes consequently were raised by about $10 billion in 1968. There was a difference, however: The 1964 tax cut was a permanent reduction, whereas the 1968 surcharge was explicitly recognized to be temporary.

This difference was not widely seen as important in 1968. Yet it may have been crucial if the implications of the modern theory of consumption

FIGURE 10.10
Long-Run and Short-Run
Consumption Functions

You saw in Figure 10.7 that the relationship over four decades was close, yet the year to year consumption/income relationship fluctuated significantly. The long-run consumption function relates consumption and disposable income over a number of years. This is the relationship between estimated permanent income and consumption. The short-run consumption function relates changes in consumption to changes in disposable income that are considered temporary. Thus if disposable income declines from Y_0 to Y_1, consumption expenditures will decline to C' if the change in disposable income is considered temporary, and to C'' if it is considered permanent.

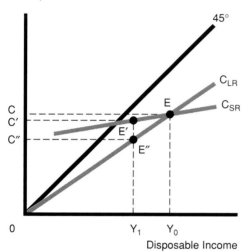

are considered. People in 1964 viewed the increase in disposable income resulting from the tax cut as permanent and increased their current consumption accordingly. The tax increase in 1968 was designed to do the opposite by reducing disposable income. It was expected that consumption spending would decline as a result. But in 1968 the increase in taxes was viewed as temporary. Households desiring to smooth their consumption over time might instead maintain their level of consumption by reducing savings.

The difference between the two outcomes can be seen in Figure 10.10. Initially, when disposable income is Y_0, consumers are in long-run equilibrium, spending amount C. A tax increase would reduce disposable income from Y_0 to Y_1. What will happen to current consumption expenditures? According to the modern theory of consumption, current consumption depends on the expected levels of present and future income. The amount of current consumption thus depends on whether the decline in disposable income is considered temporary or permanent.

If the decline is believed to be temporary, consumption expenditures will decline along the short-run consumption function from E to E′ as consumers strive to maintain their customary level of consumption until disposable income again increases. Most of the tax will be financed by a decline in savings, and consumption will decline only to C′. Similarly, if taxes were temporarily reduced and disposable income increased to a level above Y_0, consumption would increase along C_{SR} and most of the increase would be saved.

If, however, the decline in disposable income due to a tax increase is considered to be permanent, consumers will lower the level of consumption to correspond with the new lower expected level of permanent income. Consumption will decline along the long-run income/consumption function. Equilibrium will shift from E to E″, and current consumption expenditures will decline from C to C″. If, on the other hand, taxes were permanently reduced, the expected level of long-term income would increase, and consumption would increase along the long-run consumption function. Most of the increase in permanent income would be used for consumption. Thus a permanent tax change will predictably result in a greater change in current consumption than will a temporary tax increase.

Did the tax increase of 1968 work as expected by the Johnson administration or as the modern theory of consumption predicts? A real test of the effectiveness of the tax increase would require knowing what would have happened to consumption in the absence of a change in taxes. If we knew this, we could compare the two levels of consumption and see if an increase in taxes resulted in the hoped-for decline in consumption.

We cannot know what would have happened, but the facts do suggest an answer. The tax increase should have reduced consumption expenditures — that much is clear. But the question really is: Was the reduction in consumption of sufficient magnitude to reduce the inflationary gap? According to the modern theory of consumption, there is a possible way to determine whether the decline in consumption followed the short-run or the long-run consumption function. The proportion of income that is saved varies along the short-run consumption function, whereas it is constant along the long-run consumption function. Thus if consumption moves along the short-run consumption function, the savings rate, calculated as the ratio of savings to income, should decline, and if consumption moves along the long-run consumption function, the savings rate would remain the same.

TABLE 10.7
Savings Rate in Response to the 1968 Tax Surcharge

1967	1968				1969				1970
	I	II	III	IV	I	II	III	IV	
7.3%	7.2%	7.6%	6.0%	6.2%	5.3%	5.3%	6.6%	6.8%	7.9%

Source: W. L. Springer, "Did the 1968 Surcharge Really Work?" *American Economic Review* (September 1974).

Now look at Table 10.7, which presents the quarterly savings rates for 1968 and 1969 along with the annual savings rate for 1967 and 1970. The tax went into effect July 1, 1968, and lasted through the end of 1969, when it was allowed to expire. The savings rates prior to the tax were all over 7 percent. When the tax became effective, the savings rate immediately declined to between 5.3 percent and 6.8 percent, and didn't approach the before-tax rates until the tax expired, when it increased to almost 8 percent. The savings rate behaved as if consumption had followed the short-run consumption function.

It appears that the temporary tax surcharge was not as effective in reducing consumption as public officials had hoped. This interpretation is consistent with the behavior of the economy. The inflationary gap was not removed by the tax increase. The rate of unemployment remained below the natural rate, and the rate of inflation roughly doubled while the surcharge was in effect. The inability of the 1968 tax surcharge to stem inflation raised doubts about the effectiveness of temporary tax changes in influencing the level of economic activity.

These doubts were confirmed in 1975. Shortly after President Ford inherited the presidency, the economy fell into recession. The unemployment rate, which had hovered around 5 percent during 1973 and the first half of 1974, increased to 6.1 percent during the second half of 1975. It was widely believed that the level of aggregate expenditures needed to be raised. The government moved quickly to enact a temporary tax reduction, rebating 1974 taxes by 10 percent and reducing taxes for 1975.

In theory, there is no reason now to believe that a temporary tax cut will be any more effective in changing consumption expenditures than a temporary increase. Consumers will respond to a temporary increase in disposable income by attempting to spread the additional income over a number of years. Thus current consumption will be little affected, while the savings rate will increase.

Lower taxes meant an immediate increase in disposable income during the first half of 1975, but no recovery occurred. Instead the savings rate spiked upward to over 10 percent — a level that it had not reached for decades and hasn't seen since. This increase was consistent with the modern theory of the consumption function. Instead of falling as it would if aggregate expenditures had increased sufficiently, the unemployment rate rose, averaging 8.5 percent for the year, and it remained high throughout 1976.

All doubts were now removed. It became widely recognized that temporary changes in taxes have little effect on the level of aggregate expenditures. Macroeconomic theory and economic policy had advanced a step.

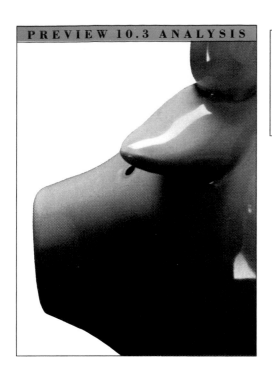

IS THE NATION'S LOW SAVINGS RATE A CAUSE FOR CONCERN?

Whenever you save five shillings, you put a man out of work for a day.
J. M. Keynes

The nation's low savings rate is a cause for concern to many economists and policymakers. Savings provide the funds for the capital goods, which increase productivity, which leads to the betterment of the standard of living that is a national goal. A prolonged decline in savings may reduce the size of the nation's future capital stock, with the possible effect of reducing future economic growth rates.

In 1981 the Japanese and West Germans saved a substantially larger portion of their national income than did Americans. The Japanese saved about 18 percent of their income and the West Germans approximately 12 percent, while the United States saved 8 percent. Thereafter the U.S. personal savings rate declined to a 40-year low in 1987, when it briefly touched 2 percent, while that of the Japanese and West Germans actually increased a bit between 1981 and 1987.

The difference in savings rates among these countries has important implications for the long-run performance of the economy. If the United States saved more, it would need to borrow less abroad to finance its federal budget deficit, or the quantity of domestic investment could be increased.

But a sudden increase in the desire to save out of current income could also have damaging short-run effects on the economy. According to the Keynesian model, sudden changes in the marginal propensity to save could have the effect, suggested by the paradox of thrift, of reducing the equilibrium level of real national income. During the recovery from the 1981–1982 recession, the personal savings rate steadily trended downward. A decline in the savings rate suggests a corresponding upward shift of the consumption function. This shift would cause aggregate expenditures to increase at a time when the economy was operating at less than potential national income. Referring to Figure 10.9, you will see that consumption expenditures in recent years have exceeded the long-run average consumption/income relationship. Increased consumption expenditures, as reflected in the declining savings rate, fueled the recovery from the recession.

Just as the decline in the savings rate may have fueled the long expansion that occurred in the middle years of the 1980s, a sudden increase in the savings rate could reduce the equilibrium level of real national income and plunge the economy into recession. It is also clear that this effect would be a short-run occurrence. In the long run the decline in aggregate expenditures and aggregate demand will result in a decline in the price level and will not affect the level of real national income.

There would be long-run benefits from increased savings. Savings are used to acquire the capital that increases the nation's productivity. A number of economists worry that the existing low savings rate is not sufficient to support in the future a high standard of living. They recommend that efforts be made to stimulate savings.

People save for a variety of reasons. They save to have a financial cushion in case of sickness or unemployment, to finance large purchases such as homes, automobiles, and vacations, for retirement, or to leave money to their heirs. The savings of an entire country will be influenced by, among other factors, the age structure of the population, the tax system, inflation, and the amount of existing wealth in the country.

The age structure of the population influences the nation's savings rate because people of different ages have different incentives to save. The higher the percentage of retired persons, the lower the amount that a nation will save. The United States has 26 retired persons for every 100 workers, while Japan has only 19. One study found that this difference alone can explain much of the difference between the two countries' savings rates.

The tax system can influence how much a nation saves. The United States and Canada had similar savings rates in 1981, but the two rates had diverged significantly by 1987. Changes in Canadian tax laws favored savings, whereas tax law changes in the United States favored borrowing. In the United States prior to 1986 interest paid was tax-deductible, so the cost of borrowing was reduced, while interest received was taxed at the taxpayer's highest rate.

Inflation and expectations of future inflation can affect the savings rate. When prices are expected to be significantly higher in the future, individuals are encouraged to consume more today. The accumulation of wealth also influences the amount a nation saves. The rise in the stock market and in housing prices that occurred in the early 1980s increased significantly the wealth of potential savers. This increase may have reduced the amount that individuals desired to save out of current incomes. An aging America, changes in the tax laws, the rise of stock prices and of the price of houses all combined to reduce the savings rate in the United States between 1981 and 1987.

Are low savings rates here to stay, or could they bounce back as quickly as they fell, perhaps dragging the economy into recession? There are indications that the savings rate might improve in the future. Some of the parameters of the consumption function are slowly changing in a way that will reduce the marginal propensity to consume, thereby increasing the marginal propensity to save. The proportion of the population aged 45 to 64, which is the age group with the highest marginal propensity to save, will increase in the future. But there are also negative factors. The proportion of the population in the 25–44 age group, which saves little and borrows a lot, is still growing. Also, the proportion of the population that is retired will continue to increase as the nation's population continues to age. The behavior of these groups will continue to put negative pressure on the savings rate.

In addition, there is the possibility that tax policy may influence the future savings rate. The 1986 tax reform act was designed in part to increase the savings rate. Time alone will tell whether it has worked as intended. Barring a change in public policy, a low personal savings rate may well remain a concern for the immediate future.

There are a number of tax policy options that might improve the savings rate, policy options that were not part of the 1986 tax reform act. A tax on consumption, which increases the relative price of consumption, could increase the proportion of the nation's income that is saved. A value-added tax, which acts like a national sales tax, would increase the price of consumption relative to saving. The higher relative price of consumption goods would create an incentive for households to save. Reducing the tax rate on interest received would also help, as would the return on individual retirement accounts (IRAs). IRAs allow individuals to defer paying income taxes on the amounts deposited in these accounts until the money is withdrawn on retirement.

HAS SOCIAL SECURITY REDUCED THE NATION'S SAVINGS RATE?

The effect of the Social Security system on the nation's savings rate and the total amount of savings is currently being debated among economists. The Social Security system is a federal government program to provide a minimum level of income to retired workers. According to one estimate, the Social Security system has substantially reduced the nation's savings rate. Because saving is the ultimate source of capital, the capital stock has consequently been reduced. A smaller capital stock means a lower level of productivity, lower real wages, and a poorer United States. Our Social Security system has as a result been singled out as one of the reasons why the United States has a lower savings rate than other countries.

Not all economists agree with this assertion. Some who have looked at the problem agree that Social Security has reduced the nation's savings rate, but only by small amounts. Others who have examined the problem find that the level of savings has been unaffected by the Social Security system. Whatever the actual amount by which

savings has been affected by the Social Security system, the economic argument provides an interesting application of the tools you acquired in this chapter.

How could our Social Security system reduce the savings rate? According to the Keynesian consumption function, it couldn't. Social Security is a transfer program. Workers are taxed, and the tax revenues are transferred to retired persons. If consumption and savings are determined by disposable income and everyone has approximately the same consumption function, then the total amount of savings will not be affected by this transfer. A dollar of Social Security tax, which will reduce the consumption and savings of workers, will be precisely offset by the increased consumption and savings of retired workers who receive the dollar.

This is precisely the case of a transfer payment being financed by an equal amount of tax payments that was discussed in this chapter. The multiplier associated with transfers is the same as the multiplier associated with taxes, except for the sign. The increase in real national income due to Social Security transfer payments will be precisely offset by the decline in national income caused by Social Security tax payments.

How then can the nation's overall level of savings be affected by the existence of a national Social Security system? The answer is to be found in the implications of the modern theory of consumption. Individuals do not receive income in an even flow over their lifetimes. The typical individual has a relatively high income during working years and a relatively low income during retirement. If the only income a worker has is from working,

then income would be positive while that person was working and zero when he or she retired. Yet everyone desires to continue consuming after retirement. The flow of income therefore does not match the desired pattern of consumption. Individuals behave as if they desire an even flow of consumption over their entire lifetimes. Saving makes this possible.

Individuals save for a variety of reasons. Among the most important is to finance their retirement years. If retirement were the only motive to save, individuals would save during their working years to finance future consumption during retirement. Thus individuals' assets will increase as they save during their working years and fall as they dissave to finance consumption during the years of retirement. In this way the flow of consumption could be spread in an even fashion over an entire lifetime.

Working individuals save for retirement by joining pension plans, contributing monthly out of their earnings or by privately saving out of earned income. These savings are invested in the economy, financing the purchase of capital goods and earning as a consequence a rate of return. As a result, wealth is accumulated that can be used to pay pensions to the workers when they retire. That is how private pension plans work.

The Social Security system is often mistakenly considered to be a national version of a private retirement plan. It is assumed that the individual's payments are invested by the government in financial assets that finance additions to the nation's capital stock, and that the amounts paid in allow wealth to be accumulated, which in turn allows the individual to collect benefits after retiring. That is

A tax policy that quickly and significantly increases the savings rate, however, runs the risk of pushing the economy into recession. The paradox of thrift provides the reason. Suppose taxes on consumption are increased at the same time that taxes on savings are reduced. The increased desire to save will, by decreasing aggregate expenditures, cause a multiplied reduction in real national income. Unless the economy is experiencing an inflationary gap, an increase in the desire to save more at every level of real national income will either cause a recessionary gap to appear (see Figure 10.8) or make an existing recessionary gap worse.

The implication of the paradox of thrift is that a tax policy to stimulate savings should be accompanied by policy changes that will also stimulate investment. Perhaps if a value-added tax is to be seriously considered in order to stimulate savings, it should be coupled with measures that will increase the rate of return on investment, thereby increasing the incentives to invest. In the short run one way to avoid a decline in real national not how the Social Security system works, and the differences are crucial to determining the effect that Social Security has on the nation's savings rate.

A working individual's contributions to the Social Security system are not invested. Instead, these contributions are transferred to retired individuals. The contributions are, in fact, a tax that finances a transfer. The nation's savings rate would be unaffected if this were as far as the analysis goes, but it is not. There is an important implication of the modern theory of consumption that bears on this situation.

All contributors to the Social Security system are guaranteed the right to receive benefits when they in turn retire. When this happens, they cease to pay the Social Security tax and instead begin to share in the proceeds of the tax. There is no need to save currently to provide the amount of income that Social Security guarantees. Persons who are still working will provide these funds in the form of their Social Security taxes. Individuals consider this guarantee to be the same thing as if their wealth had increased by the amount of saving that would generate the retirement income that Social Security will provide. This perceived increase in wealth reduces the amount of current saving and increases the amount of current consumption among the working population.

But there has not been an increase in the nation's total wealth that corresponds to the perceptions of increased personal wealth. The taxes paid into the system have been paid out to retired persons, not used to accumulate wealth. The effect of Social Security is thus to reduce personal savings and increase personal consumption over the working period of a person's lifetime.

But what becomes of the transfer payments? Retired persons do not save much out of the Social Security payments they receive. Retired persons have a much shorter life span over which to smooth consumption. As a group they thus have a high marginal propensity to consume. Thus most of the transfer payments are used to finance consumption.

The modern theory of consumption suggests that the Social Security system leads people to believe that they are wealthier than they really are. As a consequence they will save less during their working lifetimes than they would if they were entirely dependent on a private pension system. This is called the *savings replacement effect.*

There are mitigating forces at work. Social Security is a supplement to private savings. The Social Security system is designed to place a floor under the level of retirement income. The current level of benefits is generally substantially less than the level of working income. So an incentive still exists to save while working to provide a retirement income above what Social Security alone would allow.

Furthermore, there is evidence that the existence of Social Security may have induced individuals to retire earlier than they did before the system was created. Because the retirement period is therefore longer, more personally provided assets will be required to ensure an even flow of consumption over one's lifetime. The early-retirement effect thus stimulates more personal saving during working years. Called the *induced-retirement*

effect, this effect operates in the opposite direction from the savings replacement effect and could even offset it entirely.

Thus the ultimate effect of Social Security on the nation's savings rate becomes an empirical matter. The most frequently used estimate of the net effect of Social Security on personal saving is that savings have been reduced by half. If this estimate is accurate, the nation's capital stock and its people's standard of living are consequently lower than they would be if the Social Security system had been designed as a private pension program instead of a system of transfer payments.

---

income when an autonomous increase in savings occurs is to generate a corresponding offsetting autonomous increase in investment.

What can be said, on the basis of the Keynesian model, about the desire of many economists to increase the rate of savings in the macroeconomy? This desire can be restated as follows: It should be a national policy goal that (1) allows the economy to operate at full employment, and (2) allows an increased proportion of national income to be devoted to savings. When designing policies to accomplish these goals, policymakers must consider the implications of the paradox of thrift. Any new policy should be designed in a way that avoids the possibility of a recession. This requires that the resulting level of aggregate expenditures correspond to the level of potential national income. In order to accomplish this, investment demand must be stimulated by the same order of magnitude as the increased desire to save.

REQUIRED ECONOMIC CONCEPTS

Expenditure multiplier
Government expenditure multiplier
Tax multiplier
Balanced-budget multiplier
Transfer multiplier
Paradox of thrift

KEY QUESTIONS

1. What is the difference between autonomous and induced spending?
2. What is the effect of the multipliers?
3. What are three equivalent definitions for the government expenditure multiplier?
4. If the government transfer multiplier is equal in magnitude to the tax multiplier, why does it have an opposite effect on income?
5. How can you immediately determine the value of the tax multiplier if you know the value of the government expenditure multiplier?
6. What are three equivalent definitions for the tax multiplier?
7. What is the value of the balanced-budget multiplier?
8. What is the value of the balanced-transfer multiplier (the multiplier when the change in government transfers is in the same direction as the change in taxes and of equal size)?
9. What is the empirical, or measured, range of the government expenditure multiplier? Of the tax multiplier?
10. If everyone desires to save more out of income, how can everyone end up saving less? What is this situation called?
11. What are two factors that exaggerate the difference between the low U.S. savings rate and the high Japanese savings rate?
12. How does Social Security affect the nation's private savings rate?
13. What elements in the U.S. economy are indicative of the low U.S. savings rate?
14. What is the core concept in the life-cycle and permanent-income hypotheses?
15. Why does the permanent-income hypothesis predict that a temporary increase in taxes will not significantly affect consumer spending?

PROBLEMS

1. Which of the following would you classify as autonomous spending? As induced spending?

    a. Disposable income rises. More people can choose to buy expensive skiing equipment.

    b. People can afford more leisure. More videocassettes are produced.

    c. Teflon is a by-product of aerospace research. The public buys more nonstick pots and pans.

    d. The invention of the camera created employment in the film-developing industry.

2. When government or investment spending is injected into the circular flow, the multiplier operates to induce additional spending. That, in theory, proceeds for an infinite number of rounds. Why is the ultimate impact not infinitely large?

3. a.   The government spends $2 billion for a new military weapon and raises taxes by $2 billion. Explain why the effect on national income is either expansionary, contractionary, or neutral.

b.   Assume that the marginal propensity to consume is 0.8. If government increases farm subsidy payments by $30 million and raises taxes by $30 million, by how much does national income change?

4. If the marginal propensity to consume is 0.67 and investment increases by $12 million, will national income rise or fall? By how much? How much induced consumption spending will occur?

5. Taxes are raised by $3 million and the marginal propensity to consume is 0.75.

a.   By how much will national income rise or fall?

b.   By how much will savings rise or fall?

c.   By how much will consumption rise or fall?

6. a.   What is the size of the tax multiplier if the marginal propensity to consume is 0.8?

b.   What is the size of the balanced-budget multiplier if the marginal propensity to consume is 0.8?

7. Assume no government. Investment for plant and equipment is $100 billion, and firms also plan to increase inventories by $10 billion. The household consumption function is $C = \$50 \text{ billion} + 0.75Y_D$.

a.   What is the equilibrium level of income?

b.   What is the equilibrium level of consumption spending?

c.   What is the equilibrium level of saving?

8. a.   Assume the government expenditure multiplier is 3. Suppose the president intends to cut taxes by $6.4 billion and reduce government spending by $4 billion. What will be the effect on national income?

b.   What would the government expenditure multiplier have to be for the spending and tax cuts to yield no change in national income?

9. Alice wins a lottery prize of $100,000. According to the permanent-income hypothesis, would Alice be more likely to spend $80,000 soon and save $20,000 or spend $20,000 soon and save $80,000? Suppose Alice puts an $80,000 down payment on a house. Does this action contradict the permanent-income hypothesis? Explain.

10. According to the permanent-income hypothesis, will a student who skips classes one Friday to play poker put his or her winnings of $40 in the bank or blow it on pizza and beer?

11. Joe knows that if he declares himself as an exemption, he will receive an IRS refund in June. Would the refund represent temporary or permanent disposable income to Joe? Explain.

APPLICATION ANALYSIS

1.   Over the year the GNP deflator increased by 3 percent. Nominal national income was $900 billion for the year. Assume that the marginal propensity to consume is 0.6 and that real income is measured along the horizontal axis. Suppose potential real income for the economy is $860 billion for the year.

a.   Calculate real national income. Determine the size of the inflationary gap.

b.   Draw a graph illustrating the gap in part a.

c.   By how much and in what direction would government expenditures have to change to remove the gap?

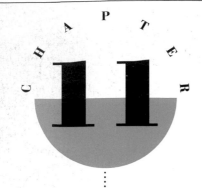

CHAPTER

11

AGGREGATE SUPPLY, NATIONAL INCOME, AND THE PRICE LEVEL

IN THIS CHAPTER YOU WILL LEARN:

The concept of aggregate
supply in both the short run
and the long run and the
role that aggregate supply
plays in the automatic
adjustment process

●

How expectations affect
aggregate supply

●

The nature of supply shocks
and how supply shocks
affect macroeconomic
equilibrium

HOW THE MACROECONOMY RESPONDS TO AN INFLATIONARY GAP

In 1966 the U.S. economy was booming, jobs were plentiful, and the unemployment rate of 3.8 percent had fallen below the full-employment unemployment rate, widely considered at the time to be 4 percent. Both the fiscal and monetary policies of the federal government provided the stimulus for further expansion. The war in Vietnam and the expanding social programs that made up President Johnson's war on poverty required significant increases in government expenditures. Monetary policy aided the expansion. The quantity of money increased at a significantly higher rate between 1966 and 1969 than in the earlier years of the decade.

Not surprisingly, as the rate of unemployment declined still further — from 3.8 percent in 1966 and 1967 to 3.6 percent in 1968 and to 3.2 percent in 1969 — the rate of inflation picked up. The rate of inflation, which had been 1.7 percent in 1965, increased to 2.9 percent for the years 1966 and 1967, and it continued to rise, reaching 4.2 percent in 1968 and 5.4 percent in 1969.

The beginning of inflation was not missed by the Council of Economic Advisors. This group recognized that an inflationary gap was developing and immediately recommended to President Johnson that he propose to the Congress a change in fiscal policy in the form of a tax increase, the purpose of which was to reduce aggregate demand by enough to eliminate the developing inflationary gap. President Johnson resisted this advice for a tax increase until the beginning of 1967. A temporary tax surcharge was enacted in June of 1968 to take effect in April of that year. The temporary tax increase failed to affect consumption significantly, and the economy continued to expand despite this attempt at restrictive fiscal policy.

Without fiscal and monetary policy to control the inflationary gap, the macroeconomy was left on its own to adjust to the situation. How does the economy adjust to the presence of an inflationary gap?

THE INFLATIONARY RECESSION OF 1973–1975

The 1973–1975 period was one of the more interesting periods in macroeconomics. Prior to 1973 the economy had enjoyed vigorous economic expansion, with the unemployment rate below the full-employment level. Inflation, as would be expected, was the result. Then late in 1973 the rate of economic growth began to slow, and in 1974 it started to actually decline — beginning slowly at first and then continuing precipitously through the second quarter of 1975. The rate of decline in real output during this recession was unprecedented since the Great Depression. The decline in real output was reflected in a rising unemployment rate, which increased from 5.6 percent in 1974 to 8.5 percent in 1975.

What was unusual about this recession was the behavior of the price level. Generally, the price level falls during a recession. That certainly had occurred during the Great Depression. But inflation did not recede during the 1973–1975 recession; it actually increased. The rate of inflation increased by 50 percent between 1973 and 1974, rising from 8.8 percent to 12.2 percent.

Economists and policymakers at the time were surprised by this development. Seemingly, the worst of all macroeconomic situations had occurred between 1973 and 1975: inflation coupled with recession. The nation's press quickly dubbed the combination of a rise in the unemployment rate and the existence of inflation as ''stagflation.'' How could the simultaneous existence of inflation and recession be explained?

• INTRODUCTION •

In our investigation of macroeconomics thus far, we have concentrated on the demand for aggregate output by examining both the aggregate demand and the aggregate expenditures schedules. Events that took place during the 1970s and 1980s demonstrated the need for a more balanced approach and promoted aggregate supply to a full partner along with aggregate demand in the theory of macroeconomics. What happens on the supply side was demonstrated by events to be very important for determining what happens to the inflation rate, the unemployment rate, and the rate of economic growth.

During the 1970s the main economic problem shifted from one of recession and unemployment to one of inflation. The 1970s was a decade of inflation as the price level doubled, but recessions were not absent. Between 1970 and 1982 the economy suffered four recessions, during each of which real gross national product (GNP) declined and the unemployment rate increased. But these recessions were different from their predecessors in one important respect — the price level, instead of falling as it is ordinarily expected to do, continued to rise. The press was quick to label this phenomenon an **inflationary recession.**

> *An inflationary recession is a recession in which real national income declines for at least two quarters but during which the price level continues to increase.*

When inflation and inflationary recessions became the nation's major macroeconomic problems, it became important for macroeconomic models to be able to deal explicitly with the price level. But changes in the price level are hidden in the aggregate expenditures model, which concentrates on the demand side.

The aggregate-demand/aggregate-supply model introduced in Chapter 7 represents a possible solution. This model overcomes these difficulties by explicitly considering the role of aggregate supply, allowing the consideration of forces that change aggregate supply, and by explicitly determining the equilibrium price level along with real national income. This consideration of aggregate supply in macroeconomic theory allows the price level to be determined within the model, allows observation of the automatic adjustment process from short-run to long-run equilibrium, and allows the prediction of how supply-side changes will affect both the price level and real GNP. •

AGGREGATE SUPPLY

In previous chapters you discovered that the SRAS schedule relates at every price level the quantity of real national income that will be supplied, the determinants of aggregate supply being held constant. The short-run aggregate supply (SRAS) schedule, when graphed as in Figure 11.1, slopes upward to the right. The quantity of real national income supplied in the short run is positively related to the price level. In Figure 11.1 the quantity of real national income supplied is Y_1 when the price level is 110, and it is less, Y_2, when the price level is 90.

There is a simple explanation for this behavior. Business firms will desire to supply more output when it becomes more profitable to do so. Profit per unit is what is left over when the costs per unit are subtracted from the selling price. When the overall price level rises, it reflects the general increase in product prices. The selling price of most goods and services will increase. Whether a business firm will attempt to supply more when the price level increases depends on what happens to the costs of production.

What happens to the costs of production as the overall price level changes will depend in large part on what happens to the prices of the factors of production. The prices that business firms have to pay for the factors of production they employ are generally fixed in the short run. Some workers are unionized and work under contracts that set wages for one to several years in the future. Even when no such formal contracts exist, employees typically bargain annually with employers over wages and salaries. The same is true for nonlabor inputs. Business firms lease facilities for relatively long periods of time at fixed rents, or they contract

FIGURE 11.1
Aggregate Supply in the Short Run and in
the Long Run

Suppose the economy is operating at a level of real national income equal to potential national income Y_P with a price level of 100. The SRAS curve slopes upward if the price level increases, because the prices of the factors of production are fixed in the short run. An increase in the price level to 110 will increase the prices of the products that businesses sell. The costs of production will not increase proportionally, because the prices of the factors of production are fixed in the short run. Because costs do not increase as much as product prices, business profits will increase. Business firms will increase production from Y_P to Y_1. Conversely, if the price level declines to 90, product prices will decline by more than the costs of production will fall, causing profits to decline and business firms to reduce output to Y_2.

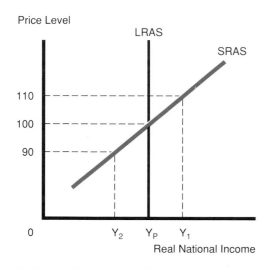

for raw materials at fixed prices for periods of months or years. These contracts last long enough to influence the short-run costs of business firms.

Suppose, however, that while the prices of the factors of production remain unchanged, the price level increases by 10 percent, which is reflected in a 10 percent increase in the price of the product a business firm produces. In this case the firm's profits will increase, and the firm will attempt to expand production. Conversely, if the price level declines, the profit margin of business firms will fall and they will attempt to reduce output.

This behavior explains why the SRAS curve slopes upward. When the price level rises, business firms will attempt to increase output because it has become more profitable to do so. Conversely, when the price level falls, business firms will reduce output because production is now less profitable.

The **short run** is a period of time in which existing supply contracts for the factors of production govern the prices that business firms pay for their inputs.

> *The short run is the period of time in which the prices of the factors of production do not change.*

All contracts exist for a specified period of time. When a contract expires, it will be renegotiated, taking into consideration the existing price level. Thus the prices of the factors of production are not fixed but are flexible in the **long run**.

> *The long run is the period of time that is sufficient for the economy to become fully adjusted to a change in the price level, and is characterized by flexible prices for both products and the factors of production.*

In the long run the prices of the factors of production are flexible and will fully adjust to changes in the price level. A 10 percent increase in the price level will be offset by a 10 percent increase in the prices of the factors of production and in the costs of production. Thus the price level, since it does not in the long run affect the profitability of production, cannot affect the output decisions of business firms. The quantity of real national income supplied in the long run will not change with the price level.

When graphed, the long-run aggregate supply (LRAS) curve is a vertical line at the level of potential national income (Y_P). This is also shown in Figure 11.1. The quantity Y_P will be supplied in the long run whether the price level is 90, 100, or 110. The potential level of real national income corresponds to full employment in the macroeconomy.

The level of potential national income is determined by the quantity of the factors of production available and the forces that determine the productivity of these inputs. These factors will be considered in Chapter 18.

In the long run aggregate demand will not affect the level of potential national income, but it will affect the price level. This is shown in Figure 11.2. In the long run the level of real national income produced is determined by the level of potential national income. The price level is determined by the level of aggregate demand. If the level of aggregate demand is AD_1, the long-run price level will be PL_1. If the level of aggregate demand increases to AD_2, the long-run price level will be PL_2. Perhaps you remember this result: It is the same as that predicted by the classical model of macroeconomics.

What, then, is the relationship between the SRAS curve and the LRAS curve? In order to understand this relationship, we need to consider the role that expectations play in aggregate supply.

RELATIONSHIP BETWEEN THE SHORT-RUN AND LONG-RUN AGGREGATE SUPPLY CURVES

The relationship between aggregate supply in the short run and in the long run is based on the role that expectations about the future price level play in determining product and factor prices.

SUPPLY OF THE FACTORS OF PRODUCTION The aggregate supply schedule in both the short run and the long run relates the quantity of real national income that will be supplied at every price level. Aggregate supply is determined by the quantity and prices of the inputs (labor, capital, and natural resources) employed in the production process and by the state of technology that determines the output per unit of input.

The quantity of aggregate output supplied, as you have seen, is responsive to changes in the price level, whereas in the long run it is not. An increase or a decrease in the price level will in the short run lead to an increase or a decrease in the quantity of aggregate output supplied. But in the long run the quantity of aggregate output supplied is fixed at the level of potential national income, a level that is itself not affected by the price level.

Conditions in the factor markets are crucial for the determination of short-run aggregate supply. To fully understand why this is so, it is necessary to investigate how **expectations** of the future price level affect the supply of the factors of production.

> *Expectations are forecasts about the future value of an economic variable.*

In this case the forecast is an estimate of the future price level. Price-level expectations affect how factor markets operate.

FACTOR MARKETS Business firms must acquire the factors of production necessary to produce the products they desire to sell. In the real world business decision makers and the owners of the factors of production do not bargain each day over the prices that will be paid and received. This would be too costly. Instead, business firms and the owners of the factors of production infrequently negotiate contracts that run for a period of time. General Motors, for example, bargains with the United Auto Workers every three years to sign a contract that will govern wages and working conditions for the next three years. IBM, a nonunion firm, annually reviews pay and performance with each worker and strikes a bargain for the next year.

Similarly, business firms enter into contracts to lease production and office facilities that run a year or more in the future. They also negotiate contracts with suppliers of parts and materials for a period of months or years. The upshot of this process is that at any point in time many prices

FIGURE 11.2
Increases in Aggregate Demand and the Long-Run Aggregate Supply Curve

The level of aggregate supply in the long run does not depend on the price level. The LRAS curve is vertical with respect to the price level. In the long run when the level of aggregate demand changes from AD_1 to AD_2, the only effect will be an increase in the price level from PL_1 to PL_2.

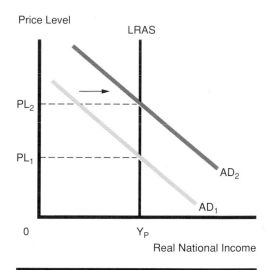

FIGURE 11.3

Short-Run Aggregate Supply and Shifts in
Short-Run Aggregate Supply

When the determinants of aggregate supply are held constant and the price level is allowed to vary, changes in the quantity of real national income supplied will trace out the SRAS curve. If the price level is held constant and one of the determinants of aggregate supply changes, the entire SRAS curve will shift.

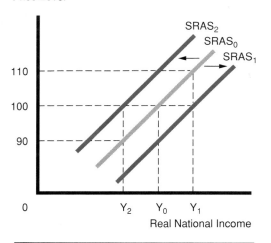

and wages are *fixed* for some period of future time. The fact that many wages and factor prices are fixed for a period of time is crucial to an understanding of how aggregate supply functions in the short run.

How are the wages and prices of the factors of production determined? They are determined in markets. The participants have made their decisions about the quantities they will supply or demand on the basis of the price expectations they hold. Thus all factor-market contracts are based on expectations of future price levels.

Economic conditions often change in ways that were not anticipated during the periods governed by such contracts. Nevertheless, while the contract is in force, the conditions of the contract will govern the exchanges between business firms and the suppliers of the factors of production. When existing contracts govern the prices of the factors of production, the economy is operating in the short run.

But as time passes each contract will expire and a new negotiation will take place. The new negotiations will take into account the changes in economic conditions that have occurred since the last contract was signed as well as new forecasts of the future. Thus over time all contracts governing the supply of the factors of production become *flexible*. When all factor prices are free to adjust to new macroeconomic conditions, the economy is operating in the long run.

SHIFTS IN THE SHORT-RUN AGGREGATE SUPPLY CURVE

The short-run aggregate supply (SRAS) curve shows how real output changes when the economy experiences an unexpected change in the price level. The SRAS curve slopes upward, suggesting that an unanticipated increase in the price level will cause the quantity of aggregate supply in the short run to increase. An unexpected decline in the price level will cause the quantity of real national income supplied to decline.

As in the case of the aggregate demand curve, factors other than the price level will affect aggregate supply. The determinants of aggregate supply in the short run are the wages and prices of the factors of production, the state of technology, and the level of expected future prices.

When these determinants are held constant and the price level is allowed to vary, an upward-sloping aggregate supply curve is generated. This can be seen in Figure 11.3. When the SRAS curve is $SRAS_0$ and the price level is 100, Y_0 of real national income will be supplied. When the price level increases to 110, real national income supplied will increase to Y_1. If, however, the price level declines to 90, real national income supplied will decline to Y_2.

When one of the determinants of aggregate supply changes, the entire SRAS curve will shift. Suppose the price of one of the factors of production increases. If this happens, the costs of production will increase, and the SRAS curve will shift to the left from $SRAS_0$ to $SRAS_2$. The amount of real national income supplied at the existing price level of 100 will decline to Y_2. If, however, the price of one of the factors of production falls, the costs of production will decline and the SRAS curve will shift to the right from $SRAS_0$ to $SRAS_1$. The amount of real national income supplied at the existing price level 100 will increase from Y_0 to Y_1.

Changes in the other determinants of short-run aggregate supply will also cause the SRAS curve to shift. If technology improves, the costs of production will decline, and the SRAS curve will shift to the right. The amount of real national income supplied at the existing price level will increase. This could occur if new improved capital goods were introduced or if the labor force became more skilled. If, however, technology deteriorates, the costs of production will increase, and the SRAS curve will shift to the left from $SRAS_0$ to $SRAS_2$, and the quantity of real national income supplied at the existing price level will decline from Y_0 to Y_2.

Changes in the expected price level will also affect the SRAS curve. If expectations about future prices change so that prices are expected to be higher in the future, the SRAS curve will shift to the left from $SRAS_0$ to $SRAS_2$. Conversely, if expectations change so that the price level in the future is now expected to be lower, the SRAS curve will shift to the right from $SRAS_0$ to $SRAS_1$.

Changes in the determinants of short-run aggregate supply are of two types: (1) regular and predictable and (2) irregular and unpredictable. Changes in the composition of the labor force and technological improvements are generally changes of the first type. They tend to occur regularly in an expected way and to cause the SRAS curve gradually to shift. Changes in the prices of the factors of production and in expectations are of the second type. These changes often come unexpectedly. When this happens, the SRAS curve will shift unexpectedly, which will have unexpected consequences for business firms and the owners of the factors of production locked into existing contracts.

THE LONG-RUN AGGREGATE SUPPLY CURVE

The long-run aggregate supply (LRAS) curve differs significantly from the short-run aggregate supply curve in that the quantity supplied in the long run is not dependent on the price level. The LRAS curve does depend on the level of potential national income. The hypothesis of the natural rate of unemployment underlies this relationship.

NATURAL RATE OF UNEMPLOYMENT The natural rate of unemployment is the approximate balance between the number of unfilled jobs and the number of qualified unemployed workers. But we can also think of it as the rate of unemployment that exists without a change in inflation.

> *The natural rate of unemployment is the rate of unemployment that can continue to exist without a change in the rate of inflation.*

This definition can be understood by considering how labor markets operate. Suppose the existing unemployment rate exceeds the natural rate so that a recessionary gap exists. Output in the long run must increase to allow the economy to operate at full employment. Labor markets will have available more potential workers than the number of jobs that exist. If the rate of inflation is zero, money wages will tend to fall until full employment is restored. The decline in money wages in this case means a fall in real wages, which is what is required to restore full employment.

If inflation exists, money wages will tend to rise less than the current rate of inflation, and real wages (money wages divided by the price level) will decline. This in turn will cause the rate of inflation itself to moderate. The costs of production of business firms will rise less rapidly. Because competition among firms will limit future price increases, the rate of inflation will moderate. When money wages rise less than prices, real wages will decline, a phenomenon that will continue until full employment is eventually restored, at which time future money wages and the price level will rise together. When this happens, the economy will be operating at the natural rate of unemployment and the rate of inflation will be constant.

When the actual rate of unemployment is less than the natural rate of unemployment, an inflationary gap exists. Real output exceeds the level of potential national income and output must fall if the economy is to operate at the level of full employment. Wages, when the economy is in this situation, will tend to rise faster than the rate of inflation. Competition among business firms will limit the rate of price increases to less than the rate at which wages are rising. This will put a profit squeeze on business firms, which will reduce production and employment so that the economy will move toward full employment.

Only when the observed unemployment rate equals the natural rate will changes in wage rates just mirror changes in the price level. The natural rate represents that point where neither an inflationary nor a recessionary gaps exists. The natural rate of unemployment represents a balancing point for the economy. When unemployment is below the natural rate, indicating that real output is above the level of potential national income, wages will rise by more than the rate of inflation until output declines to the level of potential national income and the unemployment rate rises to the natural rate. When unemployment is above the natural rate and real output is below the level of potential national income, the reverse will happen.

The natural rate of unemployment will not be zero. The economy is always in the process of reallocating resources. In a growing, dynamic economy such as exists in the United States, there will always be some people between jobs. These are persons who are leaving less productive, lower-paying jobs for more productive, higher-paying ones. Economic efficiency requires no less.

The natural rate of unemployment cannot be directly observed and must be estimated. Estimates for 1960–1987 show that the natural rate has gradually risen over the past few decades from 5 percent in the 1960s to between 5.5 and 6.0 percent during the 1980s. This increase is due partly to changes in the composition of the labor force and partly to other factors that will be examined in Chapter 17.

It is important to understand that the natural rate of unemployment does not depend on the rate of inflation. The natural rate is consistent with any rate of inflation. Comparing the existing rate of unemployment with the natural rate of unemployment provides a guide to future rates of inflation. In 1988, when the U.S. economy was operating at unemployment rates at or below the natural rate, fears were expressed by both policymakers and participants in the stock and bond markets that inflation would soon increase. It was widely believed at that time that if the existing unemployment rate fell much further, the rate of inflation would begin to accelerate.

POTENTIAL NATIONAL INCOME AND LONG-RUN AGGREGATE SUPPLY

When the economy is operating at the natural rate of unemployment, it will be producing a level of real national income that is equal to potential national income. The concept of **potential national income** was first introduced in Chapter 7. We can now extend our definition of this concept.

Potential national income is the level of real national income that is produced when the unemployment rate is equal to the natural rate of unemployment.

Only at the level of potential national income will the rate of inflation be constant. If real national income is below the level of potential national income, the rate of inflation will fall. If real national income is greater than the level of potential national income, the rate of inflation will increase.

Potential national income provides a measure of full employment for the economy as a whole. When the economy is operating at a level below potential national income, it is experiencing excess unemployment and wasting the opportunity to produce more output. You will recognize this situation as a recessionary gap. When the economy is operating above the level of potential national income, it is experiencing more than full employment and an inflationary gap will exist.

Potential national income indicates the position of the long-run aggregate supply (LRAS) curve. Since potential national income does not depend on the price level, neither does the LRAS curve. The LRAS curve is vertical at the level of potential national income and is represented graphically as a vertical straight line at the level of potential national income.

The LRAS schedule shows the quantity of real national income that the economy could supply at every price level without the rate of inflation changing. Because wages and prices are flexible in the long run, this amount of real national income will be offered in the long run regardless of the price level.

EXPECTATIONS AND THE RESPONSE TO AN UNEXPECTED CHANGE IN AGGREGATE DEMAND

The short-run aggregate supply (SRAS) curve is the schedule of real national income that all business firms are willing to supply at various price levels. The SRAS curve is constructed (see Figure 11.3) by allowing the price level to vary while holding constant the prices of the factors of production, the state of technology, and the expected price level. This last condition is very important to determining the position of the SRAS curve because the expected price level is important in determining the prices and wages of the factors of production.

The hypothesis of the natural rate of unemployment implies that when the actual change in the price level is the same as the expected change incorporated in the contracts that govern the supply of the factors of production, the economy will operate at the level of potential real national income. Thus the economy would operate above potential national income only if the actual price level were greater than the expected price level at the time the wage and price contracts of the factors of production were negotiated. The economy would operate below the level of potential national income only if the actual price level were lower than the expected price level at the time factor-price contracts were negotiated. Let us see why this would be so.

UNEXPECTED CHANGES IN AGGREGATE DEMAND: THE SHORT-RUN RESPONSE An expected price level is the result of forecasts by decision makers of the levels of aggregate demand and of short-run aggregate supply. Suppose that business firms and the owners

FIGURE 11.4
Unexpected Changes in Aggregate Demand

Part A shows that when the expected level of aggregate demand (AD_E) is the same as the actual level of aggregate demand (AD_A) and the expected level of short-run aggregate supply ($SRAS_E$) is the same as the actual level of short-run aggregate supply ($SRAS_A$), the economy will be in long-run equilibrium. Part B shows that when the actual level of aggregate demand exceeds the expected level, an inflationary gap will be created. Part C shows that when the actual level of aggregate demand is lower than the expected level, the actual price level will also be lower than expected, and a recessionary gap is created. In the long run both an inflationary and a recessionary gap will be eliminated as expectations adjust to the actual situation, causing a shift of the SRAS curve to $SRAS_{LR}$ in Parts B and C.

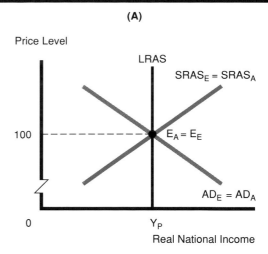

(A)

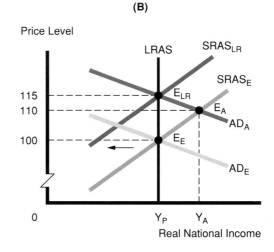

(B)

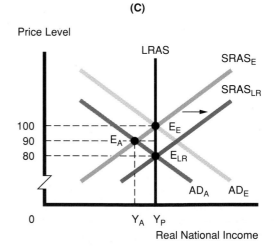

(C)

of the factors of production expected, as shown in Part A of Figure 11.4, that aggregate demand will be AD_E and the short-run aggregate supply curve will be $SRAS_E$. In this case the price level is expected to be 100. On this basis they will negotiate the contracts that govern the wages and prices of the factors of production in the short run. However, only if the actual price level turned out to be 100 would the combined output of all businesses be at the level of potential national income.

This situation is shown in Part A. The economy is expecting to produce at E_E, where the aggregate demand curve crosses the SRAS curve at a point on the LRAS curve. According to the natural-rate-of-unemployment hypothesis, when the actual level of prices turns out to be equal to the expected level of prices that governed the contracts determining factor prices, the economy will operate at the level of potential national income. In this case the actual price level will be 100, as expected, and the economy will operate at the level of potential national income Y_P.

But suppose that price expectations prove to be inaccurate because the actual level of aggregate demand exceeds the expected level ($AD_A > AD_E$). What will happen to the equilibrium level of real national income in the short run? This case is shown in Part B of Figure 11.4, where the actual equilibrium position is E_A instead of E_E. The actual price level turns out to be 110 instead of 100. Wages and prices of the factors of production are temporarily fixed according to a lower expected price level. When the actual level of aggregate demand (AD_A) exceeds the expected level (AD_E), the short-run equilibrium level of real national income will exceed the level of potential national income. The prices of the goods produced and sold by business firms will rise faster than the costs of production. Profitability will increase, and firms will increase output to Y_A, which is greater than Y_P. An inflationary gap will develop in the short run.

Suppose, however, that business firms and the owners of the factors of production enter into contracts to obtain resources based on an expected price level of 100 and the actual price level turns out to be 90, as it would if the actual level of aggregate demand (AD_A) is less than the forecasted level of AD_E, as shown in Part C. What will happen to the equilibrium level of real national income produced in the short run? In this case business firms will find that the selling prices of the goods they produce have declined more than their costs of production. Profitability will decline and business firms will reduce output. Real national income will decline in the short run to Y_A, which is less than Y_P.

It is therefore possible in the short run for actual real national income to be greater or less than potential national income, depending on whether the expected price level is lower or higher than the actual price level.

UNEXPECTED CHANGES IN AGGREGATE DEMAND: THE LONG-RUN RESPONSE A short-run equilibrium level of real national income that is different from the level of potential national income is a temporary affair. In the long run the SRAS curve will shift to eliminate either a recessionary or an inflationary gap that has resulted from incorrect expectations of the price level.

Why will the SRAS curve shift as the economy experiences either a recessionary or an inflationary gap and makes the transition from a short-run equilibrium to a long-run equilibrium? The answer is to be found in the adjustment of expectations to reality.

When experience contradicts expectations, expectations will change. If an inflationary gap exists, as shown in Part B of Figure 11.4, prior expectations of the future price level have been proved incorrect. When the contracts based on the incorrect forecasts expire, reality will win the day. The prices of the factors of production will be adjusted upward to take into account the rise in the price level that occurred while the contracts were in force and the factor prices were fixed. Moreover, recent

FIGURE 11.5
Supply Shocks

Part A shows the effect of an adverse supply shock. Initially the economy is in long-run equilibrium at E_E with the expected price level equal to the actual price level. When an adverse supply shock occurs, the SRAS curve shifts from $SRAS_E$ to $SRAS_A$. The price level increases to PL_A and real national income declines from Y_P to Y_A, creating a recessionary gap. Part B shows the effect of a beneficial supply shock, which causes the SRAS curve to shift to the right from $SRAS_E$ to $SRAS_A$. The price level unexpectedly declines from PL_E to PL_A and real national income increases from Y_P to Y_A. A beneficial supply shock will, if the economy was previously in long-run equilibrium, cause an inflationary gap to appear.

(A) Adverse Supply Shock

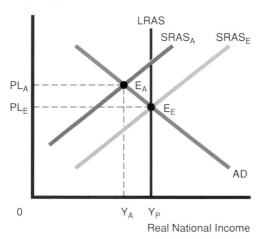

(B) Beneficial Supply Shock

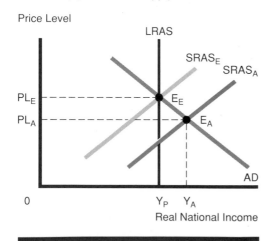

past experience will also influence currently held expectations about future price levels. Thus the shift of the SRAS curve will take into account expected future price level increases. Eventually, expectations will come into alignment with reality. When this occurs, the SRAS curve will shift to the left to $SRAS_{LR}$, where it intersects the actual aggregate demand curve AD_A at a point on the LRAS curve.

When a deflationary gap exists, as shown in Part C of Figure 11.4, it is because existing expectations of the price level were higher than turned out to be true. Expectations will adjust to reality in the long run and the SRAS curve will shift to the right to $SRAS_{LR}$ as factor prices adjust to the long-run equilibrium level.

Thus far we have been considering how expectations about the future price level adjust to reality when the expected level of aggregate demand is different from the actual level, thereby causing expectations of the future price level to be incorrect. By their very nature, expectations are forward-looking. They are forecasts made by economic decision makers. When expectations clash with reality, expectations will change until economic decision makers get it right. When expectations change, the SRAS curve will shift. It is this shift that allows the long-run adjustment process to take place.

The SRAS curve will shift in response to changes in the other determinants of aggregate supply as well. Among the most important causes of shifts in aggregate supply are supply shocks.

SUPPLY SHOCKS

A **supply shock** occurs when a determinant of aggregate supply, other than expectations, unexpectedly changes causing the aggregate supply curve to shift.

> *A supply shock is an event such as an increase in the price of imported oil, a crop failure, or a natural disaster that unexpectedly raises or lowers input prices.*

Supply shocks are *adverse* when the price of some input into the production process unexpectedly increases, and they are *beneficial* when an input price unexpectedly falls.

In the middle 1980s the United States experienced a series of beneficial supply shocks: Between 1985 and 1987 there were a series of good harvests and a decline in crude oil prices of about 50 percent. The end of the decade saw more adverse shocks in the form of higher energy prices and drought conditions in Midwestern agriculture.

Let us first consider the effects of an adverse supply shock. Perhaps weather conditions become unfavorable for agriculture. Early freezes or drought conditions reduce the size of crops. Such unfavorable changes can never be predicted. When adverse supply shocks occur, the price of some nonlabor inputs (let's call them materials prices) will increase, causing the costs of production to increase throughout the economy. Business firms will now desire to produce less at the existing price level. As a consequence the SRAS curve will suddenly and unexpectedly shift to the left.

This effect is shown in Part A of Figure 11.5. The economy is initially in long-run equilibrium at E_E, with the expected price level equal to the actual price level. When an adverse supply shock occurs, materials costs increase and the SRAS curve shifts to the left, from $SRAS_E$ to $SRAS_A$.

The equilibrium point thus moves from E_E to E_A, causing the price level to increase unexpectedly from PL_E to PL_A and the short-run equilibrium level of real national income to fall from Y_P to Y_A. An adverse supply shock thus causes a one-time increase in the price level and causes the unemployment rate to rise. If the economy had been operating at full employment, an adverse supply shock will cause the unemployment rate to exceed the natural rate of unemployment, thereby creating a recessionary gap.

Beneficial supply shocks have the opposite effect. Suppose that weather conditions are unusually favorable and harvests are more abundant than expected. The prices of agricultural commodities such as food and fiber will suddenly decline. Because materials prices are now unexpectedly lower, so are the costs of production, which causes the SRAS curve to shift to the right.

The consequences of this change are shown in Part B of Figure 11.5. The macroeconomy is initially in long-run equilibrium at E_E. A beneficial supply shock disturbs this equilibrium, causing the SRAS curve to shift to the right, from $SRAS_E$ to $SRAS_A$. A new short-run equilibrium is established at E_A. The price level falls from PL_E to PL_A and real national income increases from Y_P to Y_A. If the economy was initially in long-run equilibrium, a beneficial supply shock will have the one-time effect of reducing the rate of inflation and causing the rate of unemployment to fall below the natural rate of unemployment. A beneficial supply shock will in the process cause an inflationary gap to appear.

Both recessionary and inflationary gaps are short-run situations. Both will eventually be eliminated in the long run by an automatic adjustment process.

LONG-RUN ADJUSTMENTS RECONSIDERED: THE AUTOMATIC ADJUSTMENT PROCESS

Recessionary and inflationary gaps exist because the expectations about the future price level, on which the position of the SRAS curve is based, turned out to be incorrect. When a recessionary gap exists, the actual price level is higher than the price level that will support full employment. When an inflationary gap exists, the actual price level is lower than the price level that will allow full employment to occur. Both inflationary and recessionary gaps are short-run situations that will be eliminated as expectations about the price level are adjusted to the reality of the situation and the SRAS curve shifts accordingly.

RECESSIONARY GAP Let us consider the case of a recessionary gap. A recessionary gap can exist as a result of either an unexpected decline in aggregate demand, as shown in Part A of Figure 11.6, or an adverse supply shock, as shown in Part B. In both cases the short-run equilibrium level of real national income will fall from Y_P to Y_A. The expected price level before the changes is now inappropriate for the new situation. In the case of a deficiency of aggregate demand, the price level is now lower than expected, whereas in the case of an adverse supply shock, the price level is now higher than was expected.

In the long run, however, economic decision makers will come to realize that their previously held expectations were incorrect for the new situation. Price-level expectations will adjust to the new conditions. When

FIGURE 11.6
Automatic Adjustment Process When a Recessionary Gap Exists

A recessionary gap can exist either because of an unexpected decline in aggregate demand, as shown in Part A, or because of an adverse supply shock that suddenly reduces the level of short-run aggregate supply, as shown in Part B. In both cases the expected price level has turned out to be incorrect and a recessionary gap has appeared. In the first case the expected price level is higher than the actual price level, and in the second the actual price level is higher than the expected price level. The long-run solution is the same in both cases, as shown in Part C. The SRAS curve will shift to the right from $SRAS_1$ to $SRAS_2$ as price-level expectations change and workers accept lower money wages.

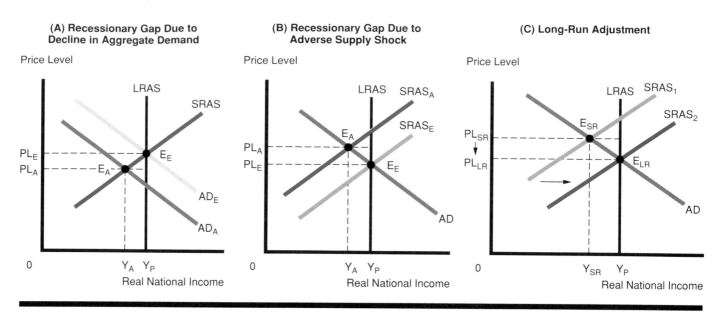

a recessionary gap exists, decision makers will adjust their price-level expectations downward, and the SRAS curve will shift down from $SRAS_1$ in Part C until it reaches $SRAS_2$ and the recessionary gap disappears. The shift in the SRAS curve causes the price level to fall and real national income to increase to the level of potential national income. When this happens, the economy has been restored to **long-run equilibrium** at E_{LR}.

> *Long-run equilibrium exists when the expected price level equals the actual price level.*

INFLATIONARY GAP The same process will work in reverse if an inflationary gap exists. Suppose an unexpected increase in aggregate demand or a beneficial supply shock occurs. In either case an inflationary gap in the short run will be created. As a result, existing price-level expectations, which govern the position of the SRAS curve, have been proven incorrect.

An inflationary gap could be created either by an unexpected increase in aggregate demand, as shown in Part A of Figure 11.7, or by a beneficial supply shock, as shown in Part B. In either case the equilibrium position moves from E_E to E_A, and real national income increases beyond potential national income from Y_P to Y_A. In the case of an increase in aggregate demand (Part A), the price level rises from PL_E to PL_A, and in the case of a beneficial supply shock (Part B), the price level declines from PL_E to PL_A. The result in either case is the creation of an inflationary gap. Real national income (Y_A) exceeds potential national income (Y_P). The expected price level formed before the surprise shift in aggregate demand, or in the short-run aggregate supply, has been proven incorrect by subsequent events.

FIGURE 11.7

Automatic Adjustment Process When an Inflationary Gap Exists

An inflationary gap can exist either because of an unexpected increase in aggregate demand, as shown in Part A, or because of a beneficial supply shock that causes the SRAS curve unexpectedly to shift to the right, as shown in Part B. In both cases the actual price level has turned out to be different than expected. In the case of an increase in aggregate demand, the actual price level turned out to be higher than expected. In the case of a beneficial supply shock, the actual price level is lower than expected. In both cases the inflationary gap that appears will be eliminated in the long run, as shown in Part C, as price-level expectations adjust and the SRAS curve shifts to the left as wages increase accordingly.

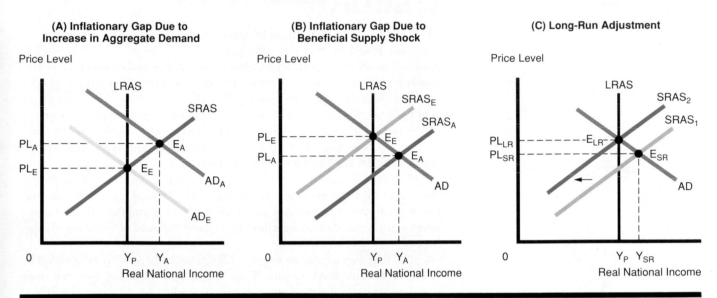

Because the existing price level is too low to allow a long-run equilibrium to occur, the price level will begin to rise. Tight labor markets and increasing prices will cause both business firms and workers to revise their price-level expectations. Once the price level is widely expected to rise, workers will insist on higher money wages when their employment contracts expire. Business firms will find that their costs of production have increased as wages rise, and they will increase prices. As prices and costs rise, the SRAS curve will shift to the left, as shown in Part C.

The equilibrium position will eventually move from E_{SR} to E_{LR}. When E_{LR} is reached, the macroeconomy will have reestablished long-run equilibrium. The aggregate demand curve intersects both the SRAS and the LRAS curves at E_{LR}. The expected price level is now equal to the actual price level, and no further incentive exists for the price level to change. Changes in the expected price level, as reflected in changes in product and factor prices, have eliminated the inflationary gap. The quantity of real national income produced is equal to the level of potential national income and the unemployment rate now equals the natural rate of unemployment.

The causes of recessionary and inflationary gaps are the unexpected events that shift the aggregate demand and aggregate supply curves in ways that were not anticipated when the contracts governing the SRAS curve were negotiated. The automatic adjustment process suggests that the effects of such surprises will not be permanent. Eventually, price expectations will adjust to reality, and the economy will return to the natural rate of unemployment and will produce at the level of potential real national income.

The automatic adjustment process suggests that in the long run the macroeconomy will operate at full employment with the rate of unemployment at the natural rate. Surprises, whether affecting aggregate demand or aggregate supply, will be automatically accommodated. But how long will this automatic adjustment take? Economists are divided on this issue. The duration of the Great Depression — over a decade — is not very reassuring in this regard.

SUMMARY

1. The explicit consideration of aggregate supply allows the basic macroeconomic model to determine the price level, to show the automatic adjustment process at work when either a short-run inflationary or recessionary gap exists, and to predict the consequences of a supply shock.

2. The short-run aggregate supply (SRAS) curve relates the quantity of real national income that will be supplied at every price level. The prices of the factors of production are generally fixed in the short run but variable in the long run. The SRAS curve will slope upward if fixed-price contracts exist for the factors of production.

3. The natural rate of unemployment is the rate of unemployment that is consistent with the economy operating at the level of potential national income with any constant rate of inflation. The natural rate of unemployment can be maintained indefinitely without the rate of inflation changing.

4. The long-run aggregate supply (LRAS) curve is vertical at the level of potential real national income. Thus the price level in the long run does not determine the level of gross national product in the macroeconomy.

5. The SRAS curve crosses the vertical LRAS curve at the expected price level. Because it is upward-sloping, the SRAS curve reveals that an unexpected increase in the price level will add more to a business firm's revenues than to costs, and hence will lead businesses to increase output in the short run.

6. Short-run equilibrium will occur where the aggregate demand curve crosses the SRAS curve. Long-run equilibrium will occur where the level of aggregate demand is equal to the level of real national income supplied in both the short run and the long run.

7. An adverse supply shock will cause the SRAS curve to shift to the left. Real national income will fall and the price level will rise. If the economy was initially in long-run equilibrium, a recessionary gap will be created.

8. A beneficial supply shock will cause the SRAS curve to shift to the right. Real national income will increase and the price level will fall. If the economy was initially in long-run equilibrium, an inflationary gap will be created.

9. A recessionary gap exists whenever real national income is below the level of potential national income. An inflationary gap exists whenever real national income exceeds the level of potential national income. Both recessionary and inflationary gaps result from incorrect price-level expectations, which arise when the actual price level is different from the expected price level.

10. Whenever either a recessionary or an inflationary gap exists, there will be an automatic adjustment process that will work to restore long-run equilibrium. This process will involve a change in price-level expectations affecting the prices of the factors of production and causing the SRAS curve to shift in the way required to restore long-run equilibrium.

HOW THE MACROECONOMY RESPONDS TO AN INFLATIONARY GAP

PREVIEW 11.1 ANALYSIS

The macroeconomy's automatic adjustment process can be seen at work eliminating an inflationary gap during the period from 1965 to 1970. Attempts to employ economic policy to stop the developing inflation failed, either because of faulty design or lack of will, and the economy's inherent stability was put to the test.

The macroeconomy was expanding rapidly between 1966 and 1967. The rate of economic growth was 6 percent during these two years. The economy, with only a temporary decline in the rate of expansion during 1967, continued to expand until 1970. The expansion was characterized by a level of real national income that was greater than potential national income, and an unemployment rate that was below the natural rate of unemployment. The result was an inflationary gap in 1966 that was equal to 5 percent of potential national income.

The existence of an inflationary gap usually signals future inflation. The 1966–1970 period was no exception, as the price level increased significantly in these years, as can be seen in Table 11.1. The year 1966 represented a clear break in the inflation performance of the economy. From 1960 to 1965 the rate of inflation was below 2 percent, generally hovering between 1 and 1½ percent. During 1966 the rate of inflation increased to around 3 percent. After 1966 the rate of inflation increased progressively, approaching 6 percent by 1970.

The initial increase in inflation did not go unnoticed by policymakers. President Johnson's economic advisors in 1966 urged a change in fiscal policy to reduce aggregate demand, but no action was taken at the time. The Federal Reserve Bank, in an attempt to halt developing inflation, did not allow the money supply to increase at all during the last three quarters of 1966. (The quantity of money in the economy, you will recall, is one of the determinants of aggregate demand.) When monetary growth halted, aggregate demand did not increase as much as had been expected.

The result was a temporary slowdown in economic activity during 1967. The short-term effects on the economy were striking. While the rate

TABLE 11.1
Macroeconomic Statistics: 1965–1970

YEAR (1)	REAL GNP (BILLIONS OF 1972 DOLLARS) (2)	POTENTIAL GNP (3)	INFLATION RATE		UNEMPLOYMENT RATE (6)	ECONOMIC GROWTH RATE (7)	INFLATIONARY GAP (PERCENT GNP) (8)
			GNP DEFLATOR (4)	CPI (5)			
1965	$ 930	$ 896	2.2%	1.7%	4.4%	6.0%	3.7%
1966	985	937	3.2	2.9	3.7	6.0	5.1
1967	1,011	978	3.0	2.9	3.7	2.7	3.4
1968	1,058	1,013	4.4	4.2	3.5	4.6	4.4
1969	1,088	1,048	5.1	5.4	3.4	2.8	3.8
1970	1,086	1,088	5.4	5.9	4.8	−0.2	0.0

Sources: *Economic Report of the President, 1985* (Washington, DC: U.S. Government Printing Office, 1985); R. Gordon, "Understanding Inflation in the 1980's."

FIGURE 11.8

Elimination of an Inflationary Gap through the Automatic Adjustment Process

The situation that existed between 1966 and 1970 in the United States is modeled in this figure. An inflationary gap has been created equal to $Y_A - Y_P$. The initial price-level expectations of workers and businesses have been proven incorrect. As expectations quickly change in the light of the new reality, and as expiring wage and factor-price contracts are renegotiated at higher rates, there is a shift from $SRAS_1$ to $SRAS_2$. The price level will increase and the inflationary gap shrink as a result. This process will continue until $SRAS_4$ is reached, completely eliminating the inflationary gap and bringing price-level expectations into agreement with reality.

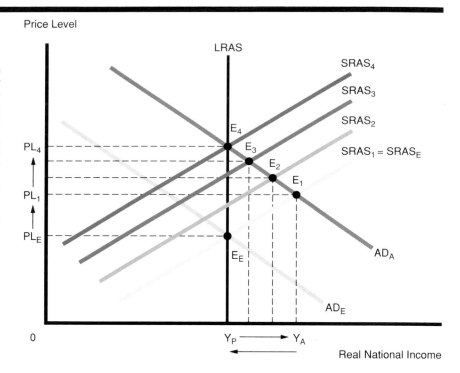

of inflation stabilized during 1967, private investment declined substantially, especially in housing construction, leading to a brief period of negative economic growth. The slowdown in economic activity raised fears of a full-scale recession. The Federal Reserve quickly relented and allowed the money supply subsequently to grow at rates actually greater than had prevailed before the decision to restrict the money supply was taken.

The economy quickly recovered, but the effect of the brief slowdown is apparent in the annual statistics of 1967. The rate of economic growth (see Table 11.1) fell from 6 percent to less than 3 percent for the year. The rate of inflation in 1968, stimulated by the return of monetary growth, once again began to accelerate, and the unemployment rate declined to a level even further below the natural rate.

President Johnson's economic advisors continued to urge a change in fiscal policy. A temporary tax surcharge was recommended in January 1967, but was not enacted until 18 months later. For reasons discussed in the previous chapter, the temporary tax surcharge failed to stem aggregate demand. Monetary and fiscal policy thus failed to remedy the inflationary gap that existed. It was left by default for the automatic adjustment process to restore real national income to the level of potential national income.

The automatic adjustment process is depicted in Figure 11.8. An inflationary gap exists because the level of aggregate demand is greater than was expected when the SRAS curve was established. Curve $SRAS_1$ exists because labor contracts were negotiated with an expected price level of PL_E, reflecting an expected equilibrium position for the economy at E_E, where the expected level of aggregate demand AD_E intersects both the SRAS and LRAS curves. The actual aggregate demand (AD_A), however, produces a short-run equilibrium at E_1 with a price level of PL_1 greater than expected. Real national income produced (Y_A) exceeds the level of potential national income (Y_P) and an inflationary gap is created.

When an inflationary gap exists, the actual price level is too low to establish long-run equilibrium at the level of potential national income. The price level will tend to rise as labor contracts expire and are renegotiated, taking into account the rise in the price level that has occurred and changes in expectations. The SRAS curve will shift to the left to $SRAS_2$, and the size of the inflationary gap will decline. This process will continue until the expected price level equals the actual price level. When this happens, assuming no further increases in aggregate demand, the SRAS curve will have shifted to $SRAS_4$, the equilibrium point will move to E_4, and the macroeconomy will be in long-run equilibrium. The inflationary gap will have been eliminated.

The automatic adjustment process working on an inflationary gap yields three implications that can be tested against the statistical evidence. The first implication is that wages and the overall price level should increase together, but that wages should rise faster than the price level. It is clear from Part A of Figure 11.9 that wages and the price level are both rising from 1965 to 1970 and that wage increases exceed the rise in the cost of living measured as the change in the consumer price index. The increase in wages is pushing the SRAS curve to the left relative to the aggregate demand curve, exactly as the automatic adjustment process predicts.

The second implication is that the inflationary gap, measured as a percentage of potential national income, should decline. Column 8 of Table 11.1 indicates that the inflationary gap was generally declining. The decline in the inflationary gap is also shown in Part B of Figure 11.9. The inflationary gap in 1966 was 5.1 percent of potential national income. By 1967, partially as a result of the abortive tight money policy, the gap had fallen to 3.4 percent. But with the abandoning of tight money, the gap increased during 1968 to 4.4 percent. Thereafter, consistent with theory, the gap declined to 3.8 percent in 1969 and was eliminated entirely in 1970. The final elimination of the inflationary gap in 1970 was due mainly to the advent of a recession during that year. But, with the exception of 1967, the trend in the size of the inflationary gap was downward and consistent with the operation of the automatic adjustment process.

The third implication is that the rate of economic growth should be falling while the price level is increasing. The information contained in Part C of Figure 11.9 measures both the rate of economic growth and the rate of inflation as the percentage change in the GNP deflator. With the exception of 1967, this predicted relationship exists in the data.

The evidence suggests that between 1966 and 1970 the automatic adjustment process was at work eliminating the inflationary gap despite the expansionary fiscal and monetary policies that existed during these years.

What can be said about the strength and duration of the automatic adjustment process? Unfortunately, very little from this evidence. The inflationary gap that existed during this period was not stagnant. The gap, with the exception of 1966, was constantly being fed by increases in the money supply. Thus the automatic adjustment process that caused the progressive shift to the left of the SRAS curve was in effect attempting to hit a moving target as aggregate demand increased throughout the period. Inflationary expectations were trying to catch up with reality.

About all that can be concluded from the experiences of the 1965–1970 period is that when monetary and fiscal policy failed to do the job intended, an automatic adjustment process was at work. In the absence of

FIGURE 11.9
Automatic Adjustment Process: 1966–1970

When an inflationary gap exists, as it did between 1965 and 1970, the automatic adjustment process would cause both wages and prices to increase, with wages increasing more rapidly than prices. This occurred between 1965 and 1970, as can be seen in Part A. The automatic adjustment process will also cause the gap between actual and potential national income to close as the price level increases. Again this was happening between 1965 and 1970, as Part B demonstrates. Finally, when the automatic adjustment process is working, the rate of growth of real GNP should decline as the price level increases. This also happened, as Part C shows.

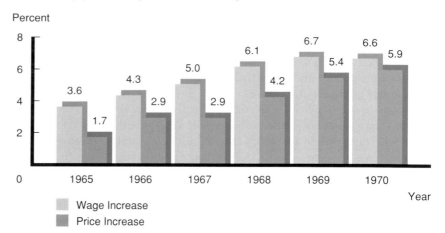

(A) Percentage Increases in Wages and Prices: 1965–1970

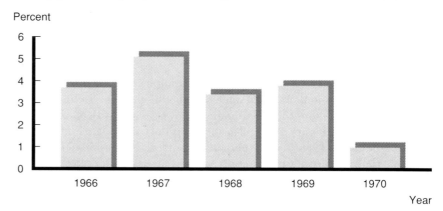

(B) Inflationary Gap as a Percentage of Potential Income: 1966–1970

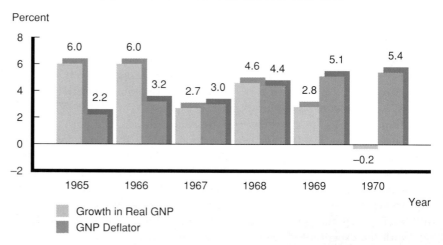

(C) Inflation and Economic Growth: 1965–1970

further changes in the rate at which aggregate demand was increasing, the rise of the price level would have eventually restored the economy to the level of potential national income. A stable rate of inflation would have developed, with the economy operating at the level of potential national income and the unemployment rate at the natural rate. By 1970 the economy was approaching this condition.

THE INFLATIONARY RECESSION OF 1973–1975

The U.S. economy suffered a severe recession in the 1973–1975 period. The unemployment rate nearly doubled within two years, rising to over 8 percent of the labor force. Real national income declined sufficiently to create a recessionary gap of about 7 percent of potential national income. This recession was unusual in that it was accompanied by an explosion of inflation. Typically, recessions in the past had been associated with a decline in the price level, not an increase. The annual increase in the price level reached double-digit levels (12 percent) in 1974, as measured by the consumer price index. Recession coupled with inflation was quickly labeled "stagflation" or "inflationary recession" by the nation's press, which considered it to be among the worst of all macroeconomic situations.

Millions of Americans agreed. During the recession a number of unusual developments simultaneously happened that spread widely the misery that a recession causes. An energy crisis swept the nation. Gasoline was in short supply, and millions of Americans waited in long lines for the privilege of buying a tank of gasoline. Nature conspired to make the situation even worse. In 1973 a severe winter damaged or destroyed many crops, and food, feed, and fiber prices rose significantly. The combination of exploding inflation, soaring unemployment, shortages of energy, and rapidly rising food prices made many Americans wonder whether their economy was in the midst of collapse.

The macroeconomic statistics of the period reveal the seriousness of this inflationary recession. Annual statistics for the period are provided in Table 11.2. The recession that began in November 1973 lasted until March 1975 before being followed by a recovery from 1976 to 1978. The definitive characteristic of a recession is a decline in real national income. This certainly happened in 1974 and 1975. The rate of economic growth was negative during both 1974 and 1975 as real GNP fell. This decline in real national income was led by a severe decline in industrial production, creating excess capacity economywide. Capacity utilization in the upper 80s is considered to be full employment. The rapidity of the decline in industrial production that occurred between 1974 and 1975 marked this recession as very serious.

What was extraordinary about this recession was the behavior of the price level. In a traditional recession the decline in aggregate output

TABLE 11.2
Macroeconomic Statistics: 1973–1978

YEAR (1)	REAL GNP (BILLIONS OF 1972 DOLLARS) (2)	PRICE LEVEL (3)	POTENTIAL GNP (4)	INDUSTRIAL PRODUCTION INDEX (5)	CAPACITY UTILIZATION INDEX (6)	INFLATION RATE (7)	UNEMPLOYMENT RATE (8)	GNP GAP (PERCENT Y_P) (9)
1973	$1,235	133	$1,249	130	88.1	8.8%	4.8%	.989
1974	1,214	148	1,258	129	84.3	12.2	5.5	.965
1975	1,192	161	1,284	118	74.4	7.0	8.3	.928
1976	1,265	171	1,325	131	80.4	4.8	7.6	.955
1977	1,370	182	1,391	138	82.6	6.8	6.9	.985
1978	1,437	195	1,439	146	84.8	9.0	6.0	.998

Sources: *Economic Report of the President, 1985* (Washington, DC: U.S. Government Printing Office, 1985); Robert H. Rasche and John A. Tatom, "Energy, Resources, and Potential GNP," *REVIEW, Federal Reserve of St. Louis*, June 1977.

FIGURE 11.10
The Inflationary Recession of 1974–1975

The significant increases in the prices of energy that occurred in 1974 represented a permanent adverse supply shock that created a recessionary gap, measured from Y_A to the new level of potential national income, Y_P'. The permanent adverse supply shift reduced the production capacity of the economy. In the long run, if government economic policy had remained unchanged, the automatic adjustment process would have caused the SRAS curve to shift to the right until it intersected aggregate demand at point E_{LR} on the new LRAS curve. What actually happened, as shown in Part B, was that government took actions that expanded aggregate demand, shifting the aggregate demand curve from AD to AD'. The new, lower level of potential national income Y_P' was approached during 1978 but at a higher price level (PL$_A$) than would have existed (PL$_{LR}$) if the automatic adjustment process had been allowed to work.

(A) Effect of Permanent Adverse Supply Shock

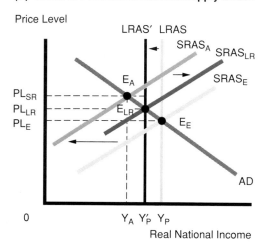

(B) What Actually Happened

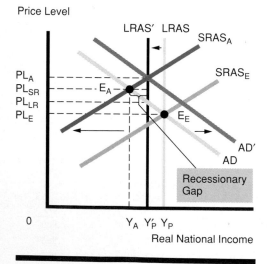

would be accompanied by a decline in the price level, or at the very least by a decline in the rate of inflation. Not so this time. Inflation actually increased significantly during the recession years.

A rise in the price level accompanied with a decline in real output cannot be explained by the usual cause of a recession: an unexpected decrease in aggregate demand. A decline in aggregate demand would produce a falling price level along with the decline in real output. This obviously did not happen during the inflationary recession of 1974–1975.

The cause of this recession is instead to be found on the supply side. A decline in short-run aggregate supply can account for a simultaneous decline in real national income coupled with a rise in the price level. This can be observed in Part A of Figure 11.10, with the economy initially in equilibrium at E_E, where aggregate demand (AD), the expected level of short-run aggregate supply (SRAS$_E$), and long-run aggregate supply (LRAS) all intersect. The initial equilibrium price level is PL$_E$ and the economy is operating at Y_P, the initial level of potential national income.

Suppose, as shown in Part A, a permanent adverse supply shift causes aggregate supply to decline. The SRAS and LRAS curves will shift to the left, from SRAS$_E$ to SRAS$_A$, and LRAS to LRAS'. Short-run equilibrium will move from E_E to E_A. The price level will increase to PL$_{SR}$. A recessionary gap will be created, as shown on the graph, measured from Y_A to Y_P', the new level of potential national income. The actual rate of unemployment now exceeds the natural rate. The behavior of real output and the changes in the price level that occurred during the inflationary recession of 1974–1975 were therefore consistent with a decline in short-run and long-run aggregate supply. Price-level expectations that existed prior to the supply shock proved incorrect and would adjust upward.

The automatic adjustment process will work on the recessionary gap. The excess unemployment will mean a weak labor market, so that the expected price level will not be PL$_{SR}$ but somewhat lower. To restore full employment, workers will accept increases in money wages that are less than the increase in the price level. As this occurs, the SRAS curve will shift down until it intersects aggregate demand at point E_{LR} on the new long-run aggregate supply curve LRAS'. Real wages will have declined at the new full employment equilibrium, because the economy reaches full employment at a lower level of potential national income than before, Y_P' instead of Y_P. The economy suffers a permanent decline in its capacity to produce.

A decline in the SRAS curve could come about in response to a change in one or more of the determinants of aggregate supply other than expectations. A decline in both the short-run and long-run aggregate supply would result, for example, when the price of one or more of the factors of production permanently increases. The price of energy mentioned above certainly fits the bill.

The price of crude oil increased from about $2 per barrel in 1973 to $10.75 per barrel in 1974 and 1975. Crude oil provides one of the main sources of energy for the U.S. industrial economy. When the price of crude oil increased, so did the prices of substitute sources of energy, such as coal and electricity, as the industrial sector attempted to adjust to the rise in oil prices. An energy crisis developed as a result. But this was not all — the dramatic rise in the price of energy was coupled with significant declines in agricultural output worldwide.

In the United States a severe winter in 1973 caused a 5 percent decline in agricultural output in 1974. The result was a substantial increase in food prices beginning in 1973 and continuing throughout 1974. The decline in agricultural output was a temporary adverse supply shock that made the impact of higher energy prices worse.

The rapid increase in energy and agricultural prices represented an adverse supply shock sufficient to propel the SRAS curve to the left during 1974 and early 1975. The effects of the adverse supply shock on the price level and on real national income are shown in Part A of Figure 11.10. The adverse supply shock created a recessionary gap. Economic growth turned negative, real national income declined, unemployment increased above the natural rate, and the price level rapidly rose.

The recession of 1974–1975 was so severe that widespread fears of another depression developed. Inflation was frightening, but the possibility of another depression was more frightening still. The president, the Congress, and the Federal Reserve decided to act to eliminate the recessionary gap through expansionary fiscal and monetary policies. An expansionary fiscal policy was enacted by March 1975, combining a temporary tax rebate, an investment tax credit, and public-service employment programs. The temporary tax cut probably wasn't very effective, for reasons that are now well known to you. But the other programs to expand aggregate demand helped to shift the aggregate demand curve to the right between 1975 and 1978. Beginning in 1976, the Federal Reserve, acting in concert with the legislature, allowed the money supply to increase more rapidly than before.

The combined result of these expansionary policies was to increase aggregate demand, shifting the aggregate demand curve to the right from AD to AD′ in Part B of Figure 11.10. Full employment was restored by 1978, but at a lower level of potential national income and at a higher price level than before the supply shock. One estimate suggests that the level of potential national income was permanently reduced by over 5 percent and the price level was increased by an equal amount due to the oil supply shock. The price level was actually increased by more than 5 percent, of course, because of the effect of increasing aggregate demand. Instead of a new equilibrium price level of PL_{LR} in Part B, a higher price level equal to PL_A resulted.

REQUIRED ECONOMIC CONCEPTS

Inflationary recession	Natural rate of unemployment
Short run	Potential national income
Long run	Supply shock
Expectations	Long-run equilibrium

KEY QUESTIONS

1. What is the name applied to the phenomenon of the simultaneous increase in the rate of inflation and the rate of unemployment?
2. What slope does the long-run aggregate supply (LRAS) curve have?
3. How does the actual level of prices relate to the expected level of prices in long-run equilibrium?
4. What is the short-run relationship between price level and aggregate output? What is the long-run relationship?
5. What is the definition of the short run in macroeconomic theory? The long run?
6. On what do business firms' demand for labor mostly depend? On what does workers' supply depend?

7. If the consumer price index is expected to rise, how will unions respond when their current labor contracts terminate?
8. What would you expect to happen to money wages during periods of high unemployment? To real wages?
9. What is the natural rate of unemployment? How is it related to potential national income? Does the natural rate depend on the inflation rate?
10. Suppose the economy is at the level of potential national income. If the actual price level were greater than the expected price level, would national income initially move below or above potential national income or remain at potential national income?
11. What parameters cause the short-run aggregate supply (SRAS) curve to shift?
12. What happens to the SRAS curve if the level of prices is expected to rise? If factor costs decline?
13. Name three possible adverse supply shocks. What would be their effect on the SRAS curve, and hence on the price level and real national income?
14. In the aggregate-supply/aggregate-demand model, what is the major source of recessionary and inflationary gaps?
15. What is meant by the automatic adjustment process of the macroeconomy?

PROBLEMS

1. Indicate the change, if any, in the short-run aggregate supply (SRAS) curve and/or the aggregate demand curve (AD) for the following:
   a. Private-sector union membership as a percentage of the labor force declined from 20 percent in 1980 to 14 percent in 1988.
   b. Real-wage increases have grown faster than productivity increases.
   c. Consumer spending has begun to shake off last quarter's doldrums. The shipment of nondefense goods is up by 20 percent. Nonresidential construction declined but not enough to stop the expansion.
   d. The increase in the number of temporary and part-time people hired accounted for more than half of the new jobs created in the 1980s. It held down labor costs relative to the inflation because of the greater labor flexibility it allowed.
   e. The federal deficit is nearly eliminated after three consecutive years of reductions in the government's budgets.

2. Consider the macroeconomic data that appears in the table to the left.
   Is this information consistent with the shape of the SRAS curve? Explain.

3. A worker earns $50 a day in money wages. Calculate the changes in a worker's real wage if he or she is locked into a union contract for a two-year period during which the economy is experiencing a rapidly increasing rate of inflation, with the price index going from 90 to 95 to 110 to 125 to 150.

4. Using the accompanying graph, answer the following questions:

CAPACITY UTILIZA- TION	UNIT COSTS OF PRODUCTION
75%	$2.00
78	2.05
81	2.12
83	2.22
87	2.35

a. Assuming that the shift in equilibrium from point 1 to point 2 is the result of a change in investment spending of $20 billion, did investment go up or down? Determine the size of the multiplier.

b. Assuming that investment spending of $20 billion occurs and shifts aggregate equilibrium from point 2 to point 3, what is the size of the multiplier in this range? Does it differ from the multiplier in Part a? Why or why not?

5. "Money wage rates depend on price-level expectations, but real wages ultimately are independent of the inflation rate." Fully explain the meaning of this quote, distinguishing the short run from the long run.

6. "In the pure Keynesian world, when aggregate demand shifts, output adjusts while the price level remains fixed. In the pure classical world, prices adjust while output remains fixed." What is the source of the fundamental difference between the Keynesian and classical views? In the real world, where money wage rates and the absolute price level rarely decline, how can the classical view be justified, since it requires both the upward and downward flexibility of wage rates and prices?

APPLICATION ANALYSIS

1. a. From the data below, gathered from the annual *Economic Report of the President*, determine for each year (1952–1953, 1974–1975, etc.) whether there was "apparently" a shift in the SRAS curve or the aggregate demand curve. Also, indicate the direction of the shift. Why was the word *apparently* used above?

b. Indicate the consecutive range of years in which the economy was either recessionary, mostly stable, or inflationary.

c. In what year(s) was stagflation in effect?

YEAR	CPI (1967 = 100)	GNP (BILLIONS OF 1982 DOLLARS)	UNEMPLOYMENT RATE
1952	79.5	$ 348.0	2.9%
1953	80.1	366.8	2.8
1954	80.5	366.8	5.4
1955	80.2	400.0	4.3
1956	81.4	421.7	4.0
.	.	.	.
.	.	.	.
.	.	.	.
1974	147.1	2,729.3	5.5
1975	161.2	2,695.0	8.3
1976	170.5	2,826.7	7.6
1977	181.5	2,958.6	6.9
1978	195.4	3,115.2	6.0
1979	217.4	3,192.4	5.8
1980	246.8	3,187.1	7.0
1981	272.4	3,248.8	7.5
1982	289.1	3,166.0	9.5
1983	298.4	3,279.1	9.5
1984	311.1	3,501.4	7.4

12 FISCAL POLICY

THE ECONOMIC RECOVERY TAX ACT OF 1981

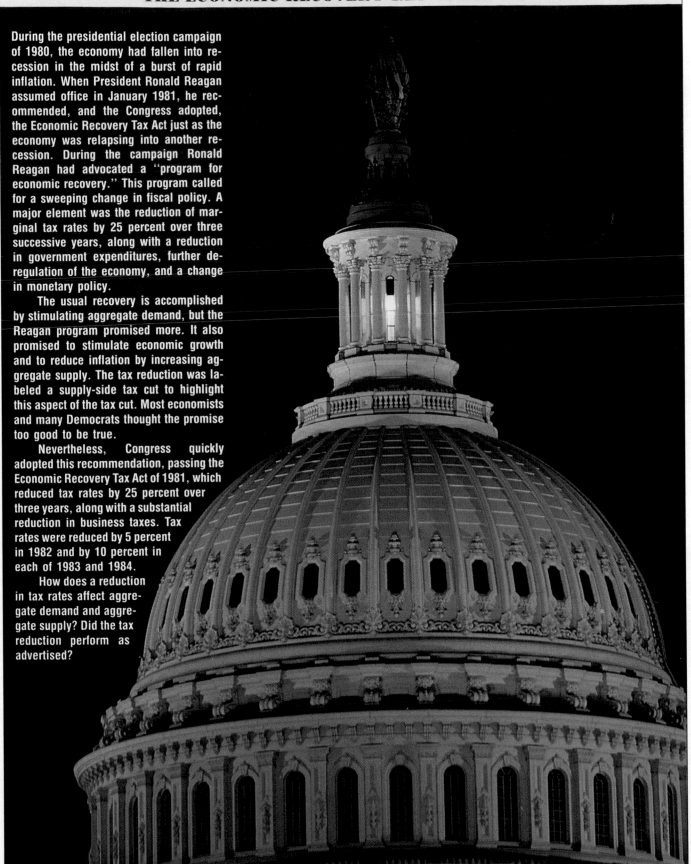

During the presidential election campaign of 1980, the economy had fallen into recession in the midst of a burst of rapid inflation. When President Ronald Reagan assumed office in January 1981, he recommended, and the Congress adopted, the Economic Recovery Tax Act just as the economy was relapsing into another recession. During the campaign Ronald Reagan had advocated a "program for economic recovery." This program called for a sweeping change in fiscal policy. A major element was the reduction of marginal tax rates by 25 percent over three successive years, along with a reduction in government expenditures, further deregulation of the economy, and a change in monetary policy.

The usual recovery is accomplished by stimulating aggregate demand, but the Reagan program promised more. It also promised to stimulate economic growth and to reduce inflation by increasing aggregate supply. The tax reduction was labeled a supply-side tax cut to highlight this aspect of the tax cut. Most economists and many Democrats thought the promise too good to be true.

Nevertheless, Congress quickly adopted this recommendation, passing the Economic Recovery Tax Act of 1981, which reduced tax rates by 25 percent over three years, along with a substantial reduction in business taxes. Tax rates were reduced by 5 percent in 1982 and by 10 percent in each of 1983 and 1984.

How does a reduction in tax rates affect aggregate demand and aggregate supply? Did the tax reduction perform as advertised?

IS A LARGE NATIONAL DEBT A THREAT TO FUTURE PROSPERITY?

The federal budget deficit and the expanding size of the national debt together form the hottest political issue since the Vietnam War. The federal budget, by official measure, has been in deficit, with expenditures exceeding revenues, in all but 8 of the last 57 years. Since 1960 only one year has seen a surplus, and the last 17 years have presented a string of unbroken deficits, with more to come. As a result the national debt doubled between 1983 and 1988 and now exceeds $2.8 trillion.

Democrats and Republicans echo each other's proclamations of looming disaster, limiting their differences to proposed remedies and to the casting of blame as to which party is responsible for this deplorable development. Political rhetoric has replaced sober economic analysis, ignoring the question: Does the size of the national debt matter, and if so, how does it matter?

• INTRODUCTION •

The federal government is a major player in the U.S. economy. Federal government spending equals 24 percent of gross national product (GNP) and tax receipts represent about 19 percent. Given its relative size, the spending and taxing actions of the federal government will have a significant effect on the economy. In this chapter we shall discuss some of the ways the fiscal actions of the federal government affect the economy.

The fiscal activities of the federal government directly affect the two basic macroeconomic variables, real national income and the price level. The spending and taxing activities of the federal government can therefore be employed to influence the macroeconomic performance of the economy. This is known as **fiscal policy.**

Fiscal policy is the conscious use of the spending and taxing powers of the federal government in pursuit of the government's macroeconomic goals.

Fiscal policy (sometimes called *stabilization policy*) generally operates through budgetary totals. It is more concerned with how much government will spend in total rather than in individual programs. The goals of fiscal policy are to influence the performance of the economy so as to allow the simultaneous existence of full employment, a stable price level, and rapid economic growth. In the United States, only the federal government has a fiscal policy. •

THE POSSIBILITIES OF FISCAL POLICY

Historically, the economy has experienced wide variations in the level of economic activity known as the business cycle, which was discussed in Chapter 8. The business cycle is composed of four phases: recession or contraction, trough, recovery or expansion, and peak. Recessions are periods of declining real national income, the trough is the low point of the contraction phase, recoveries or expansions are periods of expanding real national income, and the peak is the high point of economic activity. Fluctuations in aggregate demand and sometimes in aggregate supply underlie the business cycle.

Because the spending and taxing activities of the federal government directly influence the economy's aggregate demand curve, the government can decide to pursue a fiscal policy that will counteract recessionary and inflationary gaps.

TYPES OF FISCAL POLICY

There are two types of fiscal policy: discretionary fiscal policy and automatic fiscal policy. Discretionary fiscal policy is aimed at correcting persistent recessionary and inflationary gaps that develop from time to time. Automatic fiscal policy involves built-in stabilizers that moderate swings in aggregate demand. Discretionary fiscal policy changes happen only infrequently, whereas automatic fiscal policy is continuously in operation. First we shall discuss discretionary fiscal policy.

DISCRETIONARY FISCAL POLICY

Discretionary fiscal policy involves the conscious change in the spending and taxing behavior of the federal government in response to the recognized existence of an inflationary or deflationary gap.

Discretionary fiscal policy is policy that involves the conscious alteration of the spending and taxing behavior of the federal government to counter cyclical economic fluctuations.

FIGURE 12.1
Possibilities for Fiscal Policy

When a recessionary gap appears, as shown in Part A, it will eventually be eliminated by the automatic adjustment process, causing the SRAS curve to shift to the right until it reaches point E_{LR}', returning the economy to full employment with a lower price level, PL_{LR}'. The possibility exists for an expansionary fiscal policy by reducing taxes or increasing government expenditures to eliminate the gap more quickly than would the automatic adjustment process. This is shown by a shift of the aggregate demand curve from AD_1 to AD_2. The new equilibrium will occur at E_{LR}, with the equilibrium level of real national income at the level of potential national income. In this case the price level will be higher than with the automatic adjustment process. When an inflationary gap appears, the possibility also exists for fiscal policy to eliminate the gap more quickly than would the automatic adjustment process. In this case, shown in Part B, a contractionary fiscal policy would shift the aggregate demand curve, restoring equilibrium at E_{LR}. The price level will be lower than with the automatic adjustment process.

(A) Recessionary Gap

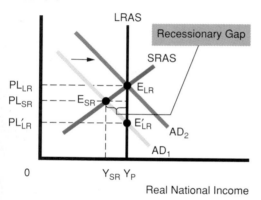

(B) Inflationary Gap

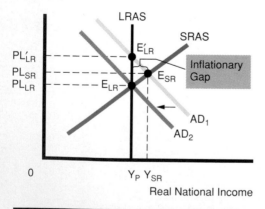

The federal government has used fiscal policy in the past in attempts to deal with both inflationary and recessionary gaps. In 1964, for example, taxes were reduced to counter a recessionary gap, in 1968 taxes were increased to offset an inflationary gap, and again in 1975 taxes were lowered to fight a recession.

The steps involved in employing discretionary fiscal policy are:

1. Identify the size of the spending gap.
2. Adjust for the probable effect on the price level.
3. Decide whether to change government expenditures or to alter taxes.
4. Apply the appropriate multiplier to determine the amount by which expenditures and/or taxes must be changed.

The first step is to identify the kind and size of the gap that exists between actual national income and the level of potential national income. If a recessionary gap exists, actual national income will be less than potential national income, and if an inflationary gap exists, the reverse will be true. The actual size of the gap must be estimated. A recessionary gap equal to $Y_P - Y_{SR}$, sometimes called the GNP gap, is shown in Part A of Figure 12.1, and an inflationary gap equal to $Y_{SR} - Y_P$ is shown in Part B.

The second step is to adjust the size of the GNP gap to take into account the short-run aggregate supply (SRAS) curve. Policymakers are primarily interested in the resulting change in real national income, but an increase in aggregate demand will affect both real national income and the price level. The short-run aggregate supply will divide the change in aggregate demand into changes in the price level and changes in real national income. So the actual change in aggregate demand required is greater in both cases than the size of the respective gaps. Aggregate demand will have to increase by the amount shown by the arrow in Part A and decrease by the amount shown by the arrow in Part B.

The third step is to decide whether to change the level of government expenditures, reduce taxes, or to do both. The fourth step is to apply the appropriate multiplier. In the case of a change in government expenditures, the value of the expenditure multiplier (1/MPS), assuming a closed economy, is divided into the adjusted GNP gap. If taxes are to be reduced, the tax-change multiplier (−MPC/MPS) is employed instead to determine how much total tax receipts must change.

EFFECT OF CHANGING TAX RATES Changes in tax rates will affect aggregate demand by a different route than will an autonomous change in fixed-amount taxes. Changing a tax rate changes the value of the multiplier itself. This occurs because an income tax changes the amount of consumption expenditure at every level of national income.

To see why this is so, consider Tables 12.1 and 12.2. Table 12.1 shows the effect on consumption spending of imposing an income tax rate of 40 percent on the level of national income. Column 1 presents various levels of national income, column 2 the associated level of consumption spending without the tax, determined by applying the consumption function $C = 100 + 0.75 Y_N$, and column 3 the amount of income taxes collected at the 40 percent rate. Disposable income is obtained by subtracting income tax receipts from national income, as shown in column 4, and consumption is reduced according to the marginal propensity to consume, as shown in column 5.

Figure 12.2 shows consumption spending without taxes (C) as a function of national income, along with consumption spending with an income

TABLE 12.1
Consumption with an Income Tax Rate of 40 Percent and a Marginal
Propensity to Consume of 0.75 (Billions of Dollars)

NATIONAL INCOME Y_N (1)	CONSUMPTION WITH NO TAX $C = 100 + 0.75Y_N$ (2)	INCOME TAX $t = 0.40$ (3)	DISPOSABLE INCOME $Y_D = (1) - (3)$ (4)	CONSUMPTION WITH TAX $C_T = 100 + 0.75Y_D$ (5)
$ 0	$100	$ 0	$ 0	$100
100	175	40	60	145
200	250	80	120	190
300	325	120	180	235
400	400	160	240	280
500	475	200	300	325
600	550	240	360	370
700	625	280	420	415
800	700	320	480	460
900	775	360	540	505
1,000	850	400	600	550

TABLE 12.2
Consumption with an Income Tax Rate of 20 Percent and a Marginal
Propensity to Consume of 0.75 (Billions of Dollars)

NATIONAL INCOME Y_N (1)	CONSUMPTION WITH NO TAX $C = 100 + 0.75Y_N$ (2)	INCOME TAX $t = 0.20$ (3)	DISPOSABLE INCOME $Y_D = (1) - (3)$ (4)	CONSUMPTION WITH TAX $C_T = 100 + 0.75Y_D$ (5)
$ 0	$100	$ 0	$ 0	$100
100	175	20	80	160
200	250	40	160	220
300	325	60	240	280
400	400	80	320	340
500	475	100	400	400
600	550	120	480	460
700	625	140	560	520
800	700	160	640	580
900	775	180	720	640
1,000	850	200	800	700

tax [C (t = 0.40)]. The slope of the consumption function with a tax is flatter than the slope of the consumption function without taxes, which is equal to the marginal propensity to consume (MPC), or 0.75. The slope of the consumption function with an income tax is equal to the MPC(1 − t), where t equals the tax rate, or 0.75(1 − 0.40) = 0.45. Thus the value of the slope of the consumption function declines and the consumption function with an income tax becomes flatter, as shown in the graph.

The multiplier is related to the slope of the consumption function. The expenditure multiplier without taxes is:

$$\text{Expenditure multiplier} = \frac{1}{1 - \text{MPC}} = \frac{1}{1 - 0.75} = 4$$

The expenditure multiplier with an income tax rate of 40 percent is:

An Income Tax Changes the Slope of the
Consumption Function

The slope of the consumption function without taxes or
imports is the same as the marginal propensity to consume, 0.75 in this case, as shown by consumption function C. When a single-rate income tax is imposed, the
marginal propensity to consume is reduced by the
amount of the tax rate. The slope of the consumption
function rotates downward around the amount of autonomous investment (100). If the single-tax rate is 20 percent, the consumption function will rotate to C (t =
0.20). If the tax rate is 40 percent, the consumption
function will rotate to C (t = 0.40). When the slope of the
consumption function changes, so will the expenditure
multiplier.

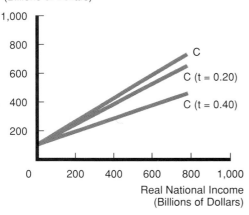

Consumption
(Billions of Dollars)

Expenditure multiplier with an income tax $= \dfrac{1}{1 - \text{MPC}(1 - t)}$

$$= \dfrac{1}{1 - 0.75(1 - 0.40)} = 1.8$$

The effect of imposing an income tax is to reduce the value of the multiplier.

What will be the effect of reducing the tax rate from 40 percent to 20
percent? This can be seen in Table 12.2. The effect of reducing the tax
rate is to reduce tax payments (compare Tables 12.1 and 12.2) and hence
to increase disposable income (column 4) and consumption spending (column 5). The slope of the consumption function becomes steeper than the
slope of the consumption function with a tax rate of 40 percent, as shown
in Figure 12.2. The multiplier also increases. When a value of 0.20 is
substituted for t in the formula above, the multiplier increases from 1.8 to
2.0.

Aggregate demand will increase, since a constant amount of autonomous expenditure will now be multiplied by a larger multiplier. This can
be seen in Figure 12.3, where the aggregate expenditure model is employed. Ignoring the effect of price-level changes, a recessionary gap
equal to $Y_P - Y_{SR}$ exists in both Part A and Part B. In Part A increasing
government expenditures or reducing taxes by a fixed amount requires
(ignoring possible price-level effects) an increase in autonomous expenditures from A to A'. The multiplier works on this increase to expand real
national income from Y_{SR} to Y_P.

Alternatively, the government could reduce tax rates, as shown in
Part B, which changes the slope of the aggregate expenditure schedule
that rotates upward from AE to AE_T. The multiplier increases so that the
existing amount of autonomous spending (A) will now generate sufficient
national income for the economy to operate at the level of potential national income.

Historically, discretionary fiscal policy has relied on changing-taxes
policy. Both fixed-amount and tax-rate changes have been employed, with
tax-rate changes being used most often. The Economic Recovery Tax Act
of 1981 reduced tax rates by 25 percent over 33 months. The Revenue Act
of 1964 also operated by reducing the tax rate for both individuals and
corporations. The Tax Reduction Act of 1975 involved a fixed-amount tax
rebate and a fixed-amount tax credit.

Federal tax laws have changed in each year since 1954, but only a
handful have been primarily motivated by the state of the macroeconomy.
Most changes had nothing to do with discretionary fiscal policy and occurred for other reasons. Taxes are levied to discourage certain activities
(e.g., alcohol and tobacco taxes), and they are reduced or eliminated to
encourage other activities (e.g., tax credits for energy-conserving activities) or to finance transfer programs (e.g., Social Security taxes have been
frequently raised to meet the financial requirements of the program).

FINE-TUNING THE ECONOMY The recognized success of the 1964
tax cut suggested the possibility of using fiscal policy on a regular basis, a
process that became known as **fine-tuning.**

> *Fine-tuning is the use of fiscal policy to maintain the economy
> at the level of potential national income by making continu-
> ous countercyclical adjustments in taxes and government ex-
> penditures.*

When a recessionary gap develops, the federal government might, in theory, adopt an expansionary fiscal policy sufficient to restore full employment. If the economy develops an inflationary gap, fiscal policy could become sufficiently contractionary to remove the gap. Fine-tuning would require fiscal policy to be altered frequently in relatively small amounts to keep the economy operating at full employment with a stable price level.

Aggregate demand is constantly changing because its components fluctuate. Investment spending fluctuates widely over time, as does the trade balance (exports minus imports). To a lesser extent consumption spending and the money supply vary over time. Aggregate supply is also frequently changing in tandem with expectations and supply shocks. Fiscal policy potentially could be used to counter these shifts.

Fine-tuning the economy in this way, however, has never been a real possibility. Such precise adjustments require accurate knowledge of the present state of the economy and its direction of change, instant identification of the policy action required, in addition to prompt and appropriate action by political decision makers. This is asking more than the system is capable of achieving.

AUTOMATIC FISCAL POLICY

Automatic fiscal policy is built into the federal government's budget in the form of **automatic stabilization**. Automatic stabilization reduces the magnitude of fluctuations in the macroeconomy by automatically stimulating aggregate demand when GNP is falling and reducing it when GNP is rising.

> *Automatic stabilization causes countercyclical changes in the spending and taxing behavior of the federal government without requiring a deliberate change in fiscal policy.*

An automatic or built-in stabilizer is anything that changes the marginal propensity to spend out of national income and thus changes the multiplier, or anything that automatically adjusts disposable income, in reaction to changes in national income. Built-in stabilizers thus reduce the fluctuations in GNP due to autonomous changes in aggregate expenditures or changes in the money supply. Moreover, they act without requiring any deliberate action by the government decision makers.

In the U.S. economy there are two principal automatic stabilizers: the tax system and the government transfer programs.

THE TAX SYSTEM The main purpose of the tax system is to spread the cost of government in a known and agreed-upon manner throughout the society. But the tax system also serves as a built-in stabilizer in that taxes tend to reduce the marginal propensity to spend out of national income. Consider the example of a single-rate income tax that we discussed above.

If you compare Tables 12.1 and 12.2, you will see how an income tax acts as an automatic stabilizer. In Table 12.2 an increase of $100 billion in national income will result in an increase of $75 billion in consumption spending without an income tax, as shown in columns 1 and 2, but will result in an increase of only $60 billion in consumption spending (column 5) if the income tax rate is 20 percent. In Table 12.1, when the income tax rate is 40 percent, the change in consumption spending relative to that in a no-income-tax economy is even more pronounced. Instead

FIGURE 12.3
Two Ways of Reducing Taxes

Two ways of reducing taxes to combat a recessionary gap are shown in this figure. The recessionary gap, ignoring the possible price-level changes, equal to $Y_P - Y_{SR}$ exists in both Part A and Part B. In Part A the effect of a fixed-amount tax reduction is shown. Dividing the recessionary gap by the fixed-amount tax multiplier reveals the amount $(A' - A)$ by which taxes need to be reduced. The multiplier will operate on this increase to expand real national income from Y_{SR} to Y_P. In Part B the effect of a reduction in tax rates is shown. In this case tax rates are reduced by the amount required to rotate the aggregate expenditures schedule from AE to AE_T. The multiplier increases in value by the amount needed to multiply the existing level of autonomous expenditures (A) sufficiently to increase real national income from Y_{SR} to Y_P.

(A) A Fixed Amount Tax Reduction

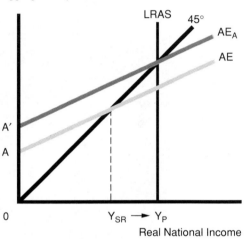

(B) A Reduction in Tax Rates

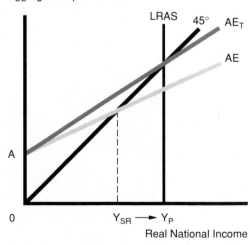

of the $75 billion increase in consumption spending that would occur in an economy without a tax, consumption spending with an income tax will increase by only $45 billion when national income increases by $100 billion.

The effect of an income tax is to reduce the magnitude of fluctuations in the economy. An economy with a low income tax rate will suffer wider swings in national income from a change in aggregate expenditures than will an economy with a higher tax rate. An income tax thus serves as an automatic stabilizer.

If a progressive income tax exists, it would function even more effectively as a built-in stabilizer. A progressive income tax, which taxes additional dollars of income at progressively higher tax rates, magnifies the effectiveness of taxes as built-in stabilizers. When GNP increases, tax collections rise more than proportionally as individuals move into higher tax brackets, and fall more than proportionally when GNP declines.

GOVERNMENT TRANSFER PROGRAMS   The federal government engages in a number of transfer programs, called *entitlement programs*, whose main purpose is to improve the welfare of particular groups within our society. Some of these programs, such as the unemployment compensation and welfare programs, also serve as built-in stabilizers.

Let us consider the unemployment insurance program. When national income declines below the level of potential national income, unemployment increases and more people become eligible for unemployment compensation. Their income and their consumption spending do not fall as much as they would if such a transfer system did not exist. When the economy revives, many unemployed workers find new jobs. They stop receiving compensation payments and begin to receive higher wage payments. Personal income increases, not from zero as would be the case without unemployment insurance, but by the difference between their earned income and the level of benefits they had been receiving. Thus the income of covered workers does not fluctuate as much with unemployment insurance as it would without it. In this way the unemployment compensation program plays the role of an automatic stabilizer.

The welfare program acts much like unemployment compensation. When the economy enters a recession, there is an increase in the number of persons who qualify for welfare payments, which cushion the fall in disposable income. When the economy revives, some of these people find jobs and leave the welfare rolls. Thus the welfare program makes net additions to disposable income when national income falls and makes net subtractions when national income increases, thereby functioning as an automatic stabilizer.

The unemployment compensation and welfare programs serve as automatic stabilizers causing fiscal policy to become more expansive during times of recession and more contractionary during boom times. Transfer programs act like automatic stabilizers, tending to stabilize disposable income and consumption expenditures during fluctuations in national income.

Although automatic stabilizers play an important role in fiscal policy, they cannot reduce fluctuations in national income to zero. Because automatic stabilizers spring into action only after a fluctuation is in process, they cannot eliminate that fluctuation; they can only reduce its magnitude.

In addition to the more or less continual minor fluctuations in the economy, there are the occasional severe and persistent recessionary and inflationary gaps that occur. The Great Depression is one example of a persistent recessionary gap, and the inflation of the 1970s is an example of a prolonged inflationary gap. Discretionary fiscal policy, despite its limitations, can potentially be used to fight such occurrences.

JUDGING THE STANCE OF FISCAL POLICY

How can economic decision makers know at any point in time whether fiscal policy is expansionary or contractionary? Often they will look to the **federal budget deficit** for the answer.

The federal budget deficit is the difference between federal government spending and total tax revenues.

Recessions cause expenditures to rise and tax receipts to fall, increasing the size of the budget deficit. During the recovery expenditures fall and revenues rise, reducing the budget deficit.

The actual deficit or surplus, because it is partially the product of the business cycle, is a misleading guide to the stance of fiscal policy. It is possible that the effect of the budget deficit on national income is actually contractionary even if the actual budget is in deficit and expansionary if the budget is in surplus, because of the cyclical forces acting on government expenditures and tax receipts.

The size of the actual budget deficit is the product of two forces — the fiscal policy of the government and cyclical fluctuations. The size cannot be used to determine the stance of fiscal policy because the amounts of tax receipts and government expenditures vary directly with the level of national income.

It would be extremely useful to be able to sort out the influence that existing fiscal policy has on the actual deficit or surplus from the influence exerted by the business cycle. One way to separate the effects of fiscal policy from those of the business cycle is to calculate the deficit (or surplus) that would exist if the economy were operating at the level of potential national income. This can be done by estimating the level of real national income when the economy is operating at the natural rate of unemployment. The federal government makes such calculations based on the assumption that the economy is operating with 6 percent unemployment, which is thought to be near the natural rate. This estimate of the budget deficit (or surplus) is known as the structural, high-employment, or cyclically adjusted budget deficit (or surplus). It is possible to separate the discretionary deficit from the **cyclical deficit** by comparing the actual budget deficit with the **structural deficit.**

The cyclical deficit is that portion of the total budget deficit that is caused by the cyclical fluctuations of the economy.

The structural deficit is the budget deficit that would occur if the economy were operating at the level of potential national income.

In Figure 12.4 both the actual and the structural deficits are charted for the years 1955–1987. In 1985, for example, the structural deficit (the deficit that would have existed if the economy were operating at full employment) was $145 billion. The actual deficit was $205 billion, so the cyclical deficit was $60 billion.

FIGURE 12.4
Actual and Structural Budget Deficits

In this figure the structural deficit is constructed by estimating the deficit or surplus that would occur if the economy was operating at the natural rate of unemployment,
which for this purpose is assumed to be 6 percent. The
structural deficit eliminates the effect that cyclical fluctuations have on the actual deficit, thereby providing a better indication of the stance of fiscal policy than does the
actual budget deficit.

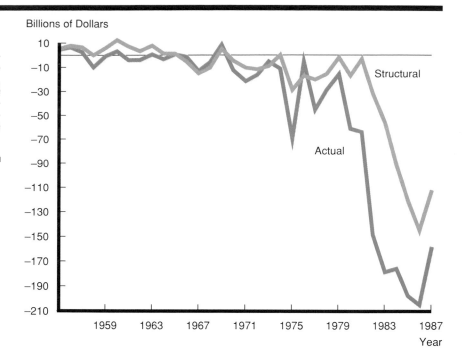

The structural (high-employment) budget deficit or surplus better
indicates the direction of the federal government's fiscal policy than the
actual budget deficit or surplus because the cyclical effects on the deficit
or surplus have been eliminated. Thus the structural deficit serves as an
indicator of the stance of fiscal policy. If a structural deficit exists, then
fiscal policy is expansionary. If a structural surplus is present, then fiscal
policy is contractionary.

If a structural deficit exists, it reveals that if the economy were operating at full employment, the actual budget would be in deficit. This suggests that fiscal policy is expansionary. If, on the other hand, the structural deficit is actually a surplus, it suggests, regardless of the level of the
actual deficit, that fiscal policy is contractionary.

In Figure 12.4 the structural (high-employment) deficit was both positive and greater than the actual budget deficit (surplus) every year between 1955 and 1965, indicating a generally contractionary fiscal policy.
From 1965 on, with the exception of 1969, the structural, or cyclically
adjusted budget, has persistently been in deficit, and since 1981 it has
been significantly in deficit.

It might be said that in a growing economy everything becomes larger.
Larger structural deficits may be the result of a bigger economy. One way
to adjust for economic growth is to present the deficits as a percentage of
GNP, as shown in Figure 12.5. The overall picture does not change much,
however. Prior to 1965 the structural deficit was always in surplus, but
after that date, with the exception of 1969, it was in deficit. Moreover, the
recent actual and structural deficits appear to be as great as when they
were presented in dollar terms.

Probably more important as a guide to the effects fiscal policy has on
the macroeconomy are the year-to-year changes in the structural deficit
or surplus. When the structural deficit expands or when the structural
surplus contracts, fiscal policy is becoming more expansionary. Conversely, when the structural deficit contracts or when the structural sur-

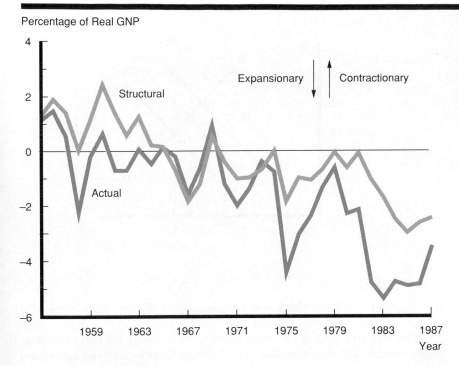

Percentage of Real GNP

Expansionary | Contractionary

Structural

Actual

Year

FIGURE 12.5
Actual and Structural Federal Budget
Deficits as a Percentage of Real National
Income

This figure presents the same basic picture as in
Figure 12.4. Changes in the structural deficit indicate a
change in fiscal policy. If the structural deficit increases,
fiscal policy has become more expansionary. If the structural deficit declines, fiscal policy has become more contractionary.

plus increases, fiscal policy is becoming increasingly contractionary. Thus
the year-to-year changes in the structural deficit or surplus measure the
change in fiscal policy.

Some of the past fiscal policy actions of the federal government can be
seen in Figure 12.5. The move from structural surplus to structural deficit in 1965 reflects the 1964 tax reduction. The 1968 tax surcharge and the
1975 tax reduction can also be seen in the chart, along with the 1981 tax
cut.

EFFECTS OF FISCAL POLICY
ON AGGREGATE SUPPLY

Fiscal policy is generally thought to work by influencing aggregate demand. In recent years some economists and politicians have suggested
that there are aggregate supply effects as well. When fiscal policy is designed to alter aggregate supply, it is often referred to as *supply-side fiscal
policy*. The 1981 Economic Recovery Tax Act was designed to be primarily a supply-side fiscal policy.

Supply-side fiscal policy is designed to influence the microeconomic
behavior of economic decision makers. A supply-side tax reduction will be
directed at reducing marginal tax rates. If the marginal tax rate is 70
percent, for example, an additional dollar in income will result in tax
revenues increasing by 70 cents while disposable income increases by only
30 cents. Such a high tax rate is thought by some to discourage both
working and saving. If the marginal tax rate is reduced from 70 percent to
33 percent, an individual will be able to keep 67 cents out of each additional dollar in income and the government will receive 33 cents.

The effect of such a marginal tax cut will be to increase individuals'
desire to work more and to save more. The reduction in tax rates is the
same as an increase in wages and in interest rates. Workers will have an
incentive to work more hours and to save more out of their earnings. If

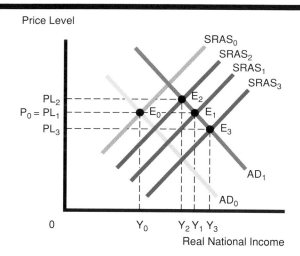

this happens, both the short-run and long-run aggregate supply will increase.

The effect of such a tax reduction, if government expenditures are
held constant, will therefore increase both aggregate supply and aggregate
demand. Aggregate demand will increase as the slope of the consumption
function changes, altering the size of the multiplier. Aggregate supply will
increase as a result of the greater incentives to work and save.

This dual effect is shown in Figure 12.6. The first effect caused by the
reduction in marginal tax rates is to raise disposable income, which increases consumption spending and thus causes the aggregate demand
curve to shift to the right (from AD_0 to AD_1). The second effect of lower
marginal tax rates is to induce workers to supply at existing prices more
labor and larger amounts of the other factors of production that they
own. This causes an increase in aggregate supply and the SRAS curve to
shift to the right. If the dual effects are of equal magnitude, then the
equilibrium will shift from E_0 to E_1, real national income will increase,
and the price level will remain constant at PL_0.

Nothing guarantees that the dual effects will be of equal strength.
Economists are divided as to which effect will dominate. It is possible that
the increase in aggregate demand will exceed the increase in the short-run
aggregate supply schedule. In this case the SRAS curve will shift only to
$SRAS_2$ and the equilibrium position will move to E_2 instead of E_1. Real
national income will still increase, but by less than in the first case, and
the price level will rise to PL_2. It is also possible that the increase in the
SRAS curve will exceed the increase in aggregate demand. In such a case
the SRAS curve will shift and the equilibrium point will move from E_0 to
E_3, real national income will still increase, but the price level will decline
to PL_3.

The supply-side effects of a tax reduction thus could nicely complement the effects of a tax cut on aggregate demand. Both the effects tend to
increase real national income, while the supply-side effects counter to
some extent the tendency for an increase in aggregate demand to raise the
price level.

Among economists there is less than universal acceptance of the actual effectiveness of supply-side tax reductions. The disagreement is more
empirical than theoretical. Many economists think the actual supply-side
effects would be small, especially in the short run, whereas others believe
that supply-side effects would be significant.

HOW FISCAL POLICY IS CONDUCTED

Fiscal policy in the United States is the product of the democratic process. The president of the United States is widely held responsible for the fiscal policy of the country. But in actuality the president is at best a partner with Congress in the budget process. The fiscal policy that emerges from this partnership must satisfy both branches of government. The president may propose the fiscal policy, but it is Congress that disposes. Congress must pass the laws that enable the federal government to spend and tax.

Congress does this by constructing and passing as a resolution an annual federal budget. The president can and does advise the Congress on the budget but needn't consent to it. A Congressional resolution, because it does not have the force of law, does not require the president's signature. What does require the president's agreement are the individual appropriations bills that provide the legal authority for the executive branch to spend money.

When the new fiscal year begins on October 1, the actions taken by Congress and the president in the individual appropriations bills allow the executive branch to begin to actually spend the money appropriated. Sometimes, however, work on the appropriations bills is not completed in time, and rather than shut down the government for lack of legal authority to spend public money, the government operates by what is known as a continuing resolution. A continuing resolution allows each government department and agency to continue to spend at the level of the preceding year's appropriation while Congress completes its work.

How well has this process worked within the political environment? The history of the budget process is the history of broken resolutions and a string of deficits that have exceeded $100 billion. Searching for a solution that would force a reduction in the deficit, Congress in 1985 passed, and the president signed into law, the Balanced Budget Act, commonly known as the Gramm-Rudman-Hollings (GRH) Act after its senatorial sponsors. This act set a strict schedule for reducing the deficit from $212 billion in 1985 to zero by 1991. The law set deadlines for Congress to follow and a schedule of automatic spending reductions to go into effect should Congress fail to pass a resolution that met the GRH Act limits in time. But the law encountered problems relating to its constitutionality and had to be passed again in modified form. In amending the GRH Act to overcome these objections, Congress took the opportunity to extend the date for a balanced budget to 1993.

How has the GRH Act worked in practice? The original 1987 limit, according to the act, was $144 billion and the actual budget deficit was $150 billion. The amended GRH limit for 1988 was $144 billion and the actual deficit was $155 billion.

What does the federal budget process imply for fiscal policy? It is clear that the president cannot by himself determine the country's fiscal policy. He is a participant in the process, but he must convince the Congress to follow his recommendations. Without Congressional approval the president cannot implement a change in fiscal policy. It is also clear that the federal budget process is very cumbersome, time-consuming, and not well suited to quickly implementing discretionary fiscal policy changes.

EFFECTIVENESS OF FISCAL POLICY

The aim of discretionary fiscal policy is to remove recessionary and inflationary gaps from the economy more expeditiously than is possible through the automatic self-correcting mechanism. Achievement of this goal requires that fiscal policy be both timely and effective. Some critics of fiscal policy believe that fiscal policy is simply too cumbersome to be timely, and others doubt that fiscal policy, even if it is timely, is actually very effective.

CHANGING GOVERNMENT EXPENDITURES

In discussing the effect that a change in government expenditures will have on real national income, it has been assumed that neither the level of autonomous consumption or of investment spending nor the marginal propensity to consume would change. Real national income would therefore be altered by the change in government spending amplified by the effect of the expenditure multiplier. But suppose the change in government spending brings about a corresponding but opposite change in consumption or investment spending. This possibility is known as the **crowding-out hypothesis.**

> *The crowding-out hypothesis is the assumption that an autonomous change in government spending induces an opposite, offsetting change in private spending.*

In its extreme form, this hypothesis suggests that when the government spends a certain amount, say $100 billion, for public goods, then private spending for consumption and investment will fall by that same amount.

The crowding-out hypothesis rests on two arguments known as *direct crowding out* and *indirect crowding out*. **Direct crowding out** occurs when government expenditures for certain goods and services replaces private spending for the same goods and services.

> *Direct crowding out exists when the government purchase of goods and services substitutes directly for households' spending.*

It is quite possible that government spending for education, health care, fire and police protection, and public roads and parks, for example, to some extent replaces private spending that would have taken place in the absence of these government expenditures.

Before local governments began to provide fire protection, for example, it was available from private fire departments. In fact, some of today's fire insurance companies got their start as private fire departments. Before the government began to build public roads, there were private turnpikes. Thus to the extent that government provides goods and services that would have been provided privately, there will be some direct crowding out. Aggregate expenditures, if direct crowding out exists, will not increase by the full amount of the increase in government spending, but by the difference between the increase in government spending and the decline in private spending.

Indirect crowding out can also occur. Consider the case of a government deficit. When the government spends more than it receives in taxes, it must borrow the difference from the private sector. Suppose the amount of savings available in the economy is fixed. In the absence of a deficit, these savings would have been lent to businesses to finance their investments in capital goods. If, instead, the government borrows part of the savings to finance a deficit, business firms will be able to borrow less. The increase in government spending is offset by a decline in investment spending.

Indirect crowding out exists when an increase in government expenditures leads to an offsetting decline in private investment spending.

When direct or indirect crowding out occurs, the aggregate expenditures curve will not shift up as much when government spending increases as it would if crowding out were not present. This can be seen in Figure 12.7. Suppose government expenditures increase in Part A. If crowding out is not present, the aggregate expenditures curve will shift up from AE_1 to $AE_1 + G$ by the full amount of the increase in government spending. Real national income will increase by the multiplier process to Y'_A and the aggregate demand curve, shown in Part B, will shift out from AD_1 to $AD_1 + G$.

But if crowding out is present, part or all of the increase in government spending will be offset by a corresponding decline in private-sector expenditures, because investment and/or consumption spending fall. Autonomous expenditures, in the case of partial crowding out, will increase only to A', the net amount by which aggregate spending has increased, instead of to A''. The aggregate expenditures curve will shift up to AE_2 instead of to $AE_1 + G$. Real national income will increase by the multiplier process to only Y_A instead of to Y'_A, because the autonomous increase in expenditures is less than the full amount of the change in government spending. Crowding out has reduced the effect of an increase in government expenditures below what would be expected by employing the expenditure multiplier to the dollar amount by which government spending has increased.

Most economists agree that crowding out does occur to some extent. There is, however, considerable dispute about how extensive it is. Some believe that it is relatively minor, others hold that it is extensive, and some say that crowding out is virtually complete. If the latter view is correct, then changing government expenditures will not affect aggregate expenditures at all, and so neither aggregate demand nor real national income will change. All that will change is the amount of government spending relative to the amount of private-sector expenditures.

CHANGING TAXES

Some economists also believe that altering tax policy will not be very effective in changing either aggregate expenditures or aggregate demand. The most frequently employed discretionary fiscal policy is tax modification, because the implementation lag is shorter than for changes in government expenditures. However, the modern theories of consumption, the life-cycle and permanent-income hypotheses, suggest that discretionary changes in taxes may have little immediate effect on consumption.

A tax change will affect consumption spending only if it shifts or rotates the consumption function. The modern theory of consumption is based on the assumption that individuals base their current consumption spending not on today's disposable income but on expected long-run disposable income. Thus changes in tax rates that are known to be temporary will not affect current consumption by very much, because such a tax change will have only a small effect on long-run disposable income.

If a change in tax policy is to be effective, it must be viewed as permanent by economic decision makers. Permanent changes in tax rates seem to be inconsistent with a discretionary fiscal policy that requires frequent changes. The more frequently tax policy is changed, the more households will consider all tax changes to be temporary whether so intended or not.

FIGURE 12.7
Crowding Out Reduces the Value of the Multiplier

If crowding out occurs when the government increases expenditures, the resulting multiplied increase in real national income will be reduced. If, in Part A, government expenditures increase and crowding out does not occur, aggregate expenditures will shift up to $AE_1 + G$. Real national income will increase from Y_0 to Y'_A via the multiplier process. Aggregate demand will increase from AD_1 to $AD_1 + G$, as shown in Part B. But if crowding out occurs, private spending will decline as government expenditures increase. This limits the amount that the aggregate expenditures curve will shift up. When government spending increases from A to A'' and crowding out equal to $A'' - A'$ occurs, the aggregate expenditures curve shifts up only to AE_2 and real national income increases only to Y_A instead of Y'_A via the multiplier process. Crowding out, to the extent it occurs, thus reduces the multiplied increase in real national income.

(A) Aggregate Expenditures

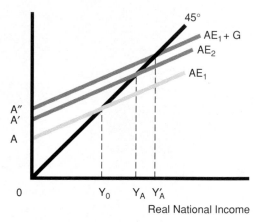

(B) Aggregate Demand

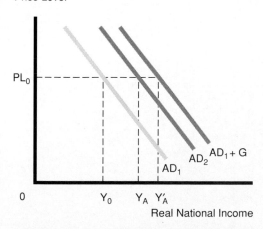

Current consumption spending will be little affected by changes in tax policy as households wait to see whether the change is really permanent.

ALTERNATIVE FISCAL POLICIES

As long as governments spend and tax, there will be a fiscal policy. But what kind of fiscal policy should the government have? We have seen that economists have differing opinions about the possibility and effectiveness of attempting to employ a discretionary countercyclical fiscal policy. They also differ in their views about the effects that government spending has on the economy, ranging from the belief that it can promote the expansion of real national income to the view that it reduces investment spending and thus leads to a reduction in the size of the nation's capital stock and to a decline in its future standard of living.

Given this diversity of views, it is not surprising that a number of alternative fiscal policies have been advocated, extending from an unrestricted discretionary policy, to a more restricted policy of balancing the budget over the business cycle, to a very restrictive policy of requiring an annually balanced budget.

The proponents of discretionary fiscal policy believe that changes in the size of the government deficit can and should play an active role in stabilizing the economy. They consider automatic stabilizers to be important but insufficient to deal with large cyclical fluctuations.

Proponents of a cyclically balanced budget believe that the federal budget should be in approximate balance over the business cycle. One way this could be accomplished, they believe, is by keeping the structural budget deficit in balance. The actual budget deficit can be allowed to vary with the cyclical fluctuations of the economy as automatic stabilizers are allowed to work. Over the business cycle the actual deficit will be in approximate balance as the economy generates surpluses during recoveries and incurs deficits during recessions.

Proponents of an annually balanced budget believe that the actual deficit should be zero every year. They believe either that fiscal policy tends to be procyclical or that it cannot affect the level of real national income. They generally also believe that deficits crowd out investment, reducing the size of the nation's capital stock and lowering future standards of living.

ARGUMENTS FOR A DISCRETIONARY FISCAL POLICY

Proponents of a discretionary fiscal policy believe that government spending and taxes should be set at the levels required to keep the economy operating at potential national income. If an increase in the budget deficit is required to achieve this goal, that is a small price to pay for full employment. The size of the budget deficit or surplus should not stand in the way of employing fiscal policy to reach this goal.

According to this view, it would be unwise to establish a goal of a cyclically balanced budget. Automatic stabilizers are important for moderating business fluctuations, but they cannot be expected to eliminate all fluctuations. When a serious recessionary gap exists, no artificial budget goal should stand in the way of adopting the fiscal policy required to restore full employment. There is nothing particularly desirable about setting the structural budget deficit at zero. The structural deficit was designed not for this purpose but to reveal the direction of fiscal policy.

Proponents of a discretionary fiscal policy are not opposed to a cyclically balanced budget, however, if that is what happens as the result of pursuing a discretionary fiscal policy. A discretionary fiscal policy advocates increasing the deficit during recessions and increasing the surplus when inflationary gaps exist. Thus a cyclically balanced budget could be the result of pursuing a discretionary fiscal policy.

It is even more unwise, from this viewpoint, to insist on an annually balanced budget. There is no virtue in a balanced budget itself, and pursuing a balanced budget is itself procyclical. When the economy suffers a recession, aggregate demand is insufficient to attain full employment. Tax revenues will decline and government expenditures will increase to the point where the budget balance becomes a deficit. If the government attempts to restore balance to the budget by increasing taxes, as it did during the depths of the Great Depression, or by cutting expenditures, then aggregate demand will decline further, making the recession worse.

When inflationary gaps appear, tax revenues will increase more rapidly than expenditures and a surplus will appear. Attempts to restore the budget to balance will require a reduction in taxes or an increase in expenditures, either of which will make the inflationary gap larger. Attempts to stick to a balanced budget will result in a procyclical fiscal policy.

ARGUMENTS FOR A CYCLICALLY BALANCED BUDGET

Proponents of a cyclically balanced budget point to the recent history of federal budget deficits. Since the middle 1960s the federal government has either balanced its budget or run a surplus only twice. Although the federal government has generally taken discretionary fiscal actions to combat recessions, it has failed to respond appropriately to inflationary gaps.

According to this view, if a cyclically balanced budget became the fiscal policy rule, the budget deficit would disappear when the economy reached full employment, as it did in 1988 and 1989. Yet in those years, instead of a surplus, the federal government showed an actual deficit exceeding $100 billion. Proponents of a cyclically balanced budget hold that such a budget can be implemented by adopting a fiscal policy that maintains the structural deficit at zero. Had this been in effect in 1988 and 1989, the budget would have been in surplus in 1989. If the structural deficit is always zero, discretionary fiscal policy would, of course, be ruled out, but automatic stabilizers would still be allowed to function in order to moderate fluctuations.

ARGUMENTS FOR AN ANNUALLY BALANCED BUDGET

Proponents of an annually balanced budget view with alarm the fiscal record of the federal government over the past 25 years. They generally do not believe that discretionary fiscal policy is either timely or effective. They tend to believe that crowding out is substantial or complete and that past budget deficits have crowded out private investment. Lower rates of investment mean less capital accumulation, which translates directly into lower economic growth rates in the future.

Among advocates of an annually balanced budget there exists the view that there is a political bias in favor of deficits. There is political advantage in enacting lower tax rates and in voting increases in government programs. Borrowing to finance the resulting deficit has proved to be an acceptable way to balance these political advantages. Although tax-payers are concerned about the size of recent federal budget deficits, the deficits do not affect citizens in as direct a way as either taxes or government spending programs. Some proponents recommend a constitutional amendment to require an annually balanced budget and the establishment of limits on government spending as the best ways to overcome this political bias.

There is no clear way to reconcile these divergent views. Each rests on a distinct view of how the macroeconomy works. If discretionary fiscal policy does not work, as proponents of a balanced budget believe, then budget deficits serve no useful purpose and may reduce future standards of living. If, however, discretionary fiscal policy does affect the level of real national income, requiring an annually balanced budget necessitates the sacrifice of a valuable tool that might prove useful in the event of an economic calamity such as the Great Depression.

SUMMARY

1.   Discretionary fiscal policy is the conscious use of the spending and taxing functions of government in the pursuit of macroeconomic goals. The objective of fiscal policy is to eliminate inflationary and recessionary gaps more quickly than is possible through the automatic adjustment process.

2.   A countercyclical fiscal policy is designed to smooth, or eliminate, the natural fluctuations of the economy. This is accomplished by increasing spending or reducing taxes so as to increase aggregate demand when recessionary gaps exist, and by doing the opposite when inflationary gaps exist. A procyclical fiscal policy has the opposite result.

3.   The tools of fiscal policy can be employed automatically either in the form of built-in stabilizers or as discretionary actions.

4.   Automatic stabilizers are fiscal programs that are in place prior to a change in macroeconomic conditions and that serve to moderate fluctuations in the economy. By bringing about an automatic countercyclical change in disposable income, automatic stabilizers moderate but do not eliminate economic fluctuations.

5.   Recent changes in discretionary fiscal policy have relied heavily on changing tax rates. Changes in tax rates operate on real national income by changing the value of the multiplier.

6.   The stance of fiscal policy cannot be determined by the actual budget deficit or surplus, because the actual deficit is the product of two forces: fiscal policy and cyclical influences. The structural, or high-employment, budget, because it eliminates the influence of cyclical factors, provides a better guide to determining whether fiscal policy is expansionary or contractionary.

7.   In recent years attention has been given to the supply-side effects of fiscal policy. A fiscal policy designed to change microeconomic behavior potentially could affect the short-run and long-run aggregate supply curves as well as the aggregate demand curve.

8.   The federal government, because it taxes and spends, will always have a fiscal policy. This fiscal policy can take several forms. The three most often proposed fiscal policies are: a discretionary fiscal policy, a cyclically balanced budget, and an annually balanced budget.

9.   The actual effectiveness of fiscal policy is a source of contention among economists.

THE ECONOMIC RECOVERY TAX ACT OF 1981

During the presidential election campaign of 1980, the U.S. economy was in a recession coupled with a burst of inflation. This recession was the product of an adverse supply shock. In his successful bid for the presidency, Ronald Reagan had proposed a "program for economic recovery." The main thrust of this proposed program evolved into the Economic Recovery Tax Act of 1981, which progressively lowered marginal income tax rates by 5 percent for 1982 and by 10 percent in both 1982 and 1983. Almost immediately upon passage of the tax cut, the economy relapsed into another recession. This time there were no time lags involved in fiscal policy. An effective tax reduction was in place at the very beginning of the recession.

The Economic Recovery Tax Act of 1981 was not the usual tax reduction designed to stimulate aggregate demand. Because it reduced marginal tax rates (the highest rate was reduced from 70 percent to 50 percent, with proportional reductions in other rates), this tax cut was designed to stimulate aggregate supply. A reduction in marginal rates, by increasing take-home wages as well as the after-tax return on savings and investment, was expected to increase the supply of productive resources and thereby stimulate aggregate supply. These changes were widely expected to cause the aggregate supply curve to shift to the right, increasing real national income and lowering the price level.

Did the supply-side tax cut work as advertised? What should have been expected? Refer back to Figure 12.6 in the discussion of supply-side tax cuts. If the increase in short-run aggregate supply is effectively equivalent to the increase in aggregate demand, real GNP will increase while the price level remains constant. If aggregate supply increases by more than aggregate demand, the price level will decline, but if the increase in aggregate demand exceeds the increase in aggregate supply, the price level will increase. So if the supply-side tax cut worked as advertised, the price level should have remained the same or fallen during the recovery.

The level of real GNP, the rate of economic growth, the price level, and the rate of change in the price level are presented in Table 12.3. The

TABLE 12.3
Economic Statistics during the Recovery from the 1981–1982 Recession

YEAR	REAL GNP (BILLIONS OF 1982 DOLLARS) (1)	GNP DEFLATOR (1982 = 100) (2)	RATE OF ECONOMIC GROWTH (PERCENTAGE CHANGE IN REAL GNP) (3)	RATE OF INFLATION (PERCENTAGE CHANGE IN GNP DEFLATOR) (4)
1982	$3,166	100.0	−2.5%	6.4%
1983	3,279	103.9	3.6	3.2
1984	3,501	107.7	6.8	4.3
1985	3,608	111.2	3.0	3.2
1988	3,713	114.1	2.9	2.6

Source: *Economic Report of the President, 1988* (Washington, DC: U.S. Government Printing Office, 1988).

FIGURE 12.8
Supply-Side Explanation of the Effects of the
Economic Recovery Tax Act of 1981

In 1982 the economy was in recession at the equilibrium
position E_{82} with aggregate demand curve AD_{82} and
SRAS curve $SRAS_{82}$. The 1981 tax reduction became effective that year, moving the equilibrium position to E_{83}.
The tax reduction, if it stimulated aggregate supply as
well as aggregate demand, must have shifted the SRAS
curve from $SRAS_{82}$ to no more than $SRAS_{83}$ when aggregate demand increased from AD_{82} to AD_{83}. Subsequent
equilibrium positions are indicated on the graph, along
with the possible shifts in aggregate demand and aggregate supply. The fact that each subsequent equilibrium
position occurred with both a higher price level and
greater real national income suggests that the increase in
aggregate demand must have been larger than the increase in aggregate supply.

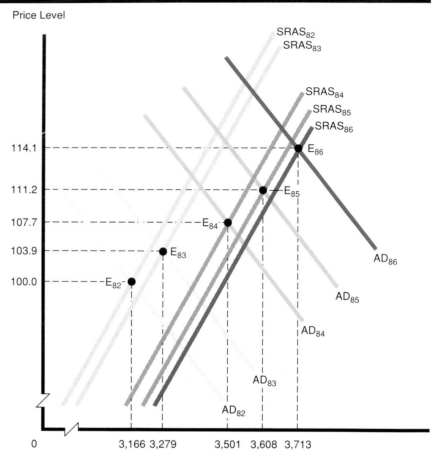

recovery began in the third quarter of 1982, the year in which the first
phase of the three-year tax reduction began and in which real GNP began
to expand. The price level, however, continued to increase throughout the
recovery. Aggregate demand had obviously increased relative to aggregate
supply (see Chapter 7 for an explanation of why this is so). The supply-
side tax cut did not eliminate inflation as suggested. In that respect its
performance was wanting.

Did the supply-side tax cut actually stimulate short-run aggregate
supply? This is a difficult question to answer. The rate of inflation did
decline and real output did increase. Moreover, the rate of economic
growth was generally higher than the rate of inflation, suggesting that the
greater portion of the increase in aggregate demand went to stimulate real
national income.

There are two contending explanations for this result. This could
have occurred either because of an increase in the short-run aggregate
supply (the supply-side explanation) or because of a movement along the
Keynesian portion of the short-run aggregate supply (SRAS) curve (the
Keynesian explanation). You will recall that the Keynesian portion of the
SRAS curve exhibits a very flat slope.

Let us consider first the supply-side explanation. The reduction in marginal tax rates increases both aggregate demand and aggregate supply. This is shown in Figure 12.8. The initial equilibrium position is E_{82}, where the aggregate demand curve AD_{82} intersects the SRAS curve $SRAS_{82}$. The result is a price level of 100 and real GNP equal to $3,166 billion. The next year, the first full year of economic recovery, equilibrium shifted to E_{83}, the price level increased to 103.9, and real GNP increased to $3,279 billion. If both the aggregate demand curve and the SRAS curve have increased (from AD_{82} to AD_{83} and from $SRAS_{82}$ to $SRAS_{83}$, respectively), then the increase in aggregate demand has clearly dominated the increase in aggregate supply. In fact, this is true for each of the years under consideration. You can readily see from the figure that the shift in aggregate demand exceeds the shift in short-run aggregate supply in each year. Even if the SRAS curve was positively affected by the tax cut, the expansion in aggregate demand was always greater.[1]

There is an alternative explanation that can explain the price-level/real-GNP pattern that occurred during the recovery without resorting to a shift in aggregate supply. During a recession the economy develops considerable slack as the rate of unemployment increases. Keynesian economists, who generally support discretionary fiscal policy, believe this translates into a very flat if not horizontal SRAS curve. Suppose the SRAS curve existing from 1982 through 1986 was as drawn in Part A of Figure 12.9. If the economy was initially in equilibrium at point E_{82}, an increase in aggregate demand such as occurred in subsequent years would shift the aggregate demand curve from AD_{82} to AD_{83}, causing the equilibrium point to move to E_{83} and both real national income and the price level to increase.

Subsequent increases in aggregate demand to AD_{84}, AD_{85}, and AD_{86} would have the same effect. The new points of equilibrium are in effect tracing out the existing Keynesian SRAS curve with points E_{82} through E_{86} marking out points on the SRAS curve. This is shown in Part B of Figure 12.9 together with a trend line that estimates the SRAS curve.

The behavior of the economy during the recovery from the 1981–1982 recession is consistent with two interpretations:

1. The supply-side hypothesis that increases in aggregate supply may have occurred but the expansion in aggregate demand from the tax cut was greater than the effect on aggregate supply. The expectations of supply-side proponents were too optimistic.
2. The Keynesian SRAS curve accurately described the shape of the existing SRAS curve. No shifts in the SRAS curve occurred. Instead, the increases in aggregate demand simply resulted in increases in the quantity of real national income supplied along the existing SRAS curve.

---

[1]Some economists credit the growth in the money supply, rather than the large structural budget deficit, with being responsible for the increase in aggregate demand. In the next part of this book you will become acquainted with their argument.

FIGURE 12.9
Alternative Explanation of the Effects of the Economic Recovery Tax Act of 1981

Part A presents an alternative to the supply-side explanation of the effects of the 1981 tax cut. When the SRAS curve is very flat (as Keynesian economists suggest it would be during a recession), an increase in aggregate demand would by itself cause the price level to increase somewhat as real national income increased. The explanation would be that an increase in aggregate demand in such circumstances would cause the quantity of real national income supplied to increase. No shift in the SRAS curve is required to understand how an expansionary fiscal policy would operate during a recession. Their argument is supported by the graph in Part B. The increase in aggregate demand that moves the economy from one equilibrium position to another has traced out the SRAS curve that existed at that time. The line constructed on the graph minimizes the distance between each equilibrium position and represents the SRAS curve.

(A) Expansion along a Keynesian Short-Run Aggregate Supply Curve

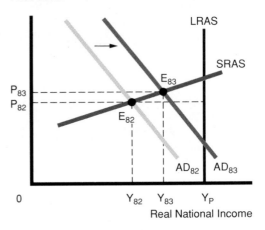

(B) Possible Short-Run Aggregate Supply Curve

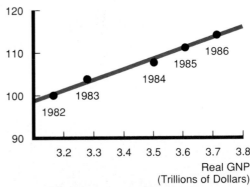

IS A LARGE NATIONAL DEBT A THREAT TO FUTURE PROSPERITY?

Since 1960 the federal government has incurred deficits in every year but one, and the last 18 years have seen an unbroken string of deficits. Moreover, the size of the deficits has been increasing, both absolutely and as a percentage of real GNP. The federal budget deficit has, in turn, a direct bearing on the national debt, which is the total amount of outstanding debt on which interest and principal payments must be made. The national debt is either increased each year by the amount of the budget deficit or reduced by the amount of the budget surplus. Between 1975 and 1980 the annual deficit (the amount by which government expenditures exceed revenue at the end of the fiscal year) averaged $70.7 billion, whereas between 1981 and 1986 it averaged $185.4 billion. As a direct result, the total national debt doubled between 1981 and 1986. It now exceeds $2.1 trillion.

Persons who are concerned about the size of the national debt generally fear that if the national debt continues to grow, it will eventually bankrupt the economy or will place an intolerable tax burden on future generations.

A baby born in 1984 inherited, along with the benefits of living in the United States, a share of the public debt that amounted to $8,779. Of this debt $6,660 was owed by the federal government and the rest by state and local governments. Over the course of the child's lifetime, he or she will have to pay taxes to pay interest on this debt and perhaps to pay it off. Critics of public deficits believe this to be an unfair burden to place on future generations.

It must be pointed out that the national debt was acquired for a purpose. The national debt was incurred in the process of the government defending the nation, as a result of acquiring a substantial stock of public capital, and during recessions. Some of the activities of government provide future as well as current benefits. It is not unfair to ask future generations to pay for the benefits they will receive from the actions of the present generation. To the extent that future benefits were created by these actions, a newborn child will be among the beneficiaries. Thus the national debt has created benefits as well as costs. Both should be taken into account.

The federal government is responsible for the vast majority of the public debt outstanding today. Is the current level of the national debt too large for the nation to carry? Do current large budget deficits threaten national bankruptcy? The ability of an individual, business, or government to carry debt is determined by comparing earning power with the extent of current liabilities. When you go to a financial institution to borrow money, your success in obtaining a loan will depend on whether the lending institution believes that you will be able to repay the loan. Your ability to repay the loan depends on how much income you earn and the amount of your existing obligations. A person who has a large income and no outstanding debts will be able to borrow more than a person with a small income and substantial debts. So too is the ability of the federal government to carry more debt determined by its income and the amount of its current obligations.

The tax revenues of the federal government are closely associated with the level of GNP. Tax revenues currently run approximately 20 percent of GNP. Should this be insufficient, the government also has the potential power to increase tax revenues as a percentage of GNP. Moreover, the federal government has the power to create money. Since the national debt takes the form of a promise to repay a certain number of dollars in the future, the right to create money implicitly gives the government the ability always to repay its debt.

One way to assess the debt-carrying power of the federal government is to compare present with past levels of the national debt expressed as percentages of GNP. The size of the nation's GNP measures the potential earning power of government. The national debt measures the extent of current debt obligations. So the ability of the federal government to carry more debt will be indicated by the percentage of GNP that the current national debt represents.

Part A of Figure 12.10 graphs the dollar amounts of the national debt for the years 1940 through 1988. From this graph it is clear why there is rising concern over the increasing size of the national debt. The national debt held by the public was three times greater in 1988 than it had been in 1980. The actual federal debt is somewhat greater than the amount held by the public, because part of the national debt is owed by the government itself or by its agencies. The national debt owed by the government is excluded because the obligation to repay, represented by the debt, is exactly offset by the value of the asset, the government bonds it holds. The net worth of the government is not affected by what happens to the bonds.

The actual amount of the debt doesn't tell anything about the ability of the government to carry this amount of debt. Absolute values are meaningless without something to compare them with. Considering the size of the national debt relative to GNP does give an indication of the debt-carrying capacity of the economy. As long as GNP increases more rapidly than the national debt, the debt/GNP ratio will decline. The debt/GNP ratio will become larger only when the national debt grows more rapidly than GNP.

In Part B of Figure 12.10 the size of the national debt as a percentage of GNP is presented for each year from 1940 to 1988. This picture of the debt is quite different from the one discussed above. Instead of constantly growing, the national debt as a percentage of GNP reached a peak at the end of World War II, when the national debt actually exceeded the level of GNP, and then declined steadily, except for the Korean War period (circa 1950) and the Vietnam conflict (1968), until 1975. Thereafter the national debt as a percentage of GNP trended upward.

During your lifetime federal deficits have become more the rule than the exception. During the 1970s the debt/GNP ratio remained fairly constant, the national debt growing at approximately the same rate as GNP. Since 1980 the national debt/GNP ratio has been rising, reflecting the severe recessions of the early years, the 1981–1984 tax cuts, and the slow recovery to full employment in 1987–1988. Still, even with the substantial deficits that have occurred since 1980, the ability of the federal government to carry more debt as measured by the debt/GNP ratio is greater today than it was at any time between the end of World War II and the early 1960s.

Another way to view the federal government's carrying capacity for debt is to compare it with debt burdens in the private sector. In 1986 18

FIGURE 12.10
National Debt of the United States:
1940–1988

Part A shows the dollar amount of the debt of the U.S. government that was in the hands of the public in the years 1940–1988. It is clear that the national debt has increased significantly since 1975. Part B shows the same information, but as a percentage of GNP. The picture is quite different. The increase in the national debt as a percentage of GNP has increased only since 1981. The relative size of the national debt today is no greater than it was in 1964 and is much lower than it was immediately after World War II.

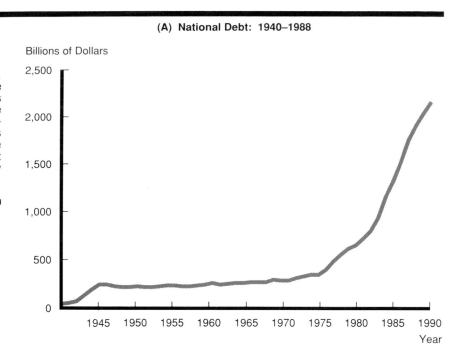

(A) National Debt: 1940–1988

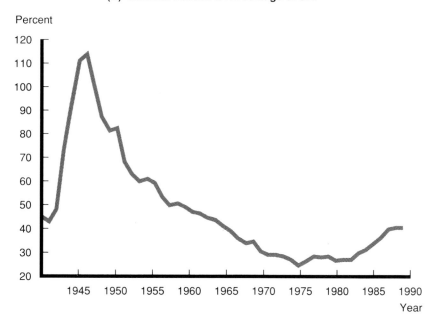

(B) National Debt as a Percentage of GNP

percent of the expenditures of the federal government went for interest payments on the national debt. In the private sector approximately the same percentage of household income was used to pay interest on household debts, most of it for mortgage interest payments. In the corporate sector approximately 20 percent of corporate income now is used for interest payments. The debt burden of the federal government does not appear to be currently out of line with that of the private sector.

Recently, however, the rate of increase in the national debt has exceeded the rate of increase in GNP, which if it continues indefinitely may give cause for alarm at some future time. It is well to remember that the federal government always has the power to raise taxes to service its debt. Individuals and businesses in the private sector do not have this ability.

What would be the signs that the federal government is approaching the limits of its debt-carrying capacity? Let us take a cue from the private sector. Recall that lenders impose discipline on borrowers. Lenders do make loans to creditors with different credit ratings, charging their more risky borrowers a higher rate of interest to compensate for the risk that they will not be paid back. This is called *default risk*. Currently, the financial obligations of the federal government are considered risk-free loans, mainly because of the government's power to tax. If the time ever comes when lenders begin to insist on a higher rate of interest from the federal government to compensate them for the risks of default, the federal government will, in the opinion of lenders, be nearing its debt-carrying capacity.

Some persons are concerned that repaying the national debt will impose a significant burden on future generations. But the national debt does not ever have to be paid off. The federal government, like corporations, expects to exist forever. These institutions can engage in perpetual refinancing of their debts. When a corporate or government bond matures, a new bond can be sold and the money raised used to pay off the previous bond. When this happens, the U.S. Treasury is said to "roll over" the debt. The British government has for several centuries serviced a perpetual bond, called a "consol," that never matures. Although the obligations of the U.S. government all expire and must be individually repaid, the total debt does not have to be repaid but can be rolled over in perpetuity. It may be prudent at times to reduce the total national debt by running annual surpluses, but nothing can ever compel the government to pay off the national debt.

What, then, can be said about the imminent threat of national bankruptcy? The possibility, at this moment, of the U.S. government becoming bankrupt because of the size of the current national debt appears to be remote.

There is another possible way in which the national debt could become a burden. Interest must be paid to service the debt. Are not the interest payments a burden to the nation? The answer to this question depends on whether the debt is internally or externally held.

The *internally held* national debt is composed of federal government obligations owned by U.S. citizens. The *externally held* debt is composed of federal government obligations owned by foreigners. This distinction is important: If the national debt is held internally, the citizens of the United States basically owe the debt to themselves. But if the debt is held abroad, the citizens of the United States are indebted to the citizens of a foreign land.

When interest is paid, one group of citizens (taxpayers) transfers income to another group of citizens (bondholders). What the first group gives up, the second group receives. Servicing the national debt in this case does not alter the amount of income in the economy; it affects only the distribution of that income. Taxpayers have less income and bondholders more. Moreover, this transfer takes place between living Americans. The national debt may have been originated by a prior generation, but it is always owned by the current generation. Thus the transfer of income affects only living Americans, and the interest payments on internally held debt do not constitute a burden on future generations.

Externally held debt affects the economy differently than internally held debt. Interest and principal payments represent transfers of income outside the domestic economy. Such payments reduce the amount of total income left for U.S. citizens to enjoy.

It does not necessarily follow that such payments are bad for the economy. Again, it is misleading to consider only costs. Costs should always be compared with benefits. Suppose the national debt sold to foreigners was used to build roads, schools, dams, and the like. Such publicly provided capital, if wisely invested, would increase the productivity of the economy and increase GNP more than enough to service the debt.

Whether the interest payments on the national debt could prove to be a burden, reducing the amount of income remaining at home, depends on who owns the debt. Who does own the national debt: citizens or foreigners? In March 1987 the total national debt held by the private sector was $1,641 billion, and of that amount commercial banks held $232 billion, leaving $1,409 billion for private investors. Foreign owners, who were not U.S. citizens, owned $264 billion. This foreign ownership constitutes the externally held debt. In 1987 the portion of the national debt held by private investors that was foreign-owned totaled about 19 percent. Thus the externally held debt does not as yet represent a significant portion of the total national debt.

REQUIRED ECONOMIC CONCEPTS

Fiscal policy   Crowding-out hypothesis
Discretionary fiscal policy   Direct crowding out
Fine-tuning   Indirect crowding out
Automatic stabilization   Cyclical deficit
Federal budget deficit   Structural deficit

KEY QUESTIONS

1. What is fiscal (stabilization) policy?
2. What is countercyclical fiscal policy?
3. What is the automatic adjustment process?
4. Why does aggregate demand change constantly?
5. What is fine-tuning? Is fiscal policy flexible enough to fine-tune the economy?
6. What is the difference between automatic (or built-in) fiscal policy and discretionary policy?
7. What is crowding out?
8. What factor determines whether fiscal policy is totally ineffective or partially effective?
9. Why might an annually balanced budget be procyclical instead of countercyclical in its effect on the movement of GNP?
10. How does an annually balanced budget differ from a cyclically balanced budget?
11. What is the structural (high-employment) deficit?
12. Historically, when has the national debt increased most rapidly?
13. What is meant by rolling over the debt? To whom is most of the national debt owed?

PROBLEMS

1. An AFL–CIO committee once declared that "public-service employment generates up to 125,000 jobs for each billion dollars spent by the federal government, compared to 15,000 jobs or so for a similar-sized tax cut." Do the relative sizes of the spending and tax multipliers in this statement sound right to you? Elaborate.

2. Which of the following are examples of (a) automatic fiscal policy, (b) discretionary fiscal policy, or (c) neither type of fiscal policy?
   a. Student loans.
   b. Social Security payments indexed to inflation.
   c. Food stamps.
   d. Farm price supports.
   e. Congressional passage of emergency funds for tornado relief in the Midwest.
   f. Significant revision of the U.S. income tax laws in 1986.
   g. A national tax amendment that limits the annual percentage increase in federal spending to the prior year's percentage increase in real GNP.

3. "An annually balanced-budget policy is like a swinging pendulum that does not come to a stop; instead it swings wider and wider." Interpret this statement for both recessionary and inflationary gaps.

4. "The basic purpose of government taxation is to finance government expenditures," says Felix. "In a recession tax revenues fall because income falls; therefore either (1) government spending must be reduced or (2) tax rates must be raised to finance the same level of government spending."
   a. What kind of budget is implied in the first statement?
   b. Is the second statement procyclical or countercyclical? From what point of view is Felix speaking? Why might you disagree with him?

5. Businesses are worried about the persistent annual federal deficits and about the growing size of the total federal debt. Since businesses borrow too, why are they concerned? Can you provide an answer for their concern? Might the answer have something to do with the children you will have someday?

6. Assuming that fiscal policy is effective, how does private saving actually increase even though the federal government, when it borrows, competes with the private sector for loanable funds? Won't crowding out depress private-sector investment? Explain why there still could be an increase in private-sector capital formation.

7. The government borrows by issuing bonds. Lower-income groups are not buyers of government bonds. Therefore, some critics argue, the federal debt presents a greater burden on lower-income groups because they are taxed to pay off the bonds purchased by higher-income groups.
   a. Is there an income transfer associated with the federal debt?
   b. Are the lower-income groups necessarily worse off when the economy is heading into a recession?

8. Was the federal debt in the 1942–1945 period greater than GNP? If so, name at least two benefits resulting from this huge debt.

9. Observed deficits during a recession are mostly due to the economy's effect on the budget, not the budget's effect on the economy. Interpret.

10. Explain how the structural deficit can show a budget surplus while the actual budget shows a deficit.

APPLICATION ANALYSIS

1. Suppose the federal government builds a dam for electric power generation, flood control, and irrigation. It borrows to build the dam, incurring a debt. The Tennessee Valley Dam is a real-world example.

a. Under what conditions in the economy would building the dam not cause crowding out and not be inflationary? When would building the dam cause crowding out and be inflationary?

b. Does the next generation of taxpayers who must pay off the bondholders unfairly absorb the cost of the dam, since they are not owners of the dam?

c. Most economists contend that the cost of the dam is borne by the generation that built the dam. In light of your answer to part b, how is the cost to the current generation determined?

d. A small minority of economists argue that future generations bear the cost of the dam and that the current generation gets off free. They reason that the current generation of bond buyers voluntarily bought government bonds instead of private-sector bonds, and that they will earn interest on the government bonds as a reward for delaying consumption. But the bondholders are indifferent between buying the public- or private-sector bonds, since the yields are the same (as they must be if the private sector is to compete for loanable funds with the government). However, future taxpayers must pay off the interest on the government bonds, interest that they would not have to pay off on corporate bonds, since the corporations do that. Therefore the burden is shifted to future taxpayers. Do you support the minority or majority (part c) view? Why?

P A R T 4

THE MONETARY SECTOR

13

MONEY, REAL NATIONAL INCOME, AND THE PRICE LEVEL

IN THIS CHAPTER YOU WILL LEARN:

What money is and the functions it performs in the economy

The desirable physical characteristics of money

The various kinds of money

What determines the value of money and the opportunity cost of money

Why people desire to hold money

The nature of the demand for money

The role money plays in both Keynesian and monetarist economic theory

THE GREAT GERMAN HYPERINFLATION

Runaway inflations, in which the purchasing power of money rapidly depreciates, are not unknown in the world today. They have recently occurred or continue to exist in some South American and African economies. Historically, few nations, Great Britain among them, have escaped at least one episode of hyperinflation. The United States, however, has suffered through two hyperinflations — the first during the American Revolution, when the phrase *not worth a continental* (referring to the value of the currency) was coined, and the second in the South during the Civil War. As runaway inflations occur and when they end, they leave permanent scars on the population.

One hyperinflation in particular has been singled out by historians as having led to events that changed history and left scars on the entire world. The great German hyperinflation, which occurred between 1919 and 1923, led to the wreckage of both the German economy and German democracy. Out of that wreckage Adolf Hitler and Nazi Germany arose, leading directly to a world war that cost millions of lives and wasted billions of dollars' worth of resources.

During this inflation the German mark became worthless. Everyone who had wealth measured in marks saw that wealth disappear. A pair of shoes that had cost 12 marks in 1913 cost 32 trillion marks in November 1923 — if a person could carry that much money to a store and if the retailer would accept it. One writer tells of how a cup of coffee rose in price from 5,000 marks to 8,000 marks while he was drinking it. No modern specialized economy can function with such an unstable price level, and the German economy was no exception.

Hyperinflations are clearly to be avoided, and if they are to be avoided, their causes must be determined. What is the relationship between the price level and the purchasing power of money?

DID THE COLLAPSE OF THE MONEY SUPPLY CAUSE THE GREAT DEPRESSION?

We have discussed the Great Depression, and you were exposed to the *spending hypothesis* as a possible historical interpretation of its cause. There is another explanation, which is widely known as the *money hypothesis*.

According to the money hypothesis, a normally short-lived recession was converted into a depression by the collapse of the money supply. The decline in the money supply during the 1930s led both to a decline in real gross national product (GNP) and to deflation. The decline in real GNP and in the price level was severe and prolonged because the decline in the money supply was severe and sustained. The direction or causation, according to this interpretation, is clear. The decline in the money supply caused nominal national income to decline. The decline in nominal national income was composed partly of a decline in real GNP and partly of a decline in the price level. How does a decline in the money supply affect the macroeconomy?

• INTRODUCTION •

By facilitating trades, money plays an essential role in an economy. Without money performing this function, most everyday trades could not take place. But the role that money plays in the macroeconomy goes beyond this vital function. By affecting the level of aggregate demand, the quantity of money also affects both the amount of real GNP and the price level. All economists agree on this point. What they disagree about is the mechanism by which the quantity of money affects the macroeconomy. In this chapter the nature of money and the functions that money performs will be discussed, along with the Keynesian and monetarist theories of the role that money plays in the macroeconomy.

Money is anything that facilitates the transfer of goods and services between persons. The main benefit of money derives from its use as a device for economizing on the resources required to carry on trades and exchanges.

> *Money is any generally accepted means of payment that will be taken in exchange for goods and services and can be used to store wealth for future use.*

Money has historically taken many forms. In the American colonies, tobacco was used as money in the southern colonies, corn in the northern colonies, and whiskey in the western territories. At some time or some place, teeth, ivory, shells, cigarettes, even large stones have served as money. Gold and silver have been used either as bullion or as coins. The form that money takes is continually changing. In the United States money is currently defined as coins, currency, and demand deposits (checking accounts in banks). Demand deposits are money because an individual's checking account deposits can be transferred to another person on demand by simply writing a check on the account. •

FUNCTIONS OF MONEY

Money performs two major functions: It serves as a medium of exchange and it serves as a store of value. It also performs two related functions: It serves as a unit of account and it serves as a standard of deferred payment.

A MEDIUM OF EXCHANGE

The role money plays as a medium of exchange is already familiar to you. Because money is generally accepted as a payment for goods and services, barter can be eliminated. Exchange in a barter economy, you will recall from Chapter 2, is burdened by the need for a mutual coincidence of wants. In using barter as a means of exchange, it is possible that a series of exchanges will be necessary before the desired exchange can be made.

Suppose, for example, you have a sheep to trade and desire champagne. But the champagne maker desires a copper pan, not a sheep. You must now find someone who wants a sheep and has a copper pan before you can trade for champagne. You see the problem. Barter makes exchanges very costly in terms of time and other resources. Money solves this problem. If you sell the sheep for money, you can use the money to buy the champagne. The champagne owner can then use the money to buy the copper pan.

The most important function of money, then, is to serve as a generally accepted means for making payments. This function eliminates the mutual coincidence of wants as a barrier to trade. The invention of money is a social innovation on a par with the discovery of fire and the invention of the wheel in its effects on human history. The establishment of a commonly accepted good as a medium of exchange allows a modern, highly specialized economy to exist.

A STORE OF VALUE

Because it is the medium of exchange, money can be employed to store wealth for future use. It can always be used to make purchases in the future. A person who holds money is taking advantage of its ability to store value.

Serving as a store of value is an important function of money because not all exchanges take place simultaneously. An individual may get paid only once a month but may desire to make purchases periodically throughout the month. This can be accomplished by holding money between paychecks. The two functions — serving as a medium of exchange and serving as a store of value — cannot be separated. Whatever serves as a medium of exchange must also serve as a store of value. A necessary function for any medium of exchange, then, is that it be able to store value so that economic decision makers can smooth out their consumption over time.

People who spend less than their income are saving, storing value, and accumulating wealth. The medium of exchange is often used to save. Money is, of course, not the only asset that stores value. Almost any good that is not perishable can be used to store value. Land, buildings, gold, silver, stocks and bonds, fine art works, and savings accounts — all can be used to store value. In fact, if you are going to store value for a long period of time, almost any physical asset would be better than money. The reason is that the value of money declines with inflation, whereas the value of most physical assets increases with inflation.

A UNIT OF ACCOUNT

How do you measure your wealth? Your wealth may be composed of assets like automobiles, clothing, records and tapes, or books, but the value of these assets is customarily measured in units of money. When we speak of millionaires or even billionaires, we are using money as a unit of account. In 1988 *Forbes* published a list of 192 billionaires from 26 different countries. The term *billionaire* means a person who owns at least $1 billion worth of **assets,** not a person who has at least $1 billion in cash.

> *An asset is anything of value that can be legally owned. The value of an asset is measured with dollars serving as the unit of account.*

Determining billionaires makes use of money as a unit of account.

What is true of individuals is, in this case, also true of the entire economy. When we discussed national income accounts in Chapter 6, we used money as the unit of account. When we calculate GNP, we end up with a figure in trillions of dollars, not the quantities of millions of separately listed goods. Unless a unit of account existed, calculating GNP would be an impossible and useless task. Calculation of both GNP and a person's wealth are possible because assets and goods can be expressed in terms of a common denominator. Thus money can serve as the common denominator in which the values of all goods and services are expressed. Because money can function as the unit of account in which prices are quoted and accounts maintained, it becomes the measure of the value of a good or service. In the United States prices are quoted in dollars. An automobile costs $12,000, for example, a pair of jeans $30, a hamburger $1.50, and a Coke $.50.

It would be possible to keep track of the prices of everything in terms of everything else, but it would be inconvenient. A new car, for example, costs 400 pairs of jeans, or 8,000 hamburgers, or 24,000 Cokes, and a Coke costs 1/24,000th of a new car, or 1/60th of a pair of jeans, or one-third of a hamburger. It is possible to do, but confusing and uneconomical. It is more economical to reckon the prices of all goods and services in terms of a common unit of account that allows relative prices to be determined quickly. By serving as the unit of account, money is a means of conserving on resources.

A STANDARD OF DEFERRED PAYMENT

A related aspect of money's role as a store of value is its use as a standard of deferred payment. Some transactions call for payments to be made in the future. Usually these payments are specified in terms of amounts of the domestic currency.

Those of you who have taken out a student loan know that you are obligated after graduation to repay the loan with interest. Sometime in the future you will have to begin making payments in dollars to repay the loan. The domestic currency (the dollar) is being used as the standard of deferred payment on your loan.

But the local currency does not have to serve as the standard of deferred payment. Anything that two parties can agree upon could serve this function. During the 1980s inflation some corporations issued gold bonds that guaranteed the repayment of the money borrowed in terms of a number of ounces of gold. When the bonds expired, the payment would be either the agreed-upon number of ounces of gold or an amount of money equal in value to the amount of gold specified in the contract.

Although money typically performs all four of the functions we have just discussed, the two functions that define money are its use as a medium of exchange and its use as a store of value. The other two functions of money — its use as a unit of account and its use as a standard of deferred payment — could be performed by other assets as well.

TYPES OF MONEY

You discovered above that at different times and in different places various things have served as the medium of exchange. Historically, there have been many kinds of money, but some goods have never been used as money. Services, such as haircuts or medical care, have never served as money, nor have perishable goods, such as peaches or fish. This suggests that there are certain characteristics a good must possess in order to perform the functions of money.

DESIRABLE CHARACTERISTICS OF MONEY

There are three desirable characteristics of money: durability, divisibility, and scarcity. Whatever is selected as a medium of exchange must be durable or it cannot serve as a store of value. Peaches and fresh seafood would make terrible mediums of exchange because they can store value for very limited amounts of time. Also, the good should be divisible so that the smallest transactions can be made along with large transactions. Again, peaches and seafood, though physically divisible, would not serve this function well. Finally, the good must be scarce or too much of the good would be required to make large transactions. Sand is durable and divisible but not sufficiently scarce. Storing enough sand to purchase a peach or fish would be very expensive.

These desirable physical requirements are met by commodity money and by monies in the form of either fiat money or bank money.

COMMODITY MONEY

Throughout recorded time there have been a number of **commodity monies** used as a medium of exchange. Gold and silver have historically been the commodities most often employed as money. Gold and silver are durable, divisible, and scarce. Gold and silver, like all commodity monies, also have significant nonmonetary uses.

> *A commodity money is an economic good that is used as money and is also bought and sold for its value as a commercial product.*

If a commodity is to serve both uses, its value as money must obviously be equal to its value as a commercial product. Also, in a competitive world the value or price of any good will be driven down to its cost of production. Thus the value of commodity money must be equal not only to its value as a commercial good but also to its costs of production.

Commodity money is subject to Gresham's Law, named after the man who first stated: "Bad money drives out good." Suppose that gold and silver coins are circulating as the medium of exchange. It will pay some persons to shave small parts off each coin and then try to pass the clipped coins in transactions at their full face value, selling the shavings to a jeweler for more gold or silver coins. This explains why many antique coins are mutilated in appearance. When this occurs, persons who receive clipped coins will immediately use them in trade, keeping any good coins they possess as a store of value. Soon only clipped coins will be in circulation. Bad coins have driven out the good.

In 1860 in the United States, for example, paper money (greenbacks) and gold, silver, and copper coins circulated together. The government issued a lot of paper currency to finance the Civil War, and its value depreciated relative to the commodity monies. Greenbacks were legal tender and everyone was obligated to accept them as payment for debts. Thus everyone used greenbacks for payment purposes and hoarded the metal coins. Bad money drove good (more valuable) money out of circulation.

Gresham's Law holds only when there is a fixed exchange rate between good (more valuable) money and bad (less valuable) money. If the relative price of the two monies can change, then the good money may drive out the bad. Persons will demand the more valuable money in exchange and will accept the less valuable money only at a discount. Therefore, to the extent that one money disappears from circulation, it will be the bad money because of its declining value.

When a commodity is used as the medium of exchange, private citizens can literally make money by producing the commodity. When tobacco was the circulating medium of exchange, growing tobacco expanded the money supply, and smoking tobacco reduced the money supply. If gold and silver are the medium of exchange, mining these precious metals adds to the quantity of money, and using the commodity to make jewelry and electronic equipment reduces the quantity of money.

The problem with commodity monies is that society must invest valuable resources in their production. Expanding the quantity of money means incurring the costs of producing the commodity. In fact, as mentioned above, the value of a commodity money will be precisely the costs of producing it. One way to conserve on scarce resources is to reduce the costs of producing money by introducing token monies.

TOKEN AND FIAT MONIES

Token money is money that costs less to produce than its value in exchange.

> *Token money is a medium of exchange whose value is greater than the value of the resources used to produce it.*

Paper money is an example of token money, as are composite metal coins. The great advantage of token monies is that the resources required to produce a commodity money are spared to be used for other purposes. The value of either a dollar bill or a 50-cent piece in exchange greatly exceeds the government's cost of producing these monies.

Token monies have alternative uses, but their use value is less than their exchange value. People do not ordinarily use dollar bills as note paper or bookmarks, nor do they use them to light fires, uses to which other forms of paper are sometimes put. There are exceptions. Runaway inflations have sometimes reduced the value of token money below its value in alternative uses. The value of Confederate dollars during the Civil War depreciated so much that people did use them for wallpaper — not for decoration but to keep the wind out. Pictures exist of children playing with piles of German marks instead of wooden blocks during the great German hyperinflation.

How can token money exist? Why would people pay more for coins or currency than it costs to produce them? The key to the successful use of token monies is that the amount of money issued must be limited. If everyone had the right to produce token monies, as they would have the right to produce a commodity money, the forces of competition would soon drive the value of the money down to the costs of production.

For token monies to exist, some control over their issuance is essential. Generally, it is believed that the issuance of token money must be monopolized, usually by the government. The monopolized producer will be concerned with maintaining the value of the currency by limiting production. Private production of token money is generally prohibited.

Modern token monies are accepted in part because the government makes them legal tender for settling debts. Token money that is legal tender for all debts and is generally acceptable in trade is called **fiat money.**

> *Fiat money is money that the government has declared to be acceptable as a medium of exchange and to be a lawful way of settling debts.*

If you closely examine a U.S. dollar, you will find in small print the words *"This note is legal tender for all debts, public and private."* This statement means that any person can settle all debts and taxes by offering the required number of dollars in exchange. Often legal tender will be the only form of money that the government will accept for taxes. This creates a demand for legal-tender money.

The advantage of fiat money is that it is relatively inexpensive to produce. The disadvantage is that this creates a great temptation to print too much money. It costs only a few cents to print a $100 bill, which the government can use to acquire $100 worth of resources. However, as

APPLICATION

13.1

GRESHAM'S LAW AND U.S. SILVER COINS

Prior to 1968 all U.S. coins, except the penny, contained real silver. The government for years had minted silver coins that were actually a mix of silver and base metals at a cost less than the nominal value of the coins it sold to the public. The difference between the mint's costs and its receipts is known as the seigniorage. Silver coins circulated in the United States because it did not pay to melt them down to obtain the silver that they contained. They were token monies even if they did contain a precious metal, because the value of the silver in the coins was less than the coins' face value in trade.

Silver as a commodity has many uses other than for coins. For centuries silver has been used in the fabrication of jewelry and decorative objects; in recent times it has come to be used for photographic and X-ray film and as a superior conductor of electricity. It was the use of silver for photographic and electronic purposes that led to an increase in the demand for silver, which in turn caused an increase in its relative price and led to the demise of silver coins in the United States.

The rise in the price of silver increased the value of the silver content in circulating U.S. coins. Eventually, the value of the silver in dimes, quarters, half-dollars, and silver dollars came to equal the coins' face value, and silver coins for a time actually became a commodity money. The U.S. government responded by discontinuing the use of silver in their coins. Instead, the U.S. Treasury in 1968 began issuing composite coins of the same size and shape that were made of copper sandwiched between two thin silver-colored metal casings. These coins cost considerably less to mint than silver coins; their cost was also considerably less than their face value. U.S. coins became token money once again, and the U.S. Treasury was able to continue to pocket the seigniorage.

The price of silver, however, continued to increase until the value of circulating coins with silver exceeded their face value. These coins were now worth more melted down than their value in exchange. People began to collect silver coins, buying rolls of coins at banks and selecting the ones with pre-1968 mint dates to sell to brokers who melted the coins down to recover the silver. Gresham's Law began to operate. The less valuable composite coins continued to circulate, while the now more valuable silver coins disappeared from circulation. Bad money drove good money out of circulation.

When two kinds of money circulate simultaneously and the exchange ratio between the two is fixed, they become subject to Gresham's Law. If one becomes worth more than the other, as coins with silver content became worth more than composite coins of equal face value, the coins that are less valuable will continue to circulate, while the coins that are more valuable will disappear from circulation.

This law holds only if the exchange ratio between the two monies is fixed, as it was between U.S. coins with silver content and composite U.S. coins without silver. If, however, the exchange ratio is free to fluctuate with the relative value of the two monies, Gresham's prediction is reversed: To the extent that one currency disappears, it will be the "bad money" that disappears, since its discount becomes so great that it is no longer practical to use it in exchange. This is what happened in Germany during the great hyperinflation, as you will see in the Preview 13.1 Analysis at the end of this chapter, and in Israel and some South American countries in recent years.

more and more fiat money enters circulation, money becomes less scarce. The price level will rise and the value of the domestic currency will fall.

The recent hyperinflations in Israel, Brazil, Bolivia, and Argentina were mainly caused by the governments' inability to resist the temptation to print too much fiat money. Israel and Bolivia have been successful in reducing high inflation rates to much more moderate levels. One element in common between the two countries' anti-inflation programs was the sharp reduction in the government deficits that reduced the pressure to issue more money. In most cases of runaway inflation the country's treasury is responsible for the money supply, enabling the government to finance budget deficits directly by printing additional money.

PRIVATE DEBT AS MONEY

Another form of money is, perhaps surprisingly, the debt or liabilities of private firms. In fact, in most developed countries this is quantitatively the most important type of money. How did the obligations of private firms become money? Why would anyone accept privately issued money? If you have ever purchased a traveler's check, you know that a traveler's check has the advantage over cash of being insured. If it is lost or stolen, the company that issued it will refund your money. Traveler's checks are therefore safer than cash. Indeed, they *are* money because people the world over will accept an American Express check in payment for goods and services. Because traveler's checks serve as both a medium of exchange and a store of value, they are money.

Traveler's checks are issued by private companies that accept money in return for their insured checks. The checks are the issuing company's debt or liabilities. American Express agrees to redeem its checks on demand for legal tender. Past performance indicates that the company is as good as its word, so people accept traveler's checks at face value. The debt of a private firm (American Express) is accepted as a medium of exchange and allows people to store value; thus it performs the essential functions of money.

BANK MONEY The debts of commercial banks in the form of **bank money** are the most frequently employed medium of exchange in the United States.

> *Bank money, in the form of checks from private financial firms, serves as a medium of exchange.*

> *A check is a written directive from the owner of a demand deposit to the bank ordering payment of legal tender to another person or firm.*

These debts take the form of **demand deposits**. A person or business firm deposits money with a commercial bank with the agreement that the money will be available on demand and can be transferred to another person by writing a check.

> *A demand deposit is an account kept at a commercial bank for the purpose of making transactions using bank money.*

If you own a demand deposit, the bank will pay you back with Federal Reserve notes and/or U.S. coins whenever you ask. Demand deposits serve as a medium of exchange in that the funds on deposit can be transferred to another party in payment for a debt or transaction by writing a check on the account. As long as the check writer has funds on deposit equal to the amount of the check, the bank will honor the request.

Not all bank deposits are checkable, however. Generally, only demand deposits can be transferred by check. Banks also offer **time deposits** (savings) that pay more interest than demand deposits.

> *A time deposit is an account kept at a bank or financial institution for the purpose of earning interest income.*

If you wish to earn interest on the money you deposit you generally put it in a time deposit. When you wish to use the funds deposited in a time deposit, you must first either withdraw the funds in cash or have them transferred to your checking account. Often a time deposit may not be withdrawn without payment of a penalty in the form of interest sacrificed.

It used to be that you held either a demand deposit or a time deposit. Recently, a number of financial innovations have occurred in banking. One is called a *negotiable order of withdrawal (NOW)*, which combined a time deposit with a limited number of transfers by check per month. Another provided *automatic transfer services (ATS)*, which allowed an automatic transfer from savings to checking whenever a check is written. Automatic transfer services now account for over $250 billion in commercial bank deposits.

The blurring of the distinction between demand deposits and time deposits complicates the problem of defining the money supply. When the two types of accounts were distinct, it was clear that demand deposits were held for purposes of making transactions and time deposits were financial assets. Demand deposits were a medium of exchange. Time deposits, on the other hand, were assets held to earn income; they were not a medium of exchange. But what about ATS and NOW accounts, which have the advantages of being checking accounts that also pay interest. Should all or part of these be considered in calculating the supply of money?

THE SUPPLY OF MONEY

Theoretically, defining the money supply would include all three types of money, commodity money, fiat money, and bank money. In the United States there currently exists no commodity money. So the **money supply** is the sum of the outstanding fiat money and bank money.

> *The money supply is, in the United States, the sum of all the fiat money (coins and currency) and the bank money held by the public.*

The difficulty in applying this definition lies in characterizing what is bank money today, since the historical distinction between demand and time deposits has blurred.

People hold their assets in a variety of forms: checking accounts, time deposits, stocks and bonds, mutual funds, real estate, or collectibles. Economists call a person's or firm's collection of assets a *portfolio*. The assets in a portfolio vary according to their ability to be converted quickly into a medium of exchange. This means that they vary according to their **liquidity**.

> *Liquidity is the ability of an asset to be converted into a medium of exchange. The degree of liquidity is influenced by the ease and cost with which an asset can be converted into a medium of exchange.*

Coins, currency, and demand deposits are perfectly liquid because they can be immediately used as a medium of exchange. There is no question that they should be included in calculating the money supply.

Other assets are less liquid. Are they money or not? Old-style time or savings accounts, for example, had first to be converted into either cash or a demand deposit before the funds could be used as a medium of exchange. Though fairly liquid, they were not perfectly so and hence not money. Since funds held in ATS and NOW accounts can be immediately transferred by check, they are perfectly liquid, but part of the funds in these accounts are seldom transferred, being an asset that earns interest. Are the funds in these accounts money? You see the difficulty in defining the existing supply of money.

If ATS and NOW accounts are money, what about money market mutual funds? Some of these funds can be transferred by check, and all of them can be converted into a medium of exchange in a matter of days if not hours. What about stocks and bonds? These can be quickly sold for money, but only during the time the markets are open; also, several days are required for receipt of the funds. Even real estate and collectibles such as antiques and fine art can be converted into cash, but not quickly unless the seller is willing to take a lower price.

There is a continuum of assets that can be ranked according to their liquidity. Demand deposits are money and real estate is not. But where do you draw the line? How do you decide that one asset is money and another is not? It is difficult to do in practice. The main characteristic of money is its ability to serve as a medium of exchange and as a store of value. Theoretically, money is composed of those assets that are perfectly liquid. But it is hard to distinguish exactly which of the new types of accounts, or which portion of them, are held to make transactions and which of the accounts, or which part of them, are held to earn income.

For this reason there are several working definitions of the money supply. The three most commonly used are known as **M1**, **M2**, and **M3**.

> *M1 is the money supply calculated as the sum of all cash (coins and paper money) held by the public as well as demand deposits at commercial banks, traveler's checks, and other checkable deposits, such as NOW and ATS accounts.*

> *M2 is the money supply that includes everything included in the M1 money supply plus all savings deposits and small time deposits of less than $100,000, and amounts invested in money market mutual funds and certain other liquid assets.*

> *M3 is the money supply that includes everything in the M1 and M2 money supplies plus time deposits over $100,000, institution-owned money market deposit accounts, time deposits held in Europe, some foreign deposits held by Americans, and certain other accounts.*

M1 was until recently the most frequently used and cited measure of the money supply. M1 is composed of the most liquid assets available in the economy, which are those that generally serve only as a medium of exchange: coins, currency, demand deposits, traveler's checks, and other checkable deposits. NOW and ATS accounts are included in M1, even though some of the funds in these accounts are held not to make immediate transactions but to earn interest for a period of time.

M2 includes assets that, though highly liquid in the general scheme of things, are less liquid than those included in M1. M2 includes all of the components of M1 plus savings deposits, small time deposits of less than $100,000, money market mutual funds, and other fairly liquid accounts. Savings accounts, for example, can be converted to a medium of exchange by a trip to the bank. Money market mutual funds can also be converted fairly easily, many by simply writing a check greater than the specified minimum amount. Time deposits, however, often have penalties for early withdrawal. They can be quickly converted into a medium of exchange, but only at some loss of interest.

The demarcation between M1 and M2 is somewhat arbitrary. The basic idea is that the most liquid assets are included in M1 and less liquid assets in M2. But NOW and ATS accounts are included in both M1 and M2, whereas money market mutual funds, which have similar characteristics, are included only in M2. Statistics are available for even broader definitions of money. M3, for example, includes everything in M2 plus

FIGURE 13.1

Components of the Money Supply: Currency, M1 Money, and M2 Money: 1959–1987

The graph reproduces the historical growth rates of currency and of the monetary components that make up M1 and M2. You can readily see that currency has historically accounted for only a small part of either definition of the money supply. Bank money in its various forms makes up the bulk of the money supply in the United States.

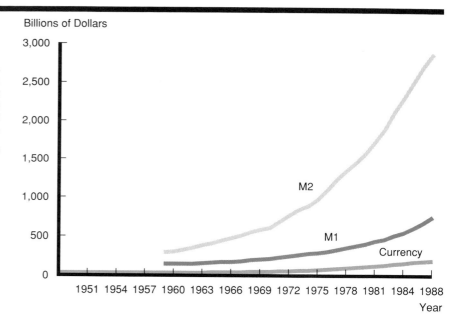

Billions of Dollars

TABLE 13.1

Money Supply of the United States: January 1, 1989 (Billions of Dollars)

COMPONENT	AMOUNT
Coins and currency	$213.4
Demand deposits	284.0
Traveler's checks	7.6
Other checkable accounts (NOW and ATS accounts)	281.3
	M1 = $786.3
Savings deposits	$427.8
Small time deposits	975.5
Money market mutual funds	331.3
Other components	548.1
	M2 = $3,069.0
Large time deposits	$544.2
Other components	308.9
	M3 = $3,922.1

Source: *Federal Reserve Bulletin*, April 1989.

large time deposits, dollar deposits of American citizens in Canadian and English banks as well as in foreign branches of U.S. banks.

The growth over time of the various measures of the money supply is shown in Figure 13.1. The relative increases in currency (coins and paper money in circulation), M1, and M2 can be read from the graph. It is clear that M1 has grown considerably faster than currency, suggesting the increasing importance of bank money. Until recently, M2 has generally grown more rapidly than M1. Table 13.1 shows the money supply in the United States as of January 1989.

The supply of money has important and wide-ranging effects on the economy. In the United States the supply of money can be controlled by the government, because the stock of money is a combination of fiat and

13.2

ARE CREDIT CARDS MONEY?

"Plastic money"—credit cards like Visa, MasterCard, Discovery Card, American Express, and Diner's Club—is today frequently used by people to make transactions. Are credit cards money? The average American household now has a half-dozen credit cards and uses most of them. Billions of dollars in transactions are racked up annually by people using their credit cards. What about the less familiar debit cards? They look like credit cards, but do they operate in the same way and are they money?

Money, you will recall, performs at least two essential functions: It serves as both a medium of exchange and a store of value. When you have a dollar bill in your wallet, you have an instrument that can be used to make a transaction at any time and that stores purchasing power while you make up your mind what to buy.

Suppose you decide to make a transaction with your credit card. The familiar statement "I put it on my plastic" accurately describes this type of transaction, highlighting the difference between credit card purchases and cash transactions. You present your credit card (instead of cash), make your purchase, and sign your name. Is this the same as using cash? Not quite, because the credit card has not served as a store of value. Until the card was used, nothing happened. Before you can spend cash, it has to be acquired through a previous transaction and the value of the transaction stored in the form of money until employed to make a trade. When a cash transaction is made, an asset (money) is exchanged for another asset (the good you acquired).

Let us examine a credit card transaction. When you use your card to pay for a purchase, you have instantly borrowed money from the bank according to a prearranged agreement. You have also instructed the bank to pay the merchant the value of the bank's loan to you. The bank pays the merchant and at the end of the month sends you a statement giving you the opportunity either to repay the loan or to continue the loan and pay interest to the bank. A credit card purchase involves creating a liability (the loan) and exchanging it for an asset in the form of the good you purchased. The transaction begins when you make the purchase. Since the credit card does not serve as a store of value, however, it cannot be said to perform the functions of money.

A debit card looks a lot like a credit card, but it works in a different way. When you make a purchase with a debit card, you instruct your bank to transfer a specified amount of your funds directly from your bank account. Using a debit card to make a transaction is just like writing a check, except that it is less time-consuming. The money that you hold in demand deposits is used to make the purchase. Debit card purchases are just another way for you to use the money you already possess.

bank money. The government thus has a tool with which it can influence the macroeconomy. However, because the effect of a 5 percent increase in M1 is likely to be different from that of a similar increase in M2, it is important that the monetary authorities know how to measure the money supply and the effect that a change in the money supply will have on the economy.

The relationship between M1 and nominal national income formerly provided the best guide to the effect of changes in the money supply on the macroeconomy. Recently, however, that relationship has broken down, because of innovations such as NOW and ATS accounts. M2 now seems to provide the better indicator. That is the reason why we shall use M2 as the measure of the quantity of money throughout the rest of this book.

The supply of money in the United States, as we shall show in a later chapter, is controlled by the Federal Reserve Bank. The Federal Reserve is not a profit-making institution. The amount of money it supplies is not determined by the desire to maximize the profits from producing money, but by other motives and desires. As a result, the quantity of money supplied does not vary with the opportunity cost of holding money—the rate of interest. The supply of money at any point in time is the vertical line S_M depicted in Figure 13.2. The supply of money is the amount that

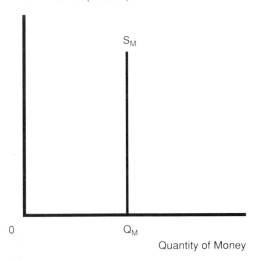

the Federal Reserve decides it will be, and it does not vary with the opportunity cost of money. The supply of money is thus determined by the federal government.

THE DEMAND FOR MONEY

Just as there is a supply of money, there is a corresponding demand for money. The demand for money, which is determined in the private sector, is instrumental in transmitting throughout the macroeconomy the effect of changes in the supply of money.

BENEFITS OF HOLDING MONEY

Money provides a variety of benefits, serving as a medium of exchange, a unit of account, a store of value, and a means of deferred payment. There is also an **opportunity cost of holding money**. If you hold money in a checking account, you are giving up the opportunity to earn more interest by owning some other less liquid asset instead.

> *The opportunity cost of holding money is the forgone interest that could have been earned by owning an asset that is less liquid but earns more interest.*

Each individual must constantly weigh the benefits of holding money against the corresponding opportunity cost.

You will recall our discussion of traveler's checks as an example of private-debt money. Traveler's checks also provide a fine illustration of the opportunity cost of holding money. Have you ever wondered *why* American Express, for example, issues traveler's checks? The fee that the buyer must pay is the obvious answer. But often traveler's checks are issued free in return for cash, and even when the customer pays a fee, it does not go to American Express but to the agent selling the checks. American Express lives on the opportunity cost of money by investing the money it receives for its checks while it waits for the checks to be spent. A firm as large and as profitable as American Express can afford to have offices worldwide to serve its customers and still earn a profit off the money its customers provide in return for traveler's checks.

That there are alternatives to holding money suggests that the demand for money will be downward-sloping. The demand for money will obey the law of demand. When the cost of holding money — the interest rate — increases, the quantity of money demanded will decline. Conversely, when the rate of interest falls, the quantity of money demanded will increase.

The benefits of holding money can be attributed to three motives: (1) the transaction motive, (2) the precautionary motive, and (3) the speculative motive. These benefits create a demand for money.

TRANSACTION MOTIVE Individuals and business firms desire to hold money because they desire to engage in trades and exchanges. Money oils the mechanism of exchange and reduces the costs of making transactions. It is less expensive to use money to make trades than to resort to barter. The cost of constantly converting less liquid assets into some medium of exchange in order to make trades exceeds the opportunity cost of holding money. All individuals and business firms will therefore desire to hold some money in order to make transactions.

As real national income expands, business firms will engage in an increasingly larger number of transactions, inducing business firms and individuals to hold more cash. The transaction demand for money will be in direct proportion to the level of real national income, rising when national income increases and falling when national income declines.

PRECAUTIONARY MOTIVE Because money will be accepted in exchange, people will desire to hold some money in case of emergencies. If you leave your car lights on and cause the battery to run down, possessing a $20 bill will ensure that you can get quickly back on the road. Wise parents see to it that their children have some money when they go out at night. Money can get you out of trouble better than any other asset. Thus economic decision makers will generally hold some money for unforeseen contingencies.

Also, the demand for money will increase when current events make the future appear to be more uncertain than usual. When economic decision makers look into their crystal balls and see clouds, they will respond by holding more money as a precaution. Business firms will hold more cash in case the firm's sales unexpectedly decline. Similarly, households will want to hold more cash to tide them over unpleasant, unforeseen events such as unemployment. Thus the demand for money will tend to expand as uncertainty increases.

SPECULATIVE MOTIVE The world is an uncertain and ever-changing place. One never knows for sure that the best investment opportunities are the ones currently available. In October 1987 the stock market crashed, falling over 500 points in one day. Many persons began to wonder whether the economy was in for an equally sharp decline, which would mean declines in the prices of financial assets. If you expect asset prices to fall, it is better to hold dollar-denominated assets rather than equities, whose prices can vary. Sometimes cash is the best investment while you wait out uncertain times.

When the future value of nonmonetary assets is expected to fall, more money will be demanded today. Conversely, when the future value of nonmonetary assets is expected to increase, less money will be currently demanded.

The factors that affect the transaction, precautionary, and speculative motives for holding money will therefore affect the demand for money.

FACTORS AFFECTING THE DEMAND FOR MONEY

The demand for money can be analyzed in theory like the demand for any other good or service — by identifying the determinants of demand. The factors that affect the quantity of money that economic decision makers wish to hold are the interest rate, the level of real gross national product, the price level, and the rate of expected future inflation.

The rate of interest measures the opportunity cost of holding money. The quantity of money demanded will vary inversely with the rate of interest. The rate of interest determines the operative point on the demand curve, the point that indicates the actual quantity of money demanded.

As real GNP increases, more transactions will be required, which translates into an increased desire to hold more money. Moreover, the higher the price level, the greater will be the amount of money required for transaction purposes. Even if the same number of transactions are

FIGURE 13.3
Demand for Money

The demand for money is a function of the rate of interest as well as real GNP, the price level, and expectations of future inflation. The last three are determinants that affect the position of the demand curve as shown in Part A, and the rate of interest determines the point on the money demand curve where the economy will operate, as shown in Part B.

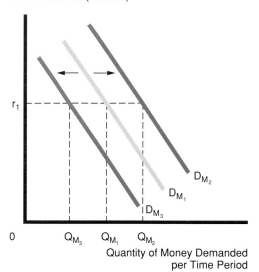

(A)

Rate of Interest (Percent)

Quantity of Money Demanded
per Time Period

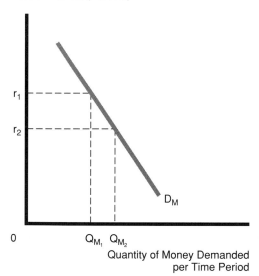

(B)

Rate of Interest (Percent)

Quantity of Money Demanded
per Time Period

made as before, if the price level increases, the total value of each transaction will increase, requiring the use of more money. Thus the transaction demand for money will be greater the higher the level of real GNP and the higher the price level.

Operating in the opposite direction is the effect that higher future expected increases in the price level have on the demand for money. When inflation increases, the purchasing power of money will decline. The higher future inflation rates are expected to be, the less adequately money will perform its task as a store of value. Decision makers will respond to these expectations by reducing the amount of money they hold, switching instead into assets whose value will increase with the price level. Thus the demand for money will decline as expected future inflation rates increase. These three influences — real GNP, price level, and expected increase in inflation — describe the demand for money, determining the position of the money demand curve.

In summary: The demand for money will increase along with real GNP and the price level, but it will decrease as expected future inflation rates increase. The quantity demanded of money will vary inversely with the interest rate, which is the opportunity cost of holding money.

The forces influencing the demand for money are shown in Part A of Figure 13.3. The determinants of money demanded are real GNP, the price level, and the rate of expected future inflation. When real GNP or the price level increases or when the expected rate of inflation declines, the demand for money will increase and the demand curve will shift to the right from D_{M_1} to D_{M_2}. The amount of money demanded at a rate of interest of r_1 will increase from Q_{M_1} to Q_{M_2}. Demand will decline and the demand curve will shift to the left from D_{M_1} to D_{M_3} when real GNP declines, or the price level falls, or the rate of expected future inflation increases. The quantity of money that will be held after this shift occurs, if the rate of interest remains at r_1, will decline from Q_{M_1} to Q_{M_3}.

When we examined the determinants of the demand for money, we held constant the opportunity cost of holding money (the interest rate). What happens if we hold constant the determinants of money demanded and allow the interest rate to vary? In this case the quantity demanded of money will obey the law of demand and vary inversely with the opportunity cost of money. This is shown in Part B of Figure 13.3. When the rate of interest declines from r_1 to r_2, the quantity of money demanded increases from Q_{M_1} to Q_{M_2}.

SUPPLY AND DEMAND FOR MONEY AND THE PRICE LEVEL

Economists have long been intrigued by the relationship between the supply of money and the price level. Economists have found that there is a close but not perfect relationship between the two. The increase in the price level over time has been accompanied by an increase in the money supply. The fact that money and prices have historically increased in tandem does not prove that an increase in the money supply causes an increase in the price level; perhaps both variables are related to some third as yet unspecified variable. What is required is a theory that explains why an increase in the money supply can be expected to cause an increase in the price level.

The model of supply and demand for money can be employed to gain useful insights into the relationship between the money supply and the aggregate price level.

A SIMPLE EXPLANATION FOR INFLATION

The opportunity cost of holding money is the interest that could be obtained by holding interest-earning assets instead. The value of money, however, is measured by its purchasing power: How many goods and services will a unit of money purchase? The value of money, therefore, changes exactly in inverse proportion to the change in the price level.

$$\text{Purchasing power of money} = \frac{1}{\text{Price level}}$$

If the price level (PL), as measured by, say, the consumer price index, rises by 5 percent, the value of the dollar will decline by exactly 5 percent.

The supply-and-demand model predicts that if the supply of money increases relative to the demand for money, the price level will rise and the value of money will decline. To see why, assume that the money market is in equilibrium. If the supply of money now increases, economic decision makers will find that they have excess money balances, since they are holding more money than they desire at the existing price level. They will respond to this imbalance by spending their excess money on interest-earning assets, and perhaps on goods and services as well.

However, what is possible for one person to do is in this case impossible for everyone to do. The private sector as a whole cannot get rid of money. What one person spends to lower his or her cash balance adds to another person's cash balance. The total amount of money will remain the same no matter who owns it. Passing money from one person to another cannot change the total amount of money in the economy.

What does change is the price level. As the excess amount of money is spent, the prices of goods and services will be bid up. There is now more money being used to purchase the same amount of goods and services as before. As the price level increases, however, so will the quantity of money demanded. More money is now required to finance the higher dollar value of total expenditures.

This is shown in Figure 13.4. Instead of the interest rate, the value of money, equal to 1/PL, is now shown on the vertical axis. The quantity of money demanded is recorded on the horizontal axis. The demand for money as a function of the price level is shown by demand curve D_M, which is downward-sloping in accordance with the law of demand.

Note that the demand curve in Figure 13.4 is a function of the value of money, which is measured by its purchasing power, and is not, as previously discussed, a function of the interest rate. Thus the value of money is measured by the quantity of goods and services a unit of money can purchase, in other words, by its purchasing power. The opportunity cost of holding money instead of an asset that pays more interest is measured by the interest rate. The demand for money (D_M) in the graph slopes downward because as the price level increases (and the purchasing power of money declines), more money will be required to make a given number of transactions because the money cost of each transaction has increased.

The initial supply of money is shown by the vertical line S_{M_1}. The supply of money is not a function of the value of money, but is rather a result of a decision by the Federal Reserve to supply at any point in time a fixed quantity of money. The economy is initially in equilibrium at E, with a value of money equal to 1/PL and a quantity of money Q_{M_1}.

Suppose that the Federal Reserve decides to increase the money supply to Q_{M_2} and that the demand for money (D_M) is unchanged. Economic decision makers now have excess money balances at the old equilibrium price level. They respond to this situation by spending the excess. This

FIGURE 13.4

Interrelationship of an Increase in the Money Supply, the Price Level, and the Value of Money

This figure shows that the quantity demanded of money is inversely related to the value of money. As the price level increases (and the value of money declines), more money will be required to finance a given quantity of trades. The supply of money is not a function of the value of money but is whatever the Federal Reserve decides it will be. When the quantity of money supplied increases, the value of money declines.

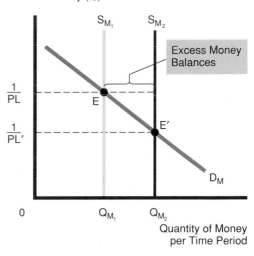

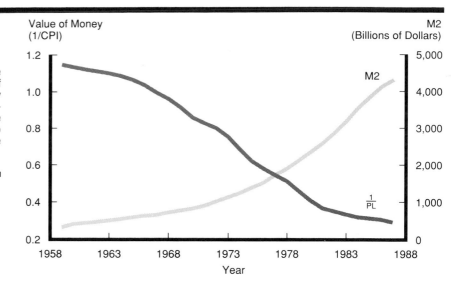

FIGURE 13.5
M2 Money Supply and the Purchasing Power
of Money: 1959–1987

According to the theory presented in Figure 13.4, there
should be an inverse relationship between the quantity of
money and the value of money. In this figure the quantity
of M2 money is compared with the value of money (measured by 1 divided by the consumer price index) for the
years 1959–1987. The predicted relationship seems to
hold: The quantity of money increases every year while
the value of money correspondingly declines.

spending process will continue until the price level rises sufficiently to
induce decision makers to hold the new quantity of money. The economy
will eventually find a new equilibrium at E'. The result of an increase in
the supply of money relative to the demand for money is a rise in the price
level and a fall in the purchasing power of money to 1/PL'.

Statistical evidence in support of this simple model is given in
Figure 13.5. Theoretically, increases in the money supply should be inversely related to changes in the purchasing power of money when measured as 1/PL. In the figure the relationship between the quantity of M2
money and the purchasing power of money, measured as 1 divided by the
consumer price index, appears to be as theory predicts. Increases in the
money supply are inversely related to the purchasing power of money.

SUPPLY AND DEMAND FOR MONEY AND NATIONAL INCOME

The simple supply-and-demand model explains inflation, but it does not
reveal the transmission mechanism by which an increase in the supply of
money relative to the demand for money affects the macroeconomy. Economists have developed two useful theories that explain how changes in the
quantity of money affect nominal national income in the short run.

The first theory of the demand for money that we shall discuss is the
Keynesian theory. The second is the modern quantity theory, which is the
basis for monetarism.

THE KEYNESIAN TRANSMISSION MECHANISM

The transmission mechanism relates the way changes in the money supply
are transmitted into changes in real national income and in the price
level. The Keynesian transmission mechanism is shown in Figure 13.6. In
the Keynesian model the influence of an increase in the money supply on
the macroeconomy is indirect. Specifically, the transmission mechanism
involves the interaction of an unchanging money demand curve, called, in

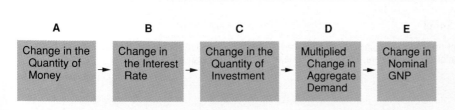

A	B	C	D	E
Change in the Quantity of Money	Change in the Interest Rate	Change in the Quantity of Investment	Multiplied Change in Aggregate Demand	Change in Nominal GNP

FIGURE 13.6
Keynesian Transmission Mechanism

Keynesian economic theory suggests that a change in the money supply operates on the macroeconomy via a change in the rate of interest, which affects the quantity of investment. The change in the quantity of investment has a multiplied effect on aggregate demand, which in turn affects nominal national income.

Keynesian analysis, the *liquidity preference schedule*, with a change in the quantity of money. The change in the quantity of money causes the interest rate to change. The change in the interest rate, along with the investment demand schedule, induces a change in investment spending. The change in investment spending has a multiplied effect on aggregate demand that causes nominal national income to change. The change in nominal national income in the short run is composed of both a change in real GNP and a change in the price level.

To see how the Keynesian transmission mechanism works in the short run, consider Figure 13.7, which depicts the effect of an increase in the money supply. The transmission mechanism begins in Part A with the liquidity preference curve (money demand curve) which reveals the amount of money that will be demanded at each rate of interest. The liquidity preference curve is D_{M_1}, the quantity of money is Q_{M_1}, and the rate of interest is r_1. In this case individuals are in monetary equilibrium, holding just the amount of money they desire.

Now suppose that the quantity of money increases to Q_{M_2}. Economic decision makers now have more money (by the amount of the increase in the money supply) than they desire to hold at the existing rate of interest. In the liquidity preference theory, the alternative to holding money is to hold **fixed-income assets** paying higher interest, such as bonds.

> *A fixed-income asset is a financial obligation that pays its owner a fixed amount of dollars in interest each year.*

According to the liquidity preference theory, people will use their excess money balances to purchase fixed-income assets paying higher interest, such as bonds. The price of bonds will be bid up, causing the interest rate in the economy to fall.

Why should the rate of interest fall when the price of financial assets increases? Suppose you purchase for $1,000 a bond that pays an annual interest payment of $100 forever. Your bond yields 10 percent per year ($100/$1000 = 10%). Now suppose that the money supply increases and persons with excess money balances attempt to buy bonds, thereby causing bond prices to increase. Suppose the price of your bond increases to $2,000 but it still pays $100 per year in interest. What is the rate of interest your bond is now paying? Divide the annual interest payment, which is still $100, by the new price of the bond, $2,000, and the rate of interest is now 5 percent.

Thus when the price of bonds or other fixed-income assets increases, the interest rate falls. Conversely, when the price of bonds falls, the interest rate rises. What does this imply for the liquidity preference curve? When the money supply increases and people find they are holding more money than they desire, they will spend the excess for bonds. The interest rate will fall as the price of these fixed-income financial assets is bid up.

FIGURE 13.7
Short-Run Effect of an Increase in the Money Supply

An increase in the money supply will cause both the level of real national income and the price level to change in the short run. In this figure real national income increases in the short run to Y_{SR} (in Part C) and an inflationary gap appears, while the price level increases to PL_{SR}.

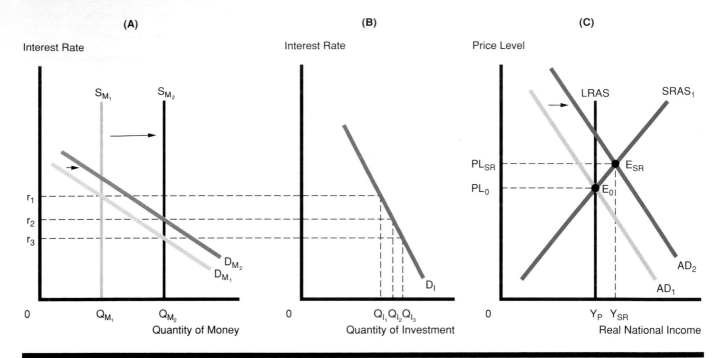

The effect of a lower interest rate on the quantity of investment is shown in Part B. The quantity of investment (Q_I) is determined by the rate of interest and the demand curve for investment (D_I). The quantity of investment demanded is inversely related to the rate of interest. When firms decide how much to spend for capital goods, they calculate the rate of return each investment project will yield and then rank the projects from highest to lowest. They will undertake only those projects with projected rates of return equal to or greater than the rate of interest. When the rate of interest increases, fewer projects will pass this test of profitability and total investment spending will decline. When the rate of interest declines, more projects will pass the test and total investment spending will increase. Thus investment spending is inversely related to changes in the rate of interest. The amount of investment spending is determined at the point where the rate of interest intersects the investment demand curve in Part B. When the rate of interest falls from r_1 to r_3, the quantity of investment spending will rise from Q_{I_1} to Q_{I_3}.

To summarize: The interest rate (shown in Part A) will initially decline from r_1 to r_3 when the money supply increases from S_{M_1} to S_{M_2}. The lower interest rate will induce business firms to undertake more investment. The amount of investment increases, as shown in Part B, from Q_{I_1} to Q_{I_3}.

So how is a change in the quantity of money transmitted into changes in real national income and in the price level? Suppose the macroeconomy is initially in long-run equilibrium. The increased amount of investment will have a multiplied effect on aggregate demand, which will increase from AD_1 in Part C. Both real national income and the price level will

FIGURE 13.8
The Long-Run Neutrality of Money

This figure shows that the overall effect of an increase in the money supply in the long run is an increase in the price level. An increase in the money supply is, in the long run, neutral with respect to the level of real national income.

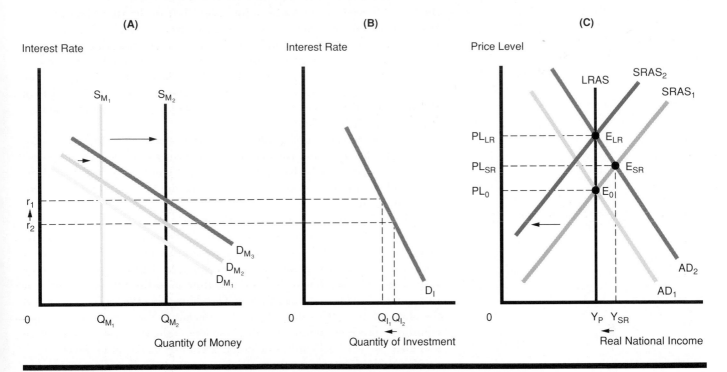

begin to increase as the short-run equilibrium moves along the SRAS curve.

The short-run adjustment process is not yet complete. The increase in real national income and in the price level will feed back, increasing the transaction demand for money. The liquidity preference curve thus shifts to the right from D_{M_1} to D_{M_2} in Part A, causing the rate of interest to rise somewhat, though not to the level r_1. The short-run equilibrium rate of interest is established at r_2, determining the short-run equilibrium level of investment spending to be Q_{I_2} (as shown in Part B) and the level of aggregate demand to be AD_2 (Part C). The new equilibrium position becomes E_{SR}, with real national income at Y_{SR} and the price level at PL_{SR}. An inflationary gap is thus created.

The increase in aggregate demand will, in the short run, cause the equilibrium to shift from E_0 to E_{SR} and the price level to increase from PL_0 to PL_{SR}. Real national income will increase to the level Y_{SR}, which is greater than potential national income, creating an inflationary gap. Thus in the short run an increase in the money supply will affect both the level of aggregate output and the price level.

NEUTRALITY OF MONEY IN THE LONG RUN   The inflationary gap that was created in Figure 13.7 by the increase in the money supply will be eliminated in the long run by a decrease in the short-run aggregate supply. This is shown in Figure 13.8, where in Part C the SRAS curve will shift from $SRAS_1$ to $SRAS_2$. Real national income will decline from Y_{SR} back to Y_P, and the price level will increase to PL_{LR}. As a result of this process, a new long-run equilibrium will be established at E_{LR}. Nominal national income will increase despite the decline in real national income, as the rise in the price level more than compensates for the decline in real output.

The rise in the price level in Part C will feed back to Part A, causing the liquidity preference curve to increase (shift to the right) from D_{M_2} to D_{M_3} and the interest rate to increase to r_1, the rate that existed prior to the increase in the money supply. The rise in the interest rate will reduce the amount of investment spending from Q_{I_2} to Q_{I_1} in Part B, which was the amount of investment before the increase in the money supply. The decline in investment spending accounts for the decline in real output. In the long run all that has changed as a result of an increase in the money supply is the price level.

We have been discussing the effects of an increase in the money supply in both the short and the long run. The process also works in reverse when the money supply declines. In the short run both real national income and the price level will decline, and in the long run only the price level will decline.

The actual effect of a change in the money supply on the macroeconomy obviously depends on many things. It depends on how much the money supply increases and on how responsive changes in the rate of interest are to a change in the money supply. It also depends on how responsive the investment demand schedule is to the fall in the interest rate and to the size of the multiplier. The short-run effect also depends on the slope of the SRAS curve, which determines the composition of the resulting change in nominal national income, indicating how much will be a change in real GNP and how much a change in the price level.

Keynesian economists generally believe that the liquidity preference curve is quite responsive to changes in the money supply. Relatively large increases in the money supply are required to change the rate of interest significantly. Moreover, Keynesians believe that investment demand is not very responsive to changes in the interest rate. So when the interest rate does change in response to an increase in the money supply, the actual affect on investment will be small. These assumptions together imply that neither real national income nor the price level will be very responsive in the short run to changes in the money supply. This explains why Keynesian economists have generally favored fiscal policy instead of proposing changes in the money supply when urging the government to intervene in the economy.

THE CLASSICAL QUANTITY THEORY

The idea that inflation is caused by the growth of the money supply dates back at least to the classical economists who first employed the equation of exchange to explain the relationship between money and the price level. The modern quantity theory of money is also based on the equation of exchange.

EQUATION OF EXCHANGE The equation of exchange begins with a truism: The expenditures by one person become the income received by another person. Expenditures and income are the opposite sides of the same coin. When you fill your car's tank with gas, the $15 you spend (expenditures) becomes the receipts (income) of the gas station owner. The same is true for the economy as a whole: The total amounts spent must equal the total amounts received.

$$\text{Value of total expenditures of final goods and services} = \text{Value of final goods and services sold}$$

Since money is the medium of exchange, if you know the quantity of money and the average number of times a dollar is exchanged each year, you will be able to determine the value of total expenditures as measured by nominal GNP.

The average number of times a dollar is used in trade is called the **velocity of circulation.**

The velocity of circulation is the average number of times per year a dollar is used to purchase final goods and services.

The velocity of circulation (V) can be calculated by dividing nominal GNP by the quantity of money:

$$\text{Velocity of circulation} = \frac{\text{Nominal GNP}}{\text{Money supply}}$$

The velocity of circulation is the ratio of nominal GNP to the money supply. The higher the velocity of circulation, the faster economic decision makers are turning over the stock of money.

Nominal GNP is composed of real GNP (call it Q) times the price level (P). Thus velocity of circulation (V) can also be expressed as:

$$V = \frac{P \cdot Q}{M}$$

where M is the money supply. Multiplying both sides by M gives the equation of exchange:

$$M \cdot V = P \cdot Q$$

The equation of exchange states that the value of the final purchases must equal the amount expended to buy them: Nominal GNP must be equal to the money supply times the velocity of circulation. The preceding statement must be true because it is an identity. The equation of exchange is not a theory, for velocity is defined in such a way that the identity always holds.

The equation of exchange can, however, be made into a theory by making assumptions about the behavior of the components of the equation. The classical economists accomplished this by assuming that velocity was a constant and that the economy was always operating at the level of potential national income. In so doing, they changed the equation of exchange into the classical quantity theory. If these assumptions are an accurate picture of reality, then the price level will change proportionally with increases in the money supply.

Suppose the quantity of money increases by 5 percent and velocity is assumed not to change. In this case nominal national income will also increase by 5 percent. Since the economy is always operating at the level of potential national income, only the price level can increase. The price level increases by 5 percent when the money supply increases by 5 percent.

The classical quantity theory provides a fairly accurate description of the economy in the long run. But in the short run the economy does not always operate at the level of potential national income, and the velocity of circulation is not a constant.

FIGURE 13.9
The Monetarist Transmission Mechanism

The monetarist transmission mechanism is more direct than the Keynesian transmission mechanism, acting directly on aggregate demand. According to monetarism, when individuals find they are holding too much money, they will spend the excess on a variety of goods and services, not just for bonds as assumed by the liquidity preference theory. As a result, consumption and investment are directly affected. The change in aggregate demand will cause nominal national income to change.

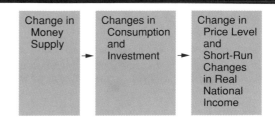

THE MODERN QUANTITY THEORY

Contemporary quantity theorists, often called monetarists, have attempted to overcome the defects in the classical theory by reexamining the demand for money. The monetarists' demand for money — the demand for cash balances to hold for transaction purposes — is similar to the demand for any other good. If, for example, you want money to hold, the way to acquire it is by not spending part of your income for other goods and services. Conversely, if you find that you are holding too much money, you will respond by purchasing a variety of goods. Thus the monetarists' money demand function is broader than that assumed by the Keynesians in the sense that any excess money balances will be spent on more than just financial assets.

TRANSMISSION MECHANISM OF THE MODERN QUANTITY THEORY How will a change in the money supply affect the rest of the economy? In the monetarist model the transmission mechanism runs directly from the monetary sector to aggregate demand. The monetarist transmission mechanism is shown in Figure 13.9. Money is considered just one of many assets that a person can use to store wealth. Therefore, when economic decision makers find that they hold too much money, they will spend it on a wide variety of goods: stock, bonds, real estate, automobiles, clothes — almost anything. When individuals find they are holding too much money, aggregate demand increases directly because both consumption and investment spending will increase, affecting in the short run both real national income and the price level.

The monetarists' money demand function stipulates that the quantity of money people demand to hold depends on:

1. The level of real GNP.
2. The price level.
3. The rate of anticipated inflation.
4. The rate of interest on alternative assets (the opportunity cost of holding money).

Modern quantity theorists argue that, although velocity is not constant, systematic determinants of velocity do exist. The modern quantity theory postulates that velocity will change over the course of a business cycle, rising during expansions and falling during contractions as the transaction demand for money changes with the level of nominal GNP. When either the price level or real GNP rises, a given quantity of money will have to finance a larger volume of trades, causing each dollar to be exchanged more often. Conversely, if either the price level or real GNP falls, a given quantity of money will have to finance fewer transactions, and so velocity will also fall.

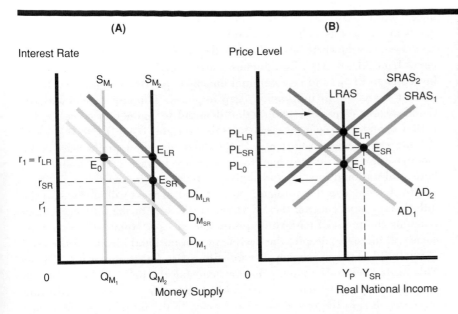

FIGURE 13.10
Effect of an Increase in the Money Supply
According to the Monetarist Model

The monetarist transmission mechanism runs directly from the money market in Part A to the macroeconomy in Part B. When the money supply is increased, the initial effect is to drive the interest rate down and to increase aggregate demand. In the short run an increase in the money supply operating through its effect on aggregate demand will cause both real national income and the price level to increase. In the long run the automatic adjustment process will operate, decreasing the short-run aggregate supply. In the long run an increase in the money supply affects only the price level and not the level of real national income.

According to the modern quantity theory, one of the most important variables affecting the demand for money is the anticipated rate of future inflation. Suppose the money supply increases and causes people to expect the rate of inflation to rise in the future, reducing the future value of money. When the value of money is expected to decline in the future, people will respond by trading money for other assets that are expected to be a better store of value. So people reduce their money holdings and velocity will increase. On the other hand, if individuals' expectations change so that they expect less inflation, or even deflation, in the future, then velocity will fall.

The modern quantity theory argues that velocity changes in a predictable way. Money supply and velocity can and do move together to cause nominal national income to change. An increase in the quantity of money fuels inflationary expectations and thereby causes the velocity of circulation to increase. The increase in nominal national income due to an increase in the money supply will be amplified by the increase in velocity. If, for example, the money supply increases by 5 percent, inducing a 5 percent increase in velocity as inflation expectations increase, nominal national income will increase by 10 percent:

$$\text{Change in M} + \text{Change in V} = \text{Change in Nominal GNP}$$
$$5\% + 5\% = 10\%$$

Monetarists also believe that changes in the quantity of money can affect the level of aggregate output in the short run, but not in the long run. In the long run a change in the quantity of money will affect only the price level. This is shown graphically in Figure 13.10. The monetarist transmission mechanism is employed. Changes in the money market shown in Part A directly affect the macroeconomy shown in Part B. The macroeconomy is initially in long-run equilibrium at E_0 in Part B, and the monetary sector, described in Part A, is in equilibrium, with the money supply at Q_{M_1}, the demand for money at D_{M_1}, and an interest rate of r_1.

Suppose the money supply now increases to Q_{M_2}. The interest rate will decline initially to r_1' as individuals spend their excess money balances. Monetarists see people spending their excess balances for other goods and assets as well as for bonds, so aggregate demand immediately increases, as shown in Part B, with the shift of the aggregate demand curve from AD_1 to AD_2. Equilibrium shifts from E_0 to E_{SR}, the price level increases to PL_{SR}, and real national income expands to Y_{SR}. Since Y_{SR} is greater than Y_P, an inflationary gap appears. The rise in nominal national income causes the transaction demand for money to increase, the money demand curve increases (shifts to the right) from D_{M_1} to $D_{M_{SR}}$, and the interest rate increases to r_{SR}. In the short run, then, an increase in the money supply will directly lead to an increase in aggregate demand, and both real national income and the price level will increase.

In the long run the automatic adjustment process will operate on the inflationary gap, causing the SRAS curve to shift to the left, eventually reaching the point of long-run equilibrium at E_{LR}. Nominal national income will increase, despite the decline in real national income to the level of potential national income, because the price level increases to PL_{LR}. This feeds back to the money market, causing the demand for money to increase. The money demand curve shifts up to $D_{M_{LR}}$ and the interest rate increases to r_{LR}, the rate that existed prior to the increase in the money supply. In the long run, then, money is neutral with respect to changes in real national income. The only long-run effect of an increase in the money supply will be an increase in the price level.

This process also works in reverse, of course, if the money supply should decline.

ANTICIPATED VERSUS UNANTICIPATED CHANGES IN THE MONEY SUPPLY

In both the Keynesian and monetarist models, the actual effect of an increase in the money supply on the economy also depends on whether or not the increase in the money supply was anticipated. If the increase was unexpected, the economy will react as described above, with the economy moving through a short-run adjustment prior to attaining long-run equilibrium. If, however, the increase was perfectly anticipated, the economy will skip directly to the long-run adjustment and the only effect of an increase in the money supply will be inflation and an increase in the price level.

SUMMARY

1. The main functions of money are to serve as a medium of exchange and to serve as a store of value. Because money performs these functions, it is considered to be perfectly liquid. In addition, money often serves as a unit of account and a standard of deferred payment.

2. The money supply could be composed of commodity money, token and fiat monies, or debt money such as bank money, or some combination of the three. Bank money consists of demand deposits. In the United States the money supply is made up of token and fiat monies as well as bank money. The value of commodity money is equal to its value as a commodity. The value of fiat money is greater than the value of the resources used to produce it and is equal to its purchasing power.

3. Economic decision makers demand money for three reasons: the transaction motive, the precautionary motive, and the speculative motive.

4. The opportunity cost of holding money is the interest that could have been earned by holding a less liquid asset instead. The value of money is equal to its purchasing power.

5. When the supply of money increases relative to the demand for money, the purchasing power of money will decline as the price level rises.

6. In the Keynesian model the quantity of money affects the macroeconomy through its affect on the rate of interest and the amount of investment spending. The Keynesian demand for money is known as the liquidity preference curve. Liquidity preference is a function of the rate of interest. When the supply of money changes, there is a change in the rate of interest, which operates on aggregate demand through its effect on investment spending.

7. According to the Keynesian model, changes in the money supply can affect both the price level and the level of aggregate output in the short run, but it can affect only the price level in the long run. This latter result is known as the neutrality of money.

8. The modern quantity theory is based on the equation of exchange. According to the quantity theory, the quantity of money demanded depends on the level of real national income, the price level, the expected rate of inflation, and the rate of interest. The quantity theory postulates that velocity behaves systematically over time.

9. In the monetarist model changes in the quantity of money can affect the level of real output and employment in the short run by directly affecting aggregate demand. In the long run an increase in the money supply affects only the price level, and so money is neutral with respect to its long-run effect on real national income.

10. The actual effect a change in the money supply has on the economy depends on whether the change was anticipated or not. If the change was unanticipated, the economy will move through short-run equilibrium prior to attaining long-run equilibrium. If the change was anticipated, the economy will move directly to the long-run equilibrium position.

THE GREAT GERMAN HYPERINFLATION

PREVIEW 13.1 ANALYSIS

What are the facts about the great German hyperinflation? Germany lost World War I and was forced to pay reparations to the victorious Allies. The German monarchy was dissolved and the weak Weimar Republic was substituted in its place. The new republic was barely able to govern and hardly able to levy and collect taxes. Yet it had to make reparation payments and pay for the costs of government. The result was persistent budget deficits. These deficits were covered by issuing paper fiat money that could not be redeemed for any other money.

As more and more German marks were placed in circulation, inflation was not far behind. Between 1919 and 1923 a rapid inflation turned into a hyperinflation. The British economist Lionel Robbins wrote of this occurrence:

It was the most colossal thing of its kind in history; and, next probably to the Great War itself, it must bear responsibility for many of the political and economic difficulties of our generation. It destroyed the wealth of the more solid elements in German society; and it left behind a moral and economic disequilibrium, apt breeding ground for the disasters which have followed. Hitler is the foster child of the inflation.[1]

---

[1]Quoted in Bresciani-Turroni, *The Economics of Inflation: A Study of Currency Depreciation in Post-War Germany*, translated by Millicent E. Savers (New York: Augustus M. Kelly, 1968), p. 5.

TABLE 13.2
The Great German Hyperinflation: Money and the Price Level: 1922–1923

DATE	QUANTITY OF MONEY (MILLIONS OF MARKS)	WHOLESALE PRICE INDEX (1913 = 1)
1922: June	295,200	70.30
July	308,000	100.59
Aug.	331,600	192.00
Sept.	451,100	287.00
Oct.	603,800	566.00
Nov.	839,100	1,154.00
Dec.	1,495,200	1,475.00
1923: Jan.	2,081,800	3,286.00
Feb.	3,588,000	5,287.00
Mar.	6,601,300	4,827.00
April	8,442,300	5,738.00
May	10,275,000	9,034.00
June	22,019,800	24,618.00
July	57,848,900	183,510.00
Aug.	196,294,700	1,695,109.00
Sept.	46,716,616,400	36,223,771.00
Oct.	6,907,511,101,800	18,700,000,000.00
Nov.	191,580,465,422,100	1,422,900,000,000.00

Source: Frank D. Graham, *Exchange, Prices, and Production in Hyper-Inflation Germany, 1920–1923* (New York: Russell & Russell, 1930).

The German economy initially suffered some inflation during World War I, which accelerated after 1919 and turned into a true hyperinflation in 1922. The hyperinflation ended in November 1923, when the currency was called in and a new currency issued, but not until severe damage had been inflicted on both the German economy and society.

The modern quantity theory provides a good starting place to analyze the great hyperinflation. The quantity theory begins with the equation of exchange:

$$M \cdot V = P \cdot Q$$

where M is quantity of money, V is velocity of circulation, P is price level, and Q is real GNP.

The cause and effect of the great German hyperinflation, according to this theory, can be seen in Table 13.2. The quantity of money increased extremely rapidly between June 1922 and November 1923. The rate of increase during the first months, which was rapid by any standard, was relatively modest compared to what was to follow. The rate of increase of the money supply accelerated, and by May 1923 it was doubling monthly, by August it was tripling, and during the fall months it was accelerating astronomically.

The increase in the price level more than kept up with the increase in the money supply. A glance at the wholesale price index suggests that the rise in the price level exceeded the growth of the money supply. Between June 1922 and November 1923 the money supply increased by 6.4 million times, while the level of wholesale prices increased by over 20 million times, suggesting that velocity also increased over the period.

TABLE 13.3
Quantity of Money and Index of Wholesale Prices in Germany: 1919–1923

DATE (END OF MONTH) (1)	QUANTITY OF MONEY (MILLIONS OF MARKS) (2)	PERCENTAGE INCREASE (3)	WHOLESALE PRICE INDEX (1913 = 1) (4)	PERCENTAGE INCREASE (5)
1919: Dec.	86,400	—	8.03	—
1920: June	113,200	31%	13.82	72%
Dec.	152,800	35	14.40	4
1921: June	185,100	21	13.66	−5
Dec.	247,100	33	34.87	255
1922: June	295,200	19	70.30	202
Dec.	1,495,200	507	1,475.00	2,010
1923: June	22,019,800	1,473	24,618.00	1,669
Nov.	191,580,465,422,100	8,708,181	1,422,900,000,000.00	57,841,463

Source: Frank D. Graham, *Exchange, Prices, and Production in Hyper-Inflation Germany, 1920–1923* (New York: Russell & Russell, 1930).

This is consistent from what we know of behavior during the German hyperinflation. Factory workers in Germany were initially paid monthly. As the inflation accelerated, they demanded to be paid weekly, then daily, and finally hourly. The workers' wives waited outside the factory gates to receive their husbands pay in order to spend it before it lost even more value. Wage rates were being renegotiated daily during 1923.

The modern quantity theory assumes that velocity will change in predictable ways. Inflation causes the opportunity cost of holding money to increase because the purchasing power of money is depreciating. As people begin to expect higher rates of inflation, they will try to hold less money by spending their excess cash balances more rapidly, which causes velocity to increase.

The modern quantity theory holds that as future inflation came to be anticipated by the German people, velocity would increase along with the price level. This would reinforce the inflationary effects of increases in the money supply. Thus the price level should have risen more rapidly than the increase in the money supply — and it did.

Look at Table 13.3. The increase in the German money supply is shown in column 2, and the percentage increase in the money supply is shown in column 3. The resulting increase in the wholesale price level is shown in column 4, and the percentage increase in the price level is given in column 5. Comparing the percentage increases in the money supply with the respective percentage increases in the wholesale price index shows that, especially after December 1922, the increases in the price level are substantially greater than the increases in the money supply. Velocity was increasing in anticipation of even higher future inflation rates.

By November 1923 the German mark had collapsed. It was no longer used for transactions. Wheelbarrows of money were required to make a simple transaction, even if someone could be found who would take the now nearly worthless currency. People reportedly left crates of money unguarded on the streets; pictures exist of children playing with piles of money as if they were wooden building blocks.

The initial effect of the increases in the money supply had been to drive the economy to full employment. In January 1919, 93.4 percent of German trade union members were employed. By December of that year employment had risen to 97.1 percent. The stimulus to aggregate demand created by the rapidly increasing money supply propelled the economy toward full employment. It didn't stop there. Employment reached a peak of 99.0 percent from April through September 1922 — the months that saw the beginning of the hyperinflation.

Thereafter, however, employment declined. The percentage of German trade unionists who were employed declined to 90.1 percent in September 1923, dropping still further to 80.9 in October and to 76.6 percent in November. The effect of the hyperinflation was to depress employment rates. Aggregate output declined with the rise in unemployment. By the end of 1923 the German economy was producing only 65 percent of the level attained when World War I began. Germans thus suffered twice: First they were cheated by the inflation and then were robbed by unemployment.

The specialized German economy could not function with an unstable price level. The rapid decline in the purchasing power of money caused sellers to begin to refuse to accept marks in trade, insisting instead on receiving foreign currencies like the U.S. dollar or goods in kind (barter). The costs of making trades increased as the payments mechanism broke down. The German mark lost its ability to function as a medium of exchange and a recessionary gap appeared. Runaway inflation was coupled with rising unemployment, and the economy fell into a depression.

What was the cause of the great overissuance of money, especially between June 1922 and November 1923? It can be directly traced to the inability of the Weimar Republic to levy taxes in proportion to its public expenditure. During 1923, for example, only a small proportion of total government expenditure was covered by tax revenues. In March 1923 only 21 percent of government expenditures were paid for by tax receipts; increases in the money supply financed the rest. This proportion dropped to 3.4 percent in July and to 1.2 percent in October.

The hyperinflation came to an end with a currency reformation in November 1923. The old currency was recalled and exchanged for a new currency at the rate of one trillion old marks for one new mark. But the damage had been done. The great hyperinflation had temporarily destroyed the economy and with it the fortunes of most Germans.

DID THE COLLAPSE OF THE MONEY SUPPLY CAUSE THE GREAT DEPRESSION?

Everyone now agrees that the Great Depression of the 1930s was caused by a decline in aggregate demand. Economists and economic historians are divided, however, over which of the determinants of the aggregate demand function was primarily responsible for the decline. In Chapter 10 you were exposed to the spending hypothesis, which asserts that it was the collapse of either investment or consumption that caused aggregate demand to decline. There is another explanation frequently employed to explain the onset of the Great Depression, which we shall term *the money hypothesis.*

The money hypothesis stipulates that it was the decline in the money supply that caused the decline in aggregate demand. The monetarist direction of causation runs from a decline in the money supply to a decline in the consumption and investment components of aggregate demand, which causes a decline in nominal national income. The decline in nominal national income was composed partly of a decline in real GNP and partly of a decline in the price level. The decline in the money supply is the causal element that led to the observed decline in the other variables.

Supporters of the money hypothesis rely primarily on the modern quantity theory of money to support their interpretation. The modern quantity theory postulates that velocity will change over the course of a business cycle, rising during expansions and falling during contractions as the transaction demand for money changes with the level of nominal GNP. When either the price level or real GNP rises, a given quantity of money will have to finance a larger volume of trades, so that each dollar will have to be exchanged more often. Conversely, if either the price level or real GNP falls, a given quantity of money will have to finance fewer transactions, and so velocity will also fall.

The behavior of the quantity of money, velocity, the price level, and real GNP for the years 1928–1934 is graphed in Figure 13.11. It is clear that all four variables reach their peak in 1929 and fall rapidly thereafter until 1934, when the recovery begins. Velocity apparently behaved as the modern quantity theory postulates, rising when the price level and real GNP rose and falling when they fell.

The close correspondence between changes in the money supply and changes in both the price level and real aggregate output is no accident, according to the money hypothesis. The Great Depression was caused by a substantial decline in the money supply, which fell by 27 percent between 1929 and 1933. The decline of the economy was prolonged and severe, because the decline in the money supply was prolonged and severe. Moreover, the recovery began only when the money supply began to increase. The money supply thus is thought by some to have exerted a powerful influence on the economy during the Great Depression decade.

According to the money hypothesis, an initial decline in the money supply led to a decline in aggregate demand, which in turn caused a recessionary gap to appear. There was nothing historically unusual about the recession at that point. But before the automatic adjustment process could restore full employment, the economy suffered a severe demand shock in the form of a bank crisis. In November and December of 1930 a number of banks failed in the Midwest, leading to numerous bank failures around the country. A bank failure at that time was a serious matter to

FIGURE 13.11
Money, Velocity, the Price Level, and Real
GNP during the Great Depression

In this figure all four variables move in concert over time,
as suggested by the modern quantity theory of money,
lending support to the hypothesis that a decline in the
money supply was responsible for the Great Depression.

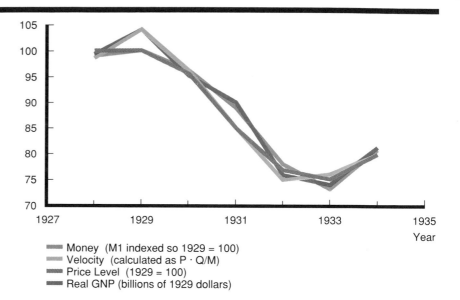

Money (M1 indexed so 1929 = 100)
Velocity (calculated as P · Q/M)
Price Level (1929 = 100)
Real GNP (billions of 1929 dollars)

depositors. When a bank failed in 1930, there was no federal deposit insurance fund to restore depositors' money. Their sole guarantee was the soundness of their banks. When a bank failed, depositors stood to lose some or all of their money.

Thus when agricultural banks in the Midwest began to fail in 1930, bank depositors throughout the nation became alarmed. The Bank of the United States, a large New York financial institution, became insolvent on December 11, 1930, the largest bank failure in history up to that time. Fear spread among depositors in other banks, leading to runs on otherwise sound banks. All in all, 1,352 banks failed in 1930, most during the last two months of the year. The number of bank failures in 1930 was more than twice the number that had occurred in 1929. Confidence in the banking system eroded.

The banking crisis affected the macroeconomy, according to the money hypothesis, through its effect on the money supply. As distrust of banks spread, individuals increasingly decided to hold their money balances in the form of cash instead of deposits. The growing distrust of banks increased the probability of bank runs. Commercial banks responded by trying to increase their cash reserves in order to be in a better position to resist a possible bank run. They did so by not renewing previously made loans, calling in existing loans, and not making as many new loans. The result of the actions of both depositors and banks resulted, as you will see in Chapter 14, in a decline in the money supply.

The effects of the bank crisis thus went further than the loss of deposits held in failed banks. In 1930 depositors lost $237 million when their banks failed, while the money supply fell by $1.8 billion. The rest of the decline was due to the actions of depositors seeking cash and banks seeking reserves. Shocks to the money supply did not stop there. Bank failures continued in large numbers in each succeeding year through 1933. The loss of confidence in commercial banks thus led to the substantial decline in the money supply between 1929 and 1933.

The money hypothesis thus runs as follows: A decline in the money supply between 1929 and 1930 led to a recession. This recession placed an unbearable strain on many commercial banks, which failed as a result.

The failure of more than 1,300 banks in 1930 caused nationwide alarm among depositors, who tried to convert their demand deposits to cash. This development led to the failure of some otherwise sound banks. Commercial banks responded by attempting to increase their cash reserves in order to meet the increased demand to convert deposits to currency. These two actions combined to reduce the nation's money supply.

The decline in the money supply did not occur all at once, but over the course of several years, from 1929 to 1933. Thus the nation's aggregate demand curve was subjected to repeated negative shocks, which were reflected in the prolonged decline in real GNP and in the price level. It was not until the bank crisis had run its course that the contraction in the money supply finally ended. Once the money supply began to expand in 1934, the recovery began. The money hypothesis thus suggests the power of the money supply in determining the performance of the macroeconomy.

REQUIRED ECONOMIC CONCEPTS

Money

Asset

Commodity money

Token money

Fiat money

Bank money

Checks

Demand deposit

Time deposit

Money supply

Liquidity

M1 money supply

M2 money supply

M3 money supply

Opportunity cost of holding money

Fixed-income asset

KEY QUESTIONS

1. What was the cause of the Great Depression of the 1930s, according to the money hypothesis?
2. What is money?
3. What are the four functions of money?
4. What three desirable characteristics should money have?
5. What are the three different kinds of money? What kind of money is the U.S. dollar? What gives it value?
6. What is liquidity?
7. What are the three official measures of the money supply as defined by the Federal Reserve? Which of them is the most liquid? The least liquid?
8. Who controls the money supply in the United States?
9. What factors influence the demand for money?
10. What is the cost of holding money?
11. What are the three motives for holding money?
12. What happens to the demand for money when the rate of inflation is expected to increase?
13. What do the supply and demand schedules for money determine?
14. What happens when the supply of money increases relative to demand?
15. What is meant by the term *transmission mechanism?* Does the Keynesian transmission mechanism differ from the monetarist transmission mechanism?
16. What is the equation of exchange?
17. What is meant by the velocity of money? Do the monetarists believe it is constant? The Keynesians?
18. What is the classical quantity theory of money? What does it predict about the relationship between GNP or national income and the price level?

PROBLEMS

1. Which function of money is best demonstrated in each of the following statements?
    a. Eggs are 90 cents a dozen.
    b. A parent sets up a college trust fund for her child.
    c. You pay cash at the store instead of using a credit card.
    d. You will receive Social Security payments on retirement.
    e. You make a deposit in your savings account.

2. A credit card is a money substitute but is not money. Why not?

3. Which is more liquid — a time deposit or a water bed?

4. Arrange the number corresponding to the following items in decreasing order of liquidity, and for each indicate the narrowest definition of money — M1, M2, or M3 — to which it belongs: (1) savings deposits, (2) traveler's checks, (3) large time deposits, (4) currency, (5) NOW accounts.

5. Using cash reduces costs. What costs? Do people in front of you in line using credit cards affect these costs for you? How does money help create efficiency in the economy by acting as a unit of account?

6. Which motive for holding money is emphasized in each of the following statements?
    a. Trina deposits $300 in her checking account on payday to cover anticipated expenses for the month.
    b. You are going to an auction and decide to carry some extra cash, just in case you get to purchase something.
    c. You transfer funds from your savings account into your checking account on Friday, intending to call your stockbroker on Monday.
    d. Firms build up their cash balances just before Christmas.
    e. Foreign banks build up their dollar reserves in the belief that U.S. interest rates are going to rise.
    f. A traveler carries extra cash on a long driving trip.

7. a. "If the fraction of its income the public desires to hold in the form of nominal M1 money is less than the public is actually holding at the moment, the public restores equilibrium between the supply and the desired demand for M1 money by reducing the amount of money it actually holds." True or false? Explain.
    b. Suppose the Federal Reserve increases the money supply so that the public is now holding more money than it wants to. Describe the adjustment of the system to a new equilibrium. What effect is there on the price level and on the purchasing power of the dollar?

8. Can you use the equation of exchange to explain how the money supply can be $200 billion while nominal GNP is $800 billion? Doesn't the money supply place an upper limit on the size of nominal GNP?

9. An identity is true by definition. The equation of exchange is such an identity. How is the equation of exchange turned into an equation that predicts something about a major macroeconomic variable and is a testable prediction? What is this equation called? What does it predict? How do you relate this prediction to the old refrain "Too much money chasing too few goods"?

10. During the early years of the Great Depression when a decline in aggregate demand set in and worsened, the Federal Reserve appeared to be increasing the money supply while output, employment, and the price level were falling. According to the equation of exchange, how could the money supply seem to be increasing when prices and output were declining?

11. The ability of monetary policy to affect the real sector (i.e., GNP, employment, and investment) depends on the sensitivity of the demand for money and investment to changes in the interest rate. The monetarists and Keynesians have differing views about the transmission mechanism. For which group is the speculative demand for money weak? How does liquidity preference explain the differing viewpoints of the monetarists and Keynesians concerning the transmission mechanism? What role does the velocity of money play in this long-standing controversy?

APPLICATION ANALYSIS

1. Assume that the economy is at full employment, the money supply is increased by 10 percent, and the velocity of money then falls by 20 percent. Using the equation of exchange, determine whether the price level will go up or down and by what percent.

2. Referring to the accompanying graphs, answer the questions below. Assume that the system is in initial equilibrium at point A. Note that the investment schedule shows investment as a function of the interest rate in Part B and as a constant function of national income in Part A, with nominal national income (or nominal GNP) playing the role of a shift parameter in Part B.

    a. What is the level of the money supply? Of the demand for money?

    b. What is the interest rate?

    c. What is the level of aggregate spending? The level of nominal national income?

    d. Determine the value of (1) the level of investment, (2) the multiplier, (3) the marginal propensity to consume, (4) the marginal propensity to save.

    e. Determine the velocity of money.

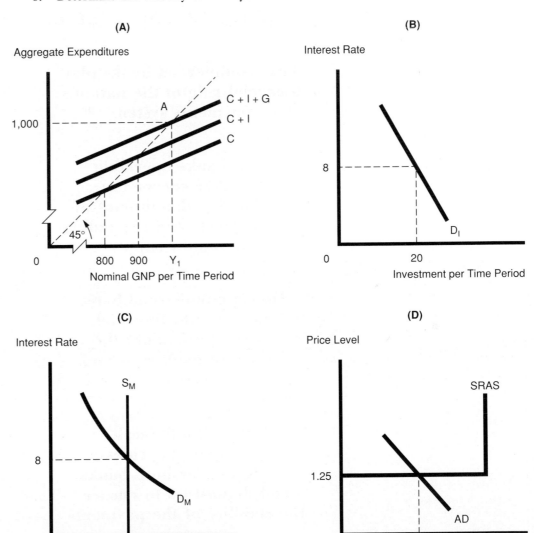

C H A P T E R

14

COMMERCIAL BANKING WITHIN THE FEDERAL RESERVE SYSTEM

IN THIS CHAPTER YOU WILL LEARN:

That commercial banks play a crucial role in the nation's payments system

•

How banks operating together succeed in multiplying the amount of total deposits and expanding the money supply

•

How a commercial bank can get into financial trouble and about the nature of bank runs and panics

•

How the federal government provides a safety net for both banks and depositors to ensure the stability of the payments system

SMALL TEXAS TOWNS ARE THE VICTIMS OF THE BIG BANKS' CRISIS

During the 1970s boom times in the oil patch, the big Texas banks in Houston and Dallas were expanding into the country-side. One of the places they reached was Lufkin Texas, an East Texas sawmill town of 32,000 persons. Dallas-based First RepublicBank and Houston-based First City Bancorp each purchased local banks and turned them into branches of the parent bank. Citizens of Lufkin were initially pleased to have the benefits of money-center banking, expanded services, and potential access to large pools of capital.

This attitude has recently changed. During the 1980s the decline in the price of crude oil led to a crisis in Texas banking. The largest banks were stung with huge loan losses as the oil industry collapsed. Their very existence became threatened. The survival of some depended on rescues from the federal government, and for others it depended on their contracting their operation and becoming smaller banks.

Banks all over Texas were forced to become leaner and, as it turned out, meaner. The golden age of easy money — with easy loans and large credit lines — was replaced by the dark age of declining money availability, when loans were inexplicably not renewed and credit lines were reduced or withdrawn. The result was that local businesses throughout Texas were squeezed. Some were even driven out of business altogether. The executive director of the Independent Bankers Association of Texas was quoted as saying that the big banks are "... just choking the entire state."

In Lufkin, this meant that a merchant that had banked for 22 years without trouble could not borrow $12,000 to repair a leaky roof, and a local doctor who routinely refinanced with his bank suddenly had a $10,000 note called in. A Lufkin egg farmer had to file for bankruptcy because his bank refused to carry him, as it had in the past, through to the fall season when egg sales typically picked up. The owner of a construction company was ordered to pay off his entire $250,000 loan when it came due despite the fact that he had never missed a payment.

Why are loan losses related to the amount of loans banks can make?

THE SAVINGS AND LOAN CRISIS

Have you ever seen on late-night TV the movie *Beau Geste?* Brian Donlevy is in command of a small unit of the French Foreign Legion that is besieged in an isolated desert fort by vastly superior numbers. Each time one of his men is hit, he props the body against the wall with a rifle at the ready. Donlevy doesn't want the enemy to know how weak his unit is becoming. In 1988 the chairman of the Federal Home Loan Bank Board (FHLBB), in dealing with the savings and loan crisis, was giving a fair imitation of Donlevy's performance. Savings and loan associations, sometimes called "thrifts," were, throughout the 1980s, losing billions of dollars. By the end of the decade over 500 were insolvent (their assets were less than their liabilities) but were still in operation. Another 450 were barely solvent, and many more would be in serious trouble if their assets were evaluated at their true market values.

The FHLBB in the meantime tried to give the impression that the situation was under control and that the Federal Savings and Loan Insurance Corporation (FSLIC, known as "Fizzlick") could handle the situation. In theory Fizzlick should either close the troubled thrifts and pay off the depositors or merge these thrifts with solvent financial institutions. But Fizzlick itself was insolvent by the end of 1987 — to the tune of $13.7 billion. So all the FHLBB could do was prop the bodies of insolvent thrifts against the ramparts and wait.

In *Beau Geste* Donlevy was expecting reinforcements and hoped to fool the enemy until those reinforcements arrived. And so was the chairman of the FHLBB. The FHLBB ultimately had to go to Congress and to the taxpayers for the funds to deal with this banking crisis. By the time the government got around to dealing with the problem, it was estimated that the final cost would be between $150 billion and $200 billion.

How did the savings and loan industry get into this situation? Why doesn't the market eliminate insolvent thrifts through bankruptcy like it eliminates an insolvent airline, waterbed manufacturer, or book publisher?

Source: H. Rudnitsky, A. Sloan, and J. R. Hayes, "Is Anybody Really Fooled?" *Forbes,* July 11, 1988, 74–76.

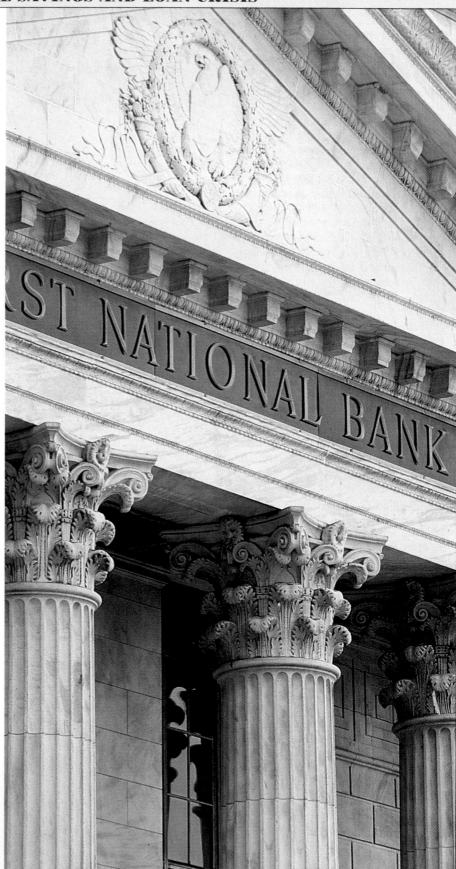

• INTRODUCTION •

In this chapter we shall examine how commercial banks function within the existing regulatory environment. We shall first discuss why banks are special, and then explain what commercial banks do and how the actions of commercial banks affect the money supply. Finally, we shall examine the federal safety net for banks. In Chapter 15 we shall examine how commercial banks are used by monetary authorities to pursue macroeconomic goals. •

COMMERCIAL BANKS IN TODAY'S WORLD

There was a time when U.S. bankers followed two rules. The first rule was 3-6-3: They borrowed from depositors at 3 percent, lent money to borrowers at 6 percent, and closed to play golf at 3 p.m. The second rule was that they would lend money only if the customer did not really need it. The first rule made banking an attractive, profitable occupation. The second meant that it was reasonably safe, for a banker could expect that most of the loans the bank made would be repaid. Few banks failed during the uneventful years when these rules could be followed.

But the times for bankers are changing. Thanks to deregulation and technological change, economic competition has revolutionized the **commercial bank.** Today banking is characterized more by innovation and change than by tradition. The new realities of banking can be seen in the statistics of bank failures presented in Figure 14.1. More banks have failed in recent years than at any time since the Great Depression.

> *A commercial bank is a financial institution, chartered either by a state or by the U.S. government, that is legally entitled to both accept deposits and make commercial loans.*

WHY ARE BANKS SPECIAL?

If gasoline stations were commercial banks, there would be several federal and state agencies whose sole function would be to supervise the stations' activities to see that they never ran out of gas. Each station would be required to maintain reserve tanks of gasoline. If the amount of gas in the reserve tanks ever fell below a certain percentage of the total amount of gas the station had, it would have to close. But one of the regulatory agencies would be ready to deliver more gas when the station ran low if its regular supplier could not, and another agency would see to it that any consumer would be able to obtain gas if the station closed down. The gasoline station would be prohibited from doing mechanical work on cars, and perhaps from selling automobile accessories like batteries and windshield wiper blades, but it could sell oil and transmission fluid. In addition, there would be a minimum amount of capital the station would have to maintain. If the station ever fell below this minimum, a regulatory agency would sell it to another service station owner or, failing that, the agency would close the station down.

Gasoline stations are not treated in this fashion, but banks are. Why are banks treated differently from gasoline stations?

FIGURE 14.1
Failures of Banks and Savings and Loan
Associations: 1934–1986

Banks failed in record numbers in the 1930s, and then
the banking industry entered a quiet period until the
1980s, when new records for bank and savings and loan
failures were set. The fabled quiet life of bankers ended in
the 1980s.

Source: *Economic Report of the President, 1989*
(Washington, DC: U.S. Government Printing Office,
1989), 201.

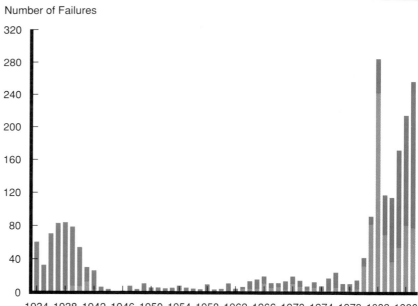

Number of Failures

■ Savings and Loan Associations
■ Commercial Banks

Year

THE PAYMENTS SYSTEM

The preceding chapter pointed out the importance of money in a modern
economy. Money serves as the medium of exchange that allows a modern,
highly specialized economy to function. The supply of money can affect
both the price level and the level of economic activity. Money is also the
means by which the country's **payments system** is operated. Every trade
creates a debt: The buyer owes the seller the money value of the goods
purchased. In cash transactions the debt is immediately extinguished by
the money payment. Many trades are settled less quickly, with the actual
settlement coming at a later time. Cash can be used to settle debts, but the
most frequently used medium for settling debts is bank money.

> *The payments system is a system based on the use of money
> to make trades and settle debts.*

The most common means of settling debts is payment by check drawn
on a demand deposit in a commercial bank. In Chapter 13 you discovered
that demand deposits are the liabilities (debts) of banks. When a check is
written, the bank's debt is simply transferred to another party in payment of the check writer's debt. The ownership of a debt is transferred to
settle another debt.

The payments system is crucially dependent on the smooth functioning of the commercial banking system. Should part of the commercial
banking system fail, households and businesses could find that debts they
thought had been settled were not, and that payments they had received
were not valid. In this event people's confidence in bank money could
disappear.

A potential problem arises from the fact that commercial banks accept deposits in order to make loans and investments. Loans and investments are not without risk. If a bank suffers large loan losses, it may not
be able to repay its depositors or settle other claims that are made on the

bank. The payments system itself could be placed in jeopardy. Consequently, a commercial bank in the United States is not free to operate as it chooses. All commercial banks must comply with both state and federal laws and regulations designed to ensure the stability of the payments system. The ultimate purpose of government regulation of the commercial banking industry is to promote the stability of the nation's payments system.

CURRENT STRUCTURE OF THE U.S. BANKING INDUSTRY

The structure of the U.S. banking system changed dramatically in the 1980s. But one thing that has not changed is that at the top sits a central bank, the Federal Reserve Bank (FRB or Fed). The Federal Reserve Bank was created by Congress in 1913 to ensure the stability of the banking industry by providing a safety net for commercial banks.

THE FEDERAL RESERVE BANK

The Federal Reserve Bank is the **central bank** of the United States.

A central bank serves as a banker's bank, accepting deposits from commercial banks and regulating their behavior; a central bank generally also serves as the banker for the government.

What does the term *banker's bank* mean? It means that the Federal Reserve Bank provides some of the same functions for commercial banks that commercial banks perform for the public. Just as commercial banks accept deposits from and make loans to the public, a central bank accepts deposits from and makes loans to financial institutions.

The Federal Reserve was created to ensure the stability of the payments system by serving as a banker's bank. During the first two decades of its history this was the sole function of the FRB, since the United States was on the gold standard and the quantity of money in circulation was determined by the amount of gold in the economy. When the Great Depression forced the United States off the gold standard, the FRB took on another function: determining the country's supply of money. How the FRB does this is the subject of Chapter 15.

Since its inception the Federal Reserve Bank has served as a banker's bank by performing the following functions:

1. Accepting deposits (called *reserves*) from financial institutions and allowing these institutions to make payments to one another using their reserve accounts.
2. Operating a nationwide check-clearing system.
3. Setting both the minimum level of reserves a bank must hold against deposits and the minimum amount of capital a bank must maintain.
4. Standing ready to make loans to financial institutions that are temporarily short of reserves.
5. Supervising, along with other federal and state agencies, the performance of commercial banks.
6. Serving as the federal government's banker by maintaining a checking account for the U.S. Treasury.
7. Supplying financial institutions with currency.

The Federal Reserve accepts deposits (reserves) from financial institutions and allows these institutions to transfer reserves to one another. This facilitates its operation of the check-clearing operation that processes checks. A bank that accepts a check drawn on another bank forwards the check to the Federal Reserve, which credits the bank's reserve account for the amount of each check, debits the account of the bank on which it was written, and forwards the check to that bank for collection. Reserves thus facilitate the check-clearing process.

Banks hold reserves for another reason. They hold reserves in order to be able to meet unexpected withdrawal requests of depositors. The Federal Reserve sets the minimum level for these reserves. It also sets the minimum amount of capital a bank's owners must have invested in the bank. The FRB serves as the lender of last resort for banks by standing ready to lend to banks caught short of reserves or in financial trouble. It thereby ensures the liquidity of the country's banks. The FRB also sets standards for safe banking practices, and by periodic audits it monitors the performance of banks. The FRB shares the monitoring responsibility with other federal agencies and with state agencies.

The Federal Reserve also serves as the banker for the federal government. The U.S. Treasury maintains an account with the FRB and uses this account to deposit tax receipts and fee revenues and to make payments. The Federal Reserve also dispenses currency to the nation's banks. When a bank's customers desire currency, the bank obtains it from the Federal Reserve and the bank's reserve account is debited for the amount of currency dispensed.

A decade or so ago it was easy to describe the nation's banking system: There were commercial banks that accepted checkable deposits and made commercial and consumer loans, and there were savings and loan associations and savings banks that accepted savings account deposits and made mortgage loans. In recent years the banking industry has undergone a number of changes as a result of technological developments and increased competition from noncommercial banks. Responding to these developments, the federal government in 1980 changed the nation's banking laws. The Monetary Control Act of 1980 and the Garn–St. Germain Act of 1982 significantly altered the restrictions placed on financial institutions.

All financial institutions are now required to hold reserves against deposits with the Federal Reserve. In return, all institutions are allowed access to the FRB's check-clearing facilities, the FRB's electronic wire service for instantly transferring funds, and the privilege of borrowing funds from the FRB when in need. Previously, these services had been available only to banks that were members of the Federal Reserve System.

In addition, all financial institutions are now allowed to offer checkable accounts, and commercial banks are allowed to offer some checkable accounts that pay interest. The level of federally supplied deposit insurance was raised from $40,000 to $100,000 per account, and all interest rate ceilings have been phased out. Savings and loans are now allowed to make consumer loans and to issue credit cards. All state usury laws (laws setting interest rate ceilings on loans) were made inapplicable. As a result, the clear legal distinction between financial institutions that had previously existed has become blurred.

REGULATORY FUNCTION OF THE FEDERAL RESERVE BANK The Federal Reserve Bank today acts in concert with the Comptroller of the Currency, the Federal Deposit Insurance Corporation

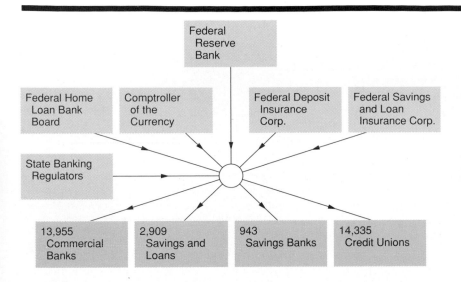

FIGURE 14.2
Structure of the U.S. Banking System

The U.S. banking system is composed of commercial banks, savings and loan associations, savings banks, and credit unions. Because these institutions play an important part in the nation's payments system, they are subject to federal and state regulatory agencies, whose task it is to provide a safety net for both banks and depositors. The Federal Reserve Bank, the Federal Home Loan Bank Board, and the Comptroller of the Currency provide the safety net for banks, and the Federal Deposit Insurance Corporation and the Federal Savings and Loan Insurance Corporation provide a safety net for depositors in insured financial institutions.

Source: Thrift data from J. Barth et al., *Contemporary Policy Issues* (Fall 1985), and J. Barth and M. Bradley, paper presented at Federal Reserve Bank of Cleveland, Nov. 3–4, 1988; bank data from Federal Deposit Insurance Corp., *1987 Annual Report.*

(FDIC), the Federal Savings and Loan Insurance Corporation (FSLIC), and state banking agencies to regulate the financial institutions that both accept deposits and make loans. The Comptroller of the Currency charters (licenses) national banks and monitors their performance, the Federal Home Loan Bank Board regulates thrifts, the FDIC and FSLIC insure depositors against loss, and state agencies charter and regulate state banks.

Figure 14.2 illustrates the regulatory structure that exists in the United States today, showing the blend of federal and state control. Each financial institution must meet minimum capital requirements and keep part of its deposits as reserves with the Federal Reserve. Any bank that fails either to meet the minimum capital requirement or to keep the legally required reserve can be closed down by a regulatory agency. If, for example, a bank fails to meet the minimum capital requirements when audited by the office of the Comptroller of the Currency, it will be declared insolvent and its assets turned over to the Federal Deposit Insurance Corporation. The FDIC can either merge the bank with a sound bank or liquidate the assets, paying off in full the depositors with accounts of $100,000 or less.

ORGANIZATION OF THE FEDERAL RESERVE   The Federal Reserve System today is composed of (1) the Board of Governors with seven members, (2) the advisory boards, (3) 12 district Federal Reserve banks, (4) the Federal Open Market Committee (FOMC), and (5) more than 18,000 commercial banks and savings and loan institutions and another 15,000 credit unions. An organization chart along with a map of the 12 Federal Reserve districts is provided in Figures 14.3 and 14.4.

Board of Governors   The Board of Governors is made up of seven members appointed by the president and confirmed by the Senate for a period of 14 years. Thus any appointed governor will serve beyond the term of the president who makes the appointment. The terms of the governors are also staggered. The Board is headed by a chairperson, who sets the agenda for the board and controls the professional staff of the Federal Reserve. But the policy actions of the FRB are determined by a majority

FIGURE 14.3
Organization of the Federal Reserve System

The Federal Reserve is headed by a seven-person Board of Governors appointed by the president and confirmed by the Senate. The Board of Governors oversees the operation of the 12 district banks. The board receives advice from various advisory boards. The Federal Open Market Committee is composed of the Board of Governors plus the president of the Federal Reserve Bank of New York and four of the other district bank presidents serving in rotation.

Source: Adapted from Board of Governors, Federal Reserve System, *The Federal Reserve System: Purposes and Functions* (Washington, DC: 1984).

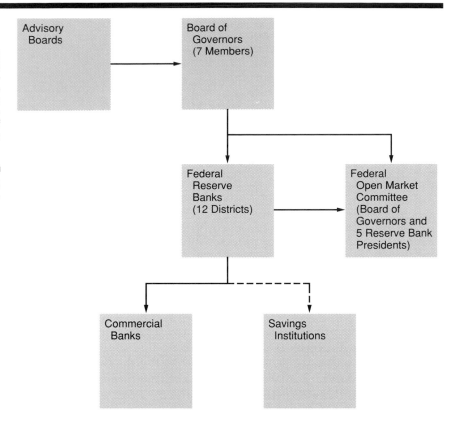

vote of the Board. The Board is responsible for directing the activities of the FRB, including the setting of monetary policy, and for exercising supervision of the district Federal Reserve banks. The Board is nominally responsible to Congress, to which it reports semiannually, but it works closely with the administration in power, especially the Treasury.

Advisory Boards   The Federal Advisory Board is composed of commercial bankers who provide the Federal Reserve Board with the views and opinions of the commercial banks about actions that should be taken to regulate the financial markets. Because the Federal Advisory Board has no administrative or decision-making powers, it has a purely advisory role. A Consumer Advisory Council and a Thrift Institutions Advisory Council also exist to provide information to the Board of Governors and to advise on consumer affairs and the particular views of thrifts and credit unions. These boards are also purely advisory.

District Reserve Banks   Commercial banking within a region is regulated by the district Federal Reserve bank. Each of the 12 district banks is owned by the commercial banks within the district. Each commercial bank must purchase a specific amount of Federal Reserve bank stock, for which it receives a fixed return, not a share of profits. Thus Federal Reserve stock is more like a bond than a share of equity ownership. The Federal Reserve Bank is self-financing, living off the interest earned on its assets and the fees earned through dealings with commercial banks, but it is not entitled to keep all the profits it makes. By law, the FRB must turn over all profits in excess of a fixed amount to the U.S. Treasury. Though privately owned and locally controlled, the district banks are, in fact, operated under guidelines set by the Board of Governors.

FIGURE 14.4
The 12 Federal Reserve Districts

The country is divided into twelve districts as shown on the map, each with a Federal Reserve Bank and several branch banks.

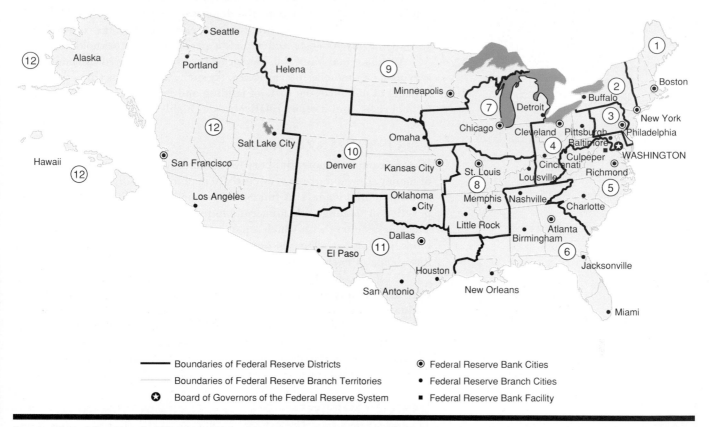

——— Boundaries of Federal Reserve Districts   ◉ Federal Reserve Bank Cities

——— Boundaries of Federal Reserve Branch Territories   • Federal Reserve Branch Cities

✪ Board of Governors of the Federal Reserve System   ■ Federal Reserve Bank Facility

Source: Adapted from Board of Governors, Federal Reserve System, *The Federal Reserve System: Purposes and Functions* (Washington, DC: 1984).

Federal Open Market Committee   The Federal Open Market Committee (FOMC) is in charge of **open-market operations.**

> *Open-market operations are the procedures undertaken by the Federal Reserve for the purchase and sale of government bonds.*

Open-market operations are the principal way the Federal Reserve regulates the amount of reserves in the banking system. This committee actually sets the monetary policy of the FRB because of the composition of its membership. The FOMC has 12 members — the 7 governors; 4 of the 12 district bank presidents, who serve in rotation; and the president of the Federal Reserve Bank of New York, who is a permanent member.

Member Commercial Banks   Each of the member commercial banks is a stockholder in its district Federal Reserve bank and elects three members of its board of directors. But the thousands of commercial banks are generally more acted upon than active participants in determining Federal Reserve policy. Though technically the owners of the FRB, the commercial banks are, in fact, the group that is regulated by the FRB. Thus in the FRB a separation exists between ownership and control. The FRB is owned by the banks it regulates, but it is controlled by governors appointed by the president.

WHAT DO BANKS DO?

As the definition of a commercial bank suggests, a bank is engaged in two activities: (1) The bank accepts deposits for which it promises to pay a rate of interest, and (2) the bank lends these funds to borrowers who pay a higher rate of interest than the depositors receive. The bank uses the difference between these two interest rates, called the *interest rate spread*, to pay its costs and return a profit for its stockholders.

A commercial bank thus performs the classic tasks of the middleman serving as a financial intermediary. As such, it performs three functions: it helps to minimize the costs of lending and borrowing, it allows lenders to pool risks, and it offers relatively safe, highly liquid assets to investors.

COST MINIMIZATION

If, for example, a potential borrower wishes to borrow a fairly large sum of money, it would prove very costly to deal individually with hundreds of small potential lenders. A financial intermediary, which makes a regular practice of dealing with numerous individuals, can do it more cheaply. The small lenders with which a particular bank regularly deals know the bank and trust it. They do not have, and cannot easily obtain, a similar knowledge of each potential borrower.

The bank, on the other hand, knows the potential borrowers; often they are already the bank's customers. The bank uses its expertise to evaluate the creditworthiness of the potential loan customers. Individual investors would find maintaining this ability to be quite costly, but the bank does it as a matter of routine business practice. Thus the existence of financial intermediaries minimizes the cost of collecting deposits from numerous small savers and of lending these sums to borrowers.

RISK POOLING

Lending always involves risk. Some borrowers inevitably cannot repay the loans they accept. The old saying "Do not put all of your eggs in one basket" applies to banking. It is wiser to spread your assets among several different activities. A commercial bank pools the deposits of many persons and in turn lends them to many different borrowers. The probability is that if the bank has done a good job of judging creditworthiness, most borrowers will be able to repay their loans, although some loans will unavoidably go bad.

Often, because of unforeseen factors unique to a specific sector or industry, loans to that sector or industry become troublesome. If a lender had concentrated its loans in one of these troubled areas, it would have suffered significant losses, but by spreading loans over many areas and activities a bank can escape serious loan losses when a particular industry declines.

Loan losses are one type of risk that banks bear. Another is the risk of loss due to interest rate changes. Commercial banks go to great lengths to avoid interest rate risk. This risk can be measured by the extent to which the interest rates earned on a bank's assets and the interest rates paid on its liabilities move together. Interest rate risk can be minimized by matching the maturities (dates of expiration) of a bank's loans and investments with the maturities of its deposits.

A savings and loan association (S&L) that makes a 30-year mortgage at a fixed interest rate and funds the loan with savings and 90-day time deposits has assumed a significant interest rate risk due to the mismatch of the maturity dates of its assets and liabilities. If interest rates increase during the 30 years, the bank's cost of funds will increase while its receipts from the mortgage will remain the same. This actually happened to

TABLE 14.1
Total Assets of Financial Intermediaries

TYPE OF INSTITUTION	TOTAL ASSETS (BILLIONS OF DOLLARS)
Commercial banks	$2,568
Savings and loan associations	955
Federal savings banks	196
Credit unions	141

Source: *Federal Reserve Bulletin.*

the troubled savings and loan industry in recent years. The hundreds of S&Ls that are currently in trouble have been hurt more by interest rate risk than by loan defaults (see Preview 14.2 Analysis at the end of the chapter).

S&Ls have a comparative advantage in originating mortgage loans, but they incur a significant interest rate risk in funding long-term mortgages with short-term deposits. There are several things an S&L can do to reduce interest rate risk. It can **securitize** a bundle of mortgages and sell the package to investors. The bank thus transfers both the default risk and the interest rate risk to others, specializing according to its comparative advantage in originating mortgage loans.

> *Securitization is the practice of packaging a bundle of loans that a bank has made and selling the entire bundle to investors in return for cash and the fees earned from servicing the loans.*

The S&L might also employ financial futures or interest rate swaps to better match the maturities of its assets and liabilities. These innovations are revolutionizing commercial banking today.

HIGH LIQUIDITY WITH SAFETY

A maxim of prudent financial management is: "Borrow long and lend short." Borrowers desire to borrow long term to ensure that they will have the use of the borrowed funds for a period of time sufficient for their purposes. Borrowing long term is insurance against the possibility that unforeseen events will require them to unprofitably interrupt their business plans. Lenders, however, prefer to lend for shorter periods of time for similar reasons. If unforeseen events occur, they are assured of having their money returned in relatively short order. These desires of borrowers and lenders stand in the way of lending funds.

Commercial banks help to bridge this gap. Commercial banks mediate between these different desires by borrowing short term, to satisfy the desires of lenders, and lending longer term to meet the needs of borrowers. Depositors are offered highly liquid accounts. Demand deposits, for example, can be withdrawn at any time and there are other types of accounts that are only slightly less liquid. The bank then uses these funds to make longer-term loans. This is possible because the bank has pooled the funds of many depositors and relies on the fact that not all of these depositors will want their money back at the same time.

KINDS OF FINANCIAL INTERMEDIARIES

Commercial banks are not the only financial institutions that play the role of intermediary, but in terms of assets they are the largest. Table 14.1

APPLICATION
14.1

SECURITIZATION, GRESHAM'S LAW, LEMONS, AND OTHER RECENT BANKING INNOVATIONS

Commercial banking is in the midst of a spate of financial innovations that are changing the way banks do business. One of the most important is securitization. Securitization involves the packaging of a bundle of loans the bank has made and selling the bundle to investors. During each quarter of 1988 the ten largest banks in the United States together sold about $200 billion in securities directly to purchasers. The next 40 largest banks were also actively engaged in this type of operation.

How does the process of securitization work? Banks make loans to customers to finance the purchase of automobiles, credit card purchases, home equity loans, and other consumer debt. Banks combine some of these loans and sell them as a package to investors in return for cash with which to make more loans. Banks in turn service these loans for a fee, collecting payments and forwarding them to the buyer of the loans, and they pursue the collection of delinquent accounts. Banks are making use of their comparative advantage in originating loans and judging creditworthiness. Investors take advantage of an opportunity, which would otherwise not be available to them, to buy securities that pay a higher rate of interest than is generally available on other financial assets. Comparative advantage thus leads to a profitable exchange.

But a higher rate of return is generally available only by assuming greater risk. One

of the risks associated with buying a bundle of loans is the risk that some borrowers will default and not repay their loans. Buyers do not have as good information about the quality of the loans in a bundle as does the selling bank that made the loans. If buyers have only the word of the seller to go on, the seller might have a strong incentive to slip some loans of questionable value into the bundle and to sell some ''lemons'' along with the ''plums.''

In fact, this incentive could cause this market to break down if there were not some way to ensure the investor of the quality of the loans being sold. This is known as the ''lemon'' problem, which was explained in the appendix to Chapter 3. The lemon problem refers to a situation in which one party to a trade (in this case the bank selling the loans) has much better information about product quality than the other party (the investor buying the loans). When this happens, the seller has the incentive to include some lemons in the loan bundle, transferring the default risk to the buyer. The buyer, recognizing his or her information disadvantage, will counter by assuming the package of loans to be of average quality and will pay a price for a bundle of loans based on this assumption. Since a bundle of loans, no matter how many plums it contains, will at most sell for the price of an average bundle, sellers will respond by including more lemons in a bundle up to the point where bad loans have completely driven good loans out of the package. The lemon problem would thus generate the results in security markets that Gresham's Law predicts in money markets. The market for a bundle of good loans (plums) disappears completely. If a market for securitized loans exists at all, it will be for lemons, not plums.

The market for securitized loans is potentially too important to banks to allow the lemon problem to stand in the way. The comparative advantage of banks is to make good loans, not bad ones. But unless the lemon problem is overcome, the market for securitized loans will not function. There are

several ways to overcome the problem. One is to offer a guarantee to the buyer. Another is to put the reputation of the seller behind the transaction. Still another way is to enhance the value of a bundle of loans by providing an independent assessment of the risks involved and/or a third-party guarantee.

In the market for securities backed by loans, all of these methods are used to assure the buyer of the loan quality of the package offered for sale. Brand names with a reputation for quality have been established: two examples are Chemical Bank Trust 1988A and First Chicago Master Trust A. Investors associate these loans with the institutions that originated the loans and that will service them. These banks are known to rely heavily on this market, so maintaining their reputation for selling good loans is important to them.

As insurance against the lemon problem, brand names may be sufficient for many buyers of consumer durables, but generally not for investors. Other players in the securitization market enter into the contractual relationship between the originating bank and the investor to either aid the buyer in judging the risk involved or to guarantee part or all of the loan bundle. These players are the trustee, credit enhancer, credit rater, and underwriter.

A typical trade involving a securitized bundle of loans is shown in Figure 14.5. The bank originates and packages the loans, has the loan bundle credit-rated, and purchases insurance against default from a credit enhancer. Finally, the bank transfers the bundle to a trustee, which is a large depository institution. The trustee issues securities against the loans and passes the securities on to an underwriter. The underwriter prices the securities and finds the ultimate buyers.

A credit-rating agency assigns, for a fee, ratings to securitized loans according to its independent estimate of the ability of the loans to generate the cash flow required to service the securities. A rating agency depends on its superior ability to judge risk based on the information it has collected. The

reveals the amount of assets controlled by the four major financial intermediaries, which can be differentiated according to their primary function. Commercial banks make short-term commercial, consumer, and real estate loans. Savings and loan associations (sometimes called thrifts) and federal savings banks generally make long-term real estate loans. Credit unions take deposits and make short-term consumer loans. In recent years all of these institutions have been given the power to offer value of a credit rating is no better than the reputation of the agency for judging quality. A credit-rating agency thus has an incentive to do its job as accurately as possible.

The credit enhancer stands behind the quality of the loan package, issuing a guarantee, also for a fee, for all of the loans in a package or for a percentage of the loans. The credit enhancer, which stands to lose if a large number of lemons are included in the package, has a strong incentive to assess accurately the risk of the loan bundle and to check on the work of the rating agency.

The trustee plays a crucial role in the trade. The trustee sets up a trust account for the bundle of loans. As borrowers make payments of interest and principal to the originating bank, the bank passes the funds on to the trustee, which in turn passes them on to the investors who have purchased the securities. If the funds are insufficient to make the promised payments, the trustee draws on the credit enhancer's guarantee. The trustee is also responsible for monitoring the performance of the originating bank in servicing the loan bundle. Once it has received the loan bundle and set up a trust account, the trustee issues securities for the loans and passes the securities on to the underwriter.

Underwriters are the original purchasers of the securities from the originating bank, buying them for a negotiated price with the intention of selling them to investors for a higher price. Typically, investment banks and securities dealers perform the underwriting function. The reputation of the underwriter for expertly pricing new securities is important to individual investors, and the underwriter's reputation for efficiently marketing securities is important to the originating bank. Underwriters depend on repeat customers. The underwriter is thus also concerned that few lemons exist in the loan bundles it resells, because the firm's reputation is at stake. In this way the lemon problem is overcome and a market for securitized bank loans can be maintained.

FIGURE 14.5
Typical Process for Securitizing Loans

A basic difficulty with creating a market for securitized loans is the lemon problem. Investors do not have as good a knowledge of the quality of the loans in the package as the bank that is selling the loans. In order to assure investors of the true quality of the loans, third parties — a rating agency, a credit enhancer, a trustee, and an underwriter — are brought into the process to provide independent evaluations of the quality of the loans.

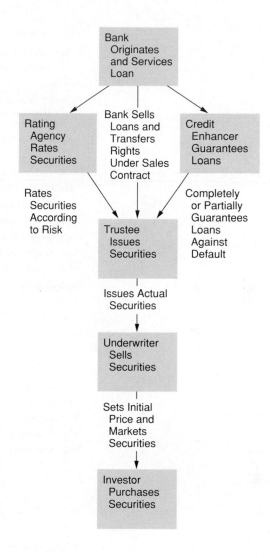

checkable accounts and to make some commercial and consumer loans as well. For this reason the distinction between banks and S&Ls and federal savings banks has blurred.

There are other financial institutions that do not meet the definition of a bank. Insurance companies do not take deposits but do make loans. Money market mutual funds do not make loans but allow investors to purchase shares, and some funds allow shareholders to write checks on

TABLE 14.2
Balance Sheet of Frontier Bank: June 30, 1988

CONSOLIDATED REPORT OF CONDITION
FRONTIER BANK
Everett, Snohomish County, Washington 98203
State Bank No. 53-0309
Federal Reserve District No. 1251
June 30, 1988

Assets		Mil. Thou.
Cash and balances due from depository institutions		
Noninterest-bearing balances and currency and coin		10,190
Interest-bearing balances		none
Securities		33,569
Federal funds sold and securities purchased under agreements to resell in domestic offices of the bank and of its Edge and Agreement subsidiaries, and in IBF's		
Federal funds sold		1,415
Securities purchased under agreements to resell		none
Loans and lease financing receivables		
Loans and leases, net of unearned income	107,707	
LESS: Allowance for loan and lease losses	1,005	
Loans and leases, net of unearned income, allowance, and reserve		106,702
Premises and fixed assets (including capitalized leases)		1,974
Other real estate owned		686
Other assets		1,546
Total assets		156,082

Liabilities		
Deposits		
In domestic offices		145,198
Noninterest-bearing	21,571	
Interest-bearing	123,627	
Securities sold under agreements to repurchase		none
Mortgage indebtedness and obligations under capitalized leases		3
Other liabilities		1,293
Total liabilities		146,494

their accounts. There are also nonbank banks that either do not take deposits or do not make loans. It is still fair to say that commercial banks are the most important of all financial intermediaries in terms of the assets they control and their role in the nation's payments system.

BALANCE SHEET OF A COMMERCIAL BANK

A good way to understand what banks do is to examine a bank's **balance sheet.**

A balance sheet is an accounting tool that summarizes the financial condition of a business, employing a T-account, which allows the comparison of a firm's total assets with its total liabilities.

Equity Capital

Common stock (No. of shares): Authorized	83,029	
Outstanding	72,600	2,723
Surplus		5,279
Undivided profits and capital reserves		1,586
Cumulative foreign currency translation adjustments		none
Total equity capital		9,588
Total liabilities, limited — life preferred stock and equity capital		156,082
MEMORANDA: Amounts outstanding as of report data:		
Standby letters of credit. Total		543

I, the undersigned officer, do hereby declare that this Report of Condition has been prepared in conformance with official instructions and is true to the best of my knowledge and belief.

F. EARL CAREY, Senior Vice President/Cashier
July 25, 1988

We, the undersigned directors, attest the correctness of this Report of Condition and declare that it has been examined by us and to the best of our knowledge and belief has been prepared in conformance with official instructions and is true and correct.

EDWARD C. RUBATINO
ARTHUR W. SKOTDAL
WILLIAM H. LUCAS

(seal)

State of Washington County of Snohomish ss: Sworn to and subscribed before me this 25th day of July, 1988 and I hereby certify that I am not an officer or director of this bank.

My commission expires Sept. 1, 1991.
LINDA K. BRIDGHAM
Notary Public

In Table 14.2 the balance sheet of an actual commercial bank is reproduced. The bank is the Frontier Bank located in Washington State. You will notice immediately that the bank's balance sheet is broken down into three categories: assets, liabilities, and equity capital. *Assets* are anything of value that is owned by the bank. *Liabilities* are obligations that are owed by the bank to others. *Equity capital*, or *net worth*, represents claims of ownership by stockholders and is equal to the difference between total assets and total liabilities.

If a bank is solvent, its total assets will exceed its total liabilities. Frontier Bank, as of June 30, 1988, was solvent. Total assets were equal to $156.1 million, total liabilities equaled $146.5 million, and total equity capital amounted to $9.6 million. Total assets are always balanced by (equal to) total liabilities plus equity capital. Frontier Bank, with assets measured in millions of dollars, is a comparatively small bank. A large commercial bank will hold assets totaling tens of billions of dollars.

ASSETS

An examination of the various assets of a commercial bank reveals much about how a bank operates. In a bank's balance sheet the total assets are broken down into constituent parts. The first item on Frontier's balance sheet is noninterest-bearing balances and coins and currency held in the vault. Why do banks hold part of their assets, which have opportunity costs, in noninterest-bearing assets? These particular assets are the bank's reserves, which prudence requires it to maintain. U.S. banks are required by law to maintain a certain level of reserves, either as a deposit with the Federal Reserve or as cash on hand.

Financial prudence requires that banks have cash on hand to meet withdrawal demands plus some highly liquid assets that can be converted to cash on short notice to meet emergencies. These requirements are met by having deposits in the regional Federal Reserve bank that can be turned into cash as quickly as an armored car can travel between the two buildings. The legal requirements of the Federal Reserve, reinforced by financial prudence, necessitate that a commercial bank have ready access to some amount of cash.

If a bank held only noninterest-bearing assets, it could never hope to earn a profit. In fact, only a small percentage of total assets are legally required to be held as cash or deposits with the Federal Reserve (in the case of Frontier Bank, only 3 percent of demand deposits and 3 percent of interest-bearing deposits). Frontier regularly holds reserves that exceed its legal requirements. Its balance sheet shows substantially larger reserves than required by law. The bank held $10.2 million in cash or in deposits (actual reserves) with the Federal Reserve when only $4.4 million was required.

The difference between required reserves and actual reserves is called *excess reserves*. Excess reserves can be loaned or invested. A bank with no excess reserves is said to be "fully loaned up." Banks with insufficient reserves are said to be "overloaned" and banks like Frontier with excess reserves are said to be "underloaned." If a bank fails to maintain the legally required amount of reserves, it can be closed by the Comptroller of the Currency.

A market, called the *federal funds market*, exists to trade excess reserves. In this market underloaned banks can lend some of their excess reserves to banks that are overloaned. The amount of Frontier's short-term interbank lendings is listed among Frontier's assets as federal funds sold. Frontier, as of June 30, 1988, was lending about 24 percent of its excess reserves ($1.4 million) to other banks. Such loans were at the time earning interest of 7.14 percent on an annual basis. The remaining 76 percent of the excess reserves was available to Frontier to lend or to invest.

Some of Frontier's assets (about 22 percent of total assets) are held in the form of interest-bearing securities, mainly the obligations of the federal government. Government obligations are free from default risk, but they are not free from interest rate risk. A bank that purchases a government bond earning 9 percent annual interest would suffer a capital loss if interest rates rose and the bank had to sell before the bond matured. Recall from the previous chapter that the market value of a fixed interest-bearing asset like a government bond or a mortgage is inversely related to the rate of interest. When the interest rate increases, the market price of a bond declines.

Frontier no doubt held a diverse portfolio of securities in terms of maturity dates. On the $33.6 million invested in securities Frontier was earning anywhere from 7.4 percent to 8.4 percent, depending on the time to maturity of the obligations. These securities are easily converted to cash by selling them in financial markets. A bank's securities portfolio serves two purposes. First, it is a secondary source of reserves. Repurchase agreements, as described in Application 14.2, allow a bank that is overloaned to acquire short term the necessary required reserves by selling some of its government securities with an agreement to buy them back at a future date. Second, the securities portfolio provides a place to store funds at interest until good loans can be made. Loans return a higher interest rate but are riskier. So until acceptable loans appear, a bank may park a portion of its assets in government securities.

Frontier Bank held most of its assets ($106.7 million, or 68 percent of total assets) as loans, along with a few leases. The interest rate earned on loans exceeds the rate earned on government securities. Provided the bank does an acceptable job of judging the creditworthiness of borrowers, loans are more profitable than securities. A small percentage of a bank's loans will always, in banking terms, "go sour." Banks provide for this contingency by establishing loan loss reserves. Frontier Bank had prudently allocated $1 million to cover projected loan losses. The bank apparently expected a little less than 1 percent of its loans (in terms of total value) to default, reflecting the advantages of risk pooling.

As a small commercial bank, Frontier Bank lends mostly to persons who live in the surrounding localities. It makes both commercial and consumer loans. The interest rate it charged for commercial loans varied between 8.5 percent and 9.5 percent in 1988, and the interest rate earned on consumer loans ranged from 10.5 percent to 13.5 percent. All loans are risky, but some business and consumer loans are more risky than others, because the amount of **collateral** behind the loan varies. This accounts for the difference in interest rates.

Collateral is the security that a borrower pledges to a lender in the case the borrower defaults; if this occurs, ownership of the collateral will pass to the lender.

When you borrow to buy a new car, for example, the title of the vehicle remains with the lender until the loan is repaid. Should you fail to make the payments on the loan, the lender will repossess the vehicle and sell it.

One way to compensate for default risk is to charge a higher rate of interest. Because the vehicle serves as collateral, new-car loans are made by banks at a lower rate of interest than unsecured personal loans where banks have only the word of the borrower that the loan will be repaid.

Some of its assets, almost $2 million worth, Frontier Bank had invested in buildings and equipment. Frontier owned a building and fixtures, including a vault, furniture, and computers. It also had a small amount of nonbank real estate and some other assorted assets. These were the bank's least liquid assets.

LIABILITIES

The balance sheet in Table 14.2 shows that the total liabilities that Frontier Bank had acquired in carrying out its role of financial intermediary were less than its assets. Remember that the difference between assets and liabilities is, in the case of a solvent bank, the positive amount of equity the owners of the bank have invested. Almost all of the liabilities of the bank (94 percent) were in the form of deposits. Most of the deposits were interest-bearing; only $21.6 million out of $145.2 million in total deposits were noninterest-bearing **demand deposits**. Because depositors generally

APPLICATION 14.2

FINANCIAL INNOVATION IN COMMERCIAL BANKING: REPOS AND SWAPS

Two financial innovations have allowed banks to manage their assets more efficiently: repurchase agreements and swaps. A repurchase agreement, called a *repo,* involves the bank's sale (or purchase) of a security to (from) another bank or dealer with an agreement to buy it back (or sell it back) at a later date at a higher price. Repos represent a very convenient way of borrowing and lending short term. Sales and purchases of repos grew during the 1980s into a huge market. In 1987 the Federal Reserve Bank alone engaged in $325 billion worth of repurchase agreements.

Swaps involve the trade of interest payments on two assets or two liabilities but not the exchange of the obligations themselves.

Such trades are called *interest rate swaps,* or when the interest payments are in two different currencies, the trade is called a *currency swap.* Banks themselves engage in swaps and even more often serve as a third party that arranges and guarantees swaps. The volume of swaps arranged by commercial banks roughly tripled every two years during the 1980s, until it involved nearly $300 billion in assets in 1989.

Let us consider the repo market first. The outline of the basic features of a repo exchange is fairly simple. A sale of an asset takes place that is really a loan of funds employing a security as collateral. A borrower sells securities through a dealer to a lender and agrees to buy them back later at a higher price, thereby implicitly paying interest on the funds. A reverse repo is the transaction viewed from the buyer's point of view. A repo is a mechanism for investing funds, and a reverse repo a mechanism for borrowing funds. The role securities play in repos is to provide the lender with collateral for the funds lent.

The convenience of using the repo market explains in part the surge in its popularity. Both banks and dealers stand ready to facilitate the trade in repos. A bank can use its investments in government securities to obtain short-term reserves. Businesses, local governments, pension funds, and school dis-

tricts with temporary excesses of cash can invest them at interest, obtaining government bonds as collateral. Repos are a way for banks to convert their securities portfolio temporarily into reserves or cash and to earn fees arranging deals.

Swaps are designed to allow firms and banks to manage portfolio risk exposure more efficiently. Two necessary conditions must exist for a swap to take place. Let us consider the case of an asset swap. First, both parties to the swap hold a financial asset from which a stream of interest payments is due. Each party has a comparative advantage in obtaining the asset but does not find desirable the income flow generated by the asset. Second, instead of selling the assets, the two parties exchange the interest payments they will receive.

There are two motivations for preferring swaps to sales: (1) Swaps allow businesses and banks to manage portfolio risk efficiently in regard to interest rate and/or exchange rate risk, and (2) swaps often allow participants to lower their financing costs. Let us consider examples of both.

Suppose a savings and loan association (S&L) has a portfolio of fixed-rate long-term mortgages and has funded these assets with savings deposits. The S&L is at risk of interest rate increases. It would have to increase the interest rate it pays in order to retain the

favor short-term deposits, most of these deposits were either **savings accounts, money market accounts,** or **time deposits** in the form of three- or six-month certificates of deposit.

> *A demand deposit is a deposit in a noninterest-bearing checking account.*

> *A savings account is an account paying a fixed rate of interest; in practice, amounts can be withdrawn at any time, but checks cannot be written on the account.*

> *A money market account is an account paying a variable rate of interest, which is pegged to some market rate of interest like the interest rate paid on U.S. Treasury bills; often checks can be drawn on the account.*

> *A time deposit is an account that bears a fixed or variable rate of interest and that is set up for a specified amount of time; the money deposited cannot be withdrawn before the end of this time period without paying a substantial interest penalty.*

deposits necessary to fund the mortgages it has made. If this happens, the profitability of the mortgages would be reduced. The S&L thus desires fixed-rate long-term financing to match its fixed-rate long-term mortgages. It is willing to swap its floating-rate funding for fixed-rate funding.

The S&L approaches a bank that knows or can find a party that has the opposite requirements. This party (often a corporation) desires to make floating-rate interest payments and currently has fixed-rate long-term financing. Suppose the corporation's chief financial officer believes that interest rates are going to decline. The S&L agrees to make fixed interest payments to the bank that will be used to service the corporate debt. The corporation agrees to make variable interest payments, depending on the current interest rate, to the bank, which forwards these funds to the S&L. Thus both parties obtain the payments stream they desire without the exchange of securities. The commercial bank that arranged the swap earns fees for its efforts, and it probably also guarantees the performance of both parties, again for a fee.

Swaps can also lower financing costs by allowing firms to specialize in borrowing. Suppose there is a large business firm with a high credit rating and a smaller business firm with a lower credit rating. The highly rated firm can borrow either short-term variable-rate funds or long-term fixed-rate funds by issuing bonds at lower rates than the smaller, lower-rated firm. The large firm has an absolute advantage in borrowing.

Suppose the lower-rated firm has the opportunity to borrow variable-rate short-term funds at the prime rate plus 1½ percent, or it can borrow long term at 13 percent. Also suppose that the larger, higher-rated firm can borrow at prime plus ½ percent, or it can borrow long term at 11 percent. A swap would involve the higher-rated firm borrowing long term and the lower-rated firm borrowing a like amount of money short term.

The two firms now swap the interest payments on the debt, but not the debt itself, after agreeing on how to split the cost savings. Suppose the small firm agrees to pay the large firm 11 percent until the maturity of the loan and the large firm agrees to pay the small firm the prime rate of interest, whatever it turns out to be, for the same period of time. The small firm thus converts its short-term variable-rate loan into a long-term fixed-rate loan, and the large firm does the opposite.

The large firm saves ½ percent on the costs of short-term funds, because it now pays the prime rate instead of prime plus ½ percent. The small firm also saves on its long-term financing costs. The small firm must pay the bank the prime rate plus 1½ percent. The large firm is now paying the small firm the prime rate, to which it must add 1½ percent, making its cost of long-term funds the 11 percent paid to the large firm plus the 1½ percent it must add. This totals 12½ percent, which is ½ percent less than the 13 percent it would have had to pay for long-term money. Swaps have become a popular means for companies to lower their financing costs by allowing them to borrow in the markets where they have a comparative advantage and then swap for the payments stream they desire.

The banks familiar with these opportunities can arrange both the initial financing and the swap in return for a fee, saving both parties financing costs on their preferred type of debt and earning a profit for arranging and guaranteeing the transaction. It is this last function that has raised some concern. If one of the parties defaults, the bank is obligated to keep up the interest payments. The rapid growth in swaps may represent a significant risk to banks that guarantee swaps. Some banks have recognized this risk by requiring swap partners to put up significant amounts of collateral to back the transaction. Nevertheless, the rapid growth in swap transactions has shown no signs of slowing. Swaps have proven to be a low-cost way to reduce portfolio risk and to lower the costs of financing.

Frontier's interest costs for money market and time deposits varied between 5.0 percent and 6.3 percent, depending on the deposit its lenders selected.

EQUITY CAPITAL

The total assets of Frontier Bank on June 30, 1988, were $9.6 million greater than its total liabilities. This was the amount for which the bank's stockholders held claims of ownership. These persons had originally invested $2.7 million in the bank, surplus (past earnings not yet counted as profits) amounted to $5.3 million, and undistributed profits (earnings determined to be profits but not yet paid out to stockholders) added another $1.6 million. Thus the total equity capital amounted to $9.6 million on the day the balance sheet (Table 14.2) was constructed.

The capital and surplus amounts stand behind the loans the bank had made. If more loans than anticipated by the loan loss reserve are not repaid, then the capital account will be drawn down to ensure that the bank can always repay its depositors. Equity capital provides a vital cushion in case the value of the bank's assets declines.

WHAT STANDS BEHIND YOUR DEPOSITS IN BANKS?

What ensures that a bank will be able to repay its depositors?[1] Two possible problems might arise: a bank can become illiquid or insolvent. The noninterest-earning reserves that the bank maintains are designed to ensure that the bank is sufficiently liquid to meet depositors' withdrawals. Frontier Bank (see Table 14.2) maintains 6.5 percent of its assets in reserves to ensure its liquidity, and it holds equity capital equal to a similar percentage of its total liabilities to protect against insolvency.

It is important to understand that Frontier, like all banks, funds most of its loans with depositors' money, not the money of the bank's stockholders. When you deposit money in a bank, most of it is quickly put back into the economy in the form of loans or securities purchases. Even though banks maintain reserves and equity capital, what really backs deposits is the quality of the loans and investments that banks make. Bank money, then, is backed by the ability of commercial banks to repay deposits when due. What stands behind the banks are the quality of the loans they have made, their reserves, their equity capital, and the Federal Reserve Bank, which serves as a lender of last resort. Generally, a bank's reserves and capital are sufficient to cover loan losses and to maintain the confidence of the public in banks.

How do Frontier's reserves and equity position compare with other banks? In Table 14.3 the consolidated balance sheet of all U.S. commercial banks is reproduced. Notice that under assets the total amount of reserves (vault cash and reserves at the FRB) totals $56.5 billion and total deposits (transaction, savings, and time deposits) total $1,891 billion. Reserves are about 3 percent of deposits. Net worth totals $175.4 billion, while total assets amount to $2,687.5 billion. Net worth, which measures the amount of owners' capital invested in commercial banks, amounted to 7 percent of assets.

HOW BANKS CREATE MONEY

So far you have discovered that commercial banks make loans, buy securities, and accept deposits. Commercial banks also play a crucial role in the creation of bank money. Individual banks do not create money, but money is nonetheless created as a result of all commercial banks acting together within a **fractional reserve system.**

> *A fractional reserve system is a procedure in which banks hold only a portion of their deposits as reserves.*

How does the money creation process operate? We shall initially assume that all money remains in the banking system, that banks desire to hold reserves equal to 10 percent of deposits, and that banks are always fully loaned up. Banks make loans by lending their excess reserves. Excess reserves equal total reserves minus the amount of required reserves, which in this case is 10 percent of deposits. If a bank has no excess reserves, it is loaned up and will not make more loans without acquiring more reserves.

---

[1] Today in the United States most individual deposits are covered by federal deposit insurance guarantees. But that does not work for society as a whole, as the recent bailout of the FSLIC demonstrates.

TABLE 14.3
Consolidated Balance Sheet of All Commercial Banks as of January 1987
(Billions of Dollars)

Assets	
Vault cash	$ 23.6
Reserves at FRB	32.9
Securities	477.3
Loans and investments	1,772.7
Other assets	381.0
Total assets	$2,687.5
Liabilities	
Transaction deposits	$ 572.6
Savings deposits	531.1
Time deposits	787.3
Other borrowings	617.5
	$2,512.1
Net worth	175.4
Total liabilities	$2,687.5

Source: *Federal Reserve Bulletin.*

The money creation process starts when money from outside the banking system is deposited in a commercial bank, creating excess reserves.

Suppose a Saudi prince (there are more than 6,000 of them) enrolls in college in the United States. He brings with him $100,000 in cash. When the $100,000 entered the country, the money supply increased by that amount. Now suppose the Saudi prince exchanges his cash for a demand deposit at Frontier Bank. The bank accepts the deposit and has a new liability in the form of a demand deposit and an offsetting asset in the form of the cash.

This transaction is duly recorded on the bank's books as shown here:

Assets		Liabilities	
Reserves		Demand deposits	+$100,000
Cash	+$100,000		

In this instance the net balance sheet records only how the balance sheet will change as a result of the transaction. The money supply has remained the same as it was: Currency in circulation has declined by $100,000, while demand deposits have increased by an offsetting amount.

We shall continue to assume that all banks desire to hold 10 percent of deposits as reserves; this percentage is known as the **reserve ratio.**

The reserve ratio is the percentage of deposits that banks hold as reserves.

When the reserve ratio is 10 percent, Frontier Bank will hold $10,000 of the $100,000 deposit in vault cash or on deposit with the FRB, leaving the bank with excess reserves of $90,000, as shown in the amended balance sheet:

Assets		Liabilities	
Reserves		Demand deposits	+$100,000
Required	+$10,000		
Excess	+ 90,000		

Frontier Bank thus has a new opportunity. If it lends out its excess reserves or uses the excess reserves to purchase securities, it can earn interest. If good loans can be made, the bank will be willing to loan up to the amount of its excess reserves. The bank will make loans by creating a demand deposit for the borrower in the amount of the loan.

Money is borrowed in order to be spent. Borrowers will quickly write checks on their demand deposits, which will probably be deposited in other banks. So the $90,000 demand deposit created by the loan will quickly be transferred from Frontier to other banks. When this occurs, Frontier will find that its balance sheet has been altered by the transaction. The T-account will now appear as follows:

Assets		Liabilities	
Reserves	+$10,000	Demand deposits	+$100,000
Loans	+ 90,000		+ 90,000
			− 90,000

Reserves now total $10,000, but a new asset in the form of the $90,000 loan has been acquired in place of the excess reserves. The bank still has the initial $100,000 in demand deposits.

Let us assume that only one loan is made by Frontier and that the entire amount of the loan is deposited in another bank, say the Midwest Bank. Midwest Bank now has a new $90,000 demand deposit and an equal amount of new reserves, of which $9,000 are required reserves and $81,000 are excess reserves, as shown.

Assets		Liabilities	
Reserves		Demand deposits	+$90,000
Required	+$9,000		
Excess	+81,000		

Total demand deposits within the banking system now equal $190,000, or $90,000 more than before the loan was made. Demand deposits have increased by the $100,000 from the original deposit and the $90,000 created by the loan. Because demand deposits are a medium of exchange, they are money. In acting together, the banks have created money in addition to the initial deposit by multiplying the amount of bank deposits. Commercial banks create money by making loans or purchasing securities. A security purchase works exactly like a loan. If the bank had not made more loans or purchased securities with its excess reserves, no new money would have been created.

Banks thus create money when they loan out their excess reserves or use these reserves to purchase securities. But the money creation process does not end there. Midwest Bank now has excess reserves of $81,000 and an incentive in the form of the profit motive to make a loan of that amount. The business or person who borrows the excess reserves will spend it. We shall assume that all loans end up as new deposits in another bank, which we shall call Northwest Bank. Northwest's balance sheet is shown below.

Assets		Liabilities	
Reserves		Demand deposits	+$81,000
Required	+ $8,100		
Excess	+$72,900		

Northwest Bank is now in the same position as were Frontier and Midwest Bank before it. It has the opportunity to make more loans. When it does, the money creation process will continue. Each bank in the sequence will be able to make additional loans as it acquires new deposits resulting from the loan activities of other banks. Each new loan will be 10

TABLE 14.4

Multiple Expansion of Bank Deposits When a New Deposit of $100,000 Is Received and the Reserve Ratio Is 10 Percent

BANK	NEW DEPOSIT FROM OUTSIDE BANKING SYSTEM	NEW LOANS	ADDED RESERVES
Frontier Bank	$100,000	$90,000	$10,000

BANK	NEW DEPOSITS CREATED BY LOANS OF OTHER BANKS (1)	NEW LOANS (2)	ADDED RESERVES (3)
Midwest Bank	$ 90,000	$ 81,000	$ 9,000
Northwest Bank	81,000	72,900	8,100
Bank 4	72,900	65,610	7,290
Bank 5	65,610	59,049	6,561
Bank 6	59,049	53,144	5,905
Bank 7	53,144	47,830	5,314
Bank 8	47,830	43,047	4,783
Bank 9	43,047	38,742	4,305
Bank 10	38,742	34,868	3,874
Sum of first ten banks	$ 651,322	$586,190	$ 65,132
Sum of remaining banks	348,678	313,810	34,868
Total all banks	$1,000,000	$900,000	$100,000

percent smaller in amount than the one before it, because 10 percent of each new deposit is held as reserves.

Where will this sequence end? We have seen that the initial deposit of $100,000 led to the creation of a series of loans, each succeeding one being 90 percent of the new deposit received. Thus the initial deposit has led to the creation of new demand deposits of $100,000, $90,000, and $81,000, respectively. Moreover, this sequence will continue until the amount of new loans approaches zero. A new deposit of $100,000 from outside the system leads to the multiple expansion of bank loans and deposit creation as reserves are redistributed throughout the banking system.

Table 14.4 keeps track of these transactions. A new deposit of $100,000 from outside the banking system has set in motion a chain-reaction expansion of deposits. Frontier Bank receives the $100,000 cash deposit and enters it on its balance sheet, creating a demand deposit liability of $100,000, assets of $10,000 in required reserves, and $90,000 in excess reserves. Frontier then loans all of its excess reserves. Loans thus expand by $90,000. Frontier itself does not add to the money supply, having merely transformed currency in circulation to a demand deposit, but its loan of excess reserves allows Midwest Bank to do so. Midwest receives a new deposit of $90,000 when it deposits the check written on Frontier Bank by the borrower. Midwest divides the deposit between required reserves ($9,000) and excess reserves ($81,000) and lends all of the excess reserves to a borrower, who in turn writes a check that is deposited in Northwest Bank, and the process continues.

Where will the process end? What will be the total of $100,000 + $90,000 + $81,000 + ···? You can obtain the answer either by logic or arithmetic. Logically, the process of money creation will come to an end when all of the new $100,000 deposit ends up as reserves in the banking system. When this happens, deposits will have expanded by 10 times this amount, so new deposits will, at the limit of the expansion, total $1,000,000. You can check your logic by looking at Table 14.4. The end of the expansion process comes when there is $100,000 in new reserves, as shown at the bottom of column 3. When this occurs, the banking system will have created $900,000 in new loans (bottom of column 2) and the total amount of deposits, when the initial $100,000 deposit is added, will be $1,000,000 (bottom of column 1).

The injection of new reserves in a fractional-reserve banking system results in the multiple expansion of demand deposits. A single bank cannot by itself expand the money supply, but the entire banking system can create a multiple expansion of demand deposits out of any addition to excess reserves.

The multiple expansion does not proceed without limit. An examination of Table 14.4 and the careful consideration of the multiple expansion process reveal that it is the reserve ratio that puts an upper limit on deposit creation. The addition of $100,000 in new reserves led to an expansion of the money supply by $1,000,000, or by a factor of 10. There is a **deposit expansion multiplier** at work, the value of which is determined by the reserve ratio.

The deposit expansion multiplier is the ratio of the expansion in total demand deposits to the change in excess reserves:

$$Deposit\ expansion\ multiplier = \frac{1}{Reserve\ ratio}$$

When the multiple expansion of deposits was completed in the example above, $10 in new deposits was created for every $1 in new reserves. Thus 10 is the value of the deposit expansion multiplier.

Had the reserve ratio instead been 20 percent, every bank would have chosen to maintain 20 percent of all deposits as reserves and been free to lend 80 percent. The resulting increase in the money supply from the multiple expansion process would have been smaller — in fact, only half as great. When the reserve ratio is 20 percent, the deposit multiplier is 5; if the reserve ratio is 5 percent, the deposit multiplier is 20, and so on.

The deposit expansion multiplier works both ways. An increase in excess reserves from outside the banking system will, as you have seen, lead to a multiplied increase in the amount of demand deposits. A reduction in reserves will work in reverse, causing a multiplied decline in the total amount of reserves.

TWO QUALIFICATIONS In the discussion above it was assumed that all banks were always fully loaned up and that all deposits remained within checking accounts in the banking system. One qualification is that banks might choose at times to hold more than the customary reserve ratio, in which case the deposit expansion multiplier would be reduced accordingly. Suppose banks were legally required to hold 10 percent of deposits in reserves, but instead banks decided to hold 20 percent. In this case the deposit expansion multiplier would be cut in half. Banks that were concerned that more depositors than usual, for example, would desire to make cash withdrawals might choose to hold excess reserves in order to meet withdrawal demands. Thus the higher the reserve ratio, the lower will be the multiple expansion of demand deposits. The actual deposit expansion multiplier thus becomes:

$$\text{Actual deposit expansion multiplier} = \frac{1}{\text{Legal reserve ratio} + \text{Excess reserve ratio}}$$

where the excess reserve ratio is the proportion of deposits held as excess reserves.

A second qualification is the effect of cash leakages. Instead of depositing a check, people sometimes cash checks and receive currency in return. What is the effect of such cash drains on the multiple expansion of deposits? Suppose that instead of $100,000 in cash, the Saudi prince in our earlier example had brought with him a check for that amount drawn on a bank in Switzerland. When the check was deposited, he asked for $5,000 in cash and deposited the rest. The amount of new reserves added to the banking system is reduced to $95,000. The expansion of the money supply would be $10 \times \$95,000$, or $950,000, instead of $10 \times \$100,000$, or $1,000,000. The actual deposit expansion multiplier never reaches its potential value because of cash leakages.

It is possible to take account of all of the potential cash leakages and calculate an actual money multiplier. This is periodically done by the Federal Reserve according to a complex formula. The simplest expression of the money multiplier is:

$$\text{Money multiplier} = \frac{\text{Money supply}}{\text{Monetary base}}$$

where the money supply is either M1 or M2 and the monetary base is composed of the total amount of bank reserves and cash in the hands of the public — both of which are elements that can be multiplied into more money. The historical average value of the money multiplier is about 2.6.

The nation's payments system is thus bound up with the business of commercial banking. Bank loans and security purchases support an expanded amount of bank money. The stability of the payments system is no greater than the stability of the banking system.

STABILITY OF THE FINANCIAL SYSTEM

Fractional reserve banking is potentially unstable. No bank would be able to repay its depositors if all of them were to attempt to withdraw their money at the same time. If this were to happen, all banks would be illiquid. This potential instability has been recognized by the federal government, which has set up a safety net for both financial institutions and depositors.

People decide to hold demand deposits because for some purposes deposits are safer and more convenient than cash. As long as depositors believe that they can withdraw their money from the bank at any time, they will want to leave it there. However, as soon as they believe that their money is in jeopardy, they will want it returned to them. This sounds paradoxical, but people will not want their bank money if they can get it, and they will want their bank money if they believe they cannot have it.

During the last decade there have been brief periods when many depositors of some banks and savings and loans decided at the same time that they wanted to withdraw their deposits. When this happens, a bank is said to be subject to a **bank run.**

A bank run is a situation in which many depositors of a bank simultaneously decide to close their accounts and withdraw their money, often asking for it in currency.

Few banks at any time will be able to meet an unexpected bank run because most of their assets are held not as cash but as securities and loans. These assets cannot be converted immediately into cash. If one bank fails to meet its obligations to its depositors, the confidence of depositors in all banks may be shaken. If this happens, a contagion may break out that can threaten otherwise sound banks. A contagion occurs when the fear of imminent bank failures rapidly spreads among the public. By causing simultaneous bank runs, a contagion could bring down the banking system and with it the payments system.

Consider Frontier's balance sheet as shown.

Assets		Liabilities	
Reserves	$100,000	Demand deposits	$1,000,000
Securities	100,000		
Loans	800,000		

Deposits equal $1,000,000. The bank holds $100,000 in cash reserves, $100,000 in securities as an interest-paying source of secondary reserves, and $800,000 in loans. If depositors unexpectedly make $100,000 in cash withdrawals, the bank loses all of its reserves.

Assets		Liabilities	
Reserves	−$100,000	Demand deposits	−$100,000

The bank must sell $90,000 of its securities to restore the level of required reserves, as shown below.

Assets		Liabilities	
Reserves	$90,000	Demand deposits	$900,000
Securities	10,000		
Loans	800,000		

Note that if depositors had withdrawn $200,000, the bank's securities holdings would be insufficient to restore the required level of reserves and the bank would have had to call in some of its loans that otherwise would have been renewed.

The buyers of the securities pay for them in checks drawn on other banks, which in turn lose reserves when the checks are cleared. A multiple contraction of the money supply thus takes place. The withdrawal of $100,000 in cash results, when the reserve ratio is 10 percent and all banks are fully loaned up, in the eventual decline in demand deposits of $1,000,000.

A bank panic occurs when numerous banks are subjected to runs at the same time. When a panic occurs, banks will have a difficult time meeting the cash demands of their customers. Their reserves will be depleted from two sources: from the cash they paid out in withdrawals and from debiting customer accounts for their purchases of securities that other banks had been forced to sell. A banking panic occurred in the early 1930s in the United States, leading to a decline in the money supply that some believe caused the Great Depression.

FEDERAL SAFETY NET FOR THE FINANCIAL SYSTEM

Commercial banking within a fractional reserve system is crucially dependent on maintaining the confidence of depositors in the financial soundness of the banks. To maintain depositor confidence, several regulatory and insurance agencies have been created by the federal and state governments to oversee and protect financial institutions. During the 1980s commercial banking sailed into rough waters, as a glance back at Figure 14.1 will show. Bank regulators have been sorely tested. Yet a contagion such as occurred in the 1930s did not break out. The federal safety net has thus far broken the fall of individual banks and thrifts.

The safety net for banks is composed of two parts: the regulation of commercial banks and the federal insurance of deposits. We shall first take up the regulation of the banking system and then consider deposit insurance.

FEDERAL REGULATION OF COMMERCIAL BANKING   All commercial banks must be chartered either by the federal government or by a state government before being allowed to operate. In return for the privilege of accepting deposits and making loans, all banks must submit to regulation. All federally chartered commercial banks, for example, must conform to applicable federal statutes as well as the regulations of the Comptroller of the Currency, the Federal Reserve Board, and the Federal Deposit Insurance Corporation. These statutes and regulations relate to capital adequacy, minimum levels of reserves, standards for securities that a bank may acquire, standards for loans, issuance of securities, mergers, acquisitions and consolidations of banks, payment of dividends, establishment of branches, and other aspects of banking operations. The purpose of such regulation is to ensure the financial solvency of the nation's banks and thereby to safeguard the payments system.

Banks, for example, are denied the right to engage in a number of activities, such as owning directly other businesses or underwriting corporate securities. These areas are considered by regulators and/or by Congress as inherently too risky for banks. The areas in which banks can participate are also subject to regulation. The extent of participation in other lines of activities, such as underwriting government securities, is limited.

The actual operations of banks are also subject to regulation. All banks, for example, must maintain a minimum level of equity capital, which is measured as a percentage of assets. In recent years the minimum level of bank capital has been increased and is scheduled to increase further in the future. By the end of 1990 a bank must have a capital-to-asset ratio of at least 7.25 percent, approximately half of which must be capital provided by shareholders. The Federal Reserve has scheduled even higher capital-adequacy standards to go into effect in 1992, at which time the capital-to-asset ratio must be 8.00 percent, of which shareholders must provide half. The office of the Comptroller of the Currency is the primary supervisory authority of national banks, regularly examining the banks to ensure capital adequacy, and it is empowered to close any bank whose capital is inadequate.

Each bank must also maintain a certain percentage of its deposits as legal reserves, either as vault cash or as deposits with the Federal Reserve Bank. In the absence of this regulation, banks would, of course, hold some level of reserves, but minimum legal reserve requirements provide a floor below which a bank's reserves cannot fall. The FRB regularly tracks the level of bank reserves to ensure compliance.

Banks are, however, not totally dependent on their own capital and assets to meet financial emergencies. The Federal Reserve Bank serves as the lender of last resort for the nation's banking system, providing banks in trouble with reserves and currency. The FRB acts as the lender of last resort by accepting sound but illiquid loans as collateral in return for reserves that banks can use to meet reserve requirements or depositors' withdrawals. This allows depositors to withdraw their funds from a troubled bank in cash or to transfer the funds to institutions thought to be safer. Such a standing offer increases the confidence of depositors in the banking system and makes runs on banks less likely.

FEDERAL SAFETY NET FOR DEPOSITORS: DEPOSIT IN-SURANCE   The Federal Deposit Insurance Corporation (FDIC) was established in the wake of the bank crisis of the 1930s. The Federal Savings and Loan Deposit Insurance Corporation (FSLIC) was established later to provide the same functions for savings and loan associations. The FDIC and FSLIC from their inception have had two functions: (1) to protect depositors of modest means from loss in the case of bank failures, and (2) to protect the payments system from the adverse effect of bank runs.

The deposit insurance agency guarantees, in return for a premium paid by each financial institution, that all deposits of less than $100,000 will be repaid in full by the insurer in the case of failure of the financial institution. The success of deposit insurance in averting bank runs is unquestioned, as is its ability to repay all depositors in case of financial failure. This is because Congress has pledged the full faith and credit of the federal government behind the deposit insurance guarantee. In 1989 the federal government made good on this commitment when it passed legislation to reform the nation's savings and loan industry and refinanced the deposit insurance funds.

Deposit insurance is not without its critics. The savings and loan crisis exhausted the FSLIC's insurance fund. The crisis also led to proposals to reform the nature of deposit insurance itself. In the opinion of some observers, the way that deposit insurance has been structured contributed to the S&L crisis. The problem lies in the nature of the incentives that deposit insurance creates for both depositors and financial institutions.

Deposit insurance removes the incentive of most depositors to monitor the performance and safety of the banks that hold their funds, because their deposits are guaranteed. It also provides an incentive for failing financial institutions to take on high-risk loans in an attempt to bail out the bank. If this high-risk strategy succeeds, the stockholders win; if it fails the taxpayers pick up the tab.

Various proposals have been made to reform the system of deposit insurance. One frequently heard proposal is to recognize the benefits that deposit insurance provides in maintaining the confidence of depositors in the banking system. This would be done by creating new regulations, such as requiring more shareholder capital and limiting financial activities, to counter the institutions' existing incentive to take on loans that are too risky. This is the approach Congress took in reforming deposit insurance. A more drastic proposal along these lines would be to require all insured deposits to be invested only in government-issued securities.

Another approach, often advocated by economists, is to charge premiums for deposit insurance based on the riskiness of a bank's assets. The more risky the activities the institution engages in, the higher would be the premium. Another proposal is to reduce the definition of a small deposit to a fraction of the existing level of $100,000 and insure only that amount. A more radical suggestion is to sacrifice the benefits of federally sponsored deposit insurance and to rely on the private sector to provide deposit insurance and on banks to purchase it.

In summary, a fractional reserve banking system, which depends on the confidence of depositors, can become unstable if depositors lose their trust in the banks' financial soundness. When this happens, bank runs can threaten the nation's payments system. In order to maintain stability, the federal government has set up a safety net for both financial institutions and for depositors that is designed to ensure the stability of the nation's payments system.

SUMMARY

1. The banking system plays an important role in the U.S. economy, facilitating the extension of credit, affecting the size of the money supply, and playing a crucial role in the nation's payments system.

2. Commercial banks in the United States are regulated by the government. The Federal Reserve Bank sits at the top of the banking system, serving as a banker's bank and as the agency that controls the money supply.

3. Commercial banks perform the function of financial intermediary, borrowing from one group and lending to another. A bank has three advantages over a person engaging in direct lending: cost minimization, risk pooling, and the offer of safe, highly liquid investments.

4. Commercial banks obtain deposits by offering safe, highly liquid investments, and they lend the deposits to borrowers they have deemed creditworthy. Commercial banks hope to earn profits from the interest rate spread. Banks accept the risk on the loans they make, thus shielding depositors from default risk, and bridge the gap between borrowers who wish to borrow long term and lenders who wish to lend short term.

5. The operations of a commercial bank can readily be seen by consulting the bank's balance sheet, which lists assets, liabilities, and equity capital. Total assets always equal total liabilities plus equity capital. Every banking transaction affects both sides of the balance sheet.

6. Commercial banks maintain reserves to ensure their liquidity. In the United States the minimum legal quantity of reserves is set by the Federal Reserve. Total reserves are less than total deposits, making commercial banking a fractional reserve system.

7. Banks acting together by using excess reserves to make loans or purchase securities create bank money through the multiple expansion of deposits. A single bank is limited in the loans it can make to the amount of its excess reserves, but the banking system as a whole can lend out a multiple of any increase in excess reserves. The size of this multiple is known as the deposit expansion multiplier.

8. Cash leakages and banks' independence in determining their own reserve ratios above the legal minimum will affect the actual value of the deposit expansion multiplier.

9. Bank runs occur when a large percentage of depositors lose confidence in a bank's ability to repay and decide they want their deposits either transferred to another bank or returned in cash. The banking system is subject to contagion in that a bank run may spread to other banks and cause a banking panic.

10. The federal and state governments have erected a safety net for banks and depositors. The Federal Reserve Bank, the Comptroller of the Currency, and the state banking agencies regulate the banking system. The Federal Reserve stands ready to serve as the lender of last resort, thereby

ensuring the continued liquidity of the banking system. The safety net for depositors lies in federally sponsored deposit insurance. Most deposits up to $100,000 are insured by a federal agency.

SMALL TEXAS TOWNS ARE THE VICTIMS OF THE BIG BANKS' CRISIS

While oil prices were high, the Texas economy flew. Energy resources make up a large portion of the Texas economy, and the income that originated there spilled over to fuel expansion in all sectors of the state's economy. The major Texas banks were heavily involved in financing the vigorous expansion. Economic growth requires new capital and investments, and all the state's banks were active in supplying the region's credit requirements. Every major Texas bank held a large portfolio of energy loans. They also were very active in real estate. During the expansion the real estate sector in particular boomed, and the banks provided construction loans and bridge financing for new office buildings and shopping centers.

When the price of oil collapsed, so did the Texas economy. It was like a roller coaster after a vigorous climb: Once the peak was reached, the economy rolled downhill even faster than it had come up. Risk pooling does not work very well when an entire region slips into a severe recession. All areas of the economy become troubled. Business firms that had expanded were caught with excess capacity. Many energy companies went bankrupt, laying off thousands of workers and leaving the banks with assets worth less than the loans they had made. Real estate projects that during the boom looked good suddenly went sour. Real estate values plummeted and projects in progress were canceled, leaving unfinished construction projects on-site. Many builders could not repay their bank loans and walked away. The banks were left holding the bag. All major Texas banks were suddenly in trouble. By the middle of 1988 only two of Texas' top ten banks had survived without either government aid or a takeover by a better-financed bank.

Consider the example of First RepublicBank of Dallas. In June 1987 First RepublicBank was formed from the merger of two Dallas banks — RepublicBank and Inter-First — and became the largest bank in Texas. Inter-First was known to be in trouble, but RepublicBank was thought to be sound. The $544 million merger fended off a possible out-of-state takeover of Inter-First and created a bank with assets of $26.9 billion. RepublicBank sold $200 million in preferred stock and bonds to support the merger.

In fact, First RepublicBank was not in appreciably better shape than the bank it acquired. After the merger the new bank held over 40 percent of its loan portfolio in real estate, much of it in Dallas, where values were still falling. First RepublicBank began immediately to slash costs in an attempt to eliminate duplication within the merged firm. While it was succeeding in this area, it was swamped by mounting loan losses. The bank's loan portfolio was souring. The bank decided to write off the worst of its loans, losing $656.8 million in 1987. This loss amounted to almost 60 percent of its equity capital. Moreover, the bank still had almost $4 billion in nonperforming loans.

This large loss and the prospect of further large losses alerted depositors and stockholders to the plight of the bank. The stockmarket reacted by marking down the value of First RepublicBank's shares, which fell from $19 at the end of 1986 to $3.75 by the end of 1987, reflecting the bank's reduced prospects.

Recall that a bank borrows short and lends long. This means that it is counting on a majority of its depositors leaving their money with the bank and on new deposits to offset withdrawals. A bank the size of First RepublicBank cannot fund all of its operations with small deposits. It must rely on wholesale deposits, called *jumbos* in the banking business. In fact, First RepublicBank obtained 8 percent of its deposits abroad. Large depositors are not guaranteed by the FDIC, although in the past the FDIC has protected the deposits of most depositors, small and large alike.

Large depositors are sophisticated investors who are well equipped to judge risk. Large depositors first reacted by demanding a premium to lend money to the bank. The bank was put in the position of having to pay more than its rivals for money and of not being able to charge more for loans than its rivals did — unless, of course, the bank took on more risky loans, of which it already had plenty. This made it difficult for the bank to fund its good loans profitably.

As the true financial position of Texas' largest bank was revealed, large depositors responded by refusing to lend at all and withdrew their deposits. First RepublicBank lost $2 billion in deposits between January and March of 1988. The bank was forced to ask seven large banks to provide a safety-net loan of $1.4 billion to maintain the bank's liquidity, which they did.

The $656.8 million loss incurred during 1987 also alerted bank regulators, who quickly found serious difficulties with the bank's loan portfolio. When rumors of their findings spread throughout the banking community, the safety-net banks demanded their money back. First RepublicBank was immediately forced to turn to the Federal Reserve Bank for funds, which were provided. This development did little to reduce the fears of the bank's large depositors, who were now joined by some small depositors in a rush to withdraw their money.

Bank runs on large banks do not take the same form today as they did prior to the advent of federal deposit insurance. Then people lined up in front of the bank to obtain their money, attracting others to join them. This sometimes still happens, as recent runs on savings and loans in Arizona, Maryland, and Ohio have demonstrated. However, when runs occur against large banks like First RepublicBank, they are curiously silent affairs, taking place through electronic communications. Large depositors simply notify the bank that they are withdrawing their deposits or not renewing prior commitments. When the deposits of a bank decline, so does the amount of its reserves. The bank's reserve account with the Federal Reserve consequently declines.

Let us use a balance sheet to reconstruct what happened to First RepublicBank. A reconstructed balance sheet for the bank is shown below.

Assets		Liabilities		
Reserves	$ 1,996	Deposits		$25,491
Loans	24,104	Noninterest	$ 6,118	
Nonperforming	3,922	Interest	19,373	
		Equity		609
Total Assets	$26,100	Total Liabilities		$26,100

This balance sheet represents a significant decline in the bank's position from the balance sheet that existed when the merged bank was created six months earlier. The bank had been forced to write off 2.1 percent of its loans, previously worth $656.8 million, as uncollectible in the last half of 1987. As a result, equity capital had declined by 59.6 percent. Moreover, almost 16 percent of the bank's remaining loans were classified as nonperforming, meaning that they were no longer paying interest or repaying the principal. It is little wonder that large depositors became alarmed.

When the bank run occurred, the bank lost reserves dollar for dollar with the decline in deposits. The net change in the balance sheet must have looked something like this.

Assets		Liabilities	
Reserves	−$2,000	Deposits	−$2,000

The consolidated balance sheet now appears as shown here.

Assets		Liabilities		
Reserves	−$ 4	Deposits		$23,491
Loans	24,104	Noninterest	$ 6,118	
Nonperforming	3,922	Interest	17,373	
		Equity		609
Total Assets	$24,100	Total Liabilities		$24,100

First RepublicBank now had a very serious problem. The bank, which had been previously fully loaned up, was effectively without reserves and the Federal Reserve would not allow it to operate without the legal minimum reserves.

Management had to scramble to find reserves. They negotiated a safety-net loan of $1.4 billion from seven large banks, which still left them short of reserves by over a half-billion dollars. To make up this amount, they began to call in previously good loans. You saw in the preview how businesses in the town of Lufkin were affected by this action. The story of Lufkin was repeated all over Texas as First RepublicBank sought to increase its reserves.

First RepublicBank was, in effect, forced to call in and not renew good loans in order to obtain reserves to make up for the decline in deposits. Good loans were sacrificed to fund the nonperforming loans on the bank's books. Some previously good loans now disappeared from its books as they were repaid. When other borrowers that had previously been meeting their payments could not repay the entire loan, these loans became problem loans, adding to the bank's problems. When an accurate picture of the bank's loan portfolio came to light, the safety-net banks withdrew their aid and the Federal Reserve Bank was forced to act as a lender of last resort and supply funds to allow the bank to meet its reserve requirements.

As a result of the audit by bank regulators, First RepublicBank was forced to announce a further loss of $1.5 billion during the first quarter of 1988 (the second highest quarterly loss ever suffered in U.S. banking history). The bank was now insolvent, all equity had been exhausted, and the bank was taken over by the FDIC, which supplied additional funds of $1 billion to keep the bank liquid. A subsequent loss of $760 million was announced for the second quarter, which brought the half-year total loss to $2.26 billion. When stockholder equity of $609 million is subtracted from the losses suffered, the bank was insolvent in the amount of $1.1 billion.

It took the FDIC four months to find a solvent bank to acquire the bankrupt bank. In August 1988 the NCNB Corporation of Charlotte,

North Carolina, assumed most of the assets of the bank in a joint owner-ship agreement with the FDIC. The FDIC agreed to keep most of the problem loans and attempt to salvage what it could. So NCNB started off with a clean bank. It was estimated that the failure of this one bank alone would cost the FDIC's insurance fund $4 billion. It agreed to forgive the $1 billion emergency loan it had made to First RepublicBank and to erase the $1.1 billion negative equity. In addition, it agreed to pump almost another $1 billion into the new bank in return for 80 percent ownership, and to assume a $5 billion pool of nonperforming loans. The FDIC esti-mated that it would eventually recover about $4 billion of this money.

In return for the $4 billion expended by the FDIC, all depositors were saved from loss, and the solvent loan customers of the now defunct bank, like many of the business persons of Lufkin, were spared the future diffi-culties of having their loans not renewed or their credit lines cut. The banking system remained solvent and depositor confidence was retained. The Federal Reserve had performed its obligation to be a lender of last resort, and the FDIC had met its obligation to insure deposits.[2]

THE SAVINGS AND LOAN CRISIS

The nation's thrift industry was in crisis at the end of the 1980s. Almost 1,000 of the nation's savings and loan associations were ei-ther insolvent or barely solvent. These institutions controlled nearly 35 percent of all assets in S&Ls (almost $450 billion), but they had liabilities, mostly the deposits of people like you and me, that were even greater. Had you been one of the depositors, you need not have worried, for the safety of your deposits was guaranteed by the full faith and credit of the U.S. government. But, though comforting to you, this was and continues to be part of the problem. The Federal Savings and Loan Insurance Cor-poration (FSLIC) in 1989 was itself insolvent. It did not have sufficient funds to close all of the sick thrifts and still pay off all of the depositors.

How did the nation's thrift industry get into this mess? Part of the problem stems from the mission that Congress assigned to savings and loans. This mission required the nation's thrifts to lend for very long periods of time and to borrow very short term. Lending institutions make profits by charging more for loans than they pay for deposits. As long as the maturities of loans and deposits of a bank are matched and the banker makes good loans, the institutions will remain solvent and profitable even if interest rates are rising. They will always be able to fully repay their depositors, keeping the spread for themselves.

Savings and loans were told by Congress to assemble short-term de-posits and use them to provide long-term fixed-rate mortgages for home buyers. This subjected the S&Ls to considerable interest rate risk. In order to attract deposits for this purpose, the deposits were to be insured by the FSLIC, and in the days of regulated interest rates the thrifts were allowed to pay a slightly higher rate of interest than commercial banks could pay. The incentive worked. In 1939 the nation's S&Ls held about 10 percent of all mortgages in the country. By 1985 they owned over a quarter of the total.

[2]Source for this analysis: *Business Week*, Mar. 28, 1988, 28, and April 1988, 92–93; *The Wall Street Journal*, Aug. 1, 1988, 1, 3, 5.

As long as interest rates were stable, or falling, savings and loans were profitable and remained solvent. But when interest rates started to rise, S&Ls got into trouble. Many families that bought houses in the mid-1960s obtained from an S&L a 30-year mortgage of about $50,000 for less than 6 percent a year. The S&Ls were paying depositors 4¾ percent to borrow the $50,000 and doing well off the spread. But interest rates did not remain at these levels; they began to rise with the rate of inflation. Short-term rates rose to 6½ percent in 1970 and trended upward thereafter, reaching 8 percent in 1974 and over 12 percent from 1980 through 1982, before falling somewhat.

The S&L that held the 6 percent mortgage was losing money in 1970 and even more in subsequent years. In 1970 it was having to pay ½ percent more for short-term funds than it was earning from mortgages that it made in 1965. By 1980 it was paying twice as much for the money it borrowed than it was earning from the funds it had committed in 1965. Mortgage holders were doing quite well. Their income was rising with inflation but their mortgage payment remained fixed. They were paying the loan back with dollars that were worth less than the S&L had expected. The S&Ls were suffering. They were losing money.

As the nation's S&Ls continued to lose money in the 1980s, some became legally insolvent: The value of their assets was less than the value of their liabilities. A financial institution is insolvent when the expected discounted cash payments due to depositors and other liabilities exceed the discounted cash receipts from loans and investments.

When interest rates rise, the value of fixed-rate assets, such as mortgages, falls. The owners of these fixed-rate assets lose money. The S&Ls could not sell the mortgages without incurring losses that would wipe out their equity and make them insolvent. So most were forced to hold on to their mortgages. Since accounting procedures allowed the S&Ls to carry the mortgages at face value rather than market value, government regulators let the S&Ls continue to operate even though many were, in fact, insolvent.

When this happens to a book publisher, the firm would not be able to pay all of its debts and no one would lend it more money or extend it credit. The company must either declare bankruptcy and have a receiver appointed to work off its debts, or liquidate the firm, selling its remaining assets to at least partially repay its creditors. In banking it does not work this way because a federal government agency has guaranteed most of the financial institutions' creditors (the depositors) from loss.

Consider what happened in Texas when the drop in the price of oil plunged the state into deep recession. The state's S&Ls, whose capital had been drained by the decade-long rise in interest rates, did not trim back their operations but plunged ahead. Texas S&Ls nearly tripled their assets to $100 billion from $36 billion between 1982 and 1986. Many of the loans and investments that were made were high-risk, desperate measures to stay afloat. How did such desperate institutions attract $64 billion for investment in an area the whole country knew was economically sick? It was easy — they offered above-market rates of interest. Individual depositors and deposit brokers from all over the country were happy to supply these funds, secure in their knowledge that the FSLIC stood behind their money.

The Federal Home Loan Bank Board did not clamp down earlier, like the Federal Reserve and the Comptroller of the Currency did in the case of First Republicbank, because the FSLIC did not have the funds to pay off all of the depositors. In 1982 the FSLIC could have solved the problem of the nation's thrifts for $10 to $15 billion, but it did not have the funds.

Instead, it allowed the sick S&Ls to stay alive and to expand in the vain hope that they would grow out of their problems. They did not. Texas thrifts alone lost $6.2 billion in 1987 and another $1.2 billion in the first quarter of 1988. In 1987 the FHLBB was finally forced by these circumstances to step in, for the FSLIC still did not have the money to solve the problem. All it could do, as suggested in the preview, was prop up the bodies on the ramparts and wait for Congress to come to the rescue. In the movie *Beau Geste* rescue eventually came. The S&Ls were eventually rescued by Congress in 1989, but not until the ramparts were stacked with bodies. Meanwhile the cost of restoring the nation's thrift industry to solvency had grown to at least a $40 billion problem by 1987, and it may be a $100 billion to $150 billion problem by the time the rescue is completely effected.[3]

---

[3] Source for this analysis: Michael C. Keeley, "Troubled Banks and Thrifts," *Weekly Letter*, *Federal Reserve Bank of San Francisco*, Jan. 29, 1988.

REQUIRED ECONOMIC CONCEPTS

Commercial bank
Payments system
Central bank
Open-market operations
Securitization
Balance sheet
Collateral
Demand deposit

Savings account
Money market account
Time deposit
Fractional reserve system
Reserve ratio
Deposit expansion multiplier
Bank run

KEY QUESTIONS

1. What is the payments system? How does the role banks play in the payments system make them special institutions within the economy?
2. What is the purpose of the regulatory function of the Federal Reserve Bank?
3. What do FHLBB, FSLIC, and FDIC stand for? What is the function of each?
4. What three advantages do banks as financial intermediaries have?
5. What is the prudent rule that banks should follow?
6. What are at least four other kinds of financial intermediaries beside commercial banks?
7. What is the word thrift a synonym for?
8. How do banks create money?
9. What are excess reserves? What does *fully-loaned up* mean?
10. What is the definition of the deposit expansion multiplier?
11. What is the relationship between the deposit multiplier and the reserve ratio?
12. Why is the actual deposit multiplier smaller than the theoretical deposit multiplier?
13. What is the Federal Reserve System? What are two of its primary functions?
14. How many members of the Board of Governors are there? What is their length of term? Who appoints them? For how long is the Board's chairman appointed? To whom is the Board directly responsible?

PROBLEMS

1. Since most money is bank debt, and since you accept checks from others, why can your debt not be money?

2. If you go to the bank and take out a loan of $1,000 in *cash*, does this transaction in itself increase the money supply? Explain. Do banks normally lend in cash? Why or why not?

3. Suppose banks expect hard times ahead for the economy. How might their subsequent behavior be self-fulfilling?

4. Indicate whether each of the following transactions in itself results in an increase, a decrease, or no change in M1 money.

   a. You find $10 on the street and deposit it in your checking account.

   b. You buy a $1,000 Treasury bond that you pay for with a check.

   c. You receive a cash loan of $200 from a friend.

   d. You receive a loan of $300 from a friend in the form of a check. You then pay your landlord, who deposits $200 in his or her checking account and spends $80 for a wool sweater at Sears and pays $20 for parking violations.

   e. You pay $400 to your landlord, who then buys $400 worth of municipal bonds.

   f. You give $20 to your nephew for Christmas in the form of two $10 bills. One falls out of his pocket while he is walking down the street.

   g. You take out a loan from the bank for $100 and then write a check to a friend for the same amount. He deposits it in his account at the very same bank.

   h. A commercial bank increases its vault cash (actual coin and currency on the premise) by $10,000 by drawing down its account at the Federal Reserve bank of which it is a member.

   i. An uninsured bank is robbed of $20,000. Does your answer change if the bank was already loaned up at the time of the robbery? Explain.

   j. You deposit $150 in currency in a noncheckable time deposit at the bank.

5. Is paper money an asset? Are all assets therefore money? Explain. If Mr. Fat Cat is a millionaire, does that necessarily mean he has $1 million in cash, including his checking account? Is net worth therefore different from money? Explain.

6. Suppose that every payday each worker deposits his or her paycheck and writes no checks for the next two weeks. Can the commercial banking system nevertheless increase the money supply during that time if the banks were fully loaned up (were holding no excess reserves) when the checks were deposited, and if no additional reserves are made available to the commercial banks by the Federal Reserve? Explain.

7. Confine this problem to the commercial banking system. Assume the banking system is fully loaned up. It is after Christmas and the public decides it wants to carry $500,000 less cash. If the reserve requirement is 20 percent, in what direction and by how much does the economy's money supply change if there are no leakages in the system? Confining this problem to the commercial banking system, set up a T-account analysis.

8. Suppose the banking *system* is fully loaned up and its reserves then fall by $3,000 because it buys $3,000 worth of government securities. The reserve ratio is 15 percent. Calculate the change, if any, in the amount of the *system's* loans. Set up a T-account analysis.

9. If a bank holds excess reserves of $20,000 when its total reserves are $100,000 and the reserve requirement is 20 percent, what is the amount of the demand deposit liabilities of the bank?

APPLICATION ANALYSIS

1. Use the bank T-account below to answer the questions that follow. (All amounts are in thousands of dollars.)

Assets		Liabilities	
Vault cash	$2,000	Demand deposits	$110,000
Reserves with Federal	25,000	Time deposits	30,000
Reserve		Net worth	20,000
Loans	50,000		
Securities	83,000		

Assume that the bank's reserve requirement is 20 percent. Calculate the following:
   a. The bank's total assets and its total liabilities.
   b. Its current level of reserves.
   c. The reserves it is required to hold against demand deposits.
   d. Its amount of excess reserves.
   e. The maximum amount of new loans it can make.
   f. The maximum increase in the money supply that the banking *system* can make if all other banks are loaned up and there are no leakages.

2. Suppose the Fed sells $50 million worth of securities to an individual who pays for it with a check against his or her account at a commercial bank. Assume that the bank is already fully loaned up, that the reserve ratio is 20 percent, and that there are no leakages.
   a. Determine the size of the deposit multiplier.
   b. In the parentheses in the accounts below enter the changes corresponding to each item.

Federal Reserve		Commercial Bank	
Assets	Liabilities	Assets	Liabilities
Government bonds	Member bank reserves	Reserves with	Demand deposits
( )	( )	Federal Reserve	( )
		( )	

   c. In what direction and by how much do total reserves change?
   d. Is there now an excess or a deficiency in reserves against the new level of demand deposits? How much?
   e. Calculate the direction of and the amount of the change in the money supply.
   f. Suppose the Federal Reserve had sold $50 million in securities directly to the bank instead. What would the parentheses in the account now show? By how much and in what direction would the money supply change?

CHAPTER

15

MONETARY POLICY

IN THIS CHAPTER YOU WILL LEARN:

How the Federal Reserve System determines monetary policy and the tools it uses to conduct monetary policy

•

How the Federal Reserve can control the money supply

•

The difference between the real and nominal rates of interest

•

The difference between the Keynesian and monetarist views of monetary policy

•

The relationship between fiscal and monetary policy in theory and in practice

IS A SOFT LANDING FOR THE ECONOMY POSSIBLE? HAS LAUNCHPAD MCQUACK FINALLY LEARNED TO FLY?

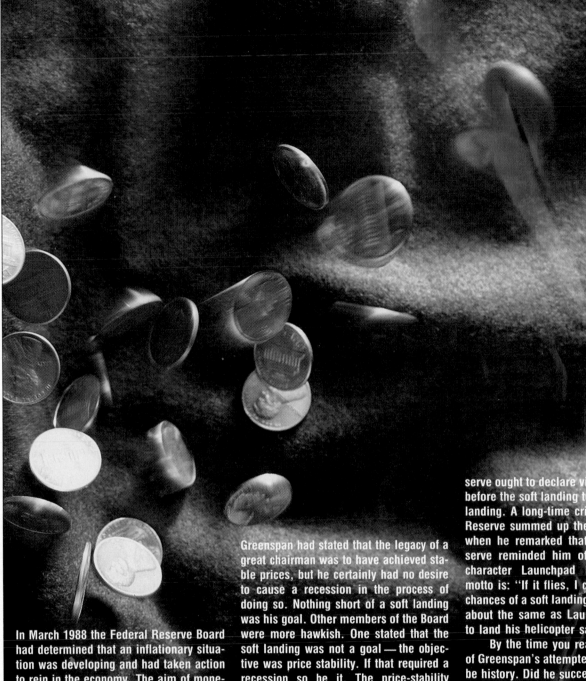

In March 1988 the Federal Reserve Board had determined that an inflationary situation was developing and had taken action to rein in the economy. The aim of monetary policy became to achieve a "soft landing" for the economy, i.e., to wring inflationary tendencies out of the economy without causing a recession. The goal was to keep the economy growing near the level of potential national income without allowing inflation to accelerate.

The Federal Reserve Board was split into at least two camps. Chairman Alan Greenspan had stated that the legacy of a great chairman was to have achieved stable prices, but he certainly had no desire to cause a recession in the process of doing so. Nothing short of a soft landing was his goal. Other members of the Board were more hawkish. One stated that the soft landing was not a goal — the objective was price stability. If that required a recession so be it. The price-stability hawks were in the minority, however, as most of the Board favored ensuring that continued economic growth, not recession, occurred. None, however, advocated a take-off.

In the summer of 1989 the Bush administration was clearly worried. The chairman of the Council of Economic Advisors openly stated that the Federal Reserve ought to declare victory and ease up before the soft landing turned into a crash landing. A long-time critic of the Federal Reserve summed up the opinion of many when he remarked that the Federal Reserve reminded him of the new Disney character Launchpad McQuack, whose motto is: "If it flies, I can crash it." The chances of a soft landing, he opined, were about the same as Launchpad's learning to land his helicopter safely.

By the time you read this, the result of Greenspan's attempted soft landing will be history. Did he succeed in engineering the fabled soft landing, or did the Federal Reserve lose its nerve and decide to circle the runway yet another time, or did the economy crash into recession?

Sources: "Greenspan's Moment of Truth," *Business Week*, July 31, 1989; Alan Murray, "The Next Recession: Just Around the Bend?" *The Wall Street Journal*, March 6, 1989; and Douglas R. Sease, "How Will Economy Hit the Runway?" *The Wall Street Journal*, May 15, 1989.

WHAT SHOULD THE FEDERAL RESERVE DO?

Most economists agree that excessive monetary growth causes inflation, and many also agree that the primary goal of the Federal Reserve Bank should be to promote price stability. The problem is how the Federal Reserve should proceed to accomplish this goal. Effects on the economy lag changes in the money supply by six months to two years. In the past the Federal Reserve has employed intermediate targets that were thought to have predictable consequences on real GNP and the price level.

At one time the Federal Reserve tried to peg interest rates, with the result, as we shall see in this chapter, that the economy became more unstable. Abandoning that goal, the Federal Reserve announced that it would target the money supply, announcing targets for the annual growth of the various definitions of the money supply, in the belief that there existed a stable relationship between the quantity of money and nominal GNP.

Unfortunately, the deregulation of the financial system and the financial innovations that occurred in the 1980s have made it more difficult to predict the effects on GNP from a given change in the money supply. As a result, the Federal Reserve Board has downgraded or abandoned money aggregates and has begun to use a variety of other indicators, refusing to announce any target in 1987 and 1988 for M1, and widening the target ranges for M2 and M3 to reflect the greater uncertainty in interpreting movements in these broader aggregates.

What should the Federal Reserve do? Some economists have suggested targeting the monetary base, others nominal GNP, still others commodity prices — and the list could go on. Recently the Federal Reserve announced a new theory, called P-star, that purports to have identified the relationship between the rate of growth of M2 and the long-run price level. This theory potentially allows the Federal Reserve to predict in advance the long-run consequences on the price level from a change in monetary policy.

SHOULD THE FEDERAL RESERVE REMAIN INDEPENDENT?

The recent 75th anniversary of the Federal Reserve witnessed a barrage of unprecedented criticism of its past performance. Numerous proposals were made for changes in the central bank that advocates thought would improve its performance. More modest proposals were limited to efforts to reform the central bank. The chairman of the Congressional Joint Economic Committee introduced legislation that would have the term of the Federal Reserve Board chairman expire at the same time as that of the president, make the Secretary of the Treasury a member of the Board of Governors, and require the Federal Reserve to release its policy decisions immediately instead of on the current delayed basis.

Should the Federal Reserve remain independent, or should it be made fully accountable to elected officials such as the president?

• I N T R O D U C T I O N •

In the United States the Federal Reserve System has for over 75 years influenced the American economy through its monetary policy. The Federal Reserve Bank, like all central banks, controls the money supply in an attempt to influence real GNP and the price level. You discovered in Chapter 13 the role that money plays in the macroeconomy. Because the money supply is a major determinant of the macroeconomy's performance, the **monetary policy** of the Federal Reserve directly affects all of our lives.

> *Monetary policy is the deliberate control of the money supply to achieve the macroeconomic goals set by the Federal Reserve.*

When the Federal Reserve undertakes to increase the money supply, it is called an *expansionary monetary policy*. A decrease in the money supply is called a *contractionary monetary policy*. •

HOW THE FEDERAL RESERVE CONTROLS THE MONEY SUPPLY

The role played by the Federal Reserve Bank (FRB) in regulating the nation's money supply can be grasped by considering the balance sheet shown in Table 15.1. The major liabilities are Federal Reserve notes (which serve as currency in circulation) and the reserve deposits of member banks. In Chapter 14 we saw that the amount of demand deposits a given level of reserves would support depended on the reserve-to-deposit ratio that banks maintain. It is through its control of the amount of reserves that the FRB controls the money supply. Anything that the FRB does that affects either the total amount of reserves or the reserve-to-deposit ratio that banks maintain will affect the quantity of money in the economy.

The FRB has three major tools for controlling the quantity of money in the economy, plus a number of minor tools. The most important tool and the most frequently employed is open-market operations.

OPEN-MARKET OPERATIONS

The main tool used by the Federal Reserve to control the level of reserves in the banking system is **open-market operations.**

> *Open-market operations are procedures that involve the purchase or sale of U.S. government securities by the Federal Reserve for the purpose of adjusting the level of reserves in the banking system.*

The consolidated balance sheet of the Federal Reserve (Table 15.1) shows that in January 1988 the FRB owned $218.4 billion worth of government bonds. In a typical year the FRB buys and/or sells hundreds of billions of dollars worth of government securities. This is a day-to-day operation. The Federal Open Market Committee instructs the New York District

TABLE 15.1
Consolidated Balance Sheet of All Federal Reserve Banks: January 1988
(Billions of Dollars)

Assets

Gold certificates and cash	$ 11.1
U.S. government securities	218.4
Loans to commercial banks	3.3
Other assets	32.4
	$265.2

Liabilities

Federal reserve notes outstanding	$209.9
Deposits of member banks (reserves)	35.3
Deposits of U.S. Treasury	10.3
Other liabilities	9.7
	$265.2

Source: *Federal Reserve Bulletin*, June 1988, Table A10.

TABLE 15.2
Open-Market Purchases and Sales by the Federal Reserve Bank: 1985–1987
(Millions of Dollars)

TYPE OF TRANSACTION	1985	1986	1987
Gross purchases	$26,499	$24,078	$37,171
minus:			
Gross sales	4,218	2,502	6,802
Redemptions	3,500	1,000	9,099
Matched transactions			
Gross sales	866,175	927,997	950,923
Gross purchases	865,968	927,247	950,935
Repurchase agreements			
Gross purchases	134,253	170,431	314,620
Gross sales	132,351	160,268	324,666
Net change in U.S.			
government securities	$20,477	$29,989	$11,235

Source: *Federal Reserve Bulletin*, June 1988, Table A9.

Federal Reserve Bank how to proceed with open-market operations. Table 15.2 provides information about the extent of open-market operations for the years 1985–1987. In each of these years the FRB was both a buyer and seller of U.S. government obligations. On balance, in each year the FRB purchased significantly more government bonds than it sold.

How does this net increase affect the money supply? We shall show how open-market operations work to change the quantity of bank money in the economy. We shall assume that all banks are fully loaned up and that no cash leakages occur as the deposit expansion process operates.

EXPANSIONARY OPEN-MARKET OPERATIONS The Federal Reserve undertakes an expansionary monetary policy whenever it decides that the economy will benefit from an increase in the money supply. In order to conduct expansionary open-market operations, the FRB buys government bonds from the public.

TABLE 15.3
Balance Sheet Changes Caused by Open-Market Purchases of Bonds
from an Individual

BALANCE SHEET: ALL INDIVIDUALS

Assets		Liabilities	
Bonds	−$1,000	No change	
Demand deposits	+ 1,000		

BALANCE SHEET: COMMERCIAL BANK

Assets		Liabilities	
Reserves	+$1,000	Demand deposits	+$1,000

BALANCE SHEET: FEDERAL RESERVE BANK

Assets		Liabilities	
Bonds	+$1,000	Reserve Deposits	+$1,000

When the Federal Reserve buys a government bond that was owned by the public, the following changes take place in the net-change balance sheets of individuals, commercial banks, and the FRB, as shown in Table 15.3. When an individual sells a $1,000 bond to the FRB, the FRB acquires an asset (the $1,000 bond) and a liability in the form of the check for $1,000 that it issued to the individual.

The assets of all individuals will be affected by the sale. The value of bonds held by the public will fall by $1,000, to be replaced by a $1,000 increase in demand deposits when the individual deposits the check in a local bank. This change takes place on the asset side of the balance sheet. The balance sheet of commercial banks will also be affected when the $1,000 check is deposited. The individual's bank account will be credited with a demand deposit of $1,000 (a liability of the commercial bank) and the check will be forwarded to the district Federal Reserve bank for collection. The commercial bank's reserve account will be credited with $1,000, which appears both as an asset on the commercial bank's balance sheet and as a liability on the balance sheet of the Federal Reserve bank.

The $1,000 demand deposit on the commercial bank's balance sheet is balanced by an asset in the form of additional reserves of $1,000. While on the balance sheet of the Federal Reserve bank, the $1,000 increase in the FRB's bond holdings is an asset that is balanced by a liability in the form of the $1,000 increase in the commercial bank's reserve account.

The banking system now has excess reserves, because of the Federal Reserve's bond purchase. Excess reserves combined with the profit motive provide both the means and the incentive for banks to make more loans. Thus when the central bank conducts an expansionary open-market operation, it buys securities on the open market, thereby increasing the reserves of the commercial banks and making possible the further expansion of bank loans and demand deposits.

Suppose that the Federal Reserve's check was deposited in a demand deposit at a large commercial bank, and that the FRB has established a reserve requirement of 12 percent on demand deposits in large institutions. The bank must reserve $120 against the $1,000 deposit. The bank thus has $880 in excess reserves. The deposit expansion multiplier for a fully loaned up bank is:

$$\text{Deposit expansion multiplier} = \frac{1}{0.12} = 8.333$$

TABLE 15.4
Changes in Table 15.3 Balance Sheets after Commercial Banks Have Become
Fully Loaned Up

BALANCE SHEET: ALL INDIVIDUALS

Assets		Liabilities	
Bonds	−$1,000	Loans	$7,333
Demand deposits	+ 8,333		

BALANCE SHEET: ALL COMMERCIAL BANKS

Assets		Liabilities	
Reserves	$1,000	Demand deposits	$8,333
Loans	7,333		

BALANCE SHEET: FEDERAL RESERVE BANK

Assets		Liabilities	
Bonds	+$1,000	Reserve Deposits	+$1,000

The $1,000 in reserves created by the deposit of the check issued by the FRB in exchange for the $1,000 bond will eventually, when all banks become fully loaned up, support additional deposits of $8,333.

As a result of selling the $1,000 bond, the balance sheet of all individuals, shown in Table 15.4, will end up holding $8,333 in additional demand deposits and $7,333 in additional loans. Assets thus rise by the same amount as liabilities. The balance sheet of commercial banks also increases: assets increase by the amount of the loans, and liabilities increase by an equal amount of new demand deposits. The Federal Reserve Bank's balance sheet remains unchanged. The effect of the open-market purchase of a $1,000 bond has resulted in an increase in demand deposits of $8,333.

What we have seen, then, is that expansionary monetary policy provides the commercial banking system with excess reserves, which makes it possible for the commercial banks to expand the money supply.

CONTRACTIONARY OPEN-MARKET OPERATIONS The Federal Reserve embarks on a contractionary monetary policy whenever the Federal Reserve Board decides the economy would benefit from a smaller money supply. A contractionary open-market operation involves the sale of government bonds to the public.

When the Federal Reserve sells government securities on the open market, the process works in reverse to the one described above. When an individual purchases a $1,000 bond that the FRB has sold, the individual writes a check in payment against his or her personal account. This is shown in Table 15.5. The FRB debits the commercial bank's reserve account $1,000 and presents the check to the commercial bank for collection. The commercial bank then debits the customer's account for the amount of the check.

The individual has traded one asset — a demand deposit — for another — a bond. The commercial bank, however, has lost $1,000 in reserves. If the bank was, as we are assuming, fully loaned up prior to the open-market operation, it will find itself short of legal reserves and will have to sell securities or call in loans. A process of deposit contraction thus begins as individuals pay for the securities they have purchased or repay their outstanding loans. Let us suppose that banks choose to reduce

TABLE 15.5
Net Balance Sheets Showing the Effect of Contractionary Open-Market Operations

BALANCE SHEET: ALL INDIVIDUALS

Assets		Liabilities	
Bonds	+$1,000	Loans	−$7,333
Demand deposits	− 8,333		

BALANCE SHEET: ALL COMMERCIAL BANKS

Assets		Liabilities	
Reserves	−$1,000	Demand deposits	−$8,333
Loans	− 7,333		
Net change	−$8,333	Net change	−$8,333

BALANCE SHEET: FEDERAL RESERVE BANK

Assets		Liabilities	
Bonds	−$1,000	Reserve Deposits	−$1,000

their loans. All commercial banks taken together will have to reduce loans by $7,333 to reduce deposits by a like amount. Thus deposits will eventually fall by $8,333 ($1,000 in payment for the bond and $7,333 in response to the decline in reserves).

Thus when pursuing open-market operations by selling government bonds to the public, some commercial banks will lose reserves. These banks will be forced to reduce their loans or securities to restore the minimum level of reserves that will reduce the amount of demand deposits. The money supply will thus decline as a result of a contractionary open-market operation.

You will observe from the data in Table 15.1 that the Federal Reserve's holdings of government bonds is considerably larger than the amount of reserves held by the banking system. This suggests that open-market operations can be a powerful tool for controlling the money supply. Comparatively small changes in the FRB's bond holdings will have a large effect on the amount of reserves in the banking system.

Generally, open-market operations are not undertaken to make drastic changes in the amount of reserves in the banking system. Rather, the Federal Reserve will, on a day-to-day basis, use open-market operations to marginally adjust the amount of excess reserves held by the banking system in a manner consistent with existing monetary policy.

In reality, since the Great Depression the Federal Reserve has hardly ever reduced the nation's money supply and then only for a short period of time. An ever-growing economy requires an ever-expanding money supply to maintain a constant price level. Thus monetary policy actually involves increases in the money supply at faster or slower rates.

In practice, then, a contractionary monetary policy involves increasing the money supply at a rate less than the rate at which nominal national income is growing, and an expansionary monetary policy involves increasing the money supply at a rate greater than the rate at which nominal national income is expanding.

OTHER TOOLS OF MONETARY POLICY

The Federal Reserve has two other major tools, besides open-market operations, with which to conduct monetary policy. These tools are changes in the discount rate and changes in the legal minimum reserve ratio.

THE DISCOUNT WINDOW Member banks have the right to appeal to the Federal Reserve as the lender of last resort. A bank whose balance sheet shows that it is short of reserves can temporarily borrow reserves from the FRB. A bank could be in this position for a number of reasons, such as a sudden, unexpected amount of deposit withdrawals or as a result of having mistakenly made too many loans or securities purchases, or because of a contractionary monetary policy.

Banks are often temporarily short of reserves. Often they borrow the excess reserves of other banks, or use repurchase agreements, or borrow dollars from abroad. If a commercial bank is unable to obtain the required reserves in other ways, it may seek a loan from the Federal Reserve's discount window. Such a request would be consistent with the FRB's role as the lender of last resort. The fact that the FRB's balance sheet (Table 15.1) shows only a small amount of bank loans suggests how infrequently this is done. More important than the actual practice of banks borrowing from the FRB, except in emergencies, is the significance of the discount rate itself.

The Discount Rate The discount rate is the announced rate at which the Federal Reserve will lend to commercial banks. The discount rate signals the intentions of the Federal Reserve. For example, a significant change in the discount rate occurred on August 9, 1988, when the FRB announced that it was raising the discount rate from 6 to 6½ percent and accompanied this action with open-market operations that drained reserves from the banking system.

The new chairman of the Board of Governors, Alan Greenspan, had told Congress in early July that he considered the threat of inflation Public Enemy Number 1 and that the Federal Reserve intended to stop it before it got out of hand. The rate at which banks could lend other banks their excess reserves in the federal funds market was hovering between 7½ and 7¾ percent. If the discount rate stayed at 6 percent, a bank could borrow from the FRB at that rate and relend the funds to other banks at the higher federal funds rate. The FRB tries to discourage such borrowings by verbally slapping the wrists of offending banks, but if the spread between the discount rate and the federal funds rate increased much more, it was feared that some banks' wrists could stand a lot of pain.

The reaction of financial markets to the announcement of the discount rate increase was quick and dramatic. The Dow Jones industrial average, which measures stock prices, lost 3½ percent of its value in two days after the announcement. The value of stocks, like bonds, varies inversely with the rate of interest and with the fear of recession that a tight monetary policy often brings. The interest rate on long-term bonds increased one-quarter of a point to its highest level in a year, and the dollar soared in value. It was widely interpreted in the nation's press that the hike in the discount rate was an indication of a tighter monetary policy in the future.

The effect of the discount rate hike was reinforced by open-market operations that were undertaken to drain reserves from the banking system. The amount of net unborrowed reserves, or free reserves, available in the banking system provides another signal of the Federal Reserve's intention to increase or decrease the rate of growth of the money supply. These net unborrowed reserves are the total reserves in the banking system minus the amount of borrowed reserves from the Federal Reserve Bank.

The amount of unborrowed reserves in the system indicates the ability of the commercial banks to create additional bank money. If the

TABLE 15.6
Reserve Requirements of Depository Institutions

TYPE OF DEPOSIT	PERCENTAGE OF DEPOSIT	EFFECTIVE DATE
Transaction accounts		
$0 million–$40.5 million	3%	12/15/87
More than $40.5 million	12	12/15/87
Time deposits		
Less than 11/2 years	3	10/6/83
11/2 years or more	0	10/6/83
Eurocurrency liabilities		
All types	3	11/13/80

Source: *Federal Reserve Bulletin*, June 1988, Table A8.

amount of free reserves is less than the legally required amount, the banking system will have to contract loans and deposits. If it is above the legally required amount, the banking system has the ability to expand loans and deposits. Between July 27 and August 10, 1988, the Federal Reserve, through contractionary open-market operations, reduced the level of free reserves from $625 million to $124 million and in response the federal funds interest rate increased to almost 8 percent. The commercial banks responded to these developments by raising the prime interest rate, which is the rate they charge their best corporate customers.

Thus the combination of an announced rise in the discount rate and contractionary open-market operations increased interest rates and signaled that the Federal Reserve was serious about applying monetary policy to counter the inflationary tendencies that the Federal Reserve Board believed were developing in the economy.

It should be pointed out that the federal funds rate actually provides a better guide to monetary policy than the discount rate, because the federal funds rate is the market rate of interest for the borrowing of reserves. Because changes in the discount rate often follow changes in the federal funds rate, they provide less information about monetary policy than is generally thought. The reaction of financial markets to the August 1988 change in the discount rate would have been less pronounced had this change not been accompanied by the other, complementary actions the Federal Reserve also took.

RESERVE REQUIREMENTS The third major tool of monetary policy is a change in the minimum legal reserve requirements. This happens so infrequently that it is literally a once in a lifetime occurrence. In 1934 Congress gave the Federal Reserve the power to set reserve requirements within specified limits. These limits were revised by the Monetary Control Act of 1980, which established uniform reserve requirements for all depository institutions. At the discretion of the Federal Reserve Board, banks' reserve requirements were set at 3 percent of the first $45 million of demand deposits and at between 8 percent and 14 percent of demand deposits in excess of that amount. Currently, the reserve requirement for demand deposits in excess of $40.5 million is 12 percent (see Table 15.6).

This law provides the Federal Reserve with a potentially powerful, if little used, tool for implementing monetary policy. The reserve requirement is the major determinant of the deposit expansion multiplier. When the reserve requirement is 3 percent, as it is for small banks, the deposit expansion multiplier is 33.3, and when it is 12 percent, as in the case of larger banks, the deposit expansion multiplier is 8.33.

A change in the reserve requirement, holding the amount of total reserves constant, will change the amount of money in the economy by affecting the amounts of loans and deposits banks can maintain. Consider the balance sheet below, which shows fully loaned up commercial banks when the reserve requirement is 12 percent and the Federal Reserve has allowed the banking system $1,000 in reserves.

Assets		Liabilities	
Reserves	$1,000	Demand deposits	$8,333
Loans	7,333		

The commercial banks can legally support $8,333 in demand deposits and $7,333 in loans.

Suppose the Federal Reserve decides to expand the money supply. This could be accomplished through open-market operations by buying bonds from the public. But it could also be accomplished by reducing the reserve ratio. If the FRB reduced the reserve requirement from 12 percent to 10 percent, the deposit expansion multiplier would increase from 8.33 to 10. Banks would now have to maintain only $100 in reserves, instead of $120, for every $1,000 in deposits. The decline in the reserve requirement has created excess reserves with which banks can expand the amount of loans and demand deposits. The final result of this expansion would be shown as follows:

Assets		Liabilities	
Reserves	$1,000	Demand deposits	$10,000
Loans	9,000		

Loans will increase to $9,000 and demand deposits to $10,000. Changing the reserve requirement thus causes the money supply to change by affecting the deposit expansion multiplier. If the reserve requirement declines, the deposit expansion multiplier will increase.

Conversely, if the Federal Reserve desired to reduce the money supply, it could sell bonds to the public or increase reserve requirements on demand deposits up to a legal maximum of 14 percent. The end result of increasing the reserve requirement from 12 percent to 14 percent is shown here.

Assets		Liabilities	
Reserves	$1,000	Demand deposits	$7,143
Loans	6,143		

The deposit expansion multiplier now decreases to 7.143. The total quantity of demand deposits that $1,000 in reserves will support is reduced to $7,143. Thus increases in the reserve requirement reduce the money supply by reducing the deposit expansion multiplier.

Small changes in the reserve requirements can have big effects on the money supply, which, perhaps, makes this tool too powerful or too clumsy for most monetary policy operations. Changes in reserve requirements are the nuclear weapons in the Federal Reserve's armory.

The tools of monetary policy available to the Federal Reserve are summarized in Table 15.7. If the Federal Reserve wishes to expand the money supply, it can buy bonds, lower the discount rate, or lower the reserve ratio required against deposits, or it can use some combination of the three tools. If, instead, it wishes to contract the money supply, it would sell bonds, raise the discount rate, raise the reserve requirement, or use some combination of the three tools.

TABLE 15.7
Major Tools of Monetary Policy Available to the Federal Reserve

EXPANSIONARY MONETARY POLICY	CONTRACTIONARY MONETARY POLICY
Open-Market Operations	**Open-Market Operations**
Buy bonds	Sell bonds
Discount rate	**Discount Rate**
Lower discount rate	Increase discount rate
Reserve Requirements	**Reserve Requirements**
Lower reserve ratio	Increase reserve ratio
Results	**Results**
Increases reserves	Decreases reserves
Increases demand deposits	Decreases demand deposits
Increases money supply	Decreases money supply

MINOR FRB TOOLS The Federal Reserve employs these major tools — open-market operations, reserve requirements, and the discount rate — along with such minor tools as moral suasion, margin requirements, and credit controls. Moral suasion is the attempt by the FRB to persuade commercial banks voluntarily to follow a specific guideline or policy. The chairman of the Federal Reserve Board has sometimes attempted to convince the nation's bankers to follow voluntarily the FRB's lead and not be fully loaned up when the FRB is pursuing a contractionary monetary policy or not to hold excess reserves when the Fed is urging expansion.

The Federal Reserve can also employ selective credit controls to pursue its aims. The use of selective credit controls is designed to alter the allocation of credit rather than affect the overall volume of credit. The FRB also has the right to regulate credit to the securities markets by setting margin requirements for the purchases of stocks and bonds. Financial markets stand ready to finance an individual's purchases of stocks and bonds just as they will finance the purchase of homes and automobiles. When it sets margin requirements, the FRB determines the minimum amount of down payment that an investor must put up to purchase stocks and bonds on credit.

These minor tools are often employed by the FRB, but they are truly of minor importance compared with open-market operations, the main tool employed by the FRB in implementing monetary policy.

Thus far we have discussed the tools with which the Federal Reserve can implement the monetary policy of its choice. Now we turn to a discussion of how monetary policy is itself formulated.

HOW MONETARY POLICY IS SET

Setting monetary policy is the process by which the Board of Governors of the Federal Reserve decides how and to what end it will control the money supply. Setting monetary policy is a complicated and difficult task, although the ultimate goals of monetary policy are clear enough. These are to achieve a stable price level along with full employment and economic

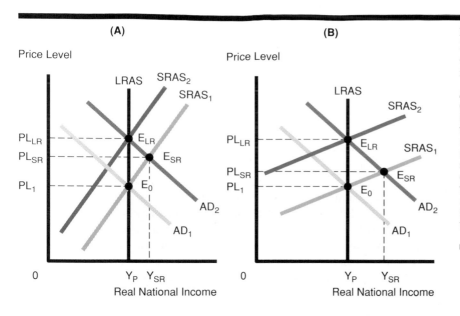

FIGURE 15.1

Effect of an Increase in the Money Supply on Real National Income and the Price Level in Both the Short and Long Run

An increase in the quantity of money will increase aggregate demand, which in turn will cause nominal national income to increase. This increase will be composed in the short run of an increase in both the price level and real national income. How much each increases is determined by the slope of the SRAS curve. In Part A SRAS₁ is steeper than SRAS₁ in Part B. In the short run the increase in real national income is less and the increase in the price level is more in Part A than in Part B. In the long run the effect is the same in both parts, because in the long run the automatic adjustment process ensures that the entire effect will be an increase in the price level.

growth at the rate at which potential national income is growing. These goals are called the **policy variables.**

> *Policy variables are the ultimate objectives of the Federal Reserve. They take the form of specific targets for the behavior of both real GNP and the price level.*

Setting a monetary policy that will achieve these goals is complicated by the inability of the FRB to directly control the policy variables.

What the Federal Reserve can control are the **policy instruments,** or targets, that affect the policy goals.

> *Policy instruments are economic variables that the Federal Reserve controls directly and that in turn affect the policy targets.*

The FRB is in the position of being able to control the money supply or the rate of interest, but not the real GNP or the price level.

The money supply and the interest rate act on aggregate demand, but how changes in aggregate demand in the short run affect real output and the price level is determined by the short-run aggregate supply (SRAS) curve, which is beyond Federal Reserve control. Consider Figure 15.1, which shows the effect that an increase in the money supply has on aggregate demand. In Parts A and B the economy is initially at full employment when an expansionary monetary policy results in an increase in aggregate demand from AD_1 to AD_2. The equilibrium position moves from E_0 to E_{SR}. The result in both cases is, in the short run, an increase in nominal GNP and the creation of an inflationary gap. The distribution of the increase between real national income and the price level is, however, different between the two panels. This difference is due to the differences between the slopes of the SRAS curve.

The flatter the SRAS curve (Part B), the greater will be the proportion of nominal GNP recorded as a short-run increase in real national income ($Y_{SR} - Y_P$) and the less will be the increase in the price level

FIGURE 15.2
Economic Growth Complicates the Problem
of Determining Monetary Policy

The level of potential national income is constantly growing. If the Federal Reserve is to maintain a stable price
level, it must constantly expand the money supply. The
rate of economic growth reflected in an increase in potential national income (Y_{P_1} increases to Y_{P_2}) probably
varies a great deal in the short run, but in the long run it
has been fairly stable, averaging between 2.5 and 3.0
percent a year.

Price Level

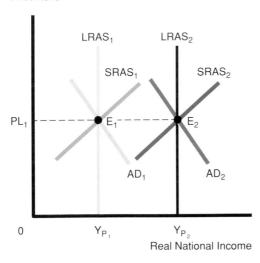

$(PL_{SR} - PL_1)$. Conversely, the steeper the SRAS curve (Part A), the greater will be the proportion of the resulting increase in nominal GNP that will occur as a rise in the price level and the less will be the increase in real GNP. Thus, given a similar increase in aggregate demand, the increase in real national income will be relatively greater in Part B and the increase in the price level relatively greater in Part A.

In the short run, then, the Federal Reserve cannot control how an increase in nominal national income brought about by an increase in the money supply will be distributed between changes in real output and changes in the price level.

In the long run there is no difference between Part A and Part B. The automatic adjustment process will cause the SRAS curve to decrease (shift to the left) to eliminate the inflationary gap. The equilibrium position in both parts will move from E_{SR} to E_{LR}. In the long run the shape of the SRAS curve no longer matters. In the long run the entire effect of an increase in the aggregate demand curve will be reflected in an increase in the price level. This implies that monetary policy designed to affect the economy in the short run will have inevitable long-term effects on the price level.

The Federal Reserve's policy-making is further complicated by the process of economic growth. In the macroeconomic real world the potential level of real national income is constantly changing. The FRB is always trying to hit a moving target. This problem is diagramed in Figure 15.2.

In the figure the long-run aggregate supply (LRAS) curve is initially $LRAS_1$, the economy is operating in both short-run and long-run equilibrium, and aggregate demand is represented by AD_1 and short-run aggregate supply by $SRAS_1$. Over time the process of economic growth will cause both the SRAS and LRAS curves to shift to $SRAS_2$ and $LRAS_2$. If the Federal Reserve wishes to maintain full employment and a stable price level, it must increase the money supply by enough to ensure that the aggregate demand curve shifts from AD_1 to AD_2, so that the equilibrium position will move smoothly from E_1 to E_2.

Successfully conducting monetary policy is also complicated by policy goals being affected by variables other than the money supply. Nonmonetary demand and supply shocks do periodically occur, and these will affect both the level of real GNP and the price level.

The task of setting targets for the policy variables is further complicated by the fact that current information about the policy variables is available only after the fact. Information about the price level is available only a month after the fact in the case of the consumer and producer price indices, but it is available only quarterly in the case of the GNP deflator. Estimates of nominal and real GNP appear quarterly and in a more reliable form fully six months later.

Monetary policy must therefore be determined on the basis of imperfect information about the policy targets. The lags involved in obtaining accurate information about policy variables forces the Federal Reserve to rely on **intermediate policy targets.**

An intermediate policy target is a variable that serves as a guide to the Federal Reserve's policy goals and that also is closely related to the policy variables and is available on a timely basis.

The two most frequently used intermediate targets are the interest rate and some measure of the money supply.

INSTRUMENTS OF MONETARY POLICY

What instruments does the Federal Reserve control that can affect the policy variables? The Federal Reserve can control the quantity of reserves in the banking system, in effect controlling the **monetary base,** and it can influence the money multiplier by setting legal reserve requirements.

> *The monetary base is the quantity of reserves in the banking system and the quantity of cash held by the nonbank public; it is sometimes referred to as* high-powered money.

It is on the monetary base that the money multiplier operates to create the money supply. You will recall from Chapter 14 that the money multiplier, though related, is not the same as the deposit expansion multiplier. Since the money multiplier can be calculated by the Federal Reserve, the ability to control the monetary base gives the FRB effective control of the money supply or aggregates.

Control over the money supply also provides the Federal Reserve with the means to control the rate of interest. But it cannot do both. The FRB must choose either to control the money supply or to control the interest rate. It does not have enough instruments to do both. If the FRB decides to control the money supply, it must accept the interest rate that the existing money demand function will determine. If, instead, it decides to control the interest rate, it must supply the appropriate quantity of money demanded by the liquidity preference function.

The nature of this choice is evident in Figure 15.3. Given the demand for money (D_M), the Federal Reserve can determine the interest rate (r) by supplying the appropriate quantity of money (Q_M), or the Federal Reserve can determine the quantity of money (Q_M) and accept the resulting interest rate (r). The interest rate is the product of two variables — the demand for money and the supply of money. The Federal Reserve controls only the supply of money, and therefore it must choose one or the other.

What difference does it make whether the Federal Reserve opts to control the interest rate or the money supply? It actually makes a substantial difference — in both theory and practice.

DIFFERENCE IN THEORY In Chapter 13 you learned of two contending monetary theories of the demand for money: the Keynesian and the monetarist theories. To refresh your memory, the basic elements of the two theories are presented in Table 15.8. In the Keynesian theory, the quantity of money together with the demand for money (the liquidity preference schedule) determines the interest rate, which in turn influences the quantity of investment spending, causing changes in nominal national income. The Federal Reserve controls only one of the variables in the Keynesian transmission mechanism — the money supply. Keynesian economists, because their postulated transmission mechanism operates through the interest rate, tend to support the use of the interest rate as the proper intermediate target.

Keynesians would argue that the Federal Reserve should determine the interest rate that is consistent with its goals for the policy variables and stick to it. Suppose the demand for money in Figure 15.3 increases from D_M to D'_M when the targeted rate of interest is r. Keynesians would

FIGURE 15.3

FIGURE 15.3
Demand for Money Together with the Supply of Money Determines the Interest Rate

The Federal Reserve can determine either the quantity of money or the interest rate, but it cannot do both. The rate of interest is jointly determined by the demand for money, D_M, and the supply of money, S_M. The point where the quantity of money supplied by the Federal Reserve intersects the demand for money determines the rate of interest. The Federal Reserve does not control the demand for money and thus must choose either to determine the rate of interest by supplying the quantity of money required, or to determine the quantity of money and allow the demand for money to determine the interest rate.

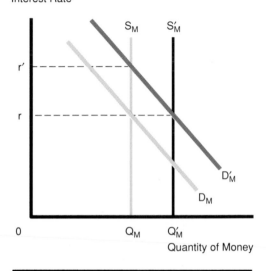

Interest Rate

TABLE 15.8
Summary of the Keynesian and Monetarist Theories of the Demand for Money

	KEYNESIAN	MONETARIST
Demand for Money	Demand for money volatile; depends on transactions, precautionary motive, and speculative motive	Demand for money stable; a function of nominal GNP, interest rates, and expected inflation rate
Interest Rate and Investment	Function of the interest rate but is unresponsive to changes	Function of the interest rate and is responsive to changes
Transmission Mechanism	Indirect; a change in money supply affects interest rates, investment, and, through the expenditure multiplier, nominal income	Direct; a change in money supply is transmitted directly to both investment and consumption and, through expenditure multiplier, to nominal national income
Velocity	Volatile	Stable

hold that the FRB should increase the money supply to Q'_M to maintain the appropriate rate of interest that would maintain the level of investment spending necessary to meet the ultimate goals.

The alternative monetarist theory derives from the modern quantity equation and postulates a broader transmission mechanism based on the equation of exchange. Changes in the quantity of money directly affect aggregate demand, because velocity behaves in predictable ways and spending will change for all goods. The monetarists thus believe that the proper intermediate target is the supply of money itself. The Federal Reserve should determine the supply of money consistent with the policy goals. If the demand for money increases from D_M to D'_M, as shown in Figure 15.3, monetarists would argue that the money supply should be held constant and the interest rate allowed to increase to r'.

The Federal Reserve Board must choose either to control the money supply and let the demand for money determine the interest rate, or to control the interest rate and supply the required amount of money. The former is called **interest rate control** and the latter **monetary base control.**

> *Interest rate control is the determination of the interest rate by the Federal Reserve, in which it supplies the quantity of money required by the money demand curve to establish the target rate of interest.*

> *Monetary base control is the Federal Reserve's regulation of the quantity of money while allowing the money market to determine the rate of interest.*

The two approaches can lead to very different results. There has been a great deal of controversy over which of the two is the proper choice.

DIFFERENCE IN PRACTICE Keynesians support the use of monetary policy (as well as fiscal policy) to smooth out the business cycle. This is known as a **countercyclical monetary policy.**

> *Countercyclical monetary policy acts to increase aggregate demand when aggregate output falls below the level of potential national income, and acts to reduce aggregate demand when aggregate output exceeds the level of potential national income.*

The opposite type of policy is a **procyclical monetary policy.**

> *A procyclical monetary policy increases aggregate demand when aggregate output exceeds the level of potential national income, and decreases aggregate demand when output falls below the level of potential national income.*

No economist, politician, or economic decision maker would advocate a procyclical monetary policy. Nor do all economists advocate a countercyclical monetary policy, not because they do not subscribe to the goal, but rather because they do not believe it is feasible.

If the Federal Reserve followed a countercyclical monetary policy, it would increase the rate of growth of the money supply whenever a recessionary gap appeared, and it would decrease the rate of growth of the money supply whenever an inflationary gap was being experienced.

However, there is evidence that the Federal Reserve in the past has actually done the opposite and has followed a procyclical monetary policy. Suppose we rewrite the quantity equation to isolate real GNP:

$$\frac{M \times V}{P} = Q$$

M2 velocity has been almost constant over time and therefore will not affect the equation. M/P thus provides a measure of the real money supply. How has the real money supply been related to real GNP over time?

A countercyclical monetary policy, if it has been followed, would reveal that the real M2 money supply increases during recessions. From Figure 15.4, where the real money supply for the years 1959–1987 is charted and the periods of recession are indicated, it does not appear that a countercyclical monetary policy has been pursued by the Federal Reserve. Instead, the picture that emerges is more consistent with a procyclical monetary policy. Note that the real money supply began to decline prior to each recession and generally continued to decline at least part of the way through the recession.

How could this happen? Monetarists believe that it can be explained as one of the implications of employing the interest rate as the intermediate target and of basing monetary policy on control of the interest rate.

HISTORICAL EXPERIENCE WITH INTEREST RATE CONTROL

Suppose that the Federal Reserve Board has decided to select interest rates as the intermediate target of monetary policy. Setting interest rates would work if the monetary authorities knew the interest rate that was consistent with the level of potential national income and could identify

FIGURE 15.4
Real Quantity of Money and Periods of
Recession: 1959–1987

Periods of recession are included on this chart. Declines
in the real quantity of money, calculated as M2 divided by
the price level, seem to lead to the advent of recession. If
you look closely it appears that the real quantity of money
begins to decline about a year prior to the onset of a
recession and often doesn't begin to increase again until
well into the recession. This suggests that monetary policy has often been procyclical rather than countercyclical.

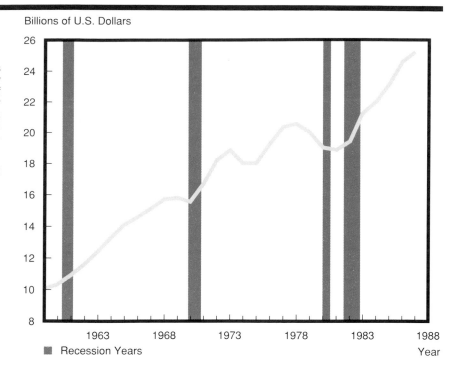

Billions of U.S. Dollars

■ Recession Years

Year

when this interest rate changed. But this is extremely difficult, if not
impossible, to do, given the state of economic knowledge.

The rate of interest that the Federal Reserve should target is the **real
interest rate** that will generate the level of investment consistent with
achieving potential national income. But the interest rate that is observed
everyday in financial markets is the **nominal interest rate.** This is also the
interest rate that the monetary authorities can affect. To obtain the real
interest rate, the expected rate of inflation must be subtracted from the
nominal interest rate.

> *The real interest rate is the nominal interest rate less the
> amount of expected inflation.*

> *The nominal interest rate is the observed market rate of in-
> terest and is composed of the real rate of interest plus a pre-
> mium to account for the expected rate of inflation.*

But nobody knows, not even the Federal Reserve, the expected rate of
inflation at any point in time. Suppose, instead, that the Federal Reserve
decided to maintain stable interest rates. This policy, since it is consistent
with its mandate to maintain orderly credit markets, is obviously an attractive one to the governors of the Federal Reserve.

Now suppose a period of rapid economic growth begins. When this
happens, the demand for credit will increase and the demand curve for
money will shift. To maintain stable interest rates, the Federal Reserve
will have to allow the money supply to expand. The increase in the quantity of money, according to the monetarist transmission mechanism, will
further fuel the boom and increase the demand for money still more. The
monetary authorities will have to increase the money supply still more to
hold down nominal interest rates.

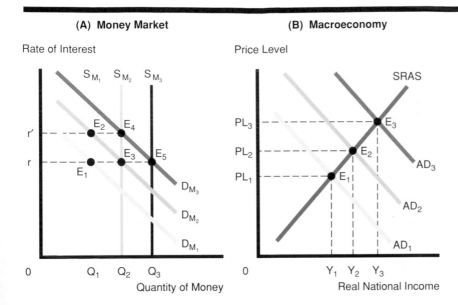

(A) Money Market

Rate of Interest

S_{M_1} S_{M_2} S_{M_3}

r'

r

E_2 E_4

E_3 E_5

E_1

D_{M_3}

D_{M_2}

D_{M_1}

0 Q_1 Q_2 Q_3

Quantity of Money

(B) Macroeconomy

Price Level

SRAS

PL_3 E_3

PL_2 E_2

PL_1 E_1

AD_3

AD_2

AD_1

0 Y_1 Y_2 Y_3

Real National Income

FIGURE 15.5
Possible Effect of Attempts to Control the
Rate of Interest

In this figure assume that the Federal Reserve has decided to maintain the rate of interest at r. In Part A the money market is initially in equilibrium at point E_1, and the macroeconomy is in equilibrium at E_1 in Part B. In Part B an autonomous increase in aggregate demand shifts the aggregate demand curve to the right, causing real national income and the price level to increase. These increases feed back to the money market, causing an increase in the demand for money and in the interest rate. To keep the interest rate from increasing, the money supply must increase. This increase in the money supply will shift the equilibrium in the money market. The increase in the money supply will itself cause aggregate demand to increase again, and the cycle repeats. Once in motion, the attempt to maintain a given rate of interest will result in a procyclical monetary policy.

Consider Figure 15.5, where both the money market (Part A) and the macroeconomy (Part B) are depicted. The Federal Reserve has decided to control interest rates by supplying the quantity of money required to maintain the nominal rate of interest at r. Initially, this is accomplished by supplying Q_1 money in Part A. In Part B the macroeconomy is in equilibrium at E_1, with aggregate demand AD_1 and short-run aggregate supply SRAS. Now suppose that an autonomous increase in aggregate demand occurs, shifting the aggregate demand curve from AD_1 to AD_2. Both real national income and the price level increase.

The increase in nominal national income will feed back to the money market in Part A, causing the demand for money to increase from D_{M_1} to D_{M_2}. Interest rates will increase from the targeted rate r to r' as equilibrium moves to E_2. To maintain the targeted interest rate, the Federal Reserve must increase the money supply to Q_2.

The increase in the money supply will in turn cause another increase in aggregate demand in Part B from AD_2 to AD_3. Both the price level and real national income will increase again. This will feed back to the money market and cause the demand for money to increase to D_{M_3}. The Federal Reserve will have to increase the money supply to Q_3 in order to maintain the targeted rate of interest, and the process will continue, with the price level rising with each increase in the money supply.

If inflation is to be controlled, the Federal Reserve must abandon its target interest rate and allow the interest rate to rise. Thus an interest rate target, if an unexpected increase in aggregate demand occurs, will have the effect of reinforcing the increase by generating increases in the money supply and causing aggregate demand to expand continuously and the price level to increase.

The opposite will happen if the economy slips into recession. When this happens, the demand for money will decline and interest rates will tend to fall. To maintain stable interest rates in the face of a declining demand for money, the Federal Reserve will have to reduce the quantity of money. Operating through a decline in aggregate demand, the reduction in the quantity of money will itself reduce nominal national income, causing interest rates to decline further. To support the targeted level of interest rates, the money supply will have to decline even more. Thus if

FIGURE 15.6
The Keynes and Fisher Effects

In Part A the growth rate of the money supply and the rate of interest on U.S. Treasury bills are charted. The Keynes effect suggests that an increase in the growth rate of the money supply will cause nominal interest rates, like the Treasury bill rate, to decline, because the real rate of interest will decline. In Part B, which shows the Fisher effect, the rate of interest on U.S. Treasury bills is plotted along with the rate of inflation measured by the change in the consumer price index. The Fisher effect indicates that when inflationary expectations increase, so will the nominal rate of interest, because the inflation premium will rise. This suggests that the nominal rate of interest should rise and fall with the rate of inflation — and it does.

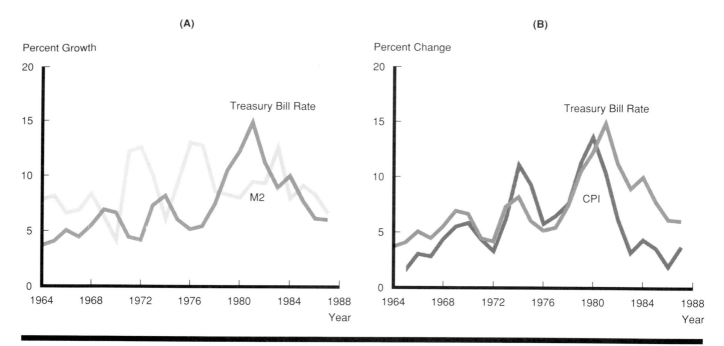

the Federal Reserve set a targeted level for interest rates and did not change the target as the macroeconomy changes, it could fall into a procyclical monetary policy.

If the Federal Reserve follows a monetary policy of rigidly targeting interest rates, economic expansions will be longer and more vigorous and more inflationary, and economic contractions will be sharper and deeper. This happened during the 1970s when the rate of inflation got out of hand, punctuated by two very severe recessions.

In Part A of Figure 15.6 the growth rate of the M2 money supply is graphed along with the rate of interest on U.S. Treasury bills. You can see that there is an inverse relationship between the growth of the money supply and the rate of interest. Each peak in the rate of growth of the money supply corresponds to a valley in the rate of interest, and each valley in the rate of increase in the money supply corresponds to a peak in the rate of interest. This relationship is sometimes known as the **Keynes effect.**

> *The Keynes effect is the prediction that interest rates will decline following an expansion of the growth rate of the money supply and that they will rise following a contraction of the growth rate of the money supply.*

Notice that each succeeding peak in the interest rate is higher than the one that preceded it. The effect of an expansionary monetary policy will be to cause the price level to rise and with it the inflation premium contained in nominal interest rates. This can be seen in Part B of Figure

TABLE 15.9
Announced and Actual Federal Reserve Growth Targets for M1 and M2
(Annual Percentages)

TIME PERIOD	TARGETED RANGE FOR M1	ACTUAL M1 GROWTH	TARGETED RANGE FOR M2	ACTUAL M2 GROWTH
1977–1978	4.0–6.5%	7.3%	6.5–9.0%	8.0%
1978–1979	1.5–4.5	5.5	5.0–8.0	7.8
1979–1980	3.5–6.0	6.7	6.0–9.0	8.9
1980–1981	3.0–5.5	5.1	5.5–8.5	9.9
1981–1982	2.5–5.5	8.5	6.0–9.0	9.0
1982–1983	4.0–8.0	10.4	7.0–10.0	12.2
1983–1984	4.0–8.0	5.8	6.0–9.0	8.0
1984–1985	4.0–7.0	11.9	6.0–9.0	8.7
1985–1986	3.0–8.0	15.6	6.0–9.0	9.4
1986–1987	3.0–8.0	6.3	5.5–8.5	4.0
1987–1988	—	5.3	4.0–8.0	7.1

Source: *Federal Reserve Bulletin*, various issues.

15.6, where the Treasury bill rate and the rate of inflation as measured by the percentage change in the consumer price index are plotted. You will notice the close relationship between the two variables. When the rate of inflation increases, so does the rate of interest, and when the rate of inflation abates, the rate of interest falls. This relationship is known as the **Fisher effect**; it was first discovered by economist Irving Fisher, a leading early quantity theorist.

> *The Fisher effect is the prediction that nominal interest rates will adjust in proportion to the change in the rate of inflation.*

When the Federal Reserve attempted in the 1970s to target the interest rate, it was forced to more or less continually increase the rate of growth of the money supply in order to counter the Fisher effect. The result was a cyclically increasing inflation rate. At least, this was the view of the former chairman of the Board of Governors, Paul Volcker, who in 1979 convinced the Board to adopt a monetary policy based on targeting the growth of the money supply rather than interest rates.

HISTORICAL EXPERIENCE WITH MONETARY GROWTH TARGETS

In October 1979 the Federal Reserve decided to abandon targeting interest rates and to target the money supply instead. Inflation was at the time approaching double-digit levels, and the new chairman of the Board of Governors argued that a policy change was needed in order to control inflation. The FRB had set targets for the various monetary aggregates since 1977, but it had not succeeded (see Table 15.9) in meeting the M1 target, then widely considered the best definition of money. After the October decision the Federal Reserve decided to consider primarily the monetary aggregates and to reduce interest rate targeting to secondary status. The Federal Reserve announced gradually reduced targets for the money supply for the years 1979–1980 to 1981–1982.

. . . .
A P P L I C A T I O N

15.1

THE FISHER EFFECT IN
ACTION

In 1981 a newly elected U.S. senator, who had become a member of the Senate Banking Committee, was invited to breakfast by the then chairman of the Federal Reserve Board, Paul Volcker. The senator took his economics advisor along to the meeting. In 1981 the main economic issues were inflation and sky-high interest rates. The rate of inflation was over 10 percent, short-term rates of interest were over 15 percent, and long-term rates were at double-digit levels. Both real and nominal interest rates were at historical highs. Small businesses were suffering, and the nation's housing market was depressed. Forest products are a major industry in the senator's home state. If new homes are not being built, lumber cannot be sold. High interest rates in 1981 had effectively shut down the forest products industry.

Breakfast was served in the Federal Reserve Board's dining room, which has a beautiful view of the flight path to Washington National Airport. After breakfast the senator raised the issue of soaring interest rates. He stated that "Interest rates are higher than that jet," pointing to a landing aircraft, "can fly!" He pressed the Board chairman to lower them immediately. Paul Volcker, sitting in front of the view with a big cigar in hand, told the senator that he agreed with him — interest rates were too high. He then turned the question back on the senator, asking him what he would do if he were chairman of the Federal Reserve Board. The senator promptly replied, "Increase the rate of growth of the money supply," because that was what his constituents had asked him to press for. An increase in the money supply, he proposed, would cause interest rates to decline.

FIGURE 15.7
The Fisher Effect in Action

The rate of interest, the rate of inflation, and the rate of increase in the money supply for the years 1980–1983 are graphed in this figure. The measured rate of inflation generally declined throughout the period, while the rate of interest both rose and fell. The rate of interest rose whenever the rate of growth of the money supply increased. Investors, with the recent past inflation of the 1970s fresh in their minds, were quick to interpret any increase in the money supply as foretelling the return of higher inflation. This happened despite the falling rate of inflation. When the Federal Reserve kept constant the growth rate of the money supply, the rate of interest generally declined, along with the rate of inflation, as inflationary expectations declined. During this period the Fisher effect dominated the Keynes effect.

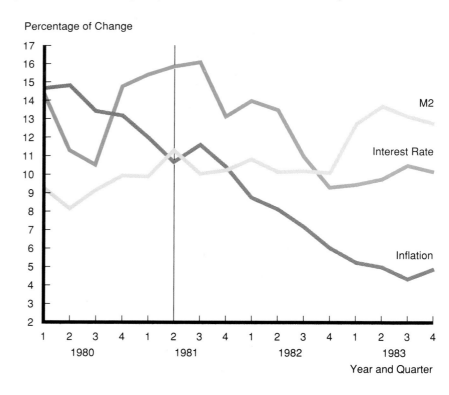

Volcker replied that he realized monetary policy had been tight. The high real rate of interest told him that. As for increasing the rate of growth of the money supply, he had been trying that for a year and it had not worked. The rate of growth of M2 had increased from 7 percent to over 10 percent during 1980, and the result had been that interest rates had shot up from 10 percent to 15 percent. They had not fallen as the senator suggested they would do. He did not expect that further easing of monetary policy would work any better.

The senator was taken aback. He had been elected to help his constituents, and they wanted lower interest rates. Now he wasn't sure what should be done. "Perhaps, then, you should reduce the rate of growth of the money supply?" the Senator said less than forcefully. "Or hold it steady," Volcker replied, rubbing out his cigar on the Federal Reserve's china breakfast plate. "Well, you have to do something! You're the chairman, not me," the senator pressured. The senator was an elected official who felt that his job, as well as the jobs of many of his constituents,

A change in the growth rate of the money supply will affect real GNP and the price level only after a time lag. The first effect is the short-run effect on real GNP. The result of the tight monetary policy of 1979–1981 was a severe recession, followed by a slowing of the rate of inflation.

FIGURE 15.8
The Fisher Effect

Ordinarily an increase in the quantity of money from Q_1 to Q_2 could be expected to lower interest rates in Part A from r to r'. But during the early 1980s when inflation fears were present, an increase in the money supply caused economic decision makers to expect that aggregate demand would increase. This expected increase is shown by the shift of aggregate demand in Part B from AD_1 to AD_E. In anticipation of this shift, the demand for money increased from D_{M_1} to D_{M_2} in Part A and thereby actually increased interest rates. So instead of falling to r', interest rates increased to r".

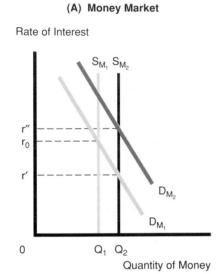

(A) Money Market

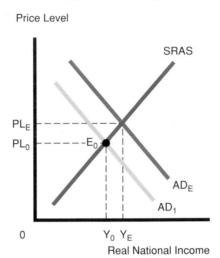

(B) Macroeconomy

depended on reducing interest rates to more normal levels. He wanted action. Volcker's job did not directly depend on public opinion. He was appointed. He also wanted lower interest rates, but he was in the position to take a longer view. He had tried increasing the money supply; now he was prepared to do something different.

Volcker was betting that the Fisher effect would eventually lower nominal interest rates. He knew that the rate of inflation was falling dramatically and that eventually the inflation premium that lenders demanded also had to decline. When this happened, nominal interest rates would fall. The changes in the growth rate of the money supply, along with the rate of interest and the inflation rate for the period under discussion, are shown in Figure 15.7. The above conversation took place during the second quarter of 1981, as indicated by the vertical line. You can see that

interest rates were near their peak at the time. If you trace the rate of growth of the money supply back one year from the second quarter of 1981, you will see that Volcker was right: The money supply had been growing. Now look at the path of interest rates over the same year and you will see that interest rates also rose significantly. In the meantime the inflation rate had been declining. But the decline in actual inflation was insufficient to overcome the inflation expectations that a further increase in the growth rate of the money supply stimulated.

After the conversation between the senator and Chairman Volcker took place, the Federal Reserve more or less held the growth rate of the money supply constant for six quarters. During this time span the inflation rate continued to fall. Moreover, so did nominal interest rates as inflationary expectations adjusted downward, reducing the inflation pre-

mium in nominal interest rates. The real interest rate, however, remained high, reflecting the continued tight monetary policy of the Federal Reserve. Suppose the Federal Reserve had taken the senator's initial advice and increased the rate of growth of the money supply. What would have happened? Look at what happened during the fourth quarter of 1982. During that quarter the Federal Reserve once again increased the growth rate of the money supply — this time to combat a recession that had developed. Note that the effect on interest rates was the opposite of what the Keynes effect would predict. Interest rates did not fall, but once again began to rise. The Fisher effect was still dominant as the memory of the previous inflation remained fresh in the minds of investors.

Figure 15.8 shows how the Fisher effect works. In Part A the money market is shown with a money supply of S_{M_1} and a money demand of D_{M_1}. The resulting nominal interest rate is r_0. This quantity of money and rate of interest correspond to the macroeconomy, shown in Part B, in equilibrium at E_0 with aggregate demand equal to AD_1 and short-run aggregate supply of SRAS. Initially, real national income is equal to Y_0 and the price level is equal to PL_0.

With a period of high inflation and high interest rates fresh in the minds of economic decision makers, the Federal Reserve increases the money supply to Q_2 as the money supply curve shifts to S_{M_2}. The public reacts by expecting aggregate demand to increase from AD_1 to AD_E. Such a shift would cause both real national income and the price level to increase in the short run, which in turn would increase the demand for money. The demand for money (Part A) increases in anticipation of these occurrences. The demand for money increases to D_{M_2} and the rate of interest increases instead of decreases.

Inflationary expectations — the Fisher effect — can overcome the Keynes effect, resulting in a rise in the nominal rate of interest instead of a decline when the money supply increases. Thus the answer to the question Paul Volcker asked the senator, "How would you lower interest rates?" would depend on which influence is stronger at the time — the Fisher effect or the Keynes effect.

In setting its targets for 1979–1981, the Federal Reserve had obviously underestimated the demand for money. The demand for money, you will recall, is a function of the level of real GNP, the price level, and expected future rates of inflation. It is possible that the reason for the increase in the demand for money (a decline in velocity) was the significant decline in inflationary expectations that occurred when the Federal Reserve announced its change in intermediate targets. Meeting the announced targets meant a monetary policy too tight to support full employment. The result was a severe recession prior to the subsequent significant decline in inflation.

The recession caused the Federal Reserve to abandon its experiment with monetary targeting. The unemployment rate in 1982 increased to 9.5 percent while the inflation rate fell to 6.4 percent. To combat the recession, the Federal Reserve abandoned its M1 target and allowed the money supply to grow by 8.5 percent. It also subsequently abandoned its 1982–1983 target, as the unemployment rate remained high, and allowed the money supply to grow by 10.4 percent.

The Federal Reserve, as Table 15.9 shows, was unable or unwilling to meet its target for M1 most of the time, but it was more successful in hitting its target for M2. Part of the explanation is probably the change in the nature of commercial bank deposit accounts (the innovation of NOW accounts, discussed in previous chapters) that occurred during these years, but part is the unexpected shift in the demand function for money.

The velocity of money, after rising at an average annual rate of 3 percent over the period following World War II, suddenly began to decline in 1981 and continued to do so through 1986. In Table 15.9 the years 1984–1985 and 1985–1986 show that the Federal Reserve missed its announced target for M1 by a mile while at the same time achieving its target for M2. Normally, such a large overshoot would raise the risk of high future inflation rates, but, as the Federal Reserve explained in its 1986 *Monetary Policy Report* to Congress, it permitted the overshoot because of the substantial decline in M1 velocity of circulation. Even though M1 increased by nearly 12 percent in 1984–1985, nominal national income increased by only 5.5 percent. Thus M1 velocity had to decline by 6.5 percent. During 1985–1986 M1 increased by over 15 percent to accommodate the further decline in velocity to 9.5 percent. M1 money demand did not behave as predicted by the modern quantity theory.

In the 1987 Federal Reserve report to Congress, it was announced that M1 targeting had been abandoned and that only targets for M2 and M3 would be declared. The relationship between M1 and nominal GNP had become, in the opinion of the monetary authorities, so erratic as to be misleading.

So what is the Federal Reserve doing now? It had tried interest rate targeting and had gotten into trouble. Its brief experiment with monetarism had not solved the problem of finding a suitable intermediate target. Currently, the monetary policy of the country is not wedded to a single theory. Monetary policy is developed by consensus: It is what the members of the Board of Governors agree it will be. In various announcements and speeches by individual governors, there have been hints that the FRB is using a number of indicators as intermediate targets: nominal national income, interest rates, commodity prices, the international value of the dollar, the spread between long-term and short-term interest rates, and the much publicized P-star (see Preview 15.2 Analysis at the end of the chapter).

HOW EFFECTIVE IS
MONETARY POLICY?

How much should we reasonably expect from monetary policy? Because of the difficulty of obtaining current information about the state of the economy and, as we shall show below, because of the existence of lags between a change in the money supply and its impact on the macroeconomy, the Federal Reserve is forced to employ intermediate targets. You have just discovered that no single intermediate target — neither the interest rate nor the quantity of money — has proved suitable or at least acceptable to the Board of Governors.

Furthermore, even if the Federal Reserve could overcome these problems, its actual control of the money supply is not exact. The Federal Reserve can supply additional reserves to the banking system, but it cannot force the banks to lend out these reserves. Nor does it have any power to force business firms to borrow to invest, or households to spend any additional amounts of money they may receive. The link between changes in the quantity of money and short-run changes in aggregate demand may at times be tenuous. Even if the Federal Reserve succeeds in affecting aggregate demand, it does not control aggregate supply and thus has no control in the short run over how an increase in nominal national income will be distributed between changes in aggregate output and the price level.

Given these difficulties, is it still possible that an activist monetary policy could be countercyclical? Only if monetary policy can correct an inflationary or deflationary gap before the automatic adjustment mechanism would solve the problem. This requires that the Federal Reserve be able to recognize the existence of an inflationary or a deflationary gap, decide to act, and have the effects of the change in the money supply on the macroeconomy occur before the automatic adjustment mechanism would solve the problem. Is it reasonable to expect the FRB to be able to do all this?

The answer to this big question depends on two lags that also affect fiscal policy: the recognition and the effectiveness lags. The **recognition lag** refers to the time required for the Federal Reserve to acknowledge the presence of an inflationary or a recessionary gap and to do something about it.

The recognition lag is the time it takes the Federal Reserve to recognize the existence of an inflationary or a recessionary gap and to change the supply of money in an appropriate way.

The FRB cannot be certain about the current state of the economy. Accurate GNP statistics are at least six months old before they are available, and unemployment and price-level statistics, though available quicker, are still a month or so behind the times. In order to know if there is a recessionary or an inflationary gap developing, the FRB also needs to know the level of potential national income and the natural rate of unemployment, neither of which can be ascertained for sure. Just as one swallow does not make a spring, one month's or one quarter's economic statistics do not reveal the existence of either an inflationary or deflationary gap.

Once the Federal Reserve has identified the need for a different monetary policy, a further period of time is necessary for the policy to be implemented and for it to affect the macroeconomy. This period of time is known as the **effectiveness lag**.

The effectiveness lag is the time required for a change in monetary policy to affect the macroeconomy.

It takes time for a change in the level of reserves to affect the money supply, and it takes still more time for its impact to be felt on the overall economy.

How long will all of this take? The two schools of monetary theory hold different views on the duration of these lags. One estimate of the recognition lag is as short as 4 months, and the estimates of the effectiveness lag for monetary policy run from 5 to 10 months, for a range of 9 to 14 months. Another estimate of the effectiveness lag alone is between 6 months and 2 years. If countercyclical monetary policy is to be effective, then, the recognition and effectiveness lags must take less time than the automatic adjustment process.

KEYNESIAN POSITION

Generally, Keynesians believe the time involved in the lags is less than the time it would take the automatic adjustment process to work, whereas monetarists believe the opposite. Even the shortest of the lag estimates involve a significant amount of time. As a result, few economists believe that the Federal Reserve should try to use monetary policy to fine-tune the economy. Many economists of the Keynesian persuasion believe that there are two roles for activist monetary policy. The first would be to affect the composition of GNP in the short run. Changes in the rate of interest will change the amount of investment spending and therefore the makeup of real GNP in the short run. Keynesians argue that monetary policy can affect the long-run aggregate supply curve by encouraging investment spending, which adds to the nation's capital stock. The second role would be for monetary policy to help correct significant inflationary or recessionary gaps.

MONETARIST POSITION

If the lags involved in monetary policy are lengthy and variable, it is, according to monetarists, asking too much to expect the Board of Governors to conduct a countercyclical monetary policy. Owing to the self-correcting mechanism, economic conditions will have changed before the impact of a monetary policy change will be felt. This is another reason, besides the defects inherent in targeting interest rates, that monetary policy historically appears to have been procyclical in effect. The inevitable lags involved in monetary policy, according to the monetarists, will always make monetary policy procyclical.

Instead, monetarists propose, the Federal Reserve should follow a **constant-growth rule** for determining the growth rate of the money supply.

> *The constant-growth rule for the money supply is the principle that monetary policy should be limited to providing each year a fixed percentage increase in the money supply.*

Monetarists argue that the monetary policy of the Federal Reserve should be confined to steadily increasing the money supply at some constant rate. Generally, the rate they propose is 3 percent, since this approximates the historical growth rate of real GNP. Increasing the money supply at this rate would cause the aggregate demand curve to shift out in tune with the average shifts in the aggregate supply curves (refer to Figure 15.2).

If a constant-growth rule were implemented, it would remove the procyclical bias in monetary policy as well as a potential source of uncertainty and instability in the macroeconomy. Moreover, the Federal Reserve, which the monetarists believe has historically failed to conduct a countercyclical monetary policy, could easily accomplish this simple task.

A constant-growth rule would eliminate the problems of both the recognition lag and the effectiveness lag. The recognition lag would be eliminated because the Federal Reserve would not have the responsibility for conducting a countercyclical monetary policy. The effectiveness lag would be eliminated because all economic decision makers could accurately anticipate the effect of a constant increase in the money supply on future economic activity.

Monetarists do not consider the 1979–1982 targeting of the money supply as a test of their theory. They believe that the Federal Reserve should follow a constant-growth rule. This did not happen between 1979 and 1982, as a glance back at Table 15.9 will confirm. The rate of growth of the money supply continued to exhibit swings as wide as had occurred in previous and subsequent years. The debate between monetarists and their Keynesian colleagues is not over.

So what can we say about the effectiveness of monetary policy? The experiences of the economy during the 1970s and 1980s have served to narrow the gap between the economic schools. There is now general agreement that the Federal Reserve's monetary policy does affect the level of real GNP as well as the price level in the short run, but that it affects only the price level in the long run. Many economists also believe that the Federal Reserve has less than absolute control over the money supply, that it certainly does not exert absolute control over aggregate demand, and that it has little control over the aggregate supply curves. Furthermore, monetary policy does suffer from both recognition and effectiveness lags.

There is less than general agreement over which intermediate targets should be employed by the Federal Reserve and over what the agreed-upon limitations on monetary policy mean for the conduct of a countercyclical monetary policy. Activist economists still see a role for the Federal Reserve in offsetting major deviations from full employment and in fighting inflation, but they do not generally believe that the Federal Reserve should try to fine-tune the economy. Monetarists, on the other hand, see an active monetary policy as inevitably procyclical in nature and still advocate tying monetary policy to a constant-growth rule.

So far the Federal Reserve Board has resisted the monetarists' suggestion that the Board limit its responsibility for setting monetary policy to providing a constant rate of increase in the money supply. Instead, each succeeding generation of central bankers has engaged in discretionary monetary policy. This, then, leads to the question of the appropriate relationship between monetary policy and fiscal policy.

RELATIONSHIP BETWEEN MONETARY AND FISCAL POLICY

In Chapter 12 we considered the effects of fiscal policy. An increase in government expenditures or a reduction in taxes had the effect of increasing aggregate demand. The extent of the increase in aggregate demand depended on the amount of crowding out of private-sector expenditures by an expansionary fiscal policy. We can now return to this topic and see how a fiscal-policy-induced expansion of aggregate demand will affect interest rates and the quantity of investment.

CROWDING-OUT HYPOTHESIS

Crowding out occurs when government expenditures replace private-sector expenditures. Investment is thought to be the sector of the economy

FIGURE 15.9
Crowding Out and the Nonneutrality of Fiscal Policy

Fiscal policy is not neutral with respect to the composition of GNP. Crowding out of investment by fiscal policy occurs as a result of a rise in the rate of interest, which in turn is caused by an increase in aggregate demand due to an expansionary fiscal policy.

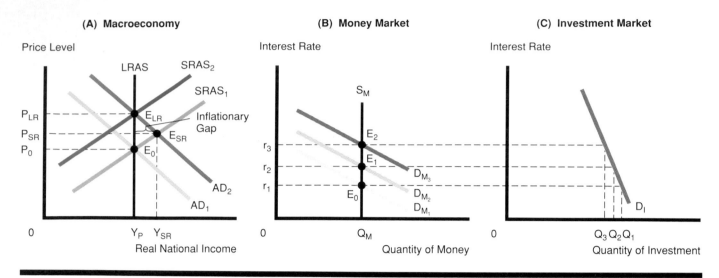

most susceptible to crowding out, but all areas of the private sector are probably susceptible to some extent. The crowding out of investment occurs because an increase in aggregate demand increases the demand for money, causing interest rates to rise and the quantity of investment to decline.

Consider Figure 15.9. In Part A, starting with a closed economy (no international trade) at full employment, an expansionary fiscal policy has increased aggregate demand, causing the aggregate demand curve to shift from AD_1 to AD_2. Such a situation existed in 1988–1989 when the federal government was pursuing an expansionary fiscal policy while the economy was near full employment. Equilibrium in the short run will shift from E_0 to E_{SR}, causing an increase in both the price level (from PL_0 to PL_{SR}) and real national income (from Y_P to Y_{SR}). As a result of the increase in the price level and real output, the demand for money will increase in Part B, shifting from D_{M_1} to D_{M_2}. Since the money supply is assumed not to change, interest rates must increase from r_1 to r_2, which in turn causes the quantity demanded of investment in Part C to decline from Q_1 to Q_2. In the short run an increase in government expenditures will crowd out private investment by causing interest rates to rise. Business investment will be affected, as will the housing market, because the purchase of a home is very sensitive to changes in the interest rate. Consumer durables such as automobiles could also be hurt when interest rates increase.

The expansionary fiscal policy diagramed in Figure 15.9 created an inflationary gap, which the automatic adjustment process will eliminate in the long run. The SRAS curve in Part A will shift to the left from $SRAS_1$ to $SRAS_2$, and the equilibrium position will move from E_{SR} to E_{LR}. The price level will increase, while real national income will decline to the level of potential national income. Nominal national income will increase as the rise in the price level exceeds the decline in real national income, and the demand for money will increase in Part B from D_{M_2} to D_{M_3}, causing interest rates to increase again, from r_2 to r_3. The increase in interest rates will, in Part C, cause a further decline in the quantity of investment demanded, from Q_2 to Q_3. The expansionary effects of fiscal policy in the long run are completely crowded out by the rise in the price level and in interest rates.

Crowding out is a reversible process. A decrease in government expenditures or an increase in taxes will, by causing a decline in aggregate demand, lead to a decline in interest rates and an increase in the quantity of investment. The increase in investment will at least partially offset the effect of a contractionary fiscal policy.

The long-run effect of fiscal policy is both similar and different from the long-run effect of monetary policy. The effect is similar in that neither an expansionary fiscal policy nor an expansionary monetary policy is capable of permanently increasing the level of real national income above the level of potential national income. Both result in a higher price level with national output at the level of potential national income. An increase in the quantity of money was shown in Chapter 13 to be neutral in the long run, because an increase in the quantity of money kept real interest rates from rising. But fiscal policy is not neutral in this respect. Fiscal policy does permanently affect interest rates and therefore the composition of real national income.

The expansionsary federal budget deficits during the second term of the Reagan administration were incurred while the economy was at or near full employment. The result, according to the model just discussed, would be to increase interest rates and crowd out private investment. There would be a smaller capital stock and lower levels of potential national income than would have been the case had the budget been balanced.

FISCAL POLICY AND FOREIGN CAPITAL

In our discussion of fiscal policy, there is an important qualification that must be made. The U.S. economy is not a closed economy, but one in which international trade is of ever-increasing importance. In an open economy the higher interest rates that result from an expansionary fiscal policy will attract foreign capital inflows to that economy. This foreign capital will augment the nation's savings and reduce the amount of investment that will be crowded out.

If foreign investment increases when the government deficit increases, the decline in domestic investment will be smaller than it otherwise would be. This happened during the 1980s. In Table 15.10, if you compare gross saving and gross investment for 1979 (a nonrecession year when the federal budget deficit amounted to 1.6 percent of GNP) and for 1986 (also a nonrecession year but with a federal budget deficit of 5.2 percent of GNP), you will see evidence consistent with the theory of crowding out. Investment in housing and by business both fell as a percentage of GNP.

The decline was cushioned by a net inflow of capital that amounted to 2.5 percent of GNP, which in 1986 was almost $140 billion. Housing and business investment was probably saved by a further decline of about this amount. Instead of its capital stock being lower by $140 billion at the end of 1986, the United States owed this much more abroad. The year 1986 was not atypical of most of the 1980s in this respect. Net foreign investment since 1984 has served as a cushion against crowding out.

TABLE 15.10
Impact of Federal Budget Deficits on Investment in the United States:
1979 and 1986

	GROSS SAVING (PERCENTAGE OF GNP)				GROSS INVESTMENT (PERCENTAGE OF GNP)		
	1979	1986	CHANGE		1979	1986	CHANGE
Personal saving	4.7%	2.9%	−1.8%	Private investment			
Business saving	13.1	13.9	0.8	Housing	5.6%	5.1%	−0.4%
Government				Business	12.6	10.6	−2.0
Federal	−0.6	−4.9	−4.3				
State and Local	1.1	1.3	0.2	Net Foreign Investment	0.1	−2.5	−2.6
Total	18.3%	13.2%		Total	18.3%	13.2%	

Source: U.S. Department of Commerce.

SUMMARY

1. Monetary policy is the process whereby the Federal Reserve regulates the money supply by controlling the quantity of reserves available in the banking system. An expansionary monetary policy aims to increase the rate of growth of the money supply, whereas a contractionary monetary policy aims to reduce the growth rate.

2. The three major tools available to the Federal Reserve for conducting monetary policy are (a) setting reserve requirements, (b) setting the discount rate, and (c) conducting open-market operations.

3. An expansionary monetary policy involves expanding reserves by purchasing government bonds in open-market operations, lowering the discount rate, or reducing the reserve requirements. A contractionary monetary policy involves reducing available reserves by selling government bonds in the open market, raising the discount rate, or increasing reserve requirements.

4. The ultimate objectives of monetary policy are called the policy variables, which are a stable price level, full employment, and economic growth at the rate of the increase in potential national income.

5. The Federal Reserve cannot directly influence these policy variables. To influence the policy variables, the Federal Reserve has to select intermediate instruments, which are variables that the Federal Reserve can affect directly and by which it can influence the policy variables. The rate of interest and the quantity of money have been used as intermediate targets in the past.

6. The nominal interest rate is composed of two elements — the real rate of interest and an inflation premium. A change in the money supply can cause the nominal rate of interest to change because of either the Keynes effect or the Fisher effect. An increase in the money supply may result in either an increase or a decrease in the nominal interest rate, depending on whether the Fisher or Keynes effect is stronger.

7. Neither monetarists nor Keynesians believe that the Federal Reserve can determine in the short run how the resulting increase in nominal national income will be divided between changes in real GNP and changes in the price level. In the long run both agree the entire effect of monetary policy is reflected in changes in the price level.

8. The use of interest rates as the intermediate target can make monetary policy procyclical, a tendency that has been reinforced from time to time by the recognition and effectiveness lags. Monetarists claim that the targeting of interest rates was responsible for allowing inflation to get out of hand during the 1970s.

9. The use of monetary targets was complicated by the instability of the money demand function during the 1980s. Monetarists believe that a constant-growth rule should supplant active monetary policy, and that it was not tried during the period of money targeting.

10. Currently, most economists recognize that there are significant limitations to the use of monetary policy as a countercyclical tool. Keynesians, however, believe that the limitations do not preclude the use of monetary policy when the situation warrants, while monetarists think that only a constant-growth rule will work.

11. Both increases in the money supply and increases in the structural deficit in the long run result in increases in the price level. Increases in the money supply, however, are neutral with respect to the composition of real national income, but changes in the structural deficit are not.

IS A SOFT LANDING FOR THE ECONOMY POSSIBLE? HAS LAUNCHPAD MCQUACK FINALLY LEARNED TO FLY?

PREVIEW 15.1 ANALYSIS

During the summer of 1989 there was much talk that the Federal Reserve, under the chairmanship of Alan Greenspan, had engineered a soft landing for the economy, reducing too rapid economic growth with accelerating inflation to a more moderate rate with a stable rate of inflation. There were a host of skeptics. Some warned that unless the FRB immediately eased monetary policy, the economy would surely hit the runway and a recession would occur. Others countered that if the FRB did ease monetary policy, inflation would take off again. Some even argued that it was already too late and that a crash landing was inevitable. Clearly, only one of these four alternative outcomes could occur, and by the time you read this, it will already have happened. So you know whether the FRB actually succeeded in bringing the economy in for a soft landing.

Why was this attempt necessary? What is wrong with a flying economy? The problem is capacity. Once the economy has reached the level of full employment and is producing at the level of potential national income, real GNP can expand only at the rate at which potential national income is growing. Most estimates place this rate at between 2.5 percent and 3.0 percent a year. If aggregate demand grows at a rate greater than this, the price level must rise. When this happens, if accelerating inflation is to be avoided, the rate of growth of aggregate demand must be reduced. The problem is that this is a delicate operation for the Federal Reserve to undertake: Tighten too much of the money supply and a recession will occur; tighten too little and inflation will accelerate.

What were the events that led up to the attempt at a soft landing in 1989? The story begins in June 1987 when Paul Volcker resigned as chairman of the Federal Reserve Board and Alan Greenspan was appointed in his place. Greenspan at the time was hailed as an inflation fighter. The economy had been flying high since taking off from the recession of 1982–

FIGURE 15.10
The Engineering of an Apparent Soft
Landing: 1986

Early in 1984 real economic growth was at excessively
high rates. The Federal Reserve decided to tighten monetary policy and drove up the rate of interest. Tight money
drove down the rate of economic growth without causing
a recession, although there was one quarter of negative
growth.

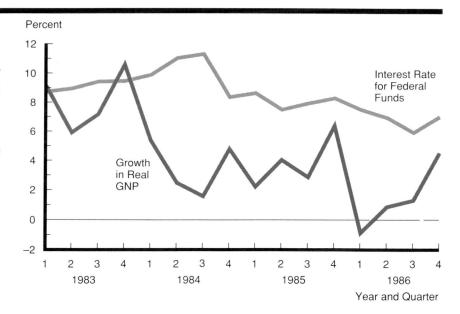

1983 and was in the midst of a record nonstop flight. The unemployment
rate during 1988 had fallen to the level of the natural rate of unemployment, and the economy had broken into a sprint with the rate of growth of
real GNP doubling the rate at which potential national income was
thought to be able to grow.

In September the Federal Reserve raised the discount rate from 5.5
percent to 6.0 percent, citing "potential inflationary pressures" that the
Board saw developing. In October 1987 the stock market crashed and the
Federal Reserve Board interrupted its anti-inflation crusade to ensure
that a financial panic did not occur. In March 1988 the Board concluded
that the economy had weathered the crash, and it returned to the anti-
inflation fight with the goal of achieving a soft landing. With the federal
funds rate rising due to the tight money policy, the Board in August 1988
and again in February 1989 raised the discount rate.

The tight monetary policy began to cause the economy to descend
rapidly in the summer of 1989 as economic growth slowed and the public
began to wonder whether the landing would be soft or hard. Many economists predicted that with Launchpad McQuack at the controls, a crash
into recession was inevitable. After all, they reasoned, neither Launchpad
nor the Federal Reserve had ever managed a safe landing before.

The problem is that the economy is difficult to direct for even the
most talented pilots. The Federal Reserve is in the position of the captain
of a huge oil tanker trying to navigate a narrow, winding channel. The
awkward tanker is difficult to pilot. It takes two miles to turn and three
miles to stop. The pilot needs to start turning a mile before a bend in the
channel in order to negotiate a safe turn. If he doesn't see the bend well
ahead of his ship, it will be too late.

Similarly, the full impact of a change in monetary policy will not be
felt for six months to two years. It is difficult to see that far ahead, so no
one knows which way the economy will be heading by that time. If inflationary pressures are still there, the Federal Reserve's action may result
in a soft landing, but if the economy is already slowing, tight money may
drive the economy into the runway.

Despite the critics' claims that the Federal Reserve Board has never engineered a soft landing, it has happened at least once before. In early 1984 the economy was growing at a rate of 10 percent, and a concerned Federal Reserve reduced the rate of growth of the money supply, driving up interest rates as shown in Figure 15.10. The rate of economic growth slowed dramatically, with one quarter of negative growth — one short of the two consecutive quarters of negative growth that define a recession. Then the FRB eased and growth resumed without a serious inflation problem developing. The FRB had apparently succeeded in wringing inflationary tendencies out of the economy without causing a recession. Supporters of the FRB point to this success as evidence that it can be done.

Did the Federal Reserve succeed a second time between 1987 and 1989? Certainly, by the summer of 1989 a similar pattern was developing: Economic growth during the second quarter was down to 1.7 percent. You now know the actual outcome. Has Launchpad McQuack finally learned to fly? Was the landing soft or did a recession occur?[1]

WHAT SHOULD THE FEDERAL RESERVE DO?

PREVIEW 15.2 ANALYSIS

Through its ability to control the money supply, the Federal Reserve can control the price level. In the long run the full effects of both fiscal and monetary policy show up as changes in the price level. Some economists believe that controlling inflation should be the FRB's sole goal, whereas others see a role for monetary policy in the short run. Whether or not zero inflation becomes the only monetary policy goal, a stable price level is the ultimate goal of Alan Greenspan, the current chairman of the Federal Reserve Board. Greenspan, while reportedly prepared to wait some years for this to happen, believes that a stable price level is the legacy of a great Board chairman.

Greenspan has helped develop a monetary theory to guide the Federal Reserve in its attempt to accomplish a goal of zero inflation. The theory has been labeled P-star, for P* (P with an asterisk), which stands for the level of expected future prices — the dependent variable of the theory. The theory is designed to predict the level of future long-run prices, which, when compared with the current price level, can be used to predict the direction of future inflation rates.

The P-star theory is a variant of the quantity theory of exchange. Its uniqueness derives from the way the variables are measured, rather than the identification of the variables themselves. The P-star theory is written:

$$P^* = \frac{M2 \times V^*}{Q^*}$$

[1]Sources for this analysis: Alan Murray, "The Next Recession: Just Around the Bend?" *The Wall Street Journal*, Mar. 6, 1989; and Douglas R. Sease, "How Will Economy Hit the Runway?" *The Wall Street Journal*, May 15, 1989.

where P* is the level of future prices, M2 is an official measure of the money supply, V* is the M2 velocity of circulation, and Q* is the future level of potential national income.

Two factors make this equation manageable: (1) the Federal Reserve's discovery that the long-run M2 velocity is a constant equal to 1.6527, and (2) an estimate that the rate at which potential national income increases is 2.5 percent per year. This leaves M2, which is controlled by the FRB, to predict the level of P*, the future (long-run) level of prices. If a stable price level is to be achieved, P* is what the FRB needs to know.

Expressing the values of the variables as percentage changes gives:

$$\%\Delta \text{ in } P^* = \%\Delta \text{ in M2} + \%\Delta \text{ in } V^* - \%\Delta \text{ in } Q^*$$

where the symbol "%Δ" stands for percent change. In the P-star theory, long-run velocity is a constant and therefore does not change, so %Δ in V* equals 0. Because the percent change in Q* is estimated to be 2.5 percent per year, the percentage change in the price level is obtained by subtracting 2.5 percent from the percentage change in the M2 money supply:

$$\%\Delta \text{ in } P^* = \%\Delta \text{ in M2} - 2.5\%.$$

The equation is designed to predict changes in the future long-run price level, which in practice means two or more years into the future.

If the predicted inflation rate P* exceeds the current inflation rate P, the rate of inflation in the future can be expected to increase. If, on the other hand, P is greater than P*, the rate of inflation can be expected to fall. During the first quarter of 1989 the calculated value of P* fell below the value of P for the first time since 1984, which predicted that the rate of inflation should not accelerate in the future. But the relationship works only in the long run. P* fell below P in 1978, but the rate of inflation did not top out until two years later. P* has been above P since 1984, and the rate of inflation did not begin to accelerate until late in 1988. So the theory is not likely to be much good for predicting the near-term consequences of monetary policy.

As a policy tool, P-star can be used to influence monetary policy. If P* equaled P and the Federal Reserve was content with the current inflation rate, it would maintain the current rate of growth of M2. If it decided that the present is a good time to reduce the inflation rate, the FRB could expect this to happen eventually if it reduced the growth rate of M2 to drop P* below the current level of P.

P-star also implies, because M2 velocity is a constant, that to attain zero inflation the Federal Reserve should increase the money supply at the same rate of growth by which potential national income is increasing. Since the FRB currently estimates that the level of potential national income increases at 2.5 percent annually, that is also the zero inflation rate of growth for the M2 money supply. As long as the actual growth of M2 exceeds this rate, the Federal Reserve will expect that the price level will continue to rise.

P-star rests on two heroic assumptions. The first is that the long-run M2 velocity will continue to be constant. M2 velocity over the previous 33 years has averaged 1.6527, which means that each dollar of M2 was spent 1.65 times each year on average. M2 velocity does change from month to month and from year to year, depending on the rate of interest and inflationary expectations, but over the long run M2 velocity has remained remarkably constant. M2, for example, has increased on average by 8.65 percent annually over the last 25 years, nearly matching the 8.52 percent average increase in nominal GNP — the closeness of these two numbers indicates that the percent change in V* was close to zero for this period.

The second assumption is that the rate of growth of potential national income will not change and has been accurately measured at 2.5 percent. However, should the growth rate of potential national income increase, a prediction of a constant price level by P-star would actually result in a deflationary situation. This would appear to be a real possibility, since several studies of the long-run growth rate in the economy report a rate of increase in potential national income of closer to 3.0 percent.

Federal Reserve research indicates that had P-star existed in the past it would have provided an accurate prediction of the inflationary experience of the 1970s and 1980s. Had the Federal Reserve Board possessed this information, history might have been different. The theory is still considered experimental, but the Board reportedly deems P-star important enough to consider reporting P* figures every quarter.

Does the Federal Reserve Board now use P-star? Members of the Board of Governors are always evasive about how monetary policy is determined. One district bank president, who at the time was also a member of the FRB's Open Market Committee, stated that there had been little discussion of P-star at the committee's meetings. He regarded such measures as of little use in setting short-term monetary policy. He apparently viewed the task of monetary policy as consisting of more than controlling the price level. If so, he was surely correct. P-star was designed to gauge the effect of monetary policy on the long-run price level. If it continues to predict accurately, its greatest usefulness will be in indicating the long-run implications for the price level of current Federal Reserve policy.[2]

SHOULD THE FEDERAL RESERVE REMAIN INDEPENDENT?

PREVIEW 15.3 ANALYSIS

The Federal Reserve's power to pursue monetary policy is independent of Congress and the president. It does not have to appeal to either for financing; it is self-supporting. Nor does the FRB have to justify its actions, other than in two semiannual reports to Congress. Its charter is perpetual. This was done purposefully to ensure the independence of the central bank from political domination.

The Federal Reserve is free to take positions that the secretary of the treasury, the president of the United States, and Congress all oppose. The members of the Board of Governors of the Federal Reserve are appointed by the president and approved by the Senate but they do not have to

---

[2]Sources for this analysis: Peter T. Kilborn, "Federal Reserve Sees a Way to Gauge Long-Run Inflation," *New York Times*, June 13, 1989; Lindley H. Clark, Jr., and Alfred L. Malabre, "Money Data Have Economists in Dither," *The Wall Street Journal*, June 28, 1989.

listen to them afterwards. The Federal Reserve is free to establish monetary policy that opposes fiscal policy, which is determined by elected officials accountable to the public at the next election. The decisions of an appointed few thus can nullify the decisions of the elected representatives of the many. Although this has happened only infrequently, it has happened. The supporters of the Federal Reserve Act of 1913 purposefully designed it this way. They believed that such a powerful institution should remain immune from the often fickle political influences that guide a democracy.

PROPONENTS OF CONTINUED INDEPENDENCE

Modern supporters of continued independence for the Federal Reserve believe that the authors of the Federal Reserve Act behaved wisely. These supporters make three arguments for continued independence based on how a representative government behaves. They suggest that if the FRB were made dependent on the prevailing political will, its performance would suffer because of (1) rational voter ignorance, (2) the influence of special-interest groups, and (3) the shortsighted effect. All of these arguments were discussed in Chapter 5.

Proponents of continued independence believe that, due to rational voter ignorance, a politically dominated central bank would exhibit a bias in favor of inflation; would exhibit unpredictable behavior if it fell under the influence of particular special-interest groups; and would not be able to adopt and carry out long-term strategies for monetary policy because of the shortsighted effect. Let us examine each argument in turn.

It is argued that rational voter ignorance would keep voters ignorant of the true effects of monetary policy and allow politicians to use the central bank for their own purposes. Elected officials like to vote for programs that generate benefits for voters, but they hate to vote for taxes to pay for the programs. A fully cooperative central bank could make it easier to vote benefits without correspondingly increasing taxes if the central bank were willing to create money to finance any deficit the federal government decided to run. Politicians, it is argued, would be presented with a golden opportunity to create new programs without the necessity to vote new taxes.

Financing deficits by expanding the money supply would, of course, be inflationary. Thus a bias toward inflation is seen as one of the consequences of making the Federal Reserve a political entity. Many countries with high persistent inflation rates have central banks that are not politically independent. It is easier, so the argument goes, for central bank officials who are not politically accountable to refuse to monetize the deficits of the government, thereby imposing some fiscal discipline on elected officials.

Second, allowing the Federal Reserve to be politically influenced could lead to its control by special-interest groups that would influence monetary policy for their narrow self-interest. Monetary policy can lead to the redistribution of income and wealth, as we have seen, which would make the FRB a tempting target. Maintaining the political independence of the central bank thus makes it less subject to the pressures of special-interest groups.

Third, proponents of continued independence point to the difficulty that democratic institutions have in devising and carrying out long-range plans. This is because of the shortsighted effect that favors programs with current benefits and delays costs until sometime in the future. The existence of the shortsighted effect could lead to politically inspired expansionary monetary policy prior to elections to ensure prosperity at election time, and to the neglect of the future costs that would have to be borne after the election. Thus a political business cycle, another potential source of economic uncertainty, could be the price of a politically controlled Federal Reserve.

Finally, proponents of continued independence suggest that the Federal Reserve is already constrained sufficiently. If the FRB consistently acted in ways opposed by a majority of the people, Congress would enact legislation to limit its behavior, which the president would sign. This possibility is sufficient to ensure consistent behavior by the Federal Reserve that is in the public's interest.

Supporters of continued independence do not argue that the Federal Reserve is perfect, only that it is better than the alternative of a politically controlled central bank. They suggest that the Federal Reserve be left as it is to determine independently the country's monetary policy.

OPPONENTS OF CONTINUED INDEPENDENCE

Opponents to the continued independence of the Federal Reserve suggest arguments countering those of the proponents, as well as two arguments of their own.

First, they counterargue that the Federal Reserve already has an inflationary bias and cite the fact that the purchasing power of the dollar in 1914 has steadily declined until today it can purchase scarcely one-tenth as many goods and services as it could then. Second, some critics of the Federal Reserve believe that the central bank is already dominated by special-interest groups, mainly those promoting the interests of the banking institutions the FRB is supposed to regulate. They argue that the FRB follows policies favored by banks and the owners of financial assets. And third, they point out that monetary policy has never been long term but has fluctuated according to the dictates of the current economic situation.

The opponents of continued independence for the Federal Reserve put forth two arguments of their own. First, they suggest that in a democracy monetary policy, like fiscal policy, should be in the hands of elected officials. There should not exist an institution controlled by nonelected officials that possesses the power to thwart the wishes of elected representatives.

Second, opponents suggest that monetary policy and fiscal policy should always be coordinated. They should never work at cross purposes, as occurred during the early years of the Reagan administration when the administration felt that the Federal Reserve was pursuing too tight a monetary policy to allow its supply-side programs to work effectively, or during the Carter administration when the switch to money targeting cut the ground from under that administration's incomes policy for fighting inflation.

An independent Federal Reserve cannot be ordered by elected officials to adopt the monetary policy they believe is required. The Federal Reserve must instead be persuaded. This may prove hard to do, especially for a new president, since the membership of the Federal Reserve's Board of Governors was appointed by the previous president. Opponents argue that an elected president should be able to choose the administration's monetary policy.

The argument of the opponents boils down to their belief that an independent central bank is inconsistent with the basic tenet of democracy that all governmental institutions should be directly responsible to the voters. The proposals of opponents range from the modest — make the term of the chairman of the Board of Governors of the Federal Reserve begin and end with that of the president, and thus enable every new president to appoint the chairman — to the more radical proposition that the Board of Governors should be disbanded and the Federal Reserve made an agency of the Department of the Treasury, thus totally ending its independence.

These, in brief, are the arguments for and against continued independence of the Federal Reserve. It is now up to you to decide for yourself.

REQUIRED ECONOMIC CONCEPTS

Monetary policy
Open-market operations
Policy variables
Policy instruments
Intermediate policy target
Monetary base
Interest rate control
Monetary base control
Countercyclical monetary policy

Procyclical monetary policy
Real interest rate
Nominal interest rate
Keynes effect
Fisher effect
Recognition lag
Effectiveness lag
Constant-growth rule

KEY QUESTIONS

1. What is the Federal Open Market Committee? What does it do?
2. Why does the public's desire to hold more of its income in the form of cash not increase the nation's money supply?
3. Which would normally cause the biggest impact on the money supply: changing the reserve ratio or daily open-market operations?
4. What are excess reserves?
5. What are policy variables? Name two.
6. As the SRAS curve becomes flatter, will the increase in nominal GNP in the short run reflect a proportionately greater increase in real GNP or in the price level? What about the long run?
7. If the economy faces a recessionary gap, what can the Federal Reserve do about aggregate demand? Aggregate supply? If it does nothing, what does the basic macro model predict? Would it be a slow or fast adjustment? Why?
8. What is one reason the Federal Reserve possesses imperfect information about policy variables?
9. What is an intermediate target?
10. Do monetarists believe that activist monetary policy as it has been carried out by the Federal Reserve is procyclical or countercyclical? What is the implication of activist policy according to the monetarists?

11. Why did the demand for money apparently increase (velocity decrease) in 1981–1982, causing the Federal Reserve to abandon its short experiment with a purely monetarist nominal money-supply target?

12. What are some of the variables that have been suggested for the replacement of M1 as an intermediate target?

13. What are four arguments supporting and two arguments against the continued existence and independence of the Federal Reserve?

PROBLEMS

1. "The Fed may control the money supply up to a point, but it doesn't determine the amount of cash in circulation." Does this statement make any sense, or is it an example of economic illiteracy? Explain.

2. How might each of the following affect the money supply?
   a. The Federal Reserve Bank raises the discount rate.
   b. The FRB engages in open-market purchases of securities.
   c. The fractional reserve requirement is lowered.
   d. The public acts to raise its holdings of cash relative to its demand deposits.
   e. The Treasury borrows from the FRB but does not immediately spend the funds.
   f. The Treasury borrows from the FRB and spends the funds.

3. These days the "discount window" of the FRB is essentially a safety valve for the banking system. Explain this. What purposes does manipulation of the discount rate by the FRB serve?

4. If you read in the newspaper that "Fed sales of securities take funds from the system because Fed dealers draw on their commercial bank accounts to pay for their purchases," what is going on?

5. Interpret this newspaper quote: "The Fed drained reserves from the banking network last Friday when the federal funds were trading at 9 11/16 percent."

6. The Federal Reserve says the money supply has been hard to control. Someone responds, "Yes, particularly when the Federal Reserve has been trying to control something else." What did the respondent mean?

7. Does the length of the effectiveness lag create the possibility of a monetary policy that is destabilizing? If so, is the automatic adjustment process better than a countercyclical monetary policy? Under what kind of timing adjustment would this be true? Which group of economists would prefer a monetary rule? Why?

8. The monetarists argue that activist monetary policy is more often than not destabilizing, and the Keynesians respond that a monetary rule could also be destabilizing. For example, assume that the demand for real balances, M/P, is constant; this is an expression of the public's preference for how much money balances it chooses to hold in order to keep its holding of real money balances constant as the price level changes. Suppose the money supply is increased 5 percent by the Federal Reserve, causing the price level to rise by 5 percent.
   a. Why does the price level rise by 5 percent?

For parts b–e, assume M/P is not constant but instead autonomously increases by 2 percent.
   b. If there is no increase in the money supply, by how much does the price level change and in which direction?
   c. By how much and in what direction should the money supply change in order to keep P level and M/P the same?
   d. Assume that a monetary rule is in effect that raises the nominal money supply 5 percent. What is the effect on the price level?
   e. Does the monetary rule cause some inflation in this situation?

9.   What is the current consensus among economists about changes in the nominal money supply and its effect on the real sector? Are the consensus and the effect different for the short run versus the long run? Does this mean that both the monetarists and Keynesians now believe there is a role for activist monetary policy, or is there still an area of disagreement? If so, where does it lie?

APPLICATION ANALYSIS

1.   Assume that you are given the following policy choices: (a) monetary policy, (b) tax policy, and (c) government spending policy. Which policy or policy combination would you choose in each of the following situations?

a.   If, to counter excess aggregate demand, you want to minimize the time between recognition of the excess aggregate demand and doing something about it.

b.   If the economy is in a deep recession, and you want stabilization policy to have a reasonably quick and significant effect on aggregate demand, and you are willing to risk an enlarged federal deficit.

c.   If the economy is in a deep recession, and you want to achieve the fastest results possible but also want to minimize the impact on the federal deficit.

d.   If the economy is experiencing excess aggregate demand and accelerating prices, and you want to cool off the economy by slowing down the influential housing and automobile industries.

e.   If the economy is experiencing excess aggregate demand, and you want all industries and geographic regions to be affected as equally as possible.

P A R T 5

MACROECONOMIC PROBLEMS: INFLATION, STAGFLATION, AND STABILIZATION POLICY

16

INFLATION

PREDICTING FUTURE RATES OF INFLATION

Why should you be interested in the future rate of inflation? The rate of interest, as you will discover in this chapter, is crucially dependent on the existing and expected future rates of inflation. Furthermore, your financial future is crucially dependent on the rate of interest.

You must save while working to enjoy your golden years — Social Security will not be enough. Your employer may offer a retirement plan to help you save, and you may have some choice of how your retirement plan is managed. The rate of return a retirement fund will earn is very important to ensuring that adequate funds will be available for retirement — a small difference in the interest rate can make a big difference in the earnings of your investments.

Some retirement funds allow you to choose the proportion of money used to buy stocks, bonds, or money market accounts. Expectations about future inflation rates and the rate of interest are critical to managing such a retirement fund. If you expect a rise in inflation, it would be best to transfer your funds out of stocks and bonds and into a money market account. Conversely, if you expect the inflation rate to fall, you should do the opposite.

When you buy a house or condominium, the rate of interest on your mortgage is very important. Both fixed-rate and variable-rate mortgages are available. Generally, variable-rate mortgages offer an initial rate of interest substantially below that of fixed-rate mortgages. If you expect the rate of inflation to rise over the next 20 years, perhaps a fixed rate is better. If you expect that inflation will remain mainly the same or even decline over the next 20 years, a variable-rate mortgage is preferable. When interest rates fall, so will your mortgage payments. If you are correct, then the real value of the dollars you pay will be less than the mortgage company expected, and you will benefit.

You can avoid making inflation forecasts only at your own peril. One way to obtain an inflation forecast is to rely on the forecasts of experts. Expert opinions abound and are readily available.

But why rely on experts? How can you forecast changes in the inflation rate the same way that experts do?

• INTRODUCTION •

During the 1970s people in the United States regarded inflation as the Number 1 macroeconomic problem. The rapid inflation of that period left a marked impression on the public.

People fear inflation for a number of reasons — some justified by experience and some not. Some nations have experienced runaway inflation, or hyperinflation, that has led to the collapse of their economies. The German economy was plagued with hyperinflation in the early 1920s, and some historians believe the rise of the Nazi Party can be traced to this economic event. Fortunately, hyperinflations have been rare in the United States, but it has not entirely escaped this menace. The United States has experienced two such hyperinflations: the first during the American Revolution, and the second in the South during the Civil War.

For the most part, however, our experience in the United States has been with inflations of a much more moderate sort. People often express the fear that inflations lead to a reduction in their standard of living. They point to their experiences during America's recent Great Inflation from 1966 to 1982. Although it is true that the standard of living did not increase during these years at the rate it had prior to the advent of inflation, it may be incorrect to blame this fact entirely on inflation. For example, productivity growth declined during this period. Inflation was only one of the possible causes for this development.

People who fear that inflation will lower their standard of living generally believe that this lowering is due to increasing prices of the things they buy. But they tend to forget that during inflations the prices of the things they sell also tend to rise. Wages also rise during inflations. For example, real hourly wages adjusted for inflation actually increased by 5 percent between 1966 and 1983, showing that inflation did not reduce the overall standard of living. Wages increase along with prices during inflations, allowing individuals to pay higher prices for goods and services.

For those who earn their living by selling labor and other resources, it is an illusion that prices always rise by more than income during an inflation. There is, however, an element of truth in this illusion. Individuals see prices rising every time they go to the store. Their paychecks increase only periodically, perhaps only once a year. If prices rise continually while your income increases infrequently, it might influence your perception. Even when the income adjustment compensates you for the rise in prices, it is perhaps natural to feel that you are not keeping up with the cost of living.

Although moderate inflation does not always lower standards of living, there are reasons to fear inflation. Inflation is not always costless. As discussed in Chapter 8, inflation can but does not always cause the following:

1. A reduction in economic efficiency.
2. Changes in the level of real national income and employment.
3. A redistribution of income among individuals in the society.

This latter fact is especially important to those living on fixed money incomes, such as those who are retired and living on pensions. Without cost-of-living adjustments, people on fixed money incomes definitely lose under inflation.

We already have some basic ideas about inflation from our previous study. In this chapter we shall study inflation in more detail and discover when inflation does and does not have substantial effects on the economy. •

FOUR FACTS ABOUT INFLATION

There is no single cause of inflation, and the effects of inflation on the economy will sometimes be substantial and will at other times be minimal. Consequently, the theories about inflation discussed in this chapter may at times be difficult to sort out. Nevertheless, these economic theories help to explain four basic facts about inflation:

1. Inflation is not certain — it is a man-made occurrence.
2. Persistent inflation is always associated with rapid growth of the money supply.
3. Inflation rates and nominal interest rates go hand in hand.
4. Whether inflation has minimal or substantial effects on the overall economy mainly depends on whether the inflation was expected or came as a surprise.

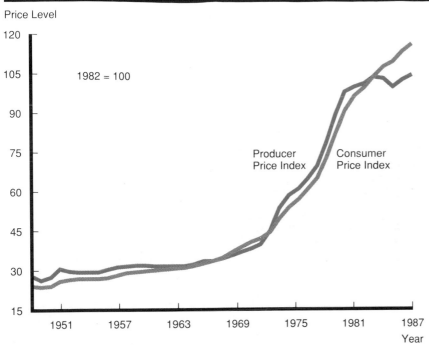

Price Level

120

105

90

75

60

45

30

15

1982 = 100

Producer
Price Index

Consumer
Price Index

1951   1957   1963   1969   1975   1981   1987

Year

FIGURE 16.1
Price Level: 1948–1987

The consumer price index (CPI) and the producer price index (PPI) are two common indexes used to measure the economy's price level and inflation. This figure shows the historical trends in these two indexes over the past four decades. In particular, notice the dramatic rises in the CPI and PPI during the Great Inflation of 1966–1982.

Before using our macroeconomic model to study the theories of inflation, let us examine each of these four facts in detail.

FUTURE INFLATION IS NOT A CERTAIN OCCURRENCE

Inflation is not certain to occur, even though recent experience seems to indicate otherwise. There have been extended periods in U.S. history when inflation was not a problem. The price level in 1940 was about the same as it had been in 1820, but in that 120 years the U.S. economy had had periods of both inflation and deflation. It was only after World War II that the price level began to rise consistently — first slowly and then much more rapidly.

Certainly, inflation has been a reality throughout your lifetime. But the inflation rate since 1983, though rapid in terms of the overall price history of the U.S. economy, has been modest in comparison with the recent past. This can be seen in Figure 16.1, which shows that the price level after 1983 has not increased at nearly so steep a rate as between 1966 and 1982.

Does this mean that inflation is no longer a cause for concern? It certainly does not. Figure 16.2 charts the inflation rate between 1949 and 1987; notice that through the 1960s and 1970s each peak in the rate of inflation as measured by the consumer price index (CPI) has occurred at a higher rate of inflation than the one that preceded it. Furthermore, the most recent inflation experience (between 1983 and 1987) shows that the rate of inflation has not returned to the level of the late 1950s and early 1960s. In fact, recent inflation rates are comparable to those seen during the period in which President Nixon imposed wage and price controls.

The inflation experience of the 1970s remains very much on the minds of investors, speculators, and policymakers. We shall show in this chapter that it is less costly to keep inflations from occurring than to stop inflations once they have gained momentum. Inflation can be cured, as you will discover below, but it is likely to be costly to do so.

FIGURE 16.2
Inflation Rate: 1948–1987

The inflation rate is calculated by taking the annual percentage change in the price index used to measure the price level. This figure shows the inflation rates over the past four decades calculated from the consumer price index (CPI) and the producer price index (PPI). Notice that the inflation rate as measured by the PPI tends to peak before that measured by the CPI. This pattern occurs because price increases are generally felt at the wholesale level before they reach the retail level.

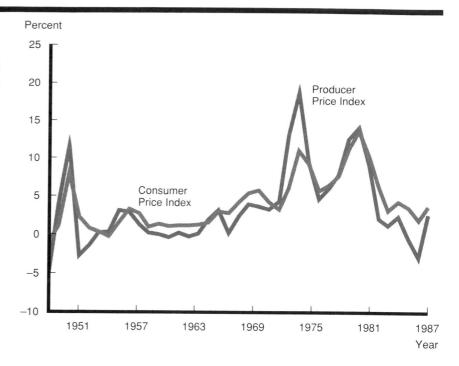

PERSISTENT INFLATION IS ASSOCIATED WITH RAPID GROWTH OF THE MONEY SUPPLY

There is a positive relationship between the money supply and the price level, as shown in Figure 16.3. The relationship is not perfect, however. The quantity of money has obviously grown more rapidly than the price level has increased. This relationship is readily explained by the quantity theory, first introduced in Chapter 13. The quantity theory states:

$$M \times V = P \times Q$$

where M is the quantity of money, V the velocity of circulation, P the price level, and Q the real GNP. Real GNP has increased due to economic growth from 1948 to 1987. If velocity is constant, the quantity theory shows that a corresponding increase in the money supply would be needed to keep the price level constant. In fact, velocity was rising over the period, so even less money was required to maintain a constant price level. The fact that the price level rose over the period suggests that the quantity of money increased at a rate in excess of what was required to accommodate the growth in real GNP and the rise in velocity.

Thus excess money growth in the long run is reflected in the rise of the price level. This gives rise to another of the qualified statements in economics: If the expansion of the money supply exceeds the amount needed to accommodate changes in real GNP and changes in the velocity of circulation, then the price level will increase.

The relationship between the expansion of the money supply and inflation can be seen in Figure 16.4, which charts the rate of inflation and the rate of growth of the money supply. You can readily see that each peak in the inflation rate was preceded by a peak in the growth rate of the money supply. Furthermore, each trough in the inflation rate was also

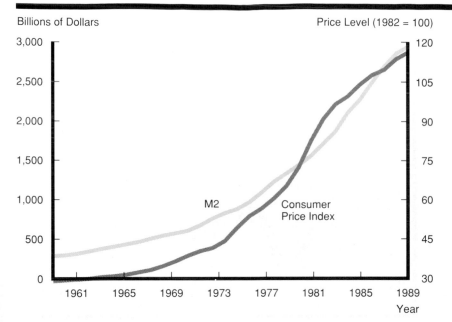

Billions of Dollars

Price Level (1982 = 100)

FIGURE 16.3
Price Level and the Money Supply:
1948–1987

This figure shows that persistent inflation is always associated with rapid money growth. This relationship is shown by a comparison of the rise in the consumer price index (CPI) with the rise in the money supply.

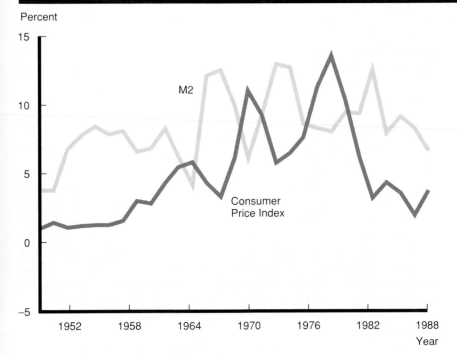

Percent

FIGURE 16.4
Rate of Growth of the Money Supply and the Rate of Inflation

This figure compares the inflation rate as calculated from the CPI with the rate of growth in the money supply. Notice that peaks in money growth usually precede peaks in the inflation rate, and troughs in money growth usually precede troughs in the inflation rate. The growth in the money supply is therefore a good, but not perfect, indicator of future inflation.

preceded by a trough in the growth rate of the money supply. The growth rate of the money supply has historically been a good — but not perfect — indicator of both future inflation rates and changes in the direction of inflation.

The money supply, though not the only possible cause of a rising price level, as you will see below, is the major cause of persistent inflations lasting for more than a brief time. An examination of the variables that make up the quantity theory shows that both velocity and real GNP do

FIGURE 16.5
Inflation Rate and the T-bill Interest Rate

This figure compares the interest rate on short-term government debt (Treasury bills, or T-bills) with the inflation rate calculated from the CPI. Clearly, the two rise and fall together.

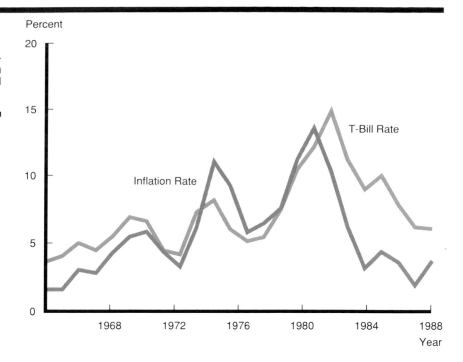

not fluctuate as widely as the money supply and the price level. The quantity theory asserts that it is the money supply that influences the price level — not the other way around.

RELATIONSHIP BETWEEN THE RATE OF INFLATION AND NOMINAL INTEREST RATES

If rapid money growth causes inflation, what does inflation cause? High nominal interest rates, for one thing. The rate of inflation and the interest paid by short-term federal government debt (Treasury bills) are charted in Figure 16.5. The close correspondence between the two is obvious.

The explanation is simple. Lenders wish to have returned to them in the future not only a rate of interest, which is the price charged for the use of money, but also the real value of the sum of money they initially lent. Thus they demand an inflation premium in the form of a higher interest rate to account for inflation. The inflation premium will rise as the rate of inflation increases.

Although the positive correlation between interest rates and the rate of inflation is there for all to see, it is not perfect. Once again, there are no unqualified economic statements. Other factors affect the interest rate, as we shall see below.

THE EFFECTS OF INFLATION DEPEND ON WHETHER OR NOT IT IS EXPECTED

Recall that inflation can reduce the efficiency with which the economy allocates resources, cause changes in the quantity of GNP and employment, and redistribute income and wealth. The occurrence of these effects depends on whether economic decision makers are surprised by the inflation. Economists use the term **anticipated inflation** to refer to inflation that does not surprise people.

> *Anticipated inflation is inflation that occurs when the future inflation rate is known in advance.*

When the future rate of inflation is perfectly anticipated, no one is surprised by the rise in the price level. If all economic decision makers correctly anticipate the rate at which the price level will increase in the future, they will all incorporate these expectations into their economic decisions. Businesses will periodically mark up their prices by the correct amount, and workers will ask for and often receive pay raises that will compensate them for the rise in the cost of living. Similarly, the owners of other factors of production will adjust their prices. Lenders will add the rate of inflation to the real interest rate, and building and land owners will adjust rents by the correct amount. Finally, if government adjusts tax rates and transfers for the expected increase in the price level, anticipated inflation will have little impact on the economy. Incomes will rise in step with prices, and relative prices will not change. There will be little incentive for decision makers to alter their behavior as long as the price level increases at the expected rate. The major exception are those on fixed incomes. Income will be redistributed away from this group unless they receive cost-of-living increases.

There will still be some costs, however. All business firms will have to mark up their prices and change their price lists accordingly. They will have to calculate and announce periodic price and wage increases. These extra costs, which would not exist if the price level were constant, are known as **menu costs.**

> *Menu costs are the costs involved in periodically changing prices to adjust for an inflationary increase in the price level.*

Besides menu costs, there is another cost of anticipated inflation. The purchasing power of money will decline, imposing a cost on persons who hold money. This expected decline in the value of money will create an incentive for economic decision makers to conserve on their money balances. This can be done by holding less money and more interest-bearing assets that cannot directly be used to make purchases. Decision makers will have to contact their banks more frequently to convert their interest-bearing assets into money when they need to make transactions. You can visualize this procedure as entailing extra trips to the bank and in the process more quickly wearing out your shoes. Thus economists refer to this effect of anticipated inflation as **shoe-leather costs.**

> *Shoe-leather costs are the costs imposed by perfectly anticipated inflation on the holders of money who incur extra costs in their attempts to conserve on their money balances.*

The menu and shoe-leather costs cannot be avoided when inflation occurs, even if the inflation rate is correctly anticipated. There is no way to avoid these costs, even if you know they will occur.

These costs are, however, likely to be small relative to the fears people hold about inflation. If menu and shoe-leather costs are the only costs of inflation, perhaps economists and policymakers would be better employed fighting fires or termites rather than inflation. The costs of an anticipated inflation are clearly trivial compared to other macroeconomic problems such as recession, unemployment, and stagnation.

A perfectly anticipated inflation does not reduce the efficiency with which the economy allocates resources, nor does it affect the level of aggregate output or employment, nor does it substantially redistribute income and wealth. A perfectly anticipated inflation does none of these things, but an **unanticipated inflation**—which comes as a surprise to economic decision makers—does all of these things.

> *Unanticipated inflation is inflation that surprises economic decision makers and that can reduce the efficiency with which resources are allocated, alter the level of real national income and employment, and result in a redistribution of income and wealth.*

When inflation is unanticipated, businesses, workers, lenders, and government do not have the opportunity to protect themselves from the higher price level in the ways discussed above. As a result, unanticipated inflation can substantially affect an economy.

INFLATION FROM THE DEMAND SIDE

Any theory of inflation must account for the four facts discussed above. The basic model of macroeconomics shows that there are two basic types of inflation theories. As we already know, an increase in the price level can arise from either the demand or the supply side. An increase in aggregate demand (i.e., a shift to the right) or a decline in aggregate supply (i.e., a shift in the SRAS curve to the left) would result in an increase in the price level. This naturally suggests that inflation can arise from either the demand side or the supply side. We shall consider both types of inflation, beginning with inflation from the demand side.

Most economists believe that persistent inflation—inflation that occurs over a relatively long period of time—is primarily a demand-side phenomenon and is due mainly to an excess supply of money. This deduction is based on the relationship between price level and real GNP that has occurred during inflations. For example, during the Great Inflation of 1966–1982, both the price level and real GNP increased. Only an increase in aggregate demand can account for this pattern of prices and outputs. If a decline in aggregate supply was the primary cause, it would produce a pattern of rising prices coupled with a decline in aggregate output. If inflation was primarily a supply-side phenomenon, real GNP would approach zero during a persistent inflation. Since we do not observe this occurrence, continual inflation is primarily a demand-side occurrence.

Moreover, the primary cause of the increase in aggregate demand is an excess supply of money. You will recall from Figure 16.4 that the money supply during recent history has increased more rapidly than the price level. Although any of the parameters of demand can cause inflation, only the money supply appears quantitatively to be the prime suspect. The money supply between 1959 and 1986, for example, increased 9.4 times while the price level increased 7.8 times. On the other hand, consumption, investment, and government spending in nominal terms increased much less rapidly than did the quantity of money, and they increased mainly in proportion to observed increases in GNP.

MONETARY THEORY OF INFLATION

Excessive growth in the money supply occurs if the money supply expands more rapidly than required to accommodate changes in real GNP and the

FIGURE 16.6

Effect of an Unexpected Increase in the Money Supply

In this figure an unexpected increase in the money supply (shown by the shift from S_{M_1} to S_{M_2} in Part A) triggers unexpected inflation. The interest rate falls to 5 percent, which stimulates consumption and investment spending. This change in turn stimulates the demand for the economy's goods, which is shown by AD shifting to AD_1 in Part B. The higher aggregate demand puts upward pressure on the economy's output (shown by real national income rising to Y_{SR}) and price level (shown by PL_2). The higher real national income stimulates the demand for money (which shifts to D_{M_1}) and causes the interest rate to rise, but not all the way back to its original level. But this short-run equilibrium is not stable. Since the economy's real income is above the potential level of national income, the automatic adjustment process will work to slow down the economy. Wages and the prices of other resources will rise, causing aggregate supply to fall (shown by SRAS shifting to the left to $SRAS_1$). The automatic adjustment process causes a higher price level (PL_3) and returns other economic variables to their original levels. In the long run the effect of a one-time increase in the money supply is limited to the price level.

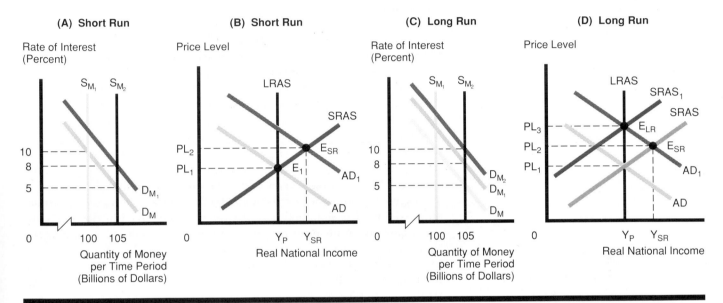

(A) Short Run   **(B) Short Run**   **(C) Long Run**   **(D) Long Run**

velocity of circulation. If GNP and velocity were constant, it would be a simple matter to predict changes in the price level: The price level would increase by the percentage change in the quantity of money.

But real GNP and velocity do vary over time, and this substantively complicates the problem of predicting the price level. If the quantity theory is to be useful, we must be able to predict how changes in the money supply affect both aggregate output and velocity.

The basic model of macroeconomics can be used to analyze the effect of an increase in the money supply on the level of GNP, velocity, and the price level, if we carefully consider the effect that changes in the money supply have on the rate of interest. To see the interaction among these economic variables, we shall study the effects of a one-time increase in the quantity of money.

UNANTICIPATED DEMAND-SIDE INFLATION CAUSED BY A ONE-TIME INCREASE IN THE MONEY SUPPLY

Suppose that the price level has been steady for a long period of time and that the macroeconomy is in long-run equilibrium. Also suppose that a one-time increase in the money supply occurs and that this increase is unexpected. In other words, economic decision makers are surprised when the money supply expands. How will they respond?

The response of the macroeconomy is shown in Figure 16.6. In Part A, the existing quantity of money ($S_{M_1} = 100$) and the money demand schedule (D_{M_1}) jointly determine the rate of interest (10 percent). The macroeconomy is at full employment and in long-run equilibrium at this interest rate.

Suppose the money supply increases by 5 percent from 100 to 105. Banks now have excess reserves and are anxious to make new loans. The result is that the rate of interest initially falls to, say, 5 percent. Business firms and consumers borrow more to acquire investment goods and consumer durables. This lower interest rate can be sustained only if the demand for money does not change.

But the demand for money will change, because aggregate demand will increase. The expansion of the money supply and the increased investment that is generated by the lower interest rate cause aggregate demand to increase from AD to AD_1. The equilibrium position will move from E_1 to E_{SR}, the price level will rise from PL_1 to PL_2, and real aggregate output will increase from Y_P to Y_{SR}. When real national income and the price level both increase, more money will be demanded to make transactions. The money demand schedule increases from D_M to D_{M_1}, and the rate of interest increases from 5 percent to, say, 8 percent.

Thus in the short run an increase in the money supply will initially result in (1) a lower interest rate, (2) an increase in investment, (3) a rise in the price level, and (4) an increase in real aggregate output above the level of potential output. The increase in nominal real national income (real GNP times the price level) will cause a subsequent increase in the rate of interest, but to a level that is below the initial level.

A short-run equilibrium is not stable. A level of real national income above the level of potential output cannot be sustained in the long run. The automatic adjustment process will work in the long run to cause the short-run aggregate supply (SRAS) curve to shift left from SRAS to $SRAS_1$ in Part D. The equilibrium position will move from E_{SR} to E_{LR}, the price level will rise to PL_3, and real national income will fall to the level of potential national income (from Y_{SR} to Y_P). The increase in nominal national income will in turn cause the demand for money to increase (from D_M to D_{M_2}) and the rate of interest to increase to its original level — 10 percent.

Looking at these results, we see that a one-time increase in the money supply will cause only the price level to increase in the long run. The rate of interest will return to its initial level, as will the level of real national income.

To summarize: In the short run an unanticipated one-time increase in the money supply will cause the rate of interest to fall, the price level to rise, and the level of real national income to increase. In the long run the effect of a one-time increase in the supply of money is limited to a rise in the price level.

ANTICIPATED INFLATIONS We have seen that the basic model of macroeconomics can help explain one of the fundamental facts about inflation — that unanticipated inflation can have real and substantial effects on the economy (in the short run). The model can also explain why anticipated inflation — inflation that economic decision makers correctly predict — has only minimal effects on the economy. We now turn to a consideration of this possibility.

First, recall why inflation will have little impact on the macroeconomy when it is perfectly anticipated. Because all wages, prices, and incomes, including interest, rise in step, relative prices are not affected. The only minor costs to the overall economy are the menu and shoe-leather costs. So it should come as no surprise that a perfectly anticipated increase in the money supply would have little impact on the economy other than to cause the price level to rise. The economy would immediately leap from the initial equilibrium to a new long-run equilibrium at a higher price level.

Such an adjustment is shown in Figure 16.7. Aggregate demand shifts to the right as the money supply increases, and simultaneously aggregate supply shifts to the left as the various cost-of-living increases received by workers and resource owners take effect to cover the anticipated inflation. The equilibrium in the macroeconomy moves from E_1 to E_2 to E_3 and the price level increases from PL_1 to PL_2 to PL_3, but the inflation does not affect the level of real national income, which remains at the level of potential national income, Y_P.

Moreover, the results remain the same if the economy is subjected to excessive money growth at a steady rate and that growth is expected. In this case the aggregate demand and SRAS curves will shift up in unison. The price level will constantly rise, first from PL_1 to PL_2, then to PL_3, and so on, but real national income will remain at the level of potential national income. Thus a perfectly anticipated increase in the money supply will cause the price level to rise but will have no impact on the real sector of the economy.

Actual inflations, it seems, never occur at a steady rate (as the data in Figure 16.2 showed us), making it more difficult to fully anticipate future inflation rates. But neither does the economy usually jump from inflation to deflation. Instead, inflation, once started, seems to fluctuate.

Whether future inflation will be anticipated or will surprise economic decision makers depends to a certain extent on how economic decision makers formulate their expectations about future inflation rates. We have seen that if expectations about future inflation rates turn out to be correct, the effects of inflation are likely to be minor, but if expectations are incorrect, the inflation will affect the real sector of the economy and substantially redistribute wealth and income.

There is no way to be certain how individuals actually form their expectations about the future. Probably it is some combination of past experience and a theory of how the world works. There are two current economic theories about how this is done that deserve your consideration: the theory of adaptive expectations and the theory of rational expectations.

THEORY OF ADAPTIVE EXPECTATIONS

The theory of **adaptive expectations** suggests that economic decision makers form expectations about future price levels by relying heavily on past experience.

> *The theory of adaptive expectations is a theory that individuals formulate their expectations about future prices on the basis of recent past experience, and that these expectations will be modified only gradually as the future unfolds.*

For example, if the inflation rate has been 5 percent for the last several years, the theory of adaptive expectations implies that decision makers will expect the inflation rate to remain at 5 percent in the future. Suppose, however, that the inflation rate doubles to 10 percent and remains steady at that higher rate. The theory of adaptive expectations suggests that individuals will be slow to appreciate this fact and will only gradually adjust their expectations upward to 10 percent.

The theory of adaptive expectations suggests that "seeing is believing" — that until the future becomes the present and possibilities become reality, decision makers will not adjust their expectations. An important implication of this view is that slowly adjusting expectations will create differences between the actual and expected inflation rates.

FIGURE 16.7
Effect of an Expected Increase in the Money Supply

In this figure, as the money supply increases, the demand for the economy's goods is stimulated (shown by the aggregate demand curve shifting right, from AD_1 to AD_2 to AD_3). If people correctly anticipate the resulting inflation, workers and owners of other resources will simultaneously require higher wages and other cost-of-living increases so that their incomes will keep up with inflation. These changes depress the supply side of the economy (shown by the SRAS curve shifting left, from $SRAS_1$ to $SRAS_2$ to $SRAS_3$). So the demand and supply sides of the economy change together, and the equilibrium moves from E_1 to E_2 to E_3. Consequently, the economy's real income and output remain at Y_P, the potential level of national income. Only the price level rises in reaction to the expected increases in the money supply.

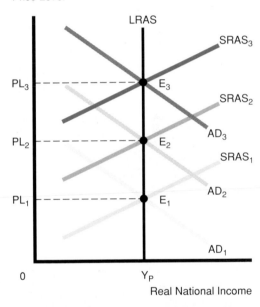

Price Level

If the actual inflation rate rises, the anticipated or expected inflation rate will be less than the actual rate until expectations fully adjust. Conversely, if the rate of inflation falls, the expected rate will for a time be higher than the actual rate. In either case the unexpectedly high or low inflation will not only influence the price level but will also affect the rate of interest, the level of GNP, and employment. The theory of adaptive expectations — through the lag time required for expectations to fully adjust — can explain why sudden changes in the supply of money will affect both real national income and the price level in the short run and will affect only the price level in the long run.

THEORY OF RATIONAL EXPECTATIONS

The theory of **rational expectations** assumes that more is involved in the formulation of expectations than just past experience — individual decision makers are assumed to use all the available information when they formulate expectations.

> *The theory of rational expectations is a theory which assumes that economic decision makers make predictions about the future state of macroeconomic variables using all available information about how the economy works, including information about past and present macroeconomic policies.*

A reader of economic and business publications and/or the financial pages of the nation's newspapers will be exposed to a large number of economic statistics and to numerous interpretations and forecasts. This information is paid for and studied by economic decision makers and helps them make economic forecasts as assumed by the theory of rational expectations. The theory of rational expectations does not imply that these predictions are correct — only that in making the predictions economic decision makers will use all of the available information.

This is the major difference between the two theories: Where the theory of adaptive expectations suggests that expectations will change gradually over time, the theory of rational expectations suggests the possibility of a quick change in expectations. It is possible, for instance, that if (1) the monetary authorities announce in advance that they are going to increase the supply of money, (2) decision makers believe this to be true and correctly predict the impact the increase in the money supply will have, and (3) fixed-price contracts and other wage and price rigidities are negligible, then expectations will immediately be revised. If this occurs, the economy will adjust as the theory of a perfectly anticipated inflation suggests, and only the price level (not the real sector) will be affected.

So whether or not inflation substantially effects the economy in the short run depends on how expectations are formed. If adaptive expectations are dominant in the economy, then changes in inflation will have real effects on employment and output. But if rational expectations are dominant, then inflation will have only minor effects when policies that change inflation are announced and decision makers correctly anticipate the effects of those policies.

INFLATION AND INTEREST RATES

Our study of demand-side inflation has shown that interest rates play an important role in explaining when the potential effects of inflation can arise. The economic theories on inflation that we have discussed can be made more practical and easier to apply by using some information about actual market interest rates.

We have talked about the interest rate as if there were just one rate, but if you peruse the pages of *The Wall Street Journal*, you will discover a bewildering variety of interest rates. Most of these are interest rates for **fixed-income securities.**

> *A fixed-income security is one that promises a fixed payment in the future. The interest rate on a fixed-income security is the annual percentage increase promised on the sum of money invested.*

Such securities are known as fixed-income securities to distinguish them from the dividends paid on common stocks. Dividends are not guaranteed but depend on the fortunes of the firm. Fixed-income securities generally mature at a specific future date, at which time a final payment is made to the investor and the principal is returned.

A **short-term security** is an asset that has a maturity date within one year of the date of purchase. The interest rate on a short-term security is called the **short-term interest rate** or **yield.** The short-term securities most often encountered are those issued by the U.S. Treasury, called Treasury bills or T-bills, and the certificates of deposit issued by commercial banks and savings and loan associations.

> *A short-term security is a security that matures within one year of the purchase date.*

> *The short-term interest rate is the interest rate on short-term (less than one year) securities; also called the short-term yield.*

Treasury bills are considered to be riskless (the U.S. government has the power to tax in order to repay its obligations), a great volume of these securities are periodically issued, and the financial markets that trade these bills are highly competitive. Consequently, T-bills are generally considered the most important short-term security, and the interest rate on T-bills is the major indicator of short-term rates.

Short-term rates are important economic indicators. Changes in macroeconomic policy and private spending decisions will have their immediate impact on the economy through changes in short-term rates. Changes in short-term interest rates thus signal coming changes in the economy as a whole.

In addition to short-term securities and interest rates, there are also **long-term securities** or **bonds,** the interest rate on which is known as the **long-term interest rate** or **yield.**

> *A long-term security or bond is an asset with a maturity date some years in the future.*

> *The long-term interest rate is the interest rate on long-term (more than one year) securities; also called the long-term yield.*

Bonds issued by the U.S. Treasury are considered the best indicator of long-term rates for the same reasons that T-bills are considered the best short-term indicator. Bonds issued by states, municipalities, and corporations are similar to Treasury bonds, but the ability of the issuer to repay the obligation is more in doubt. Hence these bonds pay a higher rate of interest.

Long-term interest rates are important to business firms concerned with making capital equipment purchases. The life span of a capital good is measured in years, not months, since machines and buildings last a relatively long time. Therefore when a firm is making the decision to invest in capital goods, the relevant interest rate is the long-term rate.

Changes in the economy are thus first reflected in short-term rates, whereas long-term rates influence business decisions. When you compare short- and long-term interest rates in the financial pages of a newspaper, they are rarely the same. What is the relationship between short- and long-term rates?

The relationship between short- and long-term rates can be explained by a theory known as the **expectations theory of interest rates.** According to this theory, current interest rates depend on expectations about the level of future interest rates. For example, an investor may have the choice of buying either a long-term security or a series of short-term assets. For example, the investor can buy either one long-term bond with a 10-year maturity or a short-term security today and a series of thirty-nine 90-day T-bills one after the other over the next 10 years. Investors will collectively buy and sell securities until they are indifferent between short- and long-term securities. When this happens, the long-term rate should reflect the sum of expected short-term rates.

> *The expectations theory of interest rates is the theory that the level of long-term interest rates reflects the sum of expected short-term interest rates. The long-term interest rate equals the average of expected future short-term interest rates from the present time until the long-term security matures.*

If the short-term rate of interest is 6 percent and short-term rates are expected to remain at the same level well into the future, then the long-term interest rate will also be 6 percent. If, however, the long-term rate is higher than the short-term rate, this suggests that short-term rates are expected to rise in the future. Long-term rates would be higher than current short-term rates only if sometime in the future short-term rates are expected to rise. Conversely, if short-term rates are lower than long-term rates, this suggests that people expect short-term rates to fall in the future. So the difference between short-term and long-term interest rates — called the **spread** — reflects the market's prediction of the direction that future short-term rates are heading.

> *The spread is the difference between short-term and long-term interest rates.*

According to the expectations theory, when expectations of the level of future short-term interest rates change, the long-term interest rate will adjust. Suppose that there is a change in current economic policy that immediately affects short-term interest rates. Long-term interest rates will change significantly only if the new policy is expected also to change *future* short-term rates.

An unexpected, one-time-only increase in the money supply will therefore only temporarily affect short-term interest rates. The long-term interest rate will not be affected because future short-term rates are not expected to rise. This was the pattern we showed in Figure 16.6 when we analyzed the effects of a one-time-only increase in the money supply.

A *permanent* increase in the rate of increase in the money supply will, however, eventually affect long-term rates as expectations of increases in the price level are taken into account. Furthermore, if the permanent increase in the growth of the money supply initially comes as a surprise, short-term rates will fall. The decline will be temporary, because the main long-run effect is to raise the inflation rate. Future short-term rates will rise to reflect the rising price level, and so will the long-term rate. When future short-term rates are expected to be higher than previously thought, long-term rates will adjust accordingly. The resulting rise in the rate of inflation from a permanent increase in the rate of growth of the money supply will therefore cause both short- and long-term rates of interest to increase.

INFLATION, INTEREST RATES, AND VELOCITY

We have discovered the positive relationship between the rate of inflation and the rate of interest. There is also a positive relationship, both in theory and in fact, between interest rates and the velocity of circulation of money. The rate of interest measures the opportunity cost of holding money. As the rate of interest increases, people expect more inflation in the future. When the opportunity cost of holding money increases, the quantity of money demanded will decline. Individuals will be less willing to hold money as the interest rate rises. They will attempt to spend their excess money balances, which will cause velocity to increase. So economic theory predicts that velocity will increase when inflationary expectations increase.

When hyperinflation exists, as in Germany in the early 1920s, the rate of interest rises through the roof — assuming anyone is willing to lend money at all. During runaway inflations people convert money into goods and services as quickly as possible, sometimes within hours of being paid. Velocity thus soars, causing the price level to increase even more rapidly than the increase in the money supply. Hyperinflation is one extreme example of how expected inflation affects velocity.

The same effect occurs from expected future inflation on a more moderate scale. An unexpected increase in the rate of expansion of the money supply will likely cause a disproportionate increase in nominal national income and inflation, because velocity will increase with the rise in inflationary expectations. This phenomenon is known as the **Friedman surge,** after the Nobel-Prize-winning economist Milton Friedman, who discovered this effect.

> *The Friedman surge is an acceleration in the growth rate of the money supply that will have a disproportionate effect on the rate of inflation, because the anticipation of future inflation will increase velocity.*

The Friedman surge explains how inflation can get out of hand. Ever-increasing rates of monetary growth will have even greater effects on the price level as velocity increases. The Friedman surge helps explain why the rate of inflation peaked at increasingly higher rates during the 1970s. Inflation can become a vicious spiral as velocity increases.

When the rate of growth in the money supply declines, the vicious spiral becomes a virtuous spiral as velocity declines with the decline in inflationary expectations. Thus the inflation rate falls by more than the decline in the rate of money expansion. When the rate of growth of the money supply declined in 1982, inflationary expectations were reduced and velocity fell significantly, having a disproportionate effect on the rate of inflation, which declined dramatically.

INTEREST RATES AND MONETARY POLICY

The strong relationships between the expected inflation rate and the interest rate and between the interest rate and velocity complicate life for the monetary authorities. When the nominal interest rate rises, reflecting an expected increase in inflation, the Federal Reserve often comes under pressure to reduce that high nominal rate. This pressure comes directly from both Congress and the president and from the public. When both short- and long-term interest rates were abnormally high in 1981, reflecting expected high future rates of inflation, the housing market collapsed. Builders responded by sending thousands of 2×4's to the Federal Reserve in protest. The nation's builders wanted lower long-term interest rates, and they wanted them immediately. Farmers, also seeking lower interest rates, formed a ring of protest around the Federal Reserve's Washington headquarters.

How can the Federal Reserve lower the interest rate through monetary policy? If the Federal Reserve increases the growth rate in the money supply and this increase is unexpected and permanent, this will reduce short-term interest rates, but only temporarily. The long-term interest rate will rise in expectation of the higher future inflation that the increase in the money supply will cause. When short-term rates are below long-term rates, it means that short-term rates are going to rise. The initial fall in short-term rates will prove temporary, as they will invariably increase as the rate of inflation rises.

If the Federal Reserve wants to lower long-term rates, it must instead reduce the rate of growth of the money supply! When the Federal Reserve unexpectedly reduces the growth rate of the money supply, the initial effect will be to increase short-term interest rates. But the effect on long-term interest rates will be in the opposite direction. A reduction in the rate of growth of the money supply means lower future inflation rates. So long-term interest rates will decline when economic decision makers recognize that a new monetary policy is in effect. When short-term rates are above long-term rates, it means that short-term rates are about to fall. And they will decline as expectations of the future rate of inflation are revised.

The difficulty with this approach is that a decline in the money supply may also bring about a decline in real national income in the short run as an inflationary recession results. Curing inflation thus presents a dilemma for monetary authorities.

INFLATION FROM THE SUPPLY SIDE

An increase in the overall price level can also be stimulated from the supply side. Anything that causes the SRAS curve to shift to the left will cause the price level to rise. A decline in technology, an increase in the prices of the factors of production, or an increase in inflationary expectations can cause such a shift. You discovered in Chapter 11 that a large increase in the price of crude oil initiated an **adverse supply shock** that had dramatic consequences for the rate of inflation in 1974–1975 and again in 1980–1981.

> *An adverse supply shock is the effect of an increase in the costs of production without a concurrent increase in aggregate demand.*

Inflation due to an adverse supply shock can be easily distinguished from inflation due to an increase in aggregate demand. When the price level rises due to an adverse supply shock, the level of real national income and employment will also decline. Inflation due to an increase in aggregate demand will produce the opposite effect on real national income and employment.

ADVERSE SUPPLY SHOCKS

You are already familiar with the effects that an adverse supply shock will have on the macroeconomy. When an adverse supply shock occurs, as shown in Figure 16.8, the SRAS curve shifts to the left. Equilibrium in the short run moves from E_1 to E_{SR}, the price level rises, and real national income declines to a level below the level of potential national income. A recessionary gap is created. This short-run equilibrium cannot be permanent — the price level is too high to sustain full employment. You will recall from Chapter 7 that if nothing is done by macroeconomic policymakers, the SRAS curve will eventually shift back to the right as wages and factor prices fall in the long run.

Suppose, instead, that policymakers, under pressure to do something about the rising unemployment caused by the supply shock, decide to expand aggregate demand by instituting either expansionary fiscal or monetary policy. What will be the effect of the change in policy? If monetary authorities decide to increase the growth rate of the money supply in order to expand aggregate demand, the results are as shown in Part B of Figure 16.8. Aggregate demand expands and the aggregate demand curve shifts to the right, from AD to AD_1, sufficiently to move the equilibrium position from E_{SR} to E_R. Full employment is restored as the equilibrium level of real national income increases from Y_{SR} to Y_P. The price level, however, rises from PL_2 to PL_3. The inflation initiated from the supply side has been made permanent — through a process called **ratification** — by an increase in aggregate demand resulting from the monetary policy.

> *Ratification is a process by which supply-side inflation is made permanent when the government adopts an expansionary policy, usually by increasing the money supply, to offset the rise in unemployment caused by an adverse supply shock.*

RATIFICATION OF THE WAGE/PRICE SPIRAL

When an adverse supply shock is ratified, it can lead to a wage/price spiral in which the inflation becomes continuous. When inflation becomes a common experience, as it did during the Great Inflation, future inflation becomes expected. The anticipated rate of future inflation will be taken into account when negotiating contracts. For example, if the rate of inflation is anticipated to be 8 percent, all prices and wages will automatically increase by 8 percent each year. The SRAS curve will shift to the left in anticipation of a similar increase in the aggregate demand curve.

This situation creates another dilemma for economic policymakers. The way to reduce inflation is to reduce the rate of growth of aggregate demand. But if this is done without an accompanying reduction in inflationary expectations, a recessionary gap will appear as real national income declines and unemployment increases.

Figure 16.9 illustrates this situation. When inflation is expected to occur at a given rate in anticipation of an increase in aggregate demand

FIGURE 16.8
Ratification of an Adverse Supply Shock

The effects of an adverse supply shock are shown in Part A. Due to higher costs of production caused by some economic event, the economy's supply of goods is depressed in the short run (shown by the aggregate supply curve shifting to the left from SRAS to $SRAS_1$). This change puts upward pressure on both inflation (shown by the price level rising from PL_1 to PL_2) and unemployment (shown by the economy's real income falling from Y_P to Y_{SR}). This supply-side inflation is ratified if the government chooses to implement expansionary policies to fight the unemployment. This situation is shown in Part B. The government's policies stimulate the demand for the economy's goods (shown by aggregate demand shifting to the right, from AD to AD_1). Although these policies restore full employment (since equilibrium real income rises from Y_{SR} to Y_P), they create more inflation (since the price level has risen from PL_2 to PL_3).

(A) Adverse Supply Shock

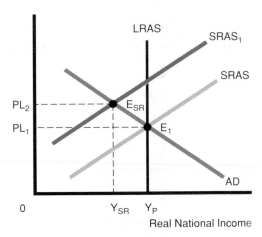

(B) Ratification of Supply Shock

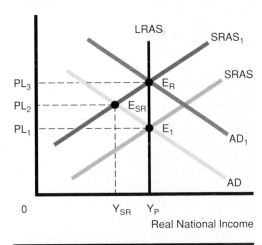

FIGURE 16.9

The Dilemma of Government Officials Trying to Stop Expected Inflation

When inflation becomes a common experience, consumers and firms expect the money supply to continue to increase to accommodate the inflation (i.e., they expect aggregate demand to continue to rise, from AD to AD_E), and they build the expected inflation rate into their wage and other contracts (so aggregate supply also shifts, from SRAS to $SRAS_E$). If the government does nothing, the wage/price spiral will continue, as the equilibrium adjusts from E_1 to E_E and the price level rises from PL_1 to PL_3. This situation puts government policymakers in a bind. If monetary authorities do not increase the money supply sufficiently to accommodate the expected inflation, aggregate demand increases only to AD_A. This policy slows down inflation, since the price level rises only to PL_2, not PL_3, but it also creates a recessionary gap as output falls from Y_P to Y_A.

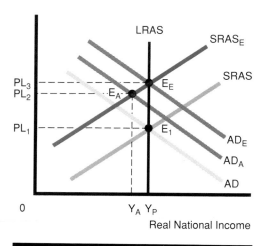

Price Level

Real National Income

from AD to AD_E, the SRAS curve will automatically shift up from SRAS to $SRAS_E$. Government officials are caught in a bind. If they allow the aggregate demand curve to shift to AD_E, the price level will increase as expected from PL_1 to PL_3. If, instead, they decide to fight inflation and allow the aggregate demand curve to shift up only to AD_A, there will be a lower level of inflation — the price level will increase only to PL_2. But real national income will fall and unemployment rise as a recessionary gap is created.

An adverse supply shock may lead to a wage/price spiral if the main economic goal of the government is to maintain full employment. When the economy suffers a supply shock, the resulting inflation will be ratified — indeed, made worse — by the expansion of aggregate demand caused by the government's policy to avoid unemployment. Once started, the wage/price spiral cannot be costlessly halted unless inflationary expectations can be reversed. On the other hand, unless the expected rate of inflation is ratified by expansionary monetary or fiscal policy, a recessionary gap will develop.

POSSIBLE SOLUTIONS TO THE PROBLEM OF INFLATION

The United States has had a varied experience with inflation. Over the last 40 years inflation has ranged from being the Number 1 economic problem to not being much of a problem at all. During the Great Inflation of 1966–1982, inflation was the major macroeconomic problem facing the country. During those years there were periods of historically high inflation, which became a thorn in the side of a series of presidents who attempted to deal with the problem in a variety of ways with varied results. Both restrictive monetary and fiscal policies were periodically tried and abandoned, only to be tried again later. Restrictive monetary policy, including credit controls, was tried at various times. Fiscal policy, in the form of tax increases, incomes policy, and even wage and price controls, was attempted during the 1970s and early 1980s.

In this section we shall examine these as well as other possible solutions to the inflation problem. As we discuss these possible cures, notice that economists can be divided into two groups according to the policies they advocate for dealing with inflation. They can be roughly divided according to their opinions about (1) the actual social and economic costs of inflation, and (2) the cost of controlling inflation, once it is under way, in the form of an increase in the unemployment rate.

THE "COLD TURKEY" CURE

Almost all economists believe that there is a "cold turkey" cure for inflation. The rate of inflation can be controlled by sharply reducing the rate of growth of the money supply. This can be seen in Part A of Figure 16.10. Inflationary expectations bring about an automatic upward shift of the SRAS curve from SRAS to $SRAS_E$ in expectation of an increase in aggregate demand from AD to AD_E, which would cause the price level to increase to PL_3. But suppose, instead, that monetary policy freezes the aggregate demand curve at AD. In this case the equilibrium position shifts from E_1 to E_{SR}, the price level rises to PL_2 (not PL_3), and real national income declines from Y_P to Y_{SR}. A recessionary gap appears.

In the long run businesses and workers will realize that the actual inflation rate is less than they expected and inflationary expectations will adjust downward. Eventually, the SRAS curve in Part B of Figure 16.10 will shift back to the right, the price level will fall to PL₁, and real aggregate output will rise to the level of potential national income. The decline in prices will eliminate the recessionary gap. The cost of revising inflationary expectations can be measured in terms of the lost output suffered while the recessionary gap exists.

THE KEYNESIAN VIEW

Not all economists believe that the results of the cold-turkey approach would be worth the cost. One group of economists, the Keynesians, believe that inflation itself is not very costly and is much less a social concern than unemployment. They believe, on the one hand, that inflation quickly becomes anticipated and that the shoe-leather and menu costs incurred, as decision makers conserve on money, are not large. On the other hand, they believe that quickly halting inflation by restrictive monetary policy would be very costly in terms of the increased unemployment that would inevitably result.

How costly will it be to eliminate inflation by the cold-turkey method? In the early 1980s, when inflation was at double-digit levels, by some estimates it would have been very costly indeed. One estimate suggested that to reduce inflation from 10 to 0 percent would take 15 years and that the unemployment rate would reach 10 percent and have to stay high for many years to accomplish this feat. Other estimates, though not quite so large, also seemed to confirm that fighting inflation would be quite costly in terms of increased unemployment.

Such large estimates convinced many economists that a cold-turkey strategy is too expensive. They advocate either living with inflation or adopting policies to bring down gradually the rate of inflation without significantly increasing unemployment.

LIVING WITH INFLATION   If inflation is costly to stop, perhaps it would be better to try to eliminate its damaging effects rather than attempt to eliminate the inflation itself. Living with inflation would require some institutional modifications to eliminate the inefficiencies that inflation might cause. Steps would have to be taken that would reduce the inefficiencies and the redistribution of income that unanticipated inflation causes.

For example, all existing price controls, such as those imposed on natural gas, would have to be removed. All tax rates and transfers would have to be automatically adjusted to account for inflation as it occurs. Wages and the prices of resources would also need to rise automatically with the price level. One way these various factors can be linked to the overall price index is through a process known as **indexing**.

> *Indexing is the process of automatically adjusting wages and prices for the effects of inflation.*

One way to achieve indexing is to include a cost-of-living escalator in all economic contracts. When inflation is reflected in the rise of the overall price index, wages and other payments that are indexed will automatically increase by the amount required to keep their real values constant. If all prices, wages, taxes, and transfers were indexed, then unanticipated inflation would neither redistribute income nor cause an inefficient allocation of resources.

Currently, a number of steps have been taken to index the economy. Some labor contracts, for example, include cost-of-living escalators that

F I G U R E   1 6 . 1 0
Cold Turkey Approach to Eliminating Inflation

During inflationary times, consumers and firms expect the monetary authorities to continue increasing the money supply to accommodate the inflation, so consumers and firms expect aggregate demand to shift from AD to AD$_E$ in Part A. In the cold turkey approach, the monetary authorities put the brakes on the money supply. Aggregate demand does not continue to rise as expected, but is frozen at AD. As shown in Part A, this creates a recessionary gap, with output falling from Y$_P$ to Y$_{SR}$. The price level, however, is not as high as expected, rising from PL$_1$ to only PL$_2$ instead of PL$_3$. In the long run, inflationary expectations adjust to the lower-than-expected inflation caused by the tight-money policy, and this is illustrated in Part B. This change stimulates the supply of goods in the economy, and aggregate supply shifts back to the right. Full employment is restored as real national income rises from Y$_{SR}$ to Y$_P$.

(A) Short Run

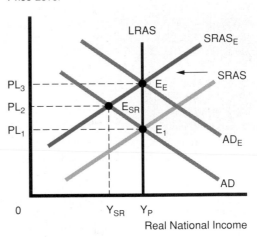

(B) Long Run

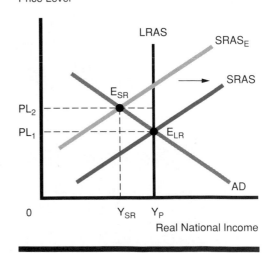

link the workers' wages to an existing price index such as the consumer price index. Social Security benefits are currently indexed, protecting recipients from being adversely affected by future inflation. Variable-rate mortgages are widely available. In these mortgages the interest rate charged on home loans rises or falls with the market rate of interest, which is, as we have seen, highly sensitive to the rate of inflation. A policy of successfully living with inflation would require that indexing be part of all transactions.

Indexing is not a cure-all for inflation, however. Indexing all transactions would be difficult, and indexing adjusts prices only after a lag. Moreover, indexing does not reduce the shoe-leather and menu costs of inflation. Finally, living with inflation may, by reducing the social costs of inflation, lead to ever-higher inflation rates. Runaway inflations could become more likely, and these hyperinflations certainly are not costless and force the economy to resort increasingly to barter.

When inflation is a major problem, indexing can reduce the social costs that inflation imposes on society. Most economists, however, do not advocate living with inflation as an acceptable alternative either to not letting inflation get started in the first place or to establishing policies that will reduce the rate of inflation.

GRADUALISM   Even economists who do not think the social costs of moderate inflation are large believe that inflation should be curtailed, provided the cost is not too high. These economists are likely to be of the Keynesian persuasion and to see inflation as the product of more than just an excess supply of money. They point to the accelerations in the inflation rate that occurred in 1974–1975 and 1980–1981 as examples that more than an excess supply of money is involved.

A comprehensive policy for fighting inflation must, in their opinion, encompass more than monetary policy if the benefits are to exceed the costs. They propose aggregate demand management using all of the macroeconomic tools available to the government, not just monetary policy. Aggregate demand should be managed to reduce the rate of inflation gradually in the hope that this could be accomplished without causing unemployment to substantially increase. This policy is known as **gradualism.**

> *Gradualism is a policy for reducing the inflation rate slowly over time by managing aggregate demand in the hope of avoiding a rise in the unemployment rate as the macroeconomy adjusts to ever-lower rates of inflation.*

The economists who advocate gradualism also recommend that the federal government, when faced with inflation, develop an **incomes policy** to use along with active aggregate demand management. An incomes policy is composed of a set of wage and price guidelines that are supposed to guide contract negotiations.

> *An incomes policy is a set of guidelines, or rules, devised by the federal government to influence wage and price increases and inflationary expectations.*

The purpose of an incomes policy is to reduce the rate of inflation and to influence inflationary expectations accordingly. To be successful, an incomes policy must include two components. First, the federal government must attempt to manage aggregate demand so that the rate of inflation gradually declines. Absent this component, an incomes policy is sure to fail. Second, the incomes policy must be announced — everyone must be aware of the changes and how they will affect the future price level so that they can act accordingly.

An incomes policy may be purely voluntary, or coupled with incentives for compliance, or legally mandated in the form of wage and price controls. Whenever a purely voluntary incomes policy is employed, the federal government tries to use moral suasion to achieve compliance. Such voluntary wage and price guidelines were tried periodically throughout much of the Great Inflation. Presidents Nixon, Ford, and Carter all employed voluntary wage and price guidelines.

These attempts to talk down the rate of inflation were characterized as "jawboning" by the nation's press and did not meet with much success. Often these incomes policies were not accompanied by the vigorous anti-inflation aggregate demand management that is necessary if an incomes policy is to succeed. When economic decision makers were faced with inflationary pressures on the one hand and the contrary suggestions of their government on the other, inflationary pressures generally won out.

A successful incomes policy therefore requires (1) that aggregate demand be regularly and gradually reduced to bring down the inflation rate; (2) that the incomes policy accurately predict what the future inflation rate will be, based on the level of aggregate demand; and (3) that the public act as if it believes the incomes policy to be effective and its predictions accurate. All three conditions were never present at the same time during the Great Inflation. As a result, the public lost confidence in incomes policies as effective weapons in the fight against inflation.

Even if the first two conditions for a successful incomes policy were met, the lack of the third would defeat any program. One way to ensure that the third condition would be met would be to create incentives to act according to the government's incomes policy. To provide an incentive for economic decision makers to take the guidelines seriously, some economists suggested that a **tax-based incomes program (TIP)** be adopted by the federal government.

A tax-based incomes program is a program that rewards workers and business firms with tax breaks if they act in compliance with the government's wage and price guidelines and penalizes them with higher taxes if they do not.

Under a tax-based incomes program, business firms would know that the amount of taxes they have to pay would depend on how much they raised their prices. If they priced their products in accord with the national price guidelines, they would pay less in taxes or, at the very least, not suffer any tax penalty. If their price increases exceeded the amount permitted by the guidelines, however, they would pay a sufficiently high tax penalty, making the excess price increase profitless.

Workers would have similar incentives under a TIP. As long as their wage increases were within allowed limits, their personal income tax bill might be lowered or, at least, would not increase. But if they demanded and received an excessive pay increase (relative to the guidelines), their tax bill would go up by enough to make the pay raise undesirable. The Carter administration tried unsuccessfully to persuade Congress to adopt a wage TIP. Tax-based incomes policies therefore remain untried. Doubtless they would be a bureaucratic nightmare to administer, but the proponents of TIP suggest that it would be less costly than the alternative of reducing inflation by the cold-turkey approach.

The most extreme form of incomes policy is legislated **wage and price controls.**

Wage and price controls set legal limits on the wages and prices that firms are allowed to pay and charge.

In wartime, wage and price controls are often used to avoid inflation as the nation devotes its resources to producing war materials. Wage and price control programs may set rules that limit future increases or may take the form of outright freezes. More recently, in 1971, President Nixon surprised the nation by imposing a wage and price freeze for 90 days in an attempt to break the back of inflation.

The principal argument for legal wage and price controls is that such controls can help to reverse inflationary expectations. Suppose that inflation has become entrenched in the economy and is expected to continue in the future. If the government suddenly adopts a restrictive macroeconomic policy without wage and price controls, the SRAS curve would shift to the left (due to the inflationary expectations), and the aggregate demand curve would also shift to the left (due to the government's contractionary policy). The result would be an inflationary recession. Wage and price controls could control (that is, fix) the SRAS curve and control inflationary expectations while the restrictive macroeconomic policies were being implemented.

The basic argument against wage and price controls is that relative price adjustments cannot occur when prices are not allowed to change. The efficient allocation of resources is therefore impeded. Virtually all economists believe that wage and price controls should not be employed over an extended period of time.

Some economists, however, think that wage and price controls for a limited period of time may be helpful in breaking inflationary expectations, provided that the controls are accompanied by an appropriately restrictive macroeconomic policy. When wage and price controls are imposed, shortages are expected and will certainly occur if aggregate demand continues to be as expansive in the future as it had been in the past. If this happens, firms and their employees will rush to raise prices and wages when the controls are eliminated. Therefore wage and price controls will be ineffective in combating inflation unless they are accompanied by a restrictive macroeconomic policy.

If a restrictive macroeconomic policy accompanies price controls, few shortages will occur and businesses and their employees will not feel that prices should be raised when the controls expire. That is how it might work *in theory*, but it has not worked that way in the past — probably because an appropriate restrictive macroeconomic policy has not accompanied controls. Controls are never a substitute but may be a possible complement for a restrictive macroeconomic policy to combat inflation.

THE MONETARIST VIEW

Another group of economists — called monetarists — believe that inflation is primarily a monetary phenomenon for which the only cure is a reduction in the rate of growth of the money supply. Inflation, they believe, cannot persist whatever its initial cause without an accommodating increase in the money supply. There is little doubt that the United States would have experienced less inflation over the last two decades if the rate of monetary growth had been slower. According to monetarists, the only way to lower future inflation rates is to lower the rate of growth of the money supply.

Monetarists offer several pieces of evidence to support their view. First, there is, as we have seen, a close historical relationship between monetary growth and the rate of inflation. The faster the rate of growth of the money supply, the higher future inflation rates will be. Second, recessions are often preceded by sharp declines in the rate of growth in the money supply. Third, the relationship between the growth in the money supply and the increase in nominal national income is lagged. This lag is not predictable but, generally, nominal national income will increase sometime between six months and two years after an increase in the money supply occurs. This increase will be composed of a temporary increase in real national income and a permanent increase in the price level.

On the basis of these observations, the monetarists suggest that inflation can be cured only by a reduction in the rate of growth of the money supply. Moreover, the fluctuations of the money supply actually cause most of the fluctuations in nominal national income that accompany business cycles. The solution to present and future inflations and business fluctuations is a steady slow growth in the money supply.

THE 4 PERCENT SOLUTION The central bank of the United States (the Federal Reserve Board) controls the money supply. The wide variations in the growth rate of the money supply are primarily due to the discretionary actions of the Federal Reserve Board. If the money supply is to be regulated, the Federal Reserve must itself be controlled. The central bank is a creation of Congress, and Congress can influence the Federal Reserve through legislation.

One way that Congress can influence the Federal Reserve is to pass a law that the Federal Reserve must limit money supply growth in the future to a constant rate. Such a mandate is known as the **constant growth rate rule.**

> *The constant growth rate rule is a policy that requires the Federal Reserve to expand the money supply at a constant annual rate in the future.*

Under such a law a policy rule would replace the discretionary monetary policy of the Federal Reserve Board, whose sole job would then be to regulate the rate of growth of the money supply within the strict limits set by Congress.

What should that rate of growth be? It really does not matter; any rate would do as long as it is constant. One suggestion has been to allow the money supply to increase annually at the rate of long-term growth of real GNP — somewhere between 3 and 4 percent. Thus, according to the monetarists, the economy would have sufficient new money to finance economic growth at constant prices. Inflation would cease to be a problem and most business fluctuations would be eliminated.

To control the growth rate of the money supply, a common suggestion in the political arena has been to fix the value of the dollar to the value of a commodity that is limited in supply. Gold has historically served this function, providing what is known as a **gold standard.**

> *The gold standard is a monetary system in which the value of the dollar is fixed in terms of a specific quantity of gold, and the government is obligated to buy and sell gold at this fixed dollar rate.*

Proponents of the gold standard believe that making the dollar convertible to gold at a fixed rate would limit the future growth of the money supply. Suppose, for example, that the dollar was made convertible to gold on demand at the rate of $500 per ounce. The U.S. Treasury would be obligated to buy gold at $500 per ounce or to sell gold at the same price. If the Federal Reserve created so much money that inflation was threatened, people would convert dollars to gold in the belief that the government could not for long keep the dollar price of gold fixed at $500 per ounce. Given the limited amount of the government's gold reserves, the Federal Reserve would have to reduce the rate of growth of the money supply to ensure that the government could meet the demand for gold at the fixed price.

Under the gold standard, the money supply is tied to the quantity of gold. Monetary authorities could no longer expand the money supply without limit. The quantity of money would rise and fall with the country's stock of gold. Consequently, inflations and deflations could still occur under the gold standard. In fact, during the period in which the United States was on the gold standard, the economy experienced both deflations and inflations. From 1880 to 1896 the price level fell nearly 50 percent, and from 1896 to 1913 it rose by over 40 percent. Under a gold standard, the economy would still experience inflation caused by the shocks of war or crop failures. Furthermore, new gold discoveries and technological changes improving the efficiency of gold mining could stimulate the money supply and cause inflation.

Many economists, both monetarists and Keynesians, are dubious about returning to the gold standard. Monetarists do not believe that the gold standard would guarantee a constant rate of increase in the money supply. When the United States operated under a gold standard, the growth in the money supply still fluctuated from year to year. Keynesians are dubious for a different reason. They are opposed to the elimination of the Federal Reserve's discretionary monetary policy, which would occur under a return to the gold standard.

MONETARISTS' ANTI-INFLATION POLICY The constant growth rate rule is a way to avoid inflation. But what should be done when inflation is already a problem? The monetarists break down into two groups according to the way they believe inflationary expectations are formulated. Both groups believe that inflation is primarily a monetary matter and that the end of inflation requires a reduction in the growth rate of the money supply. But some monetarists think that expectations are formulated out of past experiences (adaptive expectations) and believe that lower inflation rates must be experienced to be believed. Other monetarists think that economic decision makers use all available information when formulating expectations (rational expectations) and that a credible anti-inflation program could quickly reverse inflationary expectations.

The theory of adaptive expectations suggests that a program to end inflation quickly by sharply reducing the growth rate of the money supply would bring about a recession. According to those economists who hold to this theory, wide swings in the growth rate of the money supply are the main cause of economic fluctuations. They agree with the Keynesians that the cold-turkey approach would be costly and that gradualism is an appropriate strategy. Their main difference with the Keynesians is that they feel that only money matters in this case. They would advocate that the growth of the money supply be slowly reduced to a low level and then held there to avoid the return of inflation in the future.

Monetarists of the rational expectations persuasion agree that a policy of gradualism. if adhered to, would work, but they also think there could be a quicker way to end inflation without causing a recession. They do not believe that the cold-turkey approach would necessarily cause a recession. If the Federal Reserve were to announce that the money supply would grow only at a low constant rate and were determined to make it so — and everyone believed them — then inflationary expectations would quickly adjust downward and a recession would be avoided.

There are thus three essential aspects of this program: (1) a reduction of the growth of the money supply must be announced, (2) the reduction must actually happen, and (3) the announcement must be believed. To support their view, proponents of the rational expectations approach point to the quick end of the German hyperinflation of the 1920s.

SUMMARY

1. The possible effects of inflation are (1) a reduction in economic efficiency due to menu and shoe-leather costs, (2) changes in the level of real national income and employment, and (3) a redistribution of income among individuals in the society.

2. There are four basic facts about inflation: (1) Inflation is not inevitable but is man-made, (2) persistent inflation is always associated with excess growth in the money supply, (3) high inflation rates are correlated with high nominal interest rates, and (4) the effects that inflation has on the economy are minor when the inflation is anticipated but substantial when the inflation is not anticipated.

3. Persistent inflations are the result of continual rightward shifts in aggregate demand caused by rapid money growth. Rapid money growth occurs when the money supply expands faster than required to accommodate changes in real GNP and the velocity of circulation.

4. The basic macroeconomic model can be used to determine the effects of a one-time, unanticipated increase in the money supply on a full-employment economy. In the short run (1) the interest rate will first fall, then rise but remain below the initial level, (2) investment will rise, (3) the price level will rise, and (4) real output will rise above the potential level of output. In the long run the real sector of the economy will be unaffected (i.e., the interest rate, investment, and real output will have returned to their initial levels) and only the price level will have risen.

5. The effects of anticipated inflation are quite different from the effects of unanticipated inflation. As aggregate demand shifts to the right, creating inflation (due, say, to growth in the money supply), aggregate supply shifts to the left, since workers and other sellers of resources will build cost-of-living increases into their contracts to account for the anticipated inflation. Consequently, only the price level will rise; the real sector of the economy will be unaffected by anticipated inflations (save for menu and shoe-leather costs).

6. Whether inflation is unanticipated and has substantial effects on the economy or is anticipated and has minor effects on the economy depends on how expectations are formed. Adaptive expectations are expectations that are gradually modified in reaction to changing economic conditions — in this case changes in inflation will be unanticipated and will affect the economy's real sector. Rational expectations are formed by using all available information — in this case when policies that affect the inflation rate are announced and their effects are correctly predicted, the inflation will be anticipated and its effects will be minor.

7. Both short-term and long-term interest rates are published in the financial pages of major-city newspapers. A one-time increase in the price level (such as caused by a one-time, unexpected increase in the money supply) will affect only short-term interest rates. A permanent increase in inflation (such as caused by a permanent increase in the rate of growth of the money supply) will affect both short- and long-term interest rates.

8. Velocity is also affected by rising inflation. The Friedman surge predicts that an increase in the rate of growth of the money supply will create an even larger increase in the rate of inflation, because the anticipation of future inflation will also increase the velocity of circulation.

9. If interest rates are high due to high inflationary expectations, the Federal Reserve must tighten the money supply to lower those expectations, even though this will temporarily increase short-term interest rates.

10. Adverse supply shocks can also create inflation. Because unemployment rises from an adverse supply shock, the government may ratify the inflation by stimulating aggregate demand in the economy. This ratification can lead to a wage/price spiral caused by rising inflationary expectations.

11. One potential cure for inflation is the cold-turkey approach, in which the rate of growth of the money supply is sharply reduced in order to lower inflationary expectations. Keynesians and monetarists who believe in adaptive expectations fear that a recessionary gap would make the costs of the cold-turkey approach too large. Monetarists who adhere to the theory of rational expectations believe a recessionary gap can be avoided if the policy is announced and agents act accordingly.

12. Indexing can make living with inflation feasible and has already been implemented in some contracts. However, indexing would be difficult to implement in the entire economy, would suffer from lags, would not affect menu and shoe-leather costs, and could lead to further inflation.

13. Keynesian economists and monetarists who follow the theory of adaptive expectations recommend gradualism — a policy to reduce aggregate demand slowly in order to ease the economy into lower inflationary expectations without triggering a recession. Keynesians recommend using all tools available to the government to manage aggregate demand, whereas monetarists recommend steady reductions in the growth of the money supply until an adequately low level is reached and maintained.

14. Incomes policies — tax-based incomes programs and temporary wage and price controls — may be able to stabilize aggregate supply while the government conducts aggregate demand management. Although the efficacy of these policies is uncertain due to lack of experience, economists generally agree that prolonged wage and price controls are unwise.

15. Monetarists believe that inflation is primarily a monetary phenomenon. To keep inflation under control, they recommend slow, steady growth in the money supply, generally in the 3 to 4 percent range.

16. Under a gold standard, the government guarantees to buy and sell gold at a fixed dollar price. Proponents of a gold standard note that this would prevent the Federal Reserve from expanding the money supply too quickly and would therefore keep inflation under control. Most economists oppose a gold standard. Monetarists believe that a gold standard would be inadequate to guarantee a fixed growth in the money supply, whereas Keynesians believe that discretionary monetary policy is a valuable tool of the Federal Reserve that should not be curtailed.

PREDICTING FUTURE RATES OF INFLATION

Economic forecasting is one of the more challenging tasks facing a student of economics. Predicting changes in the direction of the inflation rate is especially challenging: Is the rate of inflation going to increase or decline in the future?

Fortunately, obtaining the data to predict inflation is not a serious problem. The U.S. government and the financial markets of the country are prodigious producers of economic statistics. This information is reported by the nation's press on a timely basis, generally the same day that the data are released or generated. The problem is to select from among the many economic statistics that are available the ones that are the best indicators of future changes in the price level.

There are three criteria for selecting an indicator: relevance and stability, timeliness, and availability. The first and most important criterion is relevance and stability. This is where economic theory comes in. We are looking for an economic time series (a series of data over time) that foretells changes in the price level. This time series must be stable in the sense that it does not fluctuate enough to make its path unpredictable. Besides being relevant and stable, for an indicator of inflation to be useful it must also be easily available in a timely manner. The most timely and available indicators are ones that are compiled quickly and published immediately upon release. An indicator that takes months to calculate and more months to circulate will be of limited use. Only a few of the hundreds of economic statistics available come close to meeting the tests of relevance and stability, timeliness, and availability.

There is no such thing as a perfect indicator of inflation. A few come close, however, and a few is all we need. These are (1) the producer price index, (2) the growth rate of the money supply, and (3) the commodity price index. Each of these statistics tends to foretell changes in the consumer price index, albeit imperfectly. Thus it is wise to watch all three at the same time. Let us examine each in turn.

THE PRODUCER PRICE INDEX

The producer price index (PPI) is one of the leading indicators of inflation. The PPI measures prices at the wholesale level — the prices that retailers must pay for the goods they in turn sell to you. It is released the second week of the following month, and is widely reported in the press. Price changes that begin at the commodity level and work their way through the economy will affect the PPI before they affect the consumer price index.

To see the efficacy of using the PPI as an indicator of inflation, refer back to Figure 16.2, which shows the inflation rate as measured by the PPI along with that for the consumer price index (CPI). It is clear that both show the same general pattern of inflation. When the PPI is rising, so is the CPI, and when the PPI is falling, so is the CPI. But changes in the PPI typically, but not always, lead (foretell) changes in the CPI. Increases in the inflation rate of the PPI typically lead similar increases in the CPI by a matter of months. Also, declines in the rate of inflation are likely to show up first as declines in the rate of increase of the PPI. However, the PPI is more volatile than the CPI — it changes direction more often. This is a defect in this indicator, since it allows false predictions. The PPI is generally a good indicator of changes in the overall rate of inflation, but it is not perfect. It must, like all indicators, be used with caution.

THE MONEY SUPPLY

You saw in this chapter that inflation is generally a monetary phenomenon. Increases in the price level generally follow increases in the money supply. Thus changes in the money supply should precede changes in the inflation rate. If you turn back to Figure 16.4, which showed the rate of change in the money supply and in the inflation rate, you can check this for yourself. Clearly, money growth is a leading indicator of inflation. Both the peaks and troughs of the growth rate of the money supply precede the peaks and troughs of the inflation rate.

Changes in the rate of inflation are not, however, due entirely to changes in the money supply. Changes in aggregate supply, as you know, can also affect the price level. The surges in inflation in 1974–1975 and again in 1979–1980 were partially due to adverse supply shocks that occurred during these periods. The shifts to the left in the aggregate supply curve due to the adverse supply shocks reinforced the effect of increases in the growth rate of the money supply on the overall price level. This suggests that changes in the growth rate of the money supply cannot perfectly predict future inflation rates, because a rise in the price level can come about from other sources such as supply shocks.

Another factor makes change in the money supply an imperfect indicator. When a sudden increase in the money supply occurs, it will result in a disproportionate increase in the CPI, because velocity of circulation will increase. This increase is caused by individuals attempting to conserve on money as inflation accelerates. Inflation works like a tax on money, causing the purchasing power of money to decline. Since the opportunity cost of holding money has increased, individuals will attempt to hold less money and more interest-bearing assets. The velocity of money increases, causing the price index to rise more than proportionally to the increase in the money supply.

When the increase in the money supply slows, this process works in reverse. Velocity declines as the opportunity cost of holding money falls and the rate of inflation slows.

Changes in the growth rate of the money supply foretell changes in the rate of inflation by long, variable periods of time. The lag between peaks and troughs of money supply growth and the corresponding peaks and troughs of the inflation rate is fairly long. In Figure 16.4 when you connect the peaks of money growth with the peaks of the inflation rate, the lag appears to be about two years, sometimes less and sometimes more.

You will also notice a sharp rise and peak in the growth rate of the money supply in 1983. There is no corresponding sharp rise and peak in the rate of inflation thereafter. Changes in the rate of growth of the money supply gave a false signal in 1983. In fact, many economic forecasters were misled and predicted the return of high inflation rates by 1985. In hindsight, they should not have been misled. You will recall from Chapter 13 that 1983 was the first year that banks could offer checking accounts that paid interest. These interest-bearing accounts were included in calculating the money supply. Because depositors quickly moved to take advantage of this new opportunity and funds flowed into these accounts, the money-supply numbers swelled. Much of this money came from other interest-bearing accounts, such as maturing CDs. Investors had no intention of spending these funds — they were savings, not money balances waiting to be spent. Once this surge was past, the underlying, less-inflationary growth rate of the money supply became apparent by 1985.

Changes in the institutional structure of the banking system can influence the measures of money growth, so such changes must be watched with care. They provide another reason to watch a variety of indicators to predict future inflation rates.

THE COMMODITY PRICE INDEX

The producer price index is available monthly and money supply figures are available weekly, but the commodity price index is available daily. The Dow Jones Commodity Spot Price Index is reported daily in *The Wall Street Journal*. The commodities that make up this index are the basic raw materials used by the industrial sector, such as oil, copper, lumber, food, and fiber. These are sold in competitive markets, and pressures that will cause all prices eventually to rise show up here first. The prices of individual commodities are obviously subject to specialized factors, but the prices of a mix of commodities reflect common factors that are operating to change the price level.

The commodity price index is available only from 1975. The trend in these data shows that the collapse of the inflation rate that began in 1980 was forecast by an earlier rapid decline in the commodity price index. Moreover, the recovery in commodity prices indicated a revival of the inflation rate in the last half of 1983. Thereafter the rate of change in the commodity price index was flat, suggesting that the inflation rate was not going to rise significantly. If money watchers had also been monitoring the commodity price index, they never would have predicted the return of inflation due to the surge in the money supply that occurred in 1983–1984.

The commodity price index is particularly valuable in forecasting a future increase in the rate of inflation or for predicting the end of an inflationary spiral. This index seems particularly responsive to the forces that eventually result in changes in the rate of inflation.

No single indicator of inflation is perfect. Each is likely to give false signals from time to time. Three indicators of inflation have been presented in this application for you to use as your crystal ball. If you follow them, you will have as good a sense of the direction of future inflation as anyone else.[1]

[1]Source for this analysis: Charles R. Nelson, *The Investor's Guide to Economic Indicators* (New York: Wiley, 1987).

REQUIRED ECONOMIC CONCEPTS

Anticipated inflation
Menu costs
Shoe-leather costs
Unanticipated inflation
Adaptive expectations
Rational expectations
Fixed-income security
Short-term security
Short-term interest rate (yield)
Long-term security (bond)
Long-term interest rate (yield)
Expectations theory of interest rates

Spread
Friedman surge
Adverse supply shock
Ratification
Indexing
Gradualism
Incomes policy
Tax-based incomes program
Wage and price controls
Constant growth rate rule
Gold standard

KEY QUESTIONS

1. Why is it an illusion that prices overall rise by more than income overall and reduce the standard of living?
2. What is the sole cause of a persistent inflation?
3. Are the effects from an inflation that is anticipated different from an inflation that comes as a surprise?
4. How does a one-time increase in the money supply affect the rate of interest, the price level, and the level of real national income in the short run? The long run?
5. What is the theory of adaptive expectations?
6. What is the theory of rational expectations?
7. How do the adaptive expectations and rational expectations theories view the speed of adjustment concerning expectations?
8. What is the interest rate on a fixed-income security?
9. What monetary asset is considered the major indicator of short-term interest rates?
10. Are capital formation decisions guided by short-term or long-term interest rates?
11. What is the expectations theory of interest rates? What is the yield spread?
12. Will an unexpected one-time increase in the money supply permanently affect both short-term and long-term interest rates?
13. What is the Friedman surge?
14. What is the appropriate path to achieve lower interest rates when inflationary expectations are high?
15. What does it mean to ratify a supply-side-induced inflation?
16. What are the Keynesian arguments against a cold-turkey approach to stopping a wage/price-spiral inflation?
17. How can inflation be indexed?
18. What is an incomes policy?
19. What is a tax-based incomes policy (TIP)?
20. What is the gold-standard method of controlling inflation? What are the arguments against it?

PROBLEMS

1. When the velocity of money is rising relative to an increasing real GNP, would the growth in the quantity of money have to be increased or decreased proportionately in order to keep the price level the same, that is, to maintain a zero rate of inflation?

2. "In a barter economy inflation just cannot happen." Is this statement true or false? Why?

3. Indicate whether each of the following causes of inflation is primarily demand-side (demand shock) or supply-side (supply shock).

a. Taxes were not raised sufficiently in the latter 1960s when the United States expanded its military actions in Vietnam in 1965.

b. A major Midwest crop failure occurs.

c. The Social Security payroll tax is raised.

d. An outbreak of war in the Middle East severely reduces oil shipments to the United States and Europe.

e. An economy dependent on specialized materials and highly skilled labor will experience inflation when there are sudden and sharp switches in consumer tastes.

f. Capacity and labor shortages across a broad spectrum of industries occur because of large purchases of open-market securities by the Federal Reserve.

4. Explain why a sudden slowing of the rate of inflation to 5 percent after several years of 10 percent yearly inflation will cause the unemployment rate to go up. Will the initial rise in the unemployment rate persist if the decline in aggregate demand was caused by a one-time decline in the money supply? Why or why not?

5.   Why is there a tendency for the Federal Reserve to generate unanticipated inflation? How does this affect the public's attitude about the credibility of the Federal Reserve's policy announcements? How would the monetarists solve this credibility problem?

6.   An alternative approach to Keynesian activist monetary policy and to a rigid monetarist rule is to use monetary flexibility to respond to supply shocks but to maintain the monetary rule for demand shocks. Would doing so avoid the public credibility problem the Federal Reserve may have? That is, demand shocks can be faked by the Federal Reserve to justify surprise inflations that would then serve to prevent the economy from falling below its natural rate of unemployment. Why cannot supply shocks be as easily faked? Can "productivity shocks" be easily identified?

7.   Suppose that in the past whenever the economy experienced an unemployment rate above 6 percent, the government increased spending in a successful attempt to reduce the unemployment rate to 5 percent. This time, however, before the unemployment rate can reach 5 percent, the public anticipates that this policy will raise the inflation rate from 4 percent to 7 percent.

    a.   According to the theory of rational expectations, how will unions, banks, employers, nonunion workers, and suppliers adjust their asset holdings?

    b.   Will the policy goal pursued by the government lower unemployment or will the policy goal of lowering unemployment be nullified? Explain why this problem is an example of either adaptive expectations or rational expectations.

8.   In the short run firms are inclined to respond to a decline in the demand for their products by first adjusting their output and employment levels without changing relative prices and wages downward. Why?

APPLICATION ANALYSIS

1.   Use the accompanying graph to answer the following questions, where P_E refers to the expected price level.

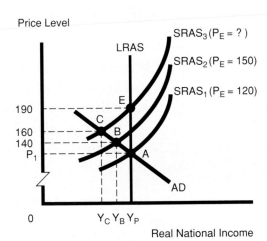

    a.   What is the actual price level at point B? What is the expected price level at point B?

    b.   Is employment higher or lower at point C compared to point B? Is the unemployment rate above or below the natural rate at point B?

    c.   What is the actual price level P_1? Can you determine the rate of inflation the economy experienced between points A and B? If so, what was it?

    d.   What expected price level P_E is applicable to $SRAS_3$?

    e.   At point C what rate of inflation is anticipated for the next period?

2.   During the recession of the early 1980s the inflation rate fell from 9.7 percent in 1981 to 3.7 percent in 1984, while the unemployment rate rose from 7.5 percent in 1981 to 9.5 percent in 1982 and 1983. It came down to 7.4 percent in 1984. Are these facts consistent with the theory of rational expectations?

17

THE INFLATION/ UNEMPLOYMENT TRADE-OFF

IN THIS CHAPTER YOU WILL LEARN:

When to expect a trade-off
between inflation and
unemployment in the short run

•

Why any inflation rate is
compatible with full
employment in the long run

•

Which factors affect the
duration of people's job
searches and how these
factors affect the
unemployment rate

•

How expectations about
inflation affect the inflation/
unemployment trade-off

•

The policies that
government can use to deal
with unemployment problems

STOPPING THE GREAT INFLATION: 1980–1986

By most accounts, inflation was the most important macroeconomic problem in 1980. Inflation had been accelerating from the 1–2 percent levels of the 1960s to around 10 percent during the presidential election year of 1980. Inflation remained high during the first year of Ronald Reagan's presidency. Unemployment was also a problem at 7.0 percent in 1980 and rising to 7.5 percent in 1981. What can be done by macroeconomic policymakers when the economy is experiencing both unacceptably high inflation and unemployment rates?

The Reagan administration and the Board of Governors of the Federal Reserve adopted an anti-inflationary program that was designed to reduce both the inflation rate and the unemployment rate. What actually happened? The rate of inflation fell substantially in every succeeding year through 1986, so the Reagan administration succeeded in half of its goals. The unemployment rate, however, first rose significantly for two years and then began to decline, but it wasn't until 1986 that the unemployment rate fell below the level seen in 1980. The rate of inflation declined as desired, but only after society paid the social costs from experiencing an extended period of excessive unemployment.

In the opinion of some economists, breaking the back of inflation ranks among the most significant economic gains of this decade. This success, however, came at a high cost in terms of the substantial unemployment that occurred, and so other economists believe that the cost paid to stop inflation was too high.

While economists are divided over the costs and benefits of the Reagan anti-inflation policy, most economists believe that the inverse relationship between inflation and unemployment that was experienced during the first half of the 1980s was no accident. The rise in unemployment was the price that had to be paid if the rate of inflation was to be significantly reduced. Why was it necessary to pay such a high price to end inflation?

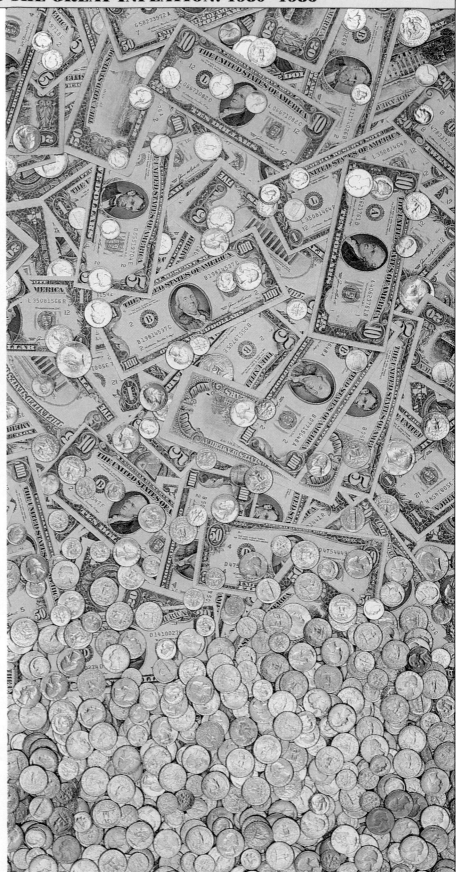

FALLING UNEMPLOYMENT: GOOD NEWS OR BAD FOR THE STOCK MARKET?

In June 1988 the stock market fell significantly on the news that the unemployment rate had declined to 5.3 percent — a 15-year low. What was going on here? A lower unemployment rate is generally considered good news, since it means that more people are working and fewer people are looking for work. Economic production in mid-1988 was, as a result, running at record levels. Why did investors react negatively to this news, which, on the face of it, appeared favorable?

The answer is simple: Investors interpreted the decline in the unemployment rate as a signal for the return of accelerating inflation. Investors, like all economic decision makers, remembered the Great Inflation of the 1970s. Both the stock and the bond markets had been badly battered during that period of substantial inflation.

The war against inflation had been the economy's great success story during the 1980s. The rate of inflation measured by the GNP deflator had declined from double-digit levels to about 3 percent in 1985 and 1986. In the last half of 1987, however, inflation increased to around 4 percent, and it rose even higher in the first half of 1988, increasing concerns about the potential for the return of accelerating inflation.

The decline in the unemployment rate was interpreted as indicating that labor markets were becoming tight. When labor markets are tight, wage rates rise. Since labor costs are a large proportion of the total costs of production, prices will also tend to rise. The conclusion from this straightforward reasoning is that lower unemployment rates should mean higher inflation rates. There should be an inverse relationship between the rate of inflation and the unemployment rate. When the unemployment rate declines, the inflation rate should, according to this logic, be increasing, and vice versa.

Why, then, did inflation remain low during most of the 1980s when the unemployment rate declined from 10.7 percent in 1982 to 5.3 percent by the middle of 1988 — in apparent contradiction to the argument made above? Moreover, the accelerating inflation that investors in the stock market feared in June 1988 failed to emerge in the following year. Why does falling unemployment not always signal rising inflation?

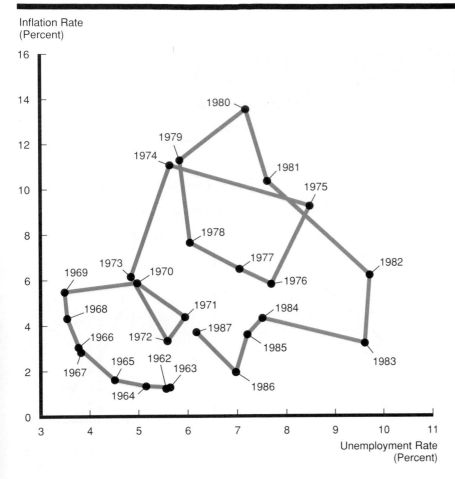

FIGURE 17.3
U.S. Inflation and Unemployment Rates: 1961–1987

The inflation/unemployment trade-off seen during the 1960s was clearly not stable in the long run. The data in this figure show that the trade-off either worsened or disappeared altogether during the 1970s and 1980s.

tion they prefer. A low level of inflation could be achieved only at the cost of a high level of unemployment; conversely, a low level of unemployment would mean a higher level of inflation. By choosing the rate of expansion in aggregate demand, government policymakers could obtain a desirable level of unemployment along with the corresponding inflation rate revealed by the Phillips curve.

Liberal economists and politicians were ecstatic, and conservatives were put on the defensive. The costs of unemployment are believed to be large when calculated as a percentage of GNP. The costs of anticipated inflation — and inflation would surely be anticipated as economic decision makers consulted the Phillips curve — are, as you know, relatively small. Weighing the benefits of low unemployment against the costs of a higher anticipated inflation, liberal economists suggested that aggressive expansions of aggregate demand were in order. The benefits of lower unemployment appeared large compared with the trivial costs of higher anticipated inflation.

Then something unexpected happened. The trade-off that existed during the 1960s worsened during the 1970s and seemed to disappear altogether in the 1980s. As shown in Figure 17.3, the Phillips curve we discovered for the 1960s seems to have totally vanished. Whatever trade-off exists between inflation and unemployment in the short run does not appear to exist in the long run.

FIGURE 17.4
Instability of the Short-Run Phillips Curve

If the economy is in a recessionary gap, as shown in Part A, there is downward pressure on wages and prices as the economy returns to full employment. So inflation and unemployment both fall when the economy recovers from a recessionary gap. In the Phillips curve in Part C, the adjustment process drives the economy from a point like A on the short-run Phillips curve PC_{SR} to a point like D, with the natural rate of unemployment (U_N) and a lower rate of inflation. The case of an inflationary gap is shown in Part B. Wages and the prices of other resources rise, causing aggregate supply to shift from $SRAS_1$ to $SRAS_2$. Both inflation and unemployment are rising. So the adjustment process takes the economy from a point like C in Part C to a point like D, with higher inflation and full employment.

   The short-run Phillips curve is not stable in the long run because the automatic adjustment mechanism drives the economy to full employment. In the long run, any inflation rate can coexist with the natural rate of inflation. This idea is shown in Part C by the long-run Phillips curve PC_{LR}, which is vertical at the natural rate of unemployment.

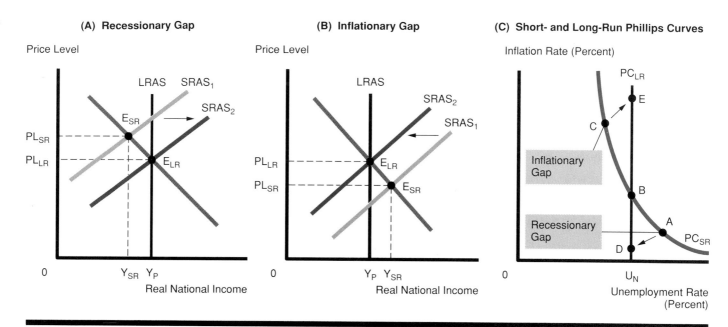

THE ORIGINAL MISINTERPRETATION OF THE PHILLIPS CURVE

Many economists initially believed that the Phillips curve provided a menu of possible long-run equilibrium positions from which to choose. Most economists now believe that this perception was incorrect. The Phillips curve, instead of presenting a menu with a variety of long-run options, is actually a short-run phenomenon that offers only one position representing a stable long-run equilibrium. That point occurs when the economy is operating at the level of potential national income and the unemployment rate is equal to the **natural rate of unemployment.**

> *The natural rate of unemployment is the rate of unemployment that corresponds to the level of potential national income.*

Most points on the Phillips curve are not sustainable in the long run because of the economy's automatic self-correcting mechanism. Whenever the economy is operating away from the level of potential national income, the automatic adjustment process will be at work to push the economy to the level of potential national income.

The automatic adjustment mechanism of the economy is reviewed in Figure 17.4. Part A shows how a recessionary gap is eliminated by an increase in aggregate supply. During a recessionary gap, unemployment exceeds the natural rate. This unemployment places downward pressure on wages as contracts are renegotiated. The decline in real wage rates reduces the costs of production, shifting the SRAS curve to the right from $SRAS_1$ to $SRAS_2$. Comparing the new long-run equilibrium, E_{LR}, with the original short-run equilibrium, E_{SR}, we see that this change puts downward pressure on both the inflation rate and the unemployment rate.

Consequently, the economy cannot remain on its original short-run Phillips curve. Part C of Figure 17.4 illustrates this. When the economy is in a recessionary gap, unemployment is higher than the natural rate (labeled U_N), so we must be at a point like A somewhere to the right of U_N. The economy's automatic adjustment mechanism returns us to full employment (the unemployment rate U_N), and it puts downward pressure on the inflation rate at the same time. Hence the economy adjusts to an equilibrium point like D, somewhere to the southwest of point A. This long-run equilibrium cannot be on the original short-run Phillips curve.

A similar process occurs if the economy is in an inflationary gap. Part B of Figure 17.4 shows the automatic adjustment process in this case. The economy is overemployed at the short-run equilibrium E_{SR}. The overemployment puts upward pressure on wages, which in turn affects the supply side of the economy. The inflationary gap is removed by the resulting decline in the short-run aggregate supply (SRAS) curve, which shifts to the left from $SRAS_1$ to $SRAS_2$. Looking at the new long-run equilibrium, E_{LR}, we see that this change in the supply side puts upward pressure on both the inflation rate and the unemployment rate. In the Phillips-curve diagram of Part C, the inflationary gap is represented by a point like C (where unemployment is below the natural rate U_N), and the self-correcting mechanism moves the economy to a situation represented by point E (where inflation is higher and unemployment has returned to the natural rate).

If either an inflationary or a recessionary gap exists, the automatic adjustment process will cause the SRAS curve to shift accordingly and return unemployment to its natural rate. Consequently, only one point on the short-run Phillips curve is stable — the point where unemployment is at its natural rate (U_N). In the long run the unemployment rate is at the natural rate, but the inflation rate could be either high or low (as shown by points D and E in Part C). These long-run equilibrium points are illustrated in the Phillips-curve diagram as the **long-run Phillips curve**.

> *The long-run Phillips curve is the graphic representation of the combinations of inflation and unemployment that can be sustained in the long run.*

The long-run Phillips curve is vertical at the natural rate of unemployment because of the economy's automatic adjustment mechanism. Consequently, no trade-off between inflation and unemployment exists in the long run. Any rate of inflation can coexist with the natural rate of unemployment in the long run.

The short-run Phillips curve is therefore not a menu from which macroeconomic decision makers can choose. It is possible for policymakers to expand aggregate demand and eliminate some unemployment in exchange for higher inflation (and, for example, move from point B to point C in Part C of Figure 17.4), but this trade-off exists only for the short run. The economy cannot sustain this combination in the long run, as the automatic adjustment process causes wages to adjust, returning the economy to the natural rate of unemployment (shown by the movement from point C to point E). The true menu of choices lies along the vertical long-run Phillips curve.

FIGURE 17.5
Shifting the Short-Run Phillips Curve

This figure shows that when the economy experiences an adverse supply shock (when aggregate supply shifts to the left), the inflation/unemployment trade-off will worsen. Any given inflation rate (like I_1) will correspond to a higher unemployment rate than before (U_2 instead of U_1). Hence an adverse supply shock will shift the Phillips curve to the right from PC_1 to PC_2.

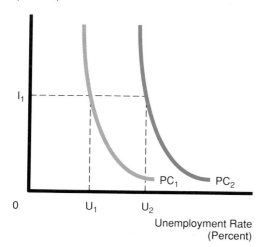

THE INSTABILITY OF THE SHORT-RUN PHILLIPS CURVE

There are two views of what happened during the 1970s to disturb the steady short-run relationship between inflation and unemployment that had existed in the 1960s. One school of thought stresses that the economic fluctuations that occurred during the 1970s were due more to adverse supply shocks than to fluctuations in aggregate demand. Since we predicted that the Phillips curve would emerge when variations in aggregate demand were the predominant factor accounting for economic fluctuations, a stable Phillips-curve relationship would not be expected to appear when economic fluctuations were due to adverse supply shocks. Instead, the entire Phillips curve would shift up in response to such shocks.

Another school of economic thought believes that the Phillips curve shows a relationship not between inflation and unemployment but between unanticipated inflation and unemployment. This turns out to be an important distinction. Let us consider each view in turn.

THE PHILLIPS CURVE AND ADVERSE SUPPLY SHOCKS

Much of the inflation of the 1970s apparently did stem from the supply side. Adverse supply shocks were caused by crop failures in 1972, 1973, and 1978 and by the large oil price increases that took place during 1973–1974 and again in 1979–1980. Each such event, if severe enough, would by itself depress the supply side of the economy, shifting the SRAS curve — and perhaps the LRAS curve as well — to the left.

Instead of an inverse relationship between the inflation and unemployment rates, a direct relationship will appear when an adverse supply shock occurs. In other words, as we have seen several times in previous chapters, both unemployment and inflation will rise when the SRAS curve shifts to the left. So when periodic supply shocks occur, a series of Phillips curves shifting up — instead of a single downward-sloping Phillips curve — would appear.

This situation is illustrated in Figure 17.5. When the SRAS curve shifts to the left, the Phillips curve will shift up and to the right, from PC_1 to PC_2. Any given rate of inflation, like I_1, is now associated with a higher unemployment rate, U_2 instead of U_1. The inflation/unemployment trade-off will therefore worsen. Conversely, an improvement in the supply side of the economy that shifts the SRAS curve to the right will cause the Phillips curve to shift down and to the left. In this case the inflation/unemployment trade-off will improve.

The supply shocks of the 1970s were interspersed with increases in aggregate demand. Various increases in aggregate demand trace out, as you now know, a Phillips-curve relationship. Thus when adverse supply shocks occurred and were interspersed with dominating increases in aggregate demand, the data should show the Phillips curve itself shifting up and to the right. If you turn back to Figure 17.3, you may be able to see a series of Phillips curves linked by years during which the adverse supply shocks shifted the individual Phillips curves upward.

Thus when a decline in the SRAS curve dominates economic fluctuations, inflation and unemployment move in the same direction. Such adverse supply shocks cause the Phillips curve to shift upward, and the inflation/unemployment trade-off appears to worsen. Many economists believe that adverse supply shocks indeed do account for the long-run instability of the Phillips curve seen in the 1970s and 1980s.

THE PHILLIPS CURVE AND INFLATIONARY EXPECTA-TIONS Many economists believe that inflationary expectations are another factor that caused the instability of the short-run Phillips curve in the 1970s and 1980s. To see this, suppose, for example, that everyone expects inflation to be 5 percent next year. Then workers will demand a 5 percent increase in their wages to compensate for the rising cost of living. Business firms know their product prices will rise by 5 percent, and competition will force them to grant this wage increase. Thus the SRAS curve will shift to the left as a result of inflationary expectations. Whenever the SRAS curve shifts, so will the short-run Phillips curve. Thus another condition for a stable short-run Phillips curve is for inflationary expectations to remain constant.

This condition was pointed out a decade after Phillips published his work. Two economists working independently, Milton Friedman and Edmund Phelps, suggested that the Phillips curve would be stable only if the anticipated (or expected) inflation rate did not change.

According to Friedman and Phelps, the Phillips curve was originally calculated using time periods during which there was no distinct trend in inflation. Consequently, inflationary expectations were steady and the resulting short-run Phillips curve was stable. If, however, the rate of inflation significantly increased, expectations of future inflation would eventually increase, causing the Phillips curve to shift.

For example, suppose economic decision makers formulate their inflation expectations on the basis of past experience. (This situation is called *adaptive expectations*, as we saw in Chapter 16.) When people see an increase in the inflation rate, it will lead to expectations of higher future inflation rates. As inflationary expectations rise, there will be larger wage increases, a reduction in short-run aggregate supply, and an upward shift in the Phillips curve.

JOB SEARCHING AND THE INFLATION/UNEMPLOYMENT TRADE-OFF

That there is a trade-off between inflation and unemployment in the short run but not in the long run is one of the most important ideas in macroeconomics. Our understanding of the inflation/unemployment trade-off is strengthened when we combine the above ideas with a study of how workers search for appropriate jobs and how firms search for appropriate employees.

First, recall that the natural rate of unemployment refers to the level of unemployment in the nation when it is producing its potential level of real income. We can also think of the natural rate of unemployment in terms of a job search — if the number of unemployed workers actively searching for jobs is approximately balanced by the number of jobs available, unemployment will be at its natural rate.

When the economy is at the natural rate of unemployment, the unemployment is caused by some mismatch. The jobs and workers may not be in the same place (due, say, to a lack of information); this is the frictional unemployment we studied in Chapter 8. Another possible mismatch is that the available workers do not have the skills required in the available jobs; we called this structural unemployment in Chapter 8. Thus unemployment is at its natural rate if there is only frictional and structural unemployment in the economy.

If the number of available unemployed workers exceeds the number of available jobs, then the actual unemployment rate would exceed the natural rate. In this case there would be the cyclical unemployment discussed in Chapter 8 — unemployment associated with general downturns in the economy. So when the economy is at the natural rate of unemployment, there is no cyclical unemployment.

JOB-SEARCHING ACTIVITIES

Persons become unemployed for a variety of reasons. In 1987, a year of economic recovery, a bare majority (52 percent) of the individuals who became unemployed had lost their jobs. Most of these, almost three-quarters, had been fired, and the remainder had been laid off. What about the other 48 percent of the unemployed? Twelve percent of the total had quit their old jobs, 25 percent had reentered the labor force after a period of not being in the labor force, and 11 percent were new entrants who had yet to find their first job.

Persons become unemployed from being fired or laid off, quitting, or from being unable to find a job upon entering the labor force. Such persons are actively searching to find the best available job for which they are qualified. These people are engaged in what economists call **searching activities**. Business firms desiring to hire workers are also engaged in searching activities. As their employment needs expand, business firms must search for the best available workers to meet their needs.

> *Searching activities are the activities conducted by unemployed workers hunting for an available job and by firms that need new employees hunting for appropriate workers.*

Examples of searching activities include placing and responding to want ads, posting and responding to "Help Wanted" signs, and using employment agencies.

Searching activities require resources. Both job searchers and employers require information to complete a search successfully. Resources are expended by firms to attract and screen job applicants. Effort is required of the unemployed to learn about and apply for jobs.

If information were free, there would be little unemployment. Each job seeker would know of all available jobs, what each job pays, and what the working conditions of each job are. Each employer would know which workers were available and the qualifications of each. Free information would thus allow unemployed workers to move quickly from one job to another.

In the real world, however, information is scarce and costly to obtain and thus is only imperfectly available. Since workers and firms have imperfect information, neither the first available job discovered, nor the first applicant interviewed, will necessarily be the best available. Passing up the first available job may lead to finding a better job, and passing up the first job applicant may lead to finding a better worker. Hence further searching can provide additional benefits. But additional job searching also incurs additional costs. Workers who pass up the first job offered in search for a better-paying one must bear the cost of the lost wages they could be earning. Employers who pass up the first applicant lose the profits from the lost production resulting from unfilled job openings. These are important ideas in the economic way of thinking, and economists refer to them as the **marginal benefit of job searching** and the **marginal cost of job searching**.

The marginal benefit of job searching is the additional benefit the job seeker (or potential employer) receives from continuing the job search (or worker search) instead of taking the job (or hiring the worker) currently available.

The marginal cost of job searching is the additional cost that the job seeker (or potential employer) incurs from continuing the job (or worker) search instead of accepting the job (or hiring the worker) currently available.

The marginal cost of searching for a job rises with time spent searching. Initially, a job search is fairly inexpensive. An unemployed worker asks friends and family, searches the want ads, and responds to "Help Wanted" signs. The cost of searching, however, is expected to rise with each succeeding week of unemployment. Not only are there the lost wages from refusing to accept the first available job, but it becomes progressively more difficult to find previously unidentified, available jobs. Employment agencies must be contacted, and perhaps fees paid. The area covered and the distance traveled mount and become increasingly costly as the job search continues. Meanwhile, the lost income from not accepting previously offered jobs multiplies.

While the marginal cost rises with extended search, the marginal benefit probably declines. As the unemployed worker identifies, with time and effort, more and more available jobs, fewer of those jobs will represent an improvement over previously discovered jobs. Thus the marginal cost of job searching will rise as more searching takes place, and the marginal benefit will decline.

As long as the marginal benefit of the job search outweighs the marginal cost, the worker will continue the search. In that situation the worker feels that the benefit of the future search will outweigh the cost. As the marginal cost continues to rise and the marginal benefit continues to fall, they will eventually become equal. Then the job seeker will feel that further searching is not worthwhile and will accept the best available job.

The employer searching for new employees also must bear the search cost, and the marginal cost of additional search can be expected to rise and the marginal benefit to decline as more effort is expended. Because business firms want to staff available positions with the best available persons, they must expend resources to attract potential employees and to gather information about their qualifications. They place want ads, contract with employment agencies, and maintain personnel offices — all to attract applicants. The longer a position remains unfilled, the greater the loss of potential output to the firm, so the marginal cost of search will generally be rising.

However, the more intensive the search, the better qualified will be the employee hired. But searching will inevitably run into diminishing returns as more effort is expended. At some point newly attracted applicants are no longer clearly better qualified than previously identified applicants, and so the marginal benefit of additional search will fall with increased efforts.

As long as the employer feels that the extra benefit of further searching outweighs the additional cost (that is, as long as the marginal benefit outweighs the marginal cost), the employer will continue the search. The job search ends when the marginal benefit becomes equal to the marginal cost, and the employer feels further searching is no longer worthwhile.

JOB SEARCHING AND THE UNEMPLOYMENT RATE

The amount of job searching that workers and business firms undertake affects the unemployment rate. The unemployment rate at any point in time is determined not only by the number of persons who are unemployed but also by the duration of their unemployment. The duration of unemployment can be measured by the average length of time an unemployed person is without work, and it is affected by the amount of time spent searching for a new position. The longer the search activity takes, the higher will be the unemployment rate at any point in time. The shorter the search, the lower will be the unemployment rate.

If for some reason the marginal cost of job searching should rise, it will tend to make people shorten their job searches. Similarly, a fall in the marginal benefit of job searching will also put downward pressure on the length of time spent in the search. Conversely, workers and employers will increase the duration of a job search when the marginal cost of searching falls or the marginal benefit rises. Any of these changes in the marginal cost and marginal benefit of searching, then, will in turn affect the unemployment rate.

Many factors affect the marginal cost and benefit of searching. Let us consider two that have important implications for economic performance: unemployment benefits and unexpected inflation.

UNEMPLOYMENT COMPENSATION BENEFITS

Unemployment compensation benefits and their utility as an automatic stabilizer were discussed in a previous chapter. Now we can see that these payments also affect the unemployment rate, because they affect the marginal cost of searching for a job. Unemployment compensation payments reduce the losses involved in being unemployed. The marginal cost of job searching thus falls, and the rational reaction of the unemployed worker is to spend more time searching. The unemployment rate will then rise as the duration of unemployment increases. The effect of creating an unemployment compensation program for the first time, as long as the program continued unchanged, would be a one-time increase in the unemployment rate.

When unemployment benefits are extended or increased, the rate of unemployment will increase as the marginal cost of job searching declines. Conversely, when unemployment benefits are restricted or reduced, the unemployment rate will fall as the marginal cost of job searching increases. For example, in 1988 the unemployment rate declined to 5.5 percent — a rate that had not been achieved since the early 1970s. In addition to the continuing economic recovery that was occurring, another factor contributing to this drop was that most states had tightened up on eligibility requirements for unemployment benefits. In fact, only one-quarter of the persons who became unemployed qualified for benefits at all. The decline in eligibility contributed to the decline in the unemployment rate by raising the marginal cost of job searching for unemployed workers.

Although the average unemployment compensation payment does not frequently change, the number of weeks an unemployed worker can receive benefits is often extended during serious recessions. Such extensions, besides providing some additional relief to the unemployed, lower the marginal cost of searching and actually increase the unemployment rate by inducing jobless workers to search longer for a new position.

INFLATIONARY EXPECTATIONS

Generally, unemployed workers have determined a **reservation wage,** which indicates the lowest wage at which a job offer would be acceptable.

> *The reservation wage is the lowest wage that an unemployed worker must be offered for the worker to accept a job offer.*

Of course, the higher a worker's reservation wage is, the longer his or her job search will be.

The reservation wage is fixed in real terms — in terms of the purchasing power of wages. But in nominal terms (in terms of the amount of money), the worker must continually update his or her reservation wage to account for expectations about inflation. For example, if the worker expects a 5 percent inflation rate, then the lowest money wage the worker will accept will also rise by 5 percent. Because inflationary expectations affect the reservation wage, they affect people's decision to terminate the job search and therefore they affect the unemployment rate.

As we saw in Chapter 16, inflation may be fully considered in people's expectations (anticipated inflation) or inflation can surprise people and be unexpected (unanticipated inflation). The effects of inflation on the job search can be quite different, depending on which of these two situations exists.

First, let us consider the case of anticipated inflation. Suppose that prices and wages are steadily rising at 5 percent and that everyone knows this is occurring. Employers seeking additional employees will adjust their wage offers according to this expected rate of inflation, and job seekers will increase their nominal reservation wages accordingly. In nominal terms, the marginal cost and marginal benefit of the job search will both be rising at 5 percent, so in real terms the marginal cost and marginal benefit remain unchanged. When inflation is anticipated, it will have no real effect on the job search.

The effects of unanticipated inflation can, however, be quite different because workers have different information about the wages they are offered and the prices of goods in the marketplace. Workers generally possess and can periodically update information on wages and employment conditions. They are paid frequently when employed, and when unemployed they have friends and acquaintances in the same occupations who can serve as sources of information about wage levels. Data about changes in money wages due to unanticipated inflation therefore are easily collected and assimilated. However, workers have less-than-complete information about prices. Workers purchase many goods relatively infrequently over a period of time. It may take some time for them to recognize that inflation is occurring at a higher or lower rate than anticipated. So the effects that unanticipated inflation has on prices take longer for workers to recognize and assimilate than do its effects on wages.

Unanticipated inflation can thus shorten the period of job searching, thereby reducing the unemployment rate. For example, suppose inflation is actually higher than anticipated. From the unemployed worker's viewpoint, his or her adjustment to the higher-than-expected wage offers will

FIGURE 17.6
The Phillips Curve and Inflationary
Expectations

In this figure the economy is in long-run equilibrium at point A with full employment, and it is assumed that people expect the current inflation rate, I_{Low}, to continue. When the government unexpectedly stimulates aggregate demand, the rate of inflation becomes higher than people anticipated. This higher-than-expected inflation causes people to terminate job searches sooner than they normally would, pushing the unemployment rate down. Thus a trade-off between unemployment and *unanticipated* inflation occurs in the short run, shown as the movement from point A to point B. In the long run, people will adjust to the new inflation and raise their inflationary expectations. This change will have two effects. The initial duration of people's job searching will return, causing unemployment to rise back to its natural rate, U_N. Also, the higher inflationary expectations will shift the short-run Phillips curve upward, to PC_{High}. In the long run the economy adjusts from point B to point C, returning to full employment and a higher permanent inflation rate I_{High}.

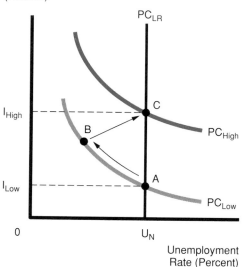

occur quicker than the adjustment to the higher-than-expected prices. The worker will be fooled into thinking that the marginal cost of job searching (from turning down job offers) is rising relative to the marginal benefit and will terminate the job search earlier. It will now be easier for the unemployed worker to find a job that pays a nominal wage equal to his or her reservation wage. Since workers, on average, end their job searches sooner, we should expect the unemployment rate to fall when there is unanticipated inflation.

In the short run, then, a trade-off should exist between unanticipated inflation and unemployment. When unanticipated inflation occurs, the unemployment rate should fall. Conversely, when the actual rate of inflation is lower than expected, the unemployment rate should increase. This trade-off exists only in the short run. Inflationary expectations will eventually adjust to unanticipated inflation in the long run. When this happens, the observed unemployment rate will approach the natural rate, and the short-run trade-off between unemployment and unanticipated inflation will disappear.

JOB SEARCHING AND THE PHILLIPS CURVE

The theory of job searching has significant implications for the Phillips curve. Suppose that the economy has been at full employment for a substantial period of time, during which inflation has been at a low, steady rate. This situation is illustrated in Figure 17.6 as point A on the long-run Phillips curve. In this long-run situation the existing inflation is fully anticipated by people. So in Figure 17.6, I_{Low} represents not only the actual inflation rate but also the anticipated inflation rate.

Now suppose that the demand for the economy's goods unexpectedly rises (perhaps due to a surprising expansionary change in fiscal or monetary policy), causing aggregate demand to shift to the left. As we know, this event will create some unanticipated inflation. Furthermore, the job-searching theory we have discussed predicts that this unexpected inflation will cause people, on average, to reduce the length of time spent in job searching, which will in turn drive down the unemployment rate. Hence the economy moves along a short-run Phillips curve, as from A to B in Figure 17.6.

We know that this short-run equilibrium cannot last in the long run. The economy's automatic adjustment mechanism will slow the economy back down and return it to full employment. Furthermore, people's expectations of future inflation will rise as they experience the higher-than-expected inflation. This change will shift the short-run Phillips curve upward. Hence the economy will move to a new long-run equilibrium like point C in Figure 17.6. The duration of people's job-searching behavior has returned to its previous level, as people now correctly anticipate the actual inflation rate, I_{High}.

Thus the intersection of the short-run and long-run Phillips curves represents the anticipated rate of inflation. The short-run Phillips curve itself shows a trade-off between unemployment and unanticipated inflation. When the actual inflation rate is greater than anticipated, the unemployment rate will decline. When the actual inflation rate is lower than anticipated, the unemployment rate will increase. This trade-off disappears in the long run as economic decision makers adjust their inflationary expectations to accurately reflect the actual rate of inflation. The long-run Phillips curve is vertical, indicating that any anticipated rate of inflation is consistent with the natural rate of unemployment.

By connecting the Phillips curve to inflationary expectations, we can now explain why economists found a Phillips curve for the United States in the 1960s, and why that inflation/unemployment trade-off apparently worsened and eventually disappeared during the 1970s and 1980s.

The short-run relationship between unemployment and inflation during the 1960s (graphed in Figure 17.2) was, in fact, a relationship between unemployment and unanticipated inflation. Inflationary expectations were low throughout the 1960s, so when the actual inflation rate exceeded the expected rate, the rate of unemployment declined, as the job-searching theory predicts. As inflationary expectations adjusted to the new reality, the short-run Phillips curve progressively shifted upward. Despite the increasing inflationary expectations, inflation during the 1970s occurred at a rate that still exceeded expectations, thus tracing out a series of Phillips curves at ever-higher expected rates of inflation. When inflationary expectations declined in the 1980s, the short-run Phillips curve shifted down, possibly confusing an observer into concluding that the Phillips curve had disappeared altogether (as we saw in Figure 17.3).

POLICIES DEALING WITH UNEMPLOYMENT

The Phillips curve contains important implications for economic policy that complicate life for macroeconomic policymakers. The Phillips curve suggests that the ideal macroeconomic world of stable prices, full employment, and rapid economic growth may not be possible to attain in certain short-run situations. If government decides to intervene and to employ monetary or fiscal policy to combat a particular short-run situation, it may be necessary at times to choose between higher unemployment and higher inflation.

The Phillips curve gives us an excellent tool to help determine the consequences of the various policies that government may use in dealing with unemployment. We shall analyze two scenarios using the Phillips curve: driving unemployment below its natural rate and fighting excessively high unemployment.

THE ACCELERATION HYPOTHESIS

The public puts pressure on elected officials to keep unemployment low. We have seen that the economy always attempts to return to the natural rate of unemployment in the long run. Suppose, however, that government officials believe that the natural unemployment rate itself is too high. What would happen if macroeconomic decision makers attempted to keep the unemployment rate permanently below the natural rate of unemployment? The answer is provided by a theory known as the **acceleration hypothesis.**

> *The acceleration hypothesis is the theory that any attempt to use monetary or fiscal policy to maintain the unemployment rate permanently below its natural rate will result in accelerating inflation.*

Using the Phillips curve, we can see that policies that try to keep unemployment lower than the natural rate will create not only inflation but ever-increasing inflation rates as well.

Figure 17.7 illustrates the acceleration hypothesis. Suppose that the economy is operating at long-run equilibrium and that unemployment is

FIGURE 17.7
The Acceleration Hypothesis

If the government tries to keep unemployment below its natural rate, the inflation rate will get higher and higher. When the government stimulates aggregate demand to lower the unemployment rate, this policy also creates unanticipated inflation. Eventually people will adjust their expectations to the higher inflation rate, shifting the short-run Phillips curve upward and returning unemployment to its natural rate. This two-step cycle will continue as long as government persists in its policy to drive unemployment below its natural rate. In this figure the economy will go from A to B to C to D to E to F as inflation continually accelerates.

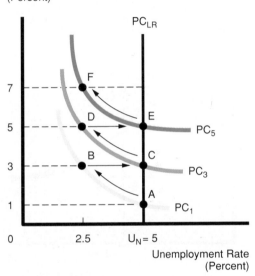

FIGURE 17.8
Fighting High Unemployment

When the economy is at E_{SR}, with a low inflation rate of 3 percent and a high unemployment rate of 9 percent, the government could respond to this situation in three basic ways: (1) The government could leave its policies unchanged and allow the automatic adjustment mechanism to eliminate the unemployment. (2) If a faster adjustment is required, the government can use an expansionary policy, the cost of which would be a higher permanent inflation rate. (3) If the government believes the current 3 percent inflation rate is also too high, it could use a contractionary policy to lower the inflation. If the policy and its effects are well-known and believed, inflationary expectations may adjust quickly. But if the fall in inflation caused by the government's policy comes as a surprise and inflationary expectations react slowly, then there would be the Phillips curve trade-off.

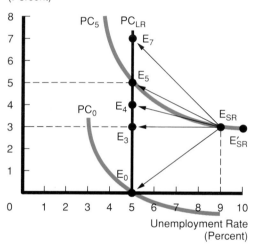

at the natural rate — assumed to be 5 percent. Also suppose that the anticipated inflation rate is 1 percent. The economy will therefore be operating at point A, the intersection of the long-run Phillips curve PC_{LR} and the short-run Phillips curve PC_1.

Now suppose that the federal government suddenly decides to reduce the unemployment rate to 2½ percent by expanding aggregate demand. Since the inflationary consequences of the increase in aggregate demand are unexpected, the economy moves to point B on Phillips curve PC_1. As usual, we shall see a short-run trade-off between unanticipated inflation and unemployment. Using the short-run Phillips curve PC_1, we find that unemployment falls to 2½ percent while inflation increases to 3 percent.

Economic decision makers are fooled temporarily by the government's action into expecting too little inflation. Business firms offer jobs too quickly and job seekers accept jobs too quickly, misinterpreting the higher money wages as higher real wages. Their inflationary expectations, however, adjust with time and experience. Let us suppose that as people become aware of the new inflation rate of 3 percent, they adjust their expectations and believe that future inflation will also be 3 percent. Thus the Phillips curve will shift up to PC_3 as inflationary expectations adjust, and the unemployment rate will return to its natural rate of 5 percent. The economy moves from point B to point C in Figure 17.7.

If the government is determined to keep unemployment at 2½ percent, it will have to increase aggregate demand even more. Aggregate demand must increase sufficiently to drive the economy to point D on the new short-run Phillips curve PC_3. The government's policy will then drive the inflation rate higher, to 5 percent. Of course, this short-run equilibrium cannot be stable. As inflationary expectations adjust to the new 5 percent inflation rate, the Phillips curve shifts again to PC_5. As this happens, the natural tendency is for the level of unemployment to return to its natural rate, rising to 5 percent at point E.

To keep this from happening, the government must increase aggregate demand still more to drive the economy to point F. The effect of the increase in aggregate demand is to keep the unemployment rate at 2½ percent, which is below the natural rate, but the price that must be paid is an even higher inflation rate of 7 percent. This process will go on and on, and inflation will continue to spiral upward, if the government insists on maintaining an unemployment rate below the natural rate.

Thus, according to the acceleration hypothesis, any attempt to maintain the unemployment rate permanently below its natural rate will lead to a steady upward shift in the Phillips curve and a constantly increasing inflation rate.

POLICIES TO FIGHT EXCESSIVELY HIGH UNEMPLOYMENT

Let us consider another macroeconomic problem. Suppose the economy is suffering from unemployment that exceeds the natural rate of unemployment. According to the Phillips curve, this situation will occur whenever the expected rate of inflation exceeds the actual rate of inflation.

Such a situation is diagrammed in Figure 17.8. When the expected level of inflation is 5 percent, the economy will be operating on the short-run Phillips curve PC_5. The precise point on PC_5 at which the economy will operate is determined by the actual rate of inflation. If the actual rate of inflation is lower than anticipated, say at 3 percent, the economy will operate at point E_{SR} on Phillips curve PC_5 with an unemployment rate of 9 percent — well above its natural rate of 5 percent.

In this case what are the alternatives available to macroeconomic decision makers? The first possibility is to not change present policies — in effect, to do nothing different — and allow the automatic adjustment process to operate. If the government holds the inflation rate steady at 3 percent, the anticipated inflation rate will adjust to this situation. The Phillips curve will eventually shift down and to the left, and the equilibrium position will move from E_{SR} to E_3. The 3 percent inflation rate will be stable at this point, as the unemployment rate will have returned to its natural rate.

Thus if economic policy remains unchanged in the face of excess unemployment, eventually the economy will return to full employment as the expected rate of inflation adjusts to the actual rate of inflation. The crucial word in this summary is *eventually*. There is substantial debate among economists as to how much calendar time *eventually* actually encompasses.

Suppose that the government believes that due to the lost output caused by the excessive unemployment, it is too costly to wait out the automatic adjustment process. What options are still available? Two basic alternatives exist: (1) Stimulate aggregate demand or (2) attempt to shift the Phillips curve down. Let us first consider what will happen if the government decides to stimulate the demand for the economy's goods.

The existing excess unemployment (at point E_{SR} in Figure 17.8) is caused by inflationary expectations that exceed the actual rate of inflation. This situation can be resolved by stimulating aggregate demand in order to increase the actual rate of inflation to the anticipated rate. If this happens, the economy will move up the existing Phillips curve (PC_5) from E_{SR} to E_5. The cost of this quick elimination of the excessive unemployment is a permanently higher inflation rate, as the new steady-state inflation rate becomes 5 percent.

Government could also adopt an expansionary policy that is either more or less stimulative than the one just discussed. A more stimulative economic policy will cause the actual inflation rate to exceed the expected inflation rate of 5 percent and thereby cause unemployment to decline. In fact, the rate of unemployment may decline to below the natural rate in the short run before returning to the natural rate as inflationary expectations adjust to the new higher actual inflation rate. If this more stimulative policy is chosen, then the economy will eventually move to a position such as E_7 as the Phillips curve shifts upward. The excess unemployment will be eliminated, but the new steady-state inflation rate will be even higher. A less stimulative policy, but one that is still more stimulative than simply relying on the automatic adjustment process, will see the economy move to a position such as E_4, with an inflation rate that still exceeds the initial inflation rate of 3 percent. Thus a stimulative economic policy designed to combat excess unemployment will result in a higher permanent inflation rate.

The second alternative is to attempt to shift the Phillips curve downward by lowering inflationary expectations. Suppose the government publicly adopts a macroeconomic goal of full employment (an unemployment rate equal to the natural rate) with a stable price level (zero inflation). This objective requires (1) that the government adopt monetary and fiscal policies that will actually reduce aggregate demand from the initial level (the level that produced E_{SR}) to just the amount that will support full employment with an unchanging price level, and (2) that the government be able to convince the public that it will follow this policy no matter what actually happens.

If — and it's a big if — the public formulates its inflationary expectations on the basis of all available information (a situation we called *rational expectations* in Chapter 16), and if economic decision makers believe the government policy will work, and if the government will stick to its announced new policy, then inflationary expectations could adjust quickly. The Phillips curve would shift to PC_0 in Figure 17.8, and the economy would move to point E_0. Inflation will drop to zero, and all excess unemployment will disappear.

If, however, the public must experience an actual fall in inflation rates to believe the government is following a new policy (the situation we called *adaptive expectations*), then unemployment will actually get worse before it gets better. The economy may first move to a position of higher unemployment, such as E'_{SR}, prior to a downward shift of the Phillips curve.

To summarize: A consistently followed, restrictive economic policy designed to lower inflationary expectations and combat excess unemployment will result in a lower permanent inflation rate. This policy can, however, worsen unemployment in the short run, depending on how quickly expectations adjust to the new policy.

This policy, which requires that the rate of growth of aggregate demand decline in the face of excess unemployment, is exactly the opposite of the usual policy recommendation, and it flies in the face of the conventional economic-policy practices of government. The federal government tried to establish several new economic policies during the 1970s to combat the existence of both high inflation rates and high unemployment rates, but it could stick to none of them. The public rightfully became skeptical of new government economic policies.

Still, even if they are only a theoretical possibility, policies to alter inflationary expectations downward could reinforce the automatic adjustment process in restoring full employment when a recessionary gap appears.

SUMMARY

1. Historically, aggregate demand fluctuates more substantially and more frequently than does aggregate supply. The basic macroeconomic model predicts that a trade-off between inflation and unemployment will be observed when aggregate demand fluctuates. The Phillips curve is a graph showing this trade-off between the inflation rate and the unemployment rate. The Phillips-curve relationship for the U.S. economy seems to have existed during the 1960s, deteriorated during the 1970s, and disappeared altogether during the 1980s.

2. Originally, economists believed that the Phillips curve represented a stable trade-off between inflation and unemployment. If this were the case, the unemployment rate could be reduced if a higher inflation rate was acceptable. Since the costs of an anticipated inflation were thought by many to be lower than the costs associated with unemployment, it was argued that a stimulative economic policy was always in order.

3. The Phillips curve was proved in theory and in fact to be unstable. It ignored the automatic adjustment process that would always tend to return the economy to the level of potential national income and return the

unemployment rate to the natural rate. A series of adverse supply shocks, along with the working of the automatic adjustment process, seemingly caused the inflation/unemployment trade-off to worsen during the 1970s.

4. The inflation/unemployment trade-off shown by the Phillips curve is a short-run relationship. In the long run any level of inflation is consistent with the natural rate of unemployment. Therefore the long-run Phillips curve is vertical at the natural rate of unemployment.

5. People are unemployed at any point in time because they either have lost their job, have voluntarily quit their job, or are entering or reentering the labor force. In the theory of job searching, unemployed persons are considered to be searching for an acceptable job offer. Each jobless person has set a reservation wage that represents his or her minimum requirement for an acceptable job offer. The marginal cost and the marginal benefit of searching for a job that meets the reservation wage affect the duration of the job search and consequently affect the unemployment rate.

6. Anticipated inflation will not affect the duration of the job search. Because business firms and workers will build anticipated inflation into their job offers and reservation wages, the marginal costs and benefits of further search are essentially unaffected. Since anticipated inflation does not affect the job search, it should not affect unemployment. Therefore we do not expect to find a Phillips curve trade-off between unemployment and anticipated inflation.

7. Unanticipated inflation can affect the length of job search and therefore the unemployment rate. When inflation is higher than anticipated, jobless individuals mistakenly interpret higher money wage offers to be higher real wage offers and will accept jobs too quickly. The unemployment rate will thus decline. When actual inflation is less than expected inflation, unemployed workers will mistakenly reject jobs that in fact are equal to their reservation wage, and the unemployment rate will rise.

8. Unanticipated inflation can exist in the short run, so the short-run Phillips curve actually shows a relationship between unemployment and unanticipated inflation. In the long run inflationary expectations will adjust to the actual rate (in other words, all inflation will be anticipated). Thus in the long run there is no trade-off between inflation and unemployment, and the long-run Phillips curve is vertical.

9. If government policymakers attempt to make unemployment permanently less than its natural rate, analysis using the Phillips curve predicts that the result will be accelerating inflation. This theory is known as the acceleration hypothesis.

10. The Phillips curve imposes a constraint on economic policymakers trying to fight excessively high unemployment. If unemployment is above the natural rate, they have three options: (1) await the working of the automatic adjustment process, (2) use expansionary policy to reduce unemployment quickly at the cost of permanently higher inflation, or (3) reinforce the automatic adjustment process by attempting to lower inflationary expectations with clearly announced, consistent restrictions on aggregate demand. Although this final option also permanently lowers the inflation rate, it runs the risk of making unemployment worse in the short run if inflationary expectations fail to adjust quickly.

STOPPING THE GREAT INFLATION: 1980–1986

In the preview at the beginning of this chapter, we asked if the severe recession of 1982–1983 that accompanied disinflation was the necessary price that had to be paid to end inflation. You now possess the economic tools to understand how the economy responded during the 1980s to the anti-inflationary policy of the federal government.

Ronald Reagan was elected, at least in part, because he promised to bring inflation under control and he initiated the anti-inflationary Economic Recovery Program at the beginning of his first term. In reality, his coequal as an economic policymaker at the time was Paul Volcker, then chairman of the Board of Governors of the Federal Reserve. Volcker had independently convinced his colleagues at the Federal Reserve to embark on a contractionary, anti-inflationary monetary policy prior to the election. The Federal Reserve proceeded to reduce the rate of growth of the money supply in accordance with its new policy.

The impact of the anti-inflationary economic policy began to be felt by the economy in 1981 and was in full force by 1982, as shown in Table 17.1. The inflation rate fell in every succeeding year between 1981 and 1986 as measured by the GNP deflator. The fall in inflation was accompanied first by a rise in the unemployment rate to 9.5 percent for two years, and then by a decline in the unemployment rate. By 1986 the unemployment rate was lower than at any time prior to 1980. The unemployment rate subsequently declined to even lower levels in 1987 and 1988, amazingly without the inflation rate accelerating. Our analysis using the Phillips curve at the end of this chapter explains why we should have expected this pattern of falling inflation with rising, then falling, unemployment.

The recession that followed the adoption of an anti-inflationary policy came about because the inflationary expectations that had been adjusting upward for 15 years were suddenly greater than the actual inflation rate. Apparently, neither the announcement by the Federal Reserve that it was going to pursue an anti-inflationary tight-money policy nor the anti-inflationary Economic Recovery Program initiated by the federal

TABLE 17.1
Inflation and Unemployment: 1980–1986

YEAR	INFLATION RATE (GNP DEFLATOR)	UNEMPLOYMENT RATE
1980	9.3%	7.0%
1981	9.3	7.5
1982	6.2	9.5
1983	4.1	9.5
1984	4.0	7.4
1985	3.7	7.1
1986	2.8	6.9

Source: *Economic Report of the President, 1987* (Washington, DC: U.S. Government Printing Office, 1987).

government was sufficient to change quickly the inflationary expectations of economic decision makers.

In retrospect, it is easy to see why consumers and business firms did not adjust their inflationary expectations in response to the new policy. Every president since Richard Nixon had announced an anti-inflation program. Despite their efforts, inflation had increased. Individuals and businesses that had believed their government and acted accordingly had suffered as a consequence, while those that acted as if they believed inflation would get worse were consistently proven right. Regarding economic policy, the credibility of the federal government and the Federal Reserve could have been at an all-time low in 1981.

But this time it was different. This time the Federal Reserve, in particular, stuck to its policy. As a result, the actual rate of inflation began to decline. You discovered in the chapter that when the actual rate of inflation falls below the level expected by economic decision makers, the unemployment rate will rise. The short-run Phillips curve explains why halting inflation in the 1980s led to a major recession with unprecedented postwar levels of unemployment.

When the actual rate of inflation began to decline in 1982, it took some time for economic decision makers to recognize that the government was serious this time about wringing inflation out of the economy, and it took even more time for the anticipated rate of inflation to come into line with the actual rate of inflation. Inflation was unexpectedly low, and the short-run Phillips curve shows us that there is a trade-off between unemployment and unanticipated inflation. Consequently, unemployment rose substantially as inflation fell. The general change seen in the economy from 1981 to 1982–1983 is illustrated in Figure 17.9 by the movement along the short-run Phillips curve from point A to point B.

Of course, this recessionary situation could not persist in the long run. Sometimes seeing is believing, and as people saw the increasingly lower inflation rates, they adjusted their inflationary expectations downward. From 1984 to 1986 inflationary expectations grew closer and closer to the actual rate of inflation. As you discovered in this chapter, there is no trade-off between inflation and unemployment when inflation is anticipated — when expectations about inflation have fully adjusted to the actual inflation rate, the economy has returned to full employment.

This long-run adjustment is also shown in Figure 17.9 by the movement from point B to point C. As inflationary expectations were falling during the 1984–1986 period, the short-run Phillips curve was shifting down. Furthermore, the gap between anticipated and actual inflation was getting smaller and smaller. So the unemployment rate was approaching the natural rate, and the economy was getting closer and closer to the long-run Phillips curve.

For the 1980s, expectations were formulated adaptively — lower inflation rates had to be experienced before they could be anticipated. The high inflation and high unemployment were both stopped, but the cure that was applied required a period of excessively high unemployment before the public's inflationary expectations changed and the economy returned to full employment.

FIGURE 17.9
A Phillips Curve Model of the 1980s

Both inflation and unemployment were high (as at point A) in the beginning of the 1980s. The government and the Federal Reserve announced new anti-inflationary policies. Past failures to curb inflation during the 1970s caused people to believe the new policies would also either fail or be abandoned, so people did not adjust their inflationary expectations downward. When the policies caused inflation to fall, we observed the Phillips curve trade-off. The lower-than-anticipated inflation caused unemployment to rise, and the economy moved from point A to a point like B in 1982–1983. From 1984 to 1986 the economy edged closer and closer to full employment while inflation continued to fall. People were revising their inflationary expectations downward, causing the Phillips curve to shift down (from PC$_{SR}$ to PC$'_{SR}$). As the gap between the actual and anticipated inflation rates narrowed, the economy approached the natural rate of unemployment. This situation in the 1984–1986 period is illustrated by the movement from point B to point C.

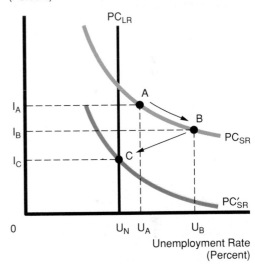

FALLING UNEMPLOYMENT—GOOD NEWS OR BAD FOR THE STOCK MARKET?

We have seen why the stock market reacted adversely to the news that unemployment had fallen to 5.3 percent in June 1988. The acceleration hypothesis that we examined in this chapter tells us that inflation will continually rise if the government attempts to keep unemployment permanently below its natural rate. In the 1970s and 1980s most economists believed that the unemployment rate lay between 5 and 6½ percent. Investors in the stock market, seeing some mild increases in inflation and a new 15-year low in unemployment, naturally feared that unemployment was falling beneath its natural rate and that accelerating inflation would soon follow.

The stock market is often considered to be an important predictor of the future state of the economy. In this situation, however, the fears of accelerating inflation were unfounded, for inflation did not substantially rise despite the low unemployment rate. An explanation for this apparent contradiction can be found by examining the natural rate of unemployment in more detail.

Recall that the natural rate of unemployment is the rate of unemployment that corresponds to the level of potential real income. Furthermore, the natural rate of unemployment is the rate that can be sustained without an increase or decrease in the rate of inflation; inflation can remain constant if the economy remains at the natural rate of unemployment. It is a kind of balance point: If unemployment is above the natural rate, inflation will tend to fall; if, instead, unemployment is below the natural rate, inflation will tend to rise.

The natural rate, however, is not fixed but fluctuates over time. Changes in the natural rate have important implications for economic performance and can be caused by changes in frictional unemployment, institutional conditions, the composition of the labor force, and structural changes in the economy. For example, economists believe that the natural rate of unemployment rose from the middle 1960s through the 1970s. This change in the economy occurred for several reasons.

First, the amount of frictional unemployment (unemployment due to the changing of jobs that would be natural for the economy to have) was on the rise during this period. The average age of the work force was declining, and since younger people tend to move more frequently than older people who have been established in their jobs for some time, more frictional unemployment would naturally occur. Also, two-income families became more prevalent, creating more frictional unemployment since a major change in the family could force one spouse to quit work and become frictionally unemployed. Unemployment compensation and welfare programs were expanded, allowing people to take more time in job searches and thereby increasing frictional unemployment.

Significant structural changes in the economy were reinforcing the effect of these changes on the natural rate of unemployment. The manufacturing sector of the economy was contracting relative to the service sector. The skills of some workers who lost their jobs were not the skills required by the expanding service sector. Thus structural unemployment increased, causing the natural rate to rise.

The adverse supply shocks suffered by the economy in the 1970s reinforced these structural changes. The significant increases in the price of oil raised the prices of energy-intensive goods, such as manufactured goods, relative to less energy-intensive goods, such as services. The economy responded by purchasing relatively more services and relatively fewer manufactured goods, thus intensifying the structural changes that were occurring and increasing the natural rate of unemployment.

The natural rate of unemployment, then, appears to have been rising during the 1970s. Since the automatic adjustment mechanism keeps the economy headed toward the natural rate, this change would have meant a rise in the observed unemployment rates during these years, no matter what economic policies were selected.

In the 1980s many of the factors that had led to the rise in the natural rate of unemployment apparently were reversed. The labor force was aging, so new entrants made up a declining proportion of it, and the new entrants of the 1970s had become the experienced workers of the 1980s. Firms showed more flexibility in dealing with two-income families and families with children; for example, working at home, flexible hours, and firm-provided day care became more prevalent. By giving workers more options in performing their jobs, frictional unemployment was reduced. The rapid structural shift to services that had occurred during the 1970s slowed during the 1980s. Consequently, economists believe that the natural rate of unemployment declined during the 1980s.

There is nothing ideal or optimal about the natural rate of unemployment. It is a positive, not a normative, concept. The natural rate of unemployment is simply the rate that is consistent with long-run equilibrium, and, like the measured unemployment rate, it can also rise or fall over time.

The stock market, when it reacted negatively to the "good" news that the unemployment rate had declined still further in 1988, was reacting to the fear that inflation would accelerate because the unemployment rate was falling below the natural rate. But, in fact, in the 1980s the unemployment rate fell along with the natural rate. In this case the good news of 1988 was that the unemployment rate, although falling, had remained steadily at or very near the natural rate of unemployment, and so accelerating inflation did not occur.[1]

---

[1]Sources for this analysis: Ellen R. Rissman, "Why Is Inflation So Low?" *Letter, Federal Reserve Bank of Chicago*, August 1988; and *Economic Perspectives, Federal Reserve Bank of Chicago*, September–October 1986, 3–18; and Adrian Throop, "Accelerating Inflation," *Weekly Letter, Federal Reserve Bank of San Francisco*, July 29, 1988.

REQUIRED ECONOMIC CONCEPTS

Phillips curve	Marginal benefit of job searching
Natural rate of unemployment	Marginal cost of job searching
Long-run Phillips curve	Reservation wage
Searching activities	Acceleration hypothesis

KEY QUESTIONS

1. What is the source of the inflation/unemployment trade-off?
2. What was the original Phillips curve? Into what relationship between variables did it evolve?
3. What kind of relationship exists between the inflation rate and the unemployment rate when an adverse supply shock occurs?
4. Why is the short-run Phillips curve unstable?
5. According to job search theory, how does a job seeker behave?
6. What two factors affect job search time?
7. When the actual rate of inflation is less than the expected rate of inflation, what should happen to the rate of unemployment?
8. Why does a trade-off exist only in the short run between unanticipated inflation and the unemployment rate?
9. What disguises the short-run trade-off between the inflation rate and the unemployment rate?
10. Why does the trade-off between the inflation rate and the unemployment rate disappear in the long run?
11. What effect do changes in inflationary expectations have on the Phillips curve?
12. What is the acceleration hypothesis?

PROBLEMS

1. "When inflation is anticipated, money wage rates will depend on price expectations, but real wage rates and the rate of unemployment will more or less be unaffected." Do you agree or disagree with this statement? Why? If the economy is at full employment, does it make any sense to say that the number of the unemployed will equal the number of job vacancies? Why or why not?

2. Use the accompanying graph to answer the questions that follow. P_E refers to the expected rate of inflation.

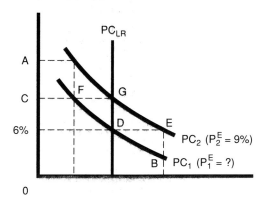

a. What is the expected rate of inflation PC_1 equal to?
b. What is the actual rate of inflation at point C?
c. What is the actual rate of inflation at point A?
d. Is the actual rate of inflation at point B greater than or less than the expected rate?

e. Does point F represent an unemployment rate above, below, or at the natural unemployment rate?

f. Is the expected inflation rate greater or less than the actual rate of inflation at point F?

g. Has job search time risen or fallen at point E relative to the natural rate of unemployment? Why?

h. What do points G and D tell you? Is the price level constant at these points?

i. Has job search time risen or fallen at point F relative to the natural unemployment rate? Why?

j. Why is curve PC_2 shifted farther to the right than curve PC_1? What is the corresponding shift in the SRAS curve in the aggregate-demand/aggregate-supply model?

3. "The temporary trade-off comes not from inflation per se, but from unanticipated inflation, which means from a rising rate of inflation. There is no permanent trade-off between inflation and employment. To say there is a permanent trade-off is a confusion between a 'high' rate of inflation and a 'rising' rate of inflation." Interpret this statement. Is your interpretation consistent with the statement that in the long run, after the economy has fully adjusted to some steady rate of inflation and regardless of whether expectations are adaptive or rational, actual and expected prices are the same?

4. How does the Phillips curve appear in both the short and long runs in an economy where adaptive expectations apply? In an economy where rational expectations apply?

5. Explain why it is important for policymakers to be familiar with the nation's natural rate of unemployment.

6. Assume that the economy is operating at the real potential national income level and that the rate of inflation is constant. Would a federal policy of disinflation bring the economy to a zero rate of inflation and be nearly costless to society? Does it depend on whether the economy is operating in an adaptive- or rational-expectations world? Explain. Roughly trace the adjustment path for each case using the Phillips-curve model.

APPLICATION ANALYSIS

1. Refer back to Figure 17.3 to answer the following questions:

a. Indicate one Phillips curve that is an extremely good fit and seems quite stable.

b. Identify two or more shifts in the Phillips curve from 1961 to 1987. What was the major economic cause for each shift?

c. Does a predictable trade-off appear between 1970 and 1987?

d. Which period indicates the occurrence of stagflation?

e. Which periods may indicate a shift of the Phillips curve to the left?

SCHOOLS OF MACROECONOMIC THOUGHT

INTRODUCTION

During our survey we have encountered several schools of macroeconomic thought that hold differing views about how the economy works. Prior to the Great Depression, one dominant view of macroeconomics — the classical school — existed. The Great Depression seemingly contradicted many of the propositions of the classical school and spawned the Keynesian revolution, which in turn was challenged by the rise of monetarism. Most recently, two new alternative views — supply-side economics and the theory of rational expectations — have developed, each with its adherents.

To help you organize your study about macroeconomics, this appendix summarizes and compares the various schools of thought. Although we shall discuss all five schools of macroeconomics, it is perhaps fair to say that most active economists today are either of the Keynesian or monetarist persuasion, or hold an eclectic position leaning to one side or the other, depending on the issue in question.

THE CLASSICAL SCHOOL

All of modern macroeconomics either is derived from or was developed to oppose the classical school of macroeconomics. Classical macroeconomists believed that the economy was basically stable and would always operate at the level of potential national income. If the economy is displaced from this level of output, flexible wages and prices will quickly return the economy to full employment through the automatic adjustment process. Thus classical economists treated aggregate supply as vertical, and aggregate output was always determined by the long-run aggregate supply curve.

Classical economists believed that inadequate demand for the economy's goods would never be a problem. This belief rested on a proposition known as Say's Law, which simply states: "Supply creates its own demand." Every dollar's worth of goods produced means a dollar earned

This appendix was written by William V. Weber of Eastern Illinois University.

and a dollar's worth of goods demanded. If private savings reduced consumer spending by an additional dollar, that dollar would be available for and be replaced by investment spending. As long as prices were sufficiently flexible to eliminate surpluses and shortages, aggregate demand would always be adequate to purchase the economy's production. Aggregate demand could not fall low enough to cause prolonged unemployment.

The classical economists' view of inflation was based on the equation of exchange:

$$M \cdot V = P \cdot Q$$

In this equation, M is the quantity of money, V is the velocity of circulation of money, P is the price level, and Q is real GNP. The classical economists believed that velocity, V, was a constant, and that Q would remain at the level of potential national income because of Say's Law and flexible wages and prices. Changes in the money supply, M, would therefore show up as similar changes in the price level, P. Inflation was a strictly monetary phenomenon.

Classical economists saw no need for the government to pursue active economic policy. The aggregate output of the economy would always be at or tending toward the level of potential national income. Since aggregate output was fixed by the level of potential national income, fiscal policy could affect only the distribution of output between the public and private sectors. An increase in government spending, for example, would result in increasing the rate of interest, which would crowd out private spending by an equal amount. Private spending would decline by precisely the amount that public spending increased.

THE KEYNESIAN SCHOOL

The Great Depression seemed to contradict the basic propositions of the classical model. For a decade the U.S. economy operated at aggregate outputs well below the level of potential national income, with unemployment as high as 25 percent. Many (but not all) economists believed the classical theory needed to be overhauled to explain why the worldwide depression was happening. The revolution in macroeconomic thought was triggered by the publication of John Maynard Keynes' *General Theory of Employment, Interest, and Money* in 1936.

Keynesian economics emphasizes the importance of aggregate demand to an economy's performance. Aggregate demand is determined by the spending desired by four sectors of the economy — consumers, firms (through investment), government, and the rest of the world (through net exports). To determine the effects of an economic event, a Keynesian will concentrate on how these four components of aggregate demand have been affected.

Keynesians disagree with the basic assumptions of the classical model. Say's Law is rejected: If savings reduced consumption expenditures, the lower demand would not necessarily be replaced by new investment expenditures. Consequently, low aggregate demand could trigger a recession; furthermore, this recession could be substantial. Keynesians believe wages and prices are not as flexible as the classical economists assumed, so the automatic adjustment mechanism could take a long time to work. The costs of unemployment during a recession could then be significant if the nonactivist policies of the classical economists are followed.

Keynesians' view of inflation is also different from that of the classical economists. The equation of exchange, they believe, does not provide much information on inflation because velocity is unstable and changes frequently. Instead, inflation can be expected when aggregate demand becomes too strong and creates an inflationary gap. However, the costs of inflation are minor compared to those of unemployment, so inflation has traditionally been a lesser problem than unemployment to Keynesian economists. Should substantial inflation become a problem, as it did during the 1970s, the policy of gradualism (discussed in Chapter 16) should be used to prevent the restrictive economic policies from putting the economy into a recession.

Keynesians view the economy as unstable, likely to fall into a recessionary or inflationary gap at any time. Keynesians have traditionally recommended activist fiscal and monetary policies, especially with regard to fighting unemployment. Fiscal policy should be used to keep aggregate demand strong, even if inflation is caused, as the result would be better than a recession. Balanced federal budgets are not a necessity (and, in fact, budget deficits can help pull the economy out of a costly recession), although most Keynesians recommend that budgets be balanced over the course of the business cycle. Keynesians believe monetary policy is weaker than fiscal policy (since it works by first affecting interest rates and then consumption and investment spending), so it is best used to keep interest rates stable.

In summary, Keynesians are activists. While they agree that it is probably impossible to conduct a perfect discretionary economic policy, they nevertheless believe that what can be accomplished is better than doing nothing at all. Fiscal policy, when properly conducted, is considered an especially effective tool that should not be limited by any restrictions on the ability of the government to run a deficit.

THE MONETARIST SCHOOL

If Keynesians are the activists among macroeconomists, then monetarists are the nonactivists. Monetarists are the intellectual descendants of the classical economists, and, like that school, emphasize the stability of the economy and the role of the money supply.

Monetarists, like the Keynesians, recognize the importance of aggregate demand to the economy. However, they have returned to the equation of exchange, $M \cdot V = P \cdot Q$, for their understanding of how aggregate demand works. When something is happening in the economy, a monetarist asks how it will affect the quantity of money, M, and/or the velocity of circulation, V. The answers to these questions allow the monetarist to predict what will happen to nominal GNP. Monetarists apply the equation of exchange by assuming that velocity, though not fixed, is stable. Velocity will change in predictable ways with the level of real output and the level of anticipated change in the price level.

Monetarists do not recommend actively implementing discretionary fiscal and monetary policy for two reasons. First, they believe that prices and wages are flexible enough to allow the automatic adjustment mechanism to do a fairly good job of keeping the economy at full employment. Second, the effects of government policies are uncertain and unpredictable due to problems in collecting adequate economic data, the lags in applying and implementing policies, and changes in the incentives and expectations of consumers and businesses. Since the economy is quick to adjust, discretionary economic policy is more likely to destabilize the economy than it is to improve its performance. Most of the economy's problems, monetarists believe, have been caused by improper actions of government and the Federal Reserve, and not by a failure of the economy to adjust.

Monetarists believe the wisest course is to build on the economy's stability by eliminating potential sources of instability where possible.

Moreover, discretionary monetary and fiscal policies are viewed as possible sources of instability instead of corrective measures for instability.

Monetarists suggest that the rate of growth of the money supply is the cause of most economic fluctuations. If these money supply fluctuations could be eliminated, then an additional source of instability in the macroeconomy would be eliminated. Thus they propose that a fixed monetary rule replace our current reliance on discretionary monetary policy. The Federal Reserve, according to monetarist doctrine, should be instructed to expand the money supply at a constant growth rate equal to the rate of growth of potential national income.

Monetarists are concerned less with fiscal policy than with monetary policy. They generally believe in the ineffectiveness of fiscal policy, for the reasons mentioned above. The amount of government spending, they suggest, should be decided on the basis of the public/private mix of goods and services appropriate for the economy, not on the basis of stabilization policy. Active fiscal policy, therefore, should not be pursued, and the federal budget should be balanced. Many monetarists are disturbed by the recent large federal deficits and have supported a constitutional amendment to require an annually balanced budget.

In summary, monetarists believe that a useful discretionary economic policy is only theoretically possible, maintaining that the requirements for such a policy are so strict that it is impossible in practice. Instead, they propose fixed policy rules. Monetarists advocate a fixed rate of growth in the money supply, arguing that this would eliminate a major existing source of economic instability. Discretionary fiscal policy should not be employed at all, and the budget should be balanced, if not annually, then at the very least over the business cycle.

THE NEW CLASSICAL SCHOOL OF RATIONAL EXPECTATIONS

Monetarists have traditionally assumed that inflationary expectations are formed adaptively on the basis of past experience, holding that major changes in inflation cannot be predicted but have to be seen to be believed. Economic theory, however, starts from the premise that individuals pursue self-interest as far as possible, and clearly it is in one's self-interest to try to predict changes in inflation instead of relying only on past experience. Many economists thus feel uncomfortable with an economic theory that assumes economic decision makers do not make use of all available information. They believe that consumers and firms would be acting irrationally if they ignored useful information.

These ideas gave rise to the theory of rational expectations. Rational expectations are predictions about the future state of macroeconomic variables using all available information about how the economy works, including information about past and present macroeconomic policies. The theory of rational expectations assumes that economic decision makers base their forecasts on the best available information interpreted in the light of the best available economic theory of how the macroeconomy actually works.

The main consequence of the rational expectations hypothesis is that *anticipated* changes in the economy cannot drive the economy away from full employment. For example, suppose that the economy is at full employment and that an expansion in the money supply (which will, of course, be inflationary) occurs. If this change in monetary policy is announced and believed, the rational expectations hypothesis implies that people will anticipate the future inflation and build it into contracts, future prices, and future wages. Consequently, the anticipated inflation will not have any *real* effects. We will not observe a trade-off between unemployment and *anticipated* inflation.

Believers in the rational expectations hypothesis claim that anticipated changes in the economy have no real effect when the economy is at full employment. This prediction is known as the *policy ineffectiveness theorem*, which states that if the economy is at full employment, anticipated economic policy can affect only the price level.

Clearly, the rational expectations school falls into the classical/monetarist tradition. Rational expectations strengthen the workings of the automatic adjustment mechanism, because wages and prices (if flexible enough) will change quickly in response to new, anticipated economic conditions. Since the policy ineffectiveness theorem indicates that discretionary monetary and fiscal policies (unless they come as total surprises) are fruitless, believers in the rational expectations hypothesis are also nonactivists.

THE SUPPLY-SIDE SCHOOL

In Chapter 12 we initially discussed supply-side economics. Supply-side economics is not a complete theory in itself but an attempt to make macroeconomics a more complete theory by explicitly introducing a consideration of aggregate supply. Supply-side economics, like the rational expectations theory, is in the classical/monetarist tradition.

Supply-siders believe that the macroeconomy is fundamentally stable, that prices and wages are flexible, and that the cause of inflation is excessive growth of the money supply. For these reasons, they do not advocate a discretionary monetary policy. Instead, they prefer a monetary rule or something even stricter, such as the return to the gold standard. (Recall from Chapter 16 that a gold standard requires all money to be backed by some quantity of gold that is freely available to economic decision makers in return for cash.)

Supply-siders generally do not favor discretionary fiscal policy, with one notable exception from which their name is derived. Supply-siders argue that marginal tax rates should be reduced as much as possible to create incentives for business firms and the owners of the factors of production to pursue more productive activities. In particular, they argue that a reduction in marginal tax rates will make it profitable for businesses to increase productivity and output, causing both the short-run and long-run aggregate supply curves to shift to the right. Such policies, if successful, would help the economy by putting downward pressure on both inflation and unemployment.

Actually, any policies that improve the economy's long-run supply (that is, shift long-run aggregate supply to the right) are supply-side policies. Job-retraining programs, tax incentives designed to stimulate capital accumulation, policies designed to improve the efficiency of economic markets by reducing market imperfections (such as monopoly power, minimum wage laws, and price supports) all qualify as supply-side policies, but in the 1980s supply-siders emphasized the reduction in marginal tax rates.

Critics of supply-side economics suggest that the effects of a marginal tax rate reduction are likely to be greater on aggregate demand than on aggregate supply, especially in the short run and perhaps even in the long run. They do not deny that there will be positive supply-side effects, stating only that they are likely to be small and perhaps insignificant.

TABLE 17A.1
A Comparison of Macroeconomic Models and Positions

ISSUE	CLASSICAL	KEYNESIAN	MONETARIST	RATIONAL EXPECTATIONS	SUPPLY-SIDE ECONOMICS
Stability of the economy	Stable	Unstable	Stable	Stable	Stable
Price–wage flexibility	Flexible	Inflexible	Flexible	Flexible	Flexible
View of velocity of circulation	Fixed	Unstable	Stable	Stable	Stable
Cause of inflation	Excess money supply	Increases in aggregate demand	Excess money supply	Excess money supply	Excess money supply
Stabilization policy	Nonactivist — unnecessary	Activist — necessary	Nonactivist — too difficult	Nonactivist — ineffective and potentially harmful	Activist — use fiscal policy to affect aggregate supply
Appropriate way to conduct monetary policy	Constant growth rate	Control interest rates	Constant growth rate	Constant growth rate	Constant growth rate
Appropriate way to conduct fiscal policy	Annually balanced budget	Discretionary or budget balanced over business cycle	Budget balanced over business cycle or balanced annually	Annually balanced budget	Budget balanced over business cycle (use to maximize economic growth)

TABLE 17A.2
Possible Compromise Positions

ISSUE	COMPROMISE POSITION
Stability of the economy	Generally stable with occasional periods of instability
Price–wage flexibility	Inflexible in the short run but flexible in the long run
View of velocity of circulation	Stable at times, but unstable at other times
Cause of inflation	Generally excess money growth, but adverse supply shocks can also cause increases in the price level
Stabilization policy	Fine-tuning impossible — discretionary economic policy should be employed during periods of extreme instability
Appropriate way to conduct monetary policy	Monitor both quantity of money and interest rates in the short run, and aim for constant growth rate in the long run
Appropriate way to conduct fiscal policy	Budget balanced over business cycle, except when extreme inflationary or recessionary gaps exist

RECONCILING THE VARIOUS SCHOOLS OF THOUGHT

The five schools of macroeconomic thought are summarized in Table 17A.1, which clearly shows the historical patterns we have discussed. Monetarism is the intellectual offshoot of the classical model and has itself spawned two offshoots, the rational expectations hypothesis and supply-side economics. Only the Keynesian model appears fundamentally different, and even this exception has more similarities than differences. For example, all of the modern schools of thought recognize the importance of both aggregate demand and aggregate supply in determining the economy's performance.

The major point of contention is whether fiscal and monetary policies should be activist or nonactivist. Classical economics and its three modern children do not see the useful possibility for discretionary economic policy in the short run, and they argue for fixed policy rules or laws. Keynesian economists alone see the possibility of successfully employing a discretionary economic policy.

Although there are some economists who can be considered strict Keynesians, monetarists, rational expectationists, or supply-siders, perhaps most economists are eclectic, preferring to be more pragmatic than dogmatic. Table 17A.2 provides a possible compromise position on the major areas of macroeconomic disagreement.

ECONOMIC GROWTH AND PRODUCTIVITY

IN THIS CHAPTER YOU WILL LEARN:

Why small differences in growth rates can cause large differences in the standard of living

•

What factors influence the rate of economic growth

•

How investment can be financed by three different types of savings

•

Why supply-side policies may or may not stimulate economic growth

•

What theories are proposed to explain the recent slowdown in economic growth in the United States

THE MYSTERIOUS DECLINE IN ECONOMIC GROWTH AND PRODUCTIVITY

An ever-increasing standard of living has become an expected part of the American way of life. Parents today, however, may be overly optimistic if they expect this trend to continue for their children. The economy is simply not growing as rapidly as it did in the past, and has not done so for 15 years. If economic growth continues at the recent slow pace, you probably will not enjoy an increase in the standard of living during your lifetime comparable to the increase your parents experienced.

Between 1929 and 1948, despite the Great Depression and World War II, real national income in the United States grew at the annual rate of 2.5 percent. Growing at this rate, the economy doubled in size roughly every 29 years. Thereafter, the economic growth rate picked up, averaging 3.6 percent from 1948 to 1973. The doubling time — the number of years it takes for the economy to double in size — declined to only 20 years. Then came a major slowdown. During the rest of the 1970s, the rate of economic growth declined by half to only 1.8 percent, and the doubling time itself doubled to 40 years. Since then, the growth rate has increased slightly but has remained below that experienced from 1929 to 1948.

Accompanying the decline in the growth rate was a slowdown in the rate at which labor productivity improved. The rate of productivity growth, which averaged 2.2 percent per year between 1955 and 1973, grew at only 0.6 percent from 1973 to 1981, and has only partially recovered to a rate of 1.25 percent during the 1980s.

The decline in the rate of economic growth and in the rate of labor productivity increase is a cause for much concern. An economy can raise the standard of living for its population over the long term only when labor productivity rises. Nothing contributes more than economic growth to a nation's ability to reduce poverty; increase leisure; improve public health, education, and the environment; and increase the quality of life in general.

What are the causes of the productivity decline? Is there anything that we as a nation can do about it?

REAGAN'S SUPPLY-SIDE POLICIES AND ECONOMIC GROWTH

Ronald Reagan won the presidency in 1980 at least partially on the promise that he had a program to reduce inflation (which was raging at double-digit levels) and spur economic growth (which had been anemic for almost a decade). The existing macroeconomic situation clearly had voters worried, and they were willing to take a chance on a new economic theory called *supply-side economics*.

Reagan had promised, if elected, to implement a program for economic recovery. This program would be based on creating positive incentives for individuals and businesses to do productive activities, to save and invest more, and to work longer and harder. The plan was to increase aggregate supply in order to both reduce the rate of inflation and increase real national income.

The cornerstone of Reagan's program was tax reform. The changes in taxes would include substantial reductions in the marginal income tax rates paid by individuals and specific inducements for businesses to increase their investment. Tax cuts had been used in the past to improve economic performance by increasing aggregate demand in times of recession. This time, however, the tax cuts were designed to promote economic growth during a period of inflation by increasing aggregate supply.

Many economists thought this proposal was the wrong policy at the wrong time, predicting that a reduction in taxes would increase aggregate demand at a time when traditional analysis suggested it should, if anything, be reduced. Cutting taxes, they warned, would make inflation worse, not better. After a decade of disappointing economic performance, however, voters were willing to try something new, even if it might be wrong. After all, it might work, and traditional policies, they felt, had not.

Ronald Reagan was given his chance. Did the new approach work?

• INTRODUCTION •

The phrase *economic growth* is often used by the media to discuss the changes in national income that have occurred over recent quarters, as in the headline "Economic Growth at 4.4 Percent in Latest Report." Economists, however, consider **economic growth** to be a longer-term phenomenon and attempt to net out cyclical variations when they investigate economic growth.

> *Economic growth occurs when both actual and potential real national income increase over the long run.*

The actual process of economic growth takes place on a more or less regular basis, but not at a constant rate. There have been decades of both higher and lower growth. Part of the variability of economic growth is due to the cyclical nature of the economy. The Great Depression obviously insured a decade of slow economic growth. But even during the 1930s, potential national income continued to increase, albeit at a reduced rate, as the labor force grew and technological change continued.

Potential national income increases during periods of economic growth. Actual real national income, however, fluctuates around the level of potential national income. Sometimes it is less, at other times more, but in the long run actual national income will tend toward the level of potential national income. So the nation's standard of living, in the long run, depends crucially on its economic growth. In this chapter, we shall discuss the factors that contribute to economic growth and how an economy can increase the rate of economic growth. •

ECONOMIC GROWTH

In terms of per capita gross national product in 1870, Great Britain was the richest nation in the world, and the United States was second. The average British citizen enjoyed an income that was 28 percent greater than the average American's ($2,000 in 1870 as opposed to $1,565). The per capita income in Britain also was substantively higher than that in France, Germany, Italy, and Japan. Over the next century, per capita income in the United States grew at only a slightly faster rate (1.88%) than it did in the British economy (1.20%). In 1980, 110 years later, this small difference in the growth rate had produced a per capita income in the United States of $12,219 — the highest in the world. In Great Britain, per capital income had increased to only $7,587. Moreover, the standard of living in Great Britain was now lower than that in Germany, France, Japan, and, by the middle of the decade, Italy. The apparently small difference of 7/10 of a percent in the growth rate had transformed Great Britain — which had been the richest country in the world — into the laggard among the developed nations of the world.

THE IMPORTANCE OF GROWTH RATES

Thus small differences in the growth rate, over a long period of time, make big differences in per capita income. In Table 18.1 the differences in the size of an economy after growing at various rates for different periods of time are shown. In the initial year (year 0), the economy's per capita income starts at $1,000. The columns of the table show how the per capita income grows when the growth rate is 1, 2, and 3 percent. The difference in income caused by these different growth rates becomes very large over time. The economy's per capita income will be 35 percent larger in 30 years when it grows at 1 percent, but 81 percent bigger when it grows instead at 2 percent, and more than 240 percent larger when it grows at 3 percent.

Another way to look at the power of compounded rates of growth is to employ the rule of 72. Divide any growth rate into 72, and the resulting

TABLE 18.1
The Power of Compound Rates of Growth

YEAR	$1,000 INCOME GROWING AT 1 PERCENT ANNUALLY	$1,000 INCOME GROWING AT 2 PERCENT ANNUALLY	$1,000 INCOME GROWING AT 3 PERCENT ANNUALLY
0	1,000	1,000	1,000
1	1,010	1,020	1,030
5	1,051	1,104	1,159
10	1,105	1,219	1,344
20	1,220	1,486	1,806
30	1,348	1,811	2,427
40	1,489	2,208	3,262
50	1,645	2,692	4,384
100	2,705	7,245	19,219

answer will be the number of years it will take national income to double. For example, an economy that grows at 1 percent per year will double roughly every 72 years. An economy growing at 2 percent per year will double every 36 years (72 ÷ 2 = 36), and an economy growing at 3 percent will double every 24 years (72 ÷ 3 = 24).

The rule of 72 helps put the recent slowdown in the growth of the U.S. economy into perspective. Between 1948 and 1973 the real output per worker increased at the rate of 2.9 percent. Using the rule of 72, the average worker's real output would double roughly every 25 years. An average worker at age 25 in 1948 would find the standard of living would have doubled when he or she turned 50, simply due to the increased productivity of the economy. But between 1973 and 1981, worker productivity in the United States increased at the rate of only 0.6 percent per year, so the average worker's real output would double only every 120 years. Since 1981, worker productivity has increased to 1.4 percent per year, but it still would require over 50 years for the average worker's output to double. Unless the rate of productivity increases in the future, a 25-year-old worker in 1973 will not see the standard of living double during his or her working lifetime. Such are the dimensions of the slowdown in economic growth. Over long periods of time, small differences in growth rates create major differences in national income.

ECONOMIC GROWTH AND THE PRICE LEVEL

Economic growth increases the productive capacity of the economy, thus increasing the level of potential national income. The effects of economic growth on the aggregate-supply curves are shown in Figure 18.1. When economic growth occurs, the long-run aggregate-supply curve (which is vertical at the level of potential national income) shifts to the right. Assuming expectations about the price level are not changing, the short-run aggregate-supply curve will also move to the right by the same amount.

The short-run effects that economic growth has on the price level and actual (not potential) real national income depend on how aggregate demand is changing. If aggregate demand increases in step with economic growth, real national income will increase and the price level will not be affected. As shown in Figure 18.2, when the short- and long-run aggregate-supply curves shift to the right from SRAS₁ and LRAS₁ to SRAS₂

FIGURE 18.1
Effect of Economic Growth on the Aggregate-Supply Curves

Economic growth causes both the short-run and long-run aggregate-supply curves to shift to the right. If people's expectations about the price level are unchanged, the intersection of the short-run and long-run aggregate-supply curves remains at the expected price level PL.

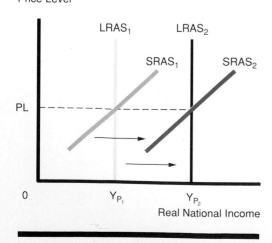

and LRAS$_2$, and these changes are accompanied by an increase in the aggregate-demand curve from AD$_1$ to AD$_2$, then the equilibrium position moves from E$_1$ to E$_2$, and the price level remains the same as before.

Economic growth will increase real national income without a change in the price level when it is accompanied by a corresponding increase in aggregate demand. If economic growth is not accompanied by an accommodating increase in aggregate demand, then the price level will be affected. When this occurs, there are two possible outcomes depending on whether economic decision makers anticipate changes that are occurring.

First consider the case where consumers and firms are surprised by the supply changes caused by economic growth. As shown in Figure 18.3, the productivity increases shift both the short- and long-run aggregate-supply curves to the right, from SRAS$_1$ and LRAS$_1$ to SRAS$_2$ and LRAS$_2$. The aggregate-demand curve does not change, remaining at AD. The equilibrium position moves from E$_1$ to E$_{SR}$, and the price level declines from PL$_1$ to PL$_{SR}$. Real national income increases to Y$_{SR}$ but not as much as the potential level of national income has increased. Potential national income increases from Y$_{P_1}$ to Y$_{P_2}$. A recessionary gap is created.

In the long run, the recessionary gap will be eliminated as discussed in previous chapters. The decline in the price level has increased the real wages earned under existing labor contracts. The level of real wages is too high to allow the full employment of the labor force. As existing labor contracts expire, the money wage rate will eventually decline, causing the short-run aggregate-supply curve to shift from SRAS$_2$ to SRAS$_3$. Equilibrium moves from E$_{SR}$ to E$_{LR}$ as this occurs. The price level will decline from PL$_{SR}$ to PL$_{LR}$, and real national income will increase to the new potential level of national income.

The second possibility is that economic growth without an increase in aggregate demand is fully anticipated by all decision makers. Consumers and firms anticipate the lower price level and automatically build this change into wages and other contracts. The resulting lower wages cause the short-run aggregate-supply curve to shift more to the right than the long-run aggregate-supply curve shifted, so in this case employment and output will not fall. The equilibrium position will move directly from E$_1$ to E$_{LR}$ without the intermediate stop at E$_{SR}$. The price level will decline from PL$_1$ to PL$_{LR}$, and real national income will remain at the potential level.

Inflation occurs during periods of economic growth when aggregate demand increases by more than the increase in the level of potential national income. Again, the short-run effects on employment and the price level depend on whether the changes in the economy are anticipated by consumers and firms.

When the changes are unanticipated, the economy will first adjust to a short-run equilibrium before the automatic adjustment mechanism returns the economy to a long-run equilibrium. In Figure 18.4, aggregate demand (AD) has increased faster than the rate of economic growth — the rightward shift from AD$_1$ to AD$_2$ is larger than the rightward shift in the supply curves. The differences in the rates of growth of the demand and supply sides cause an inflationary gap at the new short-run equilibrium E$_{SR}$. Real national income increases from Y$_{P_1}$ to Y$_{SR}$ in the short run and temporarily exceeds the new level of potential national income (Y$_{P_2}$). The price level increases from PL$_1$ to PL$_{SR}$.

The price level is higher than expected, and the automatic adjustment mechanism will work to return the economy to full employment. The purchasing power of workers' wages has been eroded; in the long run, contracts will be renegotiated to take the new higher price level into account. The higher resource prices will shift the short-run aggregate-supply curve to the left, the equilibrium position will move from E$_{SR}$ to E$_{LR}$, the price

FIGURE 18.2
Economic Growth with an Accommodating Increase in Aggregate Demand

Economic growth stimulates the supply side of the economy, shifting SRAS$_1$, LRAS$_1$ to SRAS$_2$, LRAS$_2$. If aggregate demand rises by the same amount, with AD$_1$ shifting to AD$_2$, then economic growth will not create inflation. The equilibrium will adjust from E$_1$ to E$_2$, and the price level will remain at PL.

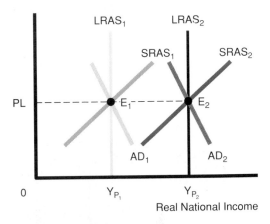

FIGURE 18.3
Economic Growth Without an Increase in Aggregate Demand

Economic growth without an accommodating increase in aggregate demand puts downward pressure on the price level and, in the short run, can result in a recession. Economic growth stimulates the supply side of the economy, shifting SRAS$_1$, LRAS$_1$ to SRAS$_2$, LRAS$_2$. Aggregate demand, however, remains at AD. If the changes in the economy are unanticipated, then the economy will adjust to a new short-run equilibrium, E$_{SR}$, with a lower price level, PL$_{SR}$, and a recessionary gap will be created. In the long run, the automatic adjustment mechanism will shift short-run aggregate supply to SRAS$_3$ and return the economy to full employment at the equilibrium E$_{LR}$.

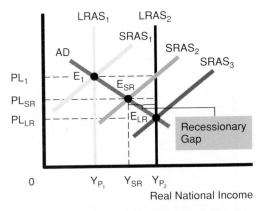

FIGURE 18.4
Economic Growth with Inflation

Economic growth can also coexist with inflation. This situation occurs when the demand side of the economy increases faster than the rate of economic growth. Economic growth has caused $SRAS_1$, $LRAS_1$ to shift to $SRAS_2$, $LRAS_2$. Aggregate demand has shifted further to the right, from AD_1 to AD_2. If these changes are unanticipated, the economy will adjust from the equilibrium E_1 to the new short-run equilibrium E_{SR}, and an inflationary gap will exist. The automatic adjustment mechanism will cause short-run aggregate supply to shift back to the left to $SRAS_3$ and restore full employment at the long-run equilibrium E_{LR}. Throughout this adjustment process, inflation was created as the price level rose from PL_1 to PL_{SR} to PL_{LR}.

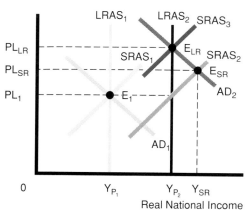

level will increase to PL_{LR}, and the level of real national income produced will decline to the level of potential national income Y_{P_2}.

If consumers and firms anticipate the changes in the economy, the intermediate short-run effects are eliminated. The short-run aggregate-supply curve will shift from $SRAS_1$ to $SRAS_3$ in anticipation of both economic growth and inflation, and the equilibrium moves directly from E_1 to E_{LR}. The price level will increase along with real national income when economic growth is accompanied with a more-than-proportional increase in aggregate demand.

You will recall the conditions of the ideal macroeconomic world discussed when you began your study of macroeconomics: rapid economic growth, full employment, and price stability. If economic growth is to proceed smoothly without causing short-run fluctuations in real national income, employment, and the price level, the increase in potential national income must be accompanied with an accommodating increase in aggregate demand. When aggregate demand increases faster or slower than the rate of economic growth, the price level will fluctuate in the long run. Furthermore, if the changes in the economy are unanticipated, short-run fluctuations in inflation and unemployment will also occur.

EXTENSIVE AND INTENSIVE GROWTH

We have seen how and why actual national income will fluctuate around the level of potential national income while it is rising during periods of economic growth. We now investigate what determines the level of potential national income. What factors cause the level of potential national income to increase? In short, what creates economic growth?

Economists divide economic growth into two types: **extensive growth** and **intensive growth.**

> *Extensive growth occurs when the quantity of the factors of production increases.*

> *Intensive growth occurs when the factors of production become more productive, increasing the average amount of output received per unit of input.*

Extensive growth occurs when the available amounts of the factors of production increase. Increases in the labor force, the capital stock, or the amount of land and natural resources available create extensive growth and increase the economy's potential national output.

The capital stock is of particular importance. Recall that capital is composed of the machines, equipment, inventories, and buildings that aid the production process. The production of capital goods requires a sacrifice — if resources are used to produce capital goods, they cannot be used to produce consumption goods. Capital formation requires that we save and postpone consumption. Thus an increase in capital formation requires either an increase in the nation's savings, or an increase in foreign investment (which allows the savings of another country to be invested in the United States).

One way for the government to stimulate extensive growth is through its structure of taxes. Tax policies can stimulate extensive growth by providing incentives for savings and investment to encourage capital formation. Tax policies also affect the resource markets, so extensive growth can be created by structuring taxes to encourage the supply and demand of labor and natural resources.

The quantity of labor can be increased in several ways, because the amount of labor available is more than simply the number of workers available. Increases in the quantity of the labor force can occur due to the growth of population or to an increase in the proportion of the population that is in the labor force; they can also occur if each worker works longer hours. The age composition of the labor force must be taken into account. A population that has a large proportion of its labor force made up of young, inexperienced persons is thought to be less productive than one with a large proportion of older, experienced workers.

The second kind of economic growth — intensive growth — occurs when the output per unit of input increases and the factors of production themselves become more productive. Technological change, economies of scale, and improvements in the efficiency with which resources are allocated can bring about increases in output that exceed the increases in the quantity of inputs.

Technological change reflects advances in knowledge that, when introduced, allow the capital and labor employed in the production process to become more productive. Any attempt to compare the present with the past would certainly include a list of technological innovations. Electricity, nuclear power, computers, telephones, television, satellite communications, automobiles, airplanes, automation, industrial robots, new chemicals, and synthetic fibers are products of technological change. Technological improvements can be entirely new production processes (such as the moving assembly line) or improvements to an existing process (such as an automated machine).

The rate of technological improvement is influenced by the research and development (R&D) expenditures undertaken by both the private sector and the government. An increase in R&D expenditures should lead to a future increase in technological change and intensive growth.

Intensive growth is also affected by **economies of scale.**

Economies of scale exist when an increase in output results in lower unit costs of production.

For example, automobiles were initially produced one at a time in small shops — which is fine if you wish to produce a small number of automobiles. However, to produce large numbers of automobiles, the capital and labor will be more efficient when employed in modern factories using a moving assembly line. Therefore, the production of automobiles exhibits economies of scale. As firms in the economy increasingly exploit economies of scale, intensive growth is created.

The efficiency with which resources are allocated is another influence on intensive growth. The shifts in resources from the farms to the factories, from rural areas to urban areas, and from heavy industries to high technological industries all represent improvements in the efficiency with which resources are allocated. As these changes occurred, the factors of production moved from less productive to more productive employments, and the average amount of output produced per unit of input increased.

Government policies and the performance of the macroeconomy can affect both extensive and intensive growth. Periods of high employment, when actual national income is close to potential national income, are more conducive to capital formation than periods of stagnation, and so are favorable for extensive growth. Periods of price stability likewise are more favorable to investment and extensive growth than periods of inflation or deflation. Regulation of the private sector may make the private sector either less or more productive depending on the individual situation, affecting intensive growth. Patent laws allow inventors and innovators to capture the economic returns their work has created. The more effective the patent laws are, the more research and development will be undertaken. Investing in the quality of the labor force — through education, job training programs, and job experience — is another way of increasing the productivity of labor, leading to intensive growth.

CAPITAL AND TECHNOLOGICAL CHANGE

Of the many factors affecting economic growth, capital and technological change are probably the most important and deserve special attention.

The advances in knowledge resulting from technological change are of two types: **basic knowledge** and **applied knowledge.**

Basic knowledge is accumulated at the scientific level and consists of a better understanding of the physical world.

Applied knowledge draws on the stock of basic knowledge to develop new products and production processes.

Nuclear science, solid-state physics, superconductivity, and genetics are examples of recent additions to basic knowledge. Nuclear power, the microchip, computers, VCRs, industrial robots, chemicals, and biotechnological drugs are examples of applied knowledge.

The private sector allocates funds for research and development in a search for profits. Business firms are interested in developing products and processes that will pay and from which the business firm will profit. Most research and development undertaken by the private sector therefore will be in the area of applied knowledge. Advances in basic knowledge do not immediately result in profitable opportunities and will not be of much interest to private firms.

The public sector must then be responsible for much of basic research. Advances in basic knowledge eventually are useful but in unpredictable ways, and the returns to advances in basic knowledge generally cannot be captured by the inventor. If sufficient resources are to be devoted to basic science, this effort must be subsidized by government or undertaken in government or university laboratories. A public sector that is mainly devoted to income transfers will undertake less basic research than one that focuses on insuring the efficiency of resource allocation.

The introduction of applied knowledge into the economy depends heavily on investment in the capital stock. As firms invest and begin to use new capital, new ways of doing things are discovered and new products and processes found. Acquiring applied knowledge through investment in this manner is called the **learning-by-doing hypothesis.**

The learning-by-doing hypothesis states that as a task is undertaken, new ways of accomplishing the task will be discovered that were not apparent when the task was begun.

Thus, capital investment does more for economic growth than simply increasing extensive growth — according to the learning-by-doing hypothesis, capital also raises intensive growth through its contribution to applied knowledge and technological change.

Learning-by-doing is also enhanced by specialization. The creative powers of individuals are naturally directed to seeking ways of improving the process in which they are engaged. As the economy becomes more specialized, each individual will perform ever narrower tasks and attention will become more finely focused. New and better ways of doing things will be discovered. Prior to the scientific revolution that began in the nineteenth century, most innovations probably resulted from the effects of specialization and learning-by-doing.

Another way the rate of technological improvement is affected by the rate of capital investment is called the **embodiment hypothesis.**

The embodiment hypothesis states that new technology is introduced in the form of new capital investment.

The embodiment hypothesis is based on the belief that it is too expensive to modify existing capital equipment to take advantage of new applied knowledge. Instead, firms find it less expensive to simply acquire new capital equipment to put new technology to use. Indeed, one reason for acquiring new capital goods is that they are more efficient than the existing capital. According to the embodiment hypothesis, new capital contributes to economic growth because it embodies (i.e., contains) the new applied knowledge resulting from technological progress.

The learning-by-doing hypothesis and the embodiment hypothesis show that the composition of spending in gross national product is important in determining the rate of technological progress. Capital investment is a more important source of economic growth than is revealed by its contribution to extensive growth — increased capital formation also results in increasing intensive growth by increasing the rate of technological improvement. Consequently, the larger that investment's share in GNP is, the stronger will be the nation's economic growth. For investment to have a larger share of GNP, some other sector — most likely consumption — must have a smaller share. Therefore, an economy that dedicates a larger percentage of its GNP to investment instead of consumption will have a higher rate of technological progress and economic growth.

THE SOURCES OF PAST ECONOMIC GROWTH IN THE UNITED STATES

Edward F. Denison has attempted to identify the sources of economic growth in the United States using the ideas we have discussed. The results of his studies are reproduced in Table 18.2 for two periods: 1929–1948 and 1948–1973. The first line of the table presents Denison's estimates for the average annual rate of growth in real national income for the two periods. (Recall from Chapter 6 that real national income differs from real gross national product by excluding a depreciation allowance for capital used up in the production process and some indirect business taxes.) Denison found that the annual average rate of economic growth increased from 2.49 percent during the earlier period to 3.59 percent during the later period. During the years 1948 to 1973, the U.S. economy experienced significantly higher growth rates — fully 1.10 percentage points greater. Applying the rule of 72, the increase in the rate of economic growth reduced the doubling time for national income from 29 to only 20 years.

The acceleration in the growth rate should not be surprising, for the period 1929–1948 encompassed the Great Depression and World War II. The Great Depression marks the nadir of macroeconomic performance, and World War II required that the economy's resources be devoted to producing war materials. Neither event was conducive to high rates of economic growth.

The sources of the higher growth from 1948 to 1973 can be found by looking at the components of economic growth. Denison separates the

TABLE 18.2
Sources of Economic Growth in the United States, 1929–1948
Compared with 1948–1973

	GROWTH RATE FOR 1929–1948	GROWTH RATE FOR 1948–1973	DIFFERENCE IN GROWTH RATES
Real national income	2.49	3.59	1.10
Growth in total factor inputs	1.52	1.60	0.08
Capital	0.10	0.57	0.47
Labor	1.42	1.03	−0.39
Employment	1.01	0.91	−0.10
Hours of work	−0.22	−0.24	−0.02
Education	0.38	0.53	0.15
Age-sex composition	0.25	−0.17	−0.42
Intensive growth	0.97	1.99	1.02
Reallocation of resources	0.28	0.37	0.09
Economies of scale	0.21	0.42	0.21
Past macroeconomic performance	0.01	−0.18	−0.19
Government policy	0.00	−0.04	−0.04
Miscellaneous	0.01	0.00	−0.01
Residual (Technological change?)	0.46	1.42	0.96

Source: Edward F. Denison, *Accounting for Slower Economic Growth* (Washington, D.C., 1979), Table 8-1; and "The Interruption of Productivity Growth in the United States," *Economic Journal* (March 1983), Table 2, p. 60.

overall growth rate into the contributions due to (1) changes in labor and capital (which is, save for the education level of the labor force, extensive growth) and (2) changes in factors that affect intensive growth.

Increases in labor and capital accounted for about the same proportion of the overall growth rate during both periods — 1.52 percent for the earlier period and 1.60 percent for the later period. The similarity between the contributions of the growth of inputs during the two periods hides a significant difference. During the higher growth period, increases in the capital stock contributed more to the growth of inputs — because the capital stock contributes to the rate of technological development, we should expect stronger intensive growth during the period 1948–1973.

Indeed, changes in intensive growth do account for most of the difference in the overall growth rate between the two periods. The rate of increase in output per unit of input more than doubled between the two periods, increasing from 0.97 percent to 1.99 percent — an increase of 1.02 percentage points. Denison attributes almost all of this increase to advances in knowledge or technological change, which accounted for 0.96 percentage points of the increase.

Technological change is not directly measured in this study, because it is difficult to measure technological change directly. Instead, all of the other factors that influence the intensive growth are measured and subtracted from the measured output per unit of input. What is left over — called the residual — is attributed to advances in knowledge or technological change.

Because a large residual remained after all of the other sources of change in intensive growth were accounted for, Denison concludes that significant advances in knowledge had occurred. Using the residual to represent technological change, during the 1929–1948 period it accounted for 0.46 percentage points of the total 2.49 percent annual increase. During the period 1948–1973, advances in knowledge accounted for 1.42 percentage points of the 3.59 percent annual growth rate — more than triple the contribution in the earlier period.

In Denison's study, advances in knowledge account for between 20 and 40 percent of economic growth and for almost all of the increase in the growth rate that occurred between the two periods. If Denison's study is accurate, technological change (and the investment in capital that contributes to it) appears to be both an important source of economic growth and responsible for much of the variation in the rate of economic growth between the two periods.

RAISING THE RATE OF ECONOMIC GROWTH

Economic growth is not a free good. We have seen that investment in capital is one of the most important factors that influences a nation's economic growth. Increasing the quantity of capital raises the rate of economic growth both directly (because increasing the quantity of a productive input creates extensive growth) and indirectly (because the learning-by-doing and the embodiment hypotheses imply that more capital will create more technological progress and intensive growth). In this section, we shall concentrate on how to stimulate investment in capital goods in order to increase economic growth.

THE TRADE-OFF BETWEEN CONSUMPTION AND INVESTMENT

One of the fundamental choices facing an economy is the choice between consumption and investment. If a country is going to place a larger emphasis on production of capital goods, fewer resources will be available to produce consumption goods. So every nation faces a trade-off when it pursues economic growth — more investment to get higher economic growth in the future requires less consumption in the present.

Figure 18.5 illustrates this trade-off between investment and consumption. Path 1 shows the growth of consumption over time if present trends continue. Path 2 shows the flow of consumption over time if policies are introduced that provide incentives to invest more and consume less starting at time T_1. Consumption drops at time T_1 as the economy begins to save and invest more. The increased rate of saving and investment, however, means that the economy will grow faster along path 2 — this change in the rate of economic growth is shown by path 2 being steeper than path 1.

Consumption along path 2 will remain below that of path 1 until the two paths cross at some future time T_2. The shaded area to the left of T_2 reflects the sacrifice of lost consumption required to achieve the higher growth rate. However, the higher growth rate allows consumption along path 2 to actually exceed the consumption along path 1 after time T_2. The shaded area to the right of T_2 shows that consumption along path 2 will eventually exceed the consumption that present trends would allow. Path 1 as compared with path 2 allows more consumption early on but less consumption after some future date.

Which path is better? The answer depends on how people in the economy evaluate the trade-off between consumption in the present and consumption in the future. The weight people place on the present relative to the future will be reflected in the rate of interest determined as people borrow and lend money.

FIGURE 18.5
Two Alternative Consumption Paths

Economic growth can be increased by increasing investment in capital goods, but this change requires a sacrifice in consumption. If more resources are to be used to produce capital goods, fewer resources will be available to produce consumption goods. Path 1 shows the growth in consumption if the status quo is continued. Path 2 shows the growth in consumption if a larger share of GNP is dedicated to capital investment at time T_1. Consumption initially falls but will grow at a faster rate, as shown by path 2 becoming steeper. The higher rate of economic growth will pay off in the long run with higher levels of consumption than would be attained on path 1.

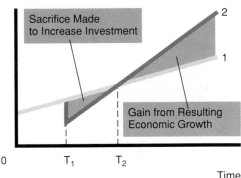

THE RELATIONSHIP BETWEEN SAVINGS AND INVESTMENT

If we wish to increase investment to stimulate economic growth, we must make a sacrifice — we must refrain from some consumption and save instead. We can use our macroeconomic model to show that there are three possible sources for savings to finance investment.

Recall from Chapter 9 that one way to describe macroeconomic equilibrium is for leakages and injections to be balanced. For an economy open to foreign trade, this condition can be written as the equation

$$S + T + M = I + G + X$$

The leakages are S, T, and M (which stand for private savings, taxes, and imports, respectively), and the injections are I, G, and X (which represent investment, government spending, and exports, respectively). By moving some terms around, this equation can be rewritten as

$$I = S + (T - G) + (M - X)$$

This equation says that actual investment (on the left-hand side) must equal the sum of three different types of savings. First, private savings (S) by consumers and firms help to finance the nation's investment. Second, government can also save, as represented by the term $(T - G)$. When the government takes in more dollars than it spends, T is bigger than G, and $(T - G)$ represents the amount government is saving through its budget expenditures. When the government runs budget deficits, government is dissaving (borrowing) and $(T - G)$ is negative. Third, $(M - X)$ represents foreign savings. When we have a trade deficit (i.e., when M is larger than X), we are in debt to other countries. Essentially, foreign agents are making loans to us, or put another way, foreign agents are saving in this country. So $(M - X)$ represents savings by foreign agents in this country and provides a third source for financing investment.

The first source of financing investment, private savings (S), is significantly affected by the structure of the tax system. For example, businesses finance their investment by borrowing and by retaining earnings that are the result of past profits (i.e., by saving). Taxes on business, particularly the corporate income tax, reduce the amount businesses have to reinvest. Reducing or eliminating business taxes would increase the amount of business savings available for investment.

The tax policies of government also affect the interest rate received by consumers who save. A tax on interest earnings will reduce the effective interest rate that savers earn. Under current tax policy, the interest earned by savers is taxed at the individual's highest marginal tax rate. Because most private saving is done by persons in the upper income tax brackets, the tax on interest income is levied at the higher tax rates and therefore probably discourages saving.

The effects of taxes on private savings and investment can, at times, be rather complicated. For example, investments in the equity market (for example, buying the stock of a corporation) are currently taxed twice. The corporation pays a corporate income tax on its earnings, and when the firm pays dividends to stockholders out of its remaining earnings, the stockholders must then pay income tax on these earnings. This double tax has the effect of shifting direct investment by savers to areas such as real estate where earnings are only taxed once.

If private-sector savings are thought to be too low, they can be stimulated by appropriate changes in the tax structure, but as we have seen, these changes may not be easy to determine or implement. Alternatively, the second source of financing investment, government savings (T − G), could be stimulated. This change could be achieved through appropriate changes in budgetary policies.

The third source of financing investment, foreign savings (M − X) has historically been an important source of domestic capital investment in the United States, especially in the nineteenth century. For most of our history, America has been a debtor nation; more foreign capital was invested here than we had invested abroad. This situation changed during World War I, and the United States became a creditor nation, having invested more abroad than foreigners invested in the United States. In the 1980s, the large federal budget deficits attracted large inflows of foreign capital, which have again made this country a debtor nation.

SUPPLY-SIDE POLICIES AND ECONOMIC GROWTH

The most ambitious attempt to use the ideas we have discussed to stimulate economic growth occurred early in the Reagan administration. A group of economists who were influential in the Reagan administration (particularly during the first term) forcefully argued for tax changes to stimulate savings and investment. These changes, they argued, would increase investment's share of potential GNP and, as we have seen, stimulate economic growth. Because economic growth results from improvements in the supply side of the economy, this group of economists became known as supply-siders.

The basic concept of **supply-side policies** is to raise the potential level of gross national product by creating incentives to save and invest and to work longer and harder.

> *Supply-side policies attempt to increase productivity and economic growth by changing the tax system to provide greater incentives to save and invest more and to work harder and more often.*

The main tool of supply-siders is the reduction of marginal tax rates which, it was predicted, would increase the returns people received from savings, investment, and work effort, and consequently, increase economic growth.

The economists who advocated supply-side policies believed that the stagnation of the 1970s was mostly due to the impact of the federal tax system. They believed that the tax system was biased against investment, saving, and work effort and that the disincentive effects of existing tax policies were significant. Supply-side economists also argued that the negative impact of federal tax policies was made worse by inflation. Taxes create distortions in the allocation of resources, and inflation, which had become increasingly worse during the 1970s, increased these distortions.

For example, the tax system and inflation combined to make returns on investment lower than initially expected. Suppose a machine cost $1,000 in 1970 and was expected to last for ten years. Also suppose that the machine was expected to return $200 a year, for a total of $2,000 in income over the life of the machine. Not all of this income was subject to taxes; the tax laws allowed the investor to deduct the price paid for the machine (called the historical cost of the machine). The investor would only have to pay taxes on $1,000 of income from the machine ($2,000 in income minus the $1,000 historical cost of the machine). So if the tax rate was 25 percent, the investor would pay $250 in taxes. The $2,000 earned from the machine would give the investor $1,000 to replace the machine and $750 (the remaining $1,000 minus $250 in taxes) as the return for investing the original $1,000. The investor expects the rate of return on the investment (ignoring the effects of discounting for the sake of clarity) to be 75 percent.

Now suppose inflation caused the price level to double immediately after the $1,000 machine was purchased. A new machine would now cost $2,000. The selling price of the goods that the machine produces would also double, so the investor would gain $400 a year, for a total of $4,000 in income. The investor would, however, be able to deduct only the historical cost of the machine ($1,000), so $3,000 would be taxed at the 25 percent rate. The tax bill would be $750, leaving the investor $2,250. After buying a new replacement machine for $2,000 the investor would have a return of only $250. So instead of receiving the expected return of 75 percent, the investor actually would receive only 25 percent, due to inflation and a tax system based on historical costs.

Inflation and the tax system, as shown by the example, reduced the real rate of return on investing, discouraging capital formation and economic growth. Supply-siders (and many other economists) also thought that the existing tax system, besides discouraging productive investment, also contained loopholes that actually encouraged wasteful investments, such as thoroughbred horse breeding or extremely risky ventures in real estate and oil exploration. Inflation, as it pushed individuals into ever-higher tax brackets, encouraged workers to consume more leisure and discouraged them from improving their skills, working overtime, or sometimes even showing up for work. All of these aspects of the tax laws, it was argued, discouraged productivity and economic growth.

The supply-siders urged that the nation's tax system be reformed. The first step would be to substantively reduce marginal tax rates, which would increase the incentives to save, invest, and work by increasing the return on all productive activities. Lower tax rates would also reduce the incentive to invest in wasteful tax shelters and other tax-avoidance schemes. Next, supply-siders urged that the capital gains tax be lowered and deductions be based on the replacement cost of capital (instead of the historical cost). Third, supply-siders suggested that the tax system be indexed so that inflation would not continually push workers into higher and higher tax brackets.

The supply-siders were not worried about possible negative effects of large budget deficits resulting from their tax changes. First, the reduction in tax rates was expected to increase the quantity of savings available should budget deficits appear. The supply-siders, however, argued that substantial budget deficits would not occur. They counted on the positive incentive effects of lower tax rates to spur work and investment, so both actual and potential national income would increase. The increase in real national income that resulted would, even at the lower tax rates, generate more tax revenues.

Furthermore, supply-siders believed that *high* tax rates actually created *low* tax revenues, because they reduced the **tax base** significantly.

> *The tax base is the amount of economic activity subject to taxes.*

This reduction had happened because high tax rates had created an incentive to either avoid activities that were taxed or not to report them to the Internal Revenue Service. For example, the effect of high marginal tax rates on the supply of labor was thought to be either a reduction of work effort or a shift to the untaxed underground economy. The effect of the income tax on the interest earned by saving was to encourage more consumption. The effect on investment was to either reduce the amount or divert investment to tax-sheltered areas. In the case of the capital gains tax, assets were retained for longer periods of time. In each case, the effective tax base is reduced.

Supply-siders argued that the reduction of tax rates would not create massive deficits because the loss in tax revenues would, at least partially (and some said totally), be offset by an expansion of the tax base. To make their case, they often employed a graph called the **Laffer curve** to illustrate the theoretical trade-off between tax rates and tax revenues (shown in Figure 18.6).

> *The Laffer curve illustrates the relationship between tax rates and tax revenues.*

The horizontal axis measures the marginal tax rate, and the vertical axis records total tax revenues that would flow from each tax rate. Initially, starting at a zero tax rate, tax revenues will rise as tax rates rise. After a maximum tax revenue of R_M is reached, total tax revenues will fall if tax rates continue to rise.

An interesting feature of this graph is that, except for the tax rate that maximizes tax revenues (t_M), the same amount of revenue could be generated by two different tax rates. Tax rates of both 0 and 100 percent will yield 0 tax revenues, because in the first instance no taxes are levied, and in the second case no taxable activities are undertaken when the government claims all of the income from a person's efforts. Tax revenues equal to R_A, for example, can be achieved by a tax rate of either t_A or t'_A.

Supply-siders argued that existing marginal tax rates exceeded the rate t_M, which would generate the maximum tax revenues. In effect, they believed that a tax rate such as t_A in Figure 18.6 was in effect. If this were the case, lowering tax rates from t_A to t_M would result in an increase in total tax revenues from R_A to R_M. This view was not widely shared among economists, most of whom believed that existing tax rates were below the revenue-maximizing rate t_M and predicted that a decline in tax rates would reduce total tax revenues.

Economists argued about the macroeconomic effects of the cuts in tax rates proposed by the supply-siders. The supply-siders believed that the changes in incentives created by lower tax rates would have a substantial effect on aggregate supply and economic growth. Most economists remained doubtful. First, critics of supply-side policies rejected the Laffer curve analysis and argued that substantial tax cuts — in the absence of equally significant reductions in government expenditures — would result in large federal budget deficits. The deficits, it was argued, would push up real interest rates and reduce the incentive to invest in capital goods — a phenomenon known as crowding out, which we discussed in Chapter 12 — and so the rate of economic growth would not substantially rise. Second, critics believed that the tax cuts were more likely to stimulate aggregate demand instead of aggregate supply — a change that could again trigger inflation.

The supply-siders got their chance. A significant part, but only part, of the supply-siders' program was actually enacted during the first term of the Reagan administration. The Economic Recovery Tax Act, stipulating lower personal tax rates, along with specific incentives designed to spur savings and investment, was passed by Congress and signed by the president in 1981. The analysis at the end of the chapter examines the

FIGURE 18.6
The Laffer Curve

The Laffer curve shows the hypothetical relationship between tax rates and tax revenues. Initially, tax revenues will increase as the tax rates are raised. Eventually, however, higher and higher tax rates will result in less and less revenue as people avoid the activities being taxed and the tax base shrinks. Supply-siders contended that tax rates were too high, such as at t_A, and actually hurt the collection of tax revenues.

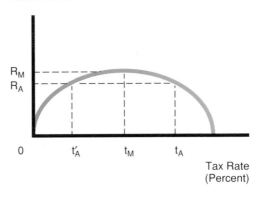

success and/or failure of these supply-side programs to stimulate economic growth.

All things considered, the lasting legacy of the supply-siders was to focus economists' attention on aggregate supply and economic growth. Hereafter, macroeconomic policymakers will be concerned with both aggregate supply and aggregate demand in formulating economic policy.

SUMMARY

1.   Economic growth occurs when the levels of actual and potential national income increase over the long run. Economic growth is a long-run phenomenon and should not be confused with quarter-to-quarter changes in the level of real national income, which may be due to short-run adjustments.

2.   Nothing affects the standard of living over the long term more than the rate of economic growth. Small differences in the percentage rate of growth will result in large differences in the size of the economy and of per capita income over the course of a few decades. The recent slow rates of economic growth for the U.S. economy are therefore of great concern.

3.   If inflation, deflation, and short-run fluctuations in real national income are to be avoided during the growth process, an accommodating increase in aggregate demand must also occur.

4.   Economic growth is of two types: extensive and intensive. Extensive growth occurs when the quantities of the factors of production increase. Intensive growth takes place when the output produced per unit of input increases and is created by technological change, economies of scale, and improvement in the efficiency with which resources are allocated.

5.   Capital makes a crucial contribution to economic growth. Not only does capital contribute to extensive growth, but (according to the learning-by-doing hypothesis and the embodiment hypothesis) capital also contributes to technological progress and intensive growth.

6.   Technological change is the most important determinant of the intensive growth. According to a study by Denison, changes in the rate of technological improvement are the most important reason the United States experienced a higher rate of economic growth between 1948 and 1973 than between 1929 and 1948. The rate of technological change is influenced by the expenditures for research and development, by investment overall, and by the state of macroeconomy.

7.   All economies face a trade-off between consumption and investment. If an economy wants to stimulate economic growth by increasing the share of GNP invested in capital goods, consumption must be sacrificed and savings increased. When this sacrifice is made, it will create lower consumption in earlier years but pay off with higher consumption in later years.

8.   Three sources of savings are available to finance investment — private savings, government savings, and foreign savings. The level of private savings by consumers and firms is especially sensitive to the structure of the tax system.

9.   Supply-side policies attempt to increase the rate of economic growth by changing the tax system to provide new incentives to save, invest, and work. Supply-siders argued that existing tax rates created a disincentive to save, invest, and work. Reducing marginal tax rates would have the effect of increasing the amounts of saving, investment, and work effort, and thus would stimulate economic growth. Critics of supply-side policies worried about large budget deficits, crowding out, and inflation caused by high aggregate demand.

THE MYSTERIOUS DECLINE IN ECONOMIC GROWTH AND PRODUCTIVITY

PREVIEW 18.1 ANALYSIS

Why did the rate of growth of the U.S. economy slow down after 1973? Economists have worked hard to answer this question, but despite their efforts, no single reason has been found. Instead, a number of plausible hypotheses have been offered. The reason for this uncertainty is that the source or sources of the decline are not to be found in the measurable elements of economic growth.

In this chapter, we introduced Denison's study, which attempts to measure various factors' contributions to economic growth. Denison's work also considered the period 1973–1981. Table 18.3 shows these results, along with those for the period 1948–1973, which we previously considered. The rate of economic growth between 1973 and 1981 was about half of the rate of growth between 1948 and 1973. The quantity of the factors of production available — extensive growth — had actually increased in the later period. This increase, however, was more than offset by a decline in intensive growth. Had intensive growth remained at the same rate between 1973 and 1981 as in the previous period, economic growth would have been higher by more than one-half of a percentage point.

Denison's study indicates that a decline in intensive growth is the cause of the decline in economic growth. Intensive growth, which provided nearly 2 percentage points of the growth rate during the period 1948–1973, actually contributed a negative 0.33 percentage points to the average annual growth rate between the years 1973 and 1981. Moreover, the factors contributing to intensive growth that Denison could directly

TABLE 18.3

Sources of Economic Growth in the United States, 1948–1973
Compared with 1973–1981

	GROWTH RATE FOR 1948–1973	GROWTH RATE FOR 1973–1981	DIFFERENCE IN GROWTH RATES
Real national income	3.59	1.80	−1.79
Growth in total factor inputs	1.60	2.13	0.53
Capital	0.57	0.46	−0.11
Labor	1.03	1.67	0.64
Employment	0.91	1.67	0.76
Hours of work	−0.24	−0.40	−0.16
Education	0.53	0.61	0.08
Age-sex composition	−0.17	−0.21	−0.04
Intensive growth	1.99	−0.33	−2.32
Reallocation of resources	0.37	0.04	−0.33
Economies of scale	0.42	0.30	−0.12
Past macroeconomic performance	−0.18	−0.22	−0.04
Government policy	−0.04	−0.21	−0.17
Miscellaneous	0.00	−0.02	0.02
Residual (Technological change?)	1.42	−0.26	−1.68

Source: Edward F. Denison, *Accounting for Slower Economic Growth* (Washington, D.C., 1979), Table 8-1; and "The Interruption of Productivity Growth in the United States," *Economic Journal* (March 1983), Table 2, p. 60.

measure accounted for only a small part of this decline. Almost all of the negative intensive growth remained unexplained in the residual term.

What could account for the unexplained residual that actually retarded the rate of economic growth? Many hypotheses exist — we consider five possible sources of the slowdown.

1. **The impact of government regulation and the poor performance of the macroeconomy.** Denison attempted to measure both of these and found that their contribution was small. Some economists argue, however, that both of these may have had indirect negative effects on other possible sources of growth, and so their contribution to the economy's slowdown exceeded Denison's estimates.

2. **The reduction in the rate of investment.** Investment provides the labor force with factories and equipment with which to work. The more capital a worker has available, the more productive he or she will be. Moreover, according to the embodiment hypothesis, new technology becomes available through the introduction of new capital investments. According to the learning-by-doing hypothesis, investment also provides the opportunity to find new ways of improving productivity.

    During the 1970s and thereafter, the rate of investment did not keep pace with the expanding labor force. As a result, workers on average had less, not more, capital with which to work. Although the magnitude of this decline is subject to question, most economists believe that the relative decline in investment is in part responsible for the decline in productivity. The decline in investment may have been caused by the rising inflation rate of the time, the periodic serious inflationary recessions, and the tax laws.

3. **The decline in research and development expenditures.** Research and development (R&D) expenditures as a percentage of gross national product declined between the 1960s and the 1970s. The number of scientists and engineers employed by industry dropped between the two decades. The decline in research and development may have been due in large part to the poor performance of the macroeconomy during the 1970s and early 1980s or to the increasing real cost of research and development. Because R&D is a major factor affecting technological change, lagging expenditures for research and development are frequently mentioned by economists seeking an explanation for the slowing of productivity growth.

4. **The extensive reallocation of resources.** The shift from farm to factory that had characterized earlier periods in American economic history was over and was replaced by a shift from heavy industry to high technological industries and from industry to services. Since the 1960s, a number of traditional industrial activities, such as iron and steel, have been declining industries. Reallocating resources from these heavy industries to expanding areas of the economy is difficult. The inability to disinvest and reinvest quickly may be an important source of the slowdown in growth. Moreover, the shift from manufacturing to services may necessarily result in declining productivity growth rates, because productivity growth in the service sector has historically been slower than in manufacturing. The increasing importance of the service sector in the economy may portend lower rates of future economic growth.

5. **The significant rise in the price of energy.** During the 1970s, the economy suffered severe supply shocks. The dramatic rise in energy prices required significant adjustments in the economy. Energy-efficient equipment was substituted for some capital goods that were

installed when energy prices were lower. Furthermore, the rise in fuel prices made it economical to substitute labor for energy-using capital, reducing labor productivity as a result. Productivity growth was also hurt by the suddenness of the energy price rises and the resulting supply shocks. Finally, every industrial nation suffered a slowdown in productivity growth during the 1970s, and the energy crisis and the significantly higher fuel costs seem to be the only elements in common among all of these countries.

The proximate causes of the slowdown in economic growth remain unknown. Probably some or all of the above factors have combined to produce a period of slow productivity growth. One economist has characterized the period as having an economy dying from a thousand cuts rather than one stab wound.

The relatively slow growth of the U.S. economy in recent years, however, is not without precedent. During the periods 1900–1916 and 1929–1948, the growth in labor productivity was about the same as our recent experience. Perhaps there is nothing unusual about a decade or so of slow growth. Decades of slow growth are often preceded by and, more importantly, succeeded by decades of faster productivity growth.

Even if the slowdown in economic growth is temporary, the policies of the federal government can aid the process of economic growth. Government policies that promote stability in the macroeconomy would go far in creating an environment that fosters economic growth. Tax policies that favor increased saving and investment could help. Government regulations, however, are not costless, and their potential impact on productivity should be taken into account along with their possible benefits.

REAGAN'S SUPPLY-SIDE POLICIES AND ECONOMIC GROWTH

PREVIEW 18.2 ANALYSIS

When Ronald Reagan became president in 1981, the inflation rate was higher than 10 percent and the rates of economic growth had been anemic for over a decade. Reagan had promised voters to solve both problems simultaneously by adopting supply-side policies, and voters were willing to give these policies a try.

As we saw in this chapter, supply-side policies attempt to stimulate economic growth. Economic growth would counter falling national income and a rising price level by causing the short- and long-run aggregate-supply curves to shift to the right.

Immediately upon taking office, Reagan took steps to introduce his program for economic recovery. As we saw in this chapter, the cornerstone of the supply-side programs was reform of the tax system. The Economic Recovery Tax Act was designed to reduce marginal tax rates, creating incentives for individuals and businesses to expand the nation's supplies of labor and capital. There were other important aspects of the supply-side program in addition to the tax cuts. Government expenditures were to be reduced to free resources for the private sector. The decline in expenditures would also balance the expansion in aggregate demand that the tax cuts would create and offset any deficit that might result, though none was expected by the supply-siders. Regulatory reform was to spur competition and productivity in the transportation, communications, and financial sectors. Environmental regulations were to be made more cost effective.

The Reagan administration and its supporters were optimistic about the possibilities of this program. Some supply-siders believed that the rate of growth of the economy could average 5 percent over the decade if this mix of policies were adopted. This expectation was fully 2 percentage points higher than the historical growth of the economy. Clearly, the supply-siders had promised much.

Did these policies deliver? Did the policies work as expected? The most optimistic predictions did not materialize, but some positive results did occur. For example, inflation did decline from double-digit levels to about 4 percent. This achievement, however, was probably due more to the Federal Reserve's monetary policy than to the supply-side policies.

On the negative side, real national income did not behave as initially expected, falling substantively as the economy entered a severe recession. The recession, however, developed before the tax cuts, which were scheduled to take effect between 1982 and 1984, were in place. The inflationary recession of 1981–1982 should not be attributed to the supply-side policies but to the anti-inflationary monetary policy that began in 1980. (The effects of this monetary policy were discussed in Chapter 17.)

In 1982, the year in which the first tax reductions occurred, the economy began a rapid recovery from the recession. There is some debate whether the stimulus provided by the tax reductions of 1982, 1983, and 1984 stimulated aggregate supply or aggregate demand. Real national income increased by 3.7 percent in 1983 and by 6.4 percent in 1984. The unemployment rate, which averaged 9.5 percent during 1982 and 1983, declined to an average of 7.4 percent during 1984. These results looked good to many supply-siders.

Moreover, the recovery proved long lasting. Real national income continued to grow thereafter, finally catching up with potential national income in 1988 when the economy experienced full employment. However, the rate of growth in real national income during this expansion was nothing spectacular. The growth in real national income was rapid in the first two years of recovery, but economic growth generally is rapid coming out of a recession. Thereafter, the annual rate of economic growth slowed to rates in the range of 2 percent. These rates were higher than the depressed rates of the 1970s, but much below the rates of economic growth enjoyed between 1948 and 1973, and certainly below the rates predicted by ardent supply-siders.

Furthermore, the expected increases in savings and investment did not occur. The private savings rate actually declined below the rates experienced during the 1970s. Moreover, the federal budget deficit increased to record levels, reducing still further the amount of savings available for investment. The national savings rate — which combines private-sector saving with the combined government surplus or deficit — fell drastically. The national savings rate, which had averaged 7 percent of gross national product during the 1970s, declined to an average of 2.6 percent between 1980 and 1985, and by 1986 averaged only 0.2 percent.

Only a massive inflow of foreign savings kept the investment rate of the economy from collapsing. The United States was converted from a creditor nation to a debtor nation as a result. Despite the inflow of foreign capital, net private investment fell by over 2 percentage points during the 1980s compared with the 1970s. During the Reagan years, total saving and investment as a percentage of gross national product declined in seeming defiance of all efforts to make them grow.

Why the disappointing results? First, not all of the recommended programs were enacted. Federal government expenditures were not reduced. Regulatory reform was only partially carried out. The timing of the programs was also different than expected, because macroeconomic conditions changed from the inflationary gap initially envisioned to a recessionary gap at the very time that the supply-side programs were being enacted.

The achievement was significantly less than the promises made, but the achievement was not insignificant. Inflation was no longer the nation's Number 1 macroeconomic problem—budget and trade deficits became Number 1. The recovery from the recession of 1981–1982, although slow, was extremely long lasting, and full employment became a reality for the first time in a decade.

There were other results. Economists and policymakers are now much more aware of the supply-side implications of economic policies than used to be the case. Second, supply-side policies are now widely recognized to require time to implement. Individuals and business firms require time to adjust fully to a new set of incentives. Supply-side policies do not provide a quick fix for inflation and slow economic growth, but they may contribute to economic growth over time as the long-lasting recovery seems to indicate.

REQUIRED ECONOMIC CONCEPTS

Economic growth
Extensive growth
Intensive growth
Economies of scale
Basic knowledge
Applied knowledge

Learning-by-doing hypothesis
Embodiment hypothesis
Supply-side policies
Tax base
Laffer curve

KEY QUESTIONS

1. What is the rule of 72?
2. What is the difference between extensive and intensive economic growth?
3. According to a famous study of U.S. economic growth by Edward F. Denison, what was the single biggest variable accounting for U.S. economic growth from 1929 to 1948 and from 1948 to 1973?
4. What is the learning-by-doing hypothesis?
5. What is the embodiment hypothesis?
6. What is the significance of the low U.S. savings rate?
7. What is the identity for macroeconomic equilibrium when the foreign sector is included? Use it to answer question 8.
8. The amount of funds available for investment depends on what three things? And how can investment be increased?
9. Give a brief definition of supply-side economics.
10. Why did supply-siders not worry about the criticism predicting that their policies would cause crowding out and not create significant economic growth?
11. What is the Laffer curve?
12. In Denison's study, why did the residual growth factor decline in the 1973–1981 period relative to the 1948–1973 period?
13. Where did supply-side economics succeed? Where did it fail to meet its goals?

PROBLEMS

1.   Approximately what would an economy's yearly growth rate have to be to double its national income in 30 years?

2.   Name the source of economic growth in each of the following.

    a.   "As the work force matures productivity rises."

    b.   "To stay competitive we must turn out more physicists, chemists, engineers, and molecular biologists, and spend more on R&D programs."

    c.   "As the size of the work force grows so will output."

    d.   "The greater the specialization of tasks the greater the output per worker."

    e.   "The newest computers to hit the market are already obsolete."

3.   The U.S. population is expected to grow more slowly over the next 20 years, hence growth in the size of domestic markets is also expected to slow down. What entry in Denison's Table 18.3 applies here?

4.   What does a nation's tax structure and savings rate have to do with economic growth?

5.   So-called primitive societies have created music and complex social structures as have industrialized societies such as the United States. Yet the former are static culturally and economically and the latter dynamic. What single factor above all others clearly distinguishes these societies? Can you relate it to Denison's Table 18.3? Is there a Table 18.3 for primitive societies?

6.   After the deaths of Elvis Presley and John Lennon, the news media rhapsodized about their influence on people's lives. Do you believe they have had more influence on your life than Thomas Edison's invention of the moving picture (also independently invented by an Englishman), the invention of the automobile, Fleming's discovery of penicillin, Enrico Fermi's construction of the first controlled nuclear chain reaction, medical scientists' development of the birth control pill, and Gutenberg's invention of the moving printing press? Do you think social change precedes or follows from technological change?

7.   An American proverb says, "It takes three generations to go from shirt-sleeves to shirt-sleeves." Beginning with the generation of the 1930s and assuming a generation spans about 30 years, do the contents of this chapter appear to confirm or contradict the proverb? Discuss.

APPLICATION ANALYSIS

1.   Consider the following example by Geoffrey Moore, an authority on business cycles. Suppose that in year 1 the population of Small Town is 100 and that 50 people are employed producing 500 widgets a year. Suppose in year 2 the town's 10 high-school graduates take jobs in the local widget factory for the first time, but the 10 new workers only produce 7 widgets each a year.

    a.   What is the town's per capita widget production in year 1? In year 2? The productivity per worker in years 1 and 2?

    b.   Has the town's productivity declined? Is this a bad thing? Why not? Would you predict that if employment were to stay at 60 in year 3, p e-worker productivity would remain the same or not? Why?

    c.   To what lines in Denison's Table 18.3 does this problem best apply?

2.   The well-known economist Mancur Olsen has asked (*The Wall Street Journal*, Dec. 22, 1988, based on an article in *The Public Opinion*, Nov./Dec. 1988), "Why do high incomes of the developed nations these days coexist with so many manifestations of discontent and despair? . . . When one looks across societies it is by no means obvious that people in the richer nations are more content with their lot than those in the poorer ones . . . higher levels of suicide rates . . . mental illness . . . do not show any tendency to diminish as incomes increase. . . . Even those who believe, as I do, that economic growth is on balance highly desirable should want to understand why it fails to bring about the reduction of discontent and social pathology that might be expected." Comment.

PART 6

THE INTERNATIONAL ECONOMY AND ECONOMIC GROWTH

19 INTERNATIONAL TRADE AND COMPARATIVE ADVANTAGE

IN THIS CHAPTER YOU WILL LEARN:

How the international role of the United States is changing

●

Why countries benefit from free trade

●

How terms of trade are set

●

Why some economists believe in protective trade measures

This chapter was written by Robert Carbaugh of Central Washington University.

CAN AMERICA COMPETE IN FOREIGN MARKETS?

In 1979 General Electric (GE) hired Ira Magaziner, an American business consultant, to help with a profit problem. Although GE's refrigerators were bringing in $1 billion each year in sales, these sales earned very little money for the company.

Magaziner was convinced the problem could be from a competitor and decided to investigate. In his research he learned that Matsushita of Japan was planning to build compressors, a major refrigerator part, and would be able to do this cheaper than GE. Later Magaziner also learned that Necchi of Italy could produce a compressor cheaper than Americans. After all, the Italians and Japanese had lower labor costs than the United States. If GE already had a profit dilemma, it now faced a problem of foreign parts competition as well.

One of the solutions Magaziner proposed was to build a new factory that could produce a new high-efficiency reciprocating compressor, because Americans excel in high-tech, high-efficiency production. This would be an expensive solution to the problem, but GE had another choice. It could buy compressors for its refrigerators from another country. This practice is known as sourcing. American businesses often agree to purchase parts (or labor) abroad because it is cheaper to do so. How did GE eventually solve the problem?

JAPAN LIMITS AUTO EXPORTS: GOOD DEAL FOR AMERICA?

American auto producers have historically been prosperous, earning profits exceeding the national average for all U.S. manufacturers. By the early 1980s, however, American auto firms faced sharp declines in output, sales, and earnings. Increased penetration of the U.S. market by foreign producers, notably the Japanese, paralleled the declining sales of U.S. producers.

Faced with the possibility of mandatory restrictions (e.g., tariffs, quotas) being placed on Japanese auto shipments to the United States, in 1981 the Japanese government voluntarily initiated a program to restrict auto shipments to the United States. In 1981 the export restriction program held Japanese shipments to the United States equal to 1.68 million vehicles; in subsequent years the restrictions were liberalized as market conditions improved in the United States.

The stated objective of the export restrictions was to allow American auto firms temporary relief from foreign competition, so that they could become more competitive in the small-car segment of the market where the Japanese were competitive.

What impact did the Japanese export restriction program have on the American economy?

• I N T R O D U C T I O N •

No nation exists in economic isolation. In fact over the past several decades, nations of the world have become increasingly economically interdependent through intensified international trade. This is true in part because of improvements in the transportation industry. Goods are shipped from one country to another far more easily than ever before. Better communications have also furthered global trade.

In this chapter the role of the United States in a world of changing international dynamics is examined. The arguments for free trade are also presented, with discussion of the benefits countries receive from trade. Terms of trade and pricing in international markets are explored. Finally, the experiences of the United States over the past two decades have caused many economists to sharpen their arguments against free trade. New reasons are given for protecting U.S. industries, products, and ideas. •

THE UNITED STATES AND INTERNATIONAL TRADE

After World War II, the large size of the U.S. economy relative to the world economy resulted in observers pointing out that "when the United States sneezed, other nations caught a cold." This saying stems from the fact that for several decades after World War II, the United States led the world as its richest nation. Yet in the past ten years, due to increased global interdependence and competition, the United States has been rivaling such nations as Japan and West Germany to keep its position.

The increasing dependence of U.S. trade on foreign nations can be seen by looking at trade data over recent years. In 1970, U.S. imports and exports were about the same. Exports amounted to $42.7 billion, while U.S. imports were $40.0 billion. These numbers changed dramatically by 1987 when U.S. imports of merchandise amounted to $406.2 billion, whereas the United States exported $254.1 billion of goods that year.

Two facts are notable from these data. First, the volume of imports and exports grew substantially over this time. Second, the disparity between exports and imports has grown. In 1970 exports were slightly greater, leading to a **net trade surplus.**

A net trade surplus occurs when a country exports more than it imports.

These data changed significantly by 1987, when the imports outstripped exports by about $150 billion, leading to a **net trade deficit.**

A net trade deficit exists when a nation's imports exceed its exports.

The significance of international trade for the American economy is also apparent when the global interdependence of America's companies is considered. For example, Exxon Corporation received 68 percent of its revenues from abroad during 1985, whereas a corresponding figure for

FIGURE 19.1
Global Manufacturing: The Component Network for the Ford Escort (Europe)

Manufacturing is not necessarily a single-country pursuit. As seen in this diagram, different countries specialized in making a part of the Ford Escort automobile in 1986. Denmark provided the fan belt, Canada the glass and radio, France the cylinder heads and brakes, and Japan the starters and alternators. Manufacture of this automobile reflects a growing global economic interdependence.

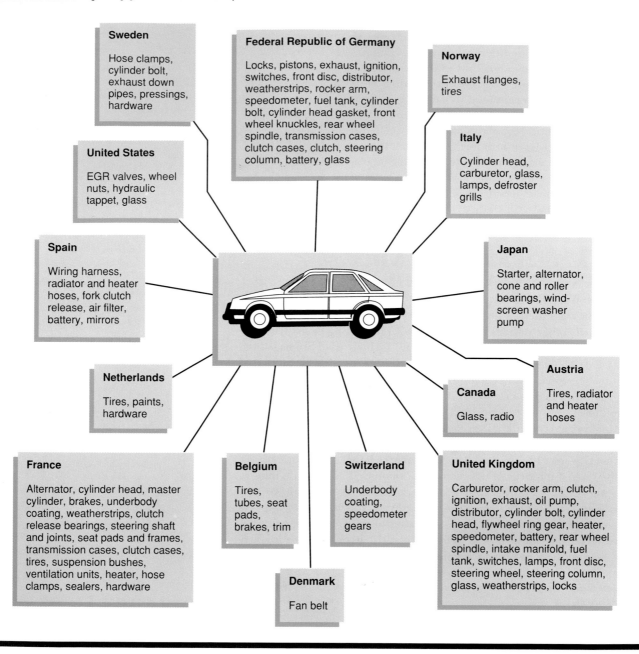

Source: Peter Kicken, *Global Shift: Industrial Change in a Turbulent World* (London: Harper & Row, 1986), 304.

IBM was 43 percent. A.C. Nielsen Company, a marketing research firm, has offices in 27 nations. In recent years, one out of every two aircraft produced by Boeing Company has been sold to a foreign customer. Most large U.S. companies do business abroad.

The Ford Escort automobile is a further example of American global interdependence. As demonstrated in Figure 19.1, this vehicle could be called "The All World Car." Its tires, tubes, seat pads, and brakes were

TABLE 19.1
Leading Trading Partners of the United States, 1986

COUNTRY	VALUE OF U.S. IMPORTS	VALUE OF U.S. EXPORTS
All countries, total	$387.1 billion	$217.3 billion
Canada	68.7	45.3
Japan	85.5	26.9
West Germany	26.1	10.6
United Kingdom	16.0	11.4
Mexico	17.6	12.4
France	10.6	7.2
Netherlands	8.0	6.3
South Korea	13.5	6.4
Hong Kong	9.5	3.0
Singapore	4.9	3.4

Source: International Monetary Fund, *Directory of Trade Statistics.*

manufactured in Belgium. Switzerland provided its underbody coating and speedometer gears. Other parts were provided by France, Austria, and Japan. The automobile is finally assembled in the United Kingdom and the Federal Republic of Germany by an American-owned company.

What has been happening to cause trade patterns to change so significantly over the past two decades? One reason is that Americans have gone abroad seeking new markets and new opportunities to do business. Among the major exports of the United States are motor vehicles and parts, computers, power-generation equipment, and agricultural commodities.

Another cause of shifting trade patterns is that Americans have lost the competitive edge in certain industries, such as the automobile parts business, the manufacture of shoes and clothing, and the computer assembly business. Labor in these industries is cheaper abroad. As an importer, the United States purchases large amounts of petroleum, automobiles, clothing, iron and steel, and office machines.

To further complicate the U.S. trade problem, the European Economic Community (EEC) was formed during the 1950s and 1960s, and the Organization of Petroleum Exporting Countries (OPEC) gained power during the 1970s. These trade blocs, from which the United States was excluded, offered cost and trade advantages to one another.

Who are the major trading partners of the United States? As Table 19.1 illustrates, Canada and Japan are at the top of the list. As of 1986, about 19 percent of total U.S. international trade (exports plus imports) occurred with Canada. Throughout the 1980s, the Newly Industrializing Countries (NICs) — including South Korea, Hong Kong, Singapore, and Taiwan — have emerged as important trading partners of the United States. The United States also has heavy trade balances with Mexico, the United Kingdom, West Germany, and France.

In comparing the amount of foreign trade in relation to total national product, however, the United States does not import nearly as much as some other industrial countries (see Table 19.2). The Netherlands, for instance, imports 64 percent of its GNP, the United Kingdom imports 26 percent, and the United States imports merely 7 percent. So although international trade is playing an increasingly important role, U.S. dependence on foreign imports is far less than in other industrialized nations.

TABLE 19.2
International Trade for Selected Countries, 1987

COUNTRY	IMPORTS AS A PERCENTAGE OF GNP
Netherlands	64%
Norway	48
West Germany	33
Canada	28
United Kingdom	26
Australia	17
Japan	12
United States	7

Source: U.S. Department of Commerce.

WHY DO NATIONS TRADE?

The previous section emphasized the growing importance of international trade in the United States. But why do nations trade? What constitutes the basis for international exchange? Stated generally, a country trades with other countries when it can improve its living standards by so doing. A country's benefits from trade can be likened to the individual who lives by specializing in producing one good and trading that good for other consumption items in the marketplace. There are gains to be gotten from specialization. An individual has no need to produce those things for which he or she has no talent or resources but can purchase with revenues from specialization. Similarly countries specialize in what they do well and trade with other countries to round out consumption needs.

Specialization implies advantages. If a country can produce something better, faster, and cheaper than other countries, it can afford to give up production of other commodities and trade. In general countries specialize in producing those commodities for which they are the **low opportunity cost** producer.

> *A country has a low opportunity cost for producing a given good or service when it gives up less of other goods and services than other countries by specializing in the production of that good or service.*

When a country is the low opportunity cost producer, it has a **comparative advantage.**

> *Having a comparative advantage means that a country can produce a given good or service more advantageously (with lower opportunity cost) as compared with other countries.*

A country gains by specializing in the production of goods for which it is the low opportunity cost producer and trading for those goods that cost relatively more for it to produce. Reflecting different resource bases, countries with warm and moist climates (e.g., Brazil) specialize in the production of coffee. With a highly skilled labor force, Japan uses its comparative advantage to produce and export electronic goods and automobiles. Canada, with abundant land, specializes in feed grains and wheat.

To demonstrate the economic gains achievable from international trade, let us examine the production possibility schedules of two commodities for two nations. We wish to show that two countries that produce and

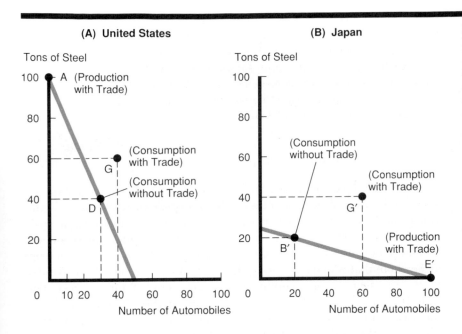

(A) United States

Tons of Steel

(B) Japan

Tons of Steel

FIGURE 19.2
Production Possibilities Schedules of the
United States and Japan for Steel and Autos

In this diagram, production possibilities for two commodities, steel and autos, are presented for the United States and Japan. The United States clearly produces steel more efficiently than Japan, but Japan has the comparative advantage in autos. It pays these countries to specialize and trade. Without trade, each nation is limited to consuming somewhere along its production possibilities frontier. Yet with trade, consumption possibilities move beyond each country's production frontier. Japan and the United States can consume at points G and G'.

trade according to principles of comparative advantage can together produce and consume more output than they can in the absence of trade. In essence trade increases world output and leaves the two countries that trade with one another with higher living standards.

Suppose that the world economy consists of just two countries, say the United States and Japan. Assume that each country is capable of producing both steel and automobiles, but at different levels of economic efficiency. Figure 19.2 shows the production possibilities schedules for the United States and Japan for autos and steel. By using all of its resources, Japan could produce 25 tons of steel, or 100 autos, or some other combination along its production possibilities curve. In similar fashion, the United States can produce 100 tons of steel, or 50 autos, or some other combination along its curve. Japan is the higher efficiency producer of autos, and the United States is the higher efficiency producer of steel.

In the absence of international trade, a country's production possibilities schedule also defines its consumption possibilities, because a nation can only consume what it produces. Assume for the sake of argument that the United States chooses to produce at point D along its production possibilities curve, and that Japan chooses to produce at point B' on its production possibilities schedule. With these levels of production for each of these two countries, total world production of steel and autos would be 60 tons of steel and 50 automobiles.

The principle of comparative advantage allows each country operating along its present production possibilities curve to choose a different combination of goods and thereby increase world consumption beyond the point shown above of 60 tons of steel and 50 autos.

According to the principle of comparative advantage, Japan will completely specialize in auto production and locate at production point E' along its production possibilities schedule, producing 100 autos and zero tons of steel. Conversely, comparative advantage suggests that the United States completely specialize in steel production and locate at point A along its production possibilities schedule, producing 100 tons of steel and zero autos. The combined (world) output of the two countries now totals 100 tons of steel (vs. 60 tons before trade) and 100 autos (vs. 50 autos before trade). This is clearly a superior world output and consumption possibilities position. Clearly we have seen the potential for making Japan and the United States better off than they were in the absence of trade.

Are the United States and Japan also respectively better off? The answer is yes, but only if each country allows its trading partners to participate in its advantage of being the lowest cost producer. To do this, countries negotiate **terms of trade.**

A country sets its terms of trade when it decides the rate at which it will exchange one good for another.

As Figure 19.2 illustrates, the opportunity cost of an auto in Japan is one-fourth ton of steel. Japan thus will not export autos unless it obtains at least one-fourth ton of steel in exchange for an auto, and it will bargain for more. This sets the lower limit to the terms of trade. American consumers, however, will be unwilling to import autos from Japan at a price higher than that which must be paid to domestic producers. In the United States, the domestic opportunity cost of each auto is 2 tons of steel. This ratio (price) stipulates the upper limit to the equilibrium terms of trade. Americans will negotiate to pay less than 2 tons of steel for an auto. Therefore, the equilibrium terms of trade must be between the two countries' opportunity costs of production.

Given these limits suppose that the Americans and Japanese agree that 1 auto should be exchanged for 1 ton of steel (Japanese get more than one-fourth ton of steel for each car, Americans pay less than 2 tons of steel for each auto). In Figure 19.2 suppose that Japan decides to export 40 autos to the United States. Starting at production point E′, say Japan trades 40 autos for 40 tons of steel and achieves a level of consumption indicated by point G′. This consumption point is not on the Japanese production possibilities curve. Specialization and trade allow Japan to consume outside of its production curve. It gains an overall increase at point G′ of 20 tons of steel and 40 autos.

Suppose the United States operates at production point A along its production possibilities schedule and desires to sell 40 tons of steel to Japan. Given terms of trade equal to one for one, 40 tons of steel exchange for 40 autos. The United States has thus achieved a consumption level indicated by point G in Figure 19.2. Compared with its consumption level in the absence of trade, consumers gain 10 autos and 20 tons of steel. These are the consumption gains from trade for the United States.

In the above example, both countries can escape the limitations of their own production possibilities schedules and attain a consumption level that exceeds the domestic production possibilities. Remember from Chapter 2 that if a country is to go beyond its production possibilities schedule it must either enjoy technological gains and higher productivity or realize a larger or improved resource base. The above example demonstrates that international trade is a third method of going beyond the output limitations of a country's production possibilities curve. International trade and specialization can be likened to a country enjoying improved technology or an expanding resource base.

DEMAND AND SUPPLY: PRICING IN INTERNATIONAL TRADE

International trade influences output and price levels in domestic markets through demand and supply. Figure 19.3 illustrates the relationship between the U.S. and world markets for wheat. In the absence of trade, the

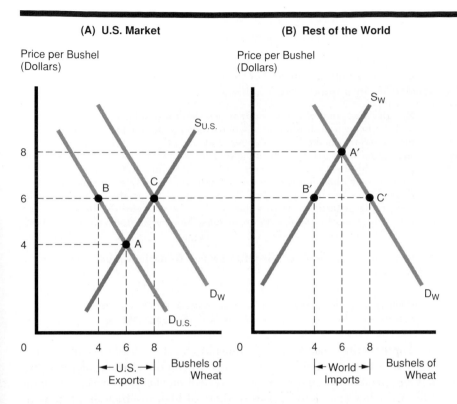

(A) U.S. Market

Price per Bushel
(Dollars)

(B) Rest of the World

Price per Bushel
(Dollars)

FIGURE 19.3
Supply and Demand:
Pricing in International Trade

This diagram shows supply and demand for wheat in the United States and for the rest of the world. The equilibrium price of $4 per bushel in the United States reflects a lower cost advantage in the United States. U.S. producers can benefit from higher world prices by selling in world markets. World customers can benefit by buying in U.S. markets. The interaction of these two forces will work toward an international price level where the surplus supply in the United States just equals the shortage in the rest of the world. In this case that price is $6.

domestic price of wheat in the United States is determined where the domestic supply curve meets the domestic demand curve at point A in Part A. The domestic price is $4 per bushel and the quantity exchanged is 6 bushels. Similarly world demand and world supply determine the world price and quantity of wheat at $8 per bushel with 6 bushels produced. In the figure the United States enjoys a cost advantage relative to the rest of the world equal to $4 per bushel; it can sell wheat at $4 per bushel less.

Because the world price is higher than the U.S. price, U.S. producers will move up along their supply curve toward greater production of wheat and greater specialization as they enter world markets. When the United States produces more wheat, two things happen: it costs more to produce per bushel because of the increasing opportunity costs implicit in the supply curve, and as the country seeks to capture the higher price level, it loses domestic customers. Yet as long as the United States can sell wheat for less than other countries, it will make up its lost revenues by replacing domestic customers with world customers. As this happens, world prices drop and world producers lower their quantity of wheat supplied.

Domestic prices stop rising and world prices stop dropping when the U.S. supply curve intersects with the world demand curve at point C in Part A at the price of $6 per bushel. At this point there is a surplus of wheat in the United States of 4 bushels, shown by the distance from B to C. Interestingly there is also a world shortage of wheat at this price, shown in Part B by the distance from B′ to C′. This is the point where the case for specialization stops for the United States. Six dollars becomes the equilibrium world price because at this price, the surplus in the United States just equals the world's shortage.

The above example illustrates that at the point of free trade, domestic and world prices become the same, and the surplus this price generates in one country just offsets the world shortage generated by this price.

THE THEORY OF FREE TRADE AND PROTECTION

In 1776, Adam Smith, an English economist, wrote a treatise on unbridled trade between nations called *The Wealth of Nations*. His arguments are summed up in a quote from his book.

> It is the maximum of every prudent master of a family, never to attempt to make at home what it will cost him more to make than to buy. The taylor does not attempt to make his own shoes, but buys them of the shoemaker. The shoemaker does not attempt to make neither the one nor the other, but employees those different artificers. All of them find it for their interest to employ their whole industry in a way in which they have some advantage over their neighbors, and to purchase with a part of its produce, or what is the same thing, with the price of a part of it, what ever else they have occasion for. (Adam Smith, *The Wealth of Nations*, New York: Modern Library, Inc., 1937, 424.)

In modern terminology, benefits accrue to nations when they engage in **free trade.**

> *Free trade between nations occurs when there are no barriers to the free flow of goods and services between them.*

The benefits of unrestricted international free trade occur because they result in lower domestic prices and an expanded range of consumption and production choices. In a free world market, resources are channeled from low productivity uses to those of high productivity. Competition from imports helps hold down prices of domestic substitutes while encouraging efficiency among domestic producers.

Although the free-trade argument tends to dominate the thinking of economics professors and scholars, virtually all nations impose some barriers on the flow of goods and services into and out of their countries. Most nations justify this policy by saying that free trade is fine in theory, but it does not apply in the real world. They argue instead for **protectionism.**

> *Protectionism is a policy of governments that restricts imports that in one way or another could harm a domestic industry.*

Countries use various means of protecting trade, among them are **import tariffs.**

> *Import tariffs are taxes imposed on goods and services brought in from another country.*

Table 19.3 provides examples of tariffs levied by the U.S. government. For example, imported wooden tool handles are taxed at 5.2 cents per pound, while a duty of 3.7 percent of import price is applied to imported steel rails. Although a major purpose of an import tariff is to make home producers more competitive with foreign producers, tariffs also provide the home government with tax dollars. The dominant motive behind the early tariff laws of the United States was to provide the U.S. government with an important source of tax revenue. In the 1980s some politicians advocated raising import tariffs as a way of helping reduce the U.S. government's budget deficits.

A second device countries use to protect domestic trade is **quotas.**

> *Quotas are used by countries to restrict the amounts of goods and services imported from another country.*

TABLE 19.3
Selected Tariffs and Import Quotas of the United States

PRODUCT	RATE OF DUTY (TARIFF)
Wooden tool handles	5.2¢ per pound
Knit fabrics (wool)	6¢ per pound
Tungsten ore	17¢ per pound
Steel rails	3.7% of import price
Sleeping bags	12.5% of import price

PRODUCT	ANNUAL IMPORT QUOTA
Milk and cream (New Zealand)	1,500,000 gallons
Cotton (Mexico)	8,883,259 pounds
Swiss cheese (Canada)	154,322 pounds

Source: U.S. International Trade Commission, 1986, *Tariff Schedules of the United States.*

Quotas act as a barrier to free trade by restricting the amount of trade between countries. In Table 19.3 we see that the U.S. government allows 154,322 pounds of Swiss cheese to be imported per year from Canada. Another example of a quota occurs when the domestic government places limits on the number of goods exported to other nations. During the 1980s the Japanese government placed restrictions on the number of Japanese autos that could be shipped to the United States to diffuse sentiments in the United States in favor of placing restrictions on Japanese autos. These are known as voluntary restrictions.

The theoretic impact of tariffs is shown in Figure 19.4. In this case the economic effects of a protective tariff for VCRs are being demonstrated. The supply and demand curves presented are domestic U.S. curves for VCRs. In the absence of trade, market equilibrium exists at point A, where the market price is $500 per unit and the market quantity is 3 VCRs. Suppose that the U.S. market becomes open to international trade and that South Korea (representing the rest of the world in this example) has the comparative advantage in the production of VCRs. Assume the free-trade price of VCRs is $300 per unit. At this price, American consumers will want 5 VCRs (see point B on the demand curve), but only one of those VCRs will be produced by American manufacturers (see point C on the domestic supply curve). Imports from South Korea, totaling 4 VCRs, constitute the difference.

To partially protect its VCR industry from foreign competition, suppose the U.S. government places a tariff of $100 on each imported VCR. This policy raises the price of imported VCRs from $300 to $400 and has several important consequences. First, with the higher prices Americans can afford to buy fewer VCRs (see point E on the demand curve). Consumers clearly have been hurt by the tariff. Second, the higher price provides American producers the incentive to expand production to 2 VCRs (see point D on the supply curve). From a political perspective, American producers see the benefits of tariff protection and thus pressure members of Congress for its enactment. Finally, South Korean manufacturers are hurt because they can sell only 2 VCRs to American consumers rather than the 4 VCRs that occurred under free trade. Although the price of VCRs to U.S. consumers has risen from $300 to $400 per unit under the tariff, South Korean manufacturers still realize a price of only $300. The other $100 is the tariff revenue collected by the U.S. government on each imported recorder. The total amount of tariff revenue cap-

FIGURE 19.4
Economic Effects of Import Tariffs and Quotas

Import tariffs make the domestic price of goods higher than they are on world markets. Consumers pay more while government gets the revenue. In this diagram the South Korean price of manufacturing VCRs is $300 per unit, and a $100 import tariff is placed on the good to protect domestic producers. Sales end up at point E. Korean merchants get $300 per unit, and the government gets $100 per unit. Quotas work in much the same way. By restricting imports, domestic prices are bid up above the world equilibrium prices.

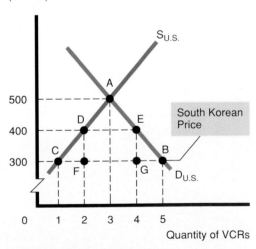

TABLE 19.4
Annual Cost of Tariffs to U.S. Consumers, 1980

PRODUCT	COST TO CONSUMERS (MILLIONS)
Aluminum	$ 286
Chemicals	829
Copper	1,589
Footwear	1,037
Furniture	926
Iron and steel	4,047
Electrical machinery	5,646
Sugar	1,742
Wearing apparel	11,795
Wood products	710

Source: Michael Munger, "The Costs of Protectionism," *Challenge* (January–February 1984): 55.

tured by the U.S. government equals $200 (2 VCRs × $100), which is indicated by the area DFGE in the figure.

These are the primary reasons free traders argue against protective tariffs. That is, although government and industry benefit from tariffs, consumers do not. Just how much do tariffs cost the American consumer? A number of researchers have attempted to answer this question. Table 19.4 provides estimates of these costs.

Quotas have a similar impact on the economy. Again referring to Figure 19.4 assume that the United States levies an import quota of no more than 2 VCRs on South Korean shipments to the United States. The free-trade equilibrium (point B on the demand curve) that would be achieved by this price is no longer feasible. That is, American producers are only willing to produce 1 VCR at a world price of $300, and domestic quantity supplied drops to 3 VCRs (2 imported, 1 domestically manufactured), while American consumers wish to purchase 5 VCRs at this price. The quota creates a shortage at the free-trade price, which forces the domestic price up to $400. Quotas tend to hurt the consumer by keeping the domestic price above the world price.

In 1981 the U.S. auto industry requested an import quota from the Carter administration that would have allowed a maximum of 1.7 million foreign autos to be imported into the United States each year. This request was denied. Estimates by the Federal Trade Commission suggested that this quota would have boosted American auto prices by an average of $527 per vehicle, resulting in an increase in consumer expenditures of $2.85 billion. Domestic auto sales would rise by 260,000 units and some 21,700 American jobs would be saved. But the cost to the U.S. consumer per job saved would have amounted to over $126,000.[1]

ARGUMENTS FOR AND AGAINST PROTECTION

The theoretical arguments are clear. Countries that have a comparative advantage gain from specialization and trade. This increases world production and consumption possibilities, and when governments intervene

---

[1]Michael Lynch, et al., *Certain Motor Vehicles and Certain Chassis and Bodies Therefore*, Federal Trade Commission, 1980.

with such trade barriers as tariffs and quotas, consumers suffer. Why then are there any arguments against free trade?

Countries that argue for protectionism and against free trade do so for many different reasons. The first is national defense. This argument asserts that certain industries (e.g., steel, petroleum, aircraft) are vital to the domestic security. Would the United States want to be entirely dependent on oil imported from the Persian Gulf? During the 1950s, the U.S. oil industry was effective in using the national security argument to persuade the president to place restrictions on oil imports. Repeatedly, the U.S. steel industry has lobbied for protectionism on the grounds that a stable supply of domestic steel is essential for production of military equipment. The American shoe industry has even tried to convince the government that growing reliance on imported footwear is jeopardizing the national security of the United States. A headline in a shoe industry press release cautioned "Military Might Go Barefoot in Case of War."

How valid is the national defense argument? Free traders would say that this position might have merit, but only if there is a threat of war. That is, unless imports of essential commodities such as oil and steel are threatened, perhaps there is no reason to attempt to limit them or produce them domestically.

A second argument against free trade stems from practices of **dumping** and from government **subsidies.**

> *Dumping is a practice whereby a nation sells large quantities of its goods in foreign markets at prices below cost or below domestic price.*

> *Subsidies are amounts of money pumped into an industry by government to help the industry.*

Domestic U.S. steel and semiconductor companies have argued that foreign manufacturers dump their products in the United States at prices below those existing in their own country, perhaps even below costs of production. They reason that if foreign industries engage in this type of practice, protectionism is warranted because technically trade is no longer at market prices and is no longer "free trade."

Free traders counter this argument by saying that selling below cost is not a reasonable market strategy. They believe no industry that needs to follow this practice can exist for long. They therefore state that the concern for dumping could be unwarranted. Further they believe that this argument could be used to disguise the fact that foreigners indeed often can produce products below U.S. costs. In this case free traders say that we need to be competitive with foreign costs and prices.

Protectionists also argue that subsidies granted by foreign governments allow producers to enjoy unfair cost advantages. For example, MITI (Ministry of International Trade and Industry), a government organization in Japan, invests heavily in various industries to build the domestic economy. In this case protectionists argue that trade barriers are needed to promote "a level playing field" based on fair competition. Alternately the U.S. government heavily subsidizes its agricultural industry, which foreign countries could call unfair.

A third argument protectionists commonly use to justify their position is the **infant industry** argument.

> *An infant industry is a new industry that has high start-up costs and limited profits due to the need for reinvestment in the early stages.*

TABLE 19.5
Hourly Compensation in U.S. Dollars per Hour Worked for Production
Workers in Manufacturing, 1988

COUNTRY	HOURLY COMPENSATION (DOLLARS PER HOUR)
West Germany	$18.07
Switzerland	17.94
United States	13.90
Japan	13.14
United Kingdom	10.56
Taiwan	2.71
South Korea	2.46
Hong Kong	2.43
Mexico	1.57

Source: U.S. Department of Labor, Bureau of Labor Statistics, "Hourly Compensation
Costs for Production Workers: All Manufacturing," 1988.

Some argue that new industries need temporary protection from the
rigors of foreign competition so they can develop to the point where they
can prosper in the world marketplace. As the new industry develops,
protectionism will gradually be dismantled. Almost a century ago, the
American steel industry successfully used the infant industry argument to
gain tariff protectionism.

Free traders argue that this might not be a viable argument against
free trade simply because infant industries often find it difficult to remove
the protection as time passes. For example, today the U.S. steel industry
is a very mature industry, yet government officials have failed to remove
trade restrictions.

Throughout the 1980s American labor unions presented a fourth argument for protectionism by saying that it is needed to defend American
jobs against cheap foreign labor. As indicated in Table 19.5, production
workers in the United States have been paid much higher wages, in terms
of the dollar, than workers in countries such as Mexico. Low foreign labor
costs have been an apparent factor that has encouraged major U.S. corporations to locate production in Mexico and other low-wage countries.
Some have argued that unless U.S. producers are protected from imports
embodying cheap foreign labor, domestic production and employment
will decrease.

The issue of jobs has become a dominant factor behind trade restriction. Union officials are quick to refer to the statistics in the left-hand side
of Table 19.6, which indicate the number of American jobs lost to import
competition during 1975–1976.

Free traders say that the protectionist view on jobs is shortsighted.
They say protectionists should see the broader view of international
trade. That is, they maintain that rather than promoting overall unemployment, imports tend to lead to jobs in other sectors of the economy.
For example, when the United States imports, say, computers, from
South Korea, Koreans gain purchasing power that eventually will be
spent on, say, Boeing aircraft. On the right-hand side of Table 19.6 the
increase in American jobs due to U.S. exports in 1975–1976 is presented.
These data show that estimated jobs gained from exports are in fact
greater than jobs lost due to imports.

TABLE 19.6
Estimated Effects of Imports and Exports on U.S. Labor Markets, 1975–1976

INDUSTRY	JOBS LOST TO IMPORTS	INDUSTRY	JOBS GAINED FROM EXPORTS
Radio and TV equipment	14,300	Transportation equipment	44,000
Automobiles	67,000	Nonelectrical machinery	58,100
Steel	17,000	Chemicals	6,800
Iron and steel foundries	6,900	Agricultural	235,900
Clothing	39,700	Scientific equipment	4,300
Footwear	19,700	Textiles	20,400
Mining	85,500		
Total	250,100	Total	369,500

Source: Clifton B. Luttrell, "Imports and Jobs: The Observed and the Unobserved," *Review*, Federal Reserve Bank of St. Louis (June 1978): 4, 8.

INTERNATIONAL EVENTS

Three major international movements are under way that are likely to have a profound impact on the future of international trade. One of these events is the General Agreement on Tariffs and Trade (GATT) talks to be held in Uruguay in 1990. A second item of interest is the implementation of the Omnibus Trade Act passed by the U.S. Congress in 1988. This act was designed to cause the United States to retain its international competitive economic status. Finally the Common Market nations of Europe are moving toward becoming a wholly unified trade bloc in 1992.

GATT

Throughout much of its history, the United States has been a high-tariff nation. Import tariffs reached their high point with the passage of the Hawley-Smoot Tariff Act of 1930, during the Great Depression. At this time the United States raised its tariffs to an average of 53 percent of import price! This led to other countries increasing their trade barriers applied to U.S. exports.

By 1934 the economic damages of an international trade war had become apparent and the United States passed the Reciprocal Trade Agreements Act, which gave the president the authority to negotiate tariff reductions on a bilateral (two-nation) basis.

In 1947 the United States and 22 other countries signed the **General Agreement on Tariffs and Trade (GATT).**

> *The GATT was designed for member nations to meet regularly to negotiate trade arrangements between countries.*

Today some 100 countries periodically meet under the GATT agreement. The purposes of this group are to work toward equal treatment for all participating countries, trade agreements that apply to many (versus two) nations, and the elimination of import quotas.

The two most recent rounds of GATT negotiations — the Kennedy Round of the 1960s and the Tokyo Round of the 1970s — each reduced tariffs nearly one-third. By 1987, import tariffs of industrial countries averaged less than 5 percent for manufactured goods. In addition, the Tokyo Round addressed the rising importance of nontariff trade barriers, including subsidies and dumping. In 1990 these countries will meet in Uruguay for a new round of negotiations. One of the major negotiating items in Uruguay will be the reduction of subsidies to agricultural exports by governments.

THE OMNIBUS TRADE ACT

In 1988 Congress passed the **Omnibus Trade Act** to address the problem of the net trade deficit described earlier in this chapter. This act gives the United States broader powers than the GATT talks, an action deemed necessary because most global trade is not covered by GATT.

> *The Omnibus Trade Act is designed to strengthen the negotiating power of the U.S. trade representative, to address unfair trade practices by other countries, to provide import relief to affected industries and workers, and to provide money for improved education in the United States.*

According to this act, the U.S. trade representative is authorized to initiate investigations of unfair trade practices and to seek agreement with other countries to reduce those practices. The bill provides the U.S. trade representative with potential powers of trade retaliation should unfair trade practices continue indefinitely.

Two unfair trade practices addressed by the bill are dumping and the piracy of intellectual property. This bill would prevent countries from getting around antidumping duties by shipping through third nations. It also contains a provision that requires the U.S. trade representative to initiate legal action against companies that infringe on U.S. intellectual copyrights. Currently, many foreign companies attempt to export goods such as videos and computer software to the United States that copy patents obtained by U.S. companies. The new law is designed to stop this practice.

The trade act also gives companies the right to petition for and to obtain assistance for import relief. It also provides retraining funding for workers adversely affected by foreign competition.

Finally, the trade act calls for funding for improved bilingual education, secondary education, and science and math education.

The bill is not designed to replace GATT. This organization will still have its traditional negotiating powers. GATT, the U.S. trade representative, and the Congress are expected to work together to achieve U.S. trade goals.

THE EUROPEAN
ECONOMIC COMMUNITY

The European Common Market was begun in 1958. Today this organization boasts membership of 13 nations and is known as the **European Economic Community (EEC).**

> *The European Economic Community was organized to help member nations remove trade barriers and to provide for an easier flow of goods and services throughout Europe.*

The EEC has engaged in massive deregulation between member nations, which has strengthened its status as a world trade entity. The EEC now has far more economic and political power to use in its negotiations with other major trading powers, such as the United States, the Soviet

Union, and Japan. Future goals of this organization include providing for a free flow of goods, workers, and services between countries, with no trade barriers, and achieving a unified currency and a unified tax system by 1992.

One of the major impacts of this deregulation is the fact that the United States, Japan, and other countries are excluded from the favored status European nations give one another, which puts these countries in a disadvantaged position. As a result foreign direct investment in Europe has increased. Foreigners do not want to be left out of growing markets and increased business opportunity.

Another impact of the EEC is to give European companies incentives to merge and become larger. With regulatory restrictions removed, companies can do business on a larger scale. Some economists fear that in 1992 Europeans will produce industrial giants excluding foreign nations from significant competition on this continent. This would amount to EEC protectionism. Executives of Europe's giant companies, however, are divided on the issue. Although some want to eliminate foreign competition, many see open markets and free trade with the rest of the world as a key to Europe's growth.

SUMMARY

1. We live in a shrinking world with no nation living in economic isolation. Nations have become increasingly interdependent on international trade and finance.

2. Compared with many other nations' imports, U.S. imports capture a relatively low portion of the U.S. gross national product. However, for selected industries — autos, steel, semiconductors, radios and TVs — foreign competitors have made significant inroads in the American market.

3. The principle of comparative advantage suggests that each country should specialize in the production of goods for which it is the low opportunity cost producer. Such specialization allows nations to consume more goods than could be achieved in the absence of trade.

4. In a two-country world, at the point of free-trade equilibrium: (1) the price of the traded commodity will be the same in both countries; (2) the quantity of the product exported by one country will equal the quantity of the product imported by the other.

5. According to the free-trade argument, open markets and competition yield gains in the form of lower domestic prices, expanded range of consumption choices, and the development of more efficient production methods.

6. An import tariff is a tax that applies to a product that is imported into the nation. By forcing up the price of foreign goods, tariffs make domestically produced goods more attractive to domestic consumers.

7. An import quota limits the number of imported goods that can enter the nation, thus shielding home producers from foreign competition.

8. Advocates of protectionism cite several arguments to defend trade restrictions: (1) national defense, (2) cheap foreign labor, (3) dumping and subsidies, and (4) job protection.

9. The General Agreement on Tariffs and Trade is a forum for the negotiation of reductions in tariff barriers on a multilateral basis.

10. The Omnibus Trade Act passed by Congress in 1988 gives the U.S. trade representative stronger powers than ever before, provides retraining and help for workers affected by imports, makes grants for math,

science, and bilingual education to keep America competitive, and tries to protect intellectual copyrights.

11. The European Economic Community is a strong trade bloc in Europe that seeks to benefit member countries with uniform trade laws.

PREVIEW 19.1 ANALYSIS

CAN AMERICA COMPETE IN FOREIGN MARKETS?

In 1982, General Electric was paying its manufacturing workers an average of $17.00 an hour to assemble and build refrigerator compressors. By comparison, a company in Brazil named Embraco paid its workers $1.40 an hour for similar work, and Japan's Matsushita hired labor for its compressors in Singapore for $1.70 an hour. How could GE compete in international markets?

One obvious answer was to purchase compressors abroad. Many American manufacturers, and for that matter worldwide manufacturers in industrialized countries, were using the option of sourcing from abroad to keep up with lower labor costs in less-industrialized countries.

Yet, GE wanted to look at the long-term picture. Buying abroad simply meant more dependence on foreign suppliers, quality, and price. Investment in a new plant could be exceptionally costly in the short run, but could provide long-term cost and supply advantages. GE knew that to give up producing something altogether when faced with foreign competition means giving it up indefinitely. Once the sourcing decision was made there was no road back.

If they decided to build a new plant, however, GE executives knew they needed to build a compressor that could be sold at prices competitive with those of Embraco and Matsushita. Their costs of raw materials and long-term costs of production would need to be far lower than those of Embraco and Matsushita to make up for the difference in labor costs.

GE's managers and engineers decided to come up with a plan for a high-speed, automated compressor plant with new high-tech features that could make the cost of the product competitive. Although it required the work of 40 engineers, 6 years, and overcoming many obstacles, GE eventually built a new plant in Columbia, Tennessee, which became operative in 1986.

Although consultants recommended that GE hire new engineers to mastermind the project, possibly from Japan, management held a firm commitment to using many workers already on board. The thinking behind this was that these people had a commitment to GE, were some of the best-trained engineers in the world, and knew the business of refrigerator manufacturing. Management reasoned that workers could prove themselves able to accept the challenge if only given a chance.

By deciding to invest, GE became one of hundreds of worldwide companies that came to believe that investment and improved technology were the best ways to meet foreign competition.

GE could not compete on the basis of high-speed, highly automated equipment and engineering skills alone. It also needed a highly trained, efficient work force. Management again wondered where it would find this work force, and once again decided to start at home in Columbia, Tennessee. With the help of the state of Tennessee, GE built a worker training center and asked workers to volunteer for training without pay. The system worked. GE workers saw the problem in much the same way as GE managers. It was time to confront the problem of foreign competition, or watch jobs go overseas, perhaps indefinitely.

It appeared that most of GE's staff pulled together on the Columbia project with a sense of teamwork, because they had a common goal. GE began to think in global terms. It realized that meeting foreign competition by making a major investment was a big risk but perhaps an essential one for survival.[2]

JAPAN LIMITS AUTO EXPORTS: GOOD DEAL FOR AMERICA?

PREVIEW 19.2 ANALYSIS

The sale of domestically produced automobiles in the United States in 1980 was more than 40 percent below the level of 1978, and U.S. autoworker employment fell to 804,000, down from the 1975–1979 average of 922,000. In the early 1980s auto company profits had turned into losses. Responding to the demand of U.S. auto companies and workers, the Reagan administration convinced the Japanese government to enter into a Voluntary Restraint Agreement (VRA) with the United States and impose an export quota of 1.68 million units on auto shipments to the United States beginning in 1981. The VRA was extended through 1985, subject to various modifications. Upon termination of the formal VRA, Japan continued to restrict auto shipments to the United States to 2.3 million vehicles per year, apparently to diffuse sentiment in the U.S. Congress for more severe protectionism.

The VRA aided U.S. auto producers greatly. Between 1981 and 1985 American auto prices rose by an average of more than $2,000 per vehicle, of which at least $440 could be attributed to the Japanese export quota. By 1984, the Big Three auto producers enjoyed profits exceeding $10 billion; GM went so far as to reward its executives with bonuses, on average exceeding $30,000 per executive. The average price of Japanese autos sold in America jumped by as much as $2,500 per vehicle. To derive more revenue from a fixed number of auto sales, the Japanese shipped cars with more expensive levels of trim, bigger engines, and more amenities such as air conditioners and deluxe stereos as standard equipment. The result was a strategy of increasing unit profit margins on the limited number of vehicles that could be exported to the United States under the quota. The United States International Trade Commission estimated that between 1981 and 1985 American consumers spent an additional $15.7 billion as the result of higher auto prices.

VRAs act as a self-imposed quota by foreign countries and affect prices in this country in much the same way as tariffs and domestically enforced quotas. The VRA has become a vehicle in the steel industry as well as the auto industry.[3]

[2]Source: Ira Magaziner and Mark Patinkin, *The Silent War* (New York: Random House, 1988), 67–100.

[3]Source: "Import Quotas and the Automobile Industry: The Cost of Protectionism," *Brookings Review* (Summer 1985).

REQUIRED ECONOMIC CONCEPTS

Net trade surplus	Quotas
Net trade deficit	Dumping
Low opportunity cost	Subsidies
Comparative advantage	Infant industry
Terms of trade	General Agreement on Tariffs and Trade
Free trade	Omnibus Trade Act
Protectionism	European Economic Community
Import tariffs	

KEY QUESTIONS

1. What are some U.S. industries that have lost jobs due to foreign trade? What are some that have gained jobs?
2. What was the effect on U.S. producers and consumers of restricting imports of Japanese automobiles?
3. Are imports a large or small percentage of U.S. GNP?
4. Name the top five trading partners of the United States. Are they primarily the underdeveloped countries?
5. What is the principle of comparative advantage?
6. Can two countries benefit from trade if their domestic exchange ratios are the same?
7. Can two countries benefit from trade if one of the countries trades at the other's domestic exchange ratio?
8. What two conditions hold at the point of equilibrium between two free-trading countries?
9. What are three benefits of unrestricted free trade?
10. What are five arguments made in support of trade restrictions?
11. What is meant by dumping?
12. Did a study of the effects of imports and exports on the U.S. labor market show a net loss or gain in U.S. jobs for the period 1975–1976?
13. What is GATT? What three conditions does GATT require of its members?
14. Has the U.S. tariff rate consistently risen or fallen since 1940?
15. What is a tariff? What three basic methods have been used to restrict free trade? What was the major reason behind the early tariff laws of the United States?

PROBLEMS

1. When it comes to infant industries, small, less-industrialized countries may have a valid argument for tariffs and quotas, because they wish to diversify their economies and not be too dependent on one commodity, which comparative advantage may force on them under free trade and the specialization it brings about. However, why might government subsidies of infant industries be a better approach than imposing tariffs and quotas? Why would an economy not want to be primarily a one-commodity producer?

2. Nobel laureate economist Milton Friedman once said, "U.S. workers who produce goods sold to Japan (and) earning yen used to buy Japanese steel, are producing steel for the U.S. just as much as the men who tend the steel furnaces in Gary, Indiana." Interpret.

3. In 1985, Lee Iacocca, chairman of Chrysler Corporation, said, "Until we fix the trade deficit, this country won't be able to compete. The USA's three major exports to Japan are corn, soybeans, and coal while Japan's three major exports are cars, trucks, and video recorders. Raw materials and food stuffs traded for manufactured goods — does the pat-

tern sound familiar? It's the classic definition of a colony. Weak-kneed U.S. trade policies are deindustrializing America." Would the head of the United Auto Workers union (UAW) agree with Iacocca? Would the head of the United Mine Workers union (UMW)? The U.S. farmers? Comment.

4. "The U.S. version of voluntary quotas on Japanese cars under a voluntary restraint agreement (VRA) is as if the U.S. is asking the Japanese to form an auto cartel with the U.S. with the obvious results." What are the obvious results?

5. The shoe and leather industries in the United States want hide exports restricted whereas the U.S. cattle and slaughter industries want export restrictions removed. Why? Does it depend on whose "hide is being gored"?

6. Many ships belonging to the United States and Canada fly under "flags of convenience" employing only foreign sailors, who are paid much lower wages than U.S. and Canadian sailors. The ships have a foreign registry. A maritime union representative said, "Those ships hurt our (Canadian) economy and deprive Canadians of jobs. We say it's time our government found the guts to tell those fat corporate welfare bums that there will be no more free lunches at the expense of Canadian voters and taxpayers." Who is better off and worse off here? Is the Canadian consumer and taxpayer hurt by Canadian ships flying under foreign flags? Will Canadian sailors who are laid off necessarily be permanently unemployed? Explain.

7. Someone says, "The national defense argument justifying tariffs and quotas is weak on both political and economic grounds." (a) Why do you think free trade is more likely to "change swords into plowshares"? Can you think of an example in the world today? (b) How could the reduction or removal of tariffs actually allow for greater expenditures for national defense?

8. The United States is a net exporter of airplanes, computers, coal, and electrical machinery among other products. The wages in these U.S. industries are the highest in the world. How can you reconcile this fact in the light of the argument about cheap foreign labor making U.S. goods noncompetitive in world markets? Consider that U.S. losses in its trade balance have been mostly gained by Japan, West Germany, France, Italy, and Canada, which are not low-wage, underdeveloped countries.

APPLICATION ANALYSIS

1. Assume Argentina and Chile are two-good economies. If Argentina devoted all of its resources per period to raising beef, it could produce 48 units per period per hour of work. If it only grew lemons, it could grow 24 units. Chile could grow either all of 20 units of lemons or all 20 units of beef per period per hour of work.

   a. Which country is the low opportunity cost producer of lemons and which one of beef? Draw the production-possibility curve for each country, assuming constant production costs.

   b. What is each country's domestic exchange ratio? Is there a basis for trade?

   c. Assume there is no trade between Argentina and Chile. Argentina produces 36 units of beef and 6 units of lemons while Chile produces 6 units of beef and 14 units of lemons. Illustrate these conditions in a figure. Pick a foreign exchange ratio halfway between the two domestic ratios. What did you pick?

   d. Now let each country specialize, with Argentina exporting 8 beef units to Chile. How many beef and lemon units does each country end up consuming? Also illustrate your answer in a figure.

   e. Suppose Argentina traded at Chile's domestic exchange rate. Who benefits and who loses if Argentina exports 6 beef units? Discuss.

2. Assume labor costs in terms of labor hours L are constant in Bolivia and Peru with both countries producing tin and lead. The labor costs are given in the table to the left. What can you conclude about the comparison of money wage rates between Bolivia and Peru?

	BOLIVIA	PERU
Tin	1L	3L
Lead	2L	5L

CHAPTER 20

INTERNATIONAL PAYMENTS SYSTEMS

IN THIS CHAPTER YOU WILL LEARN:

How currencies are valued
in international markets

●

Reasons why individuals and
institutions use foreign
currencies

●

How the value of a
country's currency is
related to its trade balance

●

Which payments systems
governments of the world
have used in the recent past

●

How the United States
keeps track of its
international payments

*This chapter was
written by Robert Carbaugh of
Central Washington University.*

THE PERSISTENT U.S. TRADE DEFICIT

Throughout most of the post–World War II era, the United States experienced trade surpluses in which U.S. merchandise exports to other nations exceeded U.S. merchandise imports from other nations. Although exports exceeded imports for the United States between 1946 and 1969, U.S. trade performance deteriorated throughout the 1970s and into the 1980s, when U.S. merchandise trade deficits became the norm.

Additionally since World War II the United States has had a history of lending more overseas than it borrows, creating net income from short-term overseas investments. In 1988 this situation changed. Payments made on foreign borrowing by the United States became greater than income from U.S. lending abroad.

The U.S. trade deficit — both the merchandise balance and the borrowing balance — is a cause of concern for economists. This situation makes the United States the largest debtor nation in the world, owing more to the rest of the world than it takes in foreign revenues. How does the United States keep track of these international transactions?

What are some of the causes, consequences, and proposed cures for the deficit?

THIRD WORLD NATIONS DEVELOP DEBT PROBLEMS

During the 1980s, the large debts of many less-developed countries (LDCs) became the headlines of major newspapers. The international debt problem goes back to the 1970s when real interest rates were low and oil prices were high. Countries such as Mexico and Brazil borrowed extensively from the United States and other Western nations to finance domestic economic development.

By the 1980s, however, the debtor LDCs were hit by several shocks that made their debt repayment situation exceptionally difficult. As a result the 1980s witnessed a series of financial crises in such Latin American countries as Mexico, Brazil, and Argentina. These nations scrambled to postpone or reduce back payments and renegotiate debt obligations to American banks.

Has this situation worsened as a result of changes in the international economic setting? What are some proposed solutions to the Third World debt problem?

• INTRODUCTION •

Governments, consumers, and businesses typically engage in foreign trade, requiring systems of payments between countries. These international payments systems are the subject of this chapter. Initially, the chapter discusses where foreign currencies are obtained and how their prices are established. Additionally, it discusses how prices of foreign currencies are related to exports and imports, and why prices of foreign currencies fluctuate.

Since World War II, major countries of the world have gotten together to determine different international payments systems. Some of the major features of these systems, their history, and their advantages and disadvantages are described in this chapter.

Finally, the chapter presents the means by which the United States keeps account of its international payments. This information is important because it yields an idea of whether we have a trade surplus or deficit and where we stand in relation to other countries of the world. •

FOREIGN EXCHANGE MARKETS

If an American wants to purchase or sell goods or services overseas, the buyer can exchange dollars for foreign currency in a **foreign exchange market.**

A foreign exchange market is a market in which people buy and sell domestic and foreign currencies.

In the United States there are a relatively small number of banks that deal in foreign exchange. These banks (called money center banks) are primarily in Chicago, New York, and San Francisco. These banks facilitate international transactions. When an American company imports from abroad, for example, it usually must pay for the goods with foreign currency. The company can purchase this foreign currency from a money center bank, buying it with American dollars.

When an American company exports goods, it wants payment from foreigners in dollars, and foreigners must go to their money center banks to exchange their domestic currencies for dollars. Such money center banks exist in locations such as London, Zurich, Frankfurt, Singapore, and Hong Kong. Bankers throughout the world thus serve as markets for foreign exchange.

To see how foreign exchange markets work, suppose a camera store in the United States orders 10 cameras manufactured in West Germany. Assuming that each camera costs 100 marks, the cost of the 10 cameras would total 1,000 marks. To pay the German manufacturer for the cameras, the U.S. camera store may need marks, so it arranges to buy them. But how much do the marks cost in American dollars? The answer to this question comes from knowing the **exchange rate.**

The exchange rate is the price of one country's currency in terms of another country's currency.

TABLE 20.1
Foreign Exchange Rates: U.S. Cents per Unit of Foreign Currency

COUNTRY/CURRENCY	1985	1986	1987	1988
Canadian Dollar	73.2¢	72.0¢	75.4¢	81.2¢
German Mark	34.0	46.1	55.6	56.9
Japanese Yen	0.4	0.6	0.7	0.78
British Pound	129.7	146.8	163.9	178.1
Hong Kong Dollar	12.7	12.8	12.8	12.8

Source: Federal Reserve Bank.

If the dollar–mark exchange rate is 50 cents for 1 mark, the camera store will need $500 to obtain the 1,000 marks needed to pay the German manufacturer.

The exchange rates of the major currencies of the world are reported in daily newspapers such as *The Wall Street Journal*. The exchange rate between two currencies, say, the dollar and the mark, can be expressed in two ways: (1) by the number of dollars needed to purchase 1 German mark — known as the U.S. dollar equivalent and (2) by the number of German marks needed to buy 1 U.S. dollar — known as the foreign currency equivalent. On August 24, 1988, the exchange rate between the two currencies was

$1 = .5322 marks (the U.S. dollar equivalent) or
1 mark = 1.8790 dollars (the foreign currency equivalent)

Table 20.1 presents data on the exchange rate between the U.S. dollar and selected foreign currencies for the period 1985–1988. The table shows how many U.S. cents it takes to purchase a single unit of a foreign currency. Between 1985 and 1988, the U.S. dollar showed **currency depreciation** against the currencies of many foreign nations.

> *Currency depreciation occurs when one country's currency loses value in relation to the currency of one or more foreign countries.*

For example, in 1985, a West German mark cost 34 cents; by 1988 a mark cost over 56 cents. Because it took more American money to buy a German mark, the dollar depreciated against the mark. Consequently, West German goods became more expensive to U.S. consumers. Table 20.1 shows that the price of the Canadian dollar, the Japanese yen, the British pound, and the Hong Kong dollar also went up for Americans from 1985 to 1988.

Table 20.1 also shows that all currencies listed had **currency appreciation** against the U.S. dollar between 1985 and 1988.

> *Currency appreciation occurs when one country's currency gains value in relation to the currency of one or more foreign countries.*

What do we mean when we say all currencies in Table 20.1 appreciated against the dollar? As an example, in 1985 a Canadian dollar was worth 73.2 American cents, and in 1988 the Canadian dollar was worth 81.2 American cents. A single Canadian dollar purchased more American goods and more American foreign exchange in 1988. While America's

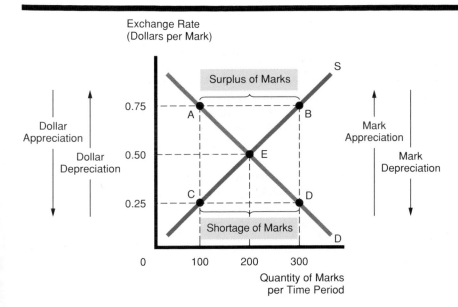

Exchange Rate
(Dollars per Mark)

FIGURE 20.1
The Foreign Exchange Market

This diagram demonstrates that the freely operating forces of supply and demand determine the equilibrium exchange rate. The exchange rate in dollars per mark is plotted on the vertical axis, and the quantity of marks on the horizontal axis. The demand curve for marks is downward sloping, because Americans want more of them (and German goods) as they become cheaper. Suppliers of marks will offer more as a single mark buys more American money. American goods thus become cheaper to West Germans. When a surplus of marks exists in the U.S.–German exchange market, there is pressure on the mark to depreciate and on the dollar to appreciate until equilibrium is achieved. When a shortage of marks exists, the mark will appreciate in value and the dollar will depreciate until equilibrium is achieved.

dollar depreciated, the currencies of the other countries listed in Table 20.1 appreciated.

The foreign exchange market is used by different people for different reasons. International businesspeople need foreign exchange for financing export and import transactions. International investors use foreign currencies to purchase foreign government securities, to engage in direct business investment in other countries, and to make investments in other types of financial assets. Many American tourists encounter foreign exchange and purchase foreign currency with dollar bills or dollar-denominated traveler's checks to pay expenses. Americans also send money to friends and relatives abroad and typically obtain foreign-currency drafts that can be bought at commercial banks.

DETERMINATION OF EXCHANGE RATES IN FREE MARKETS

When the forces of supply and demand determine exchange rates in free markets, these rates are **floating exchange rates.**

Floating exchange rates are fluctuating rates between the currencies of two or more countries freely determined by the laws of supply and demand.

When exchange rates are free to float according to the laws of supply and demand, these forces determine the prices of foreign exchange, just as they do prices of other commodities such as wheat. Figure 20.1 illustrates supply and demand in foreign exchange markets for the West German mark against the dollar. For the sake of simplicity, this is a two-country model. The price of a single mark in U.S. dollars is plotted on the vertical axis. The quantity of marks demanded is plotted on the horizontal axis.

The **demand for foreign exchange** (in this case marks) is derived from the desire of U.S. residents and firms to make payments to West Germany for goods and services and to make direct foreign investment and financial asset investment at varying exchange rates.

> *The demand for foreign exchange is a function of the desire of people in one country to make purchases or investments in another country at varying exchange rates.*

In Figure 20.1 the demand for marks is denoted by D. The demand schedule indicates that more marks are demanded as their price (in terms of American currency) goes down, all other factors remaining constant. Some of the other factors held constant for a given demand curve include income, expected interest rates, and inflation rates in the United States and West Germany.

The supply of marks (foreign exchange) results from the motivation of German firms to give up marks in exchange for dollars to finance purchases and investments in the United States at varying exchange rates. This is the **supply of foreign exchange.**

> *The supply of foreign exchange is the willingness of foreigners to give up their money at varying exchange rates to make purchases and investments in other countries.*

The supply schedule of marks, S, is upward sloping in Figure 20.1, because West Germans will make more marks available to Americans and buy more American goods as a single mark can be exchanged for a larger quantity of American money. As West Germans move up their supply curve, the mark appreciates.

Figure 20.1 brings together the demand and supply schedules of marks to determine the equilibrium exchange rate, which equals 50 cents per mark. When the price of each mark is 75 cents, there is an **exchange surplus** of marks in the U.S.–German foreign exchange market.

> *A foreign exchange surplus occurs when the quantity supplied of a foreign currency exceeds the quantity demanded for that currency.*

The surplus is shown by AB on Figure 20.1 and represents 200 marks, or the difference between the quantity supplied of foreign currency and the quantity demanded for foreign currency. At point B in Figure 20.1 the surplus of marks in the U.S.–German exchange market exists because at this favorable exchange rate West Germans will want to export more to Americans than Americans are willing to buy. As in any competitive market, the surplus of marks forces the exchange rate down toward the equilibrium rate.

Similarly, when the price of each mark in Figure 20.1 is 25 cents, there will be an **exchange shortage.**

> *An exchange shortage occurs when the demand for a foreign currency exceeds the supply of that currency.*

An exchange shortage occurs when a country's quantity demanded of a foreign currency (and goods, services, and investments in that country) is greater than the quantity supplied of foreign exchange. In Figure 20.1 the exchange shortage is represented by the distance CD, or 200 marks. In this case Americans would be exporting more to West Germany than it imports. The excess of exports over imports would lead to a shortage of marks and put pressure on the dollar to depreciate.

The market clearing (equilibrium) exchange rate in Figure 20.1 is the exchange rate of 50 cents per mark. This rate not only equates the quan-

TABLE 20.2
Currency Depreciation and Appreciation under Flexible Exchange Rates

A currency will *depreciate* when there occurs in the home country

1. An increase in the growth of income relative to the income of other countries.

2. Changes which make domestic interest rates relatively lower than those overseas.

3. An inflation rate that is relatively greater than the inflation rate of its trading partners.

A currency will *appreciate* when there occurs in the home country

1. A relative decrease of income that causes imports to fall relative to exports.

2. Changes which make domestic interest rates relatively higher than those overseas.

3. An inflation rate that is relatively less than respective inflation rates overseas.

tity demanded and quantity supplied of marks, but also promotes balance between American and German exchange of goods and services.

Proponents of floating exchange rates thus argue that flexible rates automatically adjust to eliminate excesses between imports and exports. In other words, the movement of exchange rates in response to shifts in the demand for and supply of foreign currencies automatically clears export and import markets.

WHAT CAUSES EXCHANGE RATES TO CHANGE?

Under a system of flexible exchange rates, the value of a country's currency will depreciate or appreciate in response to changing market conditions. Any force that shifts a country's demand or supply curve for foreign exchange will induce changes in a currency's exchange rates. Among the factors that forecasters consider when making predictions about exchange rate movements are: (1) changes in relative income growth between countries, (2) changes in relative interest rates, and (3) changes in relative inflation rates. Table 20.2 outlines these major forces.

CHANGES IN INCOME GROWTH RATES

Figure 20.2 again illustrates the foreign exchange market for the West German mark and the U.S. dollar, this time showing demand and supply curve shifts. The equilibrium exchange rate is initially 30 cents per mark, at point A, which is determined by the intersection of S and D. Suppose Americans enjoy an increase in income relative to West Germans and spend a portion of their additional income on imports from West Germany. In our two-country world, the increase in U.S. imports leads to a shift in the U.S. demand for German marks (and goods) from D to D_1. The increased demand for marks results in a depreciation of the dollar from 30 cents per mark to 40 cents per mark. The new equilibrium occurs at point B in Figure 20.2. Germans move up along their supply curve from A to B, because the value of the mark has appreciated relative to the dollar and because the new American demand for imports makes more foreign exchange available.

As U.S. income decreases relative to West German income, just the opposite result occurs. U.S. imports will decrease relative to U.S. exports. The relative strength of U.S. exports generates an increase in the demand for the dollar and an increase in its value relative to the mark.

FIGURE 20.2
Changing Market Conditions and Exchange Rates

There are three variables that shift demand and supply curves for foreign currencies. These are relative changes in income, interest rates, and inflation rates between countries. In this two-country model, a positive change in income in the United States with no similar change in income in West Germany will move the demand curve from D to D_1 causing the dollar to depreciate and moving equilibrium from A to B. An increase in interest rates in West Germany without a similar increase in interest rates in the United States will shift both the supply and demand curves for marks from D to D_1 and from S to S_1. The equilibrium exchange rate would move from A to C. An increase in inflation in the United States without a similar increase in West Germany would also cause both demand and supply curves to shift, resulting in dollar depreciation.

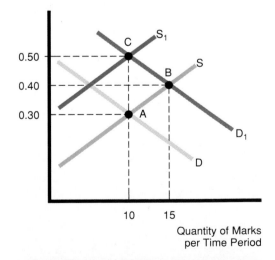

Exchange Rate
(Dollars per Mark)

CHANGES IN INTEREST RATES

Short-term financial investments (e.g., 90-day government securities) tend to be sensitive to changes in the inflation-adjusted interest rate—the real interest rate. Starting at the foreign exchange market equilibrium point A in Figure 20.2, suppose that the return on West German government securities goes up by 3 percentage points relative to yields on safe U.S. government securities. Because of the higher relative rate in Germany, American investors will respond by demanding additional German securities. The demand for German marks thus rises from D to D_1. At the same time, German investors will buy fewer U.S. government securities because the relative yield drops. The supply of marks thus falls from S to S_1 in the exchange market as German investors find investing in West Germany more attractive than ever. With the rise in the demand and the fall in the supply, the dollar depreciates against the mark, from 30 cents per mark to 50 cents per mark, with equilibrium at point C.

The U.S. dollar from 1980 to 1985 provides an example of changes in high real interest rates leading to a sharp appreciation of a currency in the foreign exchange market. During the early 1980s, large U.S. government budget deficits triggered massive borrowing by the U.S. Treasury. Combined with a restrictive, anti-inflationary monetary policy of the Federal Reserve, government borrowing kept short-term U.S. interest rates high. This encouraged foreigners to expand their investment in the United States, which added to the demand for the dollar and caused its exchange rate to appreciate. From its low in 1980 to its high in 1985, the dollar's exchange rate appreciated 47 percent on a trade-weighted basis against its major trading partners' currencies.

CHANGES IN INFLATION RATES

Other factors remaining constant, increases in the U.S. inflation rate bring about a depreciation in the value of the dollar, while U.S. deflation leads to dollar appreciation.

Again starting at equilibrium point A in Figure 20.2, suppose the United States experiences rapid inflation while no inflation occurs in West Germany. The domestic inflation leads to American consumers demanding fewer American goods and additional German goods, which results in a shift in the demand for marks from D to D_1. At the same time, West German consumers will demand fewer American goods and thus fewer dollars; the supply of marks offered in the foreign exchange market to obtain dollars shifts from S to S_1. The result of these market forces is that foreign exchange market equilibrium moves to point C, the new exchange rate being 50 cents per mark. The reader is left to determine what would happen to the value of the dollar if the United States and West Germany experienced identical rates of inflation.

An alternate way of looking at changes in the inflation rate and the exchange rate is presented in Figure 20.3. This figure illustrates the exchange value of the U.S. dollar from 1974 to 1979. As the differential of U.S. inflation over foreign inflation rose in the late 1970s, the dollar depreciated against the currencies of its major trading partners. This figure demonstrates that as inflation rates climb relative to inflation rates in other countries, exchange rates drop, because an inflated currency buys less. This leads to the concept of purchasing power parity.

PURCHASING POWER PARITY

We have seen that inflation rates in different countries play an important role in determining exchange rates. According to the **purchasing power**

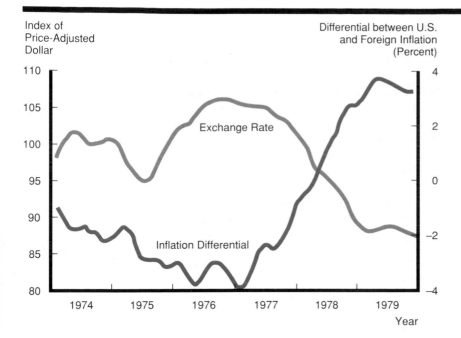

FIGURE 20.3

U.S. Dollar Exchange Rate and Inflation Differential

This diagram shows movements in exchange rates and inflation rates in the U.S. dollar between 1974 and 1979. Changes in the exchange rate mirror changes in the inflation rate. When inflation in the United States decreases relative to inflation in other countries, the exchange rate goes up reflecting the increased value of the dollar. Conversely when the relative inflation rate goes up, the exchange rate goes down reflecting decreased purchasing power of the dollar.

Source: Craig S. Hakkio, "Interest Rates and Exchange Rates — What Is the Relationship?" Federal Reserve Bank of Kansas City, *Economic Review* (November 1986).

parity theory, the exchange rate between two country's currencies adjusts to reflect differences in the price levels in the two countries.

> *Purchasing power parity occurs when a given amount of money will purchase the same market basket of goods and services when converted from one currency to another at prevailing exchange rates.*

Purchasing power parity suggests that the exchange rate between two countries reflects the difference in prices in those countries. To illustrate the workings of the purchasing power parity theory, suppose West Germany and the United States are in equilibrium with an exchange rate of $1 per 1 mark. If West Germany doubles its money supply while the United States maintains a constant money supply, there is a tendency for the prices of all German goods to double. If the price of the mark falls to 50 cents per mark, which is one-half of its previous value, German prices will appear exactly the same to U.S. consumers. A German TV that formerly cost 200 marks rises to 400 marks, but because the mark falls from $1 per 1 mark to 50 cents per 1 mark, the TV still costs U.S. consumers $200. Because the U.S. dollar buys the same goods in West Germany as before the inflation, the mark–dollar exchange rate has maintained its purchasing power parity.

Publishers of *The Economist* magazine have developed a test of their own, called the MacCurrencies test, to determine whether currencies have purchasing parity. In early 1989 they determined that the cost of the average McDonalds Big Mac was $2.02 in the United States. According to the hamburger standard, if purchasing parity exists, the Big Mac would cost the equivalent of $2.02 American dollars in all countries.

The Economist found that in early 1989 the price of a Big Mac was $2.77 in France, $2.78 in Japan, $2.27 in West Germany, $2.13 in Britain, $.98 in Hong Kong, and $1.80 in Canada.

Using the MacCurrencies index, the dollar is undervalued in relation to the currencies of France, Japan, West Germany, and Britain. If purchasing parity existed, a Big Mac would not cost more in these countries

FIGURE 20.4
Exchange Market Intervention:
Fixed Exchange Rates

In this two-country system, the official fixed rate of exchange is 50 cents per mark and initial equilibrium in the system exists at point A where D intersects S. Many different factors could conceivably shift the demand curve for marks from D to D_1. (Some of these are described as part of Figure 20.2.) Should such a demand curve shift occur, supply and demand are not in equilibrium, and the United States has a payments deficit of AC. To alter this situation under Bretton Woods, countries were obligated to use methods to shift their supply or demand curve or both to correct the trade imbalance and conform to the fixed exchange rate.

Exchange Rate
(Dollars per Mark)

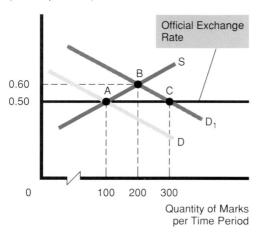

than it does in the United States. By the same token, the dollar is overvalued in Hong Kong and Canada, where the Big Mac costs considerably less than it does in the United States.

FIXED EXCHANGE RATES

Freely floating exchange rates have not always been the norm in international trade. At a conference in Bretton Woods, New Jersey, in 1944, the major nations of the world got together and implemented the Bretton Woods system. Under this system the exchange rates between major currencies were **fixed exchange rates**.

> *Fixed exchange rates are rates of exchange between currencies set by governments and international agreements.*

The Bretton Woods conference resulted in the creation of the International Monetary Fund to implement the system of fixed exchange rates. According to this system, a set rate of exchange existed between the major currencies of the world that did not fluctuate. If, for example, the dollar was worth 5 francs and 2.40 pounds, this did not change. This system was used until 1971, when currencies were once again free to fluctuate.

International investors, exporters, and importers liked having fixed exchange rates because it gave them some basis for forecasting future profits and costs. For example, suppose a foreign investor made an investment in German government securities, expecting the exchange rate to remain stable at 50 cents per mark. The investor can calculate return on investment by factoring in the rate of interest on the securities over the life of the investment. If the exchange rate remains stable, this is the extent of the return on investment. If, however, the dollar depreciates over the life of the investment, the rate of return drops. Similarly exporters and importers like stable exchange rates. Exporters like them because they know what their profits will be on sales abroad. Stable exchange rates allow importers to calculate costs of imports reliably.

To illustrate the operation of a fixed exchange rate system, suppose American and West German monetary authorities choose what they perceive to be an appropriate exchange rate between the dollar and the mark, say, 50 cents per 1 mark. By coincidence, assume that the market equilibrium exchange rate, where the supply and demand schedules of marks intersect, point A in Figure 20.4, is also the fixed rate. Because the market equilibrium exchange rate and the officially determined fixed exchange rate are identical, monetary authorities do not have to intervene in the foreign exchange market.

Suppose now that household income in the United States rises, resulting in increased American imports from West Germany and an increase in the demand for marks from D to D_1 in Figure 20.4. Under flexible exchange rates, equilibrium would move to point B. Under fixed exchange rates, the rate remains at 50 cents per mark. Along this new demand curve Americans will desire 300 marks (see point C). At this exchange rate West Germans are only willing to offer 100 marks (see point A). This results in a payments deficit in the United States of AC, because the quantity demanded for marks (and imports) is greater than the quantity supplied.

Under Bretton Woods, countries were called on to stabilize their currencies. How was this done? One way was to use reserves of international currencies to stabilize domestic currencies. Technically speaking under Bretton Woods, countries were supposed to maintain reserves of foreign currencies to use as needed. Suppose that a shortage of marks did occur in international trade between the United States and Germany, representing the U.S. payments deficit AC in Figure 20.4. In this case there would be pressure on the United States to shift the supply curve of marks to intersect with D_1 at point C. The United States could achieve this by selling marks in international markets.

During the life of Bretton Woods, this is precisely what our government did to stabilize the dollar. Government sold reserves of foreign exchange when there was a shortage of this currency and bought up reserves of foreign exchange when foreign currencies were in surplus.

A second means government had to stabilize its currency at the fixed rate was **currency devaluation.** Any given country might want to do this because its exports have become too expensive to foreigners, and the country thereby has an excess of relatively inexpensive imports over exports resulting in a trade deficit.

> *Currency devaluation refers to a decrease in the international value of a currency that occurs as the result of the actions of government. Currencies are devalued when they are made less expensive for foreigners.*

In effect currency devaluation is a one-step depreciation of a currency under a system of fixed exchange rates. A country devalues its currency by making it lose value relative to other currencies. In the two-country system we have been discussing, suppose the two countries were at the disequilibrium point C. The official exchange rate is 50 cents per mark. The dollar could be devalued by the government simply stating that the exchange rate is now 60 cents per mark. By making exports less expensive for foreign consumers and imports more expensive for domestic consumers, currency devaluation tends to reduce the excess of imports over exports and readjust trade balances.

One of the problems with the Bretton Woods agreement was the fact that the United States could not devalue its currency. Other countries could do this but not the United States, because the world used a combination of gold and the U.S. dollar under Bretton Woods as international exchange. The value of many currencies was tied to the dollar. It therefore became impossible for the United States to devalue without causing disruptions in international markets.

A third way countries could help the exchange rate remain fixed and at the same time achieve a trade balance was to initiate protectionist trade barriers and use tariffs and quotas. In Figure 20.4 this type of action could be used to shift the demand curve from D_1 back to D. This strategy was used under Bretton Woods; however, it conflicts with endeavors to have free trade between nations.

A fourth option during Bretton Woods was for countries to pursue macroeconomic policies to reduce domestic inflation and increase interest rates. This policy would make their currencies look more attractive on international markets. The problem with this strategy, however, is that it was not always consistent with domestic monetary policy needs. If, for example, the monetary authorities wanted to loosen up the money supply and make interest rates lower to control recessionary problems, this could be counter to international policy goals. This was another major drawback of Bretton Woods. The system did not allow governments to pursue domestic monetary policy goals, but put stress on achieving international ones instead. Bretton Woods eventually became unworkable and in 1973 was replaced by a system of managed floating exchange rates.

MANAGED FLOATING EXCHANGE RATES

Since 1973 the United States and other industrial nations have used what is generally described as **managed floating exchange rates.**

> *Under managed floating exchange rates, exchange rates are flexible, and for the most part the forces of supply and demand determine the rates. Under this system, however, governments intervene to prevent major disruptions in rates.*

This system is a compromise between a fixed exchange rate system and a flexible rate system. Under managed float, the currencies of the industrial countries are allowed to float in foreign exchange markets. However, the governments of the industrial countries intervene on the foreign exchange market as necessary to prevent sharp and disruptive fluctuations. Such a policy involves leaning against the wind, intervening to reduce short-term fluctuations without attempting to adhere to any particular fixed rate over the long run. For example, in 1985 the United States and other industrial countries actively sold dollars on the foreign exchange market so as to offset the appreciation of the dollar.

Advocates of managed floating exchange rates emphasize three major advantages of the system: (1) By allowing exchange rates to be flexible, the system can adjust to major shocks that affect currency values. The managed floating system was able to accommodate skyrocketing oil prices during the 1970s and plummeting oil prices during the 1980s. (2) Managed floating rates permit governments to adopt independent macroeconomic policies. Because flexible exchange rates automatically help restore balance between exports and imports, governments do not have to aim their monetary and fiscal policies at balance of payments problems. (3) Managed floating exchange rates promote balance between exports and imports without the use of tariffs or quotas that may be viewed as necessary under fixed exchange rates.

Managed floating exchange rates, however, have their critics who stress that they generate uncertainty for exporters, importers, and investors. Some argue that volatile exchange rate behavior makes it difficult for businesspeople to plan for the future. It is also argued that exchange rate fluctuations require significant time lags before they can significantly influence trade patterns. Such time lags may detract from the political attractiveness of managed floating exchange rates.

THE BALANCE OF INTERNATIONAL PAYMENTS

To know what is happening to the course of international trade and investment, governments maintain statistics of the transactions. The record of such transactions in the United States is called the **balance of payments accounts.**

> *Balance of payments accounts record all payments made to the United States by foreigners and all payments made to foreigners by the United States.*

These accounts include all payments for goods and services, loans, investment, direct foreign investment, gifts by the United States to foreign nations, and all payments made by foreigners to U.S. entities for similar

TABLE 20.3
U.S. Balance of Payments, 1987 (Billions of Dollars)

Current Account Transactions		
1. Merchandise trade balance		−160.3
(A) Merchandise exports	249.6	
(B) Merchandise imports	−409.9	
2. Services balance		19.8
(A) Military transactions (net)	−2.4	
(B) Investment income (net)	20.4	
(C) Other service transactions (net)	1.8	
3. Unilateral transfers balance		−13.4
4. Current account balance (items 1 + 2 + 3)		−153.9
Capital Account Transactions		
5. U.S. assets abroad (capital outflow −)		−76.0
(A) U.S. official reserve assets	9.1	
(B) U.S. government assets (less reserves)	1.1	
(C) U.S. private assets (net)	−86.2	
6. Foreign assets in the U.S. (capital inflow +)		211.5
(A) Foreign official assets in the U.S.	45.0	
(B) Other foreign assets in the U.S.	166.5	
7. Statistical discrepancy		18.4
8. Capital account balance (items 5 + 6 + 7)		+153.9

Source: *Statistical Abstract of the United States*, 1989, U.S. Department of Commerce.

purchases. Typically, the balance of payments is calculated over the course of a one-year period, although the financial pages of newspapers report balance of payments statistics on a quarterly basis.

As seen in Table 20.3, the balance of payments transactions for the United States in 1987 are grouped into two major categories: (1) **current account** and (2) **capital account.**

> *The balance of payments on current account transactions includes the balance of merchandise exports and imports for the United States and the balance of services imported and exported by the United States.*

> *The balance of payments on capital account transactions shows the balance of international capital flows.*

The largest portion of U.S. current account transactions typically consists of the exporting and importing of merchandise (commodities such as autos and televisions) and is called the **merchandise trade balance.**

> *The merchandise trade balance for the United States is the difference between exports and imports.*

In the popular press, the merchandise trade balance is often referred to as the trade balance. The value of merchandise exports is recorded as a plus item on the balance of payments accounts because exports lead to the receipt of payments from foreigners. The value of merchandise imports is recorded as a minus item because imports involve payments to foreigners. Thus a positive merchandise trade balance shows that exports exceed imports. A negative balance shows that imports are greater than exports.

TABLE 20.4
U.S. International Transactions, 1970–1987

YEAR	MERCHANDISE TRADE BALANCE	SERVICES BALANCE	GOODS AND SERVICES BALANCE	UNILATERAL TRANSFERS BALANCE	CURRENT ACCOUNT BALANCE
1970	2.1	1.5	3.6	−3.1	0.5
1972	−7.0	1.0	−6.0	−3.8	−9.8
1974	−5.4	9.0	3.6	−7.2	−3.6
1976	−9.4	18.7	9.3	−5.0	4.3
1978	−34.1	23.2	−10.9	−5.1	−16.0
1980	−25.3	33.6	8.3	−6.8	1.5
1982	−36.3	36.1	−0.2	−7.9	−8.1
1984	−112.5	18.2	−94.3	−12.2	−106.5
1986	−147.7	22.3	−125.4	−15.2	−140.6
1987	−160.3	19.8	−140.5	−13.4	−153.9

Source: *Federal Reserve Bulletin*, various issues.

As seen in Table 20.3, the U.S. merchandise trade balance in 1987 registered a deficit of $160.3 billion. This deficit reflected the difference between U.S. merchandise exports, $249.6 billion, and U.S. merchandise imports, $409.9 billion.

Trends in international transactions are presented in Table 20.4. This table shows that since 1970 the United States has faced deficits in its merchandise balance; this contrasts with the 1950s and 1960s when trade surpluses were common for the United States. Trade deficits are sometimes viewed as being injurious to domestic firms and labor, because sales and jobs are sacrificed to foreigners who produce our imports. Yet many economists believe that imports of goods such as new machinery and industrial goods have a positive impact on the economy.

Another portion of the current account balance is services, which includes tourism expenditures, transportation, insurance, and banking services. Services also include the income earned by U.S. investment overseas minus the income earned by foreign investment in the United States. Similar to the merchandise trade balance, the value of U.S. service exports including short-term loans is recorded as a plus item (credit) in the U.S. balance of payments, because exports lead to receipts of payments from abroad. The value of U.S. service imports is recorded as a minus item (debit) in the balance of payments, because imports involve payments to foreigners.

As seen in Table 20.3 the United States in 1987 generated a surplus of $19.8 billion on service transactions. Most of this came from the net investment income account of $20.4 billion. This is the difference between income from foreign investments and income paid out to foreigners on investments in this country. This net balance has customarily been positive; however, in 1988 this changed when payments for U.S. borrowing abroad became greater than income from U.S. lending.

The current account balance also includes an item called unilateral transfers. These are one-sided payments by the United States to the rest of the world including gifts, U.S. government grants, and military aid to governments.

Combining all elements on current account transactions shows a deficit of $153.9 billion in 1987, as seen in Table 20.3. This deficit implies that the United States realized an excess of imports over exports on current account transactions in 1987.

A second interesting feature of Table 20.3 is the composition of the capital accounts transactions. Item 5 on this part of the balance of payments shows that the United States made investments of $76.0 billion in assets abroad, resulting in a capital outflow. At the same time, item 6 shows foreigners invested $211.5 billion in this country, resulting in a capital inflow. The net capital inflow on capital account transactions is the same amount as the deficit on current account transactions (see totals 4 and 8 for the current and capital accounts).

Do the current and capital accounts really balance this easily? Is the amount of money spent abroad on current account transactions precisely equal to the net capital inflow? Generally speaking, this is not the case. In 1987, for example, capital inflow to the United States was somewhat less than the money it spent abroad on the current account balance. The United States made up for this difference by drawing down its **official reserve account** by $9.1 billion (see item 5A).

> *Official reserve accounts are stocks of foreign money held in a country's central banks.*

In the reverse case, if the United States would take in more on capital account transactions than it spends abroad, its store of reserves would grow.

Economists are not like-minded on the relationship between the balance on current account and capital account transactions. Some see a cause-and-effect relationship between the trade deficit and the buying of assets by foreigners in this country, reasoning that the excess of American dollars due to imports causes increased direct foreign investment. Other economists reason that there is simply a large worldwide demand for foreign assets in the United States, and that this could cause the strong dollar, strong import, trade deficit condition.

EXCHANGE RATES AND TRADE BALANCES

A distinct relationship exists between the trade balance and the exchange rate. When economists say that the dollar is strong, it sounds very reassuring. It means that the dollar purchases relatively more than other currencies. In this case imports from foreign countries are relatively inexpensive. The dollar buys more in foreign countries, and American importers are well served.

What does a strong dollar, however, mean to American exporters? Many economists theorize that economic growth cannot occur without a strong export sector. If the dollar is strong and buys more in relation to other currencies, then other countries can buy less in the United States, which is not good for export industries.

As we have seen, from 1981 to 1985 the dollar appreciated to record levels and imports exceeded exports in the United States. By 1985, however, the dollar had reached its peak and started to decline. Some observers predicted that the dollar depreciation would soon help the U.S. trade position by encouraging exports. Yet Figure 20.5 shows that this did not happen. The trade deficit is plotted on the vertical axis of this diagram, and time is on the horizontal axis. This figure shows that the trade balance (exports − imports) continued to decline in 1986 and 1987 despite the dollar depreciation. Why did this occur?

The pattern of net exports after currency depreciation that is shown in Figure 20.5 is known as a J-curve. According to the J-curve, the trade

FIGURE 20.5
The Exchange Rate and the Trade Deficit

Economists predict that when the value of a country's currency depreciates, its trade imbalances will eventually — but not immediately — lessen. That is, a depreciation in currency will make exports less expensive and imports more expensive, which should have a positive impact on trade deficits. This diagram shows that when a country's currency is depreciated, the trade situation worsens at first but then begins to improve over time.

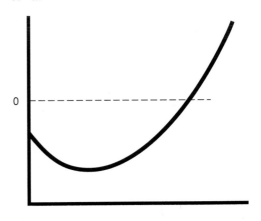

Net Exports, X − M

0

Time since Depreciation

balance continues to get worse for a while following a currency deprecia-tion (sliding down the hook of the J) before it gets better (sliding up the right side of the J). This is because the first impact of a currency depreci-ation is to increase import expenditures because the volume of imports remains unchanged due to prior contractual commitments while the price of imports rises under the currency depreciation. As time passes, the volume of imports falls in response to the currency depreciation.

What is more, our textbook illustrations assume that exchange-rate depreciations are immediately passed on to consumers in the form of higher import prices. When the U.S. dollar began to depreciate in 1985, foreign manufacturers were not willing to sacrifice their share of the American market without a struggle. Rather than permitting increases in the prices of their goods sold in the United States, they absorbed the dollar depreciation via reduced profits. They also cut manufacturing costs to hold prices down. The result was that only a portion of the U.S. dollar depreciation was passed on to American consumers in the form of higher import prices, reducing the effectiveness of the dollar deprecia-tion.

INTERNATIONAL FINANCIAL INSTITUTIONS

Several international institutions exist that lend money to countries at-tempting to undergo economic development and to countries facing bal-ance of payments difficulties. The two major institutions involved in these activities are the International Monetary Fund and the World Bank.

The International Monetary Fund (IMF) is owned by more than 100 countries and is intended to enhance the operation of the international monetary system. Using funds contributed by member countries, the IMF makes temporary loans to national central banks of countries facing bal-ance of payments difficulties and shortages of international reserves. In granting loans to member countries, the IMF adheres to the principle of conditionality — nations can borrow funds from the IMF subject to the stipulation that they initiate measures to restore balance in their imports and exports.

Borrowing nations are often asked to adopt austerity measures (e.g., slashing government spending) to shore up their economies and bring order to their muddled finances. The IMF must make a difficult decision of how tough to get with borrowers. If it is soft and lends money on liberal terms, an "easy money" policy is established for other debtor nations. But if the IMF misjudges and insists on excessive austerity policies, it risks triggering political turmoil and possibly a declaration of default by the debtor nation.

The so-called World Bank refers to both the International Bank for Reconstruction and Development (IBRD) and its affiliate, the Interna-tional Development Association (IDA). The common objective of these institutions is to help raise living standards in developing countries by channeling financial resources from the industrial countries to the devel-oping countries. Established in 1945, the World Bank is owned by the governments of some 148 countries. World Bank loans must be for pro-ductive purposes (e.g., power facilities, telecommunications, railways) and must stimulate economic growth in the developing countries where it lends. Each loan is made to a government or must be guaranteed by the government concerned.

SUMMARY

1. The foreign exchange market permits the exchange of one country's currency for another country's currency. Bankers throughout the world serve as the market makers in foreign exchange.

2. The foreign exchange rate indicates the price of one country's currency in terms of another country's currency. A currency depreciates (appreciates) when more (less) of it is needed to purchase a unit of another currency.

3. In a free market, the supply and demand schedules of foreign exchange determine the equilibrium exchange rate. Shifts in the location of these schedules cause the exchange rate to depreciate or appreciate.

4. Among the factors that forecasters consider when predicting future exchange rates are changes in relative incomes, inflation rates, and interest rates between countries.

5. Proponents of flexible exchange rates maintain that market-determined rates promote equilibrium among exchange rates, imports, and exports. Proponents of flexible exchange rates also believe that they promote purchasing power parity between nations.

6. The major nations of the world operated with a fixed exchange rate system under the Bretton Woods agreement. This system has been replaced by a system of managed float.

7. Under fixed exchange rates, a country may devalue its currency to reduce a trade deficit. In effect, a currency devaluation is a one-step depreciation initiated by a government. A country can also use protectionist trade measures, the selling of international reserves, and macroeconomic tools to deal with a trade deficit.

8. Under the Bretton Woods system, the U.S. dollar could not be devalued because it was an international reserve currency.

9. Balance of payments accounts are a record-keeping system of international payments. These accounts are grouped into transactions on current account and transactions on capital account.

10. U.S. balance of payments accounts include borrowing from abroad and lending abroad. Although income from lending abroad has normally been greater than payments on borrowing, this changed in 1988.

11. The difference between the balance on current account transactions and the balance on capital account transactions in the U.S. balance of payments is the change in international reserves held by central banks in the United States.

12. The World Bank and International Monetary Fund lend money to countries undergoing economic development and facing balance of payments problems.

THE PERSISTENT U.S. TRADE DEFICIT

The persistent U.S. trade deficit has been a cause for concern among economists because cash-rich Americans are importing more from abroad than they are exporting to foreign countries. Additionally by 1988 the United States was borrowing more from abroad than it lends, making it a net debtor nation.

How did this happen? On the merchandise trade account side, trade in manufactured goods, such as autos and steel, contributed to the majority of the trade deficit. Energy imports also added to the trade imbalance. This is due in part to the fact that in recent decades the United States has faced stiffer competition from Japan and the Common Market.

The trade imbalance is also partially worsened by trade conditions with the rest of the world. Common Market countries have a competitive trade edge with one another, excluding the United States from participation in its benefits. Japan has historically been a low-import country and does not purchase a large share of American exports.

Finally, Americans were cash rich. Until 1985, the United States was operating with a strong dollar. Foreign imports were relatively inexpensive compared with American exports. Tax cuts during the early 1980s also helped Americans find ways to make purchases abroad.

How did the balance of borrowing and lending change? In part foreign investors rushed to the U.S. to take advantage of high real interest rates, political stability, and a strong American economy. U.S. investment (lending) overseas fell due to a sluggish loan demand in Europe and loan repayment problems in Third World nations.

Is there an end in sight to the deficit on current account? Under the current exchange rate system, the U.S. dollar decreased in value against most major currencies from 1985 through 1988. A cheaper dollar should make American exports more competitive in foreign markets while making foreign goods more expensive to Americans. This could significantly help America's trade position. After devaluation America's trade deficit fell from a record of $170 billion (in 1987) to $137 billion in 1988. Devaluation made some gains in slowing down exports.

Other possible contributors to closing the trade gap would be an increase in exporting by many small businesses in America and improvement in trade negotiations with the rest of the world. Many nations restrain exports from America. According to new trade legislation, the U.S. trade representative will have power to retaliate against these nations. Additionally a bilateral trade agreement between the United States and Canada formed in 1989 is bound to help the U.S. trade position.

Yet, America has a long way to go to catch up to achieve a merchandise trade balance. Doing so by the 1990s would require U.S. industry to capture 80 percent of the new trade growth in the world.

What about deficits on the borrowing and lending accounts? The devalued dollar should discourage foreign borrowing by U.S. citizens over the long term by increasing the cost of borrowing overseas. Yet economists do not agree that the inflow of foreign money (borrowing) is necessarily a negative factor. By adding to the supply of money available for borrowing, the investment inflow from other countries in recent years helped accommodate the financial requirements of the U.S. government in running budget deficits.

THIRD WORLD NATIONS DEVELOP DEBT PROBLEMS

During the 1970s many oil-rich Latin American nations such as Mexico and Brazil borrowed heavily in the United States, because interest rates were favorable and because their revenues from oil exports made them good candidates for loan repayment. Many Latin nations borrowed ostensibly to invest in development in their nations. They borrowed from the World Bank and from private banks in the United States to help their economies.

By the 1980s, however, the debtor Latin American nations were hit by several shocks: (1) a global recession lessened foreign demand for their exports and made it more difficult for them to earn funds to pay back their loans to Western banks; (2) rising real interest rates on loans from Western banks made interest repayments increasingly difficult; and (3) Latin currencies depreciated, making their debts (which were denominated in dollars) more burdensome.

The 1980s witnessed a series of financial crises in such countries as Mexico, Argentina, and Brazil. To date a series of special financial arrangements have been negotiated by the IMF, American banks, and the governments of Latin nations.

In 1982, Mexico was hard pressed to repay $82 billion in loans from foreign countries. Creditors responded by extending the life of the loans and rescheduling repayment provisions. In Argentina, high rates of inflation and national debt forced the country to refinance its debt with major American banks. Brazil, the largest debtor among the Third Word nations, stopped making interest payments on private loans (but not World Bank loans) in 1987 due to high rates of inflation and lost revenues from exports.

In the meantime many U.S. banks suffered losses. They needed to discount the value of Third World loans and increase reserves held against these loans, adversely affecting profits.

Much of the Latin debt was incurred as a result of development loans, but instead of investing the monies from the loans in their economies, Latin American governments have used the money to finance governments and, in some cases, political patronage, and not business.

The result has been a destabilizing Latin America, both economically and politically. Honest politicians who favor loan repayment to the United States do not gain favor among the people, because loan repayment places such a burden on their economy.

At present the World Bank is reassessing its view on development planning and loans to Third World nations, seeking ways to encourage private development.

REQUIRED ECONOMIC CONCEPTS

Foreign exchange market	Purchasing power parity
Exchange rate	Fixed exchange rates
Currency depreciation	Currency devaluation
Currency appreciation	Managed floating exchange rates
Floating exchange rates	Balance of payments accounts
Demand for foreign exchange	Current account
Supply of foreign exchange	Capital account
Exchange surplus	Merchandise trade balance
Exchange shortage	Official reserve account

KEY QUESTIONS

1. What is the balance of payments account?
2. Under what exchange-rate arrangements is the current international monetary system operating?
3. How are international exchange rates determined? What role do central banks play in this? How quickly can exchange rates change?
4. Why do U.S. citizens — or any citizens — need foreign exchange?
5. When a demand curve for a currency is drawn, what are some of the variables being held fixed?
6. Why do the demand curves for marks, yen, etc., slope downward?
7. Why do the supply curves of marks, yen, etc., slope upward?
8. To what do depreciation and appreciation of currencies refer?
9. What is the purchasing power parity theory?
10. What are some advantages and disadvantages of fixed and floating exchange rates?
11. Under a fixed exchange rate system, exchange rates do not adjust. Thus what must the United States, for example, do if there is a shortage of yen at the fixed exchange rate?
12. If a country has a persistent imbalance of net imports under a fixed exchange system, what are three possible actions it can take?
13. How did some exporters in foreign countries respond in the mid-1980s to a depreciation of the U.S. dollar? Why?
14. If the current account is in debit, what can you say about the capital account in the balance of payments account?
15. Do credits and debits in the balance of payments account refer to the flow of goods or the flow of currencies between nations?
16. What is the function of the World Bank? Of the International Monetary Fund (IMF)?
17. What does it mean when the United States is said to be a net debtor nation since 1985?

PROBLEMS

1. If 1.75 U.S. dollars exchange for 1 English pound, and 130 Japanese yen exchange for 1 U.S. dollar, for how many pounds does 1 Japanese yen exchange? If a Rolls Royce sells for $100,000, how many English pounds will a U.S. importer need to buy the car?
2. When the prime interest rate (the rate banks charge their best customers, such as large corporations) rose above 21 percent in December 1980, would you expect the exchange rate of the dollar relative to foreign currencies to have appreciated or depreciated? Why?
3. Using a figure that measures the yen along the horizontal axis, explain the adjustment in the dollar–yen market if the United States experiences high inflation relative to Japan in a system of flexible exchange rates.

4. Assume a system of flexible exchange rates. Which of the following shifts the U.S. demand curve for foreign currency, and in which direction, assuming the vertical axis measures the dollar price of foreign currencies?
   a. The Federal Reserve sharply cuts the money supply.
   b. Japan buys a seafood processing plant in Seattle, Washington.
   c. West Germany's central bank enters the market to support the price of the U.S. dollar.
   d. The United States experiences a deflation relative to its major trading partners.
   e. Interest rates in Europe increase relative to U.S. interest rates.

5. Is each one of the following a debit or a credit in the balance of payments accounts?
   a. A U.S. citizen buys a Honda.
   b. West Germans reduce their holdings of U.S. Treasury securities.
   c. A relative in Poland sends you a Christmas gift.
   d. A U.S. citizen buys insurance from Lloyd's of London.
   e. The French car maker Renault buys 40 percent of American Motors Corporation's stock.

6. In which row of the balance of payments shown in Table 20.3 should each of the following be entered? Also, is each transaction entered as a debit or a credit in the balance of payments account?
   a. Royalties received from abroad by a U.S. novelist.
   b. A foreigner buys a U.S. Treasury bill.
   c. GM stock is sold to an Australian.
   d. The government sends a Social Security check to U.S. citizens who have retired to Poland.
   e. Ford Motor Company builds a factory in England.
   f. Profits earned by Ford Motor Company's factory in England.
   g. Interest paid to a U.S. holder of a German bond.
   h. A U.S. fighter plane sold to Saudi Arabia.
   i. You send a Christmas gift to a friend in France.

7. How can the balance of payments be zero if the United States has been a net debtor nation since 1985? (It may help to recognize that the U.S. dollar functions as a reserve currency for trading nations of the world.)

8. Under the gold standard, each country's currency is pegged (fixed) to gold. Under the dollar–gold standard, the dollar is pegged to gold (e.g., $35 to 1 ounce) and then other nations' currencies are pegged to the dollar. To maintain these fixed exchange rates, each country has to maintain a certain ratio of its paper money to its holdings of gold. But its gold holdings can change; hence, its money supply, for example, has to be reduced if it loses gold in order to maintain its agreed upon ratio of currency to gold. In the Great Depression of the 1930s, why do you think this gold or dollar–gold standard collapsed as unemployment surged?

APPLICATION ANALYSIS

1. In 1977 foreign central banks spent about $28 billion trying to support the value of the dollar. The $28 billion was equal to half the U.S. federal budget deficit for that year. Explain the actions of the foreign central banks. Also, what happens to Germany's domestic money supply when its central bank buys U.S. dollars with marks? Does the U.S. inflation have any connection to prices of goods in Germany?

2. a. Suppose the Federal Reserve expands the money supply causing the dollar price of the mark to rise substantially. Why does the dollar price of the mark rise?
   b. Because of the German hyperinflation experience of the 1920s, Germany has a deep fear of inflation. The German central bank can respond to part (a) by either (1) letting the value of its goods dwindle relative to the dollar or (2) enter the market and buy dollars. What is the effect of each action? Is there a conflict between the two approaches?

CHAPTER 21

ECONOMIC GROWTH AND THE DEVELOPING NATIONS

*This chapter was written
by H. Stephen Gardner
of Baylor University.*

ECONOMIC GROWTH IN INDIA

Until World War II India was under the rule of Great Britain. After the war fighting broke out in India between Muslims and Hindus, causing Britain to divide the country into two nations, Pakistan and India. By 1947 these countries had the status of independent states, and by 1950 India had adopted its own government and constitution.

This government faced special challenges because India was a typical poor, underdeveloped country. It had high population growth rates, low-yield agricultural land, high mortality rates, and an undeveloped industrial sector.

To address these problems, the new Indian government developed a growth strategy that was to follow a five-year plan. Economic development was based on government planning and involvement in the private sector. Parts of the government's plan also favored protecting domestic manufacturers from import competition. What has happened to India's population growth rates, agricultural productivity, and economic development since 1950? How has its growth strategy worked?

SOUTH KOREA — ONE OF FOUR SUCCESS STORIES

Although most of the developing world seems to revolve in a vicious circle of poverty, low productivity, and excessive population growth, a few countries have broken from the mold. Among the most remarkable of these are the East Asian Gang of Four — Hong Kong, Singapore, South Korea, and Taiwan. Since 1965, the economies of the Four Tigers have grown more than twice as rapidly as the average for other developing countries. In 1987, growth rates in these four countries ranged from 5.8 to 7.6 percent, whereas growth in 12 other developing nations selected for comparison ranged from −2.1 to 2.9 percent. Thus, the living standards in Hong Kong and Singapore are now on a par with Great Britain, the birthplace of the Industrial Revolution.

In many ways, the East Asian Gang of Four are very different from one another. They range in population from under 3 million (Singapore) to over 40 million (South Korea). Their economic systems are built on everything from unregulated free enterprise (Hong Kong) to modified central planning (South Korea). The agricultural share of the labor force ranges from 2 percent in Hong Kong and Singapore to 28 percent in Taiwan and 36 percent in South Korea. Hong Kong and Singapore had long histories of British colonialism; Taiwan and Korea were pawns of Sino-Japanese rivalry.

Despite all their differences, the East Asian Gang of Four have at least one important factor in common: while other Third World governments attempted to promote economic development by protecting domestic producers from imports, the Four opted for a strategy of export promotion. Their manufacturers are encouraged to sell on the world market rather than on protected domestic markets.

How has one of these countries, South Korea, developed and implemented an export-based growth strategy?

• INTRODUCTION •

The so-called developing nations of Africa, Asia, and Latin America account for about 75 percent of the world's population and 50 percent of its land, but only 15 percent of its production of goods and services. Thus, they have an enormous potential for economic growth and development, but their poverty represents a serious threat to world peace and security.

To see the differences in characteristics of low-income countries as opposed to industrial market economies, see Table 21.1. This table shows that poorer countries share the common characteristics of relatively high population growth rates, relatively low secondary education enrollment, and relatively poor access to medical care. These problems, along with lower life expectancy rates than industrial countries and large portions of the population engaged in agriculture, pose the true challenges for economic development. This chapter explains some of the reasons behind slower growth rates for developing nations and presents some of the theories used to explain how the growth picture could be improved. •

ECONOMIC GROWTH AND DEVELOPMENT

In Chapter 18 we said that **economic growth** occurs when actual and potential real national income rises in the long run. Nearly all economists would accept this definition.

TABLE 21.1

The Development Gap (Data Are for Selected Years Between 1965 and 1985)

	AVERAGES FOR:	
	35 LOW-INCOME COUNTRIES	19 INDUSTRIAL MARKET ECONOMIES
1985 GNP per capita ($)	828	13,227
1965–1985 growth rate of real GNP per capita (%)	0.4	2.4
1985 life expectancy at birth (years)	52	76
1980 share of labor force in agriculture (%)	71	7
1985 urban share of population (%)	20	75
1980–1985 population growth rate (%)	2.7	0.6
1985 infant mortality rate (per 1,000)	112	9
1981 population per physician	17,350	530
1984 secondary education enrollment (% of age group)	23	90

Sources: Averages for GNP per capita were calculated from Robert Summers and Alan Heston, "A New Set of International Comparisons of Real Product and Price Levels Estimates for 130 Countries, 1950–1985," *Review of Income and Wealth* 34 (March 1988): 1–25. All other data are from the World Bank, *World Development Report 1987* (New York: Oxford University Press, 1987), 202–267.

> *Economic growth is commonly defined as growth in income for a given area or nation.*

Economists do not agree, however, on a single definition of development. Certainly, an economy must grow in order to develop, but that is only the beginning. Economic development requires an improvement in the standard of living of the general population. The nation's output must grow more rapidly than its population, and the benefits of economic growth must be experienced by the majority — not by an elite few. This is indicated by an increase in income per capita, a rise in life expectancy, and a reduction in infant mortality.

Economic development is accompanied by a structural transformation of society. The labor force moves from agriculture to industry, and from rural to urban surroundings. Handicraft techniques give way to mechanization and mass production. Monetary exchange replaces barter (take another look at the development indicators in Table 21.1). Putting all of these elements together, we adopt the following definition:

> *Economic development occurs when economic growth leads to structural modernization and a sustained improvement in the general standard of living.*

To illustrate the difference between growth and development, consider the case of Kenya. From 1980 to 1985, Kenyan national income grew at an annual rate of 3.1 percent — roughly equal to the average for other poor countries. Unfortunately, the Kenyan population grew even more rapidly — 4.1 percent per year (the average rate for other developing countries was 2.7 percent). Thus, Kenyan income per capita *declined* by about 1 percent per year. As one might expect, other measures of the standard of living also deteriorated. The infant mortality rate increased from 87 deaths per 1,000 children in 1980 to 91 deaths in 1985. Average life expectancy declined from 55 years to 54 years. The share of industrial production in GNP declined.[1] Kenya's population grew, but it did not economically develop.

Regrettably, the situation in Kenya was not uncommon during the first half of the 1980s. During those years, 21 developing countries suffered a decline in GNP, and 32 others (including Kenya) experienced a reduction in GNP per capita. On the other hand, at least 33 Third World countries showed signs of economic development, with rising incomes per capita, longer life expectancies, and falling infant mortality rates. Economic growth does not guarantee economic development, but it offers the possibility.

HISTORY, GEOGRAPHY, AND CULTURE

The existing division of the world into rich and poor countries is rooted in a complex web of geographic, historical, and cultural conditions. The average developing country, for example, has only half as much land suitable for farming per capita as the average industrial country. Most of the poor countries are located in the tropics, where they are plagued by too much or too little rain, and where the winters are not cold enough to exterminate insects, parasites, and other pests.

---

[1] All of these development indicators are from the World Bank, *World Development Report 1987* (New York: Oxford University Press, 1987), 202–267.

Tradition, custom, and political factors influence economic growth as well as purely economic elements. For example, countries with longer histories of political independence typically have higher growth rates than other countries. This bodes well for the future because numerous nations have gained political independence since World War II.

Attitudes concerning wealth and land ownership also have an impact on growth. By tradition in many countries, land is owned by a wealthy few, but farmed by poor tenants. This system has an adverse effect on work incentives and productivity. In general a nation's attitudes toward investment, education, individual freedom, work, science, technology, and a range of other factors are molded by its historical and cultural traditions.

INVESTMENT, SAVING, AND ECONOMIC GROWTH

A country can usually increase its rate of economic growth by raising its rate of investment. With more machinery, equipment, and new technology at their disposal, the nation's workers are able to raise their productivity. This simple relationship is illustrated for a group of 71 developing countries in Figure 21.1. This scatter diagram illustrates that countries with large shares of investment in GNP, such as China, South Korea, and Singapore, tend to have higher rates of economic growth than countries with low rates of investment, such as Nigeria and Sierra Leone.

Domestic investment is generally financed by domestic saving, which requires abstinence from consumption. As Figure 21.2 illustrates, the countries with the highest rates of saving, such as Singapore, Algeria, and China, also have the highest rates of investment. To invest without saving, a country must rely heavily on foreign debt (as in the case of Mauritania), foreign aid (as in Burkina Faso), or direct foreign investment.

Unfortunately, the countries that need to save and invest the most are those that can afford it least. Figure 21.3 shows that saving rates tend to be lowest in countries with the smallest per capita incomes, such as Ethiopia and Burkina Faso. High saving rates allow the relatively rich developing countries, such as Singapore and Algeria, to get even richer. A few countries, such as China, Indonesia, and Cameroon, have used governmental controls and incentives to maintain higher saving rates than other countries at their income levels. Conversely, high rates of inflation discourage saving in relatively affluent Israel and Greece.

Putting all of these elements together, we have found one important **growth formula.**

> *The economic growth formula emphasizes the importance of savings and investment. The poorest countries tend to have low saving rates, which perpetuates low rates of investment and economic growth.*

It is possible for a poor country to have a high saving rate, a high rate of investment, and high rates of economic growth and development, but the odds are against it.

Savings and investment aid economic development in part because they are used for **infrastructure investment.**

> *Infrastructure investment is investment in capital goods by government. These goods are often too expensive or too general in nature to be produced by the private sector.*

FIGURE 21.1
Investment and GNP Growth, 71 Developing Countries, 1980–1985

Data in this scatter diagram show a direct correlation between investment levels and percent growth of GNP per capita. Economists hypothesize from these data that investment in business and the economy spurs economic growth.

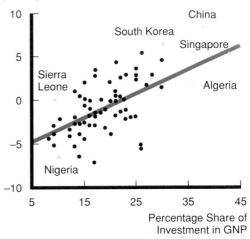

Percentage Growth of GNP per Capita

Source: World Bank, *World Development Report 1987* (New York: Oxford University Press, 1987), 202–267.

FIGURE 21.2
Saving and Investment as a Percentage of GNP in 72 Developing Countries, 1985

The data show a direct correlation between savings and investment. Economists believe investment is essential to economic growth, and high savings levels are needed for investment.

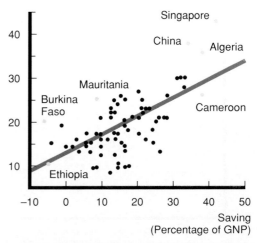

Investment (Percentage of GNP)

Source: World Bank, *World Development Report 1987* (New York: Oxford University Press, 1987), 202–267.

F I G U R E   21.3

GNP per Capita and Savings Rates in 72
Developing Countries, 1985

A statistical correlation exists between savings and GNP
growth, demonstrating that poorer countries, which need
savings to grow, have low savings rates. Growth-
oriented economies seem to be able to generate the kind
of savings that perpetuate more growth.

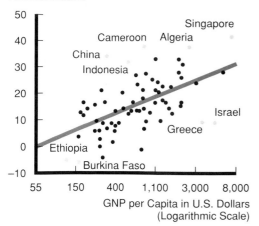

Source: World Bank, *World Development Report
1987* (New York: Oxford University Press, 1987),
202–267.

F I G U R E   21.4

Percentage Growth of GNP per Capita
and Population in 71 Developing Countries,
1980–1985

Countries with high population growth rates tend to have
low per capita GNP growth. Larger populations strain
economic resources and tend to inhibit growth. For a
long time economists believed that economic growth was
difficult in developing nations, because it was accompanied by population growth that put a strain on resources.
Now economists believe that a growing population accompanies economic growth for a time but then tapers
off.

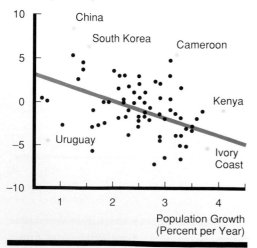

Source: World Bank, *World Development Report
1987* (New York: Oxford University Press, 1987),
202–267.

Typical types of infrastructure investment are investments in goods
and services that aid in the distribution of such economic goods as roads,
railroads, and airports. Other infrastructure investments include hydro-
electric power, water treatment systems, and waste treatment.

Other investments involve improvements in technology. Most advanced countries have highly sophisticated technologies, developed
through business investment over decades. Technologies appropriate for
advanced nations are not necessarily suited for developing countries.
These countries are in the position of needing systems that can use their
unique blend of resources, such as a large labor force. These countries
can especially benefit from ways to enhance agricultural productivity.

POPULATION PRESSURE

Excessive population growth is another problem that causes some poor
countries to remain poor. The scatter diagram in Figure 21.4 indicates
that population growth is negatively correlated with growth of GNP per
capita, although the correlation is rather weak. Thus, it is possible for a
country with a burgeoning population to have a rapid rate of per capita
economic growth (compare Cameroon and Uruguay on the diagram), but
the odds, once more, are against it.

How does population growth interfere with economic development?
Several explanations have been suggested. First, according to the simple
argument popularized by Thomas Malthus in the 1820s, the **law of diminishing returns** comes into play when the population grows more rapidly
than the other factors of production.[2]

*According to Malthus and his law of diminishing returns,
population growth will eventually outstrip the productivity of
land, leading to poverty.*

In a world of limited natural resources, population pressure under-
mines the growth of labor productivity and potentially threatens world
peace. Furthermore, it is difficult to build and maintain an adequate
stock of factories, equipment, roads, schools, houses, and hospitals to
meet the needs of a rapidly growing population.

When population growth is slow and steady, all age groups tend to
increase at about the same rate. Accelerated growth is usually caused by
an increase in the birth rate, a decline in infant mortality, or an increase
in average life expectancy. All of these tend to cause rapid growth among
the very young or the very old. Thus, accelerated population growth is
usually associated with a decline in the working-age share of the population.

Economists believe that increases in output can actually cause population growth and defeat the goal of economic growth. This is characteris-
tically true because once families are better off they tend to have more
children, of nonworking age, which causes per capita GNP to drop.

Although economists have historically believed that economic growth
can cause population growth rates to increase and thereby perpetuate
poverty, new theories have recently emerged on this subject. Many economists now believe that the initial stages of growth can cause a population
growth spurt that tapers off fairly soon. This would be true in the case
where higher standards of living improve infant mortality rates and mortality rates in general, followed by slower population growth due to increased awareness of birth control.

---
[2]This concept would be discussed in more detail in microeconomics.

GROWTH AND INEQUALITY

In 1971, Simon Kuznets won the Nobel Prize in economics for his contributions to the measurement and analysis of national income. Among his many discoveries, Kuznets noted a curious relationship between national income and inequality. He found that in very poor countries most of the population is equally poor — incomes are divided rather evenly. This is also true for relatively rich countries. Developing countries, on the other hand, have uneven distribution of income.

The scatter diagram in Figure 21.5 broadly confirms the Kuznets discovery. The countries with the most unequal distributions of income (where the poorest 20 percent of households receive only 2 percent of total income) have per capita incomes between $1,000 and $2,100. Incomes are divided more evenly in poor countries, such as India and Bangladesh, and rich countries, such as Japan and Germany. This diagram describes the **Kuznets curve.**

> *According to the Kuznets curve, incomes are divided most evenly in very poor and very rich countries, and inequality is greatest in middle-income, newly industrializing countries.*

One hypothesis that explains income inequality in newly industrializing countries is that when industrialization begins, the benefits are not divided evenly. Incomes rise for entrepreneurs, industrial workers, merchants, and financiers, but they change very slowly for the large farm population. As economic growth proceeds, the benefits finally trickle down to the entire population through rising product demand and governmental programs.

What is the practical significance of the Kuznets discovery? It tells us that economic growth can expand the gap between the rich and poor in a given country for many years. Rising income inequality, in turn, can cause political instability, which can interrupt economic progress. The most successful countries are those, such as South Korea and Taiwan, that have combined economic growth with a relatively equal distribution of income.

STRATEGIES FOR ECONOMIC DEVELOPMENT

The nations of the Third World seem to be trapped by hostile natural conditions, legacies of colonialism and cultural backwardness, feeble rates of saving and investment, population pressure, foreign debt, and income inequality. From 1965 to 1985, the average annual growth of GNP per capita was below 1 percent in 32 developing countries, and growth was negative in 16 countries.[3] At an annual growth rate of 1 percent, it would take the average low-income country about 280 years to reach the present standard of living of the average industrial market economy.[4]

What can be done to speed the rates of growth in the developing countries? Several strategies have been suggested, but none have inspired unanimous support from economists and policymakers. Let us consider a few of the options.

FIGURE 21.5
The Kuznets Curve: Income and Its Distribution in 44 Countries

The Kuznets curve relates per capita GNP to incomes of the poorest one-fifth of households in each of 44 countries. This curve demonstrates that the poor countries, such as India and Bangladesh, and rich countries, such as Japan and Belgium, have relatively even distributions of income. Countries in which families receive an uneven distribution of income are in the mid ranges of per capita GNP. The uneven distribution of income can be caused by political factors. It is also believed that newly industrializing nations have uneven income distribution because there is a newly emerging entrepreneurial class.

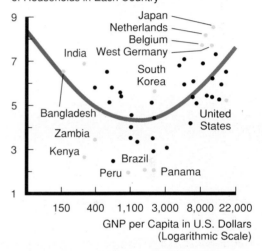

Source: World Bank, *World Development Report 1987* (New York: Oxford University Press, 1987), 202–267.

---

[3]World Bank, *World Development Report 1987* (New York: Oxford University Press, 1987), 202–203.

[4]Based on the estimates of average GNP per capita in Table 21.1.

AGRICULTURAL REFORM

In most of the low-income countries, any reasonable program to promote economic development must begin in agriculture, where about 70 percent of the labor force is employed. An improvement in agricultural productivity and food production will quickly raise the average standard of living and improve public health. In the long run, higher farm productivity will make it possible to shift more workers into industrial production, and higher farm incomes can contribute to saving and investment.

Several things can be done to improve agricultural productivity in the Third World. First, a number of Asian and Latin American countries, but few in Africa, have gained from participation in the **Green Revolution.**

The Green Revolution involves the cultivation of new high-yielding plant varieties, such as hybrid corn and rice.

Unfortunately, the new varieties require heavy applications of chemical fertilizers, which must be imported by many developing nations; heavy irrigation, when many countries are plagued by drought; and knowledge of new agricultural techniques, when much of the rural population is illiterate. Nevertheless, when properly implemented, these techniques have caused agricultural yields to increase by multiples of three to eight in India, Pakistan, Sri Lanka, the Philippines, and Colombia, and several countries have established agricultural research centers and demonstration farms to acquaint their farmers with new varieties and methods.

Rural productivity and income equity can also be improved through a program of **land reform.**

Land reform involves an alteration of land ownership arrangements.

This can take several different forms, depending on the original conditions in the host country. In many countries, for example, most of the land is owned by absentee landlords, living in the cities, and worked by tenant farmers. The tenants have little incentive to maintain and improve the land through irrigation, fertilization, and crop rotation because they never know whether their leases will be renewed from one year to the next. Even if the tenants do increase their yields through hard work and investment, all of their gains can be taken by rent adjustments.

In the most moderate version of land reform, the landlords are required to sign long-term leases, protecting the tenants from displacement and unreasonable manipulation of rents. In more radical reform programs, the land is bought or taken from the gentry, and its ownership is divided among individual farmers and/or cooperatives. Land reform can have a negative impact on productivity, even if it improves income equity, when large estates that are highly mechanized are divided into small, inefficient farms.

STRATEGIES TO INCREASE SAVING AND INVESTMENT

Earlier, we found that poor countries tend to have low rates of saving, that low rates of saving are correlated with low rates of investment, and that low rates of investment are correlated with low rates of economic growth. How can the low-income countries break out of this vicious circle? Several strategies have been attempted.

In centrally planned economies, high rates of economic growth have been achieved through a system of **forced savings.**

Forced savings occur when governments levy high taxes to pay for investment.

That is, the governments have maintained high rates of direct or indirect taxation to finance investments in nationalized industries, schools, hospitals, and other public works projects. This explains why the Chinese rate of saving was 34 percent in 1985, when the average rate was 6 percent in other low-income countries.[5] The problem with this system is that it allows the government to exercise arbitrary control over people's incomes, rather than allowing them to make their own saving decisions. Governmental investment decisions are open to politicization, graft, and corruption. Nationalized industries can operate inefficiently and ignore consumer demand if governmental support protects them from bankruptcy.

In market-oriented industrialized economies these problems are avoided because savings and investment decisions are made in well-developed financial markets. These markets are not particularly advanced or operable in lesser-developed market-oriented nations. Yet, when growth of a financial sector accompanies economic growth, investment and savings are aided.

In market-oriented developing economies, saving can be encouraged by government by strengthening financial incentives and by removing disincentives. By firmly controlling the growth of the money supply, for example, the government can maintain a low rate of inflation, which protects the purchasing power of savings. The tax system can be designed to reward saving and discourage consumption. Interest income can be exempted from taxation. Governmental control of interest rates can be abolished and competition can be encouraged between financial institutions. Unfortunately, these policies may exacerbate the problem of income inequality by rewarding the wealthy, who are able to save.

FOREIGN LOANS, INVESTMENT, AND AID

With the help of foreign loans, investment, and aid, low-income countries can maintain investment rates that exceed their domestic rates of saving. Reliance on foreign capital can be helpful or disastrous, depending on the circumstances. If the rate of return on a domestic investment is higher than the rate of interest charged by a foreign lender, it is perfectly reasonable to finance the investment with foreign credit. The credit transaction will be mutually beneficial for the foreign lender and the domestic borrower.

Unfortunately, the rate of return on an investment is seldom known with certainty when the investment is made. If money is invested, for example, to build a television factory, the actual rate of return on that investment and the borrower's ability to repay the loan will depend on future developments in the television market. If there is an unexpected decline in television prices, the borrower may be unable to repay, and the loan transaction may become mutually disadvantageous.

Reliance on foreign credit has been helpful to countries such as South Korea, where investment yields have been high and the debt burden has

---

[5]World Bank, *World Development Report 1987* (New York: Oxford University Press, 1987), 210.

been kept at a reasonable level. On the other hand, indebtedness has become an obstacle to additional growth in much of Latin America and in several African countries. From 1980 to 1986, the developing countries with recent debt-servicing problems had an average GNP growth rate of only 1.6 percent, while countries without these problems grew at an average rate of 5.6 percent.[6]

The problem of repayment can be avoided by reliance on **direct foreign investment** instead of debt.

> *Direct foreign investment is investment by foreign companies in developing nations. It has potential for stimulating growth.*

From 1980 to 1987, the developing countries obtained about $101 billion through direct foreign investment and $592 billion through foreign borrowing.[7] According to its proponents, direct foreign investment provides capital, jobs, and technology to developing countries, and it engages the active participation of experienced foreign managers. Critics of foreign investment believe that the capital stocks and workers of developing countries should not be entrusted to foreign owners and managers. Outsiders, they say, are likely to create low-skill jobs in the developing countries and send the higher-skill jobs elsewhere. They are likely to bribe public officials, introduce products and technologies that are inappropriate in the host countries, drive domestic competitors out of business, and extract excessive profits for their foreign owners.

To say the least, foreign investment by multinational corporations is a controversial subject. According to one statistical study, foreign investment contributes to the economic growth of developing countries in the short run, but continued reliance on foreign capital reduces the rate of income growth in the long run.[8] Other studies have disputed these results, and a World Bank report contends that foreign investments "can clearly be beneficial to developing countries, and it is desirable that they be increased."[9] If they choose to do so, developing countries can attract more direct investment by providing tax incentives and by maintaining a stable political, macroeconomic, and regulatory environment.

According to the data in Table 21.2, conventional lending and direct investment are important sources of foreign capital for the middle-income developing countries, but the low-income countries are more dependent on foreign aid (often called official development assistance, or ODA). In 1985, foreign aid amounted to about 8 percent of the GNP of small, low-income countries, and it financed about 40 percent of their imports.

Foreign aid can take many different forms. Almost all of the aid to low-income countries is given in outright grants, while much of the assistance to middle-income countries is given in low-interest loans with long repayment periods.

---

[6]International Monetary Fund, *World Economic Outlook* (April 1988), 116.

[7]International Monetary Fund, *World Economic Outlook* (April 1988), 160.

[8]V. Bornschier, "Multinational Corporations and Economic Growth: A Cross-National Test of the Decapitalization Thesis," *Journal of Development Economics* 7 (1980), 191–210.

[9]World Bank, *World Development Report 1985* (New York: Oxford University Press, 1985), 134.

TABLE 21.2
Net Flows of Foreign Loans, Direct Investment, and Aid to Selected
Developing Countries, 1985 (Millions of Dollars)

	LOANS	INVESTMENT	AID
Low-Income Countries:			
Haiti	49	5	153
Kenya	27	77	439
Mali	80	4	380
Pakistan	220	124	750
Rwanda	53	15	181
Zaire	27	7	324
Middle-Income Countries:			
Argentina	2,952	977	39
Brazil	1,006	1,267	123
South Korea	2,736	200	−9
Mexico	948	492	145
Singapore	−236	1,076	24

Source: World Bank, *World Development Report 1987* (New York: Oxford University
Press, 1987), 234–245.

Much foreign aid is handled bilaterally, from one nation to another.
Bilateral aid usually has many strings attached.

*Bilateral aid is foreign aid given from one country to another
to aid economic development.*

First, the distribution of bilateral aid is heavily politicized. Nearly
half of American bilateral aid, for example, goes to Israel and Egypt, two
middle-income countries. About one-third of all bilateral aid is unrestricted, allowing the recipient to use it for any purpose; the rest is desig-
nated to specific projects, such as installing water and sewer systems or
building schools, hospitals, and power-generation facilities. Over half of
all bilateral assistance is now **tied aid.**

*Tied aid requires the recipient to spend the funds on goods
produced in the donor country.*

Tying of aid is popular in the donor countries, particularly among
export producers, but it can reduce the benefit to recipients, who may be
forced to buy imports from high-priced suppliers.

About one-third of aid is extended to many nations through such
international organizations as the World Bank. The International Monetary Fund, for example, typically provides loans to developing nations for
investment purposes.

The influence of foreign aid on economic development is just as controversial as the impact of foreign debt and investment. Certainly, many
people in poor countries would face immediate hardship or starvation
without help from abroad. As previously noted, foreign aid made it possible for small, low-income countries to pay for 40 percent of their imports
in 1985.

Unfortunately, there is little evidence that aid has made a significant
contribution to the long-term growth and development of the Third
World. In a recent statistical study covering 81 developing countries, the
authors found that "aid *in the aggregate* has no demonstrable effect on

recipient countries," and they believe that these results should be a "cause for grave concern" in the donor community.[10] The problem, according to some of its critics, is that foreign aid allows poor countries to delay economic and political reforms that are needed for growth and development. Recipients can use foreign aid to cover their investment needs and squander their other income on consumption, military procurement, and civic monuments. In a word, foreign aid may allow poor countries to develop a permanent pattern of dependency.

Proponents of foreign aid can point to a number of success stories, notably in Taiwan and South Korea. They argue that domestic investment is encouraged by aid-supported construction of roads, power plants, and other public utilities. Foreign aid would have a more profound impact on economic development, they say, if more of it were distributed multilaterally, free of the political and economic strings that are attached to bilateral aid.

IMPORT SUBSTITUTION AND EXPORT PROMOTION

As noted earlier, economic development usually involves a shift from agricultural production to manufacturing. This structural transformation can occur gradually, through the spontaneous operation of the market system, or it can be pushed forward by a governmental development program. A large number of countries, including Argentina, India, and Zambia, to name a few, have adopted strategies of **import substitution.**

> *Import substitution is a strategy whereby developing countries manufacture goods currently being imported. Government protects manufacturers of these goods by tariffs and quotas.*

Import substitution elicits the following questions and answers:

Question: Which manufactured goods should our nation produce?
Answer: Products that the country is presently importing from other countries. We know that a demand exists for those products.
Question: How can we be sure that our new industries will be able to compete with foreign producers?
Answer: We will use tariffs, quotas, and other import barriers to protect our domestic producers until they become efficient and competitive.

Import substitution is a popular development strategy for many reasons. It provides simple answers to the what-to-produce and where-to-sell questions. By reducing imports, it addresses the balance of payments problem that plagues many developing countries. It gives the nation's infant industries a chance to establish themselves and to grow into maturity. Import substitution certainly is popular among workers and owners in the particular industries that are protected from foreign competition.

On the other hand, import substitution is an inward-oriented development strategy that involves restriction of foreign trade. In Chapters 2 and 19, we discussed the benefits that can be gained from trading according to comparative advantage. If import substitution causes a country to replace low-cost foreign goods with higher-cost domestic products, its people are likely to suffer a reduction in their standard of living. If domestic manufacturers are protected from foreign competition, they may *never* be forced to produce efficiently and competitively.

---

[10]Paul Mosley, John Hudson, and Sara Horrell, "Aid, the Public Sector, and the Market in Less Developed Countries," *The Economic Journal 97* (September 1987), 631 and 636, emphasis in the original.

According to its critics, import substitution cannot even be trusted to reduce a balance of payments deficit. The forced reduction of imports is likely to cause a corresponding reduction of exports. How does this happen? When individuals are not allowed to buy imports, they have no reason to exchange their currency (say, the peso) for foreign currency. This reduction in the supply of pesos on the foreign exchange market will cause the exchange rate of the peso to rise. When pesos are expensive to foreigners, the nation's goods are also expensive to foreigners. Thus, an effort to reduce imports may cause an unintended reduction of exports, leaving the trade deficit unaffected.

According to many of the critics of import substitution, economic growth and development can be supported more effectively with a strategy of **export promotion.**

> *Export promotion is a strategy that concentrates on helping the developing nations produce for export.*

A policy of export promotion causes nations to ask and answer the following questions:

Question: Which manufactured goods should our nation produce?
Answer: Products that we can sell in foreign markets.
Question: How will our producers, with their primitive technologies, and our workers, with limited education, be able to compete with foreign suppliers?
Answer: We will begin by promoting exports of simple products, such as textiles, and we will gradually raise our technological and educational levels. If necessary, we will provide governmental subsidies to help our export producers to compete in world markets.

According to its proponents, export promotion is a better strategy because it involves expansion rather than restriction of foreign trade, and it can operate with a minimum of bureaucratic regulation. Domestic manufacturers who produce for the enormous world market will benefit from economies of large-scale production and will be forced to meet world quality standards. The government is encouraged to resist inflationary policies that may weaken the nation's competitive position.

Advocates of export promotion can support their case with statistical evidence. The scatter diagram in Figure 21.6 shows that countries with the highest rates of export growth, such as Cameroon, China, and South Korea, have experienced the most rapid growth of GNP per capita in recent years. Likewise, a recent study by the World Bank found that total factor productivity increased much faster in countries with strong policies of export promotion than in strong import-competing countries. The annual growth was more than 4 percent in Hong Kong and South Korea during the 1960s and early 1970s, compared with 1.5 percent or less in Argentina, Chile, India, and Peru.[11]

Still, export promotion has its critics. Heavy reliance on foreign trade may contribute to growth when the world economy is growing, they say, but it may spell disaster if there is a serious worldwide recession. Export promotion may have worked in Hong Kong and South Korea, where about 70 percent of adults could read and write in 1960, but that does not guarantee its success in Ghana or Malawi, where only 30 percent of adults are literate today. Even if the poor countries can supply the world market with high-quality manufactured goods some day, that will raise another question: Will the rich countries react with a new wave of protectionism against "cheap foreign labor," or will they embrace the mutual benefits to be gained from expansion of foreign trade?

FIGURE 21.6
Percentage Growth of GNP per Capita and Exports in 71 Developing Countries, 1980–1985

This diagram shows the correlation between export growth and per capita GNP for 71 countries. The upward-sloping curve shows a distinct positive relationship between these two variables. GNP grows as exports grow. Faster-growing countries, such as China and South Korea, have high rates of export growth. Poorer countries, such as Nigeria and Bolivia, have low GNP and export growth.

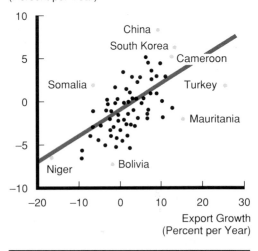

Source: World Bank, *World Development Report 1987* (New York: Oxford University Press, 1987), 202–267.

---

[11]World Bank, *World Development Report 1987* (New York: Oxford University Press, 1987), 92–93.

SUMMARY

1. The characteristics of developing nations are high rates of population growth, low per capita income, relatively poor agricultural land and medical care, large rates of population participating in agriculture, relatively high mortality rates, and relatively low levels of education.

2. Economic growth occurs when national income rises over the long run. Economic development, a broader concept, requires an improvement in the standard of living of the general population and a structural modernization of the economy.

3. The poorest countries tend to have low savings rates, which perpetuates low rates of investment and economic growth.

4. Rapid population growth seems to inhibit the growth of per capita income by reducing the growth of labor productivity. Newer economic theories hold that economic growth is accompanied by a population growth spurt that eventually tapers off.

5. According to the Kuznets curve, incomes are divided most evenly in very poor and very rich countries, and inequality is greatest in the newly industrialized middle-income countries.

6. Asian and Latin American countries, but few in Africa, have gained from the Green Revolution, which involves the cultivation of new high-yielding plant varieties.

7. Land reform is an alteration of land ownership and tenure arrangements designed to encourage work and investment in agriculture and to alter the distribution of income and wealth.

8. In centrally planned economies, high rates of economic growth have been achieved through a system of forced saving, whereby investment is financed by direct or indirect taxation.

9. In market-oriented economies, saving and investment can be encouraged by offering financial incentives, such as tax deductions, or by removing disincentives, such as inflation.

10. When a country's saving rate is not high enough to finance a sufficient level of investment, help may be obtained through foreign loans, investment, and aid. These can be most beneficial, or even necessary for the nation's survival, but they also expose the developing nation to risks of insolvency and foreign political interference.

11. In a strategy of import substitution, the government encourages production of manufactured goods that previously were imported and provides tariff protection to domestic producers. This strategy provides a market for new manufactured goods, but it may sacrifice some of the benefits of foreign trade.

12. In a strategy of export promotion, the government encourages production of manufactured goods that can be sold in foreign markets. This strategy preserves the benefits of foreign trade and has been successful in several countries, but it may not be appropriate for all developing nations.

ECONOMIC GROWTH IN INDIA

With nearly 800 million people, India is the second most populated country in the world and among the poorest. On an area one-third the size of the United States, India has a larger population than North, Central, and South America combined; it has more people than Western Europe or the African continent. Furthermore, the Indian population is increasing rapidly. Between 1980 and 1985, its annual growth rate was 2.2 percent, compared with 1.2 percent in China and 0.6 percent in the industrial world. If these rates continue, which is improbable, India will bypass China around the year 2020 to become the most populated country on earth.

In recent years, the Indian government has attempted to slow the rate of population growth by encouraging family planning and birth control. Ordinarily these measures have been voluntary, but in 1976, during a period of martial law, about 7 million men were sterilized under a compulsory program. With governmental support and pressure, the proportion of married women of childbearing age using contraception increased from 12 percent in 1970 to 35 percent in 1984. This led to a large reduction in the birth rate, but improvements in public health led to an even larger reduction in the death rate.

The density of the Indian population imposes a stern limit on agricultural productivity. Most of the farms have fewer than 2.5 acres of land and little machinery. Water shortages make it impossible to grow more than one crop per year in most regions. Thus, the market value of goods produced by the average Indian farmer is only one-fiftieth of the American average.

In the 1950s, the government initiated a program of land reform to boost agricultural productivity and equity. The percentage of owner-cultivators increased from about 40 percent to 75 percent, and the remaining tenants were given protection from eviction and rent increases. Still, population growth led to severe food shortages in the mid-1960s, and the country became heavily dependent on imports of wheat from the United States, financed by the P.L. 480 food assistance program.

The agricultural situation began to improve in the mid-1960s because of Indian participation in the Green Revolution. The government invested heavily in irrigation and agricultural research programs. In the Punjab region, the proportion of total wheat area planted in new high-yield varieties rose from 4 to 66 percent between 1966 and 1970, and national wheat production nearly doubled. Between 1970 and 1985, wheat production doubled again.

In addition to its efforts to increase agricultural output, the Indian government has spent huge sums of money to make food available to low-income consumers at stable prices. In most years, the Food Corporation of India (FCI) purchases about 10 percent of the grain crop at prices designed to encourage production and sells the grain in special "fair price shops." In the late 1970s, governmental subsidies to FCI represented about 44 percent of its total sales.[12]

The Indian government plays an even more prominent role in the industrial sector of the economy. When India gained independence from Britain in 1947, many of the Indian leaders were impressed by the Soviet

---

[12]World Bank, *World Development Report 1986* (New York: Oxford University Press, 1986), 89.

record of rapid industrialization based on central planning, nationalization of industry, price control, import substitution, and priority development of heavy industry. With significant modifications, they tried to imitate the Soviet performance.

The government began a nationalization program in 1948, and a Planning Commission has prepared a series of five-year plans since 1951. By 1970 the public sector held 60 percent of the nation's capital stock. The government's share of annual investment has typically been 50 to 60 percent; more than half of manufacturing investment has been directed to the steel and engineering sectors.

The five-year plans have supported a strict policy of import substitution. To protect new industries from import competition, foreign exchange was made available only to importers of essential products that had no domestic sources of supply. Under an industrial licensing system introduced in 1951, a governmental permit was required to establish a new plant, to add capacity to an existing plant, or to change product lines. Governmental permission was also required for a private firm to shut down or lay off workers.

In the opinions of most development economists, the Indian programs of import substitution and economic planning have yielded disappointing results. From 1965 to 1985, the growth rate of Indian GNP per capita was 1.7 percent, about half the average rate for all developing countries. Furthermore, Indian economic growth was extensive rather than intensive. That is, all of the growth was caused by expansion of the labor and capital inputs; there was no measurable growth in factor productivity.[13]

When he came to office in 1984, prime minister Rajiv Gandhi decided to reduce the role of the government in the Indian economy. He lowered the tax rate on the largest incomes from 98 percent to 50 percent. He started to dismantle many of the production quotas, import restrictions, and licensing requirements that inhibited competition, trade, foreign investment, and productivity growth. Still, few of the nationalized firms have been sold to private owners, and much of the economy remains under bureaucratic control. Some 130,000 unprofitable companies are presently receiving governmental subsidies to keep their doors open.[14] The "Rajiv revolution" has only begun.

---

[13]World Bank, *World Development Report 1987* (New York: Oxford University Press, 1987), 93.
[14]*The Wall Street Journal*, March 8, 1988, 26.

SOUTH KOREA — ONE OF FOUR SUCCESS STORIES

PREVIEW 21.2 ANALYSIS

In 1945, at the end of World War II, South Korea faced devastating circumstances. North Korea, which formerly supplied the South with electricity, minerals, and heavy industrial goods, was now a separate country and an adversary. After 35 years of occupation, the Japanese presence in Korea came to an abrupt end, cutting trade links and leaving Korea with few skilled managers. The nation's roads, bridges, and factories bore the scars of the Pacific War, and Japanese replacement parts were no longer available. The division of Korea left the South with two-thirds of the population but only half of the land. On an area smaller than 37 of the American states, South Korea had a population of 20 million in 1945 (42 million in 1987), making it one of the most densely populated countries in the world.

Under pressure from American advisors, the government initiated a program of land reform in 1947 that allowed some 1.5 million farm families to buy land formerly owned by the Japanese, the government, and absentee landlords. All holdings in excess of 3 hectares (7.4 acres) were sold at low prices to the tenants. The government provided low-interest credit and irrigation assistance. All of this led to a significant increase in rice yields, but many of the new owners still could not meet their payments and were eventually forced to sell their holdings.

The economy took another giant step backward during the Korean War (1950 to 1953), when the country became even more sharply divided. In addition to staggering civilian casualties, about half of the factories in the South were destroyed. Reconstruction, based on large inflows of aid from the United Nations and the United States, occupied the remainder of the 1950s.

In 1961, after a succession of weak and corrupt governments, General Park Chung Hee seized power in a bloodless coup. Surprising everyone, General Park gave economic development a higher priority than military power. To that end, he adopted a strategy of export promotion, based on a partnership between private and public enterprise. He devalued the won (the national currency) frequently to keep South Korean export prices competitive. He introduced a battery of tax, credit, and tariff incentives to encourage exporters and engineered a sharp increase in interest rates to stimulate personal saving.

General Park also created an Economic Planning Board (EPB) and gave it very broad powers. Private businesses are not forced to comply with governmental plans, but the EPB can offer financial aid to encourage compliance. Together with the Ministry of Trade and Industry, the EPB chooses industries to support on the basis of their export potential. Textiles and footwear were developed in the early 1960s, steel and chemicals in the late 1960s and early 1970s, shipping and machine tools in the late 1970s, and automobiles and consumer electronics in the early 1980s.[15] For the five years beginning in 1989, the target industries will be semiconductors, computers, telecommunications, aerospace, robots, and new materials (such as carbon fibers). These product categories were chosen because they are expected to account for more than 60 percent of world trade in 1995.[16]

[15]Jon Woronoff, *Asia's "Miracle" Economies* (Armonk, NY: M. E. Sharpe, 1986), 108–111.
[16]*The Wall Street Journal*, August 24, 1988, 12.

Government-owned enterprises have played an important role in South Korean economic growth. They account for about 9 percent of GNP and 23 percent of fixed capital formation. They are particularly important in heavy industry, fertilizer production, oil refining, and ship-building. Unlike government-owned enterprises in many other countries, the ones in Korea generally are profitable, but less profitable than those in the Korean private sector.

Still another important factor in the Korean development strategy is a strong commitment to public education. The government spent 18 percent of its budget on education in 1985, compared with 10 percent in the average developing country. Primary schooling is compulsory and universal. Secondary education is not compulsory in Korea, but 91 percent of that age group was enrolled in school in 1984, compared with 38 percent in the average developing country.[17] Thus, South Korea has well-educated workers, who spend a weekly average of 54 hours on the job.

The results of the Korean development strategy have been most impressive. Annual growth of GNP per capita averaged 6.6 percent from 1965 to 1985, a record matched only by other members of the East Asian Gang of Four. During the same years, life expectancy increased by 10 years and the infant mortality rate was cut in half. The Korean distribution of income is among the best in the world, but the condition of the poor is still desperate and politically explosive.

Despite his economic accomplishments, General Park was guilty of political intrigue and repression. Civil unrest mounted during the 1970s, and Park was assassinated in 1979 by one of his own intelligence officials. Since that time, the nation's leaders have moved haltingly toward political and economic liberalization. In 1988, a Presidential Commission on Economic Restructuring recommended freer importation of agricultural goods, decontrol of capital markets, reduction of support for declining industries, and expansion of social welfare programs.[18]

As they have gained new freedoms, South Korean workers have grown more assertive. There were more strikes and labor disputes in 1987 alone than in the previous decade, causing wages to rise an average of 30 percent in 18 months. This may only be the beginning. "Japanese consumers were patient — too patient, for too long," according to a Japanese banker who works in Korea. "Koreans are different. They're more demanding."[19]

---

[17]World Bank, *World Development Report 1987* (New York: Oxford University Press, 1987), 247 and 263.

[18]*The Wall Street Journal*, September 6, 1988, 23.

[19]*The Wall Street Journal*, August 1, 1988, 11.

REQUIRED ECONOMIC CONCEPTS

Economic growth
Economic development
Growth formula
Infrastructure investment
Law of diminishing returns
Kuznets curve
Green Revolution

Land reform
Forced savings
Direct foreign investment
Bilateral aid
Tied aid
Import substitution
Export promotion

KEY QUESTIONS

1. What is meant by economic development?
2. In what temperate zone are most of the poor countries located?
3. What is a major economic variable explaining why low-income countries too often remain poor? How can such countries invest when their saving rates are low?
4. Do population growth rates tend to correlate positively or negatively with growth in GNP per capita?
5. What is the Kuznets curve?
6. Is the correlation between income and income inequality across countries weak or strong? Why?
7. If a nonindustrialized country is to industrialize, in what sector of the economy must development first begin?
8. What is the Green Revolution?
9. What form must land reform take in many undeveloped countries if they are to develop economically? How does moderate land reform differ from radical land reform?
10. What is forced saving? What is often the problem with it?
11. What is a criticism of investment by foreigners in less developed countries? Why might foreign investment also be beneficial?
12. What are important sources of foreign investment for low-income countries as compared with middle-income countries?
13. What is multilateral aid? Bilateral aid? Tied aid?
14. Is there solid evidence that foreign aid has been largely effective for low-income countries' long-term growth? Are there any success stories at all?
15. What is import substitution? Export promotion? What are two countries that have successfully pursued export promotion policies?
16. Which policy, import substitution or export promotion, has India pursued since 1951 after gaining independence from Britain in 1947?

PROBLEMS

1. Formal mathematical models of economic growth abound in the economic literature but mathematical models of economic development do not. Why is this?
2. Is economic development possible without economic growth? Is economic growth possible without economic development? Discuss.
3. Industrialization has traditionally started with a shift of resources from the agricultural sector to the industrialized sector, centering initially on textiles and moving on to iron and steel production, to steel products, then on to electronics and microelectronics. But less developed countries (LDCs) today can create an engineering industry without evolving

through the intermediate stages of iron and steel production and the building of large industrial organizations. What is, therefore, more true about technical knowledge today than in the seventeenth century that makes this possible?

4. From 1960 to 1975 the amount of factor inputs grew at approximately the same rate in Argentina and Colombia, but Colombia's gross domestic product (GDP) grew about 2 percent more than Argentina's.[20] Can you explain this in terms of extensive versus intensive economic growth?

5. From 1973 to 1980 the gross domestic product (GDP) of low-income countries grew at an average annual rate of 2.5 percent compared with 2.1 percent for industrial countries. From 1980 to 1986 the rates were respectively 5.4 percent and 1.4 percent.[21] Yet in the 1980s the income disparity among families in many LDCs increased relative to the industrial countries. Can you reconcile the annual growth rates with the growing income disparity between LDCs and the industrialized countries?

6. Some economists argue that the rise in real GNP per capita is a better measure of economic growth than simply the growth in the absolute level of real GNP. Can you provide arguments supporting both kinds of measurements?

7. For purposes of economic growth and development, is it better for a country to have an educational system that produces many Nobel Prize winners (and per capita) in physics, chemistry, and medicine or to have a strong system of trade schools and apprenticeship training for the general labor force? For instance, compare England since the end of World War II (1939 to 1945) (many Nobel Prize winners) with Japan (few Nobel Prize winners). Also, compare the United States in 1960 with the United States 30 years from now given the state of precollege education today. Any conclusions, assuming the United States will likely continue to produce a number of Nobel Prize winners in the near future?

8. Labor union officials and union advocates have lauded unions as providing a major contribution to U.S. economic growth since World War II (since 1955, when labor union membership peaked at 37 percent of the nonfarm labor force, it declined to under 18 percent in 1988). Does it follow that if the LDCs were to unionize their work force economic development and prosperity would ensue? Does the Hong Kong economy suggest an answer?

9. For each entry explain the possible effect on a country's economic development.
    a.   The large debts owed by LDCs to industrialized countries that results in "capital flight," i.e., in the export of LDCs' savings.
    b.   A small 2 percent of the population owns 90 percent of the land. The landlords lease small plots to tenant farmers.
    c.   Productivity increases are small while employment grows substantially in the service sector.
    d.   A small entrepreneurial middle-class and a large low-income agricultural class.
    e.   A low-population country comes to be dominated by infant industries.

10. In many low-income countries the city population has much greater influence in government than the rural population. One common result is price controls on farm products. What do you think is the effect of this policy on (a) food production, (b) the emergence of dual food markets, (c) administrative costs, and (d) the difficulty in converting a planned economy into a free-market economy?

---

[20]World Bank, *World Development Report 1987* (New York: Oxford University Press, 1987).

[21]Ibid., 26.

APPLICATION ANALYSIS

1. Development economists are aware that the share of manufacturing (mining and construction, too) in gross domestic product (GDP) has risen in the early stages of industrialization, peaked, and subsequently tapered off as shown in the figure. Output per capita, however, has continued to improve. Moreover, the service sector's share of the economy has risen over the industrial history of industrialized nations, and for a longer time than the manufacturing sector's.

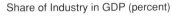
Share of Industry in GDP (percent)

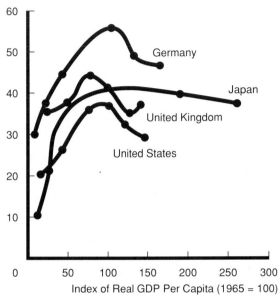

Note: The six data points shown for each country represent the following approximate time periods: (from left to right) 1870, 1913, 1950, 1965, 1975, and 1984. Industry includes manufacturing, mining, and construction.

a. What would you conclude about the trend of agriculture's share of GDP?

b. Why has the industrial sector trended upward, peaked, and then declined over time relative to the service sector?

c. In the early historical stages of industrialization before World War II, why did the textile industry play a large role? Might it have anything to do with low family incomes in the early development stage?

d. After World War II, industrialized countries began to reduce their relative amount of production of textiles and to increase, for example, iron and steel production. Economies of scale played a large part in making these basic metal operations profitable. Today these plants are smaller and more efficient. What caused scale economies to be less important, and why were they so important to begin with?

e. Has industrial growth been an *extensive* or *intensive* phenomenon?

f. Why is it possible for a country with a large population to industrialize earlier than one with a small population?

g. What is meant by infrastructure? What function does it serve for economic development?

h. Do you think the history of the Western world would have been different if southern Europe had been naturally rich in such mineral resources as coal and iron rather than northern Europe, and if southern European countries had been politically unified before the northern European countries?

CHAPTER

22

COMPARATIVE ECONOMIC SYSTEMS

....

IN THIS CHAPTER YOU WILL LEARN:

**How economic systems
differ**

•

**How central plans are
formulated in some Socialist
economies**

•

**What special incentives
Socialist governments use to
increase production**

•

**Which economic problems
the Soviet Union and China
encounter today**

*This chapter was written
by H. Stephen Gardner
of Baylor University.*

THE SOVIET BUDGET CRISIS

"At one time we believed that the outside world had its own economic processes, and we had ours. Now I think that we are just experiencing the normal economic processes." Thus, the Soviet Finance Minister, Boris Gostev, acknowledged in 1988 that the basic laws of economics are applicable to Socialist countries. Resources are scarce, choices must be made, and costs must be measured in terms of forgone opportunities.

What economic processes did Gostev have in mind? Earlier that day, in a speech to the Soviet parliament, he admitted for the first time that his government was running an enormous deficit. Indeed, he admitted that the Soviet government had been in the red for about ten years, while the published budgets had always shown surpluses.

How could this happen in a centrally planned economy? The Soviet government has direct control over production, prices, incomes, foreign trade, taxes, and expenditures. In a one-part political system, there is little need for national leaders to "buy" votes with budgetary expenditures and tax breaks.

With their broad, dictatorial power, why have central planners been unable to balance the books? What are the causes and consequences of the Soviet deficit?

WHAT'S NEXT IN CHINESE AGRICULTURE?

Since World War II, no country has suffered more twists and turns in economic policy than China. Consider, for example, the changing pattern of agricultural organizations. After the 1949 Communist takeover, land was taken from the old nobility and distributed to the poorer peasants; family farming became the dominant mode of organization. Later in the 1950s, the families were forced to merge into large collectives, and then the collectives were merged into enormous communes. Communal organization of agriculture continued through the 1960s and 1970s, but the operation of the system continued to change.

Quite suddenly, in the late 1970s, the Chinese government launched a new agricultural revolution. This time, the communes were dissolved, and control of the land was returned to individual families. By and large, the return to family farming has been a huge success, but a number of new problems have developed, and the system is still evolving. The current trend is toward creation of larger farms.

Why is this needed? Why is it difficult to find a single style of agricultural organization that is efficient for all of China?

• I N T R O D U C T I O N •

In Chapter 1, we said that an economic system is the institutional means by which scarce resources are employed to satisfy the wants of society. Every country has its own unique economic system, molded by cultural, political, and historical forces; its own blend of free markets and governmental controls; its own public and private forms of ownership and work incentives; and its own national objectives.

Different kinds of economic systems are described in this chapter, with emphasis on how each is organized. Specifically, special features of two important Communist economic systems, the Soviet economy and the Chinese economy, are described. Understanding these unique systems rounds out the picture of macroeconomics, because these two economies represent good comparisons to the free-market economies of the United States and other Western nations. •

OWNERSHIP OF RESOURCES

Typically, the owner of a farm or factory has the right to control its operation and to retain its profits. Thus, the system of ownership in a country has an important influence on the distribution of economic power, authority, income, and wealth. A useful distinction can be made between **Capitalist systems**, where resources are owned predominantly by private individuals, and **Socialist systems**, where resources are owned socially.

> *Capitalist systems are economic systems in which individuals own the factors of production. Owners earn profits in free markets.*

> *Socialist systems are economic systems in which government owns the factors of production.*

This text has studied the U.S. economy as a primary example of a capitalistic system. The Soviet Union and China exist as two extreme examples of Socialist economies. These two economies use **centrally planned socialism**.

> *Centrally planned socialism occurs in nations where governments own the factors of production and use central planning to decide what will be produced.*

In the Soviet Union, for example, public boards and ministries decide what will be produced. Consumers must buy what is available.

Some countries, such as Sweden, France, and India, use a mix of socialism and markets by having government ownership, but allowing the marketplace to determine resource allocations. These economies have **mixed economic systems**.

> *In mixed economic systems government owns the factors of production, but decisions about what will be produced are made in the marketplace.*

Most countries have a mixture of private and public property. In Western Europe, for example, private ownership is predominant, but nationalized companies account for about 5 percent of total employment. Socialism is the norm in Polish industry, but most agricultural land is owned by private farmers. In most of the world, the current trend is toward privatization, a practice through which industries, services, and businesses that have typically been owned by the state are being sold to private owners.

COORDINATION OF PRODUCTION AND EXCHANGE

An important task of any economic system is to coordinate the complex network of production and exchange of goods and resources. The output of each industry must coincide with the requirements of other industries, with demand, and with the foreign market.

In a market economy, the coordination problem is addressed by the spontaneous action of supply, demand and the price system. A gasoline shortage causes the price of gasoline to rise; that gives refiners an incentive to increase production and drivers an incentive to reduce consumption. In a centrally planned or command economy, the government attempts to coordinate production by decree. When central planners are aware of a gasoline shortage, they may order an increase in production or imports, or they may try to reduce domestic consumption of gasoline.

Typically, Communist countries rely heavily on central planning and Capitalist countries rely on the market system, but this is not always true. Yugoslavia, for example, has a market Socialist economy. The factories are owned and managed by workers' cooperatives (socialism), but they exchange products in relatively free markets, at prices set by supply and demand. The government retains control over investments and worker compensation. No country has a pure market system or a pure system of central planning; each has its own mixture of spontaneous market activity and governmental control.

INCENTIVE SYSTEMS

Economic systems differ according to the incentives they use to reward socially desirable behavior and to discourage inappropriate actions. **Material incentives**, which are based on monetary or other material rewards, are used in most modern economies, but they take many forms.

> *Material incentives are money and material rewards businesses and workers receive as compensation.*

In a market system, material rewards are regulated by the spontaneous fluctuation of prices and profit levels. In a command economy, bonus income is typically paid for fulfillment of plan assignments.

Moral incentives elicit desirable behavior by appealing to the emotions: nationalism, company pride, and compassion, to name a few.

> *Moral incentives are means by which governments attempt to cause businesses and workers to act in the nation's economic best interests.*

These incentives are manipulated with slogans, songs, peer pressure, contests, and other psychological devices. In China, Chairman Mao attempted to reduce the role of material incentives and rely predominantly on "Socialist morality" during his Cultural Revolution. Since Mao's death in 1976, the Chinese have returned to heavy reliance on material rewards.

Capitalist economies also rely on moral incentives. For example, during World War II, when the United States faced an energy crisis, Americans cooperated to save energy by shutting down Christmas lights. During the high inflation years of the 1970s, President Nixon issued wage–price guidelines, which businesses and unions could use as moral incentives to keep prices down.

Coercive incentives, such as fear of imprisonment, are used by most countries to insure compliance with laws and payment of taxes.

> *Coercive incentives are legal, police, and military means countries use to insure compliance with economic laws and statutes.*

Many countries have systems of compulsory military service, and coercion has been used pervasively by slave states and totalitarian regimes. The declining role of coercive incentives can be explained on moral grounds, or it can be explained by the rising importance of education, skill, and creativity in modern societies.

NATIONAL OBJECTIVES

Quite often, the label used to classify an economic system is inspired by the most prominent objective pursued by that society. In a free-enterprise system, a high value is placed on individual economic freedom. In a welfare state, individual autonomy may be sacrificed to some "higher" social objective, such as income equality, full employment, or public health and education. Fascism is a mixture of Capitalist ownership and coercive incentives with a goal of national military power.

Because every country has its own national objectives, culture, geography, and level of economic development, no single economic system is optimal for them all. Central planning can respond quickly to a single objective, such as mobilization for war. The market system has the advantages of microeconomic efficiency and flexibility. In countries dependent on agriculture and foreign trade, where continuous adjustments must be made to respond to the changing natural and international environment, central planning has been most unsuccessful. Governmental programs to redistribute income are more politically acceptable in Sweden, with its small, homogeneous population, than in the United States, with its racial and geographic divisions.

THE SOVIET ECONOMY

The Soviet Union has the second largest economy in the world, with a GNP slightly over half that of the United States. According to 1985 figures, GNP in the United States was $3,887 billion, and GNP for the Soviet Union was $2,129 billion. The Soviet Union's military power is second to none. Just as important, the U.S.S.R. was the first country to adopt a system of Socialist central planning. This became the prototype for new economic systems in Eastern Europe, China, Cuba, and Mongolia.

BRIEF ECONOMIC HISTORY

In 1917, under the leadership of V. I. Lenin, the Bolshevist revolutionaries (later known as the Communist party) took control of the Russian government. They immediately found themselves engaged in foreign hostilities and a civil war against forces loyal to the ruling regime.

To meet these challenges, the Bolsheviks adopted a military style of economic organization known as War Communism. To feed the troops and industrial workers, they required the farmers to surrender all "surplus" crops beyond the survival needs of their families. The farmers were left with little incentive to produce. Rapid growth of the money supply sent inflation soaring, and normal retail trade was replaced by rationing. This, in turn, encouraged graft and corruption. Nearly all industrial companies were nationalized, although the government had neither the information nor the expertise to manage them. The combination of civil war and misguided policies had disastrous consequences. Agricultural and industrial production both plummeted.

In 1921, in an effort to recover from the devastation of the civil war, Lenin adopted a system of market socialism known as the New Economic Policy (NEP). Forced requisitioning in agriculture was replaced by a progressive tax — the farmers knew that if they produced more, they could keep more. Inflation was controlled, and retail trade was revived. Many enterprises that were nationalized under War Communism were leased to independent entrepreneurs. Only the "commanding heights of industry" — fuel, heavy industry, banking, transportation, and foreign trade — were kept under direct control.

The NEP, with its improved systems of work incentives, management, and exchange, encouraged a rapid economic recovery. Prewar levels of agricultural and industrial production were restored by 1927. On the other hand, the market system produced wide income differentials, which were not easily justified in a Socialist state. The market system also perpetuated the agricultural orientation of the economy, in keeping with the Soviet Union's comparative advantage. Some Soviet leaders favored a crash program to build an industrial society and to strengthen the nation's military capabilities. This position eventually was adopted by Stalin, who came to power after Lenin's death in 1924.

In 1928, Stalin launched the First Five-Year Plan, which set wildly optimistic growth targets for all sectors of the economy, but placed the highest priority on industrial expansion. To feed the growing industrial population, Stalin revived forced requisitioning and initiated a massive drive to collectivize agriculture. The peasants violently resisted collectivization; some of them destroyed their buildings and livestock to withhold them from the government. Nevertheless, by 1932 about two-thirds of the rural population worked under Communist party control on collective farms.

Few of the targets of the First Five-Year Plan were fulfilled, but it created a new system of central planning and quickly moved resources from agriculture to industry. The growth of the military-industrial base made it possible to repel Hitler's invasion during World War II, but the Soviet Union was eventually transformed from a large exporter of food to a large importer.

CENTRAL PLANNING

The institutions and methods used to formulate Soviet central plans were developed in the 1930s, and they have changed little since that time. Based on priorities set by the Communist party leaders, the State Planning Commission, or **Gosplan**, first compiles a rough draft of a plan.

Gosplan is the organization in the Soviet Union responsible for central planning.

TABLE 22.1
A Material Balance Table

SOURCES	USES
Production	Productive uses
Imports	Exports
Beginning stocks	Ending stocks
	Personal consumption
Total	Total

This first draft of the plan sets a few targets or control figures for each industry. Based on these guidelines, the industrial ministries and their subordinate enterprises prepare detailed plan proposals, which include output targets and input requirements.

Perhaps the most difficult task performed by Gosplan is to combine the proposals of the individual ministries into a single, internally consistent plan. For this purpose, they compile a set of **material balance tables.**

Material balance tables estimate production needs for a commodity, input needed to produce that commodity, and projected consumption levels and needs.

Each of these is a statement of planned sources and used of a product (see Table 22.1), usually measured in tons or other physical units. For example, a table for gasoline would include production estimates from the Ministry of Petroleum Refining, estimates of productive uses from all of the industrial ministries that use gasoline, estimates of exports and imports from the Ministry of Foreign Economic Relations, and estimates of consumer demand from the Ministry of Trade.

If the proposed uses of gasoline exceed the proposed sources, the central planners must adjust the material balance tables to prevent a shortage. This can become very complicated, because an adjustment in one table logically requires changes in many others. An increase in gasoline production, for example, should entail an increase in productive uses of crude oil. If gasoline deliveries to farmers are reduced, planned production of agricultural goods should be cut.

In a market system, these adjustments would occur automatically, based on the interaction of supply, demand, and prices. Central planners, with limited time and information, can make only a few arbitrary adjustments to the material balances. Thus, their final plan is generally inconsistent and unrealistic. It cannot be fulfilled as it is written.

PLAN EXECUTION

How has the Soviet economy been able to operate for more than 60 years, with many outstanding achievements, on the basis of unrealistic plans? In fact, the plans are adjusted throughout the periods of their fulfillment, and they are supplemented by legal and illegal market activities. Throughout the year, when enterprises cannot obtain the raw materials they need to meet their output targets, they appeal to central planners for lower targets or additional supplies. The planners respond to these requests according to the so-called **priority principle.**

According to Soviet planners, the priority principle guarantees that resources will be available for high-priority industrial projects, with other projects receiving materials only after priorities have been met.

Resources are distributed first to the industries that are pivotal to the overall execution of the plan, such as energy and steel, and to enterprises that produce exports.

When an enterprise cannot obtain the supplies it needs through legal channels, it may resort to black-market activity. Much of this is handled on a barter basis; scarce supplies are exchanged for other scarce supplies.[1] Alternatively, the enterprise may attempt to produce the supplies for itself; a radio manufacturer may also produce wire, sacrificing the efficiency of large-scale production. Finally, if supplies cannot be obtained, the enterprise may redesign the final product, which usually means a reduction of quality. An automobile manufacturer, for example, may produce a thinner chassis or skimp on the amount of steel used to reinforce the body of the car.

Presently, the scope of legal market activity is very limited. Farm families are allowed to sell food from their small garden plot on legal markets at prices set by supply and demand. Since 1987, the Law on Individual Enterprise has allowed private provision of small-scale services, such as home repair. If implemented, more recent reforms will enhance the independence of large Socialist enterprises and expand the scope of private activity.

INCENTIVES AND PRICES

Soviet workers and managers are paid a base income related to their occupation, skill, and location, and bonus for fulfillment of plan targets. These bonuses can represent a large addition to one's income — as much as 75 percent for an enterprise director.

An incentive system that rewards plan fulfillment is necessary in a centrally planned economy, but it presents several problems. It encourages enterprise directors to bargain for easy plan targets or to falsify reports when they fail to meet their assignments. It discourages overfulfillment of plant targets by managers who fear the ratchet effect — a high level of production of this year leads to even higher plan targets next year. It emphasizes the quantity of output rather than quality, diversity, and conformity with consumer demand.

Most Soviet prices are strictly controlled by the State Price Committee and held constant for many years at a time. When they are adjusted, wholesale prices are set at levels designed to cover costs of production and provide a small profit to the average factory. The retail price of each product, when adjusted, is designed to strike a rough balance between planned production and consumer demand.

In most cases, the retail price of a product is higher than the wholesale price, and the difference between the two is pocketed by the state as a so-called **turnover tax**, similar to a sales tax.

> *In the Soviet Union, the turnover tax is the difference between wholesale and retail prices.*

In the agricultural sector, the situation is quite different. Soviet agriculture is notoriously inefficient, requiring high wholesale prices to cover costs, but retail food prices have been held down for ideological and political reasons. Consequently, the retail prices of most agricultural goods are lower than the wholesale prices, requiring the government to pay

---

[1]This allocation mechanism should be familiar to viewers of the television program "MASH." Radar, the supply officer, spends much of his time exchanging drugs, equipment, and other scarce items with other MASH units.

subsidies of about 88 billion rubles in 1980 — about 18 percent of all budgetary expenditures. To reduce these subsidies, the Soviet government has announced its intention to increase retail food prices in the early 1990s. When the state turnover tax is positive, government earns revenue. In cases where wholesale prices are greater than retail prices, however, the government subsidizes economic sectors. This creates the potential for deficits.

SOVIET ECONOMIC PERFORMANCE

Summarizing the performance of the Soviet economy in a few words is difficult. This is the country that put the first man in outer space in 1961, and it still holds most of the space endurance records, but it cannot mass produce a dependable disk drive for a personal computer. Indeed, the system of central planning has failed to provide many of the common conveniences of twentieth-century life — brooms with long handles, prepared breakfast cereals, liquid detergent, and toilet paper, to name just a few.

Unemployment and inflation are not entirely absent in the U.S.S.R., but their rates are low. Poverty exists, but its effects are ameliorated by the low prices of food, housing, health care, and other necessities. The Soviet health care system employs more physicians than the system of any other country — one for every 270 people — but the infant mortality rate is triple the U.S. rate and ranks 44th in the world, just behind Uruguay and Sri Lanka.[2]

The Soviet GNP is slightly over half of the U.S. level, and its per capita production of consumer goods is less than one-third the American level. Soviet factory workers have to work twice as long as their American counterparts to buy a loaf of bread or a pound of ground beef, five times as long for a gallon of milk or a bottle of aspirin, and ten times as long for a car or a color television.

In the past, Soviet leaders admitted that their country's standard of living was lower than that of the Western nations, but they could claim they were catching up. Indeed, Soviet GNP grew at an annual rate of about 6 percent in the 1950s, when the American growth rate was less than 4 percent. Since the mid-1960s, however, the Soviet growth rate has trended downward more rapidly than the American rate, as shown in Figure 22.1. Thus, the Soviet standard of living is still far behind the American level, and it is no longer catching up.

SOVIET ECONOMIC REFORMS

Since his assumption of power in 1985, Mikhail Gorbachev has waged an historic campaign to reform the Soviet economic and political system. His goal is to reverse the trend toward stagnation that has plagued the country since the mid-1960s. To do this, he is trying to create a system of market socialism that borrows many ideas from Lenin's New Economic Policy of the 1920s.

The basic strategy of Gorbachev's reform is to grant more independence to the farms and factories, but to hold them responsible for their actions. If the reforms are fully implemented, enterprises will be allowed to make their own production decisions, regulate the size of their work force, negotiate the prices they charge and the wages they pay, borrow

[2]World Bank, *World Development Report 1988* (New York: Oxford University Press, 1988), 278–279 and 286–287.

FIGURE 22.1
Growth Rates of Soviet and American GNP

This figure shows comparative growth rates in GNP for the United States and the Soviet Union over several decades. The United States has a higher standard of living and GNP than the Soviet Union, but during the period from 1950 to 1965 Soviets claimed their growth record was so strong that they would eventually surpass the United States. Indeed during those years the growth rate of GNP (but not actual GNP) in the Soviet Union far outstripped that in the United States. The Soviet prediction did not come true because growth slowed in the Soviet Union in the 1960s, and in the mid-1980s began to drop below the growth rate in the United States.

Sources: U.S. Central Intelligence Agency, *USSR: Measures of Economic Growth and Development, 1950–1980*, U.S. Congress, Joint Economic Committee (Washington, D.C.: U.S. Government Printing Office, 1982); and U.S. Central Intelligence Agency, "Gorbachev's Economic Program," Report to U.S. Congress, Subcommittee on National Security Economics (April 13, 1988).

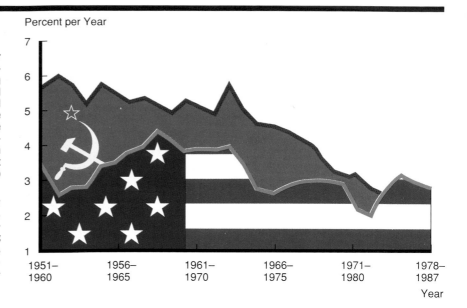

money from independent banks to finance capital investments, and sell securities to their employees. Profitable enterprises will pay a set tax and keep the rest. The 24,000 enterprises that have been unable to balance their books will face the threat of bankruptcy, and their employees will face the threat of unemployment.

Some of these ailing enterprises may be saved by the new Law on Cooperatives, which allows employees to lease factories from the state and run them on their own account. In one recent example, the money-losing Butovo Building Materials Combinat was leased by its 480 workers. Freed from the meddling of higher authorities, the cooperative quickly increased productivity by 30 percent and balanced the books with higher wages. According to the director, "In the past we didn't have any direct interest in what we did. Now we know that if we work well, we'll earn well."[3]

Leasing state property is also supposed to play an important role in agricultural reform. Late in 1988, Gorbachev called for the extension of this system to "the entire agrarian sector." Leases on agricultural land will be written for periods lasting 15, 30, and even 50 years, giving the farmers an incentive to invest in irrigation, buildings, roads, and other improvements. Still, many farmers are reluctant to abandon the fixed wages they are paid on the state and collective farms. "On the lease system, in good conditions, the pay can be many times higher" than the guaranteed wage, according to the general manager of an agricultural complex. "But in bad conditions — and that's very frequent in agriculture — you can get less."[4]

The focus of central planning is supposed to shift from microeconomic control of production and exchange to macroeconomic regulation of taxes, interest rates, and general economic priorities. Presently, the

---

[3]Peter Gumbel, "Soviets Testing Limited Private Initiative at State-Run Plants That Didn't Hack It," *The Wall Street Journal*, October 7, 1988, A10.

[4]Peter Gumbel, "Soviets Try Once More to Straighten Out Old Agricultural Mess," *The Wall Street Journal*, December 2, 1988, A8.

planners are able to control part of enterprise production through a system of compulsory state orders. These accounted for 80 to 100 percent of the output of many enterprises in 1988, but their share is scheduled to decline. In the end, state orders are supposed to apply only to capital goods, for defense needs and large construction projects. Production of consumer goods and services is to be regulated by consumer demand.

The Achilles' heel of Gorbachev's program is the price system. When the government sets prices, it does not allow the forces of supply and demand to operate. Prices that are set too low do not adequately compensate producers. To address this problem, the Soviets started a system of price reform in 1985, allowing some farms and industries to set prices for a portion of their output. For example, collective and state farms must sell at prices set by central planners unless they meet their targets. Having met these targets, they are free to sell up to 30 percent of produce at higher prices. This causes a two-level price system for some Soviet goods and popular discontent among consumers. Students of the Soviet Union wonder if price reform can work if it is done partially in this manner.

THE CHINESE ECONOMY

How do you feed 22 percent of the world's population with only 7 percent of its land? What combination of public and private ownership, market and plan, material and moral incentives, and national objectives is appropriate for this task? Through the years, the leaders of China have addressed these questions in many different ways, causing radical changes in economic policy and performance. Today, the Chinese system is still in a state of flux.

BRIEF ECONOMIC HISTORY

In 1949, after decades of civil war, world war, and political intrigue, the Chinese Communist part gained power on the mainland, led by Chairman Mao Zedong. To speed recovery, the new leaders accepted massive amounts of Soviet economic aid. In the early 1950s, the Soviets built hundreds of factories in China, provided thousands of technical advisors, and taught the fundamentals of Marxism, engineering, and central planning to tens of thousands of Chinese specialists.

Under Soviet guidance, the Chinese carried out a program of land reform from 1950 to 1952 and agricultural collectivization from 1955 to 1957. The First Five-Year Plan (1953 to 1957) reflected the traditional Soviet emphasis on industrialization, with highest priority on developing heavy industry. The goals of the plan were exceeded, but rapid growth of the industrial labor force led to urban food shortages in 1956 and 1957.

In 1958, Chairman Mao took an additional turn to the left and introduced a radical program called the **Great Leap Forward.**

> *The Great Leap Forward was an ambitious plan undertaken by Mao's government to organize China's economy for greater industrial and agricultural production.*

Wildly optimistic growth targets were set for both agriculture and industry. The large collective farms were merged into even larger communes. Massive campaigns encouraged the growth of rural, small-scale industry and the development of water resources. About 2 million so-called backyard blast furnaces were reportedly built in 1958 alone.

Because of a combination of radical policies, loss of Soviet aid, and bad weather, the Great Leap Forward was a horrible failure; agricultural and industrial production plummeted, famine reportedly caused millions of deaths, and the educational system was nearly destroyed. The authority of Chairman Mao declined between 1961 and 1965, and a group of more moderate leaders gained temporary control They tilted investment priorities toward agriculture, strengthened work incentives and technical education, reduced the sizes of communes to make them more manageable, and discourage population growth. The economy regained its former production levels by 1964, but the gap between the rich and the poor began to widen.

Chairman Mao regained power by 1966 and launched another radical program — the *Cultural Revolution.*

Mao's program had three principle objectives: (1) to overturn the existing power structure and reverse the Soviet-style trend toward bureaucratism, (2) to cleanse "New China" of all traditional Chinese and Western culture, and (3) to raise the Socialist Consciousness of the masses.

To fulfill his first two objectives, Mao recruited a revolutionary army of young people, the Red Guard, to conduct tribunals and purges against bureaucrats and "Capitalist roaders." Millions of people were persecuted, and about 34,000 were killed. To fulfill his third objective, Mao attempted to replace material incentives with moral incentives. He reduced income differences between the skilled, unskilled, lazy, and industrious, and subjected workers to peer pressure and ideological indoctrination.

The hostilities and radical policies of the Cultural Revolution did not stop economic progress entirely; the grain crop increased by about one-third between 1966 and 1976. During the same years, however, the Chinese population grew by about one-quarter, or 180 million people. Thus, production barely kept pace with the growing population. Severe restrictions on foreign trade, study, and travel isolated China from advances in foreign technology.

CHINESE ECONOMIC REFORMS

Chairman Mao died in 1976, and a power struggle erupted between the radical Gang of Four, headed by Mao's widow, and a pragmatic faction, headed by Deng Xiaoping. The pragmatists were victorious in the end, and Deng consolidated his power between 1978 and 1980. In 1987, Deng ensured that his policies would continue by installing Zhao Ziyang, another pragmatist, as new leader of the Communist party.

Under pragmatic leadership, the Chinese have enacted a dramatic series of reforms. They have discarded the Maoist emphasis on ideological purity and moved toward market exchange, material incentives, international openness, and some forms of private ownership. The new emphasis on pragmatism is best expressed by Deng's favorite slogan: "It doesn't matter whether a cat is black or white if it can catch mice."

In agriculture, most of the old communes have disappeared, and individual families are able to contract land from the state for their private use. Under a 1988 law, one peasant can sell another his right to use the land. Figure 22.2 shows comparative grain productivity for several different economic programs in China and demonstrates that Deng's program has met with success in the agricultural sector.

In industry, many of the smaller enterprises have been leased to private entrepreneurs, and about 80 percent of the larger enterprises have adopted a contract system. Under the contract system, each factory is supposed to be free of bureaucratic meddling, aside from the obligation to

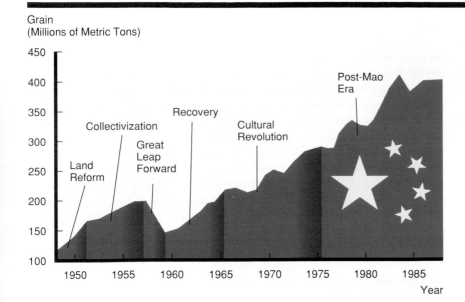

Grain
(Millions of Metric Tons)

FIGURE 22.2
Chinese Grain Production, 1949–1988

This illustration shows the increase in the production of metric tons of grain during three and a half decades and over several different eras of economic and political reforms in China. Grain production dramatically dropped during the Great Leap Forward period, which was a radical time in China's history. Clearly, the post-Mao era has been the most successful of all socioeconomic programs in terms of grain production. Students of China attribute much of the success to implementation of market incentives and forms of private ownership.

Source: Chinese State Statistical Bureau.

deliver an agreed amount of output to the state at a fixed price. Additional output can be sold to finance higher wages or capital investment.

In a daring break from Socialist orthodoxy, some Chinese enterprises have raised investment capital by selling stocks and bonds. The first issues appeared in 1980, and they could be sold only to the employees of the affected enterprises. These limits were lifted in 1984, and the nation's first stock exchange opened in Shanghai in 1986. By the end of that year, exchanges had been opened in several other cities, and securities were offered by about 7,000 enterprises. New restrictions were imposed on stock transactions in 1987, after student demonstrations provoked a backlash against liberalization. More recently, however, Chairman Zhao announced that "the shareholding system will be carried out step by step," and some Chinese economists believe that the system will extend to all state-owned enterprises by 1995.[5]

The Chinese birth control campaign has attracted international attention. Since 1980, married couples have been encouraged to have only one child. One-child families are given income bonuses, longer maternity allowances, larger pensions, and priority in housing, education, and medical care. Families with additional children are subject to fines and taxes. The government provides free contraceptives and abortions and takes an aggressive approach to family planning.

Because of these and other actions, the annual growth rate of the population fell from about 2.2 percent between 1965 and 1980 to 1.2 percent between 1980 and 1986 — the lowest rate for any low-income country.[6] In 1987, however, a large segment of the population reached childbearing age, and the growth rate climbed to 1.4 percent. If that rate continues, there will be another 22 million mouths to feed every year. Thus, the government has doubled the fine for having a second child, and

[5]Nicholas Kristof, "China, Seeking More Efficiency, Looks to a Stock Market System," *The New York Times*, December 5, 1988, 1.

[6]World Bank, *World Development Report 1988* (New York: Oxford University Press, 1988), 274.

local officials have added even more force to their family planning programs.[7]

According to a popular slogan, the Chinese reforms are supposed to create a system in which "the state regulates the market, and the market guides the enterprises" — market, that is, with strong macroeconomic management. Unfortunately, the Chinese have found it just as difficult to establish market socialism as the Soviets, and for similar reasons.

For years, the Chinese central bank has been printing money to finance the government's mounting budget deficits and to prop up unprofitable state-run enterprises. As prices have been released from control, they have reacted to the large and growing money supply. Consumer price inflation jumped from an annual rate of about 4 percent from 1980 to 1986 to over 20 percent in 1988. Accelerated inflation reduced the living standards of urban workers, and rumors of new price increases triggered bank runs and panic buying all across the country. Toward the end of 1988, the government announced a new "rectification campaign" to restore order. The state would postpone price reforms, cut investment, suspend construction projects, and maintain tighter control over the money supply.

The leaders of China and the Soviet Union are engaged in a gentle balancing act. They must reform their economies slowly enough to maintain economic and political order and quickly enough to show results and maintain momentum. "We must make sure that reform is not stopped," Chairman Zhao insists. "We must keep going despite difficulties because once we stop, we will return to the old track."[8]

SUMMARY

1. In Capitalist countries, resources are owned privately. In Socialist countries, resources may be owned by the state or by cooperatives. In mixed economic systems, resources are state owned, but the market system works to set prices.

2. Production and exchange may be coordinated by markets or by central commands.

3. All countries use a combination of material incentives, moral incentives, and coercion to encourage and enforce desired behavior.

4. The differences between a free-enterprise system, a welfare state, and a Fascist system are related to national objectives and political arrangements.

5. The Soviet Union has experimented with several economic systems since the Bolshevik Revolution. The system of central planning and forced industrialization began in 1928, but current reforms, if fully implemented, will move the country back toward more use of markets.

6. An important tool used by Soviet central planners is the material balance table, which is a statement of sources and uses of a particular product. When problems develop in execution of the plan, resources are allocated according to the priority principle.

7. Soviet incentives are based on the payment of bonuses for plan fulfillment. Thus, managers bargain for low plan targets and are tempted to emphasize quantity over quality of production.

---

[7]Cheng Gang, "China Faces Another Baby Boom," *Beijing Review* (July 4–10, 1988), 29–30; and Adi Ignatius, "China's Birthrate Rises Again Despite a Policy of One-Child Families," *The Wall Street Journal*, July 14, 1988, 1.

[8]Adi Ignatius, "Beijing, Faced With Economic Crisis, Draws Back From Liberalization Drive," *The Wall Street Journal*, September 26, 1988, 17.

8. Prices are strictly controlled in the Soviet Union. They are based on production costs at the wholesale level and on consumer demand and political criteria at the retail level.

9. The deceleration of economic growth since the 1950s has encouraged the Soviet leaders to adopt an ambitious program of reforms, granting greater autonomy and responsibility to farms and factories and limiting the central planners to macroeconomic regulation.

10. After World War II, the introduction of socialism in China was heavily influenced by the Soviet model of collectivization, planning, and industrialization.

11. The Chinese Great Leap Forward, which began in 1958, was based on wildly optimistic targets and on radical communization of the rural sector.

12. Recent Chinese economic reforms have emphasized modernization over ideological purity, stronger material incentives, international openness, some forms of private ownership, and strict measures to control population growth.

THE SOVIET BUDGET CRISIS

Since World War II, the Soviet government had never reported a budget deficit. Every year, regardless of crop failures, escalation of the arms race, or commitment of troops to Afghanistan, the finance minister would forecast a small surplus of revenues over expenditures. These budget reports were never plausible, and estimates prepared in the West revealed persistent deficits, but the veil of secrecy was never raised in the Soviet Union.[9]

Never, that is, until early 1988, when articles in Soviet newspapers and scholarly journals began to challenge the party line. In late June, in a speech to the Communist party conference, Mikhail Gorbachev gave the problem official recognition:

> Comrades, we must say frankly that we underestimated the full depth and gravity of the . . . stagnation of past years. There was a great deal that we simply did not know and are only now seeing . . . For many years, the state's expenditures grew more rapidly than revenues. The budget deficit presses on the market, undermines the stability of the ruble (the Soviet dollar) and of monetary circulation in general, and gives rise to inflationary processes . . . .[10]

Thus, Gorbachev acknowledged that Socialist countries are not immune to the laws of money and finance. If the government does not finance its expenditures through taxation or public borrowing, it must borrow money from the central bank — that is, it must "run the monetary printing press." If the money supply grows much more rapidly than the stock of goods, inflation is the likely result. In a country with price controls, "inflationary processes" may take the form of longer lines for goods, rising prices on the black market, or undesired growth of savings accounts.

In his October budget report to the Soviet parliament, Finance Minister Gostev projected a 1989 deficit of 36 billion rubles — about 4 percent

---

[9]Careful studies prepared in the West include Igor Birman, *Secret Incomes of the Soviet State Budget* (The Hague: Martinus Nijhoff, 1981); and Mark Harrison, "The USSR State Budget Under Late Stalinism," *Economics of Planning*, vol. 20, no. 3 (1986).

[10]*Pravda*, June 29, 1988, 2.

TABLE 22.2
Estimated Soviet State Budget, 1989 (Billions of Rubles)

TOTAL EXPENDITURES		495
Social Expenditures		258
Food price subsidies	88	
Pensions and social insurance	74	
Education and science	54	
Health	25	
Other price subsidies	15	
Rent subsidies	2	
Defense expenditures		111
Hardware procurement	80	
Personnel and construction	20	
Research and development	11	
State capital investments		82
Foreign aid and trade subsidies		29
Aid to unprofitable enterprises		11
State administration		3
Other expenditures		1
TOTAL REVENUES		395
Deductions from profits		121
Turnover tax		104
Foreign trade revenues		60
Personal taxes		39
Social insurance taxes		31
Other revenues		40

Sources: Compiled and recalculated from the annual budget report in *Pravda,* October 28, 1988, 4–5; and estimates in *Planecon Report*, November 4, 1988, 10. We have excluded 64 billion rubles of "loan funds" from revenues (see explanation in the text).

of Soviet GNP. After all the years of denial, this was a stunning revelation, but it still understated the problem. In his listing of budget revenues, Mr. Gostev included 64 billion rubles of "resources of the state loan fund." He did not identify the sources of these funds (i.e., borrowing from the public or the state bank), but he did say that they "involve an increase in the state debt."

As some Soviet economists have acknowledged, the loan fund is not a true source of revenue, but a source of debt financing. Properly measured, the budget deficit for 1989 seems to be 100 billion rubles — the 36 billion admitted by Mr. Gostev and an additional 64 billion of borrowing. If true, that means the deficit is an astounding 10 percent of Soviet GNP, compared with an American deficit that is about 3 percent of GNP. An estimate of the breakdown of the Soviet Union's federal budget is shown in Table 22.2.

According to the budget estimates shown in Figure 22.3, the Soviet deficit was relatively small and stable until 1985 — about 10 to 17 billion rubles per year — and then jumped by 83 billion from 1986 to 1989. This deficit is similar to the U.S. deficit in the sense that it represents an excess of spending over revenues. Significantly, 1985 was the year of Gorbachev's ascent to power, and his policies were partially responsible for the acceleration of spending and retardation of revenues.

What has caused the deficit? On the expenditure side, rising food subsidies apparently dealt the heaviest blow to the budget. In 1983, when

Billions of Rubles

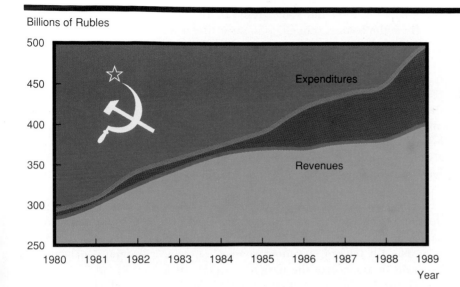

FIGURE 22.3
Estimated Soviet State Budgets, 1980–1989

In the Soviet Union, as in Western nations, the government runs budget deficits. This figure shows that expenditures have been greater than revenues for the entire decade of the 1980s. The deficit began to increase significantly in the mid-1980s when the rate of expenditures began to grow much faster than revenues. To finance the deficit, the government borrows from the public and the state bank. Part of the deficit is composed of the difference between wholesale and retail prices. When Soviet retail prices are lower than wholesale prices, the government subsidizes that industry.

Sources: U.S. Central Intelligence Agency, *USSR: Sharply Higher Budget Deficits Threaten Perestroyka*, September 1988, Table A-4; and *Planecon Report*, November 4, 1988, 10.

Gorbachev was the Communist party official responsible for agriculture, he supported the food program that increased wholesale prices paid to farmers, but left most retail prices unchanged. As you will recall from the chapter, the difference between wholesale prices and retail prices represents government revenue and a turnover tax when it is positive. When it is negative, as in the case of agriculture, it represents government debt or a subsidy. Larger subsidies on each unit of production, coupled with growing food production, caused budgetary expenditures to rise from 55 billion rubles in 1985 to 88 billion rubles in 1989. Growth in budgetary spending was also driven by Gorbachev's investment program, designed to modernize the outmoded capital stock by higher priorities for public health and education.

The largest source of revenue for the Soviet budget is a levy on over half of all enterprise profits. Profit tax receipts increased by only 2 billion rubles from 1986 to 1989, after a rise of 30 billion rubles from 1981 to 1985. One apparent reason for the slower growth of profits is Gorbachev's program to improve product quality. Traditionally, Soviet factories have employed their own product inspectors, who are vulnerable to pressure from management to approve shoddy goods. Since 1987, this function has been shifted to an independent State Inspection Office. In some cases, the new inspectors have reportedly rejected 70 percent of a factory's goods. Thus, the producers are under new pressure to raise their standards, but only at the cost of lower sales, profits, and budget revenue.

Another Gorbachev initiative that has caused the state budget to be imbalanced is his antialcohol campaign. Beginning in 1985, he slashed the production of vodka, closed more than two-thirds of the country's liquor stores, forbade restaurants to serve drinks before 2 P.M., and increased the fine for drinking at work to about one-fourth of the average monthly wage. The reduction of wine and liquor sales has reportedly led to reductions in crime, domestic violence, and divorce, but the finance minister reports that it has also caused a 36 billion ruble loss of turnover tax revenues.

Gorbachev cannot be held responsible, of course, for the budgetary impact of the disasters in Chernobyl and Armenia. Neither is he accountable for the 26 billion ruble reduction in budgetary revenues from foreign trade between 1986 and 1989 caused by the falling international price of oil. He is the leader, though, who must find a way to cope with the fiscal crisis.

Some actions have already been taken to reduce the deficit. Foreign trade reforms initiated in 1987 are designed to reduce the country's heavy reliance on energy exports. Also in 1987, the government registered the first bankruptcy of a state enterprise. "It is necessary," says the finance minister, "to repudiate the existing practice of mechanically covering losses. Unprofitable enterprises live at others' expense and incur extensive losses that have no perceptible impact on pay." The danger is that bankruptcies may create an unacceptable level of unemployment and cause opposition to the reforms.

The plan for 1989 calls for a massive shift of resources toward production of consumer goods; these are needed to reduce inflationary pressure, maintain support for the reforms, and generate turnover tax revenue. The tilt toward consumer goods, however, will delay Gorbachev's program to modernize the nation's capital stock.

To resolve their budgetary crisis, the Soviets must make hard choices between consumer goods and investment resources, education and health, housing and national defense. Scarcity is a fact of economic life in the West and in the East. "In short," Gorbachev told the 1988 party conference, "it is important to learn to live within our means."

PREVIEW 22.2 ANALYSIS

WHAT'S NEXT IN CHINESE AGRICULTURE?

early three-quarters of China's massive work force is engaged in agriculture, and more than half of the consumer budget is used for food. The health of the economy depends more on the annual grain yield than on any other variable, be it aggregate demand, interest rates, or the exchange rate. Thus, the radical shifts in Chinese agricultural policy since World War II deserve special attention.

Between 1949 and 1952, the new Communist regime redistributed about 44 percent of the arable land in China from rich landlords and farmers to poor and landless peasants. Family farming became the dominant mode of organization, and family landholdings were roughly equal in each village. The land reform provided stronger work incentives and greater income equality, and grain yields increased quickly during this period of recovery from war.

Between 1952 and 1958, agriculture was gradually collectivized into Soviet-style cooperatives, each with about 200 families. Work was performed collectively, and laborers were paid for earning work points, based on time, effort, skill, and political attitude. Work incentives were weaker under this system because the link between individual effort and income was indirect and obscure. Each household was allowed, however, to keep a small private plot, and the large collectives were able to make better use of machinery than family farms. Grain production continued to increase during these years, but at a slower rate.

During the Great Leap Forward (1958 to 1960), the collectives were merged quickly into enormous communes, each with about 5,000 families, and individual families were deprived of their private plots. A system of work points was still employed formally, but much of the food was distributed according to need. According to Mao's conception of socialism, the commune should share equally "from one big pot." As the link between effort and income grew ever more obscure, a combination of weak incentives, disruptive reorganization, and weather problems caused grain production to fall more than 25 percent between 1958 and 1960, resulting in millions of deaths.

Between 1961 and 1965, after the failure of the Great Leap Forward, the average commune was reduced in size from 5,000 to about 1,700 households, and individual incomes were linked to the performance of production teams, each with about 20 to 30 households. About 7 percent of the land suitable for farming was returned to the families in small private plots.[11] A handful of local leaders even experimented with an early version of the "household responsibility system," whereby a family was allotted a parcel of land and was required to deliver an agreed amount of output to the community. Any surplus production over the contracted amount was kept by the family.[12] Thus, work incentives improved substantially, and, together with an increase in agricultural investment, these institutional reforms helped China to recover its 1958 level of grain production by 1966.

The Cultural Revolution broke out in 1966, and Mao put an end to experimentation with responsibility systems. Otherwise, the system of agricultural organization changed very little during these years. Most importantly, the radical left did not try again to deprive peasants of their private plots. Thus, the Cultural Revolution was not as disruptive as the Great Leap Forward, and grain production increased in all but two years between 1965 and 1976. Unfortunately, however, it barely exceeded the growth of the population.

After Mao's death in 1976, some local officials returned to their secret experiments with household responsibility systems. These did not easily gain official acceptance, and they were specifically forbidden by a document issued in 1978. Nevertheless, family farming began to spread through the country, and in late 1979 it was legalized for residents of remote regions.[13] After Deng Xiaoping consolidated his power in 1980, the household responsibility system became the "mass line" of the party, and by 1984 it covered 98 percent of all farm families. In a few short years, the average size of a Chinese farm fell from 1,560 acres to less than one acre; from 13,000 people to a single family.

Initially, the return to family farming was a huge success; grain production climbed by about 44 percent between 1977 and 1984, while the Chinese population grew by 9 percent. Between 1985 and 1988, however, grain production stagnated. An editor of the *Beijing Review* declared in 1988 that "problems in agriculture are now the greatest factor restricting the development of the national economy."[14]

A number of factors, including poor weather and insufficient investment, seem to account for the recent problems in Chinese agriculture. Most importantly, however, it seems that the Chinese political system has driven the household responsibility system to an extreme. The system was adopted voluntarily where it was most appropriate — in poor villages with little agricultural machinery. When rich collectives were forced to

[11]Dwight Perkins, "Reforming China's Economic System," *Journal of Economic Literature* 26 (June 1988): 605–607.

[12]On the early development of the responsibility system, see Marshall Goldman, *Gorbachev's Challenge* (New York: W. W. Norton, 1987), 182–185.

[13]Pat Howard, *Breaking the Iron Rice Bowl* (Armonk, NY: M. E. Sharpe, Inc., 1988), 52.

[14]Wei Min, "Greater Investment in Agriculture," *Beijing Review*, December 26, 1988– January 1, 1989, 7.

divide into tiny family farms, they could no longer use their machinery efficiently.

Thus, a new movement is afoot to allow farmers to accumulate large parcels of land. This will probably lead to greater income inequality, but the *Beijing Review* has adopted a very Western analysis of the possible benefits: "The introduction of appropriate economies of scale will help raise the fertility and productivity of the land and so benefit grain production, and bring about the specialization, commercialization, and modernization of agriculture."[15]

---

[15]Ibid.

REQUIRED ECONOMIC CONCEPTS

Capitalist systems

Socialist systems

Centrally planned socialism

Mixed economic systems

Material incentives

Moral incentives

Coercive incentives

Gosplan

Material balance tables

Priority principle

Turnover tax

Great Leap Forward

Cultural Revolution

KEY QUESTIONS

1. What are the two major kinds of economic systems?
2. Are industrialized economies of the world pure Capitalist, pure Socialist, or do they combine elements of both capitalism and socialism?
3. How does a command economy coordinate production? A Capitalist system?
4. What characterizes mixed economic systems like Sweden's or India's?
5. Name three kinds of economic incentives.
6. What is one definition of fascism?
7. Who led the Bolshevik revolution in Russia in 1917?
8. What is Gosplan? A material balance table? A five-year plan?
9. What is the Soviet economy's priority principle?
10. What is one problem with the incentive system in a command economy that is based on meeting production goals? What is the ratchet effect?
11. What is the basic strategy of Gorbachev's reforms?
12. What are three major economic reform movements that have occurred in China since 1949?
13. What are some of the characteristics of Deng Xiaoping's economic reforms? What is the contract system?
14. What is the Soviet turnover tax?
15. Has the Soviet Socialist economy run budget deficits?

PROBLEMS

1. "Under capitalism prices determine the level of output. Under planned socialism the level of output determines prices." Interpret.
2. Is capitalism incompatible with planning? Is socialism incompatible with free markets? Give some examples.

3. It is said that business cycles occur in capitalistic economies because they are unplanned economies and, therefore, subject to uncertainties that derive from the interaction of many individual decisions, while planned central economies do not experience business cycles.

   a. Are capitalistic free markets disorderly and uncoordinated? If not, by what process are they coordinated?

   b. Is the Soviet economy exempt from market uncertainties? Does the fact that world crude oil prices in the early 1980s fell from $31 a barrel to $14 a barrel in less than 6 months, and that the Soviet Union is a major producer of oil, help you to answer the question?

4. The following is a partial quote from writer Michael Novak: "Socialism is a system built on belief in human goodness, capitalism on human selfishness and sin. God's heart may have been Socialist but His design was Capitalist. Capitalism, rubbing sinner against sinner, makes even dry wood yield a spark of grace, whereas socialism has an innate tendency toward authoritarianism."

   a. Do you detect echoes of Adam Smith in the quote? Comment.

   b. Vested interest plays a big role in the political and economic life of the United States. Have acts of vested interest been eliminated in Socialist Soviet Union and mainland China?

   c. Scalpers hawk scarce, high-priced tickets in the United States. Soviet factory managers sometimes resort to black markets to purchase input and meet their production goals. Are the scalpers and managers being selfish or are they serving the public interest?

5. George Orwell wrote in his novel *Animal Farm* that the new masters (the pigs) became almost indistinguishable from the former master (Jones). The outstanding Polish economist Oskar Lange (1904–1965) (pronounced Lon-ga) argued that after the institutional structuring needed to establish planning most of the other freedoms now associated with market economies can be restored. Does the Soviet experience support the Orwell or Lange forecast? Does the Chinese experience?

6. Consider the following quotes: (1) Poet Robert Browning, "Oh fancies that might be, oh facts that are." (2) A saying among Polish economists, "Under capitalism man exploits man. Under socialism it's vice versa." Can you detect any common theme in these two quotes relating to the chapter?

7. You may be at a college or university where a number of students have come from mainland China. Can you relate this phenomenon to Mao Zedong's Cultural Revolution? Explain. Did the assault on U.S. colleges and universities by Vietnam War protestors in the late 1960s and early 1970s have any long-term effect on U.S. colleges and universities that is apparent today?

8. Do you believe an imported Western philosophy — Marxism — will continue to be the dominant political ideology in China — a land with a centuries long tradition of tight family structure, Buddhism, Confucianism, and a fundamental practicality?

APPLICATION ANALYSIS

1. Have you observed whether the political attitude on your campus and in many of your classes is mostly liberal or conservative? Why do you think some college students, professors, and intellectuals in the United States seem to prefer socialism to capitalism? Is it because they have a good understanding of economics and society?

• L I S T   O F   A P P L I C A T I O N S •

• PHOTOGRAPHIC CREDITS •

Chapter One
p. 3: Art Resource. p. 4: Kobal Collection/Superstock. p. 5: David Dempster/Offshoot. p. 7: Ron Kimball. p. 15: David Edward Dempster. p. 19: Bob Daemmrich/The Image Works. p. 28: Art Resource. p. 30: Kobal Collection/Superstock. p. 33: David Dempster/Offshoot.

Chapter Two
p. 49: National Maritime Museum. p. 50: Ted Horowitz/The Stock Market. p. 51: S. Franklin/Sygma. p. 54: Adam Woolfitt/Woodfin Camp & Assoc. p. 57: David Edward Dempster. p. 59: David Edward Dempster. p. 71: National Maritime Museum. p. 72: Ted Horowitz/The Stock Market. p. 74: S. Franklin/Sygma. p. 78: David Edward Dempster.

Chapter Three
p. 83: Robert Fried. p. 84: Dallas Chang/Sygma. p. 85: David Edward Dempster. p. 93: John Pinderhughes/The Stock Market. p. 107: Robert Fried. p. 110: Dallas Chang/Sygma. p. 113: David Edward Dempster.

Chapter Four
p. 133: David Alan Harvey/Woodfin Camp & Assoc. p. 134: David Edward Dempster. p. 135: E. Cooper/H. Armstrong Roberts. p. 152: Brock May/Photo Researchers. p. 158: David Alan Harvey/Woodfin Camp & Assoc. p. 163: David Edward Dempster. p. 167: E. Cooper/H. Armstrong Roberts.

Chapter Five
p. 175: Nanoukian/Sygma. p. 176: Will & Deni McIntyre/Photo Researchers. p. 183: Rick Brady/Uniphoto. p. 202: Nanoukain/Sygma. p. 206: Will & Deni McIntyre/Photo Researchers.

Chapter Six
p. 227: David Edward Dempster. p. 228: Craig Hurness/Woodfin Camp & Assoc. p. 229: Comstock. p. 253: David Edward Dempster. p. 256: Craig Hurness/Woodfin Camp & Assoc. p. 258: Comstock.

Chapter Seven
p. 265: Alex Quesada/Woodfin Camp & Assoc. p. 266: Alex Quesada/Woodfin Camp & Assoc. p. 280: NY Daily News. p. 288: Alex Quesada/Woodfin Camp & Assoc.

Chapter Eight
p. 303: MacDonald Photography/The Picture Cube. p. 329: MacDonald Photography/The Picture Cube.

Chapter Nine
p. 345: Susan Steinkamp/Picture Group. p. 346: NY Daily News. p. 382: Susan Steinkamp/Picture Group. p. 385: NY Daily News.

Chapter Ten
p. 397: David Edward Dempster. p. 398: Jean Anderson/The Stock Market. p. 399: Comstock. p. 423: David Edward Dempster. p. 427: Jean Anderson/The Stock Market. p. 430: Comstock. p. 433: Michael L. Abramson/Woodfin Camp & Assoc.

Chapter Eleven
p. 437: Folio Inc./Eric Pogenpohl. p. 438: G. Douglas/FPG International. p. 453: Folio Inc./Eric Pogenpohl. p. 457: G. Douglas/FPG International.

Chapter Twelve
p. 463: Llewellyn. p. 464: Dennis Hallinan/FPG. p. 481: Llewellyn. p. 484: Dennis Hallinan/FPG.

Chapter Thirteen
p. 493: Comstock. p. 494: Superstock. p. 500: Brian Tumlinson/Uniphoto. p. 505: David Conklin/Uniphoto. p. 519: Comstock. p. 523: Superstock.

Chapter Fourteen
p. 529: Comstock. p. 530: Gabe Palmer/The Stock Market. p. 558: Comstock. p. 561: Gabe Palmer/The Stock Market.

Chapter Fifteen
p. 567: David Edward Dempster. p. 568: Comstock. p. 569: Robert Houser/Comstock. p. 597: David Edward Dempster. p. 599: Comstock. p. 601: Robert Houser/Comstock.

Chapter Sixteen
p. 609: Superstock. p. 635: Superstock.

Chapter Seventeen
p. 641: M. Angelo/West Light. p. 642: David Edward Dempster. p. 660: M. Angelo/West Light. p. 664: David Edward Dempster.

Chapter Eighteen
p. 673: Standard Oil Collection/University of Louisville. p. 674: Dan Connelly/Sygma. p. 691: Dan Connelly/Sygma.

Chapter Nineteen
p. 697: Courtesy of American Iron & Steel. p. 698: JP Laffont/Sygma. p. 714: Courtesy of American Iron & Steel. p. 715: JP Laffont/Sygma.

Chapter Twenty
p. 719: Brad Bower/Picture Group. p. 720: Comstock. p. 736: Brad Bower/Picture Group. p. 737: Comstock.

Chapter Twenty-one
p. 741: JP Laffont/Sygma. p. 742: Jim Brown/Offshoot. p. 755: JP Laffont/Sygma. p. 757: Jim Brown/Offshoot.

Chapter Twenty-two
p. 763: Luis Villota/The Stock Market. p. 764: JP Laffont/Sygma. p. 768: Luis Villota/The Stock Market. p. 771: JP Laffont/Sygma.

• GLOSSARY •

Absolute advantage   The ability of an individual, firm, or nation to produce more of every good than rival producers can produce, given equivalent resources and the same state of technology.

Acceleration hypothesis   The assumption that any attempt to use monetary or fiscal policy to maintain the unemployment rate permanently below its natural rate will result in accelerating inflation.

Adaptive expectations   The theory that individuals formulate their expectations about future prices on the basis of recent past experience, and that these expectations will be modified only gradually as the future unfolds.

Adverse supply shock   The effect of an increase in the costs of production without a concurrent increase in aggregate demand.

Aggregate demand   The quantity of aggregate output that is demanded at every price level; it can be expressed graphically as the aggregate demand curve.

Aggregate demand curve   A curve showing the relationship between the price level and the quantity of aggregate output demanded.

Aggregate expenditures   The total of expenditures for consumption, investment, government, and the difference between the value of exports and imports.

Aggregate output   The sum total of the final goods and services produced, evaluated in constant prices.

Aggregate price level   The average price of all goods and services included in the gross national product, expressed as a price index.

Aggregate supply   The quantity of aggregate output that will be supplied at every price level; it can be expressed graphically as the aggregate demand curve.

Aggregation   The process of combining many individual microeconomic markets into one overall market to determine the total output of the economy and the overall price level.

Anticipated inflation   Inflation that occurs when the future inflation rate is known in advance.

Applied knowledge   Knowledge that draws on the stock of basic knowledge to develop new products and production processes.

Asset   Anything of value that can be legally owned; its value is measured with dollars serving as the unit of account.

Automatic stabilization   A condition that causes countercyclical changes in the spending and taxing behavior of the federal government without a deliberate change in fiscal policy.

Autonomous consumption   The amount of consumption expenditure that would occur if disposable income were zero.

Autonomous investment   The amount of desired investment expenditure that would occur if real national income were zero.

Average propensity to consume   The amount of consumption divided by the amount of disposable income.

Balance of payments accounts   A record of all payments made to the United States by foreigners and all payments made to foreigners by the United States.

Balance sheet   An accounting tool that summarizes the financial condition of a business, employing a T-account, which allows the comparison of a firm's total assets with its total liabilities.

Balanced-budget multiplier   The multiplier obtained by dividing the change in real national income by the amount that both expenditures and taxes change.

Bank money   A medium of exchange in the form of checks from private financial firms.

Bank run   A situation in which many depositors of a bank simultaneously decide to close their accounts and withdraw their money, often asking for it in currency.

Barter exchange   An exchange in which one good is directly traded for another good.

Basic knowledge   Knowledge accumulated at the scientific level; a sound understanding of the physical world.

Bilateral aid   Foreign aid given from one country to another to aid economic development.

Business cycle   The historical pattern of up-and-down movements in real gross national product.

Capital account   A category of the balance of payments accounts that shows the balance of international capital flows.

Capitalism An economic system based on private ownership of the factors of production and on decentralized decision making in free markets.

Central bank An institution that serves as a banker's bank, accepting deposits from commercial banks and regulating their behavior. A central bank generally also serves as the banker for the government.

Centrally planned socialism An economy in which the government owns the factors of production and uses central planning to decide what will be produced.

Change in demand A shift of the entire demand curve caused by a change in one of the determinants of demand.

Change in quantity demanded A movement along a fixed demand curve caused by a change in the price of the good.

Change in quantity supplied A movement along a fixed supply curve caused by a change in the price of the product.

Change in supply A shift of the entire supply curve caused by a change in one of the determinants of supply.

Check A written directive from the owner of a demand deposit to the bank ordering payment of legal tender to another person or firm.

Classical quantity theory A theory that the change in the price level will be proportional to the change in the quantity of money.

Coercive incentives Legal, police, and military means that countries use to ensure compliance with economic laws and statutes.

Collateral The security that a borrower pledges to a lender in case the borrower defaults; if this occurs, the ownership will pass to the lender.

Command system A system that allocates resources by means of communal joint decision.

Commercial bank A financial institution, chartered either by a state or by the U.S. government, that is legally entitled to both accept deposits and make commercial loans.

Commodity money An economic good that is used as money and is also bought and sold for its value as a commercial product.

Common property Property that belongs to all citizens. All have the right to use such property resources in any way they see fit. No one can be excluded from enjoying a common-property resource.

Comparative advantage Principle that total output will be greatest when the output of each good is produced by the low-opportunity-cost producer and is exchanged for other, more desirable goods for which that individual, firm, or nation is not the low-cost producer.

Competitive (price-taker) market A market in which both buyers and sellers accept the market-determined price in making their decisions to buy or sell.

Complements Goods for which an increase in the price of one results in a decrease in the demand for the other, and vice versa.

Constant-growth rule The principle that monetary policy should be limited to providing each year a fixed percentage increase in the money supply.

Consumer price index An index that measures changes in the prices of consumption goods and services.

Consumption expenditure All of the spending by households except the purchase of housing.

Consumption function The relationship between total consumer spending and total disposable income.

Countercyclical monetary policy Policy that acts to increase aggregate demand when aggregate output falls below the level of potential national income, and that acts to reduce aggregate demand when aggregate output exceeds the level of potential national income.

Crowding-out hypothesis The assumption that an autonomous change in government spending induces an opposite, offsetting change in private spending.

Cultural Revolution In China in the 1960s, a movement aimed at removing complacency in economic and bureaucratic systems.

Currency appreciation The gain in value of one country's currency in relation to the currency of one or more foreign countries.

Currency depreciation The loss in value of one country's currency in relation to the currency of one or more foreign countries.

Currency devaluation A decrease in the international value of a currency that occurs as the result of the actions of government. Currencies are devalued when they are made less expensive for foreigners.

Current account A category of the balance of payments accounts that includes the balance of merchandise exports and imports for the United States and the balance of services imported and exported by the United States.

Cyclical deficit That portion of the total budget deficit that is caused by the cyclical fluctuations of the economy.

Cyclical unemployment The unemployment that results from a decline in aggregate economic activity, which causes a decline in the number of jobs available.

Deflationary gap A situation in which short-run equilibrium aggregate output is less than potential national income.

Demand Goods that consumers choose in the face of scarcity and for which they are actually prepared to pay a price.

Demand curve A graphic presentation of the relationship between price and the quantity demanded of a good.

Demand deposit A deposit in a noninterest-bearing checking account; an account kept at a commercial bank for the purpose of making transactions using bank money.

Demand for foreign exchange A function of the desire of people in one country to make purchases or investments in another country at varying exchange rates.

Demand schedule A tabulation of the relationship between price and the quantity demanded of a good; as price increases, the quantity demanded decreases.

Demand-side inflation Inflation that occurs when aggregate demand increases, causing the aggregate demand curve to shift to the right and the price level therefore to increase.

Deposit expansion multiplier The ratio of the expansion in total demand deposits to the change in excess reserves.

Depreciation The value of the capital stock that has been consumed or used up in a given year in the process of producing goods and services.

Depression A severe recession that lasts for a prolonged period of time.

Direct crowding out A condition that exists when the government purchase of goods and services substitutes directly for households' spending.

Direct foreign investment Investment by foreign companies in developing nations that provides capital, jobs, and technology.

Discouraged worker A person who has decided not to search for work in the belief that there are no acceptable jobs available.

Discretionary fiscal policy Policy that involves the conscious alteration of the spending and taxing behavior of the federal government to counter cyclical economic fluctuations.

Dumping A practice whereby a nation sells large quantities of its goods in foreign markets at prices below cost or below domestic price.

Economic development A condition in which economic growth leads to structural modernization and a sustained improvement in the general standard of living.

Economic efficiency A condition that exists when the economy's resources are so organized that no reallocation of resources can make one person better off without harming another person.

Economic growth A condition in which aggregate output, measured as real gross national product, increases.

Economic system The institutional means by which scarce resources are allocated to satisfy the wants of society.

Economics The study of how and with what consequences individuals and society (1) choose from among scarce goods, (2) employ scarce resources, and (3) distribute scarce goods and resources.

Economies of scale The condition that exists when an increase in output results in lower unit costs of production.

Effectiveness lag The time required for a change in monetary policy to affect the macroeconomy.

Embodiment hypothesis Assumption that new technology is introduced in the form of new capital investment.

Equilibrium (market-clearing) price Price at which the quantity demanded by buyers just equals the quantity supplied by sellers.

Equilibrium quantity The amount that equates the marginal value of the last unit of a good exchanged in the market with the marginal, or opportunity, cost of producing it. The value of the last unit traded is just equal to the value of using the same resources to produce the best alternative.

European Economic Community An organization formed to help member nations remove trade barriers and to provide for an easier flow of goods and services throughout Europe.

Excess unemployment A condition that exists when the official rate of unemployment exceeds the natural rate of unemployment.

Exchange The act of giving or taking one thing in return for another.

Exchange rate The price of one country's currency in terms of another country's currency.

Exchange shortage A condition that exists when the demand for a foreign currency exceeds the supply of that currency.

Exchange surplus A condition that exists when the supply of a foreign currency exceeds the demand for that currency.

Expansion A phase of the business cycle characterized by increasing real gross national product and total employment in the economy.

Expectations Forecasts about the future value of an economic variable.

Expectations theory of interest rates Theory that the level of long-term interest rates reflects the sum of expected short-term interest rates. The long-term interest rate equals the average of expected future short-term interest rates from the present time until the long-term security matures.

Expenditure approach An approach to calculating gross national product that sums the total dollar values of all final products sold in a given year.

Expenditure multiplier The ratio of change in real national income to change in autonomous expenditures.

Export promotion A strategy that concentrates on helping developing nations produce for export.

Extensive growth An increase in the quantity of the factors of production.

Externality External cost (or benefit) of an economic activity imposed on or received by someone other than the economic agent making the decision to engage in the activity.

Federal budget deficit The difference between federal government spending and total tax revenues.

Fiat money Money that the government has declared to be acceptable as a medium of exchange and to be a lawful way of settling debts.

Final goods and services Those goods and services that are actually consumed or retained by the ultimate user or are exported.

Fine-tuning The use of fiscal policy to maintain the economy at the level of potential national income by making continuous countercyclical adjustments in taxes and government expenditures.

Fiscal policy The conscious use of the spending and taxing powers of the federal government in pursuit of the government's macroeconomic goals.

Fisher effect The prediction that nominal interest rates will adjust in proportion to the change in the rate of inflation.

Fixed exchange rates Rates of exchange between currencies set by governments and international agreements.

Fixed investment Investment composed of the addition of new plant, equipment, and buildings to the capital stock.

Fixed-income asset A financial obligation that pays its owner a fixed amount of dollars of interest each year.

Fixed-income security A security that promises a fixed payment in the future. The interest rate on a fixed-income security is the annual percentage increase promised on the sum of money invested.

Floating exchange rates Fluctuating rates between the currencies of two or more countries freely determined by the law of supply and demand.

Flow-of-income approach An approach to calculating gross national product that sums the flow of income to the owners of all factors of production in the economy in a given year.

Forced savings Savings that occur when governments levy high taxes to pay for investments.

Foreign exchange market A market in which people buy and sell domestic and foreign currencies.

Fractional reserve system A procedure in which banks hold only a portion of their deposits as reserves.

Free good A good that is available in sufficient abundance to satisfy the wants of all who wish to consume it.

Free trade Trade between nations when there are no barriers to the free flow of goods and services between them.

Frictional unemployment The unemployment associated with the constant reallocation of resources that characterizes the U.S. economy.

Friedman surge An acceleration in the growth rate of the money supply that will have a disproportionate effect on the rate of inflation, because the anticipation of future inflation will increase velocity.

Full employment A situation in which the short-run equilibrium level of aggregate output equals the potential level of national income.

Fundamental postulate of economics Principle that as the personal gain from choosing an alternative increases, other things held constant, a person will be more likely to choose that alternative; conversely, as the cost associated with choosing a particular alternative increases, other things held constant, a person will be less likely to select that alternative.

General Agreement of Tariffs and Trade (GATT) An agreement whereby member nations meet regularly to negotiate trade arrangements between countries.

Gift giving A one-way exchange wherein one person transfers the legal ownership of a good to another person and receives in return the satisfaction resulting from making that person better off.

GNP deflator A price index that measures price changes in the economy from year to year.

Gold standard A monetary system in which the value of the dollar is fixed in terms of a specific quantity of gold, and the government is obligated to buy and sell gold at this fixed dollar rate.

Gosplan The organization in the Soviet Union that is responsible for central planning.

Government expenditure multiplier The multiplier obtained by dividing the increase in real national income by the increase in government expenditures.

Gradualism A policy for reducing the inflation rate slowly over time by managing aggregate demand in the hope of avoiding a rise in the unemployment rate as the macroeconomy adjusts to ever-lower rates of inflation.

Great Leap Forward In China, an ambitious plan undertaken by Mao's government to organize China's economy for greater industrial and agricultural production.

Green Revolution The agricultural development based on the cultivation of new high-yielding plant varieties, such as hybrid corn and rice.

Gross domestic product (GDP) The value of the final goods and services produced by all of the factors of production located within an economy regardless of who owns them.

Gross national income (GNI) The sum of all the income earned by the owners of the factors of production; it is calculated by adding together the incomes earned by labor, land, capital, and the profits received by entrepreneurs.

Gross national product (GNP) The total market value of the final goods and services produced during a year by domestically owned factors of production.

Growth formula A formula for economic growth that emphasizes the importance of savings and investment.

Imperfectly competitive (price-searcher) market Market in which either the buyer or the seller (or both) has sufficient market power to influence the market price, in which case the deci-sion maker with market power searches for the best price to charge for the good or service.

Import substitution A strategy whereby developing countries manufacture goods currently being consumed; government protects manufacturers of these goods by tariffs and quotas.

Import tariffs Taxes imposed on goods and services brought in from another country.

Income effect The change in quantity demanded of a good whose price has fallen that is caused by the increase in real income resulting from the price change. Or, change in the quantity of labor supplied that is induced by a change in the wage rate for labor.

Income-inferior good A good for which demand decreases when per capita income increases.

Income-normal good A good whose demand increases when, other things held constant, per capita income increases.

Incomes policy A set of guidelines, or rules, devised by the federal government to influence wage and price increases and inflationary expectations.

Indexing The process of automatically adjusting wages and prices for the effects of inflation.

Indirect crowding out A condition that exists when an increase in government expenditures leads to an offsetting decline in private investment spending.

Infant industry A new industry that has high start-up costs and limited profits due to the need for reinvestment in the early stages.

Inflation An increase in the overall level of prices.

Inflationary gap A condition that exists when the level of aggregate expenditures is too great and the price level too low to achieve equilibrium at the level of potential national income.

Inflationary recession A recession in which real national income declines for at least two quarters but during which the price level continues to increase.

Infrastructure investment Investment in capital goods by government.

Intensive growth An increase in the average amount of output received per unit of input.

Interest rate control The determination of the interest rate by the Federal Reserve and its supply of the quantity of money required by the money demand curve to establish the target rate of interest.

Interest rate effect The effect the interest rate has on the quantity demanded of interest-sensitive goods, thereby affecting the quantity of aggregate output demanded.

Intermediate goods Goods that are completely used up in the production of final goods and services.

Intermediate policy target A variable that serves as a guide to the Federal Reserve's policy goals and that also is closely related to the policy variables and is available on a timely basis.

Inventory investment Investment that reflects the increase or decrease over a year in the size of inventories that firms keep on hand.

Investment The purchase of newly produced capital goods — machinery, equipment, and structures — plus changes in inventories, which are the stocks of finished goods, goods in process, and materials that firms keep on hand.

Keynes effect The prediction that interest rates will decline following an expansion of the growth rate of the money supply and that they will rise following a contraction of the growth rate of the money supply.

Kuznets curve Curve indicating that incomes are divided most evenly in very poor and very rich countries, and inequality is greatest in middle-income, newly industrialized countries.

Laffer curve A curve that illustrates the relationship between tax rates and tax revenues.

Laissez-faire system A system that relies on the initiative of individual decision makers as they exchange goods and services in markets.

Land reform Alteration of land ownership arrangements.

Law of diminishing marginal value (or utility) Principle that the marginal benefit of a good declines as more of that good is consumed.

Law of diminishing returns Malthus' principle that population growth will eventually outstrip the productivity of land, leading to poverty.

Law of increasing costs Principle that as the economy attempts to produce more of a good, the opportunity cost of additional units expressed in terms of other goods sacrificed will increase.

Law of scarcity Principle that for every person and society *some* goods are scarce. These goods are not available in sufficient amounts to satisfy existing wants.

Law of supply Principle that as the price at which a good can be sold increases, more of that good will be offered for sale.

Learning-by-doing hypothesis The assumption that as a task is undertaken, new ways of accomplishing the task will be discovered that were not apparent when the task was begun.

Liquidity The ability of an asset to be converted into a medium of exchange. The degree of liquidity is influenced by the ease and cost with which an asset can be converted into a medium of exchange.

Long run The period of time that is sufficient for the economy to become fully adjusted to a change in the price level, and that is characterized by flexible prices for both products and the factors of production.

Long-run aggregate supply (LRAS) curve A curve showing the aggregate output that occurs when the macroeconomy is in full adjustment.

Long-run equilibrium The condition that exists when the expected price level equals the actual price level.

Long-run Phillips curve The graphic representation of the combinations of inflation and unemployment that can be sustained in the long run.

Long-term interest rate The interest rate on long-term (more than one year) securities; also called the long-term yield.

Long-term security (bond) An asset with a maturity date some years in the future.

Low opportunity cost The cost a country incurs for producing a given good or service when it gives up less of other goods and services than other countries by specializing in the production of that good or service.

M1 The money supply calculated as the sum of all cash (coins and paper money) held by the public as well as demand deposits at commercial banks, traveler's checks, and other checkable deposits, such as NOW and ATS accounts.

M2 The money supply that includes everything in the M1 money supply plus all savings deposits and time deposits of less than $100,000, and amounts invested in money market mutual funds and certain other liquid assets.

M3 The money supply that includes everything in the M1 and M2 money supplies plus time deposits over $100,000, institution-owned money market deposit accounts, time deposits held in Europe, some foreign deposits held by Americans, and certain other accounts.

Macroeconomic equilibrium The only price level at which the quantity of aggregate output supplied just equals the quantity of aggregate output demanded; at this price level the macroeconomic market is said to clear.

Macroeconomic law of demand Principle that when the price level falls, other things held constant, the quantity of aggregate output demanded will increase, and that when the price level increases, the quantity of aggregate output demanded will decline.

Macroeconomics The study of the economy as a whole. It is concerned with the aggregate level of employment, economic growth, and the price level.

Managed floating exchange rates Flexible exchange rates that are usually determined by the forces of supply and demand.

Marginal analysis The study of the effect of small changes relative to an existing situation.

Marginal benefit (marginal utility) The additional benefit obtained from taking an action.

Marginal benefit of job searching The additional benefit the job seeker (or potential employer) receives from continuing the job search (or worker search) instead of taking the job (or hiring the worker) currently available.

Marginal cost of job searching The additional cost that the job seeker (or potential employer) incurs from continuing the job (or worker) search instead of accepting the job (or hiring the worker) currently available.

Marginal propensity to consume The ratio of the change in consumption to the change in disposable income.

Marginal propensity to import The percentage of each additional dollar of real disposable income that is spent on imported goods and services.

Marginal propensity to save The ratio of the change in saving to the change in disposable income.

Market An institutional arrangement that brings together buyers and sellers and facilitates exchanges.

Market demand curve The horizontal summation of all individual demand curves in the market that shows the sum of the quantities demanded by all consumers in the market at each price.

Market supply curve Horizontal summation of the supply curves of all of the individual suppliers participating in the market; it is obtained by summing the quantities supplied by all suppliers at each possible price.

Material balance tables Statements of estimated production needs for a specific commodity and projected consumption levels and needs for that commodity.

Material incentives Monetary and material rewards that businesses and workers receive as compensation.

Menu costs Costs involved in periodically changing prices to adjust for an inflationary increase in the price level.

Merchandise trade balance The difference between U.S. exports and imports.

Mixed economic system An economic system in which government owns the factors of production but decisions about what will be produced are made in the marketplace.

Monetary base The quantity of reserves in the banking system and the quantity of cash held by the nonbank public; sometimes referred to as high-powered money.

Monetary base control The Federal Reserve's regulation of the quantity of money while allowing the money market to determine the rate of interest.

Monetary policy The deliberate control of the money supply to achieve the macroeconomic goals set by the Federal Reserve Bank.

Money Any generally accepted means of payment that will be taken in exchange for goods and services.

Money market account An account paying a variable rate of interest, which is pegged to some market rate of interest like the interest rate paid on U.S. Treasury bills; often checks can be drawn on the account.

Money supply In the United States, the sum of all the fiat money (coins and currency) and of the bank money held by the public.

Monopoly problem A problem that arises when, due to the lack of competition in a market, producers act as if they were a single firm and restrict output in order to increase price.

Moral incentives Means by which governments attempt to cause businesses and workers to act in the nation's economic best interests.

Movement along the consumption function A movement that occurs when disposable income changes, all other factors that affect consumption being held constant.

Mutual coincidence of wants Condition of a barter exchange requiring that each person (1) have what a potential trader wants and (2) desires what that potential trader has to exchange.

National income The total value of the payments to the owners of the factors of production.

National income accounts A set of statistics measuring aggregate output and its components; they provide a way of measuring and evaluating the performance of the whole economy.

Natural rate of unemployment The unemployment rate at which there is an approximate balance between the number of unfilled jobs and the number of qualified job seekers; the unemployment rate that corresponds to the level of potential natural income.

Negative externality A cost imposed on a third party to a trade or action without that party's consent.

Net exports The value of exports minus the value of imports.

Net national product The total value of final goods and services actually available in the economy in a given year.

Net trade deficit A condition that exists when a nation's imports exceed its exports.

Net trade surplus A condition that exists when a nation's exports exceed its imports.

Nominal gross national product (GNP) The value of final goods and services for a given year measured in terms of the prevailing market prices in that year.

Nominal interest rate The observed market rate of interest, composed of the real rate of interest plus a premium to account for the expected rate of inflation.

Normative economics The study of *what ought to be*. Normative economic statements involve value judgments and cannot be proven false.

Official reserve accounts Stocks of foreign money held in a country's central banks.

Okun's law Principle that the unemployment rate will rise by one percentage point for every two-percentage-point decline in real gross national product below 3 percent, and will decline by one percentage point for every two-percentage-point increase in real gross national product.

Omnibus Trade Act An agreement designed to strengthen the negotiating power of the U.S. trade representative, to address unfair trade practices by other countries, to provide import relief to affected industries and workers, and to provide money for improved education in the United States.

Open-market operations Procedures that involve the purchase or sale of U.S. government securities by the Federal Reserve for the purpose of adjusting the level of reserves in the banking system.

Opportunity cost The highest-valued alternative that must be sacrificed when an action is selected; it is what the decision maker could have had instead.

Paradox of thrift Principle that in the aggregate expenditures model an autonomous increase in savings without a corresponding increase in investment will result in a decline in the equilibrium level of real national income while the quantity of savings remains the same or even declines.

Payments system A system based on the use of money to make trades and settle debts.

Per capita gross national product The value per person of the final goods and services produced by domestically owned factors of production.

Personal disposable income The amount of income households have at their disposal to spend or save.

Personal income The gross amount of income available to households. It is obtained from national income by subtracting undistributed corporate profits, corporate taxes, and Social Security contributions and adding back the amount of transfers, including government interest payments.

Personal saving The proportion of personal disposable income that is saved.

Phillips curve Graphic representation of the inflation/unemployment trade-off created by a fluctuating aggregate demand curve acting on the short-run aggregate supply curve.

Policy instruments Economic variables that the Federal Reserve controls directly and that in turn affect the policy targets.

Policy variables The ultimate objectives of the Federal Reserve. They take the form of specific targets for the behavior of both real gross national product and the price level.

Political good Any good, public or private, supplied by the political process.

Positive economics The study of *what is* in the economy. Positive economic statements can, in principle, be tested and proven false.

Positive externality A benefit to a third party for which that party does not pay.

Potential national income The real gross national product that would be produced if all of the factors of production were fully employed.

Price index A mechanism relating the current year's cost of a market basket of goods and services as a percentage of the cost of the same goods in some base year.

Principle of rational behavior Rule that an economic decision maker should take any action from which there is a positive net benefit. Such a benefit exists when the addition to benefits exceeds the addition to costs.

Priority principle In the Soviet Union, a guarantee that resources will be available for high-priority industrial projects, with other projects receiving materials only after priorities have been met.

Prisoner's dilemma A framework for analyzing the choices and outcomes for a decision-making process in which the combination of the choices made by two decision makers determines the outcome.

Private saving The total of personal saving plus business saving out of retained earnings and funds set aside for depreciation expenses.

Private-property resource A resource for which the rights to use, develop, or sell that resource are granted to an individual or firm.

Procyclical monetary policy Policy that increases aggregate demand when aggregate output exceeds the level of potential national income, and that decreases it when output falls below the level of potential national income.

Production possibilities schedule A tabulation of the various combinations of the amounts of any two goods that can be produced from the resources available and given the state of technology.

Protectionism The government policy that restricts imports that in one way or another could harm a domestic industry.

Purchasing power parity A condition that exists when a given amount of money will purchase the same market basket of goods and services when converted from one currency to another at prevailing exchange rates.

Pure public good A good that is a nonrival in consumption, that is not divisible, and that nonpaying persons cannot be easily excluded from using once it has been produced.

Purely competitive market Market in which there are many buyers and sellers, a homogeneous product is traded, and there is easy entry and exit of buyers and sellers.

Quotas A device used by countries to restrict the amounts of goods and services imported from another country.

Ratification A process by which supply-side inflation is made permanent and in which the government adopts an expansionary policy, usually by increasing the money supply, to offset the rise in unemployment caused by an adverse supply shock.

Rational expectations The theory that assumes that economic decision makers make predictions about the future state of macroeconomic variables using all available information about how the economy works, including information about past and present macroeconomic policies.

Rational ignorance A condition arising from the lack of incentives for individual voters to become informed and to participate in public affairs.

Real gross national product (GNP) The actual quantity of final goods and services produced in the economy; it is determined by removing the effects of price changes.

Real interest rate The nominal interest rate less the amount of expected inflation.

Recession A phase of the business cycle that is characterized by a decline in real gross national product lasting for two or more quarters.

Recessionary gap A condition that exists when the level of aggregate expenditures is too low and the price level too high to achieve equilibrium at the level of potential national income.

Recognition lag The time it takes the Federal Reserve to recognize the existence of an inflationary or a recessionary gap and to change the supply of money in an appropriate way.

Reservation wage The lowest wage that an unemployed worker must be offered for the worker to accept a job offer.

Reserve ratio The percentage of deposits that banks hold as reserves.

Savings account An account paying a fixed rate of interest; in practice, amounts can be withdrawn at any time, but checks cannot be written on the account.

Scarce good A good that is not available in sufficient amounts to satisfy existing wants.

Searching activities The activities conducted by unemployed workers hunting for an available job and by firms that need new employees hunting for appropriate workers.

Securitization The practice of packaging a bundle of loans that a bank has made and selling the entire bundle to investors in return for cash and the fees earned from servicing the loans.

Shift in the consumption function A shift that occurs when a determinant affecting the consumption function changes.

Shoe-leather costs The costs imposed by perfectly anticipated inflation on the holders of money who incur extra costs in their attempts to conserve on their money balances.

Short run The period of time in which the prices of the factors of production do not change.

Shortage A condition in which, at the existing price, the quantity demanded exceeds the quantity supplied. A shortage occurs when the existing price is lower than the equilibrium price.

Short-run equilibrium The condition that exists at the price level at which the quantity of real national income demanded equals the quantity of real national income supplied.

Short-sighted effect The tendency for government to favor actions having immediate benefits and future costs and to neglect actions having immediate costs and future benefits.

Short-term interest rate The interest rate on short-term (less than one year) securities; also called the short-term yield.

Short-term security A security that matures within one year of the purchase date.

Socialism An economic system in which property is collectively owned and decision making is in the hands of the community, generally the government.

Special-interest group A group in which a minority of voters have a large stake in a particular political outcome. Members of this group stand to gain substantially if their position is adopted. Conversely, the majority of voters neither gain nor lose much if the special interest predominates.

Specialization The process of concentrating production in the hands of the most efficient producer.

Spread The difference between short-term and long-term interest rates.

Stagflation An economic condition characterized by the simultaneous existence of recession and inflation.

Structural deficit That portion of the total deficit that would occur if the economy were operating at the level of potential national income; it measures the existing fiscal policy of the government.

Structural unemployment The unemployment that occurs when the skills a worker possesses are no longer in demand, as when industries decline because the product produced either becomes obsolete or is replaced by a lower-cost source.

Subsidies Amounts of money pumped into an industry by government to help the industry.

Substitutes Goods for which an increase in the price of one causes an increase in demand for the other, and vice versa.

Substitution effect The increase in demand for a good whose price has fallen that is caused by the substitution of this less expensive good for other goods that are now relatively expensive. Or, a change in the quantity of labor supplied that is induced by a change in the wage rate for labor.

Substitution of foreign goods effect The effect that an increase or decrease in price level has on foreign and domestic demand.

Supply curve A graphic presentation of the relationship between price and the quantity supplied of a good.

Supply of foreign exchange The willingness of foreigners to give up their money at varying exchange rates to make purchases and investments in other countries.

Supply schedule A tabulation of the relationship between price and the quantity of a good offered for sale; as price increases, the quantity supplied increases.

Supply shock A situation that develops when the costs of production increase throughout the economy because of an increase in the price of a factor of production.

Supply-side inflation Inflation that occurs when the short-run aggregate supply declines, causing the short-run aggregate supply curve to shift to the left and the price level therefore to increase.

Supply-side policies Policies that attempt to increase productivity and economic growth by changing the tax system to provide greater incentive to save and invest more and to work harder and more often.

Surplus A condition in which, at the existing price, the quantity supplied is greater than the quantity demanded. A surplus occurs when the existing price is higher than the equilibrium price.

Tastes A reflection of consumers' preferences for and aversions to different goods; based on consumer likes and dislikes.

Tax base The amount of economic activity subject to taxes.

Tax multiplier The multiplier calculated by dividing the change in real national income by the change in taxes; it carries a negative sign.

Tax-based incomes program A program that rewards workers and business firms with tax breaks if they act in compliance with the government's wage and price guidelines and penalizes them with higher taxes if they do not.

Terms of trade Reflections of the relative prices of two goods; the rate at which one good can be exchanged for another good.

Theft An involuntary transfer in which one person confiscates a good belonging to another person.

Tied aid Foreign aid that requires the recipient to spend the funds on goods produced in the donor country.

Time deposit An account that bears a fixed or variable rate of interest and that is set up for a specified amount of time; the money deposited cannot be withdrawn before the end of this time period without paying a substantial interest penalty.

Trade The exchange of the legal right to a good or service that a person owns for the legal right to something that another person owns.

Token money A medium of exchange whose value is greater than the value of the resources used to produce it.

Transaction costs The costs involved in searching out trades, the cost of negotiating an agreement, and the cost of enforcing that agreement.

Turnover tax In the Soviet Union, the difference between wholesale and retail prices.

Unanticipated inflation Inflation that surprises economic decision makers and that can reduce the efficiency with which resources are allocated, alter the level of real national income and employment, and result in a redistribution of income and wealth.

Unemployment A condition that exists when people who wish to work are searching for acceptable job opportunities.

Unemployment rate The number of unemployed divided by the number of persons in the labor force.

Value added The amount of value contributed to a product by a firm at a given stage of the production process.

Velocity of circulation The average number of times that a unit of money is spend on final goods and services during a period of one year.

Wage and price controls Regulations that set legal limits on the wages and prices that firms are allowed to pay and charge.

Wage illusion A condition that occurs when workers wrongly equate higher nominal wages with higher real wages.

Wants The totality of goods people would have if scarcity did not exist, including all of the goods people would want if the goods were free.

Wealth Whatever people value.

Wealth and income effect The change in the purchasing power of a given amount of money-denominated wealth that results from a change in the price level, causing individuals to alter their consumption expenditures.

· INDEX ·